sixth edition

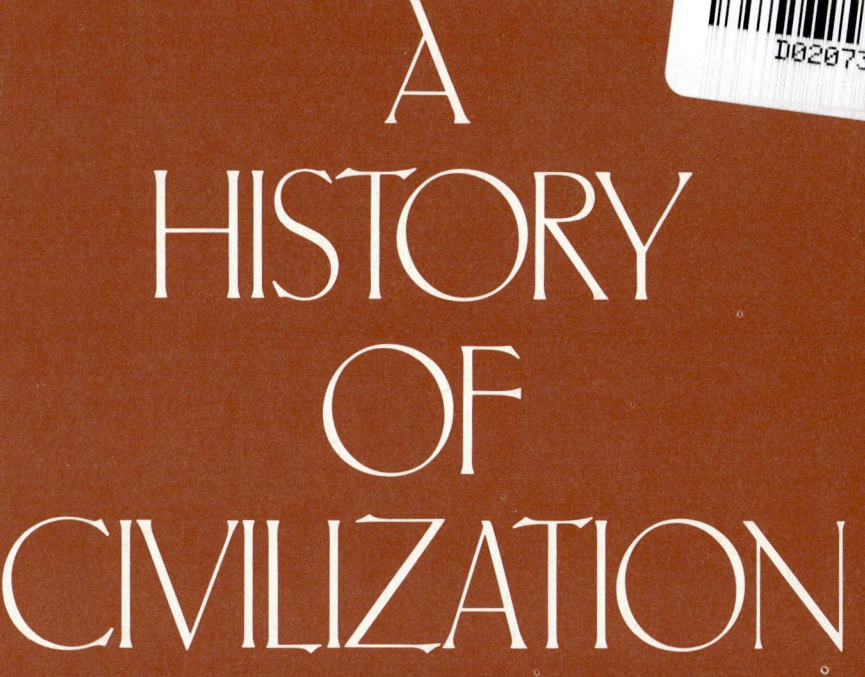

A HISTORY OF CIVILIZATION

Volume I: Prehistory to 1715

CRANE BRINTON

JOHN B. CHRISTOPHER
University of Rochester

ROBERT LEE WOLFF

ROBIN W. WINKS
Yale University

Prentice-Hall, Inc., Englewood Cliffs, New Jersey 07632

Library of Congress Cataloging in Publication Data
Main entry under title:

A History of civilization.

Rev. ed. of: A history of civilization / Crane Brinton, John B. Christopher, Robert Lee Wolff. c 1976.
Includes bibliographies and indexes.
Contents: v. 1. Prehistory to 1715 v. 2. 1648 to the present.
1. Civilization—History. I. Brinton, Clarence Crane, 1898–1968. A history of civilization.
CB69.H58 1984 909 83-13830
ISBN 0-13-389866-0 (v. 1)
ISBN 0-13-389874-1 (v. 2)

"Let us learn those things here on earth,
the knowledge of which will continue into the heavens."

Editorial supervision: Serena Hoffman
Cover and interior design: Lee Cohen
Development: Gerald Lombardi
Acquisitions editor: Stephen Dalphin
Art and photo research: Joelle Burrows
Manufacturing buyer: Ron Chapman
Cover photograph: Four By Five

Printed in the United States of America
10 9 8 7 6 5 4 3 2

ISBN 0-13-389866-0

Prentice-Hall International, Inc., *London*
Prentice-Hall of Australia Pty. Limited, *Sydney*
Editora Prentice-Hall do Brasil, Ltda., *Rio de Janeiro*
Prentice-Hall Canada Inc., *Toronto*
Prentice-Hall of India Private Limited, *New Delhi*
Prentice-Hall of Japan, Inc., *Tokyo*
Prentice-Hall of Southeast Asia Pte. Ltd., *Singapore*
Whitehall Books Limited, *Wellington, New Zealand*

contents

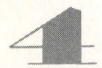

boxes

maps

preface

Each generation writes its own history and finds that the present is best decoded by a different approach to the past. By the end of World War II Americans found that they were expected to be the leaders of "the West"—which was generally taken to mean of Western civilization—and they extended their study of history to include non-Western societies in Africa and Asia, both because these societies deserved to be studied for their own sakes, and also as a simple matter of prudence. Diplomatic history moved into the space often reserved for political or administrative history, and intellectual history (most especially the history of art and of thought) also became both important and popular—which are not the same thing. As a result, a textbook used by thousands of readers in hundreds of schools, colleges, and universities, known familiarly as "Brinton, Christopher, and Wolff," went through periodic revision to keep pace with changing expectations.

The present edition represents the first wholesale revision of this text in nearly a decade. That decade has been filled with perhaps the most exceptional array of changes seen in the discipline of history since the nineteenth century—changes both in the way people think about history as well as in our knowledge of its content. Economic and intellectual history have been transformed, and social history has altered our entire way of looking at ourselves and at our past. Historical scholarship must now embrace statistics, psychohistory, geography, and the arguments usually reserved to political science, sociology, and anthropology. Yet the historian and the student must not forget that the purpose of history is to explain how we came to be as we are: why we find ourselves in our present predicaments, how we achieved our present triumphs, how we have developed across centuries through a *process* to a specific point in time—*our* specific point in time—when a savage light known as the present beats down upon us.

This present edition, therefore, is three things at once. It is, first, a body of information, argument, and interpretation that is meant to help the reader understand humanity's long search for security, for meaning, for purpose in life. Second, it is a book by which students may locate themselves in time, decoding in their own way the relevance of the past for the present. And third, it is a document that demonstrates the state of historical learning at the level of broad generalization and for the broadest general need in the 1980s. Thus, this text is intended to preserve the great strengths in breadth, depth, and grasp of the original editions of Brinton, Christopher, and Wolff, retaining for these distinguished authors (two of them no longer with us, for Robert Lee Wolff died in 1980, twelve years after the death of Crane Brinton) their many loyal readers, while also reflecting new trends in the study of history.

To summarize the significant changes in this new edition, much material has been reordered and combined in different ways and with different emphases, especially in Volume II, with a resulting total of 28 chapters instead of the fifth edition's 33. Volume I ends at 1715 with Chapter 15, "The Problem of Divine-Right Monarchy"; but that chapter also forms the first one of Volume II, which now begins at 1648. Among many other changes, nineteenth-century imperialism has received added emphasis; the chapter on events between the two World Wars has been restructured; and material on events since World War II has been compressed and brought up to date in the context of the perspectives and events of the past ten years.

A new feature, outlines at the beginning of the chapters, includes many dates in order to provide a simplified overview of a particular historical terrain before elaborating on its topographical detail. But the most obvious change to one familiar with earlier editions will be the addition of two new elements: brief boxed-off sections throughout the text that provide selections from sources and documents contemporary with the events in the text, but that also discuss matters of cultural and historiographic interest; and short summaries at the end of each chapter designed to recapitulate its major ideas and events.

A particular effort has been made to tie the illustrations more closely to the text through captions that explain and put in context the works illustrated as well as identifying them. There are several new maps, and all maps have been updated and revised with the intention of including important place names mentioned in the text. The Suggested Readings that appear at the end of each volume have been redone from scratch so as to include the most recent scholarship and to enable readers to move beyond the text as their interests dictate. In an effort to make the index more useful, the major discussion for each entry has been printed in **boldface** type. The index has been expanded to include concepts as well as events and to provide a pronunciation guide for foreign or difficult names of persons and places.

Much appreciated criticism and guidance was provided by the following reviewers, who saw rough drafts of the manuscript: Elizabeth Carney, Clemson University; Douglas McCullough, Dekalb Community College; Charles Connell, West Virginia University; David Lukowitz, Hamline University; R.V. Burks, Wayne State University; and John Donnelly, Marquette University.

The greatest challenge to the historian today is to understand movement through time, even at its most technical or controversial, without losing sight of the essential nature of history itself. History is a narrative. History is concerned foremost with major themes, even as it recognizes the significance of many fascinating digressions. Because history is largely about how and why people behave as they do, it is also about patterns of thought and belief. Ultimately, history is about what people believe to be true. To this extent, virtually all history is intellectual history, for the perceived meaning of a specific treaty, battle, or scientific discovery lies in what those involved in it and those who came after thought was most significant about it. History makes it clear that we may die, as we may live, as a result of what someone believed to be true in the relatively remote past.

A History of Civilization is about how we, as readers studying the past through the traditions and biases of the West, have come to think about civilization. Neither the title nor the content is meant to imply that there are not equally complex, challenging, and productive civilizations elsewhere. But we must recognize, even as material relating to the Far East, South Asia, or Africa is incorporated into the present edition, that we read history to understand *our own* ancient beginnings (Volume I) or *our* modern heritage (Volume II). Though this is our primary reason for studying Western civilization, we must also recognize that it is impossible to do justice to all civilizations in a single text. If these volumes enable us to understand history as a process, and if they illustrate the methodology of history, then they will surely lead us to appreciate other civilizations as well. The text is, therefore, implicitly but not explicitly comparative. Western civilization may not be typical, nor need we conclude that our ways are either "right" or "wrong" simply because they are ours and are known to us. They are the views by which we perceive our world; they are the windows on the world that our own historical experience has opened for us. And since Western societies have had so great an impact on the non-Western world in recent centuries, there is a sense in which world history is also quite legitimately viewed through the windows of Western history.

We cannot each be our own historian. In everyday life we may reconstruct our personal past, acting as detectives for our motivations and attitudes. But formal history is a much more rigorous study. History may give us some very small capacity to predict the future. More certainly, it should help us arrange the causes for given events into meaningful patterns. History also should help us be tolerant of the historical views of others, even as it helps to shape our own convictions. History must help us sort out the important from the less important, the relevant from the irrelevant, so that we do not fall prey to those who propose simple-minded solutions to vastly complex human problems. We must not yield to the temptation to blame one group or individual for our problems, and yet we must not fail to defend our convictions with vigor.

To recognize, indeed to celebrate, the equality of all civilizations is essential to the civilized life itself. To understand that we see all civilizations through the prism of our specific historical past—for which we feel affection, in which we feel comfortable and secure, and by which we interpret all else that we encounter—is simply to recognize that we too are the products of history. That is why we must study history and ask our own questions in our own way. For if we ask no questions of our past, there may be no questions to ask of our future.

Robin W. Winks
For the Sixth Edition

THE VALUE OF HISTORY AND OF HISTORICAL CONTROVERSY

History is a series of arguments to be debated, not a body of data to be recorded or a set of facts to be memorized. Thus controversy in historical interpretation—over what an event actually means, over what really happened at an occurrence called "an event," over how best to generalize about the event—is at the heart of its value. Of course history teaches us about ourselves. Of course it teaches us to understand and to entertain a proper respect for our collective past. Of course it transmits to us specific skills—how to ask questions, how to seek out answers, how to think logically, cogently, lucidly, purposefully. Of course it is, or ought to be, a pleasure. But we also discover something fundamental about a people in what they choose to argue over in their past. When a society suppresses portions of its past record, as the Soviet Union does today, that society (or its leadership) tells us something about itself. When a society seeks to alter how the record is presented, well-proven facts notwithstanding, we learn how history can become a two-edged sword.

Who controls history, it is written, controls the past, and who controls the past controls the present. Those who would close off historical controversy with the argument that we either know all that we need to know about a subject, or that what we know is so irrefutably correct that anyone who attacks the conventional wisdom about the subject must have destructive purposes in mind, is in the end intent upon destroying the very value of history itself—that value being that history teaches us to *argue productively* with each other.

Obviously, then, history is a social necessity. It gives us our identity. It helps us to find our bearings in an ever more complex present, providing us with a navigator's chart by which we may to some degree orient ourselves. When we ask who we are, and how is it that we are so, we learn skepticism and acquire the beginnings of critical judgment. Along with a sense of narrative—just as an autobiography is a narrative—history also provides us with tools for explanation and analysis. It helps us to find the particular example, to see the uniqueness in a past age or past event, while also helping us to see how the particular and the unique contribute to the general. History thus shows us humanity at work and play, in society, changing through time, in ways that we may approve, praise, share, or even comprehend. By letting us experience other lifestyles, history shows us the values of both subjectivity and objectivity—those twin conditions of our individual view of the world in which we live, conditions between which we constantly, and usually almost without knowing it, move. Thus history is both a form of truth and a matter of opinion, and the close study of history should help us to distinguish between the two. It is important to make such distinctions, for as Sir Walter Raleigh wrote, "It is not truth but opinion that can travel the world without a passport." Far too often what we read and perceive as truth—in our newspapers, on our television sets, from our friends—is opinion, not fact.

History is an activity. That activity asks specific questions as a means of arriving at general questions. A textbook such as this is concerned overwhelmingly with general questions, even though at times it must ask specific questions or present specific facts as a means of stalking the general. The great philosopher Karl Jaspers once remarked, "Who I am and where I belong, I first learned to know from the mirror of history." It is this mirror which any honest textbook must reflect.

To speak of "civilization" (of which this book is a history) is at once to plunge into controversy, so that our very first words illustrate why some people are so fearful of the study of history. To speak, as we do here, of "Western civilization" is even more restrictive, too provincial in the eyes of some historians. Yet if we are to understand history as a process, we must approach it through a sense of place: our continuity, our standards, our process. Still, we must recognize an inherent bias in such a term as "Western civilization," indeed two inherent biases: first, that we know what it means to be "civilized" and have attained that stature; and second, that the West as a whole is a single unitary civilization. This second bias is made clearer when we recognize that most scholars and virtually all college courses refer not to "Eastern civilization" but to "the civilizations of the East"—a terminology that suggests that while the West is a unity, the East is not. These are conventional phrases, buried in our Western perception of reality, just as our common geographical references show a Western bias. The Near East or the Far East are, after all, "near" or "far" only in reference to a geographical location focused on western Europe. The Japanese do not refer to London as being in the far West, or Los Angeles as being in the far East, though both references would be correct, if they saw the world as though they stood at its center. Though this text will accept these conventional phrases, precisely because they are traditionally embedded in our Western languages, one of the uses of history—and of the study of a book such as this one—is to be alert to the biases inherent in language, even when necessity requires that we continue to use its conventional forms of shorthand.

But if we are to speak of Western civilization, we must have, at the outset, some definition of what we mean by "being civilized." Hundreds of books have been written on this subject. The average person often means only that others, the "noncivilized," speak a different language and practice alien customs. The Chinese customarily referred to all foreigners as barbarians, and the ancient Greeks spoke of those who could not communicate in Greek as *bar-bar*—those who do not speak our tongue. Yet today the ability to communicate in more than one language is a hallmark of a "civilized" person.

Thus definitions of civilization, at least as used by those who think little about the meaning of their words, obviously change.

For our purposes, however, we must have a somewhat more exacting definition of the term, since it guides and informs any textbook that attempts to cover the entire sweep of Western history. Anthropologists, sociologists, historians, and others may reasonably differ about the essential ingredients of a civilization. They may also differ as to whether, for example, there is a separate American civilization that stands apart from, say, a British or Italian civilization, or whether these civilizations are simply particular variants on one larger entity, with only that larger entity—the West—entitled to be called "a civilization." Such an argument is of no major importance here, although it is instructive that it should occur. Rather, what is needed is a definition sufficiently clear to be used throughout the narrative and analysis to follow. This working definition, therefore, will hold that "civilization" involves the presence of several (though not necessarily all) of the following conditions within a society or group of interdependent societies:

1. There will be some form of government by which people administer to their political needs and responsibilities.
2. There will be some development of urban society, that is, of city life, so that the culture is not nomadic, dispersed, and thus unable to leave significant and surviving physical remnants of its presence.
3. A form of literacy will have developed, so that group may communicate with group, and more important, generation with generation in writing.
4. Human beings will have become toolmakers, able through the use of metals to transform, however modestly, their physical environment, and thus, their social and economic environment as well.
5. Some degree of specialization of function will have begun, usually at the work place, so that pride, place, and purpose function as cohesive elements in the society.
6. Social classes will have emerged, whether antagonistic to or sustaining of one another.
7. There will be a concept of leisure time—that life is not solely for the work place, or for the assigned class function or specialization—so that, for example, art may develop beyond (though not excluding) mere decoration.
8. There will be a concept of a higher being, though not necessarily through organized religion, by which a people may take themselves outside themselves to explain events and find purpose.
9. There will be a concept of time, by which the society links itself to a past and to the presumption of a future.
10. There will have developed a faculty for criticism. This faculty need not be the rationalism of the West, or intuition, or any specific religious or political mechanism, but it must exist, so that the society may contemplate change from within, rather than awaiting attack and possible destruction from without.

Not all these conditions are essential to civilization, Western or otherwise. Not all may be present in any society that we could, nonetheless, call civilized, nor do they need to arise in the order suggested here. But through its activities and beliefs the society that is becoming a civilization, or attached to a civilization, will have provided a series of declarations of intent about its aspirations. To be sure, historians lean toward what can be studied and measured through the written record, though they would be quite wrong to rely solely upon such a record. A common Western bias is to measure "progress" through technological change and to suggest that societies that show (at least until quite recently in historical time) little dramatic technological change are not civilized. In truth, neither a written record nor dramatic technological changes are essential to being civilized, though both are no doubt present in societies we would call civilized. Perhaps, as we study history, we ought to remember all *three* of the elements inherent in historical action as recorded by the English critic John Ruskin: "Great nations write their autobiographies in three manuscripts, the book of their deeds, the book of their words, and the book of their art."

The issue here is not whether we "learn from the past." Most often we do not, at least at the simple-minded level; we do not, as a nation, decide upon a course of action in diplomacy, for example, simply because a somewhat similar course in the past worked or did not work. We are wise enough to know that circumstances alter cases and that new knowledge brings new duties. Of course individuals "learn from the past"; the victim of a purse snatching takes precautions in the future. To dignify such an experience as "a lesson of history," however, is to turn mere individual growth from child into adult into history when, at most, such growth is a personal study in biography.

We also sometimes learn the "wrong lessons" from history. Virtually anyone who wishes to argue passionately for a specific course of future action can find a lesson from the past that will convince the gullible that history repeats itself and therefore that the past is a map to the future. No serious historian argues this, however: general patterns may, and sometimes do, repeat themselves, but specific chains of events do not. Unlike those subjects that operate at the very highest level of generalization (political science, theology, science), history simply does not believe in ironclad laws. But history is not solely a series of unrelated events—not simply "one damn thing after another." There are general patterns, clusters of causes, intermediate levels of generalization that prove true. History works at a level uncomfortable to many: above the specific, below the absolute.

If complex problems never present themselves twice in the same or even in recognizably similar form, if, to borrow a frequent image from the military world, generals always prepare for the last war instead of the next one, then does the study of history offer society any help in solving its problems? The answer surely is yes—but only in a limited way. History offers a rich collection of clinical reports on human behavior in various situations—individual and collective, political, economic, military, social, cultural—that tell us in detail how the human race has conducted its affairs and that suggest ways of handling similar problems in the present. President Harry S Truman's secretary of state, a former chief of staff, General George Marshall, once remarked that nobody could think about the problems of the 1950s who had not reflected upon the fall of Athens in the fifth century B.C. He was referring to the extraordinary history of the war between Athens and Sparta written just after it was over by Thucydides, an Athenian who fought in the war. There were no nuclear weapons, no telecommunications, no guns or gunpowder in the fifth century B.C.; the logistics of the war were altogether primitive, yet twenty-three hundred years later one of the most distinguished leaders of American military and political affairs found Thucydides indispensable to his thinking.

History, then, can only approximate the range of human behavior, with some indication of its extremes and averages. It can, though not perfectly, show how and within what limits human behavior changes. This last point is especially important for the social scientist, the economist, the sociologist, the executive, the journalist, or the diplomat. History provides materials that even an inspiring leader—a prophet, a reformer, or a columnist—would do well to master before seeking to lead us into new ways. For it can tell us something about what human material can and cannot stand, just as science and technology can tell engineers what stresses metals can stand. History can provide an awareness of the depth of time and space that should check the optimism and the overconfidence of the reformer. For example, millions of hours are wasted teaching children to read English, with its absurd spelling and its overrefined punctuation; yet the slightest background in history would show that societies usually resist changes like the reform of spelling, or accept them only during revolutions (as when the metric system was introduced during the French Revolution), or under dictatorships (as when the Turkish alphabet was changed from Arabic to Roman in the 1920s by the dictator Kemal Atatürk).

We may wish to protect the environment in which we live—to eliminate acid rain, to cleanse our rivers, to protect our wildlife, to preserve our majestic natural scenery. History may show us that most peoples have failed to do so, and may provide us with some guidance on how to avoid the mistakes of the past. But history will also show that there are substantial differences of public and private opinion over how best to protect our environment; or that there are many people who do not believe such protection is necessary; or that there are people who accept the need for protection but are equally convinced that lower levels of protection must be traded off for higher levels of productivity from our natural resources. History can provide the setting by which we may understand differing opinions, but recourse to history will not get the legislation passed, the angry made happy, the future made clean and safe. History will not define river pollution, though it can provide us with statistics from the past for comparative measurement. The definition will arise from the politics of today and our judgments about tomorrow. History is for the long and at times for the intermediate run, but seldom for the short run.

So, if we are willing to accept a "relevance" that is more difficult to see at first than the immediate applicability of science, and more remote than direct action, we will have to admit that history is "relevant." It may not actually build the highway or clear the slum, but it can give enormous help to those who wish to do so. And failure to take it into account may lead to failure in the sphere of action.

But history is also fun, at least for those who enjoy giving their curiosity free rein. Whether it is historical gossip we prefer (How many lovers did Catherine the Great of Russia actually take in a given year, and how much political influence did their activity in the imperial bedroom give them?), or the details of historical investigation (How does it happen that the actual treasures found in a buried Viking ship correspond to those described in an Anglo-Saxon poetic account of a ship-burial?), or more complex questions of cause and effect (How influential have the writings of revolutionary intellectuals been upon the course of actual revolutions?), or the relationships between politics and economics (How far does the rise and decline of Spanish power in modern times depend upon the supply of gold from the New World colonies?), or cultural problems (Why did western Europe choose to revive classical Greek and Roman art and literature instead of turning to some other culture or to some altogether new experiment?), those who enjoy history will read almost greedily to discover what they want to know. Having discovered it, they may want to know how we know what we have learned, and may want to turn to those sources closest in time to the persons and questions concerned—to the original words of the participants. To read about Socrates, Columbus, or Churchill is fun; to read their *own* words, to visit with them as it were, is even more so. To see them in context is important; to see how we have taken their thoughts and woven them to purposes of our own is at least equally important. Readers will find their path across the mine-studded fields of history helped just a little by extracts from these voices—voices of the past but also of the present. They can also be helped by outlines, summaries, bibliographies, pictures, maps—devices through which historians share their sense of fun and immediacy with a reader.

In the end, to know the past *is to know ourselves*—not entirely, not enough, but a little better. History can help us to achieve some grace and elegance of action, some cogency and completion of thought, some harmony and tolerance in human relationships. Most of all, history can give us a sense of excitement, a personal zest for watching and perhaps participating in the events around us which will, one day, be history too.

chapter one

THE FIRST CIVILIZATIONS

Within the lifetime of people now only in their thirties, archaeology has revolutionized what we know about the remote past of our earth and the people who live on it with new tools supplied by other sciences. Discoveries continue at a rapid pace. In the 1950s and 1960s no one could have made many of the major statements in this chapter. By the 1990s our successors will have learned enough that is new to dispute what we say here. Archaeology is, once again, at the cutting edge (as well as the beginning) of what we know about our past.

I BEFORE WRITING

History and Prehistory

It may seem strange that our concepts of the distant past are changing much faster than our concepts of the periods much closer to us in time. But when we consider the means by which we know about the past, we can quickly see that this is entirely natural. If we want to know about something that happened, let us say, during the American Revolution, we have the letters of George Washington and his contemporaries, the written records of the British government that tried to suppress the American colonists' rebellion, the proceedings of the Continental Congress, the Declaration of Independence, and literally thousands of other *written sources*—diaries, memoirs, documents, newspapers, propaganda leaflets—that open to us the minds of the people of that time and enable us to work out for ourselves what most probably happened. When we cannot go directly to these sources for history, we have hundreds of books written since the events of the Revolution by historians who have been interested in it and who have set down their views of what happened for us to accept, challenge, and consider. New sources of information may be discovered and fresh light thrown on some event we thought we understood; we may find out that Paul Revere's teacher at school had been reading radical pamphlets (something that previous students had not known) and that this helped prepare Paul as a youth for his famous ride. But the new sources probably would not force us to reject or even to reconsider all that we had learned before they were discovered.

Most of the sources we would read about the American Revolution would be written in English. If we wanted to find out about the part played by Lafayette and Rochambeau, we would soon find ourselves compelled to read documents in French. If we asked ourselves why a Pole, Tadeusz Kościuszko, joined the American side, we might have to learn Polish and Russian and German to find out. If we were interested in the ideas of Thomas Jefferson, we would have to study several of his favorite classical authors, who wrote in Greek or Latin, and though we could find translations available, we might feel it important to read them as Jefferson did, in the original. But whatever the problems of learning languages or of trying to decide which of two contradictory accounts of the same event to accept, we would be dealing with abundant written sources in languages that someone among us knows how to read.

Even for events that took place two thousand years before the American Revolution, or less well known events, or those that took place in Europe or Asia, we would still usually have written sources in Persian, Sanskrit, Greek, Latin or Chinese, sometimes fragmentary instead of full, sometimes too biased to be reliable, but written. Where possible we would supplement these with other evidence: coins with pictures or inscriptions on them that might tell us of matters we could not find out any other way; statues or paintings or poems or songs of the age that might reflect the attitudes of artists and their society more surely than a document; indeed, any remnant that we could find from the period and the place to supplement our written sources.

But suppose our written sources are written in a language that no one can read? Or suppose we have no written sources at all? As we move backward in time through human history these problems confront us more and more urgently. Over the last couple of centuries the discovery of texts written in both a known and

Years B.C.	Prehistoric Peoples
	Food-Gathering Peoples
1,000,000 and before	Australopithicenes
400,000	Homo erectus
110,000	Neanderthal man
35,000	Homo sapiens
28,000	Beginning of cave painting
10,000	Retreat of glaciers
	Food-Raising Era
8,000	Essentially modern climate
7,000	Agricultural villages in Near East
	Civilization
Just before 3,000	Cities in Mesopotamia Kingdom of Egypt

SOURCE: Chester G. Starr, *Early Man: Prehistory and the Civilizations of the Ancient Near East* (Oxford: Oxford University Press, 1973), p. 4.

a previously unknown language has enabled scholars to read the language of the Egyptians and those of the peoples of the ancient Mesopotamian river valleys in the Near East, although uncertainties often remain. Brilliant use of the techniques of cryptography in the 1950s cracked one of the two scripts commonly used in ancient Crete and on the Greek mainland. But an earlier Cretan script remains to be convincingly deciphered. Much work must still be done before scholars can confidently read Etruscan—the language, written in Greek letters, of the people that ruled in Italy before the Romans.

People lived on earth for many thousands of years before they learned to write at all. Only their skeletons, the bones of animals, and some of the things they made remain to tell us about the first humans. They are our only sources. Recent developments in science—especially the carbon-14 technique whereby radioactive carbon is used to date ancient objects within a couple of centuries—have helped straighten out chronology. But scholars will continue to find new objects and new ways of dating them that will enable our successors to write with more certainty than we can about our earliest ancestors.

The Old Stone Age

In the seventeenth century Archbishop James Ussher (1581-1656) of the Church of England carefully worked out from data given in the Bible what he believed to be the precise date of the creation of the world by God. It was, he said, 4004 B.C. If we add the sixteen hundred or so years since the birth of Christ, we could conclude that the earth is under six thousand years old. We smile now at the generations that accepted Ussher's views—although nearly everyone did so until the nineteenth century—because we now believe that the earth is billions of years old and that organic life may go back several billion years.

Beginning in 1951, a series of archaeological digs in equatorial east central Africa in and around Olduvai Gorge turned up fragments of a small creature that lived between nineteen and fourteen million years ago, for convenience called *Kenyapithecus* ("Kenya ape"), who seems to have made crude tools. Kenya ape may not be a direct human ancestor, but like us may have branched off from a primate ten million years older still, and yet more primitive. By about two million years ago a creature more like our ideas of humankind had made its appearance, *Homo habilis*, ("the skillful one"). A mere quarter of a million years later came *Zinjanthropus*, who was perhaps related to a humanlike animal about the size of a chimpanzee, though with a larger brain, called *Australopithecus*, a term derived from Greek and meaning "southern ape." *Australopithecus* may have been a vegetarian (to judge by its teeth) and seems to have ceased evolving and come to a dead end, while *Homo habilis*, who ate meat, continued to evolve in the direction of biologically modern humans, *Homo sapiens* ("the one who knows"). All these humanlike animals had larger skulls with more brains than apes. In another three-quarters of a million years (approximately a million years ago), *Homo habilis* began to look like a being long known as Java man, who lived about 700,000 B.C. First found in Java in the late 1880s, *Pithecanthropus erectus* ("apeman that walks erect") is now termed *Homo erectus*. A somewhat later stage is represented by Peking man of about 500,000 B.C., who advanced well beyond *Homo habilis*.

We need to know more about the stages by which *Homo erectus* evolved into *Homo sapiens*, who appeared first in Europe only about thirty-seven thousand years ago. *Homo sapiens* came upon a land of forests and plains that had already been occupied for perhaps a hundred thousand years by another *Homo erectus*, Neanderthal man, named for the Rhineland valley where their remains were first discovered but spread far more widely, leaving remains, for example, also in the mountains of what is today eastern Iraq. Probably far less apelike than the traditional reconstructions of its skull have portrayed, Neanderthal man was not yet *Homo sapiens*. We cannot yet locate Neanderthals accurately on a hypothetical family tree, but they probably represent another offshoot from the main trunk.

Neanderthal culture was based on hunting and food gathering. They possessed stone tools and weapons, apparently cooked their meat (their predecessors ate it raw), wore skins, and commemorated their dead through ritual burials. However, what we know remains sophisticated guesswork, based on sixty-eight specific sites. Unless scholars can prevent the destruction of these and other archaeological locations, we may never have satisfactory scientific answers to such questions as: What do we mean by "human" in such a context? Does the size of the brain—customarily used to denote evolution—really tell us much about how humans came to use tools and develop a desire for decoration? There is no point at which "humans appeared" on earth, though for convenience we generally accept *Homo sapiens*—the "wise one," or "one who knows," which means "one who thinks"—as a convenient point of departure.

We know so little about what was happening during those hundreds of thousands of years that for the historian (as distinguished from the anthropologist) almost all of this time belongs to *prehistory*—that is, history before humanity left written records. During those long, long centuries the advance of the human animal was enormously slow. The first real tools were stones that were used to chip other stones into useful instruments. And it was by those stone weapons and tools that early humans lived for hundreds of thousands of years.

Archaeologists have named the early periods of human culture from the materials used for weapons and tools. During the Old Stone (Paleolithic) Age, roughly before 8000 B.C., give or take a few thousand years according to the region being described, people used chipped stone tools. About 8000 B.C. in some places, much later in others, the development of farming and the use of more sophisticated stone implements marked the beginning of the New Stone (Neolithic) Age. Then, about 3000 B.C. the invention of bronze (an alloy of copper and tin) led to the Bronze Age and even greater transitions to new forms of human life and society. Still later, further experiments with metals ushered in the Iron Age.

Paleolithic people left remains scattered widely in Europe and Asia and took refuge in Africa from the glaciers that periodically moved south over the northern continents and made life impossible there. Wherever they went, they hunted to eat, and fought and killed their enemies. They learned how to cook their food, how to take shelter from the cold in caves, and eventually how to specialize their tools. They made bone needles with which to sew animal hides into clothes with animal sinews; they made hatchets, spears, arrowheads, awls.

They also created art. At Lascaux in southwest France and at Altamira in nearby northern Spain, Paleolithic artists left remarkable paintings in limestone caves, using brilliant colors to depict animals important to them: deer, bison, horses. The Lascaux cave paintings, found in 1940, were closed to the public in 1960 to protect them against the thousands of tourists they attracted. They are the most valuable documentation we have on the life of Cro-Magnon men and women, a type of *Homo sapiens* who apparently stood fully erect.

Ancient cave art, not having been exposed to the weather or to vandalism, has survived over thousands of years. One of the greatest series of cave paintings is at Lascaux, in present-day France. This bull from Lascaux was painted on limestone around 12,000 B.C.

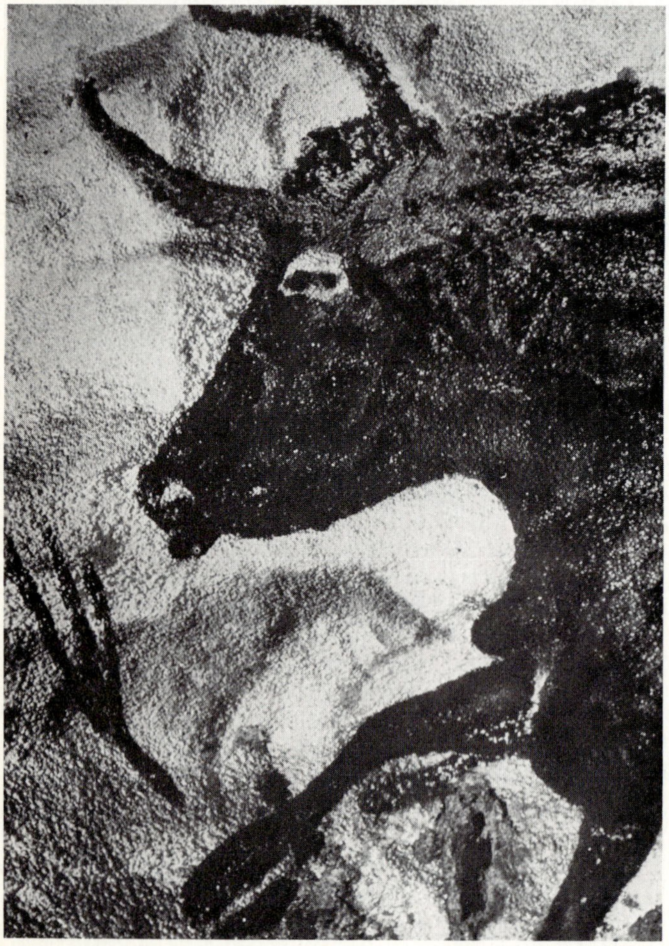

We can only guess why the Paleolithic artist painted the pictures. Did the artist think that putting animals on the walls would lead to better hunting? Would their pictures give the hunters power over them, and so ensure the supply of food? Were the different animals also totems of different families or clans? Sometimes on the walls of the caves we find paintings of human hands, often with a finger or fingers missing. Were these hands simple testimony of appreciation of one of humanity's most extraordinary physical gifts: the hand with its opposable thumb (not found in apes), which alone made tool-making possible? Or were they efforts to ward off evil spirits by holding up the palm or making a ritual gesture? Or were they prayers by hunters and warriors to avert the mutilation of their fingers or to retain their strength despite some mutilation that they had already suffered? We do not know.

Besides the cave paintings and Venuses (small female statuettes) and tools, made with such variety and with such increasing skill of manufacture from about 35,000 B.C. to about 8000 B.C. archaeology has yielded up a rich variety of other finds, especially concerning the development of the calendar, by which early people could record a sense of time. Bone tools found in Africa and Europe show markings whose sequence and intervals may record lunar periods. Sometimes only one or two lunar months had been observed, sometimes six, sometimes an entire year. Eventually, the Paleolithic craftsman learned to make the notations more complex, sometimes engraving them in a crosshatched pattern that looks like mere decoration until one learns to read it, sometimes adding extra angled marks at important dates.

Once we realize that late Old Stone Age peoples may well have been keeping a kind of calendar to enable them to predict the regular seasonal changes from year to year to year, and therefore they were presumably regulating their hunting life and their other activities, such as the preparation of skins for clothing, we get such a vivid new perspective on the quality of their minds and their perception of the importance of time in their life that the "mystery" of their extraordinary skills becomes far less mysterious. Where we find on the same piece of Paleolithic ivory from southwest France a budding flower, sprouting plants, grass, snakes, a salmon, and a seal—which appeared in spring in the local rivers—we may have an object that symbolically represents the earth's reawakening after winter. When such symbols of spring appear with the lunar calendric notation, we are looking at something very like an illustrated calendar.

In the same way, perhaps the stone female images mark the procession of the seasons, of fertility, conception, and birth. Certain animals—reindeer, bison, horses—appear on the artifacts associated with

The Tower of Babel was meant to represent the origins of diverse languages. A tower was said to have been constructed to heaven in ancient Shinar. Here the Flemish artist Pieter Brueghel the Elder uses the tower as a metaphor; he shows it in a sixteenth-century context, as a honeycomb of tiers on which an army of antlike workers swarm, while a nobleman inspects the project.

females; others—bears and lions—with males. Some representations can be interpreted as sacrifices. Late Old Stone Age people apparently had a mythology that involved tales of the hunt, successful and unsuccessful, a ritual that involved killing and sacrifice, and a deep awareness of the passing of time in the world around them and in the bodies of animals and of humans. A nude figure of a woman holding a bison horn that looks like a crescent moon and is marked with thirteen lines (the number of lunar months in a year) may be humanity's first recognizable goddess. She may be the forerunner of the bare-breasted Neolithic moon goddess long known as the Mistress of the Animals, who appears with crescent, fish, flower, plant, bird, tree, and snake, and with a consort who plays sun to her moon and hunts the animals of nature and of myth. Though the people of the Old Stone Age remain dim and remote to us, these researches for the first time make them more recognizably human.

The New Stone Age

The advance from the Old Stone Age (Paleolithic) to the New (Neolithic) was marked by certain major changes, all found first in the Near East. One of these was the domestication of animals for food. Humans had tamed dogs and used them in the hunt long before. But when they kept goats, pigs, sheep, and the ancestors of our cows in pens, they could eat them when their meat was young and tender, without having to hunt them down when they were hardest to overtake. Parallel with this went the first domestication of plants for food—a kind of wheat and barley. Finally—and this always seems to have been the last step—temporary shelter was replaced by houses with some sense of permanence. By these changes, humanity made the transition to the New Stone Age.

Accompanying these fundamental steps went the practice of a new technology, the baking of clay vessels—pots and bowls and storage jars—which were much easier to make than stone ones. It is chiefly by studying the surviving varieties of such clay vessels and their fragments, and the types of glazes and decorations the potters used, that modern scholars have been able to date the sites where ancient people lived before writing, and often even later. Recent excavations in the Near East have pushed back our previous earliest Neolithic dates. With the boundaries between periods thus in flux, it is probably better here not to try to fix any firm boundaries between late Paleolithic and early Neolithic.

At Jericho, in the Jordan Valley, during the 1950s, archaeologists excavated a town radiocarbon-dated at about 7800 B.C. that had extended over about eight acres and included perhaps three thousand inhabitants. These people lived in round houses with conical roofs—the oldest permanent houses known—and they had a large, columned building in which were found many mud-modeled figurines of animals and modeled statues of a man, a woman, and a male child. It was almost surely a temple of some kind. All this dates from a time when people did not yet know how to make pots, which appear only at a later stage.

In Çatal Hüyük in southern Turkey, discovered in 1961 and dating to 6500 B.C., the people had a wide variety of pottery, grew their own grain, kept sheep, and wove their wool into textiles. A sculpture of a female giving birth to a child, a bull's head, boars' heads with women's breasts running in rows along the lower jaws, and many small statuettes were all found together in what we can be sure was a shrine. A bull and a double ax painted on a wall seem to look forward to the main features of a better-known religion of ancient Crete, as we shall see.

Far to the east, in modern Iraq (ancient Mesopotamia, "between the rivers" Tigris and Euphrates) lay Jarmo, dated about 4500 B.C., a third Neolithic settlement. A thousand years later than Jarmo, about 3550 B.C., and far to the south, at Uruk on the banks of the Euphrates River, farmers were using the plow to scratch the soil before sowing their seeds, and were already keeping the business accounts of their temple in simple picturewriting. This was the great leap forward that took human beings out of prehistory and into history. Similar advances are also found in Egypt at roughly the same time. But archaeology seems to show that Mesopotamia took the lead, and indeed that it was from Mesopotamia that major cultural contributions—especially the all-important art of writing—penetrated into Egypt.

During the 1960s, still farther to the east in various parts of modern Iran, archaeologists found several of these early Neolithic sites, some of which seem to go back in time as far as Jericho or even before—although no city so large or complex has been found from the eighth millennium B.C. The sites are scattered, and many of them are located in the highlands, indicating that the Neolithic revolution was not necessarily confined, as had

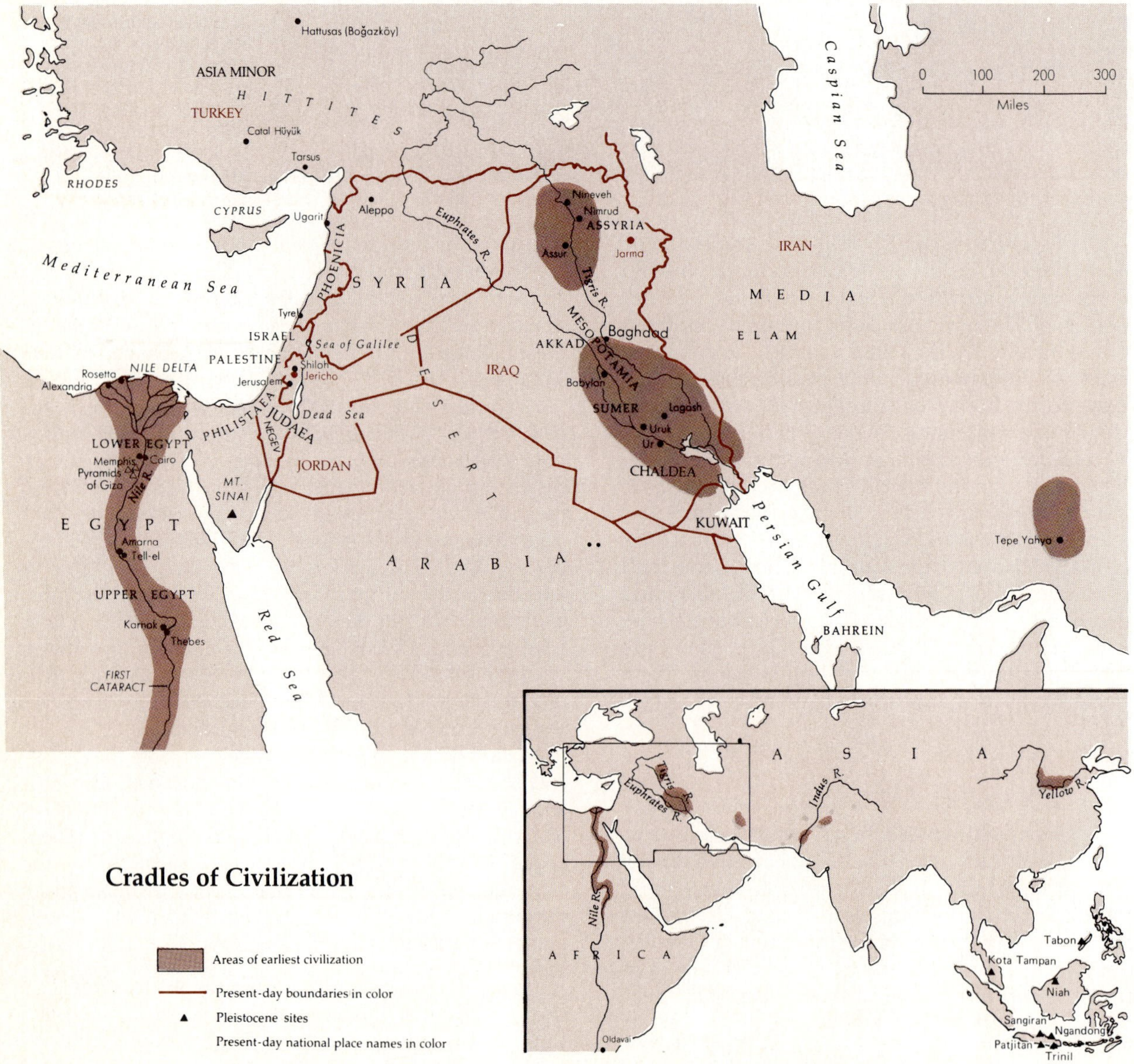

Cradles of Civilization

PLACE NAMES IN HISTORY

The mention here of Uruk provides an opportunity to discuss a special problem in history, namely that places change their names. In the Bible the city called Uruk, its ancient Sumerian name, was referred to as Erech, one of the cities of Nimrod. Today the same location appears on the map as Warka. Geographically each of the three names designates the same place; historically the names indicate different times, just as present-day Leningrad was once the czarist capital of St. Petersburg.

Furthermore, the choice of a name may suggest acceptance of one position or another in a controversy, as when the British refer to the Falkland Islands, and the Argentines (taking the name from the French) speak of Las Malvinas. Throughout this text the place name appropriate to the time under discussion will be used; for example, Russia and the Soviet Union are *not* synonymous terms. Consult a good atlas if you are not sure of how names convey political values. However, where most appropriate or essential, the text will refer to changes of name to avoid the more obvious confusions.

Pronunciation is another problem for historians because the same name takes on different pronunciations as languages change. The currently accepted pronunciation will be supplied in the index where it seems necessary. But the authors will assume that readers can pronounce, or can learn the correct pronunciation by consulting a good dictionary or encyclopaedia, names common to our culture, such as Dante, Goethe, Freud. Any student of history must, therefore, have at hand a good atlas and a substantial dictionary, for no text can adequately substitute for these tools of civilization.

usually been thought, to river valleys. Many of these Iranian discoveries are still unpublished, and much work remains to be done, especially as Iran is now closed to continued research. But from 6000 B.C. there are several sites in northwest Iran rather like Jarmo, giving plenty of evidence of domesticated animals and grains. And even earlier, perhaps around 7000, in southwest Iran very near the Mesopotamian eastern border, there are mud-brick houses and the same clear evidence of goat- and sheep-raising and cereal cultivation.

In south central Iran a fresh site was discovered in 1967 at Tepe Yahya, where the earliest settlement in a large mound proved to be a Neolithic village of about 4500 B.C. Here, along with the animal bones and cereal remains, archaeologists found in a mud-brick storage area not only pottery and small sharpened flints set in a bone handle to make a sickle, but also an extraordinary figurine sculptured of dark green stone, which in both material and subject is more complex than anything found on an earlier date. It appears that Tepe Yahya, a center of soapstone manufacturing, served to link Mesopotamia to the cultures of the Indus Valley.

The Neolithic people of the Near East were not necessarily any more intelligent than those elsewhere. Indeed, Neolithic remains also have been found in many places around the Mediterranean and far to the north. But the climate in those places was far less favorable, and even when Neolithic people managed to triumph over the environment—as in lake settlements in Switzerland, where they built frame houses on piles over the water—the triumph came later (in this case about 2500 B.C.). It was the inhabitants of the more favored regions who got to the great discoveries first. It was they who learned copper-smelting and the other arts of metallurgy, and who thus led the Stone Age into the Bronze Age. It was they who first lived in cities.

Writing, metallurgy, and urban life are among the early marks of civilization. Soon after these phenomena appeared in the Tigris-Euphrates valleys, along the Nile, and in Iran, they appeared also in the valley of the Indus, along Chinese rivers, in Southeast Asia, and in South and Central America. In North America, too, recent discoveries—first of Folsom man, who made weapons of flint, and now of the great complexities of the Chaco Canyon culture of present-day New Mexico—have carried our knowledge back twenty thousand years and more.

II THE VALLEY PEOPLES AND IRAN

Mesopotamia and Elam

Sumerians The most recent discoveries have led some scholars to believe that the first Mesopotamian inventors of writing may have been a people the later

Babylonians called Subarians. Traditionally they came from the north and coincided with Uruk in the south. In any case, by about 3100 B.C. they were apparently subjugated in southern Mesopotamia by the Sumerians, whose name became synonymous for the region immediately north of the Persian Gulf, in the fertile lower valleys of the Tigris and Euphrates. Here the Sumerians were already well established by the year 3000. They had invented bronze, an alloy that could be cast in molds, and they made tools and weapons of it. They lived in cities. They had begun to accumulate and use capital. They apparently turned the Subarians into slaves, and the word (compare the derivation of *slave* and *slav* in our Western tongues) took on precise economic and social connotations. Perhaps most important, the Sumerians adapted writing (probably from the Subarians) into a flexible tool of communication.

We have known about the Sumerians for only a hundred years. Archaeologists working at Nineveh in northern Mesopotamia in the midnineteenth century found many inscribed clay tablets. Some they could decipher because the language was a Semitic one (Akkadian), on which scholars had already been working for a generation. But other tablets were inscribed in another language that was not Semitic, previously unknown. Because these inscriptions made reference to the king of Sumer and Akkad, a scholar suggested that the new language be called Sumerian.

But it was not until the 1890s that archaeologists digging in city-states well to the south of Nineveh found many thousands of tablets inscribed in Sumerian only. Because the Akkadians thought of Sumerian as a classical language (as we think of Greek or Latin), they taught it to educated persons and they put vocabularies, translation exercises, and other aids on tablets to study in both Akkadian and Sumerian. Working from known Akkadian to previously unknown Sumerian, modern scholars since the 1890s have pretty well learned how to read the Sumerian language. Vast quantities of tablets in Sumerian have been unearthed during the intervening years from numerous excavations.

Over the thousand years between 3000 and 2000 B.C.

This group of Sumerian statuettes was found near modern Baghdad. They are from the temple to the god Abu, lord of vegetation; their height and dress indicate that they represent gods, priests, and worshipers. These Tel Asmar figures date from around 2600 B.C. This collection presents one problem of studying the ancient past, for while the group shown here was meant to be viewed together, the collection is split between the Oriental Institute in Chicago and the Iraq Museum in Baghdad.

the Sumerians developed a phonetic alphabet. With a reed pen they impressed litle wedge-shaped marks into a wet clay tablet, producing a script that we call cuneiform—a language once lost to us and now recovered—from the Latin *cuneus*, meaning a wedge. The first thousand years of Sumerian history we know from tens of thousands of these tablets, which are mostly economic or administrative records. From the second thousand years (after 2000 B.C.) we have five thousand tablets that provide us with purely literary texts, some short, some very long, some not yet transcribed or translated.

The earliest Sumerians governed themselves through a council of elders, who derived their authority in turn from a general assembly of all adult free males. This assembly, which decided on matters of war and peace, sometimes granted supreme authority to one leader for a limited time. This arrangement—which seems "modern" and even "democratic" to us—apparently did not last long and was replaced by one-man rule in each city. But the human ruler acted only as the representative on earth of the god of the city. In this capacity the ruler built temples to the god to keep him appeased and to obtain divine protection against the torrential floods that swept down the river valleys in the springtime, with disastrous results for the people in their way.

The lives and religion and literature of the people of Mesopotamia were pervaded by terror of these floods; the story of Noah and the ark in *Genesis* echoes the ancient tradition of the Sumerians that told of a single disastrous flood from which only a remnant of the people was saved, and from which (about 2900 B.C.) all subsequent events were dated. The Sumerians devised an elaborate system of canals to irrigate the fields and to control the force of the floods. Toward the south, near the Persian Gulf, the problem also became one of drainage, to halt the inward flow of salt water that would ruin the fields.

Gudea was ruler of the city of Lagash around 2100 B.C. Nearly twenty statues of him, dating from the Sumerian period, provide both artifactual knowledge—that is, knowledge derived from the physical nature of the object itself—and historical information, as derived from the inscription on Gudea's garments.

By the toil of many centuries, the Sumerians transformed the bleak marshes of the river valleys into fertile farmland, dotted with prosperous cities, each with its own political bureaucracy and religious institutions. As with all human societies, each passed through occasional oppressions, upheavals, and political overturns, many of which are recorded by surviving inscriptions. (The earliest known inscription recording the ambition of one city ruler to dominate the entire region—to be the first "universal" monarch in history—dates from about 2350 B.C.) The Sumerians also had to fight against infiltrating Semites from the Arabian deserts to the west and the hills to the north. They campaigned eastward too, against Elam, the peoples living in what today is western Iran.

About 2300, Sargon, king of Akkad, a Semite from the north, conquered the Sumerian ruler of Uruk. Sargon and his successors called themselves kings of Sumer and Akkad, perhaps indicating that a fusion of the non-Semitic Sumerians and the Semitic Akkadians had begun. By about 2100, when most scholars date the end of the early Bronze Age, Sargon's descendants had lost their power, and for a time there was no force to unify the tiny states.

Taking the lead against invaders, Gudea, ruler of the city of Lagash, united the Sumerians about 2050 B.C. Soon after he died, Ur replaced Lagash as the capital city, and for a century its rulers played the role of universal monarch. They again called themselves kings of Sumer and Akkad. Much of what we know about the Sumerians comes from the recent systematic excavation of Ur. More recently, a portion of a series of statutes promulgated by the ruler Ur-Nammu (about 2000 B.C.) has been discovered that provided fixed punishment for certain crimes, such as a fine of five shekels of silver for the rape of a virgin slave girl without her owner's consent. Ur-Nammu is thus the first known true lawgiver for an entire people, even though he did not propound a systematic code, since all the precedents in his code were expressed in the conditional—that is, the code's coverage was erratic and concerned with problems of precedents. Ur enjoyed a century of great prosperity based on farflung trade by sea in textiles and metals, a carefully recorded systematic tax system, and a revival of learning. But a decline set in, in part because Ur had taken on too many responsibilities, and outlying cities began to usurp the power they saw as overly centralized in Ur.

Sumer was a *hydraulic society*—that is, one based on the centralized control of irrigation and flood management by government. When its leaders could no longer demonstrate this control, the compact, agriculturally linked city-states began to fragment (as they also did later, in China and among the Aztecs). Ur's subject cities fell away; invading Elamites from the east destroyed it. With Ur's destruction and the end of Sumerian power, the center of political might shifted to the north.

Besides their city gods, the Sumerians worshiped a god of the heavens, a god of the region between heaven and earth (the air, hence storms and winds), and a god of earth. Another trinity included gods of the sun and moon and a goddess of the morning star, who was also associated with fertility. With this female deity was associated a young male god who died and was reborn as a symbol of the seasons.

Here, in the first religion recorded in sources that we can read and therefore interpret more fully, we find elements common to all subsequent human efforts to deal with the concept of a higher being or beings. For instance, it was Enki, god of earth and of wisdom, who poured water into the two great fertilizing rivers, Tigris and Euphrates, and stocked them with fish; who created grain, filled the land with cattle, built houses and canals, and set subgods over each enterprise.

The Sumerian gods were portrayed in human form and lived recognizably human lives, with rivalries among themselves. Sumerians also believed in a multitude of demons, mostly bad. From the beginning, they used various arts to foretell the future. The entrails of slaughtered sheep or goats were carefully observed, and meanings were ascribed to their shapes. Interpreting dreams was also important, and the stars were observed ever more scientifically, though always to obtain omens. Because the temple of the city god (and other gods) actually owned most of the land, most of the population worked as serfs of the temple. But the produce of the land was distributed as pay to them.

Life was highly diversified, if not yet truly specialized; blacksmiths, carpenters, and merchants appeared alongside the hunters, farmers, and shepherds of the older days. Fathers had many rights over their children. The society was monogamous, and women held a high position. Punishments seemed mild and specific relative to those found later in the Babylonian society that grew out of the Sumerian; in Sumer they consisted mostly of fines.

In their epic poetry the Sumerians celebrated the brave exploits of Gilgamesh, a mighty hero two-thirds divine and one third human. He undertook perilous journeys, overcame dreadful monsters, and performed great feats of strength. But even Gilgamesh, strong though he was, had to die; and ultimately a realistic tone, typical of the society, pervades Sumerian literature, its hymns, lamentations, prayers, fables, and even schoolboy compositions. A Sumerian proverb says,

THE EPIC OF GILGAMESH

One major source for the biblical account of Noah's ark and the great flood is the great epic of Gilgamesh, the king of Uruk. This epic predates the epics of Homer by 1500 years and is, in the eyes of many scholars, the first major contribution to world literature. Composed about 2000 B.C., the epic tells of the Great Flood in the following words:

For six days and six nights the winds blew, torrent and tempest and flood overwhelmed the world, tempest and flood raged together like warring hosts. When the seventh day dawned the storm from the south subsided, the sea grew calm, the flood was stilled; I looked at the face of the world and there was silence, all mankind was turned to clay. The surface of the sea stretched as flat as a roof-top; I opened a hatch and the light fell on my face. Then I bowed low, I sat down and I wept, the tears streamed down my face, for on every side was the waste of water. I looked for land in vain, but fourteen leagues distant there appeared a mountain, and there the boat grounded; on the mountain of Nisse she held fast and did not budge. A third day, and a fourth day, she held fast on the mountain and did not budge; a fifth day and a sixth day she held fast on the mountain. When the seventh day dawned, I loosed a dove and we let her go. She flew away, but finding no resting-place she returned. Then I loosed a swallow, and she flew away, but finding no resting-place she returned. I loosed a raven, she saw that the water had retreated, she ate, she flew around, she cawed, and she did not come back. Then I threw everything open to the four winds, I made a sacrifice and poured out a libation on the mountain top. Seven and again seven cauldrons I set up on their stands, I heaped on wood and cane and cedar and myrtle. When the gods smelled the sweet savour, they gathered like flies over the sacrifice. Then at last, Ishtar also came.

Quoted with permission from N.K. Sandars, *The Epic of Gilgamesh: An English Version with an Introduction*, rev. ed. (New York: Penguin Books, 1972), p. 111.

"Praise a young man, and he will do whatever you want; throw a crust to a dog, and he will wag his tail before you." In Sumerian literature we can recognize a character similar to the future Old Testament Job, and one moral is the same: glorify god and await the end of life, which may set you free from earthly suffering.

Sumerian art and architecture were largely religious, official in intent, and impersonal in style. They changed very little during more than a thousand years. The Sumerians built their temples of baked brick. In the shrine was an altar against a wall; other rooms and an outer courtyard were added later. The most striking feature of the temple was that the entire structure was set upon a terrace, the first stage toward a multiplication of terraces, each above and smaller than the last, with a sanctuary at the top, reached by stairs from terrace to terrace. This was the *ziggurat*, the typical Mesopotamian temple, whose construction itself suggests a hierarchical Sumerian social order. It was a great ziggurat that suggested the tower of Babel to the author of *Genesis*.

Sumerian tombs were simple chambers, often filled with objects intended for use in the afterlife, which Sumerians envisioned as eternally sad. Their statuary consisted of clothed human figures, solemn and stiff, with large, staring eyes. Gods were shown as larger than kings, and ordinary human beings as smaller, for many were slaves. On monumental slabs (*steles*), on plaques, and especially on seals, the Sumerians showed themselves skillful at carving in relief—clear, informative, stiff, yet human.

Akkadians: Babylonians and Assyrians The successors of the Sumerians as rulers of Mesopotamia were Akkadian-speaking Semites to whom belonged first the Babylonians and then their successors, the Assyrians, both originally descended from nomads of the Arabian desert. They owed an enormous debt to Sumer. Power first passed to them with Sargon the Great (2300 B.C.) and returned to them after an interlude (about 2000 B.C.) with the invasion from the west of a people called the Amorites.

Since 1935 excavations at Mari in the middle Euphrates valley have turned up a palace with more than 260 rooms containing many thousands of tablets, mostly from the period between 1750 and 1700 B.C. These tablets were the royal archives, and they include the official letters to the king from his own local officials scattered throughout his territories and from other rulers of local city-states and principalities. Among the correspondents was an Amorite prince named Hammurabi, who from c 1792 to 1750 B.C., by warfare and diplomacy made his own Babylonian kingdom supreme in Mesopotamia and reunited it. His descendants retained Babylon and the area around it down to 1530, but had to give up Hammurabi's great conquests.

Hammurabi's famous code of law was applied from the Persian Gulf to the Mediterranean Sea. Though modeled on its Sumerian predecessors, its punishments were much harsher. "If a son has struck his father," the code reads, "they shall cut off his hand." Yet its author, the king, boasted less of his warlike deeds than of the peace and prosperity he had brought. Inscribed on a pillar eight feet tall beneath a sculptured relief showing the king standing reverently before the seated sun god, the code reveals a strongly stratified society: a patrician who put out the eye of a patrician would have his own eye put out; a patrician who put out the eye of a plebeian only had to pay a fine. But even the plebeian had rights that, to some degree, protected him against violence from his betters. Polygamy and divorce were recognized. One clause says, "If a merchant lends silver to a trader without interest, and if the trader loses on his investment, he need return to the lender only the capital he has borrowed." (The word used for *capital* means head, just as our word *capital* is itself derived from the Latin *caput*, meaning head.) The earliest concepts of a capitalist system can also be found in Hammurabi's code. It is also significant that the scribe used not the Akkadian but the Sumerian word for *silver*, to make the language sound more learned and classical. In its vocabulary as in its concept of the social order, the code reflects the continuing Sumerian impact on the Akkadian-speaking Babylonians.

New nomads, this time from the east (Iran), the Kassites, shattered Babylonian power about 1530 B.C. After four centuries of relatively peaceful Kassite rule, supremacy in Mesopotamia gradually passed to the far more warlike Semitic Assyrians, whose power had been rising, with occasional setbacks, for several centuries in their great northern city of Assur. About 1100 B.C. their ruler Tiglath-pileser reached both the Black Sea and the Mediterranean on a conquering expedition north and west, after which he boasted that he had become "lord of the world." Assyrian militarism was harsh, and the conquerors regularly transported into captivity entire populations of defeated cities. By the eighth century B.C. the Assyrian state was a kind of dual monarchy; Tiglath-pileser III (744-727), their ruler, also took the title of ruler of Babylonia, thus consciously accepting the Babylonian tradition. He added enormous territory to the Neo-Assyrian empire. But Chaldean tribes resisted Assyrian rule over the whole of Babylonia, and in turn the mighty Assyrian Empire fell to a new power, the Medes (Iranians related to the Persians), who took Nineveh (612 B.C.) with Babylonian and Palestinian help.

For less than a century thereafter (612-538 B.C.) Chaldean Babylonia experienced a rapid, brilliant revival, during which King Nebuchadnezzar built temples and palaces, made Babylon a wonder of the world with its famous hanging gardens, overthrew Jerusalem, and took the Hebrews into captivity. But in 539 King Belshazzar, having lost the support of the priesthood, had to surrender all of Babylonia to Cyrus the Great of Persia, ending the history of the Mesopotamian empires and of the last Akkadian state after 2500 years.

In religion as in all other aspects of life, the Babylonians and Assyrians took much from the Sumerians. The cosmic gods remained the same, but the local gods were different; under Hammurabi one of them, Marduk, was exalted over all other gods and kept that supremacy thereafter. In Babylonian-Assyrian belief, demons became more numerous and more powerful, and a special class of priests was needed to fight them. Magic practices multiplied. All external events—an encounter with an animal, a sprained wrist, the position and color of the stars at a vital moment—had implications for one's own future that needed to be discovered. Starting with the observation of the stars for such magical purposes, the Babylonians developed substantial knowledge of celestial movement and the mathematics to go with it. They even managed to predict eclipses. They could add, subtract, multiply, divide, and extract roots. They could solve equations and measure both plane areas and solid volumes. But their astronomy and their mathematics remained in the service of astrology and divination. So too did jewelry-making, goldsmithing, and ivory-carving, which reached new and extraordinarily beautiful heights, as shown especially in the archaeological finds at Nimrud.

Egypt

Character of the Society What the Tigris and the Euphrates rivers did for Mesopotamia, the Nile River did for Egypt. Over thousands of years the people along the Nile had slowly learned to take advantage of the annual summer flood by tilling their fields to receive the silt-laden river waters, and by regulating its flow. About 3000 B.C., at approximately the time that the Sumerian civilization emerged in Mesopotamia, the Egyptians had reached a comparable stage of development. Much better known to us than Mesopotamia, Egypt was another ancient valley civilization that made major contributions to our own.

Egypt, though also a hydraulic society based on river-valley agriculture and its resulting slow centralization, was more dynamic, perhaps more willing—especially as its cities grew—to entertain new ideas than the Mesopotamian states had been. The Egyptians regarded life after death as a happy continuation of life on earth with all its fleshly pleasures, not as a dismal eternal sojourn in the dust. The Mesopotamian rulers—both the early city lords and the later kings who aspired to universal monarchy—were agents of the gods on earth; the Egyptian rulers from the beginning were themselves regarded as gods. The Mesopotamians were conscious of history, the Egyptians less so.

Because Egyptian territory consisted of the long strip along the banks of the Nile, it was always hard to unify. At the very beginning (3000 B.C.) there were two rival kingdoms: Lower and Upper Egypt. Lower Egypt was the Nile Delta (so called because it is shaped like the Greek letter of that name), the triangle of land nearest the Mediterranean where the river splits into several streams and flows into the sea. Upper Egypt was the land along the course of the river for eight hundred miles between the Delta and the First Cataract. Periodically the two regions were unified into one kingdom, but the ruler, who called himself king of Upper and Lower Egypt, by his very title recognized that his realms consisted of two somewhat disparate entities: one looking toward the Mediterranean and outward to other sea-girt civilizations; and the other more isolated by its deserts, more self-regarding, more inclined to resist new thoughts, using its isolation as a form of protection. The first unifier, perhaps mythical, was Menes, whose reign (about 2850 B.C.) is taken by scholars as the start of the first standard division of Egyptian history, the Old Kingdom (2700-2160).

Old, Middle, and New Kingdoms When the king is god, his subjects need only listen to his commands to feel sure they know the divine will. As each Egyptian king died, a great sepulchral monument, often in the form of a pyramid, told his subjects that he had gone to join his predecessors in the community of gods. The largest of the pyramids took several generations to build and involved the continual labor of thousands of men—a sign that the rulers of society accepted and took pride in the divinity of their lineage. A highly centralized bureaucracy carried out the commands of the king. A stratified society worked for him. His forces advanced at times westward into the Libyan desert, and at other times—drawn by the pull exerted on every ruler of Egypt from Menes to the present—eastward and northward into Palestine.

The Old Kingdom was first disturbed and eventually shattered by a growing tendency among district governors to pass their offices on to their sons, who in turn tended to regard themselves as hereditary rulers and thus to weaken the central authority. The priests of the sun had also made good their claims to special privileges that helped diminish royal power. After a disorderly interval of perhaps two centuries, a new dynasty (the eleventh of thirty in Egyptian history) restored unity in what is known as the Middle Kingdom (2134-1786), distinguished for its rulers' land-reclamation policies and its victories abroad.

To the south hostile Nubians (from the modern Sudan) were defeated and their movements controlled by the building of frontier fortresses. Palestine and Syria came under Egyptian influence. The bureaucracy flourished. Thebes ceased to be the capital, as a new city was founded south of Memphis, from which government could be exercised more effectively. The provincial governorship became hereditary, but had to be confirmed by the king, and the king's son at the age of twenty-one became co-ruler with his father. The king himself was less remote and more eager to be regarded as the shepherd of his people.

Secessionist movements and growing internal weakness combined with a foreign invasion and conquest to put an end to the Middle Kingdom. The conquerors were called Hyksos, Asian nomads of uncertain Amorite origin who imported the horse-drawn war chariot and perhaps the bow. The Egyptians hated their rule, which lasted about a century, and eventually rallied behind a new dynasty (the seventeenth) to drive out the invaders. By about 1558 and the eighteenth dynasty the task was accomplished and the New Kingdom (1575-1087) solidly established.*

The five centuries of the New Kingdom saw extraordinary advances. In foreign affairs, the Egyptians engaged in a struggle for Syria and Palestine, not only with the great powers of Mesopotamia but with the mountain and desert peoples who lived between the two great valley civilizations. The Egyptian ruler (now called pharaoh) Thutmose I reached the Euphrates on the east and marched far south into Nubia. Thutmose III (c 1469-1436) fought seventeen campaigns in the east, crossing the Euphrates to defeat his Mesopotamian enemies on their own soil. The walls of the great temple of Karnak preserve his carved account of his military achievements and the record of the enormous tribute paid him by his conquered enemies. (It is his obelisk, wrongly known as Cleopatra's Needle, that today stands in Central Park in New York.) The Egyptians established their own network of local governors throughout the conquered territories, but ruled mildly, and did not, as the Assyrians were soon to do, deport whole masses of the population into slavery. Nonetheless, the eighteenth dynasty embarked on a vast building program that depended on a ready supply of forced labor.

It was the pharaoh Amenhotep IV (1364-1350) who caused a major internal upheaval in the successful New Kingdom by challenging the priests of the sun god Amen, who had become a powerful privileged class. Amenhotep urged the substitution for Amen of the sun disk, Aten, and, even more dramatic, commanded that Aten alone be worshiped and that all the multitude of other gods be abandoned. Accordingly, Amenhotep changed his name to Akhenaten ("Pleasing to Aten") in honor of his only god. Some have seen in this famous episode an effort to impose monotheism on Egypt; others disagree. To mark the new policy, Akhenaten and his beautiful wife, Nefertiti, ruled from a new capital in Amarna, which gives its name to the "Amarna heretics" who believed in "one true god." Nearby, beginning about A.D. 1880, were found the famous Tell-el-Amarna letters (documents found in a *tell*, or ancient mound, at modern Amarna), a collection of about four hundred tablets including the diplomatic correspondence in many languages of Akhenaten and his father with the rulers of western Asia—an invaluable source for scholars.

Akhenaten's effort to overthrow the entrenched priesthood led to internal dissension and the loss of external strength. His son-in-law, Tutankhamen (1347-1338), was eventually sent to rule in Thebes, city of the priests of Amen, with whom (as his name shows) he compromised. He was the well-known "King Tut," the discovery of whose tomb with all its magnificent contents was the sensation of the 1920s. With Akhenaten's death, the new religious experiment collapsed, and the pharaohs strove to make up for the interval of weakness by resuming their foreign conquests.

The pharaoh Akhenaten is shown carrying crossed sceptres and wearing a bracelet bearing Aten's name. This statue from Karnak is a fine example of the new artistic conventions of the time, in showing the pharaoh as emaciated and almost androgenous. It may be that Akhenaten was deformed (scholars continue to debate the point), but it is more likely that the extreme stylization was meant to dramatize the break with the earlier conventions of Egyptian art.

About 1300 B.C. Ramses II (nineteenth dynasty) concluded a treaty with a people from Asia Minor, the Hittites. This treaty, of which we have texts in both Egyptian and Hittite, called for a truce in the struggle for Syria and provided for a dynastic marriage between the pharaoh and a Hittite princess. The interlude was short, however, and soon after 1200 B.C. the New Kingdom in its turn suffered severely as the result of an invasion of its eastern Mediterranean shores by mixed bands of raiders from the sea, sometimes called the Sea Peoples, possibly including ancestors of the later Greeks and Sicilians and others.

Egypt entered into a decline, marked by renewed internal struggles for power between the secular authorities and the priests, and among local and central rulers. Then came the Assyrian conquest of the seventh

*Problems of exact dating of the Egyptian kingdoms are extraordinarily difficult; those used here are the conventional ones. See Chester G. Starr, *Early Man: Prehistory and the Civilizations of the Ancient Near East* (New York: Oxford University Press, 1937), p. 101. For more detailed, complex, and exacting analysis of dates, consult William W. Hallo and William Kelly Simpson, *The Ancient Near East: A History* (New York: Harcourt Brace Jovanovich, 1971), pp. 299-302.

These giant statues of Ramses II at the rock temple of Abu Simbel were reconstructed in the twentieth century to save them from the rising waters of a new dam. Ramses wanted to show his love of the colossal, to tell all who came to view the giant sandstone figures of his greatness. Graffiti on the smooth surface of the legs in ancient Greek, Phoenician, and Persian show how strong the impulse is for each generation to leave its mark on the previous one. Restoration of the temple was completed in 1970, but the historical graffiti was left intact.

century, the Persian conquest of 525 B.C., and the conquest by Alexander the Great of Macedonia in 332 B.C.

Religion Religion—eclectic and syncretic—was the most powerful force animating Egyptian society. If one asked an ancient Egyptian "whether the sky was supported by posts or held up by a god, the Egyptian would answer: 'Yes, it is supported by posts or held up by a god—or it rests on walls, or it is a cow, or it is a goddess whose arms and feet touch the earth.'"* The Egyptian was ready to accept overlapping divinities and to add new ones whenever it seemed appropriate; if a new area was incorporated into the Egyptian state, its gods would be added to those already worshiped.

From the beginning, Egyptian cults included animals, totems perhaps; sheep, bulls, gazelles, and cats are still to be found carefully buried in their own cemeteries. As time passed, the figures of Egyptian gods became human, though often retaining an animal's head or body. Osiris, the Egyptian god who judged the dead, began as a local Nile Delta deity. He taught humans agriculture. Isis was his wife, and animal-headed Seth his brother and rival. Seth killed Osiris. Isis persuaded the gods to bring him back to life, but thereafter he ruled below (a parallel to the fertility and vegetation-cycle beliefs we have already encountered in Mesopotamia and will encounter again in Greece). Osiris was identified with the life-giving, fertilizing Nile, and Isis with the fertile earth of Egypt. Horus, the god of the sky, defeated the evil Seth after a long struggle.

But Horus was only one kind of sky god. There was also Re, later joined with Amen, and still later Aten, as we have seen. The moon god was the baboon-headed Thoth, who was god of wisdom, magic, and numbers. In great temple cities like Heliopolis, priests worked out and wrote down hierarchies of divinities. Out in the villages all the forces of nature were deified and worshiped. One local god was part crocodile, part hippopotamus, and part lion—a touching and clear revelation of what simple farmers along the river banks had to worry about. However numerous the deities, Egyptian religion itself was unified. Unlike a Sumerian temple, which was the political center of its city and for which the population toiled, the Egyptian temple had a limited religious function.

*J.A. Wilson, *The Intellectual Adventure of Ancient Man* (Chicago: University of Chicago Press, 1943), p. 44.

THE ARROGANCE OF CONQUEST

The Egyptian Pharaohs wanted succeeding generations to know of their deeds, and it was the custom to erect columns on which their exploits were shown by illustration and word. At Karnak, for example, Ramses II ordered the following said about himself (which was not, of course, literally true in any sense):

I dashed at them like the god of war; I massacred them, slaughtering them where they stood while one shrieked to the other, "This is no man but a mighty god; these are not the deeds of man; never has one man thus overcome hundreds of thousands!" I slew them all; none escaped me. . . . I caused the field of Kadesh to be white with corpses, so that one did not know where to tread because of the multitude. I fought all alone and overcame the foreigners in their millions.

Karl E. Meyer, *The Pleasures of Archaeology: A Visa to Yesterday* (New York: Atheneum, 1971), pp. 75-76.

Egyptians were preoccupied with life after death. They believed that after death each human being would appear before Osiris and recount all the evil he or she had *not* done on earth: "I have not done evil to men. I have not ill-treated animals. I have not blasphemed the gods," and so on, a negative confession to justify admission into the kingdom of the blessed. Osiris would then have the person's heart weighed to test the truth of this self-defense, and the dead person would be admitted or else delivered over to judges for punishment.

Egyptians believed not only in body and soul, but in *ka*, the indestructible vital principle of each person, which left the body at death but could return at times. That is why the Egyptians preserved the body in their elaborate art of mummification—so that the ka, on its return, would find it not decomposed. And that is why they filled the tombs of the dead with all the objects that the ka might need or take delight in on its return to the body; otherwise it might come back and haunt the living.

Literature We know Egyptian civilization so intimately because of the many inscriptions, which give us the historical materials, and of papyri (fragments of the ancient material the Egyptians wrote on, made of the pith of a water plant), which give us the literary materials. Yet what we have represents a smaller percentage of what once existed and of what may yet be found than does our collection of Mesopotamian literature on its thousands of carefully copied clay tablets.

The Egyptians used a form of picture writing (hieroglyphics, or sacred carvings), which was only deciphered in the 1820s. Scholars had possessed the key only since 1799, when a large, inscribed stone was found near the town of Rosetta in the Nile Delta. This piece of black basalt has a long text chiseled into its surface in three scripts: Greek, hieroglyphics, and another (or demotic) Egyptian script developed from hieroglyphics. Although the Greek version was imperfect, it could be read. It proved to be a decree in honor of a pharaoh named Ptolemy V, from 195 B.C., in the period after Alexander the Great's conquest. Even so, it took three decades before a French scholar, Jean-François Champollion, convinced himself that hieroglyphics were intended to be read phonetically, not symbolically, and so got beyond the mere deciphering of the name and title of Ptolemy V. Knowing the language of the Egyptian Christian church of his own day, which was close to ancient

Ramses II plays with one of his children. The medallions in the background provide a caption, to be read from right to left.

Egyptian although written differently, he gradually puzzled out the hieroglyphics on the stone. Since then, scholars have been able to read with certainty the vast number of surviving Egyptian texts. Visitors to the British Museum in London can still see the famous slab that made it possible for the nineteenth and twentieth centuries A.D. to understand ancient Egypt.

The equally famous Egyptian Book of the Dead—actually not a book but a series of papyrus chapters to be read by the living and then placed in tombs to help the dead—brings together stories of the gods with hymns and prayers and teaches us much of what we know of Egyptian religion. The Egyptian literature we have includes no epic story of a hero comparable to Gilgamesh, a mortal who cannot quite attain immortality, perhaps because the Egyptians confidently did expect to attain it. But it does include love songs, banquet songs, and what we could call fiction, both historical and fantastic. "If I kiss her," says an Egyptian lover, "and her lips are open, I am happy even without beer"*—a sentiment that seems perfectly up to date. "Enjoy thyself as much as thou canst," says a banquet song, "for a man cannot take his property with him."** The historical romance of Sinuhe tells the story of an Egyptian noble who was forced by intrigue into exile in Asia (early Middle Kingdom, c 1980 B.C.), was elected chief of a tribe there, won a magnificent single combat against a local champion, and, at the end, full of longing for Egypt, was happily recalled by the pharaoh and richly dressed, honored, and given a pyramid of his own for his future tomb. Egyptians also had their euphemisms for death—to "go to the West" was to die, and Westerners are "the dead." Thus the famous lines, "How happy is he who hath reached the West when he is safe in the hand of God."

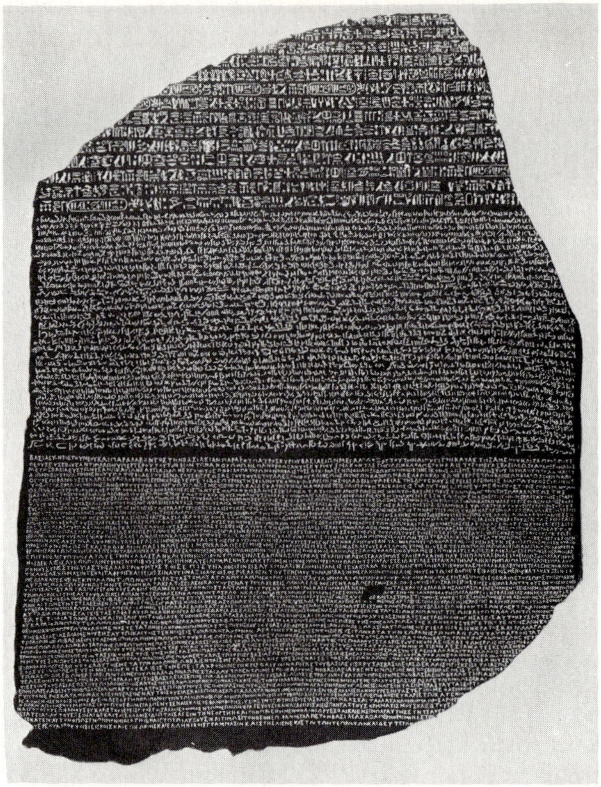

The Rosetta Stone, with its trilingual inscription, was discovered in 1799 and is now in the British Museum.

This portrait head of Queen Nefertiti dates from the fourteenth century B.C. Nefertiti was the wife of the pharaoh Akhenaten. Though this is probably the best known work of Egyptian sculpture, it is actually only a model in limestone, discovered in the workshop of the sculptor Thutmose. Nefertiti's name illustrates one of the difficulties in speaking or writing of an ancient culture; the Egyptian language contained no vowels, so her name should be written *Nfrtt.* However, today we would be unable to pronounce such a word, so conventionally vowels are inserted in Egyptian names.

III PEOPLES OUTSIDE THE VALLEYS

For well over a thousand years after their first flourishing, the peoples of the valley civilizations held the stage virtually alone. But the Hyksos invasion of Egypt, the Kassite invasion of Mesopotamia, and the Hittite attacks on both warned the river-based societies that the people of the mountains and deserts had begun to

*A. Erman, *Literature of the Ancient Egyptians*, trans. A. M. Blackman (London: Dutton, 1927), p. 244.

**J. H. Breasted, *The Dawn of Conscience* (New York, Scribner's, 1933), pp. 163-64.

THE CURSING LITANY

A litany is an incantation. The following litany, intended to quell the enemies of the sun god, is a striking example of Egyptian religious poetry that reinforces the concept of the negative confession or negative defense:

Mayest thou never exist, may thy body never exist. Mayest thou never exist.
May thy limbs never exist. Mayest thou never exist.
May thy bones never exist. Mayest thou never exist.
May thy words of power never exist. Mayest thou never exist.
May thy form never exist. Mayest thou never exist.
May thy attributes never exist. Mayest thou never exist.
May that which springs from thee never exist. Mayest thou never exist.
May thy hair never exist. Mayest thou never exist.
May thy possessions never exist. Mayest thou never exist.
May thy emissions never exist. Mayest thou never exist.
May the material of thy body never exist. Mayest thou never exist.
May thy place never exist. Mayest thou never exist.
May thy tomb never exist. Mayest thou never exist.
May thy cavern never exist. Mayest thou never exist.
May thy funeral chamber never exist. Mayest thou never exist.
May thy paths never exist. Mayest thou never exist.
May thy seasons never exist. Mayest thou never exist.
May thy words never exist. Mayest thou never exist.
May thy enterings in never exist. Mayest thou never exist.
May thy journeyings never exist. Mayest thou never exist.
May thy advancings never exist. Mayest thou never exist.
May thy comings never exist. Mayest thou never exist.
May thy sitting down never exist. Mayest thou never exist.
May thy increase never exist. Mayest thou never exist.
May thy body never exist. Mayest thou never exist.
May thy prosperity never exist. Mayest thou never exist.
Thou art smitten, O enemy. Thou shalt die,
thou shalt die.
Thou shalt perish, thou shalt perish,
thou shalt perish.

Margaret A. Murray, ed., *Egyptian Religious Poetry* (London: John Murray, 1949), pp. 64-65.

compete fiercely with the more stable valley societies. The outsiders too had centuries of history behind them, although still not well known to scholars. But by 1500 B.C. the Kassites in southern Mesopotamia, the Hurrians with their kingdom of Mitanni in northern Mesopotamia, smaller states in southeastern Anatolia (modern Turkey), and the Hittites in the remainder of Anatolia had emerged as rivals both to Babylon and to Egypt.

All of them had strong Indo-Aryan ethnic elements: that is, elements of a strain that would become predominant in Iran, and later in the Mediterranean and the West. All of them were ruled by kings, but their kings were neither the Mesopotamian agents of god on earth nor the Egyptian deified monarchs. Rather, they ruled as the most powerful among a noble class that controlled the instruments of war—horses and chariots—and shared the fruits of conquest, dividing new land among themselves. We begin now to find records, not only of war between these newly emerging peoples and the settled valley societies, but also of their diplomatic exchanges and their peace settlements.

For communication everybody used Akkadian, a Semitic tongue often foreign to both parties in a negotiation. The Egyptians, for example, corresponded in Akkadian with the peoples who ruled Syria, who did not speak it either. Even when they wrote in their own languages, some of them used Akkadian script. This enables modern scholars to pronounce the words even when they do not know what they mean, as is still often the case in Hurrian, written in Akkadian cuneiform but not related to well-known language groups and still by no means completely understood.

The Hurrians in particular transmitted Babylonian traditions to Assyria, Palestine, Phoenicia, and remotely to Greece, and they significantly shaped Hittite culture. Thus, while a more generalized culture was spread over a wider territory, the valley societies—Mesopotamia and Egypt—did not in fact succumb during the centuries from 1500 to 1200 B.C., when the threat was the greatest.

Hittites

Until the early twentieth century, scholars knew the Hittites chiefly from references in non-Hittite sources.

INTERPRETING DREAMS

Most cultures have sought to forecast the future by some means of divination. Common means have included the reading of the entrails of animals, scapulamancy (the throwing and reading of bones), and astrology (the belief that the stars influence human lives and can be used to forecast ordained events). The Egyptians developed astrology, as did the Greeks and Romans, who then prohibited its use. In the Middle Ages astrology was compounded with alchemy, or the effort to turn base metals into gold. With the introduction of printing, astrology and dream interpretation spread rapidly, and many people used horoscopes to provide a sense of security and a relationship to their place in the heavens. The Egyptian and Mesopotamian societies felt that dreams provided warnings or omens of events to come. Among accepted interpretations of the meanings of dreams were:

If, in his dreams, he often walks about naked it means: trouble will not touch this man.
If a man flies repeatedly: whatever he owns will be lost.
If he sits on the ground: honors are in store for him.
If he pours his urine into an irrigation-canal: Adad [the Weather-god] will flood his harvest.
If he eats the eye of his friend: his bad luck is straightened out, his property will prosper.
If one gives him wine: his days will be short.
If one gives him a seal of red stone: he will have sons and daughters.
If one gives him a wheel: he will have twins.

From A. Leo Oppenheim, "The Interpretation of Dreams in the Ancient Near East," *Transactions of the American Philosophical Society*, n.s., Philadelphia, XLVI (1956); as quoted in Chester G. Starr, *Early Man: Prehistory and the Civilization of the Ancient Near East.*

Uriah, for example, whom (the Bible tells us) King David arranged to have killed in battle in order to keep his wife, Bathsheba, who was a Hittite. And in Egypt a great inscription preserved the text in hieroglyphics of a treaty of 1280 B.C. between Ramses II and a Hittite king. In A.D. 1906-1908, excavations at an ancient Hittite capital, Hattusas, on the plateau of Anatolia, brought to light several thousand tablets, largely in cuneiform script and written in the Indo-European Hittite language and in many others as well. These records revealed that a strong Hittite kingdom emerged about 1700 B.C. Its Indo-European king and his aristocracy controlled a native Anatolian population. Between 1700 and c 1530, this kingdom made great conquests in Syria and resumed expansion toward Babylon. By 1500 the monarchy had become hereditary. Under Shuppiluliuma (c 1375-1335), a contemporary of Akhenaten, it reached its height, as the Hittites took advantage of Egyptian internal weakness to assert themselves.

After his intimate contact with the Egypt of Akhenaten, Shuppiluliuma began to insist that he be addressed as "my Sun" and to use the solar disk as a symbol. Thenceforth Hittite sovereigns also were deified, though only after death; it is from about this time that the written sources begin to speak of a king as "becoming a god" at death. The onslaught of the Sea Peoples that damaged the Egyptian New Kingdom about 1200 also put an end to the centralized Hittite state, although various smaller "neo-Hittite" petty principalities continued to exist in Asia Minor in the face of Assyrian expansion down to the late eighth century B.C. They wrote Hittite in hieroglyphics, whose deciphering made much progress during the 1930s, but the first major helpful bilingual text in hieroglyphic Hittite and Phoenician was not found until after World War II.

The Anatolians, the Indo-European Hittite upper class, the Mesopotamians, and the Egyptians all made contributions to Hittite religion. Foreign gods were made welcome and domesticated. No matter where they had originally come from, once part of Hittite religion these gods received homage in forms derived from Mesopotamia. But there were differences here too. Women played a more prominent role in Hittite religion and society than they did either in Mesopotamia or in Egypt; and alone among the peoples of the ancient Near East, the Hittites cremated their kings.

Though Hittite literature is full of Mesopotamian echoes, the Hittites also wrote sober official histories, which sought to determine and record the motives of rulers for their actions. The treaty, too, as a special literary and diplomatic instrument, was apparently a Hittite invention. Hittite architecture expressed itself in fortresses built on peaks, which became the nuclei of cities. The Hittite's skill at defending themselves, combined with their interest in trade and diplomacy, had given them a dominant position as far as the City of Ugarit, which having one of the best harbors on the eastern Mediterranean, became an emporium for the whole of the region, including the copper so important to Cyprus. Ugarit drew upon Hurrian and Hittite alliances with exceptional skill, enjoying a "golden age" of prosperity and growth between c 1440 and 1360 B.C.

Hurrians, Canaanites, Philistines, Phoenicians

Far less well known than the Hittites and still posing many unsolved problems are the Hurrians of Mitanni and the "Chabur triangle" on the upper Chabur River. Their language is still imperfectly read. Like the Hittites, the Hurrians had an Indo-European ruling class and worshiped some Indo-European deities. Their great importance was to act as intermediaries between the civilization of Mesopotamia and the less advanced peoples to the north and west, especially the Hittites.

Like the mountains of Anatolia and northern Mesopotamia, the deserts of Syria (the Old Testament land of Canaan) gave rise to a number of Semitic peoples who from time to time invaded the valley societies. Indeed, the Akkadians themselves—both Babylonians and Assyrians—as well as the Amorites had done the same. But there remained behind other Semitic peoples who never penetrated into the valleys and who created societies of their own along the Syrian coast of the Mediterrean and in its hinterland.

At Ugarit on the coast—where the northern portion was called Phoenicia—archaeologists in 1929 found the royal palace of a Canaanite state that flourished between 1400 and 1200 B.C., complete with cuneiform tablets in the northwest Semitic tongue of Ugaritic. They contained the archives of official correspondence, including a treaty with the Hittites written in Akkadian and showing that the Canaanites were under Hittite domination. There were also poems, including an epic about a hero named Kret, who was granted a son by divine favor—as was Abraham in *Genesis* in the Old Testament—and who also went to recapture his bride from the fortress of a king who had spirited her away—a leading theme in Homer's *Iliad*. At Ugarit, an eastern Mediterranean culture developed ties with both the Hebrews and the Greeks. Still Ugarit was only one of many Canaanite city-states, and it went down in the general chaos around 1200 B.C. caused by the Sea Peoples' invasion. Among these invading Sea Peoples were the Indo-European Philistines, who settled to the south of the Canaanites and gave their name to Palestine.

The Canaanites apparently matched their extreme political localism with extreme religious localism. They practiced human sacrifice and religious prostitution. The supreme Canaanite god was El, whose name simply means god and who is little known. Baal, on the other hand, whose name means lord, was a storm god—like the Sumerian god of the air, the region between heaven and earth. Baal and his wife Astarte—like Osiris and Isis in Egypt and parallel figures in Mesopotamia—symbolized the seasons and cyclical fertility.

After 1300 the Phoenicians (whose name comes from the word for the Tyrian purple dye made from shellfish found along the coast of their capital, Tyre) flourished along the coast south of Ugarit (in what is now Lebanon), and carried on a brisk trade with the western Mediterranean, founding Carthage (modern Tunis) as a colony about 800 B.C. The Phoenicians brought their Semitic tongue (Punic) more than halfway to the Straits of Gibraltar, through which their ships had often sailed. Many Phoenician names would appear later among the names the Greeks gave to their gods, and the Phoenician alphabet, a genuine alphabet (not, like cuneiform, a collection of signs that stood for whole syllables), perhaps inspired by Ugaritic, became the immediate ancestor of the Greek alphabet.

Land of Canaan, Baal, Phillistines. These names have been familiar to us all since childhood, for we have now come into the place and time of the Old Testament and are prepared to understand some of the regional and cultural background of the Hebrews, who were to pass on so much to the peoples of Europe and America.

Hebrews

History and the Old Testament The Hebrews were the first people to record their history in a series of books, providing a consecutive story over many centuries. Today, much changed and much debated by biblical scholars, this traditional history is contained in the Old Testament, especially in *Genesis*, *Exodus*, *Joshua*, *Judges*, *Samuel*, and *Kings*. But one also finds genealogy and ritual law (*Numbers*, *Leviticus*, and *Deuteronomy*), tales (*Ruth* and *Job*), proverbs (*Proverbs*, *Ecclesiastes*), prophetic utterances (*Isaiah*, *Jeremiah*, and the rest), and lyric poems (*Psalms*, *The Song of Songs*). For many centuries, these books were held by Jew and Christian alike to express literal and sacred truths; not until relatively recently have scholars begun to apply to them the same tests of authenticity that they apply to other works of history. Nineteenth-century scholars in particular decided that much material in the Old Testament was legendary and mythical, and they often questioned its historical accuracy.

But some doubts have been dispelled in our own time by hard archaeological evidence that has piled up in support of the general account that the Old Testament gives us. The Old Testament was not written down as the events happened; many of its earliest portions were compiled long after the events. The writings were not arranged in their present form until the second century B.C. Much is folklore. Still, the weight of the growing evidence tends to confirm the biblical story in its broad outlines, so that the Bible must be viewed not only as a work of the finest literature but also as valuable history.

Even the biblical account of the mist-shrouded beginnings of the Hebrews now seems reasonably authentic. They may well have migrated from Ur "of the Chaldees" sometime after 1950 B.C., when that Sumerian center in southern Mesopotamia was destroyed, moving northwest to the prosperous center of Harran. Abraham then may well have migrated westward into Canaan, as *Genesis* says. The accounts in *Genesis* of the origins of the universe and the racial origins of the Hebrews, and the stories of Eden, the Flood, and the Tower of Babel all indicate a northern Mesopotamian residence for the Hebrews before about 1500 B.C., when the westward migration took place. (The Flood has now been localized to either Shoruppak or Kish, well north of the once-presumed site, Ur.) Probably a racial mixture including some non-Semitic elements (Hurrian?) from the beginning, the Hebrews may well be a people called Khapiru who are mentioned beginning about 1900 B.C. in cuneiform tablets and in both Hittite and Egyptian sources as raiders, wanderers, and captives. Historians also are convinced that some of the Hebrews lived for several centuries in the Nile Delta during the Hyksos period, before Moses (whose name is Egyptian) became their leader and led them to within sight of their Promised Land about 1300 B.C. Even the miraculous crossing of the Red Sea (actually the shallow Sea of Reeds) in *Exodus* is not incompatible with the shallow waters, the reedy growth, and the winds of the region at the time.

As outsiders battering their way into Canaan against the entrenched resistance of those already there, the Hebrew confederation of tribes was held together by the new religion that Moses gave them, based on the Ten Commandments, the ark of the covenant, and the many observances that their god prescribed. Gradually, by ruthless conquest, they added to their holdings. The loose confederation became a monarchy about 1020 B.C., when the prophet Samuel chose Saul to be the first king. Saul's son-in-law, rival, and successor, David, known to us by the virtually contemporary account (1000-960 B.C.) in *Samuel*, united and strengthened the kingdom. His luxury-loving son Solomon brought the Palestinian kingdom of the Jews to new heights of prosperity at the royal city of Jerusalem, though even then his kingdom was small in size and resources compared to Sumer, Babylon, Assyria, or Egypt.

But at Solomon's death in 933 B.C., the kingdom split in two: the northern kingdom of Israel (933-722 B.C.), stronger but lacking the great center of Jerusalem, and the southern kingdom of Judah (933-586 B.C.), which despite Jerusalem had little real strength. The Assyrians destroyed Israel at Samaria in 722 B.C., and the Babylonians under Nebuchadnezzar—then, as we have seen, experiencing a brief revival—destroyed Judah in 586 and took the Jews into captivity. When the Persians under Cyrus the Great freed the Jews to return to Palestine after 538, the Jews no longer had a state but only a religious community. From then on they were held together by religion alone, and depended politically on three successive empires: the Persian, the Macedonian, and the Roman.

Religion Indeed, had it not been for the extraordinary cohesiveness of their religion, the Hebrews would have been just another people of the ancient Near East, less numerous than most at the time, less talented artistically than any. But of course we would probably not know much about them had it not been for their religion, which gave them and us the books of the Old Testament and an enduring tradition. Many of the most fundamental ideas of the Hebrew religion go back to the days when the Hebrews were still nomads, before they had adopted a settled life. His god's commandments to Moses on Mount Sinai that "Thou shalt have no other gods before me," "Thou shalt not make unto thee any graven image," and "Thou shalt not take the name of the Lord thy God in vain" determined three fundamental and permanent aspects of Judaism that were new among Near Eastern religions.

Thus, the religion of the Hebrews was monotheistic, recognizing only a single god. Despite the experiment of Akhenaten in Egypt and a few Babylonian texts that try to associate all divine power with Marduk alone, the Jews were the first to insist that their god was the only god and a universal god. Furthermore, the Jews were forbidden to represent this god in sculpture or painting—which stood in contrast to all other religions of the ancient world. More than that, they were forbidden to make *any* images of living beings, flesh, fish, or fowl—no doubt because their leaders feared that if they did make such images, they would end by worshiping them. And so from these earliest days their art was confined to nonrepresentational subjects. When they deviated from this law, as they often did, it was usually because of the influence upon them of neighbors whose traditions did not forbid animal or human representations in art. Finally, the religion of the Hebrews from the beginning regarded the *name* of God—Yahweh or Jehovah, meaning "he causes to be," or "the creator"—as literally not to be spoken, a reverence unlike any known in other ancient Near Eastern religions. From the nomadic period of Hebrew life also come the feast of Passover, with its offering of a spring lamb and of unleavened bread; the keeping of a sabbath or holy day on the seventh day of the week; an annual day of expiation (Yom Kippur); and other holy days still honored by Jews in our own time.

The Old Testament teems with episodes in which the Hebrews proved unable to keep the first commandment, broke away from the worship of their one god, tried to propitiate other gods, and were punished. Yet however often they disobeyed, the first commandment remained the central feature of their religion, though there were commandments forbidding murder, adultery, stealing, the bearing of false witness, and covetousness of one's neighbor's property or wife. Jehovah himself, both merciful and righteous, creator of all things, was human in form though not visible to the human eye. Unlike the gods of all other peoples, he did not lead a human life; he had no family; he dwelt, not in a palace, but in heaven. When he wished to speak to the leader of his people, he descended onto a mountaintop (Mount Sinai), or into a burning bush, or into the space he commanded be left for him between golden cherubim set atop a sacred wooden box in which the Ten Commandments, transcribed on two tablets of stone, were to be kept.

This box was the ark of the covenant, built by artisans to the special orders of Moses as relayed to him by his god. The covenant was the special pact between god himself and his chosen people, all the tribes of the Hebrews in confederation, held together by their regard for this most sacred of objects. Kept at first in a very special tent, a portable tabernacle, the ark moved with the Hebrews, first into the hill country of Shiloh, where the coastal Philistines captured it about 1050 B.C., and ultimately into a temple built for it by Solomon in Jerusalem—a royal chapel whose decorations incidentally included many that violated the commandment about graven images, since it was built by a Canaanite architect using Phoenician models, showing the increasing influence of non-Israelite peoples on the cult of Jehovah.

There were prophets (men called by their god) among the Jews from the beginning; they naturally multiplied during the division of the people into the two kingdoms of Israel and Judah. Summoning the people to return to the original purity of the faith, they sought to avoid the paganism that seemed to be threatening if Canaanite influences continued. In ecstasy perhaps brought on by dances, they warned of fearful punishment to come if the people did not heed them. After the punishment, however, the prophets (notably Isaiah) promised that Israel would rise again, and that a descendant of David would appear as a Messiah to usher in a new golden age. The disaster came with deportation into Babylonian captivity and the abandonment of Jerusalem. With the prophecies of evil fulfilled, the prophet Ezekiel had a vision of new life being breathed into the dead bones of Israel, and he urged all to prepare for its restoration. While in exile, in the sixth century B.C., the Hebrews selected the sacred writings and arranged them together in a form not unlike the Old Testament we know. When the captivity was over, the priests became the dominant figures in the restored community, with its rebuilt temple but without a state of its own, and they strove deliberately to return to what they believed to be the practices of their ancestors.

There was much about Hebrew society that recalls what we have already observed about the other peoples of the ancient Near East. The father exercised supreme authority within the family; polygamy and divorce were permitted; and, as among the Hittites, a widow married her dead husband's brother. The Hebrews had slaves, but a Hebrew slave could be made to serve no more than six years. A man who had injured his slave was required to set him or her free. Otherwise the law of an eye for an eye, a tooth for a tooth, held sway. Yet the general prescriptions—such as the Commandments—and even some specific regulations—not to wrong strangers, not to exact usurious interest for a loan, to help one's enemies as well as one's friends—strike an ethical note as deep as any found in earlier Mesopotamian Near East, and presage other principles that would eventually emerge from this Hebrew society, which by that time had been greatly influenced by Greek civilization.

IV CRETE AND MYCENAE

Minoans before Mycenae

Among the notable finds in Ugarit was an ivory relief of a bare-breasted goddess, holding ears of wheat in each hand and seated between two goats standing on their hind legs. She is like nothing from Mesopotamia or Egypt, but she greatly resembles the goddesses frequently found on the large Mediterranean island of Crete, on the westernmost fringe of the Near East. Cretan civilization is often called Minoan, after Minos, the legendary founder of the local dynasty.

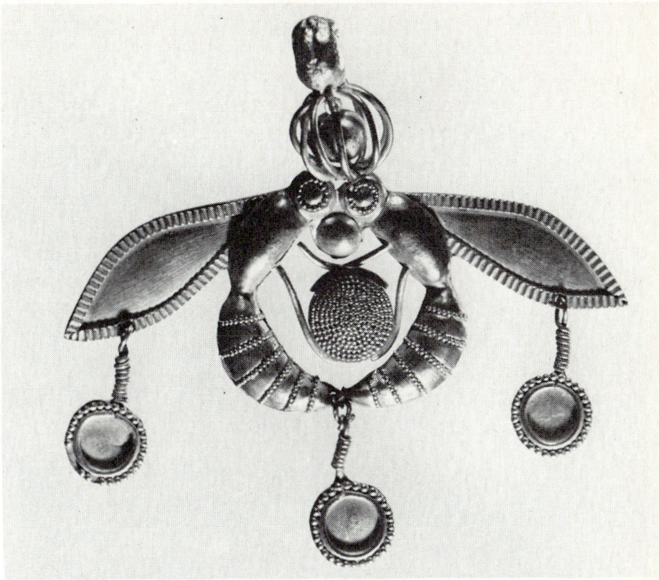

Middle Minoan culture was sophisticated, complex, and elegant, at least for those who lived at the palace. Court ladies wore embroidered dresses of gold and silver. Great rock gardens, flower beds, and flowing fountains softened the harsh landscape. The Minoans were superb craftsmen, especially in gold, as shown by this delicate pendant of a golden bee, found in the necropolis (burial place) of Malia, and dating from c 1700 B.C.

Sir Arthur Evans, a British archaeologist whose brilliant work in Crete in the first half of this century enabled modern scholars to appreciate Minoan society at its true worth, divided the culture into three main periods; today these are expressed as Early Minoan (c 2500-c 1950), Middle Minoan (c 1950-1550), and Late Minoan (c 1550-1100). Each of these three periods is further subdivided three times to enable easy discussion of the objects found. Pottery is the key for all such dating; different styles found at different levels of archaeological sites permit scholars to work out a chronological framework. In Crete such dating is of surpassing importance, partly because we have not yet learned how to read the earliest writing, some of it in hieroglyphics and some of it in a script known as Linear A.

Much is now conjectured about Linear A, and some words have been plausibly deciphered, though it cannot yet be read. There is no Rosetta stone for Linear A, which, moreover, is surely not Greek. Professor Cyrus Gordon has argued recently that it is a northwest Semitic dialect related to Phoenician, and that the Minoans who wrote it were a Semitic people who came to Crete from the Nile Delta in Middle Minoan times, about 1800 B.C. His views aroused great controversy; other scholars strongly maintained that the Minoans came from Anatolia, from the culture that produced Çatal Hüyük. Since

The ruins of the Palace of Minos, at Knossos, Crete, from which archaeologists have been able to reconstruct much of Minoan life.

This small terra cotta snake goddess was found at the Palace of Knossos and dates from 1700–1580 B.C.

we have only about two hundred Linear A texts, none of which are literary documents, it is probable that, even after scholars have learned to read it confidently, it will add little to what we have long known about the Minoans from purely archaeological evidence.

Such evidence has turned up in abundance in the palace of Minos at Knossos (modern Heraklion), found and partly reconstructed by Evans, and in other palaces and tombs in other parts of the island, of which the most recently excavated is at Kato Zakros. Pottery and seals found on Crete show that the Cretans were a busy maritime people whose ships not only plied the Mediterranean but presumably managed to defend the island against invaders, since none of the palaces was fortified. Expanding at the expense of other islanders, the Cretans had garrisons and even colonies abroad—a Bronze Age overseas empire on a small scale exacting tribute from other powers.

The palace of Minos is a Middle Minoan triumph, resting on earlier foundations, characterized by many rooms, a great staircase, strikingly beautiful wall frescoes (recovered from the ruins in fragments), massive columns, many six-foot-tall stone storage jars for olive oil or wine, and an elaborate plumbing system with pipes, running water, and ventilation. So complex was this palace that Evans believed that he had discovered the building that had inspired the ancient Athenian legend of the Labyrinth, the palace on Crete with a system of rooms and corridors so mazelike that it was impossible to find one's way without a guide or a thread to drop behind, so that one might later retrace one's steps. But perhaps the Labyrinth was a cave; Crete is full of them, and they were holy places.

Minoan craftsmen produced delicate pottery hardly thicker than an eggshell, decorated with birds, flowers, and marine animals; ivory or pottery statuettes of the bare-breasted goddess, who often holds a snake in each hand; and many paintings of bulls, some showing young athletes—girls and boys—leaping over a bull's back, in what was clearly something like a ritual game. Athenian legend held that their ancestors had been forced to send young men and maidens to be sacrificed each year by the Cretans to their Minotaur—half man, half bull. Certainly the many pairs of bull horns that have been found in Knossos and elsewhere illustrate the importance of the animal in the Cretan religion, in which a double ax, found in many sizes from fullsized models in bronze to tiny miniatures in gold, also played a role. (The word *labyrinth* means "place of the double ax.")

The reasons for the end of Cretan prosperity are still hotly debated. Was it natural catastrophes (earthquakes, tidal waves, fires) that destroyed the palace of Minos a little after 1600 B.C., again about 1500, and a third time about 1400? Or did invading Hyksos, on their way out of Egypt after their occupation, do the damage of 1600? Did mainland Greeks, crossing from the north, cause the destruction of 1500? Nobody can be quite sure about the earlier destructions, which were repaired. Since 1960 the debate has intensified rather than lessened; but the last disaster may well be attributable to actions of mainland Greeks.

Mycenaeans and Minoans

In Greece too, Bronze Age civilization had taken root. Greece was a largely barren land—mountainous and divided into small valleys and plains separated from each other, with none far from the sea. From earliest times the inhabitants took advantage of the rugged coasts and islands with their many shelters and good harbors to sail from place to place, seldom if ever losing sight of land, profiting by the exchange of olive oil and wine for grain and metal and slaves. Somewhat before 2000 B.C. the village Bronze Age culture of the inhabitants—who were not Indo-European speakers but, like the Cretans, presumably a mixture of Stone Age indigenous peoples and Anatolians who had invaded about 3000 B.C.—was interrupted by the invasion from the north of the first Indo-European speakers. The invaders first destroyed and then settled, no doubt intermarrying with the previous inhabitants, and developed early forms of the Greek language. This society had one of its chief centers at Mycenae, well situated to control land trade near the sea.

The Mycenaeans were led by warrier chieftains, but they also traded with Crete. Minoan objects have been found in the famous royal tombs at Mycenae that perhaps span the century from 1600 to 1500 B.C. In fact, the Minoan influence at work upon the arts of the mainland was so profound that scholars speak of the "Minoanization" of mainland Greece. The most celebrated objects are great gold masks of warrior princes buried in the tombs and daggers inlaid with various metals that show hunting scenes of astonishing realism and beauty. (When the famous German archaeologist Heinrich Schliemann found these objects in the 1870s, he thought that he had found the tomb of the Homeric hero Agamemnon. But, as we shall see, Agamemnon actually lived about three hundred years later.) Egypt and Anatolia also shared in the Mycenaean trade, but the chief influences in mainland Greece were Minoan.

Interchange, we now believe, went both ways. Mycenaean Greeks visited Crete as traders or even as tourists; perhaps they observed the absence of physical fortifications that left Knossos vulnerable. Then, it is conjectured, they moved in and seized power, perhaps about 1460 B.C., presumably having first built their own fleet. No longer did they need to send any tribute to Knossos. Indeed, they now controlled the very center of the civilization that had already taught them so much. Military innovations now followed in Crete; chariots were introduced, and arrows stored for large bodies of troops, but the invaders built no fortifications, presumably because they expected no new invasions. In the palace of Minos the Greeks installed a throne room of the type found in their own mainland palaces. Most important, the Minoans showed them how useful it was to keep records; and since Linear A, devised for a Semitic language, would not do, the scribes may have invented a new script—Linear B—in which to write the language

This gold Mycenaean death mask is known as the Mask of Agamemnon.

of the conquerors; namely, Greek. On the other hand, Linear B may have been developed gradually from Linear A.

Conclusive proof, worked out in 1952 by Michael Ventris, a young English scholar, showed that the language of Linear B *is* early Greek; it was this discovery that made possible the foregoing tentative reconstruction of events. Evans had found many Linear B tablets at Knossos, but no such tablets were known *from mainland Greece* until 1939, when an American scholar, Carl Blegen, discovered the first of what proved to be a large collection of them in Pylos, where he was excavating a Mycenaean palace. Since then many more have turned up elsewhere in Greece, including some in Mycenae itself. Acting on the assumption that it was probably Greek (since he now knew that Greeks were keeping records in it on the mainland), Ventris used the wartime techniques of cryptography to show that the script was not an alphabet, but that each symbol represented a syllable, and then he cracked the code. The thousands of Linear B tablets have by no means all been read even now. Nor are all readings certain. The tablets are mostly prosaic inventories of materials stored in the palaces or lists of persons in the royal services—but they are Greek.

The disappearance of Linear A in Crete and the substitution for it about 1460 B.C. of the new Linear B point clearly to a Mycenaean occupation of the island that preceded the last great violent destruction of about 1405 and lasted almost a century. We cannot be sure how independent of the mainland the new Greek rulers of Knossos were; they may have been subordinate princes. The great palace of Knossos and other major Cretan centers were burned down about 1400, apparently after looting. We do not know who did this. Perhaps the Cretans rose against their Greek masters and burned down their own cities, though it has been plausibly suggested that such an act would have invited fierce reprisals and continued occupation after reconstruction. In any event, there was no reconstruction; rather, there was permanent disruption. So perhaps it was the Mycenaeans themselves who, in revenge against Cretan rebelliousness that may have made the island ungovernable, decided to cut their losses, destroy the Cretan centers, and sail away. Or perhaps the destruction was the result of a volcanic upheaval of the seabed. The rediscovery (1967) and present active excavation of a Minoan city on the volcanic island of Santorin (Thera) to the north of Crete may enable scholars to decide the question one way or another. After the disaster of c 1400 B.C. Crete remained rich and populous but lost its Mediterranean predominance, which passed to the aggressive mainland peoples.

Mycenae, 1400-1100 B.C.

We still know relatively little about Mycenaean politics and society. We can tell from excavated gold treasures that Mycenae itself was wealthy, which is not surprising considering that it had conquered Crete. But the Mycenaeans seem not to have been overseas empire builders, even in the sense that the Cretans had been; their occupation of Crete may well have been undertaken by an invading captain who retained power for himself in Crete, however much of his revenue he sent back home. The Achaeans or Greeks of whom the Hittite sources speak may well not have been the Greeks of Mycenae at all but Greeks of Rhodes, another island principality. And there were other settlements in the southern Greek mainland (called the Peloponnesus)—Pylos, Tiryns (the latter very close to Mycenae)—which seem to have been extensive too, and perhaps under local rulers equally powerful if bound in alliance to the Mycenaeans. A loose confederacy among equals seems to fit best with the evidence.

Tombs from the period before 1400 B.C. tell us of the structure of society, for they are of two sharply distinct types: those carefully built to take the bodies of kings and nobles, and simple burial places for the rest of the population. Tombs from the period between 1400 and 1200 show a rise in general wealth; there are more chamber tombs with more gifts to the dead found in them. Similarly, at Mycenae itself, Tiryns, Pylos, Athens, and Thebes there arose great palaces as community centers, with workshops, storage areas, guardrooms, and lesser dwelling houses attached. Good roads and bridges connected the main towns, and good water-supply systems provided the towns with security. Artisans attached to the palaces built and repaired chariots, made jars to hold wine and oil, tanned leather, wrought bronze in the forges, made bricks, and sewed garments. Workmen stored goods for preservation, sale, and exchange. A Mycenaean palace was a businesslike and noisy place.

The Linear B tablets preserve records of special royal furniture elaborately inlaid in ivory, glass, and gold; like the Egyptian pharaohs, the Mycenaean rulers obviously valued objects most when they took time and effort to make. Smaller than the great palaces on Crete, those of the Mycenaeans on the mainland nonetheless testify to a vibrant life in a complex society. One of the richest hoards, containing treasures in gold, jewels, and bronze manufactured over five centuries, was found in a private house in Tiryns; it was obviously the stolen booty of a Mycenaean grave robber with a fine taste in antiques.

Mycenaean bureaucrats continually intervened in the life of the ordinary person, keeping elaborate records of how much land and livestock each subject possessed, the cash or commodities owed in taxes, the amounts of bronze issued to each craftsman to make swords and arrowheads, and how much of everything was kept in each storeroom. Such attention to detail was positively Hittite or Ugaritic, and nothing like the Mycenaean bureaucracy ever reappeared in Greece after its destruction. And yet the records do not tell us all that we want to know; although we know that there were slaves, and we know the titles of various officials, we cannot be sure of their duties or gain a clear picture of governmental organization.

Until 1968 no Mycenaean religious shrine had ever been found. There were altars. Gems discovered in

The Lion Gate of Mycenae leads into the ancient fortress, the legendary seat of Agamemnon.

Mycenaean tombs showed Cretan deities and religious scenes. The Linear B tablets from Pylos recorded offerings made to certain gods: Poseidon, god of the sea; Ares, god of war; Artemis, goddess of the moon; and even Zeus and Hera, to later Greeks the supreme ruler of the gods and his consort. Names of other gods were found who did not survive the Dark Age that lay ahead, and so did not reappear in classical Greece. But in 1968 at Mycenae, in a small storeroom, archaeologists found clay figures that suggest a religious cult—six coiled snakes and sixteen human, mostly female, hollow figures, only one of which is clothed and colored. Next door was a possible "chapel" of the cult, about which so far very little is known.

The most important episode of the three centuries 1400-1100 is the Trojan War, usually dated about 1250 or 1200 B.C., known to every Greek of the classical period from the *Iliad* and the *Odyssey*, epic poems put together about five centuries after the event, and known to all the civilized West ever since. The war was a great expedition led by the king of Mycenae, Agamemnon, in command of a fleet and an army contributed by the other towns and islands of Mycenaean Greece, against Troy, allegedly a rich city on the northwest coast of Anatolia (modern Turkey) not far from the mouth of the Dardanelles, the straits that lead from the Aegean into the Sea of Marmora. The Trojans were related to the Greeks, though they were less advanced. They did not write, and they seem to have had little contact with their neighbors in the Aegean, the Cretans, or with their neighbors in Anatolia, the Hittites. But many Mycenaean objects found in the ruins of Troy show that the Trojans traded with mainland Greece, perhaps offering in exchange for their goods woolen textiles (a great number of pottery spindles survived in the Trojan ruins) and horses, which the Trojans bred and whose bones are also numerous in the ruins.

The famous tale that the Greeks undertook their expedition to avenge the abduction by the Trojan prince Paris of the beautiful Helen, wife of Agamemnon's brother, Menelaus, prince of Mycenaean Sparta, is simply a romantic tale. The tradition that the siege lasted ten years, involving many ships and men before Agamemnon's forces won and burned Troy, may be romance too. Excavations show that the city of Troy destroyed about 1250 or somewhat later was the seventh city on the site. The first five belonged to an earlier people and had already been destroyed by 1900 B.C., when our Trojans arrived, bringing their horses and a new kind of pottery made also by the Greeks. These newcomers built Troy VI, a magnificent walled citadel enclosing a few houses for the most important people, who ruled over a larger subject population on the slopes of a hillside and in the plain below. Troy VI was ruined about 1300, probably by an earthquake. And then Troy VII, a shrivelled, partial restoration of the great Troy VI, was built in and on the ruins.

It is this shrunken city that was destroyed by enemies a few generations later. But its shabbiness is so at variance with the traditions of its splendor remembered in the *Iliad*, and the date of its destruction lies so near the date at which we know that Mycenaean Greece itself collapsed under the blows of new enemies, that a few scholars now believe that there never was a Trojan War at all. Though powerfully argued, this view will probably be slow to win acceptance because the story of Troy is so deeply embedded in our cultural traditions. Scholars who believe in the war gain comfort from the fact that the *Iliad* calls the Greeks Achaeans, and that Achaeans also almost surely are mentioned in Hittite sources as a powerful people who sometimes raided the coasts of Anatolia in the thirteenth century, when Hittite power was waning. Perhaps these "Achaeans" came from nearby Rhodes and were relatives of those whom we have always believed to have fought and won the Trojan War. Troy itself, however, went almost without mention in Hittite written sources.

Soon after the fall of Troy VII there began the upheavals in the Mediterranean world in which the so-called Sea Peoples ruined the Hittite state and the Egyptian New Kingdom and left the Philistines as new settlers on the shores of Palestine. These destabilizing changes helped generate a wave of violence that also destroyed Mycenaean Greece. Invaders from the north swept over all of Greece; the palaces and tombs vanished in the disorders, and with them went Mycenaean civilization. Scholars once called these invaders Dorians—Greeks speaking a special dialect that can be identified in later inscriptions—and attributed most of the destruction to them. We now believe that the Dorians did indeed invade about 1100, but that Mycenaean civilization had probably been pretty thoroughly destroyed before they arrived and were able to dominate most of Greece.

The Dark Age: Homer

The three centuries from 1100 to 800 B.C. are known as the Dark Age—dark because we have too little evidence to obtain a clear picture of Greek life, and dark also because civilization took dramatic steps backward. Literacy virtually vanished, and writing stopped. Some argue that Linear B had been too clumsy a script ever to have been useful for any purpose other than keeping records, that in any case only a very small percentage of Mycenaean Greeks (perhaps 5 percent) could ever have been able to read or write it, and that its disappearance was a benefit because when literacy returned, Greek was written in the convenient new alphabet adopted from the Phoenicians. But no one denies that poverty and primitive conditions prevailed in Greece, causing suffering, a loss of skills, a shrinkage of the communities, a great forgetting of the past, and a halt in progress.

After about 1050 B.C., however, iron clearly began to replace bronze as the metal for weapons and utensils. Moreover, we know that there were migrations of Greeks out of Greece to the Aegean coasts of Asia Minor; especially to the central region later called Ionia, which emerged into our consciousness again about 800 B.C. Other Greeks speaking other dialects migrated into the regions of Asia Minor to the north (Aeolic) and south (Doric) of Ionia. In the hinterland behind these seacoast regions lived the native Anatolian peoples in their own kingdoms: Lydia, Caria, Phrygia. On the mainland, the Athenians escaped the full impact of the Dorian invasions; perhaps their good fortune started them on the way to the leadership of Greece that would be theirs after the Dark Age ended.

The end of the Dark Age is closely tied to the oral composition of two epic poems, the *Iliad* (16,000 lines) and the *Odyssey* (12,000 lines). Did the same person compose both? Was it Homer? Did the *Iliad* precede the *Odyssey*? No certain answers can be given to these questions. It does seem probable that both poems took roughly the form in which we know them at some time between 850 and 750 B.C. although some say later. The *Odyssey* was almost surely composed later than the *Iliad*, though it may be a later work of the same man who composed the *Iliad* in his youth.

He was really a singer, putting together in these monumental narratives shorter songs about the deeds of heroes. Such singers, accompanying themselves on stringed instruments, sang the shorter separate songs to audiences seated at table in a princely household, or to a gathering of villagers in a public square, or to soldiers around a campfire. The *Iliad* and the *Odyssey* represent only a fraction of the epic material that existed in the Dark Age; there were many other tales of heroes that were less popular or that stood the test of performance less well. The composer of the long poems was selecting favorites that, when assembled, would make a coherent narrative. Such a singer had no written versions of his work; he learned by heart from a predecessor many thousands of lines of poetry. While he sang, he had little time to reflect on what he would sing next, so he had recourse to formulas that would fit the rhythm of the verse and that would be familiar to his hearers. From a huge stock of such formulas, he could choose and blend those that told his story. Works as long as the *Iliad* or *Odyssey* would have taken several days to recite. They may have been put together specifically for some nobleman's prolonged feast or for a religious festival. But it seems more probable that a great singer who knew many of the individual songs was inspired to assemble them "to make a complete and universal Trojan song."

For a long time after their composition, both poems continued to be transmitted orally. At Athens, in the sixth century B.C., two hundred years after the epics had been composed from the songs and seven hundred years after the Trojan War itself (always supposing that there *was* a Trojan War), the *Iliad* and the *Odyssey* were recited in public every four years at an Athenian festival; the law required that this be done in order and without omissions. By then, presumably, the poems had been written down; but it was not for another three centuries that a stable "scholarly" text was produced in Alexandria, from which the versions that have come down to us ultimately derive.

The *Iliad* deals with a single episode that took place during the siege of Troy—the wrath of the Greek hero Achilles, who stopped fighting and sulked in his tent because the commander, Agamemnon, had taken from him a captive Trojan girl. Agamemnon had allowed himself to be persuaded to restore his own captive girl to her family, and so made up for his loss by taking Achilles' prize away. While Achilles refused to fight, the great combat continued. Eventually, when Hector, a Trojan prince, had killed Achilles' best friend and comrade-in-arms, Patroclus, Achilles returned to the battle and in turn slew Hector. At the very end he returned the body to Hector's sorrowing father, old King Priam, for funeral ceremonies.

The *Odyssey* tells of the ten-year wanderings of another Greek hero, Odysseus, after the siege of Troy was over, of the extraordinary places and peoples he visited on his way back to his home on the island of Ithaca, where his faithful wife Penelope awaited him despite the attention of many suitors, and from whence their son Telemachus had set out to find his father.

Put in this summary form, the two stories seem blunt and commonplace. But a deep humanity pervades both. Despite the continual bloody fighting in the *Iliad*, the modern reader—like all before him—is moved by the terror of Hector's baby son, Astyanax, when he sees his father with his fierce plumed war helmet on, until Hector takes it off and shows the child who he really is; feels the truth of the passage when the old men of Troy admit that Helen—beautiful as a goddess—was well worth all the fuss; shares the grief and dignity of Priam as he begs Achilles to return Hector's body for a decent burial; and appreciates Achilles' courteous generosity to an enemy when he reluctantly agrees. The romantic *Odyssey*, with its lotus eaters, sirens, men turned to swine by enchantment, and fierce one-eyed giant, also provides similar moments of high human drama in the homecoming of Odysseus in disguise, in the responses of his favorite dog and his old nurse, and in the sorrow of the beautiful island princess Nausicaa, first seen playing ball on the beach with her maidens, when she finds that Odysseus will not stay and be her lover.

In both poems the gods and goddesses are standard Greek divinities—Zeus, Hera, Apollo (the sun), Artemis (the moon), Ares (war), Poseidon (the sea), Aphrodite (love), Athena (wisdom), and the rest—who play an intimate part in the affairs of mortals, intervening in the fighting to give victory to their favorites, supplying Achilles with an extraordinary shield on which are displayed many instructive scenes in cunning metalwork, saving Odysseus from the perils of his voyage. The immortals on Mount Olympus are only a little larger than the heroes; they live thoroughly human lives, quarreling over the affairs of mortals and having fits of bad temper.

It is possible that there are real links stretching backward from the *Iliad* and the *Odyssey* across the Dark Age, when the singer's art was kept alive in Ionia, to heroic songs composed by Mycenaeans themselves. Many scholars stress such links and believe in a continuous tradition. The long Catalog of the Ships in the *Iliad*, for example, lists the contingents supplied to the Greek armies at Troy by the various Greek settlements, and names their commanders. Many think it a real Bronze Age document that provides genuine, usable evidence about the diverse political organization of Mycenaean society: by city, by the captain the troops followed, and by tribe. So too, the description of Odysseus' household as including more than fifty slaves is often taken to indicate that slavery was common in Mycenaean times. And some draw conclusions from the poems about the inheritance of royal power or the existence of assemblies of elders.

Most recent scholars, however, prefer to use the poems sparingly for such purposes, or not at all. Still, whether or not *we* use the poems as history, the Greeks themselves certainly did so, forming their own conception of their ancestral past from the *Iliad* and the *Odyssey*. Together with the Old Testament, some of which was first being committed to writing at about the same time, the Homeric poems form the greatest literary and cultural legacy of ancient people. Indeed, many modern scholars maintain that both Homeric and Hebrew civilizations grew directly from a common eastern Mediterranean background and point to many parallels in action and attitude. We know so little about these people, their literature, their society. Yet we can recognize so much of ourselves in them—in their search for security, their sense of pleasure, their regard for duty and honor. Clearly, however distant from us in time, these people and their history are part of our experience.

SUMMARY

The period before humans left written records is called *prehistory*. Our knowledge of this period depends on archaeological findings. Although fossil remains of apelike human ancestors have been found that date back millions of years, the first generally accepted humans appeared in Europe and the Near East about 37,000 years ago and are called *homo sapiens*, meaning "the one who thinks."

Archaeologists call early human culture the Old Stone (Paleolithic) Age because of the crude stone implements in use at the time. Paleolithic humans have left remarkable cave paintings and carvings. About 8000 B.C. humanity advanced to the New Stone (Neolithic) Age, marked by the domestication of animals and plants and the development of more permanent dwellings.

The decisive step from prehistory to history was the invention of writing by the Neolithic inhabitants of Mesopotamia around 3500 B.C. By 3100 B.C. the Sumerians in southern Mesopotamia had invented bronze and developed writing (called *cuneiform*) into a flexible tool of communication.

Mesopotamia was what historians called a *hydraulic society*, one based on the centralized control of irrigation and flood management. There were many cities, each with its own bureaucracy and temple. Among the legacies of Mesopotamian culture are the first law codes, the first epic, *Gilgamesh*, and certain religious concepts, such as the story of a primeval flood, that have persisted in Western thought.

The Sumerian city-states gave way to the Babylonian (about 2300 B.C.) and Assyrian (about 1100 B.C.) empires. Eventually, all of Mesopotamia was absorbed by the Persian Empire in the sixth century B.C.

Another Neolithic hydraulic society developed along the Nile River in Egypt, which was first united into a single state around 2850 B.C. Egypt became a highly bureaucratic society ruled by a god-king, the pharaoh. Ancient Egyptian history is divided into three broad areas of unified rule, separated by periods of division and anarchy: the Old Kingdom (2700-2160 B.C.), the Middle Kingdom (2134-1786 B.C.), and the New Kingdom (1575-1087 B.C.). Thereafter, Egypt entered a period of political decline and foreign rule.

Religion was the most powerful force in Egyptian society. The Egyptians had many gods and were preoccupied by life after death. To ensure survival in the next world, they built elaborate tombs and mummified the bodies of the dead. Much of what we know about ancient Egypt comes from what was found in its tombs.

Egyptian writing, called hieroglyphics, was deciphered only in the nineteenth century. Egyptian literature includes love songs and what is perhaps the first fiction.

The Hebrews were nomads who established themselves in Palestine around 1300 B.C. The importance of the Hebrews lies in their religion. They were the first to insist that their god was the only god and a universal god. They were also the first people to record their history in a series of books—the Old Testament.

Cretan civilization is called Minoan after Minos, the legendary founder of the local dynasty. The Cretans ruled a maritime empire from a vast palace at Knossos. Cretan prosperity ended between 1600 and 1400 B.C., though whether because of natural disaster or foreign conquest is unclear.

Bronze Age civilization in Greece is called Mycenaean because one of its chief centers was at Mycenae in southern Greece. Mycenaean civilization was based on heavily fortified palace centers and was highly bureaucratic. Its most lasting and important legacies are the great epic poems the *Iliad* and the *Odyssey*.

chapter two

THE GREEKS

The Greeks are the first ancient civilization with which modern society feels an immediate affinity. We like to believe that they thought much as we do—that is, that they were rationalists, intensely curious about their environment, eager to acquire new knowledge and to use it to alter their condition. We recognize them as a reflective people, questioning the human condition, interested in the new, but respectful of the old. Their literature, one of the richest the world has seen, shows a feeling for history. They also believed in their gods with an intensity and good humor that humanized both the gods and the Greeks. They accepted the world of the actual—good or bad—as they understood it, and they consciously strove to understand that world through both science and religion.

We think of the Greeks as curious, given to questions: Where does the stranger I see come from? How large is your family? How much money do you make? How can we prove what we believe to be true? Why do people fall ill? How should societies govern themselves? The Greeks felt secure questioning both the specific and the general, and they recognized that people would search for security in the psychological areas that fall between such precise and such grand questions. That we recognize elements of ourselves in them—tracing our democracies remotely back to their early city-states, linking our desire for perfection to their heroes, finding in their sense of humor much that we may laugh at today—tells us at least as much about ourselves and our needs as it does about the Greeks. It is this sense of being linked in time that leads modern scholars to begin the customary history of our concept of Western civilization in the northwest corner of the ancient Near East—on the Greek peninsula, on the islands of the Aegean Sea, and in the Greek-speaking cities on the western coast of Asia Minor.

There is, of course, a special bias at work in this linkage of ourselves to the ancient Greeks. Perhaps they were not more curious about the world than other societies had been; perhaps they simply left better records behind by which we can explore their curiosity and see how it relates to our own. They too were haunted by superstition, but they had the time and courage to explore their superstitions. They too fought endless petty wars with each other, but they produced historians—Herodotus, Thucydides, Xenophon—who explained these wars in ways that make us feel we understand them. They thought deeply and well, but most of their great thinkers belonged to a leisure class that had the time to devote to thought for its own sake—to inquiry without immediate reward—because its members had slaves to assure that daily tasks did not go undone. They were not a wholly admirable people (there are no *wholly* admirable people, and, in any case, it is not the business of history to make such judgments), but they are the first people with whom we can identify. We feel that we can actually know the Greeks because we can understand their motivations.

We can also identify with the Greeks because of their art. Civilization is not the history of art. One culture is often unable to recognize the art of another culture, but art does provide objects, shapes, indications of how a culture defines beauty, at which we may look, to compare, reject, or accept into our own understanding. Art helps to embody, to objectify, an ideal of perfection—whether of reason, of justice, of balance, or of the human spirit. It attempts to express (as does religion) an ideal. We have inherited such an ideal from the Greeks, in their architecture, in their attempts to define civility, in their awareness of the tension (which they would have called "divine") between the ideal and the actual, as between the arm and the torso in the idealized figure of Greek statuary.

To have a sense of civility is to have a sense of permanence; this, in turn, means having an awareness of occupying a place in space and time; knowing that there are other cultures—now, in the past, and in the future—and knowing that the culture of which we are a part must take its place in such a continuum. This is the sense of history which the Greeks developed more acutely than any Western peoples who had preceded them, insofar as the record tells us, and it is that record, which their sense of history led them to retain, upon which we draw today.

Politically we may think of the Greeks as the fathers of democracy—that is, of government by and through the people. They also, at different times and in different places, found oligarchy to be the best government—that is, government by the few, whether those few were a natural-born aristocracy, or the rich, or the "most noble of mind." At other times they accepted tyranny—absolute rule by a single person. They did not "invent" any of these forms of government, for governmental forms evolve and are not the inventions of individuals. But they did use these various forms, for in politics as in art they experienced the tension between the ideal and the actual in terms of competition between groups who felt they alone possessed the right to define society's problems and find society's solutions. In the variety of their political thought, we also perceive ourselves as their kin.

I THE GREEKS BEFORE THE PERSIAN WARS

Modern students often derived their picture of Greek politics in general from the superb speech that Pericles, the most celebrated of the leaders of Athens, made in 431 B.C. over the Athenian soldiers killed in the first year

This figure of a charioteer from Delphi is one of the very few bronze statues to survive from the fifth century B.C.

of a great war against Sparta as reported in the history of the war by the historian Thucydides. Praising Athenian democracy, Pericles said that at Athens the law guaranteed equal justice to all, that talent and not wealth was the Athenian qualification for public service, that Athenians expected everyone to participate in public affairs. In fact, his picture corresponded more to an ideal world than to the real Athens, where the courts were often prejudiced, where wealth remained an important qualification for office, and where political ambition burned hotly and was pursued ruthlessly. In the tough world of Athenian politics, we can see strong parallels to human behavior in other, more modern democracies. The Greeks often fell far short of their ideals as expressed by Pericles, but in the expression of these ideals they also defined civility in ways for which society has striven ever since.

Revival after the Dark Age, 850 B.C.-650 B.C.

For the Greeks the Dark Age began to dissipate about 850 B.C., with the renewal of contact between the mainland and the Near East. Phoenicia, whose trade continued brisk, lay close to the Greek island of Cyprus, where Mycenaean culture had continued after the Dorians had destroyed it on most of the mainland. Objects from Phoenicia began to appear in mainland Greece; the earliest traces of the Phoenician alphabet as adapted to the writing of Greek are now dated about 825 B.C., with new letters added for peculiarly Greek sounds. New styles of pottery also testify to the renewal of communications. Greece proper now received the Homeric poems, first composed in the Ionian Greek settlements of Asia Minor, restoring to the mainland the sense of its glorious past.

In Greece, people looked back through Homer and the poet Hesiod to a time they thought of as far more heroic than their own, and this sense of a heroic past emboldened them to new acts of heroism. Hesiod, in his *Works and Days*, written in the seventh century B.C., set down proper rules for the small farmer and scolded his own brother, who had tried to grab more than his fair share of the family estate. His farm was infertile, the climate bad, and the behavior of people had degenerated, Hesiod felt, since the good old days. Hesiod also wrote a genealogy of the gods (*Theogony*), giving the traditional view of how the universe had come into being; the gods were the children of earth and heaven, and had themselves created humankind. Preaching justice, both human and divine, Hesiod's verse reflected the religious ideas of the Greeks in an early phase, perhaps partly under the influence of the oracle at Delphi, a mountain shrine of the sun god Apollo in central Greece where a divinely inspired prophetess gave advice to all comers. Hesiod's concern for the farmer also reflects the fact that the great majority of ancient populations made their living through farming.

The Polis and Colonization

For the Greeks, the prevailing social and political unit gradually became the *polis* (plural *poleis*), roughly translated as the city-state, though many were too small to be cities. The main sense of the term is that of a community of relatives, citizens all descended in theory from a common ancestor. The "kings," or local chieftains, of Mycenaean times had disappeared, and the prominent men—the richer and more noble—in each community had begun to form councils and other variously selected groups to manage public affairs. Usually the community centered upon a fortress built upon a hill, "the high city" or *acropolis*, and also possessed a public square or gathering-place for assemblies, the *agora*.

Our scanty and difficult sources give us a picture of a society in which the rich alone could afford expensive

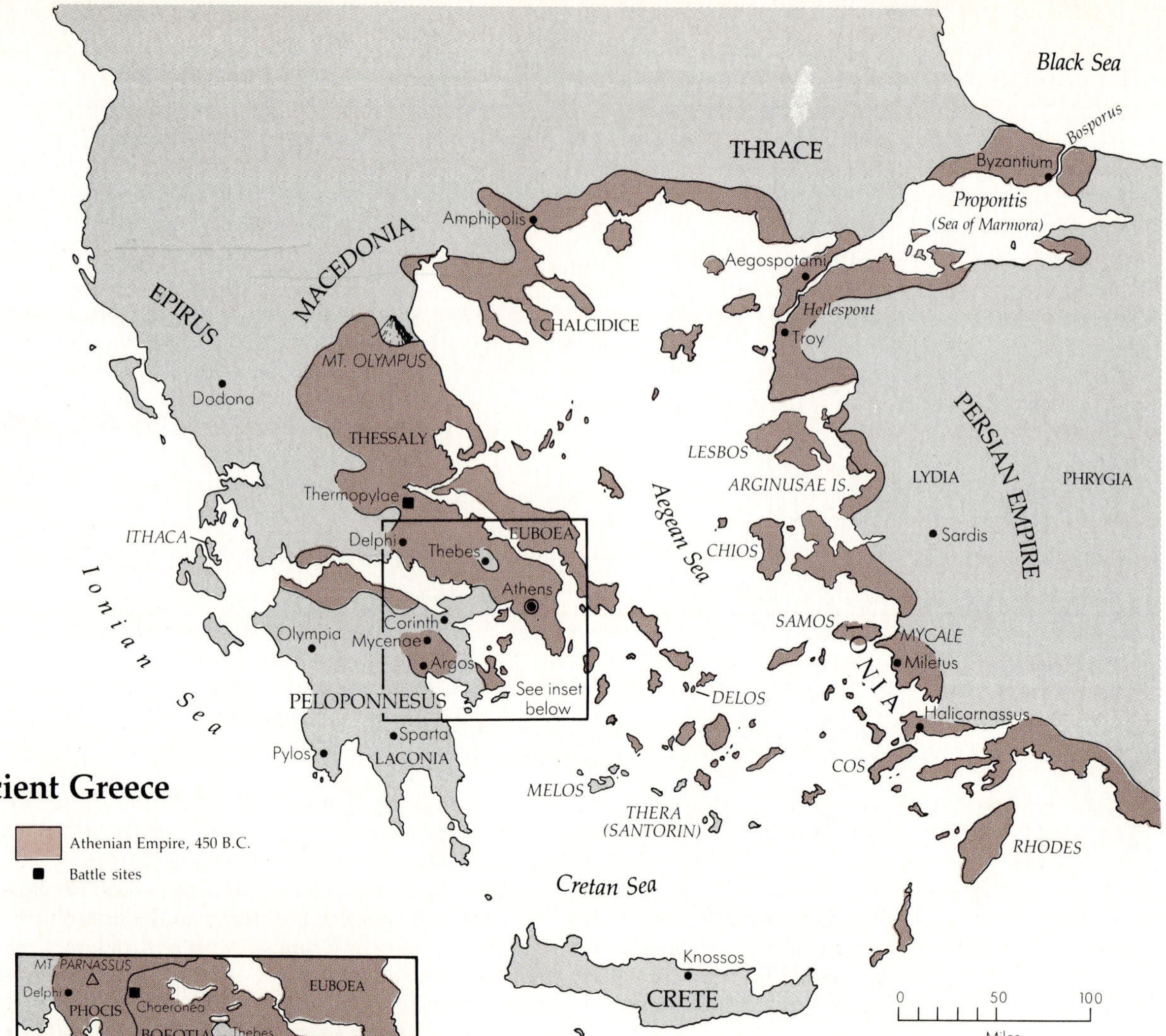

Ancient Greece

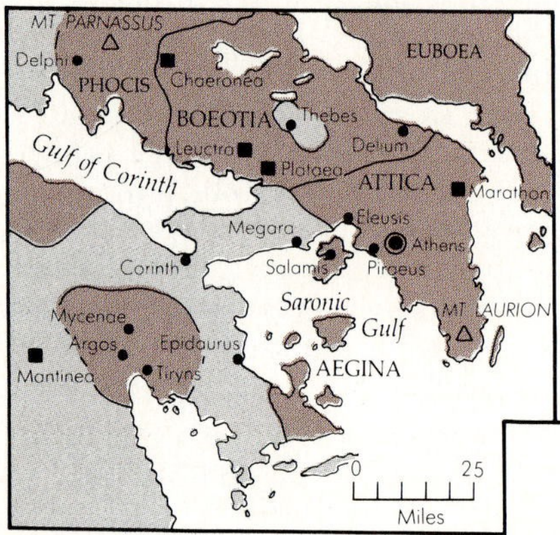

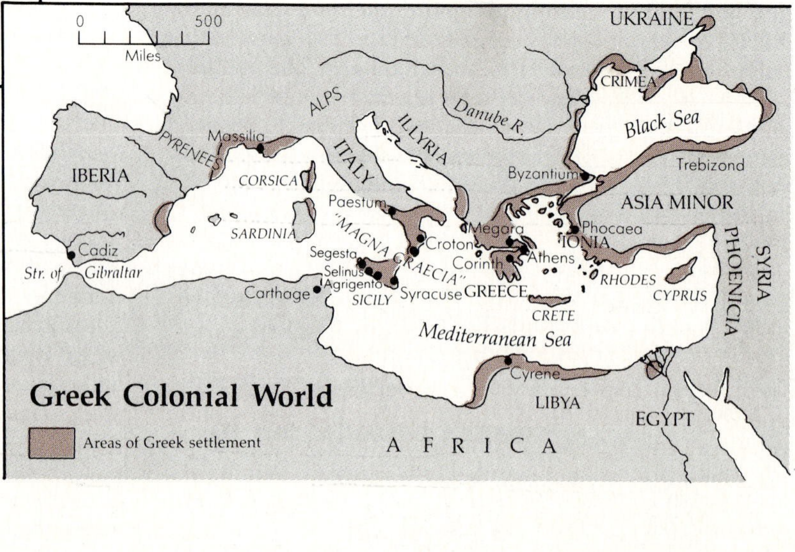

Greek Colonial World

horses and military equipment, and therefore controlled the instruments of coercion. They had organized themselves into an aristocracy of family and wealth, proud of their bloodlines, and dominated the poor who worked the land. A middle class of well-to-do farmers, merchants, and craftsmen also came into existence, and eventually formed the nucleus of the close-order infantry formations, newly developed about 650 B.C., that were more efficient than the traditional cavalry.

Social conflict within and between classes was a normal condition of life. One-man rule became the characteristic form of government within these evolving city-states beginning about 650. To some extent the conflicts were dampened, the power of the aristocracy held in check, and the lower classes protected; but in each case the personal qualities of the tyrant determined the success and decency of his rule. Usually the power of a tyrant did not last more than one or two generations at the most.

Together with the establishment of city-states, there was also large-scale Greek colonial expansion. The city-states of Asia Minor and of mainland Greece sent out naval expeditions to plant new settlements in non-Greek areas where there was no power strong enough to prevent them: around the Black Sea, along the African shore of the Mediterranean (in what we now call Libya), in Sicily and southern Italy (which the Romans later called *Magna Graecia*, "Great Greece"), and as far west as the coasts of France and Spain. Each new colony became a new city-state—independent of its mother city, though bound to it by historical and economic ties and by similar political and religious practices. Overpopulation and internal strife in the settled cities, together with the wish for trade and adventure, advanced the colonizing movement. Trebizond in Asia Minor, Byzantium (later to become Constantinople and still later Istanbul) at the Black Sea straits, Syracuse in Sicily, Naples in southern Italy, Marseilles in southern France, and Cadiz beyond the Straits of Gibraltar on the Atlantic coast of Spain are among the famous cities that began as Greek colonies.

Combined with the decline of Egypt and the Assyrian conquests in western Asia, such colonization set off a period of Mediterranean trade focusing on Greece. First one Greek city and then another would assume prominence in the busy traffic; the Dorian-founded settlements on Crete, Rhodes, Corinth, Megara all became powerful and prosperous. By the midseventh century, coins, invented in the Anatolian kingdom of Lydia, had begun to be minted on the island of Aegina in Greece, where silver was the only precious metal available. This convenient system of recording commerce soon spread westward, each city-state making its own coinage. (The coins of Aegina had turtles on them; those of Corinth, foals; those of Athens, the owl of Athena, patron goddess of the city.)

In the area of southern Greece called the Peloponnesus, a fertile, almost landlocked region, the city-state of Sparta developed. (This unique society is responsible for the overtones that the word *spartan* still has in our language.) Later called by the philosopher Aristotle "an association of villages which achieves almost complete self-sufficiency," the Spartan polis was ruled by the descendants of the Dorian conquerors, perhaps 10 percent of the total population and the only citizens, called the *homoioi*, or "equals." Most of the people belonged to the class of *helots*, farm laborers who belonged to the state, which assigned them to work the lands of the citizens. In between was a free class called *perioikoi* ("dwellers around"), descendants of the pre-Dorian residents of neighboring areas, who lived in the villages under Spartan control and had personal freedom but could not participate in politics or intermarry with the Spartans; they were also subject to Sparta in foreign and military matters. No helots were assigned to the perioikoi, but they could buy slaves abroad if they wished. The ruling Spartans lived in constant fear of revolution; they kept secret agents planted among the helots to report subversive talk, and they barely managed to put down a helot uprising in the late seventh century.

The owl, sacred to Athena, appeared on Athenian coins beginning the sixth century B.C. The original coin was struck by Pisistratus, who ruled Athens from 542 to 527 B.C.

The constitution, which the Spartans attributed to a divinely inspired lawgiver, Lycurgus, provided for two kings, perhaps descendants of two rival Dorian families. Real political power came to reside in five overseers elected annually by an assembly of all Spartan citizens over the age of thirty—excluding all women, helots, and perioikoi. There was also a kind of council of thirty elders representing the more powerful families.

War dominated Spartan thinking. The males lived under military discipline from the age of seven, when a boy was taken from his parents and taught reading, music, running, and fighting. Weak-looking babies were abandoned to die. So that there might be healthy children, girls were also given strenuous training. Adult males lived in barracks until they were thirty, though they might marry at twenty; they dined in the mess hall until they were sixty. It was a harsh, regimented life, "Spartan" in its merits and in its defects. In battle the Spartan army was excellent, and the citizens were patriotic and willing to bear misfortune. The need to control hostile neighbors and internal dissension led the Spartans to introduce iron bars as money to make ordinary commercial pursuits as unattractive, public, and difficult as possible. The result was a barracks state.

Athens, from 632 B.C.

Draco and Solon Athens—which had never undergone a Dorian occupation—did not become a polis as early as Sparta, but lingered as an old-fashioned, aristocratic tribal state, dominating the surrounding hinterland of Attica. It was divided territorially into plains, hills, and coastal land, and politically into four tribes, each of which had brotherhoods (*phratries*) or territorial subdivisions (*trittyes*). Within each phratry a further distinction was drawn between those who owned and worked their farms (the *clans*), and the *guildsmen*, later in origin, who belonged to an association of artisans or merchants. Each mature male was admitted into a phratry either as a clansman or as a guildsman. Land descended in the clan and might not be passed outside it. With the clan went a deep attachment to local religious shrines, whose priests were clansmen. The guildsmen were citizens though not aristocrats; apparently they could sell or transfer their property.

Three *archons* (leaders or chief men)—one of whom managed religious affairs, one military affairs (the *polemarch*), and one civil affairs—were joined in the seventh century by a board of six recording archons, (legal officials), making nine in all. Each was elected for a year, at the end of which all nine automatically became members of the Council of Areopagus (from the hill of Ares, god of war, in Athens), the chief judicial and policy-making body. Although a general assembly of all the males directly elected the archons and thus the future members of the Areopagus Council, only clansmen—men of birth and wealth—and not guildsmen could be elected.

These long-standing political arrangements were challenged in 632 by a young noble's plot to seize power, which led to scandal when his followers were massacred even though they had taken sanctuary at the altar of Athena. The noble family held responsible for this sacrilege was banished, and in 621 B.C. a specially appointed official, Draco, allegedly published the first Athenian law code, famous for its severe penalties (hence our term a "Draconian" measure). The harshest of all Athenian laws were those on debt; a bankrupt clansman could never sell or mortgage his land, but was compelled to mortgage its produce to his debtor. Thus he could oblige himself and his heirs to work the land indefinitely for somebody else, in effect losing his freedom. Bankrupt guildsmen thereby became the property of their creditors as slaves. In time the growing inequity of this system led to internal strife.

In the 590s a reformer, Solon, elected as the sole archon, freed both the clansmen and guildsmen then suffering these penalties for debt, canceled current debts, abolished the harsh system, and published a new constitution, or law code. He tried to improve the general prosperity by emphasizing the need to abandon complete economic dependence on agriculture and to foster a lively new commerce. He even offered citizenship to citizens of other poleis who would come to work in Athens. He opened the most important offices of state to the richest men, whatever their origin. Wealth was measured by the amount of agricultural produce a man's land provided annually; for example, 750 bushels of grain or about 4400 gallons of olive oil a year put a man into the topmost class and made him eligible for high office. A man whose land produced less than 300 bushels of grain or only about 1800 gallons of olive oil a year was eligible only for the general assembly.

Solon is also said to have founded a new body, the Council of Four Hundred, consisting of one hundred members from each of the four tribes, all named by Solon himself, to act as an inner circle of the general assembly of the people, preparing materials for discussion, and making recommendations for action. The general assembly now could not act without such a recommendation; but it could vote against it, and it still elected the archons. And Solon also made it a kind of court by selecting a panel of assembly members by lot to review the work of the magistrates.

By introducing these quasi-democratic innovations while retaining aristocratic election of the rich to magistracies and the oligarchic power of the few in the Council of the Aeropagus, Solon had introduced a radical set of compromises. In one of his own poems he says of his actions: "I stood holding my stout shield over both parties [the poor and the rich]; I did not allow either party to prevail unjustly." By justice Solon meant what we might call social justice. Though some of his fellow Athenians jeered at him for not taking advantage of his extraordinary powers to make himself rich, he answered (again in a poem) that "money flits from man to man, but honor abides forever." Urging the Athenians to abide by his laws for a hundred years, Solon then withdrew from the scene.

Pisistratus and Cleisthenes Factional strife soon began again. Athenians seem to have taken sides in accordance with both region and class. The plains people were mostly aristocrats who felt Solon had gone too far, the hill people mostly poor farmers who felt he had not gone far enough, and the coast people mostly artisans who thought he was about right. In 560 B.C. their quarrels gave Athens into the hands of a "tyrant," as the Greeks called a dictator, even if benevolent. This was Pisistratus, a noble, who had made himself leader of the hill people. In and out of office for some years, Pisistratus owed his final return in 546 to the vast wealth that he had acquired from the silver mines on his estates in the north, and to the mercenary troops from Argos whom he hired with this wealth. Pisistratus and his son, Hippias, dominated Athens until 510 B.C.

Though Solon's constitutional measures had not endured, his economic policy made Athens rich, as Athenian pottery became the best and most sought-after in Greece. Pisistratus—who collected 10 percent of all revenues for his personal fortune—pushed commercial success still further, partly by shrewd alliances with other poleis. At home, his was the only party. He exiled those aristocrats who refused to support him; he would often keep the son of a noble family as a hostage to ensure the family's loyalty. Having come to power as leader of the poor, he gave them loans, embarked on a lavish program of public works to be sure there were jobs for all, subsidized the arts, and increased the magnificence of state religious celebrations. His sons followed his policies, but the noble families whom Pisistratus had displaced continued in opposition, often from exile. When Hipparchus, one of the sons, was assassinated for personal reasons in 514 B.C., executions multiplied, government grew more tyrannical, and the exiled nobles came back in triumphant alliance with the Spartans in 510 B.C.

By 508 Cleisthenes, one of the exiles who appealed for the support of the guildsmen—already so much favored by Pisistratus—came to power on promises of constitutional reform. These he fulfilled by striking at the political influence of the clans in elections, and by giving the guildsmen equal weight. Using as a basic new political unit an old territorial division called a *deme*—a small area something like a ward in a modern city—Cleisthenes ordered all citizens to be registered as voters within their demes, irrespective of their origins, thus giving the guildsmen equal franchise with the clansmen. Whoever was a member of a given deme in 508-507 B.C. remained in it permanently, and so did his descendants, even if they moved away.

Cleisthenes also rezoned Attica into three new regions that did not coincide with the former coast, hill, and plain. He regrouped the demes into trittyes that, unlike the twelve older trittyes, were in general not compact and adjacent, but chosen from all three territorial subgroupings. Finally, by drawing lots he put every three trittyes together into a political "tribe." Instead of the four old racial (or genuinely tribal) groups, there were ten of these new political tribes whose membership cut across the old family, regional, and class lines. Each of these new, artificial tribes had members from each of the three new territorial divisions. Thus the former influence of the noble families had been effectively cut down. Cleisthenes had invented a fundamental tool of democracy—the gerrymander.

Each deme annually elected a number of its members (proportionate to its population) as its representatives, and from them the ten new tribes selected by lot fifty each to be members of the new Council of Five Hundred, replacing Solon's Council of Four Hundred. Solon had given Athenians equality before the law; Cleisthenes gave them equality at the ballot box. The four old racial or tribal tribes, the old brotherhoods, the clans, continued to play a major part in religious and social life, but their political role was virtually over.

The ten groups of fifty tribal members of which the Council of Five Hundred was made up each governed in continual session for a tenth of the year (roughly thirty-six days), and the chairman of the committee of fifty that was sitting at any given time was selected afresh by lot every day. During each continual thirty-six-day session the committee members lived in a special state building and were fed at public expense. They could summon the remaining councilors to a full session whenever they wished. No citizen between the ages of thirty and sixty could be a member of the council more than twice, or chairman of a day's session more than once. Thus, with swiftly changing large groups of citizens receiving responsibilities for short times, almost any citizen could hope to enjoy the experience of participating in government at some time during his life (for citizens were still males only). Fortified by their new constitution giving all citizens a stake in the community, the Athenians were prepared for their famous historic confrontation with the Persian Empire.

Still, Greek society and the growing economy depended upon the systematic exploitation of slaves. Dependent labor is important to any state that must be able to ensure productivity, unless that ability can be generated through other incentives. Public works, manufacture, agriculture, even trade and war production required dependent labor. Thus, in the eyes of the law, slaves were chattel. Like all ancient peoples, Greeks took slavery for granted, as their law code and their literature show. Free men who could afford slaves, if only as servants, did so, and slave women performed household chores. These slaves were even further outside the political system because most were foreigners. Athenians were not kept as slaves in Athens, though they might be in Corinth. Thus *slave* and *barbarian*, or non-Greek, came to be nearly synonymous for some Greek commentators.

We know little about the life of the slaves, for they were not in a position to leave records, and because we do not know how slavery functioned, we cannot say how basic to society it was. Their voice is best heard through their actions. Obviously, some Greeks owned no slaves and may have disapproved of slavery; some owners treated slaves as fellow workers; other owners reduced the life of the slave to a cycle of toil, punishment, and sustenance. Moreover, slaves were of different significance at different times and in different cities. At best we must recognize slavery as a basic institution in Greek society, but we cannot determine, from our present knowledge, how basic.

We know somewhat more about the role of family life in ancient Greece, though again not enough. Certainly women enjoyed political and legal rights that placed them above slaves; equally clearly, they had no political rights and few legal ones, and the personal freedom most women enjoyed depended on the social position of their husbands. Women in Athens appear to have had less significance than in Minoan society, for they were likely to be confined to their homes. There, however, they had much, though not absolute, authority over the running of the household. In Sparta alone, where young girls took part in the physical training enjoined upon all by the state, did women play roles outside the home or beyond the religious festival.

The role of women tended to be defined by social class. Among the poor, wives might well work as stall-keepers in the market. Aristophanes refers to "businesswomen," and others were courtesans. But the major badge of identity was the keys to storeroom and cellar that a wife carried with her. If she was reasonably well-to-do, she would preside over slave-girls and a substantial household to which the husband paid little attention. Nonetheless, the household would remain his; a daughter who inherited property because there was no male heir was required to marry her father's closest relative.

The secluded life of women was intensified by the fact that marriages were social or economic alliances, and that men entertained one another in the Agora, the Assembly, or in their homes. Male homosexuality was accepted, especially between an older man and a younger boy, and though these relations were at times non-physical, the presumption was that men spent their time outside the home and with each other. Even so, the role of the family was very important, for it was through the family that property was inherited, that citizenship—which was inherited through the legitimate line—continued from generation to generation, and that the moral code was transmitted.

II PERSIA AND THE GREEKS, TO 478 B.C.

The Persian Empire

We have already encountered the Medes, an Indo-European people of the Near East, who in 612 B.C. cooperated with the briefly recovering Babylonians to destroy Nineveh and bring down the hated Assyrian Empire. We have also seen the Medes' southern relatives, the Persians, conquer Babylon (538) and allow the captive Hebrews to return to Jerusalem. It was under Cyrus (c 559-530), who attacked the Medes and took their capital (Ecbatana, south of the Caspian Sea), that the Persians began a meteoric rise toward universal rule, the last and greatest empire in the ancient Near East. Official inscriptions of this Persian Empire—carved in three languages (Old Persian, Elamite, Babylonian), all written in cuneiform script—gave scholars in the early nineteenth century their first chance to learn how to read cuneiform. This led to the gradual deciphering of Babylonian (Akkadian), which in turn made possible all of the discoveries about ancient Mesopotamia discussed in Chapter 1. Inscriptions of the sixth century B.C., when deciphered, opened up more than two thousand years of history which, had it not been for the continued use of cuneiform, might still be unknown. In this way, history is reconstructed backwards on the basis of languages that have, through the consolidation of states or the diffusion of cultures, acquired widespread, if not yet universal, application.

Uniting his territory with that of the Medes and initially bypassing Babylon, Cyrus moved westward into Anatolia, absorbed the Lydian kingdom of the rich king Croesus, and conquered the Greek cities of Ionia along the Aegean coast. Next he moved east all the way to the borders of India, annexing as he went, though imposing no such tyranny as had the Assyrians. Instead of deporting whole populations, Cyrus allowed them to worship as they pleased and to govern themselves in their own way under his representatives. The fall of Babylon also led to the Persian conquest of Syria. Cyrus' son Cambyses (529-521 B.C.) conquered Egypt and died, probably by suicide, on his way home to put down a revolution, which his usurping brother-in-law Darius (521-486 B.C.) succeeded in quelling.

It was Darius who subdivided the empire into twenty provinces (*satrapies*), each with a political governor, military governor, and tax collector, with each allowed to maintain its religion and local customs. Royal agents crisscrossed the vast area from the Aegean to the Indus, collecting information for the king. Darius adopted the Lydian practice of coining money and introduced it into all his dominions. His highway system was superb, a great network whose largest thread was the royal road that ran more than sixteen hundred miles from Susa, Darius' capital, to Sardis, the chief city of Lydia. It is likely that Darius personally introduced Zoroastrianism, the religion of Zarathustra, who had died a generation earlier. In any case, he accepted the religion and honored its single god without repudiating other gods.

Zoroastrianism began as a monotheistic faith, proclaiming the one god Ahuramazda, whose identifying quality was his wisdom. (He is the only abstractly intellectual deity so far encountered.) The other divinities around him were not gods and godesses, but abstract qualities such as Justice and Integrity, which he had created. It was the existence of evil in the universe that led Zarathustra to imagine that life was a constant struggle between a good spirit and an evil spirit, both subordinate to Ahuramazda. A wise person will ponder and then choose the good way; a foolish one will choose the evil way; the supreme spirit will reward the wise and punish the foolish.

Intellectual and abstract, lacking ritual and priesthood, early Zoroastrianism was perhaps too impersonal and rarefied for a popular faith, and it was modified after its founder's death. By identifying Ahuramazda with the good spirit, the generations after Darius in effect demoted the supreme god from being the ruler over the evil spirit (Ahriman) to being a contender with

The tomb of King Darius II is high on a cliff, cut into solid rock, in present-day Iran. Nearby are the ruins of Persepolis.

him. The religion became dualistic, giving comparable power to good and evil, and revived elements of earlier polytheism, as old deities and ceremonies reappeared and a powerful priesthood asserted itself.

The Ionian Cities, The Threat to Greece, Marathon

The new Persian rulers would not allow their subjects political freedom, which was what the now-captive Ionian Greek cities most valued. Their prosperity declined, as the Persians drew toward Asia the wealth of the trade routes that had formerly enriched Aegean towns. By 513 B.C. the Persians had crossed the Bosporus, sailed up the Danube, and moved north across modern Romania into the Ukraine in a campaign against a nomadic people called Scythians. Though tentative, the new advance into Europe alarmed the Greeks, who were now receiving overtures for an alliance from the Scythians; it looked as if Darius would move south against European Greece from his new base in the northern Balkans.

Some of the Greek poleis—Sparta and her allies—were hostile to the Persians, but there were others that had pro-Persian rulers. Pisistratus' son Hippias had taken refuge at the Persian court, awaiting his return to Athens, but the Athenians refused to accept him and helped the captive Ionian cities to resist Persian rule. The Ionians rebelled in 499; with Athenian assistance, they burned down Sardis, the former Lydian capital that was now the Persian headquarters in Asia Minor. Many other Greek cities then joined the rebellion.

The Persians struck back with fury and by 495 B.C. had defeated the Ionian fleet. They burned the most important Ionian city, Miletus, massacred many of its men, and deported its women and children into slavery. By 493 B.C. the Ionian revolt was over, and in the next two years the Persians extended their authority along the northern coasts of Greece proper, directly threatening Athens. It was probably Hippias who advised the Persian commanders to land at Marathon in a region once loyal to his father, Pisistratus, about twenty-five miles north of Athens. There a far smaller Athenian force, decisively led by Miltiades, a professional soldier who had served the Persians and angered Darius, defeated his former colleagues in 490 and for ten years ended the Persian threat to Greece. Because the Spartans had been celebrating a religious festival during which military operations were forbidden, they had been unable to participate in the fighting; only the much smaller polis of Plataea had sent a thousand men to join the ten thousand Athenians. The credit for driving off the Persians therefore went primarily to Athens. Darius now planned a much greater invasion, but an Egyptian uprising and then his death prevented it. His successor, Xerxes (486-465), having subdued the Egyptians, resumed the elaborate preparations for war in 481.

The Persian Wars

By the time Xerxes was ready to attack, Miltiades was dead. A leader of the nobles, he had been brought down by a rival faction. One means of keeping factionalism under control had been introduced by Cleisthenes and, about 487, was revived: ostracism. The word comes from *ostrakon*, a fragment of a clay pot on which citizens scratched the name of any politician they wished to exile from the city for ten years. Apparently a majority of a meeting of 6,000 citizens (3,001 votes) was needed to ostracize. The 480s—the decade of preparation for Xerxes' expected attacks—was a period of frequent ostracism. (Many hundreds of the original clay potsherds still exist with the names of prominent politicians written on them, a sort of negative ballot.) In the process a leader named Themistocles emerged as the popular choice to lead the resistance to the anticipated Persian invasion.

After 487 the nine archons were no longer elected by the people but selected by lot from a preliminary list, drawn up by the demes, of five hundred candidates, who were drawn from the richer citizens. This change further limited the influence of the aristocratic clans and gradually reduced the influence of the Council of the Areopagus, since more and more of its members were

HERODOTUS AS CHRONICLER

Herodotus (c 490-425 B.C.), usually called the father of history, was a Greek from Asia Minor. Most of his information came from oral sources, though he apparently also consulted such written work as survived. Ancient references to him argue that his accounts were untruthful; modern historians are more inclined to trust his basic arguments, though they find him biased and feel that he was naive in his use of sources. If unsupported by other evidence, Herodotus' accounts are not accepted at face value; however, often other evidence does supply support. In any event, there is no doubt that his history represents great literature, as shown by the following extract, which tells of the problem of rightly interpreting the meaning to be brought back from a visit to the Oracle at Delphi:

The Athenians had sent their envoys to Delphis really to ask an oracle, and as soon as the customary rites were performed and they had entered the shrine and taken their seats, the Priestess Aristonice uttered the following prophecy:

Why sit you, doomed ones? Fly to the world's end, leaving
Home and the heights your city circles like a wheel.
The head shall not remain in its place, nor the body,
Nor the feet beneath, nor the hands, nor the parts between;
But all is ruined, for fire and the headlong God of War
Speeding in a Syrian chariot shall bring you low.
Many a tower shall he destroy, not yours alone,
And give to pitiless fire many shrines of gods,
Which even now stand sweating, with fear quivering,
While over the roof-tops black blood runs streaming
In prophecy of woe that needs must come. But rise,
Haste from the sanctuary and bow your hearts to grief.

The Athenian envoys heard these words with dismay; indeed they were about to abandon themselves to despair at the dreadful fate which was prophesied, when Timon, the son of Androbulus and one of the most distinguished men in Delphi, suggested that they should take branches of olive in their hands and, in the guise of suppliants, approach the oracle a second time. The Athenians acted upon this suggestion, "Lord Apollo," they said, "can you not, in consideration of these olive boughs which we have brought you, give us some better prophecy about our country? Otherwise we will never leave the holy place but stay here till we die."

Thereupon the Prophetess uttered a second prophecy, which ran as follows:

Not wholly can Pallas win the heart of Olympian Zeus,
Though she prays him with many prayers and all her subtlety;
Yet will I speak to you this other word, as firm as adamant:
Though all else shall be taken within the bound of Cecrops
And the fastness of the holy mountain of Cithaeron,
Yet Zeus the all-seeing grants to Athena's prayer
That the wooden wall only shall not fall, but help you and your children.
But await not the host of horse and foot coming from Asia,
Nor be still, but turn your back and withdraw from the foe.
Truly a day will come when you will meet him face to face.
Divine Salamis, you will bring death to women's sons
When the corn is scattered, or the harvest gathered in.

This second answer seemed to be, as indeed it was, less menacing than the first; so the envoys wrote it down and returned to Athens. When it was made public upon their arrival in the city, and the attempt to explain it began, amongst the various opinions which were expressed there were two mutually exclusive interpretations. Some of the older men supposed that the prophecy meant that the Acropolis would escape destruction, on the grounds that the Acropolis was fenced in the old days with a thorn-hedge, and that this was the "wooden wall" of the oracle; but others thought that by this expression the oracle meant the ships, and they urged in consequence that everything should be abandoned in favour of the immediate preparation of a fleet. There was, however, for those who believed "wooden wall" to mean ships, one disturbing thing—namely, the last two lines of the Priestess' prophecy:

Divine Salamis, you will bring death to women's sons
When the corn is scattered, or the harvest gathered in.

This was a very awkward statement and caused profound disturbance amongst all who took the wooden wall to signify ships; for the professional interpreters understood the lines to mean that they would be beaten at Salamis in a fight at sea. There was, however, a man in Athens who had recently made a name for himself—Themistocles called Neocles' son; he now came forward and declared that there was an important point in which the professional interpreters were mistaken. If, he maintained, the disaster referred to was to strike the Athenians, it would not have been expressed in such mild language. "Hateful Salamis" would surely have been a more likely phrase than "divine Salamis," if the inhabitants of the country were doomed to destruction there. On the contrary the true interpretation was that the oracle referred not to the Athenians but to their enemies. The "wooden wall" did, indeed, mean the ships; so he advised his countrymen to prepare at once to meet the invader at sea.

Herodotus, *The Histories*, trans. Aubrey de Sélincourt, revised A.R. Burn (New York: Penguin Books, 1972), pp. 488-89.

men chosen in the new way. Because the generals were still elected, the old political rivalry for the archonship now shifted to the office of general, and factional struggle continued.

When new supplies of silver were discovered in 483, Themistocles persuaded the Athenians to use the money to build a new fleet instead of passing it out among the citizens. This decision probably determined the outcome of the Persians' new effort, and incidentally suited the poor, who built and rowed the ships and whose fortunes were associated with the navy. As the leading military power of Greece, Sparta took over the leadership of the anti-Persian Greek poleis, which together formed an anti-Persian league with a congress of delegates from the individual cities and a unified command. Knowing that its forces would be greatly outnumbered, the league abandoned the northern cities, where the wide plains allowed the Persian calvary to operate freely.

In 480 B.C. Xerxes' huge army, its supply lines greatly overextended and its speed slowed down by its numbers, crossed into Europe and swung south into Greece, while a fleet, possibly of three thousand ships of various sizes, sailed along the coast. At the pass of Thermopylae in central Greece, a Greek traitor showed the Persians how to outflank the defenders, but a small army, primarily of three hundred Spartans, defended the pass to the last man, taking a deadly toll of the Persian infantry. A storm, a battle, and a second storm cut the Persian fleet in half. The historian Herodotus tells us that the Delphic oracle had mysteriously prophesied that Athens would be destroyed and had advised the Athenians to put their trust in their "wooden walls." Themistocles persuaded the Athenians that the message meant they should abandon the city to its patron goddess Athena and rely upon their fleet—their wooden ships—for their defense.

Athens was accordingly evacuated, except for the defenders of the Acropolis, whom Xerxes' men killed as they burned the city. In the narrow waters of the Strait of Salamis, near Athens, the Greek fleet awaited the Persian attack, for an engagement in the open sea would favor the larger Persian fleet. Themistocles sent a misleading message to the Persians pretending that he would betray the Greeks, and so convinced them that it was safe to attack. The Greek fleet—helped by deserters from the Persians who revealed Xerxes' battle plans—won a smashing victory, as Xerxes himself watched from a great throne set upon the shore. Xerxes had to withdraw from Greece; in 479 at Plataea united Greek forces numbering more than a hundred thousand men defeated the Persian troops once again.

Although the maintenance of Greek unity was precarious because of thousands of personal and municipal rivalries among the Greeks, members of the league had kept the oath, "I shall fight to the death, I shall put freedom before life, I shall not desert colonel or captain alive or dead, I shall carry out the generals' commands, and I shall bury my comrades-in-arms where they fall and leave none unburied." An intensely individualistic people had shown, for a time at least, that they could put the general interest ahead of all else. Soon afterward at Mycale (478 B.C.) the Greeks scored another victory on land and sea. The Persians, as it turned out, had been stopped, although peace was not formally made until 449 and at many times during those three decades the Greeks were threatened with renewed invasion.

III THE ATHENIAN EMPIRE, 478-404 B.C.

Postwar Reorganization

When the Athenians began to rebuild and refortify Athens, the Spartans advised them to stop, arguing that the new walls might be useful to the Persians if they ever again invaded Greece; but Themistocles, as ambassador to Sparta, played for time until the walls were completed. The episode serves as a symbol of Athens' unwillingness to let Sparta, the strongest military power, take the lead in planning for the future defense against Persia. It was indeed Athens, after 478 the strongest naval power, that organized the new Greek alliance, designed to liberate the Ionian cities still subject to Persia and to maintain the defenses. Athens contributed most of the ships, while the other cities were assessed contributions in both ships and money. Since the treasury of the alliance was on the island of Delos, the alliance is called the Delian League. Under Cimon it scored a major victory over the Persians in Asia Minor in 469 B.C.

About 470 Themistocles was ostracized; while in exile he was charged with corruption. In c 465 he fled to the Persians, was given rich revenues, and died in the service of Xerxes' son and successor. Themistocles accurately foresaw the great danger that lay ahead for Athens—the long-range threat from Sparta. Like Miltiades, he had lost the confidence of the Athenians after he had done them invaluable service.

In 462 a new reform further democratized Athenian government; the aristocratic Areopagus Council lost most of its powers to the Council of Five Hundred, the Assembly, and the popular courts instituted by Solon. The reform was partly inspired by a brilliant young aristocrat named Pericles. By about 457 the patriotic and incorruptible Pericles had become the leading Athenian politician, responsible for the many military and naval operations conducted simultaneously against the Persians in Egypt (an expensive failure), against the Spartans, and against certain members of the Athenian alliance itself who resented Athens' dominating ways.

At home Pericles pressed for democracy, inaugurating a system of state pay, first for jurymen (drawn from a panel six thousand strong, six hundred from each tribe), and later for those rendering other services to the state. State service was thus transformed from an activity that the poor could not afford into one that they welcomed. To limit the number of those eligible for such payment, Pericles also limited Athenian citizenship to those whose parents were both Athenian. He also saw to it that the money to pay all these people would come only from Athens' allies.

From Alliance to Empire

In fact, Pericles was gradually turning the Athenian alliance into an empire, with subject members providing the money for Athens, which would defend them all and would be able to challenge Sparta. In 454 the treasury of the alliance was moved from Delos to Athens and became in effect a major Athenian resource. Since 470 no ally had been allowed to secede. During a truce in the first Peloponnesian War with the Spartans (460-445), the Athenians, operating in the Aegean, increased the number of their allies (about 170 cities at the peak), and in 449 made peace with Persia, liberating the Ionian cities and binding the Persians not to come within three days' journey of the coast.

Athenian settlements were founded on the territories of some allied states, and Athenian coinage became standard throughout the alliance. Resentment against Athens therefore was naturally widespread among the allies. But in 445 a thirty years' treaty with Sparta provided that neither side would commit aggression against the other. Both had lost the good will of the other Greek poleis; Athens was now ruling an empire by force, and its protection against the Persians seemed less selfless; Sparta had suffered defeats and its military reputation was dimmed.

As it turned out, the peace lasted for only fifteen years (445-431). It was a prosperous period during which Pericles continued to dominate the affairs of state, being democratically elected general every year. He had at his disposal the large surpluses in the imperial treasury, which mounted in those years of peace, and which with Athens' other revenues were much more than enough to pay the ten thousand rowers of the warships, the seven hundred officials, the five hundred councilors, the six thousand jurors, and many others. Pericles embarked upon a great program of public works, of which the two most famous buildings were the celebrated Parthenon (originally the temple of Athena Parthenos, the virgin, and destroyed by the Persians in 480) and Propylaea (monumental gateway), both on the Acropolis. After one had mounted the steps that led up to the Propylaea and passed through it, one saw at the top of the hill a giant bronze statue of Athena sculptured by Phidias, a personal friend of Pericles; behind it and to the right rose the entrance portico of the magnificent new temple; inside was another statue of Athena by Phidias, in gold and ivory.

There were plenty of jobs available because of the building program, and slaves as well as freemen participated and were paid. There was money and opportunity for nearly everyone: for the *metics* (resident aliens), who had to pay a special tax and were not allowed to own land or participate in politics, but who engaged in commerce and contributed to the city's and their own good fortune; for the 80,000 slaves, whose lot was somewhat easier than it was elsewhere, and who were at times set free; and most of all for the 168,000 Athenian citizens (4,000 upper class, 100,000 middle class, and 64,000 lower class, as one rough estimate suggests). Counting children, the total population of Attica was perhaps half a million.

Relatively speaking, Athens was a democracy, though we would not consider it one today. But the Greeks often turned to demagogues who, though personally honest, manipulated the demos (or common people) to their own ends. However, what were these ends, since the function of a leader is to lead? The Greeks believed men to be unequal, not only in economic and social status, but also in moral worth, so they justified a narrow base for citizenship. They believed that because communities tend to divide into factions, a well-run state must find a means to control these factions, lest they ultimately destroy the overriding sense of a higher community.

Athens was a direct democracy, not a representative one, which meant that all 45,000 male citizens eligible for the Assembly in the time of Pericles were entitled to attend; yet we think that in general perhaps not more than six thousand took the trouble to do so. Given the problems of travel and the need for peasants to remain on their land, this group would be, on the whole, well-to-do and dominated by the aged because the young were away at war.

In its Golden Age under Pericles, Athens was a remarkable society, more complex than others among the Greek states. But we must not conclude that the Athenians had a fully articulated democratic theory, or that the irrational did not continue to play a significant role in their lives. War may be either rational or irrational, and the Peloponnesian wars were both.

The Second Peloponnesian War

The First Fifteen Years, 431-416 B.C. The complex civilization of Athens in the fifth century depended upon the continued exercise of complete control over the subject poleis in the empire. A growing number of incidents in which Athenians ruthlessly asserted their power alarmed the Spartans in particular; if they did not fight soon, they feared, they might not be able to win. They tried to force the Athenians to make concessions, but Pericles, with the support of the Assembly, said only that Athens would consent to have all disputed questions arbitrated.

In 431 began the ruinous Second Peloponnesian War (431-404 B.C.). The Spartans invaded Attica to force a military decision. Pericles countered by withdrawing the entire population within Athens' city walls, which had been extended to include the suburbs and to give access to the sea. He intended to avoid pitched battles with the superior Spartan troops on land and to go on the offensive at sea, launching seaborne raids against enemy territory and inviting naval battles.

Though these tactics worked well in the first year of

the war, in 430 plague broke out in Athens, where the population of Attica was cooped up with little sanitation. Pericles died of it in 429, leaving Athens without a trusted leader who could make unpopular but necessary policies acceptable. The plague raged until the end of 426 and cost Athens about a third of its population, including its best troops. It did not deter the Athenians from continuing the war under Cleon, however, with general though costly success at sea and even, contrary to Pericles' policies, on land.

By 424 Athens could probably have ended the war on favorable terms, and the upper and the middle classes that had suffered most from it were eager for peace. It was their lands in Attica that the Spartans ravaged, and their members who made up most of the land forces that did the heavy fighting. But the working classes, who identified with the fleet, which was still in excellent condition, hoped for even greater gains and wanted to continue the war. Since they now dominated the city's politics, the war went on.

Not until 421 could the peace party negotiate the Peace of Nicias (so called after its leader) and terminate this phase of the Peloponnesian War, which was in fact not a single war but a series of wars conventionally linked because of the title Thucydides gave to his history. The treaty provided that each side restore captured places and prisoners and remain at peace with the other for fifty years. This was soon supplemented by an actual Spartan-Athenian alliance, also concluded for fifty years but intended chiefly to give each power a chance to put its own alliance in order while secure from an attack by the other. The war had been marked by numerous acts of brutality on both sides; prisoners had been slaughtered or enslaved, and agreements broken in a way that contemporaries felt to be shameful.

Alcibiades and Failure The peace officially lasted only five years (421-416 B.C.), years which saw the gradual rise to eminence in Athenian politics of Pericles' cousin, Alcibiades, a brilliant, ambitious, dissolute, and unstable youth, who initially succeeded the demagogic Cleon as leader of the lower-class war party against the restrained and unglamorous Nicias. Athenian intrigues to support Argos against Sparta only ended in the defeat of Argos and the strengthening of Spartan prestige. By killing all the adult males of the island of Melos and enslaving the women and children as a punishment for Melos' insistence on staying neutral in the war (416), Athens underlined its ruthlessness. By deciding, against Nicias' advice, to send off a large naval expedition to Sicily to attack the great Greek city of Syracuse, the Athenian assembly once again followed Alcibiades' lead. He had said there would be great glory in it, and that all Sicily and then Greater Greece would become subject to Athens.

Yet the project bore no real relation to the politics of mainland Greece, and the Athenians had little sound military intelligence about Sicily. Just before the expedition sailed, a religious scandal broke out in Athens, and Alcibiades—who was known to have committed sacrileges when in a wild and dissipated mood—was suspected of having mutilated sacred statues. He went off to

THUCYDIDES' ACCOUNT OF PERICLES' ORATION

From the hand of Thucydides, the historian of the Peloponnesian War, we have an account of Pericles' famous speech, delivered in the winter of 431 B.C., exorting the Athenians to greater efforts by describing the ideal of an imperial democracy:

Our constitution does not copy the laws of neighboring states; we are rather a pattern to others than imitators ourselves. Its administration favours the many instead of the few; this is why it is called a democracy. If we look to the laws, they afford equal justice to all in their private differences; if to social standing, advancement in public life falls to reputation for capacity, class considerations not being allowed to interfere with merit; nor again does poverty bar the way, if a man is able to serve the state, he is not hindered by the obscurity of his condition. The freedom which we enjoy in our government extends also to our ordinary life. There, far from exercising a jealous surveillance over each other, we do not feel called upon to be angry with our neighbour for doing what he likes, or even to indulge in those injurious looks which cannot fail to be offensive, although they inflict no positive penalty. But all this ease in our private relations does not make us lawless as citizens. . . .

Our public men have, besides politics, their private affairs to attend to, and our ordinary citizens, though occupied with the pursuits of industry, are still fair judges of public matters; for, unlike any other nation, regarding him who takes no part in these duties not as unambitious but as useless, we Athenians are able to judge at all events if we cannot originate, and instead of looking on discussion as a stumbling-block in the way of action, we think it an indispensable preliminary to any wise action at all. . . .

In short I say that as a city we are the school of Hellas; while I doubt if the world can produce a man, who where he has only himself to depend upon, is equal to so many emergencies, and graced by so happy a versatility as the Athenian.

From *The Complete Writings of Thucydides: The Peloponnesian War*, trans. Richard Crowley (New York: Everyman Edition, 1951), pp. 104-6. Reprinted by permission of J.M. Dent & Sons Ltd.

MAKING A LIVING

Greek history was not all war, and neither Athens nor Sparta were always garrison states. Of course, war and politics were means of acquiring goods, for the victors could dispose of the defeated and their goods as they wished. War was a primary source of supply for the slave trade, for booty, and for new lands. But the economic order was not necessarily organized around war, even if the different classes tended to have differing attitudes toward the value of warfare itself. Manual workers and those engaged in trade went about their tasks as best they could, and the true hero of Greek life was, in a sense, the artisan who made the statue of Athena, or helped build the Parthenon, or developed the techniques of metal working.

There was a hierarchy to occupations, as there was to politics. In Athens, slaves, metics, and citizens might do the same work, though only citizens could speak in the Assembly. Even in the organization of space, Athens showed this ambivalence; there were separate quarters for specific economic functions, divided by the craft to be performed, but neither metics nor slaves were segregated into separate residential sections. Spartan warriors were contemptuous of artisans, and the retail trades were near (though not beneath) contempt on the ground that those practicing them commonly cheated. Women, too, could engage in trade, for they were not all viewed as intellectually inferior; still, though a woman was quite capable of assuming duties, of debating, and of responding thoughtfully to complex political questions, she was set apart by the fact that her conclusions did not have the force of law, unlike the conclusions of the males who met in Assembly.

This hierarchy in occupation, in methods of acquisition of property and goods, and in political authority gave structure to that portion of society not made up of children or slaves, shaped the social meanings given to how people made their living, and helped in time to distinguish the professions from artisanship. Movement between levels was difficult though possible, creating a stable value system that nonetheless was capable of gradual change.

Sicily as co-commander with the unwilling Nicias, of the greatest naval expedition ever sent out by a Greek polis, but before the fleet reached Syracuse, Alcibiades was recalled to stand trial and fled to Sparta.

The siege of Syracuse was long, drawn out (414-413), enormously expensive, and a total failure. Nicias and other leaders were captured and killed, and the Athenians lost two hundred ships. Meanwhile Sparta, now advised by Alcibiades, renewed the war at home and sent troops to help the Syracusans. The Spartans also stirred up the Ionian cities to revolt against Athens. The Persian satraps in Asia Minor, hoping to regain seacoast towns lost so long before, joined with the Spartans, and Alcibiades, who had worn out his welcome in Sparta, turned to the Persians.

Ironically enough, the balance of power between the two great Greek poleis that in 490 and 480-479 had so successfully expelled the Persians from Greece was now, in 412, held by the very same Persians. Alcibiades tried to blackmail the Athenians by telling them that if they would install an oligarchic government he would return and exercise his influence with the Persians on their behalf; meanwhile the Spartans promised the Persians that, in exchange for paying for their fleet, they would permit the cities of Ionia to fall into Persian hands once more.

Civil strife (at times accompanied by assassinations of those who opposed a change in the constitution) created a turbulent atmosphere in Athens. A group of conspirators prevailed on the Assembly to appoint a team to draft a new, though still oligarchic, constitution, and then persuaded a rump session to accept the recommendation that the existing officials be dismissed. A group consisting of five presidents appointed a hundred associates, who in turn drew in three hundred more, and this became a new Council of State, which ousted the former Council of Five Hundred by an armed but bloodless coup d'état. The new Four Hundred could summon at will a new Five Thousand, ostensibly to replace the traditional assembly of all the citizens. The democratic forces, however, still controlled the fleet.

The leading oligarchs would now have liked to proceed at once to peace with Sparta, and probably intended that the more moderate Five Thousand should never be summoned. From exile, Alcibiades, however, indicated his preference for their summoning. Frightened and angered by a naval defeat, the citizens deposed the Four Hundred and elected the Five Thousand—all from the upper class—which governed the city from 411 to 410 B.C., when, after some Athenian successes at sea, democracy was restored.

Alcibiades continued to command Athenian naval forces until the Spartan fleet defeated him in 405. He then retired to his estates along the Hellespont (the modern Dardanelles), where he was murdered by Spartan and Persian agents. His career vividly illustrates the vulnerability of the Athenian democracy to a plausible, charming, talented scoundrel and to restless factionalism and narrow competitiveness. Another weakness—the temptation to yield to impulse—was displayed soon afterward, when the Athenians had defeated the Spartan fleet at Arginusae but had suffered heavy casualties, and the Council of State was intimidated by the mourning families of the drowned soldiers into ordering the collective executions of six generals on the charge of not rescuing the troops in the water.

In the final naval action of the war, the Spartans captured most of the Athenian fleet, deserted on a beach in the Hellespont while the sailors were hunting food on shore at Aegospotami in 405. The Spartan infantry rounded up thousands of Athenian prisoners, of whom three thousand were executed as direct reprisal for recent Athenian atrocities. Starving, without money, blockaded by land and sea, its alliance in ruins as the allies had revolted or joined the Spartans, Athens had to surrender unconditionally to the Spartan leader Lysander. Some of the Spartan allies wanted to punish the Athenians as the Athenians had punished the Melians, but the Spartans refused. Instead, the Athenians demolished their long walls, abandoned their empire, surrendered their fleet, and agreed to follow Sparta's lead in foreign policy.

IV THE FOURTH CENTURY B.C. AND THE HELLENISTIC AGE

Spartan Domination

As victors, the Spartans found themselves dominant in a Greece where polis was suspicious of polis and, within each polis, where faction disputed with faction. From Ionia, which the Spartans had sold back to Persia as the price of their assistance, the Persians loomed once more as a threat to the whole Greek world. By midcentury, the new state of Macedonia in the north menaced the Greeks. Perhaps wiser or more vigorous leaders would have been able to create some sort of federation among the individual poleis that could have withstood the Persians and the Macedonians, and, still later, the Romans. But since this did not happen, it seems more likely that the polis as an institution was no longer thought to be the appropriate way for the Greek world to be organized. Perhaps it was too small, too provincial, too "old-fashioned" to keep the peace and provide scope for economic advancement and intellectual growth.

Sparta proved as unable as Athens to manage Greece. The Spartan government, suitable for a state that had no central function but war, was largely in the hands of the elders, usually too conservative to meet new challenges. Gold and silver had found their way into the simple agricultural economy whose founders had preferred to use bars of iron as exchange. Many Spartans, now, for the first time, found themselves disenfranchised for debt, and thus relegated to the status of "inferiors." They joined the helots and perioikoi as part of a discontented majority just when Sparta needed more "equals"—full,

THE MORAL DECLINE OF ATHENS

In the fifth century B.C. the Greek historian Thucydides, convinced that the Peloponnesian War had led to the moral decline of Athens by brutalizing its citizens, wrote of what he regarded as the loss of will in Athenian society by which power had passed into the hands of Sparta:

Love of power, operating through greed and through personal ambition, was the cause of all these evils. To this must be added the violent fanaticism which came into play once the struggle had broken out. Leaders of parties . . . in professing to serve the public interest . . . were seeking to win prizes for themselves. In their struggle for ascendancy nothing was barred; terrible indeed were the actions to which they committed themselves, and in taking revenge they went further still. Here they were deterred neither by the claims of justice nor by the interests of the state. . . . Thus neither side had any use for conscientious motives; more interest was shown in those who could produce attractive arguments to justify some disgraceful action. As for the citizens who held moderate views, they were destroyed by both the extreme parties. . . .

From *The Complete Writings of Thucydides: The Peloponnesian War*, trans. Richard Crowley (New York: Everyman Edition, 1951), p. 210. Reprinted by permission of J.M. Dent & Sons Ltd.

enfranchised, fighting citizens. Away from home Lysander could neither free the cities of the former Athenian Empire, in which from 404 he had installed oligarchic governments, nor rule them satisfactorily.

At Athens, for example, at the instigation of the extremist Critias, an oligarchy known as the Thirty Tyrants instituted a reign of terror not only against democrats associated with past regimes but also against moderate oligarchs. In 403 an invading force of exiled democrats killed Critias and touched off a brief civil war. At Athens they restored democracy, but the Thirty Tyrants and their sympathizers were set up as a Spartan puppet government nearby at Eleusis, and no one was allowed to move between the two separate Athenian states. In 401 the Athenians, by treachery, killed the generals of the Eleusid armies, and the two states were reunited. It would be the government of this insecurely reestablished Athens that would sentence the philosopher Socrates to death in 399 B.C.

The Spartans could not pose as the leaders of Greece and keep their bargain with the Persians to sell Ionia back to them; yet if they went back on this bargain, the Persians would start a new war. So in 401 B.C., when the younger brother of Artaxerxes II, king of Persia—Cyrus the Younger, governor of Asia Minor—rebelled against Artaxerxes and asked for Spartan aid, Sparta gave it to him. Cyrus was soon killed in a battle deep in Mesopotamia, and his Greek mercenary army was stranded in the heart of Persia. (Their disciplined march north to the Greek city of Trebizond on the shores of the Black Sea forms the substance of a book called the *Anabasis*, "The March Back," by the Athenian Xenophon, who became one of their officers.) The episode left the Spartans at war with Persia.

The Spartans failed to unite their land and sea commands, giving the Persians time to build a fleet, which they put under an Athenian admiral. The Persians also bribed Thebes, Argos, Corinth, and Athens to stir up so much trouble against Sparta that Spartan troops had to be recalled from Persia to fight a new war in Greece proper. This Corinthian War lasted eight years (to 387), saw the self-assertion of Thebes, seemed to produce the threat of a renewed Athenian Empire, and ended in stalemate, as the Persians and Spartans finally got together and imposed "The King's Peace" in 386 B.C., by which the Persians resumed control of all Greek states in Asia, and the rest were autonomous.

Thebes Rises to Leadership

Raising money from their allies and hiring mercenaries to intimidate all resistance, the Spartans systematically disciplined and punished the cities that dared resist, seizing Thebes in 382 B.C., and breaking their promise to respect the autonomy of the Greek cities. A group of Theban democratic exiles conspired to overthrow the pro-Spartan regime there, and when the Spartans tried to punish them, a new war broke out in which Athens participated as the leading power in a new anti-Spartan league of many Greek cities.

By 371 the beleagured Spartans were ready for peace, willing to guarantee independence to all Greek states and seeking disarmament. But the wording of the treaty gave Persia and Athens the leading roles as guarantors, and Epaminondas, the chief Theban delegate, refused to sign. Soon afterward he defeated the Spartans at the battle of Leuctra. Cities subject to Sparta began to oust their oligarchic governments and install democracies. Epaminondas followed up his successes with two invasions of the Peloponnesus, helped form a league of Arcadian cities, and assisted the freed helots in founding a city of their own. This destroyed Spartan power in its own homeland.

Warfare continued despite the effort of the Persians to dictate a general peace, as the Athenians returned to their former imperalist practices and installed colonies of Athenian settlers on the soil of conquered cities. The Thebans fought in the Peloponnesus, in the north, against Athens at sea, and finally in the Peloponnesus again, where an alliance of Sparta, Athens, and other poleis met them in battle at Mantinea in 362, at which Epaminondas was killed. All hope that Thebes could put an end to the interminable fighting among Greeks died with him.

Though a new Peloponnesian league of city-states was formed in 362 B.C. to end the war and to enable the Greeks as a whole to determine their foreign policy, Athens continued to act as the rival of Thebes and to play the traditional political game of alliance building within the league. Though ineffective, the league was an important effort to create something like a united states of Greece. Without its restraints, Thebes was defeated in a war against the city of Phocis, whose general had seized the shrine of Delphi and used the accumulated funds there to create a large army of mercenaries in 354. Athens strove to reconstruct its old Aegean empire, but in 357 many of its most important outposts rebelled, and Athens was forced to grant them freedom in 355. Athens was exhausted, broke, and weak.

Ironically enough, the inability of the Greek cities to give up fighting was almost surely due in part to general prosperity. Whereas during the fifth century only Athens and Sparta had been able to afford large armies and navies, during the fourth century many other cities grew rich enough to support such forces. Brisk Mediterranean commerce brought wealth to the distant Greek settlements from the Crimea to Spain; not only goods flowed, but also slaves and mercenary troops. Shortly after midcentury the Persians alone had perhaps fifty thousand Greek troops fighting in their armies.

Many devices of modern commerce to make international trade easier first made their appearance in Greece: banking and credit, insurance, trade treaties, and special diplomatic and other privileges. Private wealth grew rapidly and was more widely distributed. Slaves increased in number—Nicias appears to have owned more than a thousand of them. By 338 B.C. there may have been as many as 150,000 in Attica, working in the mines and at other more skilled occupations. All this prosperity meant that states quickly recovered from defeat in war and could afford to try again. Patriotism became increasingly a matter of cutting up real or anticipated profits. However, the poor who were not slaves grew poorer; unwilling to degrade themselves by engaging in the manual labor that was increasingly the work of slaves, they often became vagrants or mercenary soldiers. A rigid class society was increasingly confining, and the middle class was losing its sense of security between the increasingly rich and the increasingly enslaved poor.

Macedon

North of Thessaly and extending inland into what is today Yugoslavia and Albania lay the kingdom of Macedon, with a considerable coastline along the Aegean. The Madedonians were a mixture of peoples including some of Greek origin; they were organized into tribes, worshiped some of the Greek gods, and spoke a Greek dialect that other Greeks could not understand. Their kings claimed Greek descent from the hero Herakles, son of Zeus himself. The king spoke Greek as well as the native language, had title to most of the land, and ruled absolutely, though he might be deposed by the people for treason. There being no written law, he was advised by councilors who were selected from among the nobles of each tribe and felt themselves to be his social equals.

Although the Greeks had planted some poleis along the Macedonian shore, and although Greek cultural influence and Greek trade had penetrated deeply into the country by the fourth century, Macedon did not copy Greek political institutions, keeping its own, which were more like those of Mycenae. The Macedonians traditionally relied on cavalry in war, but in the fourth century they added foot soldiers to fight their neighbors from the west and north, the Illyrians (probable ancestors of the Albanians of today). From the south, both Athens and Sparta persistently interfered in internal Macedonian affairs.

The Achievements of Philip II In 359 B.C., a prince of the ruling house, Philip, became regent for his infant nephew. Having lived for three years as a hostage in Thebes, where he knew Epaminondas, Philip knew all about Greek affairs. He applied Theban military principles to his army (emphasizing infantry tactics) and led it in person. After defeating the Illyrians and other rivals for power within Macedon, Philip was made king in his own right. To get money, he exploited the rich gold and silver mines in his kingdom, minting his own coinage.

Some Athenian politicians favored Philip's advance. Others opposed him. It was not until he had won still more territory and begun to use a fleet successfully that the most famous Athenian orator, Demosthenes, began to warn against the threat from Macedon. But Philip had broken Athenian influence in Thessaly and Thrace (modern Bulgaria) and had annexed the peninsula of Chalcidice, which had been ruled by Athenian aristocrats. He also detached the large island of Euboea, close to Attica itself, from its Athenian loyalties.

At that point he suggested peace and an alliance with Athens, which in 346 B.C. was reached with the approval even of Demosthenes. Philip meanwhile had secured control over the Delphic oracle. He was moving south and consolidating his power. He made a temporary alliance with Thebes to defeat Phocis. By 342 the Athenians had acquired new allies in the Peloponnesus. In retaliation Philip moved into Thrace to cut off the Athenian grain supplies coming from the Black Sea and to avert a new Persian-Athenian alliance. Once again Demosthenes pressed for war, and Athens took military action in Euboea. By late 339 Philip was only two days' march from Attica. Demosthenes now arranged an eleventh-hour alliance with Thebes. Philip, however, totally defeated the Athenian-Theban alliance at Chaeronea in 338 with the decisive aid of a precisely timed cavalry charge led by his eighteen-year-old son, Alexander. Though Philip occupied Thebes, he spared Athens on condition that the city ally with Macedon. His leniency proved that he had never intended to destroy Athens, as Demosthenes had feared.

Philip's victories aroused in many the old hope of a unified Greece. Isocrates, an Athenian philosopher, had thought Demosthenes wrong in urging resistance to Philip, for he feared a resurgent Persia far more. At Corinth in 338 B.C., all the poleis except Sparta met to organize a league that called itself "The Greeks." Its members bound themselves to stop fighting and intervening in each other's affairs. This body immediately allied itself with Macedon and then joined with Philip in declaring war on Persia to revenge the sacrilege of Xerxes' invasion of 143 years earlier. Philip was to command the expedition. By 336 B.C. the advance forces of this army were already liberating Ionian cities from Persia. But Philip, aged only forty-six, was now mysteriously assassinated.

Philip's accomplishments greatly impressed his contemporaries. No such powerful consolidated state as his Macedon had ever existed west of Asia. Instead of allowing the resources of Macedon to be dissipated in flashy conquests, he organized the people he conquered, both in the Balkan area from the Adriatic to the Black Sea and in Greece. He kept morale high in the army and had the contingents from the various regions competing to see who would do the best job. He divided his troops into more specialized units for diverse tasks in war, and he personally commanded whichever unit had the most difficult assignment. He could appreciate the strengths of his Greek opponents, and when he had defeated them, he utilized their skills and made sure of their loyalty by decent treatment. In his final effort to unify them against their traditional Persian enemy, he associated himself with the ancient patriotic cause that, despite frequent betrayal, still had great appeal for them. Though he felt himself to be part of the Greek civilization of his own time, he centered his confederacy on Corinth, symbolic of an earlier Greek resistance to the Persians. Somehow he seemed a kind of Homeric hero in the flesh almost a thousand years after the siege of Troy.

The Achievements of Alexander Philip's son, Alexander III, or the Great, belongs to legend as much as to history. Only twenty when he came to the throne, he loved war, politics, athletics, alcohol, poetry, medicine, and science. Within a dozen years he led his armies on a series of triumphant marches that won for Macedon the largest empire yet created in the ancient world. He began by crushing a Greek revolt led by Thebes, whose entire population he sold into slavery, not massacring the males, as the Spartans and Athenians often did. Next he crossed into Asia Minor to continue the war of the Greek League against Persia and to recapture the Ionian cities. He defeated the Persians at the river Granicus in 334 B.C. and took over the coastal cities of Ionia to deny them to the Persian fleet, so that the strategy thereafter would turn upon the contending land armies. In Ionia he established democracies in the poleis. In territories belonging to the Persians, he took title to all land, thus replacing the Persian king, Darius III, whom he defeated again at Issus and so opened up Syria. He reduced Tyre by siege and refused Darius' offer of his daughter and all territory west of the Euphrates.

Next, Egypt fell easily. Here he founded the great port of Alexandria in the Nile Delta (332), a Greek city from the beginning. But he paid his respects to the Egyptian divinities and allowed himself to be treated as Amon-Re, son of Zeus. Then he marched east and defeated Darius again in Mesopotamia at Gaugamela, near Nineveh, in 331 B.C. The Persian Empire was smashed. Alexander sacrificed to Marduk in Babylon and ordered the temple the Persians had destroyed restored. Vast mopping-up operations continued in Persia proper (330-327 B.C.), as Alexander's armies seized the chief cities and all the royal treasure at the Persian capital of Persepolis, which he burned. Still, he treated the Persian royal family with great courtesy and acted toward his new subjects just as a king of Persia would have done. The Persian nobles came to acknowledge him as king by the grace of Ahura-mazda. Alexander now was king of Persia, pharaoh of Egypt, king of Babylon, king of Macedon, and *hegamon* (commander) of the Greek League.

In Central Asia, near Samarkand, Alexander fell in love with and married the daughter of a local chieftain, who joined forces with the conqueror in 327 B.C. While this marriage enhanced the loyalty of the Persians to him, it further strained the loyalty of his own Macedonian nobles, who disliked Alexander's occasional adoption of Persian dress and customs to please his new subjects. Though enjoying his role as "Great King" and claiming divine parentage, Alexander thought of himself as a Greek who paid his respects to his ancestor Achilles at Troy before he began his Eastern campaigns, and whose favorite reading was the Iliad. But tensions increased. Alexander, having executed a plotter against his life, said he was forced by Macedonian custom to execute the plotter's father also; unfortunately, the father was the most influential of the Macedonian nobles. Later, in a drunken fury, Alexander killed another of his own Macedonian generals for having taunted him for his Persian ways. There was much truth in the charge, and Alexander continued to purge Macedonians who resisted his orientalization.

The tensions of the conquest did not diminish its efficiency. New levies of troops came from Europe or were raised in Asia; new roads were built, and new towns sprang up, many named after Alexander. Believing that India was the last region in Asia, that it was small, and that beyond India lay the Ocean, via which it was possible to return to Europe by sea, Alexander next set out to conquer modern-day Pakistan from a base in what is now Afghanistan. He found himself fighting hill tribes and princes of Kashmir and Punjab. At first the Indian war elephants terrified Alexander's cavalry, but soon the Macedonians learned how to defeat them and won new victories. Alexander moved east; but India was not small, as he had thought, and his weary troops eventually mutinied. In 326 B.C. Alexander had to give in and call off any further advances; he led his troops on riverboats down the Indus toward the Indian Ocean, fighting all the way, and sacrificing a gold cup to the Greek god of the sea, Poseidon, when he reached the shore. Several new Alexandrias were founded, including the city that is now Karachi (Pakistan), before he led his forces westward across the southern Persian deserts back to Susa in 324 B.C.

Here he conducted a purge of those he suspected of treason, dramatically pursuing his plan to combine the best features of the Macedonian and the Persian nobilities by staging a mass marriage between eighty Macedonian officers and Persian noblewomen. He himself took a new Persian wife and blessed the union of ten thousand Macedonian troops with Persian women. Those Macedonians who wished to return home were sent off well rewarded; but Alexander kept their wives in Persia and planned to use their children as the nucleus of a future army of mixed blood that would owe their lives to him. A great double naval expedition from the mouths of the Tigris-Euphrates, eastward along the shore of the Persian Gulf to India and westward around Arabia (not yet circumnavigated) to Egypt, was in preparation at Babylon, where Alexander had built great dockyards. From the Greeks, who had enjoyed the longest period of internal peace for over a century, Alexander asked for divine honors; apparently he wanted to become a god. No god, in June of 323 B.C., at Babylon, he caught a fever and died at the age of thirty-three.

Ever since, scholars have speculated about what Alex-

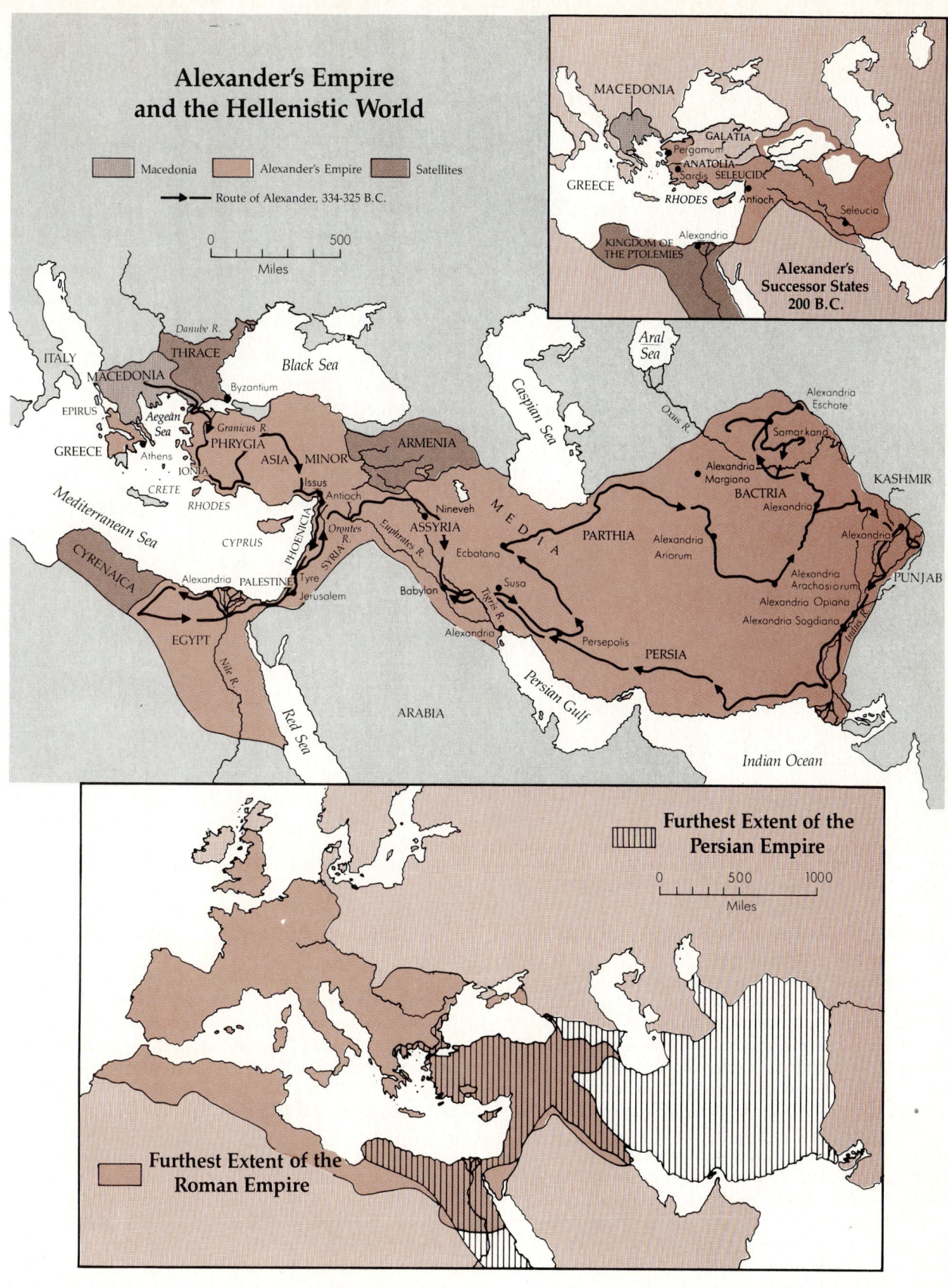

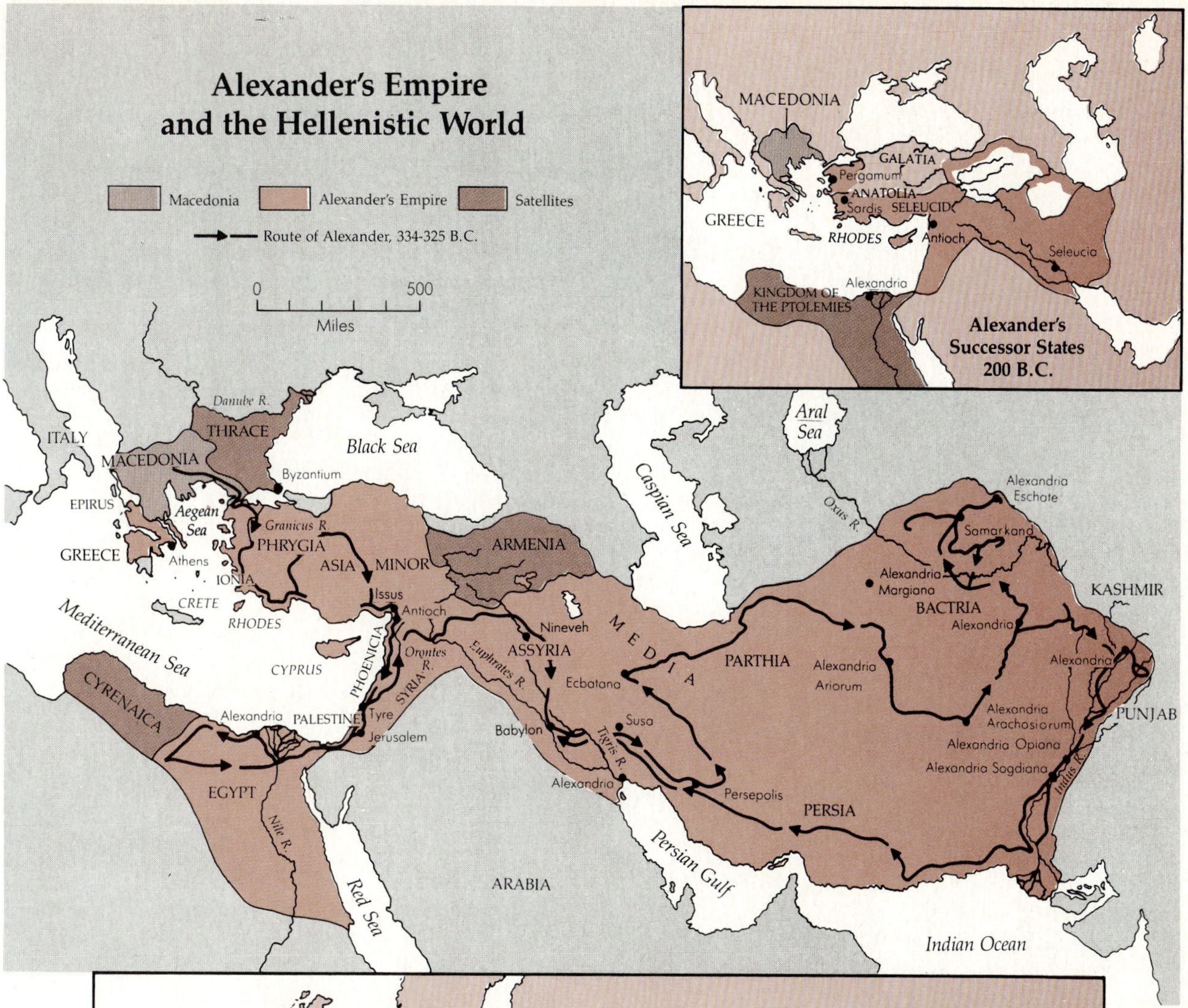
Alexander's Empire
and the Hellenistic World
Macedonia
Alexander's Empire
Satellites
Route of Alexander, 334-325 B.C.
0
500
Miles
Alexander's
Successor States
200 B.C.
MACEDONIA
GALATIA
Pergamum
ANATOLIA
Sardis
SELEUCID
GREECE
RHODES
Antioch
Seleucia
Alexandria
KINGDOM OF
THE PTOLEMIES
ITALY
Danube R.
THRACE
MACEDONIA
Black Sea
Byzantium
EPIRUS
Aegean
Sea
Granicus R.
PHRYGIA
GREECE
Athens
IONIA
ASIA
MINOR
ARMENIA
Caspian Sea
Aral
Sea
Oxus R.
Alexandria
Eschate
Samarkand
Alexandria
Margiana
BACTRIA
Alexandria
KASHMIR
Issus
Antioch
CRETE
RHODES
Mediterranean Sea
CYPRUS
PHOENICIA
Orontes
R.
SYRIA
Euphrates R.
Nineveh
ASSYRIA
MEDIA
PARTHIA
Alexandria
Ariorum
Alexandria
Ecbatana
CYRENAICA
Alexandria
PALESTINE
Tyre
Jerusalem
Babylon
Susa
Tigris R.
Alexandria
Arachosiorum
PUNJAB
Alexandria Opiana
Alexandria Sogdiana
Indus R.
Alexandria
Persepolis
PERSIA
EGYPT
Nile R.
Persian Gulf
ARABIA
Red Sea
Indian Ocean

Furthest Extent of the
Persian Empire
0
500
1000
Miles
Furthest Extent of the
Roman Empire

Alexander the Great is shown in a detailed mosiac made of hundreds of pieces of tiny inlaid stone. Originally at Pompeii, this mosaic from the National Museum in Naples shows Alexander defeating the armies of Darius at Issus in 333 B.C. Alexander, once idealized, has been the subject of extensive, often negative, revaluation by historians in recent years.

ander might have accomplished had he lived; he might well have made Greece the center of his empire, and would surely have been able to conquer the two states in the western Mediterranean already looming on the horizon as powers there: Carthage and Rome. He respected all races and religions, yet he was ruthless in pursuit of his own power and the stability of his state. Each of his new cities he settled with Greeks, to be centers for the diffusion of Greek culture. A superb general, a clever governor of subject peoples, a believer in the Greek gods, a passionate man with a streak of megalomania, Alexander astonished his contemporaries. It is little wonder that he became to later generations the hero of romances that circulated in every country, in every language, and among every people, down to our own day. Some saw in him only a drunken despot and a murderer. But to more students of his life then and now, Alexander was the first great leader to seek the security of all peoples in a single world state.

A Hellenized Civilization

As soon as the news of Alexander's death became known, his generals began a fierce scramble for portions of his empire, for his Bactrian wife, Roxane, was expecting a child, and his brother was both illegitimate and simple-minded. The generals combined against each other in various shifting alliances and arranged many intermarriages and murders in a confusing period of political and military change. By c 280-279 B.C. three dynasties had emerged as supreme, each descended from one of Alexander's generals, each in a different portion of the empire: the Ptolemies in Egypt, the Seleucids in Syria and Mesopotamia, and the Antigonids in Macedon and Asia Minor. Fighting continued almost without interruption until the rising power of Rome began to destroy them one by one.

In Egypt the Ptolemies followed the ancient pattern of government, turning themselves into successors of the pharaohs. They became gods; they sometimes married their sisters; they exploited the agricultural wealth of the country to the limit. The Ptolemies claimed title to all land, some of which was farmed by peasants directly for their own benefit and some let out to temples or to military settlers and officials. The Ptolemies' own land gave them all its produce, except what was needed to feed the farm workers; land let to others paid the Ptolemies a percentage in wheat. Oil, flax, and papyrus were royal monopolies. No tree in Egypt could be cut down without royal permission. The Ptolemies governed largely through Greek officials, who poured into Egypt for several generations after Alexander's death. Even the armies of the first three Ptolemies were wholly Greek. It was not until 217 B.C. that Egyptian troops participated in the wars of the dynasty, which were directed chiefly against the Seleucids of Asia for the possession of Palestine and against the Antigonids for the Aegean islands and the Anatolian coasts.

Alexandria, the capital, was the largest city of the ancient world, until Rome eventually overtook it. The city had harbors both on the Mediterranean and on a great lake, which was connected by canals to the Nile, and by the Nile to the Red Sea. Its towering white stone lighthouse four hundred feet high was one of the wonders of the ancient world. The city had broad streets, luxurious palaces, and a famous library of approximately a million volumes. In its "museum," scholars, freed from all duties by state subsidies, conducted their researches ("fat fowls in a coop," a skeptical poet called them). Though Alexandria was far too large to be a polis, its Greek population had its own political organization. At Alexandria also were the Ptolemies' warehouses in which all the royal grain was stored after it had come down the Nile.

The Egyptian population lived under its own law and was judged in its own courts. Those who were discontented with the system that exploited them so thoroughly—and there were many—had no escape except to take sanctuary in a temple; accordingly, the government tried to reduce the number of temples that had the right to provide sanctuary. For a long time the Greek population—with its own language, law courts, culture, and customs—did not mingle with the Egyptians, remaining a large collection of foreigners who were getting rich as fast as they could. But by the early second century, Greek immigration had tapered off. Greek-Egyptian intermarriages had begun, and the army became more Egyptian. Rome began to intervene, disorganization set in, and by 118 B.C. Ptolemy VII had to issue a series of decrees calling for reform to reunite his empire and restore public order.

Seleucus I was also one of Alexander's generals. He began as governor of Babylon and eventually won control over all of Alexander's Asian lands except northern and western Asia Minor and the Indian regions in the east, which had to be given up by 303 B.C. Seleucid territorial holdings fluctuated a good deal, however. The Seleucids' Ionian territories centered on the former Lydian capital of Sardis, their Syrian territories on the new city of Antioch-on-Orontes in northern Syria, and their Mesopotamian territories on the new city of Seleucia not far from Babylon. As the heirs of the ancient Near Eastern empires, the Seleucids used the former Assyrian and Persian administrative forms and revived Babylonian religion and literature, still written in cuneiform. Some scholars believe that, by deliberately sponsoring a Babylonian religious revival, the Seleucids were seeking a counterweight to Zoroastrianism, the Persian faith. It does appear that the Seleucids failed to achieve what Alexander had so well begun—the securing of Persian cooperation in managing the huge Asian territories.

The Seleucids could not count on deification, like the Ptolemies, nor could they create in Asia anything like the extremely centralized Ptolemaic system of exploitation. Unlike Egypt, the Asian territories were too vast to be governed; there were too many varied traditions of authority, too many local governors to be considered. Instead, the Seleucids founded Greek cities and sponsored their development. To do this they gave up large areas that were their own royal land, and they also transferred the land of powerful landowners to the cities. The lot of the peasants improved, as they ceased to be private property and gained their freedom.

These Greek cities were military colonies, given both money and land by the king. Their settlement, housing, financial, and other questions were delegated to a military governor. The settlers were required to serve in the army in exchange for the land they received. This founding of Greek cities, however, failed to solve the problem of military security, partly because there were not enough Greeks available to populate the cities and man the armies, and partly because the Seleucids did not learn how to command the loyalty of the Persian population.

In Macedon and Greece, the Antigonids, descendants of Alexander's governor of the western Anatolian province of Phrygia, had won in the struggle for succession. Even so, it was not until almost half a century after Alexander's death that Antigonus Gonatas, son of the first Antigonus, was accepted as king of Macedon. In 277 B.C. he successfully protected Greece from the raids of the Gauls, a migrating branch of Indo-European Celts, who had spread from the region north of the Alps into what is now France and Spain, and across to Britain. Herodotus mentions them only once, for they were still remote in his day. Now they were moving eastward along the Danube, raiding southward into Italy and Greece. Antigonus shunted them on to Asia Minor, where they were given a kingdom of their own, called Galatia, in a region from which their remote Neolithic ancestors may have originally come several thousand years earlier.

Though the Greek cities were now grouped together into two leagues, the Aetolian and the Achaean—larger in membership and more representative in their joint rule than the Athenian and Spartan alliances of earlier times—they fought against each other and against the Antigonid kings of Macedon with customary Greek vigor. By the 220s the Greeks were largely independent of Macedon once again. Athens had become largely a university town and usually stayed out of the perpetual feuding of other cities. But Sparta, true to its traditions, tried to take over the Achaean League, and it would have succeeded had not the Macedonians been brought back into Greece in 222, to defeat the Spartans finally. By the 220s, however, Rome had begun to intervene in the Greek world.

Alexander's heirs had begun their rule in prosperity and unity; they ended it in division, defeat, and economic decline. At first commerce had grown throughout the Hellenized world, for Greek products were widely sought. But as prosperity increased, the division between the well-to-do and the peasants grew; the cities came to be identified with wealth, the rural areas with poverty. Wars, rising inflation, and Persian gold threw the economies into disarray. Both urban laborers and peasants discovered the power they could exert over the middle class if they refused to work. Frequent debates over redistribution of land, demands for the abolition of debt, and civil wars further weakened Alexander's inheritance, so that the Hellenized states were ripe for conquest.

V RELIGION, WRITING, AND THOUGHT

The Gods

The Olympian gods, whom we first learned to know through Homer, continued to reign. The citizens of a polis had special devotion for the divinity who had founded it—Athens for Athena, Sparta for Zeus—though they worshiped the other gods as well, and all worshiped the goddess of the hearth, Hestia, the protectress of home and fireside. Poleis grouped together in special devotion to regional shrines—the temples of Apollo at Delphi and of Zeus at Olympia and at Dodona. The Olympic games, which honored Zeus, were followed by others held in honor of Apollo at Delphi and of Poseidon, the sea god, on the Isthmus of Corinth.

Two Greek cults of particular importance began outside the ordinary worship of the Olympian gods: that of Demeter at Eleusis near Athens, and that of Dionysus. Demeter (the name means literally "earth mother") was the goddess of fertility and of the harvests. Her daughter by Zeus, Persephone, was snatched away by Hades, the god of the underworld, and had to spend a third of the year with him—the months of barrenness, late autumn and winter. Every spring she returned, and the fields became fertile again. Thus, like the Sumerians and the Egyptians, the Greeks invented a story to account for the miracle of rebirth every spring.

Dionysus, the god of vegetation, fertility, and wine, originated in Boeotia, in north-central Greece, and stood for seasonal fertility in its more openly sexual aspects; his celebrants originally carried phalluses in his procession, and were often dressed as goats. In its original form the cult inspired its followers with a wild dancing frenzy in which they ate the flesh of living animals, and so acted out the eating of the god himself. The cult was tamer in Greece, where phallic songs were written for the festival, held every two years.

Tragedy

From these and other songs Athens developed the art of tragedy. (The word means "goat song" and shows the original connection with Dionysus.) At first largely sung as a choral hymn, the tragedies later began to deal with human problems, and individual actors' roles became more important. The first competition to choose the best tragedy was sponsored by Pisistratus in 534 B.C., and annual contests were held thereafter. Many hundreds of tragedies were written; comparatively few have survived in full—probably the best—but we have fragments of others. Aristotle (384-322) believed that it was the purpose of tragedy to arouse pity and terror in the spectators, and to purge or purify them by causing them to reflect on the fearful punishments that highly placed

This fifth-century bronze statue, properly called the Striding God of Artemiseion, is generally considered to be an ideal effort to represent Zeus hurling a thunderbolt; however, other scholars believe it to be Poseidon with a trident. It is now displayed in the National Museum in Athens.

OLD AGE AND DEATH

Historically poets, dramatists, and other writers have used old age and death as a theme by which they explore the nature of their own culture. In *Oedipus at Colonus* the great tragedian Sophocles reflects upon how the passage of time corrodes expectations. Oedipus is addressing Theseus:

Fair Aigeus' son, only to gods in heaven
Comes no old age nor death of anything;
All else is turmoiled by our master Time.
The earth's strength fades and manhood's glory
  fades,
Faith dies, and unfaith blossoms like a flower.
And who shall find in the open streets of men
Or secret places of his own heart's love
One wind blow true for ever?

As presented by Gilbert Murray in *The Literature of Ancient Greece* (Chicago: University of Chicago Press, 1957), p. 249.

men and women brought upon themselves by their own sins, the worst of which was *hubris*, arrogance.

The first, and some would still say the greatest, of the three chief tragedians whose works we have was Aeschylus (c 525-456 B.C.), of whose seventy-odd tragedies seven survived.

In the trilogy, *The Oresteia*, Aeschylus dealt with tragedies in the family of Agamemnon, who sacrificed his daughter Iphigenia to get a favorable wind to go to Troy, was murdered by his unfaithful wife Clytemnestra on his return, and was avenged by his son Orestes, who killed his mother on the order of Apollo. Orestes suffered torments by the Furies and was acquitted by a court presided over by Athena; but only Zeus succeeded in transforming the Furies into more kindly creatures. Crime and punishment, remorse and release, a benevolent and secure god over all—these Aeschylus portrayed in lofty, moving verse.

Sophocles, the second of the three greatest tragedians (c 496-406 B.C.), wrote many tragedies, of which only ten survive. He believed deeply in Athenian institutions and in the religion of his fellow Greeks, and he took an active part in the public life of Periclean Athens. In his *Antigone*, the niece of Creon, tyrant of Thebes, defied her uncle's harsh decision that the body of her brother, killed while leading a rebellion, must be left exposed to be devoured by beasts of prey. Proclaiming that divine law required decent burial, she disobeyed Creon and caused the proper ceremonial earth to be sprinkled on the body. Knowing she would die for her defiance, she acted in obedience to her conscience and resisted the dictator. To most interpreters, *Antigone* has carried its message of the sanctity of the individual conscience down through the centuries, proclaiming the superiority of what is eternally right and decent to any mere dictator's brutal whim.

Sophocles, who lived to be ninety, saw the ruin brought by the Peloponnesian War. His last tragedy, *Oedipus at Colonus*, produced after his death, dealt with the old age of the famous Theban king who in ignorance had killed his father and married his mother, and who had torn out his own eyes in horror when he discovered what he had done. A blind beggar, an outcast, Oedipus now knew that he could not have avoided the pollution of his unwitting crimes, and that his self-multilation too was justified. Tempered by years of suffering, he sought sanctuary to die, and received it from Theseus, king of Athens. Oedipus' tomb would forever protect the Athenians against Thebes. Reflecting upon the terrible story of Oedipus and on the trials of all human life, Sophocles' chorus sang that it is best never to be born, for all humans are but phantoms, shadows whose actions inevitably brought tragedy upon them.

Nineteen plays remain of the many written by the third and last of the great Attic tragedians, Euripides (c. 480-406 B.C.), who focused upon human psychology, with less emphasis on divine majesty. More realistic in their introduction of children, slaves, and other characters upon the scene, his plays were also more human in their exploration of the far reaches of the obsessed mind. The *Hippolytus* showed the uncontrollable sexual passion of a decent woman, Phaedra, for her ascetic stepson Hippolytus, who rejected it as he would all passion. Ashamed of her lust, she accused Hippolytus of having attacked her; he was executed, and she committed suicide. The *Medea* showed a woman so far gone in agony brought about by rejection of her love that she killed her children in a fit of madness. The *Alcestis* depicted a husband so selfish that he gladly accepted the offer of his devoted wife to die for him so that he might prolong his life. *The Trojan Women* presented the sufferings of the women of Troy at the hands of the Greeks. Staged in the same year as the Athenian atrocity at Melos, it must have caused the audience many uncomfortable moments of self-questioning. And *The Bacchae* explored the excesses of religious ecstasy, showing a frenzied queen who tore her son to bits, thinking he was a lion. Was Euripides saying that men under the impulse of strong emotion were beasts, or that the old religion had too much that was savage in it, or only that the young king had defied the god and his hubris had brought him a fate that he well deserved? The enduring beauty of all these plays is that we may discuss their meanings in the context of each succeeding century.

The ruined theater at Epidaurus, constructed about 330 B.C., still provides a superb example of theater construction from which there has been relatively little change since.

Comedy

Comedy, like tragedy, also began at the festivals of Dionysus. (The word may mean revel or village songs.) Aristophanes (c 450-c 385 B.C.) has left eleven complete plays and parts of a twelfth. By making his audience laugh, he hoped to teach them a lesson. A thoroughgoing conservative, he was suspicious of all innovation. In *The Frogs*, for instance, he brought onto the stage actors playing the parts of the two tragedians, Aeschylus (then dead) and Euripides (still alive). The god Dionysus himself solemnly weighed verses from their plays on a giant pair of scales; the solemn, didactic, and old-fashioned Aeschylus outweighed the innovating, skeptical, volatile, modern Euripides every time. A tragedian's duty, Aristophanes thought, was to teach the old truths.

In *The Clouds* Aristophanes ridiculed the philosopher Socrates, whom he showed in his "think shop," dangling from the ceiling in a basket so that he could "voyage in air and contemplate the sun." Aristophanes meant to call attention to the dangers offered to Athenian youth by the Sophists. Socrates thought the play very unfair; but, like the others, Socrates taught young men to question the existing order, and he was therefore fair game.

Aristophanes opposed the Peloponnesian War, not because he was a pacifist, but because he thought it unnecessary. In *Lysistrata* the women sexually denied themselves to their husbands until the men made peace, and in other plays Aristophanes denounced the Athenian politicians, including Pericles himself, for going to war. In *The Birds* the leading characters set off to found a Birdville (Cloud-cuckoo-land) to get away from war. In one of his later plays, the women took over the state and proposed to share all the men among them, putting prostitutes out of business; in another, Poverty and Wealth appeared in person and argued their cases. These later plays provided a transition to the "New Comedy" of the fourth century—gentler, more domestic, more respectable, conventionalized. We have portions of several New Comedies by Menander (c 342-281 B.C.) and one full text, *Misanthrope*, published for the first time only in 1958.

Drama was, of course, only one form that Greek poetic genius took. From the earliest days, the Greeks were also the masters of lyric poetry. Among the most celebrated are poems of love by the poetess Sappho, of war by Spartan poets in the very early days, and of triumph in the Olympic games by Pindar.

History

Much of what we know about the Greeks before and during the Persian Wars we owe to the industry and intelligence of Herodotus (c 484-425 B.C.), who began to write his history as an account of the origins and course of the struggle between Greeks and Persians, and expanded it into an inquiry into the peoples of the whole world known to the Greeks. Born on the Ionian coast of Asia Minor, Herodotus was a great traveler who visited Egypt, Italy, Mesopotamia, and the coast of the Black Sea, collecting information and listening to whatever stories people would tell him about their own past and their present customs. Although he loved a good story, he was both experienced and sensible. He often alerted the reader against a story that he himself did not believe but had set down only to fill out the record.

Some have tended to scoff a little, especially at Herodotus' tales of a past that was remote even when he was doing his research; but these doubters have often been silenced by archaeological finds. For instance, Herodotus said that the founder of Thebes, the semi-mythical Cadmus, was a Phoenician who had brought Phoenician letters with him to Greece, about 1350 B.C., some 900 years before Herodotus' own day. Herodotus added that Cadmus' dynasty was ousted about 1200 B.C. This was often disbelieved, but in A.D. 1964 archaeologists at Thebes found in the palace of Cadmus a collection of cuneiform seals, one of which was datable to 1367-1346 B.C., which demonstrated the high probability of Herodotus' account of Cadmus. Even the date of the ouster was verified, since the seals were in a layer of material that had been burned about 1200 B.C. and had survived because they were already baked clay. Herodotus wrote so well and so beguilingly that we would still read him with delight even if he were less reliable. Nor was he a mere collector and organizer of material. Though he wandered far, he never lost sight of his main theme—the conflict between east and west, which he interpreted as a conflict between despotism and freedom.

For his methods, his curiosity, and his sense of style, he is known as "the Father of History." One definition of civilization requires that a civilized people have a sense of history—meaning that the past counts in the present—and the Greeks showed this sense not only in their respect for their chroniclers, but in having a muse—one of nine daughters of Zeus who were patron goddesses of the arts (hence *muse* equals *music*)—for History alone, named Clio.

The equally intelligent, very different historian Thucydides (c 460-c 400), wrote of the Peloponnesian Wars. The difference between the two arose partly from their subject matter. Herodotus was dealing with events that had happened largely before his own time, and he had to accept hearsay accounts. Thucydides was dealing mainly with events in which he himself had been a participant. He was an unsuccessful Athenian general who had been punished for his defeat; but he remained impartial, scientific, and serious—collecting and weighing his information with the greatest care. Though he followed Herodotus' custom of putting into the mouths of his leading characters words that represented what they might have said rather than what he could prove they said, he told his readers that he was doing this; the actual words were not available, but the arguments on both sides of any issue could be revived and reconstructed in the form of speeches. Pericles' funeral oration, with its praise of Athenian democracy, is perhaps the most famous example (see p. 45); but Thucydides also wrote for the Melians, about to suffer terrible slaughter and enslavement at Athenian hands, all the moving arguments appropriate to those who realize they are to be massacred.

As deep a student of human psychology as any tragedian, Thucydides found the cause of war in people and nations; he knew as much about war and human behavior as anybody since has been able to learn. He wrote from the perspective of a loser, but not as a mere loser in a sporting event, where time and perhaps a return match will assuage the hurt. Thucydides had seen his own Athens, so admirable in its best qualities, brought down by the Spartan militarists. He hoped that in the future human intelligence would realize how risky war was and what damage it did to the highest human values; but he knew that human nature would always respond to certain challenges by force, and that the lessons of the past were hard to learn. He wrote in pain and in fierce detachment. His narrative of the great military events, such as the siege of Syracuse, moves with great speed and well-concealed artistry. The much less talented and more pedestrian Xenophon, author of the *Anabasis*, wrote in the *Hellenica* a continuation of Thucydides' work down to 362 B.C. And the still less talented Arrian, basing his work largely on the now lost account by Ptolemy I himself, has left us an account of Alexander's campaigns.

For the century or so that followed the death of Alexander we have no historical work comparable to these. Therefore, we know the period less intimately than any since the Dark Age. It is only with the decade of the 220s that we once again encounter a narrative history, and then its author and his purpose symbolize the change that had taken place. He was Polybius, who wrote in Greek but who had spent much time in Rome, where he had become an admirer and agent of the Romans, and the subject of his book was the rise of Roman power.

Science and Philosophy

Possessed of inquiring, speculative minds, and interested in their environment, the Greeks were keenly interested in science. Stimulated by their acquaintance with Egypt, the Ionians and later the European Greeks, though they lacked instruments to check and refine their results, correctly attributed many of the workings of nature to natural rather than supernatural causes. They knew that the Nile flooded because annual spring rains caused its source in Ethiopa to overflow. They decided that the straits between Sicily and Italy and between Africa and Spain were the result of earthquakes, not the work of gods. They understood what caused eclipses and knew that the moon shone by light reflected from the sun. Hippocrates of Cos (c 460-c 377) founded a school of medicine from which there survive the Hippocratic oath, with its high concept of medical ethics, and detailed clinical accounts of the symptoms and progress of diseases so accurate that modern doctors have been able to identify cases of epilepsy, diphtheria, and typhoid fever. Of the first, a supposedly divine disease, a practitioner wrote, "It seems to me that the disease is no more divine than any other. It has a natural cause, just as other diseases have. Men think it divine merely because they do not understand it. But if they called everything divine which they do not understand, there would be no end of divine things."

The mathematician Pythagoras (c 580-500) seems to have begun as a musician interested in the mathematical differences in the length of lyre strings needed to produce various notes. The theorem that in a right triangle the square on the hypotenuse is equal to the sum of the squares of the other two sides we owe to the followers of Pythagoras. They made the concept of numbers into a guide to the problems of life, elevating mathematics almost to a religious cult, perhaps the earliest effort to explain the universe in abstract mathematical language. Pythagoras is said to have been the first to use the word *cosmos*—"harmonious and beautiful order"—for the universe. Earlier Greeks had found the key to the universe in some single primal substance: water, fire, earth, or air. Democritus (c 460-370) decided that all matter consisted of minute, invisible atoms.

When Alexandria became the center of scientific research, the astronomer Aristarchus, in the mid-third century B.C., concluded that the earth revolves around the sun—a concept not generally accepted till almost two thousand years later. His younger contemporary, Eratosthenes, believed that the earth was round, and estimated its circumference quite accurately. Euclid, the great geometrical systematizer, had his own school at Alexandria in the third century B.C. His pupil Archimedes won a lasting reputation in both theoretical and applied physics, devising machines for removing water from mines and irrigation ditches, and demonstrating the power of pulleys and levers by single-handedly drawing ashore a heavily laden ship. Hence his celebrated boast: "Give me a lever long enough and a place to stand on, and I will move the world." In the second century, Hipparchus calculated the length of the solar year to within a few minutes.

Rhetoric also became an important study, as the Greeks reflected on the construction of their own language and developed high standards of self-expression and style. The subject began with political oratory, as politicians wished to make more effective speeches—particularly in wartime, when the population was excited and each leader strove to be more eloquent than the last. But to speak effectively, one must have something to say, and a body of professional teachers, who wrote on physics, astronomy, mathematics, logic, and music traveled about, receiving pay. These multipurpose scholars who in the fifth and fourth centuries B.C. taught people how to talk and write and think on all subjects were called Sophists ("wisdom-men"). Sophists generally tended to be highly skeptical of accepted standards of behavior and morality, questioning the traditional ways of doing things. They tended to focus on the tension between nature and law.

How could anybody really be sure of anything, they would ask? And some would answer that we cannot know anything we cannot experience through one of our five senses. How could one be sure that the gods existed if no one could see, hear, smell, taste, or touch them? If there were no gods and therefore no divine laws, how should we behave? Should we trust laws made by others like ourselves? And what sort of men were making the laws, and in whose interest? Perhaps all existing laws were simply a trick invented by powerful people to protect their position. Maybe the general belief in the gods was simply invented by clever people in whose interest it was to have the general public docile. Not all Sophists went this far, but in Athens during the Peloponnesian War many young people, troubled by the war or by the sufferings of the plague, were ready to listen to suggestions that the state should not make such severe demands upon them. Many citizens, gods-fearing and law-abiding, saw the Sophists as corrupters of youth.

It is only against this background that we can understand the career and fate of Socrates (469-399 B.C.), whose method (though not affiliation) was that of the Sophists—to question everything, all current assumptions about religion, politics, and behavior—but who retained unwavering to the end his own deep inner loyalties to Athens. Though Socrates wrote no books, we know him well from contemporary reports, chiefly those of his pupil Plato (c 427-347). Socrates was a stonemason who spent his life arguing in the Assembly, in public places, and in the homes of his friends in Athens. He thought of himself as a gadfly, challenging everything anybody said to him and urging people not to take their preconceptions and prejudices as truths. Only never-ending debate, a process of question and answer—the celebrated Socratic method—could lead human beings to truth. Reasoning led Socrates to conclude that human beings were more than animals; they had a mind, and, above all, they had a true self, a kind of soul or spirit. Their proper business on earth was to fulfill this true soul and cultivate the virtues that were proper to it: temperance, justice, courage, nobility, truth. Socrates would pursue the inquiries that led to these virtues even against the wishes of the state.

At about age seventy, Socrates was brought to trial on charges of disrespect to the gods and corrupting the young men of Athens. He argued that he had followed the prescribed religious observances and that he only wanted to make the young men better citizens; he defended his gadfly tactics as necessary to stir a sluggish state into life. But by a narrow margin, a court of 501 jurors voted the death penalty. Socrates could have escaped by suggesting that he be punished in some other way. Instead, he ironically asked for a tiny fine and, to show his respect for the law, forced the court to choose between that and death. Socrates drank the poison cup of hemlock and waited for death, serenely optimistic. He was "of good cheer about his soul." Many contemporaries and most commentators have agreed that he was the victim of hysteria following a dreadful war.

Thereafter, it was Plato who carried on his work. Plato founded a school in Athens, the Academy, and wrote several notable dialogues, intellectual conversations in which Socrates and others were shown discussing problems of life and the human spirit. Much influenced by the Pythagoreans, Plato retained a deep reverence for mathematics, but he found cosmic reality in Ideas rather than in numbers. As each person has a "true self" within and superior to the body, so the world we experience with our bodily senses has within and superior to itself a "true world"—an invisible universe or cosmos. In *The Republic*, Plato has Socrates compare the relationship between the world of the senses and the world of Ideas with that between the shadows of persons and objects as they would be cast by firelight on the wall of a cave, and the same real persons and objects as they would appear in the direct light of day. People see objects—chairs, tables, trees—of the world as real, whereas they are only reflections of the true realities—the universals—the Idea of the perfect chair, table, or tree. So human virtues are reflections of ideal virtues, of which the highest is the Idea of the Good. Human beings can, and should, strive to know the ultimate Ideas, especially the Idea of the Good.

Plato's theory of Ideas has proved to be one of the great wellsprings of Western thought and has formed the starting point for much later philosophical discussion. Moreover, in teaching that the Idea of the Good was the supreme excellence and the final goal of life, Plato (through Socrates) was advancing a kind of monotheism and laying a foundation on which both pagan and Christian theologians would build.

Politically, Athenian democracy did much to disillusion Plato; he had seen its courts condemn his master. On his travels he had formed a high opinion of the tyrants ruling the Greek cities of Sicily and Italy. So when Plato came to sketch the ideal state in *The Republic*, his system resembled that of the Spartans. He recommended that power be entrusted to the Guardians, a small intellectual elite, specially bred and trained to understand Ideas, governing under the wisest man of all, the Philosopher-King. The masses would simply do their jobs as workers or soldiers and obey their superiors. Democracy, he concluded, by relying on amateurs was condemned to failure through the fatal flaws in the character of those who would govern.

Plato's most celebrated pupil was Aristotle (384-322 B.C.), called the "master of those who know." Son of a physician at the court of Philip of Macedon and tutor to Alexander the Great, Aristotle was interested in everything. He wrote on biology, logic, ethics, literary criticism, political theory. His work survives largely in the form of notes on his lectures taken by his students. Though he wrote 158 studies of the constitutions of Greek cities, only the study of Athens survives. Despite their lack of polish, these writings have had enormous influence.

Aristotle concerned himself chiefly with matters as they are. The first to use scientific methods, he classified living organisms into groups, much as modern biologists do, and extended the system to other fields—government, for example. He maintained that governments were of three forms—rule by one man, rule by a few men, or rule by many men—and that there were good and bad types of each, respectively monarchy and tyranny, aristocracy and oligarchy, polity and mob rule. Everywhere—in his *Logic, Poetics, Politics*—he laid foundations for later inquiry. Though he believed that people should strive and aspire, he did not push them on to Socrates' goal of self-knowledge or Plato's lofty ascent to the Idea of the Good. He urged instead the cultivation of the golden mean, the avoidance of excess on either side—courage, not foolhardiness or cowardice; temperance, not overindulgence or abstinence; liberality in giving, not prodigality or meanness.

Later, in the period after Alexander, two new schools of philosophy developed, the Epicurean and the Stoic. Epicurus (342-271) counseled temperance and reason, carrying further the principle of the golden mean. Though he defined pleasure as the key to human happiness, he ranked spiritual joys above those of the body, which he recommended should be satisfied in moderation. Although the gods existed, he taught that they did not interest themselves in human affairs. This last argument led many to think that the Epicureans were atheists bent on attacking religion, though they regarded it as simply irrelevant. The Stoics, founded by Zeno (c 335-263) got their name from the columned porch (*Stoa*) in the Athens Agora from which he first taught. They preferred to repress the physical desires altogether. Since only the inward divine reason counted, the Stoics preached total disregard for social, physical, or economic differences. They became the champions of slaves and other social outcasts, anticipating to some degree one of the moral teachings of Christianity. They were often apolitical, for political debate did not help people, and thus they were thought to be fatalistic, even apathetic, in their focus on the inward life.

The Arts

The incalculably rich legacy left by the Greeks in literature was well matched by their achievements in the plastic arts. In architecture their characteristic public building was a rectangle, with a roof supported by fluted columns. Over the centuries, the Greeks developed three principal types or orders of columns, still used today in "classical" buildings: the Doric, the Ionic, and the Corinthian. Fluting gives an impression of greater height than the simple cylindrical Egyptian columns.

No matter what the order of the columns, a Greek temple strikes the beholder as dignified and simple. On the Acropolis of Athens, the Parthenon, greatest of all Doric temples, rose between 447 and 432 B.C. as the crowning achievement of Pericles' rebuilding program. By means of subtle devices—slightly inclining the columns inward so that they look more stable, giving each column a slight bulge in the center of the shaft so that it does not look concave—the building gives the illusion of perfection. In the triangular gable-ends that crowned its

This dramatic view of the Athenian Acropolis is taken from near the Pnyx. The large temple is the Parthenon. The Acropolis was a civic and religious center for Athens, completed by Pericles and those who succeeded him during the second half of the fifth century.

(left) The inside of this Attic *kylix* (drinking cup), painted by the artist Exekias about 540 B.C., shows Dionysus sailing. Greek vases and cups provide historians with knowledge about social customs, the uses of leisure time, sexual practices, and the nature of warfare. (right) This Attic *amphora* (two-handled vase used for storage) of terra-cotta shows Achilles and Ajax playing either chess or dice; it dates from c 540 B.C.

front and back colonnades (pediments) and on the marble slabs (metopes) between the beam ends above the columns, stood a splendid series of sculptured battle-scenes, most of whose remains (the so-called Elgin Marbles) are now in the British Museum. Originally, the Parthenon and its statues were brightly painted. (The building survived almost undamaged for two thousand years, until 1697, when a Venetian shell exploded a Turkish powder magazine inside.)

The achievement of Phidias and the other sculptors of the Periclean Age had gradually developed from the "archaic" statues created a century or more earlier, usually of young men rather rigidly posed, with their arms hanging at their sides and a uniformly serene smile on their lips. Probably influenced by Egyptian models, these statues have great charm for moderns, who sometimes find the realism of the finished classical work rather tiresome. Phidias' great gold and ivory statues of Athena and the Olympian Zeus long ago fell to looters, though the Parthenon frieze survived. Most of the Greeks' sculpture in bronze also was destroyed, but every so often a great bronze statue is fished out of the sea or is found beneath a modern street.

Though Greek painting as such has almost disappeared, we know from written texts that public buildings were adorned with paintings of Greek victories and portraits of political and military leaders. Moreover, the thousands of pottery vases, plates, cups, and bowls that have been discovered preserve on their surfaces—in black on red or in red on black—paintings of extraordinary beauty and of great variety. They show mythological scenes, illustrations of the *Iliad* and *Odyssey*, and the daily round of human activity—an athlete, a fisherman, a shoemaker, a miner, even a drunk vomiting while a sympathetic girl holds his head.

From left to right: Doric, Ionic, and Corinthian columns.

In the Hellenistic age sculpture became more emotional and theatrical; compare the Laocoön group, with writhing serpents crushing their victims, to a statue of

FOOD AND CIVILIZATION

History has been profoundly influenced by shifts in diets, in the migration of foods from one part of the world to another, and by discoveries concerning nutrition. Greek civilization rested to an important extent on the olive. During its height the dry Mediterranean landscape of Greece was well forested and far more green than now, since the goats that have done so much to denude the Greek coasts and mountains were not yet prevalent. By the fifth century the olive grove, interspersed among the forests on lower elevations, was providing the Greeks with a staple to their economy, an important food, and a valuable source of nutrition.

Athena and Poseidon are said to have been in competition for the loyalty of a small Greek settlement in a particularly rocky area. A jury of gods agreed to decide which would provide the inhabitants the best life: Poseidon at once struck a salt spring from the rock, to show that the fruits of the sea would belong to the villagers. Athena caused an olive tree to grow from the rocky soil, and the gods awarded the village to her. Eventually, though history does not record how, the process of soaking olives in a lye of water and wood ash, and then in brine, was learned, since olives cannot be eaten as they come from the tree. By the fifth century olives were being widely cultivated, preserved, and shipped throughout the Mediterranean world, together with grapes, figs, and wheat. Olives were also pressed to make oil, which in time made yet other foods, to which the oil was added, possible. Today the landscape of Greece is utterly different from that of the fifth century, except for the exceptional longevity of the olive orchards and the continuity of use of the fruit of the olive tree.

Two of the best known works of Hellenic Greek art are the Laocoön group and the Winged Victory of Samothrace. Laocoön and his sons, a study in terror, was done by three sculptors in the first century B.C. The family is caught in a death grip by serpents whom the gods had sent to punish Laocoön because he had urged the Trojans not to touch the wooden horse that had been brought into their midst. In contrast to this horror is the figure of Victory erected on the island of Samothrace about 200 B.C., probably to commemorate a naval victory by the Greeks over those who sought to enslave them.

the Periclean period. The Venus de Milo and the Winged Victory of Samothrace are two of the most heralded Hellenistic works of art, but there are a good many imitative and exaggerated efforts which today are regarded as comparative failures. In literature, too, beginning with Menander's New Comedy, vigor and originality ebbed, while sophistication and self-consciousness took over.

The Greeks continue to fascinate us for many reasons. They are the first people who left a record sufficiently intact to allow us to trace in some detail how their customs changed over time. Their sense of the dramatic and the human, their speculation about the universe and about individual psychology, and the divine tension they felt between the ideal and daily reality all appeal to us, for we find reflections of our own preoccupations in them. Their philosophers phrased the questions we still ask, their politicians used the techniques, both noble and ignoble, our politicians still use, and their artists strove for the sense of human perfection we want to believe attainable. The Greeks are the first people to whom modern men and women can relate, emotionally as well as intellectually.

We must recognize, of course, that we might feel a similar kinship to even remoter societies of antiquity if we knew as much about them. But we do not, and unless archaeology and history together produce new evidence, we are likely to see the Greeks as the ancient people to whom Western civilization feels closest. They worried about our worries: What does it mean to be civilized? To lead the good life? To serve the people? To retain one's own identity? How best may we attain a sense of security in a world in which chance seems to play so large a role? By denying that chance exists? By fatalistically accepting that which is? By attempting to change the future? The present? Our environment? Our past?

They asked whether god or gods exist, and, for the most part, having decided that they did, they debated how best to worship, celebrate, or propitiate those gods, individually and in groups. They asked nearly all of what we call The Big Questions, and while we have evolved many different answers to those questions (or conceived of new ways in which to state the same answers), and while our circumstances are different so that no direct parallels can be drawn from a society so far removed in time from our own, we continue to recognize in the Greeks something of ourselves.

Much of what we know about the Greeks comes from

research and discoveries in the nineteenth century. The Greeks seemed to provide answers to many questions with which nineteenth century society was concerned, and there was a tendency, especially in western Europe, to idealize Greek civilization. Only recently have new techniques and concerns among historians—especially with quantitative methods and in comparative and social history—led us to realize that there was much in Greek society which today we find deplorable. Slavery was essential to the leisure the philosophers enjoyed, and was perhaps even more prejudicial to the masters than the slaves. Women were systematically and casually kept in subordinate positions. War was used to resolve problems of population and pride as well as for territorial gain. The toilers in the fields, vineyards, and in the expanding ancient city often had no voice, in war or peace. Though professing the rational life, the Greeks could be swept up into the irrational, allowing their rituals to bring on mass hysteria.

In sum, the Greeks were—as we ought to have known before either the period of nineteenth-century romanticizing or of twentieth-century skepticism—human beings subject to the ambiguities and contradictions shown by every human society. It is this very humanness which strengthens our perception that Greek origins are so relevant to our own.

SUMMARY

The Greeks are the first ancient society with which modern society feels an immediate affinity. We can identify with Greek art, Greek politics, Greek curiosity, and the Greek sense of history. The polis, roughly translated as the city-state, was the prevailing social and political unit of ancient Greece. Athens and Sparta were the two most significant poleis.

Sparta was a conservative military oligarchy ruled jointly by two kings and a council of elders. It had an excellent army, but its society was highly regimented. Sparta produced little of artistic or cultural importance.

Athens progressed from an old-fashioned, aristocratic tribal state in the eighth century B.C. to a tyranny and then to a democracy by the fifth century B.C. Among the most important leaders of this transition from a state based on ties of kinship to one based on political citizenship were the law-givers Draco and Solon, the tyrant Pisistratus, and the reformer Cleisthenes.

Athens depended, as did all Greek states, upon the systematic exploitation of slaves. Although influential in the home, women were also a subject group. Their fathers and husbands determined the extent of their personal freedom.

By the fifth century B.C., the Persian Empire, which had subjugated all of the Near East, including the Greek cities of Asia Minor (Ionia), was extending its rule into northern Greece. Two Persian invasions of Greece were defeated: by the Athenians at Marathon (490 B.C.) and by united Greek forces at the battles of Salamis (480) and Plataea (479).

After the defeat of Persia, Athens and Sparta were rivals for the leadership of Greece. The Athenian empire that emerged from the Persian defeat was brought to its zenith by Pericles, who beautified Athens and advanced the democratization of its constitution.

Rivalry between Athens and Sparta led to the Peloponnesian Wars (460-445,431-404 B.C.) in which Athens was eventually defeated after a plague ravaged the city and a great expedition to Sicily met with disaster.

Thereafter, neither Sparta, Thebes, nor a revived Athens could successfully lead Greece. In the 330s Greek disunity led to domination by Philip, king of Macedon, a semi-Greek kingdom to the north.

Philip's son Alexander ("the Great") invaded and conquered the Persian Empire in 334-327 B.C. Alexander's conquests spread Greek colonists and culture from Egypt to the borders of India.

After Alexander's death in 324, three main successor dynasties emerged, each founded by one of his generals: the Ptolemies in Egypt, the Seleucids in Syria and Mesopotamia, and the Antigonids in Macedon and Asia Minor. All of these states were eventually absorbed by Rome.

Greek religion was centered upon the worship of the Olympian gods. Greek drama developed out of a festival at Athens in honor of the god Dionysus. The chief Greek playwrights who have survived are the tragedians Aeschylus, Sophocles, and Euripides and the comic writers Aristophanes and Menander. The principal Greek historians whose work has come down to us are Herodotus, who wrote about the Persian wars; Thucydides, the historian of the Peloponnesian Wars; and Polybius, whose subject was the rise of Roman power.

The Greeks attributed many of the workings of nature to natural rather than to supernatural causes. In medicine, geography, geometry, physics, and astronomy their achievements still command respect.

Greek philosophy had its roots in natural science and in the tendency of science to question established beliefs and traditions. Socrates taught that the truth could be found only in a never-ending debate, a process of question-and-answer—the famous "Socratic method." His pupil Plato's theory of Ideas is one of the great wellsprings of Western thought. Plato's pupil Aristotle was the first to use scientific method, classifying living things, beliefs, and systems of government. The Epicurean and Stoic schools of philosophy sought to show people how to live contented lives in a troubled world. The influence of Greek art and architecture on Western civilization is incalculable.

chapter three

THE ROMANS

The Romans cherished the legend that after the fall of Troy, Aeneas, a Trojan prince, half divine, led his fugitive followers to Italy and founded Rome on the banks of the Tiber. The poet Vergil (70-19 B.C.) immortalized the story in his *Aeneid*, written as Roman imperial glory approached its zenith. As Vergil borrowed from Homer, so Rome borrowed extensively from the older Greek and Near Eastern civilizations. The tale of Aeneas symbolizes the flow into Italy of Greeks and Near Easterners as well as Rome's debt to the Greco-oriental world. Yet Rome did not achieve greatness on borrowed capital alone. The Romans were themselves innovative builders, generals, administrators, law-givers.

Compared with Greece, Italy enjoys certain natural advantages: the plains are larger and more fertile, the mountains less a barrier to communications. The plain of Latium, south of the site of Rome, could be farmed intensively after drainage and irrigation ditches had been dug; the nearby hills provided timber and good pasturage. The city of Rome lay only fifteen miles from the sea and could share in the trade of the Mediterranean; yet its seven hills overlooking the Tiber could be easily fortified and defended. By 600 B.C. Greek colonies to the south dotted the shores of Italy and Sicily; this was *Magna Graecia*. To the north, the dominant power was held by the Etruscans—a people of whom we know little, surely foreigners in Italy, perhaps from Asia Minor (and so the source of the Aeneas legend)—who had invaded the peninsula and conquered the region north of Latium by 700 B.C. They extended their power southward, surrounding Rome, and seized it soon after 600.

Rich Etruscan remains have been discovered during the past century and a half, mostly in tombs, which show that the Etruscans had an enormous admiration for Greek art—pottery, sculpture, and painting—which they bought and imitated. They wrote their language in Greek letters, and most of the ten thousand or so existing inscriptions are very short. Many can be read, since they give, for example, only a proper name and perhaps the age at which the person mentioned died. Until 1964 no key to the Etruscan language like the Rosetta stone had turned up. Then, on the seacoast thirty miles from Rome, archaeologists found three golden tablets dated c 500 B.C. with inscriptions in both Punic (Carthaginian, or late Phoenician) and Etruscan, which, although the total number of words is only about ninety, is now throwing more light on the language.

Expert farmers, miners, and metal workers, the Etruscans built huge stone walls around their settlements. They practiced divination, foretelling the future from observing flocks of birds in flight or from examining the entrails of an animal slain in sacrifice. Their tomb decoration seems to show that, like the Egyptians, they believed in an afterlife similar to this one, and that they accorded their women a status higher than was usual in ancient society. They also enjoyed gladiatorial combat as a spectacle—a taste the Romans may have borrowed from them.

I THE REPUBLIC

When the Etruscans took over Rome, the people they conquered were apparently Latins, descendants of prehistoric inhabitants of the peninsula. Under its Etruscan kings, Rome prospered during the sixth century B.C. The Etruscans built new stone structures and drained and paved what eventually became the Forum. But the Roman population resented foreign rule and joined with other Latin tribes in a large-scale rebellion. The traditional date for the expulsion from Rome of the last Etruscan king, Tarquin the Proud, is 509 B.C. What he left behind was an independent Latin city-state, still including some Etruscan notables, much smaller than Athens or Sparta, sharing Latium with other city-states. Yet in less than two hundred and fifty years, Rome would dominate the entire Italian peninsula.

We can understand this success best by examining Roman institutions. Once they had ousted Tarquin, the dominant arisocratic forces of Rome set up a republic. Only the well-established land-owning families, the *patricians* (Latin *pater*, father), perhaps not more than 10 percent of the population, held full citizenship. The remaining 90 percent were *plebeians* (Latin *plebs*, the multitude), who included those engaged in trade or labor, the smaller farmers, and all those who were debtors as the result of the economic upheaval that followed the expulsion of the Etruscans. The plebeians had no right to hold office; they could amass as much money as they pleased, however, and wealthy plebeians would eventually lead a campaign to gain political emancipation for their class. Fifth-century urban Rome, then, was not unlike sixth-century Athens before the reforms of Cleisthenes.

The patrician class supplied two consuls, who governed jointly for a term of a year, enjoying full *imperium*, supreme political power. Each had the right of veto over the other, so that both had to support a measure before it could be put through. Ordinarily they were commanders of the army, but in wartime this power was often wielded for a period not longer than six months by an elected *dictator*, a commander who had obtained his authority constitutionally and had to surrender it when his term was over.

The consuls usually followed the policies decided on by the Senate, a body consisting of about three hundred members, mostly patricians and all ex-officials. It wielded such prestige, that it came first in the Roman

An Etruscan bronze, known as "the Capitoline wolf." Figures of Romulus and Remus were added in the late fifteenth century.

political emblem—S.P.Q.R., *Senatus Populusque Romanorum*, that is, the Senate and the People of the Romans. The reigning consuls, who were themselves senators, appointed new senators. The Romans had another deliberative body, the Centuriate Assembly, based on the century, the smallest unit (one hundred men) of the army. Although plebeians were included, the patricians also dominated the deliberations of this body. It enjoyed a higher legal prerogative but less actual power than the Senate, although it elected the consuls and other officials and approved or rejected laws submitted to it by both the consuls and the Senate.

Before a man could be chosen consul, he had to pass through a succession of lesser posts. The job that led directly to the consulate was that of *praetor* ("the one who goes in front"). Elected by the Centuriate Assembly for a term of a year, the praetor served as a judge; he also often commanded an army and later governed a province. While at first there was only one praetor, the number later rose to eight. Men seeking election as praetor or consul wore a special robe whitened with chalk, the *toga candida*, from which comes our word *candidate*. From among the ex-consuls, the Assembly elected two *censors*, for an eighteen-month term, who took a census to determine which of the population was qualified to pass for army service. They also secured the right to pass on the moral qualifications of men nominated for the Senate, barring those they thought corrupt or too luxury-loving (hence the connotation of our words *censor* and *censorship*).

The plebeians naturally resented their exclusion from political authority. As early as the 490s they threatened to withdraw from Rome and to found a new city-state of their own nearby. And when this tactic won them a concession, they continued to use it at various times with great effect during the next two hundred years. In 494 B.C. they gained the right to have officials of their own, the *tribunes* of the people, to protect them from unduly harsh application of the laws; by 457 there were ten such tribunes. In 471 the plebeians also gained their own assembly, the Tribal Assembly (named because of the subdivision of the plebeian population into tribes), which chose the tribunes and had the right, like the Centuriate Assembly, to pass on new laws. Next they complained that the patrician judges could manipulate the law for their own purposes because it had never been set down for all to read. So in 451 the consuls ordered the extremely severe laws engraved on wooden tablets—the Twelve Tables—beginning the written history of Roman law.

In the early Republic, being in debt meant that a plebeian farmer would lose his land and be forced into slavery. As a result, property steadily accumulated in the hands of the patrician landowners. In a significant advance, the plebeians were able to change the laws affecting their economic relationship with the patricians. They obtained legislation limiting the size of an estate that any one man might accumulate, abolishing the penalty of slavery for debt, and opening newly acquired lands to settlement by landless farmers. Still, the farmer-debtor problem, though eased, continued to plague the Romans to the end, even during the fifth and fourth centuries, when the plebeians won the right to hold all the offices of the state, including that of consul (366 B.C.). The plebeians also forced the repeal of the laws that forbade their intermarriage with patricians.

The fusion of wealthy plebeians and patricians formed a new class, the *nobiles*, who were to dominate the later Republic as the patricians had done earlier.

Roman Expansion, 264 B.C.-133 B.C.

This regime was well designed to carry on the chief preoccupation of the emerging Roman state—war. The Roman army at first had as its basic unit the *phalanx*—about 8,000 foot soldiers armed with helmet, shield, lance, and sword. But experience led to the substitution of the far more maneuverable *legion*, consisting of 5,000 men in groups of 60 or 120, called *maniples* (handfuls), armed with the additional weapon of an iron-tipped javelin, which could be hurled at the enemy from a distance. Almost all citizens of Rome had to serve. Iron discipline prevailed; punishment for offenses was summary or brutal. But the officers also understood the importance of generous recognition and reward of bravery as an incentive.

In a long series of wars, the Romans established their political dominance over the other Latin towns, the Etruscan cities, and the tribes of central Italy. Early in the third century B.C. they conquered the Greek cities of southern Italy. Meanwhile, in the north, a Celtic people, the Gauls, had crossed the Alps and settled in the Lombard plain. Their expansion was halted in 225 B.C. at the little river Rubicon, which was then the northern frontier of Roman dominion.

In conquered areas the Romans sometimes planted a colony of their own land-hungry plebeians. Usually they did not try to force the resident population into absolute subjection, accepting them as allies and respecting their institutions. The cities of Magna Graecia continued to enjoy home rule. Some of the nearest neighbors of Rome became full citizens of the Republic, but more often they had the protection of Roman law while being unable to participate in the Roman assemblies. So the expansion of Rome in Italy demonstrated imaginative statesmanship as well as military superiority.

The conquest of Magna Graecia made Rome a near neighbor of the Carthaginian state. Carthage (modern Tunis) was originally a Phoenician colony but had long since liberated itself and expanded along the African and

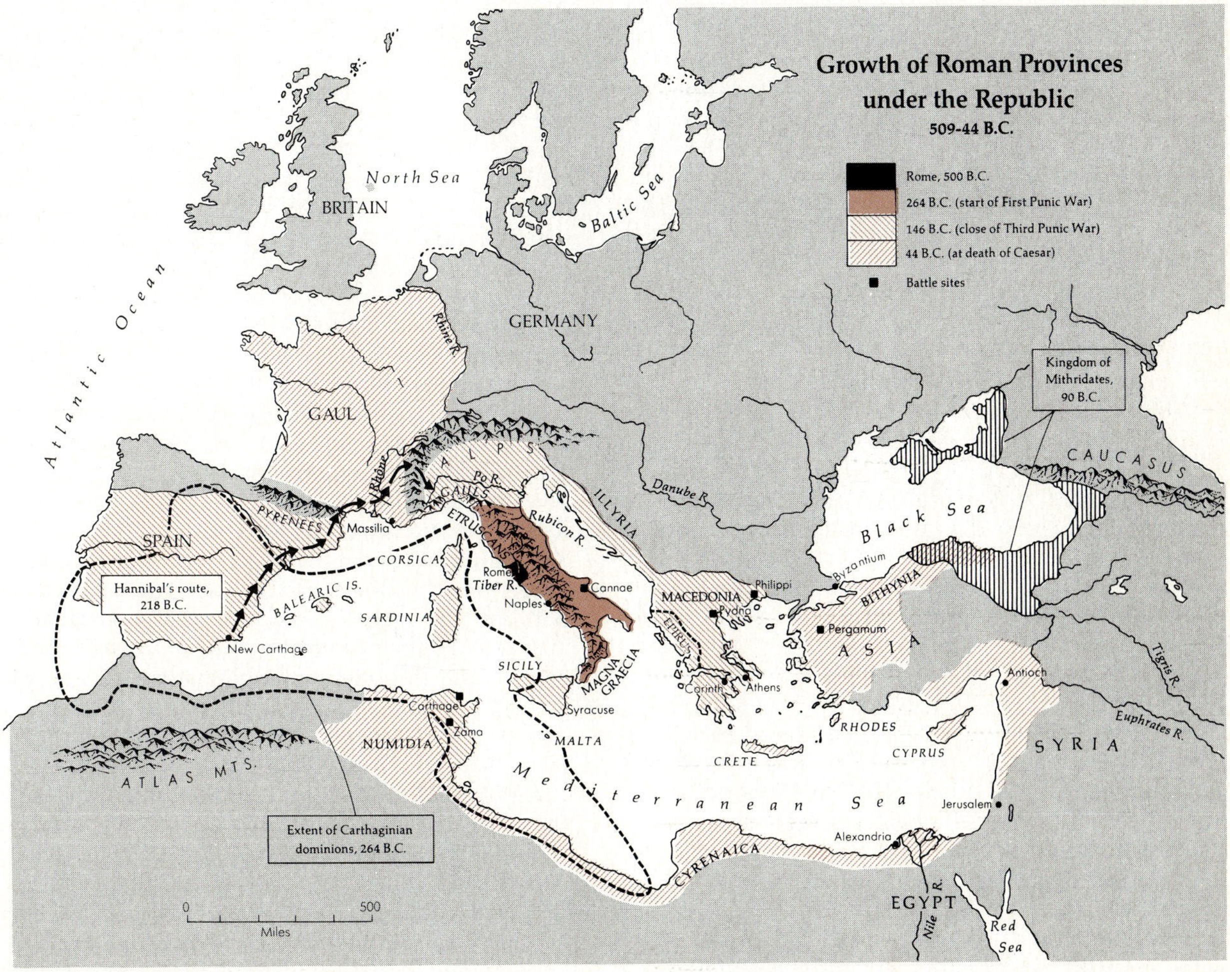

Spanish shores of the Mediterranean and into western Sicily. Ruled by a commercial oligarchy, Carthage held a virtual monopoly of western Mediterranean trade. When the Carthaginians began to attack the Greek cities in eastern Sicily, the Sicilian Greeks appealed to Rome. So the Romans launched the First Punic (from the Latin word for Phoenician) War (264-241 B.C.).

The Romans won that war by building their first major fleet and defeating the Carthaginians at sea. They forced Carthage to give up all claim to eastern Sicily and to cede western Sicily as well, thus obtaining their first province beyond the Italian mainland. Sardinia and Corsica followed in 237. Seeking revenge, the Carthaginians used Spain as the base for an overland invasion to Italy in the Second Punic War (218-202). Their commander, Hannibal (247- c 183), led his forces across southern Gaul and then over the Alps into Italy, losing in the snow many of the elephants he used as pack animals. In northern Italy he recruited many Gauls and, making brilliant use of light infantry, won a string of victories as he marched southward, notably at Cannae in 216 B.C., when the Romans suffered the most severe defeat in their history.

Gradually the Romans rebuilt their armies, and in 202 B.C. Hannibal, who had been roaming over Italy almost at will for a decade avoiding only the great walled cities, was summoned home to defend Carthage against a Roman invading force under Scipio, who had captured the Punic centers in Spain. Scipio won the battle at Zama and the title "Africanus" as a reward. The Romans forced the Carthaginians to surrender Spain (where the local population resisted Roman rule for another two centuries), to pay a large levy, and to promise to follow Rome's lead in foreign policy. Hannibal escaped to the court of the Seleucid king Antiochus III.

Though Carthaginian power had been broken, the city quickly recovered its prosperity. This alarmed the war party at Rome. Cato, a censor and senator, ended each of his speeches with the words "*Delenda est Carthago*" ("Carthage must be destroyed"). In the Third Punic War (149-146) the Romans leveled the city, sprinkled salt on the earth, and took over all its remaining territory as the province of Africa (modern Tunisia), now one of six overseas provinces.

While the Punic Wars were still going on, Rome had as early as 230 B.C. become embroiled in the Balkans and in Greece, first sending ships and troops to put down pirates who were operating in the Adriatic from bases in Illyria (modern Albania), and then intervening again in 219 to punish an unruly local ally. The Greeks were grateful to Rome and admitted Romans to the Eleusinian mysteries and the Isthmian Games. But Philip V (221-179), Antigonid king of Macedon, viewed with suspicion Roman operations on his side of the Adriatic. He tried to help Hannibal during the Second Punic War, but a Roman fleet prevented him from crossing to Italy. Many of the Greek cities—opponents of Philip, if not yet of Rome—came to Rome's aid in the fighting that ensued, helping to defeat him in the First Macedonian War (215-205).

Not eager as yet to expand on the eastern shores of the Adriatic, Rome contented itself with establishing a series of Illyrian buffer states. But Philip kept intervening in these states, and the Romans feared for their loyalty. In 202 B.C. several Hellenistic powers—Ptolemy V of Egypt; his ally Attalus, king of the powerful independent kingdom of Pergamum in Asia Minor; and Rhodes, head of a new naval league—as well as Athens, appealed to Rome to intervene once more against Philip V. Furthermore, the Romans feared the alliance struck between Philip and Antiochus III, the Seleucid king in Asia, and the Senate may have decided upon a preventive war. In the Second Macedonian War (200-197) Rome defeated Philip's armies on their own soil and forced him to withdraw from Greece altogether and become an ally of Rome. At the Isthmian Games of 196 B.C., a solemn Roman proclamation declared that the Greeks were free. Two years later, after more fighting (chiefly against Sparta), the Roman armies left Greece and its largely disillusioned population, who had learned that, though free, they were not viewed as equals by the Romans but as client states.

Antiochus III had profited by the defeat of Macedon to take over the Greek cities on the Aegean coast of Asia Minor and cross into Europe. Hoping to keep Greece as a buffer against him and worried at this advance, the Romans, preoccupied with wars in Spain, kept on negotiating with him. But Antiochus, who had with him the refugee Hannibal, opposed the Romans in Greece, unwisely hoping to win wide local support. The Romans defeated Antiochus and then invaded Asia, forcing him to surrender all the Seleucid holdings in Asia Minor in 188. Hannibal escaped but poisoned himself in 183 as he was about to be surrendered to Rome. Rome had become the predominant power in the Greek world, whether by intent, in reactive self-defense, or in pursuit of a theory of imperium.

For the next forty years the Romans felt obliged to arbitrate the constantly recurring quarrels among the Greek states. Rebellions led to or excused repeated armed intervention. In the Third Macedonian War (172-168), Perseus, Philip V's son and successor, was captured and his forces routed at the decisive battle of Pydna. Rome imposed a ruthless settlement, breaking Macedon up into four republics and exiling many who had sympathized with Perseus. Twenty years later the Romans annexed Macedon, their first province east of the Adriatic. In 146 they defeated a desperate uprising of the Achaean League and marked their victory by a brutal sack of Corinth, in which the men were killed, the women and children sold as slaves, and the city leveled. It was the same year that saw the total destruction of Carthage. The period of relatively gentle rule was over; a new harshness was now applied to allies as well as to opponents.

The Romans henceforth dominated Greece from Macedon, but did not yet annex it as a province. Internal fighting in Greece came to an end; there was a religious and economic revival; divisions between rich and poor became more pronounced. Rome's prestige was now so great that in 133 the king of Pergamum, whose family had been helpful allies of the Romans—and much hated elsewhere for that reason—left his flourishing Asia Minor state to Rome in his will. It became the new province of Asia.

II CRISIS OF THE REPUBLIC

As Roman territory increased, signs of trouble multiplied. The Republic allowed a few overseas cities to retain some self-government, but usually organized its new territories as provinces under governors appointed by the Senate. Some of the governors proved oppressive and lined their own pockets; as long as they raised recruits for the army and collected taxes, they had a free hand. In Italy pressure mounted from Rome's allies, who demanded full citizenship and a share in the new wealth flowing into the capital.

The great majority of those who lived on the Italian peninsula were farmers. By the time of the Republic, Roman farmers had advanced beyond the simple two-field system of the Greeks, in which one field was under cultivation while the other lay fallow. In the Campania the Romans cultivated the land throughout the year, having learned the merits of heavy over light plows, and the pastoral economy shifted to the production of cereal crops. By the time of the Republic Romans had learned to exploit the soil in various ways: by cereal and legume cultivation, by growing trees for timber or fruit, by animal husbandry, and by producing vegetable crops both for sustenance and sale. Such mixed intensive farming gave the farmer increased economic power, made him less dependent on the weather, and limited the tendency toward impoverishment of the soil so common in Greece—where mountains that were once covered with forest are today relatively bare. The development of sheep farms and cattle ranches on a large scale led to a division between the peasant and the larger farmer similar to the growing division between the rich and the poor that existed in the cities.

These trends in agriculture affected society as a whole. The army needed grain. When military needs increased and fewer fields were put into grain, Rome had to turn to imports, making the Republic more dependent on outside suppliers. Imported grain from Sardinia, Egypt, and Africa became essential to the growing needs of the army, as well as to those who received free grain from the state. Italian farmers who produced cereal crops, however, could thrive, because their product was regarded as superior and was nearby. The farmers tended to be politically and socially conservative, suspicious of outsiders and of new methods. They continued to sow by scattering the seed by hand (the least effective method), rather than adopting the superior method of seed-drilling (dropping seeds in furrows and covering them up)—a technique known to the ancient Sumerians and regularly practiced in China, from which it eventually came to Europe. Even with a large supply of Sicilian

SLAVERY IN THE ROMAN WORLD

Roman Italy and Sicily became a slave society as the Romans conquered the whole of the Mediterranean world. Scholars argue over how fundamental slavery has been to different cultures. Perhaps half of all societies have owned legal slaves. But if we define a slave society as one in which slaves play a significant role in production and comprise, say, 20 percent of the total population, then there have been only five slave societies in known history: classical Athens, Roman Italy (though not the remainder of the Empire), the West Indies under the British and French, the southern portion of the United States before 1863, and Brazil. This does not, of course, include other forms of forced labor.

Slavery was both fed by, and helped to feed, the expansion of the Roman Empire. The presence of slaves in Roman Italy, chiefly the captives of foreign wars, forced major changes in political and economic organization; slaves may have made up a third of the population—two million out of six million people—by the end of the first century B.C. Slaves were brought back to Rome as booty. As the rich invested in new agricultural land, angry peasants were displaced by slaves and forced into the cities, where they supported political leaders who promised to help them. Roman slaves could acquire professions and skills, however. Many were freed and assimilated as citizens, so that slavery was not fixed by unchanging status, color, religion, or origin. Slaves could purchase their own freedom, and thus emancipation meant that owners gained new sums of money produced by the newly freed slaves themselves with which they could purchase younger replacements. The system thereby became, for a time, self-perpetuating.

grain brought to Italy, there was still no surplus, for the army and the urban poor consumed the increase. Thus wheat-growing, perhaps interspersed with vines and olives, remained commonplace except in those areas where the latifundia began to take over. Latifundia were large mixed farms or cattle ranches worked by slaves. Only large landowners could afford them, and increasingly the small farmers were driven penniless into refuge among the urban poor in Rome.

Proprietors of latifundia, successful generals, governors, merchants, and contractors who had built roads for the state or furnished supplies to the army combined to form a new class of very rich men. Some of them managed to join the Senate—increasingly influential because it had managed the Punic Wars successfully—but the small inner circle, where policy was made, continued to be dominated by the nobiles. Those senators who were content with matters as they were called themselves *optimates* (the best people), while those who found themselves unable to get things done their way sometimes tried to get support from the people at large in the Tribal Assembly, and so were called by their opponents *populares*. Social tensions became acute. An old-fashioned conservative like Cato, for instance, hated the rich taste for the luxurious new ways of life imported from Greece and the East. By the time this new class of the very rich achieved real power in politics, the senators were no longer included among them. Increasingly, the political machinery of a small city-state was being used to cope with the problems of empire, of social tension, and of economic distress.

Two noble brothers named Gracchus (grandsons of Scipio, hero of the Second Punic War) emerged during the late 130s and the 120s B.C. as the champions of the dispossessed, whom they hoped to get back onto the land or into the army. Tiberius Gracchus, who served as tribune of the people in 133, and Gaius, who held the post from 123 to 121, sought to increase the role of the tribunes and the Tribal Assembly at the expense of the anti-Gracchi senators. The wild beasts, said Tiberius, had their dens, but the Romans had not a clod of earth to call their own.

The brothers wanted to resettle landless farmers either abroad or on state-owned lands in Italy that had been leased to agrarian capitalists; to give the urban poor of Rome relief by allowing them to buy grain from the state at cost; and to build roads and granaries, in part as public relief programs, so that the casually employed—who were perhaps most of the urban population—could afford to purchase bread. Politically, Gaius wanted to give certain judicial posts to the *equites* (wealthy Romans below the rank of senator), to extend Roman citizenship to all Latins, and to raise other Italians to Latin status.

The efforts of the Gracchi were not enough, and when the Senate established martial law in the face of growing public unrest and suspicion of Gaius' intentions, he was hunted down and killed. Three thousand of his followers were then condemned to death by a senatorial court. In the succeeding centuries the state had to lower the price of grain, until by 58 B.C. the poor were getting their bread free. This in itself reveals the general ineffectiveness of the resettlement program. Had the dispossessed farmers actually received new allotments, the number in the city needing cheap bread would have fallen off sharply. The agrarian capitalists, after being forced by the Gracchi to give up some of the land they rented from the state, were soon expanding their holdings once more. The latifundia had come to stay. On the political side, the Senate resented the extension of rights to the equites and balked at granting citizenship to other Italian cities until, after an uprising in 91-88 known as the Social War, it had to be done. Politics had turned unconstitutional and violent, and the deadlock between Gracchan reformism and senatorial conservatism moved Rome toward autocracy.

Political leadership now passed to generals who cared less for principle than for power. A general victorious in the chronic provincial warfare would celebrate in Rome with a great *triumph*—a parade of his successful troops and their prisoners and booty that would dazzle the public. The troops, rewarded by their commanders, became loyal to them rather than to the state. The prescription for political success in Rome was to make a record as a successful general. But instability outside Rome was increasing. In the provinces the misrule of the governors provoked uprisings. Along the frontiers, by the end of the second century B.C., Germanic tribes were threatening. In 88 B.C. Mithridates, the king of Pontus (in Asia Minor), seized the Roman province of Asia and provoked the massacre of eighty thousand Romans.

Political Generals: Marius, Sulla, Pompey, Caesar, 107 B.C.-59 B.C.

The first of the generals to achieve power was Marius, leader of the populares, who had won victories against the Numidians (led by their king, Jugurtha) in what is now eastern Algeria, and against a group of largely Celtic peoples called the Cimbri and Teutones, who had been an even graver threat before he beat them in southern France in 102 B.C. Violating the custom that a consul had to wait ten years before serving a second term, Marius had himself elected five times in succession as the savior of Rome. He began a major reorganization of the army, abolishing the requirement that a Roman citizen must pay for his own equipment—a rule that had automatically excluded the poor. Now that the state furnished the equipment, professional volunteers gradually replaced the former citizen soldiers, who in the past had gone back to their normal peacetime occupations once the fighting was over. These professionals wanted booty and a veteran's bonus, and they supported a leader who could provide them. Thus the contest in the Senate often was between a man like Marius and a contender more likely to placate the military.

When Rome went to war against Mithridates in 88 B.C., Marius emerged from retirement and demanded the command. Instead, the Senate chose Sulla, a younger general who was an optimate, and a bloody civil war broke out between the two factions. Marius died in 86, and after Sulla drove Mithridates from Greece, he returned to assume the office of dictator. On the way to and from the east, Sulla's forces plundered the treasury of Zeus at Olympia and of Apollo at Delphi, and sacked Athens for having sympathized with Mithridates. The Romans brought back Greek sculpture, painting, books, and other loot.

It took Sulla two years of bloody fighting to establish himself in power, and he had his opponents killed. He tried to move the Senate back into its ancient position as the chief force in political life. He curtailed the powers of the tribunes and the Tribal Assembly and put through laws designed to curb the rise of new, younger politicians. He broke all precedent by prolonging his tenure as dictator beyond the prescribed six months. He finally retired in 79 B.C., but the Senate proved unable to recover from the bad example he had set for it.

Within ten years Pompey, a ruthless and arrogant young veteran of Sulla's campaigns, rose to power. Having won victories first in Spain and then at home, where he worked with the millionaire Crassus to suppress a slave rebellion led by the gladiator Spartacus (73-71), in 70 B.C. he became consul before he had reached the minimum legal age. Pompey and Crassus forced the Senate to restore the tribunes and the Tribal Assembly to their previous power. After defeating troublesome pirates in the Mediterranean, Pompey took command of a new war against Mithridates for the kingdom of Bithynia (in Asia Minor) that had been left to Rome by its last king. By 65 B.C. Pompey had driven Mithridates into exile at the court of his son-in-law, Tigranes, king of Armenia. Mithridates committed suicide in 63 B.C., and Pompey, who now had imperium, reorganized Asia Minor and the entire province of Asia. Syria, where the last effective Seleucid had died in 129 B.C., had largely fallen to Tigranes by 83, and Pompey made it a Roman province as well. In 64 B.C. he took Jerusalem. The western fringe of Asia was now virtually Roman, and much new revenue soon flowed to Rome.

On his campaigns Pompey enjoyed unprecedented special powers, forced through by the tribunes of the people against much senatorial opposition. He commanded huge resources in men and money. Foreseeing a showdown on his return, Crassus tried to build up his own power by vainly calling for the annexation of Egypt. In 63 there came to light a conspiracy led by Catiline of a group of discontented and dispossessed nobles who had been the victims of Sulla's purges and who now planned a revolution and a comeback. Cicero, a consul and famous lawyer, discovered the plot and arrested the plotters, some of whom he illegally executed. His speeches in the Senate against Catiline are among the finest surviving examples of the Roman oratorical style. Cicero hoped to cooperate with Pompey in governing Rome and ending the Roman domestic quarrels, but he lacked the family background and personal following necessary to get to the very top in Rome, and Pompey was not responsive.

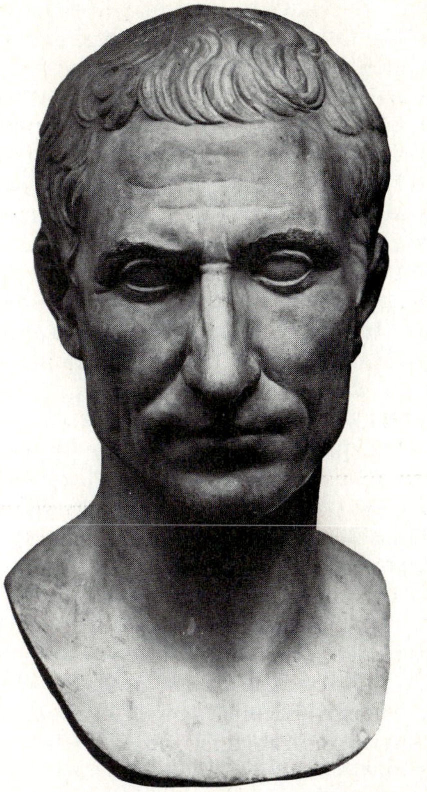

Bust of Julius Caesar (102–44 B.C.), from the Vatican Museum. Though stylized hair has been carved into the marble, Caesar was bald.

Having returned to Rome as a private citizen in 62 B.C., Pompey reentered politics because the Senate would not ratify his eastern settlement or give his veterans the usual land grants. He joined in a *triumvirate*, or team of three men, with Crassus and Gaius Julius Caesar (102-44 B.C.), a man of enormous energy, talent, and impeccable ancestry. Caesar became consul in 59 B.C.; Pompey married Caesar's daughter; Pompey's soldiers received large land grants to the south, near Naples; and the eastern Mediterranean settlement was confirmed.

The First Triumvirate, 60 B.C.-43 B.C.

Caesar became governor of the southern strip of Gaul (modern France), which Rome had annexed some sixty years earlier, and other adjacent lands rich in revenue. Between 58 and 50 B.C. he defeated the Celtic Gauls, conquering a huge area corresponding to modern France and Belgium. (These victories spread the Roman language, so that today in France and parts of Belgium and Switzerland, as in Italy, Spain, Portugal, and Romania, the languages have evolved from a Latin background and are called *Romance languages*.) Caesar also crossed the English Channel to punish the Celtic Britons for helping their fellow Celts in Gaul, though he made no effort to conquer Britain permanently.

The Gauls—distant relatives of the Celts—were predominantly a tall, fair-haired, blue-eyed people. Brave, hospitable, clean, loving bright-colored clothes, and enjoying feasts and quarrels, the Gallic tribes were governed either by kings (in the southwest and in the north) or by an aristocracy with appointed chief magistrates (in the central region). To give his achievements against the Gauls maximum publicity in Rome, Caesar wrote his *Commentaries on the Gallic Wars*, our chief written source of information about the Celts.

Caesar found Gallic society divided into three chief classes: the magicians and seers, or *druids;* the nobles, for whom he used the Roman word equites; and the common people, or plebs. As in Rome, a Gallic noble would have a group of dependents subject to his orders. A Gaul who refused to comply with the order of a magistrate was excluded from the religious sacrifices and from the company of his fellows. Mostly rural elsewhere in Europe, the Celts in Gaul were developing fortresses and urban trading centers.

They were excellent craftsmen in precious metals, bronze, iron, pottery, and textiles. For centuries they had traded with the Greeks and Etruscans, and they were familiar with Greek painted vases and weapons; they had also had contact with Iranian nomads skilled in metalwork. They expressed their own artistic ideas in mediums adapted from others, and they even struck their own coinage, inspired by Greek, Alexandrian, and Roman models. In Britain they also used as money iron bars of a fixed weight, perhaps unfinished sword blades. They fought from fast, two-wheeled, two-horse war chariots. In earlier times Celtic spear carriers had gone into battle naked, terrifying their opponents, as a means of invoking magical protection, and had beheaded their enemies and hung the heads on their saddles. They drank vast quantities of wine and beer and gorged themselves on roast pork; and while they feasted bards played and sang to them. These were people living in a heroic age.

Like most peoples in that stage of development, the Celts were obsessed with magic, celebrating seasonal changes with festivals and sacrifice. They had a rich variety of gods and goddesses, some of them animal in form or closely associated with an animal, notably Epona, a goddess-mare and great queen. Some of the gods and goddesses were threefold, and the Celts often depicted them with three heads or three faces, to emphasize their triple power rather than to suggest a trinity. Caesar reported that the Gauls worshiped the chief Roman gods and goddesses. But they seem rather to have given the most suitable Roman name to their own divinities, using "Mars," for example, in inscriptions to their own god of war, who had many attributes of his own. Sacred trees, groves, and forest shrines also played a part in Celtic religion. The Celts sometimes piled their war trophies on the ground and left them exposed to view as a present to the god who had given them the victory, but sometimes they threw the booty into a lake or a stream, and occasionally such a deposit has been found by modern archaeologists.

In Caesar's day the Gauls still performed human sacrifices, a practice the Romans had long since abandoned. Some victims were killed by a sword or spear, and their blood was then smeared on trees; others, chiefly criminals, were burned alive in groups in large wickerwork animal images, or drowned, or hanged. The druids, who were recruited from the children of the fighting nobles, foretold the future while in a frenzy or trance, preserved the secret knowledge of the magic rites, and arbitrated quarrels. Like the singers of the heroic tales of Greece, the druids also transmitted orally from generation to generation the sacred religious and legal wisdom of the tribe, including belief in the immortality of the soul. In fact, the Gauls were famous among the Romans for their eloquence, and the Romans often hired Gallic orators as tutors to their sons.

While Caesar was fighting in Gaul, the German tribes from east of the Rhine often crossed the river and made trouble. Caesar massacred two entire tribes of them, building a bridge across the Rhine for a quick punitive raid into the territory on the east bank and destroying his bridge after his return. He temporarily taught the Germans the lesson that they should stay on their own side of the river. On the Gallic side, his victories meant the spread of Roman language and civilization.

During Caesar's campaigns in Gaul, Crassus had become governor of Syria, where he was drawn into war against the Parthians, a dynasty that had risen in Persia to replace the Seleucids. At Carrhae in Mesopotamia in 53 B.C., however, the Parthians defeated and killed Crassus. The triumvirate had begun to fall apart even before that, when Pompey's wife, Caesar's daughter Julia, died in 54. Pompey, who had been commander in Spain, stayed in Rome as the most powerful politician there and became the first sole consul in Roman history in 52 B.C. A revolt in Gaul kept Caesar busy until 51 B.C. When it was over, Caesar challenged Pompey for supremacy.

In 49 B.C. Caesar defied an order from the Senate to give up his command and stay in Gaul, and he led his loyal troops south across the Rubicon River boundary, beginning a civil war. Within a few weeks Caesar was master of Italy. He then won another war in Spain, and in 48 B.C. he defeated Pompey's troops in Greece, to which most of the Senate had fled with Pompey. Pompey took refuge in Egypt, where he was murdered by troops of King Ptolemy XII. Unaware that Pompey was dead, Caesar traveled to the East and to his famous love affair with Ptolemy's queen and sister, Cleopatra. After new victories over former troops of Pompey in Asia Minor, North Africa, and Spain, he returned to Rome in triumph in 45 B.C. Less than a year later, on the Ides of March, 44 B.C., he lay stabbed to death on the floor of the Senate at the foot of Pompey's statue, the victim of sixty senators who thought of themselves as heroic tyrannicides.

During his brief dominance, Caesar had carried the subversion of the institutions of the Republic further than had Marius, Sulla, or Pompey. Unlike Sulla, he could be merciful to conquered enemies. But he was consul five times; he took the title "Liberator," and his dictatorship was twice renewed, on the second occasion

JULIUS CAESAR ON THE GAULS: THE PROBLEM OF TRANSLATION

Caesar's commentary on the conquest of Gaul is an early and vigorous account of a systematic military campaign. It has often been translated, and a comparison of two versions of its opening paragraph helps to show how translation itself can serve specific historical and even nationalistic purposes. Clearly certain nationalities, especially in the age of nationalism, would find one translation more to their liking than another:

Gaul comprises three areas, inhabited respectively by the Belgae, the Aquitani, and a people who call themselves Celts, though we call them Gauls. All of these have different languages, customs, and laws. The Celts are separated from the Aquitani by the river Garonne, from the Belgae by the Marne and Seine. The Belgae are the bravest of the three peoples, being farthest removed from the highly developed civilization of the Roman Province, least often visited by merchants with enervating luxuries for sale, and nearest to the Germans across the Rhine, with whom they are continually at war. For the same reason the Helvetii are braver than the rest of the Celts; they are in almost daily conflict with the Germans, either trying to keep them out of Switzerland or themselves invading Germany. The region occupied by the Celts, which has one frontier facing north, is bounded by the Rhone, the Garonne, the Atlantic Ocean, and the country of the Belgae; the part of it inhabited by the Sequani and the Helvetii also touches the Rhine. The Belgic territory, facing north and east, runs from the northern frontier of the Celts to the lower Rhine. Aquitania is bounded by the Garonne, the Pyrenees, and the part of the Atlantic coast nearest Spain; it faces northwest.

The first translation is from Caesar, *The Conquest of Gaul*, trans. S.A. Handford (New York: Penguin Books, 1951), p. 29.

The whole of Gaul is divided into three parts; of these one is inhabited by the Belgae, a second by the Aquitani, and the third by a people called Celts in their own language and Gauls in ours. Each differs from the others in language, customs, and laws. The Gauls are separated from the Aquitani by the Garonne, from the Belgae by the Marne and Seine. The most rugged of all are the Belgae, because they are farthest removed from the refinement and civilization of the Province and are less frequently visited by traders introducing wares which serve to slacken virility, and because they are nearest the Germans who live across the Rhine and with whom they are constantly at war. This same factor makes the Helvetii better fighters than other Gauls; they are in virtually daily battle with the Germans, either keeping them out of their own frontiers or carrying war into theirs. The sector occupied by the Gauls, as said above, starts from the Rhone and is bounded by the Garonne, the ocean, and the country of the Belgae; in the direction of the Sequani and Helvetii it touches the Rhine; and its trend is toward the north. The Belgae begin from the farthest frontiers of Gaul and extend to the lower part of the Rhine; they look to the north and east. Aquitania extends from the Garonne to the Pyrenees and the ocean which washes Spain; it looks to the northwest.

The second translation is from Caesar, *The Gallic War and Other Writings*, trans. Moses Hadas (New York: Modern Library, 1957), pp. 5-6.

for life. As dictator he arrogated to himself many of the powers that usually belonged to the consuls, the tribunes, and the high priest, and he packed the Senate with his own supporters.

Caesar showed a deep interest in the social and economic problems of Rome. He gave his veterans grants of land in outlying provinces; he tried to check the importation of slaves into Rome because they were taking work from free laborers; he made gifts to the citizens from his own private fortune and sharply curtailed the dole of grain that the Gracchi had instituted, forcing the creation of new jobs. He admitted Gallic nobles to the Senate; he issued the first gold coins; he reformed the calendar to bring it into line with the solar year. At his death he was projecting a great public works program: Tiber valley flood control, a trans-Apennine highway, and a canal through the Isthmus of Corinth in Greece.

The Roman populace seems to have regarded Caesar as a benefactor and as the restorer of order and prosperity. His opponents said he was planning to be crowned king, and they may have been right. They also accused him of wishing to be worshiped as a god, and here—so far as Rome was concerned—they were probably wrong. But he was personally autocratic and had ridden roughshod over the Roman constitution.

After Caesar's death, the assassins, to their surprise, found the public hostile. To escape punishment, they were forced to agree to accept the terms of Caesar's will. This document was in the hands of his former aide, the unscrupulous consul Mark Antony, who delivered a fiery funeral oration in Caesar's praise. He goaded the mob to fury against the conspirators, who had to flee from Rome. Antony's control proved only temporary, for Caesar had adopted his grandnephew Octavian and had left him three-quarters of his huge fortune.

Only nineteen years old, Octavian was ready to fight for his inheritance. He was supported by Cicero, who warned the Romans that Antony wanted to be a dictator. To freeze out the murderers of Caesar—Brutus and Cassius—Octavian reached an agreement with Antony and with Lepidus, a former general to Caesar, and the three formally joined in the Second Triumvirate for five years. Antony took most of Gaul; Lepidus, Spain and the rest of Gaul; Octavian, Africa, Sicily, and Sardinia.

The armies of Brutus and Cassius threatened from Macedonia and Asia Minor, and Pompey's son Sextus, another aspirant for power, had a fleet and held Sicily. Reverting to Sulla's policy of widespread proscriptions, executions, and confiscations, the triumvirs raised money by terror. Among those murdered was Cicero. With their new forces, Octavian and Antony defeated Caesar's assassins in Macedonia at Philippi in 42 B.C., whereupon Brutus and Cassius committed suicide. Antony moved to the East, and Octavian took over most of the West. Rivalry between them was postponed when Antony married Octavian's sister in 40 B.C., and in 37 the triumvirate was renewed for another five years. Sextus was defeated, Lepidus was dropped by the other two triumvirs, and Octavian ultimately controlled the entire West. He made his holdings more secure by mopping up the pirates of the Adriatic. Now calling himself Imperator Caesar, he was highly regarded in Italy as the bringer of order and justice.

In the East, meanwhile, Antony had fallen in love with Cleopatra, who bore him three children. After a victory over the Parthians in 34 B.C., Antony made his own bid for empire. He put forward Cleopatra's young son by Julius Caesar as the legitimate heir to Rome, and he assigned Roman provinces to her and to their own three children. Recognizing the threat and capitalizing on Roman distaste for these oriental arrangements, Octavian broke with Antony in 33. He cleverly roused the Romans to a war of the West against the East, which he said Antony now represented. At Actium, off the coast of Greece, Octavian's ships won a critical naval battle in 31 B.C. Antony and Cleopatra fled to Alexandria and committed suicide. Rome thus acquired Egypt, the last of the great Hellenistic states to disappear. Egypt became, not a Roman province, but the personal property of Octavian and his successors, the Roman emperors, administered for them by their agents. At thirty-two Octavian had become master of the entire Roman heritage. The Mediterranean world was now virtually united under one master, and the Republic had come to an end.

This figure of Emperor Augustus (27 B.C.-A.D. 14), known as the Augustus of Primaporta, shows him about seven years after he became the first emperor. The figures on the armor are symbolic, telling the story of the emperor's greatness. In the center of the breast plate Tiberius, who will be Augustus' successor, receives a captured Roman army standard.

III THE ROMAN EMPIRE

Augustus and his Immediate Successors, 27 B.C.-A.D. 68

Octavian was too shrewd, too conscious that he was heir to a long tradition, to startle and alienate the people of Rome by formally breaking with the past and proclaiming an empire. He sought to preserve republican forms, but also to remake the government along the lines suggested by Caesar, so that Rome would have the capacity to manage the huge territories it had acquired. After sixty years of internal strife, the population welcomed a ruler who promised order. Moving gradually, and using his huge personal fortune—now enlarged by the enormous revenues of Egypt—Octavian paid for the pensions of his own troops and settled over one hundred thousand of them on their own lands in Italy and abroad. He was consul, imperator (though not fully legally so), and soon governor in his own right of Spain, Gaul, and Syria, and *princeps* (first) among the senators. In 27 B.C. the Senate gave him the new title of *Augustus* ("revered one"), by which he was thereafter known to history, although he always said his favorite title was the traditional one of princeps, and his regime is called the *Principate.*

Augustus had far more power than anybody else, but since he called himself the restorer of the Republic, Romans could still feel that they were again living under republican rule. In 23 B.C. the Senate gave him the power of a tribune, "larger" powers than those held by any other provincial governor—the power to veto and the right to introduce the first measure at any meeting of the Senate. As censor he reduced the membership of the Senate in 29 B.C. from one thousand to eight hundred members, and in 18 B.C. from eight hundred to six hundred. He also created small inner steering committee in the Senate on which he sat. As senators, he appointed men he thought able, regardless of their birth. He created a civil service where careers were open to talent. Having endowed a veterans' pension department out of his own pocket, he created two new taxes—a sales tax of one-hundredth and an estate tax of one-twentieth—to support it. He initiated the most careful censuses known to that time, both to help in the collecting of taxes and because he simply felt it wise to have as much information about his empire as possible. His social laws made adultery a crime and encouraged larger families. He paid for the construction of splendid new buildings, boasting that he had found Rome a city of brick and had left it a city of marble. He also gave Rome its first police and fire departments, and he improved the roads throughout Italy.

The army, which at one point numbered about four hundred thousand men, was stationed in permanent garrison camps on the frontiers, where the troops in peacetime worked on public projects such as aqueducts or canals. The legions were made up of Roman citizens who volunteered to serve and who retired after twenty-six years' service with a bonus equal to about fourteen years' salary. Noncitizens in somewhat lesser number served as auxiliaries, becoming citizens after thirty years of service. Augustus also created the Praetorian Guard: nine thousand specially privileged and highly paid troops, of whom about one-third were regularly stationed in Rome.

In the East, Augustus reached a settlement with the Parthians and thus probably averted an expensive and dangerous war. In 4 B.C. Herod, the client king of Judea, died, and the Romans henceforth ruled the country through a Roman procurator, who resided outside Jerusalem as a concession to the Jews. Jews retained their freedom of worship, did not have to serve in the Roman armies, and did not have to use coins bearing "graven images"—the portrait of Augustus. Under Augustus most of Spain was pacified, and the Romans successfully administered Gaul. Roman power was extended in what is now Switzerland and Austria and eastward along the Danube into present-day Yugoslavia, Hungary, and Bulgaria, to the Black Sea.

But in A.D. 9* the Roman armies suffered a disaster in

*Note here that we have crossed the time line from B.C. to A.D.

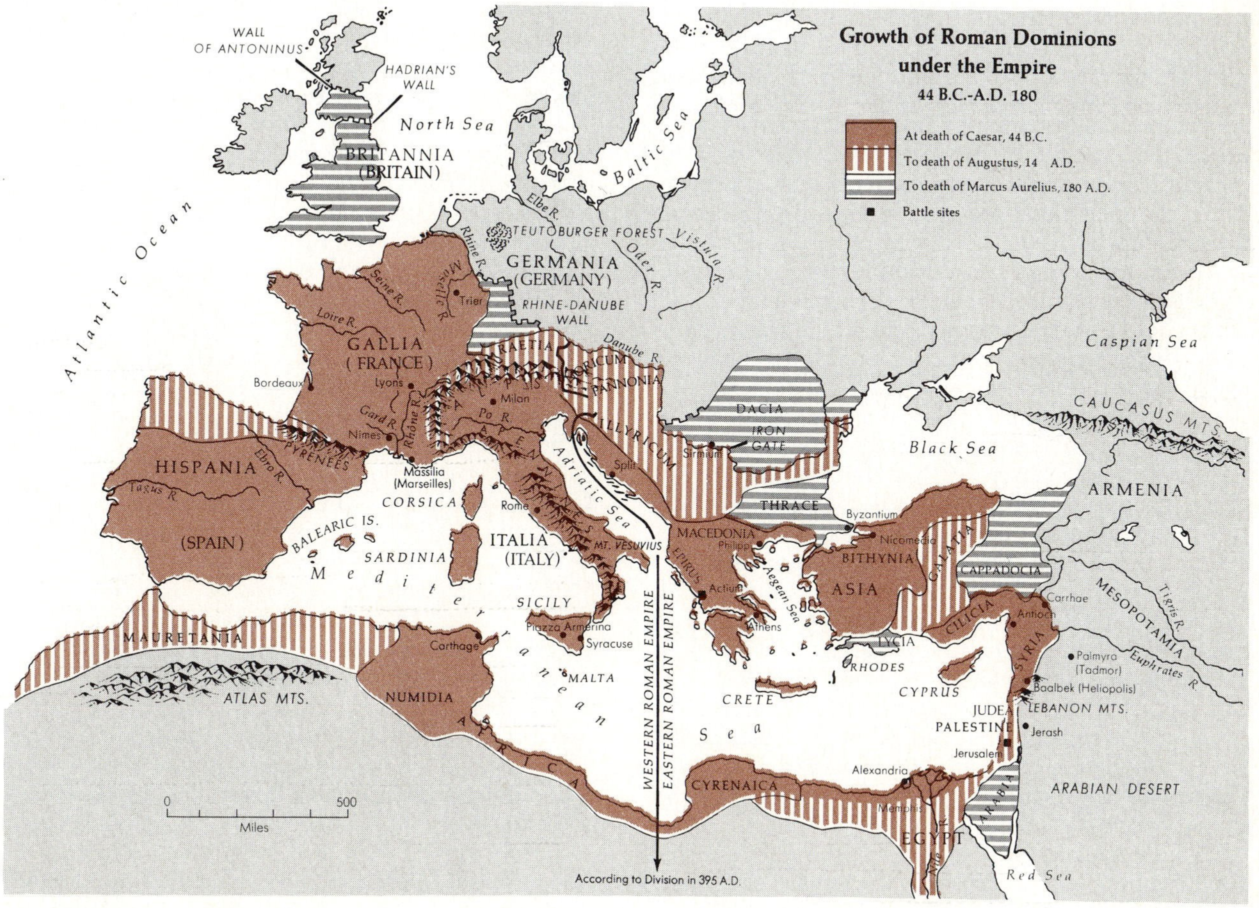

AUGUSTUS CAESAR'S RES GESTAE

As emperor, Augustus wished to be certain that history remembered him as he thought of himself. He therefore composed his own statement of his achievements (*res gestae*, "deeds"), which was to be engraved on his mausoleum after he died. He listed thirty-five specific accomplishments, of which the following were the last two:

In my sixth and seventh consulships, after I had put an end to the civil wars, having attained supreme power by universal consent, I transferred the state from my own power to the control of the Roman senate and people. For this service of mine I received the title of Augustus by decree of the senate, and the doorposts of my house were publicly decked with laurels, the civic crown was affixed over my doorway, and a golden shield was set up in the Julian senate house, which, as the inscription on this shield testifies, the Roman senate and people gave me in recognition of my valor, clemency, justice, and devotion. After that time I excelled all in authority, but I possessed no more power than the others who were my colleagues in each magistracy.

When I held my thirteenth consulship, the senate, the equestrian order, and the entire Roman people gave me the title of "father of the country" and decreed that this title should be inscribed in the vestibule of my house, in the Julian senate house, and in the Augustan Forum on the pedestal of the chariot which was set up in my honor by decree of the senate. At the time I wrote this document I was in my seventy-sixth year.

Augustus, *Res Gestae*, trans. Naphtali Lewis and Meyer Reinhold, in *Roman Civilization* (New York: Columbia University Press, 1955), II, 19.

Germany. A German chief named Hermann—who had served in the Roman army, became a Roman citizen, and had his name translated as Arminius—turned against Rome and ambushed the Roman armies, wiping out three full legions at the battle of the Teutoburger Forest. Now an old man and increasingly distrustful of foreign adventures, Augustus made little effort to avenge the defeat. The Rhine River frontier proved to be the final limit of Roman penetration into north-central Europe. Thus the Germans did not at this time become Romanized.

The Roman provinces were now probably better governed than under the Republic. Certainly, and despite occasional slave uprisings and violence in the countryside, the early Roman Empire was orderly and relatively stable economically. Regular census-taking permitted a fair assessment of taxes. In Gaul the tribes served as the underlying basis for government; in the urbanized East the local cities performed that function. Except for occasional episodes, Augustus had done his work so well that the celebrated *Pax Romana* (the Roman Peace) lasted from 27 B.C. until A.D. 180—more than two hundred years. As a second-century writer put it, "Through the Romans the world has peace, and we go wherever we like without fear, walking along the roads or sailing the sea." Whatever may have been Augustus' faults of character, he should be remembered as he wished to be remembered: he had maintained the Roman state firmly, had laid long-lasting constitutional foundations for its future, and had developed the basis for bureaucracy.

When Augustus died in A.D. 14, the only possible surviving heir was his stepson, Tiberius, son of his wife Livia by her first husband. Gloomy and bitter, Tiberius reigned until A.D. 37, emulating Augustus during the first nine years but thereafter becoming involved in the efforts of Sejanus, commander of the Praetorian Guard, to secure the succession to the throne. Absent from Rome for long periods and in seclusion on the isle of Capri, Tiberius became extremely unpopular, even though he reduced taxes and made interest-free loans available to debtors. Ultimately, he recognized the threat to his authority posed by Sejanus, whom he had executed in 31. About two years later his procurator in Judea, Pontius Pilate, allowed the execution by crucifixion of Jesus, who called himself "the Anointed" (in Greek, *Christos*), because this Messianic claim was considered seditious. Tiberius' grandnephew and successor, Caligula (37-41), was perhaps insane and certainly brutish. The number of irrational executions mounted, and the emperor enriched himself with the property of his victims. He made elaborate preparations for invasions of Germany and of England, which failed, and he convulsed Judea by insisting (unsuccessfully) that his own statue be set up in the Temple. Caligula was assassinated in A.D. 41.

His uncle Claudius (41-54)—youngest of Tiberius' nephews and the best of the first four emperors to succeed Augustus—was a learned student of history and languages who strove to imitate Augustus by restoring cooperation with the Senate. He added to the number and importance of the bureaucracy by dividing his own personal staff of bureaucrats—mostly freed slaves—into regular departments or bureaus not unlike those in modern governments. As a result, the private imperial civil service made great strides in his reign. Claudius was also generous in granting Roman citizenship to provincials. Abroad, he added to Roman territory in North Africa, the Balkans, and Asia Minor. And in A.D. 43 he invaded Britain, ninety-eight years after Julius Caesar's first invasion. Southeast England became the province of Britain, whose frontiers were pushed outward toward Wales. But the conspiracies of his fourth wife, Agrippina, to obtain the succession for her son by an earlier marriage, Nero, culminated in her poisoning Claudius in 54. Agrippina herself was murdered by Nero in 59.

Although dissolute, Nero (54-68) did not start the great fire that burned down much of Rome in 64, nor did he fiddle while Rome burned. Indeed, he personally took part in the efforts to put the fire out and did what he could for those who had been left homeless. But the dispossessed did blame him for incompetence, and to find a scapegoat he accused the new sect of Christians, now for the first time attracting attention in Rome. Their secret meetings had led to charges of immorality against them, and Nero persecuted them to distract attention from himself.

There were serious revolts in Britain in 61, led by Queen Boadicea. She was "huge of frame, terrifying of aspect, with a harsh voice. A great mass of bright red hair fell to her knees; she wore a great twisted golden torc [neck ring], and a tunic of many colors, over which was a thick mantle fastened by a brooch. She grasped a spear, and terrified all who saw her," a Roman historian reported.

But the chief threat in the provinces arose in Judea, where Roman rule had alternated between extremes of tolerance and intolerance, and where rival sects had proliferated among the Jews. Only a small upper class supported Roman rule, and the Romans had too few troops to keep order. In 66, after the Jewish high priest refused to sacrifice to Jehovah for the benefit of Nero and a group of Jewish zealots massacred a Roman garrison, there was open warfare. Faced with rebellion in Spain and in Gaul, and unable to control his armies, Nero was displaced by the Senate, and in 68 he committed suicide. The Empire appeared on the verge of disintegration.

Social tension was particularly acute, and racial prejudice was marked at this time. Fearful of the northern barbarians, the Romans depicted them as utterly without culture, even though there is now ample evidence through their pottery, ironworks, and weaponry that Germania was by no means as backward as Caesar and subsequent commentators said. The Germans were, it is true, generally illiterate, and Christianity reached them late, so that both pagan and Christian Romans found reason to think them backward. But the Romans were not content to say that they possessed a more complex technology and social structure than the Germans did. Strabo (c 64 B.C.-A.D. 14), author of one of the earliest geographies, described Rome, the barbarian regions, Asia, Egypt, and Libya, in terms that showed all at a disadvantage in comparison to the imperial center. However, he described the Iberians as a "civilized society," for they were within the Empire, while the Lusitanians (inhabitants of today's Portugal) were "strange"; they used butter rather than olive oil, drank beer rather than wine, slept on the ground, and wore their hair very long. Still, their wildness was lessened by contact with the Romans, while other northern barbarians, lacking this influence, continued to live in bestiality. Racial and cultural prejudice was thus overt—whether in persistent jokes and slurs on Celts, or in the massacre of ten thousand Jews at Damascus during the war with Nero's legions. Nonetheless, since this prejudice was based on distaste for alien or "superstitious" customs and only at times on fear, the most powerful stimulus to systematic bias in social behavior was lacking; Jews, Celts, and other barbarians continued to be assimilated into the Empire.

From Nero to Marcus Aurelius, A.D. 68-180

Augustus' first four successors are called the Julio-Claudian emperors. Each had been a member, though sometimes a distant one, of the family of Julius Caesar and Augustus. But now the line had run out wretchedly in Nero, and the Senate and people of Rome learned that emperors could be found in other families and chosen in other ways. In 68-69, four emperors, each a general supported by his own troops, ruled in rapid succession. The first three died by violence. The fourth was Vespasian, Nero's commander in Palestine, who had left his son Titus in command of the campaign there, in which the Roman troops sacked Jerusalem and destroyed the Temple in 70.

Vespasian (69-79), a professional soldier from the Italian middle class founded the second Roman imperial dynasty, the Flavian. The throne passed successively to his two sons, Titus (79-81) and Domitian (81-96). Tough and competent, Vespasian added new talent to the Senate by appointing numerous non-Romans, especially Spaniards. He put through financial reforms, subdued the rebellion in Gaul, made gains in Britain, and fought off the potential uprisings of other generals' troops against him by using some soldiers to build public works, stationing others in dangerous areas of the frontier, and keeping too few soldiers in any one place to encourage an ambitious commander to rebel. During the short reign of Titus, Vesuvius, the great volcano overlooking the Bay of Naples, erupted and wiped out the population of the provincial town of Pompeii, burying all the remains that today testify so eloquently about daily life there. Domitian was a suspicious tyrant, seeing plotters against him everywhere; in 96 he was assassinated in a palace conspiracy.

When an emperor died, the Senate—so subservient during his lifetime—had the power of appointing his successor. In 96 they chose a mild, sixty-five-year-old official named Nerva (96-98), who had no children and therefore could not found a dynasty. Called in retrospect the first of the five Good Emperors, Nerva found a method of providing for the succession: he adopted the great general Trajan (98-117) as his son and successor.

PLINY'S DESCRIPTION OF THE DESTRUCTION OF POMPEII

Pliny the Elder (A.D. 23-79) was a Roman naturalist who compiled an encyclopedic *Natural History*, in thirty-seven books (or ten modern volumes), largely based on second-hand information. He died of asphyxiation near Mount Vesuvius, having gone personally to investigate the eruption. In a letter to Tacitus, his nephew Pliny the Younger (A.D. c 62-c 113), who in 100 became consul, described the eruption:

Your request that I would send you an account of my uncle's end, so that you may transmit a more exact relation of it to posterity, deserves my acknowledgments; for if his death shall be celebrated by your pen, the glory of it, I am aware, will be rendered for ever deathless. . . .

He was at that time with the fleet under his command at Misenum. On the 24th of August, about one in the afternoon, my mother desired him to observe a cloud of very unusual size and appearance. He had sunned himself, then taken a cold bath, and after a leisurely luncheon was engaged in study. He immediately called for his shoes and went up an eminence from whence he might best view this very uncommon appearance. . . .

My uncle, true savant that he was, deemed the phenomenon important and worth a nearer view. He ordered a light vessel to be got ready, and gave me the liberty, if I thought proper, to attend him. I replied I would rather study; and, as it happened, he had himself given me a theme for composition. As he was coming out of the house he received a note from Rectina, the wife of Bassus, who was in the utmost alarm at the imminent danger (his villa stood just below us, and there was no way to escape but by sea); she earnestly entreated him to save her from such deadly peril. He changed his first design and what he began with a philosophical, he pursued with an heroical turn of mind. He ordered large galleys to be launched, and went himself on board one, with the intention of assisting not only Rectina, but many others; for the villas stand extremely thick upon that beautiful coast. . . .

And now cinders, which grew thicker and hotter the nearer he approached, fell into the ships, then pumice-stones too, with stones blackened, scorched, and cracked by fire, then the sea ebbed suddenly from under them, while the shore was blocked up by landslips from the mountains. . . .

In the meanwhile Mount Vesuvius was blazing in several places with spreading and towering flames, whose refulgent brightness the darkness of the night set in high relief. But my uncle, in order to soothe apprehensions, kept saying that some fires had been left alight by the terrified country people, and what they saw were only deserted villas on fire in the abandoned district. After this he retired to rest . . . but the court which led to his apartment now lay so deep under a mixture of pumice-stones and ashes, that if he had continued longer in his bedroom, egress would have been impossible. . . . For the house now tottered under repeated and violent concussions, and seemed to rock to and fro as if torn from its foundations. In the open air, on the other hand, they dreaded the falling pumice-stones, light and porous though they were; yet this, by comparison, seemed the lesser danger of the two; a conclusion which my uncle arrived at by balancing reasons, and the others by balancing fears. They tied pillows upon their heads with napkins; and this was their whole defence against the showers that fell round them.

It was now day everywhere else, but there a deeper darkness prevailed than in the most obscure night; relieved, however, by many torches and divers illuminations. They thought proper to go down upon the shore to observe from close at hand if they could possibly put out to sea, but they found the waves still ran extremely high and contrary. There my uncle having thrown himself down upon a disused sail, repeatedly called for, and drank, a draught of cold water; soon after, flames, and a strong smell of sulphur . . . dispersed the rest of the company in flight. . . . He raised himself up with the assistance of two of his slaves, but instantly fell. . . . When day dawned again . . . his body was found entire and uninjured, and still fully clothed as in life; its posture was that of a sleeping, rather than a dead man.

Pliny, *Letters*, trans. William Melmoth, revised by W.M.L. Hutchinson (Cambridge, Mass.: Harvard University Press, 1931), I, 475-83. Reprinted by permission of the publishers and the Loeb Classical Library.

Thus Pliny the Younger humanized the sudden death of an entire city. The first cloud from Vesuvius, he wrote, looked like "a pine-tree, for it shot up a great height . . . into several branches." The people of Pompeii fell in the streets where gas and molten lava overcame them: "a black and dreadful cloud . . . now and again yawned open to reveal long fantastic flames." Pompeii disappeared under thirty feet of ash.

When Nerva died, Trajan thus succeeded him peacefully. This was the first of a series of four successive fortunate adoptions that gave the Empire its most prosperous and peaceful years at home, A.D. 98-180. In a series of successful but expensive campaigns, Trajan moved north of the Danube to annex the gold mines of Dacia (part of modern Romania), which became a Roman province. To the east, he campaigned against the Parth-

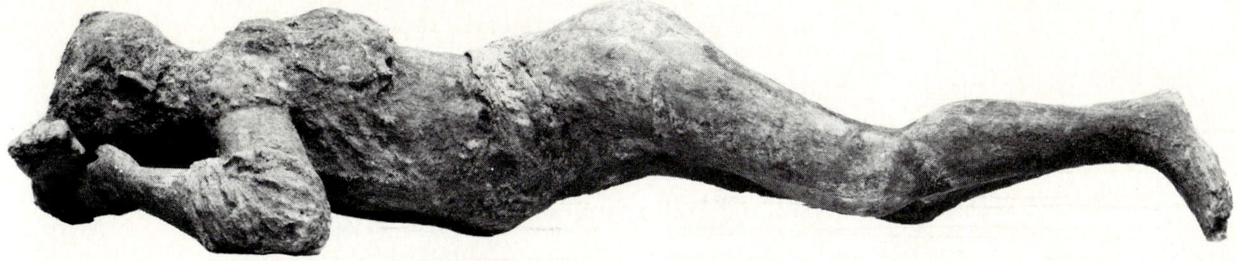

The eruption of Mount Vesuvius caught the residents of Pompeii as they slept. This figure, preserved to the present day by volcanic ash, is either asleep or trying to shield himself from the poisonous gas released by the volcano.

ians and occupied but failed to retain Mesopotamia. A massive revolt of the Jews confronted Trajan's successor, his nephew and adoptive son Hadrian, when Trajan died in 117.

Hadrian (117-138), a widely experienced soldier and administrator and a highly cultivated man, put down the Jewish uprising. Realizing that Roman communication lines became too extended whenever Roman troops tried to cross the Syrian desert against the Parthians, he abandoned Trajan's war against them and made peace. He made himself generally popular with the upper and middle classes by canceling all private debts to the government, and with the lower classes by furthering charities and putting on great spectacles in the circus. Among his advisers were some able lawyers who helped him adjust taxes and control prices in bad years and improve the legal position of slaves and soldiers. They codified all past decisions of the praetors; for the first time citizens knew when they ought to sue someone and were assured of uniform procedures under Roman law. Thorough censuses were restored, to be taken every fifteen years, both as an inventory of the Empire and to determine how many aliens there were within it (and, of course, to facilitate collecting taxes).

This relief of a Roman battle appears on Trajan's Column in Rome, set up in celebration after the conquest of Dacia.

Hadrian's Wall, which runs across present-day northern England, is the major monument to the Roman occupation of Britain. The wall was built between A.D. 122 and 130 as a defense against the Celts in Scotland. It ran for seventy-three miles, and it was garrisoned until A.D. 383.

Hadrian believed that all the provinces should be equal under Roman imperial benevolence, with himself as the "father of the fatherland." So he caused each of the armies for provincial defense to be recruited within the specific province itself. And he himself lived much of the time away from Rome touring the provinces. In Britain he built the defensive system of walls and ditches still called Hadrian's Wall, to contain invasions by the Scots and Picts to the north, and in Germania he constructed a wall of wood to link the Rhine and Danube Rivers. He resided successively in southern France, Spain, Morocco, Asia Minor, Greece, Tunisia, Libya, Greece again, Syria, Palestine (where he had to put down another Jewish uprising), and Egypt. Everywhere he inspected the troops and defenses, built buildings, and made himself known to the population, and everywhere (except Palestine) he was admired. After a decade abroad, he returned to Rome, where he began to build Hadrian's Villa at nearby Tivoli, with entire areas built in his favorite Greek and Egyptian styles. He built the great Pantheon at Rome, a temple to all the gods originally commissioned by Agrippa in 27-25 B.C., and he used the giant Colosseum, originally built by Vespasian, Titus, and Domitian, for gladiatorial combats and other spectacular entertainments.

Hadrian's successor, Antoninus (138-161), called Pius because he was so loyal an adoptive son to Hadrian, immediately adopted as his future successor his own nephew, Marcus Aurelius (161-180). The forty-two years of their combined reigns won glowing praise as an era of peace and prosperity. The eighteenth-century English scholar Edward Gibbon, whose massive history of *The Decline and Fall of the Roman Empire* influenced modern perceptions about Roman life, remarked that there had never been another period "in which the happiness of a great people was the only object of government." He was echoing Antoninus Pius' contemporary, the Greek orator Aelius Aristides, who wrote:

> *Neither sea nor land is any bar to citizenship, and Asia is treated exactly the same as Europe. In your empire, every avenue of advancement is open to everyone. No one who deserves office or responsibility remains an alien. A civil world-community has been set up as a free republic, under a single ruler, the best ruler and teacher . . . of order. From Rome, the center, there emanates thoughout the world a security that rests on a power compared with which the walls of Babylon were mere child's play and women's work. All depends on the legions, who assure the perpetual peace, because Mars, whom you have never slighted, dances his ceaseless dance upon the banks of the outer rivers [Rhine, Danube, Euphrates] and thus averts the shedding of blood.**

As Aristides said, there was little civil strife. Public buildings continued to rise, and those who lived comfortable lives had never been more comfortable. For the less privileged, in Rome itself and more widely throughout Italy, the Antonine monarchy showed great concern and softened the worst pains of poverty. However, Egypt, as always, continued to be ruthlessly exploited; slavery remained important to the economy. Stability still rested on the legions' ability to assure "perpetual peace," by fighting perpetual local wars along the borders.

Among the less privileged were the women of Rome, though they took a much more active role in affairs than women had in Greece. They were understood to be central to the *familia*, or Roman household, which in-

*Adapted and abbreviated from the edition of J.H. Oliver, "The Ruling Power," *Transactions of the American Philosophical Society* Philadelphia, XLIII (1953), part 4.

cluded relatives dependent on the head of the family and slaves. In general they were in charge of the slaves, whom they might marry, and they ran the household while their husbands managed the land. Daughters were sent to school, and at home they learned spinning and weaving, so that in the poorer households they contributed significantly to the domestic economy. Among the rich, women were expected to devote much time to their clothing and to the etiquette of social occasions, particularly dinner parties; the ability of women to engage in amusing conversation at these affairs was prized in the later Empire.

After Augustus, women who had presented their husbands with three to five children could manage their personal property, and many women engaged in business. They did not, apparently, seek to have the law altered so that they could enter politics or administration. The law's intent was to assure that women gave birth to children, preferably to sons, and this was particularly so after Romans began to think of their population as in decline. Under Augustus girls were married at twelve and boys at fourteen, both to cement an economic or political alliance and to assure early childbirth.

As there were fewer females than males in the upper class, Roman women found husbands easily and often remarried; upper-class women were probably less numerous because of deaths through childbearing and the selective infanticide of unwanted female infants. (A father was bound to raise all male children but need nurture only the first-born female.) Women could easily break across class barriers, since men of the upper classes often had to take a wife from a lower class, and this helped soften class barriers in general. The primary function of women was thus determined by the state to be biological. Once having fulfilled that function, they often were free to play other and more independent roles.

Antoninus Pius, unlike Hadrian, never left Italy, and the dance of the war god Mars along the banks of the frontier rivers was less vigorous. So Marcus Aurelius—

MENU FOR A ROMAN BANQUET

At its height, the Roman Empire put great emphasis on dining well—at least for the rich. The name of one Roman epicure, Lucullus, has given us the adjective "lucullan" to denote the most luxurious of food. A Roman chef, Apicius, produced the first surviving cookbook. Apicius' menu for one Roman banquet, which would begin in the late evening and run through the night to the accompaniment of musicians, dancers, acrobats, and poets, follows. Allowing for modern substitutions, we can see that there are some similarities to a so-called gourmet meal today:

APPETIZERS

Jellyfish and eggs
Sow's udders stuffed with salted sea urchins
Patina of brains cooked with milk and eggs
Boiled tree fungi with peppered fish-fat sauce
Sea urchins with spices, honey, oil, and egg sauce

MAIN COURSES

Fallow deer roasted with onion sauce, rue, Jericho dates, raisins, oil, and honey
Boiled ostrich with sweet sauce
Turtle dove boiled in its feathers
Roast parrot
Dormice stuffed with pork and pine kernels
Ham boiled with figs and bay leaves, rubbed with honey, baked in pastry crust
Flamingo boiled with dates

DESSERTS

Fricassee of roses with pastry
Stoned dates stuffed with nuts and pine kernels, fried in honey
Hot African sweet-wine cakes with honey

The meal also tells us something of the extent of Roman trade, for the ostrich and flamingo came from Africa, the dates from Judea, and the spices from throughout the empire. Apicius' book shows only ten lines devoted to beef and veal, three pages to pork; meat was not a main article of diet, and only pigs were raised to be eaten.

From Moses Hadas, *Imperial Rome* (New York: Time Inc., 1965), p. 85.

THE MEDITATIONS OF MARCUS AURELIUS

Marcus Aurelius (121-180), nephew and adopted son of Antoninus Pius, became emperor in 161. Much of his life was spent in military campaigns far away from Rome. During these campaigns, especially on the Danubian frontier, he wrote his *Meditations*, by which he sought to express a sense of order for his own life. In Book IV he reflected upon the transient nature of all emperors:

Consider, for example, the times of Vespasian. You will see all these things, people marrying, bringing up children, sick, dying, warring, feasting, trafficking, cultivating the ground, flattering, obstinately arrogant, suspecting, plotting, wishing for some to die, grumbling about the present, loving, heaping up treasure, desiring consulship, kingly power. Well then, that life of these people no longer exists at all. Again, remove to the times of Trajan. Again, all is the same. Their life too is gone. In like manner view also the other epochs of time and of whole nations, and see how many after great efforts soon fell and were resolved into the elements. But chiefly you should think of those whom you have yourself known distracting themselves about idle things, neglecting to do what was in accordance with their proper constitution, and to hold firmly to this and to be content with it. And herein it is necessary to remember that the attention given to everything has its proper value and proportion. For thus you will not be dissatisfied, if you apply yourself to smaller matters no further than is fit. . . .

Time is like a river made up of the events which happen, and a violent stream; for as soon as a thing has been seen, it is carried away and another comes in its place, and this will be carried away too.

Marcus Aurelius Antoninus, *Meditations*, trans. George Long, as very slightly altered in John Louis Beatty and Oliver A. Johnson, eds., *Heritage of Western Civilization* (Englewood Cliffs, N.J.: Prentice-Hall, 1982), I, 223-24.

the cultivated Stoic philosopher who found no pleasure at all in his powers as emperor, and whose melancholy *Meditations* (written in Greek) serve as a corrective to official optimism—was forced to fight in Dacia and beyond the Euphrates against the Parthians. Although he was victorious, he allowed certain barbarians to settle within the imperial frontiers and to be enrolled in the Roman armies, thus jeopardizing the unity of the traditional defensive system.

During the pivotal reign of Marcus Aurelius the ever-increasing pressure from the Germanic tribes of central Europe began. The more Germans who were allowed to settle inside the frontiers, the greater the pressure from those still outside who wanted to come in. The Empire, with perhaps sixty million people, an army of three hundred thousand, and a small and very rich upper class, could not in the long run adjust to the demands made upon it. There was no modern technology of weaponry or communications to make possible a quick settlement—through peace or war—of the frontier problem, which continued for more than three hundred years. In the end, a declining population could not cover both the farms and the frontiers. Although no one in Marcus Aurelius' entourage could have predicted it, a long downward slide was now beginning; it was signaled for a century by a catastrophic falling-off in the quality of the emperors themselves.

Why did the population of the Empire decline? We do not know, though there is abundant evidence that it did, and that the emperors took major steps to stop the decline. Augustus passed laws discouraging divorce and prohibiting abortion. His creation of charities to feed orphan children and provide emergency supplies to the poor so that their children would not die was less for humanitarian reasons than because the state required more and healthier bodies. Large families were encouraged by exempting from certain services fathers who had five or more children; women were urged to have dowries to be more attractive marriage candidates. The incorporation of barbarians into the Empire and the ready acceptance of new immigrants showed both a sense of tolerance and a desire for more peasants from whom a sturdy army could be drawn. Efforts were made to improve crop production and to reduce malaria, which was increasing, by draining swamps. Even soldiers were encouraged to marry and live in cities, where morals were more lax and the birth rate might increase.

Nonetheless, the population declined, in a vicious circle the state could not control. Barbarian raids caused more violent deaths; malnutrition and higher mortality followed economic decline; cities became more crowded, spreading disease. Debasement of coinage and general inflation led to social unrest, brigandage, and to so sharp a decline in official revenues that the emperors had to create unpopular new taxes or demand services in nonslave labor directly from the people.

Because Rome's widespread trade had created a pool of diseases, epidemics regularly ravaged the crowded cities or the unhealthy countryside. In A.D. 65 and again more devastatingly in 165 (when the plague was carried throughout the Eastern empire by troops returning from Mesopotamia) there was an outbreak of what we would perhaps call smallpox that lasted until 189 and took from seven to ten million lives. Again in c 251-266 plague struck Rome, with five thousand dying daily, while the human destruction in the countryside may have been relatively even greater. In the shortage of agricultural labor supply and recruits for the army, Rome faced the most grave demographic problems it had ever known.

We do not know for certain what these diseases that reduced the population were, although they resemble modern measles and smallpox. Malaria certainly played a chronic role (though it is probably not true, as the Romans believed, that malaria came with Hannibal; the Romans associated it with swamps, but not with the mosquitos that bred there). While both Greeks and Romans studied disease with care, they knew of no ready cures. Extensive trade was likely to introduce new diseases in any case, against which immunities were not developed. In the first century A.D. the Romans traded with the Chinese along the Silk Road (so named for the principal commodity transported from China), and fashionable women of the upper class wore semitransparent silks produced in Antioch. Such trade routes, as well as the organization of complex trading patterns by sea, helped spread diseases in patterns that are still not fully understood today.

The Downward Slide: Commodus to Diocletian, A.D. 180-284

Commodus (180-192), the true son of Marcus Aurelius, ended the line of fortunate adoptions and proved to be a throwback to Caligula, Nero, or Domitian—a tyrant without talent. In the end, his closest advisers murdered him. After two other emperors had been installed and murdered by the Praetorian Guard within a year, Septimius Severus (193-211), a North African who commanded the Roman troops in what is now Hungary, marched his army into Rome and disbanded the guard, replacing it by a new elite body chosen from his own officers. He emerged successful from the first civil strife Rome had known in more than a century. To reward his armies for their loyalty in a campaign against the Parthians in which Mesopotamia was added as a province, he provided better food, pay, and allowed his legionaries to marry native women. Married legionaries might live off the base and could keep their own flocks and grow their own crops.

Septimius Severus was succeeded by his two sons, one of whom, Caracalla (211-217), extended citizenship in 212 to all freeborn inhabitants of the Empire. This was a natural climax to the earlier acts gradually expanding the circle of Roman citizens, though it also was a money-raising device, since all new citizens would be liable to inheritance taxes from which noncitizens were exempt.

Caracalla's sixteen immediate successors were all assassinated in their turn. It was an unedifying parade. The incompetent Macrinus (217-218) was followed by Elagabalus (218-222), a fourteen-year old, immensely rich, homosexual Syrian priest of the sun god fobbed off on the Romans as a son of Caracalla. Alexander Severus (222-235), a cousin of Elagabalus, soberer and more virtuous, tried to revive cooperation with the Senate and to restore the traditional virtues to Roman life, but he too was only fourteen on his accession and was dominated by his mother. The Senate was impotent, and the army resented Alexander's neglecting to appease it by the now-traditional bribes. Though his campaign against the new Sassanian dynasty that had replaced the Parthians in Persia was a success (231-233), his military zeal was half-hearted. In Germany on another campaign, he fell victim to another military conspiracy.

During the half-century 235-284 there were twenty-six emperors, of whom twenty-five were murdered. Most of them were chosen by their troops, held power briefly, and were in turn supplanted by another ambitious military commander. But the army had been weakened by Septimius Severus' changes, for soldiers had grown accustomed to being used for nonmilitary purposes as police, tax collectors, judges, and even artisans, and they often were not ready for combat.

This sculpture shows the tetrarchs, rulers of the Roman Empire: Diocletian, Maximian, Galerius, and Constantius Chlorus. The sculpture is now in the basilica of St. Mark's, in Venice.

Attracted by Roman weakness (indeed urged on at times by the Romans themselves) and pushed from behind by other people on the move, the so-called barbarians crossed the Roman frontiers at many points. The emperor Decius was killed in battle; the emperor Valerian was captured by the Persians and died in captivity. When the plagues raged, whole provinces temporarily escaped from the central authority, population fell off, public order virtually vanished, and the Empire seemed doomed to collapse. The tide turned with the reign of Aurelian (270-275), the "restorer of the world," and definitely with the accession of Diocletian (284-305). Aurelian, a soldier, drew the best troops back from the frontiers and concentrated on the defense and restoration of Rome. Within the wider empire he turned increasingly to non-Roman mercenaries for protection. Diocletian and his successors, especially Constantine (306-337), put through numerous reforms, although we do not know exactly when some of the new measures were adopted. The result is usually called the New Empire, but what looks new about it often proves to have been instead, a return to earlier practice. The combination of all the experiments, however, was certainly new.

Under Diocletian there gradually evolved a system that when complete was called the *tetrarchy*, or rule by four men. As Augustus, Diocletian first appointed a talented officer as Caesar—an action often taken previously—and then was forced by circumstances to promote him to Augustus, or co-emperor, though it was understood that Diocletian, as the senior Augustus, was above the others. Each Augustus in turn appointed a Caesar of his own, whom he also adopted as his son; such adoption was also an old practice. It was understood that the two emperors would eventually abdicate, each to be succeeded by his own Caesar, who upon becoming Augustus would appoint a new Caesar as his son and eventual successor. The scheme was designed to assure a peaceful succession and to end the curse of military seizures of the throne. Thus the Empire, though in practice ruled by four men, still in theory remained a single unit.

This was particularly important, because accompanying the gradual establishment of the tetrarchy was a shift in territorial administration, as each of the four new rulers took primary responsibility for his own large area. Diocletian made his headquarters at Nicomedia in Asia Minor, and from there he governed Asia Minor, Syria, and Egypt, plus Thrace in Europe—the whole becoming the prefecture of the East. From Sirmium in what is now Yugoslavia, his Caesar governed the Balkans, which became the prefecture of Illyricum. From Milano, Diocletian's co-Augustus, the junior emperor Maximian, governed the prefecture of Italy, which included North Africa together with parts of what is now Austria. And from Trier in the Rhineland, his Caesar governed Gaul, Spain, and Britain, which were grouped into the prefecture of Gaul. Note that not even the prefecture of Italy was governed from Rome. The new imperial territorial reorganization exposed as a sham the ancient pretense that the emperor shared power with the Senate.

A tough Balkan soldier, Diocletian simply walked out on Rome, leaving the citizens with their free bread and circuses. It is of great importance too that he moved his own headquarters to the East, for Diocletian now adopted the full trappings of oriental monarchy. He wore silk robes of blue and gold to symbolize the sky and the sun; he sprinkled his hair with gold dust to create a nimbus when light shone upon him; his clothes glittered with jewels; he wore ruby and emerald bracelets, necklaces, and rings; his fingernails were gilded; and his boots—which were to become the new symbol of imperial power—were of purple leather. He entered his throne room carrying a golden scepter topped with a golden ball or orb—the earth—on which was seated a Roman gold eagle with a sapphire in its beak to symbolize the heavens. Servants followed, sprinkling perfume, which fan bearers spread through the air. Every person in the room sank to the floor until Diocletian was seated on his throne, after which the privileged might kiss the hem of his garment. Diocletian was making a deliberate attempt to elevate the prestige of the emperor—a divine and deified emperor—so high that it could not be shaken by the ambitions of a rival. Diocletian chose the additional surname Jovius, thus associating himself with Jupiter (Jove), the ruler of the gods.

Mechanical reorganization and geographical regrouping of forces could not have prevented the recurrence of military uprisings. Therefore, Diocletian firmly separated the military from the civil power, so that the commanders of local garrisons had no local political authority, and his new civil officials had no military authority. Moreover, Diocletian subdivided the old provinces, so that the number of new provinces rose to over one hundred, each much smaller than provinces had formerly been; these in turn were regrouped into twelve so-called dioceses, which made up the four great prefectures. Accordingly, the bureaucracy grew enormously. The various financial departments, the secret service, the post, and foreign relations each had its own structure, and the top officials became a kind of advisory body, almost a cabinet. While a Roman senator might find a place in such a system, it was independent of the Senate as such, and the Senate as a body continued only as a group of privileged magnates. Diocletian also enlarged the army, which probably reached a new high of about 600,000. He reorganized the forces and improved their pay and promotion system. He adapted military tactics to a new age, introducing a more heavily armed cavalry and developing frontier defenses that allowed troops to move rapidly to any danger point.

The new bureaucratic and military costs required new contributions from most of the population. By using as a unit of land measurement for tax purposes the amount of land that could be cultivated by a single farm laborer, and by trying to force the farm laborer to stay put, work his land, and pay his taxes, the New Empire greatly stimulated the growth of that class of rural resident called the *colonus* (plural, *coloni*), who was attached to the soil. The colonus was not a slave and could not be sold apart from the land he and his family cultivated, but when it was sold, the coloni went with it. (Slave labor was used extensively only in Italy and Spain.) Other men in other walks of life were also bound to their jobs, and sons to their fathers' jobs after them: sons of bakers had to become bakers; sons of goldsmiths, goldsmiths. To stabilize the economic situation, Diocletian also tried to fix prices, but was thwarted by black marketing and riots.

The lowest territorial administrative level was the *civitas* (a city and its surrounding countryside). The city senators (curiales) had to make up out of their own pockets any difference between the tax payments assessed for the civitas and the amount actually collected. From being an honor, the position of curialis became a burden, and curiales had to be compelled to stay in their posts, to do their duty, and to pass their jobs on to their eldest sons. Society in the New Empire became more rigidly stratified than ever before in Roman history. The combination of this increased social stratification with oriental-style despotism, a huge bureaucracy, and continuing dependence on the military made life extremely bleak for the ordinary person. Corruption, inequity, violence, and despair were frequent. The tax collector became the symbol, not of the stability of the state, but of corruption and greed, and the people seem to have been hungry for change.

Diocletian retired in 305 and left his half of the Empire to his Caesar; he forced his fellow Augustus, Maximian, to do the same. Each of the New Augusti in turn named a new Caesar; but the system broke down as the four top officials began to struggle against one another for supreme power. By 324 Constantine, son of the Western Caesar, emerged as sole Augustus, and the Empire was reunited; he ruled until 337. Though the tetrarchy did not survive, the other reforms of Diocletian and Constantine, who carried his work forward, staved off collapse.

Why Did the Empire Decline?

Few subjects have been more debated than the reasons for the long decline of the Roman Empire. The celebrated eighteenth-century historian Edward Gibbon blamed Christianity, charging that it destroyed the civic spirit of the Romans by turning their attention to the afterlife and away from their duties to the state. Michael Rostovtzeff, a Russian scholar who wrote in the 1920s and 1930s, attributed the decline in part to the constant pressure by the underprivileged masses to share in the wealth of their rulers, of which there was not enough to go around anyhow. Gibbon and Rostovtzeff each reflected his own time and experience: Gibbon the anticlerical rationalism of the eighteenth century; Rostovtzeff the bitter lesson of the Bolshevik Revolution in his native Russia. Others have emphasized the influx of Greeks and orientals into Roman society, intimating that the original Roman sense of unity was thus diluted. Still others have pointed to climatic change and disease. Most recently, archaeologists working with chemical analyses of skeletons from A.D. 79 have concluded that a generally healthy people had fallen prey to chronic lead poisoning, for apparently Roman food and wine were heavily contaminated with lead.

Economically, losses in population caused by plagues and civil war crippled an agriculture already hampered by unprogressive methods and increased soil exhaustion. The growing concentration of land in large estates and the absorption of free farmers into the status of coloni diluted Roman prosperity, which suffered from chronically feeble purchasing power and inflation. The urban middle class was declining, while psychologically the masses became alienated from their rulers. The replacement of citizen-soldiers with mercenaries testified to the decline of the old Roman patriotism. Dependence on slavery may have retarded innovation in labor organization and the application of technology. Yet even with all these factors, it would be hard to imagine the Roman decline without terrific pressure from outside forces. It was in the third and fourth centuries that the "barbarian" cultures began to expand, and it was the barbarian threat that most immediately contributed to the collapse of the Roman structure in the West, while permitting its survival in the East in a modified form.

Given all these arguable "causes" for the decline of the Roman Empire, perhaps the best summary is still Gibbon's famous judgment—"the stupendous fabric yielded to the pressure of its own weight." Rather than asking why the Empire fell, he thought, historians ought to ask why it had survived so long.

IV RELIGION, WRITING, AND THOUGHT

Greek Influences

Greece, though conquered, took her conqueror captive. Indeed, Greek influence from Magna Graecia affected the Romans long before they conquered Greece itself. In the arts, the Romans found much of their inspiration in Greek models. In literature, the Greeks supplied the forms and often much of the spirit, though the highest Roman literary achievements could not be mistaken for Greek works; they have a Roman spirit and quality. In science and engineering, the Romans accomplished more than the Greeks, as they did in law and government.

The Greece the Romans gradually conquered was not the Greece of Homer or Pericles, so that the Romans, for example, did not imitate the Greek tragedians of the fifth century B.C. There was no Roman Aeschylus, Sophocles, or Euripides. This was the Greece of the decades after the death of Alexander—of the New Comedy of Menander, not the Old Comedy of Aristophanes. Literature, much of it produced in Alexandria, was more artificial, more charming and graceful, often trivial, less grand, less concerned with the central themes of human existence. The surviving Alexandrian epic, Apollonius Rhodius' *Argonautica*, which tells of the adventures of the mythical hero Jason on his way to find the magic golden fleece, was a scholar's effort to be Homeric long after the heroic age was over. When the Romans first began to imitate the Greeks, the greatest Greek works, though deeply respected, were no longer being written. It was a lesser age.

Religion

Before the first contacts with the Greeks, the Romans had already evolved their own religion—the worship of the household spirits, the *lares* and *penates*—that governed their everyday affairs, along with those spiritual beings that inhabited the local woods, springs, and fields. Like the Greek goddess Hestia, the Roman Vesta presided over the hearth and had in her service specially trained Vestal Virgins. From the Etruscans the Romans took the belief in omens which they never abandoned. They foretold the future through observing the flight of birds (the *auspices*) and examining the entrails of sacrificed animals (the *auguries*). From Greece there came the entire Olympic collection of gods and goddesses, some of them merging their identities with existing Roman divinities, and most of them changing their names: Zeus became Jupiter; Hera, Juno; Poseidon, Neptune; and so on, although Apollo remained Apollo. But the Romans had nothing like the Greek Olympic games or the festivals of Dionysus that had led to the writing of Athenian tragedy and comedy. For the Romans religion was largely social in function.

This young Pompeian woman—a wall painting dating from A.D. 40-50 that survived the destruction of Pompeii—is shown with stylus and book to represent the leisured life of the upper class of the time.

Julius Caesar, Augustus, and many of their successors were deified after their deaths, and Augustus consented to be worshiped jointly with Rome in Gaul. Indeed, from Alexander the Great and earlier, a basis for believing in the divinity of a king, and thereby in the divine right of kings, was persistently, if unevenly, maintained. But except for certain notable social festivals each year, the individual Roman took little part either in the imperial cult or in other religious rites. The official priests performed most rites, headed by their chief priest, the *pontifex maximus*—a title and role taken over by the emperors themselves. The state religion early lost its appeal for the Romans. Moreover, there was no reason they could not worship as many other gods as they chose, after rendering due veneration to the ordinary deities, including the emperor. Rome therefore imported cults from other places, chiefly the East, which competed for popularity. (Since Christianity eventually joined and won the competition, we shall postpone discussion of it and its competitors until the next chapter, where we can more easily examine the reasons for the growth of Christianity.)

Literature

One of the great unifying forces of the Roman Empire was its language; Latin slowly became the *lingua franca*, the universal language of the Roman world. Language both unites and, there being different languages, divides. It does so at a given time, as, for example, when two merchants, unable to speak the same language, communicate in a third, more nearly universal language. And it does so across time, as when scholars of different nationalities attempt in common to reconstruct a past event. Latin became both the most widespread language of its time and the most influential language of all time, for it formed the basis of the great Romance languages of western Europe, Romania, and Latin America, and it was the language of universal scholarship until the nineteenth century. Until displaced by French, it was the language of diplomacy, and until displaced in the twentieth century by English, it was the language of technology.

A people self-consciously interested in their own civilization strive to preserve their language and to use it well. Where they borrow, as the Romans did persistently from the Greeks, they do so not only to imitate elegantly, but also to communicate effectively. To the Romans, as to the Greeks, to speak and write well and to recognize these qualities in others was a significant indication of the civilized mind. Their frequent and shared reference to the people beyond their borders as "barbarians" was more a statement about the language those people spoke than about their customs. For the Romans, their literature—in history, poetry, drama, and prose—was an indication both of their unity and their sense of a separate identity (what the nineteenth century would call the "national character"); it also posed for them intriguing questions of translation when they sought to render Greek works into Latin. For us, therefore, Latin literature takes on a dual significance; first it tells us about the Romans themselves and, second, it shows how the Romans used language to incorporate other cultures, chiefly Greek, into their own.

The figure known to us as the "father of Latin poetry," Quintus Ennius (239-169 B.C.), was born and brought up in Magna Graecia and therefore naturally turned to Homer for inspiration when he put into epic form his patriotic account, the *Annales*, of Roman successes down to his own time. Although only fragments (between six and seven hundred lines) are preserved, we have enough to appreciate Ennius' admiration for military virtues, and to understand his lasting influence on later Roman writers. And as Ennius used Homeric verse to celebrate Roman toughness and resilience, Plautus (254-184 B.C.) and Terence (190-159) took their inspiration from the Greek New Comedy of Menander. Plautus was the more raucous and knockabout. Many of his characters—the two sets of twins, masters and servants who are always being taken for each other; the rich but stupid young gentleman with an immensely clever and resourceful valet; the money-grubbing miser—recur throughout European literature. Gentler and milder in every sense, Terence remained closer to the Greek originals. He was not a success in his own day, but was a major influence during the Renaissance and later on the French playwright Molière. After Plautus and Terence, various Roman authors tried to write comedies with a native Italian inspiration, but none of their work survives. The Romans also enjoyed crude farces of the kind that had always been staged in the villages.

During the late Republic appeared two of Rome's greatest poets—Lucretius (96-55 B.C.) and Catullus (84-54 B.C.). Lucretius, a disciple of the Greek philosopher Epicurus, wrote a long poem, *On the Nature of Things (De rerum natura)*, putting into moving verse his master's beliefs that there is no human survival after death and that the gods, far from governing human affairs, do not intervene at all. He wrote that the universe is made up of atoms, whose motions and behavior are governed by fixed laws, right out to the edges, the "flaming walls of the universe," though human beings still control their own actions.

Catullus, looking to certain Alexandrian poets of the emotions, wrote passionate love lyrics recording his feelings for his mistress. Sometimes playful and charming, as in poems addressed to her pet sparrow or celebrating the first days of spring, sometimes bitter and obscene (she was unfaithful and made Catullus miserable), these brief poems seem to some readers the highest achievement of Roman literature.

In Cicero (106-43 B.C.) the late Republic produced its greatest writer of prose, who adjusted the ideas of Greek philosophy to distinctive Roman values. His oratorical skill furthered his career as a successful lawyer and politician; he won his listeners with an occasional injection of wit or irony into an otherwise somber and stately passage. He carefuly studied not only what he wanted to say, but also how to choose the most effective—sometimes the most unexpected—words in which to say it, and how to combine them into a rhythmical and pleasing pattern, so that the sound and the sense would combine to make his point irresistibly. As the recognized supreme master of oratory, he wrote treatises on the art. We also have almost a thousand letters that Cicero wrote to his friends and some of the answers to them that reveal his personal joys and sorrows.

Philosophically, Cicero largely agreed with the Stoics, as modified by Greek teachers who had adapted the originally abstract and remote concepts of Stoicism to Roman taste by allowing for the exercise in ordinary life of the Stoic virtues and admitting that one can have some virtues without possessing all knowledge. Cicero helped popularize these ideas in his essays on *Old Age*, on *Friendship*, on *The Nature of the Gods*, and on other political and social subjects; he introduced into the Latin language terms capable of conveying the meaning of the Greek concepts he was discussing.

His fellow Romans were tutored by him about the concepts of "natural law" that existed independently of all human legislation and a "law of nations" that should regulate the relationships of different people with each other. Practical, perhaps conservative, Cicero believed that law, custom, and tradition led to stability, which was essential to liberty, from which sprang a person's true security. The influence of these Ciceronian works radiated far into human history; the early Christian fathers studied Cicero, as did the humanists of the Italian Renaissance and the men who made the eighteenth-century revolutions in America and France and who wrote the Declaration of Independence and the Constitution of the United States.

Still it was the writers who came after Cicero who gave Rome its literary Golden Age. Augustus himself recruited and subsidized talent, even genius, to proclaim the glories of the new era, the Augustan Age. For example, Vergil (70-19 B.C.), in his *Georgics* and *Ecologues*, which followed the models of Greek pastoral poetry, praised the pleasures and satisfactions of rural life. Written before Augustus reached political supremacy, these poems helped him advance his later program of propaganda to get workers back to the farms. He persuaded Vergil to write the *Aeneid*, the great national epic of Rome's beginnings, in which the poet could "predict" the future glories that Augustus' rule would bring. Though designed in part to please Augustus, these passages nonetheless reveal Vergil's own sincere and intense patriotism. Vergil often reflected upon the sacrifices that necessarily accompany a rise to greatness, on sorrow, and on death.

His fellow poet Horace (65-8 B.C.) showed more humor and expressed a greater range of feelings in a greater variety of meters. He too praised the joys of rural life and the virtues of moderation, but in more solemn terms celebrated the Roman qualities of quiet toughness, the simple life, the traditional religious attitudes, while glorifying the Augustan order. Ovid (43 B.C.-A.D. 17) gave worldly, often cynical, advice on the art of love. In the *Metamorphoses* he also told of the mythical transformations reported in Greek stories in which various divinities became birds, animals, or plants. Ovid died in exile because of his involvement in a sexual scandal affecting the granddaughter of Augustus.

To match in prose Vergil's epic of Rome's early days and to reemphasize the virtues that had made Rome great, the historian Livy (59 B.C.-A.D. 17) set out to write a prose history of the city from the moment of its founding. Only thirty-five of the one hundred and forty-two books into which he divided his work have come down to us complete, but we have summaries of the missing portions. Though Livy could use as his sources many Roman writers now lost, for the earliest periods he had to fall back on legend. While he knew the difference between reliable and unreliable accounts, he often used the latter because they were the only sources available. Vividly written, his long work was soon condensed for less ambitious readers.

Such insistence on the great Roman virtues reflected the uneasy sense that they were declining. As the government after Augustus became more arbitrary and autocratic, writers began to fear the consequences of expressing themselves too freely, and disillusionment set in. Moreover, admiration for the achievements of the Augustan writers, especially Vergil, became so intense that poets were often content to imitate the authors of the Golden Age and to suppress their own originality.

The greatest Roman historian, Tacitus (c A.D. 55-c 115), himself a master of prose style, was convinced that the Romans had degenerated. His *Germania*, an essay ostensibly in praise of the rugged and still primitive German barbarians, was in fact an acid commentary on the Romans' descent into the love of luxury for its own sake. Similar disillusionment pervades his history of the period from Tiberius to Domitian. Brilliant and prejudiced, allowing his personal opinions to color his accounts (sometimes in ways we cannot check), he was the greatest writer of the period between Tiberius and Hadrian, known as the Silver Age.

Silver-Age poets included Seneca (c 5 B.C.-A.D. 65), Nero's tutor, by birth a Spaniard, a Stoic philosopher, and author of nine sensational tragedies imitating Greek originals. Seneca committed suicide at Nero's order. Seneca's nephew, Lucan (39-65), wrote an epic poem (*The Pharsalia*) about the struggle between Caesar and Pompey. Persius (34-62) and Juvenal (c 60-c 140) satirized contemporary society, and as satirists often do,

THE SATYRICON

In 1663 in Dalmatia (in present-day Yugoslavia), portions of an apparently enormously long manuscript known as *The Satyricon* were found. This bawdy satire, which cleverly mixes prose, verse, and philosophy, is attributed to Petronius, one of Nero's court officials who, like Lucan, committed suicide in A.D. 66 at Nero's orders. Though undoubtedly exaggerated, the work tells us much about contemporary attitudes and practices among the most wealthy and leisured, illustrating the theme "Eat, drink, and be merry, for tomorrow we die." One of the longest sections of what has sometimes been called "the first novel" is the wildly funny account of a lavish banquet given by the newly rich and ultra vulgar Trimalchio. Buried amidst the humor, however, is biting commentary on social perceptions:

At long last the tumblers appeared. An extremely insipid clown held up a ladder and ordered a boy to climb up and do a dance on top to the accompaniment of several popular songs. He was then commanded to jump through burning hoops and to pick up a big jug with his teeth. No one much enjoyed this entertainment except Trimalchio. . . . Just at this point the ladder toppled and the boy on top fell down, landing squarely on Trimalchio. The slaves shrieked, the guests screamed. We were not, of course, in the least concerned about the boy, whose neck we would have been delighted to see broken; but we dreaded the thought of possibly having to go into mourning for a man who meant nothing to us at all. Meanwhile, Trimalchio lay there groaning and nursing his arm as though it were broken. Doctors came rushing in. . . . [T]hey began flogging a servant for having bound up his master's wounded arm with white, rather than scarlet, bandages. . . . [I]nstead of having the boy whipped, Trimalchio ordered him to be set free, so that nobody could say that the great Trimalchio had been hurt by a mere slave. We gave this ample gesture our approval and remarked on the uncertainties of human existence.

The Satyricon, trans. William Arrowsmith (New York: New American Library, 1960), pp. 60-61.

they overstated the case. Juvenal enjoyed painting the vulgarities and wretchedness, the cruelties and greed of Rome in the harshest colors.

Law and Science

The legal code published on the Twelve Tables in the fifth century B.C. reflected the needs of a small city-state, not those of a huge empire. As Rome became a world capital, thousands of foreigners flocked to live there, and of course they often got into disagreements with each other or with Romans. But Roman law developed the flexibility to adjust to changing conditions. The enactments of the Senate and Assemblies, the decrees of each new emperor, and the decisions of the judges who were often called in as advisers—all of these contributed to a great body of legal materials.

It was the *praetors* (the chief legal officers) who heard both sides in every case and determined the facts before turning over the matter to the *judex* (a referee) for decision. Gradually, these officials developed a body of rules for deciding cases that were not covered by existing law. As they dealt with foreigners of different languages and customs, they worked out a body of common legal custom—the *jus gentium* (law of the peoples) to be applied to all of them. As each new praetor took office for a year, he would announce the laws by which he intended to be bound, usually following his predecessors and adding to the body of law as necessary. Romans also gradually acquired the benefits of the *jus gentium.*

The expert advisors (*jurisconsults*) to both praetor and judex felt an almost religious concern for equity; it was the spirit rather than the letter of the law that counted. This humane view found support in the philosophical writings of the Stoics, who believed that above all human law stood a higher natural law, which was divinely inspired and applied to all people everywhere. In practice, of course, judges were often poorly trained, the emperors brutal or arbitrary; Roman law could be used to exalt the authority of the state over the individual. Yet the law recognized the rights of the citizen, afforded legal redress even to slaves, and gave wide scope to local legal practices. Its clarity and flexibility gave it progressive authority over other legal systems; the law of much of western Europe today goes back to its provisions.

Medicine, too, advanced. Roman surgeons made a variety of ingenious instruments for special operations, including the Caesarean operation—supposed (probably wrongly) to have first been performed at the birth of Julius Caesar—for babies who could not be delivered normally. The Romans developed the first hospitals, both military and civilian. However, much superstition survived in Roman medicine, and it was the Greeks, notably Galen (c 129-199), who continued to make the major theoretical contributions, compiling medical encyclopedias and diffusing learning.

What Galen did for medicine, a contemporary, Ptolemy of Alexandria (c 85-161), did for ancient geography. Both remained the chief authorities on their subjects as late as the seventeenth century. Some learned Romans followed the Alexandrian Eratosthenes in believing that the earth was round. Pliny the Elder (23-79) made observations of ships approaching the shore to support this hypothesis; it was the tip of the mast that appeared first to an observer on shore, and the hull last—a proof Pliny felt, that the surface of the earth was curved. Pliny died when he was overcome by carbon monoxide gas while observing the eruption of Vesuvius that destroyed Pompeii (see p. 78).

Architecture, Sculpture, and Painting

Roman architecture used the Greek column, usually Corinthian, and the round arch, originated by the Etruscans; from this developed the *barrel vault,* a continuous series of arches like the top of the tunnel that could be used to roof large areas. The Romans introduced the dome, and a splendid one surmounts the Pantheon at

Detail of a mosaic pavement, c A.D. 300, showing gladiators in combat. It is now in the Borghese Gallery in Rome.

Rome. Roman structures emphasized bigness: the Colosseum seated forty-five thousand spectators; the Baths of the emperor Caracalla accommodated thousands of bathers at a time (its ruins are still used for grand opera); Diocletian's palace at Split in modern Yugoslavia contains most of the modern city within its walls. Amphitheaters, temples, villas, and other monumental remains of Roman domination can be found throughout the Middle East, North Africa, and western Europe.

Roman sculpture, though derived from Greek and Hellenistic models, had a realism of its own, especially in imperial portrait busts. A sculptured frieze running spirally up a monumental column vividly records the victories of the emperor Trajan (see p. 79). Of Roman painting we have chiefly the pretty (sometimes obscene) wall decorations of the villas at Pompeii and the mosaic floors of public and private buildings, in which a favorite subject was a hunting scene along the Nile, with crocodiles and hippopotamuses among papyrus plants. A recently discovered villa at Piazza Armerina in Sicily has a superb series of third-century floors, including a scene of women in a gymnasium tossing a ball from hand to hand. At Ostia Antica, the port for Rome, numerous mosaics tell us of art, daily life, and social customs, including for the first time evidence on the nature of tenant-landlord relations for rented houses. These ruins have only recently been uncovered and have yet to yield all their secrets.

A Final Appraisal

Tacitus was right in thinking that Rome had lost some of its traditional virtues with its conquest of huge territories, its accumulation of wealth, and its assumption of imperial responsibilities. Nevertheless, the first two centuries of the Empire mark the most stable and, for many, the most prosperous era that had yet occurred in human history. No doubt the profits of flourishing commercial life were unevenly distributed, and there were glaring contrasts between rich and poor. But many of the harshest aspects of ancient society elsewhere were softened in Rome. Slaves could obtain their freedom more easily, and once free, they enjoyed the privileges of citizenship, including that of owning slaves themselves. Women had more rights and commanded more respect (we have much evidence of harmonious family life, though there were more divorces perhaps than at any period before our own). Physical comforts were abundant for those who could afford them.

In the city of Rome itself, however, great areas were unsanitary, overcrowded slums; six- and seven-story wooden tenements often burned down or collapsed and were rebuilt, despite building codes and fire departments. Rents were exorbitantly high. Streets were narrow and dark, noisy with cart traffic, and full of crime at night, covered with hucksters' wares exposed for sale by day. Perhaps worst of all was the chronic urban unemployment; at the height of the Pax Romana perhaps half the population of the capital received free bread. The inhabitants were given free chariot races and gladiatorial combats, and the poor squandered their few pennies on betting. Bloodshed exerted a morbid fascination. Criminals were crucified and even burned alive on the stage as part of spectacles to entertain the populace; in the last century of Roman life these shows had become so popular that they superseded the theater, despite the protests of the occasional horrified citizen, like Seneca.

As we shall see in the next chapter, the structure of the Roman state did not disappear in the West until the end of the fifth century A.D. This Roman influence gave a permanent shape to western Europe. Italian, French, Spanish, Romanian, and Portuguese were all languages derived from Latin, and English has almost as many Latin as Germanic words. Roman legal concepts provided the foundations of respectability for many a chaotic society. Rome itself became the capital of Christianity and its administrative organization was the model for the structure of the church. Thus transformed into new roles, the metropolis of the Empire continued to exert power, intellectual influence, and multilayered historical fascination for each succeeding century.

SUMMARY

Early Rome was a Latin city influenced by Greek colonies in the south of Italy and by the Etruscans to the north. Rome expelled its Etruscan kings in 509 B.C. and became a republic.

Early Roman society was divided between the dominant aristocratic minority (the patricians) and the plebeians, who formed the mass of the population. The government was led by two elected consuls, who were advised by a Senate of ex-officials. At first most officials were patricians, but by the fourth century B.C. the plebeians had won the right to hold most offices, including consul.

By the third century B.C. Rome had conquered all of Italy and had come into conflict with Carthage, a former Phoenician colony that ruled much of Spain and Sicily. In three wars (264-241, 218-202, 149-146), Rome defeated and destroyed Carthage. During the same period Rome began to expand to the east, conquering Macedon and Greece and dominating Egypt and most of Asia Minor by 133 B.C..

Overseas expansion led to economic, social, and political trouble in Rome. The institutions of a small city-state could not cope with an empire. Small farms were increasingly replaced by large estates (latifundia) owned by rich generals and profiteers and worked by slaves, who made up an increasingly large share of the population. Attempts at reform failed as civil strife ultimately developed into civil war.

In the last years of the Republic, various generals either seized power or dominated the state: Marius, Sulla, Pompey. Finally in 45 B.C. Julius Caesar, who had conquered Gaul, emerged as the master of Rome. Caesar was assassinated in 44 B.C., but his nephew and heir, Octavian Augustus, was able to defeat his rivals and become the first Roman emperor.

Augustus' rule (27 B.C.-A.D. 14) inaugurated the *Pax Romana*, two centuries of relative peace, stability, and prosperity for the Mediterranean world. His successors developed the bureaucracy, extended Roman citizenship, and carried out a vast program of public works. Although the Romans failed to conquer Germany east of the Rhine River, Britain and Romania were added to the Empire during this period.

Women in Rome had many more rights and played a much more public role than in Greece, though their position depended in part on their ability to bear children. The Romans were concerned by their declining population, the result of plagues against which ancient medicine could do little.

After A.D.180 civil wars and struggles over the succession disrupted Roman society and weakened the economy. The barbarians began to push across the European frontiers. The reforms of Diocletian and Constantine staved off collapse but imposed new burdens on an overtaxed and demoralized population.

Roman culture was deeply influenced by Greece. Latin literature often imitated Greek forms. Among the greatest Roman writers were Cicero, Vergil, Horace, Ovid, Livy, and Tacitus.

Their system of law was one of the Romans' most enduring achievements. The law of much of western Europe and Latin America today goes back to its provisions.

Roman art was also heavily influenced by Greece, but the Romans also made significant contributions of their own: for example, the barrel vault and the dome in architecture, and the realistic portrayal of individuals in sculpture.

chapter four

JUDAISM AND CHRISTIANITY

The Romans constructed great buildings, baths, aqueducts, viaducts, and roads; they left behind in the writings of Vitruvius some of the earliest technical accounts from which modern technology, and especially engineering, may be dated. Hero of Alexandria, a Hellenistic inventor and writer of the first century B.C., wrote a treatise, *Pneumatics*, which set out a variety of problems in science and engineering upon which the Romans apparently drew. Between them, Hero and Vitruvius understood the cam (a disk or cylinder that can power an engine by imparting a rocking motion to an adjacent piece), surveying instruments, and how to measure the flow of water. They also had devised an early turbine that used steam to make automatic puppets turn and dance for a miniature theatre and had developed a model fire engine. Stonecutting, essential to Greek and Roman architecture, was an application of descriptive geometry. In short, both the theoretical and practical sciences were known to Greece or Rome.

Yet neither the Greeks nor the Romans systematically developed what they knew into either the practical art of engineering or into the critical mass of ideas, inventions, and technicians from which a true industrial age could develop. Hero's inventions were applied to toys rather than to productivity. Throughout the classical world, including ancient China (where trip hammers were used for hulling rice by A.D. 290, on the principle of the cam), there was no evolutionary connection between the gadgetry, the inventions, and the perceptions of education. The great inventions of Chinese technology—gunpowder, the compass, printing—did not produce the first industrial people; nor did the many clever discoveries, essentially unchallenged by the scientific world even today, which the Greeks and Romans made about their environment. Not until medieval times, for example, did the cam actually contribute to industrialization.

Why was this so? Why were there individual scientists, but no scientific community? Why were there engineers, but no profession of engineering? Hero's *Pneumatics*, written in Greek, was translated into Arabic (for the Arabs early developed a more systematic approach to science) and only then into Latin; its principles remained essentially dormant until the twelfth century A.D. Euclid's theorems, his *Elements* dating from the third century B.C., first passed into Arabic and not into Latin, in which language scholars of the Middle Ages could draw upon them most effectively, until the early twelfth century. Though known to some, the theories developed by the classical scholars did not become common knowledge, even among the educated, for well over a thousand years. From Hero's work on steam, seventeen hundred years passed before the steam engine was invented.

I THE IMPORTANCE OF RELIGION IN THE LATER ROMAN WORLD

The Failure of Science

There are many arguments as to why civilization had to wait so long before scientific knowledge was given a systematic application. Whatever the answers, the tendency to see science as being in opposition to religion—to Roman beliefs in the gods, to the cults introduced from Egypt or by way of Asia Minor, to astrology, and ultimately to the triumphant new teachings of Christianity—was already developing. Perhaps the answer lay, in part, in the attitudes of the Roman ruling groups. They considered "idle speculation" beneath them; they also looked down on commerce and industry—two of the incentives for technical inventiveness. The ruling classes who had the money to spend on developing new areas of knowledge spent it instead on warfare, on luxurious living, or increasingly on the growth of the church. While the monastic orders recognized the value of manual labor, church doctrine was developed in a period that put more emphasis on contemplation or disputation.

In any case, there were competing explanations offered by science or religion by which Romans sought to understand the world around them. Science formed no part of Roman education, and scattered statements show that the Romans scorned what we would now call research. They feared new inventions that might put more people out of work; the emperor Tiberius is said to have executed a man who had invented a process for making unbreakable glass. The prevalence of slaves and the lack of consumer markets meant that owners did not need to develop methods of mass production, even though the more thoughtful may have realized that slave labor was adaptable to mass production provided a market existed for the increased productivity. Although the earlier advance of science in the Greek and Hellenistic world had given rise to small groups of rationalists who believed in improving their lives by using their reasoning powers, even these minorities seem virtually to have disappeared.

Throughout the Roman Empire pessimism mounted, accompanied by a lack of faith in humanity's ability to work out its own future. The old gods seemed powerless to intervene, and to many, life appeared to be a matter of luck. Beginning as early as the third century B.C. and gathering increasing momentum, the cult of the goddess Fortune became immensely popular in the Mediterranean world. Chance governed everything; today's prosperity might vanish tomorrow; the best thing to do was to enjoy good fortune while the goddess smiled upon you. Closely related was the belief in Fate. What happened was inevitable because it had been fated from the beginning; when you were born, the moment of your death was already fixed. Some, like Cicero, protested that people could affect their own fate and so take advantage of fortune. Vergil attributed both fate and fortune to the will of the divine providence, but most Romans seem to have felt helpless to change their own fates or to influence events. Human beings, it was said, were slaves to two emotions, hope and fear, and sought ways of assuaging both.

Astrology

To escape from alternating between hope and fear, most Romans came to believe that the movements of the heavenly bodies influenced their fortunes and fates, and governed their decisions. Thus the science of astronomy became lost in the speculations of astrology. If one could do nothing to change one's destiny, one could at least try to find out what that destiny might be by consulting an expert astrologer. The astrologer would study the seven planets (Saturn, Jupiter, Mars, the Sun, Venus, Mercury, the Moon), each of which had its own will, character, gender, plants, numbers, and attendant animals, and each of which was lord of a sphere. Seven itself became a mystic number: there were seven ages of man, seven wonders of the world. Then too there were the twelve Houses of the Sun—constellations of stars through which the sun passed on its way around the earth; these were the signs of the zodiac, itself an imaginary belt of the heavens.

From the position of the heavenly bodies and the signs of the zodiac at the moment of conception or birth, astrologers would draw up a horoscope foretelling a person's fate. The Roman emperors, like most of their subjects, profoundly believed in astrology. Some people continue to believe in it, even to our own day. Especially valuable for the art of prophecy were so-called unnatural events—the appearance of a comet, the birth of a monster. Similarly, people believed in all sorts of magic, and tried by its power to force the heavenly bodies to grant their wishes. The *magus*, or magician, exercised enormous power.

New Cults: Cybele, Isis, Mithra, Philosophy

The state religion of the Olympian gods and of the deified emperors still commanded the loyalty of many Romans, who regarded the proper observance of its rites as the equivalent of patriotism. But by the first century A.D. the old faith no longer allayed the fears of millions of people who believed in blind fate and inevitable fortune; people increasingly sought a religion that would hold out the hope of an afterlife better than the grim reality on earth. So, along with astrology and magic, mystery religions began to appear in Rome.

These new faiths taught that the human soul could be saved by union with the soul of a savior, who in many cases had experienced death and a form of resurrection. This union was accomplished by a long initiation, marked by purifications, ritual banquets, and other ceremonies designed to overcome human unworthiness. The god would enter the candidate, who would be saved after physical death. The initiate sought a mystical guarantee against death by survival in a hereafter. One could join as many of these cults as one liked and still practice the state religion.

The Greeks had such cults in the rites of Demeter at Eleusis and in the mysteries of Dionysus. The rites of Dionysus, now called Bacchus, became popular in Rome, celebrating as they did the carnal pleasures of human nature and the abandonment of all restraint. On hundreds of late Roman sarcophagi can be seen the Bacchic procession celebrating the joys of drink and sex. But the cult of Bacchus was too materialistic to satisfy all Romans.

One of its major competitors was the cult of the great mother-goddess Cybele, which came from Asia Minor at the end of the Second Punic War. Her young husband, Attis, died and was reborn annually (like Demeter's daughter, Persephone). Attis was thus a symbol of renewed fertility. The rites of Cybele included fasting, frenzied processions, self-flagellation, and self-mutilation by the priests. The first temple to Cybele at Rome dated from 204 B.C., but the zenith of the cult was reached in the second century A.D. By that time the practices included the slaughter of a bull above a pit into which the initiate had descended in order to be bathed by the blood, with subsequent cleansing by milk and wool in a rite of purification.

Even more popular, with women as well as men, was the cult of the Egyptian goddess Isis, whose consort, Osiris, died and was reborn each year. The Isis cult was apparently first spread by sailors. All "feminine" elements—lascivious or chaste—were concentrated in an elaborate ritual of worship for Isis, the loving mother-goddess, who promised her adherents personal immortality. As Apuleius' satire *The Golden Ass* (written in the second century) makes clear, conversion to Isis worship often emphasized her purity and morality, and the prospect of salvation for her followers, in contrast to the presumed depravity and growing commercialism associated with Cybele.

From Persia about the first century A.D. came the cult of the god Mithra, allied to the supreme powers of good and light, and so connected with the sun. The male initiates passed in succession through seven grades of initiation (corresponding to the seven planets and named after animals), qualifying for each by severe tests. Baptism and communion were also part of the ritual. Unconquered, physically rough, and self-denying, Mithra became a model for the Roman soldier, to whom he held out the hope of salvation. Mithraism had no priests and welcomed the gods of other cults; it tended to absorb other sunworshiping cults, including that of

A *Taurobolium,* or Roman relief depicting the sacrifice of a bull. The act of sacrifice related both to Mithraism and to Cybele, the mother of the gods.

Apollo, into one new cult, often supported by the emperor. Temples of Mithra have been found in every province of the empire.

These cults appealed widely to the masses rather than to the educated. But there were trends in philosophy and in mysticism that were popular among intellectuals too. The older philosophical positions, somewhat altered, continued to be influential. Long before, after the death of Alexander the Great, the philosopher Epicurus had taught that unnecessary fear lay at the root of the troubles of humanity. Whatever gods might exist took no interest in what humans might do; life after death was only untroubled sleep. A quiet life and the cultivation of friendships would bring happiness; if evil came, one could endure it. Both Lucretius and Horace were Epicureans. But as ordinary people could hardly banish fear or pain or desire by following Epicurean formulas, the Epicureans were few in number.

So were the Stoics, who prescribed the suppression of human emotions; people should accept the universe and simply defy evil to do its worst. These ideas won a substantial following among the disillusioned Roman upper classes. But by compromising with astrology and with polytheism, by teaching that the universe was periodically destroyed and reconstituted, by harshly condemning human pity, Stoicism ultimately lost much of its following.

Perhaps halfway between religion and philosophy was the school of the so-called "thrice-great Hermes" (Hermes Trismegistus), who prescribed abstinence, concentration, and study as a preparation for a flash of ecstasy and a spiritual rebirth. Stronger still was Neoplatonism, whose adherents claimed to be disciples of Plato. They taught that each human soul makes a pilgrimage toward an eventual union with the divine spiritual essence—the One, the True, the Good, the last great abstraction. By contemplation, the mystic would gradually become free of material ties and achieve ecstatic vision. Though Neoplatonism soon became identified with far less lofty and rarefied rites like those of the cults, for most believers the divine reason, the *logos* (literally, "the word"), joined with the divine soul and the ultimate divinity itself as a sort of trinity. Despite its trinitarian overtones, however, it tended, like the other oriental religions, toward monotheism and pantheism—the worship of One, and the identification of that One with the universe.

No single mystery religion or philosophic movement appealed to men and women of all classes in Rome. Mithraism, which perhaps had the most adherents, especially in the army, excluded women and lacked love and tenderness. Neoplatonism had no appeal for the masses. We have already noted the presence of Christians in the Roman world, especially under Nero, who made them the scapegoat for the great fire of A.D. 64. Indeed, Christianity competed with the cults in the Roman world for more than three centuries after the death of its founder; sharing some beliefs in common with them, it also possessed qualities they lacked.

II JUDEA

History, it is said, is written by the victor. Since the Judaeo-Christian ethic came to dominate Western religious beliefs, attempts to separate precise, verifiable fact (as used by the historian) from generally held perceptions and beliefs is exceptionally difficult. Indeed, for the true believer of any faith, such an effort is felt to be unnecessary. There is, however, usually a body of material commonly accepted by believer and nonbeliever. Even so, Jewish and Christian sources present problems for the historian, for the earliest account of Jesus (by Mark) comes from about A.D. 70, and the account by John is from the end of the same century. These accounts are *Gospels*, that is, statements about the teachings of Jesus of Nazareth, so that those teachings would not be lost, and they were not written to separate religious doctrine from historical fact and myth.

We know that Jesus was born in Palestine sometime between the years we now call 8 and 4 B.C. and was crucified probably in A.D. 29 or 30 in the reign of Tiberius. He was a Jew all his life and stoutly declared that he had not come to lead a movement of secession from Judaism, but one of reform and fulfillment within it: "Think not that I am come to destroy the law, or the prophets: I am not come to destroy, but to fulfill. For verily I say unto you, Till heaven and earth pass, one jot or one title shall in no wise pass from the law, till all be fulfilled" (*Matthew* 5:17–18). But we cannot understand this apparently straightforward and uncomplicated idea without appreciating the extraordinary complexity of the Roman and Judean society in which Jesus was born, taught, suffered, died, and—as his followers declared—was raised from the dead.

The Roman Conquest: Hellenism and the Hasmoneans When, after a century of struggle between the Ptolemies and Seleucids for control of Palestine, the Seleucids won a permanent victory about 200 B.C., their monarch issued special tax privileges for the Jewish Temple and the Jews. The high priest of the Temple of Judea represented the Jews in their dealings with their Seleucid overlord and was responsible for collecting the taxes for him. The upper classes among the Jews found themselves greatly attracted by Greek culture—Hellenism—as, to varying degrees, were most inhabitants of the Near East in the wake of Alexander's conquests and the establishment of the successor kingdoms. Some Jews engaged in athletics naked in the Greek fashion; Jews discovered Greek music; Greek artistic motifs and symbols appeared on Jewish monuments and coins. In some of the later books of the Old Testament compiled in this period—notably *Jonah*—Jewish separateness, the sense of being a chosen people, so notable elsewhere, seems to have disappeared in favor of a concern for all humanity, non-Jew and Jew alike. The Greek language spread widely; many Jews took Greek names. Certain Jewish writings echo Homer, such as *Ecclesiasticus* (note that this is not the same as *Ecclesiastes*), written about 185 B.C.

This Hellenization of upper-class Jews in Judea led to conflict with the many Jews who sought to keep the traditions pure. And the poorer population—tenant farmers on the lands of the rich or humble artisans in the cities—hated their fellow Jews who oppressed them in association with the Seleucid monarchy. Party strife and civil war led to the intervention of Antiochus IV in 168 B.C., and to a concerted attempt to destroy Judaism by force. Judaism was declared illegal, and an altar on which pigs were sacrificed to Zeus was superimposed on the altar of the Temple. The Jews rebelled; the Maccabean wars (named after Judah Maccabeus, the Jewish commander) were savage. Seleucid dynastic rivalries added to the political complexity. On December 25, 160 B.C., the Maccabees restored Jewish worship at the defiled Temple in Jerusalem in a feast of dedication, or *Hanukkah.*

In 153 B.C. Judah Maccabeus' brother Jonathan became high priest, and his descendants (called Hasmoneans after a priestly ancestor, Hasmon) held the office for 117 years, until 37 B.C. The Hasmonean state of Judea was virtually independent until 63, when Pompey annexed it to the Roman Empire with the rest of Syria. The Hasmoneans made war on the territories adjoining Judea, forcibly circumcising non-Jewish men (even though in Greek, Roman, and Arab cultures circumcision was held in contempt) and adding greatly to the anti-Jewish hatred already powerful among the gentiles (originally meaning any people not Jewish) of the Mediterranean seacoast and across the Jordan River. To the gentiles' complaints, the Hasmoneans replied that they were reestablishing themselves in the lands of their ancestors.

Yet another party of Jews, highly puritanical, participated in the war against the Seleucids until the Jewish faith was secure, but opposed the Hasmonean conquests, for they were content to live under foreign rule so long as the Jewish religion was protected. They expected that the power of the gentiles would in any case pass

JONAH

The story of Jonah is best known for the passages below. They are representative of how the Bible is submitted to textual *exegesis*—that is, a critical examination of the text for its various intended meanings, which can best be understood when we understand the culture and the time from which the accounts, many of them literal and many metaphorical, are taken:

CHAPTER 1

NOW the word of the LORD came unto Jonah the son of
Amittai, saying,
2 Arise, go to Nineveh, that great city, and cry against
it; for their wickedness is come up before me.
3 But Jonah rose up to flee unto Tarshish from the
presence of the LORD, and went down to Joppa; and he
found a ship going to Tarshish: so he paid the fare
thereof and went down into it, to go with them into
Tarshish from the presence of the LORD.
4 But the LORD sent out a great wind into the sea,
and there was a mighty tempest in the sea, so that the
ship was like to be broken.
5 Then the mariners were afraid, and cried every
man unto his god, and cast forth the wares that were in
the ship into the sea, to lighten it of them. But Jonah was
gone down into the sides of the ship; and he lay, and was
fast asleep.
6 So the shipmaster came to him, and said unto him,
What meanest thou, O sleeper? arise, call upon thy God,
if so be that God will think upon us, that we perish not.
7 And they said every one to his fellow, Come, and let
us cast lots, that we may know for whose cause this evil
is upon us. So they cast lots, and the lot fell upon Jonah.
8 Then said they unto him, Tell us, we pray thee, for
whose cause this evil is upon us; What is thine occupation? and whence comest thou? what is thy country? and
of what people art thou?
9 And he said unto them, I am an Hebrew; and I fear
the LORD, the God of heaven, which hath made the sea
and the dry land.
10 Then were the men exceedingly afraid, and said
unto him, Why hast thou done this? For the men knew
that he fled from the presence of the LORD, because he
had told them.
11 Then said they unto him, What shall we do unto
thee, that the sea may be calm unto us? for the sea
wrought, and was tempestuous.
12 And he said unto them, Take me up, and cast me
forth into the sea; so shall the sea be calm unto you: for I
knew that for my sake this great tempest is upon you.
13 Nevertheless the men rowed hard to bring it to the
land; but they could not: for the sea wrought, and was
tempestuous against them.
14 Wherefore they cried unto the LORD, and said, We
beseech thee, O LORD, we beseech thee, let us not perish
for this man's life, and lay not upon us innocent blood:
for thou, O LORD, hast done as it pleased thee.
15 So they took up Jonah, and cast him forth into the
sea: and the sea ceased from her raging.
16 Then the men feared the LORD exceedingly, and
offered a sacrifice unto the LORD, and made vows.
17 Now the LORD had prepared a great fish to swallow up Jonah. And Jonah was in the belly of the fish three
days and three nights.

CHAPTER 4

10 Then said the LORD, Thou hast had pity on the
gourd, for the which thou hast not laboured, neither
madest it grow; which came up in a night, and perished
in a night:
11 And should not I spare Nineveh, that great city,
wherein are more than sixscore thousand persons that
cannot discern between their right hand and their left
hand; and also much cattle?

Authorized King James Version.

away, that the "Ancient of Days" would sit upon his eternal throne and grant to a Messiah—"one like the son of man"—an everlasting earthly dominion. To this party—the "pious people" (Hasidim or Assidaeans)—the Hasmoneans were arrogant usurpers.

Under Roman Rule As the Romans replaced the Seleucids as foreign overlord of the Jewish lands, Pompey liberated the areas the Hasmoneans had conquered and made the areas with Jewish majorities a client state (*civitas stipendiaria*) of Rome. In the mid-fifties the Roman governor of Syria divided Judea into five subareas (*synhedria*, or councils) as a step toward later dismemberment.

In 47 B.C. Julius Caesar reversed this trend, reunited Judean territory, and gave the governorship to Antipater, a convert to Judaism from one of the neighboring areas that the Hasmoneans had conquered. Rivalry and civil war between the last of the Hasmoneans and the family of Antipater (one of whose sons was Herod) was complicated by a Parthian invasion and culminated when the Roman Senate made Herod king of Judea. In 37, with the help of troops sent by Mark Antony, Herod was able to take Jerusalem. He survived the collapse of Mark

Antony after Actium by serving Augustus obediently.

Most Jews hated Herod, not so much for being an outsider and a descendant of a convert as for his subservience to the foreign ruler and his ruthlessness in wiping out not only all those who engaged in acts of violence or sabotage but all suspects, including the last of the Hasmoneans. Rome was far more powerful than the Seleucids had ever been, and was equally unacceptable to the Jews as a source of the same Hellenistic influence. Tyrannical though Herod was, he was also a thorough realist; he believed the Jews could survive only by reconciling themselves to living within the Roman Empire. Secret police, prisons, death were for resisters; for others, survival lay through abandoning exclusiveness and adapting to the Greco-Roman world.

Until his death in 4 B.C., Herod built Greek cities in Judea with splendid public buidings; he created a major new seaport at Caesarea, the provincial capital of Judea, patronized Greek artists and writers, and sponsored musical and athletic contests, to which non-Jews were invited as guests. He also began a cult of himself in the non-Jewish areas. Among Jews he represented himself as descended from the line of David, and as the restorer of the ancient glory of the kingdom. To that end he rebuilt the Temple on a grander scale than ever before.

Parties Among the Jews The Romans put down the rebellion that erupted on Herod's death, and ten years later, at the petition of the Jews, they deposed Herod's son as king of Judea and installed the first Roman prefect. By this time, there were at least three parties distinguishable among the Jews of Judea: the Sadducees, the Pharisees, and the Essenes. The Romans took advantage of this divisiveness to maintain their rule over Palestine until their empire collapsed at the center.

The Sadducees were a small, influential group of aristocrats who had long ancestral associations with the Temple priesthood; they were generally regarded as collaborationists with the Romans. What we know of their beliefs is derived from texts written by their enemies, but they apparently did not believe in the resurrection of the dead or in rewards and punishment after death. They also repudiated the belief in good and evil spirits, rejected predestination, and believed in the full responsibility of individuals for their actions.

We know much more about the Pharisees, who survived to become the prevailing force in later Judaism. They apparently originated as an Assidaean faction that, about 160, abandoned the belief that at the last judgment only they would be saved and all other Jews forever damned. The Pharisees nonetheless held themselves strictly apart (the name itself means "the separated ones") from the common people who did not observe every letter of Jewish law. They reconciled themselves to life under Herod and under the Roman prefects. They strove to achieve the Kingdom of God here on earth, and they opposed what they regarded as the unrealistic attitude that all hope must be put off until the final day.

The Pharisees' reverence for Jewish law admitted of argument and differing interpretations with respect to it. They made divorce difficult, but they did not forbid it altogether; they believed in keeping the Sabbath (or the seventh day) for rest, but they would break it to save a life. So the written law, as laid down in the first five books of the Old Testament, was supplemented by an oral law of interpretations by rabbinical sages. Pharisees conceded that there were righteous non-Jews. They believed that fate determined some human actions, though not all. Unlike the Sadducees, the Pharisees believed in a last judgment separating the righteous from the sinners.

A third school of thought among the Jews was that of the Essenes, known before 1947 only by a few ancient texts; in that year began a series of discoveries in the caves of Qumran near the Dead Sea of the so-called Dead Sea Scrolls. Dating from 200 to 70 B.C., the scrolls include fragments of the teachings of the Essenes, who lived in a monastic community nearby. Its buildings were destroyed by the Romans in A.D. 68, but we know that this was not the only Essene settlement, and that some lived in cities or other than monastic communities.

In the Essenes' monastic community, the men lived in celibacy, engaged in ritual baths and meals, and shared communal property. (Some women and children buried nearby were probably relatives of members or wives and children of members not yet fully accepted.) At the Essenes' communal meal, bread and wine were taken but were not thought of as transmuted, and the meal did not symbolize salvation. They took ritual baths and repeated them often, so the baths were not similar to the single ceremonial baptismal bath performed by John the Baptist for penitents. When the age of wickedness drew to an end, the Essenes believed that they, the "poor in spirit," would prevail.

The scrolls refer to a Teacher of Righteousness, a Suffering Just One, who had been greater than all the prophets. He was not the same as the deliverer, the Messiah, whom they still awaited, and who would be a priest and a descendant of the house of David—the same "Son of Man" who appears in the *Book of Daniel*, and in whom the Essenes' forerunners, the Assidaeans, had also believed. In one passage in the scrolls, the Teacher of Righteousness referred to himself as the father of a manchild who would have all his own powers. Thus the texts that tell us about the Essenes reveal them as a reforming movement within Judaism that apparently had much in common with the Christianity that was to appear later.

Besides the Sadducees, the Pharisees, and the Essenes, there were also groups of Jews who belonged to a "fourth philosophy," who devoted themselves to resistance against the Romans, like modern guerrillas or partisans. Though they are sometimes called Zealots by modern scholars, they may have called themselves simply Israel, to indicate that they were the only true Jews. As the Roman grip upon Judea loosened in the years immediately before the uprising that began in A.D. 66 and ended with the destruction of the Temple in 70, some of the resisters turned to terrorism and committed many murders, after which they were called "the dagger men" (*sicarii*). Many Jews had indeed been moved by zeal against the Romans, but the true Zealots, as a political party, did not exist before 67-68 as a grouping of rural peasant groups and urban militants, hostile to both the Jewish upper classes and to the Romans.

From the Roman point of view, the Jews were particularly privileged subjects whose religion was protected by the Roman state. Unlike other Roman subjects, they could become citizens of any city without forfeiting the right to their beliefs. They were exempt from military service, which would have implied for them idolatry and would have required them to break their Sabbath, since armies cannot choose a day on which not to fight. They were excused from participating in the imperial cult for the same reason, and said prayers for the emperor in the synagogues instead. Their local copper coinage was struck without the emperor's likeness. Their own judges (*sanhedrin*) acted as local administrators and handled all purely Jewish court cases.

Such privileges contributed to widespread anti-Jewish feeling among non-Jews in the Empire, who resented Jewish freedom from so many of the responsibilities of the Roman state. Non-Jews scoffed at the worship of a god who could not be portrayed and who required abstinence from pork, the most commonly eaten meat in the ancient world. They regarded Jewish abstention from emperor worship as atheism and Jewish separatism as elitism. Despite what appeared to the Romans to be generous treatment, the sense of a Jewish nationality refused to die.

The Teaching of Jesus

It was thus in a troubled and divided land that Jesus came to preach to his fellow Jews. He preached the love of one God for all people. He preached to the poor, the weak, and the simple, rather than to the priests of the Temple. His "Blessed are the poor in spirit" has an Essene echo, though Jesus was not a revolutionary like the Essenes, nor a revivalist, nor an ascetic, since he preached the enjoyment of the good things of this world, an enjoyment freed from rivalry, ostentation, and vulgarity. He was kind but stern—good intentions were not enough: "He that heareth, and doeth not, is like a man that without a foundation built a house upon the earth . . ." (*Luke* 6:49). Above all, he preached gentleness and love—humility, charity, honesty, toleration: "Judge not, that ye be not judged" (*Matthew* 7:1). He also warned that "Wide is the gate, and broad is the way that leadeth to destruction" (*Matthew* 7:13). Though he preached that the abused should turn the other cheek, he also said at another time that he came not to bring peace, but a sword. Plain people understood him and took comfort from his words.

From Jesus' preaching would arise theological conclusions of enormous importance. From the books of his disciples, the Gospels, we learn what Jesus said. He spoke of his Father in heaven, referred to himself as the Son of man, and taught that he was the Messiah whom God had sent to redeem humanity from sin. Those who hearkened and led decent lives on earth would gain eternal bliss in heaven; those who turned a deaf ear and

Carved onto the side of this fifth-century sarcophagus, or stone coffin, is a distinctly Christian scene—the Adoration of the Magi—as the three wise men present gifts to the infant Jesus. This monumental sculpture is now in Ravenna, Italy.

continued in their wicked ways would be eternally damned in hell. Jesus was the Christ, the anointed one. His followers said he was begotten by the Holy Spirit and miraculously born of a virgin mother. He was baptized by John the Baptist in the waters of the Jordan, and therefore his followers were also required to be baptized. He gave bread and wine to his followers at a feast of love and told them that it was his body and his blood, and that they should partake.

Such teaching—though not without parallel in earlier Jewish thought—aroused alarm and hostility among the Jewish authorities. Sadducees and Pharisees mistrusted all reformist efforts, of which Jesus' seemed only one more. When the Roman prefect, Pontius Pilate, asked Jesus, "Are you the king of the Jews?" and Jesus affirmed that he was, he was doomed, both by the sanhedrin and by the Romans. On the cross itself a title was inscribed to show that a leader of the resistance had

WHAT IS A GOSPEL?

The gospels are the teachings of Jesus as revealed in the first four books of the New Testament of the Bible: *Matthew*, *Mark*, *Luke*, and *John*. *Mark*, for example is referred to as *The Gospel According to St. Mark* in the King James version of the Bible. One of Mark's most powerful statements appears in the first chapter, verses 14 and 15:

> Now after that John was put in prison, Jesus came into Galilee,
> preaching the gospel of the kingdom of God,
> And saying, The time is fulfilled, and the kingdom of God is at hand:
> repent ye, and believe the gospel.

These two verses carry a host of meanings. Consider a few. "Preaching" carries a meaning beyond that understood today, for in Greek it was *Kerygma*, which meant that Jesus "proclaimed" the Kingdom of God, and in turn that the early Christians "proclaimed" Jesus. Thus preaching was not a sermon but a proclamation of the truth. That which is proclaimed is a *gospel*—that is, "good news." Not all religions have invariably brought good news, for those who preach of damnation exclusively do not bear news that can be considered good. The word here is meant to carry two meanings: that there is "good news of God" in the sense that the good news is *about* God and is *from* God. Furthermore, a gospel requires a response. Inaction nullifies the good news, but belief in the proclamation of the gospel, followed by a change in life, is the affirmative response demanded.

The second verse is similarly charged with meanings. The Greek original for "time," as used here, was *kairos*, which meant "the appropriate time"—that is, the fitness of things makes a specific moment the right time, again requiring a response. Repentance also requires a positive act. Most important, the verse indicates that which is at hand: the kingdom of God. The Jews looked toward a Messianic kingdom (Messiah and Christ both mean Anointed) of peace and righteousness ruled by the Anointed. But Jesus spoke in Aramaic, in which "kingdom" meant authority. Thus Jesus could also assert that the kingdom was already present, since he had asserted his authority.

Moreover, Jesus is said to have declared that "The Kingdom of God is within you," on the basis of a saying found on a papyrus in Egypt and incorporated into the Bible. This was not unlike the Greek concept "Know thyself." Generally scholars believe that the meanings collectively argue that the "kingdom" is an authority that is inward and spiritual, thus literally at hand. Other scholars argue that the Aramaic was mistranslated, and that a better reading is that "The kingdom of God is in the midst of you"—that is, that Jesus was moving among the people demonstrating in his actions the authority of God.

The above example of how a gospel is read in its components has been derived from John Ferguson, *What is a Gospel?* (Bletchley, England: The Open University Press, 1971), distributed by Harper & Row. The argument, however, is by Robin W. Winks.

been executed. In Christian thought the crucifixion became the supreme act of redemption: Jesus died for everyone. His followers declared that he rose from the dead on the third day and would soon return—during their lifetime, they believed—to end this world in a final Day of Judgment, when he would sit at the right hand of the Father.

Even in this bare summary we can see elements of Christian belief that are similar to Judaism and others that were present in the mystery cults. But Jesus' sacrifice of his life for humanity and the intimacy with God promised in the future eternal life gave Christianity a simplicity and a popular appeal that no mystery religion could duplicate.

The Early Christians: Judaeo-Christianity

There are no historical sources contemporary with Jesus himself from which to draw an account of his life and teaching. St. Paul's epistles to the Corinthians were written about A.D. 55, the *Acts* of the Apostles about 60-62 (though they are a chronological sequel to *Luke*), and the four Gospels that tell Jesus' story in the years that followed: *Mark* about 70, *Matthew* and *Luke* about 80-85, and *John* about 100. Late in the second century or early in the third these texts were revised in Alexandria. We have no canonical Christian text written down before this revision was prepared.

Before A.D. 60 a collection of the sayings of Jesus existed, written in Aramaic, the Semitic language that he spoke. This collection is lost. Many other texts also existed that were not regarded as authentic. Among them was a so-called *Gospel of Thomas*, written in the native Egyptian language (Coptic) in the early second century, of which fragments, including 114 sayings attributed to Jesus, were found in Egypt in 1945 and after.

All New Testament sources, then, belong to a period at least several decades after the death of Jesus. They were written in Greek for non-Jews and do not reflect the situation immediately after he died, which has only recently begun to be understood by scholars, who have studied inscriptions, monuments, and manuscripts that help tell the story. After the crucifixion of Jesus, a little group of his followers stayed together in Jerusalem; these first Christians were Jews who followed, as indeed Jesus himself had followed, the Jewish law. This was the Judaeo-Christian church, or "Church of the Circumcision," which had a succession of fifteen bishops. Because it regarded itself as the only true Israel, it was in conflict with the Pharisees and Sadducees.

But Christian belief had drawing powers that were attractive beyond the Jewish communities. Jesus had told his followers: "There be some standing here, which shall not taste of death, till they see the Son of man coming in his kingdom" (*Matthew* 16:28). This doctrine of the Second Coming, the immediacy of the emotional tie that Christianity created between the believer and Christ, and the tight bonding among members of the Christian brotherhood, explain why the *evangel*, the "glad tidings" that appealed to many gentiles as well as to Jews, was indeed dramatic and hopeful.

Saul of Tarsus (A.D. c 3 - c 67), who as a Jew had vigorously persecuted Christians and who had never known Jesus himself, was converted to Christianity by a blinding vision. He took the Greek form of his name, Paul. Apparently it was Paul and a co-worker Barnabas who, laboring together in Antioch, were the first disciples to call themselves Christians and to take the evangel to the gentiles. Problems quickly arose. Must a non-Jewish convert to Christianity be circumcised, a painful and at the time even dangerous operation? Some Judaeo-Christians were willing to exempt pagan converts from circumcision and other Jewish observances; others were not. Even those who made the concession were often reluctant or unwilling to eat in company, or mingle socially, with such converts. Paul himself went further, however, than even the more liberal Judaeo-Christians; he would have freed even former Jews from Jewish ritual requirements. Many Judaeo-Christians therefore, strongly opposed Paul's views.

The last of the Judaeo-Christian bishops of Jerusalem governed the church in the time of Hadrian, when the last of the Jewish rebellions in Judea was crushed A.D. 132-135. Thereafter Judaeo-Christianity died out in its native habitat, even though it was active in the Aramaic-speaking regions east of Palestine, and traces of it probably survived in the mighty Christian church of Roman North Africa and perhaps in that of Egypt, all areas where Paul did not labor as a missionary. But although the Judaeo-Christians held on in Jerusalem until the reign of Hadrian, it was Titus' capture of the city in 70 that ended their influence in the church. Thereafter—Paul himself was already dead—the church of the gentiles triumphed, and Christianity was separated from Judaism.

St. Paul and Gentile Christianity

Between A.D. 48 and 62 Paul traveled to Cyprus, twice to Syria and Asia Minor, twice to Greece, to Macedonia, back to Jerusalem, and eventually to Rome. Everywhere he taught that "there is neither Jew nor Greek" (*Galatians* 3:28). The Jewish Law had been a forerunner, a tutor: "For by one Spirit are we all baptized into one body, whether we be Jews or Gentiles, whether we be bond or free" (*1 Corinthians* 12:13); and most simply: "For the letter killeth, but the spirit giveth life" (2 *Corinthians* 3:6). The Christian was to be saved, not by the letter of the Jewish law, but by the spirit of the Jewish faith in a righteous God. Christianity must therefore be involved with the Hellenistic world as represented by the Roman Empire.

Paul was from the first a Hellenized Jew. He united in his person a mystic who sought to transcend the world and the flesh, a gifted spiritual adviser of ordinary men and women troubled in their everyday lives, and an able administrator of a growing church. In all Paul's writings there are passages that show him to have been ascetic in his morality and firmly convinced that Christian truth

ECCLESIASTES ON TRANSIENCE AND HISTORY

Ecclesiastes, or The Preacher, is best known for his sense of the vanity of human history:

CHAPTER 1

1 THE words of the Preacher, the son of David, king in Jerusalem.
2 Vanity of vanities, saith the preacher, vanity of vanities; all is vanity.
3 What profit hath a man of all his labour which he taketh under the sun?
4 One generation passeth away, and *another* generation cometh: but the earth abideth for ever.
5 The sun also ariseth, and the sun goeth down, and hasteth to his place where he arose.
6 The wind goeth toward the south, and turneth about unto the north; it whirleth about continually, and the wind returneth again according to his circuits.
7 All the rivers run into the sea; yet the sea *is* not full; unto the place from whence the rivers come, thither they return again.
8 All things *are* full of labour; man cannot utter *it*: the eye is not satisfied with seeing, nor the ear filled with hearing.
9 The thing that hath been, it *is that* which shall be; and that which is done *is* that which shall be done: and *there is* no new *thing* under the sun.
10 Is there *any* thing whereof it may be said, See, this *is* new? it hath been already of old time, which was before us.

CHAPTER 3

1 To every *thing there is* a season, and a time to every purpose under the heaven:
2 A time to be born, and a time to die; a time to plant, and a time to pluck up *that which is* planted;
3 A time to kill, and a time to heal; a time to break down, and a time to build up;
4 A time to weep, and a time to laugh; a time to mourn, and a time to dance;
5 A time to cast away stones, and a time to gather stones together; a time to embrace, and a time to refrain from embracing;
6 A time to get, and a time to lose; a time to keep, and a time to cast away;
7 A time to rend, and a time to sew; a time to keep silence, and a time to speak;
8 A time to love, and a time to hate; a time of war, and a time of peace.
11 He hath made every *thing* beautiful in his time: also he hath set the world in their heart, so that no man can find out the work that God maketh from the beginning to the end.

The italics of the King James Version of the Bible have been used here.

was not a matter of habit or reasoning, but of transcending faith:

> *Howbeit we speak wisdom among them that are perfect: yet not the wisdom of this world, nor of the princes of this world, that come to nought: But we speak the wisdom of God in a mystery, even the hidden wisdom, which God ordained before the world unto our glory: Which none of the princes of this world knew: for had they known it, they would not have crucified the Lord of glory (1 Corinthians 2:6-8).**

Paul was no Eastern mystic who preached denial of this world in magical ecstasy. Indeed he expressed clearly a characteristic Christian tension between this world and the next, between the real and the ideal, which firmly marks Western society. Paul's symbol for it was the mystic union of Christ with Christianity in the religious act known as communion. Christians are children of God who are destined, if they are true Christians, to eternal bliss. But on this earth they must live in the constant imperfection of the flesh, not wholly transcending it, always aware that they are at once mortal and immortal.

Much of the Pauline epistles deals with church discipline. Here we see Paul keeping a firm hand over scattered and struggling Christian congregations in the lands to which he traveled. He tried to tame the excesses to which the emotionally liberating doctrines gave rise, urging the newly emancipated not to take their new wisdom as an opportunity for wild ranting ("speaking with tongues"), but to accept the discipline of the church, to lead quiet, faithful, firmly Christian lives.

Paul was not one of the twelve apostles, the actual companions of Christ, who, according to tradition, sepa-

*Most matters touching upon religion are controversial, and summaries therefore involve choices. Readers should be aware, for example, that the version of Paul's teaching given here is from the Authorized King James Version of the Bible. It is used because it is the best known translation in modern times. However, there are other translations, including modernized ones that use present-day equivalents for old terms. The fact that this translation was produced in England means that the specific Bible from which it is drawn is rejected by many Christians, either because it is English, or felt to be Protestant, or for other reasons. Further, we have here referred to Paul by his name, though since the Christian church viewed all of the disciples as being exceptionally holy, today Paul is referred to as St. Paul. Finally, this extract from the *New Testament* does not show, as some do by using italics, that three words in the quotation were supplied later by scholars through accepted techniques intended to make the meaning clearer. Thus, like Pericles' funeral oration, the final historical document may be, and probably is, very like what Paul said but cannot be expected to be precisely as he wrote in his famous epistles (or letters) to the Christians at Corinth.

rated after the crucifixion to preach the faith in the four corners of the earth. But he has been accepted as their equal in his apostolate. Of the twelve, tradition holds that Peter (who disagreed with Paul about the purity of gentile food) went to Rome, of which he was the first bishop, and so became the first pope, and was martyred there under Nero on the same day as Paul. Thus the Church of Rome had both Peter and Paul as its founders.

In the imperial Roman capital the first Christians were a despised sect, suspected of incest, infanticide, and ritual murder. But by the year 100 the new beliefs had penetrated into many of the Eastern territories of the Empire, and had established a tenuous foothold in the West.

III CHRISTIANITY IN THE PAGAN WORLD

The Period of Persecution

What to Christians was persecution, to the Roman authorities was simply the performance of their duty as defenders of public order against those who seemed to be traitors to the Empire or irresponsible madmen. The Christians ran afoul of Roman civil law not so much for their positive beliefs and practices as for their refusal to make concessions to paganism. To cultivated Greeks and Romans of these first centuries A.D., Christians seemed wild enthusiasts; to the masses they were disturbers, cranks, revolutionaries. "Who prevents you from worshiping this god of yours also, along with the natural gods?" a bewildered Roman official of Egypt asked a Christian who insisted there was but one true faith.

The Empire was not very deeply concerned with details about the morals and faiths of its hundreds of component city-states, tribes, and nations. Scores of gods and goddesses, innumerable spirits and demons, filled the minds of the millions under Roman rule, and the rulers—themselves often Stoics with a philosophic, though scornful, toleration of mass superstitions—were willing to tolerate them all as part of the nature of things.

There was, however, a practical limit to this religious freedom, which after all was not based on any ideal of religious liberty (for freedom and liberty are different matters in the law) and certainly not on any concept of separation of church and state. To hold this motley collection of peoples in a common allegiance and give them something like the equivalent of a modern national identity, the emperor was deified. Simple rites of sacrifice to him were added to local religious customs. One more god did not offend the conscience of those who believed in the Greco-Roman pantheon, or in Isis or Cybele, or in any other conventional polytheism. Another pinch of incense on another altar was simple enough. Those who did not believe in the customary local gods—and such disbelief was widespread in the Roman Empire—had no trouble in doing what was expected of them, for they did not take any religion, new or old, with undue seriousness. The act of public worship was often essentially social, and did not signify a deeply held conviction.

The Christians, however, would not sacrifice to the emperor any more than the Jews of old would sacrifice to Baal. Indeed, they felt that, if an emperor pretended to be a god, he revealed that he was in fact a devil. The more cautious administrators of the growing Christian church were anxious to live down their reputation for

Detail from the side of a tomb of a Roman governor, depicting Christians dressed in Roman togas.

disorderliness, and they did not want to antagonize the civil authorities. These leaders may have been responsible for the familiar statement, "Render therefore unto Caesar the things which are Caesar's; and unto God the things that are God's" (*Matthew* 22:21), which historians believe is a later addition to the New Testament. But sacrifice clearly was a "thing of God's"; the dedicated Christian, then, could not make what to an outsider or a skeptic was merely a decent gesture of respect to the beliefs of others. Moreover, if he was a very ardent Christian, he might feel a sacrifice to Caesar was wicked, even when performed by non-Christians, and he might show these feelings in public, or try to prevent the practice because of its inherent wickedness.

The imperial authorities did not consistently seek to stamp out the Christian religion, and persecutions were sporadic over the course of three centuries, varying in severity at different times and different places. The first systematic persecution was under Nero in 64, who had some of the Christians torn to pieces by wild beasts and others set alight as torches in the dark. He opened his gardens to the public for the entertainments, but even the Roman mob obviously felt some doubts and compassion.

A generation or so later, in c 110-111, an imperial administrator, Pliny the Younger, wrote from his post in Asia Minor to the emperor Trajan that he was puzzled about how to treat the Christians, and asked for instructions. Should he make allowance for age, or punish children as severely as adults? Should he pardon a former Christian who now recanted? Should he punish people simply as Christians, or must he have evidence that they had committed the crimes associated publicly with their name? Up to now Pliny had asked the accused if they were Christians, and if they three times said they were, he had them executed. Pliny had interrogated the alleged Christians partly on the basis of an anonymous document listing their names. He had acquitted all who denied that they were Christians, who offered incense before the emperor's statue, and who cursed Christ, and all who admitted that they had once been Christians but had recanted. As Christians,

> *the sum total of their offense or error was this: that they were in the habit of meeting on a certain fixed day before sunrise, to sing hymns antiphonally to Christ, as to a god, and to bind themselves by an oath—not for any criminal purpose—but that they would not commit theft, robbery, or adultery, or falsify their word, or deny that they had received a deposit at the moment when they should be called upon to give it back. Then they reassembled and partook of food, a meal taken in unison, but altogether innocent. This they had given up since . . . I forbade meetings. So I felt it necessary to make a further effort to discover the truth by torture from two slave-women, who were called "deaconesses," but I could discover nothing more than superstition, shameless and excessive.*

Trajan answered with moderation that Pliny had done right. Trajan left the question of sparing children to Pliny's own judgment. He said that Christians need not be sought out, though any who were denounced and found guilty must be punished, as Pliny had done. Any who denied that they were Christians, even if they had been suspect in the past, should gain pardon by penitent prayer to the Roman gods. As for "any anonymous documents you may receive," they "must be ignored in any prosecution. This sort of thing creates the worst sort of precedent, and is out of keeping with the spirit of our times." Trajan thus established the guidelines by which the Romans dealt with the Christians under the law until the reign of Decius, in 249-251, when vigorous persecution was renewed.

Alone among the emperor's subjects, however, unrepetent Christians might be killed "for the name alone," presumably because their "atheism," as Trajan saw it, threatened to bring down the wrath of the gods on the community that tolerated it. The Jews, equally "atheist" in this sense, could be forgiven because they were continuing to practice their ancestral religion—worthy in itself in Roman eyes—and because Rome had long since officially tolerated the Jewish faith, provided that the Jews did not rebel against the Roman state. A single act of religious conformity brought acquittal.

Not until the third century, when the Roman world felt threatened from within and without, did persecutions become frequent and severe. By then Christians were far more numerous, as the faith had spread rapidly. After an anti-Christian riot in Alexandria, Decius commanded that on a given day everyone in the Empire must sacrifice to the gods and obtain a certificate to prove having done so. The dangers then threatening Rome were real enough—Decius himself would soon be killed by the Goths—and he wanted a single act of conformity from all his subjects to demonstrate that the Empire was united in the face of peril. The Pope, the bishops of Antioch and Jerusalem, nineteen Christians of Alexandria, and six at Rome are known to have been executed. No bishop in North Africa died, though there were cases of torture. In Spain two bishops recanted. Many Christians who had not obeyed the edict escaped arrest afterward for failing to have the certificate; some hid until the persecution had died down, and in parts of the Empire the edict was not enforced. In the Latin West others bribed officials to issue them false certificates saying that they had sacrificed; later they were received back into their churches with some protest. In the Greek East, the same bribery probably took place, but apparently was not regarded as sinful.

Under Valerian in 257-259, the government for the first time tried to interfere with the assembly of Christians for worship, and the clergy were ordered to sacrifice. After Valerian had been captured by the Persians, however, his successor granted toleration. But the systematic persecution begun in 303 by Diocletian was the most intense of all, especially in the East, where it lasted a full decade, as compared to about two years in the West. Churches were to be destroyed and all sacred books and church property handed over. In Palestine—for which alone we have figures—nearly a hundred Christians were martyred. A good many actively sought

TACITUS ON NERO

Tacitus said that the emperor Nero was using the Christians as a scapegoat for the great fire of A.D. 64:

But all human efforts, all the lavish gifts of the emperor, and the propitiations of the gods, did not banish the sinister belief that the conflagration was the result of an order. Consequently, to get rid of the report, Nero fastened the guilt and inflicted the most exquisite tortures on a class hated for their abominations, called Christians by the populace. Christus, from whom the name has its origin, suffered the extreme penalty during the reign of Tiberius at the hands of one of our procurators, Pontius Pilatus, and a most mischievous superstition, thus checked for the moment, again broke out not only in Judaea, the first source of the evil, but even in Rome, where all things hideous and shameful from every part of the world find their centre and become popular. Accordingly, an arrest was first made of all who pleaded guilty; then, upon their information, an immense multitude was convicted, not so much of the crime of firing the city, as of hatred against mankind. Mockery of every sort was added to their deaths. Covered with the skins of beasts, they were torn by dogs and perished, or were nailed to crosses, or were doomed to the flames and burnt, to serve as a nightly illumination, when daylight had expired.

Nero offered his gardens for the spectacle, and was exhibiting a show in the circus, while he mingled with the people in the dress of a charioteer or stood aloft on a car. Hence, even for criminals who deserved extreme and exemplary punishment, there arose a feeling of compassion; for it was not, as it seemed, for the public good, but to glut one man's cruelty, that they were being destroyed.

Moses Hadas, ed., *The Complete Works of Tacitus*, trans. Alfred John Church and William Jackson Brodribb (New York: Modern Library Edition, 1942), pp. 380-81; *Annals*, XV (44).

martyrdom by violent antipagan acts, although church officials often discouraged such "voluntary martyrdom" lest it provoke mass retaliation.

Persecution as a policy was a failure; it did not eliminate Christianity. Quite the contrary—many influential persons in the Empire had become Christians. Moreover, persecution did not avert disasters, which continued to befall the Roman state whether it persecuted Christians or not. In 311 and 313, respectively, the persecuting emperors Galerius and Maximinus officially abandoned the policy. And Constantine the Great, in agreement with his rival Licinius, in 313 confirmed the Edict of Milan, by which Christians might exist again, own property, and build their own churches, so long as they did nothing against public order. The state was to be neutral in matters of religion.

Christians had often called for universal toleration. "It is a privilege of nature," wrote the North African Christian Tertullian (c 160-230), "that everyone should worship as he pleases," and almost a century later Lactantius (d. c 325) said that, while Christians believed that their god was the god of all, whether they liked it or not, Christians did not force anyone to worship him and were not angry with those who did not. But once the Christians were free from persecution, it was not long before many forgot this view that religion was a matter of free choice. In the later fourth and in the fifth centuries the pleas for toleration would come from pagans.

The Conversion of Constantine

In 312, the year before he associated himself with the edict of toleration, Constantine had a religious experience akin to that of St. Paul. Just before going into battle against his rival Maxentius, the emperor supposedly saw in the heavens the sign of a cross against the sun and the words, "Conquer in this sign." He put the sign on the battle standards of his army, won the battle, and attributed the victory to the Christian god. Though the story has been challenged, there is little evidence for the counterargument that Constantine acted because he simply foresaw the eventual triumph of Christianity, since few at this time would have predicted such a victory, and his army remained predominantly pagan. Though he continued to appease the sun god as well as the god of the Christians, Constantine regarded himself as Christian. Before his death in 337 official policy held that confiscated church lands had to be returned, even if it was necessary to draw upon the state to do so, implying steady transfers of funds from Constantine's private imperial wealth.

One last formal attempt was made to reconstruct the old polytheism of the Empire. The emperor Julian (called the Apostate) (361-363), a pagan and philosopher much influenced by the Neoplatonists and in particular by Plotinus (205-270), sought to merge the old classical and rational philosophies with the mysticism of Egypt. However, Julian's restoration of paganism died with him, and Christianity quickly regained and extended its position. In 375 Emperor Gratian gave up the title Pontifex Maximus, so dear to Claudius and Domitian, and refused to use the public treasury to support popular pagan festivals. At last Theodosius I (379-395) made Christianity the official religion of the Empire, abolished the pagan calendar, and in 394 began to persecute pagans. Paganism continued in the countryside, in the army, and among the upper classes and the

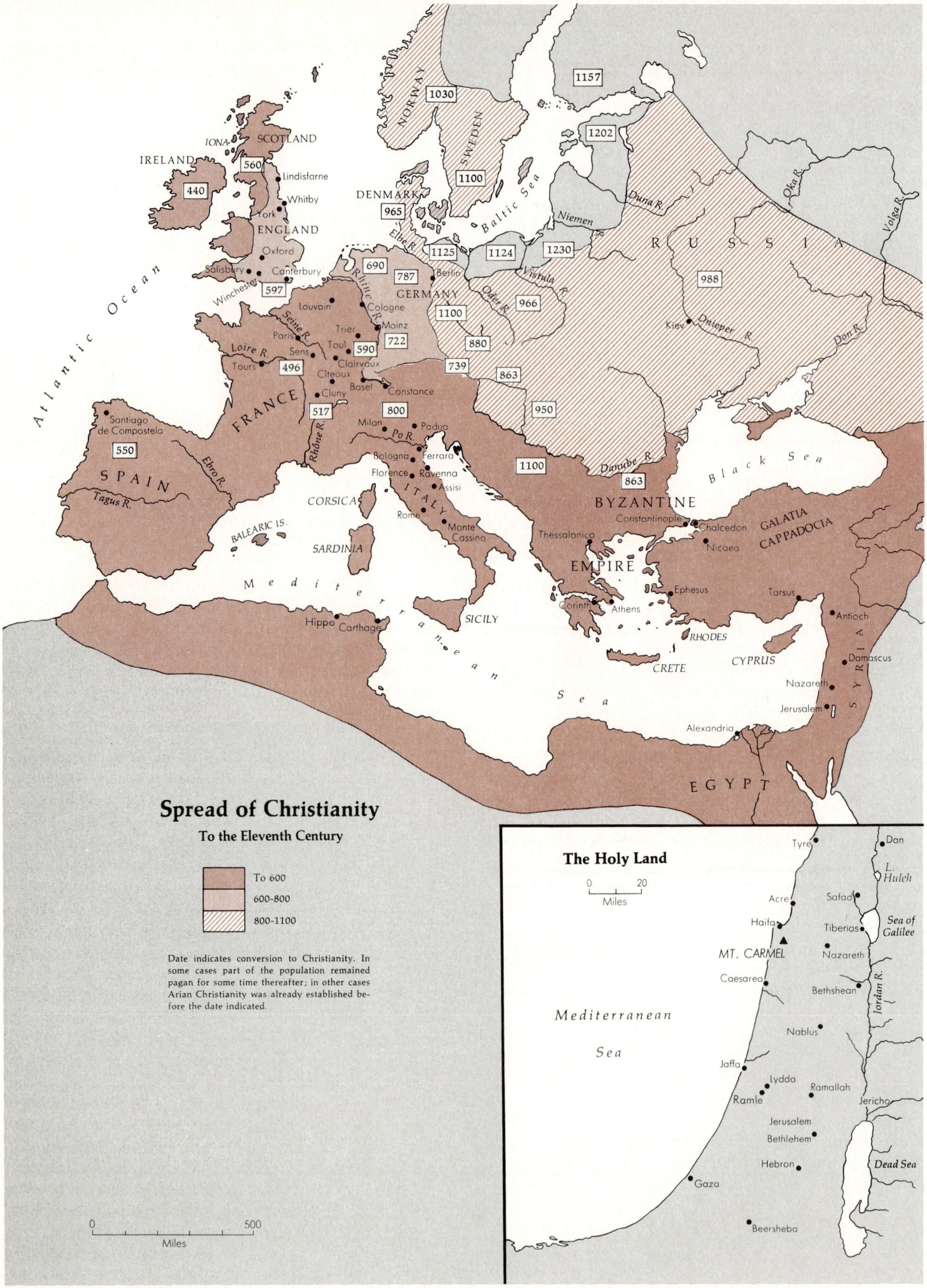

Spread of Christianity

To the Eleventh Century

Date indicates conversion to Christianity. In some cases part of the population remained pagan for some time thereafter; in other cases Arian Christianity was already established before the date indicated.

This massive bust of Constantine the Great stresses his strength and brute power. The marble sculpture is from the early fourth century A.D. The head stands over eight feet high; a hand and two feet have also survived from the original statue, which was forty feet high.

intellectuals for another century or so, but in the cities it was no longer an organized force.

IV THE ORGANIZATION OF THE CHURCH

To maintain order, the Christian community needed some authority to discipline or even oust those who misbehaved. It had to organize to survive in the midst of an empire originally committed in principle to its suppression. Prophets, or teachers, appeared in the very first churches, the informal groups of Christians organized by the missionaries; soon elders, overseers, and presidents followed.

More and more, an overseer (Greek *episkopos*) exercised authority over a compact administrative area, his *see;* this was the bishop, who became the key figure in church administration. Each see claimed to have been founded by one of the original apostles, and its bishop thus held office through apostolic succession. Since it had been Jesus himself who had chosen the apostles, every bishop, in effect, became his direct spiritual heir. Groups of bishoprics or episcopal sees were often gathered together into larger units under an archbishop, or head overseer (*archiepiskopos*). Just as the bishop often had his headquarters in a Roman *civitas*, or city-state unit, and exercised authority over the churches in the adjoining countryside, so the archbishop governed the civitates from a mother city, a *metropolis*, usually the capital of a Roman province, and his see was called a *province.*

At the top of the hierarchy stood the bishop of the imperial capital, Rome itself, the father of them all—*papa*, or pope—who claimed supreme authority. The prestige of Rome contributed powerfully to his claim. So did the association of Peter and Paul with Rome. Jesus had said to Peter, "Thou art Peter and upon this rock I will build my church"—a celebrated pun, since the Greek word for Peter is *Petros*, and that for rock is *petra.* Because Peter had been martyred in Rome, the bishops of that city could claim that Christ himself had picked Rome as the "rock" upon which to build, a claim that was embodied in the "Petrine theory." The bishops of the great cities of the eastern Mediterranean—Alexandria and Antioch—however, claimed to exercise a paternal rule equal in authority to that of the pope. They called themselves *patriarch* (fatherly governor). Still later, after Constantinople had been made the imperial capital (A.D. 330), its bishop, also a patriarch, would oppose papal claims to supremacy.

With the removal of imperial government from Rome, the popes gradually made themselves more and more responsible for the government of the great city. And as the barbarians began to pour in and Rome itself came under attack, the pope became the surviving symbol of the old Roman sense of order and certainty—a rock indeed. A succession of outstanding men became bishop of Rome, notably Leo the Great, also known as Pope Leo II (440-461). A theologian, splendid administrator, and brave man, he helped save the city from the invading Hun, Attila. By the time of the breakup of the Roman Empire in the fifth century, few in the West would have disputed the claim of papal supremacy. The papacy had emerged as the firmest institution in a new and unstable world.

The government of the church had taken shape gradually, in response to need. The church strengthened its organization by utilizing the existing political machinery of the Roman Empire, placing its major officials in centers that were already administrative capitals. Bishops and archbishops, meeting in council, determined which religious ideas or practices would be accepted and which rejected, which writings were deemed truly Christian and which false. In this way the church selected the twenty-seven canonical books of the New Testament, written in Greek, and the Old Testament writings as preserved in a Greek translation from the Hebrew. In the Greek (or Eastern) church today these orthodox versions are still in use; in the Roman (or Western) church the Latin version, called the Vulgate and made by St. Jerome after 386, is used. (Many of the writings that the church rejected have survived; though not canonical, they have much interest for the modern historian and theologian.)

Bishops and Their Duties: Church and State

Each bishop presided over several churches. Each church was under the care of a priest (Greek *presbyteros*, or elder) who had been qualified by special training and by a ceremony of ordination. The area served by each church and its priest came to be known as the parish. In the early church the office of deacon, often held by a man who had other occupations besides the service of the church, had much importance. In some of the early churches, the congregation itself elected its officers, and the church was governed by boards of elders (presbyteries); but the system of appointment from above prevailed over that of election, even if the congregation was consulted. Before long, then, a distinction between those who were merely faithful worshipers (the laity) and those who conducted the worship and administered the affairs of the church (the clergy) became well defined. Despite frequent rumbles of protest during the two thousand years of Christianity, and despite differences of degree, most Christian sects maintain some distinction between laity and clergy.

By the seventh century the broad lines of church government in both the East and the West had been established. The organization was hierarchical—that is, there was a regular series of levels from subordinate to superior, from priest to pope or patriarch, somewhat as military lines of command run from lieutenant to general. But at almost every level there were councils made up of officials who met to debate problems and to make decisions. Church government, then, was no simple relation of silent underling to commanding superior; in

The Virgin and saints, from the chapel of the Coptic monastery of St. Apollo in Egypt. From the second century until the Arab conquest in 641, Christian Copts formed the dominant religion in Egypt. Their practices probably remained the closest to the historical origins of any of the early Christian groups. This fresco dates from the sixth century.

The abbey of Monte Cassino, south of Rome, was rebuilt after being destroyed in World War II. The Benedictine monastic order was founded here in 529.

these early centuries the critical decisions were made by assemblies rather than by individuals. Once the papacy had become firmly established, however, the popes asserted—when they could—that the pope was superior even to a general council and was not bound by its decisions.

After the conversion of Constantine, the first Christian emperor, the election of bishops obviously became a matter of particular concern to the state. To retain the initiative, the officials of the church worked to put the election of each new bishop into the hands of the clergy of the cathedral (episcopal church) of the see. Practice remained uneven, however: sometimes the citizens simply gave assent to an accomplished fact by approving elections; at other times the people had real power, as when Roman mobs under the sway of rival political leaders controlled the choices for the papal throne. Since bishops often exercised actual governing power and had their own law courts, lay rulers often insisted on approving or even selecting them. The problem of the degree to which laymen could participate in the choice of the bishops remained acute in the West down to the eleventh century, as the popes strove to have the ultimate say, and this struggle was one of the major causes of debate by which present democratic institutions slowly evolved.

The point becomes most clear when we look at the very different history of church and state in the East. In the East, the emperor at Constantinople (today, Istanbul) usually acted as the real head of both church and state. No organized clerical body could tell him where to stop. Although religious disputes regularly broke out in the Eastern empire, no clear-cut moral or legal code set limits to the emperor's rights. The Russian church inherited this Eastern tradition. In the West, however, pope and emperor continually struggled over the issue. Gradually it was accepted that no single person or institution could wield both political and religious power. Such an understanding probably helped pave the way for further acceptance of the rights of smaller groups and of individuals.

Monasticism

Deacons, priests, bishops, archbishops all serve the laity and are called *secular* clergy (*sœcularis*, temporal). Early in the history of the church, however, another kind of devotee to Christianity appeared in Syria and Egypt—the monk, a man who felt that he must deny the urges of his own flesh and become an ascetic. The New Testament, in Paul's writings and elsewhere, extolled the merits of abstaining from sexual relations if possible, and from all other fleshly indulgence. Therefore, monks would leave civilization behind and go into the desert to live in solitude, meditation, and prayer, subsisting on the minimum of food and drink. By the third century there were many of these hermits, who enjoyed reputations for extreme holiness and often competed with each other in torturing themselves or in self-denial. Some lived in trees or in holes in the ground; others on the top of columns, to which they would haul up food supplied by pious followers.

To keep extremists from using the cloak of holiness to

cover un-Christian self-assertion, certain leaders, such as the Egyptian hermit St. Anthony, early drew monks to themselves and formed communities, living by a rule. The Greek St. Basil (c 330-379) wrote the most famous of these rules, which became standard in the Greek church and still regulates Greek monasticism today. Basil prescribed celibacy and poverty but combated the dangers of extreme asceticism and isolation by requiring that the monks work in the fields or elsewhere to make their communities as self-supporting as possible. Because after Basil monks lived by a rule, they are known as the *regular clergy* (Latin *regula*, rule), as contrasted with the secular clergy. In Greek monasticism, the monks not only worshiped together but also ate and worked together. Although dedicated to a life outside this wicked world, they were also required to do works of charity, such as setting up orphanages and hospitals.

In the West the problem of secular sophistication was met by the rule of St. Benedict (c 480-c 549), who founded an abbey at Monte Cassino in southern Italy. His Latin rule, like Basil's Greek rule, prescribed hard work for all and urged the monks to be tolerant of one another's interests and infirmities. In the West particularly, the monks broke new ground around their monasteries, acted as pioneers in opening up the wilderness, performed missionary service among the unconverted heathen tribes, and provided much charitable and medical work among the poor and the sick. In both East and West, scholarship early became one of the recognized occupations for monks. The monastic scribe, who copied the works of the ancients and built up the library of his foundation, helped preserve the literature of the past.

Tensions often arose between secular and regular clergy, each feeling that its own work was more valuable to Christianity as a whole. Constant care and strict government were needed to maintain the high ideals of the monasteries and of the convents for women that soon appeared. This continuing need prompted successive monastic reform movements that played a major role in Christian history. The abbots of the greater monasteries often participated, along with the bishops, in the councils of the church, and thus helped form Christian doctrine and frame the rules of church observance and discipline.

V THE DEVELOPMENT OF CHRISTIAN THOUGHT

The Christian clergy could hardly have attained their great power had they not been essential intermediaries between this visible world of actuality and an invisible other world that, to the devout Christian, is as real as this one. In Christianity certain important ideas about the other world are embodied in ritual acts called *sacraments*. These sacraments, administered by the clergy, are central to an understanding of Christian doctrine.

The central mystery (or rite known only to the initiate) of Christianity was the sacrament of the *Eucharist*, or Holy Communion. It was a mystery made available to simple men and women as part of ordinary living by the services of the church. The sacrament stems from Jesus' last supper with his disciples, where he

> *. . . took bread, and blessed it, and brake it, and gave it to the disciples, and said, Take, eat; this is my body. And he took the cup, and gave thanks, and gave it to them, saying, Drink ye all of it; For this is my blood of the new testament, which is shed for many for the remission of sins* (Matthew *26:26–28).*

By the third century, the Eucharist had become a ceremony that made the Christian believer feel a personal link with God and experience the wonder of salvation. If the sacrament of *baptism* figuratively washed away the stain of original sin and made a person a Christian, then the sacrament of the Eucharist enabled one to remain in Christian communion—subject always to good behavior—and to sustain its faith and fellowship. There were to be many grave theological disputes over the doctrine of the Eucharist, notably at the time of the Protestant revolt, but it has remained central to the drama of the Christian faith even when, as for some Protestants, it is simply a commemoration of the Lord's (or the Last) Supper.

Theological explanations were given for this symbolic act of the Mass, or Eucharist. Adam, who began with the chance for a perfect life on earth in the Garden of Eden, disobeyed God, was driven from Eden, and was exposed to death and suffering on earth. This was Adam's "original sin," and all his descendants shared his fate. But the Jews, in spite of individual or group backsliding, kept alive their faith in God; after generations of suffering, God took mercy and sent to earth his only son, Jesus. By suffering on the cross, Jesus atoned for human sins, made redemption to God the Father, and made it possible in the future for faithful Christians to be saved, despite Adam's sin, to enjoy in the other world after death the immortal happiness they could only anticipate in this one, since this world is no longer the Garden of Eden.

Even so elementary an outline of the doctrine of salvation bristles with the kinds of difficulties Christians have been arguing about for centuries. What was the relation between God the Father and his only begotten son? In this context, what does the term *begotten* actually mean? What *was* Adam's original sin? How did one attain salvation? Was it enough to belong to the church, or must there be some inward sign? This last question raises what has been for two thousand years perhaps the central point of debate in Christianity—the problem of faith versus good works.

Those who believe that salvation is primarily an inward and emotional matter for the individual Christian—a matter of faith—tend to minimize the importance of outward acts, even of the sacraments. Those who believe that a person must behave in strict accordance with God's directions to be saved put more emphasis upon good works. Either position, carried to its logical extreme, poses great dangers: on the one hand, the withering of the structure of the church and the taking over of the priestly role by the individual believer; on the other, the withering of the individual's role and dictatorship over daily behavior by the clergy.

As time passed the sacraments grew in number to seven: (1) *baptism*, by which a person was washed of the stain of original sin and brought into mystical union with Christ; (2) *confirmation*, by which one was formally brought into the discipline of the church; (3) the *Eucharist*, the central act of Christian observance; (4) *penance*, whereby a confessed and repentant sinner was granted absolution (forgiven) by the priest, having the guilt of sin and eternal punishment lifted, subject to a temporal punishment assigned as penance; this temporal punishment might or might not be sufficient to satisfy God's justice, and hence a given penance itself could not guarantee the penitent's salvation; (5) *extreme unction*, "the last rites of the Church," a ceremony performed by the priest at the dying moments of the Christian in preparation for the life to come; (6) *ordination*, the ceremony by which a candidate was made a priest; and (7) *matrimony*, holy marriage. Baptism and the Eucharist have remained as sacraments in almost all the Protestant groups. Of the other sacraments, the one that has been most heavily attacked and most vigorously rejected by Protestants generally is that of penance.

Heresy: To the Nicene Creed

The early centuries of Christianity saw a series of struggles to define the accepted doctrines of the religion—*orthodoxy*—and to protect them against the challenge of rival or unsound doctrinal ideas—*heresy*. The first heresies appeared almost as soon as the first clergy. In fact, the issue between those who wished to admit gentiles, who were outside the law, and those who wished to confine the Gospel to the Jews foreshadowed the kind of issue that was to confront Christianity in the first few centuries, when heresy followed on heresy. The points at issue sometimes seem unimportant to us today, but we must not regard these religious debates as trivial; people believed that salvation depended upon the proper definition and defense of religious belief and practice. Also, bitter political, economic, and national issues often underlay disputes that took a theological form.

It has always been difficult to understand and explain how evil can exist in a world created by a good God. The *Gnostics* (from the Greek word for knowledge) affirmed that only the world of the spirit is real and good; the physical world is evil, or an evil illusion. Thus they could not accept the Old Testament, whose god created this world; they regarded him as a fiend or decided that this world had been created by Satan. Nor could they accept Jesus' human life, work, and martyrdom in this world—an essential part of Christian belief. They could not accept baptism, because to them water was matter, or venerate a crucifix, which to them was simply two pieces of wood. Like the Zoroastrians, with their god of good and their god of evil, the Gnostics were dualists. Clearly heretical, the Gnostics focused on Christ's miracles and on other sorts of magic. Among them there arose a sharp distinction between an elite, whose members led especially pure lives, and the ordinary flock, less able to bear self-denial or the mysteries of the faith, who usually worked hard to support the elite.

Closely related to Gnosticism were the ideas of Mani, a third-century Mesopotamian prophet who called himself the Apostle of Jesus. He preached that the god of light and goodness and his emanations were in constant conflict with the god of darkness, evil, and matter and his emanations. These Manichaean dualistic views became immensely popular, especially in North Africa during the third and fourth centuries. The Christians combated them, and throughout the Middle Ages tended to label all doctrinal opposition by the generic term *Manichaean*. Yet dualist ideas persisted, more or less underground, and cropped up every few decades for a thousand years.

Within Christianity, heresy sometimes involved very practical problems. The emperor Constantine faced the so-called Donatist movement in North Africa. The movement arose because a number of priests yielded to the demands of Roman authorities during the Roman persecutions of the Christians after 303 and handed the sacred books over to them. After the edicts of toleration of 311 and 313, these "handers-over" (*traditores*) had resumed their role as priests. Donatus, bishop of Carthage, and his followers maintained that the sacraments administered by such traditores were invalid. Donatus' wish to punish collaborationist priests was understandable but divisive, because once a believer questioned the validity of the sacraments as received from one priest, he might question it as received from any other. Amid much bitterness and violence Constantine ruled that once a priest had been properly ordained, the sacraments administered at his hands had validity, even if the priest himself had acted badly. The effectiveness of the sacraments derived solely from their performance, not from the moral character of the clergy. But the Donatists persisted in their views, and North Africa was much troubled by the continued rivalry between them and their opponents.

Heresy also arose over essentially philosophical issues. One such was Arianism, named after Arius (c 280-336), a priest of Alexandria. Early in the fourth century Arius taught that if God the Father had begotten God the Son through God the Holy Ghost, then God the Son, as begotten, could not be exactly of the "same essence" (*homoousios* in Greek) as God the Father, but must be somehow inferior to, or dependent upon, or at the least later in time than his begetter, who was of a "similar essence" (*homoiousios* in Greek), but not the same. It is difficult to refute this position. Far from a quarrel over one letter (*homoousios* or *homoiousios*), Arius' view threatened to diminish the divinity of Christ as God the Son and to separate Christ from the Trinity.

Arius' bitter opponent, Athanasius (c 293-373), patriarch of Alexandria and "the father of orthodoxy," fought him passionately, disdaining logic and emphasizing mystery. Athanasius and his followers maintained that Christians simply had to accept as a matter of faith that Father and Son are identical in essence, and that the Son is equal to, independent of, and contemporaneous with the Father. Even though the Father begat the Son, it was heresy to say that there was ever a time when the Son did not exist. To Athanasius, the Arian view stood in the way of the doctrine relating to salvation, which he considered central to Christianity. In the Greek East especially, this philosophical argument was fought out not only among churchmen and thinkers, but in the barbershops and among the longshoremen. A visitor to Constantinople complained, "I ask how much I have to pay; they talk of the born and the unborn. I want to know the price of bread; they answer 'the father is greater than the son.' I ask if my bath is ready; they say 'the son has been made out of nothing.'"

After trying to stay out of the quarrel and urging the bishops to stop discussing it, Constantine realized that for political reasons it would have to be settled. In 325 he summoned the first council of the whole church, a council called *ecumenical* (from the Greek *oikoumene*, the inhabited world), at Nicaea (now Iznik) near Constantinople. A large majority of the bishops decided in favor of the Athanasian view, which was then embodied in the Nicene Creed, issued with all the force of an imperial decree by Constantine himself. The emperor had presided over the council, and against his will found himself assuming the role of head of the church, giving legal sanction to a purely doctrinal decision, and so playing the role both of Caesar and of pope. In time this "Caesaropapism" became the tradition of empire and church in the East.

But the decree of Nicaea did not dispose of Arianism. Arians disobeyed; Constantine himself wavered; his immediate successors on the imperial throne were themselves Arians. Between 325 and 381 there were thirteen more councils that discussed the problem, deciding first one way, then another. One pagan historian sardonically commented that one could no longer travel on the roads because they were so cluttered with throngs of bishops riding off to one council or another. Traces of Arianism remained in the Empire for several centuries after Nicaea. Because the missionary Ulfilas (c 311-c 383) preached the Arian form of Christianity to the Goths beyond the frontiers of the Empire, the heresy was spread among most of the Germanic peoples then being converted to Christianity, especially through his translation of the Bible into Gothic. Later, when the German tribes took over large parts of the Empire in the West, the Arian heresy would return in force.

The Debate over the Two Natures of Christ

Long before Arianism disappeared, a new and related controversy had shaken the Eastern portion of the Empire to its foundations. Exactly what was the relationship of Christ the god and Christ the man? He was both man and god, but how was this possible? And was the Virgin Mary—a human woman—the mother only of his human aspect, or, if not, how could a human being be the mother of god?

One extreme position separated the human nature of Christ from the divine and so refused to regard the human virgin as the mother of god. This view later became unfairly linked with the name of Nestorius (d. c 451), patriarch of Constantinople in the early fifth century, and its followers were called Nestorians. They

THE NICENE CREED

We believe in one God, the Father all-sovereign,
maker of all things, both visible and invisible:
And in one Lord Jesus Christ,
the Son of God,
begotten of the Father, and only-begotten,
that is from the essence [*ousia*] of the Father.
God from God
Light from light,
True God from true God,
begotten not made,
being of one essence [*homoousion*] with the Father;
by whom all things were made,
both things in heaven and things on earth;
who for us men and for our salvation came down
from heaven and
was made flesh, was made man
suffered and rose again on the third day,
ascended into heaven,
cometh to judge quick and dead:
And in the Holy Spirit.

But those who say
that there was once when he was not
and before he was begotten he was not
and he was made of things that were not
Or maintain that the Son of God is of a different
essence or substance
or created or subject to moral change or
alteration—
Them doth the Catholic and Apostolic Church
anathematize [condemn to damnation].

See Henry Bettenson, ed., *Documents of the Christian Church*, 2nd ed. (London: Oxford University Press, 1963), p. 35.

This mosaic from the fifth century shows Christ as a warrior, dressed in the uniform of a Roman legionary. His feet are planted on the heads of a serpent and a lion, and the inscription on the book he holds reads, "I am the Way, the Truth and the Life." The cross is carried over his shoulder, much as a sword. The mosaic, finished by 519, though begun earlier, is in the Bishop's Palace of Ravenna.

took refuge in Asia—Persia, and beyond to China. The other extreme view was that of the *monophysites* ("one-nature-ites"), who argued that Christ's human and divine natures were totally merged; they carried their thesis so far that they almost forgot Christ's human attributes and tended to make him a god only.

Again the dispute flared into physical violence in the East; again the decision hung in the balance; again the emperor (now Marcian, who reigned 450-457) called an ecumenical council at Chalcedon, near Constantinople, in 451. Supported by Pope Leo the Great, the council condemned monophysitism and, like the Council of Nicaea, took a mystical rather than a rational position: the true believer must believe in the two natures of Christ, human and divine, coexisting yet not distinct from each other; thus the Virgin is properly called the mother of god. The council also recognized Constantinople as having the same religious status in the East as Rome had in the West.

Like the decision at Nicaea, the decision at Chalcedon did not definitively dispose of the opposition. Monophysites were concentrated in Egypt and Syria, and they apparently expressed in their religious beliefs the resentment of the ancient Mediterranean cities of Alexandria and Antioch against the new domination by the upstart Constantinople, and the Egyptian and Syrian dislike for the Greeks who dominated at the capital. So partly because it was identified with what we would call nationalism, monophysitism did not die out, and the emperors strove to deal with it by one compromise or another. Since there were few monophysites in the West, the Roman church regarded the issue as closed; each time an emperor at Constantinople tried to appease his Egyptian and Syrian monophysite subjects, he was condemned by the pope for heresy. For two centuries the problem remained unsolved.

The disaffection of the monophysite provinces of Syria and Egypt was to facilitate their conquest in the seventh century by the new religion of Islam. To this day there are still monophysite Christians in Egypt, Syria, and Ethiopia, and Nestorian remnants in farther Asia. The continuing quarrel illustrates the lasting political impact that theological disagreement has provided.

VI THOUGHT AND LETTERS IN THE FIRST CHRISTIAN CENTURIES

Though a good deal of dislike and misunderstanding had always characterized the attitudes of most Greeks and Romans toward each other, Roman admiration for Greek literature and art deeply influenced the work of Roman writers and artists. The triumph of Christianity tended to contribute new sources of misunderstanding and tension to the relationships between Easterners and Westerners. The political divisions imposed by Diocletian and repeated by many of his successors expressed the geographic distinction between Eastern and Western provinces that corresponded roughly to the old Greece and Rome. As Germanic inroads began increasingly to disrupt communications in the fourth and fifth centuries and to threaten all the established institutions in the West, the opportunities for Westerners to know Greek and embrace the early classical tradition decreased. In the Eastern provinces few except soldiers and professional administrators had ever spoken or read Latin, though it remained the official language of legislation at Constantinople through the fifth century. Despite the growing division, however, the literature of the late Roman and early Christian world may be treated as a whole, often because of subject matter.

The Turn from Pagan to Christian Literature

In the West pagan literature declined and virtually disappeared, while in the East a few passionate devotees of the old gods still made their voices heard. Constantine's nephew Julian the Apostate was taught by a group of anti-Christian pagan scholars. As emperor he wrote satirical and moralistic essays and orations.

Christian writings increasingly took the center of the stage. In the East, writers devoted much energy to polemical writings on the burning doctrinal questions and disputes of the day. In both East and West the best minds among Christians faced the problem of how to treat Greek and Roman literature. A few thinkers, mostly in the West and especially at first, advised against reading anything but Scripture, for fear of pagan error. Later they acknowledged that one had to read the great pagans of the past to be able to refute pagan philosophical ideas. Still, there was always the danger that in the pleasure of reading a delightful classical author one might forget that the prime concern was to expose his errors and refute his arguments. The Greek Christians worried far less about this problem. In the fourth century three great Cappadocian fathers (so called for the province in Asia Minor where they were born)—Basil, author of the communal monastic rule; his brother, Gregory of Nyssa (d. c 394); and their friend, Gregory of Nazianzos (329-389)—all had excellent classical educations and used the techniques of the pagan philosophers to discuss religious ideas.

One of the most important writers in Latin was Jerome (340-420), who studied with Gregory of Nazianzos and who produced the Latin Bible (the Vulgate) as the climax of a life of devoted scholarship that had made him the master of Hebrew and Greek as well as Latin. Ambrose (c 340-397), a Roman civil servant who became bishop of Milan, wrote many theological works and commentaries. Christianizing much that he found in the classics, he transformed Cicero's Stoic concept of duty to the state into a Christian concept of duty to God. Ambrose put his own preaching into practice when he publicly humiliated the emperor Theodosius I (r. 379-395) and forced him to do penance for savagely punishing some rioters. The act symbolized the Western church's insistence that, in matters of morals and faith, church would be supreme over the state—an attitude that ran exactly counter to the practice growing up in the East.

Augustine, the Early Church's Most Influential Figure

His Early Life We know Augustine (354-430), the greatest of the Western church Fathers, intimately through his famous autobiography—*The Confessions*—written when he was forty-three and a bishop. He was born in a small market town in what is now Algeria, inland from Carthage, the administrative and cultural center of the African provinces. Here the population still spoke Punic (Phoenician), but the upper classes were Latin-speaking, wholly Roman in their outlook, and deeply imbued with the classical traditions of Rome. Prosperous planters lived on their great estates, while peasants toiled in the fields and olive groves. The Africans admired eloquence, disputation at law, and education, which they applied to religion. With a sense of irony, Augustine would reflect upon the society in which he matured, even as he grew away from it.

Of modest means and often at odds with one another, Augustine's father and his devoutly Christian and possessive mother were determined that he should be given a good education, for this was the path to advancement. But all that his teachers did was force him to memorize classical Latin texts and to comment on them in detail. Augustine was so bored that he never did learn Greek, and so was cut off from the original philosophers and forced to pick up their ideas at second hand, largely through Cicero. His parents' ambitions for him prevented him from getting married at seventeen, like most of his contemporaries. While at the university, which he left for a year for lack of funds, Augustine, barely out of his adolescence, took a concubine, as was the custom, with whom he lived happily for fifteen years, and by whom he had a son.

Disappointed with his reading of the Bible, which he found insufficiently polished and too confining, Augustine at nineteen joined the Manichaeans. Rejecting the Old Testament and its stern paternal Jehovah, and considering themselves true radical Christians, the Manichaeans were highly influential in fashionable Carthaginian society. Nonetheless, they were regarded by pagans and Christians alike as subversive and had been declared illegal. The "elect" among them fasted and abstained from sexual relations and from labor in the world, while the "hearers" learned Mani's wisdom from their secret books and supported the elite. Gone were Augustine's plans to become a lawyer, as his mother had wished; he determined to learn and teach the Manichaean "wisdom," passively keeping the good side of his nature unsullied by the encroaching baseness of the fleshly side.

When he went back to his birthplace as a teacher, his mother was so angry with him for having become a Manichaean that she would not let him into the house. But the static quality of Manichaean belief, the naiveté of its rituals, and the disappointing intellectual level of its leaders began to disillusion Augustine, and he returned to Carthage to teach rhetoric. Highly placed friends invited him to move to Italy. Steeling himself against his mother's pleas, he sailed off. At twenty-eight he was appointed professor of rhetoric at Milan, the seat of the imperial court. The job required him to compose and deliver the official speeches of praise for the emperor and for the consuls—propaganda for the official programs. He owed his advancement partly to the wishes of influential pagans to balance the orthodox Christian influence at court with that of a Manichaean.

Conversion; the Confessions But at Milan, Augustine abandoned the Manichaean faith and fell under the spell of Ambrose, the bishop of Milan, who stood staunchly against the pagan and pro-pagan elements in the city and against the Arian Goths, who formed the main force of the imperial garrison. Better educated than Augustine, a superb preacher, indifferent to the demands of the flesh, Ambrose stimulated Augustine to reexamine all his ideas. And Augustine's mother, who had followed him to Milan, eagerly drank in Ambrose's words "as a fountain of water."

Augustine toyed briefly with Stoicism. He liked the Neoplatonist idea that material things of this world were reflections of ideas in the eternal other world, and that there were means—to be painfully achieved—by which one could move away from the external world of the senses and toward the One. Augustine's world widened. Evil, instead of looming at the center of it, took a less terrifyingly prominent place; his God became more distant, more powerful, more mysterious than Mani's God. But in the end Augustine could not accept the Neoplatonist view that a person, unaided, could by reason alone attain to the vision of God; he was therefore ready for conversion to Christianity.

This was a major step, involving not only the abandonment of Augustine's promising worldly career (including his engagement to marry a girl of a rich and prominent family), but also the rite of baptism, which was then felt to be so great a spiritual ordeal that many Christians preferred to put it off until their deathbeds, as the emperor Constantine had done. At Easter 387, aged thirty-three, he was baptized by Ambrose. Soon afterward—his mother having died—Augustine returned to his native North Africa.

In his home town he soon found himself in intellectual combat with his former co-religionists, the Manichees, debating them publicly, writing pamphlets against them, arguing that evil—the central problem that worried them—was in large part simply human bad habits; once a person had derived pleasure from an evil act, the memory of the pleasure prompted doing it again. The solution was to allow God to make one take pleasure in good actions, to make one hunger for perfection. Within three years Augustine had been forced into the priesthood by the demands of a local congregation, and in 395 he became bishop of the large town of Hippo (the modern Bône) in Algeria. Here he wrote the *Confessions*, describing his spiritual journey in an effort to lead his reader to God. Augustine's great book—in its selection of individual experiences, its vivid sketches of persons and places, its communication of Augustine's familiar intimacy with God, and its honesty in reporting his past behavior and feelings—was wholly original.

Augustine's gravest practical problem was the Donatists, who regarded themselves as the only true church and who outnumbered the Catholics in Hippo. He preached against them, wrote pamphlets against them, turned out a popular set of verses satirizing them. Convinced that there could be no salvation outside the church, Augustine also persecuted the Donatists when the Christian emperors began in 399 to take severe measures to suppress paganism—itself so recently the imperial persecuting faith.

When the Goths sacked Rome in the year 410, refugees poured into North Africa with accounts of the fear that had gripped the inhabitants and the ruthlessness of the barbarians. Though no longer the imperial capital, Rome was still the symbol of the imperial tradition and of all ancient culture. The North African governors, worried about the stability of the province, issued an edict of toleration for the Donatists. Some blamed the sack of Rome on the abandonment of the old gods in favor of Christianity. Augustine protested and contrasted the City of Man, the secular world where evil was commonplace, with the City of God, toward which history was moving humanity spiritually.

The City of God In a new work, *The City of God*, written between 413 and 425, Augustine combated the pagan argument that it was Christianity that had been responsible for the catastrophic sack of Rome. It was easy to show why many pagan empires had fallen in the past, and Augustine quickly moved beyond his original subject. Virtually ignoring the recent mystery religions, he attacked the core of traditional pagan worship and of pagan interpretations of Roman history, systematically demolishing pagan philosophy, in particular the Neoplatonists who had so attracted him in earlier years. All

St. Augustine is shown dictating to a scribe in this illuminated manuscript of the Scriptures.

of them were limited to earthly values, to the mere "earthly city." Honest in seeking and generous in spending their wealth, the Romans had been allowed by God to acquire their great empire; but they became too eager for praise and glory. True glory belonged only to the citizens of the City of God, *civitas Dei.* Though apparently mixed together on earth, the community of those who served the devil in the earthly city would be separated in the afterlife from those who served God, the Christians, who even in this world lived in a heavenly community. As the demons took over Rome because the Romans had not submitted to the authority of Christ, so only in that heavenly City of God—when death itself would be defeated—could the Christian achieve the true peace. Augustine thus elaborated a complete Christian philosophy of history.

Free Will and Predestination Later in life Augustine found himself engaged in a final philosophical controversy with Pelagius (c 354-420), a British-born Christian layman who had lived for many years in Rome and who believed that humans not only could, but must, perfect themselves. He denied original sin and believed in free will. Yet such an exaltation of human possibilities, highly attractive at many times in history, is in its essence non-Christian, since it exalts human beings and diminishes God's majesty. Pelagius' ideas instantly affected questions of Christian behavior. For example, if there were no original sin, then newborn infants could not be guilty of it, and infant baptism was unnecessary. The Pelagian message, that one must simply will oneself to obey God's commandments wholly, virtually meant that every Christian must lead a monk's life. In Rome many rich upper-class Christians, who served the imperial regime, used judicial torture on prisoners, and led luxurious lives, regarded Pelagius' views as a summons to reform and purify themselves.

Augustine fought Pelagius' ideas and claims, recognizing that for the first time he had met intellectual opponents of his own caliber, skilled at disputation, and he feared for "the crisis of piety" that the Pelagians could create. On the practical level, he preferred to see zealous, rich, puritanical radicals give their property to the church rather than directly to the poor, to assure its growth and security. On the theological level, he argued that not all sins were committed willfully or could be

ST. AUGUSTINE ON THE IMMORTALITY OF THE SOUL

St. Augustine committed his writing to the proof of the goodness and ever-presence of God. For God to be omnipresent, God must be in the individual through the soul, which must be immortal. Thus St. Augustine wrote a sustained treatise "On the Immortality of the Soul," which adduced several reasons for immortality. The first reason, given here, is that the soul was the subject of *disciplina*—that is, of science—which itself is eternal:

If science exists anywhere, and cannot exist except in that which lives; and if it is eternal, and nothing in which an eternal thing exists can be non-eternal; then that in which science exists lives eternally. If we exist who reason, that is, if our mind does, and if our mind cannot reason rightly without science, and if without science no mind can exist except as a mind without science, then science is in the mind of man. Science, moreover, is somewhere, for it exists, and whatever exists cannot be nowhere. Further, science cannot exist except in that which lives. For nothing which is not alive learns anything, and science cannot be in a thing which does not learn.

Again, science is eternal. For what exists and is unchangeable must be eternal. But no one denies that science exists. And whoever admits that it is impossible that a line drawn through the midpoint of a circle is not greater than all lines which are not drawn through the midpoint, and admits that this is a part of science, does not deny that science is unchangeable. Further, nothing in which an eternal thing exists can be non-eternal. For nothing which is eternal ever allows to be taken from it that in which it exists eternally.

Now, truly, when we reason it is the mind which reasons. For only he who thinks reasons. Neither does the body think, nor does the mind receive the help of the body in thinking, since when the mind wishes to think it turns away from the body. For what is thought is thus eternal, and nothing pertaining to the body is thus eternal, therefore the body cannot help the mind as it strives to understand; for it is sufficient if the body does not hamper the mind. Again, without science nobody reasons rightly. For thought is right reasoning moving from things certain to the investigation of things uncertain, and there is nothing certain in an ignorant mind. All that the mind knows, moreover, it contains within itself, nor does knowledge consist in anything which does not pertain to some science. For science is the knowledge of any things whatsoever. Therefore the human mind always lives.

St. Augustine, *On the Immortality of the Soul*, trans. George C. Leckie, in Saxe Commins and Robert N. Linscott, eds., *Man and Spirit: The Speculative Philosophers* (New York: Random House, 1947), pp. 3-4.

willfully avoided; some came through ignorance, weakness, or even against the desire of the sinner. It was for these sins that the church existed. Baptism was the only way to salvation. For Pelagius, humans were no longer infants dependent upon a heavenly Father; they were emancipated beings who must *choose* to be perfect; the idea required true stoicism. For Augustine, human behavior was still dependent upon God, as a nursing infant upon the breast. Human beings were not stoics, not perfect, for they had sinned.

Pelagius had won a considerable following in the Holy Land. In 419 a young and brilliant successor, Julian, bishop of Eclanum, took up the contest with the aging and determined Augustine. Augustine defended the concept of original sin by citing the passage in *Genesis* in which Adam and Eve instantly cover their genitals after they have eaten of the forbidden fruit—*there* was the point, Augustine said, at which sin had arisen. All sexual feelings create guilt; only baptism and the Christian life could wipe it out. Julian answered in disgust that this imagery was blasphemous, making the devil into the true creator of humanity, destroying free will, and sullying the innocence of the newborn. Sexual power, he said, was a natural good, a sixth sense.

Both positions were held by devout Christians. Yet to Julian, Augustine's god seemed unjust, a persecutor of infants, and not the loving god who sacrificed his only son for human salvation. Justice—like the fabric of the Roman law—must underlie all society and all religion. For Augustine, God's justice was indisputable and could not be defined by mere human reason. God had said he would visit the sins of the fathers upon the children, and so Adam's sin had been visited upon all humanity. The world of the fifth century was large enough for both points of view to be heard, but it was Augustine's view that would prevail, for Julian was seen as too intellectual, too insistent on a solely rational god, while the clergy preferred a god whose mystery could not be fully grasped.

In his old age Augustine came to believe that God had already chosen those people who would attain salvation—the elect—and that a person's actions were determined beforehand, that is, predestined. Early African views of the true church as a group of saints helped Augustine arrive at his ideas of predestination. The conflict with the Pelagians—in which Augustine had been concerned to minimize free will, while they maximized it—also made an important contribution. In the face of new barbarian onslaughts—this time from the Vandals—on the hitherto safe shores of North Africa itself, predestination was a message with some comfort for those who had persevered in what was believed to be God's work. The elect would survive all earthly disaster; clearly it comforted Augustine as he faced the destruction of his life's work.

When Augustine died, a year before the Vandals devastated Hippo, a disciple listing his writings said that no one could ever hope to read them all; and yet anyone who did would still have missed the greatest experience—knowing Augustine as a human being, or seeing him in the pulpit and listening to him preach. Although the Catholic church turned away from the doctrine of predestination—always insisting that God's grace must be supplemented by good works before a person could be saved—it still considered Augustine the greatest Western Father of the church. More than a thousand years later, other non-Catholic Christians would return to his teaching of predestination.

The Christian Triumph as a Historical Problem

Why did Christianity triumph in the fourth century? It began as a despised sect of simple enthusiasts in a rich, well-organized, sophisticated society, yet it took over that society. In general, we might postulate the need for a religion of peace in the savage and insecure world of Rome. Jesus' teachings gave Christianity certain advantages over the mystery cults. The cult of Isis lacked a missionary priesthood, that of Mithra any priesthood at all. Isis was chiefly for women; Mithra, altogether for men. Apuleius, a second-century Latin novelist who followed Isis, in the eighth book of his *Golden Ass* described a troupe of eunuch priests of Isis carrying about an image of their "omnipotent and omniparent Syrian goddess" and behaving like a rowdy circus troupe. The complexity of their rites and the lack of a great leader or teacher to make clear the ideas associated with the cult gave it little sustained popular appeal.

So the evangel was really "good news"—with its promise of personal immortality, its admonition to behave with kindness and love toward one's fellow human beings, its goal of an uplifting moral code. The expanding church provided a consoling, beautiful, and dramatic ritual, and the opportunity to become part of the exciting, dangerous, and challenging task of spreading the gospel. The would-be convert could find in it ideas and rites closely related to those of Egyptians, Greeks, and Jews. In the opening of the Gospel of John—"In the beginning was the Word, and the Word was with God, and the Word was God"—the Word was identified with the Greek *logos*, the divine reason, the spark of life, the intellect celebrated by the Neoplatonists. It was at Ephesus, the shrine of the virgin mother-goddess known as Diana of the Ephesians, that quarreling Christian theologians of the fifth century would proclaim the Virgin Mary to be the mother of God. In short, the new beliefs were compatible with various already held beliefs, making possible that merging of bodies of ideas that is called *syncretism*.

From its cradle in Jerusalem, Christianity did not penetrate far into the lands of Zoroastrian, Hindu, and other Eastern faiths, nor into Africa south of the Sahara. Instead, it spread westward along the trade routes of the Mediterranean and north into Europe, essentially within the structure of the Roman Empire, for it needed the political and cultural framework of the state.

Christianity succeeded not only because it set itself

against the earthly compromises and indecencies of pagan cults and the dryness and sterility of later pagan philosophy, but also because it contained so much of Judaism and of paganism—both religious and philosophical, Hellenistic and oriental. Even more important perhaps is the extent to which Christianity allowed the old uses, the old rites and habits, the unintellectual, practical side of religion, to survive, and the extent to which it mastered and tamed pagan habits. So when the crowds of Ephesus in the fifth century hailed the victory of the theologians who were defending the Virgin's motherhood, one might almost hear an echo of the pagan cry that had been directed against St. Paul four centuries earlier, "Great is Diana of the Ephesians." Christmas celebrates the birth of Jesus, but it also marks the turning northward at last of the European winter sun, the promise of its returning warmth; and Easter is an echo of thousands of prehistoric years of celebration of the coming of spring, the resurrection of life in nature.

So Christianity appealed to men and women (though it meant a legal setback for women, since Hebraic myths, such as the story of Eve tempting Adam, replaced Roman law, in which women could own property or be granted a divorce). Christianity offered a new and believable spiritual promise, yet preserved reassuringly familiar elements; it extolled mutual love; it had a capacity for adaptation; it was well led and taught. Moreover, Christianity eventually triumphed within the Roman world because of the organization of the church, something that Jesus had not foreseen, much less planned. The Roman principle of the union of state and church, with the first predominant, was applied in reversed order of importance in the West, the better to give humanity the sense of security it needed in a period of vast and rapid change.

SUMMARY

The Romans relied on religion, not science, to explain their world. The increasing pessimism of the late Roman Empire fostered the growth of astrology, religious cults promising personal salvation, and mystical philosophy.

The Jews under Roman rule were hard to control and divided among various political and religious factions. Many Jews believed in the imminent coming of some sort of deliverer, or Messiah.

Christianity began as a Jewish movement. St. Paul separated Christianity from Judaism and spread its beliefs throughout much of the Empire.

Roman persecution of Christianity was intermittent. It arose because the Christians' refusal to sacrifice to the emperor threatened the unity of the Empire. Despite persecution, Christianity continued to spread.

Constantine ended the persecution in A.D. 312. The emperor Theodosius made Christianity the official religion of the Empire in 395.

In the West the bishop of Rome (the pope) became the surviving symbol of the old Roman sense of order and authority. He was head of the church and an important political figure. In the east the emperor at Constantinople usually acted as the real head of both church and state.

Monasticism arose out of the desire of some Christian believers to escape the temptations of the world. The rule of St. Benedict became the basis for most monasteries in the West.

The development of a complex Christian theology gave rise to many heresies in the early church, which led to both political and theological controversy.

Augustine of Hippo was the most influential figure in the early church. His writings have continued to influence Christians, and his doctrine of predestination was one of the bases of Protestantism.

Christianity had beliefs in common with its rivals, the other mystical religions and philosophic movements. Christianity succeeded because it set itself against the earthly compromises of paganism and the dryness of later pagan philosophy, and because it retained much pagan religious practice and philosophic thought.

chapter five

THE EARLY MIDDLE AGES IN WESTERN EUROPE

The period from the collapse of the Roman Empire in the West down to about A.D. 1000 provides an outstanding example of the breakdown of a whole civilization. Historians used to call the centuries from 500 to 1000 by the name still generally used for the centuries between 1100 and 800 B.C.: *the Dark Ages*. This suggests a gloomy barbarian interruption between a bright classical flowering and a later bright recovery or rebirth (*Renaissance*). But today historians prefer the more neutral term *early Middle Ages*, for they have come to believe that "dark" is a misleading exaggeration. Middle Ages accurately enough suggests a time lying *between* the ancient and the modern world, and the adjective *medieval*—meaning of the middle age—is in general use. Obviously, these terms—*medieval, modern*—are words we use about ourselves; that is, we naturally perceive historical chronology in relation to our own times. Thus there is much (generally fruitless) debate over when medieval history ends and modern history begins.

I THE BREAKDOWN OF ROMAN CIVILIZATION

Much of Roman civilization was lost in these years, but much, notably Christianity, was retained and developed, and many new ways of life and even new techniques were adopted and discovered. New kinds of social relationships arose, combining Roman and barbarian practices. New inventions, such as deeper plowing and better drainage, the horse collar (a great improvement on the old yoke), and the seaworthy Norse ships (which could face the hazards of Atlantic navigation in a way the old Mediterranean vessels never could), marked technological advances over the ancient ways of farming and sailing. Yet by the standards of classical civilization, the early Middle Ages by and large represented a catastrophic decline into a dark and barbarous age.

Viewed in the long perspective of world history, the so-called barbarian conquest of the Roman Empire is only another instance of a mature, somewhat decadent civilization falling to simpler peoples of a less complex background. Even the centuries of the *Pax Romana* had been filled with Roman combat against the tribes on the far side of the Rhine-Danube line. Tacitus had lectured his fellow Romans on the contrast between their own soft degeneracy and the simple toughness of the Germans. His account of the Germans is the fullest report we have on their tribal life before their first major breakthrough to the Roman side of the frontier, which took place in the fourth century. Despite Tacitus' fears, it was apparently not so much Roman decline that opened the way to the Germans as sheer pressure on the Germans from other tribes further beyond that drove them to try to cross the Roman borders, by force if necessary.

Indo-European in language (like the Greeks, the Romans, and the Celts), the Germans originated along the shores of the Baltic, both on the Continent and in Scandinavia. Very early in ancient times some migrated southward. When the Romans first began to write about them, they were already divided into tribes, though with no overall political unity. One group of Germanic tribes—the Goths—had settled in what we now call Romania, on the north side of the Danube boundary, and in the adjacent plains of what is now the southwestern part of the Soviet Union. In the fourth century, conditions in central Asia about which we still know very little led a fierce Asian people known as the Huns to invade the territory of the Goths.

Living on horseback for days, traveling swiftly, and reveling in warfare, the Huns started a panic among the Goths and other Germanic tribes. The shock waves, beginning in the last half of the fourth century, continued throughout the fifth into the sixth. They shattered the Roman structure in the West and left its fragments in barbarian hands. Since the Eastern territories suffered much less, the imperial tradition continued uninterrupted in Constantinople.

Besides barbarian military raids, penetrations, and conquests, there were slower and more peaceful infiltrations lasting over long periods. German laborers settled and worked on the large Roman estates, especially in Gaul. Before, during, and after the invasions, individual barbarians joined the Roman side, often rising to high positions and defending the old Empire against their fellow tribesmen. The Romanized barbarian became as familiar a figure as the barbarized Roman.

We must remember that "barbarian invasions," though a term frequently used to describe the steady encroachment upon Roman peoples by non-Romans, was also used at various stages of history to attack the origins of essentially Germanic and Asian peoples. Actually *barbarian* merely meant any people outside the Roman Empire. To speak of invasions by barbarians is redundant, in that the Empire has been invaded from outside and thus, by definition, by barbarians. Often the absorption of the Roman peoples was peaceful, with the Germanic groups establishing permanent settlements into which the Romans were then assimilated. Although there was much bloodshed and numerous genuine invasions of the land of one people by another, in general the process might more properly be thought of as a steady migration of peoples that was achieved sometimes peacefully, sometimes forcefully.

Thanks to chronicles and histories, almost all written in Latin by monks, we know a great deal about the routes

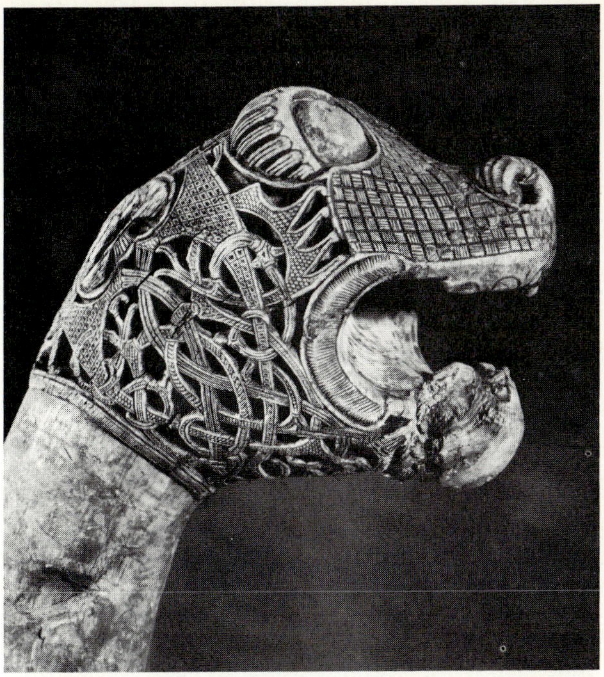

The Oseberg ship, dating from the ninth century, was excavated in 1904 and carefully reconstructed before being set up in the Viking Ship Museum in Oslo. The ship had been buried with a Viking queen, Åsa. The detail, a serpent ready for attack, is from the headpost of the ship. The work was done by the queen's carvers, probably specifically for the burial site.

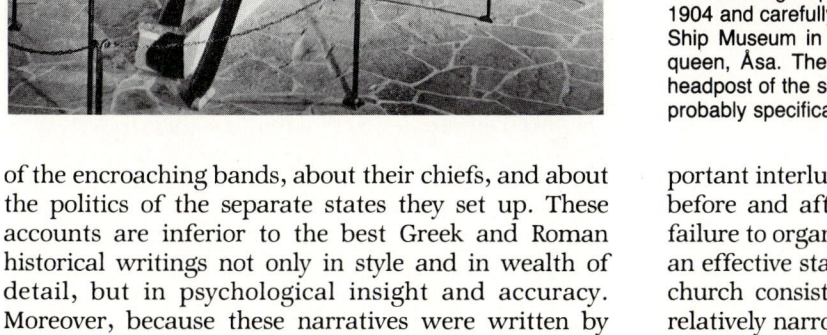

of the encroaching bands, about their chiefs, and about the politics of the separate states they set up. These accounts are inferior to the best Greek and Roman historical writings not only in style and in wealth of detail, but in psychological insight and accuracy. Moreover, because these narratives were written by clerics whose ideals and property suffered from the invaders, they almost certainly exaggerate the cruelty and destructiveness of the invasions, making it even more difficult for us to gain any sympathetic understanding of the cultures of the invaders.

As a result, our own knowledge is in a kind of dark age. We do not know how numerous the invaders were in proportion to the invaded population; we do not know to what degree the barbarians replaced peoples who were there before them; we do not know whether the total population of western Europe was greater or less under the barbarians than under the late Roman Empire. Modern research has generally tended to diminish the numerical importance of the German invaders, but we are working with only the most approximate figures. We do know that the Visigoths (or west Goths) were Christianized, but we do not know how thoroughly or to which Christian views. Though nearer to us in time, the "barbarian invasions" involve more guesswork than does the study of earlier Greek and Roman history, in part because of the lack of a retained literary record.

How complete was the breakdown of Roman civilization in the West? The loss can be seen most clearly at the level of large-scale political and economic organization. These early medieval centuries—with the brief but important interlude of Charlemagne's revived empire, just before and after the year A.D. 800—were marked by failure to organize and administer any large territory as an effective state and society. Only the Roman Catholic church consistently asserted its authority beyond the relatively narrow limits of the medieval duchy, county, or other small unit that was coming into existence and maintained an effective organization to which millions of persons adhered. And politically, even the church was subject to grave lapses of discipline and control; its local clergy were caught up in the web of lay rule, and weakness and disorder appeared in its very heart at Rome.

Roads, postal systems, and communications deteriorated from the Roman efficiency that had allowed both persons and goods to travel in freedom and ease. Thousands of little districts came to depend upon themselves for almost everything they used, and thus became relatively *autarkic* (self-sufficient). And these same little districts took to fighting among themselves. Some invading Germanic tribes did exercise loose control over sizable areas, but these areas were much smaller than the old Empire had been, and the control was uncertain and unsophisticated when compared to that made possible by the sophisticated governmental machinery of the Roman state. The network of habits of command and obedience that held a great, complex community together was rudely cut; long centuries later it had to be gradually and painfully restored.

The early Middle Ages also lost command over the classical tools of scholarship and science. Spoken Latin gradually broke down into local languages—vernaculars—French, Italian, Romanian, Portuguese, and Spanish. Even where it survived as a learned tongue, written as well as spoken, Latin was debased and simplified. The general level of cultivated literature and philosophy fell. Most writers in Latin imitated the already enshrined classics, like the works of Cicero and Vergil. Similarly, traditional skills in the arts underwent a profound change.

But much of ancient civilization did survive the early Middle Ages. People could weave, farm, use horses, and make the necessary implements of peace and war as well in the year 1000 as in the year 100; in some ways and in some places, they could do these things better. Among churchmen there survived, in the libraries of monasteries, and to some degree in the education of the cleric, an admiration for and some familiarity with the classics. The Germanic chiefs so admired the Rome they were destroying that they retained an almost superstitious reverence for its laws and institutions, even if they understood them only in part. As we shall see, the most striking political and economic event of the early Middle Ages was the revival in the West under Germanic kings of the title and the claims of the Roman Empire.

Thus generalizations about the early Middle Ages are extraordinarily difficult, in part because our knowledge is uneven. For the sixth and seventh centuries we have very few written sources (Gregory of Tours, for example, is almost the only data base for Frankish history in the sixth century), while we have a great many sources, both literate and apparently accurate, for both the ninth and the fifth centuries.

Visigoths, Vandals, Anglo-Saxons, 410-455

When the fourth-century Hunnic push began, one tribe of Goths, the Visigoths, petitioned to be allowed to cross the Danube and settle on the south bank in Roman territory, in present-day Bulgaria. The Roman border guards took cruel advantage of their fear and hunger; soon there were many desperate Goths milling about only a few miles from Constantinople. In the year 378 at Adrianople, the mounted Goths defeated the Roman legions of the Eastern emperor Valens, who was killed in battle. More and more Goths now freely entered the Empire. Unable to take Constantinople or other fortified towns, they proceeded south through the Balkans, under their chieftain Alaric, ravaging Greece (including Athens) and then marching around the Adriatic into Italy. In 410 Alaric and his Goths sacked Rome itself, an event that made a staggering impression on the inhabitants of the Empire. Pagan and Christian blamed each other for the disaster, and as we have seen, it inspired Augustine to write his *City of God*. Alaric died soon afterward, and his successors led the Visigoths across Gaul and into Spain.

Here, in the westernmost reaches of the continental Roman Empire, the Visigoths, after their long wanderings, founded a Spanish kingdom that lasted until the Muslim invasions of the eighth century. In southern Gaul a large area (Aquitaine) was given to them by the Western Roman emperor Honorius (r. 395-423), into whose family their king married; but they would lose this area in less than a century to a rival German tribe, the Franks. Since the Visigoths were Arians, they had some difficulty in ruling the orthodox Christians among their subjects.

Almost simultaneously with the Visigothic migration, another Germanic people, the Vandals, still residing in Germany, crossed the Rhine westward into Gaul and moved southward into southern Spain, where they settled in 411. The southernmost section, Andalusia (from *Vandalusia)*, still reflects their name. The Vandals entered North Africa from Spain, moved eastward across modern Morocco and Algeria—partly destroying Augustine's city of Hippo—and established their capital at Carthage in 439. Here they built a fleet and raided Sicily and Italy, finally sacking Rome (455) in a raid that has made the word *vandalism* synonymous to this day with wanton destruction of property. Like the Visigoths, the Vandals were Arians, and often persecuted the orthodox. They held on in North Africa until 533, when the emperor Justinian conquered their kingdom.

Under pressure on the Continent, the Romans early in the fifth century began to withdraw their legions from Britain. As they left, Germanic tribes from across the North Sea in what are now northern Germany and Denmark began to filter into Britain. These Angles, Saxons, and Jutes, coming from an area that had undergone little Roman influence, were still heathen. They gradually established their authority over the Celtic Britons, many of whom survived as a subject class. The barbarians soon founded seven Anglo-Saxon kingdoms, of which Northumbria, Mercia, and Wessex successively became the most important. Scotland and Wales remained Celtic, as did Ireland, which was in large measure converted to Christianity in the fifth century by Catholic missionaries from Gaul, led by a Celto-Roman, St. Patrick (c 389-c 461).

Ireland escaped the first great wave of barbarian invasions, and its Celtic church promoted learning, poetry, and the illustration of manuscripts by paintings. By the end of the sixth century, Catholic Christianity was moving into England from both Celtic Ireland and Rome. Irish monasticism became so strong that many Irish monks and scholars went out from Ireland as missionaries to convert the heathen on the Continent too; St. Columban, for example, headed missions from the Low Countries to the Frankish courts.

Huns, Ostrogoths, 451-526

Not only the Germanic peoples but the central Asian Huns also participated in the onslaught on Roman territories. Early in the fifth century the Huns conquered much of central and eastern Europe. Under their domination lived a large collection of German tribes. The

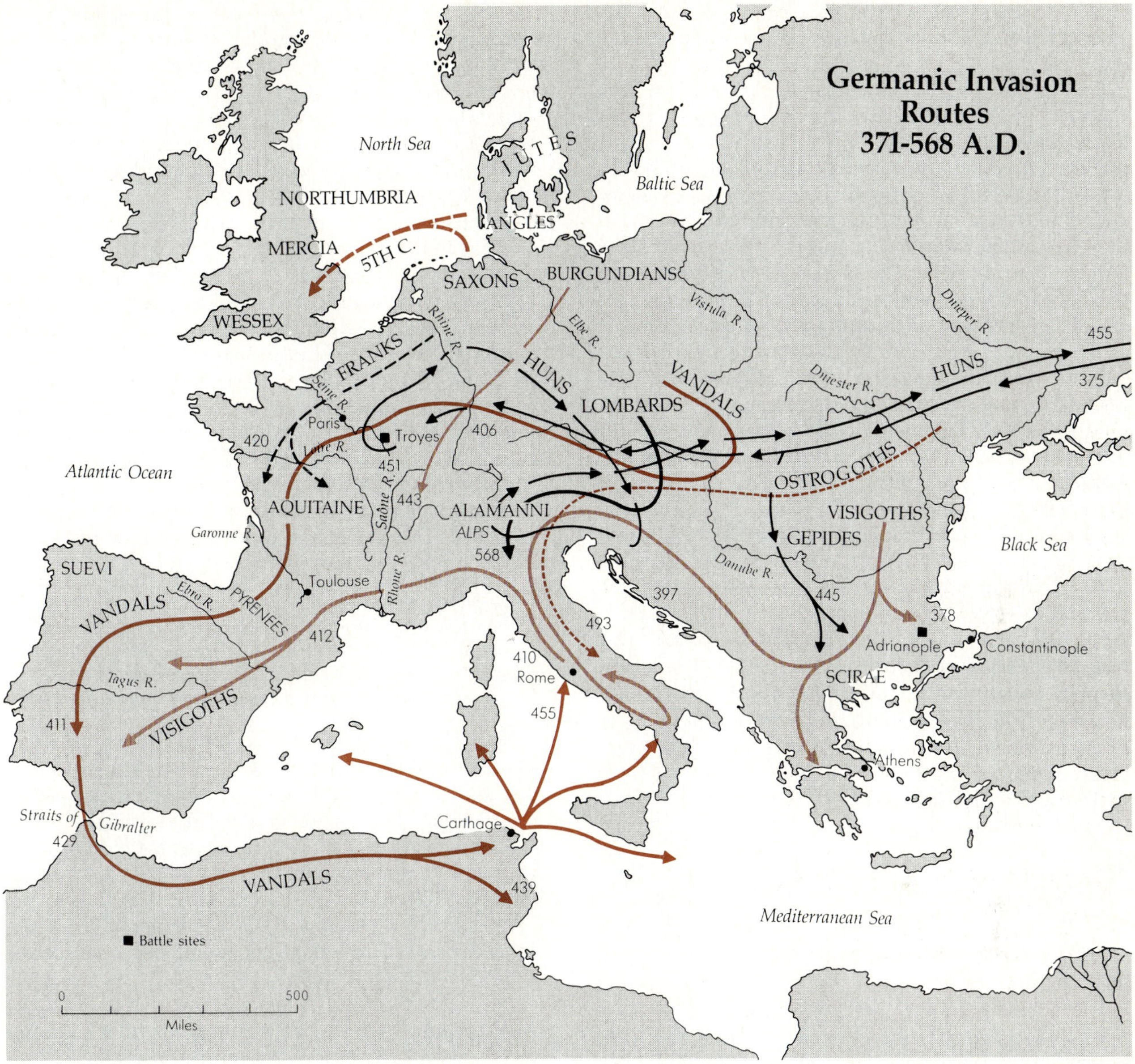

Hunnic rulers also extracted tribute money from the Roman emperors of the East at Constantinople. Under their ruler, Attila, the Huns pressed westward, crossed the Rhine, and were defeated in 451 at Châlons in northeastern France by a Roman general. Attila then invaded Italy, where Pope Leo the Great apparently persuaded him to withdraw without attacking Rome.

Like many nomad empires, that of the Huns in central Europe fell apart after the death of its founder in 453. A plague decimated their ranks and many withdrew into Asia. But other related Asian peoples—nomads and pagans like the Huns, and like them Mongol in appearance—entered Europe before the age of the barbarian invasions was over: Avars in the sixth century, Bulgars in the sixth and seventh, and Magyars in the ninth. The Magyars eventually set up a state in the Danubian plain, and their descendants still inhabit modern Hungary. As the first distant Asian invaders, the Huns had not only precipitated the invasions of the Germanic tribes, but had directly helped to smash Roman influence in central Europe.

Among the German tribes liberated after the collapse of the Hunnic empire, the first to make a major impact were the Ostrogoths (East Goths). They moved into the general disorder left in Italy after the last of the Western emperors, Romulus Augustulus (the little Augustus), was dethroned by his barbarian protector Odovacar in 476—a date often used by historians to mark the "end" of the Roman Empire in the West. Actually, like his immediate predecessors, Romulus Augustulus had been an ineffectual tool of the nearest barbarian general who could command loyal troops. Roman imperial power, however, continued uninterrupted in the East. In fact, it had been the Eastern emperor Zeno, who ruled in

Constantinople from 474 to 481, who had hired the Ostrogoths to intervene in Italy on his behalf against Odovacar.

The leader of the Ostrogoths, Theodoric, had been educated in Constantinople and admired both Greek civilization and the Roman Empire. For most of his long rule from Ravenna in northern Italy (493-526), he was content to serve as nominal subordinate to Emperor Zeno's successors in the East, as a kind of governor of Italy. Like many other Christianized German tribes, the Ostrogoths were Arians. To the popes and the Italians, they were therefore heretics as well as German foreigners. Although Theodoric hoped to impose the civilization of the Roman Empire upon his Germanic subjects, he did not have enough time to bring about any real assimilation. Moreover, toward the end of his reign, Theodoric—who had made dynastic marriages with the Vandal and other Germanic ruling houses—became suspicious of the Empire and planned to go to war against Constantinople.

Many other barbarian peoples participated in the breakup of Roman territory and power in the West during the fifth and sixth centuries but failed to found any lasting state. They remain tribal names: Scirae (from whom Odovacar came), Suevi, Alamanni, Gepides. There were two other German tribes, however, whose achievements we do remember—the Burgundians, who moved into the valleys of the Rhine and Saône rivers in Gaul in the 440s and gave their name to a succession of "Burgundies," varying in territory and government; and the Franks, most important of all, from whom France derives its name.

II THE FRANKS: THE BUILDING OF AN EMPIRE

Destined to found the most lasting political entity of any of the Germanic tribes, the Franks appear to us first as dwellers along the lower Rhine. They engaged in no long migrations, expanding gradually west and south from their territory until eventually they were to create an empire that would include most of western Europe except for the Iberian peninsula and the British isles. Clovis (r. 481-511), a descendant of the house of Merevig or Merovech (called Merovingian), was the primary founder of Frankish power. Moving into Gaul, he successively defeated the last Roman governor (486), the Alamanni (496), and the Visigoths of Aquitaine (507). Large areas of modern France, northwest Germany, and the Low Countries were now Frankish.

The most important factor in Clovis' success, aside from his skill as a general, was his conversion in c 496 to Christianity, not as an Arian heretic but as an orthodox Catholic. This gave him the instant support of the clergy of Gaul, especially of the powerful bishops of Aquitaine, who welcomed the Franks as a relief from the Arian Visigoths. Probably the greatest liability of the Franks was their habit of dividing up their kingdom among the king's sons in every generation. This meant not only a periodic parceling out of territory into petty kingdoms and lordships, but constant secret intrigues and bloody rivalries among brothers and cousins and other relatives who strove to reunite the lands. Indeed, Merovingian history forms one of the most divisive and savage chapters in Western civilization.

According to the sixth-century historian Gregory, Bishop of Tours (not an unbiased source), King Chilperic, Clovis' grandson, married Fredegund, who stopped at nothing to achieve her ambitions. She sent her husband's son by an earlier marriage into a plague-infested region in the hope of killing him off, and when that failed she stabbed him. Next, she sent an assassin to kill her sister-in-law, Brunnhild, and when the assassin returned unsuccessful, Fredegund had his hands and feet cut off. Brunnhild, nearly eighty, was dragged to her death by wild horses. Finally, Fredegund turned against her own daughter and lured her into reaching into a chest full of "necklets and precious ornaments."

> *[Fredegund] seized the lid and forced it down upon her neck. She bore upon it with all her strength, until the edge of the chest beneath pressed the girl's throat so hard that her eyes seemed about to start from her head . . . The attendants outside . . . broke into the small chamber, and brought out the girl, whom they thus delivered from imminent death.**

By the end of the seventh century, the Merovingian kings became so weak that they became known as *rois fainéants* (do-nothing kings). They delegated real power to their chief officials, the "mayors of the palace," a title showing the close connection between the household service of the monarch and the actual external government. By the eighth century one particular family, the house of Pepin, had made this office hereditary from father to son; these were the Carolingians (named for *Carolus*, Latin for Charles). One of the mayors of the palace, Charles Martel ("the Hammer") (r. 714-741), organized the Frankish nobles into a dependable cavalry and in 732 at Poitiers in western France defeated an Arab advance north from Spain. Because this was the farthest north in Europe that the Muslims ever came, the battle came to be seen as a landmark in western European history. Charles Martel's son, Pepin III, the Short (r. 751-768), assumed the title of King of the Franks and consolidated the kingdom once again. Pepin's adventurous policy in Italy initiated a new chapter in Western history, for there, in the two centuries preceding, significant new efforts had been made to reconsolidate Rome.

Italy from Theodoric to Pepin, 527-768

Soon after the death of the Arian Theodoric, the great Eastern emperor Justinian (r. 527-565) launched from

*Gregory of Tours, *History of the Franks*, ed. O.M. Dalton (Oxford: The Clarendon Press, 1927), Book IX, 34.

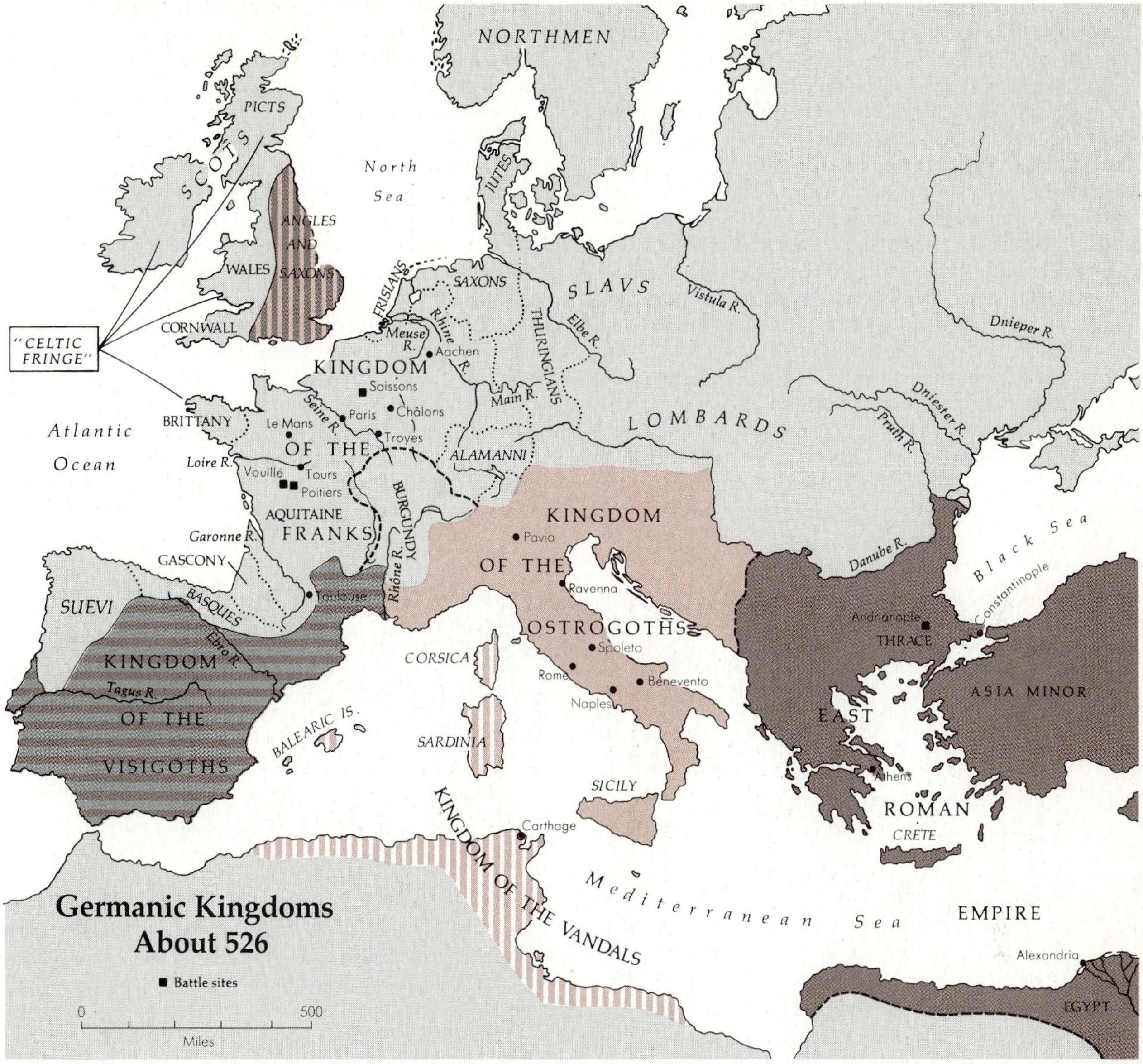

Germanic Kingdoms About 526

Constantinople an ambitious effort to reconquer the major areas of the West that had been lost to the barbarians. The imperial forces tackled the Vandals in North Africa in 533, and then, before consolidating their successes, invaded Italy from Carthage via Sicily. For almost twenty years savage and destructive warfare ravaged the peninsula, and Rome changed hands several times. The towns and countryside were decimated and the survivors reduced to misery. Justinian's proclamation of an imperial restoration in 554 was short-lived, even though in the same year imperial forces took back part of southern Spain from the Visigoths.

Three years after Justinian's death, a new Germanic tribe, the Lombards, entered Italy from the north. They easily conquered the north Italian plain that still bears their name (Lombardy) and established a kingdom with its capital at Pavia. Further to the south they set up the duchies of Benevento and Spoleto. Ravenna, Rome, and Naples remained free of Lombard rule. Italy lay once again in fragments, even though the emperor at Constantinople appointed a governor (called the *exarch*), who had his headquarters at Ravenna and was responsible for the defense of Italy.

Constantinople was far away; danger threatened the emperors from the east, and they often could not afford to pay much attention to Italy's needs or send money and troops to help the exarchs fight the Lombards. In this chaotic situation, the church emerged more and more as the protector of the Catholic population; the bishops often received privileges from the non-Catholic Lombard conquerors that conferred upon them virtual governing rights in the towns if they would keep them peaceful. Among the bishops, the pope took the lead; and among the popes, the most remarkable was Gregory I, the Great (r. 590-604).

Born into a rich and aristocratic Roman family, Gregory abandoned worldly things and became a monk—the first to become pope—and a founder of monasteries. His administrative talents were extraordinary; he served as papal ambassador to the Roman imperial court at Constantinople before becoming pope in 590. Besides his religious duties, he had to take virtually full responsibility for maintaining the fortifications of Rome, for feeding its population, for managing the great financial resources of the church and its lands in Italy, for conducting diplomatic negotiations with exarchate and Lombards, and even for directing military operations. It was he who sent the mission to Britain under Augustine of Canterbury in 597 that began the papal contribution to the conversion of the Anglo-Saxons there. Gregory had an exalted conception of papal power, and he stoutly defended its supremacy over the Eastern church in his letters to the emperor and to the patriarch at Constantinople.

During the seventh and early eighth centuries, the alienation between the Empire in the East and the papacy was greatly increased by religious disagreements and a related political and economic dispute (see Chapter 6). Simultaneously, the Lombards were gradually consolidating and expanding their power, taking Ravenna and putting an end to the exarchate. Menaced by the Lombards and unable to count on help from Constantinople, Pope Stephen II in 753 paid a visit to Pepin III of the Franks.

Pepin was unsure of his position, being only a descendant of a line of mayors of the palace. In exchange for papal approval of his new title of king, he attacked the Lombards and forced them to abandon Ravenna and other recent conquests. Then, although these lands did not truly belong to him, he gave a portion of them to the pope, as the celebrated Donation of Pepin. Together with Rome and the lands immediately around it, the Dona-

This twelfth century fresco, from the Chapel of St. Sylvester in the Church of Quattro Coronati, depicts the so-called Donation of Constantine. A fresco is painted on a moist plaster surface, and frescoes were therefore especially popular as forms of interior church art.

THE DONATION OF CONSTANTINE

In the 750s clerks of the papal chancery concocted a document in which the emperor Constantine (r. 306-337) was supposed to have given to the church the territories that came to be known as the Papal States. The forged document also had Constantine directly declare that:

inasmuch as our imperial power is earthly, we have decreed that it shall venerate and honor his most holy Roman Church and that the sacred see of blessed Peter shall be gloriously exalted above our empire and earthly throne. We attribute to him the power and glorious dignity and strength and honor of the Empire, and we ordain and decree that he shall have rule as well over the four principal sees, Antioch, Alexandria, Constantinople, and Jerusalem, as also over all the churches of God in all the world. And the pontiff who for the time being presides over that most holy Roman Church shall be the highest and chief of all priests in the whole world, and according to his decision shall all matters be settled which shall be taken in hand for the service of God or the confirmation of the faith of Christians.

Henry S. Bettenson, ed., *Documents of the Christian Church*, 2nd ed. (London: Oxford University Press, 1963), p. 140.

tion of Pepin formed the territory over which the pope ruled as temporal sovereign down to 1870. These were the Papal States, and the Vatican City is their present-day remnant. Pepin's son, Charles the Great (Charlemagne, 742-814), completed the destruction of the Lombard kingdom in 774.

The new alliance with the Franks marked the end of papal dependence upon the Empire at Constantinople and the beginning of the papacy as a distinct territorial power. The Franks—too busy to take over these Italian lands themselves and no doubt also aware of the pious responsibilities that they had acquired when they became the protectors of the church—did not try to dictate to the popes. Sometime between 750 and 760 the clerks of the papal chancery forged "proof" that Pepin had been confirming a gift of lands to the church made long ago by the emperor Constantine. For about seven hundred years, until the Italian Renaissance scholar Lorenzo Valla proved it a forgery in 1440, people believed the document on which the "donation" was based was genuine. Constantine had, after all, made many donations to the church, and there were many in the chaos that was Italy who wanted to believe in this additional donation.

Charlemagne and the Revival of Empire, 768-814

Pepin's son Charlemagne (r. 768-814)—so Einhard, his contemporary and his at times misleading biographer tells us—was a vigorous, lusty, intelligent man who loved hunting, women, and war. All his life he wore Frankish costume and thought of himself as a Frankish chieftain. Although he could read and kept pen and ink under his pillow, he could never teach himself how to write; he spoke Latin, however, and understood some Greek. A great conqueror, Charlemagne crossed the Rhine and in campaigns lasting more than thirty years conquered the heathen Saxons, who lived south of Denmark, and converted them at sword's point to Christianity. Monks and priests followed his armies.

Charlemagne also added to his domain the western areas of modern Czechoslovakia (Bohemia), much of Austria, and portions of Hungary and Yugoslavia. The eastern boundaries of his realm reached the Elbe River in the north and the Danube, where it turns sharply south below Vienna. Along these wild eastern frontiers he established provinces (*marks* or *marches*). His advance into eastern Europe also brought him victories over the Asian Avars, successors to the Huns along the lower Danube. Far to the west, Charlemagne challenged Muslim power in Spain and set up a Spanish march in what is today Catalonia. A defeat of his rear guard at the pass of Roncesvalles in the Pyrenees Mountains in 778—though only a skirmish—formed the theme of the heroic epic *The Song of Roland (Le Chanson de Roland)*, which in its most accepted surviving form was composed several centuries later.

By the end of the eighth century, Charlemagne had reunited under Frankish rule all of the western Roman provinces except for Britain, most of Spain, southern Italy, Sicily, and North Africa, but had added to his domains central and eastern European areas the Romans had never possessed. On Christmas Day, 800, Pope Leo III crowned Charlemagne emperor in Rome. So mighty was the tradition of the Roman Empire and so great its hold on people's minds that, more than three centuries after the disappearance of Romulus Augustulus, last of the Western emperors, the chief bishop of the Christian church, seeking to honor and recognize his mighty Frankish patron, automatically crowned him "Roman Emperor Carolus Augustus."

It is likely that Charlemagne himself was surprised and not altogether pleased by the coronation; he prob-

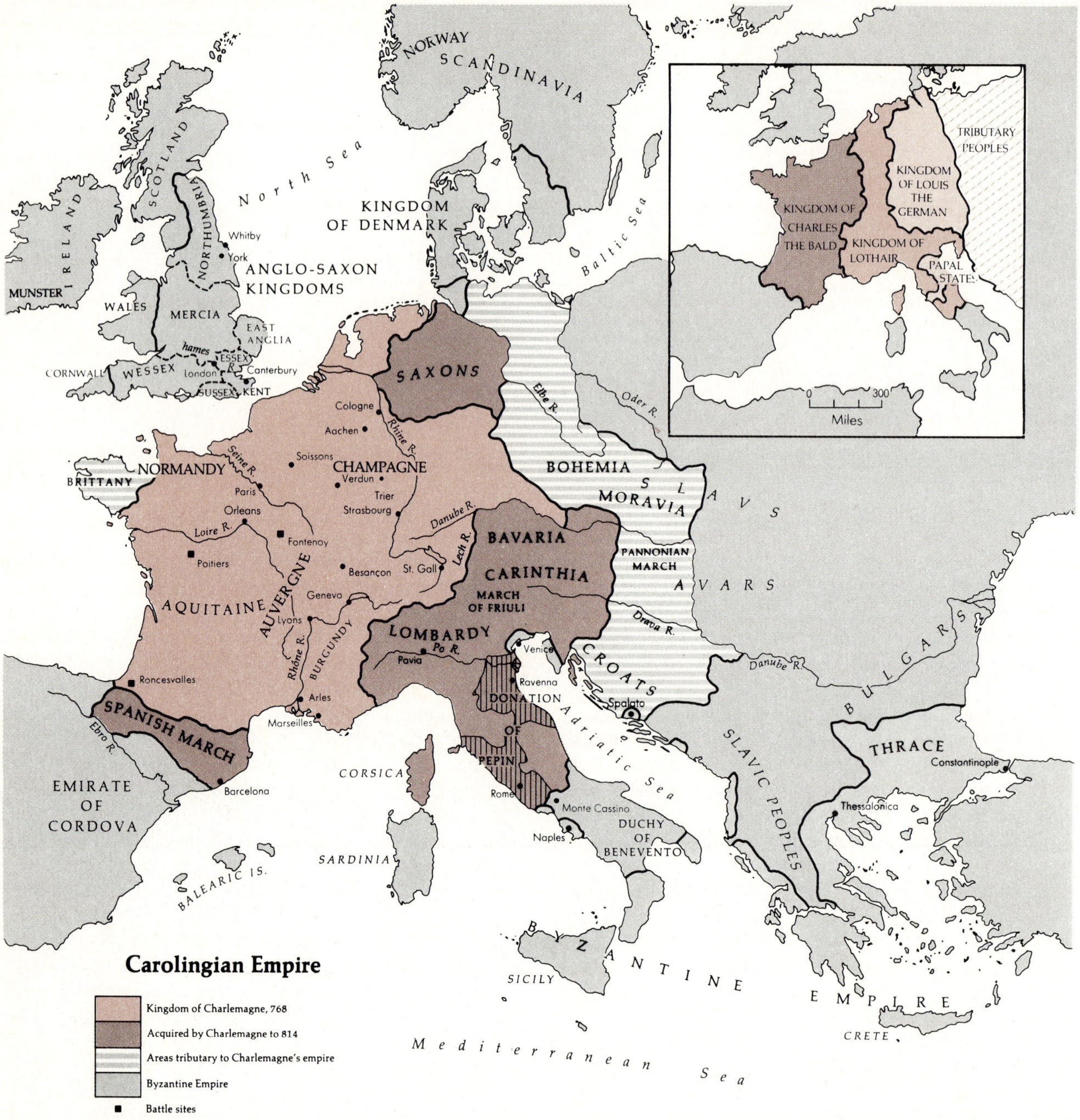

ably relished the title, but he almost surely disliked the role played by the pope and the implication that the pope had the right to choose and crown emperors. The Roman emperors at Constantinople were horrified at the insolence of the once-barbarian king of the Franks in assuming the sacred title, and considered him a usurper.

Within his territories, Charlemagne now was, by virtue of his consecration, a sacred ruler with spiritual rights and duties as well as temporal ones. His lofty concept of his office and his personal power enabled him to influence the church—even in matters of doctrine—more like Constantine or other Eastern emperors than any other Western monarch. He himself named Louis the Pious, by then his only living son, his successor in 813, and the pope played no part in the ceremonies.

Charlemagne's government was very simple. Had not all but one of his sons died before him, he would have divided the kingdom in the standard Frankish way. His personal household staff were also the government officials: the chamberlain, the count of the stable (constable), and so on. On major decisions the emperor conferred with great nobles of state and church, but he told them what he (and they) were going to do, rather than asking them for advice and permission. Since the Franks, like other Germans, believed that law preexisted and could not be made by humans, even Charlemagne could not, in theory, legislate. But he did issue instructions to his subjects, which usually dealt with special administrative problems. His was a highly personal rule. Einhard says about it:

> *When he had taken the imperial title he noticed many defects in the legal systems of his people; for the Franks have two legal systems, differing in many points very widely from one another, and he therefore determined to add what was lacking, to reconcile the differences, and to amend anything that was wrong or wrongly expressed. He completed nothing of all his designs beyond adding a few capitularies, and those unfinished. But he gave orders that the laws and rules of all nations comprised within his domains which were not already written out should be collected and committed to writing.*
>
> *He also wrote out the barbarous and ancient songs, in which the acts of the kings and their wars were sung, and committed them to memory. He also began a grammar of his native language.**

Charlemagne's territories included about three hundred counties, each governed by a count. The counties that lay in former Roman territory each corresponded to the lands of a former Roman civitas. The count had to maintain order, render justice, and recruit and command soldiers. Alongside the count, the bishop of the diocese and the various local magnates might have considerable powers of their own when on their own lands. Only a powerful king could keep the local authorities from taking too much power to themselves. Charlemagne required his counts to appoint teams of judges, whose appointment he would then ratify, and who would actually take over much of the counts' role in rendering justice. He also sent out from his own central administrative staff pairs of royal emissaries (the *missi dominici*, literally "the lord's messengers"), usually a layman and a cleric, to investigate local conditions and to correct abuses. As representatives of the emperor, they could overrule the count.

The Carolingian empire depended heavily upon Charlemagne personally—on his energy, on the brilliance that all observers attributed to him, on his administrative talents, and on the happy fact that his succession was not divisive. But he had assembled more territory than could be effectively governed, in view of the deterioration of administrative machinery and of communications since Roman days. Under his less talented successors, the Frankish practice of dividing lands and authority among the heirs to the throne continued. Quarrels over the allotment of territory raged among brothers and cousins. Although the title of emperor now descended to a single heir in each generation, it had become an empty honor by the middle of the ninth century.

Thus Charlemagne's achievement was short-lived, if brilliant. Historians have taken differing views of it; some have emphasized its brevity and denied its lasting influence. Others have stressed its brilliance and declared that the mere resurrection of the Roman imperial title in the West helped determine the future direction of European political action. The next time a new revival began, statesmen instinctively launched it by reviving the Roman Empire once again. These historians add that, as events turned out, this title lured later generations of German rulers over the Alps into Italy in search of an illusory honor, prevented them from forging Germany into early national unity, and so kept Italy and Germany tied together in an unnatural connection that helps explain why neither became a unified nation until the nineteenth century.

Some insist that Charlemagne's revival of the imperial title at least kept alive the ideal of a unified Christian

A mosaic from the Church of St. John Lateran in Rome provides an eighth-century view of how spiritual and temporal authority issued from the same source. Here St. Peter presents a *pallium*, or pope's garment, to Leo III, while handing a flag to Charlemagne.

Early Lives of Charlemagne, ed. A.J. Grant (London: Chatto & Windus, 1922), pp. 44-45. Since Einhard tells us that Charlemagne could not write, we know that this passage must mean that Charlemagne did not do this writing himself, but ordered it to be done.

The bronze statuette (above) of Charlemagne from the early ninth century appears to diminish him. Compare it with the magnificent fourteenth-century bust of Charlemagne (left) showing him dressed in his Frankish cloak.

Western society, as opposed to a collection of parochial states devoted to cutthroat competition. Others maintain that, thanks to Charlemagne's act, an ambitious secular power could oppose the temporal claims of a spiritual power, the papacy. Of course, a spiritual power well anchored in Italy could oppose the temporal power. The existence of these two claimants to supreme power—the pope and the emperor—saved the West from the extremes of secular domination of religion on the one hand and religious domination of the state on the other. This rivalry and tension helped promote such typically Western institutions and attitudes as individual rights, the rule of law, the dignity of the individual, and ultimately the separation of church and state.

All of this lies in the realm of political theory and speculation. Nevertheless, the revival of the old Roman imperial idea is clearly one of the great threads that run through all subsequent European history. With Charlemagne the "Roman" Empire became in fact largely a German one, though the name "Empire" always retained some suggestion of a common, stable, political order within which prolonged instability was somehow "unnatural," not right. In this sense, the medieval empire, reinforced by the concept of Christendom, links Roman unity with all later dreams of a united Europe. And apart from political theorizing, all students of the intellectual and artistic revival in the time of Charlemagne and his successors would agree that the period provided a dazzling flash of light after centuries that had indeed been relatively dark.

In the struggle among Charlemagne's successors, one episode deserves special notice: the Strasbourg Oaths of 842. Two of his grandsons, Charles the Bald, who held the Western regions, and Louis the German, who held the Eastern regions, swore an alliance against their brother, the emperor Lothair, whose lands lay between theirs. Each swore the oath in the language of the other's troops—Louis in a Latin-like language on its way to becoming French that scholars call Romance, and Charles in Germanic. The symbolism was a striking sign of things to come in European history. Charles and Louis could hardly have chosen a more appropriate place than Strasbourg—chief city of Alsace, in the heart of the middle zone, long to be disputed between modern France and Germany—to swear their bilingual oath.

In the ninth century, however, there were as yet no national states in Europe. Indeed, instead of coalescing into large national units, the Frankish dominions were even then breaking up into much smaller ones, despite the formal settlement reached at the Treaty of Verdun in 843. As the power of the central Frankish state was frittered away in family squabbles, smaller entities—duchies or counties—emerged as virtually autonomous units of government, many with names we still recognize as belonging to provinces of modern France or Germany: Brittany, Champagne, Bavaria, Saxony.

III AFTER CHARLEMAGNE: THE NORTHMEN

Charlemagne's conquests in Germany had for the first time brought the home ground of many of the barbarians into Christendom. Still outside lay Scandinavia, from whose shores there began in the ninth century a new wave of invasions that hit Britain and the western parts of the Frankish lands with savage force. The Northmen conducted their raids from small ships that could easily sail up the Thames, the Seine, or the Loire. Their appetite for booty grew with their successes, and soon they organized fleets of several hundred ships, ventured farther abroad, and often wintered along a conquered coast. They ranged as far east as Yaroslavl in northern Russia, as far south as Spain, penetrated into the Mediterranean through the Straits of Gibraltar, and raided Italy. To the west they proceeded far beyond Ireland to reach Iceland and Greenland. About 986 some of them almost certainly sighted Newfoundland (Vinland), Labrador, or even New England, although some scholars still question the validity of the evidence for settlement in the last.

Desire for booty does not by itself account for the Norse expansions. Polygamy was common among the upper classes of the pagan Scandinavians (the lower ones could not afford it), and the younger sons of these Viking chiefs probably had to leave home to seek more wives. Like most migrations, however, the chief motivation most likely was to find new lands to settle in the face of growing overpopulation. Cultivable land became scarce, throwing families onto marginal lands to face the fear of famine in a bad year. In addition, Scandinavian chiefs were imposing more controls, and some families chose to leave rather than submit.

The Norsemen's first captured base was along the lower Seine River, which is still called Normandy after them. In 915 the Frankish king was forced to grant the Norse leader Rolf, or Rollo (c 860-c 931) a permanent right of settlement. The Normans became an efficient and powerful ruling class—in fact, the best administrators in the new feudal age. From Normandy soon after the year 1000 younger sons would go off to found a state in the southern Italian and Sicilian territories that belonged to the Eastern Roman Empire and to the Arabs. And from Normandy in 1066, as we shall see, Duke William and his followers would conquer England. Kinsmen of these Norsemen who had settled in Normandy also did great deeds. In the 860s the first wave of Viking invaders crossed the Baltic Sea to what is now Russia and penetrated deep inland to the south along the river valleys. They conquered the indigenous Slavic tribes and, at Kiev on the middle Dnieper, consolidated the first Russian state.

While the Normans were raiding and developing Normandy, other Scandanivians were paralleling their achievements in the British isles. The Northmen were soon firmly established in Ireland, especially in the ports of Dublin, Waterford, and Limerick. But in the interior the Celtic chieftains held on. In 1014, under the leadership of Brian of Munster, these chieftains won the battle of Clontarf against the Northmen and their native allies. Eventually, the Northmen were absorbed into the texture of Irish society. But the two centuries of struggle had disastrously interrupted the brilliant development of Irish civilization, and thereafter tribal warfare was to reign unchecked until the English invasions of the twelfth century.

The Anglo-Saxon Kingdoms and the Danes, 871-1035

In England, savage Danish attacks on the northern and eastern shores soon led to settlement. The chief barrier to the Danes was the Anglo-Saxon kingdom of Wessex under Alfred the Great (r. 871-899). Although Alfred defeated the Danes, he had to concede the whole northeast of England to them, a region thereafter called the Danelaw. By the midtenth century, Alfred's successors had reunited the Danelaw to Wessex, whose royal family ruled over all England.

Soon after the turn of the eleventh century, new waves of Danes scored important successes under the command of Canute, or Knut (b. 994), the king of Denmark. In 1017 Canute was chosen king of England by the Anglo-Saxon *witenagemot*, a "council of wise men." Able ruler of a kind of northern empire (he was also king of Norway), Canute allied himself with the Roman church and brought Scandinavia into the Christian community.

Gotlandic jewelry was both precise and ornate. This shawl buckle of bronze and gold shows the complexity and skill of Viking art.

His early death (1035) without competent heirs led to the breakup of his holdings, and England reverted to a king of the house of Alfred, Edward the Confessor, who reigned from 1042 until 1066.

Like the Carolingian monarch, the Anglo-Saxon king was crowned and anointed with holy oil and ruled as God's deputy on earth, with responsibility for both church and state. His revenue came in part from an ancient practice, the *feorm*—originally a tax of food levied for the support of the monarch and his household as they moved about England, though by the time of Edward the Confessor it was often paid in money. There was also the *Danegeld*, a war tax on land first levied in 991 to bribe the Danes, which continued to be collected long after its original purpose was unnecessary. The king also had income from his own estates and from fines levied in court cases. His subjects were required to work on the building and repair of bridges and defense works and had to render military service in the *fyrd*, the ancient Germanic army.

The Anglo-Saxon king was the guarantor of law, and serious crimes were considered to be offenses against him as well as against the victims; he was also a law-giver, like the Carolingian monarch. His council of wise men, made up of important landholders, churchmen, and officials, advised him when asked on major questions of policy—war, taxes, new laws—and sometimes acted as a court to try important cases. The council also played a major role in the election and deposition of kings. In the king's personal household staff, which moved with him and did his business from day to day, lay one of the origins of future specialized governmental departments in England and the many lands ultimately influenced by it. The Anglo-Saxon monarchy resembled the Carolingian, but it flourished while that of the Carolingians declined.

Carolingian Decline: The Saxon Empire, 911-996

By the end of the ninth century, Carolingian power in the German territories had almost disappeared in the face of domestic challenges by ambitious local magnates (great lords) and foreign threats from Norsemen, Slavs, and the Asian Magyars, who poured into the Hungarian plain in the mid-890s. Their predecessors, the Huns and Avars, had vanished, but the Magyars stayed, forming the nucleus of a Hungarian state. The Hungarian language thus remains today the only non-Indo-European tongue in Europe except for Finnish and Basque.

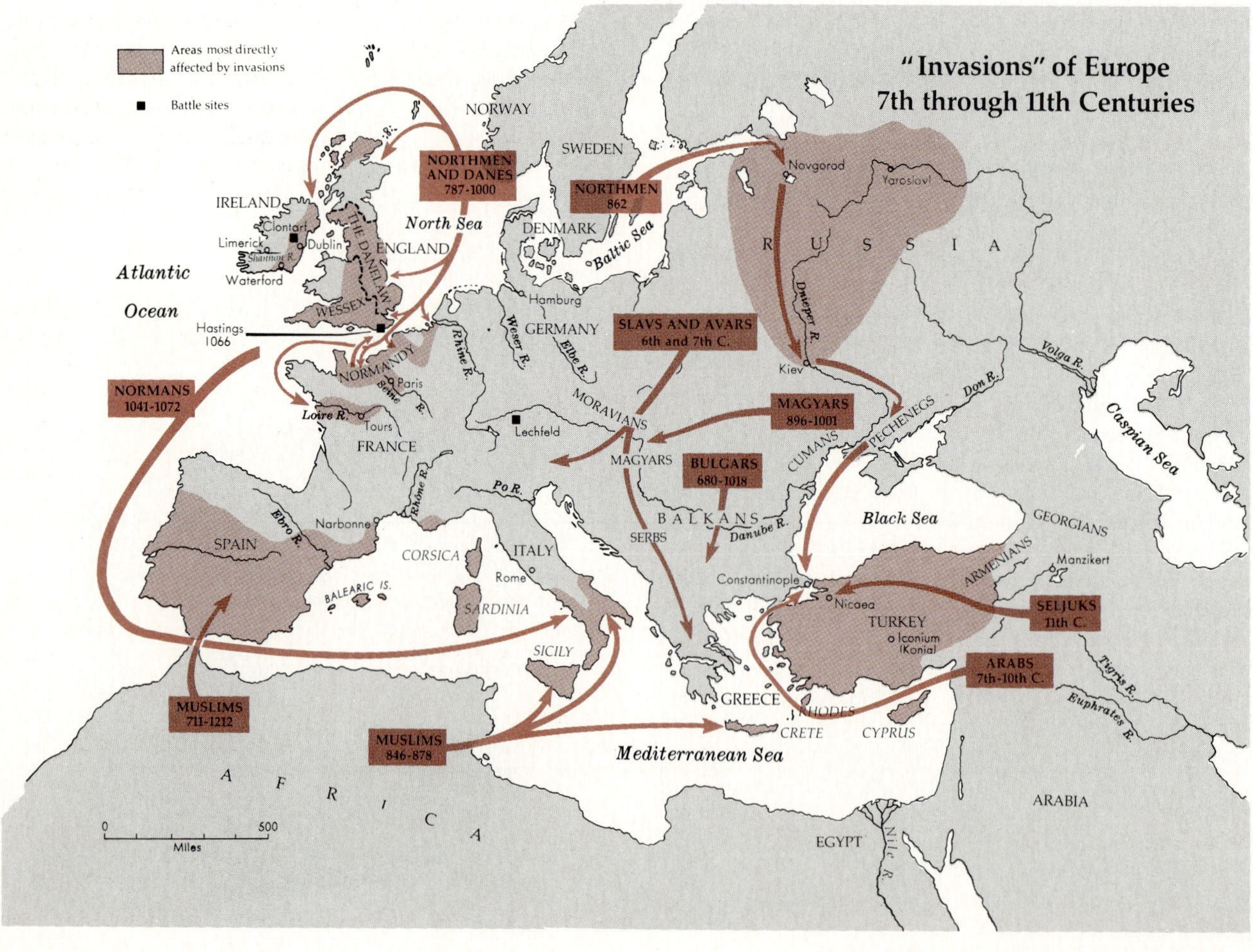

A French manuscript illumination of the eleventh century shows one of the Ottos receiving the homage of the four parts of his empire: Slavinia, Germania, Galia, and Rome. Some sources identify the figure as Otto I, other sources as Otto II. The manuscript is from the Gospel book of Otto III.

When the last nominal Carolingian ruler, Louis the Child, died in 911, the German magnates elected the duke of Franconia as King Conrad I (r. 911-918). The most important units in Germany were now duchies—Franconia, Saxony, Swabia, and Bavaria—each under an autonomous ruler. Conrad I failed to control either the other dukes or the Magyars, and he finally nominated his strongest enemy, Henry the Fowler, duke of Saxony, to succeed him as emperor. Henry's son, Otto I (936-973), checked the rival dukes and defeated the Magyars at the Battle of Lechfeld in 955, ending their threat to western Europe.

Master of his German territories, the Saxon Otto next genuinely sought to revive Charlemagne's title of Roman emperor, which had passed from one Carolingian prince to another until it had lapsed in 924. Deep in decline after the reign of the great pope Nicholas I (858-867), the papacy had fallen into the hands of rival Roman noble families, usually corrupt and ineffectual. Without strong central administration and under a two-pronged attack from Muslims in the south and Magyars in the north, Italy had become anarchic. Yet Rome, even at its lowest depths in the midtenth century, was an irresistible magnet that attracted all who sought supreme power. Like Charlemagne almost two hundred years before him, Otto therefore went to Italy and had himself crowned emperor by the depraved Pope John XII in 962. Otto then deposed John for murder and installed his own candidate on the papal throne. He forced the Roman aristocracy to promise that imperial consent would hereafter be necessary for papal elections, and he renewed the Donation of Pepin and the subsequent grants of the Carolingians to the papacy. Though the papacy for the next hundred years was hardly more than an instrument manipulated by his successors, Otto's action eventually ensured the continuity of the papacy as an independent institution; it also tightly linked the political fortunes of Germany and Italy for centuries to come. In practice, relations between emperor and pope were regulated by a pact that assured imperial supremacy.

In the western Carolingian lands, which we now call France, partitioning, strife, and feebleness led to the fragmentation of both territory and power among several ambitious landowners. As early as 887 one faction of these magnates chose a non-Carolingian, Odo, count of Paris, as king, and civil war between him and the Carolingian claimant added to the chaos. For the next century the families of the two rivals alternated in power. Finally, in 987 the magnates elected as king Hugh Capet (ruled to 996), a descendant of the early count of Paris. Though several of the nobles who chose Hugh were actually more powerful than he was, he founded the Capetian dynasty that lasted almost to our own time. (When Louis XVI went to the guillotine in 1793 during the French Revolution, his executioners would call him "Citizen Capet.")

Europe about 1000

By about the year 1000 England was a centralized monarchy; France was nominally ruled by an elected king who was feebler than his great supporters; Germany was divided into duchies, one of which, Saxony, had asserted its supremacy and claimed the old imperial title; and Italy still remained anarchic, although the papacy had begun to revive. Out of the debris of the Roman Empire, buffeted by two successive waves of barbarian incursions and held together only by their common Christian faith, these major fragments had begun to take on certain features that we can recognize today. Elsewhere, the Scandinavian kingdoms had imposed order on the turbulent peoples who had carried out the Viking expansion, and the little Christian kingdoms in the north of Spain were beginning to reconquer the peninsula from the Muslims (see Chapter 6).

In the East, the Empire, with its direct descent from Rome and its Greco-oriental character, still stood firm at Constantinople, despite many shocks. It had started its work of Christianizing the Slavic peoples nearest to it—the Bulgarians, the Russians, the Serbs. The western Slavs—Czechs, Poles, Croats, and others—and the

Magyars, lying between the Germans and the influences radiating from Constantinople, had received Roman missionaries. By the year 1000 there was already visible a fateful line of demarcation between the Western Catholic world and the Eastern Orthodox world, with a different alphabet and a different outlook.

IV FEUDAL EUROPE

If the old Roman ways of governing largely collapsed, as they did, during the centuries that we have called the early Middle Ages, what replaced them? It is all very well to speak of relative anarchy before and after Charlemagne, but what was anarchy like, and how were human relations governed? Did everyone just slaughter everyone else indiscriminately? What were the rules that enabled life to go on, however harshly?

In fact, of course, there were mutual arrangements that allowed people to work and fight, to survive if they could, to seek out some way of assuring at least temporary security. In these arrangements we find elements surviving from Roman times, innovations introduced by the barbarians, and changes linked with conversion to Christianity. The settled inhabitants of western Europe and the invaders underwent a long, slow, mutual adjustment, as new and old ways of regulating human affairs competed and often combined with each other.

Feudalism: The Rulers

To these widely varying social and political combinations scholars give the name *feudalism*. Feudal institutions were the arrangements—personal, territorial, and governmental—that made survival possible under the conditions that existed in western Europe during the early Middle Ages. The arrangements were made between important people who were concerned with maintaining order, though the customs that evolved also applied to the masses of population. Because central authority could no longer maintain itself locally, a closer, truly local authority had to be improvised to replace it. But because the processes and their results were anything but systematic, scholars seldom now use the outmoded term "feudal system."

One of the most influential arrangements among the barbarians was the war-band (or *Gefolge*) of the early Germans (or the *comitatus*, as Tacitus called it in Latin). In the war-band the leader commanded the loyalty of his followers, who had put themselves under his direction for fighting and for winning booty. It was one of the most important institutions of the Scandinavian invaders of future Russia, where it acquired the Slavic name *druzhina*. Among the Anglo-Saxons the word for chieftain was *hlaford*, the direct origin of our word *lord*. Chief and followers consulted together before a raid or before making peace; those who disagreed might go and serve another chief; booty was divided among all the fighters.

In the Roman provinces, too, local landowners often built their own private armies, while in Rome itself the magnates had long maintained their groups of *clients*, to whom they acted as *patron* and gave legal protection. When a humble man wanted to enter the client relationship, he asked for the *patrocinium* of the great man and secured it by performing the act of *commendation*, recommending or entrusting himself to the patron. He remained free, obtaining food and clothing in exchange for his services, whatever they might be. If the man was of the upper classes, he was called *fidelis*, a faithful man. By the Carolingian period, the term *vassus*, originally denoting a man of menial status, had come to mean a man who rendered military service to his patron, or lord. To be a vassus, or vassal, meant no disgrace; it was the new name for status gained by the act of commendation. So a combination of old Germanic and old Roman practices contributed to new relationships described in new terms.

A Roman patron sometimes retained title to a piece of property but granted a client temporary use of it, together with the profits to be derived from it, so long as he held it, often for life. The Romans used the term *precarium* for this kind of tenure, and the Carolingian rulers commonly adopted the old practice—sometimes using the old Roman term, sometimes the newer *beneficium* (benefice), to describe land temporarily held by a vassal in exchange for service. By the year 1000 the act of becoming a vassal usually meant that a man got a benefice; he might even refuse faithful service or loyalty unless he was satisfied with the land he received. The feeble later Carolingians and their rivals outbid each other in giving benefices to their supporters to obtain armed support and service. This was one of the practices that depleted the royal estates.

In the later Carolingian period, the benefice came more often to be called *feudum*, a fief—the term that has given us the words *feudal* and *feudalism*. When the benefice became a fief, it also became hereditary. Though title to the fief remained with the lord who granted it, the fief itself passed, on the death of a vassal, to the vassal's heir, who inherited with it the obligations to serve the lord and his heirs.

The man who received a fief often got with it certain rights to govern the farmers who lived and worked on the lands that made it up. This practice too had its precedents. In late Roman times the emperors had often granted an *immunity* to those residing on their own estates—an understanding that imperial tax collectors or other law-enforcing officials would stay away from the inhabitants. Because the immunity exempted the farmers from onerous duties, it was hoped that they would enjoy their privileged status and therefore stay put and supply the emperor with predictable quantities of badly needed produce. The Frankish kings adopted this practice, sometimes extending it to lands of the church and even to those of private proprietors. By the tenth century an immunity meant that the king undertook to keep his officials off the privileged lands, and that the holder of the lands would himself perform such governmental functions as collecting taxes, establishing police arrangements, and setting up a court of justice, from which he might keep the profits from fines or assessments.

From late Roman times too came the local offices of duke and count. Originally military commanders, they took over civil authority as the power of the central government relaxed. In Frankish times they were sometimes very powerful rulers, kings in all but name. In the disorders of the Carolingian decline, these offices gradually became hereditary; at the same time the dukes and counts were the vassals of the Carolingians. So the title and office, the duties of the vassal, and the fief (or territory that went with the office) all became hereditary.

Vassals and Lords

Feudalism and feudal practice did not extend uniformly over all of Europe. Northern France and the Low Countries were the most thoroughly feudalized areas, Germany much less so. Some pieces of land never became fiefs but remained the fully owned private property of the owners; these were called *allods.* Feudal practices varied from place to place and developed and altered with the passage of time.

Nonetheless, certain general conceptions were accepted almost everywhere. One of the most significant was that of a *feudal contract*. The lord (or *suzerain*, as he was often called) owed something to the vassal, just as the vassal owed something to the lord. When they entered into their relationship, the vassal rendered formal homage to his lord; that is, he became the lord's "man." He also promised him aid and counsel. *Aid* meant that he would appear when summoned, fully armed, and fight as a knight in the lord's wars, subject perhaps to limits on the number of days' service owed in any one year. *Counsel* meant that he would join with his fellow vassals—his *peers*, or social equals—to form the lord's court of justice, which alone could pass judgment on any one of them. He might also be required at his own expense to entertain his lord for a visit of specific length, and to give him money payments on special occasions—the marriage of the lord's eldest daughter, the knighting of his eldest son, or, later on, his departure on a crusade. The vassal also swore *fealty* (fidelity) to his lord. In his turn, the lord was understood to owe protection and justice to his vassal.

If the vassal broke this contract, the lord would have to get the approval of a court made up of the vassal's peers before he could proceed to a punishment, such as depriving the vassal of his fief (*forfeiture*). If the lord broke the contract, the vassal was expected to withdraw his homage and fealty in a public act of defiance before proceeding to open rebellion. Sometimes the contract was written; sometimes it was oral; sometimes the ceremony included a formal *investiture* by the lord in which he would give his kneeling vassal a symbol of the fief that was being transferred to him—a twig or a bit of earth. When lord or vassal died, the contract had to be renewed with the successor. The son of a vassal, upon succeeding to his father's fief, often had to pay *relief*, a special and often heavy cash payment similar to a modern inheritance tax. If the vassal died without heirs, the fief would *escheat*, or revert to the lord, who could bestow it on another vassal or not, as he saw fit. If the vassal's heir was still a minor, the lord exercised the right of *wardship*, or guardianship, until the minor came of age; this meant that the lord received the revenues from the fief, and if he was unscrupulous he could milk it dry.

Within a feudal kingdom, the king theoretically occupied the top position in an imaginary pyramid of society. Immediately below him would be his vassals, men who held fiefs directly from the king, called *tenants-in-chief*. They in turn would be feudal lords; that is, they would give out various parts of their own property as fiefs to their own vassals. These men (the king's vassals' vassals) would be the king's *rear vassals*, and so were at the next lower levels of the theoretical pyramid. But they too would often have vassals, and so on down for many more levels in a process called *subinfeudation*. But this was only theory.

Practice was more complicated still. A tenant-in-chief might hold only a very small fief directly from the king and not be a very important person at all, while a vassal's vassal's vassal might be rich and powerful. The dukes of Normandy, who were vassals to the king of France, were for some centuries much stronger than the king. A person might receive fiefs from more than one lord, and so owe homage and fealty to both. What was he to do if one of his lords quarreled with the other and went to war? Which of his lords would have a prior right to count on his military help? This happened very often; one Bavarian count had twenty different fiefs held of twenty different lords. Gradually, therefore, there arose a new concept, that of a *liege lord*, the one to whom a vassal owed service ahead of any other. But in practice the difficulties often persisted. Even though feudal law became more subtle and more complex, armed might ultimately counted for more than legality.

Manorialism

These complex arrangements directly involved only the governing class who fought on horseback as mounted knights and whose fiefs consisted of landed property known as manors or estates. Even if we include their dependents, the total would hardly reach 10 percent of the population of Europe. Most of the other 90 percent of the people worked the land. In late Roman times, as we have seen, the large estate, owned by a magnate and worked by tenant farmers, had been called a latifundium. The tenant farmers, or coloni, were often descendants of small landowners who had turned over their holdings to the magnate in exchange for a guarantee of protection and a percentage of the crop. While the coloni were personally free, not slaves, they could not leave the ground they cultivated, nor could their children.

LIFE IN THE COUNTRY

Selections from the *Capitulare de Villis* help to show what life may have been like in the countryside around the year 800. Scholars do not agree on precisely what these instructions, which were prepared for the guidance of stewards who administered royal properties in France, always meant or which part of present-day France they were applied to, though majority opinion holds that they probably were prepared by the King of Aquitaine, in southwestern France:

1. We wish that our estates which we have instituted to serve our needs discharge their services to us entirely and to no other men.

2. Our people shall be well taken care of and reduced to poverty by no one.

3. Our stewards shall not presume to put our people to their own service, either to force them to work, to cut wood, or to do any other task for them. And they shall accept no gifts from them, either horse, ox, cow, pig, sheep, little pig, lamb, or anything else excepting bottles of wine or other beverage, garden produce, fruits, chickens, and eggs.

4. If any of our people does injury to us either by stealing or by some other offense he shall make good the damage and for the remainder of the legal satisfaction he shall be punished by whipping, with the exception of homicide and arson cases which are punishable by fines. The stewards, for injuries of our people to other men, shall endeavor to secure justice according to the practices which they have, as is the law. Instead of paying fines our people, as we have said, shall be whipped. Freemen who live in our domains or estates shall make good the injuries they do according to their law and the fines which they have incurred shall be paid for our use either in cattle or in equivalent value.

5. When our stewards ought to see that our work is done—the sowing, plowing, harvesting, cutting of hay, or gathering of grapes—let each one at the proper season and in each and every place organize and oversee what is to be done that it may be done well. If a steward shall not be in his district or can not be in some place let him choose a good substitute from our people or another in high repute to direct our affairs that they may be successfully accomplished. And he shall diligently see to it that a trustworthy man is delegated to take care of this work.

6. We wish our stewards to give a tithe of all our products to the churches on our domains and that the tithe not be given to the churches of another except to those entitled to it by ancient usage. And our churches shall not have clerics other than our own, that is, of our people or our palace.

The *Capitulare* also reveal the detail in which life was administered:

40. Each steward shall always have on our estates for the sake of adornment unusual birds, peacocks, pheasants, ducks, pigeons, partridges, and turtledoves.

41. The buildings on our estates and the fences which enclose them shall be well taken care of and the stables and kitchens, bake-houses and presses shall be

If the coloni lived in groups of houses close together, the latifundium could be described as a villa. Though conditions varied widely, we are not far wrong if we think of the late Roman latifundium becoming the medieval manor, the late Roman villa becoming the medieval village, and the late Roman coloni becoming the medieval serfs. As we shall see, the early German village community also contributed to the new social structure. While the Roman landed estate had often produced its food for sale at a profit in the town and city, the centuries of disorder beginning with the Germanic invasions led to a decline of commerce, of cities, and of agriculture for profit. The medieval manor usually produced only what was needed to feed its own population.

The oldest method of cultivation was the two-field system, alternating crops and fallow so that fertility could be recovered. Later, especially in grain-producing areas, a three-field system was devised—one field for spring planting, one for autumn planning, and the third lying fallow. Elsewhere—in the mountains, in wine-growing areas, in the "Celtic fringes" of Brittany and Wales, and in the new areas of pioneer settlement in Eastern lands—there were many variant agricultural techniques and social arrangements. Here, as so often, there was no "typical" medieval way.

On the manor, oxen had originally pulled the plow, but the invention of the horse collar (so that the horse would not strangle on the old-fashioned strap around his neck) and the use of horseshoes (which allowed horses to plow stony soil that hurt oxen's feet) helped make it possible to substitute horses for oxen. So did the increasing use of tandem harnessing, enabling the horses to work in single file instead of side by side. A heavy-wheeled plow also made its appearance in advanced areas.

The pattern of agricultural settlement varied from region to region. Insofar as a "typical" manor existed, each of its peasant families had holdings, usually scattered long strips of land in the large open fields. In theory this gave each family a bit of the good arable land, a bit carefully ordered so that the workers in our service can perform their duties fittingly and very cleanly.

42. Each manor shall have in the store-room counterpanes, bolsters, pillows, bedclothes, table and bench covers, vessels of brass, lead, iron, and wood, andirons, chains, pot-hooks, adzes, axes, augurs, knives, and all sorts of tools so that it will not be necessary to seek them elsewhere or to borrow them. And the stewards shall be responsible that the iron instruments sent to the army are in good condition and when they are returned that they are put back into the store-room.

43. For our women's work-shops the stewards shall provide the materials at the right time as it has been established, that is flax, wool, woad, vermilion dye, madder, wool-combs, teasels, soap, grease, vessels, and the other lesser things which are necessary there.

44. Of the minor foods two-thirds shall be sent for our service each year, vegetables as well as fish, cheese, butter, honey, mustard, vinegar, millet, panic, dried and fresh herbs, radishes, and turnips; similarly wax, soap, and other lesser things. Whatever is left shall be made known to us in an inventory as we have said above. The stewards shall by no means neglect to do this as they have up to now because we wish to check by the two-thirds sent to us what that third is which remains.

45. Each steward shall have good workmen in his district—iron-workers, goldsmiths, silversmiths, leatherworkers, turners, carpenters, shieldmakers, fishermen, fowlers or falconers, soap-makers, brewers who know how to make beer, cider, perry or any other beverage fit to drink, bakers who can make bread for our needs, net-makers who are skilled in making nets for hunting as well as fishing or for taking birds, and other workmen whose listing would be a lengthy matter.

46. They shall take good care of our walled game preserves which the people call parks and always repair them in time and on no account delay so that it becomes necessary to rebuild them. They shall do the same for all the buildings.

47. Our hunters and falconers and other servitors who attend us zealously in the palace shall receive assistance on our estates in carrying out what we or the queen have ordered by our letters when we send them on any of our affairs, or when the seneschal or butler instructs them to do anything on our authority.

48. The wine-presses on our estates shall be well taken care of. The stewards shall see to it that no one presumes to press our grapes with his feet but that all is done cleanly and honestly.

49. The women's quarters, that is, their houses, heated rooms, and sitting rooms, shall be well ordered and have good fences around them and strong gates that our work may be done well.

50. Each steward shall see to it that there are as many horses in one stable as ought to be there and as many attendants as should be with them. And those stablemen who are free and hold benefices in that district shall live off their benefices. Similarly if they are men of the domain who hold *mansi* they shall live off them. Those who do not have such shall receive maintenance from the demesne.

51. Each steward shall see to it that in no manner wicked men conceal our seed under the ground or do otherwise with the result that our harvests are smaller. And likewise, concerning other misdeeds, they shall watch them so that they can do no harm.

52. We wish that our stewards render justice to our *coloni* and serfs and to the *coloni* living on our estates, to the different men fully and entirely such as they are due. . . .

"Capitulare de Villis," *Introduction to Contemporary Civilization in the West*, 2nd ed., eds. Contemporary Civilization Staff of Columbia College (New York: Columbia University Press, 1954), I, 5-13. Courtesy of Columbia University Press.

of the less good land, a bit of woodland, and so on. The strips might be separated from each other by narrow, unplowed *balks*, but there were no fences, walls, or hedges. The lord of the manor had his own strips, his *demesne* (perhaps a quarter to a third of the land), reserved for the production of the food that he and his household needed. It was understood that the peasants had to work this demesne land for the lord, often three days a week throughout the year, except perhaps in harvest time, when the lord could command their services until his crops were safely in the barns. Of course, the size of the lord's household varied, depending on his importance in the feudal hierarchy. The more important he was, the more armed men he had to feed, and the more dependents and servants they all had, the more numerous and bigger would be his fiefs, and the more peasants he would need to work the manors that made up those fiefs.

When a serf died, his son made the lord a payment (*heriot*) to inherit his father's right to cultivate the family strips. In exchange for permission to pasture their beasts in the lord's meadows, the serfs might perform other duties. They often had to dig ditches or maintain roads. They paid to have their grain ground at the lord's mill and their bread baked in his oven. They could not marry or allow their daughters to marry outside the manor without the lord's permission and usually the payment of a fine (*merchet*). Serfs, a hereditary caste of farm laborers, were bound to the soil. But they were not slaves; the lord could not sell them, they and their children descended with the land to the lord's heirs.

Undoubtedly the bulk of the hours of labor on the manor went directly into farming, mostly grain-farming. But some of the manor's inhabitants were also craftsmen, such as blacksmiths or tanners, and they too cultivated their own plots of land. Each manor had at least one church of its own, with its priest. If the lord was a great lord, he might have several priests, including his own chaplain for the household and a village priest for the local church.

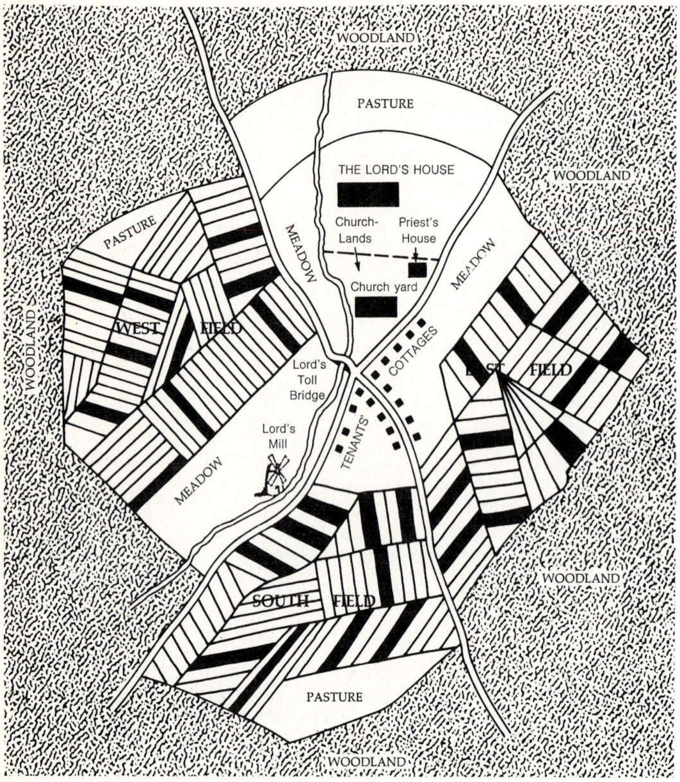

Plan of a medieval manor. The solid strips are the lord's demesne.

The organization of the countryside by manors developed earliest in eastern France and in parts of Italy and Germany. Still, even at its height, it did not include some parts of these and other European countries. In the large areas where manorialism did prevail, the old Roman landlord's economic power over his tenants had fused with the traditional Germanic village chief's political power, and by the eleventh century, with the governing rights that the lord received with his fief. The deep respect for custom often tended to prevent the lord's extorting more work from his serfs or more food than they traditionally owed him. But they had nowhere to appeal when the lord was oppressive. Custom prevailed in the lord's court of justice, where he or his steward sat in judgment on the serf-tenants, enforcing the traditional rules of the village community. Custom regulated the agreements among serfs for the use in common of plows and plow teams, which few could hope to own individually. Even though custom no doubt retarded inventiveness and stifled initiative, it was the main force that gave the serfs some sense that they were protected against unreasonable demands and cruelties.

By no means were all the peasants on every manor serfs, however. Some of them were freemen, called *franklins* in England, who virtually owned the land they worked. And between the freemen and the serfs there were probably always landless laborers who were not tied to the land as serfs, and peasants with dues so light that they were almost freemen.

The manor usually was nearly self-sufficient. Only rarely could the manorial forge have produced all the plowshares and other implements for farming and all the weapons needed for defense, the manorial quarry all the stone, its forests all the lumber needed for building, and its fields and its animals everything necessary to eat or to wear. At least the iron that went into implements had to be bought, and often such luxuries as furs or salt or occasional spices had to be bought also. The manor, then, was only comparatively self-sufficient and unspecialized. It had surpluses and deficiencies that gave it the motivation and the means for trade with outsiders. It provided something above a bare minimum of livelihood for at least a minority of the men and women who worked upon it.

Slavery also existed. All Germanic law codes prescribed enslavement as a penalty for many *delicts* (violations of laws or rights, hence *delinquents*). Since legal codes are the record of common practice, we have evidence that slavery was relatively commonplace, especially in Spain, Italy, and the Levant. The church recognized that slaves had souls, so it would intervene to some extent to protect slaves; but the church was often a major slaveholder itself and generally resisted movements for emancipation, since this would diminish its resources. However, slaves could be freed, thus adding to the ranks of freemen—as in Visigothic Spain, where they constituted a distinct legal class, indeed two classes of emancipates, or *liberti*. We have no reliable figures on the numbers of slaves or the extent of slavery, though it is believed that slavery declined after the collapse of the Roman Empire and was at its low point in the ninth century.

V THE CIVILIZATION OF THE EARLY MIDDLE AGES IN THE WEST

A General View

In letters and in the arts, the early medieval centuries saw a severe decline in the skills that had characterized the Roman Empire, even in its latest periods. Judged by comparison with the achievements of Greek, Hellenistic, or Roman civilizations, or by those of the Byzantine and Muslim East, those of western Europe in these centuries may sometimes seem feeble or primitive. But this is what one would expect in a world where life was often too turbulent to allow much leisure for the exercise of creative skills. The efficient Roman communication system had deteriorated. Cities, historically the homes of culture and of the commerce that makes culture possible and available, were often mere shells of their former splendor, where they had once been vibrant centers of communication. Technical skills were lost, as was command over Latin, the western European language of intellectuals and writers. No one spoke good Latin any

SLAVERY

A Christian prelate, Theodore, drafted a set of rules pertaining to male and female slaves in seventh-century England. The following is from the second penitential book—that is, a book on penances arising from the failure to adhere to discipline—of Theodore at Canterbury, section XIII:

1. If he is compelled by necessity, a father has the power to sell his son of seven years of age into slavery; after that, he had not the right to sell him without his consent.
2. A person of fourteen [years] can make himself a slave.
3. A man may not take away from his slave money which he has acquired by his labor.
4. If the master of a male and a female slave joins them in marriage and the male slave or the female slave is afterward set free, and if the one who is in slavery cannot be redeemed, the one who has been set free may marry a free-born person.
5. If any freeman takes a female slave in marriage, he has not the right to put her away if they were formerly united with the consent of both.
6. If anyone acquires [as a slave] a free woman who is pregnant, the child that is born of her is free.
7. If anyone sets free a pregnant slave woman, the child which she brings forth shall be [in a state] of slavery.

Early Welsh law also speaks of slavery. For example, the so-called Welsh Canons, dating from c 550-650, include entries such as these:

1. If anyone commits homicide by intention, he shall pay three female slaves and three male slaves and shall receive security.
4. If a slave kills a freeman, and this was through the freeman's fault, and if he was slain with a cudgel or an axe or a hoe or with a knife, that murderer shall be given over to the parents, and they shall have the power to do [with him] what they will.
5. If any master permits his slave to bear arms and he slays a freeman, the master shall be prepared to hand over the slave and another with him.
22. If any freeborn man or slave commits a theft by night and in the act of committing it is struck with a spear and killed, he who slays him shall have no need to make restitution.
38. If any slave kills another's slave, he shall remain alive as the joint property of the masters.

From John T. McNeill and Helene M. Gamer, eds., *Medieval Handbooks of Penance: A Translation of the Principal "Libri Poenitentiales" and Selections from Related Documents* (New York: Octagon Books, 1979), pp. 211-12, 374, 376-78.

more, and few could write it. The slowly developing vernacular languages—Romance-French or German—were written only infrequently, and usually hesitantly.

Yet a large question remains. Can we fairly use classical standards to judge the writing and art of a postclassical age, now evolving in many new directions? Most scholars would today be reluctant to do so, which is why we now reject the term *Dark Ages.* We now know enough about the original barbarian contributions to the culture of this period to dismiss old prejudices against them. Many barbarians loved and admired the Roman world that their fellow barbarians were destroying. They painstakingly kept alive, however crudely, the Roman literary and artistic tradition. Moreover, the widely traveled invading tribes brought with them art forms of their own—poetry, sculpture, and painting—that have only recently been widely appreciated by scholars.

Everywhere in the West, then, the story in general is the same, although it varies greatly in detail. The people of these centuries were gradually moving away from their Roman past, though still cherishing, and often trying with varying degrees of success to imitate, Roman models. They were also creating new and original writings and works of art that reflected their own barbarian past. While the Christian faith that the invaders took from the dwellers in the Roman Empire gave them a more permanent and firmer link with Rome itself and with its traditions than they would otherwise have had, they neither entirely absorbed the Roman heritage nor wholly abandoned their own traditions and practices.

Latin Literature: Italy

It was in Italy that the fight against the loss of the classical heritage was waged most vigorously and most successfully. Under the Ostrogothic king Theodoric (493-526), an admirer of the Greek and Latin cultural traditions, two distinguished intellectuals combated the general decline: Boethius and Cassiodorus.

Boethius (c 480-524), unlike most of his contemporaries, knew both Greek and Latin. Learned and versatile, he advised Theodoric on many points. He gave detailed directions to the king's brother-in-law, ruler of the Burgundians, for the making of a water clock. A

These sculptured figures are from the underground mausoleum at Poitiers of a seventh-century abbot, Mellebaude. Modeled on ancient tomb-chambers, this remarkable Merovingian art shows two thieves who are to be crucified with Christ, each bound to a cross of his own. In Latin on a wall nearby is painted the inscription, "Everything goes from bad to worse, and the end of time is near." This sense of pessimism and the primitive nature of the figures reinforce the later tendency to refer to the early Middle Ages as a dark period of "the barbarians."

Also preserved at Poitiers is the carved wooden bookstand owned by the Merovingian queen Radegund at the end of the sixth century. At the center of the carved reading surface is a lamb, representing Christ, and in each corner is the symbol of one of the four apostles: an eagle's head for John, a man's head for Matthew, a bull's head for Luke, and a lion's head for Mark. At the top, between two doves, is the Greek monogram for Christ, while at the bottom, also between two doves, is a cross in a circle. As in all Christian art, each decorative device carries a symbolic meaning that would have been well understood by contemporaries.

recognized authority on music, he selected the best available harpist to play at the court of Clovis, king of the Franks. He thwarted an effort of Theodoric's military paymaster to cheat the troops by showing that the paymaster had "sweated" the silver from the coins. He held the posts of consul (by then honorary, but still carrying enormous prestige) and of Master of the Offices, something very much like a prime minister and by no means honorary only.

Boethius planned a Latin translation of the works of Plato and Aristotle, and in the small portion that he completed he took care to make his translation as literal as possible. He also made the first efforts to apply to Christian theological writings the logical methods of Aristotle, writing works about the art of argument. These were to inspire scholars and thinkers who lived six hundred and more years after his death. Had Boethius survived to carry out his plans for rendering the greatest Greek philosophers into Latin, western Europe perhaps would not have been denied these materials for another five hundred years, and its intellectual development might have been speeded up. But only two years after making him Master of Offices, Theodoric imprisoned Boethius on a charge of treason. After a year in jail, Boethius was executed at age forty-four, perhaps because he was sharply opposed to the Arian Christianity practiced by Theodoric and the Ostrogoths.

In jail he wrote his most famous work, *The Consolation of Philosophy*, a dialogue between himself in his cell and the female personification of Philosophy, who appears to him. Written in excellent Latin, the *Consolation* is a moving and noble book in which the prisoner seeks—and is helped by Philosophy to find—answers not only to why he is suffering injustice, but also to the larger questions of human life and death on earth and the relationship between humans and God. Filled with reminiscences of classical authors and so sometimes criticized for its lack of originality, the book dwells on the prevalence of suffering, on the fickleness of fortune—which often unjustly punishes the innocent—and on the transitoriness and relative worthlessness of worldly triumphs. Everything we gain here on earth, even fame, will vanish. Largely owing to this book, Boethius' fame grew, for *The Consolation of Philosophy* became one of the most popular schoolbooks of the Middle Ages.

Cassiodorus (c 480-575) managed to stay in Theodoric's good graces and, like Boethius, became consul and Master of the Offices. He collected Theodoric's official correspondence. But his great ambition was to found a new Christian university in Rome, where the sadly neglected classical subjects could be taught and where a revival of learning and scholarship might take place. The terrible disorders that accompanied Justinian's recon-

THE DIALOGUES OF GREGORY THE GREAT

Gregory felt that too much emphasis had been placed on the lives of the saints who had wandered in the desert, and he sought to capture the legends of the sixth century in a new series of stories, which took place within recognizable locales, to which readers of the time could easily relate. An example comes from Book I:

It befell one day that a nun of the same convent went into the garden; there she saw a lettuce, and desired it and greedily ate it, forgetting to make the sign of the cross for a blessing. Suddenly she fell down, possessed by the devil, and sore vexed. Word was brought at once to Father Equitius, to come with all speed to her help. As soon as he came in at the door, the devil who had entered into her spoke by her mouth, as if to defend himself, and cried, *"What have I done? What have I done? I was sitting on a lettuce leaf, and she swallowed me."* Whom the man of God charged angrily to depart out of her, and to leave the handmaid of the most high God. And he departed forthwith, and had no power to hurt her more.

Translated from the Latin in W.P. Ker, *The Dark Ages* (New York: Mentor, 1958), p. 93.

quest of Italy from the Goths between 535 and 554 made this impossible. Instead, Cassiodorus founded a monastery in southern Italy where he tried to keep learning alive in its Christian form. The monks copied by hand not only the Bible but the best pagan Latin authors: Cicero, Vergil, and the rest. Cassiodorus himself wrote books on spelling, to help the monastic scribes with their task; on the *Psalms*, to provide the biblical text with a classical commentary; and on the soul, following in the footsteps of Cicero and his Greek masters. Some of his monks translated Greek works into Latin, helping turn the monasteries into centers of rote learning. When monks elsewhere encountered Greek passages in texts, they often wrote, "Greek; it can't be read," giving rise to our expression for anything incomprehensible—"It's Greek to me."

Far more typical of the period, however, were the views of Pope Gregory the Great, whom we have already encountered as the talented administrator who kept the church alive and kept Italy from falling into total chaos in the strife between the Lombards and the Eastern Empire. Practical in every way, Gregory was ready to abandon the classical past if he could bring more order into the barbarian and Christian present. "The same lips," he wrote one of his bishops, "cannot sound the praises of Jupiter and the praises of Christ," and he enjoined him to stop holding conferences where ancient literature was read. In Gregory's own writings, the same practical tendency appears; his *Dialogues* deal in four volumes with the lives and miracles of the Italian church Fathers, providing edifying anecdotes to attract Christian readers away from pagan authors and toward the proper contemplation of their own salvation.

But perhaps the most important of Gregory's writings

Contrasting details from two sculptured tombs in the crypt of Jouarre, east of Paris. Crypts (underground chapels) were common at the time. On the left is a detail from the tomb of Agilbert, of the late seventh century, with a poignant representation of men and women praying at the Last Judgment, their arms upraised. It is believed the artist was an Egyptian Christian who had fled from the Arab Muslim conquest. On the right is detail from the tomb of Theodechilde, of the eighth century, with carved shells and beautifully lettered Latin, in the Roman tradition. Thus an intense, emotional carving could be found side-by-side with the clean composition of classical art. Since Jouarre had close connections with Britain, similar sculptural styles are found in the crosses of northern England and of Ireland.

is his surviving correspondence, more than a thousand letters dating from the fourteen years of his papacy. Sent to all corners of the Christian world and dealing with every sort of problem in the management of the church and its relations with secular rulers, these letters reflect Gregory's humanity, commanding nature, enormous sense of the importance of his office, and even, at times, unexpected humor. No other pope of the early Middle Ages has left us so many letters, nor is there anything remotely resembling these documents as a vivid historical source in a period very little known to us, both before and after they were written.

Latin Literature: Gaul and Spain

Away from Italy, the center of the Roman world, the survival and cultivation of Latin letters naturally weakens. In Gaul, a highly Romanized province, there remained even during the invasions a cultivated group of Gallo-Roman aristocratic landowners and churchmen who still found it natural to communicate with each other in Latin. There were good poets among them, but perhaps the most distinguished writer of all was chiefly a prose stylist, Sidonius Apollinaris (*fl* 455-c 475).

Born of a family long prominent in imperial affairs and educated at the school of Lyon (still a major Roman provincial center), Sidonius eventually became bishop of Auvergne in south-central France during the invasions of Visigoths and Burgundians, while Huns and Franks were active nearby. Yet in 147 letters, written with a consecutive eye to preservation and future publication, Sidonius—essentially an aristocrat in his habits and tastes—writes almost as if nothing very alarming were happening in the outside world, and as if he and his fellow nobles, well born and well educated, still had control of what would happen in the future. With gentlemanly distaste, he refers to the Germanic invaders as underbred and coarse, not with the apprehension that they were bringing with them the doom of Sidonius and all his friends. He sneers at one of his fellow nobles who had learned the language of the barbarians. Still his letters correct the oversimplified view that the barbarian inroads invariably produced chaotic social upheaval.

By the time of the Frankish triumph in the next generation, the Gallo-Roman culture that Sidonius so proudly represented had virtually died. There was now very little literary activity. We have some moving sixth-century Latin hymns and descriptive poems by a writer known as Fortunatus, who deeply influenced Radegund of Poitiers, one of the first Frankish women to found and rule over a nunnery in France, and a poet in her own right. We have the history by which Gregory, bishop of Tours, chronicles the unedifying behavior of the Merovingian rulers in a Latin prose that would have shocked Sidonius. But there is a vigorous if primitive quality about Gregory, a mixture of credulity, native goodness, and calm acceptance of atrocities that gives the reader deep insight into the Merovingian age.

In Spain too, farther from Rome than Gaul though still a Romanized province, there was a good deal of writing in Latin, at least into the seventh century, which saw the *Etymologies* of Isidore (c 570-636), archbishop of Seville, a sort of encyclopedia. These *Etymologies* are outnumbered only by those of the Bible, and Isidore became perhaps the most influential and certainly the most representative literary figure of his time. His work was known in Ireland by the middle of the seventh century, and because the patristic (that is, written by eminent theologians called "Fathers of the Church") texts were often used during the Middle Ages by writers on Church liturgy and law, Isidore's listing of the cleric's duties became so well established that it was accorded semiofficial status by the middle of the twelfth century.

Besides works that can be attributed with reasonable accuracy to a specific writer, there were many accounts of the lives of the saints, known as *hagiographies.* Many people read, wrote, told, or learned about the saints through these anonymous works. Homely tales about the virtues of the saints as well as rousing exhortations to bravery in the manner of the early Christians created what may be the most influential literary sources of the period. When the church eventually canonized many hundreds of early leaders in the development of Christian theology or administration, this hagiography was heavily drawn upon.

Latin Literature: Britain, and the Continent Once More

The seventh century, then, saw the rapid decline of literary activity in the classical vein on the Continent. For a different spirit, destined eventually to restore Roman culture to the Continent, one turns to Britain, which had produced no Latin authors before the barbarian invasions. Christianity came to Britain, as we have seen, in three waves: one with the Roman troops, which virtually died out; one from Ireland, where it was of Gallic origin; and the third from Rome, at the end of the sixth century and the beginning of the seventh, in the mission sent by St. Gregory the Great. In England Christianity produced the first original writing in Latin. The combined influence of the Celtic and the Roman traditions brought such fruitful results that by the end of the eighth century missionaries from Britain stimulated a revival on the Continent—sponsored by Charlemagne himself, who provided the necessary interest and patronage.

Of several cultivated writers, the greatest was Bede (c 673-735), called the Venerable for his learning. Abbot of his own monastery, he could read Hebrew and Greek, knew the Latin writings of the church Fathers intimately, and wrote the famous *Ecclesiastical History of the English People,* the story of the spread of Christianity in England from the arrival in 597 of the missions sent by Gregory down to 731, almost to the moment of Bede's

THE VENERABLE BEDE

Bede tells us how, in 627, when the still-pagan king Edwin of Northumbria had received a letter from the pope, and a Latin missionary was at his court urging him to accept Christianity, he called his *witenagemot* (council of wise men) on the matter. One of Edwin's counselors then said:

> Man's life here on earth, O King, seems to me—so far as its uncertainties go—just the same as if, when you were sitting at dinner in the wintertime with your companions in arms and their servants, and a great fire had been kindled in the middle of the hall, and the hall was warm with its heat, but outside all about there raged the storms of winter rain and snow, a sparrow might come to the house, and fly through it swiftly, entering at one window and flying out at another. For the time while the bird is inside the house, it feels no chill from the winter blast, but after this tiny spell of fair weather has passed, that lasts only for a moment, the sparrow quickly passes again from winter to winter, and so is lost to your view. In the same way, this life of men comes into being for a brief moment, but what follows it and what went before it we certainly do not know. So if this new teaching [Christianity] has brought us anything surer to cling to, I think it should be followed.

Bede, *Historia Ecclesiastica Gentis Anglorum*, Book II, chap. xiii (London and New York: Loeb Classical Library, 1930), I, 283 ff. Translation ours.

Soon after, Edwin was converted. And the metaphor about human life on earth remains moving and effective more than thirteen centuries later.

death. Written in Latin of astonishing vigor and purity, it tells us almost everything we know of the progress of the new religion among the pagan Anglo-Saxons, about the Church's relationship with the Anglo-Saxon kings, and about the foundation of the many monastic houses, where monks found a shelter for themselves and their books. Bede's own even-tempered personality shines through the work, which sometimes rises to true poetic greatness.

Churchmen from Britain in particular helped make possible the great flowering of Latin letters that took place under Charlemagne. Alcuin of York (735-c 804), who had studied under a pupil of Bede, came to Charlemagne's court in 781 and helped to transform the palace school there into a serious and practical educational institution where men studied the seven liberal arts: grammar, rhetoric, dialectic (the art of argument), arithmetic, geometry, astronomy, and music. Alcuin wrote much prose and verse and took the lead in reviving biblical scholarship and in teaching such practical subjects as legible handwriting to the scribes, who now began to copy manuscripts in monasteries. We owe the survival of much of Latin literature to the efforts of these Carolingian scribes.

The foundations laid by scholars such as Alcuin permitted their successors in the next two generations, after Charlemagne's empire had disintegrated, to write history, poetry, saints' lives, works on theology and ethics, and vast numbers of personal letters in Latin. In new monastic centers the literary work made possible by the British immigrants who had been responsible for the "Carolingian Renaissance" went on, and the continuity of knowledge in Western civilization was assured.

Vernacular Literature: Beowulf

Britain's distance from Rome and its failure to become completely Latinized during antiquity allowed it to profit greatly from the double wave of Latin Christian missionaries—Celtic and papal—and so provide the needed stimulus for the Carolingian Latin literary revival. But the thinness of the Latin veneer probably encouraged the Angles, Saxons, and Jutes to produce a literature in their own language (called Anglo-Saxon or Old English). In contrast, the continental former Roman provinces were too inhibited by the overpowering prestige of Latin and perhaps also delayed by less stable political conditions than prevailed in Britain. Many writers in England did not hestitate to write in their own language. Sometimes they were translators; Boethius' *Consolation of Philosophy* was rendered into Old English, and King Alfred the Great himself translated Bede's *Ecclesiastical History*. Sometimes they were original writers, setting down a group of proverbs, or the life of a saint, or a chronicle, or—in verse—an account of one battle or another.

But by far the most remarkable Old English literary survival is *Beowulf*, a poem of almost 3,200 lines, preserved in only a single manuscript in the British Museum, written down about the year 1000. Hundreds of scholars have written thousands of pages about this poem; almost every statement about it might be questioned by some authority.

It is clear that the poem was composed well before the date of the surviving manuscript, perhaps as early as about 680 (it includes historical characters from the 500s), perhaps as late as 800 or even later. Until 1939

BEOWULF

Beowulf begins in Denmark, where it tells of the founding of the Danish royal line and the building of a great hall by King Hrothgar. The hall is repeatedly raided by a savage monster, Grendel, who seizes and eats the Danish warriors as they lie asleep after dinner, until from over the sea in southern Sweden comes a hero, Beowulf. He lies in wait for the monster and in single combat so severely grips his hand that Grendel has to flee, leaving his entire arm, ripped out at the socket, in Beowulf's hands. The wound is fatal, but Grendel's mother, more terrifying than her son, tries to avenge him. Beowulf has to slay her at the bottom of a wild and lonely lake. The Danes celebrate in delight. Beowulf returns home, becomes a king, and dies in a victorious combat with a dragon. Though *Beowulf* exalts heroic behavior, it is deeply concerned with the transitoriness of human life. The climax of all Beowulf's heroism, and the end of the poem, is the hero's death and funeral.

Here, in a famous passage, Hrothgar's queen, Wealhtheow, thanks Beowulf for killing Grendel:

To him she carried the cup, and asked in gracious words
if he would care to drink; and to him she presented
twisted gold with courtly ceremonial—
two armlets, a corselet and many rings,
and the most handsome collar in the world.
I have never heard that any hero had a jewel
to equal that . . . [ll. 1190-1196].

Applause echoed in the hall.
Wealhtheow spoke these words before the company:
"May you, Beowulf, beloved youth, enjoy
with all good fortune this necklace and corselet,
treasures of the people; may you always prosper;
win renown through courage, and be kind in your counsel
to these boys [her sons]; for that, I will reward you further.
You have ensured that men will always sing
your praises, even to the ends of the world,
as far as oceans still surround cliffs,
home of the winds. May you thrive, O prince,
all your life. I hope you will amass
a shining hoard of treasure. O happy Beowulf,
be gracious in dealing with my sons.
Here, each warrior is true to the others,
gentle of mind, loyal to his lord;
the thanes are as one, the people all alert,
the warriors have drunk well. They will do as I ask."

Then Wealhtheow retired to her seat
beside her lord. That was the best of banquets . . .
[ll. 1215-1234].

some scholars thought it had been composed in Northumbria, some in Mercia; but in that year a spectacular archaeological discovery at Sutton Hoo in Essex (East Anglia) turned up the ship-tomb of a king of the East Angles dating from the late seventh or early eighth century and containing a harp, jewels, and armor like those described in *Beowulf*, which also includes a description of a ship-funeral. So now some scholars think the poem may be of East Anglian origin. Some argue fiercely that the poem was written by a single author, others that it is a composite; some that it is a pagan poem with Christian interpolations, others that it breathes a wholly Christian spirit; some think that it has two parts, some six, some three. The poem has been described as "a museum for the antiquarian, a source-book for the historian, a treatise for the student of Christian thought, and a gymnasium for the philologist." It is, however, also unmistakably a poem meant for oral recitation.

The Arts

Like literature, the arts also gradually moved away from the standardized Roman forms toward newer achievements that were introduced as the barbarians merged their arts with those of the lands they settled. The early great churches of such important imperial cities as Milan or Trier were still large rectangular basilicas taken over from the secular architecture of the Romans, but innovations were tried for certain smaller Christian structures, especially baptisteries, which were detached from the main church. Some were square, others many-sided; rich mosaic decoration became common. As soon as a barbarian tribe was firmly established in its new territory, its kings, as a matter of prestige, built churches—often small, and generally imitative of the Roman models. While most of these structures have disappeared, we know from contemporary written accounts and archaeological research that they often had domes and tin or gilded bronze roof tiles that shone in the sun.

To find clear-cut examples of the kind of art the barbarians brought with them, it is easiest to turn to goldsmithing and jewelry. Fleeing before the Huns, the Germans who had settled along the shores of the Black Sea brought with them objects made by local craftsmen working in an Iranian or other Eastern tradition and characterized by brilliant color and the use of gems (often from as far away as India) or colored glass for ornamentation. In the Roman Empire, the tribes, notably the Ostrogoths, continued those arts. The Vikings also produced magnificent jewelry—sword-hilts, brooches, pendants—often embellished with gold, silver, and niello, in which silver, copper, lead, and sulfur were combined.

To understand the infuences exerted by the Byzantine outpost of the exarchate at Ravenna in particular, we must remember that between 642 and 752 virtually all the popes were of Greek or Syrian origin. These popes surely sponsored imports from the East and fostered the continued popularity of Eastern objects. The presence in the royal funeral-ship at Sutton Hoo of a massive round silver plate made at Byzantium in 491-518 and of two silver spoons with Greek inscriptions emphasizes the continuous contacts between the barbarians and the East.

The influence of the East, greatly stimulated by the influx of barbarians, led to the gradual abandonment of realistic representation of humans and beasts in art. Imported Byzantine silver, ivories, and textiles, as well as the Byzantine monuments like those of Ravenna, on Italian soil, helped speed the change in styles. The Carolingian period brought a new flowering of the arts. Surviving monuments in Italy gave the artists some of their inspiration, and Charlemagne's ability to attract the best craftsmen from anywhere in Europe enabled them to put their ideas into practice. Paintings and mosaics in Roman churches illustrated for worshipers what could be made of Christian subjects treated in the classical style.

Wall painting and mosaics are fixed monuments, and can be seen only by a traveler because they are widely separated from each other; but books are transportable,

A CELTIC FLOWERING

Historians once referred to the early Middle Ages as a "Celtic twilight," for little was known about the literature and oral traditions of the time. In more recent years medieval European thought has been extended to include areas once dismissed as the Celtic fringe. One body of material that has been reevaluated are the eleven stories collectively known as the *Mabinogion*, which were preserved in two Welsh collections, the White Book of Rhydderch and the Red Book of Hergest. Rediscovered in the sixteenth century, these stories were inaccurately edited and translated in the nineteenth century and ultimately made known in a form as near to the original as can be recovered in 1948. The title is modern—a *mabinog* was a literary apprentice, and not all the stories came down through the bards—but the stories show both the influence of other oral traditions, especially the French, and a largely idiomatic Celtic expression similar to the epic romances of the Vikings. The host of circumstantial detail is typical of tales meant to be recited. The second of the Four Branches of the Mabinogi tells of a war between the Irish and the Welsh with all the encrustations of legend:

The terms of truce were drawn up, and the house was built big and roomy. But the Irish planned a ruse. The ruse they planned was to fix a peg on either side of every pillar of the hundred pillars that were in the house, and to fix a hide bag on each peg, and an armed man was in every one of them. Efnisien came in ahead of the host of the Island of the Mighty, and scanned the house with fierce, ruthless looks, and he perceived the hide bags along the posts. "What is in this bag?" he said, to one of the Irish. "Flour, friend," said he. He felt about him till he came to his head, and he squeezed his head till he felt his fingers sink into the brain through the bone. And he left that one and put his hand upon another, and asked, "What is here?" "Flour," said the Irishman. He played the same trick on every one of them, until of all the two hundred men he had left alive but one: and he came to him and asked, "What is here?" "Flour, friend," said the Irishman. And he felt about him until he came to his head, and he squeezed that one's head as he had squeezed the heads of the others. He could feel armour on that one's head. He left him not till he had killed him. . . .

The Mabinogion, trans. Gwyn Jones and Thomas Jones (London: Everyman's Library, 1968), pp. 35-36.

Eastern influences contributed to the gradual abandonment of the realistic representation of humans and beasts in art. This change is shown by a set of stucco statues in the front of the church of Santa Maria in Valle at Cividale in northern Italy. These saints were carved by sculptors whose exceptional skills would have permitted them to do almost anything they chose. The detail is realistic, which had led scholars to date the statues from about 800 and to ascribe them to Byzantine artists working in Italy. But at the same time, art was more commonly becoming abstract, less concerned with exact detail—both cruder visually and more challenging emotionally. Compare the Cividale figures with the stone *stele,* or tombslab, from Germany, which is perhaps half a century earlier. On one side (not shown) the stele depicted a warrior; on the other, shown here, Christ was also depicted as a warrior. Contrast this with the fifth-century mosaic of Christ as a warrior in Chapter 4. The stele is now in the Rheinisches Landesmuseum in Bonn.

and it was largely through book illustration—the illumination of manuscripts—that inspirations from one region or one school could intermingle in other regions with influences from other schools. So north Italian books that embodied all these classical and Byzantine influences traveled across the Alps into Gaul and into Britain with Gregory the Great's missionaries. In due course the same influences penetrated into Germany, where artists under the Ottonian Emperors picked them up.

Charlemagne himself made five trips to Italy. Lombards from northern Italy joined Anglo-Saxons like Alcuin of York (735-804) at a court that had no permanent residence during the long years of continual campaigning, but that settled at last at Aachen in the Rhineland in 794. Here the new royal (soon imperial) residence was built at forced-draft speed. To Aachen came Romans, Lombards, Greeks from southern Italy and probably from Byzantium itself, Syrians, Anglo-Saxons, Irish, Spaniards from the Visigothic parts of Spain, Jews, Arabs, and the inhabitants of Gaul and Germany.

Charlemagne enjoyed receiving foreign travelers, many of them, especially officials, bringing rich gifts—relics, books, textiles, jewels. In 796 arrived a treasure trove captured from the Avars, who had been pillaging for two centuries. It filled sixteen oxcarts. The most sensational present was sent in 802 by the caliph at Baghdad, Harun al Rashid—a white elephant, Abu'l Abbas, who became a general favorite at Aachen and whose bones remained a wonder for many centuries after he died. Harun also sent Charlemagne a clock of gilded bronze with twelve mounted mechanical knights who, on the stroke of noon, emerged from twelve doors that shut behind them. Perfumes, silken tents, oriental robes abounded. Charlemagne had a good many beautiful daughters, whom the gentle, aging Alcuin nicknamed "the crowned doves that flit about the chambers of the palace" (and against whom he warned his stu-

A New Testament was made expressly for Charlemagne in the 780s. It was richly illustrated and was dedicated to "Charles, the pious king of the Franks with Hildegard his glorious wife. . . ." This illustrated manuscript marked the introduction of a new factor in early medieval art, the determination of a powerful royal patron to have artists work to his specific commands. In the early ninth century a book of church law was prepared at Vercelli. This illustrated page from it shows Constantine the Great on the throne at Nicaea, surrounded by the bishops who signed the Council's decrees. Below the throne, books propounding the Arian heresy are being burned. The Carolingian Renaissance was especially notable for its manuscript illumination of this type.

Charlemagne's decision to adopt southern building principles revolutionized architecture in northern Europe. Having traveled in Italy, he used Rome and Ravenna as models when he had his Palatine Chapel constructed at Aachen in 792–805. Here Byzantine sophistication was combined with dramatic and blunt geometrical strength. The chapel and Charlemagne's marble throne are still in place today.

The Church of San Apollinare in Classe, near Ravenna, shows how a sixth-century Christian church evolved from the style of the Roman basilica. Between 642 and 752 almost all the popes were of Greek or Syrian origin, and these Eastern popes sponsored many stylistic imports from the East, especially at Ravenna, the Byzantine outpost of the exarchate. The round tower shown here was added in the tenth century.

dents). The exotic atmosphere of the court remained a vivid memory for many centuries after the glory had departed.

Reflecting upon the Carolingian artistic explosion as well as upon a galaxy of writers that ranges from Boethius and Pope Gregory the Great to Isidore of Seville, the Venerable Bede, and the author of *Beowulf,* no scholar would now seriously maintain that the early Middle Ages in the West were "dark." Troubled, yes; often agonizingly wretched, yes; but certainly not dark.

SUMMARY

In the fifth century the structure of Roman government in the West collapsed under the pressure of invasion and migration by Germanic tribes. Much of the Roman heritage, however, was preserved by the church and the barbarians' own reverence for Roman civilization.

The Franks founded the most lasting political entity to arise from the ruins of Roman power. In alliance with the papacy, the Frankish king Charles the Great (Charlemagne) sought to revive the Roman Empire in the West.

In the tenth century Norse invasions severely disrupted Britain, Ireland, and northern France. By the year 1000 those invasions had died down and medieval Europe had begun to take shape.

Feudalism was the system of social and political arrangements that replaced the centralized Roman administration. Basically, it was a means of coping with the absence of strong central government. Local lords ruled over the peasants on their estates. In turn, these lords were the vassals of other lords, meaning that they owed them allegiance and services. Still other lords might be above these. This complex system varied from one part of Europe to another.

Most of Europe was organized into units called manors, owned and ruled by a noble or by the church. Most of the peasants on these manors were serfs, hereditary laborers who could not leave the land they worked. In return for protection given by the lord of the manor, the serfs were required to fulfill various obligations and hand over part of their crops. In time many lords came to prefer cash payments, so that they could purchase goods that the manor could not produce.

Early medieval culture was a blend of barbarian and Roman influences. Most serious writing was in Latin, especially in Italy and Gaul. Latin also enjoyed a revival in eighth-century England. Use of the vernacular languages was rare except in England, where the remarkable epic poem *Beowulf* was written in Old English.

The arts of this period combined Roman, German, and Byzantine elements. Under Charlemagne there was a significant artistic revival.

chapter six

BYZANTIUM AND ISLAM

At the far southeastern corner of Europe, on a little tongue of land still defended by a long line of massive walls and towers, there stands a splendid city. Istanbul it is called now, a Turkish form for three Greek words meaning "to the city." After 330, when the first Christian Roman emperor Constantine the Great made it his capital, it was often called Constantinople, the city of Constantine, but it also retained its ancient name—Byzantium. For more than eleven hundred years thereafter it remained the capital of the Roman Empire, falling to the Ottoman Turks in 1453.

The waters that surround it on three sides are those of the Sea of Marmora, the Bosporus, and the city's own sheltered harbor, the Golden Horn. A few miles to the north, up the narrow, swift-flowing Bosporus, lies the entrance to the Black Sea. To the southwest of the city, the Sea of Marmora narrows into the Dardanelles, a long passage into the Aegean, the island-studded inlet of the Mediterranean. The Dardanelles, the Sea of Marmora, and the Bosporus connect the Black Sea with the Mediterranean and separate Europe from Asia. Together, these are the Straits, perhaps the most important strategic waterway in European diplomatic and military history. The city dominates the Straits. To the Slavs of Russia and the Balkans, who owe to it their religion and much of their culture, this city has always been Tsargrad—city of the emperor. It was the center of a civilization similar in many ways to that of medieval western Europe, yet startlingly different in others.

I BYZANTIUM: THE STATE

The Emperor

After Constantine, Byzantium called itself New Rome. Its emperors ruled in direct succession from Augustus. Its population, predominantly Greek, called itself Rhomaian, Roman. Yet many non-Roman elements—Christian, Greek, Armenian—became increasingly important in Byzantine society. A Roman of the time of Augustus would have been ill at ease in Byzantium. After Constantine had become a Christian, the emperor was no longer a god; but he was ordained of God, and his power remained sacred. As there could be only one god in heaven, so there could be only one emperor on earth. The pagan tradition of the god-emperor was thus modified, not abandoned.

In theory, the will of God manifested itself in the unanimous consent of the people, the Senate, and the army to the choice of each new emperor. A reigning emperor usually followed the Roman practice and chose his heir, often his son, by co-opting him during his own lifetime. When an emperor selected someone not his son, public opinion required that he adopt him formally. Each new emperor was raised aloft on a shield as a sign of army approval, thus becoming *Imperator*, commander-in-chief. By the midfifth century, he was also formally crowned by the highest dignitary of the church, the partriarch of Constantinople, and he would swear to defend the Christian faith. In the seventh century the emperor began to call himself *Basileus*, King of Kings, in token of his military victory over the Persians. Later still he added the term *Autocrat*, for the emperor was an absolute ruler. Empresses bore corresponding feminine titles and in general played an important role. Three times in Byzantine history women ruled alone. While Byzantine dynasties sometimes lasted several centuries, politicians and the mob often intervened. They imprisoned and exiled emperors, murdered them, blinded or mutilated them (which made them ineligible to rule again), and then enthroned their own candidates. Revolution was viewed as the proper recourse against imperial tyranny.

An elaborate and rigid code of etiquette governed every movement the emperor made every day of the year. So complex were the rules of imperial life that books were written to describe them. The emperor's subjects remained silent in his presence. The emperor spoke and gave commands through simple, brief, and established formulas. When given gifts, subjects hid their hands beneath their cloaks, a Persian gesture implying that the touch of a mere human hand would soil the emperor. Those admitted to an audience approached with their arms held fast by officials and ceremoniously fell on their faces in homage when they reached the throne. On public occasions the emperor was acclaimed in song, to the sound of silver trumpets.

The "sacred palace," the emperor's residence, was the center of the state, and the officials of the palace were the most important functionaries of the state—administrative, civil, and military. All officials had a title that gave them a post in the palace as well as a rank among the nobility. At Byzantium many of the greatest and most influential officials were eunuchs (including Justinian's highly successful general Narses, who recaptured Rome, Naples, and Ravenna). This was an oriental feature of the state that astonished Westerners and made them uneasy. There was never a prime minister as such, though in practice an imperial favorite often controlled policy.

Despite such complex organization, the early emperors were at times threatened by the people of Constantinople. In the Nika revolt of 532 Justinian might have lost his throne had it not been for the coolness and bravery of his celebrated empress, Theodora, who said,

> *Now, above all other times, is a bad time to flee, even if we get away safely. Once a man has seen the light, he must surely*

These detailed mosaics from the Basilica of San Vitale in Ravenna, both from the sixth century, show the emperor Justinian and his wife, the empress Theodora. Theodora (c 500-547) played a major role in the long theological debates of the time.

*die; but for a man who has been an emperor to become a refugee is intolerable. May I never be separated from the purple [the symbol of imperial rank] and may I no longer live on that day when those who meet me shall not call me mistress. Now if you wish to save yourself, O Emperor, that is easy. For we have much money; there is the sea, here are the boats. But think whether after you have been saved you may not come to feel that you would have preferred to die. As for me, I like a certain old proverb that says: royalty is a good shroud.**

The Law

As the direct agent of God, the emperor was responsible for preserving the tradition of Roman law. Only the emperor could modify the laws already in effect or proclaim new ones. From time to time the emperor ordered the redrafting and recompiling of the statute books; thus he had on hand an immensely powerful instrument for preserving and enhancing power.

Justinian (r. 527-565) between 528 and 533 ordered his lawyers to dispose of obsolete, repetitious, and conflicting enactments, thus codifying existing Roman law. His *Code* included all legislation since Hadrian (117-138). The authoritative opinions of legal experts were collected in the *Digests*, an even bulkier work. The *Institutes*, a handbook for students, served as an introduction to both compilations. All these were set down in the Latin in which they had been issued, though Justinian's own laws, the *Novels*, or newly passed enactments, appeared in Greek. In the eighth century a new collection modified Justinian's work in accordance with Christian attitudes toward the family and with the decreasingly Roman and increasingly Greek and oriental character of the Empire. Under Leo VI, or the Wise (886-912), a new collection rejected much that dated from an earlier period, when the absolutism of the emperor had been less developed.

In the Byzantine Empire, justice could be rendered only in the emperor's name. The emperor was the supreme judge, and rendering justice was perhaps his most important function. Subordinate officials handed down decisions only by virtue of the power the emperor delegated to them, and the emperors themselves often rendered judgment in quite ordinary cases brought to them by their subjects.

The emperors of the later ninth century took great care in the systematic appointment of judges and created a kind of legal aid bureau to enable the poor of the provinces to make appeals to the capital. Judges were obliged to render, write out, and sign all decisions. New courts were set up, and new officials were created. Later, even in the provinces, side by side with the martial law administered by the local commanding general, soldiers could be tried in civil courts for civil offenses.

As defenders of the faith against hostile invaders, the Byzantine emperors fought one war after another for eleven hundred years. Sometimes the invaders were moving north and west from Asia: Persians in the seventh century; Arabs (adherents of the new Islamic religion) from the seventh century on; and Turks beginning in the eleventh century. The Empire was often shaken by these blows. Syria and Egypt, Roman for more than seven hundred years, were lost forever to the Arabs in the seventh century. But Charles Martel's victory at Tours in 732 was a far less significant check on the Muslims than was the victory of the Byzantine emperor Leo III, who had broken a major Arab siege of Constantinople in 717-718, fifteen years earlier.

*Procopius, *History of the Wars* (Cambridge, Mass.: Harvard University Press, 1961), I, xxiv, 35-38. Our translation as adapted from H.B. Dewing.

THEOPHILUS ON JUSTICE

The emperor Theophilus (r. 829-842) appeared every week on horseback at a given church and handed down judgments so fair and equitable that they have passed into legend:

One day when the Emperor appeared, a poor woman threw herself at his feet in tears, complaining that all light and air had been shut off from her house by a huge and sumptuous new palace which a high official of the police was building next door. Moreover, this official was the brother of the Empress. But the Emperor paid no heed to this. He ordered an instant inquiry, and when he found that the woman had told the truth, he had the guilty man stripped and beaten in the open street, commanded the palace to be torn down, and gave the land on which it stood to the woman. Another time, a woman boldly seized the bridel of the horse which the Emperor was riding, and told him that the horse was hers. As soon as Theophilus got back to the palace, he had her brought in and she testified that the general of the province where she lived had taken the horse away from her husband by force and had given it to the Emperor as a present to curry favor with him. Then he had sent the rightful owner of the horse into combat with the infantry, where he had been killed. When the general was haled before the Emperor and was confronted by the woman, he finally admitted his guilt. He was dismissed from his post, and part of his property was confiscated and given to the plaintiff.

Charles Diehl, "La Légende de Théophile," *Serminarium Kondakovianum*, (Belgrade: Institute Imeni N.P., Kondakova, 1931), IV, *Annales* 35. Our translation.

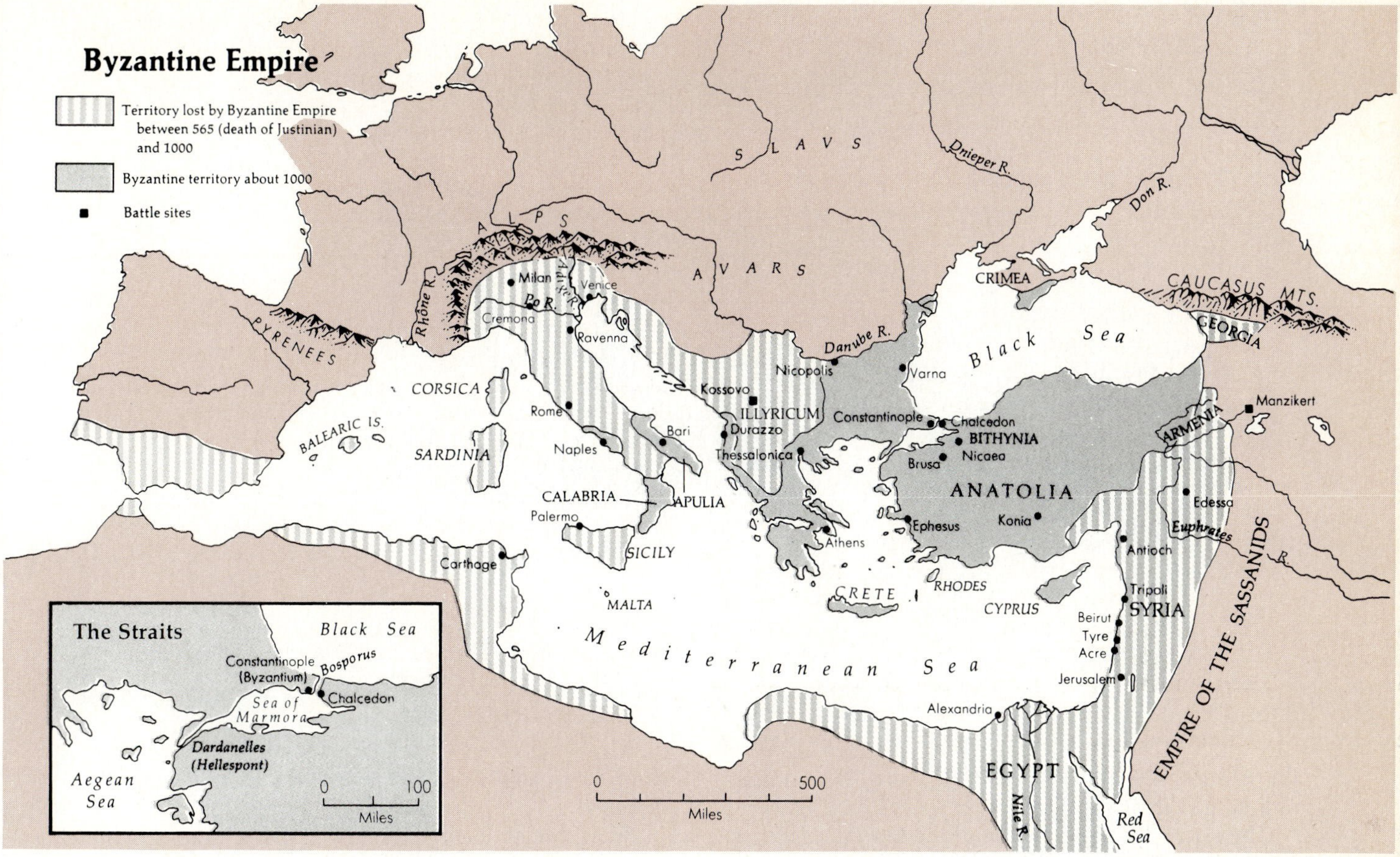

Byzantium thus absorbed the heaviest shock of Eastern invasions and cushioned the West against them. The Byzantine state was also engaged on all its frontiers in almost constant warfare against a variety of Asian enemies: the Huns of the fifth century, the Avars of the sixth and seventh, the Bulgars of the seventh and succeeding centuries, the Magyars of the ninth and later centuries, and the Pechenegs and Cumans of the eleventh, twelfth, and thirteenth centuries. All these peoples were initially Turkic, Finnish or Mongol nomads, at home for days at a time on their swift horses.

Sometimes the enemies were native Europeans, like the Slavs, who from the sixth century filtered gradually south into the Empire in a steady flow that eventually covered the entire Balkan peninsula with Slavic settlement. In the northeastern part of the peninsula just south of the Danube, the Slavs were conquered by the Hunnic tribe of the Bulgars but slowly absorbed their conquerors. These Bulgars, and much later the Slavic Serbs, fought exhausting wars against Byzantium.

So did the Russians, (or Varangians), another Slavic people, whose Scandinavian upper class was gradually absorbed into a Slavic lower class. They first assaulted Byzantium by sea in 860, having sailed across the Black Sea; they several times repeated the attack. (The Varangians, actually Vikings who moved through Russia, eventually formed the bodyguard of the Byzantine emperors.) Beginning in the eleventh century, the enemies were western Europeans: Normans from the southern Italian state in Italy and Sicily, Crusaders from France and Germany and Italy, freebooting commercial adventurers from the new Italian cities seeking to extract economic concessions by force or to increase the value of the concessions they already held.

For more than seven hundred years after Constantine, until the late eleventh century, when both Turks and Normans inflicted serious defeats, the Byzantines held their own. Though hostile forces sometimes swarmed to the foot of the land walls or threatened from across the Straits, Constantinople itself remained inviolable until 1204. In that year it was taken for the first time by a mixed force of Venetian traders eager for profit, and French, Italian, and German Crusaders, who had set out to fight the Muslims in Palestine and been detoured.

Only a state with phenomenally good armies and navies could have compiled so successful a military record. From all periods of Byzantine history, there survive studies of the art of war, discussing new ways of fighting and new weapons. The Byzantines were adaptable, learning and applying lessons from their enemies. Often commanded by the emperor in person, carefully recruited and thoroughly trained, well armed and equipped, entertained by bands playing martial music, served by medical and ambulance corps, by a signal corps with flashing mirrors, and by intelligence agencies far more competent than those of their rivals, the Byzan-

A fourteenth-century manuscript illumination illustrating the use of Greek fire.

tine armies, though occasionally defeated, by and large maintained their superiority.

The same is almost as true of the Byzantine navies. The appearance of a Muslim fleet in the eastern Mediterranean in the seventh century forced a naval reorganization by the Byzantines, who by the tenth century had recaptured their former control of these waters. In the eleventh century, like many Byzantine institutions, the navy suffered a decline from which it never recovered. Gradually, the developing Italian merchant cities replaced Byzantium as the great Mediterranean naval power; this was one of the main causes of the Empire's downfall. At its height, however, the Byzantine fleet played a major role in imperial defense. It was equipped with one of the most deadly weapons of the Middle Ages: Greek fire, a chemical compound squirted from tubes of siphons in the shape of lion's heads mounted on the prows of the Byzantine ships, which would set enemy vessels aflame, burn even when in contact with water, and strike terror into the hearts of their sailors.

Diplomacy

The Byzantines, however, preferred negotiating to fighting, and they brought diplomacy to a high level. The subtlety of the instructions given their envoys has made "Byzantine" a lasting word for complexity and intrigue. First Persia and then to some extent the Muslim caliphate were the only states whose rulers the Byzantine emperors regarded as equals. All others were "barbarians," and when they claimed an imperial title, as in the case of the Franks or the later German emperors, the claim was usually ignored in scornful silence or openly disputed.

Yet, although theory proclaimed that the Empire was universal, in their endless effort to protect their frontiers, the Byzantine emperors dealt realistically with those "barbarian" peoples whom they could not conquer. They negotiated treaties, obtaining military assistance and allowing the vassal peoples to share in imperial prestige and to enjoy the luxuries that Byzantine money could buy. A kind of "office of barbarian affairs" kept imperial officials supplied with intelligence reports on the internal conditions of each barbarian people, so that a "pro-Byzantine" party might be created among them and any internal stresses and quarrels might be turned to the advantage of the Byzantines.

As in Roman times, when the emperor sent arms to the chieftain of a foreign tribe, it was the equivalent of adoption. The Christian Byzantine emperor could make the paternal relationship even stronger by sponsoring a pagan barbarian ruler at his baptism. The son of such a chief might be invited to be educated at Byzantium, and thus introduced to all the glories of Byzantine civilization. Titles in the hierarchy of the palace, with their rich and valuable insignia, were bestowed on barbarian rulers; even a royal crown might be granted. Marriage was also a most useful instrument. Barbarian leaders were pleased to marry Byzantine women of noble family; and when it was a question of a particularly desirable alliance, the emperor himself might marry a barbarian princess or arrange to give a princess of the imperial house to a foreigner.

The Economy

Good armies and navies and impressive diplomacy always cost money. Byzantium was enormously rich. It was a great center of trade, to which vessels came from every quarter of the compass. From the countries around the Black Sea came furs and hides, grain, salt, wine, and slaves from the Caucasus. From India, Ceylon, Syria, and Arabia came spices, precious stones, and silk; from Africa, slaves and ivory; from the West, especially Italy, came merchants eager to buy the goods sold in Constantinople, including the products of the imperial industries.

The Byzantine emperors were able for centuries to maintain a monopoly of the manufacture and sale of silk textiles, purple dye, and gold embroidery—which were then not merely luxuries but absolute necessities for the dignitaries of church and state in both West and East. Long a closely guarded secret of the Persians, silk manufacture came to Byzantium in the midsixth century, when—so the story goes—two monks explained to the emperor that the mysterious cloth was the product of silkworms. Later, bribed by the promise of a great reward, they brought back silkworms' eggs hidden in a hollow cane. They taught the emperor that the worms must be fed on mulberry leaves. Great plantations of mulberries were established, especially in Syria, and a mighty enterprise was under way.

The power derived from control over the manufacture and sale of silk has been compared with modern control over such strategic materials as oil. But it was not only the imperial treasury that profited. The rich were able to embellish their persons and their homes; many middle-class merchants and craftsmen found a livelihood in the industry; and the flow of revenue into the imperial treasuries allowed the emperors to tax the lower classes less than would otherwise have been necessary for national defense and other official expenses. An elaborate system of control over manufacture (which was in the hands of carefully regulated guilds) and over sales (which were permitted only in official salesrooms) safely secured the monopoly down to the eleventh century.

Besides controlling silk, the emperor forbade the export of gold, to prevent the depletion of reserves. The *nomisma*, as the Byzantine gold coin was called, was standard all over the Mediterranean and even in the East. Until the mideleventh century it was rarely debased, and even then only gradually under the impact of a crisis brought about by civil strife and foreign invasion. For eight hundred years this money was stable.

Throughout Byzantine history the sources of state income remained much the same. Money came in from state property in land—farms, cattle ranches, gold and silver mines, marble quarries—as distinct from the money that came in from the emperor's personal estates. Booty seized in war or fortunes confiscated from rich men in disgrace provided cash. And of course there was also revenue from taxation—on land and persons, sales and profits, imports and exports, and inheritances.

From Diocletian (284-305) the Byzantines inherited the concept that land and labor were taxable together. The territory of the empire was considered to be divided into units called *yokes*, each of which was defined as the amount of land that could feed a single laboring farmer. To be taxable as a unit of land, each yoke had to have its farmer to work it; to be taxable as a person, each farmer had to have a yoke to work. The government thus had to find a person to cultivate every yoke; otherwise there would have been no revenue.

DAZZLING THE BARBARIAN

A solemn formal reception at the imperial court usually dazzled a foreign ruler or envoy, even a sophisticated Western bishop like Liudprand of Cremona (d. 972), ambassador of the king in Italy, who has left us his account from the year 948:

> Before the emperor's seat stood a tree made of bronze gilded over, whose branches were filled with birds, also made of gilded bronze, which uttered different cries, each according to its varying species. The throne itself seemed so marvellously fashioned that at one moment it seemed a low structure and at another it rose high into the air. It was of immense size and was guarded by lions, made either of bronze or of wood covered over with gold, who beat the ground with their tails and gave a dreadful roar with open mouth and quivering tongue. Leaning upon the shoulders of two eunuchs I was brought into the emperor's presence. At my approach the lions began to roar and the birds to cry out, each according to its kind. . . . After I had three times made obeisance to the emperor with my face upon the ground, I lifted by head and behold! the man whom just before I had seen sitting on a moderately elevated seat had now changed his raiment and was sitting on the level of the ceiling. How it was done I cannot imagine, unless perhaps he was lifted up by some sort of device as we use for raising the timbers of a wine-press.

Antapodosis, VI, v, in *Works of Liudprand of Cremona*, trans. F.A. Wright (London: Routledge & Kegan Paul Ltd., 1930), pp. 207-208.

This concept led to the binding of many peasants to the soil and to their slow degeneration into serfs. Large private landowners naturally flourished under such a system, since it was easier for the state to lease them large tracts of land and leave it to them to find the supply of labor. Moreover, inferior land or abandoned or run-down farms were compulsorily assigned to nearby landowners, who were then responsible for the taxes on such property as on their more productive acres. Only a landowner with rich and productive farm land could pay such taxes on the more marginal farms. So this aspect of the system also contributed to the growth of large private estates. Yet, though the large estate may have predominated in the early period, the small private freeholder seems never to have disappeared. In later centuries the balance between the two types of holding would swing one way or the other. But whether in large or small units, the economy rested primarily on agriculture, despite the glitter and sophistication of the imperial capital and it emphasis on trade.

II BYZANTINE CHRISTIANITY AND RELATIONS WITH THE WEST

Religion at Byzantium

Religion governed Byzantine life from birth to death. The church governed marriage and family relations, filled leisure time, helped determine all critical decisions. Religion also pervaded the life of the mind; the most serious intellectual problems of the age were theological and were attacked by brains second to none in power and subtlety. Religion dominated the arts and literature, economic life and politics. What the late twentieth century would call domestic issues were for the Byzantines political issues centering on theological problems. What was the true relationship of the members of the Trinity to one another? What was the true relationship of the human to the divine nature of Christ? Was it proper to worship holy images? Such problems were argued not only in monasteries and universities but also in the streets. A particular faction might riot if the emperor opposed its views. The questions were desperately important. The right answer meant salvation and future bliss; the wrong answer, damnation and eternal punishment.

Foreign policy was also pervaded by religion. When the emperor when to war, he went as the champion of the faith. Most often the enemies were infidels, heretics, or schismatics. The emperor went into battle against them with a sacred picture borne before him—an *icon* (image) of the Virgin, perhaps one of those which legend said had been painted by St. Luke, or one not even made by human hands at all but miraculously sent from heaven itself.

Contrast with the West

Yet much of this was also true in the medieval West. The real contrast is most apparent when we compare the relationship between church and state in the West with that in the East. In the West, the departure of the emperors from Rome permitted local bishops to create a papal monarchy and challenge kings and emperors. In Constantinople, however, the emperor remained in residence and no papacy developed. Constantine himself summoned the Council of Nicaea in 325; he paid the salaries of the bishops, presided over their deliberations, and as emperor gave to their decrees the force of imperial law. When he legislated as head of the Christian church in matters of Christian dogma, he was doing what no layman in the West would do. In the East the emperor regularly deposed patriarchs and punished clerics. He took the initiative in church reforms. The faith was a principle of civil law; the emperor often helped prepare canon law. Constantine's successors were often theologians themselves; sometimes they even legislated on matters of faith without consulting churchmen. In short, the church often functioned as a department of state, of which the emperor was the effective head, as he was of the other departments. One of his titles was "Equal to the Apostles."

A system in which a single authority plays the role of both emperor and pope is known as *Caesaropapism*, and this term is often, though at best only loosely, applied to Byzantium. Sometimes, for example, a partriarch of Constantinople successfully challenged an emperor. Moreover, absolute though they were, none of the emperors could afford to impose new dogma without church support or risk offending the religious beliefs of the people. The absolutism of the emperor did not apply to the inner, or "esoteric," form of the church, for the sacraments (that is, the mystery) remained the preserve of the clergy. Thus the emperor was more an "imitator of Christ"—the deputy of God on earth—with authority over both church and state.

Constantine had not wanted to intervene in the theological quarrel over Arianism, but he did so because the very structure of the Empire was threatened. The Council of Nicaea failed to impose a settlement, and the quarrel continued for another three-quarters of a century. Then, only fifty years later, new battles began over the relationship between the human and divine natures in Christ. Egyptian and Syrian Christians were monophysites—believers in a single, divine nature for Christ—as they are to this day, and they successfully resisted attempts to force them to compromise that were repeatedly made by the emperors, notably Zeno (474-491), Justinian (527-565), and Heraclius (610-641).

The Byzantines assumed, far more than did the western Europeans, that a person had very little chance of salvation. In the East, more than in the West, monasticism became an ideal of the Christian life; to become a monk was to take a direct route to salvation. Worldly men, including many emperors, became monks on their deathbeds to increase their chances of going to heaven. At Byzantium, monks enjoyed enormous popular prestige and often influenced political decisions; they provided the highest ranks of the church hierarchy. Rich and powerful laymen, from the emperor down, founded new monasteries as an act of piety. Often immune from taxation, monasteries acquired vast lands and much treasure. Though some emperors tried to check monastic growth, the monks continued to influence policies because of their hold over the popular imagination.

For the ordinary Christian, the sacraments of the church provided the way to salvation. In the East every religious act took on a sacramental quality. Every image, every relic of a saint, was felt to preserve the essence of the holy person in itself. God was felt to be *actually present* in the sanctuary; he could be reached only through the proper performance of the ritual. In the East the emphasis fell more on mystery, ritual, and a personal approach to the heavenly saviour than on the ethical teachings of Christianity. Once believers accepted the proper performance of an act as the right way to reach God, they could not contemplate any change in it; for if the old way was wrong, then their parents and grandparents were all damned.

Quarrels and Schism with the West

A difference in the wording of the liturgy, it is sometimes argued, caused the *schism*, or split between the Eastern and Western churches in 1054. The Greek creed states that the Holy Ghost "proceeds" from the Father; the Latin adds the word *filioque*, meaning "and from the son." But this and other differences might never have received much notice, and would probably not have led to a schism, had it not been for a political question at issue and for increasing divergences between the two civilizations.

More than three hundred years earlier, in the eighth century, a new religious controversy arose in the Byzantine Empire over the use of sculptured and painted sacred images (icons) and the nature and amount of reverence that a Christian might properly pay them. Something very like idolatry was widespread, and twice, for long periods (726-787 and 813-842), the emperors adopted the strict Old Testament rule that all images must be banned—*iconoclasm*, or image-breaking. The Western popes, who believed that images were educational and might be venerated (though not worshiped), were shocked and condemned iconoclasm.

In the end the emperors restored the images, but as early as the 730s an iconoclastic emperor had punished the pope by removing from papal jurisdiction southern Italy, with its rich church revenues, and Illyricum (the Balkan provinces), and placing them under the patriarch of Constantinople. The papacy was determined to recover its rights and incomes in these territories. Even more decisive than iconoclasm was the papal belief that Byzantium could not, or would not, defend Italy and the papacy against Lombards and Muslims, and the consequent decision of Pope Stephen II to turn for support to the Frankish Pepin and Charlemagne.

Competition in the 860s between papal and Byzantine missionaries to convert the Bulgarians again led to a political quarrel. It was then that the Byzantines "discovered" the Roman "error" in adding "filioque" to the creed. Though this quarrel too was eventually settled, an underlying mistrust persisted and was increased by the deep corruption into which the papacy fell during the tenth century. The Byzantines became accustomed to going their own way without reference to the bishops of Rome. When the papacy was eventually reformed in the eleventh century, the Byzantines did not at first understand that they were no longer dealing with the slack and immoral popes they had grown used to.

Under these circumstances the Byzantines were unprepared for a revival of the old papal efforts to recover jurisdiction over southern Italy. Norman adventurers began just after the year 1000 to conquer Byzantine territory in southern Italy and to restore its churches and revenues to the pope. The pope naturally welcomed this, but the Byzantine patriarch was unhappy over his losses. A violent and powerful man, he dug up the old "filioque" controversy, largely as a pretext for pushing his own grievances. In answer to his complaints, the pope in 1054 sent to Byzantium one of his most energetic and unbending cardinals. Patriarch and cardinal thereupon excommunicated each other, and the papal envoy shook the dust of Constantinople from his feet and sailed for home. From this clash we traditionally date the schism—the split between the Roman Catholic and Greek Orthodox churches. Despite numerous efforts at reconciliation since 1054, these mutual excommunications of the individuals involved were lifted only in 1965.

Eastern and Western Christians were also increasingly suspicious of and resistant to each other's cultures. To the visiting Westerner, in part jealous of the high standard of living in Constantinople, the Greeks seemed soft, effeminate, and treacherous. To the Byzantine, the Westerner seemed savage, fickle, and dangerous—a barbarian much like other barbarians. Nowhere is the Western attitude shown better than in the writings of Bishop Liudprand, who had been so impressed by the emperor's movable throne when he first visited Constantinople in 948 (see p. 155). On a second official visit in 969 as ambassador from Otto I, he describes his reception by the emperor Nicephorus Phocas:

> *On the fourth of June we arrived at Constantinople, and after a miserable reception . . . we were given the most miserable and disgusting quarters [that] . . . neither kept out the cold nor afforded shelter from heat. Armed soldiers were set to guard us and prevent my people from going out and any others from coming in. . . . To add to our troubles the Greek wine we found undrinkable because of the mixture in it of pitch, resin, and plaster. The house itself had no water, and we could not even buy any to quench our thirst. . . . Nice-*

*phorus himself . . . is a monstrosity of a man, a dwarf, fatheaded and with tiny mole's eyes; disfigured by a short thick beard half going gray; disgraced by a neck scarcely an inch long; piglike by reason of the big close bristles on his head; in color an Ethiopian, and, as the poet says, "you would not like to meet him in the dark."**

When Liudprand met the emperor's brother, they "tired [them]selves with a fierce argument over your imperial title. He called you not emperor, which is Basileus in his tongue, but insultingly Rex, which is king in his." As Liudprand left, he scrawled graffiti on the wall of his quarters, beginning

Trust not the Greeks; they live but to betray;
Nor heed their promises, what'er they say.
If lies will serve them, any oath they swear,
And when it's time to break it feel no fear.**

On the other side, the Byzantine reaction to Westerners is illustrated by the famous *Alexiad*, written by the princess Anna Comnena more than a century later, a history of her father, Emperor Alexius I Comnenus (1081-1118). She says that two Normans, Robert Guiscard and his son Bohemond

might rightly be termed "the caterpillar and the locust"; for whatever escaped Robert . . . Bohemond took to him and devoured. . . .

For by nature the man was a rogue and ready for anything; in roguery and cunning he was far superior to all the Latins [Westerners]. . . . But in spite of his surpassing them all in superabundant activity in mischief, yet fickleness like some natural appendage attended him too. . . .

He was such a man . . . as no one in the Empire had seen before. . . . for he was a wonderful spectacle . . . so tall that he surpassed the tallest man by a cubit [about eighteen inches]; he was slender of waist and flank, broad of shoulder, and fullchested; his whole body was muscular. . . . very white; his face was mingled white and ruddycolor. His hair was a shade of yellow, and did not fall upon his shoulders like that of other barbarians; the man avoided this foolish practice, and his hair was cut even to his ears. I cannot say whether his beard was red or some other color; his face had been closely shaved and seemed as smooth as chalk. . . . A certain charm hung about the man but was partly marred by a sense of the terrible. There seemed to be something untamed and inexorable about his whole appearance. . . . and his laugh was like the roaring of other men. . . . His mind was manysided, versatile, and provident. His speech was carefully worded and his answers guarded.†

The mutual dislike between Byzantines and Westerners was to grow steadily more intense after the late eleventh century, until it climaxed in tragedy in 1204.

**The Works of Liudprand of Cremona*, trans. F.A. Wright (London: Routledge & Kegan Paul Ltd., 1930), pp. 235-36.
**Ibid., p. 270.
†*Alexiad* (New York: Barnes & Noble, 1901), pp. 37-38, 266, 347. Translation partly ours, partly from Elizabeth A.S. Dawes.

III THE FORTUNES OF EMPIRE, 330-1081

When we are dealing with more than eleven hundred years of history, as with Byzantium from its dedication by Constantine in 330 to its capture by the Turks in 1453, subdivisions are useful. The late eleventh century provides the major break in Byzantine history; by then the decline in imperial strength could be plainly seen. We shall here bring the story only to 1081.

The first period runs from Constantine's dedication of his capital in 330 to the accession of the emperor Leo III in 717. Despite their efforts, the emperors at Constantinople could not reconquer the West and thus reconstitute the Roman Empire of Augustus. Indeed, theologial controversy, reflecting internal political strain, and combined with Persian and Arab aggression, cost the Empire Syria and Egypt. The internal structure was modified to meet the new situation.

From 717 to 867 the threat of Arab conquest was safely contained, the Bulgarians were converted, the major religious and political struggle over church images was fought and decided, and the large landowners began to emerge as a threat to the financial and military system.

From 867 to 1025 the Byzantine Empire was at its height. The emperors counterattacked the Arabs and regained much territory and prestige; the grim Bulgarian struggle was fought to a bloody conclusion; the Russians were converted; and the emperors made every effort to check the growth of the great landowning aristocracy. But the years 1025-1081 represented a period of decline, slow at first, accelerated as the period drew to a close. External military disaster accompanied and was related to the triumph of the landowners.

Constantine to Leo III, 330-717

The emperors immediately following Constantine were Arians until Theodosius I (379-395), who in 381 proclaimed orthodox Nicene Athanasian Christianity to be the sole permitted state religion. All those who did not accept the Nicene Creed were to be driven from the cities of the Empire. Theodosius' enactment illustrates the close relation of theology to politics and to imperial initiative. The Empire, East and West, was united under Theodosius, but his sons Arcadius (395-408) and Honorius (395-423) divided it, with Arcadius ruling at Constantinople. Although in theory it remained one empire, it was never again fully united in fact.

Until the accession of Justinian in 527, the eastern portion of the Empire successfully used Goths and other barbarians as troops and usually managed to deflect the new blows of invaders further westward. Despite the challenge from Huns and Persians, the East continued to prosper. Only the monophysite controversy warned of

Silver plate showing the emperor Theodosius with his sons Honorius and Arcadius on either side, bestowing the insignia of office on a local official. This Mass dish, made about 390, was found in the nineteenth century in Spain by two peasants, who split it in order to divide the profits, hence the clear broken line that runs across it.

internal weakness. The subtleties of theological argument partly revealed the challenge of Alexandria to Constantinople and the dangers of Syrian and Egyptian defection.

Justinian was so controversial an emperor that even his own historian, Procopius, besides several works praising him, wrote a *Secret History*, never published in his own day, that viciously denounced Justinian. We do not have to believe that Justinian was greater than Cyrus the Great or Themistocles, as Procopius says when praising him; neither do we have to believe that he was a demon who walked around the palace at night without his head, as Procopius tells us in the *Secret History*.

In an epic series of wars, Justinian's armies reconquered North Africa from the Vandals, Italy from the Ostrogoths, and southern Spain from the Visigoths, in a last desperate effort to reunite all of Rome's Mediterranean lands. But the long campaigns and a vast new system of fortifications proved extremely costly. By limiting his wars with the Persians on the eastern frontiers to defensive efforts, Justinian permitted the Persian danger to grow. His immediate successors could not check it, while in Europe Slavs and Avars crossed the Danube line and filtered into the Balkans.

The Empire did not have to pay the full bill for Justinian's policies until the early seventh century. During the reign of Phocas I (602-610), internal bankruptcy and external attacks from the Persians seemed to threaten total destruction. But Heraclius (610-641), the son of the Byzantine governor of Africa, sailed in the nick of time from Carthage to Constantinople and seized the throne. He spent the first years of his reign in military preparations, absorbing heavy losses as the Persians took Antioch, Damascus, Jerusalem, and Alexandria. After 622 Heraclius began his counteroffensive. In 626 the Persians threatened Constantinople from the Asian side of the Straits, while the Slavs and Avars were besieging it in Europe; still the Byzantines beat off the double threat. Heraclius defeated the Persians on their own territory and recaptured all the lost provinces.

But only a few years later, the new movement of Islam exploded out of Arabia and overran the very provinces that Heraclius had recaptured from the Persians. In both the Persian and the Muslim victories over Byzantium, the antagonism of the monophysite Syrians and Egyptians played a major part. From Egypt the Muslims pushed westward to Carthage in 698, putting an end to Byzantine North Africa. Muslim ships began to operate from Cyprus and Rhodes. In northern Italy the Lombard kingdom now threatened the imperial possessions. Heraclius' work and that of Justinian were seemingly undone.

Despite the desperate crisis, the emperors completely overhauled the administrative machinery of the state. Gradually they extended the system of government previously introduced into Italy to their remaining territories in Asia Minor and the Balkans. The loss of Syria and Egypt required the transformation of Asia Minor into a reservoir of military manpower; the perpetual raids of Slavs, Avars, and Bulgars into the Balkan provinces made the emergency more acute and increased still more the dependence on Asia Minor. Eventually the emperors divided Asia Minor and the Balkans into army corps areas, with the local military commanders also exercising civil authority. These new military districts were called *themes*, from a word meaning permanent garrison. In each theme the troops were recruited from the native population; in return for their military services, the independent farmers were granted land, but they were not allowed to dispose of it or to evade their duties as soldiers. Their sons inherited the property along with the obligation to fight. From the start, one of the themes was naval.

Though in theory responsible to the emperor, the commanding generals of the themes often revolted, and in the late seventh and early eighth centuries such rebellious generals seized the imperial throne. The imperial government strove to combat this danger—inevitable when military and civil powers were united in the same hands—by dividing the large original themes into smaller ones. From seven big themes at the end of the seventh century, the number mounted to about thirty smaller ones by the year 900. The emperors also asserted their direct supervision of the civil service departments.

This new system also embodied a change in concepts of taxation. As new immigration and settlement apparently ended the labor shortage of earlier centuries, it was now possible to separate the land tax from the tax on persons. The latter was transformed into a hearth tax, which fell on every peasant household without exception. For purposes of the land tax, each peasant village was considered a single unit. Imperial tax assessors regularly visited each village, calculated its total tax, and assessed each inhabitant a portion of it. The community as a whole was held responsible for the total tax, and often the neighbor of a poor peasant or of one who had abandoned a farm would have to pay the extra amount to make up the total. This obligation was onerous, and when the tax could not be collected the state itself sometimes had to take over the property and resell or rent it. Displaced officials, overburdened land owners, harried peasants, new immigrants who did not in their hearts accept the religious principles emanating from Constantinople—all these weakened the idea of unity for a common purpose.

Leo III to Basil I, 717-867

In 717-18 Leo III, who had come to the throne as a successful general, defeated the Arabs who were besieging Constantinople. Thereafter the Byzantine struggle against the Muslims gradually became stabilized along a fixed frontier in Asia Minor. But the Muslim capture of Crete and Sicily in the ninth century opened the way for repeated pirate raids against the shores of Byzantine Greece and southern Italy. In northern Italy the Lombards extinguished the exarchate of Ravenna in 751, and Byzantine rule was interrupted by the alliance between the Franks and the papacy. The Byzantine *dux* of Venetia moved his headquarters to the island of the Rialto and thus became the forerunner of the *doges* (chief magistrates) of Venice, which from 810 enjoyed considerable autonomy. And in the Balkans the Bulgarian menace reached a new peak of severity.

Under the iconoclastic emperors, the movement took on in its later phases a violent antimonastic aspect, since the monks of Byzantium were the great defenders of the images, and the monasteries, being free from taxation, were competing centers of wealth. During this phase of the struggle some of the monks challenged the right of emperors to legislate in matters of religion. But the images were twice restored by imperial decree (each time by an empress, in 787 and 843), as they had twice been banned by imperial decree. As a result of the struggle, the Byzantines drew more careful distinctions between superstitious adoration paid to images and proper reverence. When the controversy was resolved, it was tacitly understood that no more religious statues would be carved in the round.

Although the new system of small military holdings and the growth of a free peasantry retarded the development of large estates during the eighth and ninth centuries, large landlords were again beginning to accumulate big properties. One cause may have been the ruin of the small farmers in Anatolia as a result of disorders that accompanied a great rebellion under Thomas the Slav. After twice threatening to subvert the throne, this rebellion was put down in 824.

Basil I through the "Time of Troubles," 867-1081

Although intrigue and the violent overthrow of sovereigns remained a feature of Byzantine politics, the people developed a deep loyalty to the new ruling house that was established in 867 by the Armenian Basil I (867-886) and called the Macedonian dyanasty because of his birth there. Even usurpers now took pains to legitimize themselves by marrying into the imperial house. As political disintegration began to weaken the opposing Muslim world, the Byzantines counterattacked in the tenth century. They captured Crete in 961 and Antioch and much of northern Syria in 962, after three centuries of Arab domination.

A new Muslim dynasty in Egypt, which also took over in Palestine, stopped the Byzantine advance short of Jerusalem. But like the later Crusaders from the West, the Byzantine emperors still hoped to liberate Christ's city from the Muslims. While pushing back the Muslims, the Byzantines allied themselves with the Armenians and gradually annexed Armenia. This was almost surely a mistake. Armenia, which had been a valuable buffer against the Turks of Central Asia who were now beginning to raid eastern Asia Minor, lay open to direct attack. Firmly reestablished in southern Italy in the face of the Muslim threat from Sicily, the Byzantines dominated the neighboring Lombard duchies until after the advent of the Normans in the early eleventh century. From then on the emperors would find themselves under attack on three fronts—in Asia Minor, in southern Italy, and against the Bulgarians.

Under the early emperors of the Macedonian dynasty, the large landowners continued to flourish. Whole dynasties of nobles lived on their great estates. They were the powerful, who were constantly acquiring more land at the expense of the poor. The more they got, the more they wanted. They bought up the holdings of the poor and made the peasantry once more dependent upon them. The growing might of the local magnates meant that the state was losing both its best taxpayers (the free peasants) and its best soldiers (the military settlers).

During the tenth and eleventh centuries, a great struggle developed between the emperors and the powerful, parallel in some ways to the struggle between the monarchy and the feudal nobility in France though destined to end differently. The powerful thwarted all imperial attempts to check the growth of their economic and military power and eventually seized the throne itself. Laws intended to end the acquisition of land by the local magnates could not be enforced; in times of bad harvest especially, the small free proprietor was forced to sell out to his rich neighbor.

The great emperor Basil II (976-1025) made the most sustained efforts to reverse this process. He confiscated the estates of those who had acquired their estates since the rule of his grandfather. Others could keep their lands on satisfactory proof of prior ownership. As a final blow to the powerful, Basil II ordained that they would have to pay all the tax arrears of the delinquent peasants, thus relieving the village communities of the heavy burden that was so difficult for them to bear and placing it on the shoulders of the rich.

But a few years after Basil died, this law was repealed under the influence of the magnates, who thenceforth proved "more merciless than famine or plague." As the landlords got more and more of the free military peasants as tenants on their estates, their own military role grew more important and they became virtual commanders of private armies. After Basil, only the civil servants acted as a counterweight to the landowners. To reduce their power, the civil servants tried to cut down the expenses of the army, in which the landlords were now playing the leading role. Strife between these two parties weakened the imperial defenses.

The Macedonian dynasty died out in 1057, and a "time of troubles" began. The Normans drove the Byzantines from the Italian peninsula by taking the great southern port of Bari in 1071. In the same year, after three decades of raids across the eastern frontier of Asia Minor, the Seljuk Turks defeated the imperial armies at Manzikert in Armenia and captured the emperor Romanos IV. Asia Minor, mainstay of the Empire, now lay open to the Turks, who pushed all the way to the Straits and established their capital in Nicaea. Meanwhile other Turkic tribes—Pechenegs and Magyars—raided southward into the Balkans almost at will. In 1081 one of the powerful magnates of Asia Minor came to the throne, Alexius I Comnenus, who seized Constantinople.

IV BYZANTIUM AND THE SLAVS

Perhaps the major Byzantine cultural achievement was the transmission of their civilization to the Slavs. Much as Rome Christianized large groups of "barbarians" in western Europe, so Constantinople, the new Rome, Christianized in eastern Europe. Some of the problems that beset the West today in its dealings with the Soviet Union arose because the Soviet Union is first and foremost Russia—a country in the Orthodox and not in the Western Christian tradition, a country that still shows the effects of having experienced its conversion from Byzantium rather than from Rome.

Conversion of the Bulgarians

The first Slavic people to fall under Byzantine influence were the Bulgarians, product of a fusion between a Slavic population and a smaller group of Asiatic Bulgar invaders. From the time these barbarians crossed the Danube in the late seventh century, they engaged in intermittent warfare against the Byzantine Empire. The Bulgars created a powerful state and imported Greek artisans to build the palaces of the native rulers. But the Bulgarian rulers hesitated to accept missionaries from Byzantium fearing the extension of Byzantine political power.

At the same time, a Slavic people called the Moravians had also established a state in what is now Czechoslovakia. Their rulers associated Christianity with their powerful neighbors, the Germans, and feared both German and papal encroachment, as the Bulgarians feared Byzantium. To avoid German or papal influence, the king of the Moravians in 862 sent to Byzantium and asked for a Greek missionary to teach the Moravian people Christianity in their own Slavic language.

The Byzantine emperor Michael III sent to Moravia two missionaries, Cyril and his brother Methodius, called the Apostles to the Slavs. They knew Slavic and invented an alphabet in which it could be written. That alphabet, still employed by the Russians, the Bulgarians, and the Servs, is still called *Cyrillic* after its inventor. Almost at once, as a countermove, Boris, ruler of the Bulgarians, asked for Christianity from the Germans. But these efforts by the two Slavic rulers to avoid conversion at the hands of their powerful neighbors and to obtain it instead from a less threatening distant court failed. German pressure and papal dislike for church services conducted in any language but Latin proved too strong. The German clergy and Roman Christianity eventually triumphed in Moravia.

Similarly, despite Boris's long correspondence with the popes, the power of nearby Byzantium was too strong. Boris found that he could not obtain an independent church from the papacy. Byzantium, on the other hand, permitted the Bulgarians virtual ecclesiastical autonomy. Only in the fold of the Eastern church could Boris unify his country and consolidate his own autocratic power. In Bulgaria, then, from the late ninth century on, the language of the church was the native Slavonic tongue preached by followers of Cyril and Methodius.

But the ambitions of the Bulgarian rulers were ultimately too great to permit friendly relations with Byzantium. Under Simeon (893-927), second son of Boris, educated in Constantinople and called "half-Greek," there began a bitter hundred-years' war, during which the Bulgarians tried to make themselves emperors by conquering Constantinople itself. In 981 the Bulgarian ruler Samuel defeated Basil II. But in 1014 Basil captured fourteen thousand Bulgarian prisoners and savagely blinded ninety-nine out of every hundred; the hundredth man was allowed to keep the sight of one eye, so that he could lead his comrades home. At the ghastly sight of his blinded warriors, Samuel fell dead of a stroke. Basil II took the appropriate name of "Bulgar slayer," and shortly afterward Byzantine domination over Bulgaria became complete, and the country was ruled as a conquered province. But its inhabitants were never deprived of their own church, whose archbishop had as much jurisdiction as in the days of Bulgarian independence.

The great expenditures of money and manpower incurred in the long pursuit of the Bulgarian war played their part in weakening Byzantium for the military disasters that were to come at Manzikert and at Bari in 1071. But these events helped to determine where the line between East and West would be drawn for future history. The Bulgarians are an Orthodox people to this day, and their civilization throughout the Middle Ages directly reflected the overpowering influence of Byzantium. In much the same way, more than three hundred years later, the western neighbors of the Bulgarians, the Serbs, also took their faith from the Greek East after a flirtation with the Latin West.

Conversion of the Russians

To the north and east of the Balkan Bulgarians, between the Baltic and the Black Seas, lie the great plains of European Russia. Here movement is easiest by water, along rivers that flow north to the Baltic or south to the Black or Caspain Seas. Beginning in the eighth century, the Scandinavians expanded into Russia. First taking control of the Baltic shore, they moved south along the rivers to the Sea of Azov and the northern Caucasus. Their name was *Rus*, which has survived in the modern term *Russian*. Gradually they overcame many of the Slavic, Lithuanian, Finnish, and Magyar peoples who were then living on the steppe. The details of this process are obscure. The story told in the Old Russian *Primary Chronicle*, compiled during the eleventh century, is suggestive of what may have happened among the inhabitants of Russia sometime in the 850s:

> *There was no law among them, but tribe rose against tribe. Discord thus ensued among them, and they began to war one against another. They said to themselves, "Let us seek a prince who may rule over us, and judge according to the law." They accordingly went overseas to the Varangian [i.e., Scandinavian] Russes . . . [and] said to the people of Rus, "Our whole land is great and rich, but there is no order in it. Come to rule and reign over us."**

This is known as the "calling of the princes." The *Chronicle* goes on to tell how the Viking Rurik accepted the invitation in 862 and settled in the Slavic trading town of Novgorod. Scandinavian princes then moved south along the Dnieper River. They seized the settlement called Kiev, still today the major city of the Ukraine, and made it the center of a state at first loosely controlled and devoted to trade. In 860, for the first time, a fleet of two hundred of their warships appeared off Constantinople, where at first they caused panic before they were repulsed. During the next two centuries there were three further attacks as well as other wars, which the Byzantines won.

Though a brisk trade developed between the Byzantines and the Rus people, the continuing religious influence that Byzantium exercised upon the Russians was even more important. There is evidence in a trade treaty of 945 that some of the Russian envoys were already Christians, swearing by the Holy Cross to observe the provisions of the treaty. In the 950s Olga, the ruling princess of Kiev, visited the emperor at Constantinople.

> *Olga came before him, and when he saw that she was very fair of countenance and wise as well, the Emperor wondered at her intellect. He conversed with her and remarked that she was worthy to reign with him in his city. When Olga heard his words, she replied that she was still a pagan, and that if he desired to baptize her, he should perform this function himself; otherwise, she was unwilling to accept baptism. The Emperor, with the assistance of the Patriarch, accordingly baptized her. . . . After her baptism, the Emperor summoned Olga and made known to her that he wished her to become his wife. But she replied, "How can you marry me, after yourself baptizing me and calling me your daughter? For among Christians that is unlawful, as you yourself must know." Then the Emperor said, "Olga, you have outwitted me."**

The Russians were converted as a people during the late 980s during the reign of Vladimir. He felt the inadequacy of the old faith, about which we know little except that the Russians worshiped forest and water spirits and a god of thunder. According to the partly legendary story in the *Chronicle*, Vladimir was visited by representatives of the different faiths, who told him about their beliefs. He discarded the faith of Mohammad because circumcision and abstinence from pork and wine were disagreeable to him. "Drinking," said he, "is the joy of the Russes. We cannot exist without that pleasure." Judaism he rejected because the God of the Jews had not been strong enough to enable them to stay in their native Jerusalem. Roman Christianity he rejected because it required a certain amount of fasting, as of course did the Christianity of the Greeks. But the cautious Vladimir did not accept this fourth possiblity, Orthodox Christianity, until after he had sent a commission to visit various countries where all the faiths were practiced and to report back to him. Shortly after he received their report he was baptized and married a Byzantine princess. Returning to Kiev, he threw down all the idols in the city. It is said that in one day he forcibly baptized the entire population in the waters of the Dnieper.

Despite its legendary features, the story of Vladimir reflects the various cultural influences to which the Kievan state was exposed. It had Muslim, Jewish,** and Roman Catholic Christian neighbors, but the most powerful and influential neighbor was the Orthodox and Greek Byzantium. Doubtless the marriage alliance with the Byzantine princess and the resulting gain in prestige played a part in Vladimir's decision. To secure the conversion of the Russians to the Byzantine form of Christianity was also important for the Byzantines, who needed to protect their possessions along the Black Sea and their capital itself against renewed Russian attack.

The church became an important social force in

*Samuel H. Cross, *The Russian Primary Chronicle*, in *Harvard Studies and Notes in Philology and Literature* (Cambridge, Mass.: Harvard University Press, 1930), XII, 145. Reprinted by permission.

*Ibid, pp. 168-69.

**The Turkic tribe of the Khazars, settled along the lower Don River, had been converted to Judaism.

THE CONVERSION OF VLADIMIR

Vladimir (r. 980-1015) accepted Orthodox Christianity only after a commission he sent to visit the countries where it and other religions were practiced reported back to him as follows:

The envoys reported, "When we journeyed among the [Moslems] we beheld how they worship in . . . a mosque, . . . and there is no happiness among them, but instead only sorrow and a dreadful stench. Their religion is not good. Then we went among the Germans [Roman Catholics], and saw them performing many ceremonies in their temples; but we beheld no glory there. Then we went on to Greece [Byzantium], and the Greeks led us to the edifices where they worship their God, and we knew not whether we were in heaven or on earth. For on earth there is no such splendor or such beauty. . . . We only know that God dwells there among men, and their service is fairer than the ceremonies of other nations.

Samuel H. Cross, *The Russian Primary Chronicle*, in *Harvard Studies and Notes in Philology and Literature*, (Cambridge, Mass.: Harvard University Press, 1930) XII, 199. Reprinted by permission.

Kievan society, and the Slavic clergy formed a new and influential social class. Although the Byzantines always asserted theoretical sovereignty over the Russian church, and although the first archbishops of Kiev were mostly Greeks appointed from Byzantium, the Russian church early asserted its practical independence. From the first the church in Russia became an important landowner, and, as in the Byzantine Empire, monasteries multiplied. The clergy came to have legal jurisdiction over all Christians in cases involving morals, family affairs, and religious matters. The concept that crimes should be punished by the state replaced the old concept that punishment was a matter of personal revenge. For the first time formal education was established; the Cyrillic alphabet was adopted, and literature written in Russian began to appear, almost all of it ecclesiastical. Byzantine art forms were imported and imitated; the great Church of Saint Sophia at Kiev is in its way as magnificent as its namesake in Constantinople. However, the pagan faith persisted in the enormous rural areas, and the new culture was largely confined to the few cities and to the monasteries.

Yet many scholars have argued that the short-run gain was outweighed by a long-run loss. The very use of the native language in the liturgy (so great an advantage to the Byzantines when, as missionaries, they sought to spread their faith without insisting on the use of Greek) meant that the culture of Russia had little contact with Western thought. In the West, every priest and every monk had to learn Latin; as soon as he did so, he had the key to the treasures of Latin classical literature and the works of the Latin church Fathers, themselves formed in the schools of pagan rhetoric, philosophy, and literature. The educated person in the West, usually a cleric, had access to Vergil, to Ovid, to Cicero, and to the other Roman authors—some quite unsuitable for clerical reading but all giving the reader a sense of style, a familiarity with ancient taste and thought, and sometimes solid instruction. He had Jerome and Augustine. For those in the West who had the leisure, the talent, the inclination, and the luck to find themselves in a monastery with a good library, the opportunity for learning was open.

The fact that the Byzantines did not insist on the use of Greek in the liturgy meant that the Russian clergy did

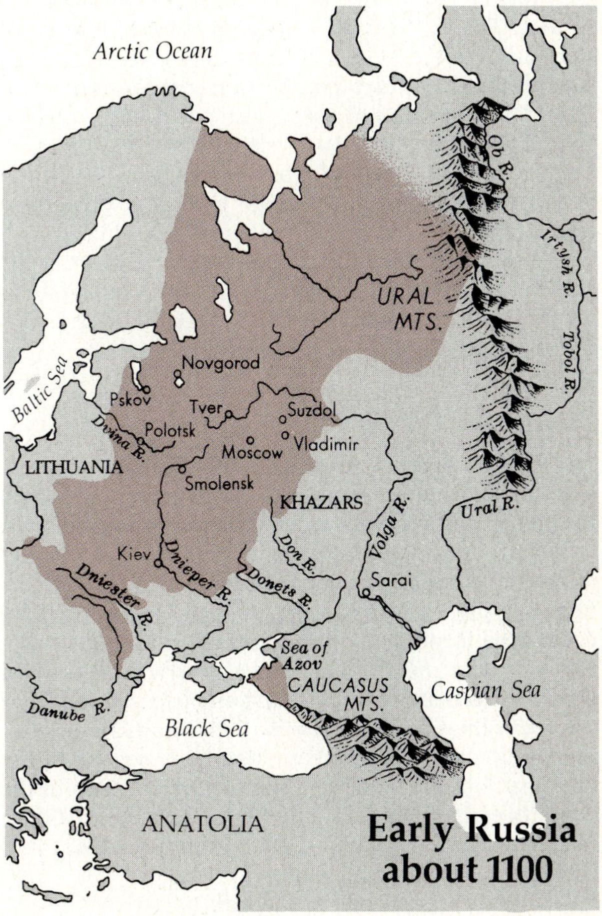

Early Russia about 1100

not automatically learn Greek, as French or English or German or Spanish priests had to learn Latin. And of course the Latin heritage was not available to the Russians either. A very few Russians did learn Greek, but by and large the great Greek classical heritage of philosophy and literature was closed to the Russians. Byzantine sermons, saints' lives, some chronicles and history, and certain other pieces of Byzantine literature were indeed translated and circulated in Slavonic. But these were no substitutes for Plato and Aristotle, Homer and the dramatists. The conversion to Christianity from Byzantium thus had the effect of stunting the intellectual and literary progress of Russia. The Kievan Russians of the tenth century were not ready for Plato and Aristotle, but when the time in their development came when the Russians were ready, they were cut off from access to the treasurehouse.

Indeed, in the nineteenth century an influential group of Russian thinkers argued that conversion from Byzantium had led Russia into stagnation and intellectual sterility, because it had cut Russia off from Rome, the fountainhead of the intellectual and spiritual life of the West, without providing a substitute. Their opponents argued just as vigorously that it was precisely the Orthodox faith accepted from Byzantium that gave modern Russia its high degree of spirituality, its willingness to bend to the will of God, and indeed all the virtues that they found in the Russian character and the Russian system. This difference of opinion persists, but most students argue that modern Russia has shown a considerable cultural lag in comparison with Western countries, that this cultural lag is partly attributable to the fact that Christianity was accepted from Byzantium, and that the very privilege of using Slavonic in the church services prevented the growth in Russia of a class educated in the wisdom of the ancient world.

It would be a grave mistake, however, to attribute the cultural lag solely to these factors. It was perhaps in even greater measure due to the effect of the Tatar invasions in the thirteenth and fourteenth centuries.

Kievan Russia

Kievan Russia developed a society different in some ways from that in contemporary western medieval Europe, despite a common emphasis on property, the law, and security. Scholars have disputed whether agriculture or commerce was economically more important in Kievan Russia; the answer appears to be commerce. In trade, with Byzantium in particular, the Russians sold mostly furs, honey, and wax—products not of agriculture but of hunting and beekeeping. Since the Byzantines paid in cash, Kiev had much more of a money economy than did western Europe. From the economic and social point of view, Kievan Russia in the eleventh century was in some ways more advanced than manorial western Europe, where markets, fairs, and industries were only beginning to develop.

Before the Tatar invasions, which started in the early 1200s, the Kievan state began to have close diplomatic and political relations with the West. Dynastic marriages were arranged between the ruling house of Kiev and the royal families of Sweden and France, and alliances were reached with the Holy Roman Empire of Germany. Merchants from the West appeared in Russia, especially at Novgorod and at Kiev. Whatever isolation was imposed by Byzantine Christianity might have been overcome had Kiev been allowed to maintain its free lines of communication and its vigorous and valuable exchange from the West. But Russia was denied this opportunity.

The Kievan state had many internal political weaknesses. It failed to make any rules for the succession to the throne, and it followed the practice (similar to that of the Franks) of dividing the land among a prince's sons. The resulting fragmentation of the Kievan state into often mutually hostile provinces weakened it in the face of outside dangers. Beginning in the eleventh century the Turkish tribe of Polovtsy, or Cumans, appeared in southern Russia. The Russian princes warring against one another made a tragic error by hiring bands of Polovtsy to fight for them. Thus when the Mongol Tatars appeared in the early thirteenth century, Kievan Russia had been softened for the blow.

Never entirely centralized politically, the Kievan state nonetheless strove for unity. It bequeathed the ideal of unity, together with a literary language and a single Christian faith, to the future Russian state of Muscovy (Moscow) that was to emerge after more than two centuries of Mongol domination. Moscow would take from the Byzantines not only their religion, already deeply entrenched in the Russia of Kiev, but also their political theory of autocracy.

V BYZANTINE LEARNING AND LITERATURE

Byzantine achievement was varied, distinguished, and of major importance to the West, though scholars have come to realize this only in the last century. Byzantine literature may suffer by comparison with the classics, but the appropriate society with which to compare medieval Byzantium is the contemporary Europe of the Middle Ages. Both were Christian and both the direct heirs of Rome and Greece. The Byzantines maintained learning on a level much more advanced than did the West, which, indeed, owes a substantial cultural debt to Byzantium.

Early Byzantium as Preserver of the Classics

In the West, the knowledge of Greek had disappeared, and no one had access to works of ancient Greek philosophy, science, and literature. During all this time the Byzantines preserved these masterpieces, copied and recopied them by hand, and studied them constantly. Again in contrast to the West, study was not confined to monasteries, although the monks played a major role. It was also pursued in secular libraries and schools. The teacher occupied an important position in Byzantine society; books circulated widely among those prominent in public life; many of the emperors were scholars and lovers of literature. Because of its strong pagan tradition. Justinian closed the university of Athens in the sixth century, but the imperial university at Constantinople supplied a steady stream of learned and cultivated men to the bureaucracy, the church, and the courts. Its curriculum emphasized secular subjects: philosophy, astronomy, geometry, rhetoric, music, grammar, law, medicine, and arithmetic. The School of the Patriarch of Constantinople, also in the capital, provided instruction in theology and other sacred subjects.

Had it not been for Byzantium, it seems certain that Plato and Aristotle, Homer and Sophocles would have been lost to us. We cannot even imagine what such a loss would have meant to Western civilization as we know it, how seriously it would have retarded us in science and speculation, in morals and ethics, how much harder it would have been to deal with the fundamental problems of human relationships. That these living works of the dead past have been preserved to us we owe to Byzantium.

Byzantine Writing: Epic, History, Theology, Hymns

In prose, Byzantium established an almost unbroken line over the long centuries of those who wrote the history of the Empire in a popular style. A great succession of Byzantine historians open up for us a world as yet little known. As we might expect, however, it is theological writing which forms the most substantial part of this prose literature. Early Byzantine theologians hotly debated the controversies that rent the Empire about the true relationship between God the Father and God the Son, or between the divine and human natures of Christ. Too difficult for most people to read or understand, such works nonetheless enormously influenced the lives of everyone. The leaders of the society were directly or indirectly affected by the answers to the problems of human social and economic life in general, or of the life of the human individual in particular, and of a person's prospects for eternal salvation or damnation. The early theologians also drew up appropriate rules for monks, balancing the need for denying the desires of the flesh by providing reasonable opportunities for work. Later, in the eleventh century, under the influence of the Neoplatonic philosophers, Byzantine theologians developed a

A BLENDING OF LITERATURE AND RELIGION

Unique among the stories of saints' lives is an extraordinary document of the tenth century, a highly polished tale of an Indian king who shuts away his only son, Ioasaph, in a remote palace to protect him from the knowledge of the world, and especially to prevent his being converted to Christianity. But the prince cannot be protected; he sees a sick man, a blind man, and a dead man. And when he is in despair at life's cruelties, a wise monk in disguise, named Barlaam, succeeds in reaching him by pretending to have a precious jewel that he wishes to show. The jewel is the jewel of the Christian faith, and the rest of the long story is an account of the wise Barlaam's conversion of Prince Ioasaph.

During the conversion, Barlaam tells Ioasaph ten moral tales illustrating the Christian life. One of these reappears in Elizabethan literature as the casket story in Shakespeare's *Merchant of Venice*; another is the tale of Everyman, which later became common in all Western literatures; other Barlaam stories were used by hundreds of Western authors and preachers of all nationalities.

What is most extraordinary about this piece of Byzantine literature is that the story originally comes from India. The life of Ioasaph is a Christianized version of the life of Buddha, the great Indian religious leader of the sixth century B.C. His life story passed through Persia via the Arabs to the Caucasian kingdom of Georgia before it was turned into Greek legend and transmitted to the West. And the stories that Barlaam tells to convert Ioasaph are also Indian in origin and are either Buddhist birth-stories (recitals of the Buddha's experiences in earlier incarnations used as comment upon what was going on around him) or Hindu moral-comic tales. Indeed the very name *Ioasaph* was once *Bodasaph*, and so is the same as the Indian word *bodhisattva*, which means a person destined to attain Buddhahood. Prince Ioasaph has been canonized a saint of both the Orthodox and the Roman Catholic churches, and thus through this legend Buddha himself became and has remained a Christian saint in the eyes of many commentators.

mystic strain in which they urged contemplation and purification as stages toward illumination and the final mystic union with God. For the ordinary person, the mysteries of faith were enhanced by the beauties of the church service, where magnificent original hymns were sung, often composed by major poets.

Saints' lives (Hagiographies), usually written for the ordinary person, depicted adventure, anxiety, deprivation, violence, and agony of various sorts before the final triumph of virtue and piety. The eyes of the reader were directed upward toward a heavenly reward, since the hero of the story was often martyred here on earth. Exciting, edifying, and immensely popular in their day, these stories supply valuable bits of information about daily life, especially among the humbler classes, and about the attitudes of the people, for which we sometimes have no other source.

The study of saints' lives, by which a saint was taken to embody an idea that could best be understood by the study of that life, became even more intense in the Latin West. The purpose and result were similar; in both, the contemplation of the saints' lives was a function of education and doctrine. Around each saint arose a cult, and the saint became a patron, protector, even friend and intimate with whom the worshiper could communicate. By projecting the real into the supernatural world—sailors, weavers, specific types of warriors each having a saint charged with their welfare—the Christian societies in the early Middle Ages found a source of authority and security close at hand, when the secular authority of the emperor seemed far away and unable to respond quickly. The rise of the saints was neither an unthinking superstition nor a mass cultural means of preserving polytheism; rather, it was a search for earthly security through the creation of new and immediately accessible heroes.

In the late fourth century, debates in East and West over the growing role of the saints and over the development of sanctuaries devoted to specific patrons reflected the tendency of the wealthy to make religious practice more private and exclusive, as opposed to the common people's desire for access by the total Christian community. The issue was not an arid one, for access to a heavenly patron depended on who was that patron's representative or intermediary on earth. The wealthy could afford to build shrines and sanctuaries to specific saints, as the poor could not. When the bishops—that is, the church—emerged victorious over the wealthy families in place after place, episcopal power became fully entrenched in the West. In the East the powerful families were generally more successful in preventing the growth of a truly mass religion, contributing another element to the growing sense of distance and lack of unity between Constantinople and the broader empire. Efforts in the late twelfth century to require that persons could be canonized only after certification that they had performed miracles became, especially in the West, a more effective means of curbing the growth in the number of cults.

The Arts

The Church of Hagia Sophia (Holy Wisdom) in Constantinople, built in the sixth century, was designed to be "a church the like of which has never been seen since Adam nor ever will be." The dome, "a work at once marvelous and terrifying," says a contemporary, "seems rather to hang by a golden chain from heaven than to be supported by solid masonry." Justinian, the emperor who built it, was able to exclaim, "I have outdone thee, O Solomon!" The Turks themselves, who seized the city in 1453, have ever since paid Hagia Sophia the sincerest compliment of imitation; the great mosques that throng present-day Istanbul are all more or less directly copied after the great church of the Byzantines.

Before Hagia Sophia could be built, other cities of the Empire, particularly Alexandria, Antioch, and Ephesus, had produced an architectural synthesis, a fusion of the Hellenistic or Roman basilica with a dome taken from Persia. This is just one striking example of how Greek and oriental elements were to be blended in Byzantine society. In decoration, the use of brilliantly colored marble, enamel, silk and other fabrics, gold, silver, jewels, and paintings and glowing mosaics on the walls and ceilings reflect the sumptuousness of the orient.

Built centuries later in Venice—first the client, then the equal, and finally the conqueror of Byzantium—the Cathedral of St. Mark's was a true Byzantine church of the eleventh century whose richness and magnificence epitomized perhaps better than any surviving church in Istanbul itself the splendor of later Byzantine architecture. Built to house the remains of the Evangelist Mark (which were said to have been carried away from Alexandria), the structure is both authentically Byzantine and a showpiece of Byzantine-influenced later styles.

Along with the major arts of architecture, painting, and mosaics went the so-called minor arts, whose level the Byzantines raised so high that the term "minor" seems almost absurd. The silks, the ivories, the work of the goldsmiths and silversmiths, the enamel and jeweled bookcovers, the elaborate containers made to hold the sacred relics of a saint, the great Hungarian sacred Crown of Saint Stephen, the superb miniatures of the illuminated manuscripts in half a hundred European libraries—all testify to the endless variety and fertility of Byzantine inspiration.

Even in those parts of western Europe where Byzantine political authority had disappeared, the influence of this Byzantine artistic flowering is often apparent. Sometimes actual creations by Byzantine artists were produced in the West or ordered from Constantinople by a connoisseur; these are found in Sicily and southern Italy, in Venice, and in Rome. Sometimes the native artists worked in the Byzantine manner, as in Spain, in Sicily, and in the great Romanesque domed churches of southern France. Often the native product was not purely Byzantine, but rather a fusion of Byzantine with local elements—a new art diverse in its genius, one of whose strands is clearly drawn from Constantinople.

Exterior and interior views of Hagia Sophia, Justinian's massive church at Constantinople. In the foreground are remnants of Roman construction. The Church of the Holy Wisdom—the English translation of *Hagia Sophia*—was built in 532 to 537 and represents a triumph of Byzantine architecture. Minarets, buttresses, and foreground tombs were added to it after the Turkish conquest of Constantinople in 1453. When finished, it was regarded as the finest church in the Christian world. Hagia Sophia served as a mosque until 1935, when it was made into a secular Turkish national museum.

VI ISLAM BEFORE THE CRUSADES

Islam (the Arabic word means submission to God) is the most recent of the world's great religions. Its adherents (*Muslims*, "those who submit" to God) today inhabit the entire North African coast, much of central and west Africa, part of Yugoslavia, and Albania, Egypt, Turkey, the entire Near and Middle East, Pakistan, parts of India, the Malay peninsula, Indonesia, and the Philippine Islands, as well as Soviet central Asia and portions of China. Relations with the Muslim world have been crucial to Western civilization since Muhammad founded Islam in the early seventh century. Islamic society rapidly joined the Latin and Greek Christian societies as the third major civilization west of India.

Muhammad, 570-632

What we know of Muhammad is derived from Muslim authors who lived some time after his death. The Arabia into which he was born about A.D. 570 was inhabited largely by nomadic tribes, each under its own chief. These nomads lived on the meat and milk of their animals and on dates from palm trees. They raided each other's flocks of camels and sheep and often feuded among themselves. The religion of the Arabs, a people known by inscriptions from the ninth century B.C., centered upon sacred stones and trees. Their chief center was Mecca, fifty miles inland from the coast of the Red Sea, where there was a sacred building called the *Kaaba* (the Cube), in which the Arab worshipers revered many idols, especially a small black stone "fallen from heaven," perhaps a meteorite. This building seems to have been the object of religious pilgrimages by the pagan Arabs.

In the sixth century Mecca was inhabited by a tribe called the Kuraish, a trading people who lived by caravan commerce with Syria. Muhammad was born into one of the clans of the Kuraish. Orphaned early, he was brought up by relatives and as a young man entered the service of a wealthy widow older than himself, whom he later married, after successfully performing several trading journeys for her. We do not know how he became convinced that he was the bearer of a new revelation, perhaps in visions when he was about forty.

Muhammad was keenly aware of the intense struggle going on between the two superpowers, Byzantium and Persia. News of the shifting fortunes of war reached him, and he apparently sympathized with the Christians, and perhaps even thought of himself as destined to lead a reform movement within Christianity. He could read no language except Arabic, and there were no religious books written in Arabic. His ideas and information on other religions must therefore have been derived

THE KORAN

The Koran is of greater significance to Islam than the Bible is to Christianity, since it supplies both the canon of the faith and also the ritual and principles of civil law. Nonetheless, until the Crusades the West had little interest in the Koran, when in 1143 a Latin version was prepared. No serious effort to study the Koran with the kind of care applied to the Gospels took place until the end of the seventeenth century, however, and the first English translation, the work of George Sale (c 1697-1736), was published in 1734. In recent years Arabic scholars have criticized the accuracy of this translation, though it remains the one through which the greatest number of Westerners first gained access to the Koran.

The Koran states that God gave revelations not only to Muhammad, but to Moses, Jesus, and other prophets, but Muslims maintain that the revelations were altered and corrupted over time so that they are no longer genuine. Reference is made to this in the following extract from Chapter II of the Koran:

There is no doubt in this book; it is a direction to the pious, who believe in the mysteries of faith, who observe the appointed times of prayer, and distribute alms out of what we have bestowed on them; and who believe in that revelation, which hath been sent down unto thee, and that which hath been sent down unto the prophets before thee, and have firm assurance in the life to come: these are directed by their Lord, and they shall prosper. As for the unbelievers, it will be equal to them whether thou admonish them, or do not admonish them; they will not believe. God hath sealed up their hearts and their hearing; a dimness covereth their sight, and they shall suffer a grievous punishment. There are some who say, We believe in God and the last day, but are not really believers; they seek to deceive God, and those who do believe, but they deceive themselves only, and are not sensible thereof. There is an infirmity in their hearts, and God hath increased that infirmity; and they shall suffer a most painful punishment because they have disbelieved. When one saith unto them, Act not corruptly in the earth, they reply, Verily, we are men of integrity. Are not they themselves corrupt doers? but they are not sensible thereof. And when one saith unto them, Believe ye as others believe; they answer, Shall we believe as fools believe? Are not they themselves fools? but they know it not. When they meet those who believe, they say, We do believe: but when they retire privately to their devils, they say, We really hold with you, and only mock at those people: God shall mock at them, and continue them in their impiety; they shall wander in confusion. These are the men who have purchased error at the price of true direction: but their traffic hath not been gainful, neither have they been rightly directed. They are like unto one who kindleth a fire, and when it hath enlightened all around him, God taketh away their light and leaveth them in darkness, they shall not see; they are deaf, dumb, and blind, therefore will they not repent.

The Koran, trans. George Sale (London: Frederick Warne, many editions and dates), pp. 2-3.

from observations on his caravan journeys and from conversations with Christians and Jews.

He seems to have spent much time in fasting and vigils, perhaps suggested by Christian practice. He became convinced that God was revealing the truth to him and had singled him out to be his messenger; these revelations came to him gradually over the rest of his life, often when some crisis arose. He probably wrote them down himself in a rhythmic, sometimes rhyming Arabic prose, and included entertaining stories from the Old Testament and from popular and current Arabian folklore, such as the legends that had come to surround the memory of Alexander the Great.

The whole body of revelation was not assembled in a book until some little time after Muhammad's death; this book is the *Koran*. The chapters were not arranged in order by subject matter, but mechanically by length, with the longest first, which makes the Koran difficult to follow. Moreover, it is full of allusions to things and persons not called by their right names. Readers are often puzzled by the Koran, and a large body of Muslim writings explaining and debating it has grown up over the centuries. Muhammad regarded his revelation as the confirmation of the Old and the New Testaments. Muslims called Jews and Christians, as they call themselves, "people of the Book." Thus Islam was a universal religion, the perfection of both Judaism and Christianity, the final revelation of God's truth.

Muhammad was a firm monotheist. His god, Allah, is the god of the Jews and Christians, yet Muhammad did not deny that his pagan fellow Arabs also had knowledge of God. He declared that it was idolatry to worship more than one god, and he believed the trinity of the Christians to be three gods and therefore polytheism. (Muslims dislike the term "Mohammadanism," once widely used in Europe, because it might imply worship of the man Muhammad.) If Judaism emphasizes God's legal covenant with the Jews and his justice, and Christianity the mercy that tempers God's wrath, Islam may be said to emphasize his omnipotence—his absolute ability to do anything he may wish to do. Acknowledgment of belief in God and in Muhammad as the ultimate prophet of God and acceptance of a final day of judgment are the basic requirements of the faith. A major innovation for the Arabs was Muhammad's idea of an afterlife, which was to be experienced in the flesh.

The demands of Islam were not severe. Five times a day in prayer, facing toward Mecca, the Muslim, having first washed face, hands, and feet, would bear witness that there is no god but Allah and that Muhammad is his prophet. During the sacred month of Ramadan—perhaps suggested by Lent—Muslims may not eat, drink, or have sexual relations between sunrise and sunset. They must give alms to the poor, and, if they can, they should at least once in their lifetime make a pilgrimage (the *hajj*) to the sacred city of Mecca. This was, and is, all, except for rules about certain aspects of daily life—for example, prohibitions against strong drink and other rules about food and its preparation, mostly taken from Jewish practice. The rest was social legislation; polygamy was sanctioned, but four wives were the most a man, save the Prophet himself, could have. Divorce was easy for the husband, who needed only to repeat a prescribed formula. Even so, the condition of women and of slaves was markedly improved by the new laws.

At first Muhammad preached this faith only to members of his family; then he preached to the people of Mecca, who repudiated him scornfully. In 622 some pilgrims from a city called Yathrib, two hundred miles north of Mecca, invited Muhammad to come to their city

A sixteenth-century Persian miniature showing the ascent of Muhammad into Paradise. It is illustrative of the style developed at the Safavid court, where artists at Tabriz and Herat produced many manuscripts and miniature paintings for the shahs. This work was prepared for Shah Tahmasp between 1539 and 1543 by a famous group of court painters directed by Sultan Muhammad.

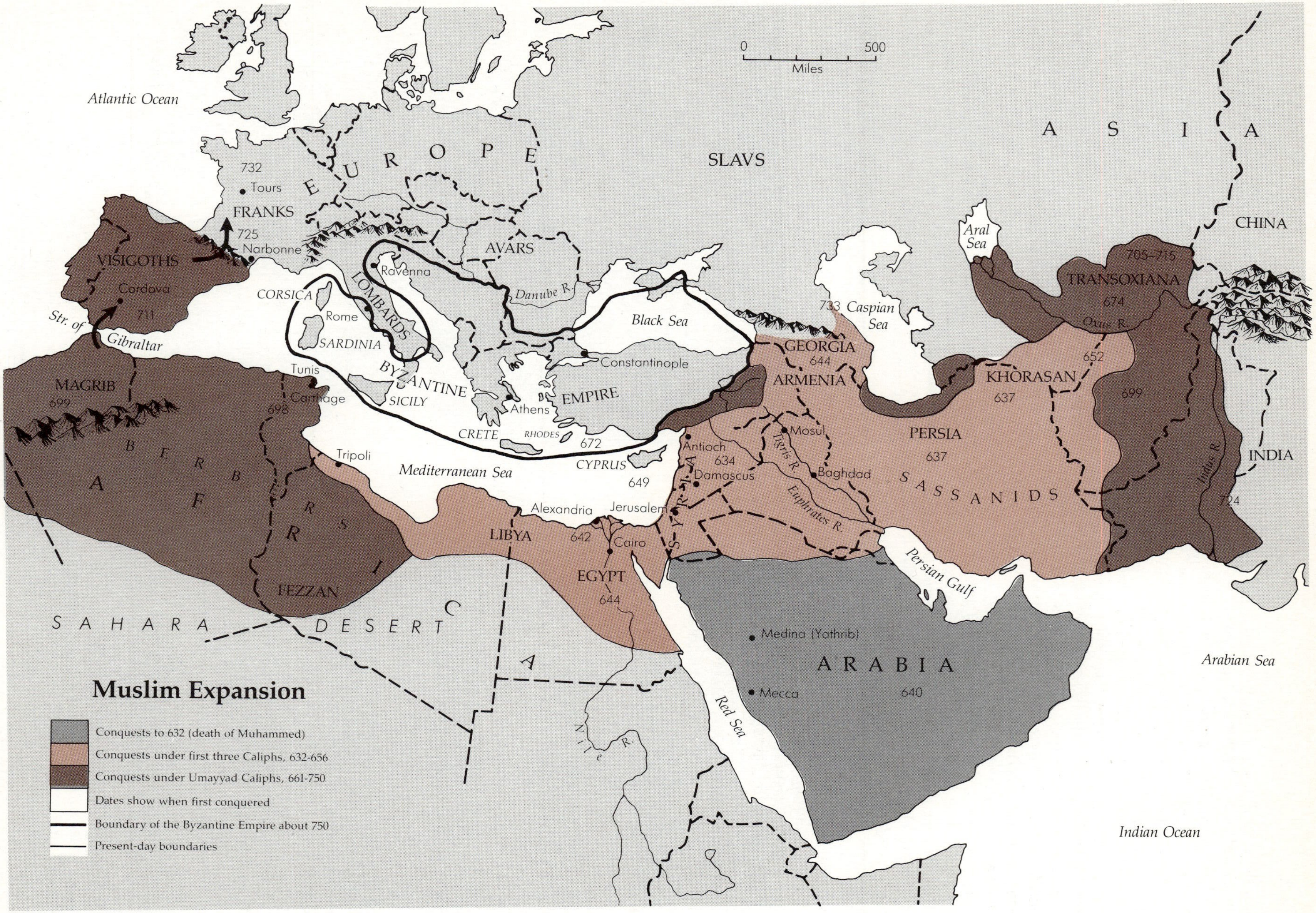
Muslim Expansion
Conquests to 632 (death of Muhammed)
Conquests under first three Caliphs, 632-656
Conquests under Umayyad Caliphs, 661-750
Dates show when first conquered
Boundary of the Byzantine Empire about 750
Present-day boundaries
0
500
Miles
Atlantic Ocean
EUROPE
SLAVS
ASIA
CHINA
INDIA
732
Tours
FRANKS
725
Narbonne
VISIGOTHS
Cordova
711
Str. of Gibraltar
CORSICA
SARDINIA
Rome
LOMBARDS
Ravenna
AVARS
Danube R.
Black Sea
Constantinople
BYZANTINE EMPIRE
SICILY
Athens
CRETE
RHODES
672
CYPRUS
649
Mediterranean Sea
Tunis
Carthage
698
Tripoli
MAGRIB
699
AFRICA
BERBERS
FEZZAN
SAHARA DESERT
LIBYA
Alexandria
642
Cairo
EGYPT
644
Nile R.
Jerusalem
Damascus
634
Antioch
SYRIA
Mosul
Tigris R.
Baghdad
Euphrates R.
GEORGIA
644
ARMENIA
733
Caspian Sea
Aral Sea
PERSIA
637
SASSANIDS
KHORASAN
637
652
Oxus R.
TRANSOXIANA
674
705-715
699
Indus R.
724
Persian Gulf
Red Sea
Medina (Yathrib)
Mecca
ARABIA
640
Arabian Sea
Indian Ocean

to settle a local war. He accepted the invitation. This move from Mecca is the *Hegira* (flight), from which the Islamic calendar has ever since been dated. Thus the Christian year 622 is the Muslim year 1.* Yathrib had its name changed to al-Medina, *the* city. Medina became the center of the new faith, which grew and prospered.

The Jews of Medina, on whose conversion Muhammad had been counting, did not convert. This aroused his hostility. He came to depend more upon the Arabs of the desert, the nomads, and became less universal in his appeal. Allah told him to fight against those who had not been converted. The holy war (*jihad*) is a concept very like the Christian crusade; those who die in battle against the infidel die in a holy cause. After Heraclius defeated the Persians (whom Muhammad considered to be pagan), Muhammad returned in triumph to Mecca in 630. Muslim historians believe that he appealed to Heraclius and other rulers to recognize him as a prophet and was disappointed when they did not do so. He cleansed the Kaaba of all idols, retaining only the black stone, and he made it a shrine of his new religion.

Two years later, in 632, Muhammad died. Much of Arabia had by then become Muslim, but it seems clear that many Arabs had not yet heard of the new faith. Yet within a century Charles Martel was battling Muhammad's coreligionists in far-off France, the great Byzantine Empire was locked in a struggle with them for its very existence, and Islam had reached India.

Expansion of Islam, 633-725

Scholars used to believe that this startling expansion was due to the religious zeal of the converts to the new faith. Now students of early Islam often argue that overpopulation of the Arabian peninsula set off the explosion of the Arabs into so huge an area. In fact, Arabs had been quietly emigrating for some time to Iraq, Palestine, and Syria. Now they had a new faith to symbolize their new unity. The first stages of their advance took them into lands already infiltrated by fellow Arabs. The movement quickly gathered momentum; Islam was its battle cry, but for many its motives included the age-old ones of conquest for living space and booty. Moreover, the organization of the Arab Muslims into armies dispatched abroad to fight surely prevented the disruption of hard-won unity inside Arabia itself. These conquering Muslims were generally tolerant toward Christians and Jews, regarding both as fellow monotheists and "peoples of the Book."

Syria, Palestine, and Persia were conquered almost simultaneously by two armies in 633-641. The Syrian province, disaffected from Byzantium by monophysitism, fell easily. And the Persians, because of their weakness after recent defeats at the hands of Heraclius, failed to put up the resistance that might have been expected.

*Throughout, this text employs the Gregorian Christian calendar for dating; the book is thus itself an artifact of a Western point of view on history. Since the Muslim calendar is a lunar one, a year takes 354-355 days; hence one may not simply subtract 622 to arrive at the date as used in the Islamic states today.

By 639 Jerusalem had been captured; in 651 the native Persian dynasty was ended. During 639-642 the Arabs added Egypt, the major Byzantine naval base, which was also monophysite in religion and ripe for conquest. Launching ships, they seized Cyprus and Rhodes and began attacking southern Italy and Sicily. Moving west across North Africa, they took Carthage in 698 and conquered the native Berber tribes, who had resisted Romans, Vandals, and Byzantines. In 711 with a mixed force of Berbers and Arabs under the command of Tariq, a freed slave, they invaded Spain across the Straits of Gibraltar. (The very name *Gibraltar* is a corruption of Arabic words meaning "Rock of Tariq.") By 725 the first Muslims had crossed the Pyrenees, to meet Charles Martel near Tours seven years later. Meanwhile, they had been spreading east from Persia throughout what is today Soviet Turkestan, and in 724 they had reached the Indus River and the western frontiers of China. They also moved south from Egypt and North Africa into the little-known desert regions of central Africa. These conquests of the first century of Islam were virtually final. Only the Mediterranean islands and Spain were permanently reconquered by Christians.

Disunity in Islam, 634-1055

The unity of such enormous and rapid conquests was more apparent than real. The Arabs had overrun a vast collection of diverse peoples with diverse customs. Moreover, internal dissensions among the Arabs themselves prevented the establishment of a permanent unified state to govern the whole of the conquered territory. After Muhammad's death, there was disagreement over the succession. Finally, Muhammad's eldest companion, Abu Bekr, was chosen *khalifa* (caliph, the representative of Muhammad). Abu Bekr died in 634, and the next two caliphs, Omar (r. 634-644) and Othman (r. 644-656), were also chosen from outside Muhammad's family, to the distress of many Muslims. Moreover, many Arabs resented the caliphs' assertion of authority over them and longed for their old freedom as nomads. In 656 Othman was murdered. By then those who favored choosing only a member of Muhammad's own family had grouped themselves around Ali, an early convert and cousin of the Prophet. This party also opposed all reliance on commentaries, or supplemental works, explaining the Koran. Fundamentalists with regard to the holy teachings, they became known as Shi'ites (the sectarians). Opposed to them was a prominent family, the Umayyads, who backed one of their members, Muawiyah, as caliph.

In 656 Ali was chosen caliph and civil war broke out. Ali was murdered in 661. His opponent, Muawiyah, had already proclaimed himself caliph in Damascus in 660. Thus began the dynastic Umayyad caliphate (661-750). On the whole, it saw ninety years of prosperity, good government, brisk trade, and cultural achievement along Byzantine lines, of which the Dome of the Rock Mosque in Jerusalem (which takes its name from the rock from which Muslims believe Muhammad ascended to heaven) is an outstanding example. The civil service was run by Greeks, and Greek artists worked for the caliph; the Christian population, except for the payment of a head tax, were on the whole unmolested and better off than they had been before.

Shi'ite opposition to the Umayyads, however, remained strong. The enemies of the Shi'ites called themselves Sunnites (traditionalists). There was little difference between the two groups with regard to religious observances and law, but the Shi'ites felt it their duty to curse the first three caliphs who had ruled before Ali, while the Sunnites deeply revered these three caliphs. The Shi'ites were far more intolerant of the unbeliever, conspired against the government, and celebrated the martyrdom of Ali's son Hussein, who was killed in battle in 680 as the result of treachery. Southern Iraq was the stronghold of Shi'ite strength, although in modern times Persia (Iran) has become the center.

From these Eastern regions came the leadership of the plot in 750 that was responsible for the overthrow and murder of the last of the Umayyad caliphs at Damascus, together with ninety members of his family.

The Dome of the Rock in Jerusalem is a fine early example of monumental Islamic building. Built in the seventh century, it continues to have great significance for two religions. Moslems believe that Muhammad ascended to heaven from this rock, while Jews maintain that Abraham prepared to sacrifice Isaac on this spot.

The leader of the conspirators was Abu'l Abbas—not a Shi'ite himself, but the great-grandson of a cousin of Muhammad. The caliphate was shortly afterward moved east to Baghdad, capital of present-day Iraq and close to the former capital of the Persian Empire, and was thereafter known as the Abbasid caliphate. The days when Islam was primarily an Arab movement under Byzantine influence were over. At Baghdad the caliphate took on more and more of the color of the Persian Empire, in whose former territory it was situated. Still, its Christian subjects were on the whole well treated.

Other groups appeared in Islam with varying views of how to interpret the Koran. Some were mystics seeking ecstatic union with God—Sufis, for example, who attempted to lose themselves in divine love and whose name was given them from *suf*, wool, for the undyed wool garment they wore, much like Christian ascetics. Politically the rest of the Muslim world fell away from its dependence upon the Abbasids. One of the few Umayyads to escape death in 750, Abd ar-Rahman made his way to Spain and built himself a state centered in the city of Cordova. Rich and strong, his descendants declared themselves caliphs in 929. Separate Muslim states appeared in Morocco, Tunis, and Egypt, where still another dynasty, this time Shi'ite, built Cairo in the tenth century and began to call themselves caliphs, though they were soon displaced by Sunnites. Rival dynasties also appeared in Persia, in Syria, and in the other Eastern provinces. At Baghdad, though the state took much of its character and culture from its Persian past, power fell gradually into the hands of Turkish troops. It was the Seljuk Turks who emerged supreme from the confused struggle for power when they took Baghdad in 1055. Although the caliphate at Baghdad lasted to 1258, during its last two centuries the caliphs were puppets in Turkish hands.

Islamic Civilization

The Arab conquerors were moving into provinces that had an ancient tradition of culture, regions which, until the Arabs appeared, had been parts of the East Roman or Persian empires. The Arabs brought their new religion and their language to the peoples they conquered. The religion often stimulated new artistic and literary development, and by requiring a pilgrimage to Mecca, it fostered mobility among the Muslims and encouraged the exchange of ideas with fellow Muslims from other parts of the Muslim world. Arabic had to be learned by everyone who wished to read the Koran, since it was forbidden for believers to translate "the Book." Since Arabic is an extraordinarily flexible and powerful literary instrument, it became the standard written language of the whole Islamic world. Indeed, Muslims were highly conscious of its merits; they felt that incessant study of it was necessary for comprehension, and they gave the highest position among the arts to composing poetry, rating it even above science.

Spreading their religion, though seldom by force, and clinging to their family and social traditions, the Arabs in the early stages of their expansion founded new cities in the conquered territories that were purely Arabic in population. But as conversions increased, the Arabs absorbed non-Arab converts. And in their way of life—houses, clothes, gardens—the Arabs borrowed much from the older urban societies they were now absorbing. So, aside from religion and language, the chief contribution to Muslim culture came from the civilizations of Persia and of the Greco-Roman world. Islamic government learned much from the Persian tradition; Islamic philosophy learned much from the classical tradition; and Islamic literature learned much from both.

Like both Roman and Greek Christianity, Islam was convinced of its superiority to all other religions and ways of life. Like the Byzantine Empire, Islam aspired to dominate the civilized world, which it thought of as divided between those lands already part of Islam and those lands still to be conquered. Like the Byzantine emperor, the caliph was an absolute autocrat, a vicar of God, chosen by a mixture of election and hereditary principle, who could not be mutilated and still keep the throne.

Christians and Muslims felt themselves to be members of religions that were on the same level of intellectual advancement and parallel in many respects—in their attitudes toward creation, human history, the last judgment, and the instability of everything mortal. When at peace with the Muslims, the Byzantines thought of them as the successors of the Persians, and as such the only other civilized nation. As a concession to the Muslim attitude toward women, diplomatic protocol prescribed that ambassadors from the caliph were not to be asked the customary questions about the health of the ladies of the caliph's household. And the caliph's ambassadors were given the highest places at the imperial table. Furthermore, each court had the highest respect for the other's attainments in science.

Science

The reign of Mamun the Great (813-833) is often said to mark the high point in the development of Arabic science and letters. In Baghdad he built an observatory, founded a university, and ordered the great works of Greek and Indian scientists and philosophers translated into Arabic. We hear of a young Byzantine geometry student who was taken prisoner by the Muslims and brought to Baghdad as a slave:

> *One day his master's conversation turned on the Caliph, and he mentioned Mamun's interest in geometry. "I should like," said the Greek youth, "to hear him and his masters discourse on that subject."... Mamun ... eagerly summoned him to the palace. He was confronted with the Moslem geometers. They described squares and triangles; they displayed a most accurate acquaintance with the nomenclature of Euclid; but they showed no comprehension of geometrical reasoning. At their request he gave them a demonstration, and they inquired in amazement how many savants of such a quality Constantinople possessed. "Many disciples like myself," was the reply, "but not masters." "Is your master still alive?" they asked. "Yes, but he lives in poverty and obscurity." Then Mamun wrote a letter to the master, Leo, inviting him to come to Baghdad, offering him rich rewards.... The youth was dispatched as ambassador to Leo. Leo discreetly showed the Caliph's letter to an imperial official, who brought the matter to the Emperor's attention. By this means Leo was discovered and his value appreciated. The Emperor gave him a salary and established him as a public teacher. ... Mamun is said to have communicated with Leo again, submitting to him a number of geometrical and astronomical problems. The solutions he received made him more anxious than ever to welcome the mathematician at his court, and he wrote to the Emperor begging him to send Leo to Baghdad for a short time, as an act of friendship, and offering in return eternal peace and 2,000 pounds of gold [about a million dollars]. But the Emperor, treating science as if it were a secret to be guarded like the manufacture of Greek fire, and deeming it bad policy to enlighten barbarians, declined.**

Although the charge that the Muslim mathematicians did not understand geometrical reasoning is surely absurd, the story nonetheless reflects a real situation—the immense eagerness of the Muslims to acquire Greek learning, which seems to have stimulated the Byzantines to appreciate their own neglected students of science. In any case, the last portion of the story, showing how jealously guarded were not only the secret weapons of the Byzantines but also what we would call today their basic research in mathematics, has a modern ring indeed.

Aristotle and the other philosophers and scientists of the ancient world were in any case available to the Arabs, whether in the original Greek or in Syrian or Persian translations. Under Harun al-Rashid (785-809), the fifth Abbasid caliph (of *Arabian Nights* fame), schools of translators were set up and manuscripts were ordered from Constantinople and elsewhere. Even more was done by Mamun.

One of the chief fields of interest was medicine, which the Muslims developed beyond the standard works of the Greek masters. They wrote textbooks, for instance, on diseases of the eye, on smallpox, and on measles, which remained the best authorities on those subjects until the eighteenth century. Al-Razi, a Persian, wrote a twenty-volume compendium of all medical knowledge, and the philosopher Avicenna (980-1037) was perhaps even more famous for his systematization of all known medical science and for his work on Aristotle and the Neoplatonists which, when translated into Latin, stimulated renewed European interest in both. In physics, al-Kindi (d. 870) wrote more than two hundred and fifty works on music, optics, and the tides.

Muslim scientists adopted Indian numerals (the ones we use today and call "Arabic"). The new numerals included the zero, a concept unknown to the Romans,

*Adapted from J.B. Bury, *A History of the Eastern Roman Empire* (London: Macmillan, 1912), pp. 437-38.

without which higher mathematical research could not be carried on. The Muslims began analytical geometry and founded plane and spherical trigonometry, and they progressed much further than their predecessors in algebra. ("*Algebra*" is itself an Arabic word, as are *alcohol, alchemy, cipher, nadir, zenith*, and others that testify to early Muslim scientific achievement.)

Philosophy, Literature, and the Arts

In philosophy, the Muslims eagerly studied Plato, Aristotle, and the Neoplatonists. Like the Byzantines and the western Europeans, they used what they learned to enable them to solve theological problems. These focused on the nature and the power of God and his relationship to the universe, or on the distinctions to be drawn between the apparent (outer) meaning and the true (inner) meaning of the Koran. Al-Ghazali (d. 1111), having written a *Refutation of Philosophy*, became a Sufi mystic for a decade before returning to his desk to write an autobiography and more theological works, all Sunni. The philosophy he sought to refute was that of the Mu'tazila, a body of theologians who had arisen under Mamun and who had carried rationalism so far as virtually to claim that reason had parity with revelation in the search for religious truth.

In opposition to al-Ghazali's dismissal of philosophy and dialectical theology, the great Spanish Muslim Averroës (1126-1198) strove to reconcile philosophy and the Koran. The debate deals with a problem present in every faith. Averroës' commentaries on Aristotle translated from Arabic into Latin were available to the Christian West by the 1240's. Thus the Muslims came to share with the Byzantines the role of preserver and modifier of the classical works of philosophy and science. And eventually, in the twelfth century and later, when the West was eager for ancient learning, it was the Muslims in Sicily and in Spain, as well as the Greeks, who could set it before them.

Indeed, the process had begun even earlier in Spain, where the physical splendor and intellectual eminence of Cordova caused its fame to spread abroad. Cordova was only dimly known to non-Spaniards, but they were deeply aware of its superiority to their own cities. In Spain itself, a Spanish Christian in 854 complained that his fellow Christians were irresistibly attracted by Muslim culture:

> *My fellow-Christians delight in the poems and romances of the Arabs; they study the works of Moslem theologians and philosophers, not in order to refute them, but to acquire a correct and elegant Arabic style. Where today can a layman be found, who reads the Latin Commentaries on the Holy Scripture? Who is there that studies the Gospels, the Prophets, the Apostles? Alas! the young Christians who are most conspicuous for their talents have no knowledge of any literature or language save the Arabic; they read and study Arabian books with avidity, they amass whole libraries of them at immense cost, and they everywhere sing the praises of Arabian lore.**

These Arabic poems of which the Spaniard spoke were derived from the pre-Islamic classical Arab tradition, and portrayed life in the desert, with its warfare and hunting, its feasts and drinking bouts. Love was a favorite subject. Composition was governed by a strict code of convention; it was customary, for example, for the poet to praise himself, but not possible for him freely to portray human character, so that nuance was very

*G.E. von Grunebaum, *Medieval Islam* (Chicago: University of Chicago Press, 1946), pp. 57-58.

THE CALAMITIES OF LOVE

A poetic treatise on the calamities of love describes the kinds of "avoidance" a lover encounters:

The first kind is the avoidance required by circumstances because of a watcher being present, and this is sweeter than union itself. Then there is the avoidance that springs from coquetry, and this is more delicious than many kinds of union. Because of this it happens only when the lovers have complete confidence in each other. Then comes avoidance brought about by some guilty act of the lover. In this there is some severity, but the joy of forgiveness balances it. In the approval of the beloved after anger there is a delight of heart which no other delight can equal. Then comes the avoidance caused by boredom. To get tired of somebody is one of the inborn characteristics of mankind. He who is guilty of it does not deserve that his friends should be true to him. Then comes the avoidance brought about when a lover sees his beloved treat him harshly and show affection for somebody else, so that he sees death and swallows bitter draughts of grief, and breaks off while his heart is cut to pieces. Then comes the avoidance due to hatred; and here all writing becomes confused, and all cunning is exhausted, and trouble becomes great. This makes people lose their heads.

G.E. von Grunebaum, *Medieval Islam* (Chicago: University of Chicago Press, 1946), pp. 269-70. Slightly adapted and abridged.

IBN KHALDUN, PHILOSOPHER OF HISTORY

The great Arab philosopher of history Ibn Khaldun (1332-1406) was the first to work out a substantial methodology for historical knowledge. Though he did not use the terms, he drew upon sociology, economics, geography, and religion. Building on the insights of Avicenna, Averroës, al-Ghazali, and others, he presented the most comprehensive statement of social philosophy in the medieval Muslim world. In the *Prolegomena* to his work he analyzed the "sources of error in historical writing":

All records, by their very nature, are liable to error—nay, they contain factors which make for error. The first of these is *partisanship* toward a creed or opinion. For when the mind receives in a state of neutrality and moderation any piece of information it gives to that information its due share of investigation and criticism, so as to disengage the truth it contains from the errors; should the mind, however, be biased in favour of an opinion or creed, it at once accepts every favourable piece of information concerning this opinion. . . .

The second factor conducive to error is *overconfidence* in one's sources. Such sources should be accepted only after thorough investigation. . . .

A third factor is the *failure to understand* what is intended. Thus many a chronicler falls into error by failing to grasp the real meaning of what he has seen or heard and by relating the event according to what he thinks or imagines.

A fourth source of error is a *mistaken belief in the truth.* This happens often, generally taking the form of excessive faith in the authority of one's sources.

A fifth factor is the inability rightly to *place an event in its real context,* owing to the obscurity and complexity of the situation. The chronicler contents himself with reporting the event as he saw it, thus distorting its significance.

A sixth factor is the very common desire to *gain the favour* of those of high rank, by praising them, by spreading their fame, by flattering them, by embellishing their doings and by interpreting in the most favourable way all their actions. . . .

The seventh cause of error, and the most important of all, is *the ignorance of the laws* governing the transformations of human society. For every single thing, whether it be an object or an action, is subject to a law governing its nature and any changes that may take place in it. . . . And it has often happened that historians have accepted and transmitted stories about events which are intrinsically impossible, as did Al-Mas'udi [a historian] when relating the adventures of Alexander the Great. Thus, according to him, Alexander was prevented by sea monsters from building the port of Alexandria. Thereupon he plunged to the bottom of the sea in a glass case enclosed in a wooden sarcophagus, made a picture of the devilish monsters he saw there, cast metal statues in the shape of these beasts, and set them up on the walls of the buildings; no sooner had the monsters emerged from the sea and seen these statues than they fled away, and thus the city was completed. All of this is related in a long tale full of impossible myths. . . .

Another cause of error is *exaggeration.* . . . The real cause of this error is that men's minds are fond of all that is strange and unusual, and that the tongue easily slips into exaggeration. . . .

Ibn Khaldun, *An Arab Philosophy of History,* trans. and arranged by Charles Issawi (London: John Murray, 1950), pp. 27-29.

important. Still, much understanding of fundamental human experience shines through.

Arabic love poetry, especially as developed in Spain, deeply influenced the poets (called *troubadours*) across the Pyrenees in Provence, in the south of France. Earthly love became an important element of medieval literature. The troubadours' songs spread to Germany, where the *minnesinger* adopted the convention. The troubadour created a revival of the theme of courtly love, and in the fourteenth and fifteenth centuries troubadour literature helped preserve and, for the aristocracy, elevate chivalric attitudes. Some of the greatest masterpieces of Western love poetry thus find their ancestry in the songs of the Muslims of Spain.

But love was not the only theme of Arabic verse. The famous blind Syrian poet al-Ma'arri (979-1057) lamented human helplessness in the face of the vicissitudes of life, sometimes in verses of a haunting beauty:

My friend, our own tombs fill so much space around us,
imagine the space occupied by tombs of long ago.
Walk slowly over the dust of this earth;
its crust is nothing but the bones of men.*

Besides poetry there is much interesting autobiography and excellent history in Arabic. Fiction is of a limited sort only—sad misfortunes of a pair of lovers, exciting incidents of urban life in the capital, with the caliph and his chief minister, the vizier, participating, or the adventures of a rogue. These stories were collected in the celebrated *Arabian Nights* between 900 and 1500. Stories of Persian, Indian, and Jewish origin are included, as well as some that derive from Greek and Hellenistic works. Thus Sinbad the Sailor's famous roc

*Wilson B. Bishai, *Humanities in the Arabic-Islamic World* (Dubuque, Iowa: Wm. C. Brown Company, 1973), p. 94. Slightly modified.

with its enormous egg came from the Greek romance of Alexander, and the *Odyssey* supplied the adventure with the blinded giant.

Deeply appreciative of secular music and dancing, the Arabs in the early Islamic period seem to have preferred the role of spectators to that of performers, most of whom were slaves or former slaves. Stringed instruments like lutes, as well as whistles, flutes, and drums, were popular in the Islamic world, whose music can be rendered only by instruments that can produce quarter tones. Many musical words we take for granted derive from Arabic. The Morris dance, for instance, is simply a *Moorish dance. Lute, tambourine, guitar,* and *fanfare* are all words of Arabic origin.

From the Muslims of Spain across the Pyrenees into France and thence to the entire western European world came not only the poetry of courtly love but the instruments the singer played as he sang of his beloved. Through Sicily and Spain came Greco-Roman and Muslim science, philosophy, and art. Understandably, only the vast body of Muslim theological disputation and treatises on the development of dogma remained unabsorbed into European thought, even though Muslims and Christians debated many of the same religious issues. When considering the contributions of the Byzantines and the Muslims to the culture of Western society, historians are altogether justified in saying that much light came from the East.

SUMMARY

The Byzantine Empire survived in the East with its capital at Constantinople until 1453. The emperors were absolute rulers chosen in theory by God and were responsible for preserving the traditions of Roman justice.

Byzantium was the buffer that cushioned Europe against frequent invasions from the north and east. The Byzantine armies and navies were well organized and led. The Byzantines also developed great diplomatic skill.

Byzantine strength was based on a rich economy. Trade and a monopoly of silk and luxury goods were important, but agriculture was the mainstay of both the economy and society. The Byzantines faced constant problems caused by the absorption of small farms into large estates.

Religion dominated Byzantine life. The emperor was also the effective head of the church, a system known as *Caesaropapism*. Religious controversies such as the iconoclast heresy were also political issues.

Differences between Latin Western Christianity and Greek Eastern Christianity multiplied after the fall of the Roman Empire in the West. In 1054 these differences came to a head in a schism between the two churches that has never been repaired.

One of the greatest Byzantine cultural achievements was the transmission of their civilization to Russia and the eastern Slavs, which were converted to Byzantine (Orthodox) Christianity in the ninth and tenth centuries. Because of its Byzantine heritage, Kievan Russia developed very differently from western Europe.

Byzantium preserved and transmitted the works of ancient Greece. Byzantine literature and art were of a high standard and were influential in the West.

Islam, a monotheistic religion, was founded in Arabia by Muhammad in the seventh century. Muhammad's teachings are collected in the Koran, the Islamic holy book. His followers are called Muslims. Their holy city is Mecca.

Muhammad converted and united most of Arabia. After his death in 632 the Muslims conquered all of the Near East, Egypt, North Africa, much of Spain, Persia, and northern India. This rapid conquest was the result of the Muslims' religious zeal, the weakness of the Byzantine and Persian empires, and the Arabs' need to expand to reduce the overpopulation of the Arabian peninsula.

In the eighth century the Arab empire split into several rival states, the chief of which was the caliphate of Baghdad.

Islamic civilization was based on religion and on the Arabic language. In government, literature, and philosophy, the Arabs borrowed extensively from the Greeks and Persians. In science, philosophy, and literature, the achievements of Arab civilization were very high.

chapter seven

CHURCH AND SOCIETY IN THE MEDIEVAL WEST

Until recently, twentieth-century historians tended to see medieval history as a period of "looking backward," well separated from a watershed such as the Renaissance, which seemed "forward looking" because of our ability to relate more closely to Renaissance figures. In recent years, however, new views of history have tended to lessen this emphasis on significant watersheds, to decrease the concern of identifying the "end of the Middle Ages" or "the beginning of modernity," and to argue that the past is one long continuum in which the Middle Ages are no less relevant to us today than times closer to us chronologically.

Our knowledge of all periods of history is changing rapidly, though not equally so. Perhaps four areas of knowledge have been transformed most in the past three decades: very early classical history, as a result of new archaeological finds and more sophisticated interpretation of old ones; the awareness of the richness of Byzantine and early Islamic history, which had been relatively dismissed by nineteenth-century historians who, for reasons of their own, sought their roots in the classical past; the reformulation of major debates and concepts about the Middle Ages; and the growth of social history in general, and the study of the family, women, ethnic communities, sexuality, and the management of disease in particular. All these subjects have influenced our view of the Middle Ages.

I THE SOCIETY AND ITS ECONOMY

In Christian Europe at the beginning of the tenth century, as the monkish biographer of the Anglo-Saxon king Alfred wrote, society was made up of those who prayed (the clergy), those who fought (the nobility), and those who worked (everyone else). These three orders of society, defined in terms of their functional contributions, were generally an accurate reflection of economic and social reality through the tenth century, but the ideas of these three orders continued long after the fact was no longer true. By the early thirteenth century it was made part of royal ideology. Thus a conception of society that was once broadly true as a generalization was given renewed life as a conservative defense against competing models of social organizations that had begun to threaten the security of orderly notions of society—whether in church or state—by the eleventh century. This three-orders view of society looked back to Augustine, Gregory the Great, and Greek ideas about the philosopher-king. However, the monasteries, various heretical movements, and the rise of a growing commercial class that was aware of competing systems of ideas originating elsewhere challenged such a scheme of things.

One major theme in the history of the Middle Ages is the growth in authority of kings. Generally this authority depended less on internal or external struggles for power, on which court chroniclers most often focused, than on religious sanctions that would provide ultimate justification. Although kings might challenge the church on specific matters, they sought to use it, and were used by it; thus, anything that weakened the church ultimately weakened the source of authority to which the monarch would turn to defend "divine right." So kings too were interested in matters of theological dispute.

Kings also governed their lands with the assistance of nobles, to whom authority was delegated and from whom obedience was expected. This created tension between central and local government that was never resolved, and since tension usually represents flux, any generalization about the relationship between central and local government is bound to be true only for a specific place and at a specific time. Yet the historian must generalize or historical narrative will become lost in detail. As authority in the name of people slowly became an alternative to authority in the name of the king, and the Crown was undermined, the language of authority began to differ more widely from place to place, so that "the state" means one thing in German history, another in Japanese history, yet another in American history. Still historians must use terms in common, and this introduces another complexity into our understanding of, for example, the emergence of the idea of national identity at the end of the Middle Ages.

These observations are necessary if we are to understand why the medieval world appears so complex, so remote, so discontinuous to us, and why it is nonetheless so significant to our understanding of Western history. For the eleventh century proved to be a major turning point in the social and economic life of the West, even though no one at the time was fully conscious of this, and the sources therefore do not speak of it directly. As the raids of Muslims, Magyars, and Northmen tapered off, most of western Europe found itself secure against outside attack. By the end of the century, western Europeans took the offensive against Islam. During the eleventh century, the population of Europe grew rapidly, which may have reflected an increase in personal life expectancy. By modern standards, of course, people were still exposed every day to unpredictable dangers from diseases that no one could cure, from undernourishment and famine that no one could assuage, and often from violence that no one could combat or police.

This larger population needed more food and more land. Pioneers felled trees, drained swamps, opened up

CLASSIFICATION IN HISTORY: THE DISAPPEARANCE OF THE WHEEL

To overcome problems of organization and argumentation, historians often turn to systems of classification to make knowledge appear systematic. The use of such systems is itself the product of assumptions about evolution, progress, orderliness, science. For example, agricultural history is extremely important to understanding the past, since over the ages most people have earned their living as tillers of the soil. Agriculture may be classified broadly into specific types: shifting agriculture, wet-rice cultivation, pastoral nomadism, Mediterranean agriculture, mixed farming, dairying, plantations, ranching, and large-scale grain production. Obviously the type of society dependent upon these types of food production will differ, but it does not follow that one type is inherently superior to another. Yet the act of classification leads some scholars to conclude that these types of agriculture represent phases, and that the phases are evolutionary, and that evolution represents progress toward some improved state. Immediately, a bias against an earlier state and the society dependent upon that form of agriculture is introduced, for that society is seen as one, three, or seven stages removed from the end of the process—that is, from "modernity."

Yet we now know that societies once possessed knowledge that was lost: Greek science, Muslim scholarship, the disappearance of the wheel and the cart from the region of their invention, the Middle East. Thus phases do not always represent a steady progression from a lower to a higher complexity, for complex knowledge and practice can be forgotten. This awareness may lead other scholars into the trap of a cyclical theory that assumes that history repeats itself. Such an assumption is, like the three orders of medieval society, most often used by those who wish to be able to predict the future, rather than by those who are studying the past for its own sake.

People have been concerned with certain questions virtually from the beginning of organized societies—questions about God, nature, human beings, society itself, and history. In contemplating these questions, philosophers sought a form of security; in acting upon their responses to these questions, rulers brought change, even as they attempted to assure continuity. Theologians who attempted to explain death, disease, sexuality, the need to labor, were contributing to the world as we know it today, for they were providing yet another set of answers to questions about God, nature, society, human beings, and the way these answers bear upon the past.

Thus all history is ultimately related to all other history, and any narrative, chronological, or classificatory system ultimately breaks down. All questions give rise to other questions. Consider the effort to explain the disappearance of the wheel and the cart from the Middle East for a thousand years, despite their diffusion around the world. To provide even a partial answer, the scholar must investigate the domestication of the camel, the invention of harnesses and saddles, the development of trade, the integration of the Arab nomads into imperial antiquity, the differing effectiveness of one-humped and two-humped camels, breeding, competing systems of commerce as discovered by the nomads, and a hundred other questions. Even then scholars are dependent upon the sources, and if these are not contemporary with the problem being investigated, they must also inquire into how the sources have been corrupted, used, abused, and manipulated over the centuries. The ultimate answer to the question about the wheel and the cart will be general at best and may contain much sophisticated though undoubted guesswork.

This example is drawn from a reading of Richard W. Bulliet, *The Camel and the Wheel* (Cambridge, Mass.: Harvard University Press, 1975).

59. BUILDING A HOUSE
Detail from a miniature, 15th century. Paris, Bibliothèque de l'Arsenal

On the left, a fifteenth-century miniature showing an artisan at work, probably in Amiens. The second miniature provides rich detail for the social historian on the variety of workers involved in building a house.

new areas for farming. When forests or marsh lay within a manor, a lord would often offer special inducements to his serfs to get them to undertake the extra heavy labor of clearing and farming it. Sometimes peasants would move into a new region that had lain empty before and would clear and farm it; if such uninhabited land belonged to a lord, he might invite peasants to colonize it and offer them freedom from serfdom and the chance to pay a money rent instead of the usual services. This would bring profit to the lord and great advantages to the freed serfs.

New technology helped to improve the farmer's life. Farmers increasingly adopted devices that had been known earlier, such as the heavy wheeled plow with horses to draw it. Windmills made their first appearance on the European landscape in the twelfth century—possibly brought from Persia but more likely developed independently—especially in flat areas like Normandy and the Low Countries, where there was no falling water to run a watermill. Slowly the anonymous inventors of the Middle Ages perfected systems of gears that would turn the millstones faster and grind more grain in less time. The growth of Christianity, the decline of slavery, the extension of the profit motive, the incorporation of knowledge gained from military campaigns, the increased supply of paid labor from the rise in population, all contributed to the first revolution in power, whether supplied by water, wind, or animal (including human).

Trade and Town

As part of the same general development, trade began slowly to revive during the eleventh century. A bad harvest year left medieval farmers helpless, and plenty or scarcity varied widely from region to region. It seemed natural to bring surpluses into areas of famine and sell them at high prices to the hungry. The first new commercial centers arose in places such as Venice and the Low Countries, where local farms could not feed the increasing population, and which trading ships could easily reach. Even in the earlier Middle Ages such trade had never disappeared altogether, but now the incentives to increase its scale were pressing.

When the owner of a manor found that year after year he could make large sums by selling a certain crop, he began to plant more and more of that crop and used the money gained by its sale to buy the things he was no longer raising. Once he had more money than he needed for necessities, he began to think of how to spend it on something extra—a luxury. Such a demand quickly creates its supply; what was once a luxury becomes a necessity. Thus, for example, the people of Flanders, living in an area that was poor for growing grain but good for raising sheep, sold their raw wool, developed a woolen-manufacturing industry, and imported the food they needed.

The recovery of commerce and the beginnings of industries stimulated the growth of towns. Old Roman towns like London and Marseilles revived. Often, a new town grew around a castle (*bourg* in France, *burgh* in England, *burg* in Germany), especially if it was strategically located for trade as well as for defense. And so the resident *bourgeois*, *burgesses*, or *burghers* enter the language as castle-dwellers, but soon become recognizable as residents of towns, engaged in commerce. Protected by the lord of the castle or sometimes by the abbot of the local monastery, the townspeople built walls around their settlement and pursued their trades. They banded together into guilds to protect themselves from brigands on the roads and to bargain with the lord of the next castle, who might be showing unpleasant signs of confiscating their goods or charging indecently high tolls whenever they crossed his land. Grouped in a guild, merchants could often win concessions; if the lord they were bargaining with seemed unreasonable, they might threaten to take a route across the lands of some less greedy lord and receive a more moderate toll.

Mutual advantage soon led landowners, including kings, to grant privileges to the townspeople by issuing a charter. Although the contents of such documents vary, most of them guaranteed free status to the townspeople; even escaped serfs within the town would acquire freedom if they could avoid capture and function as townspeople for a year. The charter might also grant the townspeople the right to hold a perpetual market, to transfer property within the town walls, and to have their lawsuits tried in a town court by town custom, which slowly developed into a whole new kind of law—the *law merchant.* Slowly there began to develop a body of commercial law for merchants and their merchandise.

Industry followed commerce into the town. The merchant, with experience of distant markets, learned how to buy raw material, how to have workers do the manufacturing wherever it was cheapest, and how to sell the finished products wherever the best price might be found. Soon the workers also began to organize into craft guilds, which provided medical care and burial for members and often fixed minimum wages, the standards of quality of a product, and even the prices to be asked.

Enterprise was neither free nor private. It was highly regulated, which not only reduced outside competition but also reflected the ideas of the age. People believed that a "just price" for a pair of shoes included the cost of the leather and the thread, the amount needed to sustain the shoemaker and family while making the shoes, and a bit more to pay the seller for time and trouble. To "make money"—in the modern sense of charging all that the traffic will bear—was in theory to cheat the customer. If many medieval customers were in fact cheated in this sense, the ethics of the time condemned such action. Finance capitalism—the use of money to make money, the investment of funds at interest—was traditionally condemned as usury. But with the help of the church's own lawyers, pressure from business modified this strict view; in practice, after 1100 there were few obstacles to the advance of trade and moneylending.

Town and Countryside

In turn, the towns greatly affected the overwhelming mass of the population who remained in the countryside, who now had a place to sell their surplus and an incentive to produce it. Some peasants saved enough cash to buy their freedom; some fled to the town in the hope of acquiring freedom, or at least in the hope that their children might acquire it. The very word "cash" suggests a most important development—the flourishing of a money economy instead of an economy of barter. Barter still continued, but as the magnates came to want more manufactured or imported or luxury items, they wanted cash rather than services. A serf's labors would produce grain, but not the money to buy armor, so the lord would let the peasant pay him cash and would forgive (commute) the serf's obligation to work on his land. More demand for money led to more money in circulation and an inflationary rise in wages and prices.

With the increase in demand for goods, large-scale fairs became a regular feature of medieval life. Some attracted traders and goods from all over Europe. In Champagne, in northeastern France, for example, there were several great annual fairs each year. The count of Champagne not only collected a fee from the towns for the privilege of holding the fair, but also received the revenues from a special court set up to try cases that arose there. As large-scale transactions grew more frequent, it became less practical for merchants to carry large amounts of cash, and during the thirteenth century they came to use a written promise to pay instead. Acceptance of these *bills of exchange*, a kind of primitive bank check, often made it unnecessary to transport money at all, since a Parisian creditor of a London merchant could call upon a Parisian debtor of the same merchant to pay the amount owed.

Historians continue to debate the causes and extent of the Western economic revival in the early Middle Ages. Many influences were at work. Muslim raids drove many people to take shelter in towns the better to resist the invaders, and these towns created a more active economy; raids and settlement by Northmen had a similar effect in what was to become Germany. In the tenth century the economy, essentially in decline since classical times, began a slow though mostly steady growth; by the twelfth century the widespread use of instruments of credit had stimulated the economy even further. Climatic change at this time substantially altered the pattern of agriculture. At the same time, the growth of more centralized monarchical states with different and evolving concepts of property rights in relation to feudal obligations led to a more efficient organization of society for production.

Population expansion, the commercial revival, agricultural growth, and the creation of a market system based on a money economy also changed the institutions of feudalism. The link between fiscal policy and property rights was especially significant in England and among the Dutch. Where an economic surplus existed, entire towns could specialize in producing one item for trade, tying themselves ever more closely to the market economy. From about 1500 the maritime expansion of western Europe would carry this economy overseas, while new products from overseas would further stimulate the European economy. Thus there was both a commercial revolution in the Middle Ages and a less heralded industrial revolution, in which agriculture, industry, construction, and mining were revolutionized and the social and physical environment were utterly changed.

Yet despite the growth of towns and of trade, society in the West did not become predominantly urban. Its rulers generally preserved the attitudes of large country landowners, interested in the productivity of their estates, on which their wealth depended; regarding the great lords and their fellow landowners as sharing their interests, even when they quarreled with them; and respecting the clergy as men of education who were often useful in administering their affairs and who were indispensable to their salvation. They spent their money ostentatiously, but felt committed to give alms to the poor and to build churches. They remained part of the country, not the town. Warriors and priests continued to be the idealized types of the time, for those who worked—the third of the estates—lacked anyone to tell their stories.

The Changing Status of Women

The status of women also reflected this idealization. Ideas of courtly love emphasized feminine nobility, while the cult of the Virgin Mary emphasized the role of the mother or glorified virginity. Marriage remained an important social institution at all levels, since it was a sacrament and also provided access to property and inheritance. But the role of women was changing. The peasant's wife worked as a partner to her husband in the fields, while the lady of the castle did not. The wife of the peasant was recognized as rendering service, and daughters could inherit land; indeed, even among the nobility, maintaining the family bloodline was felt to be more important than male dominance of inheritance. In the early Middle Ages women of child-bearing age were in short supply, and this enhanced their value in marriage, so that they could demand a larger dowry from prospective husbands.

By the fourteenth century the male-female balance in population had been reversed. Aristotle had said that men outlived women, but there were more women than men in Italy by the thirteenth century. Women of that period also controlled more wealth, and they therefore needed to know how to read and to calculate, so their education was extended beyond handicrafts, especially among the rich merchant class. As upper-class women

WOMEN OF THE GENTLE CLASS

Robert of Blois, a thirteenth-century poet, wrote of the correct behavior for women "of the gentle class":

En route to church or elsewhere, a lady must walk straight and not trot or run, or idle either. She must salute even the poor.

She must let no one touch her on the breast except her husband. For that reason, she must not let anyone put a pin or a brooch on her bosom.

No one should kiss her on the mouth except her husband. If she disobeys this injunction, neither loyalty, faith nor noble birth will avert the consequences.

Women are criticized for the way they look at people, like a sparrowhawk ready to pounce on a swallow. Take care: glances are messengers of love; men are prompt to deceive themselves by them. . . .

A lady does not accept gifts. For gifts which are given you in secret cost dear; one buys them with one's honor. There are, however, honest gifts which it is proper to thank people for.

Above all, a lady does not scold. Anger and high words are enough to distinguish a low woman from a lady. The man who injures you shames himself and not you; if it is a woman who scolds you, you will break her heart by refusing to answer her.

Women must not swear, drink too much or eat too much. . . .

Ladies with pale complexions should dine early. Good wine colors the face. If your breath is bad, hold it in church when you receive the blessing. . . .

Cut your fingernails frequently, down to the quick, for cleanliness' sake. Cleanliness is better than beauty.

From Charles-Victor Langlois, *La vie en France au moyen âge de la fin du XIIe au milieu du XIVe siècle, d'après des moralistes du temps* (Paris, 1925), as quoted in Joseph and Frances Gies, *Life in a Medieval City* (New York: Harper Colophon Books, 1961), pp. 56-57.

THE GOOD WIFE

In the fourteenth century a source known to us as The Goodman of Paris recorded what was expected of the good wife among well-to-do burgher class:

. . . [Y]ou should be careful and thoughtful of your husband's person. Wherefore, fair sister, if you have another husband after me, know that you should think much of his person, for after that a woman has lost her first husband and marriage, she commonly findeth it hard to find a second to her liking, according to her estate, and she remaineth long while all lonely and disconsolate and the more so still if she lose the second. Wherefore love your husband's person carefully, and I pray you keep him in clean linen, for that is your business, and because the trouble and care of outside affairs lieth with men, so must husbands take heed, and go and come, and journey hither and thither, in rain and wind, in snow and hail, now drenched, now dry, now sweating, now shivering, ill-fed, ill-lodged, ill-warmed, and ill-bedded. And naught harmeth him, because he is upheld by the hope that he hath of the care which his wife will take care of him on his return, and of the ease, the joys, and the pleasures which she will do him, or cause to be done to him in her presence; to be unshod before a good fire, to have his feet washed and fresh shoes and hose, to be given good food and drink, to be well served and well looked after, well bedded in white sheets and nightcaps, well covered with good furs, and assuaged with other joys and desports, privities, loves, and secrets whereof I am silent. And the next day fresh shirts and garments. . . .

Wherefore, dear sister, I beseech you thus to bewitch and bewitch again your husband that shall be, and beware of roofless house and of smoky fire, and scold him not, but be unto him gentle and amiable and peaceable. . . . And in summer take heed that there be no fleas in your chamber, nor in your bed, the which you may do in six ways, as I have heard tell. [A long passage on how to deal with fleas and mosquitoes follows, after which the document turns to flies.]

And if you have a chamber or a passage where there is great resort of flies, take little sprigs of fern and tie them to threads like to tassels, and hang them up and all the flies will settle on them at eventide; then take down the tassels and throw them out . . . have whisks wherewith to slay them by hand . . . have little twigs covered with glue on a basin of water . . . have your windows shut full tight with oiled or other cloth . . . so tightly that no fly may enter. . . .

And thus shall you preserve and keep your husband from all discomforts and give him all the the comforts whereof you can bethink you, and serve him and have him served in your house, and you shall look to him for outside things, for if he be good he will take even more pains and labour therein than you wish, and by doing what I have said, you will cause him ever to miss you and have his heart with you and your loving service and he will shun all other houses, all other women, all other services and households.

From *The Goodman of Paris*, trans. Eileen Power (London: Routledge & Kegan Paul Ltd., 1928), as excerpted in James Bruce Ross and Mary Martin McLaughlin, eds., *The Portable Medieval Reader* (New York: Viking Press, 1956), pp. 155-59.

acquired more authority, they were also seen increasingly as a force for continuity. Many apparently disliked this role, for women were to be found expressing heretical views or showing strong antagonism toward the institutions that framed their lives. Upper-class women were usually willing to play the roles assigned to them, since this would assure both salvation and inheritance.

Since Christianity associated nakedness with shame and sexual licentiousness, society developed strong dress signals to distinguish between the sexes at a glance. In the thirteenth century this need to obscure the body was combined with an aesthetic impulse to initiate through tailoring a concept of "fashion" which in turn became related to luxury. Though the role of women was ambivalent and changing, two developments brought the idea of womanhood into prominence. First was the rise of *Mariolatry* (the veneration of the Virgin Mary), which began in the ninth century and reached extraordinary heights by the eleventh century, when the Virgin was more likely to be the subject of an artist than was Jesus or the Apostles. Second was the celebration of courtly love and its accompanying forms of "manly combat" by the troubadours in France and Germany. Thus, as historians have noted, women greatly influenced two profoundly human activities—the making of love and the making of war.

Precisely when this first emancipation of women since the triumph of Christianity actually began is much debated by scholars. There is no doubt about the improved status of women by the fourteenth century; because women participated in many significant ways in the spiritual movements (heretical as well as orthodox) of the twelfth century, their role was an important one within the medieval Christian tradition. However, it is also clear that in certain places—in Saxony, for example, where noblewomen founded many religious communities—women of the aristocracy were vigorously conducting affairs of state and church as early as the tenth century. Thus these four hundred years represent an inconsistent pattern of development, though by the end of the period women could aspire to substantial achievements within the models society had set for them and against the roles society had enforced upon men.

II THE MEDIEVAL CHURCH AS INSTITUTION

The Church Universal

Down to perhaps 1600 western European society was identical with the church, as it was in Byzantium as well. The separation of church and state, the existence indeed of several, even many, different churches, was simply unimaginable for any inhabitant of medieval Europe. Everyone except the Jews belonged to the church. And the church's laws protected the Jews from being killed or converted by force or having their worship impeded, although they often suffered social or financial disabilities and sometimes persecution or worse. But the Jews were the only exception; any others who sought to leave the church or departed from its teachings were outside the law, and it was the duty of society to exterminate them.

So the medieval church had many of the attributes of the modern state. Once baptized, everyone was subject to its laws, paid its taxes, and lived at its mercy. Yet while the rulers of the church—the popes—often strove to create the machinery that would make this absolutism work, they never fully succeeded. The story of their efforts, the degree of their success, the measure of their failure, the nature of their opposition, is in some degree the political history of the western Middle Ages.

Having no armies of their own, the popes depended upon laymen—the kings and princes of Europe—to raise armies for the purposes of the church. Even a mighty secular ruler often bowed to the commands of a pope who seemed in every material respect far weaker than he. Princes were terrified of the spiritual weapons at the disposal of the pope: excommunication and interdict. *Excommunication* deprived the believer of the sacraments and threatened that person with hell-fire if he or she died while excommunicated. This Hell was a grim reality, and much attention was paid in the Middle Ages to working out the precise details of the "infernal

In medieval life, Hell was real, specific, and very much to be feared. Historians are able to trace changing conceptions of sin and punishment from the way in which both high and low art depicted Hell over the centuries. These scenes of Hell from a wall painting at the Church of St. Peter and St. Paul in Surrey, England, date from about 1200. They show the weighing of souls, the tormenting of the wicked, the infernal cauldron, and the Bridge of Dread.

journey." *Interdict* stopped all church services in a given area except baptism and the rites for the dying; none of the population could be married, take communion, confess and be absolved, or be buried with the assurance of salvation. A population under interdict sometimes became desperate, and its ruler often yielded and made his submission.

As a superstate, the medieval church gradually saw its authority diminished by the growth of secular states. Yet even rulers of those secular states who challenged the popes took it for granted that they and all their subjects and the subjects of other kings and princes were automatically Christians. Holy relics were inserted into hollows built in the throne of Charlemagne, who often disagreed with the pope. The proudest possession of Otto the Great—who deposed one pope and installed another—was the holy lance, which, legend said, had been thrust into the side of Christ, and had belonged to Constantine the Great. Such relics symbolized the total dependence of even the most powerful ruler in this world upon the will of God and served as a sign that he had God's favor. Coronation ceremonies both in the West and in the East emphasized the sacred character of the monarch being consecrated and were indispensable for public acceptance of the ruler.

But the economic expansion—it was almost an explosion—and the new drives of the eleventh century tended to diminish the sacred character of secular monarchy, as society grew more complex and more sophisticated and elaborate methods of government needed to be devised. As the king was perceived to be merely a human being doing a political job in this world and ceased to share an aura of sanctity with the churchmen, the churchmen alone, for a time, seemed to have a monopoly of spirituality. And since the secular rulers and their retainers were often unable to read and were almost always poorly educated, the tasks of secular government often fell to clerics, who performed them for both lay and ecclesiastical rulers. The western European church hierarchy of the eleventh to the fourteenth century has been well compared to a most efficient guild or labor union.

These centuries saw a sustained effort to build what has often been called a "papal monarchy," to develop a system of ecclesiastical (canon) law, and to think through an overarching theological system. They also saw the expansion and proliferation of the monasteries as new orders of monks came into being, often with reform as their aim. In a sense, these centuries were the last great period of Western unity.

Theories of the Papal Monarchy

Those who use the term "papal monarchy" believe that the papacy strove steadily to dominate the temporal as well as the spiritual government. When secular states—France, England, the Holy Roman Empire—came into being, that in itself constituted a defeat of papal purposes. Others argue that Christian theorists had always understood that human affairs must be governed jointly by a secular and a religious authority and that, even when secular rulers came into severe conflict with the papacy, the popes, though voicing strong claims of supremacy, would never have wished to see secular rulers altogether powerless. A third group maintains that, at least in the heat of battle with secular authorities, the popes did in fact voice extreme claims to complete supremacy. In the controversies that marked the period between the eleventh and fourteenth centuries, both sides expressed many extreme views. It is often difficult to judge how far such statements were put forward with complete sincerity, how far as arguments to win adherents, or how far as expressions of extreme claims that might be used as bargaining positions, and from which some retreat was always envisioned.

Christ himself had cautioned the faithful to distinguish between the things that are Caesar's and the things that are God's (*Luke* 20:25), and to Peter he gave the keys of the kingdom of heaven and the power to "bind" and to "loose" both on earth and in heaven (*Matthew* 16:19). Paul cautioned all Christians that "the powers that be are ordained of God" (*Romans* 13:1), so for Paul the secular powers were there to be obeyed. But at the time that Christ and Paul spoke, Christians were a tiny minority in the Roman world, and their precepts became difficult to interpret later when the Christian church was supreme. As early as the fourth century, St. Ambrose, as bishop of Milan, excommunicated an emperor (Theodosius I) and forced him to do penance. Augustine had conceded the necessity of a civil state with laws and police to enforce them, while cautioning true Christians to lift their eyes above the affairs of the mere earthly city. It was Pope Gelasius (r. 492-496), only two generations after Augustine, who wrote to the emperor at Constantinople that there were "two by which the world is ruled": the "sacred" *authority* of priests and the royal *power*, and that the priests had the higher responsibility, since at the last judgment they would have to answer for the behavior of kings. In Gelasius' Latin, the priests had *auctoritas*, the kings, *potestas*.

To this day scholars argue whether *auctoritas* meant "moral authority" or "the natural right to rule"; whether *potestas* meant "sovereign power" or only "a power delegated by a superior instructing church"; or even whether both words really meant essentially the same thing. Gelasius was surely thinking of the still more cryptic words of *Luke* 22:28, in which the apostles said to Christ, "Lord, behold, here are two swords," and Christ answered, "It is enough." This passage was constantly used in the Middle Ages to refer to the roles of the church and the state in human society.

Having broken with Byzantium and having been strengthened by the Frankish alliance and the protection of Pepin, Charlemagne, and their successors, the papacy in the tenth century sank into impotence, as the individual popes became instruments in the hands of rival Roman aristocratic families contesting for power in the city. Drunkenness, incest, arson, and murder were among the charges against the pope whom Otto I de-

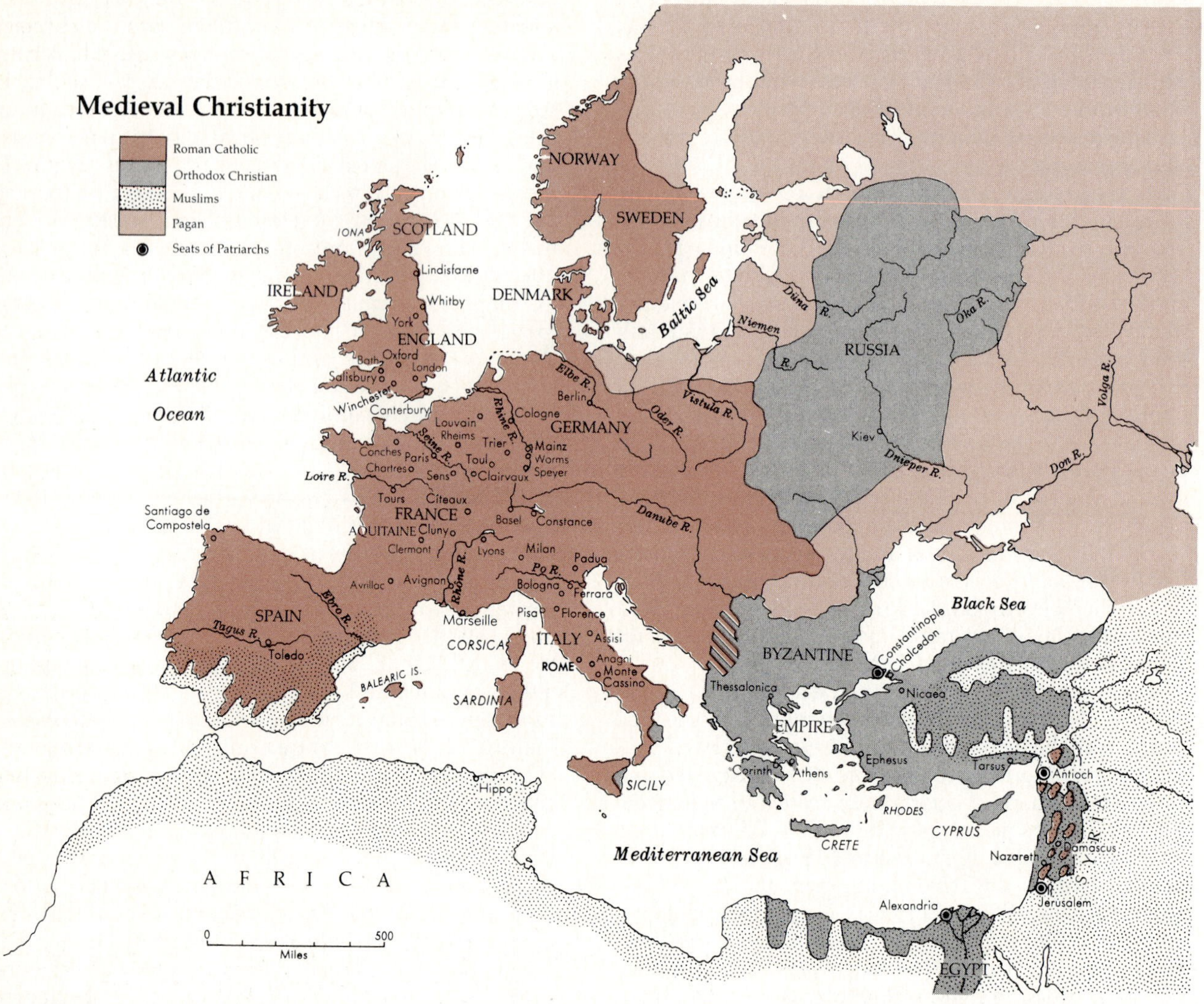

posed in 962. In such an atmosphere, the buying and selling of church offices (the sin of *simony*) was not uncommon, and immorality of other kinds—including the marriage or irregular union of priests and monks—was not curbed.

As early as the year 910, at Cluny, in eastern France, a Benedictine monastery was founded whose powerful abbots refused to tolerate, among their own flock or elsewhere, concubinage, the sale of church offices, and other abuses; they created a series of "daughter" monasteries all inspired with the same reforming principles. More than three hundred new monastic foundations were inspired by Cluny, which was probably the chief, though by no means the only, center of reforming currents in the church during the tenth and early eleventh centuries. Living in strict accordance with the ascetic rule of Benedict, the Cluniac monks acted as an organized pressure group to spread reform everywhere in the church.

Rome—home of the papacy and goal of pilgrims from all over western Europe, who believed it to be sanctified by the body of St. Peter himself in his church—remained the core of the church. Papal business continued to be conducted, even when the popes were viewed as unworthy. It was not until the mid-eleventh cventury that full-fledged reform came to the papacy itself. When it did so, the impulse was indeed partly Cluniac. But more important in papal reform, ironically enough, were the continued secular interests of the German monarchy. For this reason papal and German history became inextricably entwined.

III THE INVESTITURE CONTROVERSY

Saxon Administration and the German Church, 911-955

As the Carolingian Empire gradually disintegrated in the late ninth and early tenth centuries, five duchies (Franconia, Saxony, Thuringia, Swabia, and Bavaria) arose in the eastern Frankish lands of Germany. They were military units organized by the local Carolingian administrators, who took the title of duke (army commander). When the Carolingian dynasty became extinct, they chose one of their own number—Conrad, duke of Franconia—as their king in 911, to protect their lands against Magyar invaders. But Conrad was a military failure and a newcomer. So the dukes for the first time asserted themselves as rivals to the Crown. They built their duchies into petty kingdoms, made themselves hereditary rulers, and took control over the church in their own duchies, dominating the local administrators of the king, the counts.

Conrad's successor, the duke of Saxony, became King Henry I (919-936). He and his descendants—notably Otto I (936-973) and Otto III (983-1002)—successfully combated the ducal tendency to dominate the counts and to control the church; they made the counts serve under the Crown and regained the right to appoint bishops. In 939 the Crown obtained the duchy of Franconia; thenceforth the German kings, no matter what duchy they came from, would also have Franconia as the royal domain.

The Saxon dynasty established by Henry I relied on the church to perform much of the work of governing Germany, since bishops, unlike counts, could not pass on their offices to their sons, and bishops were better educated than laymen. The church welcomed the alliance because a strong central government was its best guarantee of stability; the papacy itself recognized the right of the German kings to appoint their own bishops. The Saxon monarchs gave church and abbey lands their special protection, exempting them from the authority of the counts and bringing them directly under the Crown. Like the former counts, the bishops obtained the right to administer justice within their own domain. In 1007, for instance, the bishops of the great sees of Bamberg and Würzburg were given all the rights that had formerly belonged to counts.

The church also supplied the German king with much of his revenue, and tenants of church lands furnished three-quarters of his army. The church participated in the German expansion to the east—the celebrated *Drang nach Osten*—in the defeat of the Magyars at Lechfeld (955), in the push into Slavic lands along the Elbe and Saale rivers, and in the advance into Silesia. New German bishoprics were set up, with Magdeburg as center, and subject sees were established east of the Elbe. Consequently, the church could impose Christianity upon the vanquished Slavs.

The Empire, 962-1075

When King Otto I took the title of emperor in 962, he created for his successors a set of problems that far transcended the local problems of Germany. In the Carolingian West, *emperor* had come to mean a ruler who controlled two or more kingdoms but who did not necessarily claim supremacy over the whole world. The kingdoms that the Western emperor was likely to control were Germany, Burgundy, and Italy. Burgundy had

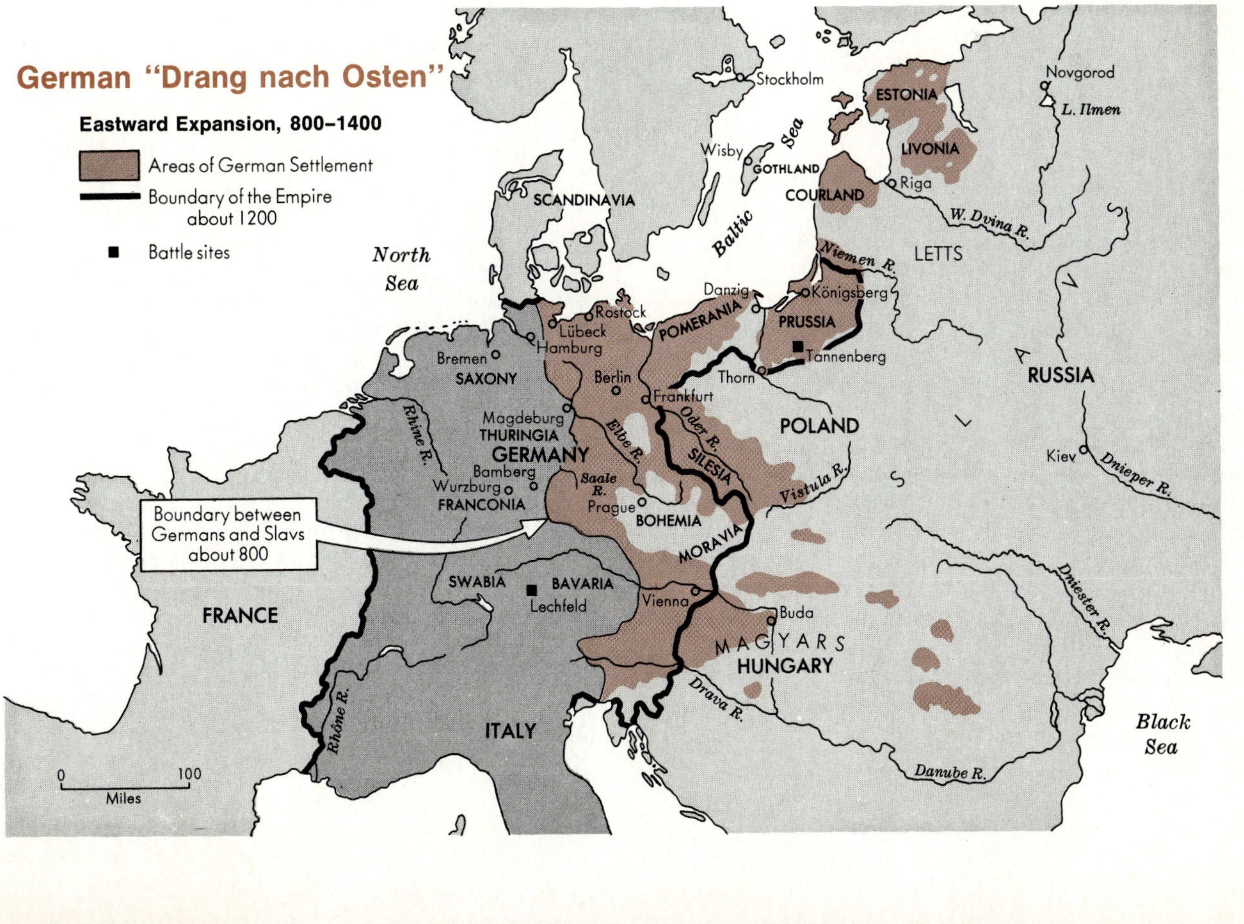

grown up under ambitious rulers in the region between the eastern and western Frankish lands. Italy, on the other hand, was weak, divided, and open to invasion. Thus the king of Germany had something to gain if he could secure the title of emperor, even in its diluted new meaning. And, if he did not make himself emperor, he faced a real danger that somebody else would.

Otto I's grandson, the brilliant young Otto III (983-1002), used a seal with the words *"Renewal of the Roman Empire."* In Rome itself he strove to restore a Roman imperial palace, Roman titles, and Roman glory, possibly acting under the influence of his Byzantine mother, and surely hoping to win the support of the Roman aristocracy. He also tried to make imperial power real in Italy by putting German officials on church lands to keep these lands out of the hands of the Italian nobility, and by appointing German bishops to Italian sees in an effort to build up the sort of government he had at home. Since Otto III did not ignore Germany but paid careful attention to relations between Germany and the Slavs, German contemporaries seem to have felt that his intervention in Italy was proper and legitimate. He was not trying to dominate the entire West, but rather to establish himself as emperor in the new sense, and to consolidate the rule of the Saxon dynasty.

German culture and trade benefited from the Italian connection. By the early eleventh century, the right of each new German king to be king of Italy and emperor was taken for granted; even if a new king had not yet been crowned emperor by the pope, he called himself "king of the Romans, still to be promoted to emperor." Italy benefited as the long period of anarchy finally came to an end. The emperors raised the level of the papacy from the degradation it had reached in the tenth century. But as the emperors sponsored reform within the church, they set in motion forces that would make the papacy a world power and bring about their own eventual ruin.

A sense of German national unity was asserting itself, as shown by the general use of the term *teutonici* (Teutons, or Germans). When the Saxon dynasty died out in 1024, the widow of the last Saxon designated Conrad II (1024-1039) of the Salian dynasty. The new dynasty, which came from Franconia, produced activist administrators, notably Henry III, or the Black (1039-1056). Conrad began training members of the lower classes to serve as administrators, the *ministeriales.* The church had long used such men to run its great estates, and now the kings used them to run the lands of the Crown. Though they often received lands as a reward, their lands were usually not hereditary and so did not become fiefs. Thus the ministeriales depended directly on the Crown, had a status that could not be described as feudal, and remained as a class peculiar to Germany. Moreover, free men in Germany did not have to choose between becoming vassals of the dukes and destruction; both large and small estates continued to be owned outright by free men. Although the social distinction between the rich and poor was great, both were more often free of feudal ties than anywhere else in western Europe.

Though the class of free landholders had no feudal ties, it had no royal ties either. So when the attack came on the increasing centralization of the eleventh-century German monarchy, it came from these free landowners, a class that had no exact counterpart elsewhere in the West. They had strengthened their position by becoming the guardians or "advocates" (German, *Vogt*) of monasteries, a process that was aided for a time by the Crown itself. In 973 there were 108 abbeys in Germany, probably all attached to the Crown; in 1075 there were more than 700, and almost all the new ones were attached to members of the landowner class. Founding a new monastery in Germany was not solely a sign of the founder's piety, for monks colonized new lands, and the resulting revenues went to the founder of the house. To keep these valuable monasteries out of royal hands, the German nobles often made them the legal property of the pope, who was far away and could not interfere as readily as the king could. Thus, side by side with what may be termed the "royal" church and its bishops, there grew up in Germany a "noble" church based largely on monastic foundations.

Opposition to the royal church, to the power of the low-born ministeriales, and to the trend toward monarchical centralization led the German nobility to revolt. In 1073 the nobles rose in Saxony against the emperor Henry IV (1056-1106); in 1075 Henry crushed the uprising. But only a few weeks later there began the open struggle with the papacy that gave the nobles new occasion to rebel. This was the Investiture Controversy, and it lasted half a century.

The Investiture Controversy, 1046-1122

The struggle originated in 1046, when Emperor Henry III found three rival popes simultaneously in office while mobs of their supporters rioted in the streets of Rome. He deposed all three. After two successive German appointees had died—perhaps by poison—Henry named a third German, his own uncle, Bishop Bruno of Toul, who became pope as Leo IX (r. 1049-1054). Leo was committed to the Cluniac program of monastic reform; the whole church hierarchy, he insisted, must be purged of secular influences, and over it all the pope must reign supreme. The emperor Henry III had thus put into power reformers whose chief target would be his own imperial system of government in Germany. Leo began to appoint *cardinals* (from the Latin *cardo,* a hinge), who now served as key advisers and administrators instead of merely ornamental dignitaries, which they had been. By 1059 the papacy had given these cardinals the power to elect new popes, depriving the German emperors of that role. And the Normans of southern Italy promised to give the cardinals military backing, so that they could do their job without fear of German intervention.

POPE GREGORY ON THE STATE OF CHRISTENDOM

In 1075 Gregory wrote to Hugh, abbot of Cluny, of his concerns for the state of Christendom:

If it were possible, I should like you fully to appreciate what great tribulation presses upon me, and what great labor, daily renewed, tires me out and increases, to my deep distress. . . . For grievous sorrow and utter sadness surround me, because the Eastern Church, by suggestion of the devil, has abandoned the Catholic Faith: and the ancient foe by his members puts Christians to death on all sides: so that, by spiritually killing the head, he causes the members carnally to perish, lest at any time by divine grace they should repent.

Then again, if I take a mental survey, and look round upon the regions of the west, south or north, I scarcely find any bishops lawfully appointed and of regular life who rule the people of God for the love of Christ and not for worldly ambition. And among all the secular princes there is hardly one who prefers the honor of God and righteousness to his own advantage. Those among whom I live—Romans, Lombards and Normans, as I often tell them, I count as worse somehow than Jews or pagans.

Returning to myself, I find myself so overburdened by the weight of my own doings, that no hope of salvation remains for me except in the sole mercy of Christ. For if I did not hope for a better life and to be of more profit to holy Church, I would not in any wise remain in Rome where, as God is witness, I have been obliged to live these five and twenty years. . . .

From Erich Caspar, *Das Register Gregors VII*, in *Monumenta Germaniae Historica: Epistalae selectae* (Berlin, 1920-1955), I, 188; trans. B.J. Kidd, *Documents Illustrative of the History of the Early Church* (London: Macmillan, 1941), III, 126. Reprinted by permission of the Society for Promoting Christian Knowledge.

In 1073 Hildebrand became pope as Gregory VII (to 1084). He was determined to push ecclesiastical reform by ensuring the canonical (legal) election of all bishops and abbots. This would mean sweeping away the system of royal selection and appointment and its subsequent ceremony of lay investiture—that is, the conferring of the prelate's insignia of office (for bishops, a ring and a staff) by a layman, the emperor. Yet the German royal administration largely depended on this royal appointment of prelates, which involved not only lay investiture but the sale of church offices and the granting of royal estates to bishops.

Gregory declared that the pope was subject to no human judgment; that the Roman church had never erred, and never could err; that the pope alone could make new laws, create new bishoprics, depose bishops, and change his own mind; that all temporal princes should kiss his feet; that the imperial insignia were his alone to use; that he could absolve the subjects of a temporal prince from their allegiance and could depose emperors. By the merits of St. Peter, he declared, all popes were saints. Such claims were a new interpretation of Pope Gelasius' words of six centuries earlier.

In 1075 Gregory forbade lay investiture. Henry IV's bishops responded in 1076 by declaring Gregory deposed. Gregory then excommunicated Henry as a usurper, declared him deposed, absolved his subjects of loyalty to him, and deprived the bishops of their offices. In a letter to the pope, Henry began, "Henry, King not by usurpation but by the pious ordination of God, to Hildebrand, now no longer Pope but false monk." The Saxon nobles, opponents of Henry, thereupon joined forces with the pope and made Henry promise to clear himself of the excommunication within four months, on pain of the loss of his crown; they also invited the pope to Germany.

To prevent this unwelcome visit, Henry secretly went to Italy in January of 1077 and appeared before the castle of Canossa, where Gregory was temporarily staying. Henry declared himself a penitent; Gregory kept him waiting outside the castle for three days, barefoot and in sackcloth. When he was finally admitted, Henry did penance and Gregory absolved him. The drama and symbolism of this famous episode have often led historians to marvel at the power of the pope. But it struck contemporaries the other way. By allowing himself to be publicly humiliated, Henry had actually forced Gregory's hand; the pope had been forced to absolve him, and once absolved, Henry could no longer be deposed.

Before Henry returned home, his German opponents had elected a new ruler, an "anti-king," Rudolf of Swabia. By refraining for three years from making a decision between the rival kings, Gregory VII did what he could to prolong the resulting civil war. When he did decide, it was against Henry, whom he deposed and excommunicated once more. But the pope's efforts failed; Rudolf was killed in battle, and a new anti-king commanded even less support. The German clergy again declared the pope deposed, and Henry marched to Italy, took Rome in 1084 after three years of bitter siege, and installed an "anti-pope," who proceeded to crown him emperor. Gregory's Norman vassals and allies did not arrive until after Henry had returned to Germany. They looted Rome and took Gregory with them to southern Italy, where he died; by 1091 the last vestige of the revolt against Henry in Germany had been stamped out.

No final settlement of the Investiture Controversy could be reached before 1122. In the Concordat of

Worms, Henry V (1106-1125) renounced the practice of investing bishops with the clerical symbols of ring and staff. The pope permitted the emperor to continue investing bishops with the *regalia* (worldly goods pertaining to the bishop's office). The investiture could take place before the bishop was consecrated, assuring the emperor of a previous oath of fealty from the bishop. Moreover, clerical elections in Germany were to be carried out in the presence of the emperor or his representatives, giving him an opportunity to exercise a strong influence over the decisions. In Italy and Burgundy the emperor retained less power; consecration was to take place *before* the regalia were conferred, and the emperor could not attend clerical elections. Thus the Concordat of Worms was a compromise that in effect ended the Investiture Controversy, despite its failure to settle many other issues.

But by 1122 Germany had become feudalized. During the years between 1076 and 1106 the princes and other nobles acted on the pretext that there was no king, since the pope had deposed him. They extended their powers and administered their lands without reference to the monarchy. Castles multiplied and became centers of administrative districts, laying the foundations for territorial principalities; free peasants fell into serfdom; the weakness of central authority drove lesser nobles to become dependent on greater nobles. In short, the familiar feudalizing process that had gone on in ninth- and tenth-century France now was operating in eleventh- and early twelfth-century Germany.

In Italy the Investiture Controversy had seen the further rise of the Norman kingdom of the south. The struggle had also been responsible for the growth of communes in the cities of the north. These communes had begun as sworn associations of lesser nobles who banded together to resist the power of the local bishops. In Lombardy, where the communes were favored by Gregory VII, they took advantage of his support to usurp the powers of municipal government. In Tuscany, where the ruling house was pro-papal, the communes allied themselves with the emperor, who granted them their liberties by charter. Thus, in Germany the Crown faced a newly entrenched aristocracy; in Italy it faced a new society of powerful urban communes.

The German nobles now controlled the election of the emperor. In 1138 they chose Conrad of Hohenstaufen, a Swabian prince, who became Emperor Conrad III (r. 1138-1152). In so doing, they passed over another claimant, Henry the Proud, duke of Bavaria and Saxony and marquis of Tuscany in Italy, a member of the powerful Welf family. Because of their ancestral estate, the Hohenstaufens were often known as Waiblings; in Italian, *Waibling* became *Ghibelline* and *Welf* became *Guelf*. Thus in the first half of the twelfth century, the Guelf-Ghibelline (or Welf-Waibling) feud—one of the most famous, lasting, and portentous in history—began. Henry the Proud, the Welf leader, refused homage to Conrad III; Conrad in turn deprived Henry of Saxony and Bavaria. Once more feudal warfare raged in Germany.

IV PAPACY AND EMPIRE, 1152-1273

With the revival of the study of Roman law during the twelfth century went a corresponding interest among churchmen in the systematization of church (canon) law. As the texts of Justinian's civil law became familiar to the students in the law schools—of which Bologna in Italy was the most important—the Bolognese monk Gratian about 1140 published the *Decretum*, a similar effort to codify for the first time past decrees of popes, enactments of church councils, and decisions of church fathers dating back a millennium. Gratian tried to reconcile apparently conflicting decisions and produced for church lawyers an indispensable tool that emphasized the papal role.

Investiture was replaced in the papal-imperial struggle by what we today call "the Italian question": How could an emperor be sovereign over Italy—including Rome—without trespassing on papal sovereignty? But if an emperor did not have effective sovereignty over Italy, did his title "Roman Emperor" become meaningless? Or was the pope in some sense the emperor's feudal overlord for his Italian possessions, and was the emperor therefore the pope's vassal? By the 1140s a mosaic picture in the papal palace of St. John Lateran showed the emperor kneeling at the pope's feet, and, as the inscription said, becoming his liege man and receiving the crown from him in return. This was not the sort of claim that a powerful or ambitious emperor would accept. And in 1152, when Frederick I Hohenstaufen (r. to 1190), nicknamed Barbarossa, "Redbeard," came to the throne of divided feudal Germany, the issue was joined again.

Frederick Barbarossa and Henry VI, 1152-1192

In 1156 Frederick married the heiress to Burgundy, which had slipped out of imperial control during the Investiture Controversy. He made Switzerland the strategic center of his policy, for it controlled the Alpine passes into Italy. In Swabia he tried to build a compact, well-run royal domain, but he needed the loyalty of cooperative great vassals. And in Lombardy he also needed an alliance with the communes in the towns.

Frederick Barbarossa made six trips to Italy. He intervened first at Rome, where in 1143 a commune had risen up against papal rule. The leader of the commune, Arnold of Brescia, strongly favored the church's return to apostolic poverty and simplicity. Barbarossa won papal good will by offering the pope assistance not only against Arnold but also against the Normans and against the Byzantine threat to southern Italy. He was crowned emperor in Rome in 1155, after an argument over whether he would hold the pope's bridle and stirrup as well as kiss his foot. (Frederick lost.) At the pope's request, the emperor hanged and burned Arnold, whose death he is later said to have regretted. The pope, however, soon reached an accommodation with the Normans and quarreled with Frederick once more in 1157; the pope seemed to be claiming that Frederick held the empire for him as a *benefice*, a fief or a "concession."

The Milanese resisted Frederick, and when a vigorous pope Alexander III (1159-1181) came to power, Frederick faced the pope, Milan, and Sicily united. They drove him back into Italy, and in 1176 their forces defeated his at Legnano. With the Peace of Constance in 1183, Frederick gave up his claims to direct imperial authority in the Lombard cities, though the Lombard League paid a special tax to support the imperial army. Frederick's claims as feudal suzerain were recognized, but the cities had gained independence over various matters.

To free himself for his Italian pursuits, Frederick Barbarossa made concessions to the German princes. His great Welf rival, Henry the Lion, obtained the right to invest the bishops of several important sees; he led a great wave of German eastward expansion into the Slavic lands across the Elbe, where he ruled independently of Frederick. Henry married the daughter of Henry II of England, received envoys from the Byzantine emperor, and conducted an almost independent foreign policy. But in the 1160s, when Henry tried to bargain with Frederick over troops needed for Italy, Frederick summoned him to his royal court. A refusal to come enabled the emperor to declare Henry a "contumacious" vassal and later to seize his property (1180).

The great territorial possessions of the Welf family were now broken up and divided among other smaller princes. The very act of parceling them out instead of adding them to the royal domain shows how feudalized Germany had become. Frederick could not hold on to these lands because he could not control his German vassals effectively. It was part of the price he paid for his Italian enterprises. In the same year (1180), Frederick recognized his immediate vassals as princes of the empire, giving formal recognition to the new feudal order in Germany by creating a new class jealous of its prerogatives.

Four years before he died, in 1186, Frederick arranged the marriage of his son, Henry, to Constance, the heiress of Norman Sicily—one of the most important dynastic marriages of the Middle Ages. The papal territories were squeezed between the heir to Germany and northern Italy and the heiress to southern Italy and Sicily. The marriage guaranteed a new round in the papal-imperial struggle.

When Henry VI (r. 1190-1197) married Constance, he acquired an extraordinary kingdom built up in less than two centuries by the descendants of the Norman adventurers. But the pope, the German Welfs, and King Richard I ("the Lionhearted") of England jointly backed a rival of Henry for Sicily. Henry captured Richard and forced him to become his vassal and to break the alliance. By 1194 Henry was supreme at Palermo, the Sicilian capital, and he refused to do homage to the pope. Rather, Henry planned to acquire the Byzantine Empire, against which the Normans had waged intermittent warfare since the early eleventh century. He was building up a fleet to invade the eastern Mediterranean when he died suddenly in 1197. Henry had widened the concept of empire, but he had sacrificed such unity as he might have achieved in Germany to the imperial dreams of union with Sicily, by which the pope would remain encircled. To persuade the German princes to recognize the hereditary rights of his son, Frederick II, to succeed him, he offered each of them hereditary rights in his own fief.

Innocent III, 1198-1216

A year after the death of Henry VI, when his infant son and heir, Frederick II, was only four years old, there came to the papal throne Innocent III (r. 1198-1216), the greatest of all the medieval popes and still one of the most controversial. His powerful intervention in the affairs of secular princes was by no means limited to the traditional papal-imperial struggle; Innocent played a major part in the politics of France, England, and the Byzantine Empire.

Pope Innocent III.

Innocent said that papal power was like the sun, and kingly power like the moon, which derives its light from the sun. While he granted that his own position was "lower than God," he maintained that it was loftier than that of any other man. But he usually made such claims outside the context of any specific controversy; in such cases he usually found some explanation for his actions that did not depend on sweeping theoretical assertions. Yet occasionally he did seem to assert the right to act as supreme judge of any dispute in Christendom.

A professional lawyer, Innocent was a practical man of affairs, and he wanted to accomplish the ends he had in view. He held the loftiest conception of the role of the church in the world, and of the pope's role in the church. He legislated widely on matters quite unconnected with politics, and he favored reform of the church. However we evaluate his ambitions, he came closer than any pope before or after to making the papal monarchy a reality.

During the minority of Frederick II, who was the ward of the pope, Innocent determined to destroy the German-Sicilian combination. He backed a Welf educated in England, Otto of Brunswick, son of Henry the Lion, against Philip of Swabia, brother of Henry VI, who initially had the support of the German princes. Innocent revived the claim of Gregory VII that no emperor could rule without papal confirmation, while Philip argued that an emperor duly elected by the princes was emperor whether the pope approved or not. To assure himself of papal support, Otto promised to give up all rights with regard to investiture that the emperors had salvaged for themselves from the Investiture Controversy. The kings of England backed their Welf nephew, Otto, while their enemy, King Philip Augustus of France, naturally opposed the English-Welf coalition by backing Philip of Swabia. The fighting continued until 1208, when Philip of Swabia was assassinated.

The German princes elected Otto IV, but once he had been crowned by the pope in 1209, Otto began to act in the interests of the Hohenstaufen. He undertook to conquer Sicily, the very thing Innocent III wanted most to prevent. So in 1210 the pope excommunicated Otto and turned to the young Frederick Hohenstaufen, son of Henry VI. Supported by the pope and given money by the French, Frederick reorganized the Hohenstaufen party in Germany and, not yet twenty, was crowned king in 1212. When Otto and the English were defeated at Bouvines by the French (1214), Frederick's position became more secure, especially after he promised Innocent III that he would never try to unite his German and Sicilian possessions into one imperial state.

In 1215 Innocent held a great council at the Church of St. John Lateran in Rome to pronounce not only on the sacraments but on church discipline. Annual confession, penance, and communion were required for all Christians; heresies were condemned, and a new holy war was proclaimed against the Muslims. Innocent seemed to have triumphed wholly. But he died the next year, and Frederick II soon gave the papacy more trouble than even Henry IV had.

Frederick II, 1212-1250

Frederick II is perhaps the most interesting medieval monarch. Intelligent and cultivated, he spoke Arabic and Greek, took a deep interest in scientific experiment, collected wild animals, and wrote poetry in Italian. He patronized the arts, wrote on the sport of falconry, and was a superb politician. He was cynical, tough, a sound diplomat, an able administrator, and a statesman with his father's vision of a Mediterranean empire. Furthermore, he felt at home in Sicily—the sophisticated society in which his mother had grown up—and greatly preferred it to Germany. Indeed, he spent only nine of his thirty-eight years as emperor in Germany.

In Sicily Frederick imposed his own completely centralized monarchical form of government upon his Italian subjects. Feudal custom was wiped out and trial by battle forbidden. At Naples Frederick founded a university, which became a state training school in which officials could be grounded in the Roman law. His army and navy were organized on a paid rather than a feudal basis. Finances were regularized and modernized, and an imperial bureaucracy collected taxes on incoming and outgoing merchandise. State monopolies like those at Byzantium controlled certain key industries, such as silk.

Germany, by contrast, suffered. The Germans felt that they had no stake in Frederick's empire. He could never extend to Germany the centralized administration that he built in Sicily. Indeed, when in 1220 he obtained for his son, Henry, election as king of Germany and a promise from the bishops and abbots that Henry would be the next emperor, he granted still more privileges to these ecclesiastical princes, who were already elected without imperial interference. Frederick abandoned his right to set up mints and customs stations in their territories, together with royal rights of justice. He promised to exclude from imperial cities any serfs who might run away from church lands to try their fortunes in the towns, and he agreed to build no new towns or fortresses on church lands. Thus he acted against the towns, failing to see that they were natural royal allies. In 1231 the secular German princes exacted similar privileges from Frederick. In Germany both the ecclesiastical and the secular princes had become virtually independent.

Yet the centerpiece of Frederick II's reign was his tremendous conflict with the papacy, beginning in the 1220s. His opponents were three successive popes—Honorius III (1216-1227), Gregory IX (1227-1241), and Innocent IV (1243-1254)—who were not only consistently determined to prevent him from achieving his aims, but were competent to fight him on even terms. Honorius did crown Frederick emperor in 1220, but before Honorius died, Frederick was already asserting himself in sensitive Lombard territory. During the emperor's absence from Italy on a crusade, Gregory IX's newly hired mercenary armies attacked his southern Italian lands. When Frederick returned, he was able to make peace temporarily, but he soon created further trouble. After he had defeated the Lombard towns in

Emperor Frederick II, on the ship on the left, watches his soldiers attack churchmen on their way to the council summoned by Gregory IX.

1237 for refusing to keep the terms of the Peace of Constance, he announced a new plan to extend imperial administration to all Italy, including Rome. So in 1239 the pope excommunicated him and war was resumed. Violent propaganda pamphlets were circulated by both sides. The pope called Frederick a heretic who was trying to found a new religion. Frederick called the pope a hypocrite and urged all monarchs in Europe to unite against the pretensions of the church. Hemmed in at Rome by the encroaching imperial system, the pope summoned a church council, presumably to depose Frederick. But Frederick's fleet captured the entire council of more than one hundred high churchmen. Just as Frederick was about to enter Rome itself, Pope Gregory IX died (1241). Frederick tried to install a new pope favorable to himself but failed. The new pope, Innocent IV, fled from Italy, summoned a council to Lyons (1245), and deposed Frederick. There followed five more years of struggle; but before the conflict had been settled Frederick died in 1250.

In its last phases, when he was locked in combat with Innocent IV, Frederick—who had hitherto always protested that he was a good Christian and had proper reverence for the papal office—wrote a letter to the princes of Europe furiously attacking the clergy for their greed. He himself, he said, would reform the church by confiscating all its wealth. Maybe a return to the poverty of the early Christian days would breed saints who would heal the sick and perform an occasional miracle, rather than clergymen who stuck their noses into political affairs that were none of their business. Although his letter was obviously a cynical piece of propaganda that seems to have startled its recipients and won over no one, it foreshadowed the days, not far off, when powerful laymen would move vigorously against the organized church. In response, Innocent IV's propagandists had to fall back on a new interpretation of the Donation of Constantine, claiming that the popes had always had the right to make and unmake emperors.

After Frederick's death, the papacy pursued his descendants with fury. In 1266 a long-maturing papal plan succeeded. Charles of Anjou, the ruthless and able brother of Louis IX, king of France, was brought into Italy as the papal candidate for the southern territories. He defeated and killed Frederick's son and grandson and established himself as king in the south.

By 1268 the Hohenstaufen line was extinct. The Holy Roman Empire, begun by Frederick Barbarossa and given an Italian rather than a German base by Henry VI and Frederick II, had been destroyed by the papacy. Yet within only forty years of Charles of Anjou's entry into Italy as the instrument of papal vengeance, Charles's grandnephew, King Philip IV of France (Philip the Fair), would puncture the temporal claims of the papacy and carry it off to "captivity" in France.

In Germany the imperial throne remained vacant from 1254 to 1273. The princes consolidated their power during this interregnum by taking advantage of the large grants made by rival candidates to the throne (all foreigners) in the hope of receiving their support. But the princes were pleased for a time not to have an emperor; their usurpation of rights that had formerly belonged to

North Sea
PRUSSIA
Danzig
Lübeck
Hamburg
Bremen
Elbe R.
Weser R.
POMERANIA
Vistula R.
FRIESLAND
SAXONY
BRANDENBURG
HARZ MTS.
Magdeburg
Goslar
Oder R.
POLAND
Meuse R.
KINGDOM OF GERMANY
Elbe R.
Cologne
THURINGIA
SILESIA
LOWER LORRAINE
Aachen
Rhine R.
Saale R.
Bouvines
Frankfurt
Main R.
Bamberg
Prague
Trier
Mainz
Würzburg
Worms
PALATINATE
FRANCONIA
BOHEMIA
MORAVIA
UPPER LORRAINE
Ratisbon
Strasbourg
Danube R.
Augsburg
AUSTRIA
Vienna
SWABIA
BAVARIA
FRANCE
Constance
STYRIA
Saône R.
KINGDOM OF BURGUNDY
(KINGDOM OF ARLES)
CARINTHIA
TYROL
CARNIOLA
Trieste
Danube R.
Drava R.
Danube
HUNGARY
Rhône R.
Legnano
Brescia
LOMBARDY
Milan
Adige R.
Venice
Pavia
Po R.
Roncaglia
Alessandria
Ferrara
Genoa
Canossa
Bologna
Ravenna
Avignon
Arles
KINGDOM OF ITALY
ROMAGNA
Zara
Pisa
Florence
Ancona
Siena
Assisi
TUSCANY
SERBIA
Adriatic Sea
Ragusa
CORSICA
(to Pisa)
PAPAL STATES
Tagliacozzo
Rome
Anagni
0 100 200
Miles
Bari
Melfi
Naples
APULIA
Amalfi
Salerno
Taranto
SARDINIA
(to Pisa and Genoa)
KINGDOM OF THE TWO SICILIES
(Hohenstaufen, 1194)
CALABRIA
Palermo
SICILY
Syracuse
Mediterranean Sea
Battle sites
Boundary of the Holy Roman Empire
Kingdom of the Two Sicilies
Papal States
Claimed by papacy
Venetian possessions

Medieval Germany and Italy

At the Death of Frederick II, 1250

the monarchy was now well on its way to completion. Meanwhile, the old links with Italy were virtually broken, and the earlier form of the imperial idea vanished. Imperial preoccupation with Italy had ensured that the princes would emerge as the real rulers of Germany. Thereafter *particularism,* an intense localism, would dominate in Germany until the nineteenth century, while united nation-states were rising in the West. Ultimately, the monarchical papacy and the German kingdom would destroy each other.

V THE CHURCH IN SOCIETY

Frederick II's denunciation of the church was a partisan document issued for his own selfish purposes. Yet he was right in believing that the church needed reform. For example, Innocent IV, in fighting Frederick, had approved the appointment to a bishopric in German territory of an illiterate and dissolute young man of nineteen just because he was a member of a powerful anti-Hohenstaufen noble family; this bishop was forced to resign after twenty-five years, when the last Hohenstaufen was dead, but only because his public boasting about his fourteen bastards (some by abbesses and nuns), all of whom he had provided with ecclesiastical benefices, had become a scandal. Because the church had an efficient bureaucracy in each bishopric, it probably did not matter much if the bishop were incompetent or even wicked; in the end the papacy, which had installed him, removed him. The need for reform was constantly felt in the church itself, and successive waves of reforming zeal manifested themselves, especially in monastic movements.

Cluny, within the Benedictine order, continued in its determination to rid the church of abuses, and its centrally organized rule over daughter-houses was its strength and its weakness. Reforming enthusiasm is difficult to sustain over a long period, especially after the particular abuses that arouse it begin to yield. The effectiveness of centralized control depends on the personality of the abbot of the ruling house; weak or selfish or cynical abbots endanger the whole enterprise. Those who started out determined to leave the world and live in poverty and humility found themselves admired by the rich and often took gifts that in turn transformed their order into worldly men of business all too concerned with the things of this life. Thus, by the late eleventh century, the Cluniac houses had become wealthy and their rule had relaxed.

Augustinians and Cistercians

One newly founded order broke with the rule of Benedict, finding its inspiration in a letter of Augustine that prescribed simply that they share all their property, pray together at regular intervals, dress alike, and obey a superior. Some of the "Augustinians," as they called themselves, interpreted these general rules severely, living in silence, performing manual labor, eating and drinking sparingly, and singing psalms; others ate meat, conversed among themselves, and did not insist on manual labor. Beginning often as small informal foundations without large endowments, the Augustinians helped the sick and did useful, if humble, actions in the world, rather than leaving it altogether. They attracted modest donations from relatively modest donors. Unlike Cluny, with its vast collections of buildings crowned by a great and splendid church, the Augustinian foundations were simple and humble. The Augustinians wore neither splendid vestments nor hairshirts and ropes; but they preached, baptized, heard confessions, and helped the poor unobtrusively. They multiplied rapidly, and in the thirteenth century there were thousands of Augustinian houses in England and on the Continent.

Founded only a little later, the Cistercians abandoned the world instead of living in it. Their original house, Cîteaux (Cistercium) in Burgundy, lay in a dismal wasteland far from the distractions of the world. They considered themselves the only true Benedictines, aggressively declaring that the rule of Benedict, when lived purely, was identical with the message of the Gospels—life as Christ himself had lived it. Yet the self-denial, poverty, and wholly spiritual life in retirement that the Cistercians adopted was often seen by their contemporaries as arrogant, militant, worldly, and even greedy.

The most celebrated Cistercian leader was St. Bernard of Clairvaux (c 1091-1153), who in 1115 led a small band of Cistercians to Clairvaux, a spot as unpromising as Cîteaux itself. From here the ostensibly unworldly Bernard influenced the affairs of the world to a degree almost beyond modern understanding. He not only upbraided clergymen for their laxity in observing ecclesiastical rules, but also helped to organize a crusade to the Holy Land, advised the kings of France, and chastened even the greatest feudal nobles.

In the end, the Cistercians too changed. Display conquered austerity, and aristocratic traditions quenched humility. By the thirteenth century, great Cistercian monasteries—Fountains Abbey in Yorkshire, for instance—were wealthy centers of production. The expensive arts of architecture and sculpture—scorned initially by Bernard as devilish devices that took men's attention from worship—were lavished on their buildings. These Cistercian monasteries had become great corporations, thoroughly tied into the increasingly complex web of medieval economic life.

Friars: Dominicans and Franciscans

In the early thirteenth century, the reforming movement within the church took on new aspects. As town populations grew, the new urban masses—often neglected by the church and hostile to the rich and worldly clergy—were eager to "get religion" in a revivalist sense, and they were sometimes subject to waves of mass hysteria and guilt. These outbreaks and the terror that led to them were a cry for spiritual help, and two famous new orders of friars—Dominican and Franciscan—arose in response.

Dominic (1170-1221) was a Spanish Augustinian canon who saw richly dressed Cistercian abbots wholly failing in their mission to convert heretics in southern France in 1206. He revived the idea of apostolic simplicity that had given birth to the Augustinians, founded the "Order of Preachers" within the Augustinian rule, and until his death directed them in their work of preaching and living the life of simple, primitive Christians.

Francis (1182-1226), the son of a wealthy Italian merchant, gave his possessions to the poor in 1206, and with a few followers, who had also given up their property, obtained Pope Innocent III's approval of his new order of the Friars Minor (little brothers) in 1210. Poverty was not new, but the heavy emphasis that Francis placed upon it—the brothers were to be dependent for their daily bread upon alms from the charitable—was new. Much against his will, Francis was soon the head of a large, loosely structured organization.

Dominic subordinated all other duties to the obligation to preach, while Francis of Assisi led a truly grass-roots urban movement of protest against wealth and show. They were rivals in a sense, and both orders were soon borrowing from each other's principles. The Franciscans adopted the more efficient organizing principles of the Dominicans; the Dominicans took over the Franciscan emphasis on poverty. From the first the Dominicans had emphasized the need of study as a fundamental duty; the Franciscans, who began by repudiating book learning, soon imitated the Dominicans, moved into the universities, and became distinguished scholars. Both orders divided Europe into "provinces" and spread widely.

Education

The church alone directed and conducted education in medieval Europe. Unless destined for the priesthood, young men of the upper classes had little formal schooling, though the family chaplain often taught them to read and write. Young women had no more and usually less education. But the monastic schools educated future monks and priests, and the Cluniac reform, with its increased demand for piety, stimulated study and the copying of manuscripts.

Medieval scholars divided knowledge into the seven liberal arts: the trivium (grammar, rhetoric, dialectic) and the quadrivium (arithmetic, geometry, astronomy, music). The first three included much of what we might call humanities today; the last four corresponded to the sciences. In the eleventh century only a few monastic schools taught all seven. In general monks sought to preserve rather than to advance knowledge.

The cathedral schools, on the other hand, whose teachers were often less timid about studying classical pagan writings, fostered a more inquiring spirit. In France during the eleventh century, at the cathedral schools of Paris, Chartres, Rheims, and other towns, distinguished teachers were often succeeded by men whom they themselves had trained, and distinguished pupils went on to join or found other schools. In Italy, where the connection with cathedrals was less close, the medical school at Salerno had existed since the early Middle Ages. At Bologna law became the specialty, beginning as a branch of rhetoric and so within the trivium. Students were attracted to Bologna from other regions of Italy and even from northern Europe. In the early twelfth century, as education became fashionable for young men ambitious for advancement in the church or in the royal service, the number of students grew rapidly.

The student body at Bologna organized itself into two associations—students from Italy and students from beyond the Alps—and the two incorporated as the whole body, the *universitas*, or university. As a corporate body they could protect themselves against being overcharged for food and lodging by threatening to leave town; having no property, they could readily have moved. They depended on their own work, or their parents to meet their fees:

> *Well-beloved father, I have not a penny, nor can I get any save through you, for all things at the University are so dear: nor can I study in my Code or my Digest, for they are all tattered. Moreover, I owe ten crowns in dues to the Provost, and can find no man to lend them to me; I send you word of greetings and money.**

If the students did not like a professor, they simply stayed away from his lectures, and he starved or moved on, for he depended on their tuition fees for his living. Soon the students fixed the price of room and board in town and fined professors for absence or for lecturing too long. The professors organized too and admitted to their number only those who had passed an examination and so won a *license* to teach, remote ancestor of formal academic degrees.

In Paris and elsewhere in the north the cathedral schools were the immediate forerunners of the universities. It was the teachers, not the students, who organized first, as a guild of those who taught the seven liberal arts and who got their licenses from the cathedral authorities. By the thirteenth century pious citizens had founded in Paris the first residence halls for poor students, who might eat and sleep free in these "colleges." The practice crossed the Channel to Oxford and Cambridge, where the university authorities stoutly resisted control by the secular powers. The friction of "town and gown" dates from medieval times, a friction to which the students contributed when they played, drank, sang, hazed freshmen, organized hoaxes and practical jokes, and rioted. University authorities passed many ordinances, usually in vain, against student sports and brawls.

*Quoted in G.G. Coulton, *Life in the Middle Ages* (Cambridge: Cambridge University Press, 1929), III, 113.

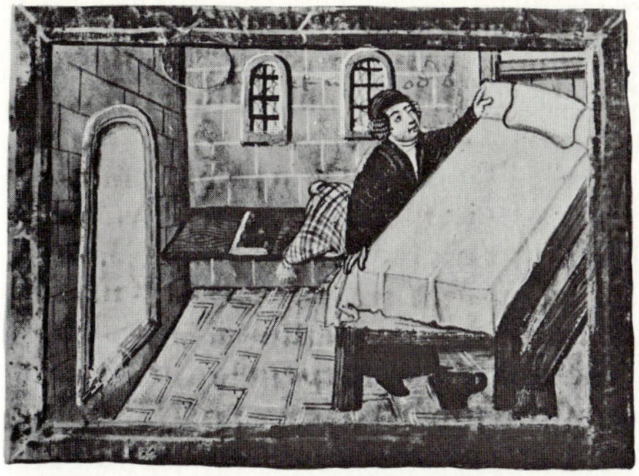

Scenes of student life in the Middle Ages.

The Question of Universals

Much of the study at that time consisted of mere memorizing by rote, since in the days before printing ready reference works were scarce. Though the formal rules of scholarly debate were fixed, there was, nonetheless, lively discussion available for those who worked to sharpen their minds, not just to load their memories. Discussion and learning were particularly taken up with defining systems by which people could live faithfully within the expectations of Christendom.

At the turn of the eleventh century, Gerbert of Aurillac, who became Pope Sylvester II (999-1003), stood out as the most learned man of his day; the smattering of mathematics and science that he had been able to pick up caused his contemporaries to suspect him of witchcraft. Because he was interested in logic, he turned to the work of Boethius. His probing mind delved into the portions of Aristotle that Boethius had translated and discovered in logic a systematic means of approaching the writings of the church fathers. By the end of the century, churchmen could debate whether it was proper to use human reason to consider a particular theological question (for example, was Christ actually present in the sacramental wafer and wine?), and in all efforts to explain away inconsistencies in the Bible and in the writings of the church fathers in general. Even those who attacked the use of reason used it themselves in making new definitions that enabled them to argue that bread and wine could, in a certain way, become flesh and blood.

Once the new method became available, the dogmatists of the late eleventh and early twelfth centuries employed it in a celebrated controversy over the philosophical problem of *universals.* A universal encompasses a whole category of things; when we say "dog" or "table" or "person," we mean not any specific dog or table or person, but the idea of *all* dogs, tables, or people—dogdom, tabledom, humanity. The question that concerned medieval thinkers was whether universal categories exist: Is there such a thing as dogdom, tabledom, or humanity apart from the aggregate of individuals?

If you said no, you were a *nominalist*; that is, you thought dogdom, tabledom, humanity were merely *nomina*—names that people give to a general category from their experience of individual members of it. You experience dogs, tables, persons, and so you infer the existence of dogdom, tabledom, humanity because the individual members of the category have certain points of resemblance; but the category, the universal, has no existence in itself. If you said yes, you were a *realist*, that is, you thought that the general categories did exist. Many realists took this view a large step further and said that the individual dog, table, or person was far *less* real than the generalizing category or universal, or even that the individual dog, table, or person was a mere reflection of one aspect of the category and existed only by virtue of belonging to the category: a person exists only by partaking of the nature of humanity, a dog because it partakes of the nature of dogdom.

If we transfer this question to politics and think of the state and the individual, we can see at once how great its practical importance may be. A pure nominalist would say that the state is just a name and exists only because the individuals who make it up are real. It could therefore be argued that the state must then serve its subjects, since after all it is only the sum of their individualities. A pure realist would say that the state is the only real thing, that its individual subjects exist only insofar as they partake of its general character, and that the state, by virtue of its existence, properly dominates the individual. In religion, an extreme nominalist, arguing that what we can perceive through our senses is alone real, might even have trouble believing in the existence of God. An extreme realist would tend to ignore, or even to deny, the existence of the physical world and its problems.

Moderate realists have to start with faith—to believe so that they may know, as St. Anselm (1033-1109) put it. Anselm, a philosopher and theologian, was the archbishop of Canterbury, and likely to be listened to. He founded the approach to knowledge known as *Scholasticism*, which is based in part on his ontological proof for the existence of God. According to Anselm's "proof," that which exists in reality *as well as* in the mind must be greater than that which exists in the mind alone, and since the mind can conceive the idea of a being greater than all else, it logically follows that this being *must exist in reality* as well as in the mind, or it is not in fact greater than anything else.

Peter Abelard (1079-1142), a popular lecturer at the University of Paris, tried to compromise the question. He argued that universals were not merely names, as the nominalists held, nor did they have a real existence, as the realists held. They were, he said, *concepts* in people's minds, and as such had a real existence of a special kind in the mind, which had created them out of its experience of particulars: humanity from individuals, dogdom from dogs, and so on. Abelard's compromise between nominalism and realism is called *conceptualism*.

Abelard insisted on the importance of understanding for true faith. He put reason first, and thus a person must understand in order to believe, instead of the other way around. His most famous work, *Sic et Non (Yes and No)*, lists over one hundred and fifty theological statements and cites authorities both defending and attacking the truth of each. When Scripture and the Fathers were inconsistent, he seems to argue, how could a person decide what to believe without logical thought? A rationalist and lover of argument, Abelard was nonetheless a deeply pious believer. St. Bernard the Cistercian, who was a mystic and suspicious of reason, believed Abelard heretical and had his views condemned and denounced repeatedly.

Clearly, these various positions on universals were and are important, not only in the concept of the state or in a person's relationship to God, but in terms of how abstract concepts govern daily life. Obviously, an idea such as "God is Love" takes a position in this debate; so too does any person's application of the *idea* of "love" to an individual circumstance.

Thomas Aquinas

By Abelard's death, the Greek scientific writings of antiquity were starting to be recovered, often through translations from Arabic into Latin. In the second half of the century came the recovery of Aristotle's lost treatises on logic, which dealt with such subjects as how to build a *syllogism* (an expression of deductive reasoning), how to prove a point, and how to refute false conclusions. With these instruments, medieval thinkers for the first time could systematize and summarize their entire philosophical position.

Yet the recovery of Aristotle posed certain new problems. For example, the Muslim philosopher Averroës, whose comments accompanied the text of Aristotle's *Metaphysics*, stressed Aristotle's own view that the physical world was eternal; since the soul—a nonphysical thing—was essentially common to all humanity, no individual human soul could be saved by itself. Obviously this ran counter to fundamental Christian teaching. Some scholars tried to say that both views could be true—Aristotle's in philosophy and the Christian in theology. But this led directly to heresy. Others simply tried to forbid the reading of Aristotle, though without success. It was the Dominican Albertus Magnus (1193-c 1280) a Swabian, and his pupil Thomas Aquinas (1225-1274), an Italian, who, in massive multivolume works produced over a lifetime, succeeded in reconciling the apparent differences between Aristotle's teachings and those of the Christian tradition. They were the greatest of the Schoolmen, exponents of Scholasticism.

Aquinas' best-known writings were the *Summa Theologica* and the *Summa contra Gentiles*. He discussed God, humans, and the universe, arranging his material in systematic topical order in the form of an inquiry into and discussion of each open question. First he cited the evidence on each side, then he gave his own answer, and finally he demonstrated the falsity of the other position. Although Aquinas always cited authority, he also never failed to provide his own logical analysis. For him, reason was a most valuable instrument, but only when it reasonably recognized its own limitations. When unaided reason could not comprehend an apparent contradiction with faith, it must yield to faith, since reason by itself could not understand the entire universe. Certain fundamentals must be accepted as unprovable axioms of faith, although, once they had been accepted, reason could show that they were probable. If a person put a series of arguments together and came out with a conclusion contrary to what orthodox Christians believed, the logic had been faulty, and the correct use of logic could readily show the error.

Thus the "Angelic Doctor," as Aquinas was called,

TRUTHS WHICH ARE ABOVE NATURE

Aquinas delighted in the game of inventing arguments against accepted beliefs, matching them with a set of even more ingenious arguments, and then reconciling the two with dazzling intellectual skill. Here is an example of a relatively unimportant part of the *Summa Theologica* which is fairly easy to follow; it brings out clearly how close to "common sense" Aquinas could be.

He is discussing the specific conditions of "man's first state"—the state of innocence before the Fall. He comes to the question of what children were like in the state of innocence. Were they born with such perfect strength of body that they had full use of their limbs at birth, or were they like human children now, helpless? In the Garden of Eden, we might think that any form of helplessness would detract from perfection, and that God might well have made the human infant strong and perfect, or might even have had men and women born adult. Aquinas did not think so; even Eden was as "natural" as he could make it:

By faith alone do we hold truths which are above nature, and what we believe rests on authority. Wherefore, in making any assertion, we must be guided by the nature of things, except in those things which are above nature, and are made known to us by Divine authority. Now it is clear that it is as natural as it is befitting to the principles of human nature that children should not have sufficient strength for the use of their limbs immediately after birth. Because in proportion to other animals man has naturally a larger brain. Wherefore it is natural, on account of the considerable humidity of the brain in children, that the sinews which are instruments of movement, should not be apt for moving the limbs. On the other hand, no Catholic doubts it possible for a child to have, by Divine power, the use of its limbs immediately after birth.

Now we have it on the authority of Scripture that *God made man right* (*Ecclesiastes*, vii.30), which rightness, as Augustine says, consists in the perfect subjection of the body to the soul. As, therefore, in the primitive state it was impossible to find in the human limbs anything repugnant to man's well-ordered will, so was it impossible for those limbs to fail in executing the will's commands. Now the human will is well ordered when it tends to acts which are befitting to man. But the same acts are not befitting to man at every season of life. We must, therefore, conclude that children would not have had sufficient strength for the use of their limbs for the purpose of performing every kind of act; but only for the acts befitting the state of infancy, such as suckling, and the like.

The Summa Theologica of St. Thomas Aquinas, (New York: Benzinger, 1947), Article 495, Quest. XCIX.

This apparently trivial passage contains much that is typical of *Thomism*, as the philosophy of Aquinas is termed. It reveals the supremacy that is granted to "truths which are above nature," which are held by faith and received through divine authority: the belief that God usually prefers to let nature run its course according to its laws; the belief that there is a "fitness" in human action conforming to these laws of nature; and, finally, the appeal to authority, in this case the Old Testament and Augustine. Notice also that Aquinas never even brings up the kinds of questions anticlerical rationalists were later to ask, such as: Just how were children procreated before the Fall? Or, were there any children, anyone but Adam and Eve, in Eden before the Fall? Such questions clearly fell outside the realm of faith on which the passage was posited.

worked out a systematic theology on rational principles, declaring that, since truth was indivisible, there was no contradiction between faith and reason, theology and science. In 1879 Pope Leo XIII would declare Thomism to be the official philosophy of Roman Catholicism.

Political Thought

In dealing with problems of human relations, medieval thinkers used a vocabulary that is different from ours, yet they came fairly close in many ways to modern democratic thinking. Except for extreme realism, medieval political thought was emphatically not autocratic. To the medieval thinker the perfection of the kingdom of heaven could not possibly exist on earth, where compromise and imperfection were inescapable.

Nor could full equality exist on earth. Medieval political thought accepted as its starting point an order of rank in human society. The twelfth-century *Policraticus (Statesman's Book)* of the English Scholastic philosopher John of Salisbury (c 1115-1180) provided a complete statement of this social theory. The prince (or king) is the head of the body of the commonwealth; the senate (legislature) is the heart; the judges and governors of provinces are the eyes, ears, and tongue; the officials and soldiers are the hands; the financial officers are the stomach and intestines; and the peasants "correspond to the feet, which always cleave to the soil." This "organic" theory of society was a great favorite with those who opposed change, for obviously the foot does not try to become the brain, nor is the hand jealous of the eye. The whole body is at its best when each part does what nature meant it to do. The peasant, the blacksmith, the merchant, the lawyer, the wife, the priest, and the king had all been assigned a part of God's work on earth.

While medieval thought thus distinguished among vocations, it also insisted on the dignity and worth of all vocations, even the humblest. It accepted the Christian doctrine of the equality of all souls before God, and held that no person could be a mere instrument of another. Even the humblest person on this earth could hope to enjoy bliss as full and eternal as any king's in the next world. Furthermore, medieval political theory by no means opposed all change on earth. Medieval thinkers were certainly not democratic in the sense of believing that the people had a right to, or could, "make" their own institutions. But they did not hold that, since God had arranged authority as it was in this world, humanity should preserve existing conditions, come what may. Bad conditions probably meant that good conditions had been perverted. The thing to do was to try to restore the original good conditions—"God's own plan."

Thomas Aquinas repudiated Augustine's views that the state was a necessary evil and the result of human sin. He concluded that kings were needed; good kings obviously were best; limited monarchy logically had the least chance of becoming a tyranny. Though the pope was at the peak of both temporal and spiritual power, he had "an indirect rather than a direct authority in temporal matters"—another example of Aquinas's moderation.

Later Marsiglio of Padua (c 1290-1343), the author of *Defensor Pacis (Defender of the Peace)*, found the only true source of authority in a commonwealth to be the *universitas civium*, the whole body of the citizens. Marsiglio probably did not mean to be as modern as this may seem. He still used medieval terms; the constitutionalism and popular sovereignty that have been attributed to him are a long way from any notion of counting votes to determine political decisions. But like many other medieval thinkers, Marsiglio believed that no one's place in the order of rank—even at the top—is such that those of lower rank must always and unquestioningly accept what is commanded of them. If worse came to worst, medieval political thinkers—even in autocratic Byzantium—were willing to approve tyrannicide. To the medieval mind, even to that of the lawyer, law was not made but found. Law for common everyday purposes was custom. But beyond custom lay the *law of nature*, or natural law—something like God's word translated into terms that made it usable by ordinary persons on earth. It was the ethical ideal, the "ought to be," that was discernible by those who were thinking rightly.

The medieval intellectual assumed that the universe was static; the modern intellectual assumes that it is dynamic. The one assumed that laws for right human action had been designed for all time by God in heaven, and that those laws were discoverable and clear to the good Christian. The other assumes that laws for right human action are worked out in the process of living, that no one can be sure of them in advance, and that new ones are constantly being created. The medieval thinker, if puzzled, tended to resolve problems by an appeal to authority—the best or the natural authority people had been trained to believe in, such as Aristotle or Aquinas or the customary law of the land. And medieval thinkers usually believed that no perfectly satisfactory solution of their problems would be available until they went to heaven. The modern thinker, if puzzled, tends at least to consult several different authorities and to compare them before deciding. Modern thinkers may also try to experiment. If the inquiry is conducted in the right way, that could solve the difficulty. The right way for the medieval person already existed and had, at most, to be *found;* the right way for the modern person may have to be *invented, created.*

Mysticism

Although Scholasticism set faith above reason, it nevertheless held that the instrument of thought is a divine gift, and that it must be used and sharpened here on earth. Mystics who distrusted reason and intellect could never accept this view. There were many mystics in the Middle Ages. St. Bernard, mystic and activist, denounced Abelard, thinker and rationalist teacher. St. Francis also distrusted formal intellectual activity. For him, Christ was no philosopher; Christ's way was the way of submission, of subduing the mind as well as the flesh.

> *My brothers who are led by the curiosity of knowledge will find their hands empty in the day of tribulation. I would wish them rather to be strengthened by virtues, that when the time of tribulation comes they may have the Lord with them in their straits—for such a time will come when they will throw their good-for-nothing books into holes and corners.**

The quality of Francis's piety comes out in this fragment of a work which is almost certainly by his own hand, the *Canticle of the Brother Sun:*

> *Most High, omnipotent, good Lord, thine is the praise, the glory, the honour and every benediction.*
>
> *Praised be thou, my Lord, with all thy creatures, especially milord Brother Sun that dawns and lightens us.*
>
> *Be praised, my Lord, for Sister Moon and the stars that thou hast made bright and precious and beautiful.*

*Quoted in H.O. Taylor, *The Mediaeval Mind* (Cambridge, Mass.: Harvard University Press, 1949), I, 444-45.

In those lands that became France and England, a series of strong monarchs emerged to provide the state with another center of authority that could contest with the Church for the loyalties of the people. While open conflict with the papacy was not yet contemplated, and no state in Western Europe was secular in the sense of placing the monarch above the papacy, both France and England were experiencing a rise of collective identity that would lead to a succession of royal triumphs. Both would achieve unity as nation-states earlier than most other areas of Europe, in part because of the balance of force represented by the monarchies. In both an emerging tradition of scientific inquiry—not yet hostile to religion though not following overtly religious modes of thought—and the development of a lively, highly imaginative vernacular literary tradition would provide additional sources of controversy and discussion, sources, which though rooted in a churchly tradition, did not invariably support churchly policy.

I THE DEVELOPMENT OF FRANCE: FROM HUGH CAPET TO PHILIP THE FAIR

The central thread of French history during the period between 987 and 1314 is royal success. The French monarchy grew in power and prestige from small beginnings until it dominated the machinery of government. France became the first large and unified state in the medieval West, a state built largely by the French monarchy.

The Capetians, 987-1226

When Hugh Capet (c 938-996) came to the throne of France in 987, there was little to distinguish him from the last feeble Carolingians. Yet he was different, if only because he was the first of a male line that was to continue uninterrupted for almost 350 years. Like the Byzantine emperors, but with better luck, the Capetians had procured the election and coronation of the king's eldest son during his father's lifetime. When the father died, the son would already be king. After two centuries, when the king decided for reasons of his own not to follow this practice, the hereditary principle had become so well established that the succession was no longer questioned.

For a hundred years before the accession of Hugh Capet, his ancestors had been rivals of the Carolingians for the throne. As king of France, Hugh was recognized by all the feudal lords as their suzerain, but they were actually more powerful than he. Thus he might not be able to collect the aid (military service), the counsel, and the feudal dues that his vassals in theory owed him. He was also, of course, lord of his own domain, the Ile de France. This was a piece of land including Paris and the area immediately adjacent, and extending south to Orléans on the Loire River. It was far smaller than the domain of any of the great feudal lords: the dukes of Normandy or Burgundy or Aquitaine, the counts of Flanders, Anjou, Champagne, Brittany, or Toulouse. It may indeed have been for this very reason that Hugh was chosen to be king; he seemed less likely to be a threat than any of the better-endowed lords. Yet the Capetian domain was compact and central, easy to govern and advantageously located. Unlike the Hohenstaufens, who were preoccupied with lands far afield, Hugh and his immediate successors concentrated on consolidating the administration of their center of power.

The Capetians also enjoyed the sanctity of kingship that came with coronation and unction (anointing) with holy oil, which tradition said a dove had brought down from heaven for Clovis at his baptism. In the eyes of the people, this ecclesiastical ceremony brought the king very close to God. He could work miracles, some believed. In this way the king was raised above all other feudal lords, however powerful.

Furthermore, the church was his partner. He defended it, according to his cornonation oath, and it assisted him. In the great sees near Paris, the king could nominate successors to vacant bishoprics and archbishoprics, and he could collect the income of bishoprics during vacancies. As in Germany, these royal powers aroused the opposition of the papacy, but the French kings abandoned lay investiture without a prolonged struggle. The king retained his right of intervention in episcopal elections, and the bishops still took oaths of fealty to the king and accepted their worldly goods at his hands. This unbroken partnership with the church greatly strengthened the early Capetian kings.

The history of the Capetians during their first two centuries of rule in France is, on the surface, far less eventful than the contemporary history of several of their great vassals, such as the dukes of Normandy, who were conquering England, and whose vassals were establishing a great state in Sicily, or the dukes of Burgundy, whose relatives were taking over the throne in Portugal. The Capetian kings stayed at home, made good their authority within their own domain, and, piece by piece, added a little neighboring territory to it. Within the royal domain, the Capetians increased their control over the *curia regis*, the king's court, which consisted of an enlargement of the royal household. The great offices had at first tended to become hereditary, thus concentrating power in the hands of a few families. Under Louis VI (r. 1108-1137) one man held the key household offices of chancellor and *seneschal* (steward) as well as five important posts in the church. Louis VI, however, ousted this man and his relatives from their posts and made appointments of his own choosing. These new men were lesser nobles, lower churchmen, and members of the middle classes that were now emerging in the towns. Since they owed their careers to the Crown alone, they were loyal and trustworthy royal servants, not unlike the ministeriales in Germany. Most important among them was Suger (1081-1151), the abbé (abbot) of St. Denis, a man of humble origin and learned attainments who efficiently served both Louis VI and Louis VII (r. 1137-1180) for decades.

The most important single factor in the development of Capetian France, however, was the relationship of the kings with their most powerful vassals, the dukes of Normandy. By the mideleventh century, these dukes had centralized the administration of their own duchy, compelling their vassals to render military service, forbidding them to coin their own money, and curbing their rights of justice. The *viscounts*, agents of the ducal regime, exercised local control. After Duke William conquered England in 1066 and became its king, he and his successors were still vassals of the Capetians for Normandy. But they became so much more powerful than their overlords that they did not hesitate to conduct regular warfare against them. Norman power grew even greater during the early twelfth century, when an English queen, Matilda, married another great vassal of the French king, Geoffrey IV, count of Anjou. In the person of their son, King Henry II of England (r. 1154-1189), England was united with the French fiefs of Normandy, Anjou, Maine, and Touraine in what is sometimes called the Angevin, or English-French Empire.

But this was not all. King Louis VII of France had married Eleanor, the heiress of Aquitaine, a great duchy in the southwest of France. When he had the marriage annulled (1152) for lack of a male heir, Eleanor lost no time in marrying Henry II and adding Aquitaine to his already substantial French holdings. So when Henry became king of England in 1154, he was also lord of more than half of France. He added Brittany and still other French territories. This Angevin threat was the greatest danger faced by the Capetian monarchs, and it was their greatest achievement that they overcame it.

The first round in the victorious struggle was the achievement of Philip II, Philip Augustus (r. 1180-1223), who quadrupled the size of the French royal domain. Shrewd and calculating, Philip first supported Henry II's rebellious sons against him. Then, after Henry's death, Philip plotted with Henry's younger son, John, against John's older brother, Richard the Lionhearted—Philip's former companion on the Third Crusade and now (1192-1194) a captive in Austria. Philip married a Danish princess with the idea of using the Danish fleet against England and making himself heir to the Danish claims to the English throne. He later divorced her, but the mighty pope Innocent III was able to force him to take her back in 1198. Even Innocent, however, could not force Philip to accept papal mediation in his English quarrel. When John succeeded Richard in 1199, Philip Augustus supported a rival claimant to the English throne—John's nephew, the young Arthur of Brittany.

Through legal use of his position as feudal suzerain, Philip managed to ruin John. In 1200 John married a girl who was betrothed to someone else. Her father, vassal of the king of France, complained in proper feudal style to Philip, his suzerain and John's. Since John would not come to answer the complaint, Philip declared John's fiefs forfeit and planned to conquer them with Arthur's supporters. John murdered Arthur and played right into Philip's hands. He lost his supporters on the Continent, and in 1204 he had to surrender Normandy, Brittany, Anjou, Maine, and Touraine to Philip Augustus.

Only Aquitaine was now left to the English, who had been expelled from France north of the Loire. In 1214, at the battle of Bouvines in Flanders, Philip Augustus, in alliance with Frederick II, now supported by the pope, defeated an army of Germans and English under the emperor Otto IV, John's ally. Unable to win back their French possessions, the English finally confirmed this territorial settlement by treaty in 1259. Though England's remaining possessions in France were to be the cause of much future fighting, John's great losses were now added to the French royal domain. The French kings had possession of the efficiently run duchy of Normandy, which they could use as a model for the rest of France.

The Winning of the South

The Capetians next moved to take over the rich Mediterranean south. Its people spoke a dialect different from that of the north of France, and many of them belonged to the heretical church of the Cathari (Greek for "pure ones"), with its center at the town of Albi. The Albigensians, as the Cathari were therefore called, believed that the history of the universe was one long struggle between the forces of light (good) and the forces of darkness (evil). The evil forces (Satan) created man and the earth, but Adam had some measure of goodness. Jesus was not born of a woman, nor was he crucified, because he was wholly good, wholly light. The Jehovah of the Old Testament was the god of evil. The Albigensians had an elite of their own ("the perfect"), who devoted themselves to pure living. Some of them forbade the veneration of the cross; others forbade infant baptism, the celebration of the Mass, or the holding of private property. Many of them denied the validity of one or more of the sacraments. Some even said the Catholic church itself was Satan's. While Albigensians were strongest among the lower classes, they often had the support of the nobles who adopted their views to combat the church politically. The church proclaimed a crusade against the Albigensians and a related heretical group, the followers of Peter Waldo (Waldensians), in 1208.

Philip Augustus did not at first participate in the expeditions of his nobles, who rushed south to plunder in

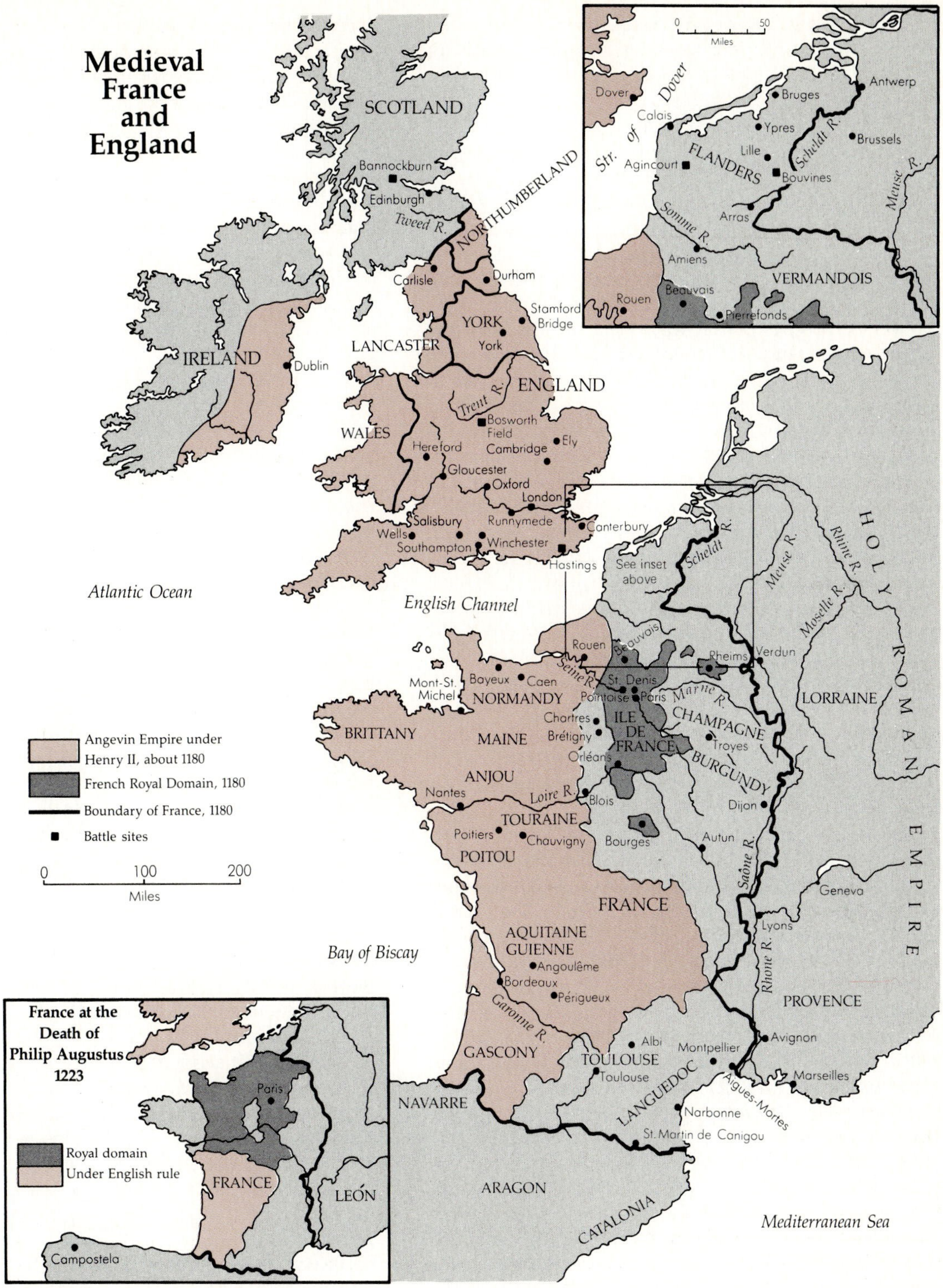

Medieval France and England

the name of the Catholic church. Northern French nobles were soon staking out their claims to the lands of southern French nobles who embraced the heresy. By the year of Philip's death (1223), after the war had gone on intermittently for fourteen years, the territorial issue had become confounded wth the religious one. So Philip sponsored an expedition led by his son, Louis VIII (r. 1223-1226). Assisted by a special clerical court called the *Inquisition*, which was first set up to root out this heresy, Louis VIII and his son Louis IX (r. 1226-1270) carried on the campaign, which by the 1240s had ferociously driven the heresy underground. The south was almost entirely taken over by the Crown, and it was arranged that the lands of the count of Toulouse, the greatest lord in the region, would come by marriage to the brother of the king of France when the last count died, as he did in 1249.

Royal Administration

Administrative advances kept pace with territorial gains. Indeed, it is doubtful if Philip Augustus and his successors could have added to the royal domain if they had not overcome many of the disruptive elements of feudalism, and if they had not asserted their authority effectively in financial, military, and judicial matters. Philip Augustus systematically collected detailed information on precisely what was owed to him from the different royal fiefs. He increased the number of his own vassals, and he reached over the heads of his vassals to their vassals, in an attempt to make the latter directly dependent on him. He exacted stringent guarantees—such as a promise that if a vassal did not perform his duties within a month, he would surrender his person as a prisoner until the situation was resolved. Moreover, if a vassal did not live up to this agreement, the church would lay an interdict upon his lands, which the people feared above all else.

Philip and his officials were alert to increase the royal power by purchasing new estates, by interfering as much as possible in the inheritance of fiefs upon the death of their holders, and by providing husbands of their own choosing for the great heiresses. A lady would sometimes outlast three or four husbands, inheriting from each; thus she became a more desirable prize each time and offered the king a chance to marry her off with profit to himself.

The local officials of the Crown, the *prévôts* (provosts), who administered justice and taxation, had regularly been rewarded by grants of land, which together with the office tended to become hereditary. The Crown lost both income and power as well as popularity when a local provost imposed taxes on his own behalf. Early in his reign Philip Augustus held an investigation and heard the complaints to which the system had given rise. He appointed a new sort of official—not resident in the countryside, but tied to the court—who would travel about, enforcing the king's will in royal lands, rendering royal justice, and collecting moneys due to the king. This official received no fiefs to tie him to a given region; his office was not hereditary; he was a civil servant appointed by the king, who paid him a salary and could remove him at will. In the north, where this system was introduced, he was called a *bailli* (bailiff), and his territory a *baillage* (bailiwick). In the south, to which the new system was extended, he was called a *sénéchal* (not to be confused with the old officer of the household) and his district a *sénéchausée.*

Like any administrative system, this one had its drawbacks. A *bailli* or *sénéchal* far from Paris might become just as independent and unjust as the old *prévôt* had been, without the king's being aware of it. Louis IX had to limit the power of these officials. He made it easy for complaints against them to be brought to his personal attention, and he appointed a new kind of official to take care of the caretakers. These were the *enquêteurs*, or investigators—royal officials not unlike Charlemagne's *missi*. The enquêteurs had supervisory authority over the baillis and sénéchals and traveled about the country inspecting their work. This complex of new civil servants introduced in the late twelfth and thirteenth centuries meant that the king could interfere with almost all local and private transactions to collect what was due him and to supply royal justice at a price.

Naturally the curia regis was so swamped with new business that the old haphazard feudal way of attending to it could no longer be followed. The king's household slowly differentiated itself into departments, most of which had little to do with government. Rather, they attended to the needs of the king and the curia regis. This court consisted not only of retainers but of clerics and others who served as advisers on day-to-day problems. When a major policy question affecting the realm was up for decision or when a major legal case needed to be tried, the king was entitled to summon his vassals (both lay and clerical) for counsel, and those he summoned were obliged to come. They then joined the rest of the curia regis in a kind of enlarged royal entourage.

When the curia regis sat in judgment on a case, it came to be known as the *parlement*—a high judicial tribunal. Naturally, as the laws grew more complex, trained lawyers had to handle more and more of the judicial business. At first they explained the law to the vassals sitting in judgment, and then, as time passed, they formed a court of justice and arrived at decisions themselves in the name of the king. By the fourteenth century this court of justice was called the *Parlement de Paris*, since Paris was its headquarters. When the curia regis sat in special session on financial matters, auditing the reports of income and expenditure, it acted as a kind of government accounting department. By the fourteenth century, this was called the *chamber of accounts.* Naturally enough, it engaged professional full-time employees, clerks, auditors, and the like.

Cash flowed to the Crown from the lands of the royal domain—from customs dues and special tolls, from fees for government services, and from money paid by vassals in order to avoid rendering such outmoded feudal services as entertaining the king and his court. But despite this varied revenue, the king of France could not levy regular direct taxes on his subjects. During the twelfth century the regular collection of feudal aids had accustomed the nobles to paying money to the Crown. Then a special levy was imposed on those who stayed home from the Crusade of 1145. In 1188 Philip Augustus collected one-tenth of the movable property and one-tenth of a year's income from all who failed to join in a crusade. These extraordinary imposts, however, aroused a storm of protest.

St. Louis, 1226-1270

Further advances in royal power came with Louis IX, viewed as a perfect ruler, who stood in sharp contrast to his contemporary, Frederick II of Germany. Deeply pious, almost monastic in his personal life, Louis carried

THE SAINTLY ST. LOUIS

Jean de Joinville (c 1224-1317) tells this characteristic story about St. Louis in his memoirs:

He was so temperate in his appetite that I never heard him, on any day of my life, order a special dish for himself, as many men of wealth and standing do. On the contrary, he would always eat with good grace whatever his cooks had prepared to set before him. He was equally temperate in his speech. I never, on any single occasion, heard him speak evil of any man; nor did I ever hear him utter the name of the Devil—a name in very common use throughout the kingdom—which practice, so I believe, is not pleasing to God. He used to add water to his wine, but did so reasonably according as the strength of the wine allowed it. . . . [He] asked me why I did not mix my wine with water. I replied that this was on the advice of my doctors, who had told me that I had a strong head and a cold stomach, so that I could not get drunk. He answered that they had deceived me. . . . Moreover, if I went on drinking undiluted wine when I was old, I should get drunk every night, and it was too revolting a thing for any brave man to be in such a state.

Jean de Joinville, *The Life of Saint Louis*, in *Joinville & Villehardouin: Chronicles of the Crusades*, trans. Margaret R.B. Shaw (New York: Penguin Books, 1977), pp. 167-68.

In the middle of the court of the devout St. Louis, connected to his apartments, was the Gothic Sainte-Chapelle, consecrated in 1248.

his own high standards over into his role as king. He wore simple clothes, gave alms to beggars, washed the feet of lepers, built hospitals, and created in Paris the Sainte-Chapelle (Holy Chapel), a small church that is now a jewel-box of glowing stained glass, to hold a reliquary containing Christ's Crown of Thorns. The church made Louis a saint in 1297, less than thirty years after his death, for personally leading two crusades against the Muslims.

St. Louis did not let his own devotion to the church stop him from defending royal prerogatives against every attempt of his own bishops or of the papacy to infringe upon them. For example, when the popes tried to enforce the theory that "all churches belong to the pope," and to assess the churches of France for money and men for papal military campaigns, the king declared that church property in France was "for the requirements of himself and his realm" and was not to be despoiled by Rome (1247). Yet when he himself became deeply interested in the crusading movement, he needed papal support to enable him to tax the French clergy. The clergy then complained to the pope about the king's demands for funds.

With the townspeople too—those old allies of the Capetian dynasty—there were difficulties during Louis's reign. These difficulties arose in large measure out of internal conflicts between the small upper class of rich merchants, who kept city government a kind of oligarchy, and the lower class of tradespeople and artisans, who felt oppressed and excluded from their own government. When the Crown intervened, it was out of concern not so much for the poor and humble as for the maintenance of order and the continued flow of funds to the royal coffers. Louis began to send royal officials into the towns, and in 1262 issued a decree requiring that the towns present their accounts annually.

This decree itself was a further instance of the king's assertion of royal prerogative. It was a new sort of enactment, an *ordonnance*, or royal command issued for all of France without the previous assent of all the vassals. Royal power and prestige had now so progressed that Louis did not feel the need to obtain all his vassals' consent each time he wished to govern their behavior; ordonnances signed by some vassals governed all. Examples of Louis's ordonnances were his prohibition of private warfare and his law providing that royal money was valid everywhere in France; both show his reformist views, as well as his determination to strengthen the power of the monarchy.

Royal justice had now become widely desired, and appeals flowed into the parlement from the lower feudal courts. The royal court of justice alone came to be recognized as competent to try cases of treason and of breaking the king's peace. The extension of royal justice to the towns was secured by bringing into the parlement's deliberations representatives of the middle classes—the king's *bourgeois*. So fair and reasonable was the king's justice felt to be that his subjects often applied to him personally for it. He made himself available to them by sitting under an oak tree in the forest of Vincennes near Paris, and listening to the case of anyone, high or low, who wished to appeal to the king. He maintained no royal protocol on these occasions, and there were no intermediaries. His justice was prized not only in France but also abroad; he settled quarrels in Flanders, Navarre, Burgundy, Lorraine, and elsewhere. He reached a reasonable territorial settlement with England in 1259, and in 1264 was asked to judge a dispute between King Henry III of England and the English barons.

Louis was a remarkable and representative man of the thirteenth century. In his devotion to the crusading enterprise, for instance, he was wholeheartedly embracing the highest ideals of the period. But he never seemed to realize that the Holy Lands could not be won by more crusades. Moreover, it cost France a great deal to have the king delayed abroad for years and to have him languish in captivity from which he was redeemed only at great expense. Yet for all his human failings, St. Louis typifies the medieval ideal that the divine law of God's revelation was mirrored in human law. As God ordered the universe, so human law established the proper relationships of individuals to one another in society. The king had his special role in society, and St. Louis, in his conception and enactment of that role, reached heights that had not been attained by other monarchs.

Philip the Fair, 1285-1314

After the death of St. Louis, the French monarchy experienced the same general change that was coming over the entire Western world in the thirteenth and fourteenth centuries. Conventions and forms persisted and seemed to be hardening. In the political history of France, this tendency began with the reign of St. Louis's grandson, Philip IV (1285-1314). Called "the Fair" because he was handsome, Philip ruthlessly pushed the royal power and consolidated the royal hold; the towns, the nobles, and the church suffered further invasions of their rights from his agents. Against the excesses of Philip the Fair, the medieval checks against tyranny—which had been effective against many other aggressive kings—failed to operate. His humiliation of the papacy alone helped as much as any other event of the Middle Ages to end the Christian commonwealth to which St. Louis had been so devoted. The vastly increased *gens du roi*, "the king's men," used propaganda, lies, and trickery to undermine all authority except that of the king. This undermining went on in a series of small engagements in local courts of justice, with the king's lawyers pushing his rights. Members of the parlement now traveled to the remotest regions of France, bringing royal justice to all parts of the king's own domain, and more and more taking over the machinery of justice in the great lordships. The system of royal justice was thereby gradually swallowing up the system of feudal justice.

In the same period, the most intimate advisers of the king in the curia regis, whom he regularly consulted, became differentiated as the "narrow" or "secret," while the larger group of advisers, consisting of the remaining lords and high clerics, was called the "full council." In 1302, apparently for the first time, representatives of the towns attended a meeting of this larger council. At the moment when townspeople first participated, there began the long transition to a new kind of assembly, the Estates-General (though the term would not be used in France for some time). An *estate* is a social class; traditionally, the clergy is considered the first estate, the nobility the second, and the townspeople the third. When all three estates are present, an assembly is therefore an *Estates-General*. Though the clerics and nobles acted as individuals, the townspeople were a collective body representing the corporations of their municipalities.

War with England and Flanders kept Philip pressed for cash during much of his reign. He summoned the estates to explain his need for money and to obtain their approval for his proceeding to raise it. He usually asked for funds in a general way but did not fix the amount, since the groups he was asking to contribute had the right to bargain. Since medieval lords felt that no action was proper unless it was customary, whenever the king wanted to do anything new he had to try to make it seem like something old. A protest that such and such attempt to get money was an *exactio inaudita* (an unheard-of exaction) often was enough to frustrate the king's efforts. Philip tried all the known ways of getting money. One of the most effective was to demand military service of a man and then permit him to buy himself off. When protests arose, the king usually had to retreat to more orthodox methods. Still, requests for revenue that had hitherto been irregular were made regular. Forced loans, debasement of coinage, additional customs dues, and royal levies on commercial transactions also added to the royal income.

Although the need for money lay behind the most famous episode of Philip's reign—his fierce quarrel with the papacy—its importance and the significance of its outcome had a major impact on the medieval world. In his papal opponent, Boniface VIII (r. 1294-1303), Philip was tangling with a fit successor to Gregory VII and Innocent III. A Roman aristocrat and already an old man when elected pope, Boniface suffered from a malady that kept him in great pain and probably partly accounted for his undoubted bad temper and fierce language. During his fight with Philip, for instance, he said that he would rather be a dog than a Frenchman, whereupon Philip's pamphleteers charged Boniface with heresy for implying that Frenchmen, like dogs, had no souls.

Philip claimed the right to tax the clergy for the defense of France in his wars against England; but the English monarch was also taxing his clergy on the other side of the Channel to pay for the fight against France. Boniface issued an edict (known as a *bull* from the papal seal, or *bulla*, on it) declaring that kings lacked the right to tax clerics, and that clerics should disobey them, the bull *Clericis laicos* (1296). Philip the Fair answered not with theory but with action. He slapped an embargo on exports from France of precious metals, jewelry, and currency, which threatened the elaborate financial system of the papacy severely. Under pressure from his distressed bankers and from a hostile group of cardinals who were accusing him of heresy, simony, and even murder, the pope retreated, saying in 1297 that in an emergency the king of France could tax the clergy without papal consent, and that the king would decide when an emergency had arisen. Boniface also canonized Louis IX.

But a new quarrel arose in 1301. Boniface had held a Jubilee in Rome in 1300, and the display of popular religiosity had given him renewed confidence. When Philip ordered Boniface's legate to Paris to be arrested, tried, and convicted of heresy and treason, he asked for papal approval of the sentence. But Boniface flatly refused and declared that when a ruler was wicked, the pope might take a hand in the temporal affairs of that realm. The meeting of the Estates-General in 1302 backed Philip.

Boniface pushed his claims still further in the famous bull *Unam sanctam*, which declared that it was necessary for salvation for every person throughout the world to be subject to the pope. When he also threatened to excommunicate the king, Philip issued a series of extreme charges against Boniface and sent a gang of thugs to kidnap him. They burst into the papal presence at the Italian town of Anagni and threatened the pope brutally, but did not dare put through their plan to seize him. Nonetheless, Boniface, who was over eighty, died not long after this humiliation.

In 1305 Philip obtained the election of a French pope, Clement V (1305-1314), who never went to Rome at all. Instead, in 1309 Clement went to Avignon, on the border between France and the Holy Roman Empire, and two years later made this city his permanent residence. Thus began the "Babylonian captivity" of the papacy at Avignon (1309-1377). Moreover, Clement issued bulls

This large statue of Pope Boniface VIII (1294-1303), sculpted in 1300, bestows upon him the dignity appropriate to the person who issued the single strongest statement concerning the authority of the church over the state, the papal bull *Unam sanctam.*

ONE GOD, ONE CHURCH, ONE SOURCE OF SALVATION

According to Boniface VIII, there is but *one* church, and all Christ's sheep are committed to it:

That there is one Holy Catholic and Apostolic Church we are impelled by our faith to believe and to hold—this we do firmly believe and openly confess—and outside of this there is neither salvation or remission of sins. . . . The Church represents one mystic body and of this body Christ is the head; of Christ, indeed, God is the head. In it is one Lord, and one faith, and one baptism. In the time of the flood, there was one ark of Noah, prefiguring the one Church, finished in one cubit, having one Noah as steersman and commander. Outside of this, all things upon the face of the earth were, as we read, destroyed. . . .

Therefore, in this one and only Church, there is one body and one head,—not two heads as if it were a monster—namely, Christ and Christ's Vicar, Peter and Peter's successor, for the Lord said to Peter himself, "Feed my sheep": *my* sheep, he said, using a general term and not designating these or those sheep, so that we must believe that all the sheep were committed to him.

"The Bull *Unam Sanctam* of Boniface VIII," in *Translations and Reprints from the Original Sources of European History* (Philadelphia: The Department of History of the University of Pennsylvania, 1912), pp. 20-23. Courtesy of the Department of History of the University of Pennsylvania.

reversing Boniface's claims, lifted the sentence of excommunication from Boniface's attackers, and praised Philip the Fair for his piety.

The last installment of this long story—which had begun in 1046 when Henry III had installed his reforming pope Clement II, whose successors fought the German emperors for two centuries—thus took the form of a quarrel between the pope and the king of France. The efforts of the papacy to use the spiritual authority of the church to govern the policies of national states had failed. In Avignon for three-quarters of a century the papacy instead was seen as a tool of the French monarchy.

In another notorious affair, Philip IV used the weakness of the papacy at Avignon to attack the Knights Templars, a crusading military order that had evolved into a rich banking house. He wanted their money and brought them to trial on a series of charges of vicious behavior, using as evidence against them confessions extorted by the increasingly brutal court of the Inquisition. The Templars were abolished, and Philip took over their funds, while a rival order was allowed to annex the Templars' lands. Philip also arrested the Jews, stripped them of their property, and expelled them from France in 1306. In 1311 he expelled the agents of Italian bankers. All debts owed to the Jews and Italians were collected by royal agents, and the Crown kept the money.

Just before Philip died in 1314, the towns joined with the lords in protest against the king's having raised money for a war in Flanders and then having made peace instead of fighting. Louis X (r. 1314-1316) calmed the unrest by revoking the aid, returning some of the money, and making scapegoats of the more unpopular bureaucrats. He also issued a series of charters to several of the great vassals that confirmed their liberties. The episode resembled in many ways the protest that had arisen in England a century earlier and had culminated there in one great charter, the Magna Carta.

But taxation was still thought of as inseparably connected with military service, and military service was an unquestioned feudal right of the king. So the king was still free to declare a military emergency, to summon his vassals to fight, and then to commute the service for money, just as Philip the Fair had done. For this reason the charters of Louis X did not effectively halt the advance of royal power, and there was no committee of barons (as there had been in England) to make sure that the king lived up to his promises. Because the French barons did not defend their corporate interests, the French monarch would continue to enjoy a position unique among the kings of western Europe.

II THE DEVELOPMENT OF ENGLAND

The Norman Conquest, 1066

The England that for so long threatened the security of France had first become a major power as the result of the Norman Conquest of 1066. In that year William, duke of Normandy (c 1027-1087), defeated the Anglo-Saxon forces at Hastings near the south coast of England. The Anglo-Saxon monarchy had, since the death of Canute in 1035, fallen prey to factions. Upon the death of Edward the Confessor (r. 1042-1066), a pious but ineffectual monarch who had been brought up at the Norman court speaking French, his brother-in-law Harold, half-Danish son of a powerful upstart earl, Godwin, had succeeded to the throne. But William of Normandy also had an excellent competing claim to the English crown.

After a troubled minority, William had successfully asserted his rights in Normandy over the vigorous and tough Norman nobility. He allowed no castle to be built without his license, and insisted that, once built, each castle be put at his disposal on demand. Mideleventh-century Normandy was a unified duchy, overloaded with younger sons, even though many had gone off on the great south Italian adventure half a century earlier. The Norman cavalry was formidable and early perfected the technique of charging with the lance held couched, so that all the force of horse and rider was concentrated in the point of the weapon at the moment of shock. Infantry and bowmen supported the charge. As a result of trade with Scandinavia and England, Normandy was prosperous even beyond the norms of the eleventh-century revival. It enjoyed a flourishing agriculture, growing towns, a flowering of monastic learning and church building under ducal patronage, and an effective fiscal administration. Moreover, because William put down private warfare and efficiently dispensed justice, there was peace and order.

While facing England across the Channel, Normandy had always maintained contact with the Scandinavian lands of Norman origin. After the Danish invasions of England all three regions were closely involved in commercial relations and often in strife. Emma, daughter of a Norman duke, married first the Anglo-Saxon king Ethelred II (r. 978-1016), by whom she was the mother of Edward the Confessor, and then married the Danish king Canute (r. 1016-1035), by whom she had a son, Harthacnut (r. 1040-1042). Wife of two English kings and mother of an English king by each of them, she apparently dominated all four. And she remained close to her Norman ducal relatives. William was her great-nephew. In the tangled English-Danish-Norman royal politics there were dark crimes, including the murder in 1036 of Edward the Confessor's older brother Alfred. Earl Godwin, Harold's father, was in part guilty, and the Normans at Hastings were in part revenging Godwin's act on his son Harold. It was Norman nobles, favorites of Edward the Confessor, who built the first castles in England shortly before the conquest. Edward gave important posts in the English church to Norman clerics, and as early as 1051 Edward had recognized William as his rightful heir.

In England pro- and anti-Normans intrigued and squabbled for two decades before 1066. Norman sources report that probably in 1064 Harold went to Normandy and affirmed the promise of William's succession to the English throne, in exchange for a confirmation of Harold's English lands. If the sources are accurate, in taking the throne in 1066 Harold was breaking his oath. But some Anglo-Saxon sources say that on his deathbed Edward the Confessor had made Harold his heir after all; however, even if he did, it may have been under duress. And nothing can alter the fact that Harold, although his sister was married to Edward, was not of royal blood, English or Danish. Furthermore, there was a third claimant to the English throne: the king of Norway.

William the Conqueror was depicted in a thirteenth-century manuscript illumination in The British Museum as sharing out England among his followers. Feudal rights stemmed from the king, who theoretically owned the entire kingdom. This miniature shows William granting his nephew Alan title to land.

Just before William's victory in 1066, the Norwegians landed and Harold defeated them at Stamford Bridge in Yorkshire.

William's invasion had the blessing of the papacy, which recognized his claim to the throne of England. His fleet had to be built in nine months; he had to weld an army of seven thousand men, mostly Norman but including adventurers from many parts of France and from southern Italy, into a fighting unit; he had to wait for favorable weather. But he landed and established two fortified beachheads on the Sussex coast before Harold could get back from defeating the Norwegians. All was over in one hard day's fighting. Norman horsemen and bowmen slaughtered Harold's close-packed warriors fighting on foot with battle-axes.

William was crowned on Christmas Day, 1066, by the archbishop of York. The joyous Norman accounts stress the new master's clemency. The Anglo-Saxon accounts echo the bitterness of defeat and of having to accept an alien master, who took vast quantities of loot from his victims to reward his triumphant Norman supporters.

The Bayeux Tapestry is a work of art; it is also one of the most significant documents of early medieval history. Made only a few years after the event, the tapestry is rich in detail concerning the Norman Conquest. In this segment, showing the troops of William the Conqueror in battle with those of King Harold, William is on horseback.

Yet William seems to have taken special pains to prevent disorders. *The Anglo-Saxon Chronicle*, a collection of contemporary vernacular histories, says of him:

> *Amongst other things the good security that he made in this country is not forgotten—so that any man could travel over his kingdom without injury, with his bosom full of gold; and no one dared strike another, however much wrong he had done him.**

This was after William had taken possession of the whole of England, which took two campaigns in the far southwest and expeditions to the north in which William punished pro-Danish English rebels by destroying the crops and causing widespread famine. The last uprising in England was crushed in 1071 on the Isle of Ely, and in 1072 the Conqueror won the submission of the king of Scotland, who became his vassal. There were political troubles even after this, but the conquest was essentially complete. Each stage was marked by the building of new castles to hold the region and enforce order; the former ruling class of England was replaced by Norman and French nobles, perhaps a total of ten thousand newcomers in a population of not more than one and a half million.

All of England belonged to William by right of conquest. He kept about one-sixth as royal domain, gave about half as fiefs to his great Norman barons, and returned to the church the quarter that it had held before. Although many of his barons subinfeudated their lands (gave part of them as fiefs to their own followers), these vassals owed military service only to William, and they swore primary allegiance to him in the Salisbury Oath of 1086, giving him authority that no French king would ever enjoy. The bishops and abbots also held of him and owed him feudal services. He alone claimed all castles, and none could be built without a license from him. He forbade private war and allowed only royal coinage. He continued to levy the Danegeld, to impose judicial fines, and to summon the *fyrd*, or national militia. He kept the Anglo-Saxon system of courts and bound local officials closely to the Crown by giving them wide local authority at the expense of bishop and earl. As on the Continent, Latin now became the language of administration.

The Conqueror thus maintained old English custom and law, while superimposing on it Norman feudal structure with its mounted knights and castles. The sheriffs provided continuity. The Norman curia regis superseded the Anglo-Saxon witenagemot; it met regularly three times a year, but could be summoned at any time to give counsel and try the cases of the great vassals. Its members also could be asked to perform special tasks in the *shires*—local administrative units which had begun in the early eleventh century and which were divided into smaller units known as *hundreds*—for adjusting taxation, maintaining the peace, and settling local pleas.

In 1086 William ordered a careful survey of all landed property in England. The record of that survey is the Domesday Book, which included a full statement of ownership, past and present, for every piece of land, and a listing of all resources, so that the royal administration

*Dorothy Whitelock, D.C. Douglas, and S.I. Tucker, eds., *The Anglo-Saxon Chronicle* (London: Oxford University Press, 1961), p. 164.

might learn whether and where more revenue could be obtained. Tenants, plows, forest land, fish ponds—all were listed in Domesday Book, which became an indispensable source for later historians. Contemporary accounts reveal the thoroughness of William's inquiry and the resentment it caused:

> *So very narrowly did he have it investigated, that there was no single hide nor a yard of land, nor indeed (it is a shame to relate but it seemed no shame to him to do) one ox nor one cow nor one pig was there left out, and not put down on his record: and all these records were brought to him afterward. . . .*
>
> *Other investigators followed the first; and men were sent into provinces which they did not know, and where they themselves were unknown, in order that they might be given the opportunity of checking the first survey and, if necessary, of denouncing its authors as guilty to the king. And the land was vexed with much violence arising from the collection of the royal taxes.**

Those who collected the information from the old Anglo-Saxon territorial subdivisions of vill and hundred arranged it under the new Norman divisions of royal demesne and fiefs of the king's tenants-in-chief. The Domesday Book, then, was a formal written record attesting to the introduction of feudal landholding and law into England. No such monumental survey was ever compiled for any other country in the Middle Ages.

With the assistance of an able Italian, Lanfranc (d. 1089), whom he made archbishop of Canterbury, William established continental practices in the English church. Norman churchmen gradually replaced the English bishops. To commemorate the victory at Hastings, William founded Battle Abbey on the site of the battlefield; other monastic foundations followed, notably in the north. Norman abbots brought Latin books and learning from the Continent, and for a time vernacular writing in English ceased. William refused the pope's demand that feudal homage be done to him as overlord of England; rightly maintaining that none of his predecessors on the English throne had ever acknowledged papal suzerainty, he agreed only to pay the accustomed dues to the Church of Rome. The English church recognized no new pope without the king's approval and accepted no papal commands without his assent. When William died in 1087, the English monarchy was stronger than the French was to be for more than two hundred years.

Henry I and Henry II, 1100-1189

William's immediate successors extended his system. They made their administrators depend on the king alone by paying them fixed salaries, since payments in land (fiefs) often led the recipient to try to make his office hereditary, and since clerical administrators might feel the rival pull of papal authority. Household and curia regis grew in size, and special functions began to develop. Within the curia regis the king's immediate advisers became a "small council" and the full body met less often. The royal *chancery*, or secretariat, also grew, since the king was also duke of Normandy and had much business on the Continent.

Henry I (r. 1100-1135) allowed his vassals to make payments (*scutage*, shield money) to buy themselves off from military service. He also exempted the royal towns or boroughs from Danegeld while collecting still heavier payments from them. To handle the increased income, the first specialized treasury department came into existence, the *exchequer*—so called because the long table on which the clerks rendered to the officers of the curia regis their semiannual audit of the royal accounts was covered with a cloth divided into checkerboard squares representing pounds, shillings, and pence.

Because Henry's only legitimate son drowned, the succession was disputed between Henry's daughter, Matilda, wife of Geoffrey IV of Anjou, and Henry's nephew, Stephen of Blois. A civil war (1135-1151) between their partisans produced virtual anarchy in England and did great harm to the prosperity of the realm. Yet when Henry II (r. 1154-1189), son of Matilda and Geoffrey, succeeded to the throne, he found the foundations of a powerful monarchy to add to the half of France under his rule.

Stormy and energetic, Henry II systematically cut at the roots of the anarchy; he had more than 1,100 divisive, unlicensed castles destroyed. From the contemporary *Dialogue Concerning the Exchequer*, written by his treasurer, we learn how the money rolled in: from scutage plus special fees for the privilege of paying it, from fines, from aids, from tallage paid by the boroughs, and from a new tax collected from the knights who did not go on crusades. Even more important than this reestablishment and strengthening of the financial institutions was Henry's contribution to the law of England, built on that of Henry I.

New law could not, in theory, be made at all. Law was what had always existed, and it was the job of the lawyers and government officials to discover what this was and to proclaim it. Henry I and Henry II therefore did not fill statute books with new enactments; instead Henry I asserted that he was ruling in accordance with the law of the Saxon king Edward the Confessor, and the law books issued in this period contain a mixture of Anglo-Saxon and other materials, including, for example, fixed schedules of money payments imposed as penalties for crime. It was not by issuing laws that Henry I and Henry II transformed the legal practices of England. Rather, by developing old instruments in new combinations, they created the new *common law*—law common to all of England because it was administered by the royal courts. Though hundred and shire courts had continued to exist, their jurisdiction had been diluted by competing courts, baronial and ecclesiastical; only the king could provide better ways of settling

*Op. cit., and a note by the bishop of Hereford in D.C. Douglas and G.W. Greenaway, eds., *English Historical Documents, 1042-1189* (New York: Oxford University Press, 1953), II, 161, 851.

An illuminated manuscript showing the murder of Archbishop Thomas à Becket in Canterbury Cathedral on December 29, 1170. This version, dating from about 1200, is probably the earliest surviving representation.

quarrels than the old trial by ordeal or trial by battle.

The chief royal instruments were writs, juries, and traveling justices. If, for example, someone seized a subject's property, by the middle of Henry II's reign the victim could buy a royal writ: an order from the king directing a royal official to give the plaintiff a hearing. The official would assemble a group of twelve neighbors who knew the facts in the case; they took an oath, and were therefore called a jury (from *juré*, "man on oath"). They then told the truth as they knew it about whether dispossession had taken place, answering yes or no, and thus giving a verdict (from *veredictum*, "a thing spoken truly"). These early juries were not trial juries in the modern sense, but men who were presumed to be in the best position to know the facts already. By similar machinery of writ and jury, inheritances unjustly detained could be recovered, and a person unjustly held as a serf could be freed. Although the use of a jury or sworn inquest dated back to the ninth-century Carolingians and had come to England with the Conqueror, its application to civil cases between individuals was new, as was the flexibility permitted by the variety of writs. No matter who won, the royal exchequer profited, since the loser had to pay a fine. Also, judgments rendered by royal judges became new law without any legislation.

Building on the practice begun by Henry I, Henry II also regularly sent justices out to the shires. On their travels they were instructed to receive reports in each shire from the local officials and to try all cases pending in the shire court. Moreover, the sheriffs (or *shire reeves*, the king's chief executives in local government) had to bring before the justices from each hundred and township a group of sworn men to report under oath all crimes that had occurred since the last visit of the justices, and to indicate whom they considered to be the probable criminal in each case. This was another use of the jury, the jury of *presentment*, since it presented the names of suspect criminals. (It is the ancestor of the modern grand jury—"grand" in the sense of large—consisting of more men than the twelve that took part in the petty juries.) Again the treasury profited, as the justices imposed heavy fines. Again blatant innovation was avoided, and refinements and combinations of existing instruments produced new legal conditions. Even so, the usual means of proof in a criminal trial under Henry II was still an ordeal by cold water. If the accused, with hands and feet tied, floated in a pool blessed by the church, he was guilty; if he sank, perhaps to drown, he was innocent.

Henry II, however, failed to limit the competing system of canon law. He had appointed his friend and chancellor Thomas à Becket (1118-1170) archbishop of Canterbury. But once he had become archbishop, Becket proved inflexibly determined not to yield any of the church's rights, but rather to add to them whenever he could. A great quarrel between the two broke out over the question of clerics convicted of crime. In publishing a collection of largely earlier customs relating to the church (Constitutions of Clarendon, 1164), Henry included a provision that clerics charged with crimes should be indicted in the royal court before being tried by the bishop's court, and then, if convicted, returned to the royal authorities for punishment. Becket refused to agree to this part of the document and appealed to the pope for support.

Although the issue was compromised after a dispute that lasted six years, Henry, in a fit of temper over Becket's Christmas Day excommunication of bishops who supported the king, asked whether no one would rid him of Becket. Four of his knights responded by murdering Becket in his own cathedral at Canterbury. Henry swore to the pope that he was innocent of complicity in the murder, but he had to undergo a humiliating penance and, more important, he had to yield on the issue. The Church in England won the sole right to punish its clergy—*benefit of clergy*, the principle was called. Moreover, Henry had to accept the right of litigants in church courts to appeal to Rome directly, without royal intervention of any sort. This meant that the papacy had the ultimate say in an important area of English life. It was a severe defeat for Henry's program of extending royal justice. Yet the other clauses in the Constitutions of

Clarendon were not challenged, and the king continued to prevent the pope from directly taxing the English clergy. Becket was made a saint only two years after his death, and pilgrimages to his tomb at Canterbury became an important scene in English life.

Henry's reign was also notable for the reorganization of the old Anglo-Saxon fyrd by the Assize of Arms in 1181, which made each free man responsible, according to his income, to maintain suitable arms for the defense of the realm.

Richard I and John, 1189-1216

Henry II's son, Richard the Lionhearted (r. 1189-1199), spent less than six months of his ten-year reign in England, but thanks to Henry II, the bureaucracy functioned without the presence of the king. Indeed, it functioned all too well for the liking of the population, since Richard needed more money than had ever been needed before to pay for his crusade, for his ransom from captivity, and for his wars against Philip Augustus of France. Heavy taxes were levied on income and on personal property; certain possessions, including silver plate, were simply confiscated; many charters were sold to cities. Thus it was that Richard's brother John (r. 1199-1216) succeeded to a throne whose resources had been squandered. John had the misfortune to face three adversaries who proved too strong for him: Philip Augustus, who expelled the English from France north of the Loire; the pope Innocent III; and the outraged English barons.

In 1206 the election to the archbishopric of Canterbury was disputed between two candidates, one of whom was favored by John. The pope refused to accept either, and in 1207 procured the election of a third, Stephen Langton (c 1155-1228), who was a learned English scholar at Paris. John exiled the monks of Canterbury and confiscated the property of the see. Innocent responded by putting England under an interdict and by excommunicating John. He threatened to depose John and thought of replacing him with a Capetian; he corresponded with Philip Augustus, who prepared to invade England. Fearing with good reason that such an invasion would strain the loyalty of his own vassals, John gave in (1213). Not only did he accept Langton as archbishop of Canterbury and promise to restore church property and to reinstate banished priests, but he also recognized England and Ireland as fiefs of the papacy and did homage to the pope for them. He also agreed to pay an annual tribute to Rome. Here was a startling papal victory. Thereafter Innocent sided with John in his quarrel with a large faction of the English barons—a quarrel that became acute after the French had won the Battle of Bouvines.

Magna Carta, 1215

A quarrel with perhaps a third of the English barons arose from John's ruthlessness in raising money for the campaign in France and from his practice of punishing vassals without trial. At the moment of absolution by the pope in 1213, John had sworn to Stephen Langton that he would "restore the good laws of his predecessors." But he violated his oath. After Bouvines, the barons hostile to John renounced their homage to him and drew up a list of demands, most of which they forced him to accept on June 15, 1215, at a meadow called Runnymede on the banks of the Thames. The document that he agreed to send out under the royal seal to all the shires in England had sixty-three chapters, in the legal form of a feudal grant or conveyance, known as *Magna Carta*, the Great Charter.

Magna Carta was a feudal document, a list of specific commissions drawn up in the interest of a group of barons at odds with their feudal lord, the king. The king promised reform in his exactions of scutage, aids, reliefs, and in certain other feudal practices. He made certain concessions to the peasantry, the tradespeople (uniform weights and measures, town liberties), and the church (free elections to bishoprics and maintenance of liberties).

This medieval special-interest document is often called the foundation stone of present liberties in Britain and North America largely because some of its provisions could be given new and expanded meanings in later centuries. For instance, the provision that "No scutage or aid, save the customary feudal ones, shall be levied, *except by the common consent of the realm*" in 1215 meant only that John would have to consult his great council (barons and bishops) before levying extraordinary feudal aids. Yet this could later be expanded into the doctrine that all taxation must be by consent, that taxation without representation was tyranny—which would have astonished everyone at Runnymede. Similarly, the provision that "No freeman shall be ar-

A fourteenth-century manuscript illumination showing King John hunting deer.

MAGNA CARTA

The Magna Carta reaffirmed traditional rights and personal liberties against royal authority. Many of its provisions became the basis for specific civil rights enjoyed in Western democracies today:

20. A freeman shall be amerced [fined] for a small offence only according to the degree of the offence; and for a grave offence he shall be amerced according to the gravity of the offence, saving his contenement [property necessary for sustenance of his family and himself]. And a merchant shall be amerced in the same way, saving his merchandise; and a villein in the same way, saving his wainage [harvested crops needed for seed]—should they fall into our mercy. And none of the aforesaid amercements shall be imposed except by the oaths of good men from the neighbourhood.

28. No constable or other bailiff of ours shall take grain or other chattels of any one without immediate payment therefor in money, unless by the will of the seller he may secure postponement of that payment.

29. No constable shall distrain [require] any knight to pay money for castle-guard when he is willing to perform that service himself, or through another good man if for reasonable cause he is unable to perform it himself. And if we lead or send him on a military expedition, he shall be quit of castle-guard for so long a time as he shall be with the army at our command.

30. No sheriff or bailiff of ours, nor any other person, shall take the horses or carts of any freeman for carrying service, except by the will of that freeman.

31. Neither we nor our bailiffs will take some one else's wood for repairing castles or for doing any other work of ours, except by the will of him to whom the wood belongs.

39. No freeman shall be captured or imprisoned or disseised [deprived] or outlawed or exiled or in any way destroyed, nor will we go against him or send against him, except by the lawful judgment of his peers or by the law of the land.

41. All merchants may safely and securely go away from England, come to England, stay in and go through England, by land or by water, for buying and selling under right and ancient customs and without any evil exactions, except in time of war if they are from the land at war with us. And if such persons are found in our land at the beginning of a war, they shall be arrested without injury to their bodies or goods until we or our chief justice can ascertain how the merchants of our land who may then be found in the land at war with us are to be treated. And if our men are to be safe, the others shall be safe in our land.

54. No one shall be arrested or imprisoned upon the appeal of a woman, for the death of any other than her husband.

Carl Stephenson and Frederick George Marcham, eds., *Sources of English Constitutional History* (New York: Harper & Brothers, 1937), pp. 119-21.

rested or imprisoned, or dispossessed or outlawed or banished or in any way molested; nor will we set forth against him, nor send against him, unless by the lawful judgment of his peers and by the law of the land" in 1215 meant only that the barons did not want to be tried by anybody not their social equal, and they wished to curb the aggressions of royal justice. Yet it was later expanded into the doctrine of due process of law, that everyone is entitled to a trial by "his peers".

Although medieval kings of England reissued the charter with modifications some forty times, it was to be ignored under the Tudors in the sixteenth century, and it was not appealed to until the revolt against the Stuarts in the seventeenth century. By then the rebels against Stuart absolutism could read into the medieval clauses of Magna Carta many of the same modern meanings that we, just as inaccurately, see in them at first glance. Thus Magna Carta's lasting importance lies partly in what later interpreters were able to find in its original clauses. It also lies, perhaps even more, in two general principles underlying the whole document: that the king was subject to the law and that he might, if necessary, be forced to observe it. This is why this document—over seven and a half centuries old, dealing with a now obsolete social system—is still important for the twentieth century.

As soon as John had accepted the charter, he tried to break his promises. The pope declared the charter null and void, and Langton and the barons opposed to John now took the pope's former place as supporters of a French monarchy for England. Philip Augustus' son actually landed in England and occupied London briefly; but John died in 1216 and was succeeded by his nine-year-old son, Henry III (r. 1216-1272), to whose side the barons rallied. The barons then expelled the French from England. It was not until 1258 that the king found himself again in an open clash with a faction of his own barons.

Henry reissued Magna Carta, formally ratifying it. Nonetheless, the barons felt that he did not fully adhere to it, and they were increasingly disturbed by his appointment of French administrative officials. The clash came to a head in 1258, a year of bad harvest, when Henry asked for one-third of the revenues of England as an extra grant for the pope. The barons came armed to the session of the great council and secured the appointment of a committee of twenty-four of their number, who then issued a document known as the Provisions of

Oxford. This document, an effort to restore the charter, created a council of fifteen without whose advice the king could do nothing. The committee put its own men in the high offices of state, and it replaced the full great council with a baronial body of twelve. This provision clearly contained the seeds of a baronial tyranny as bad as the king's own.

But the barons could not agree among themselves, and Henry III resumed his personal rule. Open civil war broke out in 1263 between the king and the baronial party headed by Simon de Montfort (c 1208-1265). When in the next year Louis IX was called in to arbitrate, he ruled in favor of the king and against the barons. Simon, however, would not accept the decision. He captured the king and set up a regime of his own, based on the restoration of the Provisions of Oxford. This regime lasted fifteen months. In 1265 Simon called an assembly of his supporters, which was a step in the evolution of Parliament. But the heir to the throne, Prince Edward, defeated and killed Simon and restored his father, Henry III, to the throne. For the last seven years of Henry's reign (1265-1272), as well as for the next thirty-five years of his own rule (1272-1307), Edward I was the true ruler of England.

The Origins of Parliament, 1258-1265

The revolts of the thirteenth century had given the barons experience in the practical work of government, and many of their reforms had been accepted by the royal governments that followed. Still more important, during the struggle the local communities of England had emerged as significant elements in the central administration. Indeed, it is to these years under Henry III that historians turn for the earliest signs of the major contribution of the English Middle Ages to the West—the development of Parliament.

The Parliament of Edward I. This picture is one of the oldest views in existence of Parliament in session. To the right of Edward is Alexander III, king of the Scots, and to his left is Llewellyn, prince of Wales. In the center members are seated on the original woolsacks; on the left are the lords spiritual (archbishops, bishops, and abbots), and on the right are the lords temporal. In fact, neither Alexander nor Llewellyn was ever present, and the arrangement of the figures, probably painted about 1524, was meant to make a political point.

The word *parliament* comes from French and simply means a talk or parley—a conference of any kind. The French vernacular historian Geoffrey de Villehardouin (c 1150-1212) refers to a discussion between the French and Venetian leaders in the Fourth Crusade (1204) as a *parlement*. Joinville, the biographer of St. Louis, refers to his hero's secret conversations with his wife on the palace staircase as *parlement*. And the word was applied in France to that part of the curia regis which acted as a court of justice. In England during the thirteenth century, the word often refers to the assemblies summoned by the king, especially those that were to hear petitions for legal redress. In short, a parliament in England in the thirteenth century was much like the parlement in France—a session of the king's large council acting as a court of justice.

The Anglo-Saxon witenagemot had been an assembly of the great churchmen and laymen of the kingdom who advised the king on taxation and on matters of policy, and who could also act as a supreme court in important cases. In these respects the great council of the Norman kings was not much different from the witenagemot. Feudal law simply reinforced the king's right to secure from his chief vassals both aid (that is, military service and money) and counsel (that is, advice on law and custom and a share in judicial decisions). The Norman kings made attendance at sessions of the great council compulsory; it was the king's privilege, not his duty, to receive counsel, and it was the vassal's duty, not his privilege, to offer it.

But by requiring the barons to help govern England, the kings unconsciously, and contrary to their own intentions, strengthened the assembly of vassals, the great council. The feeling gradually grew that the king must consult the council; this feeling is reflected in the scutage and aid provision of Magna Carta. Yet the kings generally consulted only the small council of their permanent advisers; the great council met only occasionally and when summoned by the king. The barons who sat on the great council thus developed a sense of being excluded from the work of government in which they felt entitled to participate. It was baronial discontent that led to the troubles under Henry III. When the barons took over the government in 1258, they determined that the great council should meet three times a year, and they called it a parliament. When Henry III regained power, he continued to summon the feudal magnates to the great council, to parliament.

The increasing prosperity of England in the thirteenth century had enriched many members of the landed gentry who were not necessarily the king's direct vassals. The inhabitants of the towns had also increased in number and importance with the growth of trade. Representatives of these newly important classes in country and town now began to attend parliament at the king's summons. They were the knights of the shire, two from each shire, and the burgesses of the towns. Accustomed since Anglo-Saxon times to compulsory participation in their local hundred and shire courts, the knights were landholders with local standing, and they were often rich men. By the time of Richard the Lionhearted, some were occasionally selected to bring court records to the judges. At royal command, the towns had chosen representatives to bring documents proving titles before the royal justices, either on circuit in the shires or in London. In 1254 knights of the shire were summoned for the first time to a meeting of the great council. Meanwhile, burgesses or townsmen were also being summoned by the king to appear before his justices, either on circuit in the shires or in London.

Although controversy on the subject still rages, recent research has made it seem probable that the chief reason for the king's summons to the shire and town representatives was his need for money. By the thirteenth century the sources of royal income, both ordinary and extraordinary, were not enough to pay the king's ever-mounting bills. Thus he was obliged, according to feudal custom, to ask for "gracious aids" from his vassals. These aids were in the form of percentages of personal property, and the vassals had to assent to their collection. So large and so numerous were the aids that the king's immediate vassals naturally collected what they could from their vassals to help make up the sums. Since these subvassals would contribute such a goodly part of the aids, they, too, came to feel that they should consent to the levies. The first occasion for which there is clear evidence of the king summoning subvassals for this purpose was the meeting of the great council in 1254.

The towns also came to feel that they should be consulted on taxes, since in practice they could often negotiate with the royal authorities for a reduction in the levy imposed on them. Burgesses of some towns were included for the first time in Simon de Montfort's "parliament" of 1265. Knights of the shire also attended this meeting because Simon apparently wanted to muster the widest possible support for his program. But only known supporters of Simon were invited to attend the parliament.

This parliament proved, in time, to be a precedent, for the presence of shire and town representatives made it the first true ancestor of the modern House of Commons. Not all subsequent parliaments had representatives from shire and town, and not all assemblies attended by knights and burgesses were parliaments. Knights and burgesses had no "right" to come to parliament; no doubt, they often felt it a nuisance and an expense to come, and not a privilege. But gradually they came to attend parliament regularly.

Edward I, 1272-1307

By the late thirteenth century the earlier medieval belief that law is custom and that it cannot be made was fading, and Edward I enacted a great series of systematizing statutes, for which he is sometimes called "the English Justinian." Edward's statutes were framed by the experts of the small council, who elaborated and expanded the machinery of government, and under whose rule Parliament's function was more judicial than legislative or consultative. Each of the statutes was really a large bundle of different enactments. Taken together, they reflect a declining feudalism and show us an England in which the suzerain-vassal, relationship was becoming a mere landlord-tenant relationship, and in which the old duties of fighting were becoming less important than financial obligations. The Second Statute of Westminster (1285), for example, was designed to assure the great landowner that an estate granted to a tenant could not be disposed of except by direct inheritance; this is what we could call *entail.* Similarly, the Statute of Mortmain (1279) prevented transfer of land to the church without the consent of the suzerain. The church placed a "dead hand" (*mortmain*) on land and could hold on forever to any land it received; lay landlords, therefore, found it highly unprofitable to see portions of their holdings transferred to clerical hands. Besides these statutes, which protected the interest of the landlord, Edward I, in a statute of 1290, commanded the barons to show by what authority (*quo warranto*) they held any privilege, such as the right to have their own court of justice. Some privileges (franchises) he revoked, but his chief aim was to assert the principle that all such franchises came from the king, and that what he had given he could take away.

Under Edward the business of royal justice increased steadily, and specialized courts began to appear, all offspring of the central curia regis. The Court to Common Pleas, which handled cases that arose between subjects, had begun to take shape earlier, but now it crystallized into a recognizable, separate body. The new Court of King's Bench handled criminal and Crown cases, and a special Court of Exchequer dealt with disputes about royal finance.

Edward I also regularized and improved existing financial and military practices. He made permanent the king's share in export duties on wool and leather, the burden of which fell mostly on foreigners, and in customs dues on foreign merchandise, which soon became the most important single source of royal income—eloquent testimony to the flourishing commerce of the period. At the request of Parliament, Edward expelled an important source of loans, expelling the Jews from England in 1290; they were not allowed to return until the midseventeenth century. After this expulsion, the Italians assumed the role of money lenders.

Edward I's parliament of 1295 is traditionally called the Model Parliament because it included all classes of the kingdom—not only barons, higher clergy, knights of the shire, and burgesses, but also representatives of the lower clergy. In the royal summons of 1295 appeared a celebrated clause: "What touches all should be approved by all." This basic principle would be repeated two years later, even though the lower clergy soon turned to their own convocations and ceased attending.

Edward also required all freemen to equip themselves for military service. The less wealthy served as foot soldiers. But those with a certain minimum amount of property were compelled to become knights (this was called distraint of knighthood) and serve on horseback, in part for financial reasons; once they had achieved knight's status, the king could collect feudal dues from them.

Edward's vigorous extension of royal power aroused the same sort of opposition that had plagued John and undone Henry III. In 1297 both the clergy (under the influence of Pope Boniface VIII) and the barons refused to grant the aid that Edward wanted; they were able to make him confirm Magna Carta and promise not to make any nonfeudal levy without first obtaining consent. Unlike the French monarchs, the English kings had encountered a corporate baronial opposition, which by forcing consultation upon the king had begun to create new institutions.

In France, the Capetian kings, beginning as relatively powerless and insignificant local lords, had by 1300 extended their royal administration into the lands of their great vassals and created the institutions of a powerful centralized monarchy. The question of the English claims to large areas on the Continent remained to be settled in the grim struggle of the Hundred Years' War. In England, on the other hand, the Norman conquerors proved able to make the most of existing Anglo-Saxon institutions and to superimpose effective feudal monarchy, while they and their successors developed the common law, bringing not only money and power to the monarch but relative security to the subject.

Whereas in France the vassals were unaware of the danger to their position until it was too late, and were too divided among themselves to unite in opposition to the monarch's aggressions, in England the vassals early recognized the need for presenting a united opposition if they were to preserve their rights. Out of their opposition emerged the guarantees that limited the king: promises given in the first instance on behalf of the great vassals, though later subject to much broader interpretation. By the early fourteenth century, out of the king's need to obtain assent for taxation and out of the custom of consultation between king and subject, there was beginning to emerge a recognizable parliament that would have a major impact on the world. The English and French were launched upon contrasting historical paths.

III SCIENCE, LITERATURE, AND THE ARTS IN THE WEST

Although these historical paths diverged, there was throughout the West a growing interest in scientific inquiry that also served to unite peoples. Science has always been international, since ideas cannot be restrained within the borders of a state, but technology—that is, the application of science to practical ends—may for a time be held within the confines of a single nation through legislation or restrictions on immigration. Thus England and France, and most especially England, were cautiously setting themselves apart from the mainstream of ready acceptance of all logic as deriving from churchly authority. Literature too contributed to this sense of inquiry and artistic experimentation.

Science

The Middle Ages saw considerable achievement in natural science. Modern scholars have revised downward the reputation of the Oxford Franciscan Roger Bacon (c 1214-1294) as a lone, heroic devotee of "true" experimental methods; but they have revised upward such reputations as those of Adelard of Bath (twelfth century), who was a pioneer in the study of Arab science; William of Conches (twelfth century), whose greatly improved cosmology was cited for its particularly elegant clarity; and Robert Grossteste (c 1175-1253) at Oxford, who clearly did employ experimental methods. No doubt much medieval theological and philosophical thought was concerned with forms of human experience that natural science is not concerned with; but in many ways even modern Western science goes back at least to the thirteenth century.

First, especially in the late Middle Ages, real progress took place in the technologies that underlie modern science—in agriculture, in mining and metallurgy, and in the industrial arts generally. Accurate clockwork, optical instruments, and the compass all emerged from the later Middle Ages. Even such sports as falconry and such dubious subjects as astrology and alchemy helped lay the foundations of modern science. The breeding and training of falcons taught close observation of the birds' behavior; astrology involved close observation of the heavens and complicated calculations; alchemy, though it was far short of modern chemistry, nevertheless brought the beginnings of identification and rough classification of elements and compounds. Second, mathematics was pursued throughout the period. Thanks in part to Arab influences, it had been fashioned into a tool ready for the use of early modern scientists. Through the Arabs, medieval Europeans learned Arabic numerals and the symbol for zero—a small thing, but one without which the modern world could hardly get along. Try doing long division with Roman numerals—dividing, say, MCXXVI by LXI. The process is difficult and time-consuming.

Finally, and most important, the discipline of Scholasticism, antagonistic as it often was to experimental science, formed a trained scholarly community that was

Popular interest in astronomy during the Middle Ages is demonstrated by the inclusion in the Bayeux Tapestry of Halley's Comet passing over Normandy in 1066.

THE CONFESSION OF GOLIAS

Much verse was still written in Latin in the medieval West, even extremely colloquial or satirical verse, such as the famous student songs of the twelfth century, still preserved in a single manuscript found in a German monastery.

These songs, all anonymous, are called Goliardic because the authors—mostly, we imagine, wild young renegade clerics wandering about Europe from one lecturer to another—claimed to be in the service of a certain Golias, a kind of satanic figure perhaps deriving originally from the Old Testament giant, Goliath, whom David slew with a stone from his sling. Their verses mocked the form and the values of the serious religious poetry of the time and satirized the clergy and the church and even the Bible. No doubt the Goliardic verses in praise of wine, women, and song shocked the virtuous, as they were intended to do.

Here is the way in which the Confession of Golias defined the highest good:

My intention is to die
In the tavern drinking;
Wine must be on hand, for I
Want it when I'm sinking.

Angels when they come shall cry
At my frailties winking:
"Spare this drunkard, God, he's high,
Absolutely stinking."

George F. Whicher, *The Goliard Poets* (New York: New Directions, 1949).

accustomed to a rigorous intellectual discipline. Natural science uses deduction as well as induction, and early modern science inherited from the deductive Scholasticism of the Middle Ages the meticulous care, patience, and logical rigor without which all the inductive accumulation of facts would be of little use to scientists. Without the Aristotelian revival of the thirteenth century, science could not have developed along the path it took.

Literature

In literature and the arts, as in science and in social and economic life, Latin continued to be the language of the church and of learned communication everywhere in western Europe. In fact, by the eleventh century it was written better than in the earlier Middle Ages. All the churchmen—John of Salisbury, Abelard, Bernard, Aquinas, and the rest—wrote Latin even when corresponding informally with their friends. Children began their schooling by learning it. It was also the language of the law and of politics; all documents, not only important ones like Magna Carta but private ones like a deed to a piece of property, were written in Latin. Sermons were delivered in Latin, and church hymns and popular songs were written and sung in it.

But if Latin was widely used for all literary purposes, the period after the eleventh century marks the gradual triumph of the vernacular languages all over Europe for the literature of entertainment, of *belles lettres*. Whereas *Beowulf*, coming from a Britain never thoroughly Latinized, was the only important literary vernacular poem during the early Middle Ages, now such poems began to appear in ever greater numbers everywhere except Britain, where English was in temporary eclipse. A particularly celebrated one in Old French is *The Song of Roland*, whose earliest surviving manuscript was probably written down a little after the year 1100, and which survives in hundreds of versions, the variations of which can tell the scholar much about the culture from which the version originated.

The poem was known from oral tradition earlier, as it was sung by William's men at Hastings in 1066. It deals with a historic episode far in the past, the defeat of Charlemagne's rear guard by the Muslims in 778 in the mountain pass of Roncevaux in the Pyrenees. In *The Song of Roland* human beings, not monsters, are the enemy; the landscape has brightened; a more intense Christian piety softens some of the worst violence; Roland sees to it that comrades slain by the infidel receive a Christian blessing. It is human treachery that brings tragedy down on the heroic forces of Charlemagne, leaving Roland and

THE SONG OF ROLAND

The military feeling of this poem is apparent in its description of a single clash between Archbishop Turpin and the Saracen Abisme (or Abyss, for "sink of iniquity"):

And so the battle begins with Turpin's charge
He rides a horse he took from King Grossaille,
That time in Denmark he fought him to his death.
The horse is swift and spirited and proud;
His hooves are hollow, slender and strong his legs,
Short in the thigh, his quarters large around,
His chest is deep, his back set straight and high.
White is his tail, yellow his flowing mane,
His ears are small, his head of tawny gold;
No charger set to race him has a chance.
Archbishop Turpin spurs on against Abisme—
And with what valor! Nothing can stop him now.
He strikes the shield a superhuman blow;
Its surface sparkles with topaz, amethyst,
Stones of great virtue, rubies that hotly glow—
(In Val Metas a devil gave that shield
To the emir, who gave it to Abisme).
But Turpin's spear accords it no respect:
After his blow it isn't worth a cent.
Right through that pagan his spear thrusts like a spit;
He throws the body into an empty space.
The Frenchmen say, "Against him no one stands!
The holy staff is safe in Turpin's hands."

The Song of Roland, trans. Patricia Terry (Indianapolis: Bobbs-Merrill, 1977), pp. 58-59.

the king grief-stricken. The highest virtue in the poem is loyalty to one's lord—a quality that was the first necessity in a feudal society where, it was felt, only the knight's loyalty to his suzerain saved all from anarchy. In Roland's deep loyalty to his lord, Charlemagne, there is something new—a love for "sweet France," a patriotic note of love of country that was struck at about the earliest moment that we can speak of Europeans as having "a country."

As the knight was always defined as a mounted man, a man on a horse, so the unwritten but generally accepted code that came to govern his behavior in elaborate detail was called *chivalry*, from the French word *cheval*, a horse.

The literature of chivalry and courtly love developed with particular complexity at the court of Eleanor of Aquitaine, who left Henry II of England in 1170 to live with her daughter Marie, countess of Champagne, at the court of Poitiers in western France, where the two became patrons of writers and poets. The hopes of aristocratic women were revealed through the tales of courtly love, and such tales were commentaries on the domestic life of the aristocracy under the strict tenets of feudal relations. The most distinguished court literature was the work of Marie de France, Chrétien de Troyes, and Andrew the Chaplain. De Troyes' *Chevalier de la Charette* expressed the doctrines of courtly love in their most developed form, and his work has been called "the perfect romance" for its presentation of a Lancelot who would cast aside all conventions for the love of Queen Guinevere. Marie wrote simpler tales about the physical attraction exerted by youth and beauty, while Andrew wrote, in *De Amore*, a most extensive treatise on courtly, carnal, profane, and platonic love and the attitudes of the church toward the subject.

These stories, like the *Song of Roland*, were told, sung, and written in *cycles*, added to by troubadours (wandering minstrels) as they spread the tales to other lands, rewritten and glossed by subsequent generations. Perhaps the best known cycle were the stories that evolved in the same period around King Arthur of Britain, far more legendary than Charlemagne. The exploits of Arthur's knights (of whom Lancelot was one) became part of the vernacular literature in most of western Europe. Taken up in France, these stories were passed in the thirteenth century into Germany, where Wolfram von Eschenbach wrote a long poem about Arthur's knight Sir Percival, and thus gave new impetus to an old tradition that would not culminate perhaps until Richard Wagner's opera *Parsifal* in the nineteenth century. Writers of both elite and popular culture drew upon the Arthurian cycle, as did Alfred Lord Tennyson in nineteenth-century Britain and a host of moderns, including detective and science fiction writers (of which the "Star Trek" cycle of the late twentieth century might be the best known). Thus have the weavers of tales always been ready to retell a well-known story in a way that would speak afresh to the psychological attitudes of new generations.

The elaborate and artificial game that became courtly love flourished through lyric poetry. The Roman poet Ovid was rediscovered and misunderstood; he wrote of carnal appetites rewarded, while the code of *courtoisie* (courtly love, from which would develop modern concepts of "courtesy") required that the singer's lady almost always prove unattainable. The wife of another, made inaccessible by the obligations of feudal vassalage, the lady was to be worshiped from afar. Thus the singer celebrated in ecstasy even the slightest kindness she might offer him. Her merest word was a command, and her devoted knight undertook without question even the most arduous mission she might propose to him, without hope of a reward. But a lady who failed to reward him, at least to some degree, was not playing by the rules of this elaborate and artificial game. The twelfth-century troubadours who sang in the southern French language (called Provençal after the large region of Provence, and quite a different dialect from that spoken in the north) were often half-humorous as they expressed their hopeless longings for the unattainable lady.

Needless to say, few medieval nobles behaved according to the code, and yet some of the ideals fostered by the troubadours did become part of the developing notions of chivalry. St. Louis was as close to a truly chivalrous figure as may have existed.

In Italy, the original home of Latin, a vernacular language was somewhat slower to develop. But here too, at the sophisticated and cosmopolitan court of the emperor Frederick II in Palermo, some of Frederick's chief advisers began to write love poetry in what they themselves called the "sweet new style," and soon the fashion spread northward. It was not until somewhat later, with Dante Alighieri (1265-1321) of Florence, that the vernacular Italian tongue scored its definitive triumph. It is significant to note that Dante himself, among his other books, felt impelled to write (in Latin) a stirring defense of vernacular Italian: *De Vulgari Eloquentia* (*Concerning the Speech of Every Day*). For his own greatest work, *The Divine Comedy*, he chose Italian.

Among writers in the Western tradition, Dante belongs with Homer, Vergil, and Shakespeare as a supreme master. As a towering intellectual figure, he heralds the new age of rebirth at least as loudly as he sounds the now-familiar medieval note. But *The Divine Comedy* was a medieval book, perhaps the most famous and in some ways the most typical of all medieval literary expressions.

Lost in a dark wood, in his thirty-fifth year, "halfway along the road of our human life," Dante encounters the Roman poet Vergil, who consents to act as his guide through two of the three great regions of the afterlife: Hell and Purgatory. Descending through the nine successive circles of Hell, where the eternally damned must remain forever, the two meet and converse with souls in torment, some of them historic persons like Judas or Brutus, others recently deceased Florentines of Dante's own acquaintance, with whose sins he was familiar. In Purgatory less sinful human beings are being punished before they can be saved. The souls of the great pagan figures, born too early to have become Christians, are neither in Hell nor in Purgatory, but in Limbo—a place of rest on the edge of Hell where Vergil himself must spend eternity. Here he introduces Dante to the shades not only of such ancients as Homer, Plato, and Socrates, but of characters in ancient myth and poetry such as Hector, Odysseus, and Aeneas. According to Dante, even the Muslim scholar Averroës and the Muslim hero Saladin are in Limbo, not in Hell.

When the poet comes to the gates of Paradise, Vergil cannot continue to escort him; so the guide to the final region of the afterlife is Beatrice, a Florentine girl with whom Dante had fallen desperately in love as a youth but whom he had worshiped only at a distance. Here Dante was consciously transforming one of the central experiences of his own life into literature in accordance with the traditions of the code of courtly love. In Paradise he finds the Christian worthies and the saints—Benedict, Bernard, Aquinas, and others—and at the climax of the poem he sees a vision of God himself.

This voyage through the afterlife is designed to show in new pictorial vividness a traditional Christian concept: that people's actions in this life determine their fate in the next. From the lost souls in Hell, who have brought themselves to their hopeless position ("Abandon Hope, All Ye Who Enter Here" reads the inscription over the gates of Hell), through those who despite their sufferings in Purgatory confidently expect to be saved, to those whose pure life on earth has won them eternal bliss, Dante shows the entire range of human behavior and its eternal consequences. It is a majestic summary of medieval Christian moral and ethical ideas, and it has often been compared in its completeness and its masterful subordination of detail to general vision with the philosophical work of Aquinas.

Another late medieval giant was Geoffrey Chaucer (1340-1400). By Chaucer's day the vernacular had long since recovered in England, and the Old English of the pre-Conquest period had evolved into a new form of the language usually called Middle English, recognizable today as an archaic version of the present language. Chaucer is the supreme poet of Middle English and surely the most brilliant English literary voice before Shakespeare. An experienced man of affairs who served his king at home and abroad, Chucer left behind many literary works, including a long and moving poetic narrative love story, *Troilus and Criseyde*, deriving its characters from the Trojan War stories then fashionable in western Europe.

Chaucer's most celebrated work, however, is *The Canterbury Tales*—tales told by a group of pilgrims on their way to the tomb of Thomas à Becket, the sainted archbishop of Canterbury murdered under Henry II. The pilgrims come from all walks of English life except the high nobility and include a knight, a squire, a prioress, a clerk, a monk, a friar, a sailor, a miller, and others. On the way from London each tells at least one story, fully consonant with his or her personality and experience.

The knight tells a romantic story of chivalric love. Two cousins fall in love with a maiden whom they have barely glimpsed from the window of their prison cell. Deadly rivals thereafter, they cherish their mutual strife, in prison and out, without the lady's being aware of them. In the end, one kills the other and wins her as his own—a story of courtly love. The miller tells a raw story of a young wife's deception of her elderly husband with a young lover—a barnyard anecdote full of liveliness and good humor. The prioress tells a saint's legend, the squire an unfinished story full of semiscientific marvels, and so on. Chaucer does not hesitate to satirize his churchmen. The fourteenth century was a period of much discontent with the English church, and the poet was striking a note that was sure to be popular. The sophistication, delicacy, power, passion, and humor that Chaucer commands put him in the same class with Dante and with no other medieval writer in any country.

The Arts

The arts also changed notably in this period. The Romanesque style dominated the eleventh and most of the twelfth centuries. The Gothic style, following it and developing from it, began in the twelfth century and prevailed down to the fifteenth. Among the great Romanesque churches were those built at Mainz, Worms, and Speyer in western Germany by the Holy Roman emperors of the Salian line. Another great Romanesque monastery church, with its surrounding buildings, was the complex at Cluny, and yet another was the pilgrimage church of St. James (Santiago) at Compostela in northwestern Spain. To Compostela from all over western Europe, and especially from France, came crowds of pilgrims to worship at the shrine of the saint, since access to Jerusalem was perilous. In the twelfth century from five hundred thousand to two million pilgrims a year made their way to this site, using what may be the first "tourist guide" ever written, the Pilgrim Guide of 1130.

All art forms evolve, and beginning in the late twelfth century Romanesque structures began to change substantially. From being round, the arches now gradually rose to points at the peak. Similarly, the roofs also rose more and more steeply as the smooth flow of the arch was sharply broken and two loftier curves met instead at a point. This pointed arch was the chief feature of the newer medieval architecture known as Gothic. It enabled the builder to carry his buildings to soaring heights. The vaulted ceilings of Romanesque churches now rested upon a series of masonry ribs in groups of four, two rising from each side of the wall, and each group supported by a massive pillar. Four pillars therefore could now be made to take the place of a whole section of solid Romanesque wall, and the spaces between the pillars could be used for windows. Outside, too, increased lightness and soaring height was achieved by arched support, called "flying buttresses."

Into the new window spaces the craftsmen of the thirteenth century fitted a new form of art: windows in multicolored (stained) glass, glittering with gemlike colors in ruby, sapphire, and emerald, and showing biblical episodes or episodes from the life of the saint whose church they illuminated. The first were commissioned by Suger for the chapels of the choir of St. Denis and at Chartres cathedral in the midtwelfth century.

Gothic architecture flourished for at least two centuries everywhere in Europe. Its first and perhaps greatest moments came in northern France, between the 1190s and about 1260, with the building of the cathedrals of Chartres, Rheims, Amiens, Notre Dame of Paris, and other celebrated churches. Open and vast, solidly built, soaring upward according to carefully calculated mathematical architectural formulas, the Gothic cathedral terminated in aerial towers. Though its great windows let in the light, the stained glass kept the interior dim and awe inspiring. In the fourteenth and fifteenth centuries ornamentation grew richer, decoration became more intricate and flamelike (or "flamboyant"), and Gothic architecture on the Continent moved toward its decline. In England, however, the later, richer Gothic produced such marvels as King's College Chapel in Cambridge and the Henry VII Chapel at Westminster Abbey in London.

In the years between 1180 and 1220, complex lifelike forms of sculpture were rendered in exquisite stonework that revealed respect for architectural form, combined with mastery of the craft of stonecutting, a high idealism, and a readiness to attempt realism. Physiques were

The Cathedral of St. Peter's at Worms, in western Germany, begun in the eleventh century.

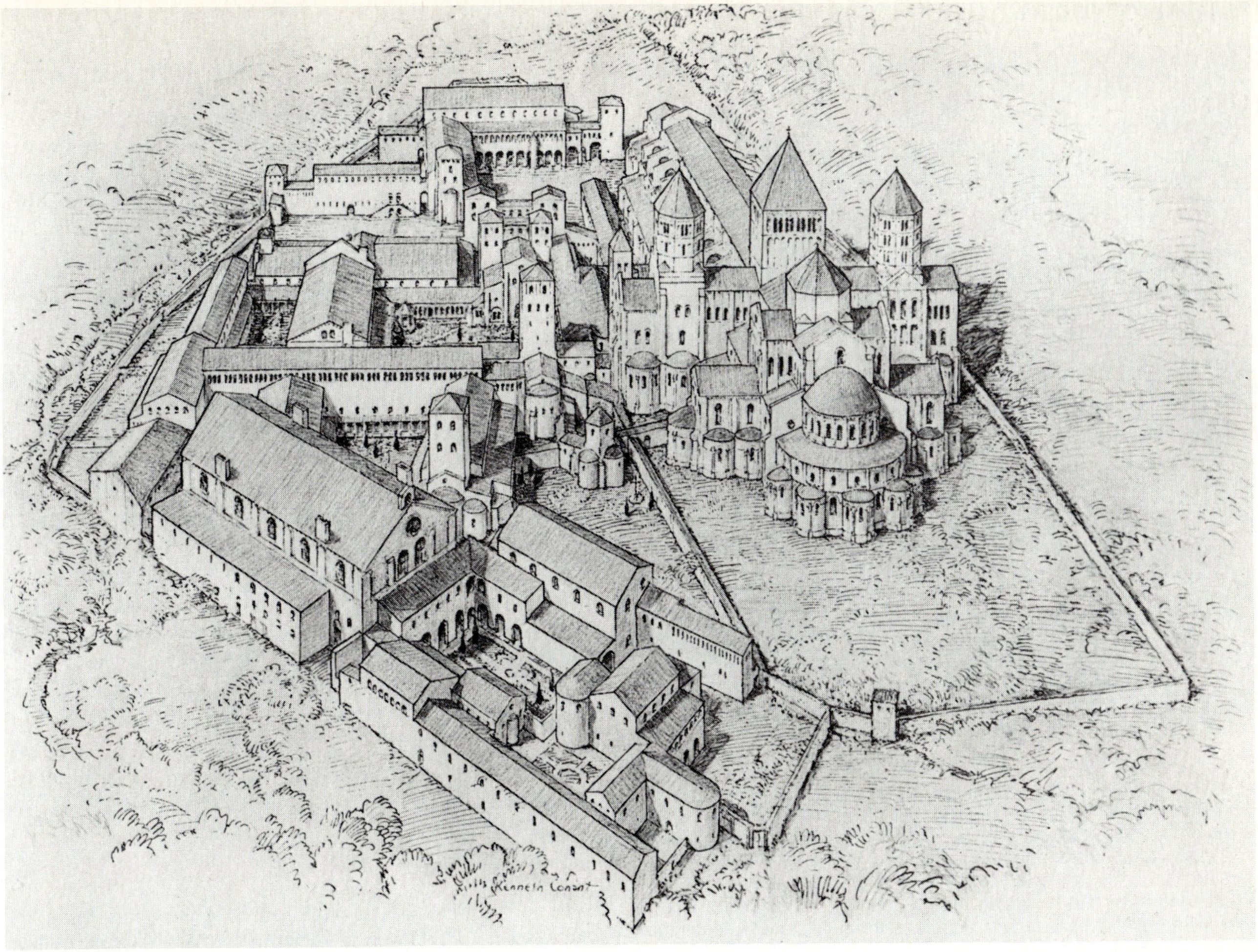

not camouflaged or ignored but were studied; gestures developed an entirely new form of their own.

Gradually sculpture in the round became more common. Lifelike representation of drapery and the firm balance of the figures on their feet are principal characteristics of these new statues, occurring chiefly in northern France. Similar influences are shown elsewhere in metalwork and in manuscript illumination, rather than in monumental sculpture, and the influences from outside that helped make the development possible came through Byzantine art, then undergoing a kind of classical renaissance, which became available to Western eyes through renewed and intensified contacts between East and West by pilgrims, travelers, and warriors during the period of the Crusades. Thus an artistic revival was launched as a result of matters of state as well as of religion. For most of those living in the West in the Middle Ages, there were, in any case, no such distinctions; life was a whole, its customs and practices focused on the ideals and precepts of Christianity.

Perhaps no one figure can represent how art connected one conventionally named period—the Middle Ages—to another—the Renaissance. Still, the "rebirth" of the arts implied by the latter term was already in progress well before the dates normally assigned to the Renaissance, though not all the characteristics associated with Renaissance art were yet present. The Florentine architect, sculptor, and painter Giotto di

(above) A drawing of a model of the monastery of Cluny in 1157. (below) Santiago de Compostela, goal of western European pilgrims. This drawing shows a restoration of the church to its medieval state.

Variations on the typical Romanesque church can be found today throughout southwestern France. Domed roofs are representative of the style, sometimes with the domes in a row above the nave or, as shown above at St. Front of Pèrigueux, built 1120-1160, in a Greek (equal-armed) cross pattern. The effect upon a worshiper standing under a roof made up of a series of domes was quite different from that produced by the ordinary Romanesque barrel vaulting, as exemplified by the interior of the cathedral of Angoulème shown below.

Bondone (c 1266-1337) is particularly illustrative of how one stage of artistic development is father to the next. A friend of Dante, Giotto often followed the Byzantine models so popular in his day, but he also sought to make his paintings more lifelike and emotional. He learned from Italian sculptors who had studied the sculptures on the portals of Gothic cathedrals, especially at Chartres. Giotto executed similar forms in frescoes, creating the illusion of three dimensions by the use of foreshortening and perspective, in the chapel of Madonna dell'Arena in Padua, a great university and commercial center. Between 1304 and 1306 Giotto painted thirty-eight frescoes depicting the lives of the Virgin and of Christ. His scenes of the Kiss of Judas and of the Entombment became highly influential in the development of Renaissance art, as did Joachim and the Shepherds, which makes brilliant use of dramatic positioning of figures by forcing the viewer to "read" the picture from left to right, and by employing *chiaroscuro*, the use of light and shade to enhance the effect. He would be much copied.

Even before the Renaissance, Giotto exemplified the Renaissance artist's approach to his work—individualistic, intent upon fame and success, expecting lucrative art commissions, and engaging in business activities (in this case as a debt-collector and a landlord to weavers) for further profit. The richest man in Padua had commissioned Giotto to decorate the Arena chapel

Durham Cathedral in northern England, showing the view of the nave facing toward the east window, with typical Norman Romanesque rib vaulting. Romanesque had become an international style, and this same type of interior could be found in the cathedral of Pisa, in Italy.

These fine figures of Melchizedek, Abraham, and Moses from the north portal of the cathedral of Chartres date from about 1238, and they illustrate the movement toward sculpture in the round.

Romanesque Burgundy moved away from the Cluny style (of which Autun was an example) with the consecration of La Madeleine at Vézelay in 1104. Here the pointed barrel vault was replaced by a groined vault with transverse arches, creating a high, airy effect.

The exterior of Chartres Cathedral. On the left is the New Tower (which is the oldest, being from 1134), capped with a spire added in the sixteenth century. This contrasts with the simpler Old Tower to the right. Chartres became famous as the finest repository of stained glass on the Continent.

on behalf of his father's soul, for Dante had placed him in Hell as a usurer. Thus money and art were wed through patronage, as when the great banking families of the Bardi and Peruzzi of Florence employed Giotto to apply his art to the Church of Santa Croce, later to be the resting place of Michelangelo, Machiavelli, and Galileo—symbols of the Renaissance to come.

Dante, Chaucer, Giotto, the soaring Gothic spire—all attested to the primacy of the Christian God. Each sought to show life as a pilgrimage, a search for salvation in an ever more complex world; each sought to draw the eye upward, literally to follow the Gothic tower toward Heaven. Each was lively, energetic, fond of exquisite detail. The complexity of one of Chaucer's pilgrim's tales, the intricacy of an inner circle of Purgatory in Dante's vision of a netherworld, the carefully rendered individuality of one of Giotto's figures spoke to the desire to see the individual in relation to God. The Renaissance would place heavier emphasis on individualism, worldly

(above) The Cathedral of Amiens, showing the nave, begun in 1220: a superb example of Gothic architecture. (below) King's College Chapel, in Cambridge, England, is perhaps the finest example of Gothic architecture in Britain. The fan vaulting is exceptionally intricate: it was completed between 1446 and 1515. The delicate windows and glass were calculated to give the sense of being open to air.

Shortly before 1100 a revival of European sculpture began. The tradition had never been lost, as demonstrated by early medieval Irish and English crosses, but the finest surviving examples of the art of sculpture before the Romanesque revival were in ivory and metal work. Now the stone of the churches began to blossom out with rosettes, palm-leaf ornaments, and grapevines, and hiding behind the foliage would be mythical beasts, some of them illustrating the popular bestiaries of the time—collections of anecdotes about real and mythical animals, usually with a Christian allegorical explanation of the animals' fantastic characteristics. Scenes from the Bible also appeared on the capitals above the columns, now often interpreted individually by the artist. Above is one such capital, from the Cathedral of Autun, about 1120, showing Judas hanging himself while winged demons pull on the rope. Relief sculpture next appeared in the large flat surfaces available to the artist in a Romanesque church, for example, the space over the outside of the front portal, called the *tympanum.* Also at Autun, and sculpted between 1130 and 1140, Christ is shown on opposite page, enthroned, with the Virgin and saints nearby, while beneath them is a depiction of the Last Judgment. Such large-scale compositions gave the sculptor an opportunity to show his versatility and to portray more broadly the Christian conception of the universe.

success, the fascinating diversity of life. But the outward expression of the inward search for glory, individually and collectively, for spiritual and physical adventure, would best be found in the several Crusades by which the Christian monarchs and their followers in the West sought to carry once again to the East, where the origins of Christianity lay, the authority of the church and of the states that supported that church.

SUMMARY

Between 987 and 1314 the French monarchy grew in power and prestige until it dominated the machinery of government. France became the first large, unified state in the medieval West.

The Capetian kings made good their authority over their own territory and piece by piece added to it. By 1214 at the battle of Bouvines they had overcome the Norman-Angevin threat; in the south under Louis IX (St. Louis) they drove the Albigensian heresy underground and took over Mediterranean lands. They increased their control over the curia regis, the king's court, and under Philip IV, the Fair, they consolidated the royal hold on power against the towns, the nobles, and the church.

After the Norman conquest of England in 1066, English kings developed existing Anglo-Saxon institutions into a strong and unified state. Henry I and Henry II extended William the Conqueror's system of administration. The development of common law brought power to the monarch and security to the subject.

However, the united opposition of the English barons limited the royal power. The guarantees first given to the great vassals in Magna Carta were in time broadened to include most of the population. By the early fourteenth century a recognizable parliament began to emerge.

Progress took place in the technologies that underlie modern science, and the discipline of Scholasticism formed a trained scholarly community that was accustomed to a rigorous intellectual discipline.

Although Latin was still widely used, the vernacular languages were increasingly employed for the literature of entertainment, as in the French tales of chivalry, *The Song of Roland*, Dante's *Divine Comedy*, and Chaucer's *Canterbury Tales*.

The Romanesque style gave way to the Gothic in the twelfth century, and Gothic dominated down to the fifteenth. Among its greatest achievements are the cathedrals of Chartres, Notre Dame in Paris, Rheims, and Amiens. The Florentine architect, sculptor, and painter Giotto best bridges the styles of the late Middle Ages and the Renaissance that was to follow.

chapter nine

THE LATE MIDDLE AGES IN EASTERN EUROPE

The idea of a holy war was not new in 1095. In Spain the fighting of Christian against Muslim had been virtually continuous since the Muslim conquest in the eighth century. Just after the year 1000 the Cordovan caliphate weakened, and the Spanish Christian princes of the north won the support of the powerful French abbey at Cluny. Under prodding from Cluny, French nobles joined the Spaniards in warring on the Muslims. Soon the pope offered an indulgence to all who would fight for the Cross in Spain. In 1085 the Christians took the city of Toledo, though a new advance by Muslim Berbers from North Africa set them back for a time. The Christian movement continued into the twelfth century, recovering a large area of central Spain. It was itself a *Crusade*—a holy war against the infidel supported by the papacy. So too were the wars of the Normans against the Muslims of Sicily.

I THE CRUSADES

Origins of the Crusades

From the third century on, Christians had visited the scenes of Christ's life. In Jerusalem Constantine's mother, St. Helena, had discovered what was believed to be the True Cross and other relics of the Passion, and her son built the Church of the Holy Sepulcher there. Before the Muslim conquest in the seventh century, pilgrims came from Byzantium and the West, often seeking sacred relics for their churches at home. For a while after the Muslim conquest, pilgrimages were very dangerous and could be undertaken only by the hardiest pilgrims. During the reign of Charlemagne, conditions had improved for Western pilgrims, largely because of the excellent relations between Charlemagne and the caliph Harun al-Rashid. The caliph made Charlemagne a present of the actual recess in which Christ was believed to have been buried and allowed him to endow a hostel in Jerusalem for the use of pilgrims. So deep was Charlemagne's interest that there sprang up a legend that he had somehow acquired from Harun a "protectorate" over the Holy Land, and another that he had actually made a pilgrimage to the East in person. By the tenth century the belief had grown that pilgrimage would procure God's pardon for sins—a Western form of the Muslim *haj*. Santiago of Compostela in Spain, and of course Rome itself, had become favorite places of pilgrimage, but no place could compare in importance with the shrines of Palestine.

Obviously, stable conditions in both Muslim and Byzantine dominions were essential for the easy and safe continuance of pilgrimages. But in the early eleventh century the able though eccentric Egyptian ruler of Palestine, Hakim (r. 996-1021) abandoned the tolerant practices of his predecessors and began to persecute Christians and Jews and to make travel to the Holy Places unsafe. He destroyed the Church of the Holy Sepulcher and declared himself to be God incarnate. Moreover, with the death of the last ruler of the Macedonian house in 1057, an open struggle began at Byzantium between the civil servants of the court and the military led by the great landowners of Asia Minor. Simultaneously came Pecheneg invasions of the Balkans, Norman attacks on Byzantine southern Italy, and the rise in Asia of the Seljuk Turks.

By 1050 the Seljuks had created a state centering on Persia. In 1055 they entered Baghdad on the invitation of the Abbasid caliph and became the champions of Sunnite Islam against the Shi'ite rulers of Egypt. In the 1050s Seljuk forces raided deep into Anatolia, almost to the Aegean. Their advance culminated in the catastrophic Byzantine defeat of Manzikert in 1071, followed by the occupation of most of Asia Minor and the establishment of a new sultanate with its capital at Nicaea. Jerusalem fell in the year of Manzikert and became part of a new Seljuk state of Syria.

In 1081, amid disorder and palace intrigue, with the Empire reduced in territory and the capital in danger, Alexius I Comnenus, general and great landowner, came to the Byzantine throne (ruled to 1118). He held off the Norman attack on the Dalmatian coast through an alliance with Venice, and he played one local Turkish potentate off against another, slowly reestablishing a Byzantine foothold in Asia Minor. Civil wars among the Turks and the multiplication of brigands on the highways in Anatolia and Syria made pilgrimage in the two decades after Manzikert ever more dangerous.

The schism between Eastern and Western churches provided the papacy with an additional incentive for intervention in the East. To the vigorous reforming popes of the later eleventh century the disunity of Christendom was intolerable. In 1073 Pope Gregory VII sent an ambassador to Constantinople who reported that the emperor was anxious for a reconciliation. Gregory VII planned to reunite the churches by extending the holy war from Spain to Asia. He would send the Byzantines an army of Western knights, which he would lead himself. It was only the quarrel over investiture with the German emperor that prevented the pope from carrying out this plan.

The First Crusade, 1095

Pope Urban II (1088-1099) carried on the tradition of Gregory VII. To his Council of Piacenza in 1095 came envoys from Alexius, who asked for military help against the Turks. Turkish power was declining, and now would be a good time to strike. The Byzantine envoys also seem to have stressed the sufferings of the Christians in the East. Eight months later, at the Council of Clermont, Urban preached to a throng of the faithful. He emphasized the appeal received from the Eastern Christians, brothers in difficulty, and painted in dark colors the hardships that now faced pilgrims to Jerusalem. He summoned his listeners to form themselves, rich and poor alike, into an army, which God would assist. Killing each other at home would give way to fighting a holy war. Poverty at home would yield to the riches of the East (a theme especially important in view of the misery in which so many Europeans lived). If a man were killed doing this work of God, he would automatically be absolved of his sins and assured of salvation (a *plenary indulgence*). The audience greeted this moving oration with cries of "God wills it." Throngs of volunteers took a solemn oath, and sewed crosses of cloth onto their garments. Recruitment was under way. The First Crusade had been launched.

On the popular level, a certain Peter the Hermit, an unkempt, barefoot old man who lived on fish and wine and was a moving orator, proved the most effective preacher of the crusade. Through France and Germany he recruited an undisciplined mob of ignorant peasants, including women and children, many of them serfs living wretched lives, suffering near-starvation as a result of crop failure. Often they believed that Peter was leading them straight to heaven, the New Jerusalem, flowing with milk and honey, which they confused with the Jerusalem on earth.

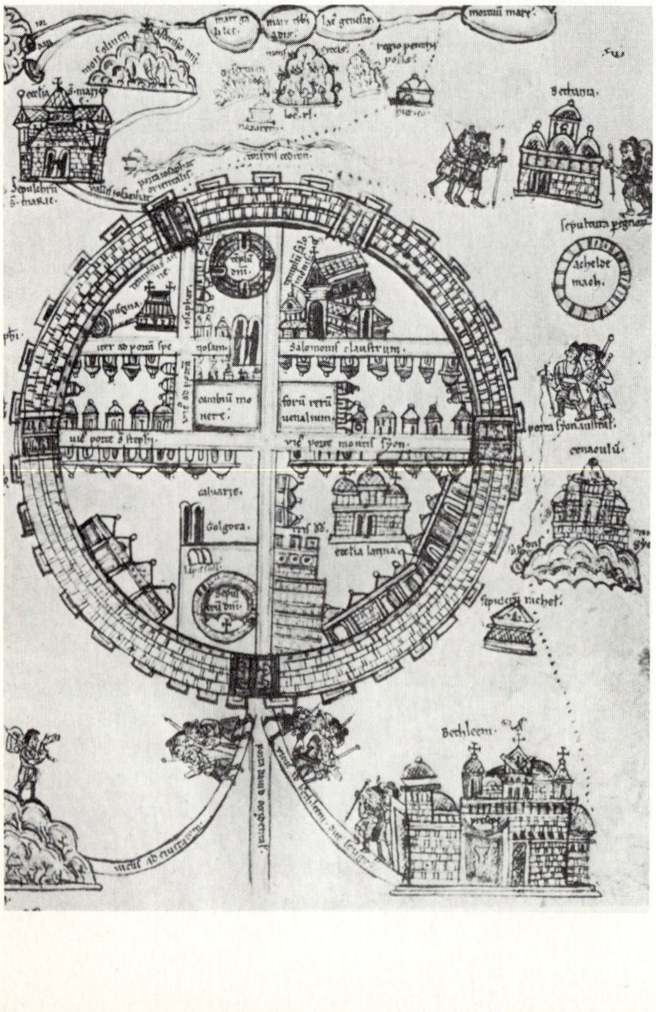

The Crusader's map of Jerusalem, with the principal Christian sites clearly marked.

In two installments, they poured up the Rhine, across Hungary, where four thousand Hungarians were killed in a riot over the sale of a pair of shoes, and into Byzantine territory at Belgrade. The Byzantines, who had hoped for the loan of a few hundred well-trained knights, were appalled at the prospect of the enormous armies of human locusts about to descend on them from the West. They proceeded to arrange military escorts and to take all precautions against trouble. Despite their best efforts, the undisciplined Crusaders burned houses and stole everything that was not chained down, including the lead from the roofs of churches.

Once in Constantinople, they were graciously received by Alexius Comnenus, who shipped them across the Straits as quickly as possible. In Asia Minor they quarreled among themselves, murdered the Christian inhabitants, scored no success against the Turks, and were eventually massacred. The trouble brought upon the Byzantines by this first mob of Crusaders was a sample of future difficulties.

Meanwhile, at the upper levels of Western society, no kings had enlisted in the Crusade, but a considerable number of great lords had been recruited, including a brother of the king of France, the duke of Normandy, and the count of Flanders. The most celebrated, however, were Godfrey of Bouillon (duke of Lower Lorraine), and his brother Baldwin, Count Raymond of Toulouse, Count Stephen of Blois, and Bohemond, a Norman prince from southern Italy. Better equipped and better disciplined, the armies led by these lords now began to converge on Constantinople by different routes, arriving at intervals. Still, there was plenty of trouble for the people on the routes. "My lips are tight," wrote the distressed Byzantine archbishop of Bulgaria, through whose see so many of the Crusaders passed. "The passage of the Franks, on their invasion, or whatever you want to call it, has upset and gripped us all. . . . As we have grown accustomed to their insults, we bear trouble more easily than we used to. Time can teach a person to get used to anything."*

The emperor Alexius was in a very difficult position. He was ready to have the Western commanders carve out principalities for themselves from Turkish-occupied territory. But he wanted to assure himself that Byzantine lands would be returned to his control, and that whatever new states might be created would be dominated by him. He knew of the Western custom of vassalage and the importance attached to an oath taken to an overlord. So he decided to require each great Western lord to take an oath of liege homage to him on arrival. To obtain these oaths, Alexius had to resort to bribery with splen-

*J.P. Migne, *Patrolgia census completus: Graeca* (Rome: Lutetiad Parisiorum, 1857-1903), CCXXVI, 324-25. Our translation.

A fourteenth-century miniature illustrating a French account written in 1337 of the Crusader assault on Jerusalem in 1099. Leading the assault is Godfrey of Bouillon; to the far left is Peter the Hermit.

did gifts and to all sorts of pressure, including in some cases the withholding of food from the unruly crusading armies.

The armies were all ferried across the Straits. There was no supreme command, but the armies acted as a unit, following the orders of the leaders assembled in council. In June of 1097 at Nicaea, the Seljuk capital, the Turks surrendered at the last minute to Byzantine forces rather than suffer an assault from the Crusader armies. This the Crusaders bitterly resented, since they had not been informed of the negotiations for surrender, and had been looking forward to plundering the town. Crossing Asia Minor, the Crusaders defeated the Turks in a battle at Dorylaeum, captured the Seljuk sultan's tent and treasure, and opened the road to further advance. Godfrey's brother Baldwin, leaving the main army, marched to Edessa, a splendid ancient imperial city near the Euphrates, strategically situated for the defense of Syria from attacks coming from the east. Here, after negotiations with the local Armenian rulers, he became count of Edessa—lord of the first Crusader state to be established (1098).

The Crusader States, 1098-1109

Meanwhile, the main body of the army was besieging the great fortress city of Antioch, which finally was conquered by treachery after more than seven months. Antioch became the center of the second Crusader state under the Norman Bohemond. The other Crusaders then took Jerusalem by assault in July 1099, followed by a slaughter of Muslims and Jews, men, women, and children.

The Lorrainer Godfrey of Bouillon was chosen, not king, for he would not consent to wear a royal crown in the city where Christ had worn the crown of thorns, but "defender of the Holy Sepulcher." The third Crusader state had been founded. When Godfrey died not long afterward, his brother Baldwin of Edessa became first king of Jerusalem in 1100.

Venetian, Genoese, and Pisan fleets now assisted in the gradual conquest of the coastal cities, ensuring sea communications with the West and the vital flow of supplies and reinforcements. In 1109 the son of Raymond of Toulouse founded the fourth and last of the Crusader states, centering around the seaport of Tripoli. The king of Jerusalem was the theoretical overlord of the other three states but was often unable to enforce his authority. The Byzantine emperors never relinquished the rights that had been secured to them by the oath that the Crusaders had made to Alexius, and were, especially in the case of Antioch, occasionally able to assert those rights successfully.

The holdings of the Westerners lay within a long narrow coastal strip extending from the Euphrates River to the borders of Egypt, more than five hundred miles

Crusader States

long and seldom as much as fifty miles wide. From the Muslim cities of Aleppo, Hamah, Emesa (Homs), and Damascus, just inland from the strip, and from Egypt to the southwest, danger constantly threatened. The Westerners failed to take obvious measures for the common defense. The great lords built superb castles at strategic places but often fought with one another, sometimes in alliance with neighboring Muslims.

The Assizes of Jerusalem—not written down until the thirteenth century, when the Muslim reconquest was nearly complete—record the governmental practices of the Crusader states. The great officers of the realm were the officers of the king's household: seneschal, constable, marshal, and the like. The high court of barons not only settled disputes but acted as council of state for the king's business. The lords had rights of justice on their own fiefs. Police and civil cases were under the direction of *viscounts*, royal officers in the towns, and there were special commercial and maritime courts. The Italian commercial cities, as colonial powers, had quarters of their own in the coastal cities, with privileged status. Revenues were raised by carefully collected customs dues, by monopolies on tanning and similar industries, by a poll tax on Muslims and Jews, and by a land tax on the native population. Yet money was scarce, and the kings raided Muslim caravans or married rich wives in an effort to bolster their shaky finances. Ecclesiastical organization was complex: the two Latin patriarchs of Jerusalem and Antioch each had a hierarchy of Roman Catholic archbishops and bishops subject to them, but Greek, Syrian, and Armenian churches continued to exist, each with its own clergy, in addition to the Muslim and Jewish faiths.

The Military Orders, 1119-1798

Early in their occupation of the eastern Mediterranean, the Westerners founded the military orders of knighthood. The first of these were the Templars, started about 1119 by a Burgundian knight who sympathized with the hardships of the Christian pilgrims, and who banded together with several others to protect the helpless on their way to pray at the Holy Places. These knights took vows of poverty, chastity, and obedience, and were given headquarters near the ruins of the Temple of Solomon—hence the name Templars. St. Bernard himself inspired their rule, based on the rules for his own Cistercians and confirmed by the pope in 1128. A second order, founded shortly after, was attached to the ancient Hospital of St. John of Jerusalem, and was therefore called the Hospitalers. Made up of knights, chaplains, and serving brothers under the command of a grand master, with branches both in the East and in Europe, the two orders were the most effective fighting forces in the Holy Land. Each had a special uniform; the Templars wore red crosses on white, the Hospitalers white crosses on black. Later a third, purely German group became the order of the Teutonic Knights with headquarters at Acre; they wore black crosses on white.

The orders rapidly grew wealthy; they had fortresses and churches of their own in their own Holy Land and villages from which they obtained produce. Moreover, Western monarchs endowed them richly with lands in Europe. Their original purposes were soon dimmed or lost sight of, and they became another element in the complicated political, military, and ecclesiastical tangle in the Crusader states. They often allied themselves with Muslims and so completely forgot their original vows of poverty that they engaged in banking and large-scale financial operations. In the early fourteenth century the Templars were destroyed by Philip IV of France for political reasons of his own. The Teutonic Knights, most of whose fighting was done against the pagans of the eastern Baltic shore, were disbanded only in 1525 and transmitted some of their lands and much of their outlook toward the world to the modern state of Prussia. The Hospitalers moved first to Cyprus and then to Rhodes in the early fourteenth century; they were driven to Malta by the Turks in 1522 and continued there until Napoleon's seizure of the island in 1798.

The Muslim Reconquest and the Later Crusades, 1144-1291

Tormented as the Crusader states were by the political disunity characteristic of feudal society at its height, it is a wonder that they lasted so long. It was not the castles or the military orders that preserved them so much as the disunion of their Muslim enemies. When the Muslims did achieve unity under a single powerful leader, the Christians suffered grave losses. Thus, beginning in the late 1120s, Zangi, governor of Mosul on the Tigris (the town that gives its name to our muslin cloth), succeeded in unifying the local Muslim rulers of the region. In 1144 he took Edessa, first of the Crusader cities to fall. It was never to be recaptured. Two years later Zangi was assassinated, but the Muslim reconquest had begun.

As an answer to the loss of Edessa, St. Bernard himself preached the so-called Second Crusade in Europe. He aroused enormous enthusiasm, and for the first time Western monarchs—King Louis VII of France and King Conrad III of Germany—came to the East. But the Second Crusade proved a shattering failure. As the German and French armies passed through Constantinople, relations with the Byzantines were worse than ever. It is quite likely that the emperor, Manuel I Comnenus (1143-1180), whose capital the Crusaders seriously considered attacking, mixed chalk with the flour that he sold them before he managed to get them across the Straits, and altogether possible that he was in touch with the Turks.

The Western armies were almost wiped out in Asia Minor. When the remnants reached the Holy Land, they found themselves in hopeless conflict with the local lords, who feared that the newcomers would take over the kingdom, and who sabotaged what might otherwise have been a successful siege of the key Muslim city—Damascus. The Crusaders' failure to take Damascus in 1149 brought its own punishment. In 1154 Zangi's son, Nureddin, took it, and Muslim Syria was united against the Latins. St. Bernard had boasted of his success in

The *Krak des Chevaliers*, or Castle of the Knights, a Crusader fortress built by the Hospitalers and taken by Saladin in 1188. Saladin later adapted its architecture to his own defenses.

ANNA COMNENA DESCRIBES BOHEMOND

Emperor Alexius Comnenus' reign was described by his daughter, Anna Comnena, in an important source known to us as *The Alexiad*, which dates from the early twelfth century. In *The Alexiad* she described Bohemond:

Now the man was such as, to put it briefly, had never before been seen in the land of the Romans, be he either of the barbarians or of the Greeks (for he was a marvel for the eyes to behold, and his reputation was terrifying). Let me describe the barbarian's appearance more particularly—he was so tall in stature that he overtopped the tallest by nearly one cubit, narrow in the waist and loins, with broad shoulders and a deep chest and powerful arms. And in the whole build of the body he was neither too slender nor overweighted with flesh, but perfectly proportioned and, one might say, built in conformity with the canon of Polycleitus. He had powerful hands and stood firmly on his feet, and his neck and back were well compacted. An accurate observer would notice that he stooped slightly, but this was not from any weakness of the vertebrae of his spine but he had probably had this posture slightly from birth. His skin all over his body was very white, and in his face the white was tempered with red. His hair was yellowish, but did not hang down to his waist like that of the other barbarians; for the man was not inordinately vain of his hair, but had it cut short to the ears. Whether his beard was reddish, or any other colour I cannot say, for the razor had passed over it very closely and left a surface smoother than chalk; most likely it too was reddish. His blue eyes indicated both a high spirit and dignity; and his nose and nostrils breathed in the air freely; his chest corresponded to his nostrils and by his nostrils . . . the breadth of his chest. For by his nostrils nature had given free passage for the high spirit which bubbled up from his heart. A certain charm hung about this man but was partly marred by a general air of the horrible. For in the whole of his body the entire man shewed implacable and savage both in his size and glance, methinks, and even his laughter sounded to others like snorting. He was so made in mind and body that both courage and passion reared their crests within him and both inclined to war. His wit was manifold and crafty and able to find a way of escape . . . in every emergency. In conversation he was well informed, and the answers he gave were quite irrefutable. This man who was of such a size and such a character was inferior to the emperor alone in fortune and eloquence and in other gifts of nature.

From *The Alexiad*, trans. Elizabeth A.S. Dawes (New York: Barnes & Noble, 1967), pp. 37, 38, 266. Translation modified by the authors.

recruiting the Crusade: "Because of my preaching, towns and castles are empty of inhabitants. Seven women can scarcely find one man." He now lamented:

> *We have fallen on evil days, in which the Lord, provoked by our sins, has judged the world, with justice, indeed, but not with his wonted mercy. . . . The sons of the Church have been overthrown in the desert, slain with the sword, or destroyed by famine. . . . The judgments of the Lord are righteous, but this one is an abyss so deep that I must call him blessed who is not scandalized therein.**

The next act of the Muslim reconquest was carried out in Egypt by a general of Nureddin's who was sent to assist one of the quarreling factions in Cairo. This general became vizier of Egypt and died in 1169, leaving his office to his nephew, Saladin, celebrated in both history and legend, who became the greatest Muslim leader of the Crusade period. A vigorous and successful general, often moved by impulse, Saladin was also often chivalrous and humane.

Saladin brought the Muslim cities of Syria and Mesopotamia under his control and distributed them to faithful members of his own family. By 1183 his brother ruled Egypt, his sons ruled Damascus and Aleppo, and close relatives ruled all the other important centers. Internal decay in the kingdom of Jerusalem and a squabble over the throne gave Saladin his chance, and a violation of a truce by an unruly Crusader lord gave him his excuse. In 1187 Jerusalem fell, and soon there was nothing of the kingdom left to the Christians except the port of Tyre and a few castles.

These events elicited the Third Crusade (1189-1192). The Holy Roman emperor, Frederick Barbarossa, led a German force through Byzantium, only to be drowned in Asia Minor (1190) before reaching the Holy Land. Some of his troops, however, continued to Palestine. There they were joined by Philip Augustus of France and Richard the Lionhearted of England, deadly rivals in the West. Each was at least as interested in thwarting the other as he was in furthering any common cause. The main operation of the Third Crusade was a long siege of the seaport of Acre, which was finally captured in 1191. Jerusalem itself could not be taken, but Saladin signed a treaty with Richard allowing Christians to visit the city freely.

*Quoted in A.J. Toynbee, *Civilization on Trial* (New York: Oxford University Press, 1948), p. 171.

When Saladin died in 1193 his dominions were divided among his relatives, and the Christians obtained a respite. Reinforcements from the West, however, had dwindled away to a small trickle. The failures in the East were partly balanced by successes in Spain, where, by the end of the thirteenth century, the Christians had restricted the Muslims to the kingdom of Granada in the southeastern corner of the peninsula; far to the northeast, the pagan Lithuanians and Slavs received the attention of the Teutonic Knights in the Baltic region.

Innocent III came to the papal throne in 1198 and called for a new crusade, the Fourth. Several powerful lords responded and decided to proceed to their goal by sea. The Venetians agreed to furnish transportation and food—at a price that proved higher than the Crusaders could pay—and also to contribute fifty armed warships on condition that they would share equally in all future conquests. The shrewd, blind old doge (duke) of Venice, Enrico Dandolo (c 1108-1205) agreed to forgive the debt temporarily if the Crusaders would help him reconquer Zara, a town on the Dalmatian side of the Adriatic that had revolted against Venetian domination and had gone over to the king of Hungary. So the Fourth Crusade began with the sack and destruction of a Roman Catholic town in 1202. Angrily, the pope excommunicated the Crusaders, who settled down to pass the winter in Zara before pressing on. Their primary worry was finance; the leaders had badly overestimated the number who would join the crusade and had committed themselves to a larger contract with the Venetians than needed, a contract to which the Venetians intended to hold them.

During the winter the Crusaders turned their attention to a new goal: Constantinople. The German king, Philip of Swabia—who was Barbarossa's son and brother to the late emperor Henry VI, and who thus had a large following—proposed that the massed army escort Alexius, a young prince with a strong claim to the Byzantine throne, to Constantinople and enthrone him in the place of a usurper. If successful, Alexius would finance the subsequent expedition, whose goal was actually Egypt, though the organizers of the crusade had hoped to keep this secret. The idea had much to recommend it, for it would serve to pay off the debt, would restore the unity of Christendom by bringing Byzantium under its rightful and friendly heir, and would most likely (as Dandolo knew) vastly expand Venice's power. Most of the knights agreed to this plan.

In the spring of 1203 a greatly augumented Crusader fleet, with enthusiastic Venetian support, attacked Constantinople. Despite advance warning, the usurper, Alexius III, had done little to prepare the capital. After all, no one had successfully attacked Constantinople in nine hundred years. In the initial onslaught the attackers won a resounding naval victory, though the city held. A second attack on land and sea broke through the defenses, and Alexius III fled the city. The young Alexius was then crowned as Alexius IV. While he was away pursuing Alexius III, the city was badly damaged by the worst fire in its history, probably begun when a group of

Twelfth-century Spanish Muslim warships, showing both decorative and technological details borrowed from the Normans and from the Byzantines. Each vessel had up to one hundred and thirty galley slaves at the oars.

Franks set fire to a mosque in the Saracen quarter. Angry, Alexius IV declined to make the promised payment. Certain that he could neither bring peace with the increasingly impatient Crusaders nor defeat them in battle, a group of senators, clergy and the populace deposed Alexius IV. He was murdered in prison by another usurper, who showed such qualities of leadership as to convince the Crusaders that they must attack quickly before the city was fully prepared against them.

In March 1204 the Crusaders and Venetians agreed to seize the city a second time, to elect a Latin emperor (who would receive a quarter of the empire and its booty), and to divide the other three-quarters equally between Venetians and non-Venetians. The second siege ended in a second capture and a systematic three-day sack of Constantinople, Byzantium's darkest hour.

The pope himself criticized the outrages committed by the Crusaders. What was destroyed in the libraries of the capital is untold. Despite general destruction, the Venetians salvaged much of great value and beauty, shipping it all back to their city. Among the booty were the four great bronze horses that had been a symbol of the city since Constantine, a host of sacred relics the Greek emperors had been collecting (including a fragment of what was identified as the True Cross and a part of the head of St. John the Baptist), and hundreds of works of Byzantine art. The Crusaders now paid their debt in full to the Venetians and chose not to continue on to their professed goal.

The zeal that had driven men toward the Holy Land was thoroughly tainted by the Fourth Crusade, which

THE SACK OF CONSTANTINOPLE

A contemporary Greek historian who was an eyewitness to the sack of Constantinople described atrocities of which he had thought human beings incapable:

How shall I begin to tell of the deeds done by these wicked men? They trampled the images underfoot instead of adoring them. They threw the relics of the martyrs into filth. They spilt the body and blood of Christ on the ground, and threw it about. . . .

They broke into bits the sacred altar of Santa Sophia, and distributed it among the soldiers. When the sacred vessels and the silver and gold ornaments were to be carried off, they brought up mules and saddles horses inside the church itself and up to the sanctuary. When some of these slipped on the marble pavement and fell, they stabbed them where they lay and polluted the sacred pavement with blood and ordure. A harlot sat in the Patriarch's seat, singing an obscene song and dancing lewdly. They drew their daggers against anyone who opposed them at all. In the alleys and streets, in the temple, one could hear the weeping and lamentations, the groans of men and the shrieks of women, wounds, rape, captivity, separation of families. Nobles wandered about in shame, the aged in tears, the rich in poverty.

Nicetas Choniates, *Historia*, ed. Immanuel Bekker (Bonn, 1835), pp. 757 ff. Condensed; our translation.

horrified Innocent III. Perhaps most of all, their zeal was further diluted by the continuing worldly struggle between the papacy and its European opponents: first, the Albigensian heretics of southern France between 1208 and 1240; and second, the emperor Frederick II between 1220 and 1250. In these affairs the popes were offering those who would fight against a European and nominally Christian enemy the same indulgence they offered those who fought Muslims. All these developments brought disillusionment when combined with the spectacle of repeated military failure and internal Christian dissension in the Holy Land itself.

Perhaps the high point of tragic futility was the so-called Children's Crusade in 1212, when throngs of French and German children went down to the Mediterranean, expecting that its waters would divide before them and open a path to the Holy Land along which they could march to a bloodless victory. When this failed to happen, several thousand pushed on to Marseilles and other seaports. There many were sold into slavery.

The rest was a history of short-term victory measured against long-term defeats. In the Fifth Crusade (1218-1221) the Christians attempted the conquest of Egypt, on the sound theory that this was the center of Muslim strength. They failed. Emperor Frederick II personally led the Sixth Crusade (1228-1229). The papacy excommunicated him once for not going on the crusade and a second time for going on it. No fighting was involved, partly because the Syrian Christians would not support a ruler at odds with the pope, partly because Frederick was too sophisticated to fight when he could get what he wanted by diplomacy. Speaking Arabic and long familiar with the Muslims from his experience in Sicily, he secured more for the Christians by negotiation than any military commander since the First Crusade had secured by war. In 1229 he signed a treaty with Saladin's nephew that restored Jerusalem to the Latins again, except for the site of the Temple. Bethlehem and Nazareth were also handed over, and a ten-year truce was agreed upon. But the Egyptian ruler now took into his service several thousand Turks from central Asia who took Jerusalem in 1244 and shortly thereafter thoroughly defeated the Latins in battle at Gaza. Jerusalem thus remained in Muslim hands until 1917.

Now St. Louis, king of France, launched the first of his two crusades, sometimes called the Seventh (1248-1254), aimed at Egypt. Louis himself was taken prisoner and had to pay a very heavy ransom. In 1250 the household troops of the Egyptian sultan (called Mamluks, or slaves) took power into their own hands in Egypt. Soon after, the Mongols, fresh from their victories in Asia, where they had finally ended the Abbasid caliphate in Baghdad (1258), invaded Syria and were defeated in battle by the Mamluk general Baibars, who immediately made himself sultan. Baibars reduced the number of strongholds remaining to the Crusaders, taking Antioch in 1268. He delayed his advance in fear of a new crusade (the Eighth) by St. Louis in 1270, then resumed it when the king landed in Tunis and died there. The Muslims took Tripoli in 1289 and Acre in 1291, massacring sixty thousand Christians.

The century-long, partly secular sequel to the first hundred years of more pious crusading fervor was now over, and the Christian settlements were wiped out. They were not deeply mourned even in western Europe, from which so much blood and treasure had flowed for their establishment and defense. They had proved divisive, had distracted attention from the building of states in Europe, and had produced little of spiritual value.

Impact of the Crusades on the West

The number of Crusaders and pilgrims who went to the East and returned home was large. From Marseilles alone the ships of the Hospitalers and the Templars carried six thousand pilgrims a year—so many that the shipowners of the port sued the knightly orders for unfair competition. Ideas flowed back and forth with the people. Arabic words in Western languages testify to the concepts and products borrowed by the Westerners—in commerce: *bazaar, tariff,* the French *douane,* and the Italian *dogana* (a customs house, from the Arabic *diwan,* the sofa on which the officials sat); in foods: *sugar, saffron, rice, lemon, apricot, shallot, scallion, melon,* and *pistachio;* in manufactured goods: *cotton, muslin, damask* (from Damascus), and many others.

The new products stimulated the markets and fairs and the growing commercial life of the West. Venice and Genoa, the ports from which much of the produce of the East was funneled into Europe, prospered exceedingly. So did the cities of Flanders, whose own manufacture of woolen goods was stimulated by the availability of Eastern luxuries for trade. Letters of credit and bills of exchange became a necessity in an ever more complex commercial and financial system, stimulated by the vast numbers traveling and making financial arrangements for a journey and a long absence from home. Italian banking houses sprang up with offices in the Holy Land. The orders of knighthood—especially the Templars—played their own role in the money trade.

Thus the Crusades contributed to the introduction of new products, first luxuries and then necessities, and helped create the conditions that led to modern methods of finance. In the long run, they probably also stimulated the movement of population from the country to the towns, which in turn permitted the smaller rural population to live better on their lands and perhaps to improve their methods of agriculture. Yet these changes, though surely speeded by the Crusades, were under way before they began, partly because of earlier contact with Islam in Spain and Sicily.

Historians can only speculate about the political and religious impact of the crusading experience upon Western society. Some believe that the Crusades helped to weaken and impoverish the feudal nobility, and therefore benefited the monarchies. Certainly, kings could tax directly for the first time as a result of the need to raise money for expeditions to the Holy Land. The papacy was strengthened in its climb to leadership over all Western Christendom by sponsoring so vast an international movement. Yet this short-term gain may have been outweighed by a long-term loss. The religious motive was diluted more and more by worldly considerations. The spectacle of churchmen behaving like laymen, the misuse of the crusading indulgences for purely European papal purposes, and the cumulative effect of failure and incompetence contributed to a disillusionment with the original concept of the Crusades. Moreover, the discovery that all Muslims were not savage beasts, that profit lay in trade with them, and that coexistence was possible must have broadened the outlook of those who made the discovery and must have led them to question statements to the contrary, even when these statements came from Rome.

The fourteenth- and fifteenth-century Europeans who explored the coasts of Africa and Asia and crossed the Atlantic were the direct descendents of the Crusaders. It is perhaps as a medieval colonization movement, inspired, like all else in the Middle Ages, largely by the church, that the Crusades are best understood. The Westerners called the Crusader states in Syria *Outremer,* the "land beyond the sea." The failure of the Crusades meant that these eastern Mediterranean lands, once a significant part of Western history and self-awareness, were increasingly thrust away from the mainstream of European thought, until they were no longer seen as a natural part of the story of Western civilization.

II THE FALL OF BYZANTIUM, 1081-1453

During its last 372 years, the fate of the Byzantine Empire increasingly depended upon western Europe. The increasing economic power of the Italian merchants robbed the emperors of their independence on the sea. The flood of Crusaders first made the Byzantines uneasy and ultimately destroyed them. From 1204 to 1261, while the Byzantine government was in exile from its own captial, its chief aim was to drive out the hated Latins. But even after the Byzantine leaders had recaptured Constantinople in 1261, they still could not shake off the West. The economic and military dominance of Westerners was such that twice (1274 and 1439) the Byzantine emperors actually concluded a formal "union" with the Church of Rome, only to have it repudiated by Greek public opinion.

The Western attitude is revealed in the crisp words of the great fourteenth-century Italian poet Petrarch:

> *I do not know whether it is worse to have lost Jerusalem or to possess Byzantium. In the former Christ is not recognized; in the latter he is neglected while being worshiped. The Turks are enemies but the schismatic Greeks are worse than enemies. The Turks openly attack our Empire [the Empire of the West]; the Greeks say that the Roman Church is their mother, to whom they are devoted sons; but they do not receive the commands of the Roman pontiff. The Turks hate us because they fear us less. The Greeks both hate and fear us deep in their bellies.**

The Greek attitude is revealed by a fifteenth-century Greek churchman who said that he would rather see the turban of the Turk in Constantinople than the red hat of a cardinal. Those who shared this opinion got their wish in 1453. One of the great ironies of history is that the fate of Eastern Christendom was settled by Western Christendom, and that the Muslim rule that the Latin West had sought to roll back was vastly extended by Western Christians.

*H.A. Gibbons, *Foundation of the Ottoman Empire* (New York: Century, 1916), p. 133. Our translation.

Byzantine Decline, 1081-1204

The drama of Byzantium's last centuries was played out to the accompaniment of internal decay. "The powerful," in the person of Alexius I Comnenus, had captured the throne in 1081. Thereafter the accumulation of lands and tenants—who could serve as soldiers in the landlords' private armies—seems to have gone unchecked. With the weakening of the central government and the emergence of the local magnates, a form of feudalism became the characteristic way of life, as free peasants increasingly were forced by economic decline to sell their lands to the great landowners and sink into serfdom. Severe depopulation of the countryside followed, while in the cities imperial police officials or local garrison commanders acted as virtually independent rulers.

Economic ruin and social misery mounted steadily in the twelfth century. The tax collectors demanded food and lodging, presents and bribes. They would seize cattle on the pretext that they were needed for work on state projects, and then sell them back to the owners and keep the money for themselves. Irregular taxes for defense gave further chances to oppress the population. With the decline of the navy, piracy became a major problem. The coasts of Greece and the Aegean islands became nests of raiders, preying not only on merchant shipping but upon the population on shore. Bands of wandering monks, at odds with the secular clergy, swarmed everywhere; with no means of support they also often acted like bandits.

In 1171 Emperor Manuel I Comnenus made a desperate effort to rid the capital of Venetian merchants by suddenly arresting all he could lay his hands on in one day; more than ten thousand were imprisoned. But the economic hold of Venice was too strong, and the emperor was soon forced to restore its privileges, though its rulers remained angry with the Byzantines. In 1182 a passionate wave of anti-Latin feeling led to a savage massacre by the Constantinople mob of thousands of Westerners living in the capital. In 1185 the Normans of Sicily, pursuing their century-old wars against the empire, avenged the Latins by sacking Thessalonica, second city of the Byzantines. The last of the Comnenian dynasty, Andronicus I (r. 1182-1185), was tortured to death by the frantic citizens of Constantinople as the Norman forces approached the city walls. The weak dynasty of the Angeloi succeeded, and in 1204 Constantinople fell to the Latin West.

The Latin Empire, 1204-1261

After the sack of Constantinople, the Latins set about governing their conquest. They elected Baldwin of Flanders as the first Latin emperor (1204-1205), and the title continued in his family during the fifty-seven years of Latin occupation. The Venetians chose the first Latin patriarch and kept a monopoly on that rich office. The territories of the Empire were divided on paper, since most of them had not yet been conquered. The Venetians secured for themselves the long sea route from Venice by claiming the best coastal towns and strategic islands. A hybrid state was created in which the emperor's council consisted half of his own barons and half of Venetian merchants. Although in theory the Latin emperors were the successors of Constantine and Justinian, and although they wore the sacred purple boots, in practice they never commanded the loyalty of the Greek population and could not make important decisions without the counsel of their barons.

In Asia Minor Greek refugees from Constantinople, under Theodore Lascaris (d. 1222), son-in-law of the deposed Alexius III, set up a state in Nicaea and constantly threatened to recapture Constantinople. Outnumbered, incompetent as diplomats, slow to learn new military tactics, miserably poor after the treasures of Byzantium had been wasted, the Westerners could not maintain their Latin Empire, especially after its main sponsors ceased to assist it. When the popes became deeply involved in their quarrel with the Western emperor Frederick II, the Latin Empire was doomed. In 1261 the Greeks of Nicaea seized Constantinople and reestablished the Byzantine Empire.

Meanwhile, however, the Latins had fanned out from Constantinople. Greece was divided into a series of feudal principalities and French dukes of Athens worshiped in the Parthenon. The Peloponnesus became the principality of Achaia, with twelve feudal baronies and many minor lordships. Thessalonica became the capital of a new kingdom, which, however, fell to the Greeks in 1224. In the Aegean a Venetian adventurer established the duchy of Naxos, and other barons, mostly Italian, founded their own tiny lordships among the islands. The Venetians held Crete and other islands. These feudal states of Greece lasted for varying periods, but most of them were wiped out during the long process of Turkish conquest in the fifteenth century; none existed after the sixteenth.

Byzantium after 1261

When the Greeks of Nicaea under Michael VIII Palaeologus (1259-1282) recaptured Constantinople, they found it depopulated and badly damaged and the old territory of the Empire mostly in Latin hands. It was impossible for Michael and his successors to reconquer all of Greece or the islands, to push the frontier in Asia Minor east of the Seljuk capital of Konia, or to deal effectively with the Serbians in the Balkans. Therefore, Michael VIII's diplomacy was distinguished for its subtlety, even by Byzantine standards. He staved off the threat posed to his empire by Charles of Anjou, younger brother of St. Louis, to whom the popes had given the south Italian kingdom of the Normans and Hohenstaufens. Just as a new and powerful force seemed headed for Byzantium from Sicily in 1282, a revolt known as the Sicilian Vespers forestalled invasion. The French were massacred by the population, Charles of

A view of the Piazza San Marco in Venice, looking toward St. Mark's Cathedral. Much of the cathedral dates from the eleventh century and was intended to house the remains of the Apostle Mark. This painting by Canaletto (1697-1768) was completed about 1730.

Anjou's plans had to be abandoned, and the way was open for the conquest of Sicily by the Aragonese from Spain.

So incompetent and frivolous were most of the successors of Michael VIII, however, that they contributed materially to the decline of their own beleaguered Empire. Wars among rival claimants for the throne tore the Empire apart internally just when the preservation of unity in the face of external enemies seemed of the utmost necessity. The social unrest characteristic of the period before the Latin conquest reappeared in even sharper form, as Thessalonica was torn by civil strife. The value of the currency was allowed to decline. New theological controversy, which barely concealed political disagreements, divided the clergy, already tormented by the choice between uniting with Rome or, it appeared, perishing.

In a theocentric empire, religious controversy continued to be important. From about 1330 a new movement was reviving monasticism throughout the whole of eastern Europe, a revival associated with *Hesychasm* (Greek *hesychia*, quietude). In the tenth century monks of the Orthodox Eastern church had founded at Mount Athos, isolated in northern Greece, a remarkable monastery from which females, human or animal, were forbidden. Responsible directly to the patriarch of Constantinople, these monks preserved their independence of Byzantine emperors, Ottoman sultans, and modern Greek rulers alike, governing themselves and devoting their energies to self-sufficiency, the preservation of an exceptional library of Byzantine illuminated manuscripts and icons, and to scholarship. From Mount Athos many monks founded other movements. One of these, St. Gregory of Sinai, set up a monastery in southeastern Bulgaria that emphasized the Hesychast views: a mystical state of recollection and inner silence that would be achieved after man's victory over his passions. Only contemplative prayer could lead to God, though bodily exercises meant to aid spiritual concentration were also important. From Mount Athos and from Bulgaria cosmopolitan Hesychast monks covered all of eastern Europe.

In the early fourteenth century monastic churches within the walls of Constantinople were restored under the patronage of wealthy men. Byzantine churchmen took a renewed interest in scholarship, in the maintenance of libraries, and in the Greek heritage, preserving for future generations the knowledge of the past. Byzantine society recognized both the life of the world and the life of the spirit. Some monks emphasized Greek literature and philosophy, known as the "outer" wisdom, which prepared one for the truth; others, often illiterate, emphasized the "inner" knowledge that came from the "divine light" that illuminated the soul. This illumination was said to be the uncreated Light of the Transfiguration, the Metamorphosis. Humans were deified through this divine light, through a direct experience that involved the body and the soul. Obviously such teachings posed grave problems for the traditional views of the Orthodox church, and many commentators ridiculed the Hesychast movement. Nonetheless, the mystical movement, the growing and regenerated monasteries, and the heated discussion that arose initiated a renaissance of learning and spirituality in fourteenth-century Byzantium.

As the Turks pressed against Constantinople, pious Byzantines increasingly believed that their downfall at the hands of the infidels was the result of their sins; only repentance might save Byzantium from Turkish conquest. Long before the fall of Constantinople in 1453, the patriarchs had been preaching that the Second Coming of Christ was near. Science, superstition, and theology tended to merge; though able to foretell eclipses through scientific principles, astronomers nonetheless interpreted the eclipses as signs of future disasters. Much controversy took place over the approaching end to the world—over its nature, over who would be saved, over when it would occur. There came to be a reasonable consensus on the likely date of the event: 1492. Thus when the Turks poured into Constantinople, the patriarch could take comfort in the thought that the final victory would, in a few years, be his.

The Advance of the Ottoman Turks, 1354-1453

By the fourteenth century the Ottoman Turks had begun to press against the borders of Byzantine Asia Minor. Economic and political unrest led the discontented population of this region to prefer the Ottomans to the harsh and ineffectual Byzantine officials. Farmers willingly paid tribute to the Turks, and as time went on many of them were converted to Islam to avoid payment. They learned Turkish and taught the nomadic Turkish conquerors the arts of a settled agricultural life; the Turks, in turn, adopted Byzantine practices in government.

The *Anastasis,* a fourteenth-century fresco in the Church of the Chora, a restored monastic church in Istanbul. Christ is shown raising Adam and Eve from the dead. Below are the locks, bolts, and hinges of the smashed gates of Hell.

Having absorbed the Byzantine territories in Asia Minor, the Turks built a fleet and began raiding in the Sea of Marmora and the Aegean. In 1354 one of the rivals for the Byzantine throne allowed them to establish themselves in Europe. Soon they had occupied much of Thrace. In 1363 they moved their capital to the city of Adrianople, well beyond the European side of the Straits. Constantinople was now surrounded by Turkish territory and could be reached from the west only by sea. To survive it all, the later emperors had to make humiliating arrangements with the Turkish rulers—in some cases becoming their vassals.

Although the Byzantine Empire lasted to 1453, its survival was no longer in its own hands. The Turks chose to attack much of the Balkan region first, conquering the Bulgarian and Serbian states in the 1370s and 1380s; the final defeat of the Serbs occurred at the battle of Kossovo in 1389. A French and German "crusade" against the Turks on behalf of the Hungarians was wiped out at Nicopolis on the Danube in 1396.

But further Turkish conquests were delayed for half a century when a new wave of Mongols under Timur the Lame (celebrated in literature as Tamerlane, c 1336-1405) emerged from central Asia in 1402 and defeated the Ottoman armies at Ankara, the present-day capital of Turkey. Like most Mongol military efforts, this proved temporary, and the Ottoman armies and state recovered. In the 1420s and 1430s the Turks moved into Greece. The West, now thoroughly alarmed at the spread of Turkish power in Europe, tried to bolster the Byzantine defenses by proposing a union of the Eastern and Western churches in 1439 and by dispatching another "crusade," this time to Bulgaria in 1444. Both efforts proved futile.

The walls of Constantinople now stand in ruins. Originally begun in the fifth century, these fortifications were added to until the fifteenth century.

CONSTANTINOPLE FALLS TO THE TURKS

After seven weeks of siege, the Sultan's armies took up positions along the land walls of Constantinople, and after ten days of preparation began a direct assault against the walls on April 18. After the city fell on May 29, a Turkish chronicler, Ashikpashazade, described the events in a straightfoward manner:

For fifty days the battle went on by day and night. On the fifty-first day the Sultan ordered free plunder. They attacked. On the fifty-first day, a Tuesday, the fortress was captured. There was good booty and plunder. Gold and silver and jewels and fine stuffs were brought and stacked in the camp market. They began to sell them. They made the people of the city slaves and killed their emperor, and the *gazis* [frontier fighters] embraced their pretty girls. . . .

A century later, when the passage of time lessened the immediacy of the brutal events, a famous Ottoman historian, Sa'd ed-Din, described what had happened in more literary terms:

That wide region, that strong and lofty city . . . from being the nest of the owl of error, was turned into the capital of glory and honor. Through the noble efforts of the Muhammadan sultan, for the evil-voiced clash of the bells of the shameless misbelievers was substituted the Muslim call to prayer, the sweet five-times repeated chant of the Faith of glorious rites, and the ears of the people of the Holy War were filled with the melody of the call to prayer. The churches which were within the city were emptied of their vile idols, and cleansed from their filthy and idolatrous impurities; and by the defacement of their images, and the erection of the Islamic prayer niches and pulpits, many monasteries and chapels became the envy of the Gardens of Paradise. . . .

Both extracts are quoted in Bernard Lewis, *Istanbul and the Civilization of the Ottoman Empire* (Norman: University of Oklahoma Press, 1963), pp. 8-9.

With the accession of Muhammad II (also called Mehmed the Conqueror) to the Ottoman throne in 1451 (ruled to 1481), the doom of Constantinople was sealed. New Turkish castles on the Bosporus prevented ships from delivering supplies to the city. In 1453 strong forces of troops and artillery were drawn up in siege array, and the Turks even dragged a fleet of small boats uphill on runners and slid them down the other side into the Golden Horn itself. As final defeat grew more and more certain, the Greeks and Latins inside the city took communion together in the Hagia Sophia for the last time, and the last emperor, Constantine XI (ruled from 1448), died bravely defending the walls against the Turkish attack.

On May 29, 1453, with the walls breached and the emperor dead, the Turks took the city. Muhammad II gave thanks to Allah in Hagia Sophia and ground the altar of the sanctuary beneath his feet; thenceforth, it was to be a mosque. Shortly thereafter, he installed a new Greek patriarch and proclaimed himself protector of the Christian church. On the whole, during the centuries that followed the Orthodox church accepted the sultans as the secular successors to the Byzantine emperors.

III THE OTTOMAN EMPIRE, 1453-1699

Part of the Ottomans' inheritance no doubt came from their far-distant past in central Asia, when they had almost surely come under the influence of China and had lived like other nomads of the region. Their language, their capacity for war, and their rigid adherence to custom may go back to this early period. From the Persians and the Byzantines, the Turks seem to have derived their exaltation of the ruler, their tolerance of religious groups outside the state religion, and their practice of encouraging such groups to form independent, separate communities inside their state. Persian was always the literary language and the source of Turkish literature. From Islam, the Turks took the sacred law and their approach to legal problems, the Arabic alphabet in which they wrote their Turkish tongue, and the Arabic vocabulary of religious, philosophical, and other abstract terms. All the wellsprings of their inheritance—Asiatic, Persian, Byzantine, and Muslim—tended to make them highly traditional people.

The Ottoman System

Until the sixteenth century, the Ottomans showed tolerance to their infidel subjects, permitting Christians and Jews to serve the state and allowing the patriarch of Constantinople and the Grand Rabbi to act as leaders of their own religious communities, or *millets*. The religious leader not only represented his flock in its dealings with the Ottoman state but also had civil authority over them in civil, judicial, and financial matters that affected them alone. Non-Muslims paid a head tax and lived in comparative peace. Thus, the patriarch of Constantinople exercised far more power than he ever had under the Byzantines.

From 1280 to 1566 ten able sultans ruled the Ottomans. In theory, the sultan possessed the entire wealth of his dominions, and his object was to exploit it to the full. To do so he maintained an elaborate system of administrators whose lives and property belonged absolutely to him. All of them were considered his slaves (*kullar*) and at the same time members of the ruling class (Ottomans). To belong to the ruling class, a man had to be loyal to the sultan, a Muslim, and a true Ottoman; that is, he had to master the "Ottoman way" of speaking and behaving. Anyone who lacked one or more of these attributes was not a member of the ruling class but a subject (*raya*, literally "cattle"). Any raya could become an Ottoman by acquiring the necessary attributes. Beyond collecting, spending, and increasing the imperial revenues, and defending and adding to the imperial possessions, the Ottomans had no duties, and rayas could, in their own millets, take care of everything else.

The Ottoman ruling class included four subdivisions: the men of the emperor, the men of the sword, the men of the pen, and the sages. The first—the imperial class—comprised an inner service, embracing the sultan himself and his wives, sons, servants, private purse, and palace attendants, including the entire harem; plus an outer service, including the grand viziers and the other highest officers of the state, those who directed all the other branches of the service. A grand vizier presided over the council of state, and if the sultan trusted him might exercise great influence; but the sultan too, could depose or kill him. As a slave, the vizier was completely subject to the sultan's whim.

In the early days of the Ottoman Empire the Turkish princely families from Anatolia virtually monopolized both the inner and the outer services of this imperial class. But by the fourteenth century the sultans had learned to balance their influence by recruiting new talent from among their Christian subjects. Some entered the system as prisoners of war; some the sultan bought or received as presents. But most he obtained through the regular levying of a tribute of male children between the ages of ten and twenty that took place every four years. The recruits had to accept Islam, and so these recruits, all originally Christian, competed with the older Turkish artistocratic families for the honor of staffing the imperial class.

The men of the sword included all those connected with the Ottoman armies. Besides the usual irregular troops and garrison forces, these were the cavalrymen who predominated in early Ottoman history. They received fiefs of land in exchange for service and could administer these fiefs as they wished, collecting taxes

Sultan Muhammad II of Turkey, painted by Gentile Bellini (1429-1507). Muhammad ruled from 1451 to 1481; he is seen here shortly before his death. Most famous for painting Venetian ceremonial occasions with exceptional detail, Bellini lived in Constantinople from 1476 until 1481.

from their tenants and keeping order and justice among them. The infantrymen, at first far less important, received fixed salaries from the treasury. But with the introduction of gunpowder and the development of artillery and rifles, the Ottomans founded a special new corps to use these weapons, the *janissaries*. Most of the janissaries came from the recruits who were not selected for training for the imperial class. The janissaries lived in special barracks in the capital and enjoyed special privileges. They were both a source of strength and a constant potential danger to the state.

The men of the pen performed the other duties of government, striving to see that all land was tilled and that all trade was carried on as profitably as possible, so that the sultan might obtain his share in taxes. Once the money came in, these officials spent it on the necessary expenses of state, including salaries for troops and other employees. To keep an official honest and zealous, the Ottoman system often rewarded him by giving him in place of a salary a portion of the sultan's property as a kind of fief to exploit for himself. In the country every farm and village, in town every business and trade, in government every job thus became a kind of fief. As the Ottoman system declined in the seventeenth and eighteenth centuries, the transformation of these fiefs of land or money into private possessions without obligations signaled the loss by the sultan's administration of its former power to extract wealth from all its resources.

The sages (*ulema*) included all those connected with religion: the judges who applied Muslim law in the courts, the teachers in the schools, and the scholars of the Koran and the holy law (*Shariya*), the *muftis*. The muftis, or jurists, answered questions that arose from lawsuits and that were submitted to them by the judges. They applied the sacred law of Islam and usually gave short replies without explanation. The Grand Mufti in Istanbul, the former Constantinople, whom the sultan himself consulted, was known as *Sheikh-ul-Islam*, The ancient or elder of Islam, and outranked everyone except the grand vizier. Since he could speak the final word on the sacred law, he exercised a kind of check on the absolute power of the sultan himself. He alone could proclaim the beginning of war or denounce a sultan for transgressing the sacred law. The opinions of the muftis were collected as a body of interpretative law, lying between the changeless, age-old sacred law of Islam and the current enactments of the sultans. The general acceptance by all Muslims of the supremacy of the sacred law and the reluctance of the muftis to elaborate upon change were two of the factors that accounted for the failure of the Ottoman system to develop to meet the needs of the times. There were no "reformations" in Turkish history until the twentieth century.

Ottoman Expansion and Retraction to 1699

By the end of the 1460s most of the Balkan peninsula was under Turkish rule. Thus the core of the new Ottoman state was Asia Minor and the Balkans—the same area around which the Byzantine Empire had been built. From this core before the death of Muhammad II in 1481 the Turks expanded across the Danube into modern Romania and seized the Genoese outposts in the Crimea. They also fought the Venetians and landed forces in Italy. The limits of their expansion were marked by the great Hungarian fortress of Belgrade, key to a farther advance into central Europe, and the island fortress of Rhodes in the Aegean, stronghold of the Hospitalers and key to a farther naval advance westward.

Sultan Selim I, the Grim (1512-1520), nearly doubled the territories of the Empire in Asia at the expense of the Persians and in Africa at the expense of Egypt, which was annexed in 1517 and the rule of the Mamluks ended. From them the sultan inherited the duty of protecting the Muslim holy cities of Mecca and Medina. He also assumed the title of caliph, with the sacred insignia of office. It is doubtful whether this alone greatly enhanced his prestige, since the title had for centuries been much abused. At one moment in his reign, Selim contemplated

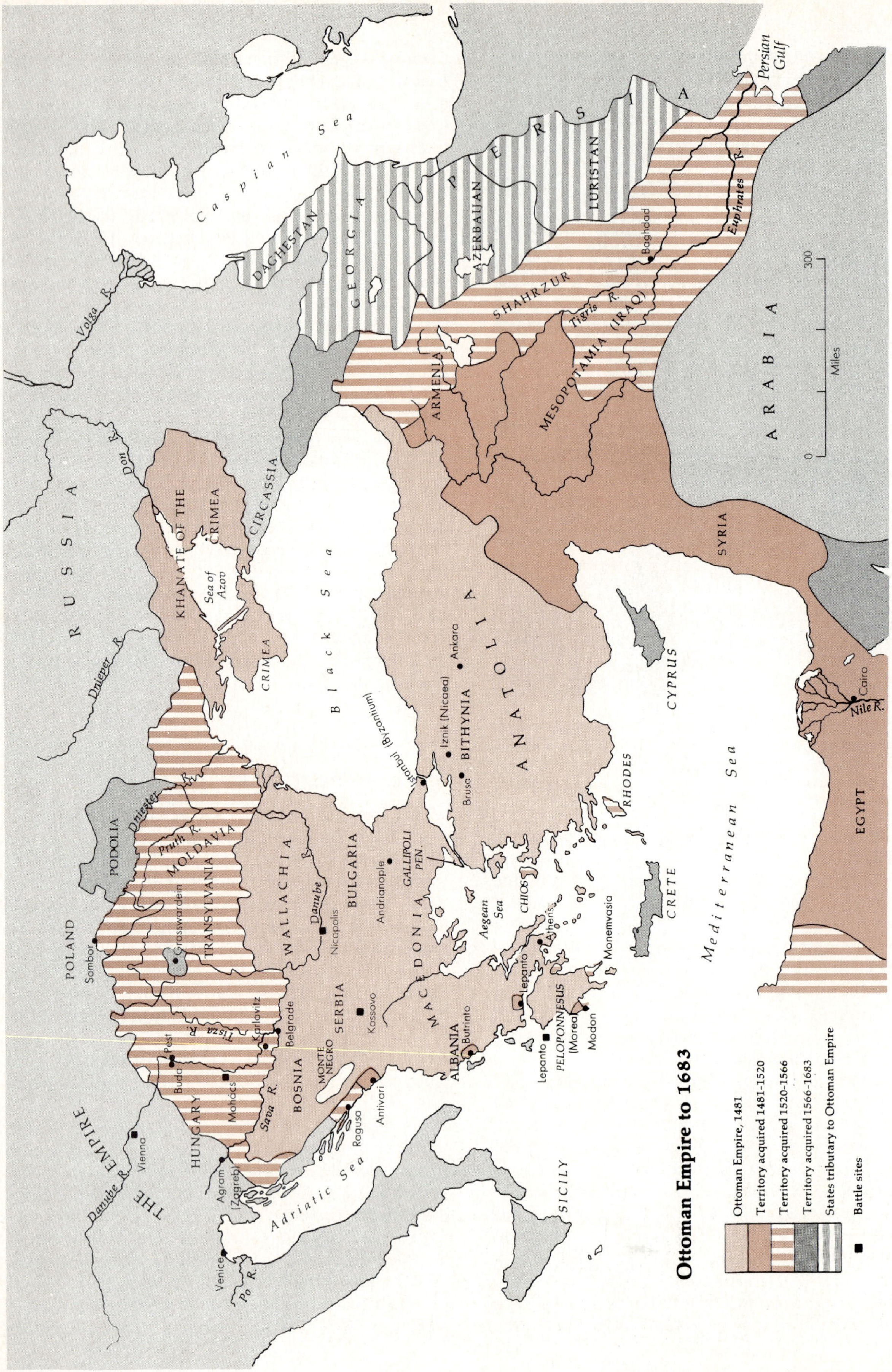

Ottoman Empire to 1683

a general massacre of all his Christian subjects; only the refusal of the Sheikh-ul-Islam to grant consent saved the Christians. This episode vividly illustrates the insecurity of Christian life under the Turks. It also demonstrates that the character of the Ottoman state was substantially altered by the acquisition of so much territory. It was now no longer necessary to appease the Christians by generous treatment because most of the population was Muslim. Moreover, most of the newly acquired Muslims were Arabs, more intent upon enforcing widespread conversion to Islam than the Ottoman Turks had hitherto been.

Suleiman I, the Magnificent (1520-1566), resumed the advance into Europe. The Ottoman Empire thus became deeply involved in western European affairs. It participated in the wars between the Hapsburgs and France and affected the Protestant Reformation in Germany by the threat of military invasion from the southeast. The newly consolidated national monarchies of the West had begun to be more of a danger to the Turks than the Venetians and Hungarians were.

Suleiman took Belgrade in 1521 and Rhodes in 1522, thus removing the two chief obstacles to westward advance. In 1526 at Mohács in Hungary, he defeated the Christian armies, and the Turks entered Buda, the Hungarian capital on the middle Danube. In September 1529 Suleiman besieged Vienna but had to abandon the siege after two weeks. In the years that followed, Suleiman acquired Algeria, which remained an Ottoman vassal state in the western Mediterranean until the nineteenth century. In Asia he defeated the Persians, annexed modern Iraq, including Baghdad, and secured an outlet on the Persian Gulf from which he fought naval wars against the Portuguese in the gulf and on the Indian Ocean.

In 1536 a formal treaty was concluded between France and the Ottoman Empire, the first of several so-called "capitulations." It permitted the French to buy and sell throughout the Turkish dominions on the same basis as any Turk. In Turkish territory, the French were to enjoy complete religious liberty and were also granted a protectorate over the Holy Places, the old aim of the Crusades. This was a great advance in prestige for the Roman Catholic church.

These "capitulations" contributed to the wealth and prestige of France and gave it a better position in the Ottoman Empire than that of any other European power. They also brought the Turks into the diplomatic world of western Europe. And they are parallel to the Byzantine trade treaties with Venice and Genoa, which granted them virtually the same privileges beginning at the end of the eleventh century. In this respect, the Ottoman sultans were behaving as the successors of the Byzantine emperors.

The sixteenth-century mosque of the emperor Suleiman the Magnificent, in Istanbul.

SULEIMAN THE MAGNIFICENT REFLECTS ON HIS POWER

By 1538, when Suleiman ordered the following inscription placed on a fort as a reminder of his power, the Ottomans figured deeply in all European diplomatic and military calculations:

I am God's slave and sultan of this world. By the grace of God I am head of Muhammad's community. God's might and Muhammad's miracles are my companions. I am Süleymân, in whose name the *hutbe sermon* is read in Mecca and Medina. In Baghdad I am the shah, in Byzantine realms the Caesar, and in Egypt the sultan; who sends his fleets to the seas of Europe, the Maghrib and India. I am the sultan who took the crown and throne of Hungary and granted them to a humble slave. The voivoda [a local ruler in Transylvania] Petru raised his head in revolt, but my horse's hoofs ground him into the dust, and I conquered the land of Moldavia.

Michail Guboglu, *Paleografia si diplomatica Turco-Osmana* (Bucarest: Editura Academici Republicii Populaire Romaine, 1958), as quoted in Halil Inalcik, *The Ottoman Empire: The Classical Age 1300-1600*, trans. Norman Itzkowitz and Colin Imber (New York: Praeger, 1973), p. 41.

After Suleiman the Ottoman system, already manifesting signs of weakness, deteriorated despite occasional successes. The Ottoman capture of Cyprus was preceded by the formation of a Western Holy League headed by the pope against the Turks, an enterprise as near to a crusade as the sixteenth century produced. In 1571 the League won a great naval battle (Lepanto) off the Greek coast, destroying the Ottoman fleet. However, the Spanish and Venetians failed to follow up the victory, and the Turks rebuilt their fleet.

In 1606 the Turks signed a peace treaty with the Hapsburgs. Previously all treaties with Western states had been cast in the form of a truce granted as a divine favor from the sultan to a lesser potentate and had required the other party to pay tribute to the sultan. This time the Turks had to negotiate as equals; they gave the Hapsburg emperor his proper title and were unable to demand tribute. Had western Europe not been preoccupied by the Thirty Years' War, the Ottoman Empire might have suffered even more severely in the first half of the seventeenth century than it did. As it was, internal anarchy disturbed the state; janissaries rebelled, troops rioted, and several sultans were deposed within a few years. The Persians recaptured Baghdad, and rebellion raged in the provinces.

Yet a firm sultan, Murad IV (1623-1640), temporarily restored order through brutal means. He reduced the janissaries, initiated a new military system, reorganized military fiefs, and abolished tribute in Christian children. Despite renewed revolts after Murad's death, the revival continued under a family of viziers, the Köprülü of Albania. The first Köprülü executed thirty-six thousand people in five years (1656-1661), hanged the Greek patriarch for predicting in a private letter that Christianity would defeat Islam, rebuilt the army and navy, and suppressed revolt. Between 1661 and 1676 the second Köprülü took Crete from Venice and temporarily won large areas of the Ukraine from the Russians and Poles. In 1683 the Turks again penetrated the heart of Europe and besieged Vienna. All Europe anxiously awaited the outcome. But for the second time in two centuries the Turkish wave was broken, this time by a German and Polish army, and Europe began a great counteroffensive. The Turks remained fearsome warriors, but the Ottoman Empire was decaying from the center, for the Köprülü had been unable to effect the kinds of domestic reforms essential to future stability.

The Hapsburgs drove the Turks out of Hungary, the Venetians seized the Peloponnesus, and the Russians appeared for the first time since the Tatar invasion on the shores of the Sea of Azov, which opens into the Black Sea. In 1699, after an international congress at Karlowitz on the Danube, most of the gains of the European counteroffensive were recognized by the Turks. The extensive territorial losses suffered by the Turks, the strengthening of the Hapsburgs to the east, and the appearance of Russia as an important enemy of the Turks made this settlement a landmark. The western European powers could stop worrying about the Ottoman menace, which had preoccupied them since the fourteenth century, and which had replaced the Crusades as a great cause for which Christendom could occasionally be united. Thereafter, Turkey was a power in decline over whose possible disintegration and division the states of Europe began to squabble and negotiate. With Karlowitz, what is called the "Eastern question" in European diplomacy had begun.

IV RUSSIA FROM THE THIRTEENTH TO THE END OF THE SEVENTEENTH CENTURY

Western and Northern Lands, 1386-1478

The collapse of Kievan Russia about the year 1200 led to the formation of a series of virtually independent petty

Medieval and Early Modern Russia

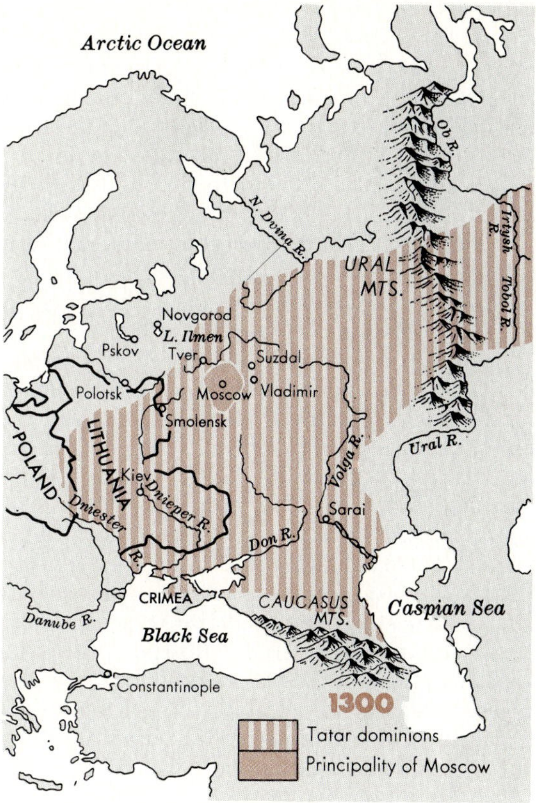

principalities. These states were too weak and disunited to resist the constant pressure from Poland and Lithuania. By the early fourteenth century, the grand duke of Lithuania, with his capital at Vilna, ruled nominally over most of western Russia. The Lithuanians, still mostly pagan, gradually took over the language and manners of their Russian vassals. But in 1386 the grand duke married the heiress to the Polish throne and became king of Poland. As a result, the Polish Roman Catholic church and the Polish nobility came to the fore in Lithuania.

Had it not been for the antagonism between Orthodox Russians and Catholic Poles and for the conflicting interests of the nobles of different religions and languages, the original Lithuanian-Russian combination might have proved to be the center around which Russia could reunite. Yet even before the connection with Poland, this region had become so feudal that its potential ability to unify Russia is doubtful. Even under the grand duke of Lithuania, most of the lands nominally affiliated with his duchy were ruled without interference by local nobles who were bound to him only by an oath of fealty and by their obligations to render military service. An assembly of nobles also limited the political authority of the grand duke. As in the West, the economic basis of society in western Russia was manorial, and restrictions were placed on the freedoms of the peasant farmer quite early.

In the north the town commonwealth of Novgorod came to rule over the vast, empty, infertile regions that were explored by armed merchants and pioneers in search of furs and other products. Even before the collapse of Kiev there grew up in Novgorod a tradition of municipal independence. The town council, or *veche*, became very strong. The lifeblood of the city was its trade with the Germans, who had their own quarter in Novgorod, which they maintained for centuries despite constant friction with the Russians.

Internally, Novgorod had a rigid class system. The representatives of the richer merchants came to control the veche, and a few powerful families concentrated the city's wealth in their hands and vied for political power. The gap between rich and poor grew wide. A man who could not pay his debts would be made a slave, and slaves frequently revolted and became brigands. Because the surrounding countryside had little good soil, the city depended upon the region to the southeast, around Moscow, for its grain. When in the fifteenth century the Polish-Lithuanian state and the state of Moscow were competing, the struggle inside Novgorod was reflected in the allegiances of the population. The upper classes favored the Poles and Lithuanians; the lower favored Moscow. In 1478 the ruler of Moscow conquered Novgorod and deported the upper classes to central Russia. While Novgorod may be compared with Venice and other commercial patrician oligarchies in the West, its inability to solve internal problems deprived it of any chance to unify Russia.

The Tatars, 1223-1400

By the early thirteenth century Genghis Khan had consolidated under his command the Mongolian nomads of central Asia—Huns, Avars, and Polovtsky—who had repeatedly erupted into Europe. Having conquered northern China and Asia from Manchuria to the Caspian Sea, Genghis Khan led his Tatars across the Caucasus Mountains and into the steppes of southern Russia, defeating Russians and Polovtsky together near the Sea of Azov in 1223. He then retreated to Asia, where he died in 1227. Batu Khan (d. 1255) brought the Tatars back again in the 1230s, sacked Moscow in 1237 and Kiev in 1240, and moved into the western Russian regions and into Poland, Hungary, and Bohemia.

Tatar success seems to have been due largely to excellent military organization: unified command, general staff, clever intelligence service, and deceptive battle tactics. Though Batu defeated the Poles and the Germans in 1241, political affairs in Asia drew him eastward, and the Tatars never again appeared so far to the west. Batu retreated across Europe, and at Sarai, near the great bend of the Volga, he founded the capital of a new state—the Golden Horde—which accepted the overlordship of the far-off central government of the Mongols in Peking.

Other Mongol leaders ended the Abbasid caliphate in 1258 and were defeated by the Mamluks in 1260. The enmity between Mongols and Muslims led the popes, St. Louis, and other leaders of western Europe to hope that they could convert the Mongol rulers to Christianity and ally with them against the Muslims. Several embassies were sent to Mongolia and China during the thirteenth and fourteenth centuries with this end in view. Nothing came of it except a great increase in geographical knowledge derived from the accounts of the European ambassadors, who were usually Franciscans or Dominicans.

The most lasting effect on Europe of the Tatar invasions was in Russia. Here the Tatars' main purpose was the efficient collection of tribute. Although they ravaged Russia while they were conquering it, after the conquest they shifted to a policy of exploitation. They took a survey of available resources and assessed tribute at the limit of what the traffic would bear. They did not disturb economic life as long as their authority was recognized. They did draft Russian recruits for their armies, but they made the local Russian princes responsible for the delivery of manpower and money, and they stayed out of Russian territory except to take censuses, survey property, and punish rebels. Each tributary Russian prince traveled to Sarai or to China on his election to do homage. Although no part of Russia was exempt from Tatar attacks during the conquest, the expensive burden of tribute and the humiliating sense of subservience fell most heavily upon Moscow.

Toward the end of the fourteenth century, as the Mongol Empire itself grew feebler, the Russians grew bolder. The first Russian victories over the Tatars, scored by a prince of Moscow in 1378 and 1380, were fiercely avenged. Yet they showed that the Tatars could be defeated. The Golden Horde did not disintegrate until the early fifteenth century, and even then the Tatars did not disappear from Russian life. Three separate khanates, or Tatar states, were formed from the debris of the Golden Horde: one at Kazan on the middle Volga, where it blocked the full use of the river for another century and a half to Russian trade; one at Astrakhan at the mouth of the Volga on the Caspian; and one in the Crimea, which became a vassal of the Ottoman sultan.

Historians have long debated the effect upon Russia of the "Tatar yoke." Some have argued that the experience was beneficial because it eventually enabled the centralizing influence of the prince of Moscow, successor of the Tatar khan, to prevail, and further, that trade with Asia helped Russia. They minimize the devastation wrought by the Tatar forces and emphasize that, except for an occasional punitive expedition, the Russian people never saw a Tatar after the conquest was over. Yet the Tatar conquest also had negative effects on Russia. As the great nineteenth-century Russian poet Alexander Pushkin remarked, the Tatars brought to the Russians "neither algebra nor Aristotle." By this he meant to contrast the cultural impact of the Tatars on Russia with that of the Muslims on, let us say, Spain.

There was no inherent reason why Russia in the late twelfth century should not have developed as a European state with characteristics of its own. After two centuries of Tatar domination, however, it had not advanced, as measured against the material progress of western Europe. Contemporaries felt that the Tatar yoke was a calamity, and historians have yet to prove otherwise. When the Tatar power was finally shattered in the fifteenth century, Russian civilization was far less complex than that of the West. To the retarding effect of Byzantine Christianity, there had been added the tremendous handicap of two centuries of cultural stagnation.

The Development of the Muscovite State

During these two centuries, the princes of Moscow assumed leadership. Moscow lay near the great watershed from which the Russian rivers, always the great routes for trade, flow north into the Baltic or south into the Black Sea. It was richer than the north, could provide enough food for its people, and had flourishing forest industries. Thus, when the Tatar grip relaxed and trade could begin again, Moscow was advantageously located. Moreover, Moscow was blessed with a line of remarkably able princes—shrewd administrators, anxious to increase their holdings and to consolidate their own authority within the steadily expanding borders of their principality. They married into powerful families, acquired land by purchase and by foreclosing mortgages, and inherited it through wills. Moreover, unlike the princes of Kiev, they did not divide their domain among their sons in each generation.

They also developed useful relations with their Tatar overlords. It was the princes of Moscow whom the Tatars chose to collect the tribute from other neighboring princes and deliver it to Sarai. Soon the princes could point to their success in excluding the Tatar agents from Russia, and could attract settlers to their lands. They scored the first victories over the Tatars and could truthfully claim to be the champions of Russia.

Finally, and very possibly most important, the princes of Moscow secured the support of the Russian church. In the early fourteenth century the metropolitan archbishop made Moscow the ecclesiastical capital of Russia. When the effective line of Muscovite princes temporarily faltered, it was the metropolitan who administered the principality loyally and effectively until the ruling house recovered. Thus the Russian church cast its lot with Moscow.

By the middle of the fifteenth century, Moscow was a self-conscious Russian national state that could undertake successful wars against both the Polish-Lithuanian kingdom and the Tatars. Ivan III (r. 1462-1505) put himself forward as the heir to the princes of Kiev and declared that he intended to regain the ancient Russian lands that had been lost to Poles and Tatars—a national appeal, although a purely dynastic one. Many nobles living in the western lands came over to him with their estates and renounced their loyalties to the Lithuanian-Polish state. In 1492 the prince of Lithuania was forced to recognize Ivan III as sovereign of "all the Russias." This new national appeal was fortified by a religious appeal as well, for Ivan was also the champion of Orthodoxy against the Catholic Poles and the now Muslimized Tatars.

In 1472 Ivan had married Zoe, niece of the last Byzantine emperor, Constantine XI, who had been killed fighting against the Turks in Constantinople in 1453. Ivan adopted the Byzantine title of Autocrat, used the Byzantine double eagle as his seal, and began to behave like a Byzantine emperor. He sometimes used the title *Czar* (Caesar) and no longer consulted his nobles, reaching decisions in solitude. Italian architects built him an enormous palace, the Kremlin (or fortress), a building set apart like the palace at Byzantium. When the Holy Roman emperor in the 1480s decided to make an alliance with Ivan III and to arrange for a dynastic marriage, Ivan responded that he already had unlimited power derived directly from God—a claim that a Byzantine emperor might have made.

When a rebellious noble fled Russia under the reign of Czar Ivan IV, the Terrible (1533-1584), he wrote the czar from abroad, denouncing him for failing to consult his nobles on important questions, as had been the custom in the days of Kievan Russia. Ivan replied that he was free to bestow favors on his slaves or inflict punishment on them as he chose; the czar thought of Russian nobles as his slaves. The first to formally take the title of czar, Ivan broke the power of the Tatars, conquered Kazan, Astrakhan, and Siberia, and systematically and brutally suppressed the most powerful nobles to establish a thoroughly autocratic government.

Members of the Muscovite cavalry in the early sixteenth century. The cavalry formed the bulk of the army, but it performed badly in warfare and was generally ill-equipped.

Part of the explanation for this rapid growth of autocratic theory is that Russia lived in a constant state of war or preparation for war; a national emergency prolonged over centuries may lead to a dictatorship. Perhaps more significant is that in Moscow, feudalism had not developed a united class of self-conscious nobles who would fight against the rising monarchy for their privileges, as it had in the West. Instead of uniting against the pretensions of the monarch, the Muscovite nobility produced various factions with which the monarch could deal individually.

But most important of all was the ideology supplied by the church and taken over largely from Byzantium. In the West, the church itself was a part of feudal society and jealous of its prerogatives. In Russia it became the ally of the monarchy and something like a department of state. Russian churchmen were entirely familiar with Rome's claim to world empire and to Constantinople's centuries-long position as "new Rome." They knew many written Byzantine claims to world domination, and they were conscious of many historical legends that could be useful to them. With the fall of Constantinople (Czargrad) to the Turks, they elaborated a theory that

Moscow was the successor to the two former world capitals:

> *The Church of Old Rome fell because of its heresy; the gates of the Second Rome, Constantinople, have been hewn down by the axes of the infidel Turks; but the Church of Moscow, the Church of the New Rome, shines brighter than the Sun in the whole Universe. . . . Two Romes have fallen, but the Third stands fast; a fourth there cannot be.**

Russian churchmen spread the story that Rurik, the first political organizer of Russia, was descended from the brother of Augustus. They claimed that the Russian czars had inherited certain insignia and regalia not only from the Byzantines but even from the Babylonians. All the czars down to the last, Nicholas II (r. 1894-1917), were crowned with a cap and clothed with a jacket that were of Byzantine manufacture, though of uncertain history. Thus the church supplied the state with justification for its acts. Imperial absolutism became one of the chief political features of modern Russia.

Nobles and Serfs

Between the accessions of Ivan III in 1462 and Peter the Great in 1689, the autocracy overcame the opposition of the old nobility. This was done in part by virtually creating a new class of military-service gentry who owed everything to the czar. Their estates, at first granted only for life in exchange for service, eventually became hereditary, like the western European fief. The estates of the old nobility, which had always been hereditary but for which they had owed no service, became service estates, and thus like fiefs too. By the end of the period the two types of nobles and the two types of estates had by a gradual process become almost identical: the hereditary nobles often owed service; the military-service nobles often had hereditary land. Under Peter the Great (1689-1725) this process was to be completed, and state service was to become universal. A central bureau in Moscow kept a census of the service gentry and of their obligations in time of war.

This important social process was accompanied by the growth of serfdom. Economic factors and political unrest in Russia had forced more and more peasants to ask large landowners for protection. The peasants would accept contracts that required payment of rent in produce and performance of service on the landlord's own land, in return for a money loan that had to be repaid over a period of years with interest or with extra services. By the early seventeenth century the peasant could not leave his plot until he paid off his debt; but since the debt was often too great for him to repay, he could in fact never leave.

The process was speeded up when the czars gave estates to the new military-service gentry. An estate was not much good unless there was farm labor to work it. In the bitter agrarian and political crises of the sixteenth and seventeenth centuries, the government helped the service gentry to keep their farmers where they were. And since the peasants paid most of the taxes, it was easier for the government to collect its own revenues if it kept the peasants where they were. Gradually it was made harder for a tenant to leave his landlord, until by 1649 the avenues of escape were closed, and the serf was fixed to the soil. The landlord administered justice and had police rights on the estate; he collected the serfs' taxes; he could sell, exchange, or give away his serfs. The status of serf became hereditary; children of serfs were enrolled on the estate's census books as serfs like their fathers.

Russian serfs were not emancipated until 1861. Together with absolute autocracy, the institution of serfdom is the most dramatic feature of Russian society. It affected every Russian for the centuries it existed. Russian serfdom became a fixed custom much later in time than did western European serfdom; it was extended most widely during the eighteenth century, when the serfs in western Europe had long been on their way to complete liberation. Thus once again Russia went through the same processes as the West, but with greater intensity and at a later time.

The Reign of Ivan the Terrible, 1533-1584

Many of the disorders that characterized Russian history in the sixteenth and seventeenth centuries began in the long reign of Ivan IV, the Terrible. Pathologically unbalanced, Ivan succeeded to the throne as a small child. When strong enough in 1547 to throw off the tutelage of the nobles, he embarked upon a period of sound government and institutional reform. He regulated the greediness of the imperial administrators in the provinces, who had oppressed the population. He convoked the first *zemski sobor* (land assembly), a consultative body consisting of nobles, clerics, and representatives from the towns, to assist with imperial business, particularly with important questions of war and peace. Though comparable in social composition to the various assemblies of medieval western Europe, the zemski sobor under Ivan appears to have met only once and cannot be regarded as a parliamentary body.

When Ivan fell ill in 1553, the nobles refused to take an oath of allegiance to his son. This refusal apparently reawakened his savagery. Upon his recovery he created a new institution—the *oprichnina*, or "separate realm"—to belong to him personally, while the rest of Russia continued to be administered as before. The men Ivan appointed to run the oprichnina (called *oprichniks*), dressed grimly in black and riding black horses, bore on their saddlebows a dog's head (for vigilance) and a broom (symbolizing a clean sweep). They were the forerunners of the secret police forces that have long

*Quoted in T.A. Archer and C.L. Kingsford, *The Crusades* (London: T.F. Unwin, 1919) p. 220.

A contemporary icon portrait of Ivan the Terrible dating from 1500-1550. It now hangs in the National Museum of Denmark, in Copenhagen.

characterized Russian society. They waged a fierce, relentless war on the nobles, confiscating their estates, exiling them, killing them. The oprichniks took over the estates of the men they were destroying. By Ivan's death, many of the oprichniks themselves had been murdered at his orders, and Russian administration was close to chaos. Yet Ivan had extended Russian authority far to the east against the Kazan and Astrakhan Tatars, thus for the first time opening the whole Volga waterway to Russian commerce.

The Time of Troubles, 1584-1613

Though the territory was wide and the imperial rule absolute, ignorance, illiteracy, and inefficiency weakened Russian society. The few foreigners who knew the Russia of Ivan could foresee chaos ahead. Though the old nobility had been weakened, the new gentry had as yet no sense of corporate entity and therefore was not firmly in control of the machinery of government. Ivan's son and heir, Fëdor (1584-1598), was an imbecile, and with his death, the Moscow dynasty, descended from the rulers of Kiev, died out. Cliques of rival nobles intrigued for power. Fëdor's brother-in-law, Boris Godunov (1598-1605), emerged as the dominant figure in the state.

Though Boris Godunov was probably a man of talent, he could not overcome his handicaps: Ivan's legacy of disorder, the intrigues of the nobility, and a famine and plague that began in 1601. Bandits roamed the countryside, and when in 1603 a pretender arose under the protection of the king of Poland and falsely declared that he was a son of Ivan the Terrible (thus he is known as "the false Dmitri"), he won the support of many of the discontented. Russia was launched on the decade known as the "Time of Troubles" (1603-1613).

After Godunov's death, the pretender ruled briefly as czar. But within a year he was murdered and was succeeded by a representative of the ancient aristocracy. New pretenders arose; the mobs of peasants and bandits were rallied once again; civil war continued, as Poles and Swedes intervened; and Polish forces took Moscow. It soon appeared that the king of Poland intended to reign in Russia himself. It was this specter of foreign and Catholic dominaton that aroused the national sentiments of the Russians. In answer to a summons from the patriarch, there assembled a kind of national militia, drawn largely from prosperous free farmers of the middle Volga region. They were organized by a butcher named Kuzma Minin and led by a nobleman named Dmitri Pozharski, the national heroes of the Time of Troubles. Under their command the militia won the support of other rebellious elements and drove the Poles from Moscow in 1612-1613.

The Role of the Zemski Sobor, 1613-1653

A zemski sobor now elected as czar Michael Romanov, grand-nephew of Ivan IV. The Romanov dynasty reigned from the election of Michael in 1613 to the Russian Revolution of 1917. Michael succeeded with no limitations placed upon his power by the zemski sobor or by any other body; he was an elected autocrat. For the first ten years of his reign, the zemski sobor stayed in continual session. Since it had picked the new czar in the midst of a crisis, it had indeed performed a constitutional function. It even included some representatives of the free peasantry. It assisted the uncertain new dynasty to get under way by endorsing the policies of the czar and his advisers, thus lending them the semblance of popular support. But after 1623 the zemski sobor was summoned only to help declare war or make peace, to approve new taxation, and to sanction important new legislation. It endorsed the accession of Michael's son Alexis (r. 1645-1676), and in 1649 confirmed the issuance of a new law code. After 1653 Alexis did not summon it again, nor did his son and successor, Fëdor III (r. 1676-1682).

No law abolished the zemski sobor and none had created it. The dynasty was entrenched and no longer needed it. Autocratic czardom was taken for granted. No czar needed to consult with any of his subjects unless he wanted to. No subject had the right to insist on being consulted, though all subjects had the duty to give advice when asked. The Romanovs no longer felt the need to consult anyone except their court favorites.

The Role of the Church

The church remained the partner of the autocracy. The czar controlled the election of the patriarch of Moscow, a rank to which the archbishop was elevated in 1589. In the seventeenth century there were two striking instances when a patriarch actually shared power with the czar. In 1619 the father of Czar Michael Romanov, Filaret, who had become a monk, became patriarch and was granted the additional title of "Great Sovereign." He assisted his son in all the affairs of state. In the next generation Czar Alexis appointed a cleric named Nikon to the patriarchal throne and gave him the same title and duties. Nikon proved so arrogant that he aroused protests from clergy as well as laity, especially when he revised Russian church ritual to bring it into line with Greek practice. (Those who thereupon seceded from the Russian church, taking the name of Old Believers, were condemned as schismatics.)

Nikon also argued that the authority of the patriarch in spiritual affairs exceeded that of the czar and that, since the spiritual realm was superior to the temporal, the patriarch was actually superior to the czar. This was a claim parallel to that made regularly in the West by the more powerful popes but seldom made in Byzantium or in Russia. In 1666 a church council deposed Nikon, who died a mere monk. These two experiments with two-man government (*dyarchy*, it was called, in contrast with monarchy) were never repeated. Thereafter, the church accepted that it depended upon the state. Peter the Great was to abolish the patriarchate itself, largely because he did not wish Nikon's claims ever to be repeated.

The church, almost alone, inspired the literature and

St. Basil's Cathedral in Red Square, Moscow, built 1555-1560.

art of the Muscovite period. History was written by monks in the form of chronicles. Travel literature took the form of accounts of pilgrimages to the Holy Land. Theological tracts attacked the Catholics and later also the Protestants, whose doctrines were known in the western regions. This literature is limited, and it was still dominated by the church several centuries after the West had begun to produce secular writing. Almost all of it was written in Old Church Slavonic, the language of the liturgy and not the language of everyday speech. Though stately and impressive, Old Church Slavonic was not an appropriate vehicle for innovation. There was almost no secular learning, no science, no flowering of vernacular literature, no philosophical debate, despite the presence of immensely rich monasteries that owned perhaps a third of the cultivatable land.

The Expansion of Russia, to 1682

The sixteenth and seventeenth centuries saw tremendous physical expansion of the Russian domain. Russian pioneers, in search of furs to sell and new land to settle, led the way, and the government followed. Frontiersmen in Russia were known as Cossacks (*kazakh* is a Tatar word meaning "free adventurer")—Russians living on the frontiers organizing themselves for self-defense against the Tatars. Cossack communities gradually became more settled, and two Cossack republics, one on the Dnieper River, the other on the Don, were set up. These republics had a kind of primitive democracy relatively independent of Moscow. As time passed, more Cossack groups formed along the Volga River, in the Ural Mountains and elsewhere.

The frontier movement took the Russians eastward into the Urals and on across Siberia—one of the most dramatic chapters in the expansion of Europe. Far more slowly, because of Tatar, Turkish, and Polish opposition, the Russians also moved southeast toward the Caucasus and south toward the Black Sea. Repeated wars were fought with Poland over the Ukraine. Sometimes the Cossacks favored the Poles and sometimes the Russians. By 1682 the Poles were weakening and were soon to yield. On the European frontiers it was the Swedes, still controlling the Baltic coast, against whom Russia's future wars would be fought. There were also constant struggles with the Tatars of the Crimea. The Ottoman Turks, overlords of the Tatars, held the key fort of Azov and controlled the Black Sea. But in 1681 they abandoned most of their holdings in the Ukraine to the czars.

Russia and the West

A final development of these two centuries was to prove of the utmost importance for the future Russia. This was the slow and gradual penetration of foreigners and foreign ideas, a process welcomed—as in most societies—with mixed feelings by those who prized the technical and mechanical learning they could derive from the West while fearing Western influence on society and manners. This ambivalent attitude toward Westerners and Western ideas became characteristic of later Russians; they sought what the West could give, but they often feared the giver.

The first foreigners to come were the Italians, who helped build the Kremlin at the end of the fifteenth century. But they were not encouraged to teach the Russians their knowledge, and they failed to influence even the court of Ivan III in any significant way. The English, who arrived in the midsixteenth century as traders to the White Sea, were welcomed by Ivan the Terrible. He gave the English valuable privileges and encouraged them to trade their woolen cloth for Russian timber and rope, pitch, and other naval supplies. These helped build the great Elizabethan fleets that sailed the seas and defeated the Spanish Armada. The English were the first foreigners to penetrate Russia in any numbers and the first to teach Russians Western industrial techniques. They got along well with the Russians and supplied many officers to the czar's armies. Toward the middle of the seventeenth century the Dutch were able to displace the English as the most important foreign group engaged in commerce and manufacturing, opening their own glass, paper, and textile plants in Russia.

After the accession of Michael Romanov in 1613, the foreign quarter of Moscow, always called "the German suburb," grew rapidly. Foreign technicians of all sorts—textile weavers, bronze founders, clockmakers—received enormous salaries from the state. Foreign merchants sold their goods, much to the distaste of the native Russians; foreign physicians and druggists became fashionable. By the end of the seventeenth century Western influence was fully apparent in the life of the court. A few nobles began to buy books and form libraries, to learn Latin, French, and German. The people, meanwhile, distrusted and hated the foreigners, looted their houses when they dared, and jeered at them in the street.

Suspicion of foreign influences had divided the Russian church, cut the people off from sources of change, smothered the development of even modest representative institutions, assured the continuation of serfdom, and, together with the impact of the Ottoman Empire, left the East under medieval conditions to the end of the seventeenth century—long after Renaissance and Reformation, exploration and discovery, and a commerical revolution had transformed society in the West. The Middle Ages came to have quite different dates in East and West, reflecting the different pace of development.

SUMMARY

By the late eleventh century, instability in the Muslim and Byzantine empires and the expansion of the Seljuk Turks had made pilgrimages to Palestine unsafe for Christians. When Byzantine envoys asked Pope Urban II for military aid against the Seljuks, the pope responded by calling for a crusade. Crusades, or holy wars supported by the papacy against the infidel, had been waged in Spain since the Muslim invasions of the eighth century.

People responded to the pope's call for both religious and secular motives. During the First Crusade, feudal lords established four Crusader states: Edessa, Antioch, Jerusalem, and Tripoli. The Templars, Hospitalers, and Teutonic Knights, orders of military knights, were established to protect pilgrims traveling to Palestine, but as the orders grew in wealth and power, they were diverted from their original purpose.

During the Second and Third crusades, monarchs of France, Germany, and England tried to repel Muslim advances in the East. The Fourth Crusade, which resulted in the sack of Constantinople, and other later crusades showed how far the Crusaders had strayed from the original crusading spirit.

Increased trade and travel during the Crusades resulted in the introduction of new products, ideas, and methods of finance. The Crusades also helped foster the explorations of the fourteenth and fifteenth centuries. The failure of the Crusades, however, meant the closing of the eastern Mediterranean to western Europe.

The Byzantine Empire had been in decline even before Crusaders looted its palaces and churches in 1204. Official corruption had contributed to economic and social decay. Under the Latin emperors, the Byzantine Empire was divided into feudal states, but in 1261, the Greeks of Nicaea ousted the Latin emperors from Constantinople.

Rival claims to the throne, social unrest, and religious controversy led to further decay in the Empire. Thus weakened, the Byzantine Empire could not withstand the advance of the Ottoman Turks in the fourteenth century. Finally, in 1453, even the supposedly impregnable city of Constantinople fell to the invaders and was renamed Istanbul.

Ottoman rulers were generally tolerant of other religions, including Christianity. They organized their state based on a strong ruling class that included men of the emperor, men of the sword, men of the pen, and the sages. The Turks expanded their empire into Africa, Persia, and Europe. Twice, Ottoman armies besieged Vienna, but each time, they were turned back. By the seventeenth century, however, the Ottoman Empire entered a long decline.

In the thirteenth century, Genghis Khan and his successors invaded Russia. For two hundred years, Tatars collected tribute from the Russians although they allowed Russian princes to rule themselves. In the fourteenth and fifteenth centuries the princes of Moscow challenged Tatar rule and eventually, with the support of the church, established an absolute autocratic state.

Historians have debated the impact of Tatar rule on Russia, which resulted in Russia's falling behind the West. Not until the seventeenth century after the accession of Michael Romanov was Russia exposed to Western ideas and learning. During this period Russia expanded eastward to the Urals and into Siberia, south toward the Caucasus and Black Sea, north toward the Baltic Sea, and westward into territory ruled by Poland.

chapter ten

THE RISE OF THE NATION

In eastern Europe medieval institutions continued to flourish long after the Turks captured Byzantium in 1453—the date often cited for convenience as the turning point from medieval to modern. Indeed, in Russia the Middle Ages ended comparatively recently, with the emancipation of serfs in 1861. In western Europe, by contrast, the Middle Ages ended about five centuries ago. No one year or event can be singled out; rather a series of crucial developments took place over half a century in the late 1400s and early 1500s: the consolidation of royal authority in France, England, and Spain; the discovery of America; the virtual disappearance of serfdom in the West; and the revolt of Martin Luther against the medieval church. The Renaissance and the Reformation disrupted the Christian cultural synthesis and the religious unity of the Middle Ages.

I THE PASSAGE FROM MEDIEVAL TO MODERN

During the fourteenth and fifteenth centuries old forms and attitudes persisted in Western politics but, in a manner characteristic of an era of decline, became less flexible and less creative. Political leaders sometimes acted as though they were living centuries earlier. The Holy Roman emperor Henry VII in the early 1300s sought to straighten out the affairs of Italy in the old Ghibelline tradition, even though he had few of the resources that had been at the command of Frederick Barbarossa, who had reigned a century and a quarter before. The nobles of France and England, exploiting the confusion of the Hundred Years' War, built again the private armies and the great castles of the feudal heyday and attempted to transfer power back from the monarch to themselves. Their movement has been called *bastard feudalism*, for service in these neofeudal armies hinged upon money, not upon the genuinely feudal elements of personal loyalty and mutual respect and guarantees.

Manifestations like these have been interpreted as symptoms of senility, a hardening of the arteries of the body politic; but they may also be viewed as expedients or experiments in the adjustment of old institutions to new demands. The nobles who practiced bastard feudalism were not only taking selfish advantage of a prolonged war; they were also putting soldiers in the field when neither French nor English monarchies could sustain a military effort decade after decade. The importance of the monetary factor to the individual—the soldier hired for money, the ex-serf paying rent in money, the banker earning his livelihood handling money—was characteristic of the passage from medieval to modern.

By the close of the fifteenth century, it was evident that the future lay not with neofeudal lords but with the so-called new monarchs, who had little interest in reviving old glories and were committed to power politics. Although politics and power had always gone hand in hand, the "new" monarchs were distinguished from their predecessors by the candor and the professionalism of their operations. They did not hide their pursuit of power behind the church, and they were served by better instruments of government, better equipped and trained soldiers, diplomats, and bureaucrats. Outstanding representatives of the new professionalism were Louis XI of France, Henry VII of England, and Ferdinand and Isabella of Spain—all of them monarchs of developing national states. On a local or regional scale, the princes of the various German states and the despots of the Italian city-states also often exemplified the new businesslike political behavior.

Meanwhile, the economy and society of western Europe had been undergoing even more strain and upheaval than the political institutions had experienced. In the countryside the traditional patterns of manorialism, serfdom, and payment in kind coexisted with new patterns of a free peasantry producing for a cash market and paying rents and taxes in cash. The economy and society showed some of the same symptoms of rigidity and senility affecting political life. Former serfs, for example, who thought they were legally free peasants, often found that a lord could still oblige them to use his oven or flour mill or wine press and pay a stiff fee for the privilege. But they also found that they could no longer turn to a lord for protection in time of trouble. The uncertainty and insecurity of a world no longer wholly medieval nor yet wholly modern underlay the numerous outbreaks of rural violence in the fourteenth century, such as the French *Jacquerie* or the English Peasants' Revolt. Crises also convulsed urban life in the 1300s. Civil war broke out in the prosperous woolen-manufacturing towns of Flanders, and chronic strife developed between the wealthy and poorer classes in another woolen center, Florence, where the rigid old institution was the guild and the unsettling new element was the aggressive businessman.

Life for the peasant—man or woman—was circumscribed, harsh, and on the whole, short. Rural life showed a bewildering variety, however, particularly in England, and broad generalization is difficult, beyond a slow increase in the value of labor in western Europe and a slow descent into serfdom in eastern Europe. The towns often were a political and economic buffer between nobles and peasants, and where there was no growth in towns or rise in urban class consciousness, the gap between the rich and the poor was particularly great.

Men continued to be warriors and priests. Medieval

women were, if of the upper class, placed on a pedestal, to be admired for their attainments in conversation, embroidery, or household management; if of the lower class, they were sent with their husbands into the field. There was a growing gap between the few women who led brilliant lives of state at court or plotted the triumphs of their business-oriented families, and the drudgery of the great majority. The arranged marriages of royalty and nobility typically took place in childhood; the arranged marriages of the peasantry came at a later age, and many peasant women did not marry because of a shortage of eligible land-holding males. Daughters were, therefore, frequently put out to service, creating a class of permanent domestic workers on the manorial estate who often were outside the protection of feudalism. Initially, women's wages were less than men's, though by the late Middle Ages female laborers received the same wages as men for the same jobs in many places. Childbirth was always a hazard from which riches did not protect one, for many women were injured in labor, by abortion, or by the diseases that accompanied childbirth. Infanticide of girls was not uncommon, for a daughter's contributions in work might be thought to be less than the cost of raising her. Despite the great risks men faced in frequent warfare, simple survival remained a major problem for females.

Two social traumas particularly undermined the morale and resiliency of fourteenth-century Europe. The first was the great famine of 1315-1317, probably caused by the combination of a long spell of bad weather and the gradual end of the long medieval process of clearing forests and draining marshes for new farmland. With Europe unable to grow enough grain to supply its population with bread (then the mainstay of the diet), starvation was widespread. For example, about 10 percent of the inhabitants of the Flemish town of Ypres died in one six-month period. The second and greater trauma was the Black Death of 1346-1350, which is estimated to have killed one-third of the European population. This ghastly epidemic apparently marked the first appearance in Europe of bubonic plague, introduced by ships coming from the Crimea. Propagated by flea bites, prevalent wherever there were rats, and also carried in the air by sneezing and coughing, the plague wiped out entire communities and penetrated to faraway Greenland. Recurring in the 1360s and 1370s, the persistence of the plague altered the socioeconomic pyramid and initiated a steady decline in population that lasted to 1480. The plague continued to recur in the western Mediterranean until the 1720s. A major social consequence of the plague was a severe shortage of labor, which depressed the economy for several decades and emboldened the peasants and workers who had survived the epidemic to press for greater rights, usually with only limited success.

The Black Death also had far-reaching psychological effects. Attitudes toward death became more morbid, and fascination with the rituals of death and dying grew, until by the fifteenth century the horror of physical death and of bodily decay had become an obsession, with particular attention devoted to the corruption of the physical body by worms. The Black Death returned for a fourth time in 1388-1390, and with this visit the cult of death developed even greater strength. Dance, decoration, art, and public ceremony used death as a centerpiece, for it was a central fact of life. Cemeteries were surrounded by charnel houses that displayed the bones of the deceased, both to make room for new ones and because people were fascinated with returning to the gravesite.

In enclosed places, the infection of one person meant the likely death of all, and entire monasteries were wiped out. Not knowing the cause of such sweeping disasters, people looked to demons, superstition, and the wrath of God for explanation. They also tried to keep their distance from anything Asian, since rumor had it that the plague had begun in China and had so severely struck India as to depopulate it utterly. At Avignon, the pope declared that nearly twenty-four million people had died. Since no one knew the real statistics, the sense of fear was even greater.

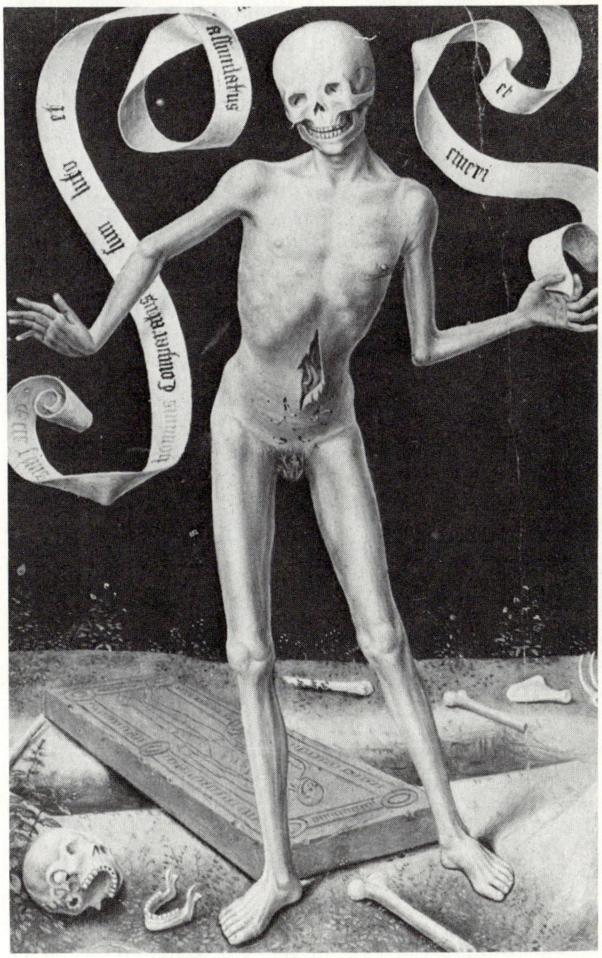

This figure of Death, from the studio of Hans Memling (c 1430-1494), is representative of the preoccupation of the late fifteenth century with the physical manifestations of disease and dying.

The fourteenth century was particularly frightening, for even the climate turned against the rural population. In the midst of one of the earth's great climatic swings from an earlier time when wheat was grown in Sweden and there were vineyards in Newfoundland, Europe passed through a long succession of wet years when crops rotted, and panic, famine, and death were common in the countryside. No one was outside this cycle of hardship, for rich as well as poor died in the plague, suffered from the climatic changes, and faced the Inquisition for charges of heresy as they attempted to account for the remarkable intensity of God's anger. Hygiene was generally lacking, even at court; disease was the normal state of things, even when there was no plague, for antisepsis was unknown, and simple injuries easily led to death. Even the presumed innocence of childhood was no joy, for neither medieval thought nor art knew of childhood as a separate stage of development, and while the children of the well-to-do certainly had toys, children were often seen simply as small adults. Not until the seventeenth century could one speak of "the discovery of childhood."

To the average citizen, then, these late Middle Ages must have seemed a time of incredible calamity and hardship. The Black Death ravaged the streets and the countryside, and no one could count on the security of awakening the next morning. The Hundred Years' War brought political and social collapse to much of western Europe, sweeping aside old ways. Soldiers experienced an unprecedented death rate, as gunpowder and heavy artillery came into widespread use for the first time. The great schisms within the church forced Christians to take sides in a complex dispute that involved competing popes. The Turks were on the march, threatening the gates of Europe, as the powerful armies of the West fought one another, and yet, although the time may have seemed one of exceptional decline and instability, it also presaged rebirth.

II THE EMERGING NATIONAL MONARCHIES

At the death of Philip the Fair in 1314, the Capetian monarchy of France seemed to be evolving into a new professional institution staffed by efficient and loyal bureaucrats. Philip Augustus, Louis IX, and Philip the Fair had all consolidated royal power at the expense of their feudal vassals, who included the kings of England. Soon, however, France became embroiled in a long conflict with England—the so-called Hunred Years' War of 1337-1453—that crippled the monarchy for well over a century.

The Outbreak of the Hundred Years' War, 1337

The nominal cause of the war was a dispute over the succession to the French throne. For more than three hundred years son had followed father as king of France. This remarkable succession ended with the three sons of Philip the Fair, none of whom fathered a son who survived infancy. The crown then passed to Philip of Valois, Philip VI (1328-1350), a nephew of Philip the Fair. But the king of England, Edward III (1327-1377), whose mother Isabella had been a daughter of Philip the Fair, claimed that as the nephew of the last Capetian kings he had a better right to succeed than their first cousin, Philip of Valois. To settle the question, French lawyers went back to the Frankish Salic law of the sixth century, which said that a woman could not inherit land. Although the Salic law had not been applied in France for centuries, the lawyers now interpreted it to mean that a woman could not transmit the inheritance to the kingdom. This legal quibble was to serve Edward III as the pretext for beginning the Hundred Years' War.

Edward's claim to the French throne was not the only reason for the outbreak of war. England's continued possession of the rich duchy of Aquitaine, with its lucrative vineyards and its prosperous wine-shipping port of Bordeaux, was a glaring exception to an increasingly unified France. As suzerains over Aquitaine, the kings of France encroached upon the feudal rights of the kings of England. The English, for their part, wished to keep what they had and to regain Normandy and the other territories they had lost to Philip Augustus.

The most pressing issue arose farther north, in Flanders. This small but wealthy area, which today straddles the frontier between Belgium and France, was ruled by the count of Flanders, a vassal of the king of France. The thriving Flemish cloth manufacturers bought most of their wool from England and sold much of their finished cloth there; the English crown collected taxes both on the exported wool and on the imported woolens. Inside Flanders the artisans and tradespeople of the towns were in almost constant conflict with the rich commercial ruling class. The rich sought the backing of the count of Flanders, and he in turn sought that of his overlord, the king of France; the workers got the help of the English, who feared the disruption of their lucrative trade. Warlike incidents multiplied during the early fourteenth century, culminating in a victorious invasion of Flanders by French armies. Edward III thereupon allied himself with a flemish merchant of Ghent, Jacob van Artevelde, who expelled both the ruling Flemish oligarchy and the French and organized his own government of Flanders. It was in response to pressure from these Flemish allies that Edward III put forth his claim as king of France and started a war in 1337.

The first major operation of the war was an English naval victory at Sluys in 1340, which gave the English command of the Channel until 1372. When their Flemish ally, Van Artevelde, was killed in 1345, the English invaded northern France and gained a great victory at Crécy in 1346. Despite inferior numbers, the English profited by incompetent French generalship and by their own successful experiments in relying upon large numbers of infantrymen armed with the longbow. From higher ground English archers poured arrows down on a

The Cloth Hall and Belfry in Ypres, Belgium. Its Gothic architectural style surrendered to the prosperity of the Renaissance.

confused crowd of mounted French knights and mercenaries armed with the crossbow, a cumbersome weapon rather like a giant slingshot. Next the English took Calais, which gave them a port in France that they would hold for over two hundred years. When open warfare was resumed after the Black Death, the English not only defeated the French again, at Poitiers in western France (1356), but also captured the French king, John III (1350-1364), and carried him off to luxurious captivity in England. John's teenage son, Charles, the future King Charles V, the Wise, became regent for his father in France.

In 1360 the Hundred Years' War paused when Edward III virtually renounced his claim to the French crown by treaty in exchange for all southwestern France and lands bordering the Channel near Calais. When the war was resumed in 1369, the French made impressive gains under Charles the Wise and his capable advisers. By his death in 1380 they had driven the English from French soil except for a string of seaports, including Bordeaux and Calais. The French fleet now could sail freely in the Channel and raid the English coasts. At home Charles kept the upper hand over the Estates General, securing their agreement that existing taxes would be made permanent and not require further approval by the Estates.

The war dominated the history of France for a troubled century. The Valois kings, with the notable exception of Charles V (1364-1380), were far less effective rulers than the Capetians had been. The English, who showed military superiority, won the main battles and gained much French territory by treaty. France was racked by the Black Death and swept by social crisis and civil war. Yet the English were overextended, and the French ultimately drove them out and completed the unification of their country under a strong national monarchy. Necessity obliged the Valois kings to develop a standing army, finance it by direct taxation, and enlist the support of the middle classes, on whose assistance the whole accomplishment depended.

The Estates General

In these years the French monarchy faced increasingly hostile criticism at home, focused in the central representative assembly. This assembly was the Estates General, to which the three estates or social classes of the realm—the clergy, the first estate; the nobles, the second; and the commoners, the third—sent deputies. When summoned in 1355 to consent to a tax, the Estates General insisted on fixing its form—a general levy on sales and a special levy on salt—and demanded also that their representatives rather than those of the Crown act as collectors. Moreover, the Estates for the first time scheduled future meetings "to discuss the state of the realm." After the defeat at Poitiers, they demanded that the regent, Charles, dismiss and punish the royal advisers and substitute for them twenty-eight delegates chosen from the Estates. When Charles hesitated, the leader of the Estates, the Paris merchant Etienne Marcel, led a general strike and revolution in the capital, the first of many in French history, and forced the regent to consent. But Marcel made two cardinal mistakes. He allied himself with a rival claimant to the throne, and he assisted a violent peasant revolt, the *Jacquerie,* (so called from the popular name for a peasant, Jacques Bonhomme—James Goodfellow).

Already harrowed by the Black Death, the peasants endured fresh suffering from bands of soldiers living off the land and from demands for more taxes and money to ransom nobles taken prisoner with King John. The peasantry felt harassed by the Estates General, which required them to repair the war-torn properties of the nobility, and they were freed from their fear of the army as an organized force by its collapse at Poitiers. In several regions they rose up in 1358, without a specific program or effective leadership, murdering nobles and burning châteaux. The royal forces, in disarray though they were, put down and massacred the peasants; the death toll has been estimated at twenty thousand. The outcome of the Jacquerie showed that, put to the test, the country failed to support either the more radical Parisians or the mobs in the countryside. (This, too, was to be a familiar pattern in French history.) In the final flare-up, Marcel was murdered and Charles repressed the revolt.

Although the Estates had in effect run France for two

England and France During the Hundred Years' War

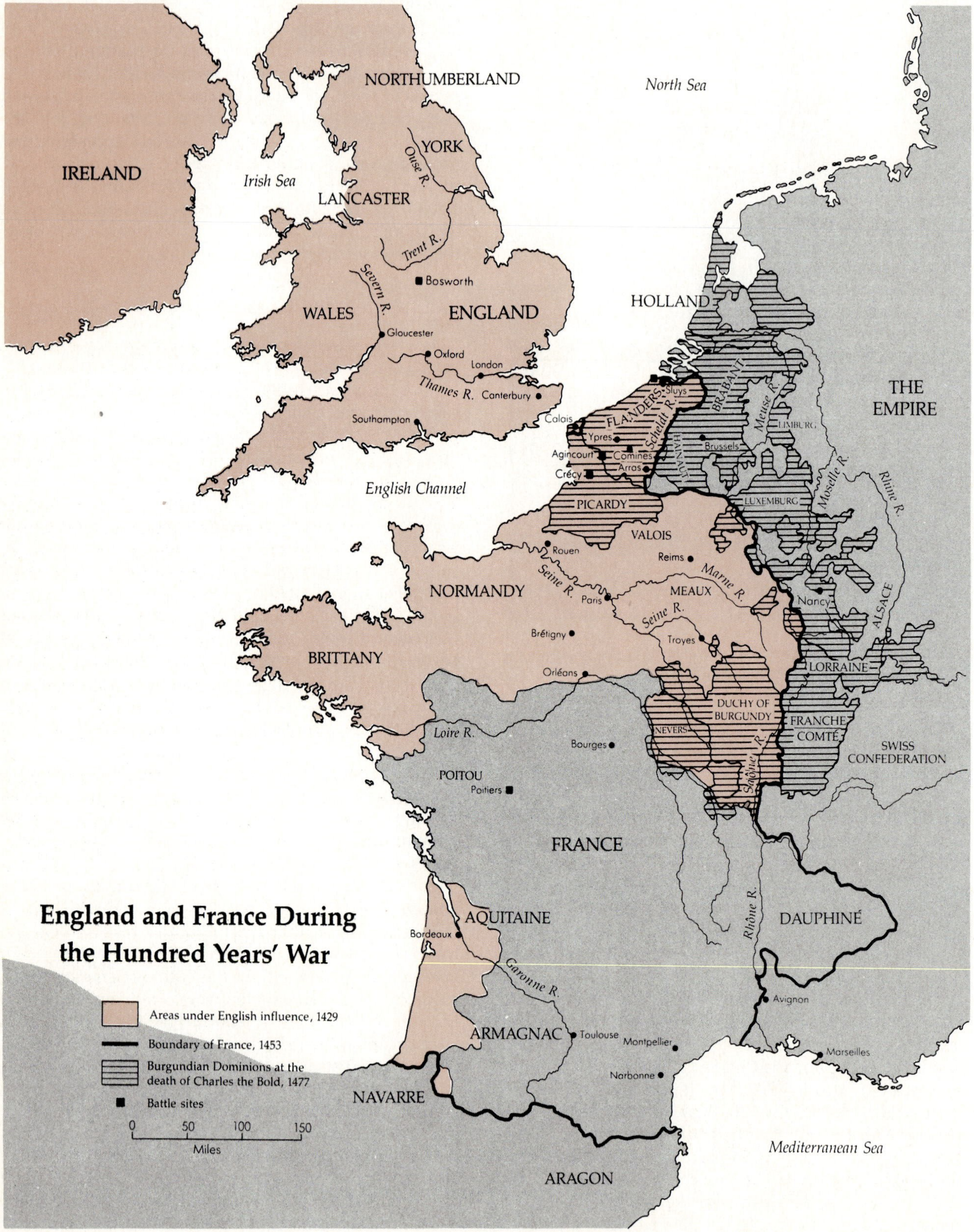

years, they had imposed no principle of constitutional limitation upon the king. With the country in chronic danger of invasion, even rebels wished to meet the emergency by strengthening rather than weakening the monarchy. Moreover, the critics of the Crown—clergy, nobles, townsmen—mistrusted one another because of conflicting class interests. Even members of a single estate were divided by the differing interests of the provinces from which they came. Charles the Wise was quick to exploit the advantages that these class and local antagonisms gave the Crown.

Burgundians and Armagnacs, 1380-1467

However, the successes of Charles the Wise were followed by still worse suffering. The new King, Charles VI (1380-1422), was intermittently insane. During his reign the monarchy was threatened by the disastrous results of the earlier royal policy of assigning provinces called *apanages* to a king's younger sons. Such a son might himself be loyal, but within a generation or two his heirs would be remote enough from the royal family to become its rivals. It was essentially this pattern that had ruined the Carolingians. In 1363 King John II revived the practice and opened the door to bastard feudalism by making the important duchy of Burgundy the apanage of his youngest son, Philip. Charles the Wise compounded the danger of giving the duchy of Orléans as an apanage to his younger son, Louis.

During the reign of Charles VI the two dukes, who were the king's uncle and brother respectively, engaged in a bitter rivalry for influence and power, which was continued by their successors in the duchies. In 1407 John, who followed his father, Philip, as duke of Burgundy, arranged the assassination of Louis, duke of Orléans. All France was now torn by the factional struggle between the Burgundians and the Orléanists, who were called Armagnacs after their leader, Count Bernard of Armagnac, father-in-law of the new duke of Orléans. The Armagnacs commanded the loyalty of much of southern and southwestern France, while the Burgundians controlled the north and east. The Armagnacs were strongest among the great nobles and were anti-English; the Burgundians, whose duke had inherited Flanders and had thus become immensely rich, were pro-English and had the support of the upper bourgeoisie in the towns. The careful English king Henry V (1413-1422) reopened the war and won the battle of Agincourt, where the heavily armored French knights were mired in the mud in 1415. The Burgundians took over in Paris, killing partisans of the Armagnacs, whose factions fled south of the Loire River to set up a rival regime. The English took Rouen, the capital of Normandy, in 1419; the Burgundians tried to patch up a truce with the Armagnacs, but John, the duke of Burgundy, was assassinated, ostensibly to avenge the murder of the duke of Orléans a dozen years earlier.

Next, the unstable Charles VI declared his own son, the dauphin, to be illegitimate. (The title of dauphin and the right to hold the province of Dauphiné in southeastern France were reserved for the eldest son of the king.) By the Treaty of Troyes (1420), Charles adopted Henvy V of England as his heir and made him his regent during his lifetime. Henry married Charles's daughter and was allowed to retain the conquests he had made north of the Loire until he should inherit all of France on the death of Charles. This incredible settlement, which threatened to extinguish French national sovereignty, was supported by the Burgundians, the Estates General, and the University of Paris. Had Henry V lived, it is possible that the entire future of France might have been changed. But in 1422 both Charles VI and Henry V died, the English crown passed to the infant Henry VI, and England too was torn by factionalism and was unable to supply enough troops to hold down conquered northern France.

In France the dauphin, excluded from Paris by the Burgundians, ruled at Bourges in central France as King Charles VII (1422-1461) with Armagnac support. When the regent for Henry VI of England prepared to move south against Charles, the mystic Joan of Arc (c 1412-1431) saved France. The demoralized forces of Charles

BIAS IN PLACE NAMES

Not only do historic place names change, but places often simultaneously have two or more names and pronunciations. For example, *Biscay Bay*, referred to in the text, is the English form for *Viscaya*, its Spanish name; *Napoli* is the Italian form for *Naples*. Were this book written in a language other than English, these other forms would be used. One is not more "correct" than the other. The choice simply reflects the bias of language.

Behind this bias may lie serious distortions of history, however, for the use of one term, spelling, or pronunciation for a place or person tends to reflect how "the victor writes the history." The pronunciation of *Agincourt* is another example, for the English call it *ag'-in-kort;* properly, in French, the pronunciation is *ä-zhan-koor'*. By the choice of pronunciation one may implicitly take sides in a dispute.

Joan of Arc, as visualized by the romantic artist Jean-Auguste-Dominique Ingres (1780-1867) in 1854. As time passed, Joan was shown as more militant and more mature, becoming a symbol of France itself.

VII were inspired by the visionary peasant girl from Lorraine who reflected the deep patriotism of the French at a moment when all seemed lost. Joan told the pitiful dauphin how saints and angels had told her that she must bring him to be crowned at Rheims, traditional coronation place for the kings of France. She was then armed and given a small detachment that drove the English out of Orléans. The king was crowned in 1429 but the next year Joan was taken prisoner by the Burgundians, sold to the English, turned over to the French Inquisition, and burned at the stake for witchcraft and heresy in Rouen in 1431. The papacy itself undid the verdict against her in 1456 and made her a saint in 1920.

Against heavy odds, the French monarchy managed to sustain the impetus provided by the martyred Joan. In 1435 Charles VII and Burgundy concluded a separate peace that made it impossible for the English to win the war. Although Charles recovered Paris, for ten years the countryside was ravaged by bands of soldiers; moreover, leagues of nobles, supported by the new dauphin, the future Louis XI, revolted in 1440. Fortunately for the Crown, the Estates General in 1439 granted the king the permanent right to enjoy two essential neofeudal resources: to keep a standing army and to levy the *taille* (from a French word meaning "cut"), a direct tax collected by royal agents.

With these instruments available to him and with loans from the wealthy merchant, Jacques Coeur, Charles VII reformed his inadequate military forces. Twenty companies of specialized cavalry were organized, twelve hundred men to a company, under commanders of the king's personal choice; these companies were assigned to garrison the towns. Professionals supervised the introduction of artillery, which became the best in Europe. The new French force drove the English out of Normandy and Aquitaine (1449-1451), so that only Calais remained in English hands when the Hundred Years' War finally ended in 1453. The standing army, based on direct taxation that had been granted by the Estates as a royal right, had enabled France to overcome the English threat.

Meantime, Charles had acted against another institution that might have weakened the Crown. In 1438 he regulated church-state relations by the Pragmatic Sanction of Bourges (the term refers to a solemn royal pronouncement), which laid down the policy known as *Gallicanism,* claiming for the Gallican (French) church a virtually autonomous position within the Roman Catholic church. It greatly limited papal control over church

Charles VII, King of France, as painted by Jean Fouquet (c 1420-c 1481), probably about 1444.

appointments and revenues in France and asserted the superiority of church councils over popes.

The Burgundian Threat and King Louis XI, 1419-1483

Against one set of enemies, however, Charles VII was not successful—his rebellious vassals, many of them beneficiaries of the new bastard feudalism, who still controlled nearly half of the kingdom. The most powerful of these vassals was the duke of Burgundy, Philip the Good (1419-1467), whose authority reached far beyond the duchy of Burgundy in eastern France and the adjoining Franche-Comté (Free County of Burgundy—still technically part of the Holy Roman Empire) and extended to Flanders and other major portions of the Low Countries. Though divided, this sprawling Burgundian realm was almost an emerging national state. Its two main territorial blocs in eastern France and the Low Countries were separated by the non-Burgundian lands of Alsace and Lorraine. And it was also a personal state, for Duke Philip had assembled it as much by good fortune as by good management, inheriting some lands and acquiring others by conquest or negotiation. Yet it was also a menacing state that might have interposed itself permanently as a middle kingdom between France and Germany. Philip had defied Charles VII by allying with the English in the Hundred Years' War and behaved in general as though he were a monarch of the first magnitude. The wealth of the Flemish and Dutch towns enabled him to maintain the most lavish court in Europe, and his resources at least equaled those of the king of France and the Holy Roman emperor.

The decisive trial of strength between France and Burgundy took place under the successors of Charles VII and Philip the Good; King Louis XI (1461-1483) and Duke Charles the Bold (1467-1477). Although the new French king had repeatedly intrigued against his father while he was dauphin, he now energetically pursued the policies that Charles VII had initiated. At his accession Louis was already a crafty and practiced politician who despised the pageantry of kingship and preferred secret diplomacy to open war. He returned to the strong monarchical tradition of Philip Augustus and Philip the Fair. He forced his protesting subjects to pay higher taxes, but gave men of the middle class responsible posts

LOUIS XI AND CHARLES THE BOLD

One of Charles's approving aides, a Fleming, Philippe de Commynes, of Comines (c 1445-1511), drew a portrait of him in his *Mémoires*, a notable work of contemporary history:

> Amongst all those I have ever known, the most skillful at extricating himself out of a disagreeable predicament in time of adversity was King Louis XI . . . , the most humble person in terms of speech and manner and the prince who worked more than any other to gain to his cause any man who could serve him or who could be in a position to harm him. And he was not discouraged if a man he was trying to win over at first refused to cooperate, but he continued his persuasion by promising him many things and actually giving him money and dignities which he knew the other coveted. . . .
>
> He was naturally a friend to those of middle rank and an enemy of all the powerful lords who could do without him. No man ever gave ear to people to such an extent or inquired about so many matters as he did, or wished to make the acquaintance of so many persons. For indeed he knew everyone in a position of authority and of worthy character who lived in England, Spain, Portugal, Italy, in the territories of the Duke of Burgundy, and in Brittany, as well as he knew his own subjects. These methods and manners . . . saved the crown for him, in view of the enemies he had acquired for himself at the time of his accession to the throne.

Commynes also assessed the temperament and policies of Charles the Bold whom he had served before he shifted his allegiance to Louis:

> I have not seen any reason why he should have incurred the wrath of God, unless it was because he considered all the graces and honors which he had received in this world to have been the result of his own judgment and valor, instead of attributing them to God, as he should have. For indeed he was endowed with many good qualities and virtues. No prince ever surpassed him in eagerness to act as patron to great men. . . . No lord ever granted audience more freely to his servants and his subjects. . . . He was very ostentatious in his dress and in everything else—a little too much. He was very courteous to ambassadors and foreigners; they were well received and lavishly entertained. . . . He desired great glory, and it was that more than anything else which made him engage in these wars.

Samuel Kinser, ed., *The Memoirs of Philippe de Commynes*, trans. Isabelle Cazeaux (Columbia, S.C.: University of South Carolina Press, 1969) I, 130-31, 135. Reprinted by permission of the University of South Carolina Press.

in his administration. He appeased the pope by withdrawing the Pragmatic Sanction of 1438, but in practice continued most of its restrictions on papal control over the Gallican church. He enlarged the army bequeathed him by his father, but conserved its use for the direst emergencies.

Where Louis XI was cautious, Charles the Bold was audacious to the point of folly. He was determined to build a true middle kingdom by bridging the gap between Burgundy and the Low Countries and seizing Lorraine and Alsace. Since Alsace was a confused patchwork of feudal jurisdictions overlapping northern Switzerland, his designs threatened the largely independent Swiss confederation. Subsidized by Louis XI, the Swiss defeated Charles three times in 1476 and 1477; in the last battle, at Nancy, Charles was slain.

Since Charles left no son, his lands were partitioned. The Duchy of Burgundy passed permanently to France. The Low Countries went to Mary, the daughter of Charles, who married Maximilian of Hapsburg, later Holy Roman emperor. Their son was to marry the daughter of Ferdinand and Isabella of Spain, and their grandson, the emperor Charles V, was to rule Germany, the Low Countries, and Spain, and to threaten France.

Though Louis XI did not keep all the Burgundian inheritance out of the hands of potential enemies, he shattered the prospect of a middle kingdom. He broke the strength of the Armagnac faction as well, recovered most of the territory held as apanages, and doubled the size of the royal domain. At his death, French bastard feudalism was virtually eliminated. The only major region still largely independent of the Crown was the Duchy of Brittany, and this passed to royal control during the reign of Charles VIII (r. 1483-1498), Louis's son and successor. The France of Louis XI was not yet a full-fledged national monarchy, but by his consolidation of territory and by his competent central administration, Louis laid the foundations for a proud, cohesive, confident nation in subsequent centuries.

England: Edward II and Edward III, 1307-1377

England was also emerging as a national monarchy. Here too social and political dissension had accompanied the Hundred Years' War, and bastard feudalism flourished until Edward IV and Henry VII reasserted royal power in the later fifteenth century, much as Louis XI did in France. But however close the parallels between the two countries, there was also an all-important difference. Whereas the French Estates General was becoming the servant of the monarchy, the English Parliament was slowly setting precedents and acquiring powers that would one day make it the master of the Crown.

In England, after the death of the strong and successful Edward I in 1307, the political tide turned abruptly against the monarchy. His son, Edward II (1307-1327), was a bored, weak, and inept ruler, dominated by his favorites and by his French queen, Isabella. In 1314 he lost the battle of Bannockburn to the Scots, and with it a short-lived English rule over Scotland. Meantime, Edward II faced baronial opposition much like that which had harassed his grandfather, Henry III. In the Ordinances of 1311 the barons set up as the real rulers of England twenty-one *lords ordainers*, who had to consent to royal appointments, to declarations of war, and to the king's leaving the realm. Parliament repealed the Ordinances in 1322, and noble malcontents gathered around Queen Isabella, who led a revolt against her husband. Imprisoned, then murdered, Edward II was succeeded on the throne by his fifteen-year-old son, Edward III, a knightly and vigorous figure.

The reign of Edward III (1327-1377) was marked by stunning English victories in the early campaigns of the Hundred Years' War and by the great economic crisis following the Black Death. This plague created a devastating shortage of labor; crops rotted in the fields for lack of harvesters, and good land dropped out of cultivation. English agricultural laborers, aware of their suddenly increased bargaining power and of the wealth gained by their masters from the French war, demanded better working conditions or left home for the towns. In 1351 Parliament passed the Statute of Laborers, forbidding workers to give up their jobs and attempting to fix wages and prices as they had been before the plague. The law was not a success, and the labor shortage hastened the end of serfdom and paved the way for the disorders that took place under Edward's successor. The cause of the peasants was defended effectively in a vernacular verse satire of Edward's reign, *The Vision Concerning Piers Plowman*, which denounced the corruption of officials and of the clergy. Probably written by William Langland (c 1332 -c 1400), the poem has become an invaluable source for social history.

Attempts to enforce the Statute of Laborers were made by the justices of the peace, a notable English institution first appearing under Edward III. The justices were all royal appointees, selected in each shire from the landed gentry, who were accustomed to exercising local leadership. Since they received no pay, they accepted office from a sense of duty or for prestige. As the old shire and hundred courts disappeared, the justices of the peace became the chief local magistrates and the virtual rulers of rural England, often to the displeasure of the peasants.

The reign of Edward III also witnessed the growth of English national feeling, fostered by the long war with France. The papacy was a particular target of nationalist suspicion because the popes now resided at Avignon and were thought to be under the thumb of the French. In 1351 Parliament passed the Statute of Provisors restricting the provision (that is, the appointment) of aliens to church offices in England. Two years later Parliament checked the appeal of legal cases to the papal curia by the Statute of Praemunire (a Latin term that refers to the prosecution of a legal case). Meantime, increased use of the English language reflected the developing sense of national identity. In 1362 Parliament declared English the official language of the courts, although the Norman

PIERS THE PLOWMAN

Piers the Plowman was a popular writer roughly contemporary to Chaucer. His poetry has come down to us in three quite distinct versions written between about 1362 and 1398. The poem is a series of allegorical dreams that show the relationship of the individual to society in the fourteenth century. Piers, a simple plowman who works because he finds it good to do so, encounters lust, sloth, and greed around him. Traditionally, the author is said to have been named William, probably Langland, and though the poem is set in the west of England, the dialect (from which the following translation was made) was that of London:

Askers and beggars fast about flitted,
Till their bags and their bellies brimful were
  crammed;
Feigned for their food, fought at the ale-house;
In gluttony, God wot, go they to bed.
And rise up with ribaldry, these bullying
  beggar-knaves;
Sleep and sloth follow them ever.
Pilgrims and palmers pledge themselves together
To seek the shrine of St. James and saints at Rome;
Went forth in their way with many wise tales,
And had leave to lie all their life after.
Hermits in a band with hooked staves
Went to Walsingham, and their wenches after.
Great lubbers and long, that loath were to work,
Clothed themselves in capes to be known for
  brethren,
And some dressed as hermits their ease to have.
I found there friars, all the four orders,
Preaching to the people for profit of their bellies,
Interpreting the gospel as they well please,
For covetousness of capes construes it ill;
For many of these masters may clothe themselves at
  will,
For money and their merchandise meet oft together.
Since Charity hath turned trader, and shriven chiefly
  lords,
Many wonders have befallen in these few years.
Unless Holy Church now be better held together
The most mischief on earth will mount up fast.

Paul Robert Lieder, Robert Morss Lovett, and Robert Kilburn Root, eds., *British Poetry and Prose* (Boston: Houghton Mifflin, 1938), I, 61-62. This is a translation of the first version.

French of the old ruling classes persisted in some legal documents. As the years passed, English was taught in the schools and in 1399 was used to open Parliament.

Nationalism, dislike of the papacy, and widespread social and economic discontent were all involved in England's first real heresy, preached during Edward's reign by the Oxford scholar John Wycliffe (c 1320-1384). Advocating a church without property in the spirit of the early Christians, Wycliffe called for direct access by the individual to God without priest as intermediary. He denied that in the Mass the bread was transubstantiated into the body of Christ. He and his followers were also responsible for an English translation of the bible, despite the church's insistence that the Scriptures be read only in the Latin of the Vulgate, and not in the vernacular. Though his views, called Lollardy, were condemned as heretical, Wycliffe was not sentenced until well after his death, when his body was dug up and burned.

The most significant constitutional development of Edward III's long reign was the evolution of Parliament. Division of Parliament into two houses was beginning to appear in the fourteenth century, although the terms "House of Commons" and "House of Lords" were not used until later. Edward I's Model Parliament of 1295 had included representatives of the lower and higher clergy, barons, knights of the shire, and burgesses. While the lower clergy had dropped out, the other groups continued to attend. The higher clergy—the lords spiritual—came to Parliament as vassals of the king. In time, the lords spiritual joined with the lords temporal—the earls and barons—to form the House of Lords; the knights of the shire and the burgesses merged to form the House of Commons.

This gradual merger of knights and burgesses was an event of major significance that laid the social foundation for the future greatness of the House of Commons. It brought together two elements, the one representing the gentry, the lower level of the second estate, and the other representing the third estate, which had always remained separate in the assemblies of the continental states. In the fourteenth century the knights of the shire had little sense of social unity with the burgesses, feeling closer to the great lords with whom they had many ties of blood and common interests. But some of the smaller boroughs were represented by knights from the countryside nearby. By the end of the fourteenth century the Commons began to choose one of their members to report to the king on their deliberations, and this position developed into the important office of Speaker of the House. This parliamentary coalition of knights and burgesses evidently came into existence well before any sense of social closeness had developed.

Meantime, the political foundations of the future greatness of the House of Commons were also being laid. In the fourteenth century the chief business of Parliament was judicial. From time to time the knights and burgesses employed the judicial device of presenting petitions to the king; whatever was approved in the petitions was then embodied in statutes. This was the faint beginning of parliamentary legislative power. The growth of parliamentary power was further stimulated by Edward III's frequent requests to Parliament for new grants of money to cover the heavy expenses of the Hundred Years' War. Slowly Parliament took control of the purse strings, while Edward, who had little interest in domestic affairs other than finances, let the royal powers be whittled away imperceptibly. Significantly, then, the responses to the major economic and nationalistic grievances of the midfourteenth century took a parliamentary form, in the Statutes of Laborers, Provisors, and Praemunire.

Richard II and Bastard Feudalism, 1377-1399

When Edward III died, his ten-year-old grandson succeeded as Richard II (1377-1399). Richard's reign was marked by mounting factionalism by royal relatives and their noble followers and by an outbreak of peasant discontent. Both conflicts strongly resembled their French counterparts—the strife between Burgundy and Armagnac, and the Jacquerie of 1358.

The social disorders arose out of protests against the imposition of poll (head) taxes, which fell equally upon all subjects; the poorer classes bitterly resented paying their shilling a head for each person over fifteen. Riots provoked by attempts to collect the tax led to the Peasants' Revolt of 1381. Under the leadership of John Ball, a priest, and Wat Tyler, a day laborer, the peasants burned manor records to destroy evidence of their obligations, murdered the archbishop of Canterbury, and demanded the end of serfdom and the seizure of clerical wealth—a program that showed the widespread influence of Wycliffe's teaching. When they marched on London, the fifteen-year-old king promised to settle their grievances and saved his own life by offering to lead the peasants himself. But Richard failed to keep his promises and permitted severe reprisals against the rebels. Indeed, king and Parliament would have restored serfdom had it been economically possible.

The most long-standing popular statement of the grievances of the rural population is probably the legend of Robin Hood. The first written reference appears in *Piers Plowman*, though it is clear that Langland assumed his readers already knew the story. The legend became firmly entrenched in the fifteenth century and was revived briefly in 1812. Probably a thirteenth-century Yorkshire criminal, Robin Hood became part of the *gest*, some thirty ballads accompanied by lute and harp. These ballads spoke of economic and social grievances, of the constant savaging of open lot and woodland by the followers of noblemen and gentry, of fears of both tyrants and towns—that is, of resistance to change in the countryside. Just as the Jacquerie opposed attempts to regulate life in ways ultimately bound to benefit the nobility and the entrepreneur, so did the Peasants' Revolt of 1381. The tales of Robin Hood attest to the persistence of popular demands for freedom, as defined neither by barons nor philosophers but by those who saw themselves as belonging to an underclass. All were precursors of the peasant revolts of the seventeenth century.

Under Richard II and his successors, factional strife assumed critical dimensions. During the fourteenth century the baronage had become a smaller and richer class of great magnates, whose relationship to their vassals grew to be based more on cash and less on military service and protection. These great lords recruited the armed following they still owed to the king, not by bringing into his increasingly professional army their tenants duly equipped as knights, but by hiring small private armies to go to war for them. Soldiers in these armies, while often members of the country gentry, were bound less by the old feudal ties than by "written indenture and a retaining fee." This custom was known as livery and maintenance, since the lord provided uniforms for his retainers, who, in turn, maintained others, usually "bachelors" who were closely attached, often through money, without holding land. Though forbidden by statute in 1390, this practice continued to flourish. The danger from private armies became greater during each interlude of peace in the war with France, when mercenaries used to plundering in a foreign country returned to England.

The trouble had begun during the last years of Edward III, when effective control of the government passed from the aging king to one of his younger sons, John of Gaunt, duke of Lancaster, and his corrupt entourage. John of Gaunt could mobilize a private army of fifteen hundred men, and his faction persisted under Richard II. New factions also appeared, centered on two of the king's uncles, the dukes of York and Gloucester. After defeating Richard II's supporters in battle, Gloucester had royal ministers condemned for treason in a packed Parliament (1388). The barons put their own people onto royal administrative commissions and seemed to control the Crown. Richard II waited a few years and then in 1397 arrested Gloucester and moved against his confederates. The king packed Parliament in his own favor, had it pass retroactive treason laws, and imposed heavy fiscal exactions on his subjects. Richard's confiscation of the estates of his first cousin, Henry of Bolingbroke, son of John of Gaunt, set off a revolution. Its success rested not so much on the popularity of exiled Bolingbroke as in the great alarm created by Richard's doctrine that the king could control the lives and property of his subjects. After Bolingbroke's landing in England, Richard was forced to abdicate in 1399 and was murdered. Bolingbroke became Henry IV (1399-1413), first monarch of the House of Lancaster.

Lancaster and York, 1399-1485

To recover from the upheavals of Richard II's reign and to check the growth of bastard feudalism, England needed a long period of stable royal rule. But this the Lancastrian dynasty was unable to provide. Henry IV owed his position in part to confirmation by Parliament, and Parliament, in turn, mindful of its experience with Richard II, was sensitive about allowing any assertion of royal authority. Moreover, Henry faced a series of revolts—by dispossessed supporters of Richard, by the Welsh aristocracy under Owen Glendower, and by the great family of the Percies in Northumberland on the Scottish border. The last years of his reign were troubled by his own poor health and by the hostility of his son, Henry V (1413-1422). Henry V renewed the Hundred Years' War with spectacular victories and reasserted royal power at home, tempered by his need to secure parliamentary support to finance his French campaigns. He also vigorously persecuted the Lollards in an attempt to suppress the social and religious discontent shown by the Peasants' Revolt.

The untimely death of Henry V in 1422 from dysentery contracted while personally leading the seige of Meaux on the River Marne, ended the brief period of Lancastrian success, for it brought to the throne Henry VI (1422-1461), a nine-month-old infant who proved mentally unstable as he grew up. The reign of this third Lancastrian king was a disaster for England. As English forces were defeated in the last campaigns of the Hundred Years' War, the feebleness of Henry VI strengthened both the hand of Parliament and the growth of private armed retainers. While corrupt noble factions competed for control of government, a quarrel broke out between Henry VI's queen, Margaret of Anjou (with whom he was united in an arranged marriage in 1444) and her English allies on the one side, and on the other, Richard, duke of York, a great-grandson of Edward III, once regent of France and heir to the English throne. The quarrel led directly to the Wars of the Roses (1455-1485), so named for the red rose, badge of the House of Lancaster, and the white rose, badge of the House of York.

In thirty years of dreary, sporadic fighting, Parliament became the tool of rival factions, and the kingdom changed hands repeatedly. In 1460 Richard of York was killed, and the ambitious Earl of Warwick, the "kingmaker," took over the leadership of the Yorkist cause. Warwick forced the abdication of Henry VI and placed on the throne the son of Richard of York, Edward IV (1461-1483). King and kingmaker soon fell out, and Warwick briefly restored the House of Lancaster to the throne (1470-1471). Edward IV quickly regained control, however, and Henry VI and Warwick were killed. With Edward securely established, firm royal government returned to England, seemingly on a permanent basis.

Again, however, the prospect of stability faded, for Edward IV died in 1483 aged only forty-one. His twelve-year-old son, Edward V, was soon pushed aside by his guardian and uncle, brother of the older Edward, Richard III (1483-1485), last of the Yorkist kings. Able, courageous, and ruthless, Richard III continues to be the focus of much controversy, having been indelibly depicted as a villain by Shakespeare. There is still debate over whether Richard was responsible for the death of the "little princes of the Tower"—Edward V and his younger brother. In any case, factional strife flared up again as Richard's opponents found a champion in the Lancastrian leader Henry Tudor. In 1485, on Bosworth Field, Richard III was slain, and the Wars of the Roses came to an end. The battle gave England a new monarch, Henry VII, and a new dynasty, the Tudors.

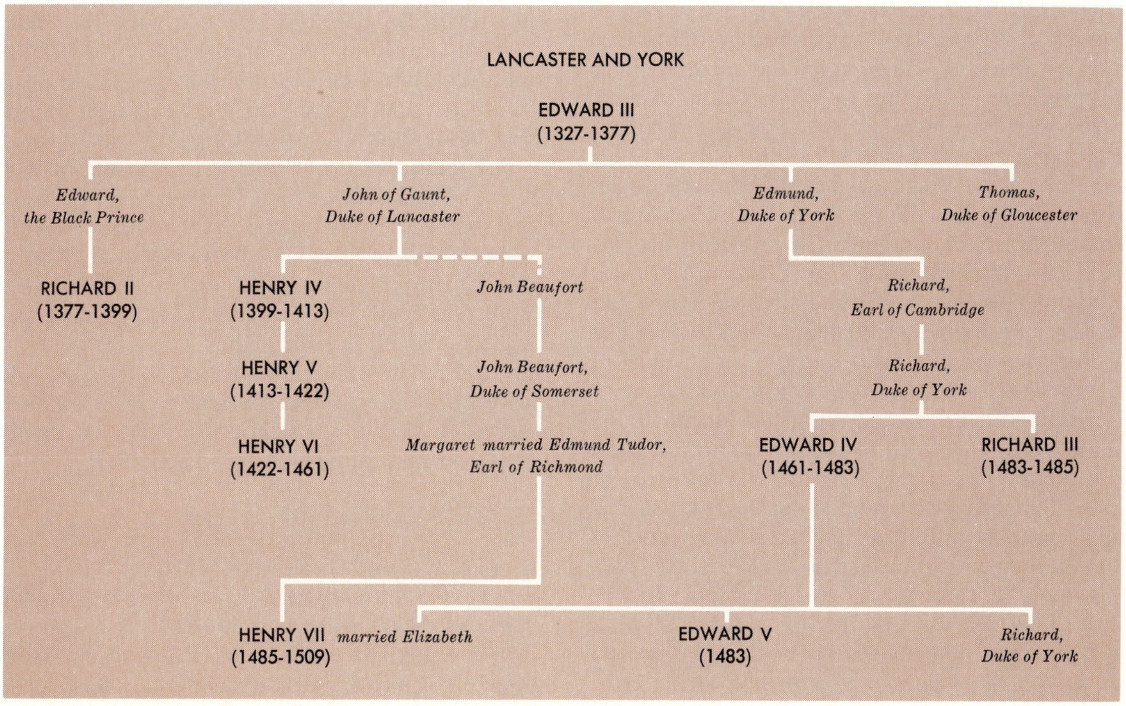

THE ACT OF SUCCESSION, 1485

To assure the legitimacy of Henry VII's succession, Parliament passed an act by which Henry could set about the task of reestablishing the authority of the crown:

Henry, by the grace of God, king of England and of France and lord of Ireland, at the parliament holden at Westminster the seventh day of November, in the first year of the reign of King Henry VII after the Conquest. To the pleasure of Almighty God, the wealth, prosperity, and surety of this realm of England, to the singular comfort of all the king's subjects of the same and in avoiding of all ambiguities and questions: be it ordained, established, and enacted by authority of this present parliament that the inheritances of the crowns of the realms of England and of France, with all the preeminence and dignity royal to the same pertaining, and all other seignories to the king belonging beyond the sea, with the appurtenances thereto in any wise due or pertaining, be, rest, remain, and abide in the most royal person of our now sovereign lord, King Henry VII, and in the heirs of his body lawfully coming, perpetually with the grace of God so to endure, and in none other.

For those interested in the language of the law, this text is especially useful. It is taken from the *Statutes of the Realm*, II, 499, and is reprinted in Carl Stephenson and Frederick George Marcham, eds., *Sources of English Constitutional History* (New York: Harper & Brothers, 1937), pp. 298-99.

Henry VII, 1485-1509

Henry VII (1485-1509) was descended from a bastard branch of the Lancastrian family. His right to be king, however, derived not from this tenuous hereditary claim, but from his victory at Bosworth and a subsequent act of Parliament. The new monarch had excellent qualifications for the job of tidying up after the divisiveness of civil war; shrewd, able, working very closely with his councilors, waging foreign policy by diplomacy and not by arms, Henry VII had much in common with Louis XI of France. Unlike Louis, however, Henry was devout and generous, maintaining a lavish court and endowing Westminster Abbey with a magnificent chapel in elaborate late Gothic style. Henry formally healed the breach between the rival houses of the roses by marrying the Yorkist heiress Elizabeth, daughter of Edward IV. He deprived the nobles of their private armies by forbidding livery and maintenance, and also banned the nobles' intimidation of litigants in the royal courts.

Henry pursued new fiscal policies. Although he depended heavily on the country gentry and other traditional mainstays of monarchical government, he also welcomed new men from the prosperous urban merchant class or from the ranks of churchmen who had worked their way up and owed their careers to him, like the able lawyer Morton, who became archbishop of Canterbury. Henry rewarded many of his advisers with lands confiscated from his opponents at the end of the Wars of the Roses. The king and his councilors more than doubled the revenues of the central government, at times by such high-handed methods as "Morton's Fork," attributed (probably unfairly) to Archbishop Morton. When prelates were summoned to make special payments to the king, those who dressed magnificently to plead exemption on the grounds of the cost of high church office were told that their rich apparel proved their ability to make a large payment. The other tine of the fork caught those who dressed shabbily to pretend poverty, for their frugality argued that they, too, could afford a large contribution. Such practices enabled Henry to avoid a clash with Parliament because he seldom needed its sanction for taxes. The king's obvious efficiency, his avoidance of costly wars, and his assistance to English merchants in gaining trading privileges abroad won his support in the increasingly significant business community.

Henry VII reestablished prosperity as well as law and order in an England weary of rebellion, civil war, and insecurity. His policies set the stage for the more dramatic reign of his successors, Henry VIII and Elizabeth I. He restored the prestige of the monarchy, making it the rallying point of English nationalism, especially after the Statute of Drogheda in 1495 made it clear that no Irish parliament could meet, bring bills, or resist the application of English law in Ireland, the "other island." He fixed the pattern for Tudor policy toward the English Parliament, a policy often given the misleading label of "Tudor absolutism." While Henry VII and his successors were indeed strong monarchs, they were not absolute in the sense that they attempted to ignore Parliament. Henry asked Parliament for money as seldom as possible; during the last dozen years of his reign he had to summon only one Parliament, which met for a few weeks in 1504. Even so, when it refused to give him all the monies he wanted, he yielded gracefully and avoided a confrontation. Henry VII was well aware that precedents for limiting a monarch's authority lay at hand, ready for use against an arbitrary ruler.

Spain, to 1492

The accomplishments of Henry VII and Louis XI, impressive though they were, were overshadowed by those of their Spanish contemporaries, Ferdinand and Isabella. Henry and Louis ruled kingdoms that, however racked by internal dissension, had long been well-

Queen Isabella

King Ferdinand

defined states with established central institutions. Ferdinand and Isabella inherited a Spain that had never been united; they had to build the structure of central government from the foundations.

The decisive event in the early medieval history of the Iberian peninsula was the conquest by the Muslims, who brought almost the whole of the peninsula under their control. In the eighth and ninth centuries, Christian communities free of Muslim domination survived only in the extreme north. Starting in the ninth century, these Christian states had pressed southward until the last Muslim stronghold at Granada fell in 1492. This slow expansion by Catholic Spaniards has often been likened to a crusade more than five hundred years long. It was indeed a crusade, and the proud and militant spirit of the crusader left a permanent mark upon the Spanish "style." The reconquest of Spain, however, like the great Crusades to the Holy Land, was a disjointed movement,

The effigy of King Henry VII on his tomb in Westminster Abbey, London.

undertaken in fits and starts by rival states that sometimes put more energy into combating each other than into fighting the Muslims.

Three Christian kingdoms dominated the Iberian peninsula in the middle of the fifteenth century. Castile, the largest and most populous, had assumed the leadership of the reconquest. The capture of Toledo in central Spain (1085) and a great victory over the Muslims at Las Navas de Tolosa (1212) were landmarks in its expansion southward. But the power of the Castilian kings did not grow in proportion to their territory. The powerful organization of sheep-ranchers, the *Mesta*, controlled vast stretches of Castilian territory and constituted a virtual state within the state. Both the nobility and the towns, which played a semi-independent part in the reconquest, maintained many rights against royal authority. Both were represented, together with the clergy, in the *Cortes*, the Castilian counterpart of the English Parliament and the French Estates General which had originated in the Visigothic council of nobles. The Cortes was, however, largely powerless by the fifteenth century.

To the west of Castile, along the Atlantic coast, lay the second Christian kingdom, Portugal, a former Castilian province that had won independence in the twelfth century. Though still retaining close links with Castile, the Portuguese had developed their own distinctive language and pursued their own national interests, especially in exploration and overseas commerce, in which they brilliantly exploited their Atlantic seacoast.

The third kingdom, located in northeastern Spain, was Aragon, which was as much a Mediterranean power as an Iberian one. Its kings controlled the Balearic Islands, ruled lands along the Mediterranean on the French side of the Pyrenees, and had an important stake in southern Italy. In the breakup of the Hohenstaufen Empire, Aragon took the island of Sicily (1282) and King Alfonso V, the Magnanimous (1416-1458), added Naples in 1435. In Aragon, as in Castile, the oldest established political institutions were those limiting the Crown—the nobility, the towns and the Cortes, which was much more powerful than in Castile. Moreover, two territories of the Crown of Aragon on the Spanish mainland, Valencia and Catalonia, the latter centered on the prosperous port of Barcelona, had Cortes of their own and so many other autonomous privileges that they were, in effect, separate states.

In 1469 Ferdinand, later king of Aragon (1479-1516), married Isabella, later queen of Castile (1474-1504), and thus made the dynastic alliance that eventually unified Spain. The obstacles confronting them were enormous. Not only was the royal power weak in both states; the inhabitants of Castile and Aragon did not speak the same language, a difference still evident today in the distinction between the Castilian Spanish spoken in Madrid and the Catalan of Barcelona, whose closest linguistic relative is the Provençal once spoken in the south of France. Aragon looked toward the Mediterranean, Castile toward the Atlantic, so that a union of Castile with Portugal might have been more natural. Even today, Spanish nationalism is diluted by strong regional loyalties, especially in Catalonia and among the Basques.

Ferdinand and Isabella made a good political partnership. He was a cautious realist like Louis XI and an ardent promoter of Aragon's interests in Italy; though given the honorific title of "The Catholic" by the pope, he was skeptical and tolerant in religion. Isabella, on the other hand, was devout to the point of fanaticism, adored the pomp and circumstance of the throne, and in politics was wholly absorbed in consolidating her power in Castile. She vested much authority in a new body staffed by royal appointees, the Council of Castile. She allied herself with the middle class of the towns against the nobles and drew military support from town militias, rather than from feudal levies. Finding her sovereignty weakened by three large military brotherhoods founded in the twelfth century to advance the reconquest and controlled by the Castilian nobility, she

Christian Reconquest of Spain

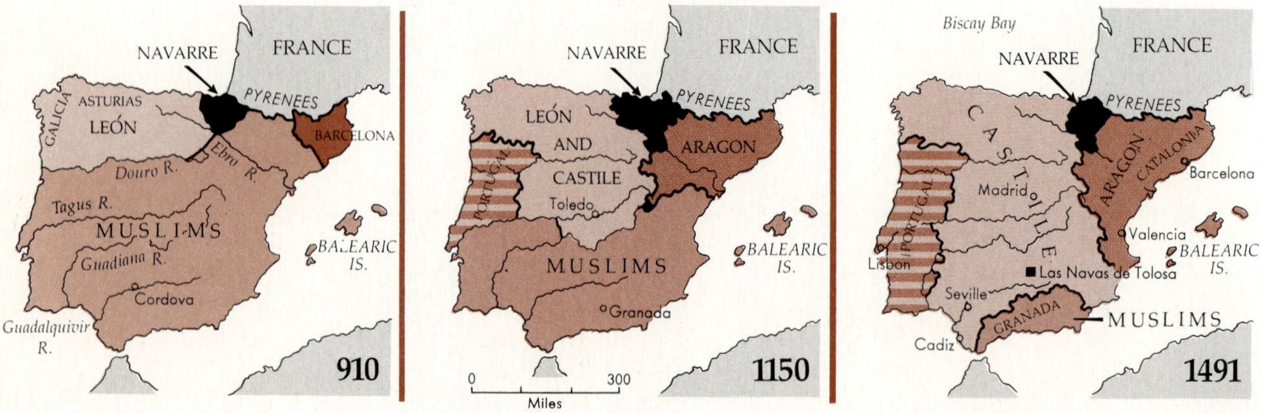

insisted that Ferdinand become head of each brotherhood. Isabella was more indulgent toward the Mesta, since payments made by the sheep interests were the mainstay of royal revenue until the wealth of the New World began to pour in.

Ferdinand and Isabella relied heavily on the church in advancing the royal power. Though pious, the Queen was determined to bring the Church under royal discipline, and she prescribed a much-needed purge of ecclesiastical corruption. The Spanish monarchs also obtained from the papacy the right to appoint Spanish bishops and to dispose of parts of church revenue. Like the Gallican church of France, the Spanish church was half-independent of Rome; far more than the Gallican church, it was the prop of royal absolutism. The ranking Spanish prelate, Cardinal Jiménez de Cisneros (1436-1517), the archbishop of Toledo, became Isabella's chief minister and executed her policies of purifying the church, curbing the aristocracy, and courting the towns.

When the Inquisition was introduced into Spain in 1478, it was from the first a royal rather than a papal instrument. The Spanish Inquisition sought to promote Spanish nationalism by enforcing universal Catholicism, and to create loyal subjects of the Crown by obliging all people to be obedient children of the church. Its chief targets were two religious minorities—the Muslims and the Jews—who had long enjoyed toleration and who owned some of the most productive farms and businesses in Spain. The Jews, because they had accumulated substantial economic resources and showed political reliability, were favorite agents of the Crown until Isabella's alliance with the Christian townspeople. Earlier, however, fear and envy of Jewish success had promoted popular anti-Semitic outbreaks that led many Jews to become converts to Christianity.

The Inquisition was established to check backsliding among these New Christians, or *Marranos*—Jews secretly practicing their old faith. The persecution was so menacing, with its tortures and burnings at the stake, that more than one hundred thousand New Christians fled the country. In 1492 unconverted Jews were confronted with the alternatives of baptism or exile with the loss of their property; about one hundred fifty thousand chose exile. Ten years later, it was the turn of the Muslims, who received no choice except baptism. Catholicism thereby won many nominal new adherents who conformed only because they dreaded what the Inquisition had in store for those who wavered in their new faith. Isabella and Jiménez had secured religious uniformity at the cost of alienating some of the most productive groups in Spanish society.

The year 1492, accordingly, may be viewed as the most crucial date in Spanish history. It began, on January 2, with the triumphal entry of Ferdinand and Isabella into Granada, marking the conquest of the last fragment of independent Muslim Spain. Later in the year, the way was opened for immense new conquests when Columbus sailed from a Castilian port on the first of his voyages to the New World. But in that same year persecution on a grand scale was confirmed as national policy. The new Spanish monarchy already bore the stamp of the intolerant nationalism that was to be at once its strength and its weakness in generations to come.

III PARTICULARISM IN GERMANY AND ITALY

The Princes and the Empire, 1254-1493

In contrast to the new national monarchies of western Europe, power in Germany shifted steadily from the emperor to the princes of the particular states. Once, for almost two decades, there was no emperor at all. This

Illustrations from the fourteenth-century *Mirror of Saxony*. The top panel represents the five cities in which the Saxon king could hold court. In the center the pope receives the key from St. Peter as the emperor watches. At the bottom the pope and emperor embrace, symbolizing the coordination of spiritual and temporal power.

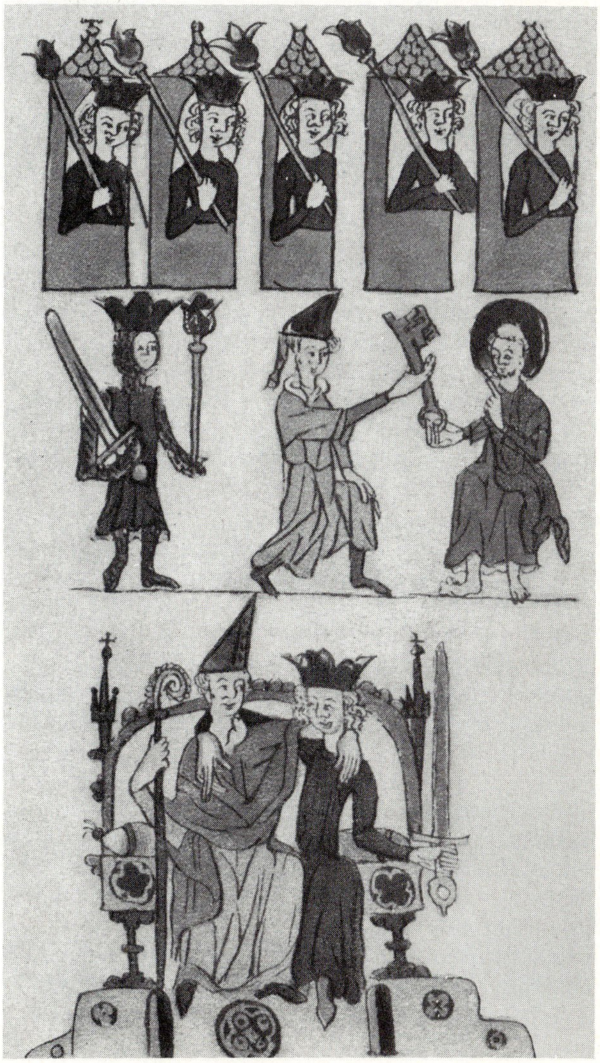

THE GOLDEN BULL

The bull was named for its gold seal, and it established the means for electing emperors, recognized the powers of the seven electors, and excluded popes from what would thereby become a German administration of the empire:

1. Mass shall be celebrated on the day after the arrival of the electors. The archbishop of Mainz administers this oath, which the other electors repeat:

2. "I, archbishop of Mainz, archchancellor of the empire for Germany, electoral prince, swear on the holy gospels here before me, and by the faith which I owe to God and to the holy Roman empire, that with the aid of God, and according to my best judgment and knowledge, I will cast my vote, in this election of the king of the Romans and future emperor, for a person fitted to rule the Christian people. I will give my voice and vote freely, uninfluenced by any agreement, price, bribe, promise, or anything of the sort, by whatever name it may be called. So help me God and all the saints."

3. After the electors have taken this oath, they shall proceed to the election, and shall not depart from Frankfort until the majority have elected a king of the Romans and future emperor, to be ruler of the world and of the Christian people. If they have not come to a decision within thirty days from the day on which they took the above oath, after that they shall live upon bread and water and shall not leave the city until the election has been decided.

4. Such an election shall be as valid as if all the princes had agreed unanimously and without difference upon a candidate. If any one of the princes or his representatives has been hindered or delayed for a time, but arrives before the election is over, he shall be admitted and shall take part in the election at the stage which has been reached at the time of his arrival. According to the ancient and approved custom, the king of the Romans elect, immediately after his election and before he takes up any other business of the empire, shall confirm and approve by sealed letters for each and all of the electoral princes, ecclesiastical and secular, the privileges, charters, rights, liberties, concessions, ancient customs, and dignities, and whatever else the princes held and possessed from the empire at the time of the election; and he shall renew the confirmation and approval when he becomes emperor.

Oliver J. Thatcher and Edgar H. McNeal, eds., *A Source Book for Medieval History: Selected Documents Illustrating the History of Europe in the Middle Ages* (New York: Scribner's, 1905), pp. 288-89.

was the Great Interregnum (1254-1273), following the death of the last Hohenstaufen emperor, Conrad IV. During this time the princes grew even stronger at the expense of the monarchy, and the old links between Germany and Italy were cut. The earlier idea of an emperor who ruled lands outside Germany vanished.

The imperial title, however, survived. It went to Rudolf of Hapsburg (1273-1291), from a family of lesser German nobility whose estates lay mostly in Switzerland. Rudolf cared nothing for imperial pretensions; he wanted to establish a hereditary monarchy for his family in Germany and make this monarchy as rich and as powerful as possible. He added Austria to the family holdings, and his descendants ruled at Vienna until 1918. Since Hapsburg interests were focused on the southeastern part of the empire, Rudolf made concessions to the French in the west to get their support for the new Hapsburg monarchy.

After 1270, consequently, the French moved into imperial territories that had once belonged to the old Carolingian middle kingdom, thereby securing lands east of the Rhone and a foothold in Lorraine. The German princes, however, especially the great archbishops of the Rhine Valley, opposed the Hapsburg policy of appeasing the French. Thus, during the century following the Interregnum two parties developed in Germany. The Hapsburg party, eastern-based and pro-French, favored a strong hereditary monarchy. The opposition party, western-based, and anti-French, was against a strong hereditary monarchy. This division frustrated the development of German national unity.

Toward the middle of the fourteenth century, when the principle of elective monarchy finally triumphed, the princes as a class secured a great victory, which was embodied in the Golden Bull of 1356, issued by the emperor Charles IV. It affirmed that the imperial dignity was of God, that the German electoral princes chose the emperor, and that the choice of the majority of the electors needed no confirmation by the pope. The electors were to number seven: three ecclesiastical princes—the archbishops of Mainz, Trier, and Cologne—and four secular princes—the count palatine of the Rhine, the duke of Saxony, the margrave of Brandenburg, and the king of Bohemia. The rights of the four secular electors were to pass to their eldest sons, and their territories could never be divided. Each of the seven electors was to be all but sovereign in his own territory, with full rights of coinage and of holding courts from which there was no appeal. Thus, the Golden Bull has been termed "the Magna Carta of the German princes."

Throughout the fourteenth century, the German princes faced the threat of new political fragmentation,

especially from their administrative officials, the *ministeriales*, who were originally from the lower classes but who had turned their lands and powers into feudal rights, assumed knighthood, and virtually merged with the old nobility. To levy taxes, the princes had to obtain the consent of the nobles and knights, along with that of the other two estates—the clergy and the towns. The estates regularly won privileges from the princes in exchange for money. This period also saw the rise of the *Hansa* (guild of merchants) of North German commercial towns and the increasing prominence of sovereign "free cities," such as Hamburg and Frankfurt, all over Germany.

After about 1400 the power of the estates slowly yielded to the implications of the Golden Bull. The princes who were not electors gradually adopted for their own principalities the rules of primogeniture (inheritance by the first born) and indivisibility that the Golden Bull had prescribed for the electoral principalities. The princes were assisted in their assertion of authority by the spread of Roman law, which helped them make good their claims to absolute control of public rights and offices. Gradually, in dozens of petty states, orderly finance, indivisible princely domains, and taxation granted by the estates became typical.

With numerous sovereign princes firmly established in their particular states and with a long roster of free cities enjoying virtual political independence, the empire itself had become almost meaningless. It had lost control not only over the western lands taken by France but also over other frontier areas, notably Switzerland. In 1291 three forest cantons in the heart of the country had won effective self-rule. By the early sixteenth century there were thirteen confederated cantons, and the Swiss, backed by France, had checked both Burgundian and German attempts to subjugate them. The Swiss Confederation, though nominally still subject to the empire, was in fact an independent entity with boundaries beginning to resemble those of present-day Switzerland. Thus, another national state was emerging, though one without a strong central authority, for the Swiss federal government was extremely weak.

In 1438 the Holy Roman emperorship, though still elective, passed permanently to the house of Hapsburg. Forty-five years later the able Hapsburg Maximilian I (1493-1519) became emperor. He had acquired great riches by marrying Mary of Burgundy, daughter of Charles the Bold and heiress of the Low Countries. Under his weak predecessors the Hapsburg position in central Europe had deteriorated; Maximilian reestablished firm Hapsburg power in Austria and its dependencies. He also arranged marriages for his children and grandchildren that promised to add vast new territories to the family possessions and that would make his grandson, Charles V, ruler of half of Europe. On the other hand, Maximilian's projects for reforming the empire came to little, not only because of the vested interests of German particularism but also because of Maximilian's own dynastic concerns.

Despots and Condottieri in Italy, 1268-1513

The Italians too lacked a central authority to give effective political expression to any potential national awareness. With the disintegration of the Hohenstaufen empire in the thirteenth century, Italy, like Germany, witnessed the emergence of powerful local rulers. In Germany the fifteenth century was the Age of the Princes; in Italy it was the Age of the Despots—brilliant, ruthless, cultivated rulers who did much to set the style of the Renaissance.

Despots had not always ruled in Italy. The medieval struggle between popes and emperors had promoted the growth of independent communes or city-states, particularly in northern Italy. In the twelfth and thirteenth centuries the communes were oligarchic republics dominated by the nobility and by rich businessmen. The ruling oligarchies, however, were torn by the strife between the pro-papal Guelfs and the pro-imperial Ghibellines. Meantime, something close to class warfare arose between the wealthy, on the one hand, and the small shopkeepers and wage earners, on the other. Dissension grew so bitter that arbitrary one-man government seemed the only remedy. Sometimes a despot seized power; sometimes he was invited in from outside by the contending factions; often he was a *condottiere*, a mercenary commander the states had hired under contract to fight their wars. (*Condotta* is Italian for "contract," whence *condottiere*, "contractor".) One of the first great condottieri was an Englishman, Sir John Hawkwood, who went to Italy during a lull in the Hundred Years' War and, as a soldier of fortune, sold himself to various communes. In the fifteenth century the most celebrated condottieri were drawn from noble dynasties like the Gonzaga of Mantua, or ambitious plebeians such as Francesco Sforza, who became duke of Milan (1450-1466).

By the fifteenth century the fortunes of war and politics had worked significant changes in the map of Italy. Especially in the north, many city-states that had been important a century or two earlier were sinking into political obscurity. Pisa, Siena, and Lucca, for example, were subjugated or eclipsed by stronger neighbors, though they continued to participate vigorously in economic or cultural life. Half a dozen states now dominated Italian politics—Naples in the south, the States of the Church in the center, and the duchy of Milan and the republics of Florence and Venice in the north.

The kingdom of Naples, which included Sicily, had long been subject to foreign domination—Byzantine, Arab, Norman, and Hohenstaufen. In 1268 Charles of Anjou, brother of Louis IX of France, conquered them from the grandson of the emperor Frederick II. Sicily revolted (1282) and passed to the control of Aragon, and eventually to the Spain of Ferdinand and Isabella. Naples remained under Angevin rule until 1435, when it was taken by Alfonso the Magnanimous of Aragon. On his death it became independent once more under his illegitimate son Ferrante (Ferdinand I, 1458-1494), a particularly unscrupulous despot. Under Angevin and Aragonese rule the area never fully recovered the prosperity and cultural leadership it had earlier enjoyed, although Naples was significant in Renaissance culture.

The Florentine Andrea del Verrocchio's dramatic monument (1488) of the condottiere Bartolommeo Colleoni, who became generalissimo of Venice in 1454.

Leonardo da Vinci's forceful drawing of a condottiere.

The States of the Church also experienced a material decline in the fourteenth and early fifteenth centuries. While the papacy was at Avignon, the city of Rome suffered severe economic losses and passed to the control of rival princely families; outlying papal territories fell to local lords or despots. In 1377 Pope Gregory XI paid a visit to Rome and died there in the following year before he could make his planned return to Avignon. The angry Romans, determined to bring the papacy back to their city permanently, intimidated the French-dominated College of Cardinals into electing an Italian as Urban VI. The new pope alarmed the cardinals by plans for drastic reform, and thirteen of them proceeded to declare his election invalid and chose a rival to rule the church from Avignon, "Clement VII" (1378-1394). (The quotation marks indicate that he does not rank as a legitimate pope and distinguish him from the sixteenth-century Pope Clement VII.) These events inaugurated the Great Schism (1378-1417), when there were two popes, each with his own college of cardinals—one at Rome, the other at Avignon. International alliances and enmities largely determined which states recognized which claimant to the papal title; for example, since France and its ally Scotland were pro-Avignon, England was pro-Rome.

Against the scandal of the Great Schism, the church rallied in the Conciliar movement, which began when both colleges of cardinals agreed to summon a general council of five hundred prelates and representatives from European states. The Council of Pisa (1409-1410) deposed both papal claimants and elected an Italian, who was more a condottiere than a spiritual leader, "John XXIII" (1410-1414). Since neither of the rival popes accepted the council's actions, there was now a triple split. A second general council, meeting at Constance (1414-1417), finally ended the Great Schism and elected Martin V (1417-1431), a Roman aristocrat, who restored the formal unity of Western Christendom.

On other issues, however, the Conciliar movement was less successful. The Council of Constance tried the Bohemian reformer John Hus (c 1369-1415), a professor at the University of Prague, for doctrinal heresy and had him burned at the stake in violation of a guarantee of his safety. The movement Hus had started continued until the Hussites were again granted communion at the Council of Basel in 1436. Neither this council nor its successors, which met sporadically until 1449, managed to purge the church of corruption and worldliness. And their efforts to transform the papacy from an absolute monarchy into a constitutional one by making general councils a permanent feature of ecclesiastical government were thwarted by determined papal opposition. Some European states were courted by the pope to strengthen his hand against the councils. Nevertheless, important limitations were placed on his authority. A notable example was France, where the Pragmatic Sanction of Bourges in 1438 gave the Gallican church a large measure of autonomy.

With the Conciliar movement defeated, the popes concentrated their attention once more on central Italy. Beginning with Sixtus IV (1471-1484), the papacy was held by a series of ambitious men. They were often highly cultivated and very secular as well, openly acknowledging their children and lavishing favors on them and on other relatives. They restored Rome as a center of art and learning and began the reconquest of the papal dominions outside Rome. A Spanish pope from the Borgia family, Alexander VI (1492-1503), made notable progress in subjugating the lords of central Italy and breaking the power of the Roman princely families. Alexander was greatly aided by his son Cesare, the alleged hero of Machiavelli's *Prince*, who employed violence, treachery, and poison to gain his ends. The most redoubtable of these condottieri popes was Julius II (1503-1513), who commanded papal armies in person. The pontificate of Julius II marked the summit of papal temporal power, which receded thereafter because of the wounds inflicted on the church by the Reformation and the damage sustained by Italy as the battleground in wars between the Hapsburgs and France.

Milan, 1277-1535

One of the three great northern Italian states, Milan lay in the midst of the fertile plain of Lombardy, the breadbasket of Italy. It was the terminus of trade routes through the Alpine passes from northern Europe and was also a textile and metal-working center, famous for its velvets and brocades, its weapons and armor. Milan

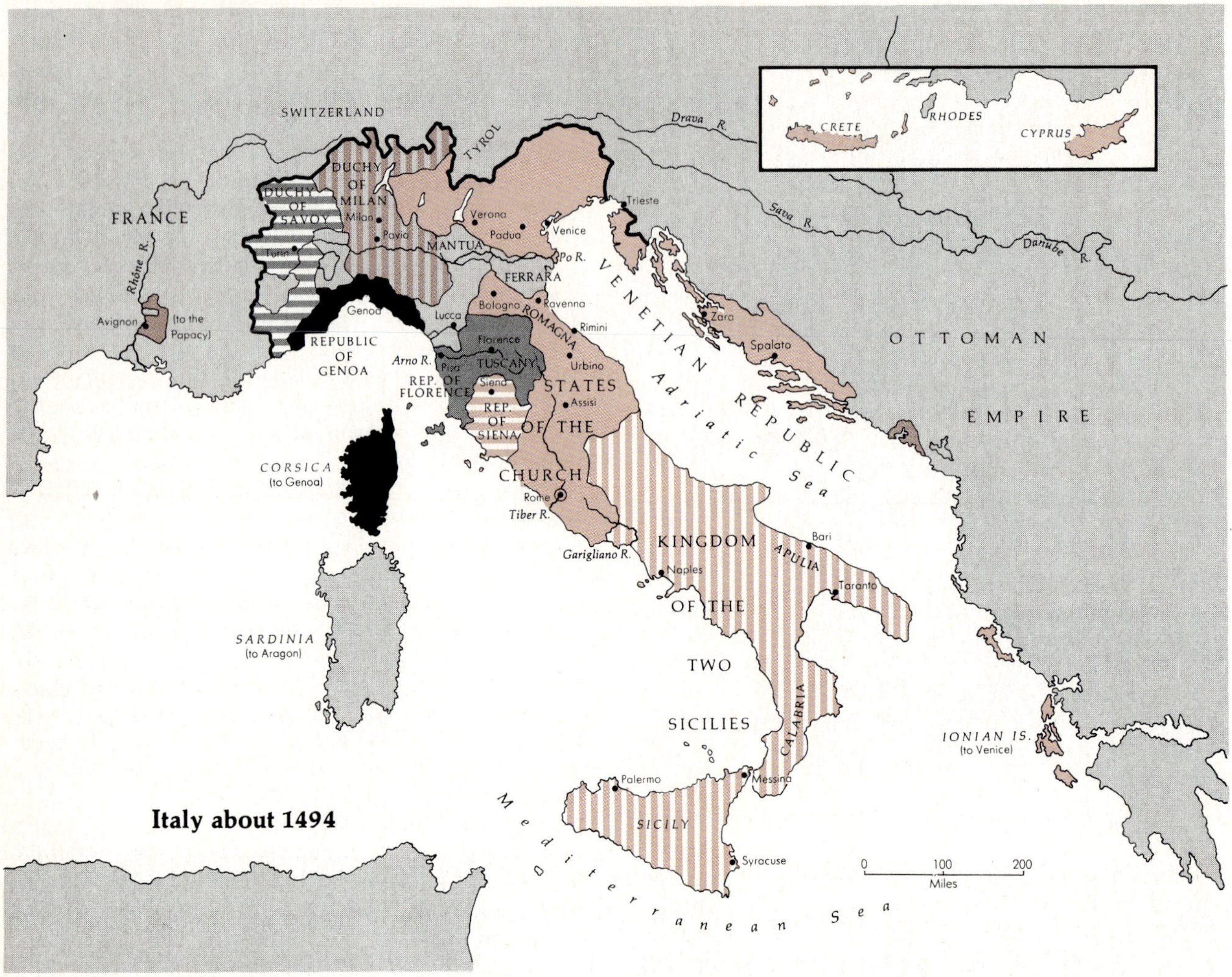

Italy about 1494

had played a major political role since the twelfth century, when it headed the Lombard League in successful contest with Frederick Barbarossa. Milan was then a republic, run by the nobility in conjunction with a *parlamento*, or great council, in which all citizens of modest means could participate. This precarious balance between aristocracy and democracy was upset by outbreaks of Guelf and Ghibelline factionalism. In 1277 authority was seized by the noble Visconti family, who soon secured recognition from the emperor as dukes of Milan.

When the direct Visconti line died out in 1447, Francesco Sforza usurped the ducal office in 1450. The most famous of the Sforza dukes was a younger son of Francesco, Ludovico Il Moro (1451-1508)—the nickname derived perhaps from his dark "Moorish" appearance. Ludovico made the court of Milan possibly the most brilliant in Europe by assembling a retinue of outstanding artists and intellectuals, headed by Leonardo da Vinci (1452-1519). Although he had the reputation of being the craftiest diplomat of the age, Ludovico's craftiness could not protect him against the armies of France and Spain, which invaded Italy in the 1490s. Driven from his throne in 1500, Il Moro died in French imprisonment eight years later. The duchy of Milan came under Spanish control in 1535 and remained there for almost two hundred years.

Florence, to 1569

Midway between Milan and Rome lay the city of Florence, on the banks of the Arno River in Tuscany. The Republic of Florence, like that of Milan, was a fragile combination of aristocratic and democratic elements. It was badly shaken by Guelf-Ghibelline rivalries and by the emergence of the city as a pioneering center of industry and finance, which created an ambitious wealthy class of bankers and merchants. In the twelfth century the commune had acquired a dominant position, though historians cannot reconstruct precisely how, since the written record is notably sparse.

Florence exemplified the growth of social mobility, new wealth, extensive trade, and complex credit operations. These changes were mirrored in religious thought, as society slowly shifted from gift-exchange to holy poverty and practical charity. The result was a society based on a desire to work cooperatively, as best shown by the widespread use of credit in both public and private finance. A willingness to rethink the miracles of the Virgin, like a willingness to take risks with coinage and credit, forced individuals and groups to step outside the bounds of security as it had been defined earlier. The result was a productive tension between the cult of poverty (and insecurity) that was deeply rooted in monastic and philosophical Christian thought and the desire for wealth (and security) that lay at the base of the growth of the Italian cities. The factionalism, therefore, was not simply petty, for it expressed very major concerns in a changing society.

In the thirteenth century two noble factions contended for power: the Guelfs, who were ready to open their ranks to newly rich commoners, and the Ghibellines, who were reluctant to do so. In the late 1200s Guelf capitalists prevailed over the Ghibelline aristocrats and revised the constitution of the republic so that a virtual monopoly of key government offices rested with the seven major guilds, which were controlled by the great woolen masters, bankers, and exporters. They denied any effective political voice to the artisans and shopkeepers of the fourteen lesser guilds, as well as to Ghibellines, many nobles, and common laborers. But feuds within Guelf ranks soon caused a new exodus of political exiles, including the poet Dante, whose attempts to heal Guelf divisions resulted in his permanent banishment in 1302.

Throughout the fourteenth century and into the fifteenth, political factionalism and social and economic tensions tormented Florence, though they did not prevent a remarkable cultural growth of the city. The politically unprivileged—almost everyone outside the dominant Guelf oligarchy—sought to make the republic more democratic; they failed in the long run because of the oligarchy's resilience and also because the reformers themselves were torn by the hostility between the lesser guilds and the poor day laborers, often termed *Ciompi*, which literally meant wool carders. The English king Edward III's repudiation of his debts to the Florentine bankers, followed in the 1340s by disastrous bank failures, weakened the major guilds enough to permit the fourteen lesser guilds to gain supremacy.

Unrest persisted, however, compounded by the catastrophe of the Black Death, reaching a climax with the revolution of the Ciompi in 1378. Wool carders, weavers, and dyers gained the right to form their own guilds and to have a minor voice in politics. Continued turbulence permitted the wealthy to gain the upper hand over both the Ciompi and the lesser guilds. The prestige of the reestablished oligarchy rose when it defended the city against the threat of annexation by the aggressive Visconti of Milan. Finally, in the early 1400s, a new rash of bankruptcies and a series of military reverses weakened

The Catena Map of Florence in 1490 shows the rapid changes that overtook the city during the preceding century.

MACHIAVELLI DESCRIBES LORENZO THE MAGNIFICENT

A celebrated Florentine, Niccolò Machiavelli, drew an admiring portrait of Lorenzo the Magnificent:

His purpose was to keep the city rich, the people united, and the nobility honored. He greatly loved whoever was excellent in any profession. . . . For this reason, Count Giovanni Pico della Mirandola [philosopher who sought to combine Greek and Christian ideas into a Platonist humanism], a man almost divine, rejected all the other parts of Europe he had visited and made his abode in Florence, because of Lorenzo's liberality . . . . His way of living and his prudence and good fortune were observed with admiration and highly respected not merely by the princes of Italy but by those at a distance. . . . His reputation, because of his prudence, daily increased, since in discussing affairs he was eloquent and penetrating, in settling them wise, in carrying them out prompt and courageous. Nor can any vices be brought up against him that soiled his great virtues, even though in affairs of love he was wonderfully involved, and he delighted in witty and keen men and in childish play more than seemed fitting for so great a man, so that he was often seen among his sons and daughters, taking part in their sports. Hence, observing both his frivolous and pleasure-seeking conduct and his serious conduct, we see him in two different persons joined in an almost impossible combination.

The History of Florence, in *The Chief Works and Others*, trans. Allen Gilbert (Durham, N.C.: Duke University Press, 1965), III, 1433-34.

the hold of the oligarchy. In 1434 some of its leaders were forced into exile, and power passed to a political champion of the poor, Cosimo de' Medici.

For the next sixty years (1434-1494) Florence was run by the Medici, who had large woolen and banking interests and were perhaps the wealthiest family in all Italy. The Medici were rather like some tyrants of ancient Greece, who did much to benefit the lower classes. Their application of the graduated income tax bore heavily on the rich, particularly on their political enemies, while the resources of the Medici bank were employed to weaken their opponents and assist their friends. They operated quietly behind the facade of republican institutions. Cosimo, for example, seldom held any public office and kept himself in the background.

The grandson of Cosimo was Lorenzo, the most famous of the Medici, ruler of Florence from 1469 to 1492 and known as the Magnificent for want of a formal title. Though possessing in full measure the zest for living and the wide-ranging interests admired by his contemporaries, Lorenzo was not without flaws. His neglect of military matters and his financial carelessness, which contributed to the failure of the Medici bank, left Florence poorly prepared for the wars that were to engulf Italy in the late 1400s. After Lorenzo's death in 1492 at the age of forty-three, the Florentines made two short-lived attempts to restore a genuinely republican government. In 1569 the Medici converted the republic of Florence into the Grand Duchy of Tuscany, with themselves as hereditary grand dukes, but by then the city had forfeited any claim to grandeur.

Venice in the Fifteenth Century

The third great north Italian state, Venice, enjoyed a political stability that contrasted with the turbulence of Milan and Florence. By the fifteenth century the Republic of Saint Mark, as it was called, was in fact an empire, that controlled the lower Po valley on the Italian mainland, the Dalmatian coast of the Adriatic, the Ionian islands, and part of mainland Greece. The Po territories had been annexed to secure the defenses and food supply of its island capital, and the others were the legacy of its aggressive role in the Crusades and the symbol of its predominance over the Eastern trade, unchallenged after the Venetians outdistanced their Genoese competitors in the fourteenth century.

Unlike Florence and Milan, Venice had no landed nobility, so that its government reflected the city's commercial interests. The Venetian constitution assumed its definitive form in the early fourteenth century. Earlier, the chief executive had been the *doge*, or duke, first appointed by the Byzantine emperor, then elected; the legislature had been a general assembly of all the citizens, somewhat resembling the parlamento of Milan. However, the Venetian merchants feared that a powerful doge might establish a hereditary monarchy, and they found the assembly unwieldly and unbusinesslike. Accordingly, they relegated the doge to a ceremonial role like that of a constitutional monarch today. The merchants also transformed the old assembly into the Great Council, whose membership of two hundred and forty men was limited to the families listed in a special Golden Book. The Great Council, in turn, elected the doge and the members of the smaller councils, which really ran the government. Foremost among these was the Council of Ten, charged with maintaining the security of the republic.

The Venetian elite was much more compact than that of Florence, where aggressive newcomers could gain membership in one of the greater guilds. The Venetian system gave a permanent monopoly of political power to the old merchant families listed in the Golden Book, about two percent of the total population. Yet the oligarchs of Venice, while denying the majority a voice in politics and sternly repressing all opposition, instituted many projects that served the general welfare, from neighborhood fountains to a great naval arsenal. They treated the subject cities of the empire with fairness and generosity, and they were pioneers (at least in the Western world) in developing a corps of diplomats to serve the far-reaching concerns of a great commercial power. Though they could not prevent the eventual decline of the city, they did pursue their business aims with single-minded efficiency for several prosperous centuries, so that Venice was unique among Italian states for its political calm and order. Seldom in history have political means been so perfectly adapted to economic ends.

"The School of Europe"

The Italian states of the fifteenth century have been called "the school of Europe," instructing the rest of the Continent in the new realistic ways of power politics. Despots like Il Moro, Cesare Borgia, Lorenzo the Magnificent, and the oligarchs of Venice might well have given lessons in statecraft to Henry VII of England or Louis XI of France. In international affairs, the experiments with diplomatic missions made by Venice, by the Visconti of Milan, and by the Gonzaga family in Mantua were soon copied by the national monarchies. They marked an early stage in the development of permanent diplomatic embassies. Italian reliance on condottieri in warfare foreshadowed the increased use of mercenaries and the abandonment of the old feudal levies. Finally, the rival Italian states, though their competition often led them into open conflict, learned to coexist in a precarious balance of power, which was to be a precedent for the major European states.

This very example, however, also reveals that Italy was the school of Europe in a negative sense, for Italy also furnished an object lesson in how not to behave politically. By the close of the fifteenth century it was evident that the balance established among the Italian states was too precarious to preserve their independence. Beginning with the French invasion of 1494, Italy became a prize for the new national dynastic imperialists of France, Spain, and the Hapsburg realm; in the end the Spanish dominated. The national monarchy was the wave of the future, at least of a successful political future; the city-state was not, even when it was run by an efficient despot, or when, like Venice, it ruled an empire. The Italians of the Renaissance, like the Greeks of antiquity whom they resembled, were victimized by stronger neighbors and penalized for their failure to form a united Italy.

These lessons from "the school of Europe" were first drawn by Niccolò Machiavelli (1469-1527), a diplomat who served the restored Florentine republic in the early 1500s and was exiled when the Medici returned in 1512. Soon after, he wrote *The Prince* and dedicated it to the Medici ruler in the vain hope of regaining political favor. *The Prince* had a low opinion of human beings in general:

> *They are ungrateful, changeable, simulators and dissimulators, runaways in danger, eager for gain; while you do*

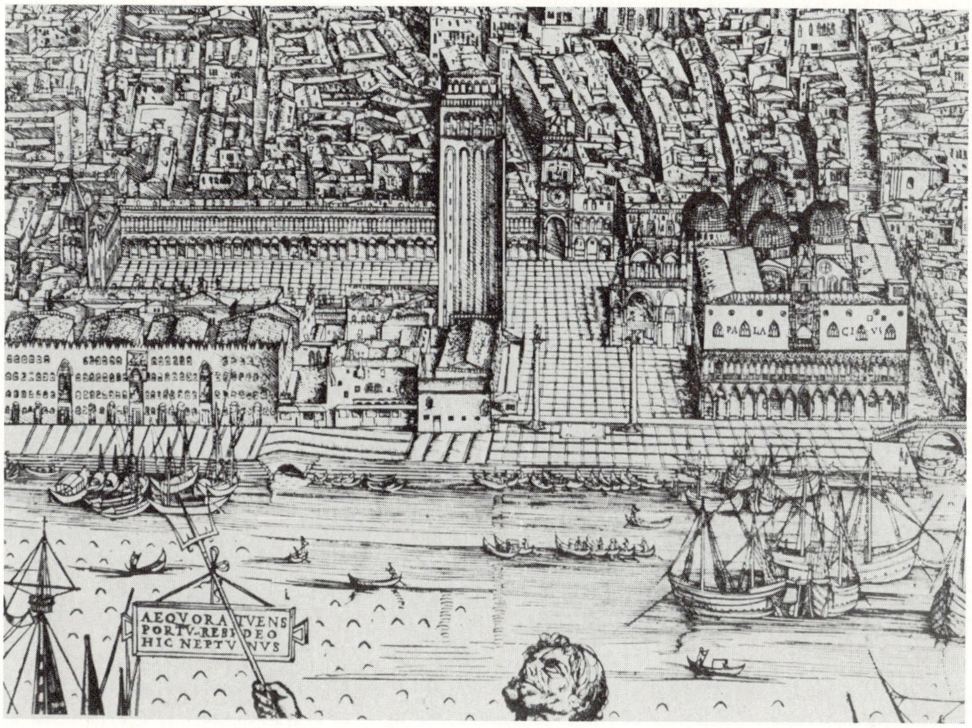

A panoramic view of the city of Venice in 1500 from a woodcut by Jacobo de Barbari (c 1440-c 1511). The Doge's palace is in the right foreground, with the Cathedral of Saint Mark beside it. That Venice was ruled from the sea and also ruled the sea is shown by the inclusion of Neptune's head at the bottom of the scene.

*well by them they are all yours; they offer you their blood, their property, their lives, their children . . . when need is far off; but when it comes near you, they turn about.**

One might term this a secular adaptation of original sin, a transfer of doubts about humanity from religion to social and political psychology. The politics of *The Prince* follow directly from its estimate of human nature:

*Since . . . a prince is necessitated to play the animal well, he chooses among the beasts the fox and the lion, because the lion does not protect himself from traps; the fox does not protect himself from wolves. The prince must be a fox, therefore, to recognize the traps and a lion to frighten the wolves. . . . By no means can a prudent ruler keep his word—and he does not—when to keep it works against himself and when the reasons that made him promise are annulled. If all men were good, this maxim would not be good, but because they are bad and do not keep their promises to you, you likewise do not have to keep yours to them.***

Accordingly, Machiavelli praised the vigorous and unscrupulous absolutism of Francesco Sforza and Lorenzo de' Medici and, above all, the bad faith and deception practiced by Cesare Borgia to tighten his hold on the States of the Church.

The Prince was a prescription against the severe political maladies afflicting Italy in the early 1500s. But what precisely was Machiavelli's diagnosis of Italy's ills, and what precisely was his recommended prescription? Scholars do not entirely agree. Most believe that *The Prince* is to be taken literally, and that Italy's desperate plight in the face of foreign invasion—"without head, without order, beaten, despoiled, lacerated,"† as Machiavelli wrote in his emotional final chapter—required a desperate remedy. Others argue that Machiavelli's intention was satirical, and that he was warning Italians against relying on excessive despotism, even during a national emergency.

This last view gains some plausibility when *The Prince* is compared with Machiavelli's longer work, *The Discourses on the First Ten Books of Titus Livius* (the Roman historian Livy). Here he addressed not the immediate Italian crisis, but the universal problem of building a lasting government, and he argued that the state required more than a single prince endowed with still more power. In a chapter entitled "The Multitude Is Wiser and More Constant Than a Prince," Machiavelli wrote:

It also appears that in choosing magistrates a people makes far better choices than a prince, nor will a people ever be persuaded that it is wise to put into high places a man of bad repute and of corrupt habits—something a prince can be persuaded to do easily. . . .

Besides this, we see that cities where the people are in control grow enormously in a very short time, and much more than those that have always been under a prince, as Rome did after she expelled the kings and Athens after she freed herself from Pisistratus. This comes from nothing else than that governments by the people are better than those by princes.††

In *the Discourses* Machiavelli presented both an estimate of human nature and a political program seemingly in conflict with *The Prince*. But the conflict is perhaps more apparent than real. *The Discourses* con-

*Niccolò Machiavelli, *The Prince*, in *The Chief Works and Others*, trans. Allen Gilbert (Durham, N.C.: Duke University Press, 1965). I, 62. © 1965 Duke University Press.
**Ibid., I, 65.

†Ibid., I, 93.
††Ibid., *The Discourses*, I, 316.

MACHIAVELLI ON THE CHURCH

Machiavelli blamed the Italians' loss of civic spirit on the church, attacked the temporal interests of the papacy for preventing Italian unity, and questioned the values of Christianity itself. Machiavelli evidently believed that the purpose of government was less to prepare people for the City of God than to make them upstanding citizens of this world—ready to fight, work, and die for their earthly country.

Pondering, then, why it can be that in those ancient times people were greater lovers of freedom than in these, I conclude it came from the same cause that makes men now less hardy. That I believe is the difference between our religion and the ancient. Ours, because it shows us the truth, and the true way makes us esteem less the honor of the world; whereas the pagans, greatly esteeming such honor and believing it their greatest good, were fiercer in their actions. . . . Ancient religion . . . attributed blessedness only to men abounding in worldly glory, such as generals of armies and princes of states. Our religion has glorified humble and contemplative men rather than active ones. It has, then, set up as the greatest good humility, abjectness and contempt for human things; the other put it in grandeur of mind, in strength of body, and in all the other things apt to make men exceedingly vigorous.

The Discourses, in *The Chief Works and Others*, trans. Allen Gilbert (Durham, N.C.: Duke University Press, 1965), I, 330-331. © 1965 Duke University Press.

cerned people like the Athenians and Romans of old, who had great civic virtues and were demonstrably capable of self-government. *The Prince* concerned people, Machiavelli's Italians, who in his judgment had lost their civic virtues and therefore required the strongest kind of government from above. The one was a reading from history, the other a judgment on current events—two modes of analysis that must not be confused.

In defending national identity, Machiavelli was exalting a doctrine that was to help shape the modern world. In defending secularism and power politics, Machiavelli preached what others had already practiced; Henry VII, Louis XI, Ferdinand of Aragon, and the Italian despots, in their different ways, were all good Machiavellians. And all were, again in their different ways, exemplars of the phenomena grouped together under the label of the Renaissance. These figures were Renaissance men. Their lives demonstrate how life had changed during the late Middle Ages. They illustrate how a person, a body of thought, or a social custom is a bridge between periods of time customarily treated as distinct, though in fact blending imperceptibly into one another.

SUMMARY

The transition from medieval to modern times was marked by the consolidation of royal power, the decline of serfdom, the revolt against the medieval church, and the increasing importance of a money economy. These changes were hastened by the calamity and hardships of the late Middle Ages, including the Hundred Years' War, the Black Death, the Great Schism in the church, and the threat of Turkish invasion.

In France, the consolidation of royal power was interrupted by the Hundred Years' War (1337-1453). The war broke out after Edward III of England laid claim to the French throne. England gained early victories at Crécy (1346) and Poitiers (1356) and captured the French king.

A peasant revolt, the Jacquerie, and factional strife between Armagnacs and Burgundians contributed to French inability to unify against the English. After the battle of Agincourt (1415), the French king, Charles VI, adopted Henry V of England as heir to the throne. Rallying behind Joan of Arc, whose mystical faith inspired French patriotism, French armies began to drive the English back. Although Joan was burned at the stake for witchcraft, the new French king Charles VII regained control of his lands.

By the end of the Hundred Years' War, the French monarch had gained important powers from the Estates General: the right to keep a standing army and the right to collect the taille. Louis XI (1461-1482), a crafty politician, centralized royal administration, eliminated bastard feudalism, and laid the foundations for absolutism in France.

In England, a strong national monarchy also had emerged by the late 1400s. However, unlike France, where the Estates General was subservient to the Crown, the English Parliament had power to grant money and thereby exert control over the monarch.

During the fourteenth and fifteenth centuries, England was affected by social and economic dislocations as a result of the Black Death. The emergence of English nationalism was reflected in the official use of English in place of Norman French. In Parliament, two houses began to emerge, and a significant alliance evolved between knights and burgesses in the House of Commons.

Henry VII (1485-1509), a shrewd ruler who established the Tudor dynasty, restored property, law, and order after the factional strife of the Wars of the Roses (1455-1485). He also centralized royal authority and inaugurated new fiscal policies.

In Spain, three Christian kingdoms had emerged by the fifteenth century: Castile, Portugal, and Aragon. A dynastic marriage between Ferdinand of Aragon and Isabella of Castile led to the consolidation of royal power in Spain. With the support of the church, Spain imposed religious uniformity, forcing tens of thousands of Spanish Jews and Muslims to convert. By 1492, Ferdinand and Isabella had ousted Muslims from their last stronghold in Granada and embarked on a policy of religious and national intolerance that would mark the Spanish monarchy for centuries to come.

In Germany, the principle of an elective monarchy triumphed in the fourteenth century and was confirmed in the Golden Bull of 1356. Sovereign princes and free cities ruled their own territories. In the west, the Swiss Confederation became virtually independent of the Holy Roman Empire. After 1483, Hapsburg princes were always elected Holy Roman emperors.

In Italy, individual city-states rather than any central authority prevented the development of national awareness. Of the three most powerful states of northern Italy—Milan, Florence, and Venice—only Venice enjoyed political stability under merchant oligarchs. Venice introduced the idea of establishing diplomatic embassies throughout Europe.

The Florentine diplomat Niccolò Machiavelli (1469-1527) wrote two books, *The Prince* and *The Discourses*, which embodied ideas that would shape the modern world: the primacy of secular over religious interests, the realities of power politics, and the importance of national identity.

chapter eleven

THE RENAISSANCE

Renaissance—rebirth—is the name traditionally bestowed upon the remarkable outpouring of intellectual and artistic energy and talent that accompanied the passage of Europe from the Middle Ages to the modern epoch. The term is also often extended to politics and economics. However applied, the Renaissance raises basic problems for the historian. Some difficulty even arises in deciding when and where the Renaissance began, how far it spread, and for how long it continued; that is, questions of chronology are not fully settled. Most scholars accept that the Renaissance started in Italy around 1300 and continued for three centuries, during which the economic, intellectual, and cultural currents flowing from its homeland eventually reached France, the Low Countries, Germany, England, and also, though with diminished force, Spain and Portugal. By 1600, with Europe increasingly preoccupied by the great Protestant-Catholic antagonism issuing from the Reformation, it had virtually ended, giving way to the culture called *baroque*.

Few scholars would date the start of the Renaissance later than 1350. Many argue for two "Renaissances": one a period of revival based on the old learning and spread through traditional methods; the other a period of innovation in which much new knowledge was generated that would become the foundation of modern thought, and spread by a new medium, print—which meant that a far wider community could share in and debate the changes. Still other scholars find three distinct periods to the Renaissance, coinciding roughly with the "three ages of mankind": youth, maturity, and decline.

Indeed, debate over what the Renaissance was and when it began is a good example of the entire problem of "periodization": how the present generation, looking back, relates earlier periods to the present through labels, through the notion that there are watersheds between periods, and through the belief that certain events or inventions clearly distinguish one period from another. The common error of equating phases in the development of a culture to stages in human life—the use of biological metaphors about birth, growth, maturity, and death—obscures the way in which most historical development is a tightly woven fabric, each thread carrying equal tension in relation to another, however distinct.

Thus it is extremely difficult to establish the degree to which the term *Renaissance* should be interpreted literally. Were the classical values of ancient Greece and Rome in fact reborn at the close of the Middle Ages? If so, for whom? Only for an elite group with the money and time to explore the meanings of the classics? Or for a far broader part of the population, though in ruder and less evident ways? Could such a rebirth alone account for the extraordinarily productive careers of Renaissance writers, sculptors, painters, architects, musicians, and scientists? Until the middle of the nineteenth century most educated people would have answered yes to all these questions, for such a view was important to their own sense of cultural roots and achievements. The chief reason for the classical revival appeared to be the capture of Constantinople by the Turks in 1453 and the flight of Greek scholars to Italy and other countries of western Europe.

Today, this simple answer no longer suffices. We know that, long before 1453, knowledge of Greek writings was filtering into the West from Muslim Spain, from Sicily, and from Byzantium itself. Moreover, Greek influence was by no means the only catalyst of the Renaissance. In an influential study first published in 1860, the Swiss historian Jacob Burckhardt insisted that much of the credit for Renaissance productivity must also go to the genius and individualism of Italians. Burckhardt, however, accepted the traditional contrast between medieval darkness and Renaissance light that had first been drawn by the men of the Renaissance themselves.

Today it is almost universally agreed that a great Christian civilization had, in fact, matured during the Middle Ages, and that the cultural heritage from classical antiquity had never disappeared from the medieval West. During this time European society had gradually shifted from an oral to a print culture, from Gothic to Italic ways of writing, and from the preservation of knowledge to the expansion of knowledge through the immensely explosive power of printing. Some historians contend that the cultural rebirth had begun in the "Carolingian Renaissance," or that the "Renaissance of the twelfth century" centered at the court of Eleanor of Aquitaine. But to claim that the germ of the Renaissance had been planted and, indeed, had sprouted long before 1300—to deny originality to the Renaissance, as some historians do—is to go too far.

The thinkers and artists of the Renaissance owed much to their medieval predecessors, and they were often as religious, as credulous, as caste-conscious, and as "feudal" as their forebears. Yet they were also materialistic, skeptical, and individualistic to a degree almost unknown in the Middle Ages. The Italian historian Federico Chabod has observed that the new secular credo could be summed up as "art for art's sake, politics for politics' sake, . . . science for science's sake."* Human beings were attempting to create things, to do things, to study things as ends in themselves because they enjoyed them, derived a sense of accomplishment from them, felt they were contributing to their own security and well-being, rather than doing things as a means to the glorification of God and to salvation—

*Federico Chabod, *Machiavelli and the Renaissance*, trans. David Moore (New York: Harper & Row, 1971), p. 184.

much as Machiavelli had divorced political thought from theology. Yet there was a strong sense of the past in Renaissance writers like Machiavelli, Erasmus, or Castiglione.

I A MONEY ECONOMY

Trade

During the Renaissance the more developed areas of Europe that are loosely termed the West—that is, the areas to the west of the Adriatic Sea and the Elbe River—were changing from the subsistence economy of the early Middle Ages to a money economy, from an economy based on home-grown produce paid for in kind to one relying heavily on imports paid for in money or letters of credit. By the fifteenth century the West had long been importing salt from the mines of Germany or the sea-salt pans of the Atlantic coast to preserve food; to make food tasty after it had begun to spoil, the West had long sought the spices of the East; to wash it down, western Europeans had developed a taste for the wines of the Rhine, of Burgundy, and of Bordeaux. The furs of eastern Europe, the wool of England and Spain, and the woolen cloth of Flanders and Italy commanded good markets among those who had to live in cold medieval buildings. At the close of the Middle Ages supplies of palatable food and warm clothing were steadily increasing. Salt fish, for example, was cheap and did not spoil; in the fourteenth century, such a boom occurred in the herring fisheries along the narrow waters between Denmark and Sweden that the Baltic fisheries employed thousands of people in catching fish, salting them down, making the barrels to pack them in, and shipping them out.

Trade slumped during the serious economic depression of the early 1300s and the prolonged aftermath of many wet summers, the Black Death, and the Hundred Years' War. Recovery came in the fifteenth century, and by the late 1400s the trade of the West could, for the first time, be compared in relative volume and variety with that of the Roman Empire, of Byzantium at its peak, and of Norman and Hohenstaufen Sicily. Meantime, Western merchants developed more elaborate commercial procedures and organizations, of which the Hanseatic towns of the Baltic and the trading cities of Italy provide the most important illustrations.

In the fourteenth and fifteenth centuries the membership of the *Hansa* (the German word means league) included almost a hundred towns, among which Lübeck, Hamburg, Bremen, and Danzig were the leaders. Its policies were determined by meetings of representatives from the member towns, usually held at Lübeck. The weakness of the Holy Roman Empire and the fact that many of the Hanseatic towns began as autonomous frontier outposts east of the Elbe enabled the Hansa to play a virtually independent political and military role, besides exercising great economic power.

The Hansa was not the first important confederation of commercial towns in Europe, nor was it the first to resist control by a higher political authority. Alliances of communes in Lombardy and in Flanders had blocked the ambitions of Hohenstaufen emperors and French kings, respectively. The Hansa, however, operated on a grander scale; its ships carried Baltic fish, timber, grain, furs, metals, and amber to western European markets and brought back cloth, wine, and spices. For a time, Hanseatic vessels controlled the lucrative transport of wool from England to Flanders. Hanseatic merchants, traveling overland with carts and pack trains, took their Baltic wares to Italy. The Hansa maintained large depots at Bruges, London, Venice, Novgorod and Bergen on the Norwegian coast. These foreign establishments enjoyed so many special rights of maintaining their own German officials and laws that they were colonial outposts of a Hanseatic empire. The Hansa itself had its own legal code (the Law of Lübeck), its own diplomats, and its own flag.

After 1500, however, the fortunes of the Hansa declined rapidly. The shift of trade routes from the Baltic to the Atlantic ended the prosperity of many Hanseatic towns, to the advantage of Holland and England. The loosely organized Hansa was no match for the stronger monarchical governments growing up along the rim of its Baltic preserve in Sweden, Russia, and some of the German princely states. Internally, the Hansa was weakened by the mounting conservatism and restrictiveness of its merchants and by rivalries among member towns and competing merchant families. Only a minority of the member towns usually sent representatives to the deliberations in Lübeck, and very few of them could be counted on for men and arms in an emergency. Moreover, Hanseatic trading activities were carried on in a relatively primitive fashion by a multitude of individual merchants who entered temporary partnerships for a single venture rather than establishing permanent firms.

The truly big business of the last medieval centuries was to be found not along the Baltic but in the cities of the Mediterranean, many of which were already thriving veterans of trade, enriched and toughened by the Crusades: Venice, Genoa, Pisa, Lucca, Florence, Milan, and a dozen others in Italy; Marseilles, Montpellier, and Narbonne in France; and Barcelona in Spain. Venice furnishes an excellent case study. It was the East-West trade that brought wealth to Venetian merchants: from the East, spices, silk, cotton, sugar, dyestuffs, and the alum needed to set colors; from the West, wool and cloth. The area of Venetian business was enormous, from England and Flanders to the heart of Asia, which the thirteenth-century Venetian Marco Polo (1254-1324) crossed to reach China.

The main carrier of Venetian trade was the galley. By 1300 the designers of the Venetian arsenal (originally a government-operated shipyard) had improved the traditional long, narrow, oar-propelled galley of the Mediterranean into a swifter and roomier merchant vessel, relying mainly on sails and employing oarsmen chiefly to get in and out of port. In the fifteenth century these merchant galleys had space for 250 tons of cargo—big enough for lucrative shipments of spices and other items that were small in bulk and large in value. Records from the early fifteenth century show about forty-five galleys sailing from Venice annually, including four to Flanders, two to southern France, three to the Black Sea, three to Alexandria, four to Beirut, and two or three transporting pilgrims to Jaffa in the Holy Land. The Flanders fleet, which touched also at London and Southampton, was an important economic institution because, from its start in 1317, it provided a service between Italy and northwestern Europe that was cheaper and more secure than the overland route.

The state supervised the activities of these galleys. Since the average life of galleys was ten years, government experts periodically tested their seaworthiness, and the arsenal made needed replacements. The government provided for the defense of the galleys and their cargoes by requiring that at least twenty of the crew be bowmen. The captains of the Flanders galleys were directed to protect the health of the crew by enlisting a physician and a surgeon, and to maintain the prestige of the city with two fifers and two trumpeters. The Venetian republic also maintained an ambassador in England to smooth the way for its merchants.

As is often the case, changes in technology led to changes in the economy and society. Ever more expert knowledge about ship construction, rigging, and propulsion was demanded by governments. Ship design changed slowly, since the sea did not change, but as more and more galleys ventured out into the Atlantic, the differences between northern European and Mediterranean designs began to disappear. The great medieval ship was the full-rigged three-master that could be adapted to carracks (ships that carried bulk cargoes in the Mediterranean or journeyed outward to the Indies), to caravels (ships that crossed the Atlantic), to galleons (ships that brought heavy loads of treasure back from the newly discovered Americas to Spain, and eventually sailed the Pacific), to merchantmen for the Baltic trade, and finally to the *fluyt*, a late-sixteenth-century Dutch ship best used for grain, wine, and alum, which became the model for Europe's rapidly expanding commerce.

With these changes went better instruments, improved charts, and clearer lines of authority for ships' captains. Improved navigation was all-encompassing; it tied the world of commerce closer together, sped cargoes that otherwise might spoil, increased shipboard specialization, created a new scientific community of instrument makers, and made possible western Europe's pursuit of cargoes around Africa. Sailing in tropical waters brought changes in ship design, new cargoes, knowledge of disease, and new forms of finance. For example, ship-worm, which rotted the bottoms of wooden ships, was far more active in the tropics; ships sailing in those waters therefore had to be replaced far more often. This, together with the increase in sailing distances and the need to carry cargoes further and to sail at greater speeds, led to ever more complex commercial arrangements. Europeans hoisted sail before they saddled horse, and watercraft became the first tool for the European conquest of the world.

Industry

The expansion of trade stimulated the industries that furnished the textiles, metals, and ships required by merchants. The towns of Flanders and Italy developed the weaving of woolen cloth, with many workers and high profits for relatively few entrepreneurs. In the early fourteenth century perhaps two hundred masters controlled the wool guild of Florence, which produced nearly one hundred thousand pieces of cloth annually and employed thirty thousand men. By and large, only those two hundred had saved enough capital to finance the importation of raw wool from England and put it through the long process that ended with finished cloth.

The earlier practice of grouping in a single guild all artisans engaged in making a single product was giving way to the modern division (and tension) between capital and labor, and, within the ranks of labor, between the highly skilled and the less skilled—divisions by which the workers were alienated or increasingly removed from the means of production. In late fourteenth-century Florence, the strife was intense among the seven great guilds, the fourteen lesser guilds, and the *Ciompi* (workers excluded from the guild membership).

Despite the growth of capitalism, Europe had not yet experienced a full industrial revolution, and most "manufacturing" continued to be what the Latin roots of the word suggest—a "making by hand"—though many hand tools were ingenious and efficient. But a few advanced crafts showed modern trends: increase in output, mass production of standardized articles, and specialization of the labor force. In Lübeck Hanseatic capitalists promoted the mass output of rosaries by hiring beadmakers and supplying them with materials; in the Hapsburg lands of central Europe the silver mines inaugurated round-the-clock operations by dividing their workers among three eight-hour shifts; in Florence twenty or more different specialized crafts participated in woolen production—washing, combing, carding, spinning, weaving, dyeing, and so forth. But the actual work was subcontracted to small domestic shops according to the *put-out* system; instead of the worker's going to a mill or a factory, the work went to the worker's home.

The largest industrial establishment in Europe was probably the Venetian arsenal, which normally employed a thousand men and during emergencies many more. These workmen, called *arsenalotti*, formed a pyramid of skills, with unskilled laborers at the bottom; at the next level, sawyers, who cut the timbers for the galleys, and caulkers, who made the wooden hulls seaworthy; then pulleymakers and mastmakers; and at the top, highly skilled carpenters, who shaped the lines of the hull. Supervisors disciplined the arsenalotti, checking on their presence at their posts during the working day; anyone who reported late forfeited a day's pay. By the sixteenth century, the process of adding a superstructure to the hull and outfitting the vessel was so efficient that it took the arsenalotti only two months to complete and equip a hundred galleys for a campaign against the Turks.

Banking

The expansion of trade and industry promoted the rise of banking, as merchants invested their accumulated capital in trading enterprises, and kings, popes, and lesser rulers borrowed money to meet the expenses of war and administration. The risks of lending were great—rulers, in particular, were likely to repudiate their debts—but so too were the potential profits. Florentine bankers were known to charge 266 percent annual interest on an especially risky loan! In 1420 the Florentine government vainly tried to put a ceiling of 20 percent on interest rates. Bankers were also money-changers, for only experts could establish the relative value of the hundreds of coins in circulation, varying enormously in reliability and precious metal content and minted by every kind of government unit from the national monarchy down to the tiny feudal principality.

Bankers also facilitated the transfer of money over long distances. Suppose an English exporter, A, sold wool to an Italian importer, Z; it would be slow and dangerous for Z to pay A by shipping coins to him. Suppose that two others then entered the transaction: Y, an Italian woolen manufacturer who sold cloth to B, an English importer. It was safer and speedier if Z paid Y in Italy what he really owed to A in England, and if B paid A what he really owed Y. This sort of transaction was facilitated by bills of exchange, which bankers bought and sold and on which they took a commission. Letters of credit, which represented sums of money not physically transferred, were also safer, since they could easily be hidden and carried from, say, Rome to London by a cleric or other unsuspected person.

The great European bankers were Italians—the "Lombard" bankers, though many of them came not from Lombardy but from Florence, Siena, and other towns in Tuscany. By the late 1200s Italian bankers had become the fiscal agents of the pope, charged with the transfer of papal revenues from distant countries to Rome. The florins minted by Florence were the first gold coins made outside Byzantium to gain international currency because of their reliability. The Florentine banking families of the Bardi and the Peruzzi financed imports of English wool and the export of finished cloth; both firms advanced large sums to the kings of England and France at the outbreak of the Hundred Years' War, and both failed in the 1340s when Edward III defaulted on his debts. The repercussions of this banking failure, felt for more than a generation, included new attempts to democratize the Florentine government and the revolt of the Ciompi against the tyranny of the wool guild in 1378. Florentine banking rallied in the fifteenth century under the dynamic Cosimo de' Medici, whose activities involved companies for woolen and silk manufacture, as well as Medici bank and branch firms in Venice, Rome, Milan, Avignon, Geneva, Bruges, and London. However, the inefficiency of branch managers together with the extravagance of Lorenzo the Magnificent caused the failure of the Medici bank before the end of the century.

Meanwhile, money and banking were thriving elsewhere. The golden ducats of Venice joined the florins of Florence in international popularity, and the Bank of St. George, founded at Genoa in 1407, eventually took over much of the Mediterranean business done by Spanish Jews before their persecution in the late 1400s. In London the merchant and moneylender Sir Richard (Dick) Whittington (d. 1423) was lord mayor for three terms between 1397 and 1420. In France, Jacques Coeur of Bourges (1395-1456) used private wealth to secure public office and was master of the mint and superintendent of royal expenditure for Charles VII. In Germany powerful banking families flourished in the cities of Augsburg and Nuremberg. The most famous was the Fugger family of Augsburg, whose founder was a linen weaver and trader in the late fourteenth century; his sons and grandsons imported textiles and luxuries from Venice and began buying silver and lead mines. In the late 1400s the Fuggers became bankers to the Hapsburgs and, after the failure of the Medici bank, to the papacy as well. With the Fuggers, as with Coeur, wealth bred more wealth, power, and eventual ruin. Through Hapsburg favor they secured silver, iron, and copper mines in Hungary and the Tyrol, and in the 1540s the family fortune may have exceeded half a billion of present-day dollars. Thereafter it dwindled, as the flood of gold and silver from America ended with the central European mining boom, and as the Fuggers themselves made extensive loans to the Hapsburg Philip II of Spain, who suffered repeated bankruptcies. In 1607 the family firm went bankrupt; by then they were so famous that the term *Fuggerei* meant businessmen.

Town and Countryside

Yet Augsburg's total population at the height of Fugger power probably never exceeded twenty thousand. None of the centers of international economic life was a city at all. One set of estimates for the fourteenth century puts the population of Venice, Florence, and Paris in the vicinity of one hundred thousand each; that of Genoa, Milan, Barcelona, and London at about fifty thousand; and that of the biggest Hanseatic and Flemish towns between twenty and forty thousand. Most Europeans still lived in the countryside.

The urban minority, however, was beginning to bring important changes to the life of the rural majority. Ties between town and countryside were especially close where towns were numerous: Lombardy, Tuscany, Flanders, the Rhine valley, and northern Germany. Merchants often invested their wealth in farm properties; nobles who acquired interests in towns usually retained their country estates; and peasants often moved to town as workmen or became artisans on the farm. Town governments sometimes improved adjacent farmland on the pattern established by the medieval communes of Milan and Siena, which had drained nearby marshes to increase the amount of cultivable land in order to assure a more dependable food supply. But individuals, whether of town or country, were more closely drawn together into wider communities by the changes in economic, social, and political organization; thus they had less time and desire to respond to the calls of the wider, theoretically all-encompassing community of Christian society.

The development of a money economy also greatly altered the agrarian institutions of the West, as well as being a symptom of the ongoing changes that influenced agriculture. Money became important for the exchange of surpluses that resulted from many causes, including technical improvements that were applied to the fields. Many manors could specialize in a single crop, like grain or wool, olives or grapes, and therefore could purchase items they no longer produced. The lords of these one-crop manors, depending increasingly on a monetary income, became capitalists on a modest scale. The more enterprising wanted to sweep away what seemed to them inefficient medieval survivals, demanding that their peasants pay rent in money rather than in commodities or in work on the lord's land. The sheep-raising capitalists of sixteenth-century England won the right of *enclosure*—fencing off for their own flocks common lands where peasants had traditionally pastured their own livestock. In Spain the *Mesta* secured rights to vast tracts of pasture. Urban businessmen wanted property in a form that they could readily buy and sell, free from the restrictions of feudal tenure; they wanted laborers they could hire and fire, free from the restrictions of serfdom. All these desires, together with the labor shortage and peasant unrest created by the Black Death, spelled the end of serfdom, which had virtually disappeared in most of western Europe by 1500.

Thus, at the heart of economic and social relationships, the cash network of the capitalist was beginning to replace the medieval complex of caste and service. These new developments blurred the old lines between classes. The ordinary person probably earned more by becoming a wage-earning worker or rent-paying tenant farmer instead of a serf. Yet something was also lost—the tenuous security, the inherited job, the right to certain lands—which the serf had generally possessed in the days of manorialism. Despair and discontent had surfaced in the Jacquerie and the English peasant uprising of 1381, and they continued as undercurrents in the more prosperous Europe of the fifteenth century. In towns and cities pressures also mounted, as the guilds became more exclusive and the separation between wealthy master and ordinary worker widened.

One important political result of these economic changes was the expanded role of the business class, the

Bust of Lorenzo de Medici by Andrea del Verroccheo (c 1435-1488).

bourgeoisie. Sometimes the bourgeois themselves ruled, as did the Medici in Florence and the merchants of Venice and the Hansa; sometimes they provided monarchs with money or professional skills to further dynastic and national interests. These leaders made their mark on the whole style of the age. The bourgeois were beginning to invade the church's near-monopoly of the support of culture; the Medici, the Fuggers, Coeur, and the well-to-do were generally patrons of art and learning and financed public monuments. The palace or library of the rich now challenged the monastery or the church-dominated university as a center of scholarship. By the late fifteenth century the intellectual life of Florence revolved around the Platonic Academy subsidized by Lorenzo the Magnificent. There was little to distinguish the rich and cultivated prelate from the rich and cultivated layman. Such Renaissance popes as Sixtus IV, Alexander VI, and Julius II were admirers and amassers of material wealth and great connoisseurs of art; so too were their business contemporaries.

II PRINTING, THOUGHT, AND LITERATURE

The rising capitalism and secularism of the Renaissance centuries did not mean that all medieval values were rejected or all medieval customs replaced. Old values always survive in certain places, occupations, or classes, and a cultural lag between those who represent the cutting edge of change and those who are the sheet anchor of tradition is to be found in all cultures at all times. A good case in point is linguistic; the new vernaculars—the native or local languages—became important media of literary expression without seriously undermining the traditional preeminence of Latin as the learned language. Linguistically, the Renaissance had a kind of split personality, with the vernaculars dominating the world of popular culture and Latin that of "serious" or learned thought. Before 1500 about 77 percent of all books were in Latin, and the presses first reproduced large editions of Aesop and Cato, Cicero and Boethius, the latter representing the ideal blend of classical and medieval thought.

The history of printing well illustrates Francis Bacon's warning that too often facts of life that actually belong together are kept apart. The communications revolution brought on by the printing press, the enormous significance of the book as a force for change, the simple fact that printing preceded the Protestant revolt on which the Reformation fed, are all aspects of a profound shift in perspective which, perhaps more than any other change, defines the transition between medieval and modern. Humanity began to secularize, to particularize, to conceive of knowledge as growth rather than as discovery when it entered upon the long transition from "the great book of nature"—which included both human experience and the teachings of the Bible—to "the little books of men"—the scientific inquiries that were made widely known and were thus liberated from the scribes of the monasteries and the libraries of the very rich by the dramatic shift from script to print.

Those historians who most emphasize the significance of technology in promoting human change and who see the development of print as perhaps the most sweeping technological revolution between the wheel and the steam engine also argue that there were essentially two stages to the Renaissance: the earlier, which preceded the printing press, being only one more classical revival that looked backwards in an essentially imitative way; and the later, which accompanied the spread of print, being expansive, new, intellectually comprehensive, and permanent—the true Renaissance celebrated for ushering in modernity. However, we need not choose, for human ingenuity arises from the known and moves on to the unknown, and the Renaissance clearly did have two phases, the difference between the two being a matter of degree. Printing was the revolutionary event that made possible the diffusion of scientific knowledge, so that scholars could better judge which problems needed attention, turning science into a revolutionary force rather than a systematic curiosity, closing the gap between the practice of artisans and the theories of scholars.

The introduction of print slowly filtered down to the peasants. Perhaps as many as 10 percent could sign their names, though even they were basically illiterate; but some learned their letters and how to keep accounts from printed materials, and a few sons of laborers found their way to a university. More important was the change brought about by print to the custom of the *veillée*—the gathering of villagers together two or three nights each week, or farm families telling each other stories about ghosts or werewolves, such gatherings eventually turning into dances or an interchange of gossip, that is, of news. These social meetings helped create a sense of traditional life, of shared worries and of disagreements openly discussed, that continued in France in particular until the eighteenth century. To the evening gathering was added, in the sixteenth century, the practice of listening to traditional story-tellers who enriched their repertoire by referring to a few books. In time someone—often the rural schoolteacher—would use the veillée for reading aloud to the village. *Aesop's Fables*, the *Romance of the Rose*, or the vernacular Bible were thus spread and altered, for the reader usually had to render the printed work into the local dialect, in effect translating and editing it. The *Shepherds' Calendar*, full of practical agricultural advice illustrated by woodcuts, was also read aloud, and in time it was changed to deal with religious issues (especially Protestant) or to tell peasants something of "history": a list of dates that revealed God's way to humankind. Print also made possible anonymous *calendriers historials*, Protestant calendars that were stripped of saints and used to transmit peasant lore, proverbs, and Calvinist theology.

The Vernaculars and Latin

The vernaculars of the western European countries emerged gradually, first as the spoken languages of the people, then as vehicles for popular writing, finally achieving official recognition. Many vernaculars—Spanish, Portuguese, Italian, and French—developed from Latin; these were the Romance (Roman) languages. Castilian, the core of modern literary Spanish, attained official status in the thirteenth century when the king of Castile ordered that it be used for government records. In Italy the vernacular scarcely existed as a literary language until the eve of the Renaissance, when Dante employed the dialect of his native Tuscany in the *Divine Comedy*, and it was not until the early sixteenth century that Tuscan Italian won out over the rival dialect of Rome as the medium for vernacular expression.

In medieval France two families of vernaculars appeared: southern Frenchmen spoke the *langue d'oc*, so called from their use of *oc* (the Latin *hoc*) for "yes"; their northern cousins spoke the *langue d'oïl*, in which "yes" was *oïl* (the modern *oui*). The epic verses of *The Song of Roland*, the rowdy *fabliaux*, and the chronicles of Villehardouin and Joinville were composed in the *langue d'oïl*, while the troubadours at the court of Eleanor of Aquitaine sang in Provençal, a form of the *langue d'oc*. By 1400 the *langue d'oïl* of the Paris region was well on its way to replacing Latin as the official language of the whole kingdom; Provençal eventually died out. Another offshoot of the *langue d'oc* survives in Catalan, used in both Spain and France at the Mediterranean end of the Pyrenees, and the name *Languedoc* is still applied to southern France west of the Rhone.

In Germany and in England the vernaculars were derived ultimately not from Latin but from an ancient Germanic language. The *minnesingers* of thirteenth century Germany composed their poetry in Middle High German, predecessor of modern literary German. The Anglo-Saxons of England has spoken a dialect of Low German, which incorporated some words of Scandinavian or Celtic origin and later added many borrowings from Norman French and Latin to form the English vernacular. English achieved official recognition in the fourteenth century; meantime, it was coming into its own as a literary language with such popular works as *Piers Plowman* and Chaucer's *Canterbury Tales* (see Chapter 10).

Use of a common language undoubtedly heightened a common sense of national purpose and a common mistrust of foreigners. The vernaculars also accelerated the emergence of distinctive national styles in France and Spain. Yet the triumph of particularism in fifteenth-century Germany and Italy demonstrated that the vernaculars could not by themselves create national political units. Nor did the vernaculars divide Western culture into tight national compartments. Translations kept ideas flowing across national frontiers, and some of the vernaculars themselves became international languages. In the Near East the Italian that had been introduced by the Crusaders was the *lingua franca*, the Western tongue most widely understood; by the seventeenth century it would be replaced by French and in the twentieth by English.

Meantime, Latin remained the international language of the church and of the academic world. Scholars worked diligently to perfect their Latin and, in the later Renaissance, to learn the rudiments of Greek and sometimes of Hebrew. They called themselves *humanists*, that is, devotees of what Cicero had termed *studias humanitatis*, or humane studies, which still included rhetoric, grammar, history, poetry, and ethics. Humanism was more than a linguistic term, and humanists were usually more than philologists. Their studies of the classical past led them to cherish the values of antiquity, pagan though they might be; Machiavelli found greater virtue in pre-Christian Greece and Rome than in the nominally Christian society of his own day. Other humanists sought a kind of highest moral denominator in the best ancient doctrines and loftiest Christian aspiration.

Altogether, humanism drastically changed attitudes toward the classical heritage. The medieval schoolmen had not disdained this heritage; they admired and copied its forms but transformed or adapted its ideas to fortify their own Christian views. They fond in Vergil's *Aeneid*, for instance, not only the splendor of epic poetry but also an allegory of human life on earth. The humanists of the Renaissance transformed their medieval heritage in the more secular spirit of their own age and in the light of their own more extensive knowledge of the classics. They revered both the style and the content of the classics and began to study them as an art form, not to strengthen or enrich their faith. Reverence for the classics did not prevent some humanists from becoming enthusiastic advocates of the vernacular; the reverse was also true, as vernacular writers studied Cicero to improve their own style.

Writers of the Early Italian Renaissance

Dante Alighieri (1265-1321) was the first major Italian writer to embody some of the qualities that were to characterize Renaissance literature. Much of Dante's writing and outlook bore the stamp of the Middle Ages, and the grand theme of the *Divine Comedy* was medieval, the chivalric concept of disembodied love inspiring his devotion to Beatrice, whom he seldom saw. His hostility to the political ambitions of Boniface VIII did not express Machiavellian anticlericalism but the reaction of a Christian who wanted the pope to keep out of politics. Vergil, Euclid, Plato, Socrates, Caesar, and other virtuous pagans dwell forever in Limbo on the edge of Hell, suffering only the hopelessness of the unbaptized who can never reach God's presence. Yet Dante not only chose the vernacular for the *Divine Comedy* but also wrote a treatise in Latin urging others to follow his example. Furthermore, he modeled the style of the *Comedy* on the popular poetry of the Provençal troubadours and achieved a remarkable popular success during his lifetime.

Popular fame and classical enthusiasm obsessed the

Portrait of Dante, attributed to the school of Giotto, now in the Bargello Museum in Florence. The scene is meant to show Dante in the Paradise of his own making.

next major Italian literary figure, Petrarch (Francesco Petrarca, 1304-1374). Since his father was a political exile from Florence, the young Petrarch lived for a time at the worldly papal court in Avignon and attended the law school at the University of Bologna. As a professional man of letters he collected and copied the manuscripts of ancient authors, produced the first accurate edition of the Roman historian Livy, and found in an Italian cathedral forgotten letters by Cicero that threw new light on Cicero's political activities. Petrarch so admired the past that he addressed a series of affectionate letters to Cicero and other Roman worthies; he also composed a Latin epic in the style of the *Aeneid* to celebrate Scipio Africanus, the hero of the Second Punic War. Petrarch's attainments led the senate of Rome (then a kind of municipal council) to revive the Greco-Roman recognition of excellence and crown him with a wreath of laurel in an elaborate ceremony.

Ironically, the writings of Petrarch most admired in modern times are not those in his cherished Latin but those he esteemed the least—vernacular love poems he addressed to his adored Laura, whom he courted in vain until she died during the Black Death. In these lyrics Petrarch perfected the verse form known as the Italian sonnet—fourteen lines long, divided into one set of eight lines and another of six, each with its own rhyme scheme. The word *sonnet* means "little song," and Petrarch developed his sonnets from vernacular folk songs. Almost despite himself, therefore, he proved to be one of the founders of modern vernacular literature.

Petrarch is an excellent instance of the intermixture of old and new in the Renaissance. He exemplified emerging humanism by his devotion to the classics and his deep feeling for the beauties of this world; for him Laura was a real woman, not a disembodied chivalric heroine. He criticized medieval schoolmen because of their rationalism, their dependence on Aristotle as an infallible authority, and their preoccupation with detail, all of which led them, in his judgment, to miss the true spirit of Christianity in their concern with its letter. But he admired Augustine almost as much as he admired Cicero, believing that the religious teachings of the one and the Stoic morality of the other could counter the materialism he observed around him. "I am filled with bitter indignation against the mores of today," he wrote in a letter addressed to the ancient Roman historian Livy, "when men value nothing except gold and silver and desire nothing except sensual pleasures."*

Petrarch's friend and pupil, Giovanni Boccaccio (1313-1375), shared his master's estimate of humanity, but not his confidence in the possibility of human improvement. Boccaccio, son of a Florentine merchant, spent part of his youth at the frivolous court of Naples and turned to letters after his apprenticeship in banking left him disillusioned by the sharp business practices of wealthy Florentines. He became a humanist scholar and eventually held the Dante memorial lectureship at Florence; meantime, he learned Greek and aided his master in tracking down old manuscripts, finding a copy of Tacitus in the Benedictine abbey on Monte Cassino. His distress at the clergy's neglect of manuscripts and their corruption made him strongly anticlerical.

Anticlericalism is a recurrent theme in Boccaccio's *Decameron,* the first major prose work in the Italian vernacular, which recounts stories told by a group of young Florentines who have moved to a country villa during the Black Death. Most of the plots in the *Decameron* were not original with Boccaccio, who borrowed freely from classical and Eastern sources and from the *fabliaux* of medieval France. He retold these earthly tales in a graceful and entertaining way and with a lighthearted disenchantment based on his own worldly experience.

Classical Scholarship

The men of letters of this period may be divided into three groups: first were the conservers of classical culture—scholars, cultivated despots, and businessmen—heirs of Petrarch's humanistic enthusiasm for the classical past; second were the vernacular writers—many of them not Italians—who took the path marked out by the *Decameron,* from Chaucer at the close of the fourteenth century down to Rabelais and to Cervantes in the sixteenth; and third were the synthesizers—philosophical humanists, headed by Pico della Mirandola and Erasmus, who tried to fuse Christianity, classicism, and other elements into a universal human philosophy.

The devoted antiquarians of the fifteenth century uncovered a remarkable number of ancient manuscripts. They ransacked monasteries; they pieced together the works of Cicero, Tacitus, Lucretius, and other Latin authors; they collected Greek manuscripts through agents in Constantinople both before and after 1453. They did their work so thoroughly that almost all the Greek classics now known reached the West by 1500. To preserve, catalog, and study these literary treasures, the first modern libraries were created. Cosimo de' Medici supported three separate libraries in and near Florence and employed forty-five copyists. Humanist popes founded the library of the Vatican, today one of the most important collections in the world, and even the minor duchy of Urbino in northern Italy had a humanist court and a major library, assembled by its cultivated dukes.

Greek scholars as well as Greek manuscripts made the journey from Byzantium to Italy. One of the earliest of them, Manuel Chrysoloras (1368-1415), came to Italy to seek help for the beleagured Byzantines against the Turks and remained to teach at Florence and Milan. He did literature a great service by insisting that translations into Latin from the Greek should not be literal, as they had been in the past, but should convey the message and spirit of the original. The revival of Greek studies reached maturity in the 1460s with the emergence of the

*Myron P. Gilmore, *Humanists and Jurists* (Cambridge, Mass.: Harvard University Press, 1963), p. 6.

informal circle of Florentine humanists known as the Platonic Academy. The Greek language, however, never equaled Latin in popularity because of its difficulty, a fact that discouraged interest in the Greek drama and led most humanists to study Plato in Latin translation.

The classicists of the fifteenth century made a fetish of pure and polished Latin. They composed elaborate letters designed less for private reading than for the instruction of their colleagues. Papal secretaries began to make ecclesiastical correspondence conform to what we should call a manual of correct style. At their worst, these men were pedants, exalting manner over matter, draining vitality from the Latin language. But at their best, they were keen and erudite scholars who sifted out the inaccuracies and forgeries in defective manuscripts to establish definitive texts of ancient writings.

Lorenzo Valla (c 1407-1457) represented classical scholarship at its best. One of the few important figures of the Italian Renaissance not identified with Florence, Valla passed much of his adult life in Rome and Naples. Petty and quarrelsome, fond of exchanging insults with rival humanists, he also commanded both immense learning and the courage to use it against the most sacred targets. He even criticized the supposedly flawless prose of Cicero and took Thomas Aquinas to task for his failure to know Greek. His own expert knowledge of the language led him to point out errors and misinterpretations in the Vulgate (St. Jerome's Latin translation of the Bible), as compared to the Greek New Testament, and thereby to lay the foundation for humanist biblical scholarship.

Valla's fame rests above all on his demonstration that the Donation of Constantine, one basis for justifying papal claims to temporal dominion, was a forgery. He proved his case by showing that both the Latin in which the Donation was written and the events to which it referred dated from an era several centuries after Constantine. When Valla published this exposé in 1440, he was secretary to Alfonso the Magnanimous, king of Aragon, whose claim to Naples was being challenged by the papacy on the basis of the Donation itself. The credibility of the Donation had long been in question, and Valla was not punished for completing the destruction of this ancient myth; rather, he was rewarded as a major textual critic by being commissioned by the pope to translate the Greek historian Thucydides.

The philosophical humanists aspired not only to universal knowledge but also to a universal truth and faith. They were centered at Florence, attracted by the Platonic Academy founded in 1462 by Cosimo de' Medici, who entrusted the commission of translating Plato to Marsilio Ficino (1433-1499), a medical student turned classicist who also translated some of the Neoplatonists' works. These followers of Plato cultivated the search for god through mystical experiences. The opportunity for stressing the compatibility of Neoplatonism with Christianity exerted a strong attraction on Ficino and his circle.

Ficino, who was also a priest, argued that religious feeling and expression were as natural to humanity as barking was to dogs. Humanity, he wrote, has the unique faculty called intellect, which he described as an "eye turned toward the intelligible light," or God. He coined the term *Platonic love* to describe the love that

THE RENAISSANCE IDEAL

The Renaissance ideal was that the individual had the freedom to become whatever ability allowed. In speaking of the dignity of man, Pico della Mirandola summarized this ideal:

The best of artisans [God] ordained that that creature (man) to whom He had been able to give nothing proper to himself should have joint possession of whatever had been peculiar to each of the different kinds of being. He therefore took man as a creature of indeterminate nature and, assigning him a place in the middle of the world, addressed him thus: "Neither a fixed abode nor a form that is thine alone nor any function peculiar to thyself have we given thee, Adam, to the end that according to thy longing and according to thy judgment thou mayest have and possess what abode, what form, and what functions thou thyself shalt desire. The nature of all other beings is limited and constrained within the bounds of laws prescribed by Us. Thou, constrained by no limits in accordance with thine own free will, in whose hand We have placed thee, shall ordain for thyself the limits of thy nature. We have set thee at the world's center that thou mayest from thence more easily observe whatever is in the world. We have made thee neither of heaven nor of earth, neither mortal nor immortal, so that with freedom of choice and with honor, as though the maker and molder of thyself, thou mayest fashion thyself in whatever shape thou shalt prefer. Thou shalt have the power to degenerate into the lower forms of life, which are brutish. Thou shalt have the power, out of thy soul's judgment, to be reborn into the higher forms, which are divine." O supreme generosity of God the Father, O highest and most marvelous felicity of man! To him it is granted to have whatever he chooses, to be whatever he wills.

From Giovanni Pico della Mirandola, *Oration on the Dignity of Man*, in *The Renaissance Philosophy of Man*, ed. Ernst Cassirer et al. (Chicago: University of Chicago Press, 1961), pp. 224-25.

BIBLICAL HUMANISM

Erasmus wanted everyone to be able to read the Bible rather than learn of it through an intermediary. In the *Paraclesis* (1516), his preface to his Greek and Latin edition of the New Testament, he exhorted the Christian to study Holy Scripture, which alone provided the teachings of Christ. The essay became a classic of biblical humanism, best known for its definition of "the philosophy of Christ" and for its plea for vernacular Bibles:

Only bring a pious and open mind, possessed above all with a pure and simple faith. Only be docile, and you have advanced far in this philosophy. It itself supplies inspiration as a teacher which communicates itself to no one more gladly than to minds that are without guile. . . . This doctrine in an equal degree accommodates itself to all, lowers itself to the little ones, adjusts itself to their measure, nourishing them with milk, bearing, fostering, sustaining them, doing everything until we grow in Christ. . . .

I disagree very much with those who are unwilling that Holy Scripture, translated into the vulgar tongue, be read by the uneducated, as if Christ taught such intricate doctrines that they could scarcely be understood by very few theologians, or as if the strength of the Christian religion consisted in men's ignorance of it. The mysteries of kings, perhaps, are better concealed, but Christ wishes his mysteries published as openly as possible. I would that even the lowliest women read the Gospels and the Pauline Epistles. And I would that they were translated into all languages so that they could be read and understood not only by Scots and Irish but also by Turks and Saracens. Surely the first step is to understand in one way or another.

John C. Olin, ed., *Christian Humanism and the Reformation: Selected Writings of Erasmus*, rev. ed. (New York: Fordham University Press, 1975), pp. 96-97. Translated by John C. Olin from the Latin text edited in 1933 by Hajo Holborn.

transcends the senses and may lead to mystical communion with God. He supported his arguments with appeals to a wide range of authorities: the wise men of the ancient Near East, the prophets of the Old Testament, the apostles of the New, and the Greek philosophers. Ficino seemed to be attempting a synthesis of all philosophy and religion.

The attempt was pressed further by Ficino's pupil, Giovanni Pico della Mirandola (1463-1494). Pico crowded much into his thirty-one years: he knew Arabic, Hebrew, Greek, and Latin; he studied Jewish allegory, Arab philosophy, and medieval Scholasticism, which, almost alone among humanists, he respected. Pico's tolerance was as broad as his learning. In his short *Oration on the Dignity of Man*, he cited approvingly Chaldean and Persian theologians, the priests of Apollo, Socrates, Pythagoras, Cicero, Moses, Paul, Augustine, Muhammad, St. Francis, Thomas Aquinas, and many others.

Together with Ficino, Pico helped to found the humane studies of comparative religion and comparative philosophy. He strengthened Ficino's idea that humanity was unique—the link between the mortal physical world and the immortal spiritual one. This concept of the uniqueness of humanity's central position in the universe lay at the core of Renaissance style. Yet among the Platonic humanists, the medieval element also remained strong; in his final years, Pico gave away his worldly possessions and became a supporter of a fanatical preacher, Savonarola.

However, the "Prince of Humanists," the person who epitomized the most mature expression of the impulse to draw on all wisdom, was not Italian but Dutch: Desiderius Erasmus (1466-1536). He might also be called the foremost citizen of the western European Republic of Letters, for he studied and taught at Oxford and Cambridge, at Paris, and in Italy, and he particularly relished the free atmosphere of small city-states like Louvain in the Low Countries, Basel in Switzerland, and Freiburg in the Rhineland. Building on Valla's scholarship, Erasmus published a scholarly edition of the Greek New Testament. He carried on a prodigious correspondence in Latin and compiled a series of *Adages* and *Colloquies* to give students examples of good Latin composition. Most influential was his satirical *The Praise of Folly*, in which Erasmus employed the female Folly, as many of his contemporaries used the jester or fool, to contrast the spontaneous natural reactions of the supposedly foolish with the studied and self-serving artificiality of those who claimed to be wise. Erasmus mocked any group inflated by a sense of its own importance—merchants, philosophers, scientists, courtiers, clerics, and kings.

Erasmus possessed most of the main attributes of Renaissance humanism. He coupled a detached view of human nature with faith in the dignity of humanity, or at least of a few persons. He joined a love of the classics with respect for Christian values. While at times testy, vain and indecisive, he had little use for the fine-spun arguments of Scholasticism and was a tireless advocate of what he called his "philosophy of Christ"—the application of the doctrines of charity and love taught by

Jesus. Yet, although Erasmus always considered himself a loyal son of the church, he nevertheless helped to destroy the universality of Catholicism. His edition of the Greek New Testament raised disquieting doubts about the accuracy of the Latin translation in the Vulgate and therefore of Catholic biblical interpretations. His repeated insistence on elevating the spirit of piety above the letter of formal religious acts seemed to diminish the importance of the clergy, and his attacks on clerical laxity implied that the wide gap between the lofty ideals and the corrupt practices of the church could not long endure.

A sixteenth-century epigram stated, "Where Erasmus merely nodded, Luther rushed in; where Erasmus laid the eggs, Luther hatched the chicks; where Erasmus merely doubted, Luther laid down the law." When Luther did lay down the law in the Protestant revolt, however, the growing dogmatism and belligerence of the rebels alienated Erasmus, who chose a middle way between siding with the church and a direct break with it. Both his fidelity to the Christian tradition, as he understood it, and his humanist convictions committed Erasmus to the position that the only worthy weapons were reason and discussion. Perhaps because he sought compromise, he has also become enormously popular with twentieth-century humanists. The very ambiguity of his life was with him at death. Erasmus died on July 11, 1536, just before midnight, in the suburbs of Basel. His tomb states that he died on July 12, for in Basel, where he is buried, the clocks were an hour ahead. The development of standardized time is an innovation of worldwide commerce in the nineteenth century, and until then there was no agreement on date or even time. In so simple a matter, we find illustrated the complexity of life in an unstandardized age.

The medieval values still evident in some writings of the period, vanishing with Erasmus, were gone in the words of the Frenchman François Rabelais (1490-1553). Rabelais contributed far more to literature than the salacious wit for which he became famous, for as a secular priest he made an original contribution through wit to the "philosophy of Christ." He studied the classics, particularly Plato and the ancient physicians, practiced and taught medicine, and created two of the great comic figures of letters—Gargantua and his son Pantagruel. The two are giants, and everything they do is of heroic dimensions. The abbey of Theleme (the Greek word for will), which Gargantua helps to found, permits its residents a wildly unmonastic experience:

> *All their life was spent not in lawes, statutes or rules, but according to their own free will and pleasure. They rose out of their beds, when they thought good; they did eat, drink, labour, sleep, when they had a mind to it and were disposed for it. . . . In all their rule, and strictest tie of their order there was but this one clause to be observed,*
>
> *DO WHAT THOU WILT.**

*Rabelais, *Gargantua and Pantagruel*, trans. Sir Thomas Urquhart and Peter Anthony Motteux (London: Gibbings, 1901), I, pp. 165-67.

Erasmus, as painted by Hans Holbein in 1523.

To Rabelais free will meant self-improvement on a grand scale. Gargantua exhorts Pantagruel to learn *everything;* he is to master Arabic in addition to Latin, read the New Testament in Greek and the Old in Hebrew, and study history, geometry, architecture, music, and civil law. He must also know "the fishes; all the fowls of the air; all the several kinds of shrubs and trees, . . . all sorts of herbs and flowers that grow upon the ground; all the various metals that are hid within the bowels of the earth . . ." "In brief," Gargantua concludes, "let me see thee an abyss, and bottomless pit of knowledge."** Both his insatiable appetite for knowledge and the exuberance with which Rabelais wrote about it represent important aspects of Renaissance style.

Rabelais leaned heavily on oral traditions and other forms of popular culture, for he used the language of the marketplace. He discovered the people who spoke and wrote, if they wrote at all, in the vernacular; he enjoyed the carnival atmosphere of ordinary life, which he had observed in his travels, and he put popular forms together with his knowledge of the classics, theology, medicine, and law. He drew upon folksongs, ballads, German and French chapbooks, which ignored the traditional upper-class values, mixing literary traditions

**Ibid., II, pp. 32-35.

with less than customary respect for the barriers between types of audiences. He understood that there was an under-culture of wanderers, sailors, women, who desired and created their own literary forms. By depicting them in his writings, he was at once a humanist who truly saw the unity between all people, an innovator producing a new genre, and a subversive whose language brought popular culture to academic respectability.

In a sense Rabelais personified the tension between the carnal and the spiritual in Renaissance life, for he drew upon both. He saw himself as an exponent of the "philosophy of Christ," yet the very word *Rabelaisian* came to mean bawdy, vulgar, even obscene. He understood how the peasantry, in particular, ritualized the tension in their lives in both Lent and Carnival. Carnival was a time of holiday, an end in itself, with emphasis on food, violence, and sex. (*Carne* meant that meat could be eaten before the long Lenten fast; *carne* also meant the flesh, in the sexual sense.) Symbols of lust were openly displayed at Carnival, aggression was expressed toward animals, women, and Jews, and the widespread use of costumes during Carnival freed men and women to reverse roles, to justify disorder, and to do things for which they would not be blamed, since, even if recognized behind their masks, they were not "themselves."

Against Carnival, traditional popular culture set Lent, as shown in a famous painting by Pieter Brueghel (see p. 297, *Combat of Carnival and Lent*, 1559). While Carnival was represented as a gross man eating and drinking licentiously, Lent was depicted as a thin woman, going without food or sex, that is, depriving

THE PRAISE OF FOLLY

Prince of humanists, Erasmus used gentle satire to make his points about how conventional wisdom often prevented original thought. *The Praise of Folly*, written in 1509, gave him international fame when it was published in Paris in 1511:

At what rate soever the World talks of me (for I am not ignorant what an ill report Folly hath got, even amongst the most Foolish), yet that I am that She, that onely She, whose Deity recreates both gods and men, even this is a sufficient Argument, that I no sooner stept up to speak to this full Assembly, than all your faces put on a kind of new and unwonted pleasantness. So suddenly have you clear'd your brows, and with so frolique and hearty a laughter given me your applause, that in troth, as many of you as I behold on every side of me, seem to me no less than Homer's gods drunk with Nectar and Nepenthe; whereas before, ye sat as lumpish and pensive as if ye had come from consulting an Oracle. And as it usually happens when the Sun begins to shew his Beams, or when after a sharp Winter the Spring breathes afresh on the Earth, all things immediately get a new face, new colour, and recover as it were a certain kind of youth again: in like manner, by but beholding me, ye have in an instant gotten another kind of Countenance; and so what the otherwise great Rhetoricians with their tedious and long-studied Orations can hardly effect, to wit, to remove the trouble of the Mind, I have done it at once, with my single look. . . .

But, by the way, I hope that Sexe is not so foolish as to take offence at this, that I my self, being a woman, and Folly too, have attributed Folly to them. For if they weigh it right, they needs must acknowledg that they owe it to Folly that they are more fortunate than men. As first their Beauty, which, and that not without cause, they prefer before every thing, since by its means they exercise a Tyranny even upon Tyrants themselves; otherwise, whence proceeds that sowre look, rough skin, bushy beard and such other things as speak plain Old age in a man, but from that Disease of Wisdom? whereas women's Cheeks are ever plump and smooth, their Voice small, their Skin soft, as if they imitated a certain kind of perpetual Youth. Again, what greater thing do they wish in their whole lives, than that they may please the Men? For to what other purpose are all those Dresses, Washes, Baths, Curlings, Slops, Perfumes, and those several little tricks of setting their Faces, painting their Eye-brows, and smoothing their Skins? And now tell me, what higher Letters of Recommendation have they to men than this Folly? For what is it they do not permit 'em to do? and to what other purpose than that of pleasure? wherein yet their folly is not the least thing that pleaseth; which how true it is, I think no one will deny, that does but consider with himself, what foolish Discourse and odd Gambals pass between a man and his women, as oft as he has a mind to be gamesome? And so I have shown ye whence the first and chiefest delight of man's life springs. . . .

But I forget my self and run beyond my bounds. Though yet, if I shall seem to have spoken any thing more boldly or impertinently than I ought, be pleas'd to consider that not only Folly but a Woman said it; remembring in the mean time that Greek Proverb, "Sometimes a fool may speak a word in season", unlesse perhaps you'll say this concerns not Women. I see you expect an Epilogue, but give me leave to tell ye you are much mistaken if you think I remember any thing of what I have said, having foolishly bolted out such a hodg podg of words. 'Tis an old Proverb, "I hate one that remembers what's done over the Cup". This is a new one of my own making: I hate a man that remembers what he hears. Wherefore farewell, clap your hands, live, and drink lustick, my most excellent Disciples of Folly.

Erasmus, [*Moriae Encomium*, or,] *The Praise of Folly*, trans. John Wilson, 1668, ed. Mrs. P.S. Allen (Oxford: Clarendon Press, 1925), pp. 7-8, 33-34, 187-88. By permission of Oxford University Press.

Brueghel's *Combat of Carnival and Lent* (1559). The original is in the Vienna Kunsthistorisches Museum.

herself of whatever was most valued for pleasure. Religious reformers increasingly sought to distinguish Lent from Carnival, to use the popular pastimes of the peasantry for didactic purposes. The Catholic reformers sought to modify, the Protestant reformers to eliminate, Carnival. In this tension between the mortification of Lent and the release of Carnival, both so intense in Rabelais, the diversity of Renaissance life is well revealed; in the triumph of Lent in the seventeenth century, the success of the Reformation would be demonstrated.

III SCIENCE AND RELIGION

Humanism both aided and impeded the advance of science—a term not widely popularized until the nineteenth century. The Renaissance was less a dramatic rebirth of science than an age of preparation for the scientific revolution that was to come in the seventeenth century of Galileo and Newton. The major contribution of the humanists to this preparation was increased availability of ancient scientific authorities, as works by Galen, Ptolemy, Archimedes, and others were for the first time translated from Greek to Latin. An important contribution also came from the Scholastic tradition, which survived robustly throughout the Renaissance centuries, notably at the universities of Paris and Padua. For despite the scorn the humanists heaped upon them, the Scholastics' insistence on systematic work habits and their enthusiasm for Aristotle promoted scientific studies.

Humanism thwarted the advance of science by putting old authorities beyond the reach of criticism. Few scholars of the Renaissance believed it possible to improve on the astronomy taught by Ptolemy or the medicine taught by Galen in the second century A.D. Galen for example, had taught that the blood moved from one side of the heart to the other by passing through invisible pores in the thick wall of tissue separating the two sides of the organ; actually, as William Harvey (1578-1657) was to show in 1616, the blood gets from the one side to the other by circulating through the body and lungs. Galen's theory of invisible pores kept Leonardo da Vinci from anticipating Harvey; when his anatomical investigations led him to the brink of discovery, he backed away because he could not believe that Galen might have erred.

Da Vinci (1452-1519) exemplifies both the shortcomings and the achievements of Renaissance science. Taking notes in a hit-or-miss fashion and in a secretive left-handed writing that had to be held up to a mirror to be read, he had little concern for systematic cataloging of observations and the publication of his findings and speculations. Yet Leonardo also showed remarkable inventiveness, drawing plans for lathes, pumps, war machines, flying machines, and many other contraptions, not all of them workable but all highly imaginative. He had a passionate curiosity about almost everything concerning human beings and nature. His accurate drawings of human embryos differed radically from the older notion of the fetus as perfectly formed miniature human being. Moreover, Leonardo did not always bow before established authority, as he did before Galen. His geological studies convinced him that the earth was far older than the scholars of his time thought it to be. The Po river, he estimated, must have been flowing for two hundred thousand years to wash down the sediments forming its alluvial plain in northern Italy.

Invention, Technology, Medicine

The most important invention of the Renaissance—the technology for printing books—furnishes a case history of how many individual advances contribute to an end result. The revolution in book production began in the twelfth century, when Muslims in Spain introduced a technique first developed by the Chinese and began to make paper by shredding old rags, processing them with water, and then pressing the liquid out of the finished sheets. The cost of the new product was only a fraction of that of the sheepskin parchment or calfskin vellum employed for manuscripts. The next step came when engravers, adapting another Chinese technique, made a mirror image of a drawing on a wood block or copper plate that could make many identical woodcuts or engravings. Sentences were then added to the plates or blocks to explain the drawings. Finally, movable type was devised (the first known attempt to print in movable type was also in China, in 1041-1048), each piece of type representing a single letter on a minute bit of engraving that could be combined with other pieces to form words, sentences, a whole page, and then salvaged to be used over and over again. This crucial invention was perfected during the 1440s, almost certainly in the Rhineland; Johann Gutenberg (c 1397-1468), who used to receive the

Gutenberg examining a proof from his press, as shown on the pedestal of the Gutenberg statue in Mainz, Germany.

credit for its invention, has been the focus of a scholarly controversy that has deflated his reputation. Though the first printed Bibles are still referred to by his name, others may have done the printing while he was plagued by creditors.

The new invention gained wide popularity because printed books were not only much cheaper than manuscripts but also less prone to copyists' errors. By 1500 the total number of volumes in print had reached the millions, and Italy alone had some seventy-three presses employing movable type. The most famous of them, the Aldine Press in Venice (named for its founder, Aldus Manutius, 1450-1515), sold inexpensive editions of the classics printed in a beautiful typeface that was said to be modeled on the handwriting of Petrarch and is the source of italics, first cut in 1501. Without the perfection of printing, Erasmus might not have become the acknowledged arbiter of European letters. Without it, Luther could not have secured the rapid distribution of his antipapal tracts, and the Protestant Reformation might not have torn Christian Europe apart.

Although no other single invention can be compared with printing for quick and decisive effects, many innovations ultimately had comparable influence. Gunpowder, for example, brought from China to medieval Europe, was used in the later campaigns of the Hundred Years' War. Improved firearms and artillery were to doom both the feudal knight and the feudal castle. In navigation important marine aids came into general use, particularly the magnetic compass and sailing charts, which for the Mediterranean possessed a high level of accuracy. By the close of the fifteenth century, Europeans had the technical equipment needed for world discovery.

On land the engineers of the late medieval centuries solved some of the problems of extracting and smelting silver, iron, and other ores. Then, in 1556, a German physician and mining expert published a comprehensive treatise on the practices of the industry—*De re metallica*

(All about Metals). Following the sixteenth-century custom, its author called himself Georg Agricola, a Latinized version of his German name, Bauer (peasant). Agricola's treatise was an early specimen of those handbooks that are indispensable to the engineer, and its detailed observations on soil structure also made it a pioneer study in geology.

The wide publication of printed books with clear anatomical illustrations also advanced medical skills, which were further improved by the partial lifting of the old ban against dissection of human cadavers. Pharmacology also progressed, thanks to experiments with the chemistry of drugs made by an eccentric Swiss physican Paracelsus (Theophrastus Bombastus von Hohenheim, c 1493-1541). He rejected Galen's theory of disease—that illness was caused by an imbalance in bodily fluids—and proposed that chemical remedies be applied to specific diseases. The French surgeon Ambroise Paré (c 1510-1590), who also had little reverence for antiquity, laid the foundations for modern surgery by developing new techniques, notably that of sewing up blood vessels with stitches rather than cauterizing them with a hot iron. Yet many so-called physicians were quacks, and many teachers of medicine merely repeated the demonstrations that Galen had made more than a thousand years earlier, without attempting to confirm the truth of his findings.

A striking exception to this rule was furnished by the physicians and scholars of the University of Padua. Because Padua was ruled by Venice, they were protected against possible ecclesiastical censorship. They maintained a tradition of scientific inquiry that presaged the seventeenth-century triumphs of the experimental method. In 1537 a young Belgian named Andreas Vesalius (1514-1564), trained at Paris, took a teaching post at Padua. Vesalius repeated the dissection of Galen and watched for possible errors; thus he rejected Galen's notion of invisible pores in the wall of tissue within the heart because he simply could not find such pores. In 1543 Vesalius published *De humanis corporis fabrica* (Concerning the Structure of the Human Body), prepared with concern for anatomical accuracy and detail, and illustrated with elaborate woodcuts.

Growth in medical knowledge probably had little direct impact on life span, however. Until the early eighteenth century, the typical operating theater in a hospital—if there was one—was much like a butcher shop. Indeed, patients were often led to an operation blindfolded so that they would not be frightened by seeing the operating instruments, which were only modified butcher's tools. As in a butcher shop, the floor was covered with sawdust to soak up the flow of blood, and most operations involved amputations by sawing. The patient was drugged with opium or alcohol. The operation was performed quickly to forestall surgical shock, and perhaps half of the patients died—either from the operation itself or from infection afterwards.

The Black Death coincides with the customary dates for the beginning of the Renaissance. The idea of quarantine was introduced in 1346, based on the biblical injunction to separate out lepers, and regulations concerning the quarantine of suspected carriers of disease were fully in place in Venice by 1485. Nonetheless, plagues continued until the last major outbreak in Marseilles in 1720; London was swept by plague in 1665. Until rats were understood to be the transmitters of the disease, the prevalence of thatched roofs from which rats or fleas might fall assured a high level of infection. Leprosy, commonplace in Europe from the sixth century, declined in part for ecological reasons and in part because of changing patterns of disease competition. As tuberculosis became more common in the Renaissance, the infectious chain of Hansen's disease (the proper name for leprosy) may have been interrupted, as the one called forth antibodies that forestalled the slower-moving bacillus associated with the other. Yaws, classified with leprosy, declined dramatically, while syphilis broke out equally dramatically in the fifteenth century.

Disease patterns were influenced more by social and economic conditions than by medical knowledge. Expanding use of woolens (intensified by a prolonged period of cold weather), changes in household sanitation—especially in the kitchen—and the introduction of a virtually free interchange of infections between the Old and the New Worlds by the Spanish after the discovery of America altered the balance of disease and immunities. The Old World introduced bluegrass, dandelions, daisies, and measles, for example, to the New, while taking from it exotic foods and, ultimately, the plant louse (*phylloxera*), that virtually destroyed European vineyards in the 1880s—all in ignorance of the effect of such introductions. At the same time, the rise of the city, the growth of closer communities, and easier communication throughout Europe between 1500 and 1700 lessened the probability of devastating epidemics, as the frequent circulation of disease also quickened the adaptability of the human species to them. By the end of the Renaissance many once-virulent diseases that had systematically struck adults had been reduced to the category of childhood diseases—that is, diseases that generally struck only the very young or newcomers from abroad who had not developed immunities. Despite the growth of scientific knowledge about disease, the general public continued to rely on magic, witchcraft, alchemy, and astrology for protection against the unpredictable.

Astronomy

The year 1543 marked the launching of modern astronomical studies, with the publication of Copernicus' *De revolutionibus orbium coelestium* (Concerning the Revolutions of Heavenly Bodies). Born in Poland of German extraction, Nicolaus Copernicus (1473-1543) studied law and medicine at Padua and other Italian universities and spent thirty years as canon of a cathedral near Danzig. His work in mathematics and astronomy led him to attack the hypothesis of the geocentric (earth-centered) universe derived from

Ptolemy and other astronomers of antiquity. In its place he advanced the revolutionary new hypothesis of the heliocentric (sun-centered) universe.

The concept of the geocentric universe generally accepted in the sixteenth century included an elaborate system of spheres. Around the stationary earth there revolved some eighty spheres, each, as it were, a separate sky containing some of the heavenly bodies, each moving on an invisible circular path, each transparent so that mortals could see the spheres beyond it. This imaginative and symmetrical picture of the universe had already come under attack before Copernicus, for observers could not make it tally with the actual behavior of heavenly bodies. Copernicus used these earlier criticisms and his own computations to arrive at the heliocentric concept, which required that the earth move around the sun rather than remain stationary.

The Copernican hypothesis had radical implications. It destroyed the idea of the earth's uniqueness by suggesting that it acted like other heavenly bodies, and thus opened the way to attacks on the uniqueness of the earth's human inhabitants. Nevertheless, once Copernicus had reversed the roles of the sun and the earth, his universe retained many Ptolemaic characteristics. Its heavens were still filled with spheres revolving along invisible orbits, only now they moved about a stationary sun, and Copernican astronomy required thirty-four of them, not eighty. The revolution in astronomy begun by Copernicus did not reach its climax for a hundred and fifty years. The circular orbits of Copernicus yielded to elliptical orbits; the scheme of thirty-four spheres was modified, and a theory explaining the forces that kept the universe together had to be put forward. These developments all turned on the genius of Galileo and Newton and the observations made possible by the invention of the telescope.

Music

In the medieval curriculum music was grouped with the sciences because mathematics underlies musical theory and notation. The mainstay of medieval sacred music was the Gregorian chant or *plainsong,* which relied on a single voice and thus did not involve harmonizing two or more voices. At the close of the Middle Ages more intricate innovations appeared. Musicians in the Low Countries and northern France developed the technique of *polyphony* (from the Greek, "many voices"), which combined several voices in complicated harmony. When French and Flemish musicians journeyed to Italy in the fifteenth century, they introduced polyphonic music and borrowed in return the popular tunes of the dances and folk songs they encountered in southern Europe. Flemish composers even based masses on rowdy popular tunes. The end products of the interaction were the sacred and secular polyphonic compositions of the internationally renowned Fleming Josquin des Pres (c 1450-1521) at the court of Louis XII, and the masses of the Italian Giovanni Palestrina (c 1526-1594), choirmaster in the Vatican. Much of this music sounds quite otherwordly today, since it lacks dissonances, strong rhythms, and clear climaxes.

Michelangelo Caravaggio (1565-1609) shows *The Musicians* with their instruments: a lute, a fiddle, and a cornet.

The secularism and individualism of the Renaissance and its taste for experimentation also affected music. New instruments were developed or imported: the violin, doublebass, and harpsichord; the organ, with its complement of keyboards, pedals, and stops; the kettledrum, which was adopted from the Polish army; and the lute, which originated in medieval Persia and reached Italy through Spain. Composers and performers began to lose the anonymity associated with the Middle Ages, although the era of prima donnas had not quite arrived. Paid professional singers staffed the choirs of Antwerp cathedral and of the Vatican; a retinue of musicians became a fixture of court life, with the dukes of Burgundy, Philip the Good, and Charles the Bold leading the way. German artisans, calling themselves mastersingers, organized choral groups; the most famous of them, Hans Sachs (1494-1576), a cobbler and poet in Nuremberg in the 1500s, was later immortalized in Wagner's opera *Die Meistersinger.* And music had also become part of popular culture; the French *cabaret*, the Spanish *venta*, the German *Wirtshaus*, the Polish *gospoda*, the English *pub*, all rang to popular folk songs. Indeed, Sachs was unusual in accepting credit for songs, for the customary attitude was that the performer did not admit to authorship, since popular songs and stories were regarded as traditional—belonging to all.

The Renaissance and the Church

Renaissance science as a whole aroused discord within the church. Even though Copernicus dedicated his great book to the pope, Christendom did not welcome a theory that questioned the belief in an earth-centered, human-centered universe. By Copernicus' time, Western Christendom was preoccupied by its division into the warring factions of Catholic and Protestant. To what extent was the Renaissance responsible for the Reformation?

First, the Renaissance did not make the Reformation inevitable. (Indeed, very little in history can be said to be inevitable.) It is an oversimplification to suppose that the religious individualism of Luther arose directly out of the more general individualism of the Renaissance. In the checkered culture of the age, there were many elements—materialism, self-indulgence, power politics—that are hard to reconcile with traditional Christian values. If pushed to extremes, these elements could indeed become anti-Christian—but they were seldom pushed to extremes. Even the most ruthless politicians and financiers—men like Cesare Borgia and Jacob Fugger—remained nominal Christians. Even a pronounced anticlerical like Machiavelli reserved his most stinging criticism for the pope's claim to temporal authority, not his claim to be head of the church.

Second, the most characteristic intellectual movement of the Renaissance—humanism—proposed to enrich or purify Christianity, not subvert it. Erasmus, perhaps the most representative thinker of humanism, was too strongly attached to Catholicism and too moderate in temperament to be a revolutionary.

Finally, although a religious crisis was indeed gathering during the Renaissance, it was more internal than external. That is, the church was only to a limited extent moved by outside forces operating beyond its control, such as the challenge presented to its old international dominion by the new national monarchies. If the church of the 1400s had been strong and healthy, it might have met such external challenges successfully. Except in Spain, however, the church set a flabby example, even though honorable exceptions to the prevailing laxity and backwardness could be found. Priests were often illiterate, untrained, underpaid, and immoral; many bishops acted like politicians, not churchmen.

Perhaps the worst shortcomings existed at the top, in the papacy itself. In the fourteenth and early fifteenth centuries the papacy had abandoned Rome for Avignon and gone through the crisis of the Great Schism and the Conciliar Movement. It emerged from these ordeals with its power reinvigorated, notably by its victory over the reformers who sought to make church councils a check against unlimited papal absolutism. But its spiritual prestige was gravely damaged. For three-quarters of a century after 1450 the papacy was occupied by men who scored political and military successes and lavished money on learning and the arts. While they bequeathed to posterity the Vatican Library, the Sistine Chapel, and the early parts of the Basilica of St. Peter, they also increased the burden of ecclesiastical taxation. Papal indifference to spiritual functions enfeebled the church at a time when it needed firm control and reform.

Intellectually, too, the clergy were losing the vitality they had possessed in the age of Abelard and Aquinas. Some of the monks and friars on university faculties hardly qualified as teachers; they blindly defended Scholasticism against the new humanist studies and provoked an illustrative satire, *The Letters of Obscure Men.* Johann Reuchlin (1455-1522), a German humanist working with Pico at Florence, learned Hebrew in order to read the great books of Judaism. On returning to Germany he aroused the wrath of theological faculties by suggesting that a knowledge of the sacred Jewish writings might enable a Christian to be better informed. Arraigned in an ecclesaistical court, Reuchlin assembled in his defense testimonials from leading humanists, *The Letters of Eminent Men;* then, in 1516 and 1517, two of his friends published *The Letters of Obscure Men*, supposedly exchanged between Reuchlin's clerical opponents, though actually a hoax designed to laugh the opposition out of court by mocking the futility of theological hair splitting. Reuchlin lost his case and was sentenced to pay the cost of the trial but managed to avoid making any payment.

IV THE FINE ARTS

Even more than the writers and preachers of the Renaissance, its artists displayed an extraordinary range of originality in their interests and talents. They found

RENAISSANCE SATIRE: THE LETTERS OF OBSCURE MEN

For you must know that we were lately sitting in an inn, having our supper, and were eating eggs, when on opening one, I saw that there was a young chicken within.

This I showed to a comrade; whereupon quoth he to me, "Eat it up speedily, before the taverner sees it, for if he mark it, you will have to pay for a fowl."

In a trice I gulped down the egg, chicken and all. And then I remembered that it was Friday!

Whereupon I said to my crony, "You have made me commit a mortal sin, in eating flesh on the sixth day of the week!"

But he averred that it was not a mortal sin—nor even a venial one, seeing that such a chickling is accounted merely as an egg, until it is born.

Then I departed, and thought the matter over.

And by the Lord, I am in a mighty quandary, and know not what to do.

It seemeth to me that these young fowls in eggs are flesh, because their substance is formed and fashioned into the limbs and body of an animal, and possesseth a vital principle.

It is different in the case of grubs in cheese, and suchlike, because grubs are accounted fish, as I learnt from a physician who is also skilled in Natural Philosophy.

Most earnestly do I entreat you to resolve the question that I have propounded. For if you hold that the sin is mortal, then, I would fain get shrift here, ere I return to Germany.

Adapted from Francis Griffin Stokes, ed., *Epistolae obscurorum virorum* (New Haven: Yale University Press, 1925), pp. 445-47. The two authors were Ulrich von Hutten and Crotus Rubianus.

patrons both among the princes of the church and among merchant princes, condottieri, and secular rulers. They took as subjects their own patrons and the pagan gods and heroes of antiquity, as well as Christ, the Virgin, and the saints. Although their income was often meager, they enjoyed increasing status both as technicians and as creative personalities. They boasted of their skills and attainments, for in the arts, too, the anonymous or community stamp of medieval culture was yielding to the individual ego.

The artists liberated painting and sculpture from subordination to architcture, which had been the "queen of the arts" during the Middle Ages. The statues, carvings, altarpieces, and stained glass contributing so much to Romanesque and Gothic churches had usually been only parts of a larger whole. In the Renaissance the number of free-standing pictures and sculptures—each one an independent work of art—steadily increased.

Important advances in painting came with the further development of *chiaroscuro* (in Italian, "bright-dark"), stressing contrasts of light and shade, and with the growing use of perspective—both of which enhanced the three-dimensional quality of a picture. In the early Renaissance painters worked in fresco or tempera; in fresco they applied pigments to the wet plaster of a wall, and the painters had to work swiftly before the plaster dried; in tempera they mixed pigments with a sizing, often of eggs, which allowed them to work after the plaster had dried but gave the end-product a muddy look. Oil paints, developed first in Flanders and brought to Italy in the last half of the fifteenth century, overcame the deficiencies of fresco and tempera by permitting leisurely, delicate work and ensuring clearer and more permanent colors.

The Flemish origin of oil paints serves as a reminder that modern scholarship has exploded the old idea that the artistic Renaissance was exclusively Italian, existing in isolation from the rest of Europe or from the medieval centuries. An older, Gothic strain persisted even in Italy, as evident in Milan where, throughout the Renaissance centuries, much money went into building the cathedral, a celebrated example of the Gothic "wedding-cake" style. Late Gothic artists, especially those in the Low Countries during the Burgundian ascendancy of the fourteenth and fifteenth centuries, contributed to the Renaissance not only by introducing oil paints but also by stressing decorative richness and an almost photographic realism in depicting the details of nature. Botanists can identify dozens of flowers and plants in the Ghent altarpiece (*The Adoration of the Mystic Lamb*) of the Van Eyck brothers, Hubert (c 1366-1426) and Jan (c 1385-1441). The commercial links between Flemish and Italian cities promoted cultural interchange, and Italians were eager to buy paintings by the Van Eycks and other Flemish masters and also admired the tapestries, the music, and the fashions of the rich Burgundian court.

Yet without Giotto earlier, and Masaccio, Leonardo, Michelangelo, and other Italian artists of genius, the Renaissance could never have become one of the great ages in the history of art. In sculpture it rivaled the golden centuries of Greece; in painting it transformed a rather limited medium into a dazzling new instrument. It is no wonder that historians often use Italian designations for these centuries; *trecento*, *quattrocento*, and *cinquecento* (literally, 300s, 400s, and 500s, an abbreviated reference to the 1300s, 1400s and 1500s).

Florence was the artistic capital of the Renaissance in Italy. Lorenzo the Magnificent subsidized the painter Sandro Botticelli (c 1444-1510) as well as the humanists

Although religious themes continued to be popular during this period, figures became more fleshy and lifelike. Here the Florentine Masaccio (1401-1428), who revolutionized art during his short lifetime, provides his version of *The Expulsion of Adam and Eve* from the Garden of Eden. Light slants in sharply from an outside source to create a sense of distance; the figures are caught in motion and despair. Deprived of God, Eve cries out, and both Adam and Eve hide their nakedness, having learned of evil. Neither figure attempts to resist the angel who expels them.

of the Platonic Academy. Court painters were commonplace in other states, both in Italy and elsewhere. In Milan Il Moro made Leonardo da Vinci in effect his minister of fine arts and director of public works; after Sforza's fortunes collapsed, Leonardo found new patrons in Cesare Borgia, the pope, and the French kings Louis XII and Francis I. The Renaissance popes, who also employed Botticelli, Raphael (1485-1520), Michelangelo, and other luminaries, had a keen artistic appreciation, coupled with a determination to have Rome surpass Florence in artistic eminence.

The mixture of worldly and religious motives among patrons also characterized the works they commissioned. Artists applied equal skill to scenes from classical mythology, to portraits of their secular contemporaries, and to such religious subjects as the Madonna, the Nativity, and the Crucifixion. Often the sacred and the secular could be found in the same picture; for example, in the *Last Judgment,* in the Arena Chapel, Giotto portrayed Scrovegni, who had commissioned the work, on the same scale as the saints. His successors sometimes included the whole family of the donor in the picture, as in Botticelli's *Adoration of the Magi* (1482), which showed Cosimo and Lorenzo de' Medici as well as the artist himself.

Patronage, like art, was a complex matter, for the commissioning of a "work of art"—a modern phrase arising from art galleries and museums—required the means, the taste, the sense of permanence, and the desire to exercise authority that arose differently in different places and times. Many patrons were lay men and women who wanted a religious painting for their house; many were corporate and ecclesiastical, such as religious brotherhoods who wished a painting on the theme of the saint after whom their church was named; many were corporate and secular, such as the wool guild (which was responsible for the cathedral in Florence), who might wish to illustrate a specific theme; many were individual and ecclesiastical, such as the popes, archbishops, and bishops of the church; and there was always the state, as when the Florentine government commissioned Michelangelo to make a bronze David (as opposed to his marble David). Patrons could and did dictate the trends in themes, the use of materials, the placement of finished objects. Thus commerce, prestige, a sense of place, the desire to honor an occasion, and social customs all shaped art and were in turn shaped by the artists' responses to their commissions. Church art obviously would not promote belief in magic; government art might promote a historical sense of the greatness of the past, as in a battle scene, to encourage citizens to fight for the present greatness of the state. Artists who did not fully accept the explicit purpose behind their commissions were in some sense social deviants, promoting the idea of the ultimate independence of the artist's work.

Renaissance artists at first painted classical and pagan subjects like Jupiter or Venus as just another lord and lady of the chivalric class. Later they restored the sense of

Botticelli's *The Birth of Venus* and *Primavera,* also called *Allegory of Spring.* Both are in the Uffizi Gallery in Florence.

historical appropriateness by using classical settings and painting the figures in the nude; at the same time, however, they also created an otherworldly quality. When Botticelli was commissioned by the Medici to do *The Birth of Venus* (1485), he made the goddess, emerging full grown from a seashell, more ethereal than sensual, and he placed the figures in the arrangement usual for the baptism of Christ. In *Primavera* (c 1478), Botticelli's allegory of spring, the chief figures—Mercury, Venus, The Three Graces, Flora (bedecked with blossoms), and Spring herself (wafted in by the West Wind)—are all youthful, delicate, and serene.

Leonardo da Vinci completed relatively few pictures, since his scientific activities and innumerable odd jobs for his patrons consumed much of his energy. Moreover, his celebrated fresco, *The Last Supper* (1495-1498), began to deteriorate during his own lifetime because the mold on the damp monastery wall in Milan destroyed the clarity of the oil pigments he used. Luckily, Leonardo's talent and his extraordinary range of interests can also be studied in his drawings and notebooks. The drawings include preliminary sketches of paintings, fanciful war machines, and doodles, along with realistic portrayals of human embryos and of deformed or suffering individuals.

In composing *The Last Supper* Leonardo departed dramatically from previous interpretations, which depicted the solemn moment of the final communion, with the treachery of Judas suggested only by placing him in isolation from the others. Leonardo divided the apostles into four groups of three men around the central figure of Christ—an innovation that was most effective psychologically, even though it would have been physically impossible for the thirteen men to have eaten together at the small table depicted. Leonardo's second departure was to choose the tense moment when Jesus announced the coming betrayal, and to place Judas among the apostles, relying on facial expression and bodily posture to convey the guilt of the one and the consternation of the others.

Michelangelo Buonarotti (1475-1564), though best known as a sculptor, ranks among the immortals of painting as a result of one prodigious achievement—the frescoes he executed for the Sistine Chapel in the Vatican. Pope Sixtus IV had built the chapel, and his nephew, Pope Julius II (1503-1513), entrusted the commission of decorating its walls and ceiling to Michelangelo. He covered a huge area with three hundred and forty-three separate figures and spent four years working almost single-handed, assisted only by a plasterer and a color mixer, painting on his back atop a scaffold, sometimes not even descending for his night's rest. He began over the chapel entrance with *The Drunkenness of Noah* and ended over the altar with *The Creation*. God appears repeatedly, draped in a mantle, an ever-changing patriarch: hovering over the waters, he is benign; giving life to the motionless Adam or directing Eve to arise, he is gently commanding; creating the sun and the moon, he is the formidable, all-powerful deity. In this vast gallery of figures, nude and draped, Michelangelo summed up all that Renaissance artists had learned about perspective, anatomy, and motion.

A self-portrait of Leonardo da Vinci, from the Royal Library in Turin.

Both Michelangelo and Leonardo had received their artistic training in Florence. Titian (1477-1576) was identified with Venice, and the rich reds and purples that are his hallmark exemplify the flamboyance and pageantry of that city. Titian's longevity, productivity, and success were extraordinary. At the start he was engaged to do frescoes for the Venetian headquarters of German merchants, and he went on to portraits of rich merchants, Madonnas, altarpieces for churches and monasteries, and a great battle scene for the palace of the doge. He was offered commissions by half the despots of Italy and crowned heads of Europe, including the emperor Charles V, shown burdened with all the problems of the vast Hapsburg domains.

Painting in Northern Europe

In northern Europe the masters of the fifteenth century were influenced by their Gothic traditions as well as by Titian and other Italians. The ranking northern paint-

Dürer was interested in the intellectual life of his times, and he chose to show St. Jerome at work in his study rather than in a monastery. Erasmus had just completed a translation of St. Jerome's letters, so Dürer's theme was timely. Erasmus had also written a *Manual of the Christian Knight*, and Dürer's engraving, *The Knight, Death and the Devil,*could easily be taken as a commentary on it.

ers included two Germans, Albrecht Dürer (1471-1528) and Hans Holbein (c 1497-1543), and two from the Low Countries, Hieronymus Bosch (c 1450-1516) and Pieter Brueghel (c 1525-1569). Dürer received commissions from the emperor Maximilian (the grandfather of Charles V), and Brueghel from wealthy businessmen of Antwerp and Brussels. Holbein, who was armed with an introduction from Erasmus when he went to England, executed portraits of Henry VIII and his courtiers as well as a likeness of Erasmus that catches the humanist's wit and intelligence.

Dürer, who became identified with Lutheranism in his later years, created what has been termed the first great Protestant art, in which he simplified traditional Christian themes by pruning them of what Lutherans regarded as Catholic trimmings. But this was only one facet of Dürer's many-sided talent; his fascination with nature led him to include wild creatures in many pictures; his realistic and compassionate portrait of his aged mother might almost have been taken from Leonardo's notebooks; and his improvements in the techniques of woodcuts and engravings enabled him to mass produce his own drawings as illustrations for printed books. Dürer was the first artist in history to become a best seller.

Northern art was fascinated with the monstrous and supernatural. Dürer depicted this Gothic strain in a series of woodcuts of the Four Horsemen and other grim figures of the Apocalypse. Bosch, who reflected the piety and reforming spirit of the Brethren of the Common Life, made his paintings graphic sermons filled with nightmarish apparitions illustrating the omnipresence of sin and evil and foreshadowing the techniques and effects of the surrealists of the twentieth century. Brueghel's works contained coats-of-arms that fight, shellfish that fly, and monstrous hybrids that have insect wings, artichoke bodies, and flower heads. Other paintings of Brueghel were realistic and sensitive comments on human misery in a time long before social services, such as *The Blind Leading the Blind*, with its file of stumbling wretches. Brueghel also favored two types of painting otherwise neglected in the period. One was the landscape; his series illustrating farming activities through the year was in the tradition of late medieval books of hours, but with new attention to the changing light and atmosphere of the seasons. The other was the densely populated scene of everyday life and popular culture—children's games and peasant weddings, dances and festivals—depicted with Rabelaisian gusto yet suggesting that people were doomed to repeat endlessly the same simple pleasures and obvious follies. On the whole, northern art was more concerned with moralizing than was its Italian counterpart.

Sculpture

Renaissance sculpture and painting were closely related, and Italian pictures owed some of their three-dimensional quality to the artists' study of sculpture. Leading painters like Michelangelo and Leonardo were accomplished sculptors, the latter, for example, producing miniature anatomical horses stripped of their hides to show bones and muscles. The first Renaissance sculptor was Donatello, whose statue of the condottiere Gattamelata in Padua was even then a landmark in the history of art. The subject is secular, the treatment classical (Gattamelata looks like the commander of a Roman legion), and the medium bronze, not the stone of medieval sculpture. Donatello created the first statue of a nude male since antiquity, a bronze David who, however, looked more like a handsome youth than the inspired slayer of Goliath. Yet Donatello's wooden statue of Mary Magdalene, all lank hair and emaciated skin and bones, was a saint who looked the part (see p. 308).

Bosch shows John the Baptist in the desert, perhaps hallucinating.

Brueghel's *The Blind Leading the Blind* illustrates Christ's parable of how false prophets have led mankind astray.

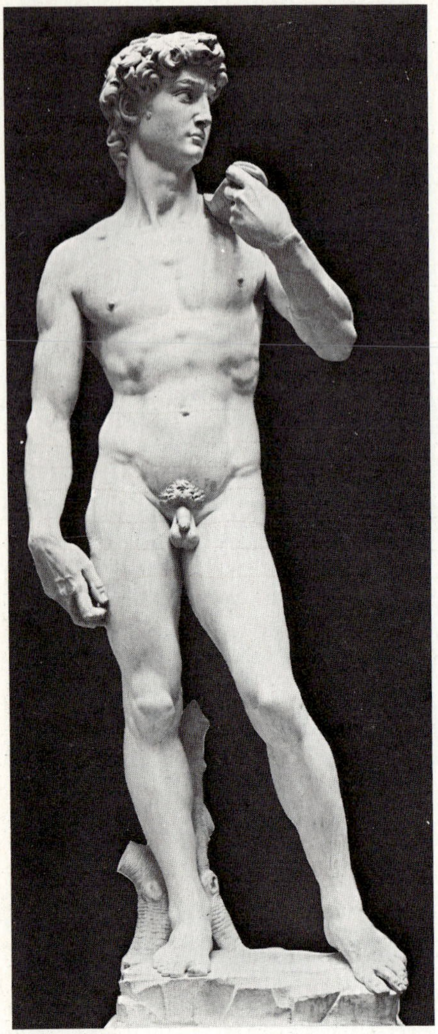

Michelangelo's marble statue of David, 1501-1504, in the Galleria dell' Accademia in Florence contrasts sharply with the detail from Donatello's statue of Mary Magdalene, c 1457, in the Bapistry of Florence. Donatello (1386-1466) set many themes on which subsequent artists commented.

Still another gifted Florentine, Andrea del Verrocchio (1435-1488), extended the concern for social and political realism. His *David* looks like a plebeian lad and was created in obvious criticism of Donatello. His statue of the condottiere Colleoni in Venice, mounted on a muscular horse, is more dynamic than Donatello's Gattamelata. Painter, goldsmith, teacher of Leonardo, and student of architecture, geometry, music, and philosophy, Verrocchio ranked among the universal men of the Renaissance. So did Benvenuto Cellini (1500-1571), goldsmith, engraver, devotee of high living, and author of a noted autobiography. Cellini boasted as patrons two popes as well as King Francis I of France and the Medici grand duke of Tuscany, who commissioned an elegant statue of Perseus (1533) holding aloft the head of Medusa, which commands a place of honor overlooking the Piazza della Signoria in Florence.

On that same piazza is a replica of Michelangelo's colossal statue of David, a muscular nude more than sixteen feet high, fashioned from an enormous block of marble abandoned by another sculptor. Michelangelo went on to carry sculpture to a summit it had not attained since the age of Pericles. He showed his ingenuity in solving technical problems with his *Pietà* (c 1499), in St. Peter's, which shows the Virgin mourning the dead Christ. It was exceedingly difficult to pose a seated woman with a limp adult body across her lap, yet Michelangelo succeeded triumphantly; the face of Mary is sorrowful yet composed and younger than that of Christ, for Michelangelo explained that she was the eternal Virgin and would not grieve as an earthly mother would.

BENVENUTO CELLINI ON CREATIVITY

While the workshop for executing my Perseus was in building, I used to work in a ground-floor room. Here I modelled the statue in plaster, giving it the same dimensions as the bronze was meant to have, and intending to cast it from this mould. But finding that it would take rather long to carry it out in this way, I resolved upon another expedient, especially as now a wretched little studio had been erected, brick on brick, so miserably built that the mere recollection of it gives me pain. So then I began the figure of Medusa, and constructed the skeleton in iron. Afterwards I put on the clay, and when that was modelled, baked it.

I had no assistants except some little shopboys, among whom was one of great beauty; he was the son of a prostitute called La Gambetta. I made use of the lad as a model, for the only books which teach this art are the natural human body. Meanwhile, as I could not do everything alone, I looked about for workmen in order to put the business quickly through; but I was unable to find any. . . . I set about to do my utmost by myself alone. The labour was enormous: I had to strain every muscle night and day; and just then the husband of my sister sickened, and died after a few days' illness. He left my sister, still young, with six girls of all ages, on my hands. . . . So I went home with despair at heart to my unlucky Perseus, not without weeping. . . . At the end of three days news was brought to me that my only son had been smothered by his nurse, which gave me greater grief than I have ever had in my whole life. However, I knelt upon the ground, and, not without tears, returned thanks to God, as I was wont, exclaiming, "Lord, Thou gavest me the child, and Thou has taken him; for all Thy dealings I thank Thee with my whole heart." This great sorrow went nigh to depriving me of reason; yet, according to my habit, I made a virtue of necessity, and adapted myself to circumstances as well as I was able. . . . Nevertheless, I felt convinced that when my Perseus was accomplished, all these trials would be turned to high felicity and glorious well-being.

From *The Autobiography of Benvenuto Cellini*, trans. John Addington Symonds (New York: Modern Library Edition, 1942), pp. 382-83, 399-401, 412.

Benvenuto Cellini's *Perseus*, 1553.

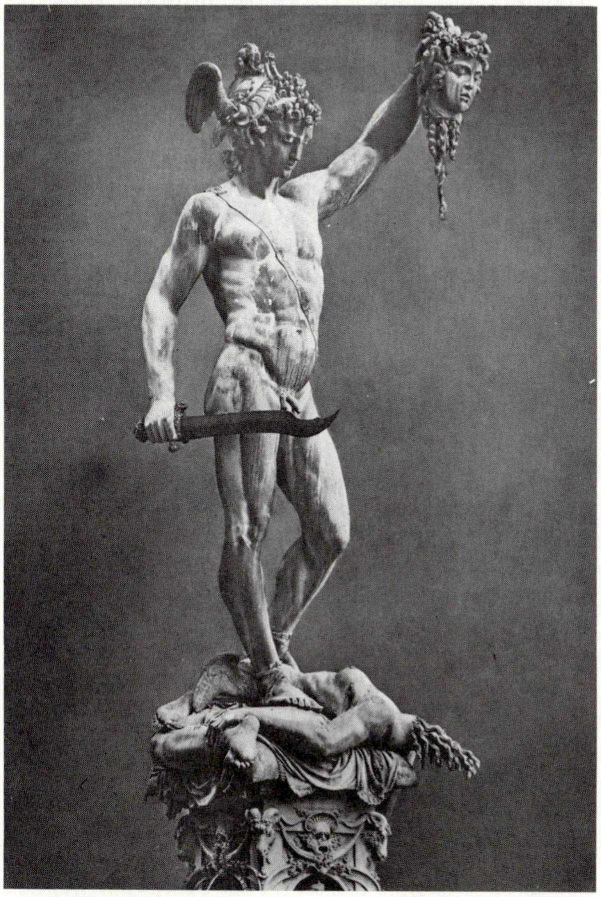

Michelangelo's *Pietà*.

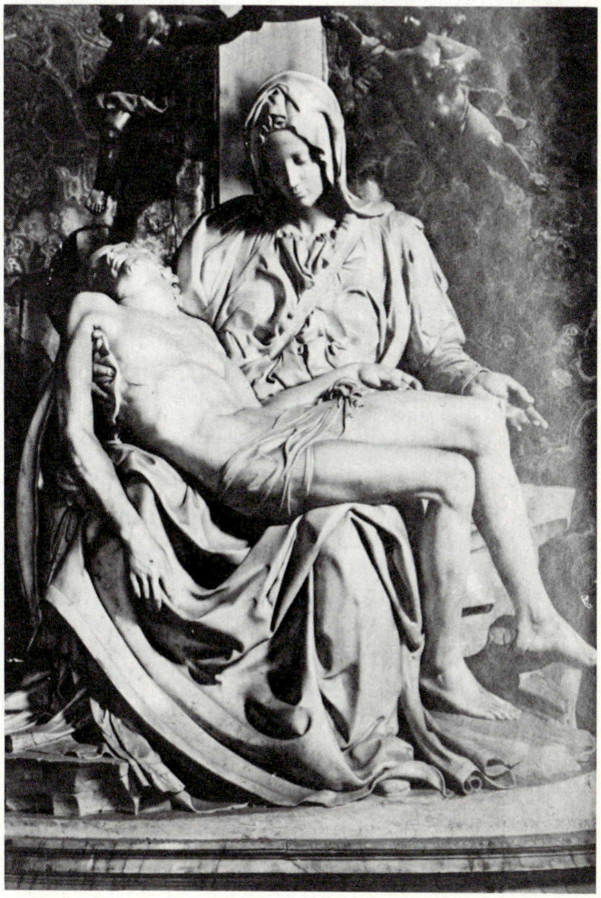

Architecture

In 1546, at the age of seventy, Michelangelo agreed to become the chief architect of St. Peter's in Rome. Though he died long before the great church was completed in 1626, and though his successors altered many details of his plan, the huge dome, which was the key feature of the structure, followed his basic design. St. Peter's exemplifies many of the features that distinguish Renaissance architecture from Gothic. Gothic cathedrals were topped by great spires and towers; St. Peter's was crowned by Michelangelo's massive dome, which rises 435 feet above the floor. Gothic buildings, with their great windows, pointed arches, and high-flung vaults, create an impression of strain and instability; St. Peter's appears indestructible because of its heavier walls, stout columns, and round arches.

Renaissance architects shared the humanists' enthusiasm for Platonic concepts of perfect ideas and perfect geometrical forms. Andrea Palladio (1508-1580), the leading architectural theorist of the cinquecento, stressed the symbolic value of designing churches on the plan of the Greek cross, which had four arms of equal length, in contrast to the Latin cross used in Gothic churches, which had one long arm forming the nave. If the ends of the arms of the Greek cross were rounded and the spaces between the arms filled with rounded chapels, then the structure became a circle. Some scholars have interpreted the new popularity of the Greek-cross design as a shift from the medieval emphasis on the sacrifice of Christ to the Renaissance celebration of the perfection of God. Palladio himself designed many elegant structures: the Church of San Giorgio Maggiore on an island at the mouth of the Grand Canal in Venice, palaces, public buildings, villas, and a Greek theater in the area of Vicenza, his home town, in the hinterland of Venice. He also wrote a four-volume study on architecture which spread the influence of the Palladian style.

In Renaissance Europe private individuals could afford lavish residences, and the increasing prevalence of law and order meant that a home no longer needed to be a fortress. Elaborate villas dotted the Italian countryside; in the cities the characteristic structure was the *palazzo*, an imposing townhouse combining business and residential apartments; many examples survive throughout Italy.

V THE ART OF DAILY LIVING

Indoors, Renaissance buildings reflected the improving standard of life among the affluent. The small classical rooms were easier to heat than the vast drafty halls of the Middle Ages, and items of furniture began to multiply beyond the medieval complement of built-in beds, benches, cupboards, and tables. Although chairs were still largely reserved for the master of the house and important guests, chests, benches, or stools on which people could perch were becoming more common. Chests, which were used not only for storage and sitting

Palladio's Palazzo Chiericati, in Vicenza.

A ROUNDEL BY CHRISTINE DE PISAN

A roundel was a popular form of poetry, written to a prescribed length and format and intended to be recited or sung. Christine de Pisan wrote the following one:

Laughing grey eyes, whose light in me I bear.
Deep in my heart's remembrance and delight,
Remembrance is so infinite delight
Of your brightness, O soft eyes that I fear.

Of love-sickness my life had perished here,
But you raise up my strength in death's respite,
Laughing grey eyes, whose light in me I bear.

Certes, by you my heart, I see full clear,
Shall of desire attain at last the height,
Even that my lady, through your sovereign might,
May me continue in her service dear,
Laughing grey eyes, whose light in me I bear.

From *The Book of the Duke of True Lovers*, trans. Alice Kemp-Welch (London: Chatto & Windus, 1908), p. 36. Reprinted by permission of the author's Literary Estate and Chatto & Windus.

but also as trunks on a journey, were often elaborately painted or carved, sometimes on the model of ancient sarcophagi—another instance of the Renaissance passion for the classical. New articles of furniture served more specialized purposes: the bookcase to house the new printed books (medieval manuscripts had been kept in chests), the writing desk, and the jewel cabinet, a miniature chest on high legs often encrusted with ivory or inlaid work.

The popularity of brooches, pendants, and other forms of jewelry with intricate gold settings attested both to the wealth and to the taste of upper-class Renaissance men and women. The fact that silversmiths made elaborately etched helmets, shields, and suits of armor better suited for show than for military use was a sign of the vanishing medieval preoccupation with security. Along with gold and silver work, fine glass was highly esteemed, particularly the elaborate and delicate work of that was made in Venice. Both the less-affluent and the rich had embroidered household linens and brass and pewter utensils. One great luxury was a mirror, small and made of polished metal, for mirror glass had not yet been perfected.

When Italians of the Renaissance looked into the mirror they saw a gown or tunic surmounted by a cape or cloak, the whole made of increasingly colorful and elegant material. Personal cleanliness advanced with the custom of the weekly bath and change of body linen; bodily wastes were disposed of in an outside privy or in a "close-stool" (commode) indoors. In Italy table manners became more complex, with the substitution of the fork for the fingers, the fading out of the custom of tossing bones and other debris from a meal onto the floor beneath the table, and the use of easily cleaned tiles or mosaics for flooring. Elsewhere changes came more slowly. In England the fork was not in common use until the seventeenth century, and the floor of the great hall in many houses was still covered with rushes; a fresh layer of rushes and fragrant herbs was added from time to time to counter the stench and insects from the lower layers.

Such apparently small changes often brought major alterations in life, particularly for the less affluent. The peasantry probably lived better after the Black Death than before, for those who survived could demand higher wages and use those wages to buy better food, including meat for special occasions. By the midfifteenth century, however, white bread and meat were again exclusively for the rich, and the peasant was once again reduced to hard bread and gruel as population increased and the bargaining power of labor declined. The worker in the field expected to wear dirt as though it were clothing; insects slept, ate, and worked with men and women. Some men sold themselves as galley slaves to escape the cold. The hungry would eat stones or dirt to lessen the pain of a collapsing stomach. Privacy did not exist for any purpose, and even the rich used corridors and decorative bushes to urinate or defecate. The world stank. Furthermore, at nightfall people were deprived of their sense of sight, for candles were very expensive.

For the rich, luxury did not mean comfort. Travel was difficult, for roads were bad and highway robbers common. There was neither underwear nor soap in any quantity. The perfumes of the fabled East were used to cover the body odors of the West. There was much concern for fashion among men as well as women; the size of a bow, the length of a sleeve, the nature of a ruffle were important matters, commented on at court, by writers, and in paintings. Yet, as social historians have pointed out, such matters were not entirely trivial; style of dress did not change in Persia between the fourteenth and seventeenth centuries at all, while it changed constantly, with debate and controversy, in France and Italy. Those who would invest energy and argument in the cut of garments would also consider remaking the social order; to break tradition in small matters could prepare the way to breaking them in large.

In the Renaissance women lost many of the privileges they had gained in the era of chivalry; yet in an age of war they also gained, since they were spared from direct participation in battle. Divorce became more frequent in newly Protestant lands. But the quest for beauty, like the quest for God and the quest for knowledge, was now largely a male prerogative. Women were thought to be themselves disorderly and also the cause of disorder; medical theory in the sixteenth century held that the female was composed of cold and wet humors, males of hot and dry humors, and the first made for unpredictable behavior. This disorderliness made women likely to practice witchcraft, according to church authorities. They were dominated by their womb, which was believed to affect their speech and senses.

To control her animal appetites, a woman was encouraged to study, to learn practical arts, and to become physically exhausted working in the home and fields. As printed books became more available, the wealthy woman became a primary consumer. The Christian humanists urged that women be educated, though only enough to fill subordinate positions. As one learned woman writer, Christine de Pisan (c 1363-1431), wrote in 1405, "Alas, God, why was I not born into this world as a member of the masculine sex?" She and many male writers were much interested in sexual symbolism, for such symbolism was, and is, used to make comments about social experience and, when possible, to note contradictions within the social order through tales based on an inversion of the roles traditionally assigned to the sexes. Since economic relations were seen as a matter of service—artist to patron, mercenary to state, bureaucrat to doge, lay clerk to archbishop—and since society was often convulsed by discussions of sovereignty, political rule, and the fundamental roots of power, women were symbolically employed to indicate hierarchical values. Thus, the relation of wife to husband reflected the general concern for identifying the relationship between subordinates and superiors in law, family function, and social attitude.

Regard for the importance of a person's actions in the

CASTIGLIONE'S COURTIER

Many of the changing values and ideals of Renaissance men and women can be seen in *The Courtier*, a dialogue on manners published (on the Aldine press) by the Italian Baldassare Castiglione (1478-1529) in 1528. An elegant aristocrat, Castiglione had spent years on diplomatic missions and at the highly civilized court of Urbino. Castiglione was said to be "one of the finest gentlemen in the world."

Over many years he wrote out the code of the Renaissance patrician—the universal man, or *uomo universale.* The ideal courtier should know Greek and Latin, the Italian poets, horsemanship and military skills, music and painting. In love, the perfect gentleman should adore in his lady "no less the beauty of the mind than of the body"; in duels and private quarrels, he should be far more moderate than the medieval knight thought honorable. He should excel in sport, like the knight of old, should hunt, wrestle, swim, "play at tennis." He should also receive a good education in "orators and historiographers, and also in writing both rhyme and prose, and especially in this our vulgar tongue." On love Castiglione wrote:

[I]t is not unreasonable to say also that the old can love without blame, and more happily than the young; taking this word old, however, not in the sense of decrepit or as meaning that the organs of the body have already become so weak that the soul cannot perform its operations through them, but as meaning when knowledge in us is in its true prime. I will not refrain from saying this also: I think that, although sensual love is bad at every age, yet in the young it deserves to be excused, and in some sense is perhaps permitted. For although it brings them afflictions, dangers, toils, and the woes we have said, still there are many, who, to win the good graces of the ladies they love, do worthy acts, which (although not directed to a good end) are in themselves good; and thus from that great bitterness they extract a little sweetness, and through the adversities which they endure they finally recognize their error. Hence, even as I consider those youths divine who master their appetites and love according to reason, I likewise excuse those who allow themselves to be overcome by sensual love, to which they are so much inclined by human weakness: provided that in such love they show gentleness, courtesy, and worth, and the other noble qualities which these gentlemen have mentioned; and provided that when they are no longer youthful, they abandon it altogether, leaving this sensual desire behind as the lowest rung of that ladder by which we ascend to true love. But if, even when they are old, they keep the fire of the appetites in their cold hearts, and subject strong reason to weak sense, it is not possible to say how much they should be blamed. For like senseless fools they deserve with perpetual infamy to be numbered among the unreasoning animals, because the thoughts and ways of sensual love are most unbecoming to a mature age.

Castiglione, *The Book of the Courtier*, trans. Charles S. Singleton (Garden City, N.Y.: Doubleday Anchor, 1959), pp. 339-40.

mortal sphere helped establish the sense of confidence and inner security that has led historians to find in the Renaissance the transition to the modern. A Renaissance scholar had written of a child, "To him it is granted to have whatever he chooses, to be whatever he wills." The unlimited horizon, the hungry quest for knowledge, the sense that the world was a vast encyclopaedia to be roamed for experience as an end in itself, underlay the vigor associated with Renaissance humanity. As one of Florence's foremost contemporary historians, Francesco Guicciardini (1483-1540), wrote in a series of maxims and reflections on history, "It is a remarkable fact that we all must die, and yet we all live as if we were to live forever." The Renaissance canvas was vast and disorderly, for it was a time of contradiction and tension—as is the twentieth century—between ideals of the state versus the individual, of luxury versus asceticism, and of instinct versus discipline.

SUMMARY

Scholars have debated what the Renaissance was and when it began. However, most accept that it began in Italy about 1300 and lasted for about three centuries. The outpouring of intellectual and artistic energy was not only marked by a revival of interest in classical Greek and Roman values but also owed a debt to medieval Christian civilization.

During the Renaissance, the economy of western Europe changed from one based on barter to one based on money. Improvements in ship design and better navigational instruments resulted in the expansion of seaborne trade. Industry, especially textiles, metals, and shipbuilding, also grew.

Early forms of capitalism such as mass production and specialization emerged. To finance growing trade and industry, banking expanded. Kings, popes, and merchants borrowed large sums from Italian bankers. Banking families, such as the Fuggers in Germany, gained power and wealth.

Towns expanded, bringing change to people in surrounding areas. The money economy led to the raising of cash crops on the manor and the payment of rent in money. Lines were blurred between classes as money replaced the medieval social system based on caste and service. Moreover, the bourgeoisie arose as a new business class and generously supported Renaissance learning and art.

During the Renaissance, vernacular, or popular, literature emerged, although Latin remained the language of scholarship. The development of printing brought on a communications revolution in which the printed book became a profound force for change.

Petrarch exemplifies the mixture of the old and the new in the Renaissance. In France, the language of the Paris region replaced Latin as the official language.

Renaissance scholars such as Lorenzo Valla, who revealed the forgery of the Donation of Constantine, uncovered, preserved, and studied ancient manuscripts. Humanists expressed the secular spirit of the Renaissance. Yet philosophical humanists fused Christian and classical traditions and helped establish the studies of comparative religion and comparative philosophy. Erasmus had faith in the dignity of humanity and encouraged individuals to read and study the Bible for themselves.

The uncovering of classical works both helped and hindered science. Leonardo da Vinci explored scientific subjects but was still largely influenced by the erroneous theories of classical writers.

With the perfecting of moveable type in the 1440s and the development of the printing press, books became cheaper and had fewer errors. Printed handbooks became available on many specific subjects.

Copernicus launched a revolution in astronomy in 1453 by putting forth the heliocentric theory of the universe. Within one hundred and fifty years, however, the Copernican revolution was confirmed by the work of Galileo and Newton.

Music reflected the Renaissance emphasis on secular and individual concerns. New instruments were developed, and music became part of popular culture.

The Babylonian Captivity and Great Schism had damaged the prestige of the church. In addition, the burden of church taxation to support the lavish Renaissance papacy and indifference to the need for reform left the church open to attack.

In the fine arts, an extraordinary outpouring of creativity occurred in painting and sculpture. Botticelli, Michelangelo, Leonardo, and Raphael found patrons among Renaissance popes and rulers and produced works reflecting a mixture of worldly and religious themes.

In the fifteenth century northern European painters such as Dürer, Holbein, Bosch, and Brueghel were influenced by Gothic as well as Italian Renaissance styles. Notable in some of their works were elements of the monstrous and supernatural.

Many leading painters such as Michelangelo and Cellini were also sculptors and masters of other arts. The great work of Renaissance architecture was St. Peter's in Rome, crowned by Michelangelo's massive dome.

The wealthy enjoyed great luxury though not comfort, but daily life for the peasants was not much changed. Women lost some privileges they had enjoyed in the era of chivalry although divorce became possible in Protestant lands. In printed works, women were portrayed as the cause of disorder.

chapter twelve

THE PROTESTANT REFORMATION

In October 1517, at Wittenberg in the German electorate of Saxony, the Augustinian monk Martin Luther drew up ninety-five theses for theological disputation, and thereby touched off the sequence of events that produced the Protestant Reformation. Luther's provocative theses were soon translated from Latin into German and, when printed, were read and debated far beyond the local academic and religious community for which he originally intended them.

The term *Protestant* dates from 1529, when a meeting of the Diet of the Holy Roman Empire at Speyer rescinded a grant of toleration to followers of Luther that it had made three years earlier. A minority of delegates—six Lutheran princes and fourteen Lutheran city delegates—thereupon lodged a formal "protest" with the Diet. In Europe the term *Reformed* is often used synonymously with *Protestant*, and *Reformation* is the accepted word for the Protestant movement, except in Catholic tradition, which refers to the Protestant *revolt*. The difference in language is, as always, significant, because early Protestant leaders like Luther and Calvin did not conceive of themselves as rebels or founders of new churches, but as teachers trying to return the faithful to the one true church from which they felt the church in Rome had long deviated.

In fact, however, the Protestant leaders did prove to be revolutionaries. The Reformation not only created a major schism in the church, but also constituted a major social, economic, and intellectual revolution.

In the Middle Ages, the Catholic church had faced many reform movements: the Cluniac, the Cistercian, the Franciscan, and, in the century or so before Luther, movements like those of Wycliffe and Hus that anticipated Protestant doctrines and had almost set up separate or schismatic religious bodies. The Reformation came after the Conciliar Movement had made papal authority a subject of open discussion.

More important, the Reformation came in a time when people were groping to replace the old values and institutions being changed by the Renaissance. It came in a time of great religious ferment, of economic innovation, of violence, uncertainty, even a sense of doom—a time well described in the phrase of the Dutch historian Johan Huizinga as "the autumn of the Middle Ages." People everywhere were seeking something—not necessarily specific political or economic reforms so much as spiritual salvation, renewal, the better, more secure world of Christian promise. Against what he held to be evident evil, Luther appealed to the good deep in the soul, or at least potentially present there; hence the Lutheran emphasis on *faith*, on something not visible but inside us all if we could but see it, rather than on *works*, the performance of the established (and still significant) conventions of religion.

Although when he drew up his theses Luther had no clear intention of setting up a separate religious body, he soon helped to organize a church outside the Catholic communion. The Lutheran church proved to be the first of many "protesting" or Protestant churches—Anglican, Calvinist, Anabaptist, and dozens more. By the middle of the sixteenth century, the medieval unity of Catholic Christendom had given way to the multiplicity of denominations common today. Hence the Reformation, or revolt, however it is labeled, was (along with the Renaissance) central to a definition of "modernity."

Many Christians, lay and clerical, had long been aware that the church needed cleansing. Papal opposition, however, persistently blocked fresh attempts to increase the powers of representative church councils. The great renovation fostered by Queen Isabella and Cardinal Jiménez was restricted to Spanish lands. Meantime, a quiet Catholic renewal had been advanced by the activities of the Brothers and Sisters of the Common Life. Founded in the Low Countries in the 1370s, they consisted of lay people who pooled their resources in communal living and followed the spiritual discipline of a monastic order without taking religious vows. They also emphasized service to others as a way of practicing Christian ideals.

Opposed to Scholasticism, the Brethren of the Common Life started schools of their own, which had a high reputation in fifteenth-century Europe. Erasmus, who was educated in one of them, complained that the curriculum was too orthodox and rigid, yet he adopted the goals of the Brethren in his own "philosophy of Christ," with its belief that the example of Jesus should be a guide to daily lives. A similar theme, expressed in more mystical terms, ran through the enormously popular *Imitation of Christ*, written by Thomas à Kempis (c 1379-1471), one of the Brethren. However, its message was addressed to the inner life of the individual rather than to the reform of the Christian community or its institutions.

A more radical and sweeping reform was launched by the Dominican friar Girolamo Savonarola (1452-1498), who won the favor of the Medici. His eloquent sermons and reputed gift of predicting the future soon made him the most popular preacher in Florence. Sparing no one in his denunciations of what he regarded as un-Christian conduct, he delivered tirades against the Florentine nobles and many of the bishops. He particularly hated Pope Alexander VI of the Spanish Borgia family, whom he cursed for "a devil" and "a monster" presiding over a "harlot church."

In the political confusion following the death of Lorenzo the Magnificent (1492), Savonarola gained power and prestige in Florence, attracting many enthusiastic supporters, including the artists Botticelli and Michelangelo. By 1494 he was virtual dictator of the

Florentine republic and organized troops of children to collect all "vanities"—from cosmetics to pagan books and paintings—and burn them on public bonfires. This hysterical zeal could not last for long, and when Alexander VI placed Florence under an interdict and excommunicated Savonarola, his popular following began to disperse, especially after he failed to work a promised miracle. In 1498 Savonarola was condemned for heresy, hanged, and his body burned. Savonarola perished at the hands of his political and ecclesiastical enemies, but also because of his own fanaticism. He was, in a sense, too unworldly to survive; but the church that he sought to purge was too worldly to survive without undergoing the major crisis of the Reformation.

I PROTESTANT FOUNDERS: MARTIN LUTHER, 1483-1546

Martin Luther (1483-1546) was a professor of theology at the University of Wittenberg. In 1517 he was undergoing a great religious awakening, in effect a conversion after prolonged spiritual despair. Luther's parents were of peasant stock; his authoritarian father became a miner and in time a prosperous investor in a mining enterprise. Ambitious for his son, he sent him to the University of Erfurt, then the most prestigious in Germany, to study law. Luther yearned instead to enter the religious life and took the decisive step in 1505 as a result of a traumatic experience. On his way back to Erfurt he was terrified by a severe thunderstorm and vowed to the patron saint of miners that he would become a monk. Against his father's opposition, Luther joined the Augustinian friars, an elite order both socially and intellectually.

A portrait of Martin Luther by Lucas Cranach (1492-1553) in the Uffizi Gallery in Florence, Italy.

After ordination, however, Luther underwent a prolonged and intense personal crisis. He was convinced that he was lost—literally lost. (As the psychoanalyst Erik Erikson points out in his *Young Man Luther*, modern psychology calls his predicament an identity crisis.) None of Luther's good works, neither the discipline of his order nor his pilgrimmage in 1510 to Rome, could free him of the gnawing feeling that he could not attain God's grace and was destined for hell. Finally a confessor advised the desperate young man to study the Bible and to become a teacher of Scripture. Through his reading in the Epistles of Paul and the writings of Augustine, Luther gradually found an answer to his anxiety: that he should have faith in God and in the possibility of his own salvation. This answer had indeed long been the answer of the Roman church; what later separated Luther doctrinally from this church was his emphasis on faith alone, to the exclusion of good works.

Fortified by his intense conviction of the great importance of faith, Luther questioned Catholic practices that in his view were abuses that tended to corrupt or weaken faith. He cast his questions in the form of his Ninety-five Theses, written in the medieval Scholastic manner as a challenge to academic debate. The specific abuse that the theses sought to prove un-Christian was what Luther called the "sale" of indulgences, in particular the activities of a talented fund-raiser, a Dominican named Tetzel. Tetzel was conducting a "drive" for voluntary contributions to help fill the treasury of a great institution that could not extend its taxing powers sufficiently to keep up with the rising costs of an era of inflation and luxurious living. He was raising money to rebuild St. Peter's in Rome, and he had papal authorization for his campaign. One of the great German ecclesiastical princes also had a stake in the indulgences; this was Albert, brother of the elector of Brandenburg, who held two major sees, the archbishoprics of Mainz and Magdeburg. Albert had paid a very large sum to the papacy for a dispensation permitting him to grant indulgences. To get the money, he had borrowed heavily from the Fuggers; to repay them he would use his share in the proceeds of the indulgences.

Indulgences made possible the remission of temporal punishment for sins. Only God can forgive a sin, but repentant sinners also must undergo punishment on earth in the form of penance, and after death in Purgatory, where they atone by painful but temporary punishment for their sins and are prepared for heaven. According to the theory advanced by the medieval schoolmen, indulgences could not assure the forgiveness of sins, but they could remit penance and part or all of the punishment in Purgatory. The church claimed authority to grant such remission by drawing on the Treasury of Merit—a storehouse of surplus good works accumulated by the holy activities of Christ, the Virgin, and the saints. Only the priest could secure for a layman a draft, as it were, on this heavenly treasury.

The use of the word *sale* in connection with indulgences became a form of Protestant propaganda. The Catholics insisted that an indulgence was not "sold," that it was "granted" by the priest, and any monetary contribution made by the recipient was a freewill offering. However, the highly successful Tetzel had virtually advertised indulgences with a slogan, "As soon as coin in coffer rings, the soul from purgatory springs." Those learned in church matters understood that only indulgences imposed by priests were valid, but it was widely believed by the faithful that an indulgence could also secure total remission of penalties in Purgatory. The doctrine of indulgences was too complex for the ordinary person to grasp completely, and it must have looked as though a sinner could obtain forgiveness of sin as well as remission of punishment if only one secured enough indulgences.

In the Ninety-five Theses Luther vehemently objected to the whole procedure and the doctrine behind it:

> 23. *If any remission of all penalties whatsoever can be granted to anyone, it can only be to those who are most perfect, in other words to very few.*
>
> 24. *It must therefore follow that the greater part of the people are deceived by that indiscriminate and high-sounding promise of freedom from penalty.**

At the theological level Luther's quarrel with his ecclesiastical superiors was over one of the oldest and most abiding tensions of Christian thought: the tension between faith and good works. Faith is an inward and emotional belief, and good works are the outward demonstration of that belief as expressed by a person's good deeds, partaking of the sacraments, and submitting to the discipline of penance. Indulgences held out the promise that one might secure extra good works by drawing on those stored up in the Treasury of Merit. While Christian practice usually insisted on the need for *both* faith and works, in times of crisis one extreme or the other was emphasized.

In response to Luther's Theses, the challenged papacy stiffened its resistance, which in turn drove the Lutherans to further resistance. Moreover, Luther's own increasing hostility to things as they were in Germany drove him to emphasize things as they ought to be. He was driven to minimize the importance of works and, at his most extreme moments, to deny their validity altogether. In the Ninety-five Theses he attacked not all works but only those, like indulgences, that he felt to be wrong; yet in his theses he had also made harsh statements about the pope. Soon thereafter, under pressure of combat, Luther rejected good works entirely and declared that people were saved by faith alone. He went on to deny that priests were necessary intercessors and to affirm the priesthood of all true believers: "every man his own priest."

*E.G. Rupp and Benjamin Drewery, eds., *Martin Luther* (London: E. Arnold Publishers Ltd., 1970), p. 20.

Luther and Hus as portrayed by Lucas Cranach, court artist to Elector Frederick of Saxony. Cranach was a personal friend of Luther.

The Defiance of Papacy and the Empire

The Roman church was quickly alerted to the importance of the issues that Luther had raised. Tetzel had aroused such indignation that he dared not appear in public, and the archbishop of Mainz complained to the pope of the disastrous financial implications. Pope Leo X (1513-1521), son of Lorenzo the Magnificent, possessed little of the Medici family's intelligence or decisiveness. He soon had to recognize the gravity of the storm over the Ninety-five Theses. Accordingly, in 1518 at Augsburg, Luther was summoned before the papal legate and general of the Dominican order and was directed to recant some of his propositions on indulgences. Luther would not. In 1519 at Leipzig, a learned theologian, John Eck, charged Luther in debate with disobeying the authoritative findings of popes and church councils. Luther denied that popes and councils were necessarily authoritative and, carrying his revolt further, explicitly declared his adherence to some of Jan Hus's teachings that had been declared heretical by the Council of Constance a century earlier.

The complete break between the rebel and the church was now at hand. Late in 1520 a papal bull condemned Luther's teachings; Luther burned the bull. In January 1521, he was excommunicated. In April 1521, after a dramatic session of the imperial Diet at Worms, the

MARTIN LUTHER: ALL CHRISTIANS ARE ONE

In 1520 Luther brought his defiance to its highest pitch by publishing a pamphlet, *To the Christian Nobility of the German Nation on the Improvement of the Christian Estate*, which said, in part:

It has been devised that the Pope, bishops, priests and monks are called the spiritual estate; princes, lords, artificers and peasants are the temporal estate. This is an artful lie and hypocritical device, but let no one be made afraid by it, and that for this reason: that all Christians are truly of the spiritual estate, and there is no difference among them, save of office alone. As St. Paul says (*I Corinthians* 12), we are all one body, though each member does its own work, to serve the others. This is because we have one baptism, one Gospel, one faith, and are all Christians alike. . . .

E.G. Rupp and Benjamin Drewery, eds., *Martin Luther* (London: Edward Arnold Publishers Ltd., 1970), p. 43. The verses from *I Corinthians* are actually 11 and 12.

Luther's adherence to justification by faith alone had led him to reject the central Catholic doctrine of works, that only the priest had the God-given power to secure for the layman remission of punishment for sin. In his appeal, *To the Christian Nobility*, he declared the priesthood of all believers by sweeping aside the distinction between clergy and laity.

emperor Charles V placed him under the ban of the empire, which made him an outlaw and was the civil consequence of excommunication. Shortly before the ban was imposed, Luther was asked in front of the Diet if he would recant. He replied:

*Since your serene Majesty and your lordships request a simple answer, I shall give it, with no strings and no catches. Unless I am convicted by the testimony of scripture or plain reason (for I believe neither in Pope nor councils alone, since . . . they have often erred and contradicted themselves), I am bound by the scriptures I have quoted, and my conscience is captive to the Word of God. I neither can nor will revoke anything, for it's neither safe nor honest to act against one's conscience. Amen.**

The empire and the papacy took their drastic actions in vain. Luther was already gathering a substantial following and becoming a national hero. He had the protection of the elector Frederick the Wise of Saxony (1493-1525) and was soon to secure the backing of other princes. Frederick arranged to "kidnap" the outlaw on his way back from Worms, and Luther vanished into seclusion at the castle of the Wartburg, where he began work on his translation of the Bible into vigorous and effective German. In the next year Luther returned to Wittenberg to begin reshaping the church in Saxony.

The Reasons for Luther's Success

More than theology was at issue in Luther's revolt and in its success. The church that he attacked was, especially in Rome, under the influence of the worldly Renaissance, with its new wealth and new fashion of good living. The papacy, triumphant over the councils, had become embroiled in Italian politics. The Rome Luther visited as a young man, when the warlike Julius II was pope, was to him a shocking spectacle of intrigue and ostentation. One reason for Luther's success was his attack on practices already abhorrent to many; another was his specific attack on the exploitation of Germans by Italians. In *To the Christian Nobility*, he claimed:

*For Rome is the greatest thief and robber that has ever appeared on earth, or ever will. . . . Poor Germans that we are—we have been deceived! We were born to be masters, and we have been compelled to bow the head beneath the yoke of tyrants. . . . It is time the glorious Teutonic people should cease to be the puppet of the Roman pontiff.**

As always in human affairs, ideas and ideals worked together with material interests and such powerful emotions as patriotism. The princes who supported Luther stood to gain financially, not only by ending the flow of German money to Italy, but by confisating Catholic property, especially monastic lands, which the Lutherans did not need. Luther gave them a new weapon in their struggle against their feudal overlord, the emperor. While the princes were moved by Luther's German patriotism, some, like Frederick the Wise of Saxony, also genuinely sympathized with many of his religious ideas.

What Luther started was soon taken out of his hands by princes who joined the reform movement—in part to strengthen their political power and fill their treasuries. Yet the momentum of Lutheranism without Luther is inconceivable. Though dismayed when his Ninety-five

*Ibid., p. 60.

*H.S. Bettenson, ed., *Documents of the Christian Church*, 2nd ed. (Oxford: Oxford University Press, 1963), p. 196.

Theses were translated into German without his authorization, he wrote *To the Christian Nobility* in German to reach the largest possible number of readers; that his expectations were fulfilled further demonstrates the combined power of the vernacular and the printing press. Luther's defiance of the papal legate, of the papal champion Eck, and of the pope himself was well known among Germans, deepening their nationalistic emotions; his marriage to a former nun and their rearing of a large family dramatized the break with Rome; his translation of the Scriptures and the hymns he composed—"Ein feste Burg" (A Mighty Fortress) above all—became part of German culture and made Luther's language one of the bases of modern literary German. Behind all this was Luther's conviction that he was doing what he had to do.

Moreover, Luther's doctrine of justification by faith alone had been attractive to many, responding in a more general way to the same needs that the Brethren of the Common Life had tried to meet. At the very beginnings of Christianity, St. Paul set up the contrast between the Spirit—invisible, in a sense private to the believer—and the Letter—visible and public. Established churches have always tended to balance spirit and letter, invisible and visible, internal and external, faith and works. But to the ardent, crusading Luther, even a successful balance of this sort seemed a surrender to materialism. To him, the established Roman church had lost its medieval balance. The Lutherans felt that their new church offered something not to be found in Rome—a return to the original intentions of Christ.

Yet another reason for Luther's success also applies to many other revolutionary movements: the relative weakness of the forces opposing him. Religious opposition centered in the top levels of the Catholic bureaucracy. There were many moderate Catholics, anxious to compromise and avert a schism, both within the church and on its margin among the humanist scholars, notably Erasmus. The great liberal Catholic historian Lord Acton (1834-1902) claimed that if the Catholic church had been headed by a pope willing to reform to preserve the unity of the church, even Luther might have been reconciled. Luther's ablest associate, Phillip Melancthon (1497-1560), was a moderate and a humanist. Yet once Luther had been excommunicated and outlawed and had gained powerful political backing, compromise was unlikely, for Luther's new associates could have been won away from him only by concessions too great for the papal leadership to make.

Politically, the opposition to the Lutherans was centered in the youthful Charles V, who became Holy Roman emperor in 1519. The combined inheritance of his Austrian Hapsburg father and his Spanish mother made Charles the ruler not only of the German empire but also of Hungary, the Low Countries, Spain, Spanish America, and parts of Italy. On the map this looked like the largest European superstate since Charlemagne, and Charles wanted very much to make it such a state in reality. The activity of Luther's princely supporters in Germany threatened Charles's power there and might have been enough to turn him against Luther. But he was also a cautious, conventional man and was unwilling to exert his great influence on the side of the moderate Catholics. Instead of seeking a compromise, he decided to fight the Lutherans.

But Charles did not lead the fight personally. Though he bore the Hapsburg name, he had little cultural interest in things German; he spoke French, not German, and felt most at home in the Belgian lands of his Burgundian grandmother. In 1521 he entrusted the government of Germany to his younger brother, who formed alliances with Bavaria and other Catholic German states to oppose the Lutheran princes. Thus began a long series of alliances, which bore fruit in the religious wars of the next generations and the division of Germany into a Protestant north and east and a Catholic south and west, which has endured to this day. Moreover, Charles had too many other problems to concentrate on Germany. Spanish

The emperor Charles V, by Titian.

cities revolted early in his reign, the Low Countries were chronically restless, and the Ottoman Turks, who annexed most of Hungary in the 1520s and then besieged Vienna, continued to threaten Charles's frontiers in central Europe and his lines of communication on the Mediterranean. Above all, Charles's huge inheritance encircled the only remaining great power on the Continent, France, which was already engaged with the Hapsburgs in a struggle for control of Italy. The struggle broadened into an intermittent general war between Charles V and the French king, Francis I (r. 1515-1547), which outlasted both monarchs and prevented any sustained pressure on the German Protestants by imperial Hapsburg power.

The military arm of the Protestant princes and cities was the League of Schmalkalden (named for the town where it was founded in 1531), led by Philip Landgrave of Hesse (1504-1567). When Charles finally crushed the League with Spanish troops in 1547, his victory was short lived because it threatened to upset the balance of power and alarmed both the papacy and the German princes, Catholic as well as Protestant. In 1555, in the twilight of his reign, Charles felt obliged to accept the Peace of Augsburg, a religious settlement negotiated by the German Diet.

The peace formally recognized the Lutherans in the German states where they already held power. Its guiding principle was expressed in the Latin phrase *cuius regio eius religio* (he who rules establishes the religion), which meant in practice that since the elector of Saxony was Lutheran, all his subjects should be too; and since the duke of Bavaria was Catholic, all Bavarians should be Catholic. No provision was made for Catholic minorities in Lutheran states or Lutheran minorities in Catholic states. The settlement also failed to recognize any Protestants except Lutherans; the growing numbers of Calvinists and still more radical Protestants were certain to press for equal treatment in the future. More trouble was also bound to arise from the failure to deal with the question of "ecclesiastical reservation," that is, what should be done with church property in a German state headed by a prelate who had turned Protestant. Yet with all these deficiencies, the Peace of Augsburg did make possible the permanent establishment of Protestantism on a peaceful basis in Germany.

A Conservative Revolutionary

While Luther was a great revolutionary, he was also in some respects a conservative. For example, he did not push his doctrines of justification by faith and the priesthood of all believers to their logical conclusion, namely, that if religion is wholly a matter between "man and God," an organized church would be unnecessary. When radical reformers inspired by Luther attempted to apply these potentially anarchical concepts to the churches of Saxony in the early 1520s, there was immense confusion, rioting, and vandalism. Luther, who had no sympathy with such experiments, left his sanctuary in the Wartburg and returned to Wittenberg to drive out the radicals. He and his followers then organized a Saxon church that permitted its clergy to marry and put increased emphasis on sermons, but that also included ordained clergymen, ritual, dogmas, even some sacraments—an entire apparatus of good works.

The Lutherans did not found their separate church as an alternative to the Roman Catholic, but as the one true church. Where a Lutheran church was founded, a Catholic church ceased to be; the Lutherans usually just took over the church building. Stimulated by Luther and his clerical and academic disciples, this process at first went on among the people of Germany without the intervention of political leaders, though certain lay rulers soon took a hand. In Saxony, Hesse, Brandenburg, Brunswick, and elsewhere in northern Germany, princes and their administrators superintended the process of converting the willing to Lutheranism and evicting the unwilling. Much excitement was caused in 1525 when the head of the Teutonic Knights, the crusading order controlling Prussia at the eastern corner of the Baltic, turned Lutheran, dissolved the order, and became the first duke of Prussia. Meantime, many of the free cities also opted for Lutheranism, usually not on the initiative of the municipal government but as a result of pressure from the guilds.

A major debate among historians today centers on the role of the cities in the growth of Protestantism. Some have argued that the free imperial cities of the Holy Roman Empire tended to find Lutheran teachings attractive because their civic institutions already emphasized those elements of Christianity that Luther found most important. There was a clear drift toward Protestantism in those regimes—whether city-state or emerging centralized monarchy—which were developing a limited centralism, for the idea of a transcendental God was compatible with emphasis on a single approach to God, as opposed to a complex and trinitarian one. Furthermore, centralizing governments, and perhaps especially those in which guild representatives were most important, found it easier to identify with religious thought that taught that humanity was essentially corrupt. Luther's view of the depravity of human nature supported the burghers' fear of an undisciplined mob, "a great beast." Thus Luther's success was greatest in areas already politically predisposed toward his view of humanity.

Other scholars contest this view, which makes political or social structure more important than ideas, and specifically religious ideas, for they argue that even structure develops from and reflects a pattern of beliefs. Thus debates over the Reformation, and specifically over Luther, reveal the tensions between historical materialists and historical idealists. Virtually all agree, however, that the cities played a crucial role. Since population was concentrated in them, the new power of the printing press could be effective more quickly in an urban setting. Also, they were predisposed toward a capitalist formulation of economic questions, as was Luther, and even more, as we shall see, Calvin.

Other social groups also used the Lutheran revolt to

assert themselves. Just beneath the lay and ecclesiastical princes in the German social pyramid (and, like them, a legacy of the Middle Ages) were the knights—the lesser nobility. Some of them held a castle and a few square miles from the emperor and were in theory as sovereign as the elector of Saxony or Brandenburg; others were simply minor feudal lords. Many knights were younger sons, gentlemen without land, whose only career could be that of arms. The knightly class as a whole was losing power to the princes and was caught in the squeeze between rising prices and the need to maintain an aristocratic lifestyle. Luther's challenge to the established order and the opportunity it gave to take over ecclesiastical holdings was too good a chance to be missed. The knights rose in war in 1522 and were eventually put down by the larger lords.

The most bitter social conflict of the early German Reformation, however, was not this Knights' War but the Peasants' Rebellion of 1524-1525. In many ways it resembled the peasant revolts of the fourteenth century in England and France. The rebellion was directed against attempts by money-poor lords, lay and ecclesiastical, to increase manorial dues. It lacked coordination and effective military organization and was cruelly put down by the propertied classes—perhaps one hundred thousand peasants were killed. It was a rebellion, not of the most oppressed peasants, but of those who were beginning to enjoy some prosperity and who wanted more—what is known as a "revolution of rising expectations." In Germany the Peasants' Rebellion centered not in the east, where serfdom was most complete and the status of the peasant lowest, but in the south and southwest, where the peasantry were beginning to become free landowning farmers.

Yet in one very important respect this sixteenth-century German uprising looks more modern than its medieval counterparts in western Europe. Even more clearly than the English Peasants' Revolt, which had been influenced by Wycliffe and his followers, the Peasants' Rebellion was led by educated men who were not themselves peasants and who had a program—a set of revolutionary ideas of what the new social structure should be. Their leaders drew up a series of demands known as the Twelve Articles. They demanded that each parish have the right to choose its own priest, that the tithes paid to the clergy and the dues paid to the lord be reduced, and that peasants be allowed to take wood and game from the forests.

Although the Twelve Articles were relatively moderate, Luther was horrified at what the peasants' leaders

MARTIN LUTHER ON CHRISTIAN LIBERTY

In 1520, the same year that he wrote his *Address to the Christian Nobility*, Martin Luther also wrote *On Christian Liberty*. Considered to be "the most beautiful" of Luther's writings, the *Treatise on the Liberty of a Christian Man* (its correct formal title) was an affirmation rather than a protest. This long essay was sent as a "gift" to Pope Leo X a little over a month after the thunder of Luther's *Babylonian Captivity of the Church:*

Many have thought Christian faith to be an easy thing, and not a few have given it a place among the virtues. This they do because they have had no experience of it, and have never tasted what great virtue there is in faith. For it is impossible that anyone should write well of it or well understand what is correctly written of it, unless he has at some time tasted the courage faith gives a man when trials oppress him. But he who has had even a faint taste of it can never write, speak, meditate, or hear enough concerning it. For it is a living fountain springing up into life everlasting, as Christ calls it in John 4. For my part, although I have no wealth of faith to boast of and know how scant my store is, yet I hope that, driven about by great and various temptations, I have attained to a little faith, and that I can speak of it, if not more elegantly, certainly more to the point, than those literalists and all too subtle disputants have hitherto done, who have not even understood what they have written.

That I may make the way easier for the unlearned—for only such do I serve—I set down first these two propositions concerning the liberty and the bondage of the spirit:

A Christian man is a perfectly free lord of all, subject to none.

A Christian man is a perfectly dutiful servant of all, subject to all.

Although these two theses seem to contradict each other, yet, if they should be found to fit together they would serve our purpose beautifully. For they are both Paul's own, who says, in I *Corinthians* 9, "Whereas I was free, I made myself the servant of all," and *Romans* 8, "Owe no man anything, but to love one another." Now love by its very nature is ready to serve and to be subject to him who is loved. So Christ, although Lord of all, was made of a woman, made under the law, and hence was at the same time free and a servant, at the same time in the form of God and in the form of a servant. . . .

Martin Luther, *Christian Liberty*, trans. W. A. Lambert (Philadelphia: Muhlenberg Press, 1943), pp. 5-6. Used by permission of Fortress Press.

had found in his German translation of the Bible. He burst into impassioned abuse in a tract *Against the Murdering, Thieving Hordes of the Peasants.* Luther thereupon turned to the princes, and his church became an established church, respectful toward civil authority. He is quoted as saying, "The princes of the world are gods, the common people are Satan." In the face of one interpretation of his own views, that Christianity preached the equality of all, he wrote, "Baptism does not make persons and property free, but only the soul."

Luther's conservatism in social, economic, and political matters was by no means inconsistent with his fundamental spiritual position. To Luther, if the visible external world was really wholly subordinate to the invisible spiritual world, the most one could hope for in the world of politics was that it be kept in as good order as possible, so that the spiritual could thrive. Authority, custom, law, existing institutions combined to provide this orderliness. Kings and princes were better for the wretched world than democratically chosen representatives of the people; obedience in temporal matters was better than discussion.

Luther's views brought him increasing support from kings and princes. By the midsixteenth century, Lutheranism had become the state religion in most of northern Germany and in Scandinavia. The Scandinavian kings, in particular, appear to have been attracted to the Reformation for secular reasons: the opportunity to curb powerful bishops and to confiscate monastic wealth. Because of this and Luther's increasing conservatism, the initiative in the radical Reformation was transferred from the Lutherans to other Protestants.

II ZWINGLI, CALVIN, AND OTHER FOUNDERS

Zwingli, 1484-1531

Among the other founders of Protestantism, the first in importance is Calvin, but the first in sequence was Ulrich Zwingli (1484-1531). At about the time of Luther's spectacular revolt, Zwingli, a German, began a quieter reform in the Swiss city of Zurich that soon spread to Bern and Basel in Switzerland and to Augsburg and other south German cities. His movement produced no great single organized church, and when it was only a decade old its founder died in battle against the staunchly Catholic areas of central Switzerland. Zwingli's reform extended and deepened some of the fundamental theological and moral concepts of Protestantism. A scholarly humanist trained in the tradition of Erasmus, Zwingli sought to combat what seemed to him the perversion of primitive Christianity that endowed the consecrated priest with a miraculous power not shared by the laity. But where the doctrine of the priesthood of the true believer drove Luther to the edge of anarchism, Zwingli preached a community discipline

Ulrich Zwingli, painted by Hans Holbein the Younger.

that would promote righteous living. This discipline would arise from the social conscience of enlightened and emancipated people led by their pastors.

Zwingli believed in a personal God, powerful and real, yet far above the petty world of sense experience. Because his God was not to be approached by mere sacraments, Zwingli was more hostile to the sacraments than Luther was. He distrusted belief in saints and the use of images, incense, and candles, which he thought likely to lead to superstition among the ignorant. In the early 1520s Zwingli began to abolish the Catholic liturgy, making the sermon and a responsive reading the core of the service and simplifying the church building into an undecorated hall, in which a simple community table replaced the elevated Catholic altar. He thus started on the way toward the puritanical simplicity of the later Calvinists.

A good example of Zwingli's attitude is his view of communion. The Catholic doctrine of *transubstantiation* held that by the miraculous power of the Christ and elements in the Eucharist, the bread and the wine became in substance the body and blood of Christ, although their "accidents," their chemical makeup, remained those of bread and wine. Luther refused to eliminate the miraculous completely; in a hostile meeting with Zwingli, he insisted that Christ had meant himself to be taken literally when he offered bread to his disciples and said, "This is my body." In rejecting transubstantiation, Luther put forward a difficult doctrine called *consubstantiation,* which held that in communion the body and blood were mysteriously present in the bread and wine. Zwingli, however, adopted what became the usual Protestant position: that partaking of the elements in communion commemorated Christ's

CALVIN REFUTES THE IDEA OF FREEDOM OF THE WILL

Calvin's rigorous prose style proved to be attractive, especially since he often engaged in debate and commentary on those writers about church doctrine who had preceded him. In discussing freedom of the will, he turned to St. Augustine:

Then man will be said to possess free will in this sense, not that he has an equally free election of good and evil, but because he does evil voluntarily, and not by constraint. That, indeed, is very true; but what end could it answer to decorate a thing so diminutive with a title so superb? Egregious liberty indeed, if man be not compelled to serve sin, but yet is such a willing slave, that his will is held in bondage by the fetters of sin. I really abominate contentions about words, which disturb the Church without producing any good effect; but I think that we ought religiously to avoid words which signify any absurdity, particularly when they lead to a pernicious error. How few are there, pray, who, when they hear free will attributed to man, do not immediately conceive, that he has the sovereignty over his own mind and will, and is able by his innate power to incline himself to whatever he pleases? But it will be said, all danger from these expressions will be removed, if the people are carefully apprized of their signification. But, on the contrary, the human mind is naturally so prone to falsehood, that it will sooner imbibe error from one single expression, than truth from a prolix oration; of which we have a more certain experiment than could be wished in this very word. For neglecting that explanation of the fathers, almost all their successors have been drawn into a fatal self-confidence, by adhering to the original and proper signification of the word.

But if we regard the authority of the fathers—though they have the term continually in their mouths, they at the same time declare with what extent of signification they use it. First of all, Augustine, who hesitates not to call the will a slave. He expresses his displeasure in one place against those who deny free will; but he declares the principal reason for it, when he says, "Only let no man dare so to deny the freedom of the will, as to desire to excuse sin." Elsewhere he plainly confesses, that the human will is not free without the Spirit, since it is subject to its lusts, by which it is conquered and bound. Again: that when the will was overcome by the sin into which it fell, nature began to be destitute of liberty. Again: that man, having made a wrong use of his free will, lost both it and himself. Again: that free will is in a state of captivity, so that it can do nothing towards righteousness. Again: that the will cannot be free which has not been liberated by Divine grace. Again: that the Divine justice is not fulfilled, while the law commands, and man acts from his own strength; but when the Spirit assists, and the human will obeys, not as being free, but as liberated by God. And he briefly assigns the cause of all this, when in another place, he tells us, that man at his creation received great strength of free will, but lost it by sin. Therefore, having shown that free will is the result of grace, he sharply inveighs against those who arrogate it to themselves without grace. "How, then," says he, "do miserable men dare to be proud of free will, before they are liberated, or of their own strength, if they have been liberated?" Nor do they consider that the term *free will* signifies liberty. But "where the Spirit of the Lord is, there is liberty" [II *Corinthians* 3:17]. If, therefore, they are the slaves of sin, why do they boast of free will? "For of whom a man is overcome, of the same he is brought in bondage" [II *Peter* 2:19]. But if they have been liberated, why do they boast as of their own work? Are they so much at liberty as to refuse to be the servants of him who says, "Without me ye can do nothing" [*John* 15:5]? Besides, in another place, also, he seems to discountenance the use of that expression, when he says that the will is free, but not liberated; free from righteousness, enslaved to sin. This sentiment he also repeats and applies in another place where he maintains that man is not free from righteousness, but by the choice of his will, and that he is not made free from sin, but by the grace of the Saviour. He who declares that human liberty is nothing but an emancipation or manumission from righteousness, evidently exposes it to ridicule as an unmeaning term. Therefore, if any man allows himself the use of this term without any erroneous signification, he will not be troubled by me on that account: but because I think that it cannot be retained without great danger, and that, on the contrary, its abolition would be very beneficial to the Church, I would neither use it myself, nor wish it to be used by others who may consult my opinion. . . .

Calvin, *Institutes of the Christian Religion* (Chicago: Henry Regnery, 1949), pp. 13-15.

last supper in a purely symbolic way. There was no miracle, only a renewed sharing of the memory of Christ's stay on earth.

Calvin, 1509-1564

Another Swiss city ripe for Protestant domination was French-speaking Geneva, where the citizens in 1536 won a ten-year struggle with their new Catholic bishop. who was also their political ruler. A new religious and political regime developed there under the leadership of the French-born Jean Chauvin—John Calvin (1509-1564). Calvin shaped the Protestant movement as a faith and a way of life in a manner that gave it a more broadly European and not solely German and Scandinavian basis. Particularly in early Protestant history, *Reformed* meant Calvinist, as opposed to the more conservative Lutheran.

Jean Calvin in 1534.

Calvin's career had many parallels with Luther's. Both men had ambitious fathers who had made their way up the economic and social ladder; the senior Calvin had risen from an artisan to perform clerical and legal services for the municipal and ecclesiastical authorities in a French town, and had eventually been admitted to citizenship in the town, a considerable distinction. Both fathers gave their sons superior educations; the young Calvin studied theology and, to please his father, law. Both young men experienced spiritual crises, Calvin's resulting in his conversion to Protestantism in his early twenties, though apparently with little of the storm and stress experienced by Luther. Both men married. In temperament, however, the two men differed markedly. In contrast to the emotional, outgoing Luther, Calvin was a very private man, an intellectual, a humanist scholar much interested in Roman Stoic philosophy, austere, earnest, high-minded, very certain of his convictions and of his vocation to convert others to them.

In 1536 Calvin published in Basel his *Institutes of the Christian Religion*, which laid the doctrinal foundation for a Protestantism that, like Zwingli's, broke completely with Catholic church organization and Catholic ritual. The very title, *Institutes*, suggested Justinian's code. Calvin's system, reflecting his legal training, had a logical rigor and completeness that gave it great conviction and attractiveness in a time of growing chaos. Also in 1536 Calvin passed through Geneva and was invited to remain. There he set about organizing his City of God and made Geneva a Protestant Rome—a magnet for Protestant refugees from many parts of Europe who were indoctrinated in Calvin's faith and then returned, sometimes at the risk of their lives, to promote his teachings in their own countries. Within a generation or two Calvinism had spread to Scotland, where it was led by a great preacher and organizer, John Knox (c 1510-1572); then to England, whence it was brought to Plymouth in New England; to parts of the Rhineland; to the Low Countries, where it was to play a major role in the Dutch revolt against Spanish rule; and to Bohemia, Hungary, and Poland.

In France, where concern over the worldliness of the Catholic church was very great, Calvin's ideas also found ready acceptance. Soon there were organized Calvinist churches, called Huguenot, especially in the southwest. But France was a centralized monarchy, and King Francis I was not eager, as so many of the German princes were, to challenge Rome. In 1516 he had signed with the pope the Concordat of Bologna, which increased royal authority over the Gallican church in exchange for certain revenues that went to Rome. In the midsixteenth century few people could conceive of the possibility of subjects of the same ruler professing and practicing differing religious faiths. In France, therefore, Protestantism had to fight not for toleration, but to succeed Catholicism as the established faith. The attempt failed, but only after wars of religion lasting for a generation in the later 1500s (see Chapter 13) and after Calvinism had left its mark on French thought.

Henry VIII, 1509-1547

In England, by contrast, the established church became Protestant. The immediate introduction of an English Reformation arose from the desire of King Henry VIII (b. 1491; r. 1509-1547) to put aside his wife, Catherine of Aragon (1485-1536) because she had not given him the male heir he felt that the recently established Tudor dynasty required. In 1529 Henry decided to rest his case on the grounds that Catherine had been married first to his deceased brother Arthur, and that marriage with the widow of a brother was against canon law; but Henry's case was hardly strengthened by the fact that he had taken twenty years to discover the existence of this impediment. Moreover, Catherine was the aunt of the emperor Charles V, whom the pope could not risk offending by granting an annulment, especially since Charles's troops had sacked Rome in 1527. Nevertheless, Henry pressed his case through his minister, Thomas Cardinal Wolsey (c 1471-1530), whom he dismissed in disgrace for his failure. In 1533 Henry married Anne Boleyn (1507-1536), whom he had made pregnant; Thomas Cranmer (1489-1556), the obliging archbishop of Canterbury recently appointed by Henry, annulled the marriage with Catherine. When the pope excommunicated Henry and declared the annulment invalid, Henry's answer was the Act of Supremacy of 1534, which made the king supreme head of the church in England.

Much more than the private life of Henry VIII was involved in the English Reformation, however. Henry could not have secured the Act of Supremacy and other Protestant legislation from Parliament if there had not been a considerable body of opinion favorable to the break with Rome, particularly among the prosperous middle classes. Many English scholars were in touch with reformers on the Continent, and one of them William Tyndale (c 1492-1536), studied with Luther and published an English translation of the New Testament. Antipapal sentiment had long existed as part of English nationalism; it had motivated the fourteenth-century statutes that limited the right of the pope to intervene in the affairs of the English church. Anticlericalism went back to the days of Wycliffe; under Henry VIII it was aimed particularly at the monasteries, which still had great land holdings but had often degenerated since their medieval days. In the eyes of many in England, the monasteries had outlived their purpose and needed to be reformed or abolished. There were 563 religious houses, and charges of financial irregularity, lack of discipline, and immorality were commonplace; not more than 5 percent of their income went to charity.

Between 1535 and 1540 Henry VIII closed the monasteries and confiscated their property; the larger establishments were persuaded to "dissolve" voluntarily. During the 1540s the Crown sold much of the land, usually for twenty times its yearly income. The principal purchasers, aside from short-term speculators, were members of the rising merchant class, of the nobility, and above all, of the country gentry, or squirearchy. By greatly increasing the wealth of the landed gentry, the dissolution of the monasteries amounted to a social and economic revolution. It contributed to the high rate of economic growth in Tudor England and also to the social dislocations accompanying that growth, and it provides another illustration of how closely the religious and the secular threads were interwoven in the Reformation.

Yet Henry VIII, though he must be numbered among the founders of Protestantism, did not consider himself a Protestant. The Church of England set up by the Act of Supremacy was in his eyes—and remains today in the eyes of some of its communicants, the High Church Anglicans—a Catholic body. Henry hoped to retain Catholic doctrines and ritual, doing no more than abolish monasteries and deny the pope's position as head of the church in England. Inevitably, his policies aroused opposition, in part from English Roman Catholics who greatly resented the break with Rome, and still more from militant Protestants. Henry had hardly given the signal for the break with Rome when Low Church Anglicans began to introduce within the Church of England such Protestant practices as marriage of the clergy, use of English instead of Latin in the ritual, and abolition of confession to priests and the invocation of saints.

Henry VIII, much-married king of England, displays determination and strength in this portrait done in 1540 by Hans Holbein the Younger.

Henry used force against the Catholic opposition and executed some of its leaders, notably John Fisher (1459-1535), a cardinal and bishop of Rochester who had defended Catherine of Aragon, and Sir Thomas More, author of *Utopia*, who had succeeded Wolsey as chancellor. Henry then tried to stem the Protestant tide by appealing to Parliament, many members of which had already been enriched by the confiscation of church properties. In 1539, at Henry's behest, Parliament passed the statute of the Six Articles, reaffirming transubstantiation, celibacy of the priesthood, confession to priests, and other Catholic doctrines and ritual, and making their denial heresy. But there were now far too many heretics to be repressed. England was to become a great center of religious variation and experimentation; the Anglican church, much more Protestant than Henry had intended, became a kind of central national core. Henry had sought to hold to a middle path, and he appealed to Christian unity. No Protestant, he nonetheless broke the authority of Rome. By the time of his death, the Bible, the Creed, the Lord's Prayer, the Ten Commandments, all were used in English. Though he most likely thought of himself as its preserver, Henry was really the founder of the Church of England.

Anabaptists and Other Radicals, 1521-1604

Socially and intellectually less "respectable" than the established Lutheran and Anglican churches or the sober Calvinists was a range of radical sects, the left wing of the Protestant revolution. In the sixteenth century most of these were known as Anabaptists (from the Greek for "baptizing again"). Some of Zwingli's followers had come to hold that the Catholic sacrament of baptism of infants had no validity, since the infant was too young to "believe" or "understand." Here again Luther's doctrine of faith as a direct relation between the believer and God was involved—only for the Anabaptist it was a relation of rational understanding by the believer. At first, the Anabaptists baptized members again when the believer voluntarily joined the company of the elect. (Later generations were never baptized until they came of age, so the prefix *ana-* was dropped, leading to the Baptists of modern times.) The assumption that the beneficiaries of adult baptism were in effect "saved" could lead to exclusiveness and smugness, a kind of spiritual snobbery that brought accusations of self-righteousness against radical congregations.

Baptism, however, was but one of many issues separating the radicals from other Protestants. The issue of what the primitive church had been like in the days of the apostles had become intense in 1521, when the extremists tried to impose their convictions on the church at Wittenberg during Luther's absence. Anabaptist preaching of the need to reform both church and society also contributed to the demands put forward by the rebellious German peasants in 1524-1525.

The Anabaptists split under the pressure of persecution and as a result of the spread of private reading and interpretation of the Bible. Some observers saw the increasing number of Protestant sects as the inevitable result of the Protestant practice of seeking in the Bible for an authority they refused to find in the established dogmas of Catholic authority. The Bible contains an extraordinary variety of religious experience, from rigorous ritual to intense emotional commitment and mystical surrender. Especially the apocalyptic books of the Old Testament and the *Revelation* of Saint John the Divine of the New Testament can be made to yield almost anything a lively imagination wants to find. Many of the leaders of these new sects were uneducated people with grievances against the established order who were seeking to bring heaven to earth immediately. They were in large part landowning farmers, miners, and artisans; yet they felt themselves to be have-nots because they were pinched by inflation.

The most spectacular manifestation of extreme Anabaptism gave both conservatives and moderates as great a shock as had the German Peasants' Rebellion. In 1534-1535 a group of Anabaptists led by Jan Bockelson of Leiden, a Dutch tailor, took control of the city of Münster in northwest Germany, expelled its prince-bishop, and tried to set up a biblical utopia. They preached polygamy (Jan was reported to have taken sixteen wives). The Anabaptists pushed the Lutheran doctrine of justification by faith to its logical extreme in anarchism, or, in theological language, *antinomianism* (from the Greek "against law"). Each person was to find God's universal law within the private conscience, not in written law and tradition. They did not believe in class distinctions or in the customary forms of private property. The established order—an alliance between the Catholic bishop of Münster and the Lutheran landgrave of Hesse—put them down by force; their leaders were executed, and the troops hunted the members of the sect down to the last man and woman.

The great majority of Anabaptists were far removed from the fanaticism of Münster. Many sought to bring the Christian life to earth in quieter and more constructive ways. They established communities in accordance with their beliefs about how the primitive Christians had lived—in brotherhood, working, sharing, and praying together. These communities bore many resemblances to monasteries, though their members had taken no vows and did not observe celibacy. This sober majority of Anabaptists also met violent persecution in the sixteenth century but survived, thanks to the discipline and submissiveness insisted upon by their gifted leader, Menno Simmons (c 1496-1561), a Dutch ex-priest whose followers became Mennonites.

Two other radical strains in Protestantism were the mystical and the Unitarian. The first was exemplified by one of the few aristocratic reformers, Caspar von Schwenkfeld (1489-1561), a former Teutonic Knight and convert to Lutheranism who believed that the true church was to be found solely in the inner spirit of the individual. His stress on the spiritual and the mystical and his antagonism toward formalistic religion contributed later to the development of German pietism in reaction against the established Lutheran church. Some of his eighteenth-century followers settled in the New World in eastern Pennsylvania, as did the Mennonites.

Unitarianism is usually identified with rejection of the Trinity as an irrational concept, and the view that Christ was simply an inspired human being. But this version of Unitarianism derives largely from the rationalistic Enlightenment of the eighteenth century; sixteenth-century Unitarianism was a very different matter and much more mystical in outlook. Its most famous advocate, the Spanish physician Michael Servetus (1511-1553), believed that Christ was the son of God, yet at the same time he denied the existence of the Trinity and its doctrine that father and son were coeternal. Thereby Servetus hoped to make it easier for humanity to acquire a mystical identification with Christ; he also hoped that it would be possible to reconcile the Jewish and Muslim traditions of Spain with the Christian. His teachings and the uncompromising way he presented them greatly alarmed many Protestants and Catholics. He was prosecuted for heresy at Geneva by Calvin himself, and burned at the stake in 1553.

Other antitrinitarian victims of persecution were the Socinians, named for the Italian theologian Fausto Sozzini (1539-1604), who preached in eastern Europe. The Socinians were mainly found in Poland, Hungary, and Transylvania, areas where the weakness of central government and the power of local landlords had permitted Protestantism to make great inroads before the Catholic Counter-Reformation was launched.

III PROTESTANT BELIEFS AND PRACTICES

Common Denominators

The most obvious characteristic of the Protestant churches, especially in their formative period, was the wide gap that separated one from another. Yet there were certain common beliefs and practices that linked all Protestant sects and set them apart from Catholicism. The first of these common denominators was the Protestant repudiation of Rome's claim to be the one true faith. The difficulty here was that each Protestant sect initially considered itself to be the one true faith, the legitimate successor to Christ and his apostles. Some early Protestants were confident that their particular belief would eventually prevail through the slow process of education and conversion. Others, however, could not wait, and though they had once been persecuted themselves, they did not hesitate to persecute in their turn when they rose to power

The humanist Sebastian Castellio (1515–1563) attacked Calvin's action against Servetus in a book on "whether heretics are to be persecuted" (1554), which asserted that force should not be used to change religious ideas. "To kill a man is not to defend a doctrine, but to kill a man," he wrote. This, however, was a minority opinion. In the sixteenth and seventeenth centuries few Europeans accepted the separation of church and state and the coexistence of many creeds tolerated by an impartial government. Religious toleration would be widely advocated only with the eighteenth-century Enlightenment.

A second common denominator of Protestantism was that all its churches placed less emphasis on organization, ritual, and other religious externals than the Catholic church did. All the sects relaxed the requirement of clerical celibacy and either banned or sharply curtailed monasticism. All reduced the seven sacraments; a general Protestant minimum was to retain baptism and communion. But theological justification of these sacraments ranged widely, from Lutheran consubstantiation to the view that the Eucharist was purely symbolic. Veneration of saints declined and pilgrimages and the use of rosaries and amulets disappeared among all Protestants. The more radical also banished musical instruments, sculpture, painting, and stained glass—indeed all the arts except the oratorical—for distracting attention from the contemplation of God.

Beneath these outward signs, Protestants were all rebels in origin. They had almost always protested in the name of a purer, primitive church, maintaining that Rome was a wicked innovator. This appeal to the past to justify revolt recurs often in Western history, indicating the strong need to base a vision of the future on an interpretation of the past.

The Conservative Churches

The divergent beliefs and practices that separated the Protestant churches one from another may be arranged most conveniently in order of their theological distance from Catholicism, beginning with those nearest to it. The Church of England managed to contain almost the whole Protestant range, from High Church to extreme Low Church. It permitted its clergy to marry, and although it did retain some religious orders, it put little emphasis on the regular clergy. Yet the Church of England retained a form of the Catholic hierarchy, with archbishops and bishops, though without acknowledging the authority of the pope. Perhaps the central core of Anglicanism became a tempered belief in hierarchy and authority from above, a simplified ritualism, and a realistic acceptance of an imperfect world—a moderate attitude not far from the outlook of Thomas Aquinas.

But there has also been a strong puritanical current in the broad stream of Anglicanism and ultimately its North American counterpart, Episcopalianism. Puritanism, which may be defined as a combination of plain living and high thinking with earnest evangelical piety, was an important variant of the Low Church attitude. While some Puritans reluctantly left the Anglican communion in the late sixteenth and early seventeenth century, many others remained within it.

The Church of England assumed its definitive form during the reign of Elizabeth I (1558-1603), daughter of Henry VIII and Anne Boleyn. The Thirty-nine Articles enacted by Parliament in 1563 were a kind of constitution for the church. The Articles rejected the more obvious forms of Romanism: the use of Latin, confession to a priest, clerical celibacy, the allegiance to the pope. They also affirmed the Protestant stand on one of the great symbolic issues of the day—the Eucharist—by giving both the bread and the wine to communicants, as the reformers had long demanded, in contrast to the Catholic custom of giving only the wafer. In interpreting the Lord's Supper, the Articles rejected both Catholic transubstantiation and Zwinglian symbolism and attempted to find a compromise somewhere in between. Finally, the Thirty-nine Articles sought emphatically to avoid the anarchistic dangers implicit in the doctrines of justification by faith and the priesthood of the believer.

The Church of England has always seemed to its enemies, and even to some of its friends, a bit too acquiescent in the face of civil authority. In what was once a word of abuse, the Church of England has seemed Erastian, so called after Thomas Erastus (1524-1583), a Swiss theologian and a disciple of Zwingli who objected to the theocratic practices of the Calvinists. To check abuses by the religious authorities Erastus wanted to increase the power of the political authorities. The term *Erastianism*, however, has come to imply that the state is all-powerful against the church and that the clergy should be simply a moral police force. While Anglicanism seldom went this far in practice, a touch of subservience to the political powers that be, a modified Erastianism, does remain in the Church of England, and we shall encounter it in the English civil and religious strife of the seventeenth century.

To outsiders the Lutheran church has appeared even more Erastian than the Anglican. As the state church in much of northern Germany and in Scandinavia, it was often a docile instrument of its political masters. And in its close association with the rise of Prussia (though Prussia's Hohenzollern rulers later became Calvinist), it was brought under the rule of the strongly bureaucratic Prussian state.

Luther, like so many others upon whom character and fate have thrust rebellion, was at heart a conservative. He wanted the forms of Lutheran worship to recall the forms he was used to. Once it had become established, Lutheranism preserved many practices that seem Catholic in origin but that to Luther represented a return to early Christianity before the corruption by Rome. Lutheranism preserved the Eucharist, now interpreted by the doctrine of consubstantiation, and it also preserved bishops, gowns, and something of the plastic arts. The tradition of good music in the church was not only preserved but greatly foritified. The Lutheran church, however, had a strong evangelical party, the germ of the later pietist movement, as well as a conservative High Church party.

Calvinism and Predestination

For Calvinists the main theological concern was not so much Luther's problem of faith against good works as the related problem of predestination against free will. The problem was already evident in the fifth-century struggle over the heresy of Pelagius, who believed in human goodness and in complete free will, whereas his opponents stressed human sinfulness and God's goodness.

The problem arose from the concept that God is all-powerful, all-good, all-knowing; this being so, he must determine all that happens, even willing that the sinner must sin. For if he did not so will, a person would be doing something God did not want, and God would not be all-powerful. There is a grave difficulty here. If God wills that the sinner sin, the sinner cannot be blamed for it. Logical argument appeared to be at a dead end. People can always claim, no matter what they do, that they are doing what God makes them do. Such a position cuts the ground from under individual moral responsibility.

Theologians however, preserve the moral responsibility of the individual by asserting the profound distance between God and humanity, a distance that the miracle—the grace—of faith alone can bridge. This means that for a person to claim that whatever is done is what God wants done is to make a presumptuous claim to knowing God's will. Petty human understanding is never on a par with God's; a person can never be certain of what God wants done; therefore, one should look for signs of God's intentions. Such signs are found in Christian tradition and history. A person tempted to commit adultery will not say that God wants it; Christian tradition indicates that adulterous desire is a temptation to sin, which, if committed, will prove that that person is damned.

Calvin himself, though he certainly would not have put it this way, would have reached the same conclusion. But he was a logician. Both his temperament and his environment led him to reject what he believed to be the Catholic emphasis on easy salvation. He emphasized the hard path of true salvation, the majesty of God and the insignificance of humanity; therefore he evolved an extreme form of the doctrine of predestination.

In Calvin's system Adam's original sin was unforgivable. God, however, in his incomprehensible mercy, sent Jesus Christ to this earth and let him die on the cross to make salvation possible for some—but emphatically not all or even most—of humanity, stained though they were by original sin. Very few—in fact, only the elect—could attain salvation, and that through no merit of their own, and certainly not on the scale the Roman Catholic church of the sixteenth century was claiming. The elect were saved only through God's free and infinite grace, by means of which they were given the strength to gain salvation. Grace, Calvin said, is not like anything else that touches human life on earth. It is not of a piece with law, morals, philosophy, and other human ways of relating to the environment, but neither is it wholly divorced from these earthly relations. The elect actually tend to behave in a certain way, an identifiable way, a way that could be called "puritanical." This mode of behavior will reveal the inward grace through outward signs.

Where the Calvinists were in complete control of an area (as in sixteenth-century Geneva) or in partial control of larger areas (as in England, Scotland, the Netherlands, or Puritan Massachusetts), they censored, forbade, banished, and punished. Particularly in Geneva, where all trace of the Roman hierarchy had vanished along with the prince-bishop, the local Catholic tradition of scrutinizing the morals of the populace continued on an intensive scale. Every week a consistory composed of pastors and lay elders appointed by the city council passed judgment on all accused of improper behavior. The members of the Geneva consistory and other representatives of the Puritan spiritual police saw themselves as God's agents, doing God's work. Paradoxically, these firm believers in the inability of human efforts to change anything worked most ardently to get people to change their behavior.

The Calvinists did not seek to eliminate physical pleasures, but sought rather to select among worldly desires those that would further salvation, and to curb or suppress those that would not. The Calvinists believed that for most people the world was the prelude to hell and eternal suffering. The Calvinists thought that Satan fostered human pleasures—music, dancing, gambling, fine clothes, drinking, playgoing, and fortune-telling, among others. Although the Calvinists did not hold that all sexual intercourse was sinful, they believed that God provided sex to continue life and not to give pleasures; such pleasures were all the more dangerous since they might lead to sex outside of marriage, which was a very great sin.

Calvinism appeared in pure or diluted form in many sects: Presbyterian and Congregational in Britain, Reformed on the Continent. It influenced even the Anglicans and the Lutherans. Theologically its main opponent was a system of ideas called *Arminianism*, from Jacobus Arminius (1560-1609), a Dutch professor at Leiden. Arminianism may be classified among the freewill theologies, for Arminius held that election and damnation were conditional in God's mind—not absolute as Calvin had maintained—and that therefore what a person did on earth could change that person's fate. Generally, Arminianism was more tolerant of the ways of the world than Calvinism, less puritanical, more Erastian. Though at first condemned by the Dutch Reformed church, it later exerted a strong influence on other protestant churches, notably the Baptist and the Methodist.

Calvinism can hardly be accused of being Erastian. Where it did become the established state church—in Geneva, in the England of the 1650s, in Massachusetts, for instance—the Calvinist church ran or tried to run the state. However, this theocracy was never fully realized, even in Geneva, where the city council refused to surrender all of its authority. Where Calvinism had to fight to exist, it preached and practiced an ardent denial of the domination of the state over the individual. Later generations turned these affirmations of popular rights to the uses of their own struggles against both kings and churchmen. In this sense, Calvinism helped create modern democracy. Its basic original concepts were not, however, democratic, if democracy is based on principles, equality, and on a generally compassionate and hopeful view of human beings.

The Radicals

The radical Protestant sects were greatly influenced by Calvinist theology and example. Their practices, however, varied widely; sometimes the congregation shouted, danced, and sang hymns with fervor; others, like the Mennonites, stressed silent prayer and meditation. Among the radicals, preaching was even more important than in other forms of Protestantism, and more emotionally charged with hopes of heaven and fears of hell. Many sects expected an immediate Second Coming of Christ and an end of the material world. Many were economic equalitarians, communists of a sort; they did not share wealth, however, so much as they shared the poverty that seemed to them, as it had seemed to Francis of Assisi, an essential part of the Christian way.

Almost all of them had some beliefs that alarmed conventional men and women. Many refused to take oaths on grounds of conscience. Most distrusted the state, regarding it as an institution from which true Christians should remain aloof. What is most striking about these sects is the extraordinary range of their ideals and behavior. Some of them really behaved badly as their conservative enemies have charged. John of Leiden—crowned at Münster as "King David," with two golden jeweled crowns, one royal, one imperial, with his "Queen Diavara" and a whole harem in attendance—seems a mad parody of the Protestant appeal to the Bible. Yet most Anabaptists were shocked by what went on at Münster and were for the most part pious and earnest pacifist Christians, living simply and productively, as do their modern successors, Baptists, Mennonites, and Quakers.

These left-wing sects often displayed a remarkable combination of pacifist principles with readiness to fight (so long as the weapons were not ones to inflict bodily injury). These men were fighting to end fighting. Here is Jacob Hutter, who founded the Hutterite sect of Moravian Anabaptists, addressing the governor-general of Moravia, Ferdinand of Hapsburg, a good Catholic who was ruling the Germanies for his brother Charles V:

> *Woe, woe! unto you, O ye Moravian rulers, who have sworn to that cruel tyrant and enemy of God's truth, Ferdinand, to drive away his pious and faithful servants. Woe! we say unto you, who fear that frail and mortal man more than the living, omnipotent, and eternal God, and chase from you, suddenly and inhumanly, the children of God, the afflicted widow, the desolate orphan, and scatter them abroad. . . . God, by the mouth of the prophet, proclaims that He will fearfully and terribly avenge the shedding of innocent blood, and will not pass by such as fear not to pollute and contaminate their hands therewith. Therefore, great slaughter, much misery and anguish, sorrow and adversity, yea, everlasting groaning, pain and torment are daily appointed you.**

Such men were also martyrs, and they were persecuted by more moderate reformers with as much violence as that which Protestant tradition attributes to the Catholic Inquisition.

Not all sectarians of the left were as violently nonviolent as Hutter. An even stronger and more lasting note is that sounded by the English John Bunyan (1628-1688), whose *Pilgrim's Progress* has long been read far beyond the circles of the Baptist sect in which he was a lay preacher. This book is an allegory of life seen as a pilgrimage, which, while full of trials, leads toward a happy end.

*Tieleman Jans van Braght, *Martyrology of the Churches of Christ, commonly called Baptists*, I:151-53, (London: J. Haddon, 1850), quoted in R.J. Smithson, *The Anabaptists* (London: J. Clarke, 1935), pp. 69-71.

IV THE CATHOLIC REFORMATION

The first Catholic response to the Protestant challenge was to suppress the rebels; that was the papal policy toward Luther. Yet the religious ferment from which Protestantism emerged was originally a ferment within the Catholic church, to which many who remained Catholics had contributed. Erasmus and other Christian humanists greatly influenced the early stages of what came to be called the Catholic Reformation. Particularly in Spain, but spreading throughout the Catholic world, there was a revival of mysticism and of popular religion.

The Catholic church rallied its spiritual and material forces and achieved a large measure of reform from within. By winning back areas in Germany, Bohemia, Hungary, the Netherlands, and Poland, it limited the spread of Protestantism in the West. This Catholic Reformation (which Protestants usually call the Counter-Reformation) was a positive spiritual renewal that reinvigorated fundamental Catholic beliefs and practices.

They could not have been preserved, however, without secular aid. Both the Catholic and the Protestant reformations were inseparably tied to domestic and international politics (see Chapter 13). The powerful house of Hapsburg, both in its Spanish and its German branches, was the active head of political Catholicism in the next generations. The French monarchs, though their support was often more political than religious, helped to keep France Catholic, and in the seventeenth century the French participated in a many-sided Catholic revival. In southern Germany and in Italy the reigning princes were powerful supporters of the old religion.

The only authentic portrait of Ignatius Loyola, by the Spanish artist Claudio Coello (c 1630-1693).

Moreover, following medieval precedent, new orders of clergy greatly aided the Catholic renewal. This reforming current was already gathering strength when

LOYOLA ON OBEDIENCE

The following extracts from Loyola's *Spiritual Exercises* bring out the Jesuit emphasis on total obedience, together with the realistic Jesuit estimate of what could be expected of ordinary human beings on the subjects of predestination, free will, and good works:

1. Always be ready to obey with mind and heart, setting aside all judgment of one's own, the true spouse of Jesus Christ, our holy mother, our infallible and orthodox mistress, the Catholic Church, whose authority is exercised over us by the hierarchy.

13. That we may be altogether of the same mind and in conformity with the Church itself, if she shall have defined anything to be black which to our eyes appears to be white, we ought in like manner to pronounce it to be black. For we must undoubtedly believe, that the Spirit of our Lord Jesus Christ, and the Spirit of the Orthodox Church His Spouse, by which Spirit we are governed and directed to Salvation, is the same. . . .

14. It must also be borne in mind, that although it be most true, that no one is saved but he that is predestinated, yet we must speak with circumspection concerning this matter, lest perchance, stressing too much the grace or predestination of God, we should seem to wish to shut out the force of free will and the merits of good works; or on the other hand, attributing to these latter more than belongs to them, we derogate meanwhile from the power of grace.

H.S. Bettenson, ed., *Documents of the Christian Church*, 2nd ed. (Oxford: Oxford University Press, 1963), pp. 259-60.

This eighteenth-century print, published in London, was titled *View of the Principal Place and Manner of Execution of Persons condemned by the Inquisition of Spain.*

the papacy was still in the lax hands of Leo X, Luther's opponent. During Leo's pontificate an earnest group formed at Rome the Oratory of Divine Love, dedicated to the deepening of spiritual experience through special services and religious exercises. In the 1520s the Oratory inspired the founding of the Theatines, an order aimed particularly at the education of the clergy. A new branch of the Franciscans, the Capuchins, appeared, to lead the order back to Francis's own ideals of poverty and preaching to the poor. During the next decade half a dozen other new orders were established, among them the Ursuline nuns, pioneers in the education of young women.

The Jesuits and the Inquisition 1540-1556

The greatest of these clerical orders by far was the Society of Jesus, founded in 1540 by the Spaniard Ignatius Loyola (1491-1556). Loyola, who had been a soldier, turned to religion after receiving a painful wound in battle. From the first the Jesuits were the soldiery of the Catholic church; their leader bore the title of general, and a military discipline was laid down in Loyola's *Spiritual Exercises*, which set the rules for the order. Born in controversy, the Jesuits have always been a center of controversy. To their hostile critics, who have been numerous both within and without the Catholic church, the Jesuits have seemed unscrupulous soldiers of the pope, indulging in dirty fighting, and not just on the battlefield, if such tactics seemed likely to bring victory. They have been accused of preaching and practicing the doctrine that the end justifies the means and also of pursuing worldly power and success. Yet Jesuit devotion to Catholic tradition was too deep for them to make Machiavelli's mistake of underestimating the hold the moral decencies have on human beings. And the historical record leaves no doubt of Jesuit success in bolstering the spiritual as well as the material credit of Catholicism in the critical days of the sixteenth and seventeenth centuries. Jesuits seemed to be everywhere, in Hungary, in Poland, in England, in Holland, trying to win back lands and peoples from the Protestants. They were winning new lands and peoples on the expanding frontiers of the West, in India, in China, in Japan, in North America. They were martyrs, preachers, teachers, social workers, counselors of statesmen, almost always disciplined, not lapsing into the kind of fleshly worldliness that had been the fate of other orders. As realists they particularly sought to influence the politically powerful and to mold the young men who would later become leaders. Their schools rapidly acquired great fame, not

THE INQUISITION

In the sixteenth century the Inquisition inquired into the faith and correctness of view of many people who considered themselves to be Christians. In 1583 Domenico Scandella, called Menocchio (1532-1599), was denounced for heresy, was tried twice, and in 1599 was burned at the stake. Menocchio had been asked about the relationship of God to chaos, and he had answered "that they were always together, that they were never separated, that is, neither chaos without God, nor God without chaos." This led to further efforts on the part of the inquisitor to clarify Menocchio's views:

Inquisitor: It appears that you contradicted yourself in the previous examinations speaking about God, because in one instance you said God was eternal with the chaos, and in another you said that he was made from the chaos: therefore clarify this circumstance and your belief.

Menocchio: My opinion is that God was eternal with chaos, but he did not know himself nor was he alive, but later he became aware of himself, and this is what I mean that he was made from chaos.

Inquisitor: You said previously that God had intelligence; how can it be then that originally he did not know himself, and what was the cause that afterwards he knew himself? Relate also what occurred in God that made it possible for God who was not alive to become alive.

Menocchio: I believe that it was with God as with the things of this world that proceed from imperfect to perfect, as an infant who while he is in his mother's womb neither understands nor lives, but outside the womb begins to live, and in growing begins to understand. Thus, God was imperfect while he was with the chaos, he neither comprehended nor lived, but later expanding in this chaos he began to live and understand.

Inquisitor: Did this divine intellect know everything distinctly and in particular in the beginning?

Menocchio: He knew all the things that there were to be made, he knew about men, and also that from them others were to be born; but he did not know all those who were to be born, for example, those who tend herds, who know that from these, others will be born, but they do not know specifically all those that will be born. Thus, God saw everything, but he did not see all the particular things that were to come.

Inquisitor: This divine intellect in the beginning had knowledge of all things: where did he acquire this information, was it from his own essence or by another way?

Menocchio: The intellect received knowledge from the chaos, in which all things were confused together: and then it [chaos] gave order and comprehension to the intellect, just as we know earth, water, air, and fire and then distinguish among them. . . . I believe that it is impossible to make anything without matter, and even God could not have made anything without matter. . . . The Holy Spirit is not as powerful as God, and Christ is not as powerful as God and the Holy Spirit.

Inquisitor: Is what you call God made and produced by someone else?

Menocchio: He is not produced by others but receives his movement within the shifting of the chaos, and proceeds from imperfect to perfect.

Inquisitor: Who moves the chaos?

Menocchio: It moves by itself.

Quoted in Carlo Ginsburg, *The Cheese and the Worms: The Cosmos of a Sixteenth-Century Miller*, trans. John and Anne Tedeschi (New York: Penguin Books, 1982), pp. 54-56. Reprinted by permission of The Johns Hopkins University Press.

Here, then, was the moment of clear heresy.

only for the soundness of their Catholic doctrines, but also for their humanistic classical teaching and their insistence on good manners, adequate food, and exercise.

While the Society of Jesus was the chief new instrument of the Catholic Reformation, an old instrument of the church was also employed—the Inquisition. This special ecclesiastical court in its papal form had been started in the thirteenth century to put down the Albigensian heresy, and in its Spanish form in the fifteenth century to bolster the efforts of the new Spanish monarchy to force religious uniformity on its subjects. Both papal and Spanish inquisitions were medieval courts that used medieval methods of torture, and both were employed against the Protestants in the sixteenth century.

Protestant tradition sometimes makes both the Inquisition and the Jesuits appear as the promoters of a widespread reign of terror. Certainly the Jesuits and their allies made full use of the many pressures and persuasions any highly organized society can bring to bear on nonconformists. And the Inquisition did perpetrate horrors against former Muslims in Spain and against Catholics-turned-Protestants in the Low Countries. But it was not a major force in stemming the Protestant tide. It was most active in countries of southern Europe—Italy, Spain, Portugal—where Protestantism was never a real threat. And where the Catholic

Reformation succeeded in winning back large numbers to the Roman faith—in Germany and eastern Europe—persecution was not the decisive factor.

The Council of Trent, 1545-1564

The Catholic Reformation was neither a change of dogma nor of spiritual direction. If anything, revulsion against the Protestant tendency toward the "priesthood of the believer" hardened Catholic doctrines into a firmer insistence on the miraculous power of the priesthood. Protestant variation promoted Catholic uniformity. Not even on indulgences did the church yield; interpreted as a spiritual rather than a monetary transaction, indulgences were reaffirmed by the Council of Trent. The Catholic Reformation reformed practice, not doctrine.

The council met in Trent on the Alpine border of Italy in 1545 at the call of Paul III (1534-1549), the first of a line of reforming popes. Paul was in many respects a secular Renaissance figure, but he also realized that reform of the church was overdue and that it was imperative, despite the earlier Conciliar Movement, to risk convoking another general council. To liberal Catholics, the Council of Trent seemed an instrument in the hands of the popes and the Jesuits, a mere rubber stamp. In theory it was meant to provide at least a chance for reconciliation with the Protestants, and leading conservative Protestants were invited but did not attend. The French clergy, with Gallican suspicion of papal power, did not cooperate freely, and part of the work of the Council of Trent was not accepted in France for fifty years. The council was caught in the web of the religious wars and intrigues of high politics, and its work was several times interrupted. Nevertheless, it continued to meet off and on for twenty years until it completed its work of reaffirming and codifying doctrine in 1564.

The Council of Trent took a stand on doctrine that ruled out all compromise with Protestants on the major issues. It reaffirmed the essential role of the priesthood, of all seven sacraments, and of the importance of both faith and works, and it maintained that both the Scriptures and the spokesmen of the church were authorities on theology.

The council and the reforming popes of the later sixteenth century effected in Catholic practice the kind of change that had been achieved under Cluniac auspices five hundred years earlier. The council insisted on the strict observance of clerical vows and on the end of such abuses as absentee bishops and the sale of church offices. It called for seminaries to give priests better training. It imposed censorship on a large scale to promote discipline among the laity, issuing the *Index*—a list of books that Catholics were not to read because of the peril to

A session of the Council of Trent, meeting in 1555.

TRENT PROFESSION OF FAITH

The uncompromisingly traditional stand taken by the Council of Trent was evident in the Trent Profession of Faith, which for long was subscribed to by converts to Catholicism:

I profess . . . that true God is offered in the Mass, a proper and propitiatory sacrifice for the living and the dead, and that in the most Holy Eucharist there are truly, really and substantially the body and the blood, together with the soul and divinity of our Lord Jesus Christ, and that a conversion is made of the whole substance of bread into his body and of the whole substance of wine into his blood, which conversion the Catholic Church calls transubstantiation.

H.S. Bettenson, ed., *Documents of the Christian Church*, 2nd ed. (Oxford: Oxford University Press, 1963), p. 267.

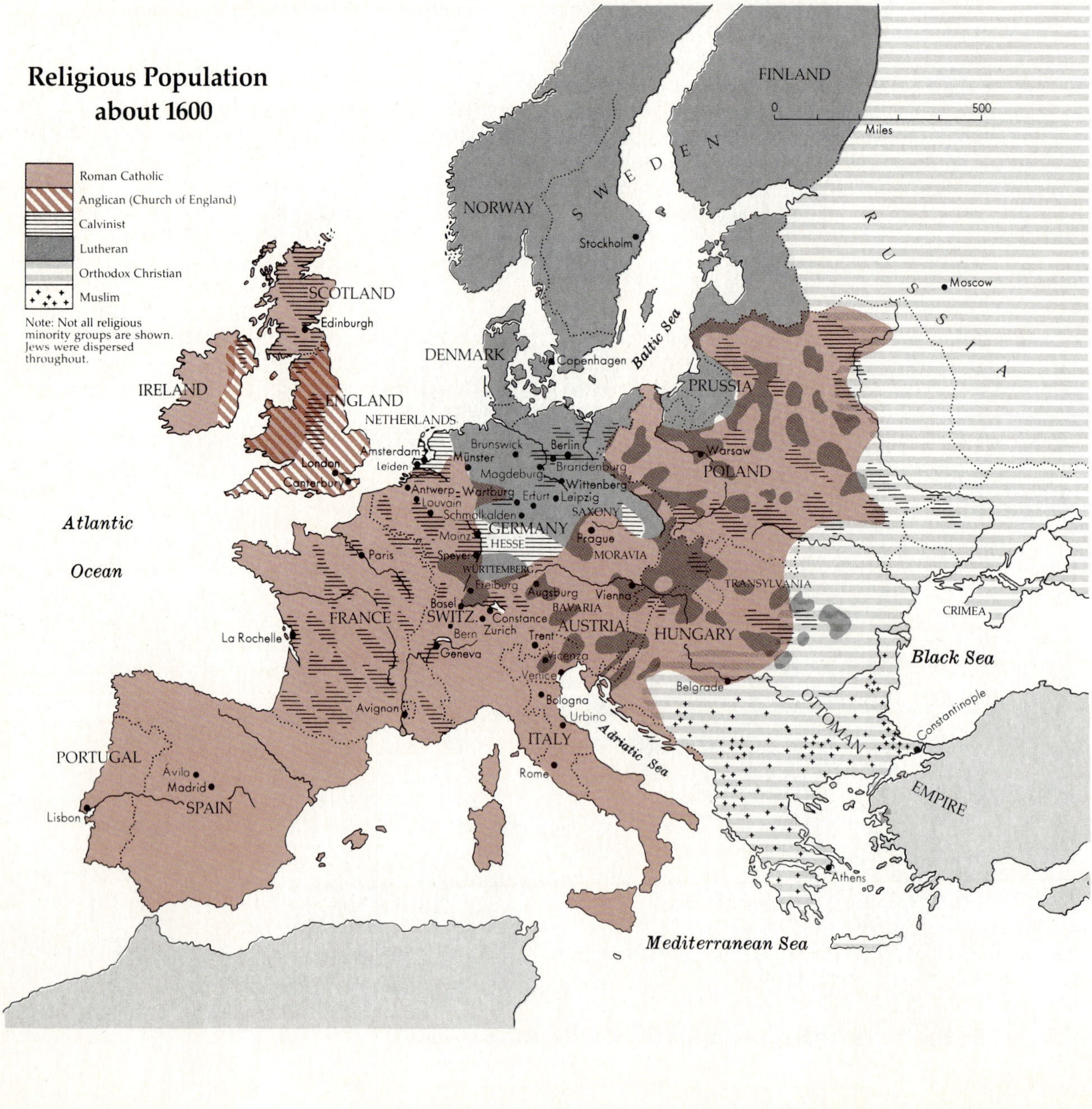

Religious Population about 1600

their faith, including the works of such anticlericals as Machiavelli and Boccaccio and the writings of heretics and Protestants.

Under Pius V (1566-1572), a standard catechism, breviary, and missal were drawn up embodying the work of the Council of Trent. In short, the whole structure of the church, both for the training of the priesthood and for the training of the laity, was tightened and given a new spirit. The papal court was no longer just another Italian Renaissance court. It is true that, especially among the upper clergy and in the monasteries, laxity would again creep in by the eighteenth century; that same century would witness the spread of rationalism, especially among the teaching clergy in France, Italy, and in the Hapsburg domains. But the widespread corruption that Luther and his fellows attacked never again prevailed in the West.

The strength of the Catholic Reformation is shown by the fact that, once it was well launched, the Protestants made few further territorial gains. Within a century of Luther's revolt, the broad lines of the territorial division in the West between areas dominantly Roman Catholic and areas dominantly Protestant were established. No significant part of Europe turned Protestant after 1580—when the United Netherlands was created—and much of central Europe had changed from Protestant to Catholic by 1650, either by persuasion (as in Poland) or by direct force (as in Bohemia). England, Scotland, Holland, northern and eastern Germany (with a southward projection toward Switzerland), and Scandinavia thereafter were predominantly Protestant. Ireland, Belgium, France, southern Germany (with a northern projection in the Rhine valley), the Hapsburg lands, Poland, Italy, Spain, and Portugal were predominantly Catholic. There were strong Catholic minorities in England, Scotland, and Holland, and the two faiths mingled confusedly in Germany. There were Protestant minorities in Ireland, France, and some of the Hapsburg lands, notably Hungary, that the Jesuits had won back.

V PROTESTANTISM AND PROGRESS

How "Modern" Was Protestantism?

The Reformation has often been interpreted, especially by Protestants, as peculiarly modern, forward-looking, and democratic—as distinguished from the stagnant and class-conscious Middle Ages. This view seems to gain support from the fact that those parts of the West that in the last three centuries have been most prosperous, that have seemed to have worked out democratic government most successfully, and that have often made the most striking contributions to science, technology, and culture were predominantly Protestant. Moreover, the states that since the decline of Spain after 1600 rose to power and prestige in the West—France, the British Empire, Germany, and the United States—were, with one exception, predominantly Protestant. And the exception, France, had since the eighteenth century a strong element that, though not in the main Protestant, was strongly anticlerical.

The contention that Protestantism is a cause or at least an accompaniment of political and cultural leadership in the modern West needs to be examined carefully. It has what modern philosophers have called "the truth of the myth," that is, many Protestants and secularists in these prosperous countries have long believed that Protestantism was a major part of what made them thrive. To the average Victorian, for instance, at the height of British power and wealth, the fact that Britain had gone Protestant in the sixteenth century was at least as important as Magna Carta—and the existence of good deposits of coal and iron—in producing the prosperous England of which the Victorians were so proud. Historians must record the acceptance of the myth; they must also attempt to go back to the events that were used to construct the myth.

Protestantism in the sixteenth century was in many ways quite different from Protestantism in the nineteenth and twentieth centuries, just as Magna Carta in the thirteenth century was quite different from Magna Carta viewed from the twentieth. First, sixteenth-century Protestants were not rationalists; they were almost as "superstitious" as the Catholics. It is said that Luther threw his ink bottle at the devil, and Calvinists hanged witches. The Protestants for the most part shared with their Catholic opponents fundamental Christian concepts of original sin, the direct divine governance of the universe, the reality of heaven and hell. Most important, they did not have, any more than the Catholics did, a general conception of life on this earth as capable of progressing toward a better life for future generations, since the point of life was not to improve the temporal world but to prepare for the spiritual one.

Second, the early Protestants were by no means tolerant and did not believe in the separation of church and state. When they could, they used governmental power to prevent public worship in any form other than their own. Many of them persecuted those who disagreed with them, both Protestants of other sects and Catholics; that is, they banished, imprisoned, or killed them.

Third, the early Protestants were not democratic. Logically, the Protestant change from the authority of the pope, backed by Catholic tradition, to the conscience of the individual believer and a reading of the Bible fits in with developing ideas about individualism, the rights of man, and liberty. Some historians have found a correlation between the Protestant appeal to the authority of the text of the Bible and the later American appeal to the authority of a written constitution. But most early Protestant reformers did not hold that all men are created equal. Rather, they believed in an order of rank, a society of status. In this sense, Lutheranism and Anglicanism were clearly conservative in their political and social doctrines. Calvinism can be made to look very undemocratic indeed if a critic concentrates on its conception of an elect few chosen by God for salvation and a majority condemned to eternal damnation. In its early years in Geneva and in New England, Calvinism came close to being a theocracy—an authoritarian rule of the elect, that is, of the "saints."

In the long run, however, Calvinism favored domination by a fairly numerous and prosperous middle class, especially in the cities. The most persuasive argument for a causal relationship between Protestantism and modern Western democratic life proceeds less from the ideas of the early Protestants about society than from how Protestant moral ideals strengthened a commercial and industrial middle class. Even in the sixteenth century, the Anabaptists and other radical sects issued demands for political, social, and economic equality; but these demands were cast in biblical language and rested on concepts of direct divine intervention. Moreover, many of these sects tended less toward active social revolt to improve earthly standards of living than toward a more Protestant form of withdrawal from things of this earth—toward pacifism, mysticism, and a spiritual exclusiveness quite compatible with leaving the sinful majority in possession of an unworthy physical world.

The Protestant Reformation did not create modern society. But it did challenge those in authority in many parts of Europe and did start people, some of them in humble circumstances, thinking about fundamental problems of life in the temporal world as well as in the spiritual one. Its educators and propagandists, using the printing press as a weapon, began a drive for widespread literacy. Thus, the Protestant revolt was one of the great destroyers of the medieval synthesis. The ideas associated with the Reformation helped form the way of life of the middle classes, who were to lay the foundations of modern Western democracy.

Contesting Views

The German sociologist Max Weber explored this question in *The Protestant Ethic and the Spirit of Capitalism*, first published in 1904. His thesis aroused a storm of controversy, in part over historical method, in part over the general problem of the history of ideas (about which there may be more differences of opinion than over fields of history that deal more directly with verifiable events), and in part because of the implications for present policy that arise more readily from the work of a sociologist than from that of a conventional historian. Though many historians reject his conclusions, Weber's thesis remains a stimulating and suggestive contribution to an issue that can never be fully resolved.

What started Weber's exploration was evidence suggesting that in his own day German Protestants had a proportionately greater interest in the world of business, and German Catholics a proportionately smaller interest, than their ratio in the German population would lead one to expect. Why was this so? Weber's answer—his celebrated thesis—may be summarized as follows: the accumulation of capital requires some sacrifice of immediate consumption; true capitalists must plow some of their profits back into their businesses so that they can produce more and make higher profits, with a higher potential for future capital; to achieve this, they must not only curb expenditures but also work very hard, spending most of their time making money.

Protestantism, especially in its Calvinist form, encouraged this sort of life. It encouraged hard work because, as the maxim put it, "The devil lies in wait for idle hands." Work keeps one from sexual temptation, from playing silly games, from drinking, or acting in other ways displeasing to the Calvinist God. Moreover, work is a positive good, a kind of tribute paid to the Lord. Luther also glorified work of all kinds and preached the dignity of whatever vocation a person is called to, be it ever so humble. In almost all forms of Protestantism this feeling of commitment to a "calling" contrasts with the contempt for manual labor and commerce evident in the tradition of chivalry.

On the negative side, Protestantism, and in particular Calvinism, discouraged many kinds of consumption that took energies away from the large-scale production that became the essence of the modern economic system. The Calvinists discouraged the fine arts, the theater, the dance, expensive clothes—conspicuous consumption generally. But the Calvinists encouraged the satisfaction of the simple needs of solid, substantial food, adequate shelter, clothing, and the like—needs most readily supplied by large-scale industry serving a mass demand. The Calvinists thus represented a new development in Christian asceticism. A society with many Calvinists tended to produce much, to consume solidly but without waste or ostentation. Therefore, under competitive conditions, its business leaders accumulated capital, which they could invest in the methods of production that enriched the West. Much work and little play made Calvinist society prosperous. Merchants in government tended to emphasize economic growth, prudence, and a desire for predictable (that is, steady) work conditions.

The Scots, Dutch, Swiss, the Yankees of New England—all Calvinistic peoples—acquired a popular reputation for thrift, diligence, and driving hard bargains. The Protestant societies at once cut down the number of holy days—*holidays* without work. With Sunday rigorously observed as a day without work, the other six were all the more clearly work days. The Calvinists eliminated Christmas, and since there were as yet no national secular equivalents of the old religious festivals—no Fourth of July or Labor Day—the early modern period in most Protestant countries had a maximum of work days per year. This may be a marginal matter, but it is partly by such margins that economic growth is won.

Many Protestant theologians rejected the medieval Catholic doctrine that regarded interest on investments beyond a low or "just" rate as usury, and they also rejected most of the medieval attitudes suggested by the term "just price" in favor of something much closer to the ideas of free competition in the market. In the marketplace, God would take care of his own. Wealth became a sign of the good life—that is, the moral life—well lived.

Finally, the firm Calvinist insistence on the other world as the supreme, but never certain, goal helped shield the newly rich from the temptation to adopt the standards of a loose-living, free-spending upper class. Prosperity might be a token that a person was predestined to election, but so too was a cautious husbanding of profits. Among Calvinists, family fortunes founded by hard work and inconspicuous consumption tended to hold together for generations.

Weber's thesis must not be taken as the sole or sufficient explanation of capitalism in early modern times; it is but one variable in a complex situation. Indeed, the stirrings of modern economic life began long before Luther and Calvin and were first evident in regions that were never won over to Protestantism: Italy, southern Germany, Belgium. Banking began in Florence and other northern Italian cities under Catholic rulers in an era when usury was still prohibited in theory. Almost certainly rules against usury would have been relaxed by the Catholic church even if there had been no Protestant Reformation. Moreover, there is no perfect correlation between Protestantism and industrial development, on the one hand, and Catholicism and industrial backwardness or notably slower development, on the other. Belgium, the German Rhineland, and northern Italy are striking examples of productive and prosperous Catholic regions. Finally, no sensible explanation for the rise of a modern industrial economy can neglect the simple facts of geography and natural resources. Even if Italy had turned Calvinist, it would still have lacked the coal and iron deposits that contributed to Protestant Britain's industrial head start.

Yet the Protestant ethic did perhaps provide the extra push that started the West on its modern path—along with the expansion of Europe overseas, which favored the Atlantic over the Mediterranean nations; along with the natural resources of northern and western Europe; along with the damp, temperate northern climate conducive to hard work and longer hours, especially indoors, in contrast to the milder Mediterranean climate; along with free enterprise, freedom for science and invention, relatively orderly and law-abiding societies, and whatever else went to produce that still not fully understood phenomenon, economic growth.

Nationalism, Modernity, and the Reformation

Another generalization about the Reformation is much less open to dispute than attempts to tie Protestantism to modern individualism, democracy, and industrialism. After the great break of the sixteenth century, both Protestantism and Catholicism became important elements in the formation of modern nationalism. Here again the trap of one-way causation must be avoided. Neither Protestants nor Catholics were always patriots. French Protestants sought help from the English enemy, and French Catholics from the Spanish enemy. But where a specific religion became identified with a given political unit, religious feeling and patriotic feeling reinforced each other. This is most evident where a political unit had to struggle for its independence. Protestantism heightened Dutch resistance to the Spanish; Catholicism heightened Irish resistance to the English. But even in states already independent in the sixteenth century, religion strengthened patriotism. Despite the existence of a Catholic minority, England from Elizabeth I on proudly held itself up as a Protestant nation; with equal pride Spain identified itself as a Catholic nation. In the wars of early modern Europe, religion and politics were inextricably combined.

As scholars look more and more closely into the local aspects of religious change during the Reformation, they find generalization more and more difficult. They also find the differences between Catholics and Protestants on purely doctrinal matters less great than at first appeared. Both believed in witchcraft and persecuted witches. Both drew a distinction between a crime and a sin, that is between civil and church law—increasingly the one applied to the market-place and public matters, and the other to private (and by the seventeenth century more specifically sexual) matters. Both recognized the necessity to work within the temporal world. And both were compatible, though to different degrees and for different reasons, with the rising capitalism. The Protestants emphasized educational indoctrination and moral controls, but so did the Jesuits in the Catholic Reformation. Both originally defined madness in individuals as "a different form of reason" and set those deemed mad apart because of a presumption that they possessed a special kind of spirituality; and both experienced a shift in attitudes toward madness in the seventeenth century, seeing the "mad" as ill, no longer to be kept at a "sacred" distance by which they might reach salvation, but instead to be confined in order to protect society. In matters of charity (which was taken increasingly from the hands of monasteries), of religious practice, of marriage, the family, and sex—in short, in a vast range of changes in human attitudes and practices—Protestants and Catholics differed, but those differences generally appear more minor now than scholars once supposed.

Thus the question of the "modernity" of the Reformation is being asked differently. In many matters both Protestants and Catholics appear quite "modern," in the sense that their views were, by the early seventeenth century, often much like those of today. Yet there were significant exceptions, as in the witchcraft trials, which appear to place great distance between the beliefs of the Reformation and of the twentieth century. Indeed, historians no longer find the debate over modernity very productive, for today they are more interested in exploring the connections between political and religious experience, the concept of an exchange between spheres of human experience that were often analyzed separately by earlier historians. The Reformation is a superb example of the growing emphasis in history on the incredibly complex interconnectedness of all human activities.

SUMMARY

In 1517 Martin Luther touched off a revolution when he drew up Ninety-five Theses for debate. In them he questioned church practices, specifically the practice of granting indulgences—popularly believed to grant forgiveness of sin and remission of punishment. Luther himself had come to believe in the primacy of faith over good works and in the priesthood of individual believers.

Luther's challenge produced a storm within the church that eventually drove him to reject some Catholic doctrine and organize his own church. Excommunicated in 1521, Luther became a national hero under the protection of the elector of Saxony, and soon other German princes joined the revolt.

Luther owed his success partly to religious sentiment and partly to political issues. Luther's doctrine of justification by faith had widespread appeal. Moreover, many Catholics sympathized with the need for reform.

Although the Holy Roman emperor Charles V fought Protestantism, he was distracted by the many other concerns of his huge empire. In 1555 he was obliged to accept the Peace of Augsburg that recognized the right of each prince to determine whether his lands would be Catholic or Lutheran. The peace did not, however, recognize any other Protestant groups.

Ulrich Zwingli led a quiet reform in Switzerland. He reinforced fundamental principles of Protestantism, especially the emphasis on the simplicity of primitive Christianity and rejection of Catholic liturgy. John Calvin shaped the Protestant movement as a way of life and was instrumental in its spread across Europe to France, Scotland, and England.

The English Reformation was carried out by royal authority. By the Act of Supremacy in 1534, Henry VIII became head of the English church. He retained Catholic doctrine and ritual but ended the authority of Rome. Henry enjoyed the support of the middle class in his action. His seizure of monastic lands and dissolution of monasteries fostered an economic and social revolution.

Although beliefs differed among Protestants, they shared in common a repudiation of Rome, relaxation of ritual and organization, a limit on the number of sacraments, and their rebel origins.

Calvinists rejected the Catholic emphasis on salvation and emphasized instead the belief that only a very few had been chosen by God to be saved. Although Calvinism was not originally democratic, its preaching set the individual above the state and may have contributed to modern democratic thought.

At first the Catholic church responded to the Protestant challenge by trying to suppress the revolt. Then it rallied to reform itself from within, an effort known today as the Catholic Reformation. Hapsburg rulers in Spain and Germany actively led the Catholic Reformation. The Jesuits, founded by Ignatius Loyola and organized on military discipline, won back some lands from Protestantism and made new converts overseas.

The Council of Trent, convened in 1545, brought about reform but also reaffirmed Catholic doctrine, ending the hope of some Catholics for compromise with Protestants. The Catholic Reformation succeeded in stemming the tide of Protestantism. Thus, by 1580 the lines of Catholic and Protestant lands in Europe were drawn.

Interpretations vary as to the causal relationship between Protestantism and the rise of modern Western democracy. Most historians agree that Protestant moral ideas strengthened the commercial and industrial middle class and led people to reexamine old ideas and institutions. In 1904, German sociologist Max Weber advanced the much debated thesis that Protestantism, especially Calvinism, established precepts and values that created a society predisposed to hard work, an essential of modern economic life. A more widely accepted generalization is that the Protestant and Catholic reformations, along with other currents, were important elements in the rise of modern nationalism.

chapter thirteen

THE GREAT POWERS IN CONFLICT

There is no general agreement on which date, or even which development, best divides the medieval from the modern. Those historians who argue most strongly for a single date usually reveal that they value either economic, political, or religious developments over all others. Thus some make a strong case for a date associated with the emergence of the great, ambitious monarchs who ushered in the modern state system: Louis XI in France in 1461; or Ferdinand of Aragon and Isabella of Castile, who were married in 1485; or the advent of Henry VII and the Tudors in England, also in 1485—all dates favored by political historians. Scholars who value international relations tend to choose 1494, when Charles VIII of France began what is often called "the first modern war" by leading his army over the Alps to Italy, initiating the concept of "the balance of power" between states. Other historians find 1492 a convenient date, for the discovery of America began the great age of European expansion overseas. Still others would emphasize 1517, when Martin Luther opened his attack on the Roman Catholic church. In any event, "becoming modern" was a process, and there were subsequent "first modern wars" (depending on which aspect of war the historian emphasizes) and other major intellectual developments than the Reformation and Counter-Reformation; the formal presentation of the heliocentric (sun-centered) hypothesis by Copernicus in 1543 is one such date of convenience.

All such dates are arbitrary, for, as our discussion of the Renaissance has shown, the dividing line between medieval and modern culture cannot be placed in a single country or a single year. Moreover, it can be argued that what really makes the modern world modern is the combination of rationalism, natural science, technology, and economic organization that has given us new power over natural resources. By this standard, the great change came in the eighteenth century, and the sixteenth and seventeenth were but preparation. Still, for the historian of international relations, a difference between the medieval and modern organization of the European state system is noticeable as early as the late 1400s.

Identifying when modern history began is really only a matter of convenience. Modern history turns upon the presence of activities and customs that seem less strange or remote today than do certain events closer to us in time, or certain very ancient customs. Consider the range of such changes. In the Renaissance astrology was an accepted branch of learning; religious objections to it, largely because its concept of human actions as being governed by the heavenly bodies threatened the doctrine of free will, lessened its significance, until Pope Sixtus V condemned it in 1586. The plague, which brought vast changes to the pattern of population, sets two major periods off from each other: the Black Death in 1347-1348 and the great Venetian outbreak of 1575-1577. Social historians find significance in the changing nature of slavery. Until about 1450 slaves were commonly used as domestic servants and might be of any race. After the Ottoman advance cut off the usual sources of non-European slaves, and the plantation economy of the New World gave rise to the need for large-scale slave labor, slavery began to change and was generally limited to only one race by the seventeenth century. Still other historians note the growing emphasis during the Renaissance on individualism, while others find no less individualism in the Middle Ages, whether in William the Conqueror or Peter Abelard. Nor does a general theory of individuality necessarily apply to an entire society; an elite group may emphasize individualism for itself while repressing it among the lower classes.

A shift in the meaning of "glory" also helps set the periods apart, though there can be no agreement on when this occurred. In the Middle Ages, glory was attached to the afterlife; modernity argues for the significance of having one's deeds recognized during one's lifetime and also commemorated posthumously—a shift reflected in literature, portraits, political rhetoric, and tombstones. Clearly changes in banking, business methods, taxation, industry, and the economy generally also set the periods apart, though these changes were gradual. Depending upon one's perspective, the primary determining date for modern history may turn on attitudes toward the environment, the status of women, or a scientific discovery that takes on new significance when reinterpreted by a future generation.

I A LONG DUREE

In the long struggle between the European nations for hegemony, in which kings and battles dominated the historical narrative, creating a sense of historical chaos, there was an enduring theme—a "long sixteenth century," or *long durée,* of population growth and price inflation during which the Mediterranean basin largely remained the economic and military heart of Europe. When population increases, the space that population occupies is altered and the economy changes. In the past a steady increase in population tended to exceed the capacity of a society to feed the new mouths. This was true until the eighteenth century in Europe and remains true in certain parts of the world today. The great population rise between 1450 and 1650 was followed by regression, while that after 1750 was not, for society had changed in ways that made it possible to feed the increase. These changes—in political, social, family, and economic structure—were in progress during the long durée, but their impact was not felt for over a century.

However, since the first genuine census was not taken until 1801, and then only in England, all population figures are guesswork for the sixteenth century. The lowest estimate of world population for 1300 is 250 million people, and the highest estimate for 1780 is 1380 million people. Conservatively, historians accept that from the fifteenth to the eighteenth century world population at least doubled, despite economic and physical disasters. As Europe entered into an industrial revolution, the Far East experienced an agricultural revolution, and both grew enormously. Furthermore, both Europeans and Chinese expanded during this time into vast new lands that had not been systematically tilled by their native populations. While the specific interpretations remain controversial, historians today generally agree that this systematic extension of agriculture and industry into new areas was made possible by a combination of social and technological changes, and by rhythms of climate variation upon which people who had come to identify themselves by nationality were able to seize.

Renaissance Monarchies, 1450-1650

In early modern times, Western society was a group of states, each striving to grow, usually by annexing other states or at least bringing them under some sort of control. At any given moment some states were on the offensive, trying to gain land, power, and wealth; others were on the defensive, trying to preserve what they had. The units in this competitive system are usually termed *sovereign states,* which means in practice that their rulers had armed forces to carry out their policies and could take initiatives independently of other states. After the height of feudal disintegration, perhaps in the tenth century, a continuous though irregular process of reducing the number of sovereign states lasted down to World War I.

By the end of the Middle Ages, most smaller feudal units had been absorbed into bigger states over much of the West, with the exceptions of Germany and Italy. When local wars occurred, they were seldom wars between states but rather civil wars, uprisings of dissident nobles or peasants against their sovereigns. The shadowy unity of Western Christendom was destroyed at the end of the Middle Ages, but so too was the real disunity of numerous local units capable of organizing war among themselves.

As the modern state system began to take shape in the fifteenth and sixteenth centuries, the three well-organized monarchies of Spain, France, and England dominated western Europe; Scotland, Portugal, and the Scandinavian states generally played subordinate roles. In central Europe, the Holy Roman Empire, with its many semi-sovereign member states, did not have the kind of internal unity enjoyed by the Atlantic powers. Yet under the leadership of the Austrian Hapsburgs, the Empire was a leading international competitor. Between France and the Empire lay a zone of small states where the fifteenth-century dukes of Burgundy had tried to build a revived middle kingdom. Out of this zone would eventually come Holland, Belgium, Luxembourg, Switzerland, and Italy, which at this period were divided into several sovereign states. In southeastern Europe the new and expanding Ottoman Empire extended to the central Danube valley. To the east, Muscovite Russia was beginning to become a great state, and Poland-Lithuania was already great in size if not in power.

Over the last five hundred years certain states have threatened to disrupt or to stabilize this state system in their own favor: sixteenth-century Spain; the France of Louis XIV in the seventeenth century and of the Revolution and Napoleon a century later; Britain during the long *Pax Brittanica* of the nineteenth century; the Germany of the Kaiser and Hitler. They tried to reduce or obliterate the sovereignty of other states. Each time this happened, the threatened units sooner or later joined together in a coalition against the aggressive power to maintain the system and, in a time-honored phrase, to restore the "balance of power." The phrase is a descriptive one, not a moral principle, and it is a convenient thread through the intricacies of international politics in the modern West from 1494.

Many political units made up the competitive state system: dynastic states to about the end of the eighteenth century, and nation-states thereafter. This distinction may be found in the change of title imposed on Louis XVI by the Revolution in 1791—from "King of France," which suggests that the kingdom was real estate belonging to his family, to "King of the French," which suggests that he was the leader of the French nation. Some early modern states were groupings of formerly independent units that might be separated from each other by foreign territory, that sometimes spoke different languages, and that were tied together almost solely by the ruling dynasty—the widely scattered Hapsburg realm, for example. Early modern wars were not total wars, and, except in their disastrous effects on government finances and on taxes, they scarcely touched the lives of the common people if those people were not in the way of contending armies trying to live off the land. In the peace settlements, no one worried greatly about transferring areas and populations from one dynasty to another.

However, the distinction between dynastic states and nation-states must not be overdrawn. Especially in the great Atlantic monarchies, a degree of national patriotism existed in the sixteenth century, and in England and France it had already been evident during the Hundred Years' War, when the English referred scornfully to the French as "frogs," and Frenchmen retaliated by calling the English *les godons*, the French mispronunciation of "goddams." At the time of the great Spanish Armada

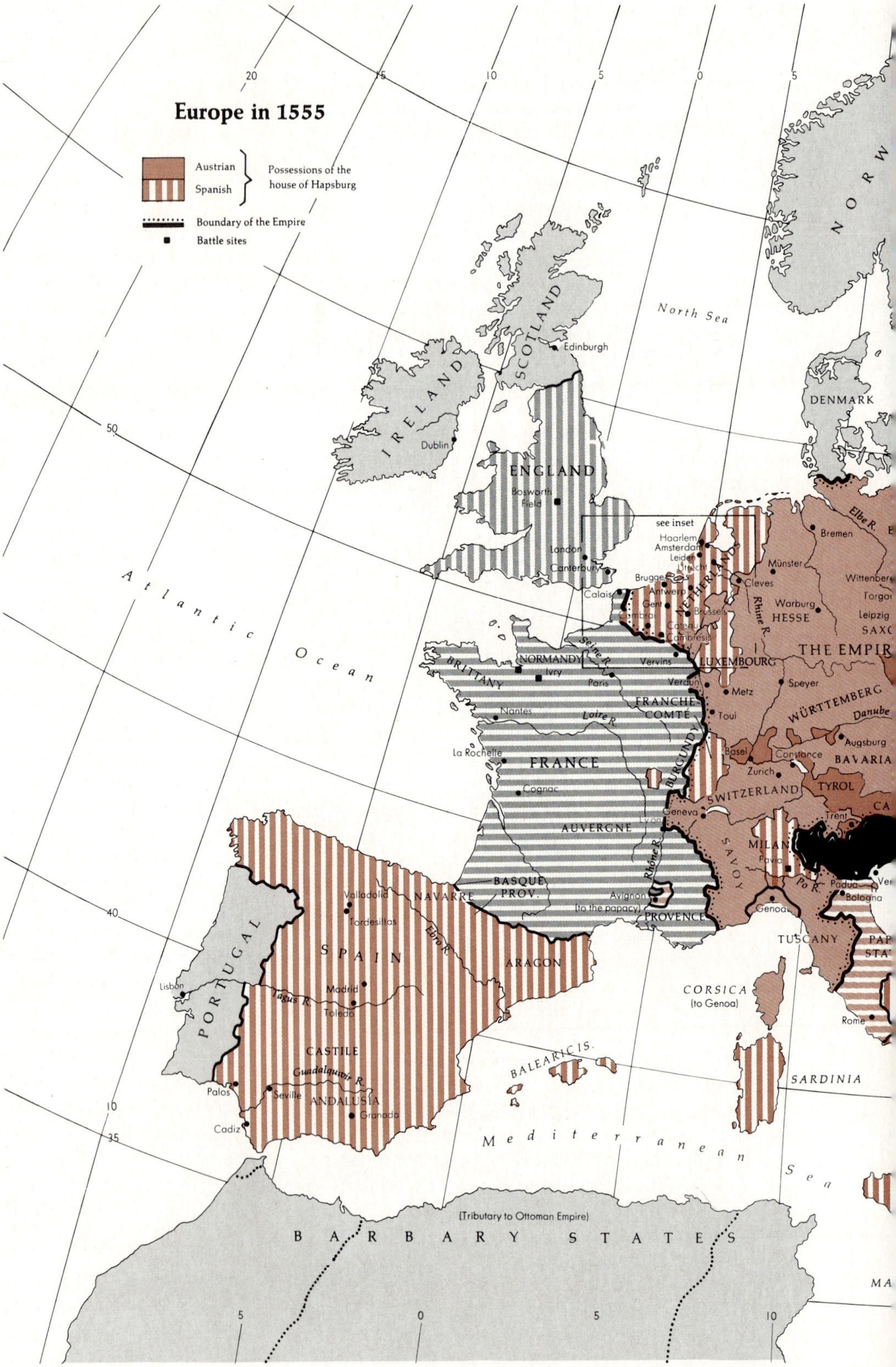
Europe in 1555
Austrian
Spanish
Possessions of the house of Hapsburg
Boundary of the Empire
Battle sites
North Sea
NORW
DENMARK
SCOTLAND
Edinburgh
IRELAND
Dublin
ENGLAND
Bosworth Field
London
Canterbury
Calais
see inset
Haarlem
Amsterdam
Leiden
Utrecht
NETHERLANDS
Bruges
Antwerp
Gent
Brussels
Cambrai
Cateau-Cambrésis
Bremen
Elbe R.
Münster
Cleves
Rhine R.
Wittenberg
Torgau
Warburg
HESSE
Leipzig
SAXO
THE EMPIR
LUXEMBOURG
Atlantic Ocean
BRITTANY
NORMANDY
Ivry
Seine R.
Paris
Vervins
Verdun
Metz
Toul
Speyer
WÜRTTEMBERG
Danube
Augsburg
BAVARIA
Nantes
Loire R.
FRANCHE-COMTÉ
BURGUNDY
Basel
Constance
Zurich
La Rochelle
FRANCE
Cognac
SWITZERLAND
TYROL
Geneva
Trent
AUVERGNE
Lyon
SAVOY
MILAN
Pavia
Rhône R.
Po R.
Padua
Bologna
BASQUE PROV.
NAVARRE
Valladolid
Tordesillas
Avignon (to the papacy)
PROVENCE
Genoa
TUSCANY
PAPAL STATES
Ebro R.
SPAIN
ARAGON
PORTUGAL
Lisbon
Madrid
Tagus R.
Toledo
CORSICA (to Genoa)
Rome
CASTILE
Guadalquivir R.
BALEARIC IS.
SARDINIA
Palos
Seville
ANDALUSIA
Granada
Cadiz
Mediterranean Sea
(Tributary to Ottoman Empire)
BARBARY STATES
MA

(1588) the English showed intense patriotic emotion, hating and fearing the Spanish both as foreigners and as Catholics. Even in divided Germany, Luther could count on Germans to dislike Italians. Hatred of the foreigner bound groups together at least as effectively as love of one another.

The Instruments of Foreign Policy

By 1500 almost all European sovereign states possessed, at least in rudimentary form, most of the social and political organs of a modern state, lacking only a large literate population brought up in the ritual and faith of national patriotism. Notably they had two essential instruments: a professional diplomatic service and a professional army. The fifteenth and sixteenth centuries saw the steady development of modern diplomatic agencies and methods. Governments established central foreign offices or ministries, sent diplomats and regular missions to foreign courts, and organized espionage under cover of open diplomacy. Formal peace conferences were held and formal treaties were signed, with elaborate ceremony and protocol. To govern these formal relations a set of rules or expectations began to take shape that is sometimes termed "international law," but often proved impossible to enforce.

The apparatus of interstate politics was developed most elaborately in Renaissance Italy, especially in the diplomatic service of the Republic of Venice. The detailed reports Venetian ambassadors sent back to the senate from their residences abroad are among the earliest documents of intelligence work historians have. They are careful political and social studies of the personalities and lands involved, in which the relative merit of gossip and rumor—the latter often used by diplomats to further their ends—was weighed. The diplomat was often an important maker of policy in his own right. With travel very slow, his government could not communicate with him in time to direct him in detail, and he often had to make important decisions on his own. Good or bad diplomacy, good or bad intelligence about foreign lands, made a vital difference in a state's success or failure in the struggle for power.

The armed forces made still more difference. The early modern centuries were the great days of the professional soldier, freed from the restrictions of feudal warfare and not yet dominated by the immense economic requirements and inhuman scale of modern warfare. The officer class in particular could plan, drill, and campaign on a fairly large yet manageable scale; it could, in effect, view warfare as a skill, an art, or an adventure. The common soldiers for the most part were mercenaries. (The word *soldier* comes from *solidus*, Latin for "piece of money.") Some of these mercenaries were recruited at home, usually among the poor and dispossessed, sometimes by impressment. Others were foreigners who made a career of soldiering, particularly the Swiss and Germans; thousands of them served in the armies of Francis I of France, together with contingents of Englishmen, Scots, Poles, Italians, Albanians, and Greeks.

Early modern armies showed many feudal survivals in organization and equipment. The officer class continued to preserve many of its old habits of chivalry, such as the duel, which often seriously menaced internal discipline. If the feudal lord no longer brought his own knights for the forty days of allotted time, his descendant as regimental colonel often raised his own regiment and financed it himself. Desertion was common, as was whipping as punishment. Each regiment might wear a prescribed uniform, but entire armies did not, so that in battle it was difficult to tell friend from foe, sometimes leading to indiscriminate slaughter at close quarters. Weapons were of a great variety. Reminders of hand-to-hand fighting survived in the sword and in the pike, a long shaft used by foot soldiers against the armored knight and his mount. Hand firearms—arquebus, musket, pistol, and many others—were slow loading and slow firing and could seldom be accurately aimed. The cannon, unstandardized as to parts and caliber and hard to move, fired solid balls rather than exploding shells. Armies on the march lived mostly off the land, even when they were in home territory. But they were beginning to organize their supply and to use engineers.

Both the growth of military technology and the differences of national temperament were reflected in the shift of military predominance from Spain to France about 1600. Spain, the great fighting nation of the sixteenth century on land, excelled in infantry, where the pike was a major weapon. France, the great fighting nation of the seventeenth and early eighteenth centuries on land, excelled in artillery, engineering, and fortification—all services less suited to the formal feudal nobility than infantry and calvary. By the sixteenth century France was overpopulated in relation to its resources, as Spain and England were not, so that many Frenchmen sought to be mercenaries and were content to learn the less romantic military tasks.

A sixteenth-century woodcut of an army besieging a city.

Meanwhile, the first modern navies were also being developed. In the later Middle Ages, Venice, Genoa, and Pisa had all begun to assemble fleets of galleys disciplined to fight both as individual ships and in fleet maneuvers. In the Renaissance Venice took the lead with its arsenal and its detailed code of maritime regulations. Naval organization, naval supply, the dispatch and handling of ships, all required more orderly centralized methods than an army; they could not tolerate survival of feudal individualism, lack of discipline, and lack of planning.

As in the armies, the officer class was predominantly aristocratic. During the sixteenth century, naval supremacy passed from the Mediterranean to the Atlantic, where it rested briefly with Spain and then passed in the seventeenth century to the northern maritime powers of Holland, France, and England. These shifts were the result of changes in marine architecture, maritime technology and knowledge, and alterations in both the balance of power and the organization of centralized states by which monies could be spent on navies.

Of course, these instruments of foreign policy were both shaped by, and helped to shape, the economic developments of the "long sixteenth century." The upswing in population, trade, and prices made war more likely. New commercial trends that first appeared in port cities, where new money entered the European economy, gave the municipal governments of these cities greater say in the affairs of state and made the ports increasingly attractive targets of diplomacy or battle. Italian business practices in particular laid the institutional foundations for the expansion of trade, and as northern Europe adopted the bill of exchange, the joint-stock company, and marine insurance—all of which originated in the Italian cities—business practices became sufficiently general to be recognizable as modern commerce.

Still, failures in diplomacy and in military strategy were most important in the decline of the Hanseatic League, in the disruption of trade between Italy and the Levant, in the rise of English competition in the Mediterranean cloth trade (which contributed to the decline of Lyons and the very slow growth of Marseilles), and in the reshaping of the political and religious (and thus economic and social) map of Europe. After the midcentury it was apparent that the Dutch and English were moving into a dominant position at the expense of the Spanish, French, and the Hapsburg (or Holy Roman) Empire.

II A COMPLEXITY OF WARS

The Italian Wars of Charles VIII and Louis XII, 1483-1515

Charles VIII of France (r. 1483-1498) inherited from his father Louis XI a well-filled treasury and a good army. He continued Louis's policy of extending the royal domain by marrying the heiress of the duchy of Brittany, hitherto largely independent of the French crown. Apparently secure on the home front, Charles decided to expand abroad. As the remote heir of the Angevins (who had seized the throne of Naples in the thirteenth century), Charles disputed the right of the Aragonese, then led by Ferrante (1458-1494), to hold that throne. He chose to invade Italy, however, not only because of his family claim but also because Renaissance Italy was rich and was divided into small rival political units. It looked, in short, easy to conquer. And so it was at first, for in the winter of 1494-1495 Charles paraded his army through Italy to Naples in triumph. But his acquisition of Brittany had disturbed his neighbors, and his possession of Naples threatened the balance of power in Italy.

The French intrusion provoked the first of the great modern coalitions, the so-called Holy League composed of the papacy (as an Italian territorial state), the Holy Roman Empire, Venice, Milan, Spain, and soon England. This coalition forced the French armies out of Italy in 1495. Thereafter, various changing coalitions would seek to prevent the domination of Italy by any one power. (At the same time, foreign forays into the Italian states facilitated the transmission of Renaissance thought to France and the other countries whose armies campaigned in Italy.)

Charles was followed on the French throne by his cousin of the Orléans branch of the Valois family, Louis XII (r. 1498-1515). Louis married Charles's widow to make sure of Brittany, and then tried again in Italy, reinforced by another family claim, this time to Milan. Since his grandmother came from the Visconti family, Louis regarded the Sforza dukes as usurpers, and he drove Ludovico Sforza from Milan in 1499. In this second French invasion the play of alliances was much more complicated—quite worthy of the age of Machiavelli. Louis tried to insure himself against the isolation that had ruined Charles by allying in 1500 with Ferdinand of Aragon, with whom he agreed to partition Naples. Then in 1508 Louis helped form the League of Cambrai, in which Louis, Ferdinand, Pope Julius II, and the emperor Maximilian joined to divide up the lands held in the lower Po valley by the rich Republic of Venice.

All went well for the allies until Ferdinand, having taken the Neopolitan towns he wanted, decided to desert Louis. The pope, frightened at the prospect that France and the Empire might squeeze him out entirely, in 1511 formed another Holy League against France with Venice and Ferdinand, joined later by Henry VIII of England and the emperor Maximilian. The French could not hold out against such a coalition, for they now faced war on two fronts. Henry VIII attacked the north of France, and Louis XII, like Charles VIII, was checkmated.

Francis I of France.

Francis I versus Charles V, 1515-1559

These two French efforts were, however, merely preliminaries. There were now really two aggressors: the French house of Valois, still bent on expansion, and the house of Hapsburg. When the Hapsburg Charles V (who was Charles I in Spain), succeeded his grandfather Maximilian as emperor in 1519, he was a disturber by the mere fact of his existence, rather than by temperament or intent. He had inherited Spain, the Low Countries, the Hapsburg lands in central Europe, the Holy Roman Empire, and the new preponderance in Italy. He apparently had France squeezed in a vise, which he sought to close. Louis XII's successor, Francis I (r. 1515-1547), was badly defeated by the largely Spanish Hapsburg forces at Pavia in 1525 and was himself taken prisoner and held in Madrid until he signed a treaty giving up all the Valois Italian claims and ceding the duchy of Burgundy. He repudiated this treaty the moment he was safely back in France.

One of the imperial commanders at the battle of Pavia in which the French were so severely beaten was the Constable de Bourbon (1490-1527), a French noble at odds with his king. The same Bourbon next commanded the emperor's Spanish and German mercenaries in the sack of Rome in 1527—the date conventionally used for the end of Rome's preeminence in the Renaissance. Pope Clement VII (1523-1534), a Medici, had turned against Charles V after Pavia. In the League of Cognac (1526) he had allied himself with the other main Italian powers and with Francis. Charles had besieged Rome, but he did not intend the sack, which took place when his mercenaries became infuriated by delays in pay and supplies. By the end of the decade Charles had made peace with the pope and with Francis, and in 1530 he was crowned by the pope as emperor and as king of Italy—the last ruler to receive this double crown, the inheritance of Charlemagne. But the world over which Charles symbolically ruled was very different from that of Charlemagne, and Charles was in fact a new dynast in a new conflict of power.

France was still in the vise between the Spanish and the German and Netherlands holdings of Charles. Francis I, a proud Renaissance prince, was not one to accept so precarious a position. He used the death of the Sforza ruler of Milan in 1535 to reopen the old claim to Milan and to begin the struggle once more. Neither Francis nor Charles lived to see the end of this phase of the Hapsburg-Valois rivalry. Neither side secured a decisive military victory. In 1559 the important Treaty of Cateau-Cambrésis confirmed Hapsburg control of Milan and Naples. France failed to acquire a real foothold in Italy, but the Hapsburgs also failed to reduce the real strength of France, which retained the important bishoprics of Metz, Toul, and Verdun on its northeastern frontier, first occupied during the 1550s. The Hapsburg vise had not closed, primarily because France proved militarily, economically, and politically strong enough to resist the pressure. But the vise itself was a most imperfect instrument; Charles's German arm was paralyzed by the political consequences of the Reformation and the stubborn resistance of Protestant princes.

The last phase of the personal duel between the aging rivals, Charles and Francis, shows how many variables affected the balance of power. To gain allies, Francis did not hesitate to turn to Charles's rebellious German subjects. Although head of a Catholic country whose king had long been called "the eldest son of the Church," he allied himself with the Protestant duke of Cleves and even concluded an alliance with the Muslim Ottoman emperor, Suleiman the Magnificent, who attacked Charles from the rear in Hungary.

One other participant in the complex struggles of the first half of the sixteenth century was England, which, though not yet a great power, was already a major element in international politics. The men who set English policy were probably not guided by a consciously held theory of the balance of power, but they knew that one contestant must not get all the power and that they should intervene on behalf of whoever was losing. Moreover, England had on its northern border an independent Scotland, which tended to side with France, the hereditary English enemy. Yet the English were quite capable of supporting France if they thought Charles V too strong. After Charles had won at Pavia and taken Rome, the English minister Cardinal Wolsey worked out an alliance with France in 1527. The English were also capable of reversing themselves. In 1543, when Charles was beset by Protestants and Turks, Henry VIII came to his aid against France, but not so vigorously that Paris, which was threatened by a German army, would be lost to Francis.

The Wars of Philip II and the Dutch Revolt, 1556-1598

The first great Hapsburg effort to dominate Europe ended with the Peace of Augsburg and the Treaty of Cateau-Cambrésis. The second effort at domination was less Hapsburg than Spanish. In 1556 Charles V abdicated both his Spanish and imperial crowns and retired to a monastery, where he died two years later. His brother, who became Emperor Ferdinand I (r. 1556-1564), secured the Austrian Hapsburg territories; his son, Philip II of Spain (r. 1556-1598), added the Spanish lands overseas (Mexico, Peru, and in the Caribbean), the Burgundian inheritance of the Netherlands, and Milan and Naples in Italy. Even without Germany, Philip's realm was a supranational state, drawing much gold and silver from the New World and threatening France, England, and the whole balance of power. Aware of the potential of such power, contemporary Italians were saying that "God has turned into a Spaniard."

Like his father, Philip II found Protestantism intolerable, a divisive force that must be wiped out by any means necessary. His attempt to invade England and restore Catholicism would make him one of the villains of Anglo-Saxon and Protestant tradition, the cold-blooded "devil of the south." In fact, he was no lover of war for its own sake, but was a serious, hard-working administrator who was both the most powerful monarch and the greatest civil servant of the age.

Philip could not have escaped involvement in European affairs had he wanted to, for any one of five arenas would have drawn him in: (1) So long as Italy remained divided into the five major units of Milan, Venice, Tuscany, the Papal States, and Naples, it was to be a stake in the balance of power, a temptation to expansionist states. (2) In France Philip was bound to appear as the Catholic champion in the civil and religious strife that prevailed during the second half of the sixteenth century. (3) In the Mediterranean, which Ottoman naval power was threatening to turn into a Muslim lake, the Spanish fleet, under Philip's illegitimate half-brother, Don John of Austria, participated in the Christian victory over the Ottoman fleet at Lepanto in 1571. This battle checked but did not immediately roll back Ottoman expansion. (4) In the New World and on the seas connecting it with the Old World, England and France were beginning to challenge the monopoly Spain and Portugal had tried to set up. (5) In the Netherlands the revolt of the Dutch Protestants soon involved Philip in a struggle with their champion, Tudor England.

The Dutch revolt was the dramatic focus of Philip's wars. Charles V had come to count heavily on the wealth of the Netherlands, estimated to be the highest per capita in Europe, to finance his constant wars. But he joined into a unified state the seventeen provinces of the Netherlands, which were jealous of their traditional autonomy. Each province had its own medieval Estates or assembly, dominated by the nobility and wealthy merchants, which raised taxes and armies. In the mid-sixteenth century the area was still overwhelmingly Catholic, with small minorities of Anabaptists and Lutherans; Calvinism was just starting to move northward across the French border.

Whereas Charles V had liked the Netherlands and made Brussels his favorite place of residence, Philip II was thoroughly Spanish in outlook and never left Spain after the early years of his reign. Not only Philip's temperament antagonized his subjects in the Low Countries, but also his ideas about centralized efficient rule, which led him to curtail their political and economic privileges. The inhabitants cherished their traditional autonomy, and, as a commercial and seafaring people, they were intent on conducting business without the restrictions imposed on trade and industry by Spanish regulations. The Protestants among them resented and feared Philip's use of the Inquisition in the Netherlands.

This explosive mixture of religion, politics, and economics produced a revolt. Philip sent Spanish garrisons to the Netherlands and attempted to enforce edicts against heretics. Opposition, which centered at first in the privileged classes who had been most affected by Philip's political restrictions, soon spread downward. In 1566, when two hundred nobles petitioned Philip's regent to adopt a more moderate policy, an official sneeringly referred to "these beggars." The name stuck and was proudly adopted by the rebels. The political restlessness, combined with an economic slump and the growing success of the Calvinists in winning converts, touched off riots in August 1566 that resulted in severe destruction of Catholic churches in Ghent, Antwerp, and Amsterdam. Philip responded to this "Calvinist fury" in 1567 by dispatching to the Netherlands an army of ten thousand Spaniards headed by the unyielding, politically clumsy duke of Alva.

The Spanish infantry was the best in Europe, and the rebels were ill armed and ill prepared. Their eventual success was achieved against great odds. Alva set up a Council of Troubles—later dubbed the Council of Blood—which resorted to large-scale executions, confiscations, and fines. The number of victims executed under the Council of Blood totaled about fifteen hundred, yet repression only heightened the opposition to Spanish policy. In 1573 Alva was recalled to Spain.

Meantime, the rebel "Beggars" turned to naval guerrilla warfare, gaining control of the ports of the populous northern province of Holland, which became a refuge for Protestants, especially Calvinists, from other provinces. A split was developing between a largely Catholic south and a mainly Protestant north—to use popular terminology, between Belgium and Holland. (Holland, the name of one province, is often, though inaccurately, applied to all seven northern provinces.) It was to be a religious, not a linguistic split, for Dutch was the language of both the north and of Flanders in the south; French was spoken only among the Walloons of the southeast. North and south had much to unite them, and union of all seventeen provinces was the goal of the rebel leader, Prince William of Orange, the Silent. William, who got his name because his silences could be discreet or deceptive by turn, had firm political convictions but few religious ones; he was, at different periods, a Lutheran, a Catholic, and a Calvinist.

William's goal of unification seemed almost assured in the wake of widespread revulsion at the "Spanish Fury" of 1576, when Spanish troops, desperate because their pay was two years in arrears, sacked the great Belgian port of Antwerp and massacred several thousand inhabitants. But in 1578, when the duke of

This marble bust of Philip II of Spain is from the workshop of Leone Leoni (c 1509-1590), a Tuscan bronzeworker who served both Charles V and Philip II, especially at the Escorial, the great palace and monastery that was a monument to the Golden Age of Spain. That the bust is now in the Metropolitan Museum in New York City is in itself an indication of an emerging trend in art patronage and purchasing by the New World that would profoundly affect European artists from the nineteenth century onward.

Parma arrived to govern the Netherlands, Philip at last appeared willing to compromise. The cost of the war was becoming intolerable, and Spanish executions in Haarlem and other cities had made the Dutch resolve to fight to the last man. By restoring old privileges of self-rule, Parma won back the ten southern provinces, which remained largely Catholic after the exodus of many Calvinists to the north. It was too late to win back the northern provinces (which formed the Union of Utrecht in 1579), except perhaps by radical religious concessions, which Philip would not make.

In 1581 the Dutch took the decisive step of declaring themselves independent of the Spanish Crown. They made good that declaration by courageous use of their now much better organized land forces, and also because Philip faced grave internal economic problems just when he was being drawn into fighting on other fronts. He had to cope with the Turks, the French Protestants, and the anti-Spanish moderate wing of French Catholics. In 1584 William the Silent was assassinated. But his death did not profit the Spanish cause, since it created a hero-martyr not only for the Dutch but for all Protestants.

In 1585 the English queen, Elizabeth I, after long hesitancy came out on the side of the Dutch and sent an army to their aid. The English had been sympathetic to the Dutch all along, but Elizabeth had feared that, with France in the midst of civil war, a Franco-Spanish alliance against English and Dutch was quite possible. But here again Philip showed himself incapable of subtle diplomacy; he permitted France to maneuver into neutrality, and he provoked England by fomenting Catholic plots against Elizabeth. The English in turn provoked Spain; for years they had been preying on Spanish commerce on the high seas, and Sir John Hawkins, Sir Francis Drake, and other sailors had been raiding Spanish possessions in the New World.

The great armada of unwieldy men-of-war that Philip sent out to invade England was defeated in the English Channel in July 1588 by a skillfully deployed lighter English fleet, and was further battered afterward by a great storm. This battle was the beginning of the end of Spanish preponderance, the start of English greatness in international politics, and the decisive step toward Dutch independence. These portentous results were not as evident in 1588 as they became later, but even at the time the defeat of the Spanish Armada was viewed as a great event, and the storm that finished its destruction was christened the "Protestant wind."

In 1598 Philip II died in the austere, mathematically precise palace of the Escorial he had built in Madrid. Save for the seven northern provinces of the Netherlands—and even these he had never officially given up—the great possessions that had been his when he began his reign were intact. In 1580 he had added Portugal by conquest and brought the whole Iberian peninsula under a single rule. Yet after over forty years of rule he had left his kingdom worn out, drained of men and money, only sluggishly able to attend to the needs of a vast empire. And whatever his goals in international politics had been—whether Spanish hegemony, a revived Western empire, or the extinction of the Protestant heresy—he had realized none of them. The fierceness of his Inquisition, his unrelenting stubbornness, the ever-

The Escorial was a combined palace, monastery, and burial place for Spanish kings. It was built for Philip II between 1563 and 1584 by Juan Bautista de Toledo (d. 1563) and Juan de Herrera (1530-1597).

increasing burden of taxation placed on his people, the rise of efficient contending states, the long war against the Dutch, and the effective exploitation of "the Black Legend" (that the Spanish were cruel, lascivious, and "tainted" with Jewish and Moorish blood) by the Italians, Dutch, and English, had all defeated him in the end.

III THE CATHOLIC MONARCHIES: SPAIN AND FRANCE

The states that took part in these dynastic and religious wars experienced an uneven working out of the new businesslike aims and methods characterizing the passage of domestic politics from the medieval to the modern world. Both their armies and their civilian bureaucrats were paid professionals. They had a central financial system, a central legal system that made some attempt to apply the law uniformly to all subjects, and a central authority—whether king, king and council, king and parliament, estates, cortes, or other assembly—that could make new laws.

Such labels as Age of Absolutism and Age of Divine-Right Monarchy are frequently applied to the early modern centuries; over most of Europe the ultimate control of administration rested with a hereditary monarch who claimed a God-given right to make final decisions. But while the greater nobles were losing power and influence to the monarchy, the lesser nobles continued to dominate the countryside, where medieval local privileges survived vigorously almost everywhere, together with local ways of life quite different from those of the court and the capital.

The Renaissance monarchies had many characteristics in common: splendid courts, some form of representative assemblies, complex diplomatic policies and foreign services to pursue those policies, expensive armies, and, above all, growing bureaucracies. For Spain, efficiency in government turned upon the bureaucracy nurtured by Philip II. For France, torn by religious and civil wars, bureaucracy depended more upon the personal popularity of the monarch. For England, the Tudor monarchs achieved a new balance between the reality and the appearance of royal and parliamentary powers. Localism remained strong, and true national patriotism had not yet developed. But a growing emphasis on the structure of government that flowed outward from the monarch and the assemblies—from identification with a single seat of government, though not yet a "national" capital, and from a shared interest in nationalist propaganda—meant that a divided Europe sought security and stability in the concept of the state.

Spanish Absolutism, 1516-1659

Spain in its Golden Age, 1516-1659, offers a case study of the clash between the ideal of absolutism and the persistence of the varied groups on which the monarchy sought to impose its centralized, standardizing rules. The reigns of two hard-working monarchs, Charles V (1516-1556) and Philip II, span almost the entire century. Charles did little to remodel the government he had inherited from his grandparents, Ferdinand and Isabella. Brought up in the Low Countries, he came to Spain a stranger, with a Flemish entourage that already had the northern European contempt for the "backward" south. Charles's election to the imperial throne in 1519 made him further suspect in Spain; the aristocrats were restless in the face of the distractions of his Hapsburg responsibilities, and the municipalities disliked the growth of imperial fiscal controls. In 1520 a league of Spanish cities led by Toledo rose up in the revolt of the *Comuneros*. The Comuneros—about whom there is still much debate, though they appear to have represented the urban bourgeoisie of Castile and converts of Jewish origin who hoped to have the Inquisition curbed—were put down in 1521 with assistance from Andalusia. But Charles had been frightened out of what reforming zeal he may have had, and in the future he did his best not to offend his Spanish subjects openly. Nonetheless, with the defeat of the Comuneros the Spanish monarchy had become absolute, at least in theory.

Unlike his father, Philip II grew up as a Spaniard and was much more willing to build a professional, centralized regime in Spain. He devised a system of councils, topped by a council of state, which were staffed by great nobles but had only advisory powers. Final decisions rested with Philip, and details were worked out by a series of private secretaries and local organs of government that were not staffed by nobles. Philip also reduced the Cortes, the representative assemblies, to practical impotence. In Castile nobles and priests, because they did not pay direct taxes, no longer attended the sessions of the Cortes, and the delegates of the cities were left as a powerless rump. The Cortes of Aragon, while retaining more power, was seldom convoked by Philip. Above all, Philip began with assured sources of income: his tax of a fifth of the value of the precious cargoes from America, direct taxes from the states of his realm, revenues from the royal estates and from the sale of offices and patents of nobility, and revenues from the authorized sale, at royal profit, of dispensations allowed by the pope, such as permission to eat meat on Fridays and during Lent. Philip, like most continental monarchs of his time, had no need to worry about representative bodies with control of the purse. Yet he was always heavily in debt and on three occasions suspended payments on his obligations; it was his bankruptcies that triggered the fall of the famous Fugger bank in Augsburg.

Even in this matter of revenue, the limitations of the absolute monarch were clear. Except by borrowing and hand-to-mouth expedients like the sale of offices, he could not notably increase his income at home; he could not summon any representative group together and get them to vote new monies. In the first place, the constituent parts of his realm—Castile, Aragon, Navarre and the Basque provinces, the Italian lands, the Low Countries, the Americas, and the newest Spanish lands named after the monarch himself, the Philippine Islands—had no common organs of consultation. Each had to be dealt with as a separate entity, and the slowness of communication with his far-flung domains further delayed the always deliberate process of decision making. For the most part the nobility and clergy were tax exempt and could not be called upon for unusual financial sacrifices. The difficulty of collection, the opportunities for graft, and the lack of long-accumulated administrative and financial experience were additional reasons why Philip could not introduce more systematic general taxation and had to look to windfalls and expedients.

Outside the financial sphere, the obstacles to really effective centralization were even more serious. The union of the crowns of Aragon and Castile, achieved by the marriage of Ferdinand and Isabella, had by no means made a unified Spain. Even today, regionalism is more intense in Spain than in most of western Europe. In the sixteenth century, some of the provinces would not even extradite criminals within the peninsula, and many of them levied customs dues on goods from the others. The northern regions, which had never been totally conquered by the Muslims, preserved all sorts of ancient privileges known as *fueros*, and Aragon still kept the office of *justicia mayor*, a judge nominated by the Crown for life and entrusted with enormous public authority.

What the house of Austria, as the Hapsburg dynasty was termed in Spain, might have accomplished had it been able to expend its full energies on uniting and developing its Spanish lands can never be known. What actually happened was that it exhausted the peninsula and weakened its lands overseas in trying to secure hegemony over Europe and to subdue the Protestant heresy. This was indeed the great age of Spain, when both on land and on sea the Spanish were admired as the best fighters, when Spain seemed to be the richest of states, destined to rule over both the Americas; it was also the age of Loyola and Cervantes, the golden age of Spanish religion, literature, and art. And yet it was a brief flowering, for Spanish greatness largely vanished in the seventeenth century.

The Spanish Economy

Spain is a classical instance of a great state's failure to maintain a sound economic basis for its greatness. The Iberian peninsula is mountainous, and its central tableland is subject to droughts, but its agricultural potential is considerable, more than that of Italy, for example; and it has mineral resources, notably iron. Spain was the first major European state to secure lands overseas and to develop a navy and merchant marine to integrate the vast resources of the New World with a base in the Old World. Yet all this wealth slipped through Spain's fingers in a few generations. An important factor here was the immense cost of the wars of Charles V and Philip II; in particular, the Low Countries, which had brought much revenue to Charles, became a drain on Philip's overburdened finances.

Sixteenth-century Spain drew from the New World immense amounts of silver and many commodities—sugar, indigo, tobacco, cocoa, hides—without which it could hardly have fought its European wars. But all this revenue was not enough to pay for world dominion. The bullion passed through Spanish hands into those of bankers and merchants in other European countries, partly to pay for the Spanish armies and navies, and partly to pay for the manufactured goods sent to the New World. These goods, which the colonies were forbidden to make for themselves, Spain could not supply from its own meager industrial production. Although a royal decree gave Spanish merchants a monopoly on trade with the Indies, as the century wore on they became mere middlemen, sending to the Indies items imported from the rest of Europe. Also, the English, Dutch, and other competitors invaded this theoretical monopoly by large-scale smuggling of goods into Spain's colonies. Thus Spain's governmental expenditures primed foreign economies, not the Spanish one, and by 1600 Spain's home industry was declining.

Free-trade economic historians of the nineteenth century attributed Spain's failure to exploit its economic opportunities to the prevalence of monopoly under governmental supervision. Sixteenth-century Spain was certainly moving toward the economic policy called *mercantilism* (referring not to individual merchants but to the "mercantile" or commercial system) which was to reach its fullest development in seventeenth-century France. Although Spain lacked the true mercantilist passion for building national wealth under government auspices, it used many mercantilist techniques: close regulation in general, and narrow channeling of colonial trade in particular. In Castile a single institution, the *Casa de Contratación* (House of Trade) in Seville, controlled every transaction with the Indies and licensed every export and import. The paperwork was staggering, slowing the flow of trade and encouraging smuggling to avoid frustrating delays and high taxes.

The vast riches of the New World were not an unmixed blessing. Competition for gold and silver bullion increased the probability of war with other European powers. The obsessive need to control the monopoly in the movement of bullion, coin, and goods drained many able civil servants into a potentially stagnant area of administration. The flow of bullion in unprecedented quantity (in 1577 alone a fleet of fifty-five ships arrived at Seville from the Indies with over two million ducats in bullion for the king) may well have stimulated a rate of inflation that Philip's sluggish bureaucracy could not control. Certainly inflation was a persistent problem throughout the sixteenth century, and unabated inflation usually revolutionizes economic life. Castilian prices more than doubled in the first half of the century in sharp spurts, and doubled again in a steady rise in the second half of the century; such a rate of increase was unheard of before then.

Sometime between 1600 and 1620 Spain moved from an expansionist to a stagnant economy. Furthermore, climatic changes severely affected Spain during the sixteenth century, and while neither the New World nor the policies of Philip could be blamed for the vagaries of nature, the inability to adjust to the change from a dry and sunny climate at the beginning of the century to a cycle of wet, cold years marked by exceptionally harsh winters toward the end of the seventeenth century reflected the conservative nature of Spanish agriculture.

In any case, the story of Spanish inflation is more complicated and not yet fully understood. The crucial precious metal from the New World was not gold, which first came to a Europe already well supplied with it, but silver, which became more plentiful than gold in the 1530s. The actual movement of the silver cannot be fully known; much of it apparently went to buy Asian luxury goods like spices and porcelain, and most of it may not have entered the Spanish monetary system. Any direct relationship between the influx of silver and the movement of prices is impossible to demonstrate, though if silver was not the original stimulus to a price revolution, it helped maintain prices at a high level. The American trade also entered into the inflationary cycle, though by the seventeenth century Europe appeared not to need American silver so much. What can be said is that the New World trade, and the conventional belief at the time that bullion was the best form of wealth, no doubt did attract men (and some women) of enterprise who saw the silver of the New World as a windfall by which they, more as a class than as a nationality, might change their individual fortunes. Thus the question of the significance of New World silver in the Old World raises in classic form the historian's traditional quandary over cause and effect.

Still, it was Philip's imperialist wars that brought Spain nearer to destruction. The cost of the lost Armada alone was ten million ducats; the war in the Netherlands was eating up another two million ducats annually, while three million were sent as subsidies to French Catholic leaders. In 1589 the Cortes voted a new, expedient tax, the *millones*, which brought in eight million ducats over a decade. Even before this, it is estimated that peasant farmers in Castile were surrendering half their income in taxes, tithes, and feudal dues.

Yet all of this income was still insufficient. Philip II had to borrow heavily, quadrupling the public debt. Eventually debt interest absorbed at least half the Crown's income, so that funds were not sufficient to meet military needs, thus leading to a vicious circle of more borrowings. Furthermore, the outlay of public money did not remain in Spain, for the wages of those in military service were spent where the soldiers were: in Italy, France, or the Netherlands. By the 1590s Spain was in the midst of an acute crisis of capital starvation and overtaxation, made worse by a series of harvest failures across all of western Europe. In 1598-1599 the great plague struck an undernourished population, killing perhaps six hundred thousand in Castile alone; in some areas half the population died.

Still Philip had not retreated from his wars, for he felt that the religious issue—turning the New World Catholic, putting down Moriscos and Jews in Spain, supporting the Catholics of France against the Protestants, crushing the Dutch and holding the English off from the Continent or the New World—was paramount. After 1596 Philip was often ill, and his pleasure at the *auto de fé* (public burning of heretics) and his anti-Semitism were unabated. Worse was to come for the Spanish economy after Philip's death, however, for while his policies may have started the Spanish downward slide, his attention to detail, his ability to get through mountains of work, and the fact that, except for the Netherlands, he had held the empire together until his death, had prevented the general decline from becoming fully evident. By 1640 Spain, and in particular Castile, had fallen into economic disaster, resulting in a major revolt in Catalonia that would continue until 1659 and so weaken Spain as to make her dependent on France.

"The Spanish Century"

Yet Spanish supremacy, though shortlived, was real enough, and it helped shape the present-day world, where half the Americas speak Spanish or Portuguese and carry a cultural inheritance from the Iberian peninsula. The Spanish character, the Spanish "style," was set in this Golden Age, which has left the West magnificent paintings, architecture, and decoration, and one of the few really universal books, *Don Quixote* by Miguel de Cervantes (1547-1616). This Spanish style is not at all like those of France and Italy, even though they are often tied with Spain as "Latin"—a term that is very misleading if the "Latin" peoples are grouped together as "sunny." For many historians see the Spanish spirit as among the most serious, most darkly passionate, most unsmiling in the West—a striving spirit, carrying to an extreme the chivalric concept of honor.

In religion, during the generations following Ignatius Loyola, the Spanish style was expressed most strikingly in the careers of St. Teresa of Avila (1515-1582) and St. John of the Cross (1542-1591), who brought back the tortured ecstasies of the early Christian ascetics and added a dark, mystical note of their own. Theirs was no attempt to withdraw into monastic isolation, but a heroic effort to do combat with this world of the senses and thus transcend it. Together they worked vigorously to reform Spanish monasticism, and John, in particular, was harshly persecuted by established religious interests. They were both familiar figures to the Spanish common people, who identified with these saints in their struggle.

The creations of Cervantes, in their very different way, likewise carry the mark of the Spanish style. Don Quixote tilts with windmills, aflame with passion for Dulcinea, the woman he has invented—quite mad. The

El Greco, the great artist of Spain's Golden Century, depicted the city of Toledo with a heightened sense of drama, just as he would reveal the tension, asceticism, and bigotry in those who sat for portraits by him. *A View of Toledo* is not only the first Spanish landscape painting of note; it is one of the most famous paintings in the world. Its elongated structures, the ectoplasmic clouds that fill the nighttime sky and reflect the lightning, and its rearrangement of the city's landmarks in accordance with the artist's sense of composition and drama (a dramatic rearrangement of which contemporary viewers were well aware) gave the painting a sense of eeriness and foreboding.

knight's servant, Sancho Panza, is conventional, earthy, unheroic, and sane enough, though his sanity fails to protect him from sharing his master's misadventures. Cervantes almost certainly meant no more than an amusing satire of popular tales of chivalry, but his story was caught up in a web of symbolism, and the Don and his reluctant follower became a Spain forever racked between fantasy and common sense.

Extreme pride—pride of status, of faith, of nation—was often the mark of Spain. El Cid (c 1040-1099), the legendary hero of the reconquest from the Muslims, is fatalistic and proud in these verses as he goes off to his Crusade:

> I fight by necessity:
> But once I am in the saddle,
> Castile goes widening out
> Ahead of my horse.

These writers and saints were representative of the Golden Age of Spain, though perhaps the painter El Greco expressed most that was important to the Spanish leaders of the time. El Greco, "the Greek" (1541-1614), was born on Crete. After studying in Venice, he settled in the 1570s in Toledo, the religious capital of Castile. He was a professional, an artist trained in Italy. His work showed the influence of other cultures; Titian and Tintoretto in particular were of great importance to his early development. Yet he also developed his own independent voice, infused with Byzantine, Iberian, and Counter-Reformation concerns. He was an intellectual who developed the arguments of the Catholic Reformation explicitly in his art. The famous picture of St. Peter in tears, painted between 1580 and 1585, emphasized the importance of penitence, even for the founder of the church, precisely because the Protestants had disparaged penitence. He personalized the saints, encouraging a personal attachment to a specific saint, and he glorified the Virgin Mary in his work. To bring the church fathers and the saints closer to the people, he depicted them in sixteenth-century dress. In El Greco the ideas of the Catholic Reformation spoke as clearly as in the teachings of Loyola.

Historians loosely speak of great world powers as having possessed, or been dominant in, a particular century: the twentieth century has often been referred to as "the American century"; certainly the nineteenth was "the British"; and the seventeenth century the "French." The sixteenth century, the Golden Age of Spain, while no more entirely the "possession" of one nation than any other century would prove to be, was nonetheless distinctively marked by the Spanish sense of style and by Spain's initiatives in western European affairs.

El Greco's Byzantine and High Renaissance training served as a foundation for his highly personal way of dealing with religious themes. This approach is best illustrated in his masterpiece, *The Burial of the Count of Orgaz,* which is in the church of Santo Tomé in Toledo. Orgaz, a fourteenth-century nobleman, had made generous gifts in honor of St. Augustine and St. Stephen, both of whom, it was said, miraculously appeared after his death to bury his body. The painting shows both the earthly and heavenly realms; the saints gently lift the corpse as the aristocratic mourners gaze upward toward the angel bearing the count's soul to heaven. There the Virgin and St. John are waiting to intercede for him with Christ and St. Peter. The slender, elongated figures have tapering fingers, narrow heads, and unnaturally large eyes. Stretching toward heaven like a Gothic pinnacle, *The Burial of the Count of Orgaz* is an effort to record a mystic's unrecordable experience.

France: Toward Absolutism, 1547-1588

The long-established French monarchy began to move toward more efficient absolutism after the Hundred Years' War, particularly under Louis XI. In this development, France had certain advantages. None of its provinces—not even Brittany or Provence—showed quite the intense regionalism that could be found in Catalonia or among the Spanish Basques. Moreover, unlike the Iberian peninsula, Italy, or Greece, most of France is not cut up by mountain ranges into compartments isolated by problems of transport and communications. Yet despite these assets, France was still only loosely tied together under Francis I. Many provinces, especially Brittany and others that had recently come under direct royal rule, retained their own local Estates, their own local courts (parlements), and many other privileges. The national bureaucracy was only a patchwork, and the nobility held on to feudal hopes and social attitudes, even though most of its old governmental functions had passed to royal appointees.

Nonetheless, the kingdom of Francis I had been strong enough to counter the threat of encirclement by Charles V. The king himself was not another Louis XI, however. Self-indulgence weakened his health and distracted him from the business of government; his extravagant court and, far more, his frequent wars drained French finances. In many respects Francis was a good Renaissance despot: good-looking (until his health broke down), amorous, lavish, courtly, Francis lived in the grand manner. It is reported that it took eighteen thousand horses and pack animals to move the king and his court on their frequent journeys. He built the châteaux of Chambord and Fontainebleau, and in Paris he remodeled the great palace of the Louvre and founded the Collège de France, second only to the old

TILTING AT WINDMILLS

A tension runs all through *Don Quixote;* its hero struggles against reality, and in his aspirations he is ennobled even in a world where evil often triumphs:

"I would inform you, Sancho, that it is a point of honor with knights-errant to go for a month at a time without eating, and when they do eat, it is whatever may be at hand. You would certainly know that if you had read the histories as I have. There are many of them, and in none have I found any mention of knights eating unless it was by chance or at some sumptuous banquet that was tendered them; on other days they fasted. And even though it is well understood that, being men like us, they could not go without food entirely, any more than they could fail to satisfy the other necessities of nature, nevertheless, since they spent the greater part of their lives in forests and desert places without any cook to prepare their meals . . ."

"Pardon me, your Grace," said Sancho, "but seeing that as I have told you, I do not know how to read or write, I am consequently not familiar with the rules of the knightly calling. Hereafter, I will stuff my saddlebags with all manner of dried fruit for your Grace, but inasmuch as I am not a knight, I shall lay in for myself a stock of fowls and other more substantial fare."

Don Quixote, trans. Samuel Putnam (New York: Viking, 1949), I, 78-79.

Sorbonne as an educational center. He patronized Leonardo, Cellini, and other artists and men of letters.

At the beginning of his reign he had extended the royal gains first made in 1438 at papal expense in the Pragmatic Sanction of Bourges; through the Concordat of Bologna in 1516 the pope had granted the king increased control over the Gallican church, including the important right to choose bishops and abbots. In adversity, Francis had courage: witness his successful recovery after the disaster at Pavia in 1525. In diplomacy he was unscrupulous and flexible: witness his alliances with the Turks and with the German Protestants.

But Francis was the last strong monarch of the house of Valois. After his death in 1547, his son Henry II and his grandsons could barely maintain the prestige of the Crown in the face of crippling disorders. The second half of the sixteenth century was the age of French civil and religious wars, a time of crisis that almost undid the centralizing work of Louis XI and his successors.

The religious map of France in the 1550s showed a division by class as well as by territory. While Protestantism scarcely touched the French peasantry except in parts of the south, the Huguenots were strong among the nobility and among the rising classes of capitalists and artisans. Paris, Brittany, most of Normandy, and the northeast remained ardently Catholic. Protestantism was gaining in the southwest, where the Old Albigensian heresy had arisen. Even in these regions, however, the employer class was more likely to be Protestant, the workers to be Catholic.

The French nobility took up Protestantism partly in response to a missionary campaign directed toward them from Geneva and partly for political reasons. The old tradition of local feudal independence among the nobles encouraged resistance to the centralized Catholic monarchy and its agents. The German princes in revolt had everything to gain in a worldly way by confiscation of church property and establishment of an Erastian Lutheran church. But after the Concordat of 1516, the French kings had everything to lose by a Protestant movement that strengthened their restive nobility and that in its Calvinist form elevated the power of the church above that of the Crown.

Sporadic warfare began soon after the death of Henry II in 1559, who was fatally wounded in a tournament celebrating the Treaty of Cateau-Cambrésis. Thereafter, the crown passed in succession to Henry's three sons—Francis II (1559-1560), Charles IX (1560-1574), and Henry III (1574-1589)—and France was torn by civil and religious strife. Since Charles IX was a boy of ten at his accession, authority was exercised by his mother, Catherine de' Medici, who shared the humanistic and artistic tastes of her Florentine family and had no particular religious convictions. Catherine was determined to preserve intact the magnificent royal inheritance of her sons, however, which seemed threatened by the rapid growth of the Huguenots. What especially worried Catherine was the apparent polarization of the high nobility by the religious issue; the great family of Guise was zealously dedicated to the Catholic cause, and the powerful families of Bourbon and Montmorency to the Huguenot.

Success in scattered fighting during the 1560s netted the Huguenots some gains. Their ambitious leader, Gaspard de Coligny (1519-1572), who was linked to the Montmorencys, gained great influence over the unstable Charles IX and hoped to control the government. Panicky at the danger to the prospects for her sons and to her own position, Catherine threw in her lot with the Guises and persuaded Charles to follow suit. The result was a massacre of Huguenots on St. Bartholomew's Day (August 24, 1572). Six thousand Protestants were killed in Paris, including Coligny, many of them dragged from their beds in the early hours of the morning according to a prearranged plan; thousands more perished in the provinces. Yet despite St. Bartholomew's Day and subsequent reverses in the field, the Huguenots remained strong. As warfare continued, the Catholic nobles organized a threatening league headed by the Guises, and both sides negotiated with foreigners for help—the Catholics with Spain and the Protestants with England. Thus the French Crown found itself pushed into opposition to both groups.

French civil and religious strife culminated in the War of the Three Henrys (1585-1589)—named for Henry III, the Valois king and the last surviving grandson of Francis I; Henry, duke of Guise, head of the Catholic League; and the Bourbon Henry of Navarre, Protestant cousin and heir-presumptive of the childless king. The threat that a Protestant might succeed to the throne pushed the Catholic League to propose violating the rules of succession by making an uncle of Henry of Navarre king, the Catholic cardinal of Bourbon. But this attempt to alter the succession alienated moderate French opinion, already disturbed by the extreme positions taken by both Catholics and Protestants.

Paris was strongly Catholic, and a popular insurrection there (May 1588) frightened Henry III out of his capital, which triumphantly acclaimed Henry, duke of Guise, as king. Henry III responded by conniving in the assassination of the two great leaders of the Catholic League, Henry of Guise and his brother Louis. Infuriated, the Catholic League rose in full revolt, and Henry III took refuge in the camp of Henry of Navarre, where he was assassinated by a monk.

The First Bourbon King: Henry IV, 1589-1610

Henry of Navarre was now by law Henry IV (r. 1589-1610), the first king of the house of Bourbon. In the decisive battle of Ivry in March 1590, he defeated the Catholics, who had set up the aged cardinal of Bourbon as "King Charles X." But Henry's efforts to besiege Paris were repeatedly frustrated by Spanish troops sent down from Flanders by Philip II. Philip planned to have the French Estates General put Henry aside and bestow the crown on the Spanish infanta, Isabella, daughter of Philip II and his third wife, Elizabeth of Valois, who was

THE EDICT OF NANTES

By this edict Henry IV recognized Huguenot religious freedom. Its key provisions follow:

We have by this perpetual and irrevocable Edict pronounced, declared, and ordained and we pronounce, declare and ordain:

I. Firstly, that the memory of everything done on both sides from the beginning of the month of March, 1585, until our accession to the Crown and during the other previous troubles, and at the outbreak of them, shall remain extinct and suppressed, as if it were something which had never occurred. . . .

II. We forbid all our subjects, of whatever rank and quality they may be, to renew the memory of these matters, to attack, be hostile to, injure or provoke each other in revenge for the past, whatever may be the reason and pretext . . . but let them restrain themselves and live peaceably together as brothers, friends, and fellow-citizens. . . .

III. We ordain that the Catholic, Apostolic, and Roman religion shall be restored and re-established in all places and districts of this our kingdom and the countries under our rule, where its practice has been interrupted. . . .

VI. And we permit those of the so-called Reformed religion to live and dwell in all the towns and districts of this our kingdom and the countries under our rule, without being annoyed, disturbed, molested or constrained to do anything against their conscience, or for this cause to be sought out in their houses and districts where they wish to live, provided that they conduct themselves in other respects to the provisions of our present Edict. . . .

XXI. Books dealing with the matters of the aforesaid so-called Reformed religion shall not be printed and sold publicly, except in the towns and districts where the public exercise of the said religion is allowed. . . .

XXII. We ordain that there shall be no difference or distinction, because of the aforesaid religion, in the reception of students to be instructed in Universities, Colleges, and schools, or of the sick and poor into hospitals, infirmaries, and public charitable institutions.

XXVII. In order to reunite more effectively the wills of our subjects, as is our intention, and to remove all future complaints, we declare that all those who profess or shall profess the aforesaid so-called Reformed religion are capable of holding and exercising all public positions, honours, offices, and duties whatsoever . . . in the towns of our kingdom . . . notwithstanding all contrary oaths.

Church and State through the Centuries: A Collection of Historic Documents, trans. and ed. S. Z. Ehler and John B. Morrall (New York: Biblo and Tannen, 1967), pp. 185–87.

the child of Henry II and Catherine de' Medici. In the face of this new threat, Henry was persuaded that if he would formally reject his Protestant faith, he could rally the moderate Catholics and secure at least toleration for the Protestants. He turned Catholic in 1593 and Paris surrendered to him, giving rise to the tale that he had remarked, "Paris is well worth a Mass." Henry thereupon declared war against Spain and brought it to a successful conclusion with the Treaty of Vervins (1598), which essentially confirmed the Cateau-Cambrésis settlement in 1559.

Within France the Edict of Nantes, also in 1598, endeavored to achieve a lasting religious settlement. While it did not bring complete religious freedom, it did provide for a large measure of toleration. The Huguenots were granted substantial civil liberties and were allowed to exercise their religion in certain towns and in the households of great Huguenot nobles. Public worship by Huguenots was forbidden in cities that were the seats of bishops, and most particularly in Paris. In the two hundred towns where Huguenots could worship, they were to fortify and garrison one hundred soldiers at government expense as symbols of safeguard.

The intellectual preparation for the Edict of Nantes and for the revival of the French monarchy under Henry IV had been in large part the work of a group of men known as *politiques*, a term that comes closer to meaning political moralist than politician. The greatest of them, Jean Bodin (1530-1596), and his colleagues stressed the need for political unity to maintain law and order; yet they were moderates who by no means preached that the king must be obeyed blindly. The politiques were convinced that under the supremacy of the French state, French citizens should be allowed to practice different forms of the Christian religion. They believed that the basic aim of the belligerents in the religious wars—to put down by force those who disagreed on matters of faith—was un-Christian.

Henry IV was particularly fortunate in arriving on the French scene when the passions of civil war were nearing exhaustion and the nation was ready for peace. The casualty rate in war had become catastrophic; commonly a third of those engaged in battle died. Slowly a general revulsion against the excessive destructiveness of war offset the fanaticism displayed on both sides in the succession of religious wars. Henry balanced concessions to the Huguenots with generous subsidies to the Catholic League for disbanding its troops, and he declined to summon the Estates General because of its potential for proving troublesome. Other kings in other days—Louis XI of France and Henry VII of England—had restored law and order, but because of his personal qualities, only Henry of Navarre became a genuinely popular hero. He was the most human king the French had had for a long time and the best-liked monarch in their history, for he convinced his subjects that he was truly concerned for their welfare. Henry IV is still remembered as the king who remarked that every peasant should have a chicken in the pot on Sunday.

The range of efforts to improve the economy was extensive and innovative. Henry's economic advisers reclaimed marshes for farmland, encouraged luxury crafts in Paris, and planted thousands of mulberry trees to foster the manufacture of silk. They extended canals and built roads and bridges that eventually gave France the best highways in Europe. Faced with a heavy deficit when he took office, Henry's chief minister, the Huguenot Maximilien Sully (1560-1641), systematically lowered it until he balanced government income and expenditure. His search for new revenues had some unhappy consequences, however. He not only continued the old custom of selling government offices, but permitted the beneficiary to transmit the office to his heir on payment of an annual fee—a lucrative new source of royal income but an even greater source of future difficulty; officeholders became more concerned with enjoying and protecting their vested interests than with the faithful execution of their duties. And the distribution of taxation remained lopsided, with some provinces much more heavily burdened than others, and with the poor paying much more than their share. Collection remained in the hands of contractors, called *farmers*, and the treasury suffered loss of revenue from entrusting this public function to often unscrupulous private businessmen. Fiscal instability was to remain the greatest weakness of the French monarchy for the next two centuries.

IV THE PROTESTANT STATES: TUDOR ENGLAND AND THE DUTCH REPUBLIC

Henry VIII, 1509-1547

In England Henry VII had already established the new Tudor monarchy on a firm footing. That Henry VIII did not run through his heritage and leave an exhausted treasury and discredited monarchy was not because he lacked the will to spend lavishly. He loved display, elaborate palaces (Hampton Court, near London, is the best known), and all the trappings of Renaissance monarchy. His "summit conference" with Francis I, a kindred luxurious spirit, near Calais in 1520 has gone down in tradition as taking place on the Field of the Cloth of Gold. Democratic critics have often accused European royalty of ruinous expenditures on palaces, retinues, pensions, mistresses, and high living in general, and yet such expenditures were usually a relatively small part of government outlays. War was really the major cause of disastrous financial difficulties for modern governments. Henry's six wives, his court, his frequent royal journeys did not beggar England; the wars of Charles V and Philip II did beggar Spain.

Henry VIII made war prudently, never really risking large English armies on the Continent, and contenting himself with playing a cautious game of balance of power. He used the English Reformation to add to royal revenues by confiscating monastic property and, even more important, by rewarding his loyal followers with the lands so confiscated. Henry thus followed in the footsteps of his father in helping create a new upper class, which soon became a titled or noble class. In contrast to France, the new nobles were on the whole loyal to the Crown and yet, in contrast to some of the German states, by no means subservient to it. The result was a "balanced monarchy," with substantial power to which there were, nonetheless, limits.

Under Henry VIII and his successors the newly rich continued to thrive, and many others also prospered. But Tudor England also had a class of the newly poor as a result of the enclosing of land for sheepfarming. These small farmers, who lost their right to pasture animals on former common lands now enclosed in private estates, lost the margin that had permitted them to make ends meet.

Lacking the patience to attend to administrative details, Henry relied heavily on members of the new Tudor nobility as his chief assistants—Wolsey in the early part of his reign, then Thomas Cranmer (who as archbishop of Canterbury enabled Henry to marry Anne Boleyn), and above all, Thomas Cromwell (c 1485-1540), later made earl of Essex, who superintended the break with Rome. Cromwell exploited the printing press to spread propaganda favoring the royal point of view. He was a master administrator who endeavored to make the royal administration more loyal, professional, and efficient, and less tied to the king's household and to special interests. In achieving much he antagonized other ambitious royal servants. Discredited by his enemies in the eyes of the king, Cromwell was executed for treason in 1540. Wolsey too had been disgraced and died awaiting trial.

Henry could be ruthless, yet he could be tactful and diplomatic, as in his handling of Parliament to get everything he wanted, including statutes separating the English church from Rome and grants for his wars and conferences. Henry's parliaments were far from being elected legislatures based on wide suffrage. The House of Lords had a safe majority—titled nobles and, after 1534, bishops of the Anglican church—who were of Tudor creation or allegiance. The evolving and complex House of Commons was composed of the knights of the shire, chosen by the freeholders of the shires, and of the burgesses, representatives of incorporated towns or boroughs (not by any means all towns). In most boroughs a very narrow electorate chose these members of Parliament. Since most of the people of the shires were agricultural workers or tenants, rather than freeholders of land, the county franchise was also limited. The knights of the shire were chosen from among, and largely by, the squires and the lesser country gentlemen. It was assumed that royal favor and royal patronage, as well as the patronage of the great lords, could still mold a particular sitting of the House of Commons.

Still, even the Tudor parliaments were nearer a modern legislative assembly than the assemblies on the Continent. The great difference lay in the composition of the House of Commons, which had emerged from the Middle Ages not as a body representing an urban bourgeoisie, but as a blend of the rural landed gentry and the ruling groups in the towns. On the Continent the assemblies corresponding to the English Parliament usually sat in three distinct houses: one representing the clergy, another all the nobles, great and small, and a third the lay commoners. Some countries, as for instance Sweden, had four estates: clergy, nobles, townsmen, and peasants. However, in England town and country were joined.

Historians today emphasize that the political differences between England and the Continent reflected differences in social structure. England had its nobility or aristocracy ranging from barons to dukes. These nobles, plus Anglican bishops, composed the House of Lords. But in England, the younger sons of nobles were not themselves titled nobles, as they were on the Continent. Still, they were members, usually top members, of a complex social and political group that also included the squires and rich bankers and merchants, who almost always acquired landed estates and became squires themselves. It also included leading lawyers and civil servants, the Anglican clergy, professors at Oxford and Cambridge (who at first were usually Anglican clergymen), officers in the army and navy, and a scattering of others in the liberal professions. This large and diverse group was never a closed caste and remained open to the socially mobile from the lower classes. (The imprecise terms *gentry* and *gentlemen* are sometimes applied to this group, although the former is too exclusively rural in connotation and the latter is not always accurate in its implication that gentlemen invariably own enough property or capital so that they do not have to work for a living. Perhaps "ruling elite" or "establishment" would be as good names as any for this uniquely English class.)

By the beginning of the Tudor era, Parliament had already obtained much more than the purely advisory powers that were all that the French Estates General really had. Parliament emerged from the Middle Ages with the power to make laws or statutes, though these did require royal consent. The Tudor parliaments could have quarreled as violently with the Crown as the Stuart parliaments were to do in the next century. Yet, although the Tudor monarchs had their difficulties with Parliament, they usually got what they wanted without serious constitutional crises. This was particularly true of Henry VIII and Elizabeth I, who succeeded in part because their parliaments were generally recruited from men indebted to the Crown for their good fortune. But the Tudors also succeeded because they were skillful rulers, willing to use their prestige and gifts of persuasion to win the consent of Parliament, careful to observe the constitutional and human decencies, and aware that courtesy is often the highest form of efficiency. Both Henry and Elizabeth were self-aware, hearty persons, sure of themselves and their dignity, immensely popular with all classes of their subjects. Both were fortunate to be able to identify with and to use strong national feelings of patriotic resistance to the two most hated foreign foes: the Roman church and the Spanish monarchy.

Edward VI and Mary, 1547-1558

The course of Tudor domestic history, however, did not run with perfect smoothness. Henry VII had faced two pretenders; Henry VIII met opposition to his religious policy. A Catholic minority, strong in the north, continued throughout the sixteenth century to oppose the Protestant majority, sometimes with arms, sometimes with plots. The death of Henry VIII in 1547 marked the beginning of a period of extraordinary religious shifts.

Henry was succeeded by his only son, the ten-year-old Edward VI (r. 1547-1553), borne by his third wife, Jane Seymour. Led by the young king's uncle, the duke of Somerset, as lord protector, Edward's government pushed on into Protestant ways. The Six Articles, by which Henry had sought to preserve the essentials of Roman Catholic theology, worship, and even church organization, were repealed in 1547. The legal title of the statute commonly called the Six Articles had been "An Act for Abolishing Diversity in Opinion." The goal was still uniformity, and in the brief reign of Edward VI an effort was made to prescribe uniformity of religious worship through a prayer book and articles of faith imposed by Parliament. Cranmer, as archbishop of Canterbury, was much influenced by Zwingli and had committed himself by marriage—as did Luther—to a clear symbolic break with Roman Catholicism. Under his supervision the English were pressed toward Protestant worship.

Then in 1553, the young king, Edward VI, always a frail boy, died. Protestant intriguers vainly attempted to secure the crown for a Protestant, Lady Jane Grey, a quiet, scholarly great-granddaughter of Henry VII. But Edward VI was followed by his older sister Mary (r. 1553-1558), daughter of Catherine of Aragon, whom Henry VIII had divorced. Mary had been brought up a Catholic and began at once to restore the old ways. Rebellion flared into the open when Mary announced her marriage to Philip II of Spain. Mary prevailed against the rebels, and Lady Jane Grey was executed for a plot in which she had never really participated. A Catholic cardinal replaced Cranmer as archbishop of Canterbury, and two thousand married clergy were ejected from their churches.

Catholic forms of worship came back to the parishes, though, significantly, the church land settlement of Henry VIII remained undisturbed. In 1554 three statutes on heresy were reenacted, and vigorous persecution of Protestants followed; nearly three hundred people, mostly from the lower classes and including women, were burned. The queen was given the lasting name of "Bloody Mary," and the foundations of the English Protestant hatred and suspicion of Catholicism, traces of which still survive today, were laid. Cranmer submitted to the Catholic church and declared Luther and Zwingli heretics; but on the day he was burned he reverted to Protestantism and became (with five former bishops who were also burned to death) the symbol of Mary's persecutions.

Elizabeth I, 1558-1603

When Mary died in 1558, Henry VIII's last surviving child was Elizabeth, daughter of Anne Boleyn. She had been declared illegitimate by Parliament in 1536 at her father's request; Henry's last will, however, had rehabilitated her, and she now succeeded as Elizabeth I (1558-1603). She had been brought up a Protestant, and so once more the English churchgoer was required to switch religion. This time the Anglican church was firmly established; the prayer book and Thirty-nine Articles of 1563 issued under Elizabeth have remained to this day the essential documents of the Anglican faith.

The Elizabethan settlement, moderate though it was, did not fully solve the religious problem. England still had a large Catholic minority, Catholic Spain was a serious enemy, and independent Scotland could always be counted on to take the anti-English side. The new queen of Scotland was Mary Stuart (1542-1567), granddaughter of Henry VIII's sister Margaret, and therefore heir to the English throne should Elizabeth die without issue. Mary, who was Catholic and whose mother was a member of the Catholic Guise family of France, did not wait for Elizabeth's death to press her claim. On the ground that Elizabeth was illegitimate, she assumed the title of queen of England as well as Scotland.

Meantime, numerous Protestant groups not satisfied with the Thirty-nine Articles were coming to the fore.

The *Armada Portrait of Queen Elizabeth I,* by Marcus Gheeraerts (c 1525-1599), shows the Queen with her hand on globe, dominating the Atlantic Ocean, as the Armada sinks (upper right-hand corner) before the "Protestant Wind."

QUEEN ELIZABETH AT TILBURY

Queen Elizabeth reviewed her troops at Tilbury Fort as they prepared to resist the expected Spanish invasion. She found the camp cheerful and clean, and the troops determined that they would remain loyal in the face of the gravest danger. She slowly moved through the camp, inspecting, encouraging, seeking to set an example of calm. She repeated the inspection the next day and then spoke to her people:

My loving people, we have been persuaded by some that are careful for our safety, to take heed how we commit ourselves to armed multitudes, for fear of treachery. But I assure you, I do not desire to live to distrust my faithful and loving people. Let tyrants fear. I have always so behaved myself that, under God, I have placed my chiefest strength and safeguard in the loyal hearts and good will of my subjects; and therefore I am come amongst you as you see, at this time, not for my recreation and disport, but being resolved, in the midst and heat of the battle, to live or die amongst you all, and to lay down for my God and for my kingdom and for my people, my honour and my blood, even in the dust. I know I have the body of a weak and feeble woman, but I have the heart and stomach of a king, and of a king of England too, and think foul scorn that Parma or Spain, or any prince of Europe should dare to invade the borders of my realm; to which, rather than any dishonour shall grow by me, I myself will take up arms, I myself will be your general, judge, and rewarder of every one of your virtues in the field. I know already for your forwardness you deserve rewards and crowns; and we do assure you, in the word of a prince, they shall be duly paid you.

Quoted in Garrett Mattingly, *The Armada* (Boston: Houghton Mifflin, 1959), pp. 349-50, from J. E. Hales, *Essays in Elizabethan History*.

Collectively, they were called nonconformists or Puritans, since they wished to purify the Anglican church of what they considered papist survivals in belief, ritual, and church government. In practice, their proposals ranged from moderate to radical. The moderates would have settled for a simpler ritual and retained the office of bishop. The Presbyterians would have replaced bishops with councils (synods) of elders, or *presbyters*, and adopted the full Calvinist theology. The Brownists, named for their leader Robert Browne (c 1550-1633), would have gone still further and made each congregation an independent body; from this group would emerge the Congregationalists.

Thus Elizabeth had a religiously divided kingdom at the start of her reign. The troubles of Edward and Mary had undone some of the work of the two Henrys. Dissension seemed all around her, yet she was to reign for nearly fifty years. Her personality was hardly heartwarming. She was vain (or simply proud), not immune to flattery, but too intelligent to be led astray by it in important matters. She was a Renaissance realist who personally set English policy, while accepting that it

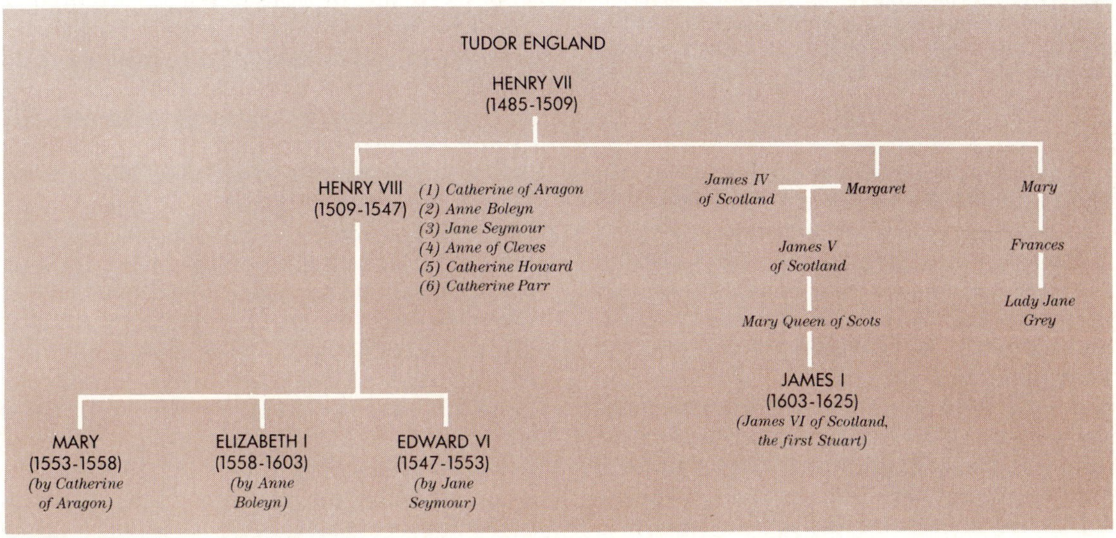

Queen Elizabeth, the most consistently successful ruler of the sixteenth century, gave her name to an entire age. Here she appears before Parliament. This engraving is taken from *Nobilitas Politica vel Civilis,* published in London in 1608. The book depicted the major dignitaries and nobles of England.

would be widely discussed. She was loved by her people, if not by her intimates. She never married, but played off foreign and domestic suitors one against another with excellent results for her foreign policy. She sought to avoid the expense and danger of war, always trying to get something for nothing. When policy appeared to require it, she appeared to be ready to marry a Valois, the duke of Anjou. Most important, she realized that engaging in open war with Spain to protect the Netherlands, an ally that might soon no longer exist, could be disastrous.

Mistrusting the great English aristocrats, Elizabeth picked most of her ministers from the ranks just below the nobility, talented men who put her government in splendid order. Thanks to skillful diplomacy that made full use of the French and Dutch opposition to Spain, the final confrontation with Philip was postponed until 1588, when the kingdom was ready for it. Mary, as queen of Scots, proved no match for her gifted cousin, not merely because she was a poor politician, but even more because she had no firm Scottish base to work from. Mary was Catholic, and Scotland under the leadership of John Knox was on its way to becoming one of the great centers of Calvinism. Mary managed everything wrong, including—and perhaps most important in a puritanical land—her love affairs. The Scots revolted, and Mary was forced in 1568 to take refuge in England, where Elizabeth had her put in what was to prove a long confinement. Mary alive was a constant temptation to all who wanted to overthrow Elizabeth. Letters, which Mary declared were forged and over which historians still debate, apparently involved her in what was certainly a real conspiracy against Elizabeth. She was tried, convicted, and executed in 1587, to become a romantic legend.

The dramatic crisis of Elizabeth's reign was the war with Spain, resolved in the defeat of the great Spanish Armada in 1588. But her old age was not to be altogether serene. Forced to turn frequently to Parliament for approval of financial measures, she met mounting criticism of her religious policy from Puritan members of the House of Commons. She got her money, not by making concessions to the Puritans, but by grudgingly conceding more rights to the Commons. But the Commons responded with bolder criticism of the queen's policy, and at what proved to be the last meeting of Parliament Elizabeth attended, they failed to salute her appearance with the usual salvo of applause. The stage was being set for the great seventeenth-century confrontation between the Crown and Parliament in the gradual emergence of what another generation would call party leaders—politicians who shaped policy below the level of the Crown.

During Elizabeth's final years the stage was also being set for a drama that was to have an even longer run—the Irish question. The half-English (Anglo-Irish) ruling class was out of touch with the local population, mostly peasants. In 1542 Ireland had been made a kingdom, but hardly an independent one, since the crowns of England and Ireland were to be held by the same person. Earlier, in 1495, a statute had put the Irish Parliament firmly under English control and had made laws enacted by the English Parliament applicable to Ireland as well. Attempts to enforce Protestant legislation passed by the English Parliament outraged the native Irish, who had remained faithful Catholics. In 1597 the Irish revolted under the earl of Tyrone. The favorite of Elizabeth's old age, the earl of Essex, lost influence by his failure to cope with the Irish rebels; Essex then became involved in a plot against the queen and was executed. The rebellion was put down bloodily in 1601, but the Irish issue remained unresolved. Elizabeth's successor, James I, sought to further the conversion of the Catholic Irish by implanting Protestant settlers in the northern part of the island, known as Ulster.

The English Renaissance

Elizabeth's reign was marked by intrigue, war, rebellion, and personal and party strife. Yet there were solid foundations under the state and society that produced the wealth and victories of the Elizabethan Age and its attainments in literature, music, architecture, and science. The economy prospered in an era of unbridled individual enterprise that was often unscrupulous and, in raids on the commerce of foreigners such as the Spaniards, piratical. The solid administrative system was based on a national unity made possible by the absence of the extreme local differences and conflicts encountered on the Continent. A common sentiment kept the English together and set limits beyond which most of them would not carry disagreement. Elizabeth herself played a large part in holding her subjects together. Her religious policy, for example, was directed at stretching the already broad principles and practices of the Church of England so that they would cover near-Catholicism at one extreme and near-Congregationalism at the other. There was a limit to this flexibility, however, and Elizabeth did not grant either Catholics or Brownists the right to practice their religion publicly. But, in contrast to Mary's severity, Elizabeth's persecution was largely a matter of fining offenders.

The age of Elizabeth was marked by a great flowering of culture that extended beyond the chronological limits of her reign (1558-1603), back to the reign of Henry VIII and forward to that of James I. This was the English Renaissance, when ladies and gentlemen cultivated all the muses, played the lute, sang madrigals, admired contemporary painting, and sought to dress as their counterparts did in the pacesetter of European style, Italy. The glory of the English Renaissance resided in its literature, in the works of Thomas More, William Shakespeare, Francis Bacon, Edmund Spenser, Ben Jonson, and many others who became part of the formal higher education of English-speaking people all over the world.

Their writings have suffered from both uncritical popular admiration and from neglect, as well as from the thorough academic working-over that goes with their status as established classics. They belong to a culture now four centuries old, and their authors wrote English before its structure and its word order were set—partly by the influence of French prose—in their present straightforward simplicity and relative uniformity. Shakespeare, notably, continues even outside the English-speaking world to be a giant of letters, above the limitations of a national language, read by more of the literate world than any other secular writer.

These Elizabethans were overwhelmingly exuberant; they were exuberant even in their refinement, full-blooded even in their learning. To a later generation, to the polite, orderly admirers of quiet measure and a calm sensibility in the late seventeenth and eighteenth centuries, these Elizabethans were uncouth, undisciplined, too full of the gusto of life. To the nineteenth-century romantics, they were brothers in romance, and nineteenth-century scholars rediscovered the Elizabethan age. The love of excess is obvious in much Elizabethan writing: in the interminable, allusion-packed, allegory-mad stanzas of Edmund Spenser's *Faerie Queene*, in the piling up of quotations from the ancient Greeks and Romans, in Shakespeare's fondness for puns and rhetorical devices, in the extraordinarily bloody tragedies and exuberant comedies that made Elizabethan drama second only to that of the ancient Greeks. Except for the Bible, more phrases from Shakespeare's plays—from *Hamlet*, *Othello*, *King Lear*, or *The Tempest*—have become part of common speech than have the words of any other writer in any other Western language.

The Dutch Republic, 1602-1672

The great age of the Dutch extended from the late sixteenth century through the first three-quarters of the seventeenth. The United Provinces of the Northern Netherlands gained effective independence from Spain before the death of Philip II, though formal international recognition of that independence came only in 1648. The Dutch state was a republic amid monarchies, but it was an aristocratic merchant society that was far from being a truly popular democracy. It was the first significant middle-class state in Europe with virtually no landed aristocracy, built on the instabilities of commerce alone. Despite its small size, it was a great power, colonizing in Asia, Africa, and the Americas, trading everywhere, and supporting an active and efficient navy.

The Dutch were the economic pacesetters of seventeenth-century Europe, and Amsterdam succeeded Antwerp (as Antwerp had earlier succeeded Bruges) as the major trading center of northwestern Europe. Dutch ships played a predominant role in the international carrying trade; in the midseventeenth century the Dutch probably operated between half and three-quarters of the world's merchant vessels. The Dutch also controlled the very lucrative North Sea herring fisheries. Their East India Company, founded in 1602, assembled and exploited a commercial empire. It paid large regular dividends and was a pioneer instance of the joint-stock company, sponsored by the state and pooling the resources of many businessmen who could not have risked such a formidable undertaking on an individual basis. The Bank of Amsterdam, founded in 1609, was also a model, minting its own florins and so innovative in its services to depositors that it made Amsterdam the financial capital of Europe.

The Dutch instituted life insurance and perfected the actuarial calculations on which it is based. Specialized industries flourished in particular cities and towns; diamond cutting, printing, and bookbinding at Amsterdam; shipbuilding at Zaandam; gin distilling at Schiedam; ceramics at Delft; woolens at Leiden; and linens at Haarlem. The Dutch, together with their Catholic cousins under Spanish rule in Flanders, were in the forefront of European agricultural progress; they created new farm plots called *polders* by diking and draining lands formerly under the sea, and they experi-

Jan Vermeer (1632-1675) was one of "the little Dutch masters" whose crystal clear sense of lighting had a simple beauty that led to his rediscovery in the twentieth century. His *View of Delft,* painted c 1658, is now in the Mauritshuis in The Hague.

mented with new techniques of scientific farming and with new crops. Among the latter were tulips, imported from the Ottoman Empire; the growing of tulip bulbs in the fields around Haarlem set off a wild financial speculation—the Tulipomania of the 1630s.

In government, the Dutch republic was no model of efficiency, for the United Provinces were united in name only, fragmented by Dutch deference to traditional local home rule. The seven provinces sent delegates (*Hooge Moogende,* "High Mightinesses") to the Estates General, which functioned like a diplomatic congress rather than a central legislature. Each province did have a chief executive, the *stadholder,* originally the local lieutenant of the Spanish king in the days of Hapsburg rule. Most of the provinces chose as stadholder the incumbent prince of the house of Orange, which made him a symbol of national unity. Twice in the seventeenth century, however, the preponderance of the Orange stadholder was challenged by the ranking local official of the most important province, the grand pensionary of Holland. In the first quarter of the century the grand pensionary, Jan van Olden Barneveldt (1547-1619), who was also the organizer of the East India Company, dominated Dutch politics until he was executed because of his support for Arminian doctrines of free will against Calvinist predestination. The grand pensionary, Jan De Witt (1625-1672), an actuarial expert, ran the republic until he was lynched by a mob when the soldiers of Louis XIV overran an ill-prepared Holland in the 1670s.

In religion, the Dutch practiced wide toleration. By the middle of the seventeenth century a general theory of toleration was being worked out. The colonial pioneers in the New World, the increasingly broad-minded groups in England, and the liberal Calvinists in Holland felt that religious fanaticism retarded the growth of commerce and of the state. Though there was a marked decline of tolerance by the end of the seventeenth century, the United Provinces generally remained relatively benign toward the Dutch Catholic minority. In particular Johannes Althusius (1557-1638), a Westphalian who was a chief magistrate in the United Provinces from 1604, set forth clear arguments from doctrine, reason, and expediency for permitting relatively free selection of religious worship. He would not tolerate atheists, but he extended his arguments to embrace Jews, who ought to be allowed their synagogues. Althusius was followed by

Baruch Spinoza (1632-1677), a Dutch Jew, who began with the premise that personal liberty was the foundation of civil peace, obedience, and stability in the state, and that on matters of religion all persons must have absolute freedom of conscience. Under the influence of such theorists on the relationship of church and state, Amsterdam in particular became a haven for religious dissenters, and it would be to the Netherlands that the English Puritans came first, before going on to America.

In the Netherlands, the beneficiaries of religious toleration were the large Catholic minority, Jewish refugees from Spain, Portugal, Poland, and Lithuania, and various Protestant dissidents escaping from Calvinist orthodoxy elsewhere on the continent: Lutherans, Anabaptists, and in time even Arminians. As the southern Netherlands (present-day Belgium) became rigorously Catholic under Philip II and his successors, Calvinist refugees from the south also added to the vigor and commercial growth of the north. Dutch freedom made Holland a major publishing center of works in French and English and carried Dutch universities, especially that at Leiden, to the top of the European learned world.

The style of Dutch civilization in its great age was solid, reasonable, sober, but far from colorless, and by no means puritanical in any ascetic sense. This little nation, through intelligence, hard work, hard trading, and adventurous exploration—and exploitation—overseas, won a high place in the world. But by 1700 the great days of the Dutch republic were ending, as it was eclipsed by its larger and more powerful neighbors: Britain, France, and Prussia. Like the Swedes, who won a brief supremacy in the Baltic at about the same time, the Dutch did not have the resources at home to be a great power abroad. Though at times competitors with the English, Dutch fate was linked to Tudor policy, and the interchange between the countries—in diplomatic judgment, in trade, in technology, in manpower, even in artists—was close and would persist to the present day.

V GERMANY AND THE THIRTY YEARS' WAR

Like the great wars of the sixteenth century, the Thirty Years' War of 1618-1648 was in part a conflict over religion, and like them it had a Hapsburg focus. This time, however, the focus was more on the Austrian than the Spanish Hapsburgs, and so most of the fighting took place in Germany. While the Hapsburg emperor, Ferdinand II (1619-1637), did not aspire to universal control, he did make the last serious political and military effort to unify Germany under Catholic rule. The Thirty Years' War began as a conflict between Catholics and Protestants; it ended as an almost purely political struggle to reduce the power of the Hapsburgs in favor of France and Sweden. Though the physical devastation of war, which was exceptional even by the standards of the times, was limited to certain areas in central Europe, the war finally involved most of the European powers and their colonies. It was, in the context of the times, the first "world war," and one of exceptional political and religious complexity.

The Peace of Augsburg in 1555 did not bring complete religious peace to Germany. It did not recognize Calvinism, to say nothing of the more radical Protestant sects, and it did not settle the problem of ecclesiastical reservations. On this issue, imperial decree stated that if a Catholic prelate was converted to Protestantism, the property formerly under his control should remain in Catholic hands. But this proclamation had not been formally negotiated with the Protestants, who greatly resented it.

By the opening of the seventeenth century, the religious situation in Germany was becoming increasingly unsettled. Calvinism had spread rapidly since 1555; Calvinist princes sponsored active missions in both Lutheran and Catholic regions, and they also banded to-

The Hanging, by Jacques Callot (1592-1635), who developed etching to virtuoso heights, is taken from his series *The Miseries of War,* which emphasized the savagery of the Thirty Years' War.

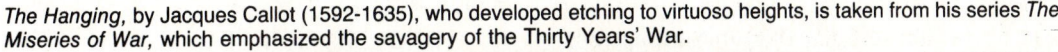

gether in the Protestant Union (1608). This led Catholic German states to form the rival Catholic League (1609). More than religion was involved. Both the Union and the League also had political ambitions, representing the interests of German particularism—that is, of the individual states—against those of the Holy Roman Empire, even though the Catholic League and its leader, Maximilian, duke of Bavaria, were eventually to ally with the emperor Ferdinand.

The German religious situation concerned the Spanish Hapsburgs as well as the Austrians. After the Dutch revolt, the Spaniards wanted to stabilize a line of communications between their Belgian and Italian lands traversing the Rhine valley and the Alps—the so-called Spanish Road to Flanders. The Dutch and the French both wanted to thwart Spanish plans for securing this overland route. The French Bourbons did not relish being encircled by Hapsburg territory any more than their Valois predecessors had. A major physical obstacle blocking Spanish communications was the Palatinate, a rich area in the Rhineland ruled by a Calvinist prince, the Elector Palatine.

The Struggle over Bohemia and the Palatinate, 1618-1625

In 1618 the Elector Palatine Frederick V, who was married to the daughter of James I of England, also headed the Protestant Union. Frederick hoped to break the Catholic hold on the office of emperor upon the death of the incumbent, the emperor Matthias (1612-1619), who was old and childless. The electors of Saxony and Brandenburg were also Protestants. If there could be four Protestant electors instead of three when the emperor died, the majority could then install a Protestant. Because three electors were Catholic archbishops, the only way to elect an additional Protestant was to oust the one lay Catholic elector, the king of Bohemia—a position filled in name by the emperor and in practice by his heir, Ferdinand, who was styled "king-elect."

Bohemia, today a part of Czechoslovakia, was then a Hapsburg crown land; its Czech inhabitants wanted local independence from the rule of both Germans and of Vienna. Some Czechs expressed their national defiance of the Germans by following the faith that John Hus had taught them two centuries earlier, called *Utraquism* (from the Latin for both) because it gave the laity communion in both bread and wine. While Utraquists, Lutherans, and Calvinists were all tolerated in Bohemia, Catholicism was the official state religion. The prospect of Ferdinand becoming king of Bohemia and then emperor, with the added obligations of religious orthodoxy this would force upon him, alarmed Czech Protestants. When Protestant leaders opposing the erosion of Czech religious liberties were arrested, a revolt broke out, beginning with the "defenestration of Prague" (May 23, 1618), in which two Catholic imperial governors were thrown out of a window into a courtyard seventy feet below. Landing on a pile of dung, they escaped with their lives.

The Czech rebels offered the crown of Bohemia to Frederick of the Palatinate, as he had hoped. Frederick went off to Prague without insuring the defense of his home territories in the Rhineland, which the Spaniards occupied in 1620. Meantime, Catholics in Bohemia, Spain, and Flanders rallied against the Czech rebels with money and men. On the death of the emperor Matthias in 1619, the imperial electors duly chose the Catholic Hapsburg Ferdinand II as his successor. Maximilian of Bavaria, head of the Catholic League, supported Ferdinand's cause in Bohemia in return for a promise of receiving Frederick's electoral vote. The Lutheran elector of Saxony also supported Ferdinand. Both the Protestant Union and England remained neutral.

In Bohemia, Maximilian and the Catholic forces won the battle of the White Mountain (1620). Derisively nicknamed the "winter king" because of his brief tenure, Frederick now fled, and Ferdinand made the Bohemian throne hereditary in his own family. He also abolished toleration of Czech Utraquists and Calvinists, but granted it temporarily to Lutherans because of his obligations to the elector of Saxony. He executed the leaders of the rebellion, confiscated their lands, and sanctioned destruction of Protestantism in Bohemia.

The continued presence of Spanish forces in the Palatinate, however, had upset the balance of power. The Lutheran king of Denmark, Christian IV (r. 1588-1648), feared that the Hapsburgs would move north toward the Baltic; the French faced a new Hapsburg encirclement; the Dutch were threatened by an immediate Spanish attack. The Dutch therefore made an alliance with Christian IV, and another with the fugitive Frederick, agreeing to subsidize his attempt to reconquer the Palatinate. When fighting resumed, Frederick was defeated again, whereupon the emperor Ferdinand transferred the Palatine electorate to Maximilian of Bavaria (1625).

In France, meantime, Cardinal Richelieu, chief minister of Louis XIII (1610-1643), recognized the Hapsburg danger and took steps to counter it. He was ready to arrange a dynastic marriage between the future Charles I of England and Louis XIII's sister, Henrietta Maria, and to make an alliance with other Protestants: Frederick, the Dutch, Christian IV, and Gustavus Adolphus, the Lutheran king of Sweden. By the summer of 1624 the new coalition was taking shape, when it was shattered by Spanish victories in Holland and by the unwillingness of Gustavus to serve under the Danes, traditional enemies of the Swedes. Christian IV thus had to defend the Protestant cause alone.

Intervention by Denmark and Sweden, 1625-1635

A vigorous and ambitious monarch, King Christian IV had taken full advantage of the increased authority that Lutheranism gave to royalty. When he intervened in the war, he sought not only to defend his coreligionists but also to extend Danish political and economic power over northern Germany. To check the Danish invasion, the

German Catholics enlisted the help of the private army of Albert of Wallenstein (1583-1634). Wallenstein recruited and paid an army that lived off the land, sometimes even at the expense of Catholic and imperial sympathizers. He had bought huge tracts of Bohemian real estate confiscated from Czech rebels and was in essence a German condottiere, a private citizen seeking to become a ruling prince, perhaps even emperor of a rejuvenated Germany. Though he never came close to success, his army was a major factor in the war at its most critical period. Together with the forces of the Catholic League, Wallenstein's army defeated the Danes and invaded Denmark.

Then, at the height of the imperial and Catholic success, the emperor Ferdinand and his advisers overreached themselves. In the Edict of Restitution (1629) they attempted a one-sided resolution of the long-vexing question of ecclesiastical reservation by demanding the restoration of all clerical estates that had passed from Catholic to Lutheran hands since 1551, three generations earlier. The Edict also affirmed the Augsburg exclusion of Calvinists and radical Protestants from toleration. The Treaty of Lübeck, two months later, allowed Christian IV to recover his Danish lands but exacted from him a promise not to intervene again in Germany. This seemed to those concerned with maintaining the balance of power a sign that Hapsburg power was actually spreading to the Baltic, a region thoroughly Protestant and hitherto only on the margin of imperial control.

Furthermore, Ferdinand's heavy-handedness contrasted with Cardinal Richelieu's handling of the Huguenots at the seige of their stronghold, La Rochelle, which ended in 1628. There, after the Protestant residents had been reduced to eating first their carriage horses and then the leather harnesses, the city had fallen, and despite the unprecedented length and ferocity of the seige and the wide acceptance that fallen cities could be sacked, the royal army was kept under absolute discipline and food was provided to the starving inhabitants of the city. Richelieu acted throughout with magnanimity, making it clear that while La Rochelle must abandon its political independence, and every church be returned to the Catholics, the price of heresy need not be paid in blood. What concerned Richelieu was maintaining a balance of power. The Hapsburgs were now pressing into the Baltic, well beyond their spheres of influence, and although fellow Catholics, they were trespassers who ought to be forced to withdraw.

The more the emperor Ferdinand became indebted to the ambitious Wallenstein, the less he could control him. Wallenstein planned to found a new Baltic trading company with the remnants of the Hanseatic League, and by opening the Baltic to the Spaniards make possible a complete victory over the Dutch. Thus, when Ferdinand asked him for troops to use in Italy against the French, Wallenstein, intent on his northern plans, refused; and he persisted in such brutal execution of the Edict of Restitution and such wholesale extortion of supplies from Catholics that he lost much of his support. Ferdinand dismissed Wallenstein, leaving the imperial forces under the command of the count von Tilly and of Maximilian of Bavaria, who had been alarmed by Wallenstein's activities and was placated by his departure. If Ferdinand had also placated the Protestants by revoking the Edict of Restitution, peace might have been possible. But he failed to do so, and the war was resumed with Gustavus Adolphus as the Protestant champion.

Called the Lion of the North, Gustavus Adolphus (r. 1611-1632) was a much stronger champion than Christian of Denmark had been. Like Christian, he had ambitions for political control over northern Germany, and he hoped that Sweden might assume the old Hanseatic economic leadership. A Lutheran but tolerant of Calvinists, Gustavus brought a large well-disciplined army equipped with hymn books and added to it all the recruits, even prisoners, that he could induce to join him. Sharing the hardships of his troops, he usually restrained them from plunder. Richelieu agreed to subsidize his forces, and Gustavus agreed not to fight against Maximilian and to guarantee freedom of worship for Catholics. The Protestant electors of Brandenburg and Saxony denounced the Edict of Restitution and mobilized, both to revive the Protestant cause and to protect the Germans against the Swedes.

German Protestant hesitation ended after a Catholic victory that probably did more to harm the Catholic cause than a defeat—the fall and sack of Magdeburg, a great symbol of the Protestant cause. Stormed by the imperialists in May 1631, it was almost wholly destroyed by fire and pillage. The imperial general Pappenheim, who commanded at the storming of the walls, estimated that twenty thousand people were killed. Each side sought to blame the sack on the other and used the printing press to enlist public opinion in its cause throughout Europe. The Protestants accused the imperial commander-in-chief, Tilly, of planning the destruction of the city and its inhabitants—an accusation from which most historians absolve him, for the imperial troops clearly got out of hand. The Catholics countered by accusing the Protestants of setting the fires themselves as a scorched-earth tactic. But in the long run, as the outpourings of the press took effect, the Protestant cause was strengthened.

The Protestant electors of Brandenburg and Saxony now allied themselves with Gustavus. In September 1631 Gustavus defeated Tilly. Combined with a defeat of the Spaniards off the Dutch coast, this turned the tide against the Hapsburgs. The Saxons invaded Bohemia and recaptured Prague in the name of Frederick of the Palatinate, while Gustavus invaded the Catholic lands of south-central Germany, achieving an alliance of many princes and free cities. In the crisis, Ferdinand turned again to Wallenstein.

Gustavus had been more successful than Richelieu, his sponsor, had expected—indeed too successful, since not only the Hapsburgs, but Maximilian and the Catholic League, still friends of France, were now suffering at the hands of the Swedes. Gustavus was planning to reorganize all Germany, to unite the Lutheran and Calvinist churches, and to become emperor—aims opposed by all

The seige of Magdeburg in 1631.

the German princes, Catholic and Protestant alike. But the strength of Gustavus's position declined. In the face of his ambitions, his allies proved untrustworthy, and his enemies, Maximilian and Wallenstein, drew together. In November 1632 the Swedes defeated Wallenstein at Lützen, but Gustavus Adolphus was killed.

Peace might now have been possible, yet the fighting and the plague, famine, and death accompanying it continued. The pope wanted peace. Richelieu preferred war to further advance French aims in the Rhineland; the Swedes needed to protect their heavy investment and come out of the fighting with some territory; the Spaniards hoped that Gustavus's death meant that the Hapsburg cause could be saved and the Dutch at least defeated. Gustavus's chancellor, Axel Oxenstierna (1583-1654), an able diplomat, was recognized by the German Protestants in 1633 as chief of the Protestant cause.

As Wallenstein negotiated with the enemies of the Empire, hoping the French would recognize him as king of Bohemia, his army began to fade away, and he was again dismissed by the emperor Ferdinand. In February 1634 an English mercenary in the imperial service murdered Wallenstein and won an imperial reward. In September 1634 the forces of Ferdinand defeated the Protestants, thereby lessening the influence of Sweden and paradoxically making Cardinal Richelieu the chief strategist for the Protestant cause, which was now also the Bourbon cause.

The Hapsburg-Bourbon Conflict, 1635-1648

The remainder of the Thirty Years' War was a Hapsburg-Bourbon conflict, a sequel to the Hapsburg-Valois wars. The Protestant commander had to promise future toleration for Catholicism in Germany, and to undertake to fight on indefinitely in exchange for a guarantee of French men and money. The original religious character of the war became transformed into a dynastic and political struggle between emerging national identities. The armies on both sides were a mixture of men from every nationality in Europe; they fought as professional soldiers, changing sides frequently and taking their women and children with them everywhere. As these armies ranged across central Europe, the land was laid waste in their wake.

In 1635 the emperor Ferdinand at last relinquished the Edict of Restitution and made a compromise peace with the Protestant elector of Saxony. Most of the other Lutheran princes signed also. Alarmed by the imperial gains and by Spanish renewed activity in the Low Countries, Richelieu made new arrangements with Oxenstierna for Germany and a new alliance with the Dutch. No longer confining himself to the role of subsidizer, he openly declared war on Spain. The war would go on, though the only German allies the French and Swedes still had were a few Calvinist princes.

A great Dutch naval victory over Spain in the battle of

the Downs in 1639 ended the power of the Spanish navy, which had been declining for years. Spanish strength was further sapped by the unrest in Catalonia and by a revolt in Portugal. Preoccupied by Catalonia, the Spanish allowed the election of John of Braganza (r. 1640-1656), a dynasty that would reign until 1910. Nor did the death of Richelieu (1642) and of Louis XIII (1643) alter French policy. A few days after the death of Louis, the French defeated the Spaniards so thoroughly at Rocroi that Spain was permanently removed from effective competition for European hegemony. Another factor making for a negotiated settlement of the war was the accession of the peace-loving Christina, daughter of Gustavus Adolphus, as Swedish queen in 1644. What had begun as religious wars were, by now, basically dynastic wars, much like those of Charles V and Francis I.

Peace conferences were already under way in Westphalia—between Hapsburgs and Swedes at Osnabrück and between Hapsburgs and French nearby at Münster. The problems to be settled were many and delicate, and the differences between the allies that had been unimportant during open warfare proved critical when it came to negotiating a religious settlement. The conferences dragged on for several years while fighting and destruction continued. The Dutch made a separate peace with the Spaniards and pulled out of the French alliance after they learned of secret French negotiations with Spain that were hostile to their interests. French victories forced the wavering emperor Ferdinand III (r. 1637-1657) to agree to the terms that had been so painstakingly hammered out, and on October 24, 1648, the Peace of Westphalia put an end to the Thirty Years' War.

The Peace of Westphalia, 1648

In religion, the terms of the peace extended the Augsburg settlement to Calvinists as well as to Lutherans and Catholics. Princes could still "determine" the faith of their subjects, but the right of dissidents to emigrate was recognized. In most of Protestant Germany multiplicity of sects was in fact accepted. On the question of ecclesiastical reservation, 1624 was designated by compromise as the base year for establishing the status of church property. For Protestants this was a great advance over the Edict of Restitution, since states forcibly converted to Catholicism during the war won the right to revert to Protestantism. For Protestants in Hapsburg territories, however, there was no toleration.

Territorially, though some of the separate German states came out well, Germany itself was a victim. France secured part of Alsace and sovereignty over the bishoprics of Metz, Toul, and Verdun—all on the western margins of the Holy Roman Empire. Sweden received much of Pomerania, along the Baltic shore of Germany, plus three votes in the German Diet and a large cash indemnity to pay the one hundred thousand troops (chiefly non-Swedish mercenaries) still under the Swedish flag. As recompense for the loss of Pomerania, Brandenburg received the archbishopric of Magdeburg and several other bishoprics. The family of Maximilian of Bavaria kept the electoral vote of the Palatinate and a part of its territory; the rest was returned to the son of Frederick, who was restored as an elector, thus raising the total number of electors to eight.

German particularism gained, as the individual German states secured the right to conduct their own foreign affairs, making treaties among themselves and with foreign powers if these were not directed against the emperor. This principle of *Landeshoheit* was a face-saver for the Hapsburgs, for the fact that the constituent states now had their own foreign services, their own armies, their own finances—three signs of independent sovereignty—showed that the Holy Roman Empire of the German nation was no longer a viable political entity. The Westphalian settlement also formally recognized the independence of the Dutch republic, already independent for over half a century, and of the Swiss confederation, the nucleus of which had broken away from Hapsburg control during the later Middle Ages.

For more than two centuries after 1648, the Thirty Years' War was blamed for everything that later went wrong in Germany. The economic decline of Germany had begun well before the war started in 1618, and, though great, the figures of deaths and destruction recorded in contemporary chronicles were inflated and are highly unreliable. Yet even when allowance is made for such exaggerations, scholars estimate that the German population declined from about twenty-one million in 1618 to less than thirteen and a half million in 1648. Some historians also trace to this destructive war aspects of modern Germany that they believe have made it a disturbing influence in the modern world. They discern a national sense of inferiority heightened by the delayed achievement of national unity, a lack of slow ripening in self-government that a more orderly growth in early modern times might have encouraged, a too strong need for authority, security, and obedience, fostered by the anarchic conditions of the seventeenth century. These are dangerously broad generalizations that are at most suggestive; they can, of course, by no means be proved, and like all generalizations based on the idea of "national character," they have also been used to score propaganda points in subsequent conflicts.

Certainly, the final outcome of the war raised almost as many problems as it solved. It did not end hostilities between two of the chief belligerents, France and Spain, who continued to fight for another eleven years, until the Treaty of the Pyrenees in 1659. The Peace of Westphalia satisfied neither the pope, who denounced it, nor many Protestants, who felt betrayed by it. Politically, the fresh successes of German particularism limited the Hapsburgs' direct power in Germany to their family lands and enabled such states as Bavaria, Saxony, and above all, Brandenburg-Prussia to move to the fore in German affairs. Non-Austrian Germans also harbored bitter resentment against the Hapsburgs for having fought this most terrible of dynastic and religious wars to protect

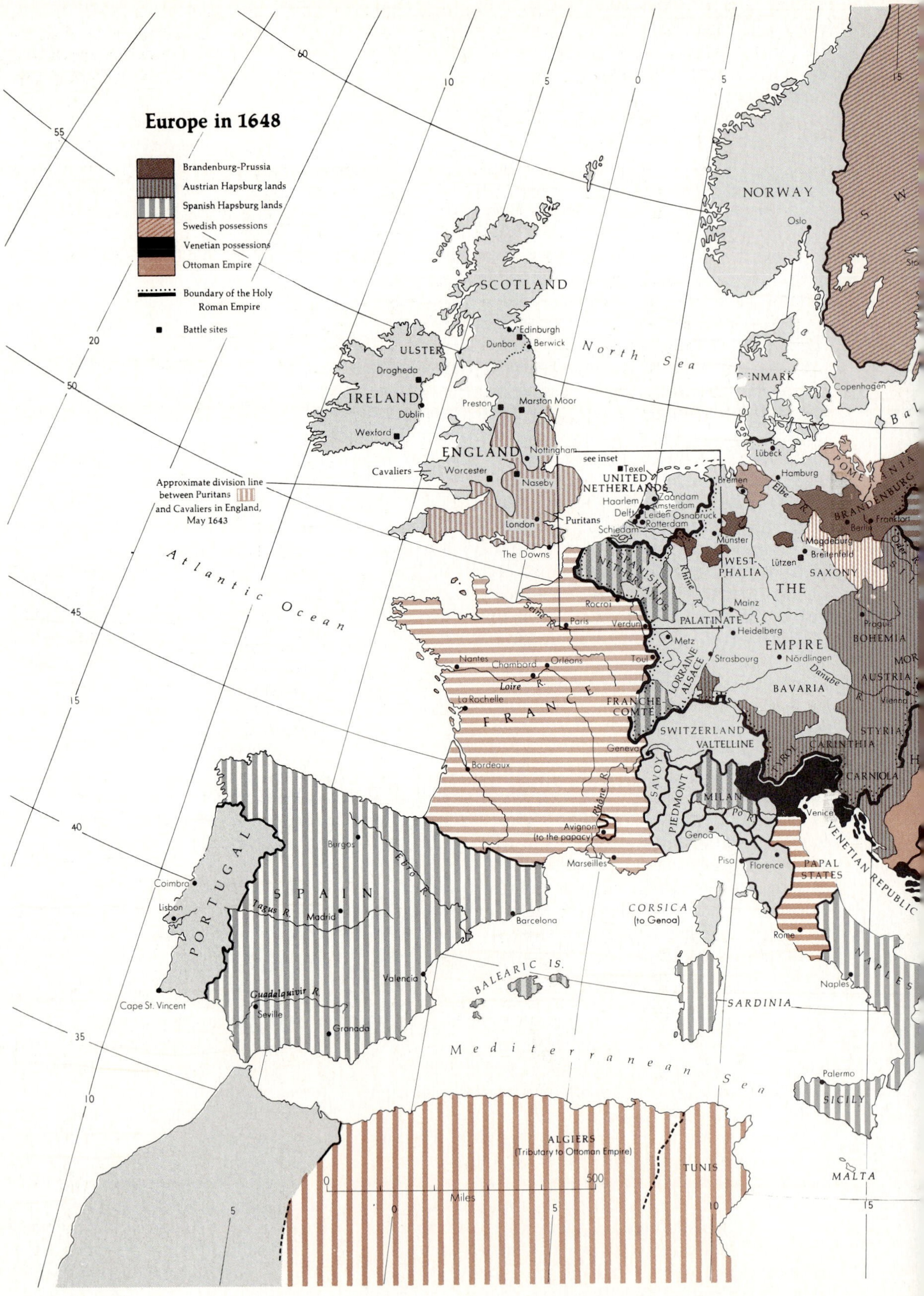
Europe in 1648
Brandenburg-Prussia
Austrian Hapsburg lands
Spanish Hapsburg lands
Swedish possessions
Venetian possessions
Ottoman Empire
Boundary of the Holy Roman Empire
Battle sites
Approximate division line between Puritans and Cavaliers in England, May 1643
NORWAY
Oslo
SCOTLAND
Edinburgh
Dunbar
Berwick
North Sea
ULSTER
Drogheda
IRELAND
Dublin
Wexford
DENMARK
Copenhagen
Preston
Marston Moor
ENGLAND
Nottingham
Cavaliers
Worcester
Naseby
London
Puritans
The Downs
see inset
Texel
UNITED NETHERLANDS
Zaandam
Amsterdam
Haarlem
Delft
Leiden
Osnabrück
Schiedam
Rotterdam
Lübeck
Hamburg
Bremen
Elbe R.
POMERANIA
BRANDENBURG
Berlin
Frankfort
Munster
Magdeburg
Breitenfeld
Lützen
WESTPHALIA
SAXONY
SPANISH NETHERLANDS
Rhine R.
THE
Atlantic Ocean
Rocroi
Mainz
Seine R.
Paris
Verdun
PALATINATE
Heidelberg
Metz
EMPIRE
Prague
BOHEMIA
Toul
LORRAINE
ALSACE
Strasbourg
Nördlingen
Danube R.
AUSTRIA
Vienna
Nantes
Chambord
Orléans
Loire R.
BAVARIA
La Rochelle
FRANCE
FRANCHE-COMTÉ
SWITZERLAND
Geneva
VALTELLINE
TYROL
CARINTHIA
STYRIA
CARNIOLA
Bordeaux
SAVOY
PIEDMONT
MILAN
Po R.
Venice
Rhône R.
Avignon
(to the papacy)
Genoa
VENETIAN REPUBLIC
Burgos
Ebro R.
Marseilles
Pisa
Florence
PAPAL STATES
Coimbra
PORTUGAL
SPAIN
Lisbon
Tagus R.
Madrid
Barcelona
CORSICA
(to Genoa)
Rome
NAPLES
Valencia
BALEARIC IS.
Naples
Guadalquivir R.
Cape St. Vincent
Seville
SARDINIA
Granada
Mediterranean Sea
Palermo
SICILY
ALGIERS
(Tributary to Ottoman Empire)
TUNIS
MALTA
0
500
Miles

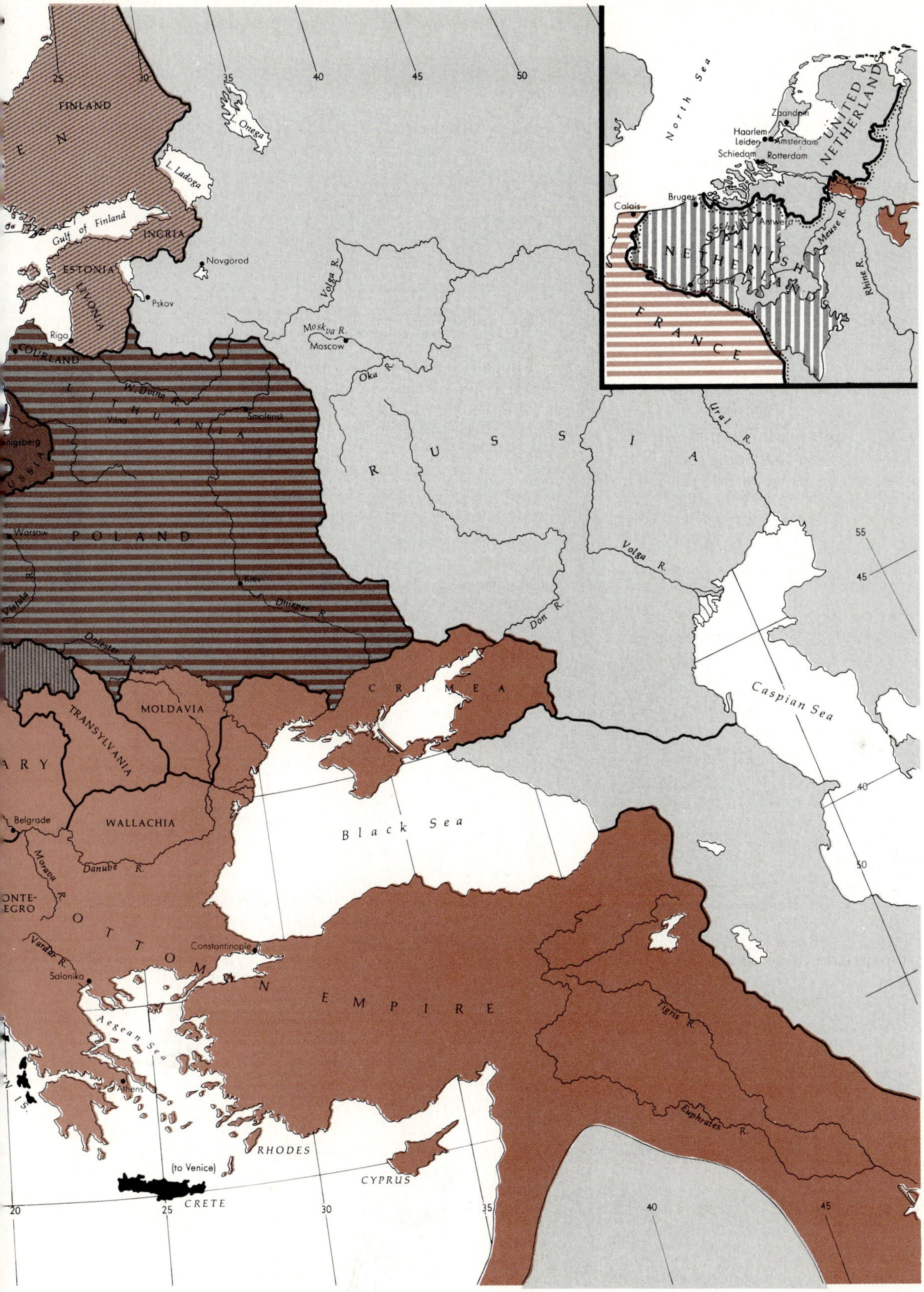

FINLAND
L. Onega
L. Ladoga
Gulf of Finland
INGRIA
ESTONIA
LIVONIA
Novgorod
Pskov
Riga
COURLAND
Volga R.
Moskva R.
Moscow
Oka R.
W. Dvina R.
LITHUANIA
Vilna
Smolensk
RUSSIA
Ural R.
POLAND
Warsaw
Vistula R.
Kiev
Dnieper R.
Dniester R.
Don R.
Volga R.
Caspian Sea
CRIMEA
MOLDAVIA
TRANSYLVANIA
WALLACHIA
Belgrade
Danube R.
Morava R.
Black Sea
OTTOMAN EMPIRE
Constantinople
Vardar R.
Salonika
Aegean Sea
Athens
Tigris R.
Euphrates R.
RHODES
(to Venice)
CRETE
CYPRUS
North Sea
UNITED NETHERLANDS
Zaandam
Haarlem
Leiden
Amsterdam
Schiedam
Rotterdam
Bruges
Calais
Antwerp
Scheldt R.
SPANISH NETHERLANDS
Cambrai
Meuse R.
Rhine R.
FRANCE

family interests. And it was a most terrible war, not just because of its length, but because of its savage character and the large armies involved. The Swedish force alone numbered two hundred thousand at its peak and was the largest to be put in the field since Roman days. Despite the enormous loss of life, however, the war made little change in the social hierarchy of Germany. Once the fighting was over, the nobility often succeeded in forcing the peasants back onto the land by denying them the right to leave their village or engage in home industry.

One can appreciate why several modern historians have pronounced the Thirty Years' War a crucial event in the development of a "crisis" in seventeenth-century Europe that was extensive enough in itself to constitute a unifying theme, as the Renaissance had been for an earlier time. Whether the problems stemming from the Thirty Years' War induced, prolonged, or merely revealed a crisis in European societies, there can be no question that it made Europeans aware of the need for stability in matters of state and concerned with issues that could create the stability and security they lacked.

VI SCIENCE AND RELIGION

During the long sixteenth century and deep into the seventeenth, a slow transition from societies based on religious certainties to societies derived from secular concerns was taking place throughout western Europe. The pace was uneven; it differed markedly from place to place, and for most people religion remained at the root of human concern, since salvation was still the desired end of life. But religion was receding from the foreground toward the background, and security and stability seemed to be a matter for the state rather than the church. The long religious wars had discouraged many and repulsed some; the general weakness of church institutions in the face of the rising state system made it clear where a person's first source of protection lay, at least in this life. The general compatibility between Protestantism and absolutism in politics and the more specific compatibility between Calvinism and commerce brought secular issues further into the foreground. Wars and monarchies that had turned upon religious issues had by 1648 been settled largely in dynastic, military, and secular terms.

Contemporary with these developments was the rising influence of philosophers and writers whose primary concerns were related to science. Indeed, though science had always been a separate branch of knowledge, it was now becoming a profession; and while no conflict necessarily existed between science and religion, the scientific revolution launched by the Italian Galileo, the Englishman Newton, the Frenchmen Descartes and Pascal, and others, moved steadily in a secular direction. As the twentieth-century philosopher of science Alfred North Whitehead remarked, since the time of Galileo and Newton we "have been living upon the accumulated capital of ideas provided . . . by the genius of the seventeenth century."*

The Scientific Revolution

A major role in the cultivation of a new scientific attitude was taken by the English thinker and politician Francis Bacon (1561-1626). Though not himself a successful practitioner of science, Bacon was a tireless proponent of the need to observe and to accumulate data. By relying on "the empirical faculty," which learns from experience, Bacon was promoting what he called induction, which proceeds from the particular observed phenomenon to the general conclusion to be drawn. By contrast, deduction, the medieval mode of reasoning still in fashion in Bacon's day, proceeds from the general expectation to the particular example as proof. Deduction is not necessarily antiscientific, for it sometimes produces the guesses that advance theoretical science. What Bacon particularly attacked was the inclination of deductive reason to accept general opinions as "settled and immovable." Ranking high among such established opinions were the views of the universe associated with two authorities of antiquity, Aristotle and Ptolemy. Bacon's contemporary, Galileo Galilei (1564-1642), ridiculed blind accceptance of ancient authorities and thereby became embroiled with the church.

Galileo was also one of many—some famous, some unknown even then or now forgotten—who contributed to the invention of new instruments that permitted the more exact measurements and more detailed observations needed by inductive science. It is probable, for example, that Dutch glassmakers first put two lenses together and discovered that they could thus obtain greater magnification; by 1610 Galileo was using the new device in the form of a telescope to study the heavens. Later in the century two Dutchmen employed it in the form of a microscope—Jan Swammerdam (1637-1680) to analyze blood (he probably discovered red corpuscles), and Anthony Van Leeuwenhoek (1632-1723) to view and describe protozoa and bacteria. Working from the experiments of Galileo, other technicians developed such instruments of measurement as the thermometer and the barometer. Using the barometer, the French mathematician Blaise Pascal (1623-1662) proved that air pressure diminished with altitude; from this he went on to counter the old adage, "Nature abhors a vacuum," by showing that a vacuum is possible.

King Charles II of England roared with laughter on being told that members of his Royal Society were weighing the air. Yet the Royal Society for Improving Natural Knowledge, founded in 1662, and its French counterpart, the Académie des Sciences (1666), were important promoters of scientific investigation. The one was a private undertaking, though with a royal charter; the other, sponsored for the greater glory of Louis XIV,

*A.N. Whitehead, *Science and the Modern World* (New York: Signet, 1948), p. 58.

THE EMPIRICAL AND THE RATIONAL FACULTY

In *The Great Instauration* (the word means restoration) Francis Bacon wrote:

For all those who before me have applied themselves to the invention of arts but cast a glance or two upon facts and examples and experience, and straightway proceeded, as if invention were nothing more than an exercise of thought, to invoke their own spirits to give them oracles, I, on the contrary, dwelling purely and constantly among the facts of nature, withdraw my intellect from them no further than may suffice to let the images and rays of natural objects meet in a point, as they do in the sense of vision. . . . And by these means I suppose that I have established for ever a true and lawful marriage between the empirical and the rational faculty, the unkind and ill-starred divorce and separation of which has thrown into confusion all the affairs of the human family.

M.T. McClure, ed., *Bacon: Selections* (New York: Harcourt, 1928), pp. 14-15.

was a governmental institution whose fellows received salaries—and were also ordered not to discuss religion and politics.

An international scientific community arose through the formal exchanges of the corresponding secretaries and the publications of such academies, and also through the extensive private correspondence among members and their acquaintances. Both professionals and aristocrats joined learned societies, and many a gentleman and an occasional lady worked in a private laboratory or observatory. One, Robert Boyle (1627-1691), son of an Irish earl, discovered the law of physics named after him—that under compression the volume of a gas is inversely proportional to the amount of pressure. While many scientists still published in Latin, their discoveries were popularized in books and articles in the vernacular. The publication of these discoveries and the diffusion of scientific argument helped bridge the gap between theory and practice, for it showed scientists where their work related to that of others and helped indicate which problems most needed attention.

Meantime, the basic language of science—mathematics—was taking a great leap forward. In 1585 Simon Stevin (1548-1620), a Fleming, published *The Decimal, Teaching with Unheard-of Ease How to Perform All Calculations Necessary among Men by Whole Numbers without Fractions.* Another great timesaver was devised by the Scot John Napier (1550-1617) with his *Marvelous Rule of Logarithms* (1616), which shortened the laborious processes of multiplying, dividing, and finding square roots. René Descartes (1596-1650) worked out analytical geometry, which brought geometry and algebra together through the Cartesian coordinates, as in the plotting of an equation on a graph. The mathematical achievements of the century culminated in a method for dealing with variables and probabilities. Pascal made a beginning with studies of games of chance, and Dutch insurance actuaries devised tables to estimate the life expectancy of their clients. The Englishman Sir Isaac Newton (1642-1727) and the German baron Gottfried Whilhelm von Leibniz (1646-1716) invented calculus, apparently quite independently of each other. Without Cartesian geometry and calculus, Newton could never have made the calculations supporting his revolutionary hypotheses in astronomy and physics.

In astronomy the heliocentric theory advanced by Copernicus in the sixteenth century proved to be only a beginning. It raised many difficulties, notably when observation of planetary orbits did not confirm Copernicus' belief that the planets revolved about the sun in circular paths. The German Johannes Kepler (1571-1630) proved mathematically that the orbits were in fact elliptical. Then Galileo's telescope revealed the existence of spots on the sun, rings around Saturn, and moonlike satellites around Jupiter. All this evidence led Galileo to publish a book in 1632 defending the heliocentric concept and ridiculing supporters of the traditional geocentric (earth-centered) theory. But the church, headed by traditionalists, brought Galileo before the Inquisition, which placed his book on the *Index* of prohibited works and sentenced him to perpetual house arrest. Despite a public recantation, Galileo is reported to have had the last word—"And yet it does move"—the Earth is not stationary, as the church insists, but a planet behaving like other planets.

An even more celebrated story recounts Galileo's experiment of dropping balls of different weights from the Leaning Tower of Pisa to test Aristotle's theory that objects fall at velocities proportional to their weight. While the story itself may not be true, Galileo did disprove Aristotle. Galileo's studies of projectiles, pendulums, and falling and rolling bodies helped establish modern ideas of acceleration and inertia, which Newton later formulated mathematically.

In 1687 Newton published the laws of motion together with other great discoveries in *Philosophiae Naturalis Principia Mathematica (Mathematical Principles of Natural Philosophy).* He had made many of these findings two decades earlier, when he was still an undergraduate at Cambridge; he was recognized in his later years, gaining a professorship at Cambridge, a knighthood, the presidency of the Royal Society, and the well-paid post of Master of the Mint. But Newton's greatest contribution was the law of gravitation. It followed from his laws of motion, which picture bodies moving not in straightforward fashion of themselves but only in response to forces acting upon them. These forces are at work in the mutual attraction of the sun, the planets, and their satellites, which are thereby held in their orbits. Newton stated the formula that the force of gravitation is proportional to the product of the masses of two bodies attracted one to the other, and inversely proportional to the square of the distance between them. Newton also promoted the development of optics by using a prism to separate sunlight into the colors of the spectrum. He demonstrated that objects only appear to be colored, and that their color is not intrinsic but the result of reflection and absorption of light.

Meanwhile, the mechanistic views of the physicists were invading geology and physiology. In 1600 the English physician William Gilbert (1540-1603) in a study of magnetism suggested that the earth itself was a giant magnet. In 1628 William Harvey (1578-1657), the physician of Charles I, published his demonstration that the human heart is a pump driving the blood around the body through a single circulatory system. Harvey's theory, confirmed a generation later by the discovery through microscopic observation of the capillary connections between arteries and veins, discredited the hypothesis handed down from Galen in classical antiquity that the blood in the arteries moved quite separately from that in the veins. And in 1679 the Italian anatomist Alphonso Borelli (1608-1679) showed that the human arm is a lever and that muscles do mechanical work.

Portrait of Descartes by Frans Hals.

World-Machine and Rationalism

All these investigations in the various sciences tended to undermine the older Aristotelian concept of a thing's being "perfect." Instead of perfect circles, post-Copernican astronomy posited ellipses; instead of bodies moving in straightforward fashion of themselves, Newton pictured bodies responding to forces acting upon them. All these investigations, in short, suggested a new major scientific generalization, a law of uniformity that simplified, explained, and coordinated many separate laws into one general law. Galileo almost made this step but got into trouble with the church. It was Newton who finally drew everything together in the grand mechanical concept that has been called the Newtonian world-machine.

The Newtonian world-machine and the new science of which it was the product had obvious theological and philosophical implications. Natural science of itself does not deal with theology and philosophy; it does not explore human ends or purposes but rather means, and its theories are explanations, not moral justifications. Yet historically the rise of modern science was associated with a definite world view and a system of values for which the best name is probably *rationalism* This is a broad term. It is possible to be both a rationalist and a believer in a supernatural God, like Thomas Aquinas and other medieval schoolmen. In the early modern West, however, rationalism tended to banish God entirely from the universe, or to reduce him to a First Cause that started the world-machine going but then did not interfere with its operation. The new mechanistic interpretation of the universe regarded God not as the incomprehensible Creator and Judge but as the architect of a world-machine whose operations men and women could grasp if only they could apply their reason properly.

The rationalism and materialism engendered by the scientific revolution found a most articulate spokesman in René Descartes. When he was a young man, as his *Discourse on Method* (1637) relates, he resolved to mistrust all authorities, theological or intellectual. His skepticism swept everything aside, until he concluded that there was only one fact that he could not doubt: his own existence. There must be reality in the self that was engaged in the process of thinking and thus of doubting:

MAKING HASTE SLOWLY: RENÉ DESCARTES

Descartes began his *Discourse on Method* with the first principle of all methodology—that progress is best achieved through the careful application of a discipline of thought:

Good sense is, of all things among men, the most equally distributed; for every one thinks himself so abundantly provided with it, that those even who are the most difficult to satisfy in everything else, do not usually desire a larger measure of this quality than they already possess. And in this it is not likely that all are mistaken: the conviction is rather to be held as testifying that the power of judging aright and of distinguishing truth from error, which is properly what is called good sense or reason, is by nature equal in all men; and that the diversity of our opinions, consequently, does not arise from some being endowed with a larger share of reason than others, but solely from this, that we conduct our thoughts along different ways, and do not fix our attention on the same objects. For to be possessed of a vigorous mind is not enough; the prime requisite is rightly to apply it. The greatest minds, as they are capable of the highest excellences, are open likewise to the greatest aberrations; and those who travel very slowly may yet make far greater progress, provided they keep always to the straight road, than those who, while they run, forsake it.

Descartes, *Discourse on Method* (New York: Scribner's, 1928), p. 1.

"Cogito ergo sum" (I think, therefore I am). Building from this one fact, Descartes reconstructed the world until he arrived at God—a deity poles apart from older patriarchal concepts, a supreme geometer whose mathematical orderliness foreshadowed the great engineer of the Newtonian world-machine.

But where Newton would proceed inductively, at least in part, by relying on the data of scientific observations and experiments, Descartes proceeded deductively, ultimately deriving the universe and God from his initial formulation. The world that Descartes reconstructed proved to be two separate worlds—that of mind and soul, on the one hand, and that of body and matter, on the other; this was Cartesian dualism. He claimed competence to deal in detail only with the material world; yet the way in which he dealt with it intimated that it was the only world that counted—witness his boast that, if given matter and space, he could construct the universe himself.

As yet, these scientists were not specialists, for their speculations ranged across all fields of inquiry. But as Ferdinand was initiating his Edict of Restitution and Wallenstein was laying seige to Magdeburg, at least nominally for reasons of religion, men like Descartes were shifting the long-held bases for perceived reality. The scientific revolution of the sixteenth and seventeenth centuries was a decisive turning point in history. It was not the first such "revolution," but it was the one by which science in the twentieth century is still governed. Perhaps more than all other changes of the long durée, it defined the shift to what we recognize as "modern." While most people were not concerned with the work of these scientists, their influence was substantial: on puritanism, on capitalism (and vice versa, for Protestantism and mechanistic science were compatible), on political philosophy, on the literary imagination, in time on both religion and daily life.

To be sure, rationalism had not pervaded daily life by the seventeenth century, which would see the most severe outbreak of the periodic witchcraft madness, nor had it lessened the hardships for the villager or peasant. But the drama inherent in the life of a scientist such as Galileo, a scientist who was not prepared to reject almost any possibility without testing it, marked the conflict between two great powers—science and religion—which carried no flags and were identified with no language (except, perhaps, the once-convenient language of science, Latin) or nationality.

As Francis Bacon wrote in his *Novum Organum* in 1620, two years before the beginning of the Thirty Years' War:

> *"By far the greatest obstacle to the progress of science and to the undertaking of new tasks and provinces therein, is found in this—that men despair and think things impossible. . . . And therefore it is fit that I publish and set forth those conjectures of mine which make hope in this matter reasonable; just as Columbus did, before that wonderful voyage of his across the Atlantic, which he gave the reasons for his conviction that new lands and continents might be discovered besides those which were known before; which reasons, though rejected at first, were afterwards made good by experience, and were the causes and beginnings of great events."**

*As quoted in Franklin Le Van Baumer, ed. *Main Currents of Western Thought* (New Haven: Yale University Press, 1978), p. 287, aphorism XCII.

SUMMARY

By the sixteenth century, changes in political, social, family, and economic structure were underway that marked the beginning of what historians call the modern period. In the fifteenth and sixteenth centuries, the modern state system took shape as well-organized states competed for power in western Europe. With the emergence of Spain, France, and England came the growth of national patriotism. European states developed diplomatic services and professional armies. The first modern navies were also built. Increases in populations, trade, and prices fostered conditions that led to warfare.

Some historians have called the invasion of Italy by Charles VIII of France the "first modern war." The invasion enmeshed France in a long and complex power struggle with the Hapsburgs.

Philip II of Spain (1556-1598), a powerful, hardworking monarch, waged a battle on many fronts: against Protestantism, against France, against the Ottoman Turks, and against his subjects in the Netherlands. The Dutch revolted against Philip's attempt to limit their autonomy and to use the Inquisition against Protestants. During a long, costly war, the northern provinces declared their independence from Spain. When Elizabeth I helped the Dutch, Philip launched an armada to invade England. The destruction of the armada marked a turning point for Spain—a gradual international decline—and for England—an increase in international standing.

In Spain, as elsewhere, the growth of absolutism was marked by persistent struggles against local centers of power. Philip centralized administration and reduced the power of the Cortes, the representative assemblies. Yet Spain failed to establish a sound economic footing for its power. Despite the influx of New World gold bullion, the Spanish economy stagnated, while Philip's wars drained the treasury.

During Spain's Golden Age (1516-1659) Cervantes penned *Don Quixote,* a landmark in literature. In religion, St. Teresa of Avila and St. John of the Cross became important figures to the common people. The paintings of El Greco embodied the ideas of the Catholic Reformation.

In the late sixteenth century France was plunged into civil and religious strife which finally subsided after Henry of Navarre took the throne, the first Bourbon king. By the Edict of Nantes (1598), Henry IV assured the Huguenots of some religious toleration. He tried to improve the economy but did not solve the problem of fiscal stability.

In England, Henry VIII moved cautiously in war and added to the treasury by his seizure of monastic property. Tactful in handling Parliament, which had the power to enact laws, Henry and later Elizabeth I moved against the enemies of England: Spain and the Catholic church. Elizabeth firmly established the Protestant religion in England and scored success in war with Spain.

But she had to concede rights to the House of Commons, foreshadowing the struggle between the Crown and Parliament of the next century. The Tudor period also saw the beginning of the Irish question. In literature, William Shakespeare expressed the exuberance of the Elizabethan Age, a period of significant achievement in music, architecture, and science.

The Thirty Years' War (1618-1648) began as a religious conflict but ended as a political power struggle between France and the Hapsburgs. During the war, armies ravaged the land. The final settlements, negotiated at the peace conferences of Westphalia and Münster, extended the Peace of Augsburg to include Calvinists, made territorial concessions to France, Sweden, and Brandenburg, and recognized the right of individual German states to conduct their own foreign policies.

In the sixteenth and seventeenth centuries, secular concerns replaced religious certainties. Galileo, Newton, Descartes, and Pascal were in the forefront of the scientific revolution. Francis Bacon furthered the new scientific attitude by his reliance on the empirical faculty.

The rise of modern science helped create a new world view known as rationalism—a mechanistic interpretation of the universe that maintained that all things could be understood if people applied their reason. Rationalism would have a profound impact on ways of thinking in Europe.

chapter fourteen

EXPLORATION AND EXPANSION

During the early modern centuries, when Europeans were experiencing the Renaissance and the Reformation and their long aftermath of traumatic conflict, some nations took part in a remarkable expansion that carried European sailors, merchants, missionaries, settlers, and adventurers to almost every quarter of the globe. What Westerners rather parochially called "the known world"—meaning known to them—spread outward at a breathtaking pace, although relatively few Westerners, then or now, realized that non-Western peoples—the Chinese or American Indians, for example—had their own equally valid concept of the "known world." In the age of Homer the known world of the West had encompassed little more than the eastern Mediterranean and its fringes; under Alexander the Great and the Romans it was still centered on the Mediterranean and the western fringes of Asia, with much of the interior of Europe and Africa hazy or blank. Then the explorations of the late Middle Ages launched a continuous process that culminated in rapid advances in Western geographical knowledge.

I EXPLORATION AND EXPANSION

Westerners were not the first people to migrate over vast reaches of water. Even before the Viking voyages in the Atlantic, the Polynesians, for example, had settled remote Pacific islands. But the Polynesians and other early migrants kept neither written records nor significant ties with their places of origin. They were not societies in expansion, but groups of individuals on the move. The expansion of the West was different. From its beginning in ancient Greece and Rome, records were kept, maps were made, and the nucleus always remained in touch with its offshoots.

Modern Western expansion, which began in the midfifteenth century, differed also in four important ways from the expansions that had carried the cultures of the ancient Near East as far as western and northern Europe. First, this modern expansion was much faster and covered more ground. Although some secrets of the Arctic and the Antarctic, some details of the wilder interiors of the world, were not known until the twentieth century, the whole world was broadly revealed to Europeans within the three centuries after 1450—within four long lifetimes. Second, this modern expansion was the first time Western society crossed great oceans. Ancient and medieval Western navigation had clung to the narrow seas and the shorelines; the ancients had even commonly drawn their boats up on land to spend the night. Now Westerners crossed the Atlantic and the Pacific, far from the protecting land for weeks at a time. Third, this expansion carried Westerners well beyond the familiar orbit of relations with Byzantines and Muslims, who were also successors to the cultures of Socrates and Christ, into relations with a bewildering variety of races, creeds, and cultures. Fourth, and of very great importance, Europe possessed a margin of superior material and technological strength that enabled Western society to do what no society had ever done before—extend its influence around the world. An important element of that margin was the possession of firearms; yet firearms could be acquired by non-Europeans, and very soon were.

The strength by which Europeans overcame the world was a compound of technological and economic power plus political and social organization, which permitted superior military enterprise. This material advantage was not applied from a common Western center, but rather by half a dozen competing Western nations, each anxious to cut the others' throats, and each quite willing to arm and organize the local population against its Western competitors. The French in North America armed the indigenous peoples against the British, and the British armed them against the French. Not even the locally powerful Iroquois could maintain themselves against the encroaching technology. In the Far East, the French, British, Portuguese, Dutch, Spanish, and later the Germans and Americans intrigued against one another, and yet not until the early twentieth century did an Asian nation really compete successfully in war and politics with a Western state. So great was the Western advantage that the rivalries of competing powers did not delay the process of expansion as much as stimulate and hasten it.

The motives for expansion were, of course, mixed. Though the power of the new states was at stake, sincerely held beliefs were also being tested. Though often moved by greed, by sheer despair over their lot at home, or by the Renaissance enthusiasm for new things, those who carried out the expansion were also convinced that they were doing God's work, the work of civilization, that they were carrying with them a better way of life. They wished to convert the heathen, to win glory for the church or for a particular Christian state, and to save souls. The acquisition of empire is usually laid to four primary motivations: the human desire for glory, the desire to serve God, the hunger for gold in all its forms, and the strategic need to seize certain areas or resources to achieve the other three ends. While specific empire builders may have held one of these motives uppermost, all were compatible.

Why did those living on the Atlantic coasts of Europe in the second half of the fifteenth century venture out onto an ocean that ancient and medieval mariners had not seriously tried to explore before? So small a matter as the magnetic compass helped make ocean voyages possible. Without the compass, earlier mariners had been helpless, except when clear weather gave them sun or stars as guides. The actual origins of the compass are obscure, but the Chinese were long aware of magnetic polarity, and the compass itself was used in Mediterranean navigation by the end of the Middle Ages. Not only were better instruments and better methods of determining a ship's position at sea available by the fifteenth century, but shipbuilders were constructing vessels that were longer and narrower than the traditional Mediterranean ships and better able to withstand the long swells of the ocean. Technologically, the way was ready for the great explorations.

Moreover, the rising political and economic power of the Atlantic states—Portugal, Spain, France, and England—led their merchants to search for new routes to India, since the old Near Eastern route was controlled by the Ottoman Turks and by the Italians, especially the Venetians and the Genoese. Historians who interpret developments first in terms of economics also suggest that Renaissance Europeans discovered new worlds because the aggressive drives inherent in rising capitalism sent them on their way.

Yet the technology and the politics of the trade routes could only be taken advantage of by persons in the state of mind that sent Columbus out across the unknown ocean—to see with his own eyes what was there, to test his theory that because the earth was round one could travel westward from Europe and reach Asia. The explorations of the Europeans were guided by the new spirit of empirical science. For instance, if they heard about unicorns they would feel impelled to go out and try to find some; their medieval predecessors did not need to see a unicorn to believe in its existence. The new scientific spirit, however, did not immediately banish unicorns, mermaids, and sea serpents. The first reports of newly discovered worlds resulted in a whole new set of wonders, some quite unreal and others merely exaggerated, which the published accounts of travel spread to all Europe.

Nothing makes more clear the consecutive, planned, deliberately scientific nature of these early modern explorations and settlements than the contrast with the sporadic, unplanned, and often mythical nature of earlier oceanic navigations. Tradition is full of tales of these early voyages and of Atlantis, a lost continent now sunk beneath the waves but once inhabited, on which Plato and later commentators remarked. The Phoenicians, the Irish, the Norse, the Welsh, and Breton fishermen had all been credited with the "discovery" of America—discoveries that were never widely reported in the medieval West. Of all these tales of pre-Columbian discovery, that of the Vikings' reaching the North American continent about the end of the tenth century is supported by the firmest evidence. There is no doubt that the Norse reached Iceland and settled it, and that they had outposts in Greenland. Their heroic sagas credit Leif Ericson with reaching a Wineland (or Vinland), which almost certainly was somewhere along the present New England or Canadian coasts. It is quite possible that all during the Middle Ages, more probably toward their close, fishermen from northwest Europe fished the Grand Banks off the coast of Newfoundland and wintered on that great island. Yet even if hundreds of Europeans reached the New World before Columbus, they did not establish a permanent link between the two worlds; they were not explorers supported by a state or a group of merchants expecting a full report, and they were, above all, not urged on by an organized social purpose or scientific expectation.

II EAST BY SEA TO THE INDIES

Prince Henry and the Portuguese

The first of the great names in modern expansion is that of an organizing genius who directed the work of others. Prince Henry of Portugal (1394-1460), known as "the Navigator," was a deeply religious man who may well have been moved above all by a desire to convert the populations of India and the Far East, whose existence had been well known to Westerners since the travels of the Venetian Marco Polo (1254-1324) in the thirteenth century. Indeed, many in the West were convinced that these distant peoples were already Christian, and for true salvation needed only to be brought in direct contact with the Roman Catholic church. One of the great medieval legends told of a Prester (that is, Priest) John, a powerful Christian ruler somewhere out in the East, or perhaps Africa. Prester John was never found, and the Portuguese in India were soon disabused of their notion that the Hindus, since they were not Muslims, must therefore be Christians.

Prince Henry and his associates wanted to promote Portuguese commerce and national power as well as the Christian faith. They hoped to break the North African Arabs' monopoly over the trade in gold from sub-Saharan Africa. They went about their work carefully, sending out frequent, well-equipped expeditions. They were also favored by geography and knew it; the Portuguese referred to Cape St. Vincent as "the end of the world," but on a globe the Cape could equally be "the center." Their vessels discovered Madeira and the Azores, uninhabited islands in the Atlantic where the Portuguese and other Europeans then began to settle, the first about 1420—the conventional date for the beginning of "the age of Discovery." The main thrust southward gradually crept along the harsh desert coast of Africa where the Sahara meets the Atlantic, until in 1445 the Portuguese moved eastward past Cape Verde, where the land did begin to grow greener, thus arousing false hopes that the southernmost point of the continent was near. Whether Henry himself believed that Africa could be circumnavigated with the right technology is not certain, but according to legend the Phoenicians had done it, and Greco-Roman geographers had argued that

Expansion of Europe, 1529

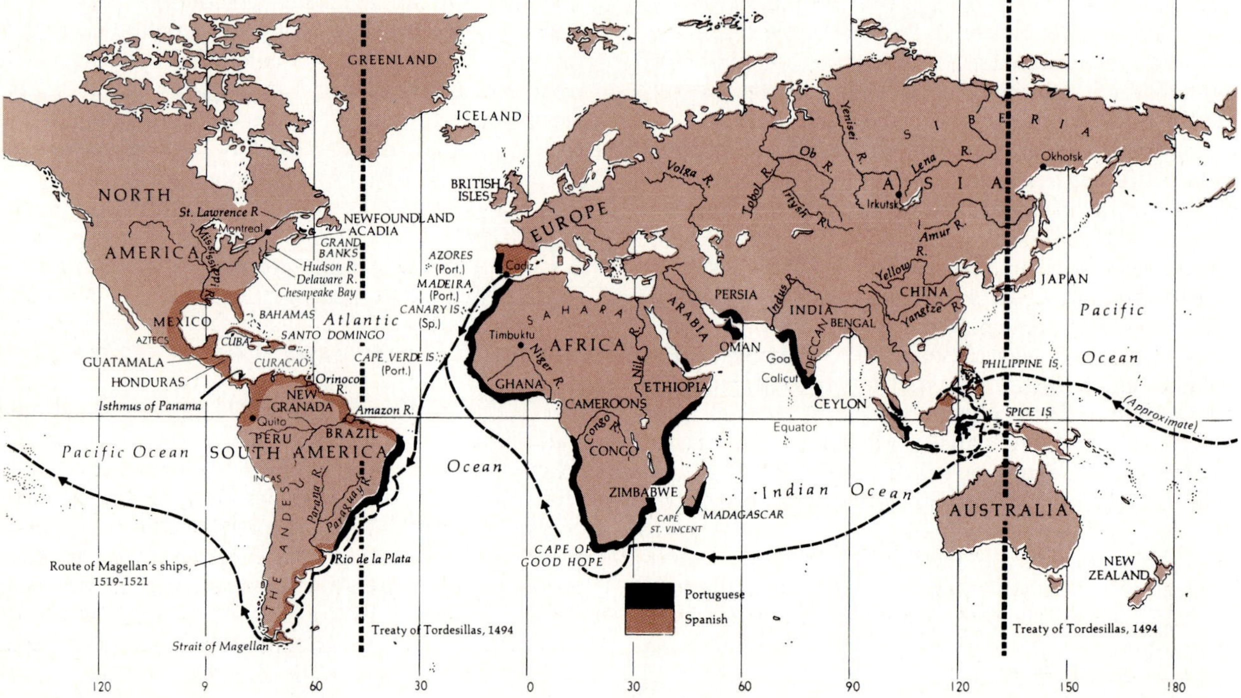

Expansion of Europe, 1715

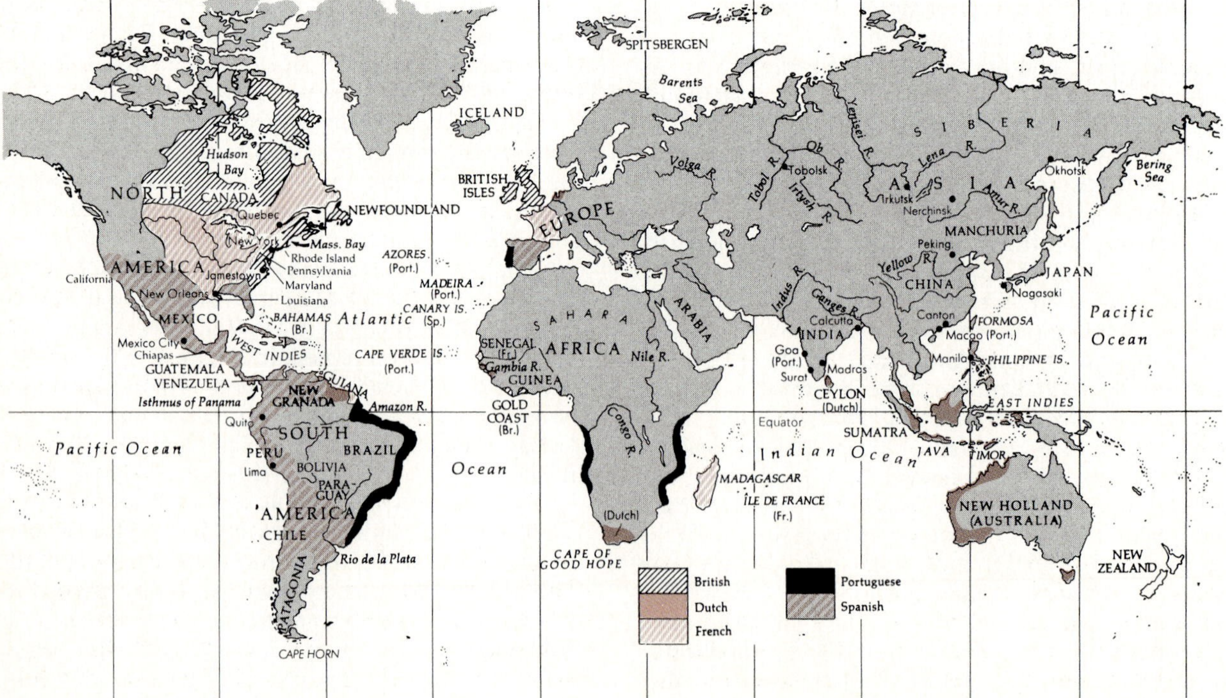

Africa was surrounded by ocean. The risks, they knew, were less from the reported torrid zone through which the ships had to pass, or the Sea of Darkness (said to be too shallow for navigation), or from sea monsters, than from the very real problem that a return voyage was almost impossible against the winds and currents unless a huge arc could be plotted out into the Atlantic, and vessels—adopted from Arab and Mediterranean sailors—could be developed to withstand such waters.

By 1472, after Prince Henry's death, the Portuguese reached the end of the bulge of West Africa at the Cameroons and were disheartened to see that the coast was once more trending southward, no longer eastward. But they kept on, stimulated by royal patronage, and in the next generation two great explorers finished the task. In 1488 Bartholomeu Dias (1450-1550), blown far south by a great storm, turned northeast and found that he had rounded the great cape later called Good Hope. He was followed by Vasco da Gama (c 1460-1524), who set out in 1497 with four ships to reach India and worked northward along the east coast of Africa, coming soon to an area of Arab trading where the route to India was well known. Despite Arab jealousy of the intruder, da Gama secured a pilot and reached the Malabar coast of India at Calicut ten months and fourteen days out from Lisbon. The Portuguese now had an ocean route to the East.

On the next great voyage toward India, the Portuguese made a lucky strike that was to break the Spanish monopoly in South America and ensure that one of the great Latin American states would be Portuguese in language and culture. Pedro Cabral (c 1464-c 1520) started out in 1500 to repeat da Gama's voyage to India. But by now the Portuguese were used to long voyages on the open ocean. Cabral kept boldly southward from the bulge of Africa and then bore westward to make a landfall on the bulge of the South American continent in what is now Brazil. He at once detached a ship to Portugal to announce his discovery. Since the voyages of Columbus were well known to navigators by this time, some geographers think that Cabral set out deliberately to see what he could find south of the route Columbus had taken. Six years previously, by the Treaty of Tordesillas (1494), Spain and Portugal had agreed to partition their newly discovered lands along a north-south line about a thousand miles west of the Azores, so that eastern Brazil, when discovered, fell within the Portuguese sphere.

The main Portuguese push, however, continued toward India and the Far East. Explorers were followed by that other characteristic agent of European expansion, the trader, who by no means worked alone. He was aided and protected by the power of his state, which aimed to set up for its nationals a monopoly of commerce with the newly found lands. The great figure of early Portuguese imperialism was Affonso de Albuquerque (1453-1515), governor of the Indies from 1509 to 1515, under whom the Portuguese founded their capital at Goa in India. From Goa they organized regular trade routes toward southeast Asia and China. By 1557 they had established a base at Macao on the Chinese coast near Canton and had begun to trade with the Japanese. By then they dominated the trade routes, and kings Manuel I (1495-1521) and John III (1521-1557) could take the somewhat inflated title "Lord of the Conquest, Navigation, and Commerce of Ethiopia, India, Arabia, and Persia" (assumed in 1501) seriously.

New Encounters: Africa

The two new worlds thus opened to Europeans were very different both from Europe and from each other. Africa—excluding North Africa, from Morocco to Egypt, which had long been part of the Mediterranean world—was humid, relatively thinly populated, and was thought to be poor by European standards, despite the active trade in gold. India, China, and much of southeast Asia were even then thickly populated, with great wealth accumulated in a few hands, and with much that Europeans wanted in the way of spices, silks, and other luxuries. Africa was temporarily bypassed, though the many coastal stations that the Europeans founded in West Africa soon carried on a flourishing trade in slaves. East Africa had been trading with the Arabs since the first century, especially with Oman, and a slave trade had developed long before the arrival of the Europeans.

The African tribes on the great westward bulge of the continent had already left their mark on history, for they had set up two empires whose names have been revived by present-day African states after gaining their independence. Medieval Ghana controlled a much larger area than its modern namesake until it was overthrown by Muslim invaders from North Africa in the eleventh century. When the Portuguese reached West Africa, parts of the interior were controlled by the empire of Mali, centered at Timbuktu, on the upper Niger River. Caravans organized by North African traders came to Timbuktu to buy gold and slaves and to sell some of the wares from the Mediterranean.

In the interior of central and southern Africa there were politically complex tribal states, especially at Zimbabwe and among the kingdoms of the Kongo, Luba, Lunda, and Kuba. But these cultures were little known to the Europeans, who judged Africa by what they encountered near the coasts, where the societies were much less complex. These cultures were so different from those of Europe that few Europeans made any effort to understand them. Nor did the Europeans, at least in these centuries, do much to undermine these indigenous cultures. Except for the enforced mass migration of slaves, largely to the Americas, and for some trade in ivory and other tropical goods, Africa had for years little effect on Europe. Except for the southern tip of Africa, where the Dutch began settlement in the seventeenth century, Africa south of the Sahara was not directly subject to colonialism until the annexations and partitions of the nineteenth century.

The French explorer René Caillié (1799-1838) was obsessed with the desire to find the fabled city of Timbuktu on the upper Niger River. To do so he learned Arabic and studied Moorish culture. Learning that the Geographical Society of Paris was offering a prize of ten thousand francs to the first European to reach Timbuktu, he raised the money for his expedition. In 1828 he reached his goal, only to find a rather ordinary village of earthen dwellings. This drawing is from Caillié's own manuscript.

India

The India that Europeans reached after sailing around the Africa they ignored had been marginally in touch with Europe for several thousand years. Alexander the Great had campaigned in northern India, and throughout the Middle Ages the Arabs had served as a link in trade and in transmitting such Indian inventions as "Arabic" numerals, which were actually Hindu in origin. In the sixteenth century a direct link was forged between the West and India, never to be loosened. West and East, however, hardly communicated at the higher levels of cultural interchange. The Portuguese were contemptuous of the Indians once they discovered that they were not Christians; and among the Dutch, French, and British who later went to India, this attitude of contempt became set in the racist notion of white superiority. Actually, Western superiority was at bottom a superiority of technology and organization on the battlefield. Even long after the initial European monopoly of firearms had ended, a European army or navy, or a native one trained and commanded by Europeans, could always prevail over a purely local force.

European domination in India was greatly helped by political and military disunity on the subcontinent itself. When the Portuguese reached India, Muslim invaders were consolidating foreign rule that for thousands of years had periodically brought comparative stability to northern India. The Muslim empire was misleadingly called Mogul (Mughal or Mongol), for its rulers were Turks from central Asia and its founder was a descendant of Tamerlane. It had little hold over the regions of southern India where Europeans first established their footholds. Local Indian rulers, whether Muslim or Hindu, were intense rivals and were ready prey to European promises of aid against each other. All the European powers found it easy not merely to win Indian princes to their side but to raise and train native armies to fight under Portuguese, French, Dutch, or British flags. Perhaps this lack of extensive political and social cohesion in India is basically why a few thousand Europeans could dominate the vast area until 1945.

The extraordinary variety and range of Indian life fascinated Europeans. Some of the more isolated parts of India in the Deccan or southern peninsula were inhabited by tribes that seemed to Europeans to have stepped out of the Stone Age. Some on the northern edges were warrior tribes, much like those who had invaded Europe from the highlands of Central Asia. In the great valleys of the Indus and the Ganges and in the richer parts of the Deccan, there was a wealthy, populous society basically Hindu in culture—though when the Europeans arrived it was dominated in many areas by Muslim invaders.

Hindu society was the result of a mix between earlier native groups and invaders from the north who spoke a language closely related to Greek and Latin and who were probably Indo-Europeans or Aryans. The early history of India, however, is still controversial, and there is no full agreement on how numerous these invaders were or just where they came from, though the invasion apparently took place between 2000 and 1200 B.C.

According to the Indian laws of caste, men and women were by the fact of birth settled for life in a closed group that pursued a given occupation and occupied a fixed social position. When the Europeans reached India there were apparently over a thousand castes, plus a group at the bottom without caste, "untouchables." The ruling groups were of two main castes, the *Brahmins*, or priests, and the *Kshatriya*, or warriors. Most other castes were in the third group, the *Vaisya*, or common people, and were based largely on vocation or trade. In theory, marriage between members of different castes was forbidden, as was change of caste through social mobility. In fact, however, in the centuries since the invasion by the Indo-Europeans, considerable human intermixture had undoubtedly occurred. Yet color prejudice was still important, for the upper classes were generally much lighter than the lower.

The priestly caste, the Brahmins, enjoyed exceptional prestige and authority. The Brahmin faith had strains of an otherworldly belief in shunning the evils of the life of the flesh and in seeking salvation through mystic and ascetic denial. With this went a doctrine of the transmigration of souls, in which a sinful life led to reincarnation as lower animal life, and a virtuous life led, at least in some forms of Hindu belief, to ultimate freedom from flesh of any sort and reunion with the All-perfect. Official Brahminism acquired a series of rigid and complicated rituals, but the religion of the common people carried over from earlier times an elaborate polytheism of gods and goddesses who were fleshly indeed by post-Greek European standards. Against all this worldliness there had arisen in the sixth century B.C. a great religious leader, Gautama Buddha, himself of noble stock. Buddhism accepts the basic Brahmin concept of the evil of this world of the flesh, but it finds salvation—the *nirvana* of peaceful release from the chain of earthly birth and rebirth—in a life that is ascetic but not withdrawn, a life of charity and good works.

Although Buddhism died out in India, it spread with great power to China, Japan, and southeastern Asia. In these lands it took two forms that still exist. In Tibet, China, and Japan, the *Mahayana* (Great Vehicle) continued to emphasize Buddha's strong ethical desire to make nirvana available to all. In southeastern Asia and Ceylon (present-day Sri Lanka), the *Hinayana* (Lesser Vehicle) prevailed; in theory, the Hinayana relies more on ritual, and its monks are wholly detached from the world. Buddhism remains one of the world's great religions and has made some converts among Western intellectuals, especially in an altered form known as Zen Buddhism, originally a kind of stoicism of Japanese origin.

The religious thought of India has left a firmer imprint of otherworldliness, of greater emphasis on the mystical subjugation of the flesh, of a revulsion from the struggle for wealth and from the satisfaction of human appetites, than has Christianity or Islam. In practice, Indian life, even before the Europeans came, displayed its measure of violence, greed, cruelty, and self-indulgence. To some observers, the educated classes of India seemed to take refuge in otherworldly doctrines as a psychological defense against the growing technological superiority of the West. Over the five and a half centuries of contact between India and the West, the idea grew that the cultures were so different that no real reconciliation was possible. As the British writer Rudyard Kipling was to declare in 1889, in lines somewhat misrepresented as racist rather than religious and fatalistic:

> Oh, East is East, and West is West, and never the
> twain shall meet.
> Till Earth and Sky stand presently at God's great
> Judgment Seat. . . .

This Mogul painting from late sixteenth-century India shows Portuguese naval mercenaries attacking a local population. One man wears armor in the hot climate. One vessel carries a horse for the commander to use after landing. As this picture is a non-Western rendition, it provides a clear sense of how Westerners were viewed through Eastern eyes.

China

China too resisted the West, in many ways more successfully than did India. China also saw its armed forces beaten whenever they came into formal military conflict with European or European-trained armies or fleets. It too was forced to make many concessions to Europeans—to grant treaty ports, and above all, extraterritoriality, that is, the right of Europeans to be tried in their own national courts for offenses committed on Chinese soil. Yet China, unlike India, was never annexed by a European power and never lost its sovereignty, for China preserved a fairly strong central government and had many strands of ethical and political unity that India lacked.

Like the other civilizations bordering the great nomadic Eurasion heartland—the Mesopotamian, the Indian, the European—this ancient civilization was subject to periodic incursions by nomadic tribes; it was against such incursions that the Great Wall was built in the third century B.C. On the whole, the Chinese protected their institutions against the victorious nomads, whom they absorbed after a few generations. The last of these "barbarian" conquests occurred when the first Europeans were setting up permanent trade relations with China. Early in the seventeenth century Mongolian tribes established a state of their own in eastern Manchuria, to the north of China proper. In 1644 they seized the Chinese capital of Peking and established a dynasty that lasted until 1911. But the Manchus, like other outsiders before them, left Chinese institutions almost untouched.

A stone carving at Angkor Wat. The great *wats,* or temples, at Angkor in southeast Asia had been built by the Khmers, particularly in the eleventh century. Mysteriously abandoned in 1432, the great city was reclaimed by the jungle, only to be found again by the French naturalist Henri Mouhot (1826-1861) in 1860.

Chinese history is by no means the uneventful record of a "frozen" and unchanging society that Westerners of the prenineteenth century thought it to be. It is filled with the dynamic rise and fall of dynasties; with periods of effective governmental centralization and periods of "feudal" disintegration; with wars, plagues, and famines; and with the gradual spread of Chinese culture to Canton, Vietnam, Korea, and Japan. Viewed very broadly, many of the same trends found in European history also marked Chinese development.

Within this flux were many elements of continuity. At the base of Chinese social life was a communal village organization held together by very strong family ties, a

CONFUCIUS ON THE MORAL LAW

Confucius argued that all of humanity was bound by one moral law:

The moral law is to be found everywhere, and yet it is a secret.

The simple intelligence of ordinary men and women of the people may understand something of the moral law; but in its utmost reaches there is something which even the wisest and holiest of men cannot understand. The ignoble natures of ordinary men and women of the people may be able to carry out the moral law; but in its utmost reaches even the wisest and holiest of men cannot live up to it.

Great as the Universe is, man is yet not always satisfied with it. For there is nothing so great but the mind of the moral man can conceive of something still greater which nothing in the world can hold. There is nothing so small but the mind of the moral man can conceive of something still smaller which nothing in the world can split.

The Wisdom of Confucius, trans. and ed. Lin Yutang (New York: Modern Library, 1938), p. 108.

A section of the Great Wall of China, which was first built in the third century B.C. to encourage Chinese isolation and was later restored by the Ming Dynasty.

cult of ancestor worship, and a tradition of hard work on farms. The Chinese village, basically unchanged until the midtwentieth century, was one of the oldest socio-economic organizations in the civilized world. At the top of this society was an emperor, the Son of Heaven, whose subjects were conditioned to at least formal imperial unity in somewhat the same manner as early medieval Westerners were conditioned to the unity of Roman Catholic Christendom.

The business of running this vast empire was entrusted to the mandarins, one of the most remarkable ruling classes history has recorded, a bureaucracy of intellectuals, or at least of those who could pass examinations in literary and philosophical classics requiring a rigorously trained memory. The mandarin class, though it was susceptible to graft and to nepotism and proved not very adaptable to new European ideas, had served the state for thousands of years, and its existence was one of the reasons for the extraordinary stability of Chinese society. Although in theory this class was open to talent, the necessary education was too expensive and too difficult for any but a few gifted, lucky, and persistent poor boys. Just as in India, China had a small upper class that enjoyed a style of living hardly available to the aristocracy in the medieval West, and an immense population near the margin of tolerable existence.

In China the upper class took little interest in mysticism and otherworldliness. They accepted the world and were concerned with human relations, with politeness and decorum; their conventional Confucianism was a code of manners and morals, not a sacramental religion. Confucius (551-479), a sage who flourished in the fifth century B.C., was not a prophet but a moralist who taught an ethical system of temperance, courtesy, and obedience to those who were wise and good. This lack of commitment to an otherworldly religion may have made the Chinese less receptive to Western ideas.

The Growth and Decline of the Portuguese Empire

The Portuguese empire in Asia and Africa was a trading empire, not one of settlement. Along the coasts of Africa, India, and China, the Portuguese established a series of posts over which they hoisted their flag as a sign that these bits of territory had been annexed to the Portuguese crown. Such posts were often called factories after the *factors*, or commercial agents, who were stationed there to trade with the local population. As all the European colonial powers were to do, the Portuguese offered guns, knives, cheap cloth, and fascinating items of all sorts which provided access to a new technology. In

The variety and technical superiority of Western vessels for long distance travel with both passengers and cargo helped speed contacts between European nations and the East. This contemporary illustration shows the different types of vessels the Portuguese had available for use in the Indian Ocean.

return they got gold and silver (which did not have the same value in non-Western societies), pepper and other spices—still essential for making meat palatable in a prerefrigeration technology—silks and other luxuries, and finally, raw materials such as cotton and, in Brazil, tobacco and sugar.

Two guiding principles of this trade were accepted by almost all contemporaries, whether in the "mother country" or in the colonies. First, in this trade the mother country was the dominant partner and would provide manufactured goods and services, while the colony produced raw materials. Second, nationals of other European lands were excluded from this trade; they could not deal directly with the colony or share in the commerce between mother country and colony. The Portuguese, in sum, followed a policy of mercantilism, symbolized by Lisbon's virtual monopoly over European imports of pepper and cinnamon in the sixteenth century.

Armed forces were essential to this colonial system. Relatively small land forces proved sufficient both to keep "the natives" under control and to ward off rival Europeans from the trading posts. A large and efficient navy was also necessary to protect the sea routes of a colonial power, for the easiest way to raid a rival's trade was to wait until its fruits were deposited in the hold of a merchant vessel, and then take it at sea as a prize. Pirates were often an unofficial adjunct of a navy, called privateers and operating only against enemies or neutrals, never against their own nationals. The Portuguese fleet, therefore, was not simply a merchant fleet. Under the command of governors like Albuquerque, it was a great military machine that swept aside Arab opposition and for a few decades ruled the known oceans.

Few Portuguese settled either in the hot coastlands of Africa or in the already heavily populated lands of India and the Far East; nor, with one exception, did they attempt to transform these populations into pseudo-Portuguese. Many local residents were enlisted in the armed forces or used as domestic help or in subordinate posts such as clerks, and they inevitably learned something of the language and culture of the colonial power without abandoning their own. But neither among the tribes of Africa nor among the Indian and Chinese masses did the process of Europeanization go very deep. The Portuguese left the old ruling chiefs and classes in local authority much as they had found them. The local upper classes monopolized most of the limited European wares, for Europe could not yet flood non-European markets with cheap manufactured goods made by power-driven machinery. Very little that was Western touched the masses in the sixteenth century, or tempted them away from their traditional ways in anything like the degree with which the twentieth-century West would attract and tempt Africa and Asia.

There was one exception. The Portuguese and the Spanish, and even their relatively secular-minded rivals, the English, Dutch, and French, did attempt to Christianize the indigenous groups they encountered. Some of these attempts involved force, as at Goa, where the Portuguese pulled down all the temples and made it impossible to practice the traditional religion. From the first, the earliest missionaries underestimated the obstacles they were to encounter. Many missionaries were in a sense partly converted themselves; that is, they came to be very fond of their charges and were convinced that they were almost Christians already. The Jesuits in China, the first European intellectuals to live in that very civilized country, believed that a full reconciliation between Christianity and Confucianism could be achieved with just a bit more effort.

From the start, difficulties arose between the missionaries, anxious to protect those they regarded as their charges, and the traders and colonial officials, driven by material incentives to exploit the local population. To local chiefs and monarchs converts were potential traitors, likely to be more loyal to their Western faith than to their own rulers. Money and manpower were always serious problems for the missionaries, with so many to convert and tend, and with so few people and so

AN EPIC FOR A CONQUEROR

Camões sailed for India in 1553, and in 1556 he was sent to Macão, on the China coast. He traveled widely, seeing much of the Portuguese overseas empire, and he decided to write an epic poem to record the deeds of those he had seen in action. He changed his mind, however, and modeled his account upon the exploits of Vasco da Gama. When he returned to Lisbon, he published *The Lusiads:*

I say to you, O Lusian generation,
Yours in this world is but a little place,
Not in this world, but in His congregation.
Whose rule doth the round firmament embrace;
You, in whom risk quelled not determination
Wholly to subjugate a loathsome race,
Or greed, or an allegiance incomplete
To Her Whose Essence hath in Heaven Her seat;
You Portuguese, so strong, though you are few,
Who your weak powers never stop to weigh,
Who, though you pay the price of death, ensue
The law of life that shall endure for aye,
Such was the die which Heaven cast for you,
That, be your numbers little as they may,
For Christendom you act a mighty part.
So dost Thou, Christ, exalt the meek in heart!

From *The Lusiads of Luiz de Camões*, trans. Leonard Bacon (New York: The Hispanic Society of America, 1950), p. 249.

little money to do the work. Measured in statistical terms, the effort to convert India and the Far East to Christianity did not make a serious impression on the masses; there were fewer than a million converts by 1600. The greatest missionary successes tended to occur in areas of Buddhism, then in a state of decay comparable to that of Catholicism on the eve of the Reformation, and the greatest failures in areas of Islam, for Muslims seldom abandoned their faith for any other. Yet the influence of Christianity cannot be measured in terms of actual church memberships in the East; its effect was far greater on the upper and intellectual classes than on the masses and became an important part of the Western impact on Asia.

The Portuguese, though first in the field, very soon had to yield to newer rivals. Like the Spaniards, they suffered from an inadequate home industry; their banking, their business methods, their initiative were not equal to competition with the aggressive, expanding powers of northwest Europe. Though monopolizing the import of pepper from the East, they sought the assistance of the more knowledgeable merchant community of Antwerp in distributing the pepper to European markets. The cloth and other wares that they traded in the East were often imported from competing European countries with more developed industries. After the sixteenth century the Portuguese ceased to add to their empire and to their wealth, and they sank back to a secondary place in international politics. A great epic poem, the *Lusiads* (1572) of Luiz de Camões (c 1524-1580), was their monument, written at the height of empire.

The sixty years of union between the Spanish and Portuguese monarchies, 1580-1640, accelerated the decline of Portugal's imperial fortunes by involving it in prolonged worldwide warfare with Spain's great adversary, the Dutch republic. Better equipped and better disciplined Dutch forces drove the Portuguese from most of their posts in present-day Indonesia and from Ceylon and parts of the Indian coast. Yet a Portuguese empire did survive along the old route around Africa to Goa, on the island of Timor off southeast Asia, and at Macao. It survived in fact to 1974, when the overthrow of an authoritarian regime in Lisbon ended the stubborn Portuguese effort to resist the increasingly determined attempts by Africans to expel the Portuguese from their colonies: Portuguese Guinea and Angola on the west coast, and Mozambique on the east.

Thus the first colonial empire in Africa was also virtually the last. It endured so long because the Portuguese never voluntarily relinquished any territories; the Republic of India had to seize Goa by force in 1961. Another reason for the longevity of the Portuguese empire in the face of such active and hungry competitors as the French, Dutch, and British was that while Portugal's most successful rivals took away its leadership, they did leave Portugal a role in the competition. Finally, the survival of Portugal's empire was greatly aided by an alliance with the greatest of the European imperial powers, Britain, an alliance that lasted into the twentieth century.

III WEST BY SEA TO THE INDIES

Columbus and Later Explorers

In the earliest days of concerted effort to explore the oceans, the rulers of Spain had been too busy disposing of Muslim Granada and uniting the separate parts of Spain to patronize scientific exploration as the Portu-

COLUMBUS REFLECTS UPON WHAT HE HAS SEEN

As Columbus neared the end of his first voyage, he prepared a letter for the king of Spain to describe some of what he had seen:

Sir:

As I know that you will have pleasure of the great victory which our Lord hath given me in my voyage, I write you this, by which you shall know that, in twenty days I passed over to the Indies with the fleet which the most illustrious King and Queen, our Lords, gave me: where I found very many islands peopled with inhabitants beyond number. And, of them all, I have taken possession for their Highnesses, with proclamation and the royal standard displayed; and I was not gainsaid. On the first which I found, I put the name San Salvador, in commemoration of His high Majesty, who marvellously hath given all this: the Indians call it Guanahani. The second I named the Island of Santa Maria de Concepcion, the third Ferrandina, the fourth Isabella, the fifth La Isla Juana [Cuba]; and so for each one a new name. When I reached Juana, I followed its coast westwardly, and found it so large that I thought it might be the mainland province of Cathay. And as I did not thus find any towns and villages on the seacoast, save small hamlets with the people whereof I could not get speech, because they all fled away forthwith, I went on farther in the same direction, thinking I should not miss of great cities or towns. And at the end of many leagues, seeing that there was no change, and that the coast was bearing me northwards, whereunto my desire was contrary since the winter was already confronting us, I formed the purpose of making from thence to the South, and as the wind also blew against me, I determined not to wait for other weather and turned back as far as a port agreed upon; from which I sent two men into the country to learn if there were a king, or any great cities. They travelled for three days, and found interminable small villages and a numberless population, but nought of ruling authority; wherefore they returned. I understood sufficiently from other Indians whom I had already taken, that this land, in its continuousness, was an island; and so I followed its coast eastwardly for a hundred and seven leagues as far as where it terminated; from which headland I saw another island to the east, ten or eight leagues distant from this, to which I at once gave the name La Española. And I proceeded thither, and followed the northern coast, as with La Juana, eastwardly for a hundred and seventy-eight great leagues in a direct easterly course, as with La Juana. The which, and all the others, are very large to an excessive degree, and this extremely so. In it, there are many havens on the seacoast, incomparable with any others that I know in Christendom, and plenty of rivers so good and great that it is a marvel. The lands thereof are high, and in it are very many ranges of hills, and most lofty mountains incomparably beyond the Island of Centrefrei; all most beautiful in a thousand shapes, and all accessible, and full of trees of a thousand kinds, so lofty that they seem to reach the sky. And I am assured that they never lose their foliage; as may be imagined, since I saw them as green and as beautiful as they are in Spain during May. And some of them were in flower, some in fruit, some in another stage according to their kind. And the nightingale was singing, and other birds of a thousand sorts, in the month of November, round about the way that I was going. There are palm-trees of six or eight species, wondrous to see for their beautiful variety; but so are the other trees, and fruits, and plants therein. There are wonderful pinegroves, and very large plains of verdure, and there is honey, and many kinds of birds, and many various fruits. In the earth there are many mines of metals; and there is a population of incalculable number. Spañola is a marvel; the mountains and hills, and plains and fields, and land, so beautiful and rich for planting and sowing, for breeding cattle of all sorts, for building of towns and villages. There could be no believing, without seeing, such harbours as are here, as well as the many and great rivers, and excellent waters, most of which contain gold. In the trees and fruits and plants, there are great differences from those of Juana. In this, there are many spiceries, and great mines of gold and other metals. The people of this island, and of all the others that I have found and seen or not seen, all go naked, men and women, just as their mothers bring them forth; although some women cover a single place with the leaf of a plant, or a cotton something which they make for that purpose. They have no iron or steel, nor any weapons; nor are they fit thereunto; not because they be not a well-formed people and of fair stature, but that they are most wondrously timorous. They have no other weapons than the stems of reeds in their seeding state, on the end of which they fix little sharpened stakes. Even these, they dare not use; for many times has it happened that I sent two or three men ashore to some village to parley, and countless numbers of them sallied forth, but as soon as they saw those approach, they fled away in such wise that even a father would not wait for his son. And this was not because any hurt had ever been done to any of them. . . .

As extracted in John Louis Beatty and Oliver A. Johnson, eds., *Heritage of Western Civilization*, 5th ed. (Englewood Cliffs, N.J.: Prentice-Hall, 1982), I, 371-72.

guese had done. But Spanish traders were active, and Spain was growing in prosperity. When Portuguese mariners found the three groups of Atlantic islands—Azores, Madeira, and Canaries—a papal decree assigned the Canaries to the crown of Castile and the others to Portugal. Once the marriage of Ferdinand and Isabella had united Aragon and Castile, Queen Isabella wanted to catch up with the Portuguese. So in 1491, when the fall of Granada seemed imminent, she commissioned Christopher Columbus to try to reach India by sailing west.

Columbus (1451-1506), born in Genoa, was essentially self-educated and, in navigation and geography, had educated himself very well. He was an experienced sailor and had gone at least once to the Gold Coast of Africa; he may also have sailed to Iceland. His central obsession, that the Far East ("the Indies") could be reached by sailing westward from Spain, was not unique. No educated person in 1492 seriously doubted that the earth was round, but as it turned out most scholars had greatly underestimated its size, and Columbus believed that it was even smaller. The major problem was a practical one; if one accepted Ptolemy's ancient estimate of the circumference of the earth, as most educated people did, no ship of the time could complete so great a voyage. But Columbus insisted that the wealthy island of Cipangu (Japan) was only 2,400 miles due west, a distance easily within the range of ships and crews. Thus, mistaken geography made possible a voyage that would never have been undertaken otherwise.

Columbus might not have been able to set out with the sole aim of reaching the Indies. But he was also charged to discover and secure for the Spanish crown new islands and territories—a mission that may reflect ancient and medieval legends about Atlantis, St. Brendan's Isle of the Blessed in midocean, and other lands beyond the Azores. Therefore, even if he did not reach the Indies, there seemed a chance that he would reach something new.

He reached a New World. Setting out from Palos near Cadiz on August 3, 1492, in three very small ships, he made a landfall on an island in the Bahamas on October 12, and eventually discovered the large islands we know as Cuba and Santo Domingo (Haiti). Since he assumed that he had reached the Indies, he called the people he encountered there "Indians"—a particularly dramatic instance of how the vocabulary of the explorer and the conqueror came to dominate the maps of geography, ethnography, and natural science. On a second voyage in 1493, Columbus went out with seventeen ships and some fifteen hundred colonists, explored further in the Caribbean, and laid the foundations of the Spanish Empire in America. On his third voyage, in 1498-1500, he reached the mouth of the Orinoco River in South America, but he encountered difficulties among his colonists and was sent home by the royal governor, who took over the administration of the Indies for the Crown. Columbus was released on his return to Spain, and in 1502-1504 he made a fourth and final voyage, in which he finally reached the mainland at Honduras in August 1502. He died in comparative obscurity in Spain, totally unaware that he had reached, not Asia, but a new continent that was, by a caprice of history, not destined to bear his name.

News of Columbus's voyage soon spread by word of mouth in Europe, for printing was still in its infancy. There were as yet no newspapers or geographical institutes; the international learned class was more interested in Greek manuscripts than in strange lands; and, in any case, from the early Portuguese voyages on, governments had done their best to keep their discoveries as

THE RENAISSANCE SENSE OF CURIOSITY AND ADVENTURE

The deep urge the explorers felt to discover and tell of new sights was evident from their reports. Ludovico Varthema (c 1465-1510) wrote of this Renaissance sense of curiosity and adventure by which he hoped great fame could be won:

> There have been many men who have devoted themselves to the investigation of the things of this world and by the aid of divers studies, journeys, and very exact relations have endeavoured to accomplish their desire. Others again of more perspicacious understandings, to whom the earth has not sufficed, such as the Chaldeans and the Phoenicians, have begun to traverse the highest regions of Heaven with careful observations and watchings: from all which I know that each has gained most deserved and high praise from others and abundant satisfaction to themselves. Wherefore, I, feeling a very great desire for similar results, and leaving alone the Heavens as a burthen more suitable for the shoulders of Atlas and Hercules, determined to investigate some small portion of this our terrestrial globe; and not having any inclination . . . to arrive at my desire by study or conjectures, I determined, personally, and with my own eyes, to endeavour to ascertain the situations of places, the qualities of peoples, the diversities of animals, the varieties of the fruit-bearing and odoriferous trees of Egypt, Syria, Arabia Deserta and Felix, Persia, India and Ethiopia, remembering well that the testimony of one eye-witness is worth more than ten hearsays.

As quoted in J.R. Hale, *Renaissance Exploration* (London: British Broadcasting Corporation, 1968), p. 91; modernized from Robert Kerr, *A General History and Collection of Voyages and Travels* (Edinburgh: William Blackwood et al., 1812), VII, 43-44.

Under this impulse Varthema would leave Venice in 1502 for Egypt, reach India by the Red Sea route, probably attain the Spice Islands, and return via the Cape of Good Hope, the first free-lance traveler of such scope in history.

THE HAZARDS OF EXPLORATION

A routine entry from the journal of Antonio Pigafetta (c 1491-c 1536), who completed the circumnavigation of the globe begun by Magellan, tells of daily pain and deprivation:

On Wednesday the twenty-eighth of November, one thousand five hundred and twenty, we issued forth from the said strait [of Magellan] and entered the Pacific Sea, where we remained three months and twenty days without taking on board provisions or any other refreshments, and we ate only old biscuit turned to powder, all full of worms and stinking of the urine which the rats had made on it, having eaten the good. And we drank water impure and yellow. We ate also ox hides which were very hard because of the sun, rain, and wind. And we left them four or five days in the sea, then laid them for a short time on embers, and so we ate them. And of the rats, which were sold for half an écu [French silver coin] apiece, some of us could not get enough. Besides the aforesaid troubles, this malady was the worst, namely that the gums of most part of our men swelled above and below so that they could not eat. And in this way they died, inasmuch as twenty-nine of us died. . . . For during this time we had no storm, and we saw no land except two small uninhabited islands, where we found only birds and trees. Wherefore we called them the Isles of Misfortune. . . . And I believe that nevermore will any man undertake to make such a voyage.

Pigafetta, *Magellan's Voyage: A Narrative Account of the First Circumnavigation*, trans. and ed. R.A. Skelton (New Haven: Yale University Press, 1969), I, 57. Another version of this manuscript adds that the men ate sawdust from planks; the disease referred to was scurvy.

secret as possible. The most effective spreading of the word in print about the New World was done by another Italian navigator in the Spanish service, Amerigo Vespucci (c 1454-1512), who wrote copiously about his own alleged explorations in the immediate wake of Columbus. Scholars doubt that Vespucci really made all the discoveries from the southeastern United States to the tip of South America that he claimed to have made, though many accept as authentic his report of a voyage in 1499-1500 in which he may have seen the mouth of the Amazon. Vespucci's letters came to the attention of a German theoretical geographer, Martin Waldseemüller (c 1470-c 1522), who in 1507 published a map blocking out a landmass in the southern part of the New World that he labeled, from the Latinized form of Vespucci's first name, America.

After Columbus, discoveries multiplied. Juan Ponce de León (c 1474-1521) reached Florida in 1513, and Vasco Nuñez de Balboa (1475-1519) in 1513 crossed the Isthmus of Panama and saw a limitless ocean on the other side of which the Indies did indeed lie, for it was the wide Pacific. Many other Spaniards and Portuguese in these first two decades of the sixteenth century explored in detail the coasts of what was to be Latin America. It was now quite clear that an immense landmass lay across the westward route from Europe to Asia.

Maritime exploration then turned to the problem of getting around the Americas and into the Pacific by sea. North America proved an obstacle indeed, for the great rivers—the Chesapeake, Delaware, Hudson—promising though they looked to the first explorers, barely penetrated the great continent, the breadth of which was totally unknown. The St. Lawrence River looked even more promising, and to its first French explorers it seemed like the sought-for strait; but it too gave out, and the rapids near Montreal that showed it was only another river received the ironic name of Lachine (China). Not until 1903-1906 was the ice-choked "Northwest Passage" in the Arctic finally traversed by an English expedition.

However, the "Southwest Passage" was found only a generation after Columbus, by an expedition that is the most extraordinary of all the great voyages of discovery. Ferdinand Magellan (c 1480-1521), a Portuguese in the Spanish service, set out in 1519 with a royal commission to find a way westward to the Spice Islands of Asia. Skirting the coast of South America, he found and guided his ships through the difficult, fog-bound passage that bears his name, the Straits of Magellan, reached the Pacific, and crossed it by a route not precisely known in a voyage of incredible hardship. Scurvy alone, a disease now known to be caused by a lack of vitamin C, meant that he and his men had to suffer torturing illness. After he reached the islands now known as the Philippines, Magellan was killed in a skirmish with a hostile chief. One of his captains, however, kept going along the known route by the Indian Ocean and the coast of Africa. On September 8, 1522, the *Victoria* and a crew of eighteen men—out of five ships and two hundred and forty-three men that had sailed in 1519—reached Cadiz. For the first time, circumnavigation of the earth had proved empirically that the world was round.

The Growth of the Spanish Empire

As a by-product of Magellan's voyage, the Spaniards got a foothold in the Far East. By the Treaty of Tordesillas

Spain and Portugal had divided the world open to trade and empire along a line cut through the Atlantic, so that Brazil became Portuguese. This same line extended across the poles and cut the Pacific, so that some of the islands Magellan discovered came into the Spanish half. Spain conveniently treated the Philippines as if they too were in the Spanish half of the globe, though they were actually just outside it, and colonized them from Mexico.

The Spaniards in the New World soon explored and acquired thousands of square miles of territory. The original explorers by sea were followed by the *conquistadores*, often of the now-impoverished lesser nobility—half explorer, half soldier-administrator, and all adventurer. Of the conquistadores, two in particular—Hernando Cortés (1485-1547) and Francisco Pizarro (c 1478-1541)—conquered vast territories. With a handful of men they seized the two most civilized regions of the New World: the Aztec empire of Mexico, taken by Cortés with six hundred men in 1519-1521, and the Inca empire of Peru, taken by Pizarro with one hundred and eighty soldiers in 1531-1533. These conquests are among the most fascinating, disturbing, and brutal chapters of Western history; the death of the Aztec emperor Montezuma and the execution by treachery of the Inca emperor Atahualpa set the tone for the conquest of two continents.

Other Spaniards in search of gold, salvation, glory, and excitement toiled up and down these strange new lands: Francisco Vasquez de Coronado (c 1510-1554), Hernando de Soto (c 1500-1542), and Alvar Cabeza de Vaca (c 1490-c 1556) in the southwest of what became the United States; Sebastian Cabot (c 1484-1557) on the great Paraguay and Parana river systems; Pedro de Valdivia (c 1502-1553) in Chile; Pedro de Alvarado (1485-1541) in Guatemala; and Pedro de Mendoza (c 1487-1537), a Basque who with many Austrians, Flemings, and Saxons reached La Plata (the area around the River Plate in present-day Argentina and Uruguay) in 1536 and founded Buenos Aires.

The toll in lives of Spanish exploration was staggering, especially in South America. A single expedition to Peru in 1535 lost 150 Spaniards, 150 slaves, and 11,000 Indians. The sea passages were often horrendous; by 1540 over 2,000 men and twelve ships had been lost trying to find the route ultimately mapped out by Magellan. As late as 1925 an entire expedition disappeared in the interior of Brazil. No continent, including Africa, cost so much to discover, explore, and map.

Unlike the great cultures of India and the Far East, the pre-Columbian cultures of the Americas crumbled under the impact of the Europeans. From Mexico to Bolivia, Paraguay, and Patagonia (in southern Argen-

Machu Picchu, ancient Inca city in the Andes of Peru, was at 7,000 feet elevation. Corn and potatoes were grown on the terraces. It was rediscovered by the American Hiram Bingham (1875-1956) in 1911.

tina), millions of people survive today who are of American Indian stock. Any understanding of Latin America requires some knowledge of their folkways and traditions. Mexican artists and intellectuals, for example, proudly uphold their Indian heritage against the Yankees and against their own Europeanized nineteenth-century rulers. But the structure of the Aztec and the Inca empires has totally disappeared. The sun god in whose name the Inca ruled and the Aztec god of War are no longer a part of the lives of people today, as are Confucius and Buddha. Yet the existence in Peru and Central America of large civilized states with remarkable achievements in art, architecture, and science is further evidence against naive Western notions of racial superiority.

Well before the end of the sixteenth century, the work of the conquistadores was over, and the first of the true European colonial empires—in contrast to the trading empires in Africa and Asia—had been established in Latin America. Nowhere, except in northern Argentina and in central Chile, was the native Indian population eliminated and replaced by a population almost entirely from the Old World—something that happened in North America except for a tiny Native American minority. Over vast reaches of Mexico and Central and South America, a crust of Spanish or Portuguese formed at the top of society and made Spanish or Portuguese the language of culture. A class of "mixed blood," the *mestizos*, was gradually formed from the union of Europeans and the indigenous population, and in many regions the Indians continued to maintain their old ways of life almost untouched. Finally, where the Indians were exterminated, as in the Caribbean, or where they proved insufficient as a labor force, as in Brazil, African slaves added another ingredient to the racial mixture.

Moreover, geography and the circumstances of settlement by groups of adventurers in each region created several separate units tied together only by their dependence on the Crown and destined to become the independent nation-states of nineteenth-century Latin America. Geography alone was a fatal obstacle to any subsequent union of the colonies, such as was achieved by the English colonies that became the United States of America. Between such apparently close neighbors as present-day Argentina and Chile, for instance, lay the Andes, crossed only with great difficulty through high mountain passes; between the colonies of La Plata and those of Peru and New Granada lay the Andes and the vast tropical rainforests of the Amazon basin, still almost unoccupied in the twentieth century. The highlands of Mexico and Central America were invitations to local independence, as were the mountains of Hellas to the ancient Greeks. Cuba and the other Caribbean islands had the natural independence of islands.

Nonetheless, the Spaniards transported to the New World the centralized administration of Castile. At the top of the hierarchy were two viceroys: from Lima, Peru the viceroy ruled for the Crown over the Spanish part of South America, except Venezuela; from Mexico City the viceroy ruled over the mainland north of Panama, the West Indies, Venezuela, and the far-away Philippines. Each capital had an *audiencia*, a powerful body staffed by professional lawyers and operating both as a court of law and as an advisory council. During the sixteenth century audiencias were also established in Santo Domingo, Guatemala, Panama, New Granada, Quito, Manila, and other major centers. A special Council of the Indies in Madrid formulated colonial policy and supervised its execution.

This centralized, paternalistic government was less rigid in practice than in theory; given the vast areas and the varied peoples under its control, it had to be. The rudiments of popular consultation of the Spanish colonists existed in the assemblies of citizens in the towns. Moreover, in time the bureaucracy itself came to be filled largely with colonials who had never been in the home country, and who developed a sense of local patriotism and independence. Madrid and Seville were simply too far away to enforce all their decisions. It proved especially impossible to maintain the rigid monopolies of mercantilistic theory, which sought to confine trade wholly to the mother country, and to prohibit or severely limit domestic industry in the colonies. Local officials connived at a smuggling trade with the English, Dutch, French, and North Americans, which reached large proportions in the eighteenth century.

The hand of Spain was heaviest in the initial period of exploitation, when the rich and easily mined deposits of the precious metals in Mexico and Peru were skimmed off for the benefit both of the Spanish crown, which always got its *quinto*, or fifth, and of the conquistadores and their successors. This gold and silver did the local population no good, but in the long run it also did Spain no good since it financed a futile bid for European supremacy, created inflation, and paid other countries for wares needed by the colonies that Spain did not produce. By the early seventeenth century, when the output of precious metals began a long decline, the economy and society of Spanish America had stabilized. The economy was not progressive, but neither was it hopelessly backward. Colonial products—sugar, tobacco, chocolate, cotton, hides, and much else—flowed out of Latin America in exchange for manufactured goods and for services. Creoles (American-born subjects of European descent) and mestizos were the chief beneficiaries of this trade. Above the African slaves in the social pyramid, but well below the mestizos, was the native population. This was a system of social caste based on color rather than race, one that never became as rigid as that in North America.

Everywhere, but especially in the Caribbean, the whites tried to use native labor on farms, in the mines, and in transport. The results were disastrous, for epidemics of smallpox and other diseases new to the area that had been introduced by the Europeans took a terrible toll of the native population. In the West Indies the Carib Indians were wiped out. In central Mexico the total population fell from about nineteen million when

Cortés arrived to only some two and a half million eighty years later. Conquest may have been preceded by a "disease frontier" in which smallpox and influenza had so weakened the Indian groups that they could not resist the major European military attacks. However, a biological exchange also took place; although the origin of syphilis is still disputed, many historians of medicine believe that it was brought from the West Indies, where it was mild, to western Europe, where it became virulent.

Attempts to regiment native labor in a plantation system or to put it on a semi-manorial system of forced labor, known as the *encomienda,* proved almost as disastrous. The encomiendas, which had been developed in Spain itself for lands reconquered from the Muslims, grouped farming villages whose inhabitants were "commended" to the protection of a conquistador or colonist. The "protector" thereby acquired both a source of income without engaging in demeaning labor and an economic base for potential defiance of central authority. The shortage of native labor made recourse to slaves from Africa seem essential.

Against these forces making for harshness and cruelty, there were counteracting forces. In its aims Spanish imperial policy toward the native population was reasonably generous; even in practice, it holds up well in comparison with the long and harsh record of relations between Europeans and non-Europeans all over the globe. For example, the New Laws of 1542 forbade the transmission of encomiendas by inheritance, thereby inhibiting feudal decentralization. These laws also forbade the enslavement of Indians, who were regarded as wards of the Crown. The central government in Spain passed many laws to protect the Indians (as did the government in England later), but the European settlers on the scene quite often ignored the laws, and the imperial authorities were unwilling to commit the resources necessary to enforce them. In the Spanish empire the cause of the indigenous people was championed by men of great distinction, notably by Bartolomé de las Casas (1474-1566), "Father of the Indians" and bishop of Chiapas in Mexico.

Unlike their counterparts in Africa and Asia, the Indian masses in the New World were converted to Christianity. More than Spanish pride was involved in the grandiose religious edifices constructed by the colonists and in their elaborate services; many priests wished to fill the void left by the destruction of the Indians' temples and the suppression of complex pagan rituals. Church and state in the Spanish and Portuguese colonies in the New World worked closely together, undisturbed for generations by the troubles caused in Europe by the Protestant Reformation and the rise of a secular anti-Christian movement. The Jesuits in Paraguay tried to set up a remarkable society—a benevolent despotism and paternalistic utopia of good order for the Guarani Indians. On the northern fringes of the Spanish world, where it was to meet the Anglo-Saxons, a long line of

The Pyramid of the Sun at Teotihuacán. (Teotihuacán means "Abode of the Gods" in Nahuatl, which was the Aztec and Toltec language.) Larger in volume than the Great Pyramid of Egypt, this huge structure dominated a stone city that perished in the ninth century. The city was excavated by the Mexican government in the 1960s so that the present generation might know how the Aztecs lived and worshiped.

Much of our knowledge of life in North America at the time of the arrival of the European comes from the work of the English artist John White (*fl.* 1585-1590), who was one of the first settlers in Virginia. Sixty-three of his watercolors have survived, and they provide much historical and anthropological detail. This one shows an Indian village as seen by Sir Walter Raleigh's expedition in 1585.

missions in California and the Southwest held the frontier. Everywhere save in Amazonia, the Roman Catholic church brought a veneer of Western tradition.

In their close union of church and state, in their very close ties with the home country, in their mercantilist economics, and in other respects, the Portuguese settlements in Brazil resembled those of the Spaniards elsewhere in Latin America. Yet there were significant differences. The Portuguese settlements were almost entirely rural; Brazil had nothing to compare with the growing urban splendor of Mexico City or Lima. Many black slaves were imported into tropical Brazil, and both because there were more slaves and because the white males often drew no sexual color line, the races became more thoroughly mixed in colonial times than they did in most Spanish colonies except Cuba. Finally, perhaps because of the relative proximity of Brazil to Europe, the Portuguese had more troubles with rival nations than the Spaniards did. The French, Dutch, and British all made serious efforts to acquire colonies on Brazil's northern fringe.

IV THE NORTH ATLANTIC POWERS

Spain and Portugal enjoyed a generation's head start in exploration and a head start of nearly a century in founding empires of settlement, in part because of their position as heirs of the Mediterranean trade. The northern Atlantic states soon made up for their late start, however. As early as 1497 John Cabot (d. c 1498) and his son Sebastian, Italians in English service, saw something of the North American coast and gave the English territorial claims based on their explorations. In the first half of the sixteenth century the explorations of another Italian, Giovanni da Verrazzano (c 1485-1528), and a Frenchman, Jacques Cartier (1491-1554), gave France competing claims, which were reinforced in the early seventeenth century by the detailed exploration of Samuel de Champlain (c 1570-1635). Dutch claims began with the voyages of Henry Hudson (d. 1611), an Englishman who entered Dutch service in 1609.

English, Dutch, and Swedes in North America

The English did not immediately follow up the work of the Cabots. Instead, they put their energies into the profitable business of interloping, that is, of breaking into the Spanish trading monopoly. In 1562 John Hawkins started the English slave trade; his nephew, Francis Drake, reached the Pacific and claimed California for England under the name of New Albion. Drake returned to London by the Pacific and Indian oceans, completing the first English circumnavigation of the globe (1577-1580), an act for which he was knighted by Queen Elizabeth I. Under Sir Humphrey Gilbert (c 1539-1583) in 1583 the English staked out a claim to Newfoundland, which gave them a share in the great fishing grounds off northeastern North America.

In 1584 Sir Walter Raleigh (c 1552-1618) unsuccessfully attempted to found a settlement on Roanoke Island (in present-day North Carolina) in an area the English named Virginia, after their Virgin Queen, Elizabeth. Early in the next century the English established two permanent footholds at Jamestown in Virginia (1607) and at Plymouth on Massachusetts Bay (1620). Both were to become colonies of settlement in which the sparse local population was exterminated and replaced by the British; but in their inception both were nearer the pattern of trading posts set by the Spanish and Portuguese. Both were established by chartered trading companies with headquarters in England; both, and especially the Virginia colony, cherished high hopes that they would find, as the Spaniards had, great stores of precious metals. Both were disappointed in these hopes and only just managed to survive the years of initial hardship. Tobacco, first cultivated in 1612, and John Smith (1580-1631), explorer and propagandist for colonization, saved the Virginia colony; furs (notably beaver), salted cod, and Calvinist determination saved Plymouth. Both colonies gradually built up an agricultural economy supplemented by trade with the mother country and the West Indies. Neither received more than a few tens of thousands of immigrants from abroad. Yet both these and the later colonies expanded by natural increase in a country of abundant and productive land. By 1763 there were fourteen mainland British colonies with nearly three million inhabitants.

Before these English mainland colonies were secure, two foreign groups had to be pushed out. The Dutch, following up the explorations of Henry Hudson, had founded the colony of New Amsterdam (1626) at the mouth of the river that bears his name and had begun to push into the fur trade. This made them rivals of the English and of the French, farther north in Canada. In their wars with England in the 1660s, however, the Dutch lost New Amsterdam, which was annexed by the English in 1664 and renamed New York. The Dutch, though few in number, left descendants prominent in the future United States, as such family names as Stuyvesant, Schuyler, and Roosevelt suggest.

The Swedes, who were minor competitors, founded Fort Christiana (1638) on the Delaware near present-day Wilmington. But New Sweden was never a great enterprise and in 1655 was absorbed by the Dutch. Pennsylvania, chartered to the wealthy English Quaker William Penn (1644-1718) in 1681, replaced the Swedes and Dutch on the Delaware.

The arch of colonies, in which Pennsylvania formed the keystone, reached from Nova Scotia to Georgia and numbered fourteen, each founded separately and each with its own charter. Partly as the result of a vast civil war in the midnineteenth century, American tradition perhaps exaggerates the differences between the southern and northern groups of colonies. Massachusetts was not wholly settled by democratic plain people, "Roundheads," nor was Virginia settled wholly by great English landowners, gentlemen or "Cavaliers" and their retainers. All the colonies were settled by a varied human lot, which ranged from the gentry at the top down to members of the poorest classes.

New England was for the most part settled by Calvinist Independents (Congregationalists), committed to local self-government and distrustful of land-owning aristocracy. The southern colonies, especially tidewater Virginia, were settled for the most part by Anglicans used to the existence of social distinctions and to large estates. In Virginia the Church of England became the established church; in Massachusetts the Puritan Congregationalists set up their own state church. Geography, climate, and a complex of social and economic factors drove the South toward plantation monoculture of tobacco, rice, indigo, or cotton even in colonial days (despite the presence of many small landholders and farmers) and drove New England and the Middle Colonies toward small-scale farming, industry, and commerce by independent farmer-owners and artisans. Yet the small farmers in the Piedmont sections of Virginia and the Carolinas represented an otherwise rather northern mixture of Presbyterians, Scotch-Irish, and Germans. The natural environment, and not original differences of social structure and religious belief, accounted mainly for the diverging cultures of North and South and their eventual armed conflict.

These colonists came from an England in which the concept of freedom of religion was only beginning to emerge. It was quite natural for the Virginians and the New Englanders to set up state churches. Yet these immigrants represented too many conflicting religious groups to enforce anything like the religious uniformity that prevailed in the Spanish colonies or in French Canada. Even in Calvinist New England "heresy" appeared from the start, with the presence of Baptists, Quakers, and some Anglicans. Moreover, some of the colonies were founded by groups that from the first practiced religious freedom and separated church and state. In Pennsylvania, founded by Quakers who believed firmly in such separation; in Maryland, founded in part to give refuge to the group most distrusted at home, the Catholics, and named after their queen, the French-born Catholic wife of Charles I; in Rhode Island, founded by Roger Williams (c 1603-1683) and others unwilling to conform to the orthodoxy of Massachusetts Bay—in these colonies there was something like religious freedom.

The seeds of democracy existed, although the early settlers, not only in Virginia but also in the North, readily accepted class distinctions. No formal colonial nobility ever arose, however, partly because land was relatively cheap; and the early tendency to develop a privileged gentry or squirearchy in the coastal regions was balanced by the freedom of the frontier and by careers open to talent in the towns. Government by discussion was firmly planted in the colonies from the start, and all of them had some kind of legislative body.

This was the critical difference between the English colonies in the New World and the Spanish and French colonies. In Spain and France the home governments were already centralized bureaucratic monarchies; their representative assemblies were no more than consultative bodies with no power over taxation. Royal governors in Spanish America and in New France could truly dominate their provinces—counting upon men they appointed and recalled, and raising funds by their own authority. But England was a parliamentary monarchy, torn by two revolutions in the seventeenth century. Though the Crown was represented in most colonies by a royal governor, the English government had no such extensive bureaucracy as the Spanish and French had. Royal governors in the English colonies had hardly even a clerical staff and encountered great difficulty in raising money from their legislatures. Furthermore, in all the colonies the established landowners, merchants, and professionals (every colony had property qualifications to vote and hold office) participated not only in colonial assemblies but also in local government—called towns in New England and counties elsewhere. Finally, the settlers brought with them the common law of England, with its trial by jury and its absence of a highly bureaucratic administrative code.

The French in North America

To the north and west of the fourteen colonies, in the region of the St. Lawrence basin, the French built upon the work of Cartier and Champlain, and New France was to be a serious threat to its southern neighbors for a century and a half. The St. Lawrence River and the Great Lakes gave the French easy access by water to the heart of the continent, in contrast to the Appalachian ranges that stood between the English and the Mississippi River. The French were also impelled westward by their search for furs, which are goods of great value and comparatively small bulk, easily carried in canoes and small boats. Trappers depended upon migratory animals, especially the beaver, that retreated further inland as the fur trade progressed, drawing the French increasingly into the interior. Moreover, led by the Jesuits, the Catholic French showed far greater missionary zeal than did the Protestant English. The priest, as well as the *coureur des bois* (literally, rover of the forest, or fur trapper), led the push westward. Finally, the French in North America were guided by a conscious imperial policy, a grand design directed from Bourbon France at the height of its prestige and power.

In this great age of exploration, the French were second only to Spanish (or Spanish-sponsored) explorers in finding new lands, and in North America they were second to none in their exploration of the interior of the continent. The Sieur de La Salle (1643-1687) discovered the mouth of the Mississippi River, which dissected the continent from north to south and broke the pattern of eastward-flowing rivers. In 1682 he took formal possession of a vast region for France. His work was built upon that of a young American-born Frenchman, Louis Joliet (1645-1700), a fur trader, and Father Jacques Marquette (1635-1675), one of six Jesuit missionaries in the vast interior who had passed far enough down the great river before turning back to prove that it flowed into a great sea. Able French colonial governors—of New France, especially the comte de Frontenac (governed 1672-1692, 1689-1698), and of Louisiana after its founding in 1699 by the Canadian-born Sieur Pierre de Moyne d'Iberville (1661-1706)—further enhanced French strength, prestige, and authority among the Indians, who soon found themselves being used by French and English alike in a series of local colonial wars. By 1712 the French had built up a line of isolated trading posts, with miles of unoccupied land between, thinly populated by Indians who were coerced or persuaded into cooperation, so that the territory of New France and that of Louisiana (named after Louis XIV) were linked, and the English colonists on the Atlantic coast thought of themselves as encircled by a "Gallic peril."

Impressive though this French imperial thrust looked on the map, it was far too lightly held to be able to push the English into the sea. It was a trading empire with military ambitions, and except in Quebec it never became a true colony of settlement; even there it never grew in the critical eighteenth century beyond a few thousand inhabitants. Enough French settlers simply did not go overseas, and those who did spread themselves out over vast distances as traders and adventurers. The French who might have come, the Huguenots, were excluded by a royal policy bent on maintaining a total monopoly for the Catholic faith in New France.

The Two Indies, West and East: Areas of Conquest

The northwestern Europe maritime powers intruded upon the Spanish and Portuguese in the New World as in the Old. The French, Dutch, and English all sought to gain footholds in South America, but had to settle for the unimportant Guianas. They thoroughly broke up the Spanish hold on the Caribbean, however, and ultimately made that sea of many islands a kaleidoscope of colonial jurisdictions and a center of constant naval wars and piracy. In early modern times these islands were one of the great prizes of imperialism, the "cockpit of empire." Cheap slave labor raised great staple crops: tobacco, fruits, coffee, and, most profitably, cane sugar. (There was then no competition from beet sugar, which northern countries only began to produce around 1800.)

By 1715 the French, Dutch, and English had also laid the bases of trading and colonial empires in Asia and Africa. India proved to be the richest prize and the most ardently fought for. The Mogul empire could not keep the Europeans out of southern India, but it did confine them mainly to the coastal fringes. Gradually during the seventeenth century both the French and the English established themselves in India, on the heels of decaying Portuguese power and wealth. The English defeated a Portuguese fleet in 1612 and immediately got trading rights at Surat on the western coast. Although the able and active Mogul emperor Aurangzeb (r. 1658-1707) tried to revoke their rights in 1685, he soon found their naval and mercantile power too much to withstand. In 1690 the English founded in Bengal in eastern India the city they were to make famous—Calcutta. Meanwhile, the French had gotten a foothold in 1674 on the south coast near Madras at Pondichéry, and soon had established other stations. By the beginning of the eighteenth century the stage was set in India, as in North America, for a decisive struggle for overseas empire between France and Britain—a struggle now known as the Great War for Empire—which lasted until 1763.

Both countries operated in India, as they had initially in North America, through chartered trading companies: the English East India Company (1600) and the French Compagnie des Indes Orientales (1664). The companies were supported by their governments when it was evident that the whole relationship with India could not be purely commercial, and that some territories around the trading posts had to be held. Although both countries became involved in Indian politics and warfare to support their trading companies, neither attempted extensive permanent settlement in the East.

The Dutch entered even more vigorously into the competition, founding their own East India (1602) and West India (1621) companies. In sharp contrast to the close government supervision exerted by Spain and Portugal over colonial activities every step of the way, the Dutch granted these private business ventures full sovereign powers. They had the right to maintain their own fighting fleets and armies, declare war and wage it, negotiate peace, and govern dependent territories. The Netherlands East India Company succeeded in pushing the Portuguese out of Ceylon and then concentrated on southeastern Asia, especially the East Indies. Here again they pushed the Portuguese out and effectively discouraged interlopers. Through it all the company paid its shareholders an annual dividend averaging 18 percent. Despite their rapid decline as a great power in the eighteenth century, the Dutch had so firm a hold in Java and Sumatra that their empire in Indonesia was to last until the midtwentieth century.

Africa and the Far East: Areas of Influence

To reach the East all three of the northern maritime powers used the ocean route around Africa that the Portuguese had developed in the fifteenth century. All three secured African posts, with the Dutch occupying the strategic Cape of Good Hope at the southern tip of the continent in 1652. While the Cape was at first a repair and replenishing station for Dutch ships on the long voyage to the East, it had a temperate climate, and a small colony of settlement grew up peopled by Dutch and by French Huguenots, together the ancestors of the Afrikaners of twentieth-century South Africa. In West Africa the Dutch took the Portuguese posts on the Guinea and Gold Coasts and won a share of the increasingly lucrative slave trade.

The French too worked down the Atlantic coast, taking Senegal (1626) at the westernmost point of the African bulge, and later reaching the large island of Madagascar and taking the smaller one of Mauritius in the Indian Ocean, from the Dutch. The British secured a foothold at the mouth of the Gambia River near Senegal (1662) and made further acquisitions at the expense of the French and the Dutch. Thus by the eighteenth century a map of Africa and adjacent waters would show a series of coastal stations controlled by various European powers. The interior remained for the most part unexplored, untouched except by slavers and native traders. Not until the nineteenth century was "the Dark Continent," as it was romantically called, opened to European expansion.

The Far East too was not truly opened to Western imperialism until the nineteenth century. In China the Portuguese clung to Macao, and the Dutch, on their heels as always, obtained a station on Taiwan (1624), an island that the Portuguese had named Formosa (beautiful). The Jesuits were tolerated by the Chinese as scientists and technicians in the seventeenth century, but they made few converts. At bottom the Chinese, convinced that their empire was the Middle Kingdom—the spiritual and cultural center of the world—considered most Europeans barbarians who should be paying them tribute.

In Japan the reaction against European penetration was even stronger than in China. The Portuguese had won trading privileges in the sixteenth century, followed

A JAPANESE FOLK TALE

Once upon a time there was a man who did nothing all day long—he just waited and hoped that suddenly he would meet with unexpected good fortune and become rich in an instant without any effort.

And thus he lived for many a year, until one day he heard tell that there was a certain island inhabited by people who had only one eye.

"At last! That will be my good fortune," thought the man to himself. "I'll travel to that island, I'll catch one of these one-eyed creatures and bring him back and show him in the marketplace for a penny a look. In a short while I shall be a rich man."

And the more he thought about it, the more he liked the idea.

Finally he made up his mind. He sold the little that he had, bought a boat and set off. After a long journey he reached the island of the one-eyed creatures and, indeed, hardly had he stepped ashore when he saw that the people there really had only one eye each.

But of course the one-eyed people noticed that here was a man with two eyes, and a few of them got together and said:

"At last! So this will be our good fortune! Let's catch him and show him off to the marketplace for a penny a look. We'll soon be rich men!"

No sooner said than done. They seized the two-eyed man and carried him off to the marketplace, where they showed him for a penny a look.

And that's the sort of thing that happens to people who sit and wait for unexpected good fortune.

From *The Fairy Tale Tree: Stories from All Over the World*, retold by Vladislav Stanovsky and Jan Vladislav, trans. Jean Layton (New York: Putnam's, 1961), p. 242.

by the Dutch in 1609. Meantime, the great Jesuit missionary Francis Xavier, "the Apostle of the Indies" (1506-1552), began preaching in 1549. Many Japanese became Christians. The Tokugawa family, the feudal rulers of Japan from 1600 to 1868, feared Christianity. They saw it as a threat both to national traditions and to their own rule because of the opportunities it might give European powers to intervene in Japanese politics and intrigue with their enemies. They therefore decided to close their land entirely to foreign dangers. In the early seventeenth century they suppressed Christianity with brutal force and sealed off Japan. Foreigners were refused entry, and Japanese were refused exit. Even the building of ocean-going ships was forbidden. The Dutch, who had persuaded the Japanese that Protestants were less subversive than Catholics, were allowed under strict supervision to retain an island in Nagasaki harbor, where after 1715 they were limited to voyages by two ships a year. Not until the American commodore Matthew Perry came to Japan in 1853 was this unusual self-imposed blockade really broken.

V RUSSIA

East by Land to the Pacific

The expansion of Europe in the early modern centuries was not restricted to the maritime powers. Russian exploration and conquest of Siberia matched European expansion in the New World, both chronologically (the Russians crossed the Urals from Europe into Asia in 1483) and politically, for expanding Muscovite Russia was a "new" monarchy, newer in some ways than the Spain of Charles V and Philip II or the England of Elizabeth I. This Russian movement across the land was remarkably rapid—some five thousand miles in about forty years. Thus the Russian advance left vast unabsorbed areas behind the line of formal settlement. The enormous flatlands of the Siberian river basins made movement relatively easy and, unlike the resistance put up by indigenous peoples in other areas into which settlers moved, as in North America, the tribal population of Siberia appears on the whole to have cooperated with the Russians.

The victories of Ivan the Terrible over the Volga Tatars led to the first major advances, with private enterprise leading the way. By the end of the sixteenth century the Stroganov family had obtained huge concessions in the Ural area, where they made a great fortune in the fur trade and discovered and exploited Russia's first iron mines. The Stroganovs hired bands of Cossack explorers, who led the eastward movement; Yermak, "Conqueror of Siberia" (d. 1585), whose exploits took on legendary proportions, extended control to the mouth of the Tobol. At a suitable point on a river basin, the spearhead of the advance party would build a wooden palisade and begin to collect furs from the surrounding area. Almost before the defense of each new position had been consolidated, the restless advance guard would have moved hundreds of miles farther eastward to repeat the process, until the Pacific was reached at Okhotsk in the 1640s.

The government followed with administrators and tax collectors, soldiers and priests, as each new district was opened up. A Siberian bureau in Moscow had nominal responsibility for government of the huge area, but decisions had to be made on the spot because of slow communications, despite an efficient postal service. Thus the Siberians always tended to have the independence traditionally associated with the wide open spaces, reinforced by their Cossack traditions. Because Okhotsk and its surrounding area along the Pacific were intensely cold and the ocean frozen for much of the year, the Russians were soon looking enviously southward toward the valley of the Amur River, which flowed into the Pacific at a point where the harbors were open year round.

Explorations in this area brought the Russians into contact with the Chinese, upon whose outer lands they were now casually encroaching. But the Chinese government of the period had little interest in these regions, which, from its point of view, were distant northern outposts. In 1689 the Chinese signed with Moscow the Treaty of Nerchinsk, the first they concluded with any European state. The treaty stabilized the frontier, demilitarized the Amur valley, and kept the Russians out of Manchuria, the home territory of the ruling Manchu Chinese dynasty, though it recognized the Russian advances farther north. It also provided the two powers with a Mongolian buffer zone that acknowledged Chinese overlordship. Thus, with great speed the Russians had acquired an empire with extensive natural resources and had staked out a future as an Asian power with interests in the Pacific just when the English were eliminating the Dutch as competitors in that other vast frontier land, the New World.

North by Sea to the Arctic

By 1715 European expansion was beginning to affect almost every part of the globe. European explorers, missionaries, traders—the proconsuls of empire—had spread out in all directions. Even Arctic exploration, stimulated by the hope of finding a passage that would shorten the route to the Far East, had gone a long way by the beginning of the eighteenth century. Henry Hudson had found not only the Hudson River, but also Hudson Bay in the far north of Canada. In 1670 English adventurers and investors formed an enterprise that still flourishes—the Hudson's Bay Company, originally set up for fur trading along the great bay to the northwest of French Quebec. In the late sixteenth century the Dutch had penetrated far into the European Arctic, had discovered the island of Spitsbergen to the north of Norway, and had ranged eastward across the sea named after their leader, William Barents (d. 1597). Early in the eighteenth century the Russians also explored most of the long Arctic coasts of Siberia, and a Dane in their service, Vitus Bering (1681-1741), discovered the Aleutian Islands and the sea and strait that now bear his name separating northeastern Siberia from Alaska, proving conclusively that Asia was not connected with North America.

VI THE IMPACT OF EXPANSION

The record of European expansion contains pages as grim as any in history. The African slave trade—begun by the Africans and the Arabs and turned into a profitable sea-borne enterprise by the Portuguese, Dutch, and English—is a series of horrors, from the rounding up of the slaves by local chieftains in Africa, through their transportation across the Atlantic, to their sale in the Indies. The slaves were treated as so much livestock.

American settlers virtually exterminated the native Indian population east of the Mississippi. There were, of course, exceptions to this bloody rule. In New England missionaries like John Eliot, the "Apostle of the Indians" (1604-1690), did set up little bands of "praying Indians," and in Pennsylvania relations between the Quakers and the Indians were excellent. Yet the European diseases, which could not be controlled, together with alcohol, did more to exterminate the Native Americans than did fire and sword.

Seen in terms of economics, however, the expansion of Europe in early modern times was more complex than simple "exploitation" and "plundering." There was robbery, murder, and enslavement. There was, in dealing with the native populations, much giving of "gifts" of nominal value in exchange for land and goods of great value. The almost universally applied mercantilist policy kept money and manufacturing in the home country. It relegated the colonies to producing raw materials—a role that tended to keep colonies of settlement relatively primitive and economically dependent.

While Europeans took the lion's share of colonial wealth in the early modern centuries, some of the silver from America financed European imports of spices and luxuries from Asia. Not many European mercantilist monopolies were watertight in practice, and enterprising locals shared in the new trade and its profits. Although few Europeans settled in India or Africa, their wares, and especially their weapons, gradually began the process that would ultimately produce a worldwide "revolution of rising expectations" in the twentieth century. By the eighteenth century this process was only beginning; in particular, few of the improvements in public health and sanitation that Europeans would bring to the East later on had yet come about, nor had greater public order come to India or Africa, as it

THE SLAVE TRADE

The Dutch slave ship *St. Jan* started off for Curaçao in the West Indies in 1659. Its log recorded deaths of slaves aboard, until between June 30 and October 29 a total of 59 men, 47 women, and 4 children had died. There were still 95 slaves aboard when disaster struck, thus matter-of-factly recorded:

Nov. 1. Lost our ship on the Reef of Rocus, and all hands immediately took to the boat, as there was no prospect of saving the slaves, for we must abandon the ship in consequence of the heavy surf.

Nov. 4. Arrived with the boat at the island of Curaçao; the Hon'ble Governor . . . ordered two sloops to take the slaves off the wreck, one of which sloops with eighty four slaves on board was captured by a privateer.

And here is the governor's report to his board of directors in Holland:

What causes us most grief here is, that your honors have thereby lost such a fine lot of negroes and such a fast sailing bark which has been our right arm here.

Although I have strained every nerve to overtake the robbers of the negroes and bark, as stated in my last, yet have I not been as successful as I wished. . . .

We regret exceedingly that such rovers should have been the cause of the ill success of the zeal we feel to attract the Spanish traders hither for your honors' benefit . . . for the augmentation of commerce and the sale of the negroes which are to come here more and more in your honors' ships and for your account. . . .

I have witnessed with pleasure your honors' diligence in providing us here from time to time with negroes. That will be the only bait to allure hither the Spanish nation, as well from the Main as from other parts, to carry on trade of any importance. But the more subtly and quietly the trade to and on this island can be carried on, the better will it be for this place and yours.

Elizabeth Donnan, ed., *Documents Illustrative of the History of the Slave Trade to America* (Washington, D.C.: Government Printing Office, 1930), I, 143, 150-51.

eventually would. Most fundamentally, colonialism undermined lifestyles and social arrangements that had survived for centuries without offering equally stabilizing substitutes. As a result most native societies were rendered chronically unstable and insecure, and their leaders became more and more dependent on trade and technology from the West.

The West has in its turn been greatly affected by its relations with other peoples. The list of items that have come into Western life since Marco Polo and Columbus is long. It includes foodstuffs above all. Tobacco, brought into Spain in the midsixteenth century, became essential to the pleasure of many Europeans. Maize, or Indian corn (in Europe corn refers to cereal grains in general), was imported from the New World and widely cultivated in Spain and Italy. Potatoes, on the other hand, though they are cheaper to grow in most climates than the staple grains, did not immediately catch on in Europe; in France they had to be popularized in a propaganda campaign that took generations to be effective. Tomatoes, or "love-apples," were long believed to be poisonous and were cultivated only for their looks. Tea from China, coffee from Arabia, and chocolate from the New World—which Europeans took for granted by the eighteenth century—revolutionized taste.

Among Westerners, knowledge of non-European beliefs and institutions eventually penetrated to the level of popular culture, where it was marked by a host of words—*powwow, kowtow, taboo, totem*, for instance. In religion and ethics, however, the West took little from the new worlds opened after Columbus. The first impression of Westerners, when they met the cultures both of the New World and of the East, was that they had nothing to learn from them. Once the process of interchange had gone further, some Europeans were impressed with the mysticism and otherworldliness of Hindu philosophy and religion, and with the ethics of Chinese Confucianism. Others came to admire the dignity and apparent serenity of the lives of many simple peoples. But for the most part, what struck the Europeans—when they bothered to think beyond profits and empire building—was the poverty, dirt, and superstition they felt they found among the masses in India and China—unaware that their own institutions might seem no less superstitious.

Yet exposure to these very different cultures stimulated Western minds and broadened intellectual horizons. The first effect only increased the fund of the marvelous and incredible; early accounts of the New World are full of giants and pygmies, El Dorados where the streets were paved with gold, fountains of eternal youth, wondrous plants and animals. Soon, however, genuine observation was encouraged. The collection of early accounts of voyages edited in English by Richard Hakluyt (c 1552-1616) in 1589 shows the realistic sense and careful observation of these travelers—modern geography on its way to maturity, the foundations of the modern social sciences of anthropology, comparative government, even of economics.

The intellectual effects of the great discoveries were on the whole unsettling, disturbing. Along with the new astronomy, the new mechanics, and the Protestant Reformation, and much else, they helped to break the medieval "cake of custom." They helped, literally, to make a New World of ideas and ideals. Such changes are always hard on human beings, for they demand that people change their minds—something that most find hard to do.

The great discoveries helped to revolutionize the economy and society of Europe. In the long process of inflation and expansion, which has continued with ups and downs to the present, some groups gained and others lost. In general, merchants, financiers, and business people enjoyed a rising standard of living. Those on relatively fixed incomes suffered, including landed proprietors, unless they turned to large-scale capitalist farming. Governments also suffered unless they could find new sources of income. Wage earners, artisans, peasants, and the general majority of people usually did not find their incomes keeping pace with the rise in prices. In short, the effects of expansion were unsettling, even harsh, as well as stimulating. The opportunities for expansion that the overseas discoveries gave to Europeans were obviously one factor in the rapid growth of productivity, population, and technical skills. But, by the midseventeenth century, the beneficial effects of expansion were fading, as silver became scarcer and more costly, colonial manufacturing began to increase, and the colonial market for European goods began to diminish, in defiance of mercantilist strictures.

For Spain the vast empire acquired in the New World both helped and hurt. Perhaps alone among the great powers, Spain was permanently put into decline by the so-called "general crisis" of the seventeenth century. The Catalonian revolt, the Portuguese insurrection of 1640, and the revolt of the Spanish territories in Italy in 1647 successfully challenged the Spanish monarchy, already hurt by the inflationary spiral induced by the flow of precious metals from the New World. These revolts made it increasingly difficult for Spain to defend its far-flung empire against other European powers. Britain in particular began to encroach steadily on that empire. By 1670 England and France were negotiating secretly over the future of the Spanish-American colonies, for England's Charles II regarded his nation as the natural heir of the Spanish overseas legacy.

The death of Philip IV in 1665 brought to the Spanish throne his four-year-old son, and Philip's widow acted as regent; she was preoccupied with religious questions, and the royal armies were being systematically destroyed in an attempt to defend Flanders against Louis XIV of France. In 1670 Spain agreed by treaty with England to admit the English to the New World trade and recognized British conquest of Jamaica; two years earlier the formal independence of Portugal and its colonial possessions had been conceded. Spain's European dominance was ended, and with this collapse went the rapid decline of the empire of Philip II, Spanish

THE FIRST TRAVEL BOOK

A mixture of curiosity, precise observation, and fascination with the new ran through Richard Hakluyt's *Voyages and Discoveries.* A typical example was the extraction of cotton—a fiber that would be at the heart of the Industrial Revolution, would create a revolution in clothing, and would help assure the enslavement of millions of people. Of "bombasine cotton" he recorded:

> . . . this groweth on a certain little tree or briar, not past the height of a man's waist, or little more: the tree hath a slender stalk like unto a briar, or to a carnation gillyflower, with very many branches, bearing on every branch a fruit or rather a cod, growing in round form, containing in it the cotton: and when this bud or cod cometh to the bigness of a walnut, it openeth and showeth forth the cotton, which groweth still in bigness until it be like a fleece of wool as big as a man's fist, and beginneth to be loose, and then they gather it as it were the ripe fruit. The seeds of these trees are as big as peas, and are black, and somewhat flat, and not round; they sow them in plowed ground, where they grow in the fields in great abundance in many countries in Persia, and divers other regions.

Richard Hakluyt, *Voyages and Discoveries: The Principal Navigations, Voyages, Traffiques and Discoveries of the English Nation,* ed. Jack Beeching (New York: Penguin Books, 1972), pp. 230-31.

Cotton had been known from time immemorial in Egypt, India, and China; it was introduced into Spain in the ninth century, but it was hardly known in England until the fifteenth century. Only in the seventeenth century was it introduced extensively from India, and then into other "divers regions," including the southern colonies of English North America, and, in time, Africa. Empire thus made cotton the world's best known, most important plant fiber.

mastery of the seas between the New World and Asia, and effective Spanish control over South American colonies. In 1678 Spain accepted France's terms for peace.

As European powers expanded into Africa, Asia, and the New World, they left their mark so indelibly as to "Europeanize" the world. This does not mean that indigenous cultures were radically changed, for traditional ways of life continued little altered. Rather, it means that European ideas dominated the way in which history was written, for example, the notion that Europeans were "discovering" people—people who, from the vision of their own history, had no need to be "discovered." In a sense, a New World was made as well as found, invented by European literature and thought. This is one other definition of the modern world: a world seen as a unity brought on by expansion, whether Spanish, Portuguese, French, English, or Russian.

The transition from medieval to modern history was marked by European expansion. Indeed, the making of one vast new nation in North America—at first a product of European history, then an independent piece of that history, and ultimately a major power within that history—was one of the prime results of the colonial empires and one of the hallmarks of the move from medieval to modern times. Even as Spain declined, the fact that its empire would in part be inherited by another centralizing monarchy—though not one of religious (or even political) absolutism—meant that the world was drawing more into one.

"There is only one world, and although we speak of the Old World and the New, this is because the latter was lately discovered by us, and not because there are two."* These words were written by a Spaniard in sixteenth-century Peru. By the eighteenth century—although there were still blank spots on the map, especially in the African interior and the Pacific northwest of America, and although Japan and China still tried to exclude European influence—it was already clear that one system of international politics dominated the world. European wars increasingly tended to be "world wars," fought, if only by privateers, on the seven seas and on distant continents. Sooner or later, any considerable transfer of territory overseas and any great accession of strength or wealth in any quarter of the globe affected the international balance of power with which European monarchs were so concerned.

The one world of the eighteenth century was not one world of the spirit; the great mass of Europeans were ignorant of other cultures. But already Western goods penetrated almost everywhere, led by firearms and liquor but followed by a great many other commodities, not all of them "cheap and nasty," as later critics of imperialism would charge. Already an educated minority was appearing, from professional geographers to journalists, diplomats, and business people, who dealt

*J.H. Elliott, *The Old World and the New* (New York: Cambridge University Press, 1970), p. 59.

with what were now quite literally the affairs of the world. Perhaps the most powerful act of imperialism was that the history of the world and the history of Western civilization increasingly seemed to overlap, and that the history of the non-Western world came to be written in the language of the West, with Western place names imposed upon it.

The conventional date for the end of the great Age of Discovery is 1779—the year in which the English explorer Captain James Cook (1728-1779) was killed on the Sandwich (or Hawaiian) Islands. It was Cook who, in three great voyages, made known the full shape of the Pacific Ocean, from Cape Horn to the Bering Strait, from new Holland (present-day Australia) and New Zealand to Japan, and deep into the Antarctic Ocean. There was, of course, much yet to discover, much fame yet to be won, but from now on it would be more in the interior of the continents and not on the seas. The age of maritime exploration had knit the globe together as one intellectual construction, just as it had also set peoples against one another, for the pursuit of gold, for the glory of God, and for the satisfaction of their hunger for knowledge and adventure.

SUMMARY

In the early modern period explorers representing western European nations crossed vast oceans to discover other civilizations. With superior material and technological strength, especially firearms, Europeans were able to win empires. The motives for European expansion varied from desire to serve God to glory, gold, and strategic need.

Prince Henry directed early Portuguese exploration in order to promote commerce, national power, and Christianity. In 1488 Bartholomeu Dias rounded the Cape of Good Hope, and by 1497 Vasco da Gama had reached India by sea. Soon afterwards, Portugal acquired a dominant position in trade with the East.

Europeans were generally contemptuous of Eastern civilization. Taking advantage of military and political disunity in India, western Europeans were able to dominate the subcontinent with relatively few people. In India, Europeans found an entrenched caste system. Further east, in China, they found an ancient civilization that had weathered many changes. The Chinese emperor, with the aid of a bureaucracy run by mandarins, ruled a huge empire that was firmly built on communal villages.

Portugal established its trading empire on mercantilist principles that held that the mother country should supply manufactured goods in exchange for raw materials from its colony. Other nations were excluded from the trading monopoly the mother country established. Despite their head start, the Portuguese were challenged in the sixteenth century by the French, Dutch, and English, and they eventually lost their dominance in the East.

In 1492 Columbus, an experienced voyager, discovered a "New World" for Europeans that he claimed for Spain. Discoveries multiplied after Columbus, especially as explorers hunted for a northwest or southwest passage around the Americas.

The conquests of Cortés and Pizarro gave Spain a vast empire in the Americas. Spain established a centralized administration in its New World colonies with a viceroy representing the Crown. Indians were converted to Christianity and were protected by the New Laws of 1542. Nevertheless, millions died of European diseases and harsh treatment.

In the seventeenth century England established permanent colonies in North America, overrunning earlier Dutch and Swedish colonies. Although New England was largely settled by Calvinists and the southern colonies by Anglicans, differences among the colonies were influenced by geography and climate as well as by social and economic factors. Unlike the colonies of Spain and France, where royal governors represented centralized bureaucracies, English royal governors lacked extensive bureaucracies.

In the St. Lawrence region explored by Cartier and Champlain, the French established New France. The search for fur led to exploration of the interior of North America, but the region was not heavily settled by colonists.

Both the Spanish-held West Indies—where sugar, tobacco, fruit, and coffee crops were profitable exports—and the East Indies became battlegrounds for imperialist powers. France, England, and the Netherlands established coastal posts in Africa but did not expand inland. In China and Japan, rulers imposed restrictions on foreigners. By the midseventeenth century, Japan had virtually sealed itself off from the West, a self-imposed isolation that lasted until 1853.

At the same time that Western European nations expanded overseas, Russia explored and conquered a vast Asian empire that stretched across Siberia to the Pacific.

The age of European expansion resulted in the horrors of the slave trade, the extermination of Indian populations, and the undermining of social arrangements that had existed for centuries. New products as well as knowledge of other beliefs and institutions created a new world in the West. Expansion revolutionized economies and societies in Europe. As Portugal, Spain, France, Britain, and Russia explored Africa, Asia, and the New World, they set the stage for international politics for centuries to come.

chapter fifteen

THE PROBLEM OF DIVINE-RIGHT MONARCHY

The Peace of Westphalia in 1648 ended the Thirty Years' War but also marked the end of an epoch in European history. It ended the Age of the Reformation and Counter-Reformation, when wars were both religious and dynastic in motivation, and the chief threats to a stable international balance came from the Catholic Hapsburgs and from the militant Protestants of Germany, the Netherlands, and Scandinavia. After 1648 religion, though continuing to be a major source of friction in France and the British Isles, ceased to be a significant international issue elsewhere. The main force jeopardizing the European balance thereafter was the entirely secular ambition of Bourbon France on the Continent and abroad. For seventy-two years (1643-1714) France was under a single monarch, Louis XIV, who inherited the throne when only four.

Louis was the embodiment of the early modern form of royal absolutism—monarchy by divine right—and he was the personification of royal pride, elegance, and luxury. To the French, Louis XIV was the *grand monarque*. His long reign brought to an end the *grand siècle*, that great century begun under Cardinal Richelieu in the twenty years before Louis's accession that was marked by the international triumph of French arms and French diplomacy and, still more, of French ways of writing, building, dressing, eating—the whole style of life of the upper classes in France, which called itself *la grande nation*.

While French culture went from triumph to triumph, Louis XIV's bid for political hegemony was ultimately checked. His most resolute opponent was England, still in the throes of the greatest political upheaval in its history, an upheaval that resulted from the collision between the forces of the Stuart monarchy and High Church Anglicanism, on the one hand, and those of Parliament and the Puritans, on the other. The final settlement, after decades of violence and change, was a compromise weighted in favor of the parliamentary side, with one English king executed and another forced into exile. While France appeared stable, England was racked by revolution and insecurity.

The seventeenth century, during which the struggle for stability could be seen in most societies of early modern Europe, was an age of crisis. In England the aristocracy faced unique challenges; a steady decline in population in war-ravaged Germany and in Spain changed society drastically, and the years after 1648 were marked throughout most of Europe by a severe depression, by social upheavals, and by a struggle between the capitalism espoused by the rising middle class and the agrarian traditions of the landed classes, who feared displacement. Revolution seemed almost commonplace—successful, abortive, plotted, rumored—in England, France, Portugal, Spain, and elsewhere. Still, since the province or an even smaller local unit generally remained relatively self-sufficient economically, these broad generalizations about trends are open to many exceptions. And as always, amidst change there was continuity.

It was also a century of intellectual ferment, as writers, philosophers, theologians, painters sought to justify monarchy by divine right or revolution by various groups that saw themselves as "the people," and as the basic intellectual underpinnings of society were changed. The seventeenth century is often called "the century of the genius," for so many innovative ideas sprang forth during it: from explorers and conquerors, from simple sailors and soldiers, from figures like Bacon, Descartes, Pascal, Newton, or Locke, as well as from inventors who drew upon the theories of Galileo and others. According to different historians, "modern history" began with a different event or development, but nearly all agree that the 1600s were the century when Western civilization passed into what is known as the Modern Age.

The intimations of popular revolution in the seventeenth century, the impact of new ideas on a broader public, and the slow but certain change of even traditional peasant culture, which was becoming more articulate, more observable through the printed record, were yet another dividing line between the Middle Ages and the modern period. Before 1700 most people apparently were basically illiterate; a century later, literacy was apparently far more widespread.

I BOURBON FRANCE

Louis XIII and Richelieu, 1610-1643

In 1610 the capable and popular Henry IV was assassinated in the prime of his career by a madman who was believed at the time to be working for the Jesuits—a charge for which there is no proof. The new king, Louis XIII (1610-1643), was nine years old; the queen mother, Marie de' Medici, served as regent but showed little political skill. Her Italian favorites and French nobles, Catholic and Huguenot alike, carried on a hectic competition that threatened to undo all that Henry IV had accomplished. During these troubles the French representative body, the Estates General, met in 1614 for what was destined to be its last session until 1789. Significantly, the meeting was paralyzed by tensions between the noble deputies of the second estate and the bourgeois of the third. Meanwhile, Louis XIII, though barely into his teens, tried to assert his personal authority and reduce the role of his mother. Poorly educated, sickly, masochistic, and subject to depression, Louis needed expert help.

This illustration from Abraham Bosse's "Le Palais Royal" (1640) provides a good picture of French fashions and tastes. Bosse (1602-1676) took a particular interest in etchings that showed how the upper middle class dressed. Furniture also evolved in new styles to accommodate the new clothing.

He was fortunate in securing the assistance of the remarkably talented duc de Richelieu (1585-1642), who was an efficient administrator as bishop of the remote diocese of Autun. Tiring of provincial life, Richelieu moved to Paris and showed unscrupulous skill in political maneuvering during the confused days of the regency. He emerged as the conciliator between the king and his mother and was rewarded, first, by being made a cardinal and then, in 1624, with selection by Louis as his chief minister. While the king maintained a lively interest in affairs of state, Richelieu was the virtual ruler of France for the next eighteen years. He proved to be a good Machiavellian, subordinating religion and every other consideration to *raison d'état* (reason of state)—a phrase that he may have coined himself.

Richelieu had four goals for the France of Louis XIII: to eliminate the Huguenots as an effective political force; to remind the nobles that they were subordinate to the king; to make all of France conscious of a sense of national greatness; and, through these measures, to make the monarchy truly rather than only theoretically absolute. *Raison d'état* made the ruin of the Huguenots the first priority, for the political privileges they had received by the Edict of Nantes made them a major obstacle to the creation of a centralized state. The hundred fortified towns they governed, chiefly in the southwest, were a state within the state, a hundred centers of potential rebellion. Alarmed, the Huguenots rebelled. The fall of La Rochelle, their chief stronghold, in 1628 and Richelieu's unexpectedly humane approach—by which the political and military clauses of the Edict of Nantes were revoked while partial religious toleration continued—helped Richelieu neutralize the Huguenots.

The siege of La Rochelle was prolonged because France had no navy worthy of the name. Over the next

LE GRAND MONARQUE

At age twenty-two Louis XIV already displayed an impressive royal presence, as reported by Madame de Motteville (d. 1689), an experienced observer of the French court:

> As the single desire for glory and to fulfill all the duties of a great king occupied his whole heart, by applying himself to toil he began to like it; and the eagerness he had to learn all the things that were necessary to him soon made him full of that knowledge. His great good sense and his good intentions now made visible in him the rudiments of general knowledge which had been hidden from all who did not see him in private. . . . He was agreeable personally, civil and easy of access to every one; but with a lofty and serious air which impressed the public with respect and awe . . . , though he was familiar and gay with ladies.

Memoirs of Madame [Françoise Bertaut] de Motteville on Anne of Austria and Her Court, trans. Katherine Prescott Wormeley (Boston: Hardy Pratt, 1902), III, 243.

As she noted, the young king never laughed in games or at play, and he said of himself that he must be "perfect in all things" and never be found "to fail in anything."

ten years Richelieu created a fleet of warships for the Atlantic and a squadron of galleys manned by European slaves for the Mediterranean. Meanwhile, he guided France expertly through the Thrity Years' War, committing French resources only when concrete gains seemed possible and ensuring favorable publicity by supplying exaggerated accounts of French victories to the *Gazette de France*.

Few official portraits from this period have survived. The only ones about which knowledge is certain are those of Louis XIII and Richelieu. Philippe de Champaigne (1602-1674) often depicted Richelieu, and in this triple portrait he sought to emphasize the rationalism of the age. The painting is now in the National Gallery, London.

Next Richelieu tried to humble the nobles, with only partial success, by ordering the destruction of some of their fortresses and forbidding private duels. More effective was his transfer of supervision of local administration from the nobles and officeholders of doubtful loyalty who had purchased their posts to more reliable royal officials called *intendants*. These officials had existed earlier but had performed only minor functions; now they were given greatly increased powers over justice, the police, and taxation.

Richelieu made possible *la grande nation* of Louis XIV by building an efficient, centralized state. But in a sense he built too well, making the French government so centralized, so professionally bureaucratic, that it became too inflexible for the give and take of politics. Moreover, Richelieu did little to remedy the chronic fiscal weakness of the government, particularly the corruption in tax collection and the recurrent deficits. His concentration on *raison d'état* led him to take a callous view of the subjects on whose loyal performance of their duties the strength of the state depended. He believed that the masses were best kept docile through hard work, that leisure led to mischief, and that the common people ought to take pride in the splendors of the monarchy, in the accomplishments of French literary culture, and in victories over the monarch's enemies. Individual hardship, especially among the lower classes, was to be accepted in the interests of national glory—a common ingredient of nationalism.

Mazarin

The deaths of Richelieu in 1642 and Louis XIII in 1643, the accession of another child king, and the regency of the hated queen mother, Anne of Austria (actually a

Hapsburg from Spain, where the dynasty was called the house of Austria), all seemed to threaten a repetition of the crisis that had followed the death of Henry IV. The new crisis was dealt with by the new chief minister, Jules Mazarin (1602-1661), a Sicilian who had been picked and schooled by Richelieu himself and was exceptionally close to Anne. Mazarin, too, was a cardinal (though not a priest, as Richelieu had been) and a supreme exponent of *raison d'état*. Mazarin was also careless about the finances of France, but, unlike Richelieu, he amassed an immense personal fortune during his career. He antagonized both branches of the French aristocracy: the nobles of the sword, descendants of feudal magnates, and the nobles of the robe (the reference is to the gowns worn by judges and other officials), descendants of commoners who had bought their way into government office. The former resented being excluded from the regency by a foreigner; the latter, who had invested heavily in government securities, particularly disliked Mazarin's casual way of borrowing money to meet war expenses and then neglecting to pay the interest on the loans.

In 1648 discontent boiled over in the *Fronde* (named for the slingshot used by Parisian children to hurl pellets at the rich in their carriages), one of several midcentury uprisings in Europe. Some of the rioting involved the rural peasantry and the common people of Paris, impoverished by the economic depression accompanying the final campaigns of the Thirty Years' War and deeply affected by the peak famine years of 1648-1651. But the Fronde was essentially a revolt of the nobles, led first by the judges of the Parlement of Paris, a stronghold of the nobles of the robe, and then, after the Peace of Westphalia, by aristocratic officers returned from the Thirty Years' War. Various "princes of the blood" (relatives of the royal family) confusingly intervened with private armies. Though Mazarin twice had to flee France and go into exile, and though the royal troops had to lay siege to Paris, and despite concessions Mazarin felt forced to make, the end result of what was in reality two revolts in one—of the Parlement and of the nobles—was to weaken both. The Fronde prepared the way for the personal rule of Louis XIV, with the mass of ordinary citizens in Paris supporting the queen and her son when they returned in triumph in October of 1652. Essentially, the Fronde failed because it had no real roots in the countryside, not even in the rising middle classes of the provincial cities. Rather, it was essentially a struggle for power, pitting Mazarin and his new bureaucracy against the two privileged groups of nobles, each of which distrusted the other. All Mazarin had to do was to apply the old Roman maxim, "Divide and rule."

Louis XIV, 1643-1714

When Mazarin died in 1661, Louis XIV began his personal rule. He had been badly frightened during the Fronde when rioters had broken into his bedroom, and he was determined to suppress any challenge to his authority, by persuasion and guile if possible, and by force if necessary. In 1660 he married a Spanish princess for political reasons; after a succession of mistresses, he married again, in 1685, to a devout former Huguenot, Madame de Maintenon, the governess of his illegitimate children, and she did much to assure dignified piety at court for the rest of his reign.

Louis XIV, the Sun King, succeeded as the *grand monarque* because by education, temperament, and physique he was ideally suited to the role. He had admirable self-discipline, patience, and staying power. He never lost his temper in public and went through long daily council meetings and elaborate ceremonials with unwearied attention and even enjoyment, to which his conspicuous lack of a sense of humor may have contributed. He had an iron physical constitution, which enabled him to withstand a rigorous schedule, made him indifferent to heat and to cold, and allowed him to survive both a lifetime of gross overeating and the crude medical treatment of the day.

He was five feet five inches tall (a fairly impressive height for that day) and added to his stature by shoes with high red heels. To provide a suitable setting for the Sun King, to neutralize the high nobility politically by isolating it in the ceaseless ceremonies and petty in-

Engraving was a particularly important art form in the seventeenth century, for acids and etching tools had been greatly improved. The French were proud of their public buildings, which were often used as subjects for engravings, as with this work by P. Menant, showing the Palace of Versailles. The foreground emphasizes that the palace was in the countryside, well outside Paris.

trigues of court life, and also to prevent a repetition of the rioters' intrusion into his bedroom in Paris, he moved the capital from Paris to Versailles, a dozen miles away. There, between 1668 and 1711, he built a vast palace more than a third of a mile long, set in an immense formal garden with fourteen hundred fountains, supplied by water which had to be pumped up from the River Seine at great expense. Versailles housed, mainly in cramped, uncomfortable quarters, a court of ten thousand, including dependents and servants of all sorts. This was self-conscious government by spectacle, and it would be copied by every monarch who could afford it—and some who could not.

Divine-Right Monarchy

The much admired and imitated French state, of which Versailles was the symbol and Louis XIV the embodiment, is also the best historical example of divine-right monarchy. Perhaps Louis never actually said, "*L'état c'est moi*" (I am the state), but the phrase clearly summarizes his convictions about his role. In theory, Louis was the representative of God on earth—or at least in France. He was not elected by the French, nor did he acquire his throne by force of arms; rather, he was born to a position God had planned for the legitimate male heir of Hugh Capet who had been king of France in the tenth century. As God's agent his word was final, for to challenge it would be to challenge the structure of God's universe; disobedience was a religious as well as a political offense. Thus the origins of divine right were a logical extension of Gallicanism.

In some ways the theory that justified divine-right monarchy looked back to the Middle Ages, to the view that right decisions in government are not arrived at by experiment and discussion, but by "finding" the authoritative answer provided for in God's scheme of things. In other ways the theory was "modern" or forward-looking, in that it derived from expectations about national loyalties and the growth of a sense of nationalism. Henry IV, Richelieu, and Louis XIV sought to fuse the sixteen million inhabitants of France into a single national unit. The problem was to make these millions think of themselves as French and not as Normans, Bretons, Flemings, Alsatians, Burgundians, Gascons, Basques, and Provençaux. The makers of the Bourbon monarchy could not rely on a common language, for only a minority spoke the standardized French that the French Academy tried to foster. Nor could they rely on a common education, a common national press, or a common participation in political life. They could, and did, attempt to set the king up as the symbol of common Frenchness. The king collected taxes, raised armies, and touched the lives of his subjects in a hundred ways. The French had to believe that the king had a right to do all this, and that he was doing it for them rather than to them.

Divine-right monarchy, with its corollary of unquestioning obedience on the part of subjects, was thus one ingredient in the growth of the modern centralized nation-state. It was an institution that appealed to old theological ideas, such as the biblical admonition to obey the powers that be, for "the powers that be are ordained of God." But it was also inspired by the newer ideas of binding people together in a productive, efficient, and secure state. Naturally, in practice the institution did not wholly correspond to theories about it. Louis XIV was not the French state, and his rule was not absolute in any true sense of that word. He simply did not have the physical means to control in detail everything his subjects did; but his policies could touch their daily lives by bringing relative prosperity or hardship, peace or war. And Louis XIV could endeavor, in the majesty of his person, to act out the theories of those like Bishop Jacques Bossuet (1627-1704), who provided the intellectual foundations for a universal history that justified divine-right arguments.

Increasingly, the chief opposition to such ideas came not from the various religions but from the feudal nobles, so that in both France and England the seventeenth century brought a crisis to the aristocracy. The degree to which the nobility was integrated into the new state machinery was of crucial importance in the development of modern Europe. In Hapsburg Spain and in the Hapsburg lands of central Europe the old nobility generally accepted the new strength of the Crown, but maintained many of their privileges and all of their old pride of status. In Prussia they were more successfully integrated into the new order, becoming servants of the crown, yet with a social status that set them well above bourgeois bureaucrats. In England the nobility achieved a unique compromise with the Crown. In France the nobles of the sword were deprived of most major political functions, but they were allowed to retain social and economic privileges and important roles as officers in the king's army.

This process of reducing the old French nobility to relative powerlessness in national political life had begun during the fifteenth century and had been hastened by the religious and civil wars of the next century. An important part of the nobility, perhaps nearly half, had become Protestant, in large part from sheer opposition to the Crown. The victory of Henry IV, purchased by his conversion to Catholicism, was a defeat for the nobility. Under Richelieu and Louis XIV the process was completed by the increasing use of commoners to run the government, from the great ministers of state, through the intendants, down to local administrators and judges. These commoners were usually elevated to the nobility of the robe, which did not at first have the social prestige of the nobility of the sword. But the Fronde had shown that these new nobles could not be counted upon as loyal supporters of the Crown, and among the old nobles they aroused contemptuous envy. Though at times they were able to work together, they posed no long-term threat to the Crown.

Louis XIV was sixty-three and at the height of his power when Hyacinthe Rigaud (1659-1743) painted this strikingly posed portrait. In the background Rigaud has invoked memories of another great empire, Rome, while showing Louis's strength and sense of elegance in the flowing robe, the great ceremonial sword of office, and the coiffed wig. This portrait hangs in the Louvre in Paris.

Nor did the church. Under Louis XIV the French clergy continued to possess important privileges; they were not subject to royal taxation; they contributed a voluntary grant of money that they voted in their own assembly. Carefully the Crown fostered the evolution of a national Gallican chuch, firmly Catholic though controlled by the monarchy. The Gallican union of throne and altar reached a high point in 1682, when an assembly of French clerics drew up the Declaration of Gallican Liberties, asserting in effect that the "rules and customs admitted by France and the Gallican church" were just as important as the traditional authority of the papacy. Louis XIV thereupon took as the goal of his religious policy the application of a French motto—*un roi, une loi, une foi* (One king, one law, one faith).

Where Richelieu had attacked only the political privileges of the Huguenots, Louis attacked their fundamental right of toleration and finally revoked the Edict of Nantes in 1685. Fifty thousand Huguenot families fled abroad, notably to Prussia, Holland, the Dutch colony in southern Africa, England, and British North America. The practical skills and the intellectual abilities of the refugees strenghtened the lands that received them, and the departure of industrious workers and thousands of veteran sailors, soldiers, and officers weakened France. Some Huguenots remained in France, worshiping secretly despite persecution.

Within the Catholic church itself, Louis had to contend with two important elements that refused to accept Gallicanism. Both groups saw themselves as countering the Counter-Reformation while remaining within the Catholic church. The Quietists, a group of religious enthusiasts led by Madame Jeanne Marie Guyon (1648-1717), sought a more mystical and emotional faith and believed in direct inspiration from God and perfect union with him, so that a priesthood was not needed; but their tendency to exhibitionism and self-righteousness combined with their zeal for publicity belied their name and offended the king's sense of propriety. The Jansenists, sometimes called the Puritans of the Catholic church, were a high-minded group whose most distinguished spokesman was the scientist and philosopher Blaise Pascal. Named for Cornelius Jansen (1585-1638), bishop of Ypres, the Jansenists took an almost Calvinistic stand on predestination. They stressed the need to obey God rather than man, no matter how exalted the position of the particular man might be. They therefore questioned the authority of both king and pope, and attacked the pope's agents, the Jesuits. On the surface, Louis repressed both Quietists and Jansenists, but the latter survived two papal bulls of condemnation (1705, 1713) to trouble his successors in the eighteenth century.

The Royal Administration

Of course, in a land as large and complex as France, even the tireless Louis could do no more than exercise general supervision. At Versailles he had three long conferences weekly with his ministers, who headed departments of War, Finance, Foreign Affairs, and the Interior. The king kept this top administrative level on an intimate scale; he usually had only four ministers at one time and gave them virtually permanent tenure. Jean Colbert (1619-1683) served as controller general for eighteen years, and Michel Le Tellier (1603-1685) was secretary of state for the army for thirty-four years, a post later entrusted to his son, who had been ennobled as the marquis de Louvois (1639-1691). All told, only sixteen ministers held office during the fifty-four years of Louis's personal reign. Yet in practice the royal administration was full of difficulties and contradictions. There were many conflicting jurisdictions, survivals of feudalism; the officials of Louis XIV, being nobles of the robe, had a privileged status they could hand down to their heirs. The thirty key provincial administrators, the intendants, were agents of the Crown, but many of them exercised considerable initiative on their own, despite being moved about from one administrative unit to another.

A particularly important potential for trouble existed in the parlements, the supreme courts of appeal in the various provinces. The Parlement of Paris enjoyed special prestige and power from its place in the capital and from the size of its territorial jurisdiction—almost half of France. The judges who staffed these courts headed the nobility of the robe, owned their offices, and could not be removed by the king. Besides the usual work of a court of appeals, the parlements also had to register royal edicts before they went into force. They thus claimed the right to refuse an edict if they thought it not in accord with the higher law of the land. Although this claim negated theoretical royal absolutism, Louis got around it in his own lifetime by using another old institution, the *lit de justice* (literally, "bed of justice"), in which he summoned the Parlement of Paris before him in a formal session and ordered the justices to register a royal edict. In this way, for instance, he enforced measures against Jansenism, which was strong among the judges. But the parlements were also to continue to plague his eighteenth-century successors.

Mercantilism and Colbert Divine-right monarchy was not peculiarly French, of course, nor was the mercantilism practiced by the France of Louis XIV. But like divine-right rule, it flourished most characteristically under the Sun King. Mercantilism was central to the early modern effort to construct strong, efficient political units. The mercantilists aimed to make their nation as self-sustaining as possible, as independent as possible of the need to import goods from other nations, which were its rivals and potential enemies. The mercantilists held that production within a nation should provide all the necessities of life for a hard-working population, and also provide the power needed to fight and win wars. They believed that these goals required planning and control from above. They wished to sweep away such medieval remnants as the manor and the guild, which, they felt, reduced the energies and abilities needed in an expanding economy. But they did not believe, as free-trade economists would later argue, that people should be free to do whatever they thought would enrich themselves. Instead, the mercantilists would channel the national economic effort by protective tariffs, by government subsidies, by grants of monopolies, by industries run directly by the government, and by scientific and applied research.

The mercantilists viewed overseas possessions as a particularly important part of France that should be run from the homeland by a strong government. Many foodstuffs and raw materials were more easily available overseas than in Europe. Colonies therefore should be encouraged to provide necessities, so that the mother country need not import them from competitors. In return, the mother country would supply industrial goods to the colonies and have a monopoly over colonial trade. This mercantilistic approach to colonies was followed not only by France and Spain but by the less absolutist governments of England and Holland.

The great French practitioner of mercantilism was Colbert, who had served his apprenticeship under Mazarin and advanced rapidly to become controller general early in the personal reign of Louis. He never quite attained the supremacy reached by Richelieu and Mazarin; he was the collaborator, never the master, of Louis XIV, since other great ministers, especially, Louvois for military affairs, stood in the way of his supremacy. Yet Colbert was influential in all matters affecting the French economy, most interested in foreign trade and in the colonies, and therefore in the merchant marine and in the navy. His hand was in everything: in invention, in technological education, in designing and building ships, in attracting foreign experts to settle in France.

Among the industries Colbert fostered were the processing of sugar, chocolate, and tobacco from the colonies; the production of military goods by iron foundries and textile mills; and the manufacture of the luxuries for which the French soon became famous. The fifteenth-century Gobelins tapestry enterprise in Paris was taken over by the state and its output expanded to include elegant furniture, for which the king was a major customer. Glassblowers and lacemakers were lured away from Venice, despite strenuous efforts by the Venetian republic to keep their valuable techniques secret. In a blow against French competitors, Colbert imposed heavy tariffs on some Dutch and English products. To promote trade with the colonies and also with the Baltic and the Mediterranean, he financed trading companies, of which only the French India Company eventually succeeded.

At home, Colbert encouraged reforestation, so that iron foundries could have abundant supplies of charcoal (then essential for smelting); he also promoted the planting of mulberry trees to nourish the silkworms vital to textile output. He even attempted—vainly, as it turned out—to control quality by ordering that defective goods be prominently exhibited in public, along with the name of the offending producer, and that the culprit be exhibited for a third offense. He also endeavored, again for the most part in vain, to break down the barriers to internal free trade, such as provincial and municipal tariffs or local restrictions on the shipment of grain to other parts of France. He did, however, successfully sponsor the construction of important roads and canals; the Canal du Midi, linking the Atlantic port of Bordeaux with the Mediterranean port of Narbonne, reduced transport charges between the two seas by three-fourths and was described as the greatest engineering feat since Roman days.

Whether the great prosperity France achieved in the first thirty years of Louis's reign came about because of, or despite, the mercantilist policies of Colbert is difficult to decide. Under the mercantilist regime France did attain undoubted leadership in European industry and commerce. That lead was lost in part because the last two wars of Louis XIV were ruinously expensive, in part because in the eighteenth century France's rival, England, introduced new methods of power machinery and concentrated on large-scale production of inexpensive goods, while France clung to the policies set by Colbert, favoring relatively small-scale production of luxuries and other consumer goods. But the difference between French and English industry was also a difference in the focus of national energies; France, like Spain before it, spent an exceptional proportion of its national product in an unfruitful effort to dominate through the force of arms both Europe and the known overseas world.

French Expansion

France was the real victor in the Thirty Years' War, acquiring lands on its northeastern frontier. In a postscript to the main conflict, it continued fighting with Spain until the Peace of the Pyrenees in 1659, securing additional territories. Prospering economically, France was ready for further expansion when the young and ambitious Louis XIV began his personal rule in 1661. Louis hoped to complete the gains of 1648 and 1659 and secure France's "natural frontiers" along the Rhine and the Alps. As his sense of confidence grew, he waged a mercantilist war against France's major economic competitors, Holland and England. At the height of his prestige, Louis probably wanted to revive the multinational empire that Charlemagne had ruled nine hundred years earlier. He was also keenly aware of cultural imperialism, and he wanted the French language, French taste in the arts, and French customs to spread their influence over Europe.

Louis XIV and his talented experts fashioned splendid instruments to support this aggressive foreign policy. In 1661 half a dozen men made up the whole Ministry of Foreign Affairs; half a century later it had a large staff of clerks, archivists, coders (and decoders) of secret messages, secret agents, and great lords and prelates who lent their dignity to important embassies. The growth of the French army was still more impressive, from a peacetime force of twenty thousand to a wartime one almost twenty times larger. Louis and his lieutenants almost revolutionized the character of France's fighting forces. At the Ministry of War the father and son team of Lė Tellier and Louvois grouped regiments in brigades under a general to bring them under closer control. They also introduced two new ranks of officer, major and lieutenant colonel, to give more opportunity to talented commoners; these new commissions were awarded only for merit and were not available for purchase, like the ranks of colonel or captain. Supplies were more abundant, pay was more regular, and an effort was made to weed out the lazy. The inspector general of infantry, Jean Martinet (d. 1672), was so rigorous in drilling and discipline that his name added a word to the modern vocabulary. The armies showed particular strength in artillery, engineering, and siege techniques, all important in the days when armies moved ponderously and did much fighting in the waterlogged Low Countries. The French boasted an engineer of genius, Marshal de Vauban (1633-1707), of whom it was said that a town he besieged was indefensible and a town he defended was impregnable. And though military medical services remained crude and sketchy, a large veteran's hospital, Hôtel des Invalides, was built in Paris.

The First Two Wars of Louis XIV The main thrust of this vast effort was northeast, toward the Low Countries and Germany. Louis XIV sought also to secure Spain as a French satellite with a French ruler. Finally, French commitments overseas in North America and in India drove him to attempt, against English and Dutch rivals, to establish a great French empire outside Europe.

The first war of Louis XIV was a minor one, with Spain, and it ended quickly with the peace of Aix-la-Chappelle in 1668. Furious at the Dutch because of their economic ascendancy, their Calvinism, and their republicanism, Louis resolved to teach them a lesson for entering into an alliance with England and Sweden against him. He bought off Sweden and England, and in 1672 French forces invaded Holland. The terrified Dutch turned to the youthful William III of Orange (1650-1702), great-grandson of the martyred hero of Dutch independence, William the Silent. But the French advance was halted only by the extreme measure of opening the dikes.

Thereupon, Spain, the Holy Roman Empire, and Brandenburg-Prussia joined against France and her allies. French diplomacy separated this ineffective coalition at the six treaties of Nijmegen (Nimwegen) in 1678-1679. Holland was left intact at the cost of promising to remain neutral, and the French gave up Colbert's tariff on Dutch goods; Spain ceded to France the Franche Comté (county of Burgundy), part of the Hapsburgs' Burgundian inheritance, plus some towns in Belgium; Prussia, which had defeated Louis's ally, Sweden, at Fehrbellin (1675), was nonetheless obliged by French pressure to return Swedish lands in Germany. The power and prestige of France were now at their peak, as rulers all over Europe, and in particular the host of minor German princes, tried to copy the standards of Versailles.

The Last Two Wars But in the last three decades of Louis's reign most of his assets were consumed. Not content with the prestige he had won in his first two wars, Louis took on most of the Western world in what looked like an effort to destroy the independence of Holland and most of western Germany and to bring the Iberian peninsula under a French ruler. As a prelude to new military aggression special courts, "chambers of reunion," were set up by the French in the early 1680s to tidy up the loose ends of the peace settlements of the past generation. And there were loose ends aplenty on the northern and eastern frontiers of France, a zone of political fragmentation and confused feudal remnants, many of which were technically within the Holy Roman Empire. After examining the documents in disputed cases, the chambers of reunion "reunited" many strategic bits of land to territories controlled by France. In this way the former free city of Strasbourg, the chief town of Alsace, passed under French control.

Continued French nibbling at western Germany and Louis's assertion of a dynastic claim to most of the lands of the German elector Palatine set off the third of his wars, the War of the League of Augsburg, 1688-1697. This league against Louis was put together by his old foe, William of Orange, who after 1688 shared the throne of England with his wife, Mary, daughter of James II. Thereafter England was thoroughly against Louis. The League also included Spain, the Holy Roman Empire, and Savoy, which was threatened by Louis's tactics of "reunion." The English won a great naval victory at Cape La Hogue in 1692, but William was repeatedly defeated on land in the Low Countries, though never decisively crushed. In Ireland, French (and thus Catholic) attempts to restore the deposed English king, James II, were foiled at the battle of the Boyne in 1690. France and England also exchanged blows in India, the West Indies, and North America, where the colonists called the conflict King William's War. The Treaty of Ryswick ended the war in a peace without victory, an agreement to hold to the status quo.

In 1701 Louis XIV took a step that led to his last and greatest conflict, the War of the Spanish Succession (1701-1714). Charles II, the Hapsburg king of Spain and Louis's brother-in-law, had died in 1700 without a direct heir. For years diplomats had been striving to arrange a succession that would avoid putting on the throne either a French Bourbon or an Austrian Hapsburg. Although they had agreed on a Bavarian prince, he had died in 1699, and plans were made to partition the Spanish inheritance between Hapsburgs and Bourbons. Charles II left his lands intact to Philip of Anjou, grandson of Louis XIV. Louis accepted on behalf of Philip, even though he had signed the treaty of partition. This threat to the balance of power was neatly summarized in the remark a gloating Frenchman is supposed to have made, "There are no longer any Pyrenees." England, Holland, Savoy, the Holy Roman Empire, and many German states formed the Grand Alliance to preserve a separate Spain.

In the bloody war that followed, the French were gradually worn down. In North America they lost Nova Scotia to the English, and in Europe they were beaten by the allies in four major battles, beginning with Blenheim in 1704 and concluding with Malplaquet in 1709. The allied armies were commanded by two great generals, the French-born Prince Eugene of Savoy (1663-1736) and the English John Churchill (1650-1722), first duke of Marlborough. But the French were not annihilated, and Malplaquet cost the allies twenty thousand casualties, at least as many as the French suffered. By scraping the bottom of the barrel for men and money, the French still managed to keep armies in the field.

Moreover, the Grand Alliance was weakening. The English, following their policy of keeping any single continental power from attaining too strong a position, were almost as anxious to prevent the union of Austria and Spain under a Hapsburg as to prevent the union of France and Spain under a Bourbon. At home they faced a possible disputed succession to the throne, and the mercantile classes were sick of a war that was injuring trade and seemed unlikely to bring any compensating gains. In 1710 the pro-peace party won a parliamentary majority and began negotiations that culminated in a series of treaties at Utrecht in 1713.

Utrecht was a typical balance-of-power peace, which contained France without humiliating it. France lost Newfoundland, Nova Scotia, and the Hudson Bay territories to England, while preserving Quebec, Louisiana, and its Caribbean islands. In a sense Louis gained what he had gone to war over, for Philip of Anjou was formally recognized as King Philip V of Spain and secured the Spanish lands overseas. However, the French and Spanish crowns were forbidden ever to be held by the same person, so the allies too had won their point. Furthermore, England took from Spain the Mediterranean island of Minorca and the great Rock of Gibraltar guarding the Atlantic entrance to the Mediterranean. The English also gained the *Asiento*, the right to supply slaves to the Spanish colonies—a right that also gave them opportunities for smuggling. The Austrian Hapsburgs were compensated with Belgium and the former Spanish possessions of Milan and Naples. In Belgium—now the Austrian Netherlands—the Dutch were granted the right to garrison certain fortified towns, "barrier fortresses," for better defense against possible French aggression. For faithfulness to the Grand Alliance, the duke of Savoy was eventually rewarded with Sardinia and the title of king. The elector of Brandenburg was also rewarded with a royal title, king *in* (not *of*) Prussia, which lay outside the Holy Roman Empire.

Yet the rivalry between France and England for empire overseas was undiminished. After Utrecht, in India, as in North America, each nation would continue to try to oust the other from land and trade. In Europe the Dutch did not feel secure against the French, while the Austrian Hapsburg emperor, Charles VI (1711-1740), never gave up hope of becoming "Charles III" of Spain. The distribution of Italian lands satisfied no one, Italian or outsider, and the next two decades were filled with acrimonious negotiations over Italy. In short, the peace was fatally flawed.

French Aggression in Review

Proponents of the view that Europe underwent a severe crisis during the seventeenth century can find much evidence in the horrors resulting from Louis XIV's aggressions. The total cost of his wars in human lives and economic resources was very great, especially in the deliberate French devastation of the German Palatinate during the War of the League of Augsburg. The battle of Malplaquet, which left forty thousand men wounded, dying, or dead in an area of ten square miles, was not surpassed in bloodshed until Napoleon's Russian campaign a century later. There was also much suffering behind the lines notably in the great famine that struck France in 1693-1694. And the year of Malplaquet, 1709, was one of the grimmest in modern French history, as bitter cold, crop failures, famine, skyrocketing prices, and relentless government efforts to stave off bankruptcy by collecting more taxes caused almost universal misery. The Parisians complained bitterly in a mock *Paternoster:* "Our Father which art at Versailles, thy name is hallowed no more, thy kingdom is great no more, thy will is no longer done on earth or on the waters. Give us this day thy bread which on all sides we lack. . . ."*

Louis set himself up as a champion of Catholicism, especially after the revocation of the Edict of Nantes in 1685, and William of Orange was hailed as a Protestant champion. Yet Louis, unlike his predecessor in aggression, Philip II of Spain, had no real hope of stamping out Protestantism among the Dutch. William's Protestant victory at the Boyne brought new hardship to Irish Catholics, and in England and New England the French were hated because they were Catholics. In the end, however, the Grand Alliance against Louis was a complex mixture of Catholic and Protestant in which religion played a comparatively minor role. Louis XIV had achieved no permanent stability for Europe or France, and his authority would die with him; his funeral procession was mocked as it passed through the streets of Paris, though he remained a figure of veneration to the rural masses who made up the majority of France.

II STUART ENGLAND

To the extent that English government utilized the new methods of professional administration developed in the fifteenth and sixteenth centuries, it was potentially as absolute as any divine-right monarchy. But the slow growth of representative government checked this potential, generating a set of rules not to be altered easily by the ordinary processes of government. These rules might be written down, but they might also be unwritten, being a consensus about certain traditions. These rules came to be regarded as limiting the authority not only of the king but even of a government elected by a majority of the people—a guarantee to individuals that they had "civil rights" and might carry out certain acts even though those in authority disapproved. Without such rules and habits of constitutionalism, and without the powerful and widespread human determination to back them up, the machinery of English parliamentary government could have been as ruthlessly absolute as any other government.

*G.R.R. Treasure, *Seventeenth Century France*, 2nd ed. (London: John Murray, 1981), p. 441

French kings and ministers could govern without the Estates General. In England, however, King Charles I, who had governed for eleven years without calling Parliament, felt obliged in 1640 to summon it and, though he dismissed it at once when it refused to do his bidding, he had to call another in the same year. This was the Long Parliament, which sat—with changes of personnel and with interruptions—for twenty years, and which made the revolution that ended the threat of absolute divine-right monarchy in England.

Charles was ultimately obliged to call Parliament for two basic reasons that go back to medieval history. First, in the English Parliament the House of Commons represented two different social groups not brought together in one house elsewhere: the aristocratic knights of the shire and the burgesses of the towns and cities. The strength of the Commons lay in the practical working together of both groups, which intermarried quite freely and, despite economic and social tensions, tended to form a single ruling class, with membership open to talent and energy from the lower classes. Second, local government continued to be run by magistrates who were not directly dependent on the Crown. True, England had its bureaucrats, its clerks and officials in the royal pay, but where in France and in other continental countries the new bureaucracy tended to take over almost all governmental business, especially financial and judicial affairs, in England the gentry and the higher nobility continued to do important local work. The Elizabethan Poor Law of 1601 put the care of the needy not under any national ministry but squarely on the smallest local units, the parishes, where decisions lay ultimately with the amateur, unpaid justices of the peace, recruited from the local gentry. In short, the privileged classes were not, as in France, thrust aside by paid agents of the central government; nor did they, as in Prussia, become agents of the Crown. Instead, they preserved secure bases in local government and in the House of Commons. When Charles I tried to govern without the consent of these privileged classes, when he tried to raise money from them and their dependents to run a bureaucratic government, they had a solid institutional and traditional basis from which to resist his unusual demands.

Because Elizabeth I was childless, she was succeeded by the son of her old rival and cousin, Mary, Queen of Scots, in 1603. James Stuart, already king of Scotland as James VI, became James I of England (1603-1625), thus bringing the two countries, still legally separate, under the same personal rule. James was a well-educated pedant, sure of himself, and above all certain that he ruled by divine right. As a Scottish foreigner, he was an object of distrust to his English subjects. He totally lacked the Tudor heartiness and tact, the gift of winning people to him. His son Charles I (1625-1649), under whom the divine-right experiment came to an end, had many more of the social graces of a monarch than his father, but he was still no man to continue the work of the Tudors. Although he was quite as sure as his father had been that God had called him to rule England, he could neither make the compromises the Tudors made nor revive their broad popular appeal. Thus an accident of personality was also important in shaping the outcome of divine-right theories in England.

The business of state was also gradually growing in scope and therefore in cost. The money required by the Stuarts—and indeed by the Bourbons, Hapsburgs, and all monarchs—did not only go for high living by royalty and to support hangers-on; it also went to run a government that was beginning to assume many new functions. Foreign relations, for example, were beginning to take on modern forms, with a central foreign office, ambassadors, clerks, travel allowances, and the like, all requiring more money and personnel. James I and Charles I failed to get the money they needed because those from whom they sought it, the ruling classes, had succeeded in placing the raising and spending of it in their own hands through parliamentary supremacy. The Parliament that won that supremacy was a kind of committee of the ruling classes; it was not a democratic legislature, since only a small fraction of the population could vote for members of the Commons.

In this struggle between Crown and Parliament, religion helped weld both sides into cohesive fighting groups. The struggle for power was in part a struggle to impose a uniform worship on England. The royalist cause was identified with High Church Anglicanism, that is, with bishops and a liturgy and theology that made it a sacramental religion relatively free from left-wing Protestant austerities. The parliamentary cause, at first supported by many moderate Low Church Anglicans, also attracted strong Puritan or Calvinist elements; later it came under the control of Presbyterians and then of extreme Puritans, the Independents or Congregationalists. The term *Puritanism* in seventeenth-century England is confusing because it covered a wide range of religious groups, from moderate evangelical Anglicans all the way to radical splinter sects. But the core of Puritanism went back to Zwingli and Calvin, to the repudiation of Catholic sacramental religion and the rejection of most music and the adornment of churches; it emphasized sermons, simplicity in church and out, and "purifying" the tie between the worshiper and God.

James I, 1603-1625

In the troubled reign of James II there were three major points of contention—money, foreign policy, and religion. In all three issues the Crown and its opposition each tried to direct constitutional development in its own favor. In raising money James sought to make the most of revenues that did not require a parliamentary grant; Parliament sought to make the most of its own control over the purse strings by insisting on the principle that it had to approve any new revenues. When James levied an import duty without a parliamentary grant, an importer of dried currants refused to pay; the case was decided in favor of the Crown by the Court of Exchequer, and the decision attracted much attention because the judges held the king's powers in general to be absolute. Then a royal appeal for a general "benevolence"—a euphemism for a contribution exacted from an individual—was resisted with the support of the chief justice, Sir Edward Coke (1552-1634). James summarily dismissed Coke from office for asserting the independence of the judiciary and thereby drew attention once again to his broad use of the royal prerogative.

The Tudors had regarded foreign affairs as entirely a matter for the Crown. The delicate problem of a marriage for Elizabeth I, for instance, had concerned her Parliaments and the public; but Parliament made no attempt to dictate a marriage, and Elizabeth was careful not to offend her subjects in her own tentative negotiations. On the other hand, when James I openly sought a princess of hated Spain as a wife for his son Charles, the Commons in 1621 petitioned publicly against the Spanish marriage. When James rebuked them for meddling, the House drew up the Great Protestation, the first of the major documents of the English Revolution, in which they used what they claimed were the historic privileges of Parliament to assert what was in fact a new claim for parliamentary control of foreign affairs. James responded by dissolving Parliament and imprisoning four of its leaders. The Spanish marriage fell through, but the betrothal of Charles in 1624 to the French princess Henrietta Maria, sister of Louis XIII, who was also Catholic, was hardly more popular with the English people.

Though refusing to permit public services by Catholics and Puritans, Elizabeth had allowed much variety of practice within the Anglican church. James summed up his policy in the phrase "no bishop, no king"—by which he meant that the enforcement of the bishops' authority in religion was essential to the maintenance of royal power. James at once took steps against what he held to be Puritan nonconformity. He called a conference of Anglican bishops and leading Puritans at Hampton Court in 1604, at which he presided in person and used the full force of his scholarship against the Puritans. After the conference dissolved with no real meeting of minds, royal policy continued to favor the High Church, anti-Puritan party.

Despite James's failure to achieve anything like religious agreement among his subjects, his reign is a landmark in the history of Christianity among English-speaking peoples, for in 1611, after seven years' labor, a committee of forty-seven ministers authorized by him completed the English translation of the Bible that is still the most widely used. The King James version was a masterpiece of Elizabethan prose, perhaps the most remarkable literary achievement a committee has ever made.

Charles I, 1625-1642

Under Charles I all his father's difficulties came to a head very quickly. England was involved in a minor war against Spain, and though the members of Parliament hated Spain, they were most reluctant to grant Charles funds to support the English forces. Meanwhile, despite his French queen, Charles became involved in a war against France, which he financed in part by a forced loan from his wealthier subjects and by quartering troops in private houses at the householders' expense. His financial position was tenuous; as a French observer remarked, "They wish for war against heaven and earth, but lack the means to make it against anyone." The military preparations were the greatest since 1588, when there had been a visible enemy; in 1626-1628 Charles's subjects were less certain of the need for extraordinary measures. Consequently, in 1628 Parliament passed the Petition of Right—"the Stuart Magna Carta"—which for the first time explicitly stated some of the most basic rules of modern constitutional government: no taxation without the consent of Parliament; no billeting of soldiers in private houses; no martial law in time of peace; no imprisonment except on a specific charge and subject to the protection of regular legal procedures. All these principles were limitations on the Crown.

Charles consented to the Petition of Right to secure new grants of money from Parliament. But he also collected duties not sanctioned by Parliament, which thereupon protested not only against his unauthorized taxes but also against his High Church policy. The king now switched from conciliation to firmness. In 1629 he had Sir John Eliot (1592-1632), mover of the resolutions, arrested, together with eight other members. He then dissolved Parliament, in part for refusing to vote supplies to the king, in part because he felt Parliament was meddling in matters of religion beyond its authority, and in part because Eliot intended to appeal over the king's head to the country. Eliot died a prisoner in the Tower of London, the first martyr in the parliamentary cause, having in effect driven Charles I to take a calculated risk.

For the next eleven years, 1629-1640, Charles governed without a Parliament. He squeezed every penny he could get out of royal revenues that did not require parliamentary authorization, never quite breaking with precedent by imposing a wholly new tax but stretching precedent beyond what his opponents thought reasonable. For example, ship money had been levied by the Crown before, but only on coastal towns for naval expenditures in wartime; Charles now imposed ship money on inland areas and in peacetime. John Hampden (1594-1643), a rich member of Parliament from inland Buckinghamshire, refused to pay it. He lost his case in court (1637) but gained wide public support for challenging the king's fiscal expedients.

In religious matters Charles was guided by a very High Church archbishop of Canterbury, William Laud (1573-1645), who systematically enforced Anglican conformity and deprived even moderate Puritan clergymen of their pulpits. Puritans were sometimes brought before the Star Chamber, an administrative court that denied the accused the safeguards of the common law. In civil matters Charles relied on an opportunist conservative, Thomas Wentworth, first earl of Strafford (1593-1641), who had deserted the parliamentary side and went on to become Lord Lieutenant of Ireland, a source of continued conflict and expense.

England was seething with repressed political and religious passions underneath the outward calm of these years of personal rule. Yet to judge from the imperfect statistics available, the relative weight of the taxation that offended so many Englishmen was less than on the Continent, and far less than taxation in any modern Western state. The members of Parliament who resisted the Crown by taking arms against it were not downtrodden, povery-stricken people revolting out of despair, but self-assertive people defending their concept of civil rights and their own forms of worship, as well as seeking power and wealth.

Why, then, was there a revolution? Historians are not agreed, especially about the economic motivations of the English revolutionaries. There is evidence that the more capitalistic gentleman farmers—rural bourgeois—supported the Puritans; but other scholars argue that the elements from the gentry who supported the Puritans were those who saw themselves sinking on the economic scale, because of inflation, because of the enclosure of once common lands for sheep farming, and because of competition by the new secular owners of the old monastic lands. This debate about the nature and role of the gentry illustrates two problems faced by the historian: first, that of definitions, since the debate turns in part on how social classes are defined, or defined themselves in the past; second, that two historians examining the same evidence, or different evidence that overlaps at certain points, may arrive at quite different conclusions about the meaning of that evidence. Was the English Revolution caused by despair—a declining gentry seeking to turn the clock back, so that the revolution was actually conservative in its goals—or was it caused by the perception of the need to modernize, to change the institutions of governments to more rational, efficient purposes—that is, the final stage of the long movement away from feudalism?

The English Revolution did not, in fact, greatly alter the face of England. The laboring poor played almost no role in the Revolution. Nonetheless, a precedent of great significance was established, for a king was brought to trial and executed and his office abolished; an established church was disestablished and its property taken; less emphasis was placed on deference. All this would later be undone, the monarchy and the established church restored. Yet in the process, many would perceive that human beings could alter their world if they chose, and many would see the importance of the political process. And they would see that the Crown was neither rational nor truly responsible in various aspects of finance: in government credit, in the use of improper taxes for purposes considered immoral, and in placing the government's financial interest before its social responsibilities. Thus religion, economics, and politics would prove inseparable, a linked chain of causation.

Charles I could perhaps have weathered his financial

Sir Anthony Van Dyck (1599-1641) painted King Charles I hunting. Probably completed in 1638 and now in the Louvre, this portrait shows the king informally dressed, having dismounted from his horse. The arrogant pose, with hand on hip and cane, was used from medieval times to represent nobility. Contrast the dress and compare the pose with Rigaud's portrait of Louis XIV (p. 407).

difficulties if he had not had to contend with the Scots. Laud's attempt to enforce the English High Church ritual and organization came up against the three-generations-old Scottish Presbyterian "kirk" (church). In 1638 a Solemn League and Covenant bound the members of the kirk to resist Charles by force if need be. Charles marched north against the Scots and worked out a compromise with them in 1639. But even this mild campaign was too much for the treasury, and in 1640 Charles had to call Parliament back into session. This Short Parliament denied him any money until the piled-up grievances against Charles and his father were settled; it was dissolved almost at once. Then the Scots went to war again, and Charles, defeated in a skirmish, bought them off by promising the Scottish army £850 a day until peace was made. Since he could not raise the money, he had to call another Parliament, which became the Long Parliament of the revolution.

Since the Scottish army would not disband until it was paid off, the Long Parliament held it as a club over Charles's head and put through a series of reforms striking at the heart of the royal power. It abolished ship money and other disputed taxes and disbanded the unpopular royal administrative courts, such as the Star Chamber, which had become symbols of Stuart absolutism. Up to now Parliament had been called and dismissed at the pleasure of the Crown; the Triennial Act of 1640 required that Parliament be summoned every three years, even if the Crown did not wish to do so. Parliament also attacked the royal favorites, whom Charles reluctantly abandoned; Archbishop Laud was removed, and Strafford was declared guilty of treason and executed in May 1641.

Meanwhile, Strafford's harsh policy toward the Irish had led to a rebellion that amounted to an abortive war for national independence by Irish Catholics and caused the massacre of thirty thousand Protestants in the northern Irish region of Ulster. Parliament, unwilling to trust Charles with an army to put down this rebellion, drew up in 1641 a Grand Remonstrance summarizing all its complaints. Charles now made a final attempt to repeat the tactics that had worked in 1629. Early in 1642 he ordered the arrest of five of his leading opponents in the House of Commons, including Hampden of the ship-money case. The five took refuge in the privileged political sanctuary of the City of London, where the king could not reach them. Charles left for the north and in the summer of 1642 rallied an army at Nottingham. Parliament simply took over the central government, and the Civil War had begun.

During these years of political jockeying, signs were already evident that strong groups in England and in Parliament wanted something more than a return to the Tudor balance between Crown and Parliament, between religious conservatives and religious radicals. In politics the Nineteen Propositions that Parliament submitted to the king in June 1642 would have established parliamentary supremacy over the army, the royal administration, the church, and even the rearing of the royal children. Charles turned down the propositions, and they became the principal foundation of the war that followed. In religion a Root and Branch Bill, introduced in 1641 but not enacted into law, would have radically reformed the Church of England, destroying "root and branch" the bishops and much of what had already become traditional in Anglican religious practices. In the midst of such extreme contentiousness, a middle path seemed impossible to find.

The Civil War, 1642-1649

England was split along lines that were partly territorial, partly social and economic, and partly religious. Royalist strength lay largely in the north and west, relatively less urban and less prosperous than other parts, and largely controlled by gentry who were loyal to throne and altar. Parliamentary strength lay largely in the south and east, especially in London and in East Anglia, where Puritanism commanded wide support. The Scots were a danger to either side, distrustful of an English Parliament but equally distrustful of a king who had sought to put bishops over their kirk.

In the field, the struggle was at first indecisive. The royalists, or Cavaliers, recruited from a class used to riding, had the initial advantage of superior cavalry. What swung the balance to the side of Parliament was the development of a special force recruited from ardent Puritans in the eastern counties and gradually forged under strict discipline into the Ironsides. Their leader was a Puritan, Oliver Cromwell (1599-1658), who won a crucial battle at Marston Moor in 1644. The parliamentary army, reorganized into the New Model Army and staffed by radicals in religion and politics, stood as Roundheads (from their short-cropped hair) against the Cavaliers. At the battle of Naseby in 1645, the New Model Army was completely victorious, and Charles in desperation took refuge with the Scottish army, who turned him over to the English Parliament in return for their £400,000 back pay.

A situation now arose that was to be repeated, with variations based on time and place, in the French Revolution in 1792 and the Russian Revolution in 1917. The moderates who had begun the revolution and who controlled the Long Parliament were confronted by a much more radical group who controlled the New Model Army. In religion the moderates, seeking to retain some ecclesiastical discipline and formality, were Presbyterians or Low Church Anglicans; in politics they were constitutional monarchists. The radicals, who were opposed to churches disciplined from a central organization, were Independents or Congregationalists, and they already so distrusted Charles that they were thinking about a republican England. The situation was further complicated by the Presbyterian Scots, who regarded the Roundheads as religious anarchists.

The years after 1645 were filled with difficult negotiations, during which Charles stalled for time to gain Scottish help. In 1648 Cromwell beat the invading Scots at Preston, and his army seized the king. Parliament, with the moderates still in control, now refused to do what the army wanted—to dethrone Charles. The Roundhead leaders then ordered Colonel Thomas Pride (d. 1658) to exclude by force from the Commons ninety-six Presbyterian members. This the Colonel did in December 1648, with no pretense of legality. After "Pride's Purge" only some sixty radicals remained of the more than five hundred original members of the Long Parliament; this remnant was known thereafter as the Rump Parliament. The Rump brought Charles to trial before a special high court of radicals, fifty-nine of whom condemned him to death. On January 30, 1649, Charles I was beheaded. To the end he insisted that a king could not be tried by any superior jurisdiction on earth, that his cause was the cause of the people of England, and that if he could be silenced, so might all others. The monarchs of Europe now had their own martyr, and Parliament was, in the eyes of many in England, stained by a clearly illegal act.

Cromwell and the Interregnum, 1649-1660

The next eleven years are known as the Interregnum, the interval between two monarchical reigns. England was now a republic under a government known as the Commonwealth. Since the radicals did not dare to call a free election, which would almost certainly have gone against them, the Rump Parliament continued to sit. Thus, from the start, the Commonwealth was a dictatorship of a radical minority come to power through the tight organization of the New Model Army. From the start too, Cromwell dominated the new government. In religion an earnest and sincere Independent, a patriotic Englishman, strong-minded, stubborn, if now power-mad, still by no means unwilling to compromise, Cromwell was nevertheless a prisoner of his position.

Cromwell faced a divided England, where the majority was royalist at heart and certainly sick of the fighting, the confiscations, the endless confusing changes of the last decade. He faced a hostile Scotland and an even

Oliver Cromwell is invariably depicted as stern and dedicated, staring into the future. This painting by Samuel Cooper (1609-1672), who specialized in miniature portraits of figures from the Commonwealth and Restoration, emphasizes Cromwell's sense of force by focusing solely on the head, devoid of background or distracting detail.

By 1651 the House of Commons was depicted on the Great Seal of England as used by the Commonwealth—testimony to the symbolic significance that Cromwell attached to the House. This scene is a Dutch rendition of Cromwell's dissolution of Parliament in 1653. The owl and small lion made to look like a dog are intended as a satirical commentary on the debate and the dissolution.

more hostile Ireland, where the disorders in England had encouraged the Catholic Irish to rebel once more in 1649. In 1650 Charles II, eldest son of the martyred Charles I, landed in Scotland, accepted the Covenant (thereby guaranteeing the Presbyterian faith as the established Scottish kirk), and led a Scottish army against the English. Once more the English army proved unbeatable, and young Charles took refuge on the Continent after a romantic escape in disguise. Cromwell then faced a war with Holland (1652-1654) brought on by the Navigation Act of 1651, which forbade the importation of goods into England and the colonies except in English ships or in ships of the country producing the imported goods, thus striking at the Dutch carrying trade.

In time Cromwell mastered all his foes. He himself went to Ireland and suppressed the rebellion with extreme bloodshed. In the so-called Cromwellian Settlement of 1652-1654, he dispossessed rebel Irish landholders in favor of Protestants, achieving order in Ireland but not peace. He brought the naval war with the Dutch to a victorious close in 1654. Later Cromwell also waged an aggressive war against Spain (1656-1658), from whom the English acquired the rich Caribbean sugar island of Jamaica. Even in this time of troubles, the British Empire kept growing.

Cromwell, however, could not master the Rump Parliament, which brushed aside his suggestions for an increase in its membership and a reform of its procedures. In April 1653 he forced its dissolution by appearing in Parliament with a body of soldiers. In December he took the decisive step of inaugurating the regime called the Protectorate, with himself as lord protector of England, Scotland, and Ireland, and with a written constitution—the only one Britain has ever had—as the Instrument of Government. It provided for a Parliament with a single house of four hundred and sixty members, who were chosen solely by Puritan sympathizers since no royalist dared vote. Even so, the lord protector had constant troubles with his parliaments, and in 1657 he yielded to pressure and modified the Instrument to provide for a second parliamentary house and to put limits on the lord protector's power. Meanwhile, to maintain order, Cromwell had divided the country into twelve military districts, each commanded by a major general.

Oliver Cromwell died in 1658 and was succeeded as lord protector by his son Richard, who was a nonentity. The army soon seized control, and some of its leaders regarded the restoration of the Stuarts as the best way to end the chronic political turbulence. To ensure the legality of the move, General George Monck (1608-1670), commander of the Protectorate's forces in Scotland, summoned back the Rump and readmitted the surviving members excluded by Pride's Purge. This partially reconstituted Long Parliament enacted the formalities of restoration, and in 1660 Charles Stuart accepted an invitation to return from exile and reign as Charles II.

The Revolution in Review

At the height of their rule in the early 1650s some Puritans had attempted to enforce on the whole population the austere life of the Puritan ideal. This enforcement took the form of "blue laws": prohibitions on horse racing, gambling, cock fighting, bear baiting, dancing on the greens, fancy dress, the theater, and a host of ordinary pleasures of daily living. Yet this attempt to legislate morality, coming too early for modern techniques of propaganda and regimentation, was not entirely effective. Many an Anglican clergyman, though officially "plundered"—that is, deprived of his living—continued worship in private houses, and many a cock fight went on in secluded spots. Nevertheless, the strict code was there, with earnest persons to try to enforce it and with implacable enemies to oppose it. The remark of the great Victorian historian T. B. Macaulay (1800-1859)—that the Puritans prohibited bear baiting not because it gave pain to the bear but because it gave pleasure to the spectators—showed the deep hostility that survived in England toward the reign of the Puritan "saints" two centuries later.

Despite this negative judgment, the events of 1640-1660 are of major importance in the history of the West. For the first time a monarch was challenged in a major revolt by politically active private citizens. Though the Stuarts were ultimately restored, no English king could ever hope to rule again without a Parliament, or revive the Court of Star Chamber, or take ship money, benevolences, and other controversial taxes. Parliament thereafter retained that critical weapon of the legislative body in a limited monarchy, control of the public purse by periodic grants of taxes.

Another basic freedom owes much to this English experience. Freedom of speech was a fundamental tenet of the Puritans, even though at the height of their power they did not observe it themselves. It received its classic expression in 1644 by the poet John Milton (1608-1674), who was the secretary of the Commonwealth, in his *Areopagitica*. While Milton defended free speech principally for an intellectual and moral elite, one of his arguments was characteristically pragmatic and English, namely, that attempts to curb free expression just would not work.

The voluminous pamphlet literature of the early years of the great turmoil was a lively manifestation of free speech in action. The extraordinary rise of radical minorities foreshadowed modern political and social thought. One such group, the Levelers, found many sympathizers in the revolutionary army and advanced a program later carried by emigrants to the American colonies. They called for political democracy, universal suffrage, regularly summoned parliaments, progressive taxation, separation of church and state, and the protection of the individual against arbitrary arrest. There were even hints of economic equality, a goal then closely tied to biblical ideas. The Diggers, for example, were a small sect that preached the sharing of earthly goods in a kind of communism. They advocated plowing up common and waste land throughout England, regardless of ownership, in the interests of social reform. Fifth Monarchy advocates, Millenarians, and a dozen other radical sects preached the Second Coming of Christ and the achievement of a utopia on earth.

Still more important, there emerged from the English Revolution, even more clearly than from the religious wars on the Continent, the concept of religious tolera-

BLACKSTONE ON THE LAW

By the eighteenth century the English recognized that a unique constitution had evolved from the period of their Civil War. Basically unwritten, rooted in the common law, this constitution would contribute to a remarkable period of political stability. In 1765 an English jurist, William Blackstone (1723-1780), would prepare a lengthy set of commentaries on the laws of England in which the process dramatically accelerated by the English Revolution was described by him:

And herein indeed consists the true excellence of the English government, that all the parts of it form a mutual check upon each other. In the legislature, the people are a check upon the nobility, and the nobility a check upon the people; by the mutual privilege of rejecting what the other has resolved: while the king is a check upon both, which preserves the executive power from encroachments. And this very executive power is again checked and kept within due bounds by the two houses, through the privilege they have of inquiring into, impeaching and punishing the conduct (not indeed of the king, which would destroy his constitutional independence; but, which is more beneficial to the public,) of his evil and pernicious counsellors. Thus every branch of our civil polity supports and is supported, regulates and is regulated, by the rest. . . . Like three distinct powers in mechanics, they jointly impel the machine of government in a direction different from what either, acting by itself, would have done . . . a direction which constitutes the true line of the liberty and happiness of the community.

Blackstone, *Commentaries on the Laws of England*, 15th ed. (London: A. Stralan, 1809), I, 153.

MILTON ON FREEDOM OF EXPRESSION

An early, and ringing, defense of freedom of expression was written by John Milton in his *Areopagitica* in 1644. He argued that liberty took three forms: ecclesiastical, domestic, and civil. The first would come through reform of the church. The second and third became merged in Milton's personal concerns, for he wrote a series of tracts defending divorce as a private matter not to be regulated by the state, since he was deeply unhappy in his own marriage. In August 1644 Parliament reapplied, through a new ordinance, the old principle of censorship of the press, and ordered that the author of the tracts on divorce should be found. Milton replied in November with his "Speech for the Liberty of Unlicensed Printing, to the Parliament of England," phrasing his defense of freedom of expression as though he were a Greek orator, addressing the representative Athenian assembly of the Areopagus, hence the title, *Areopagitica:*

There have been not a few since the beginning of this Parliament, both of the Presbytery and others, who by their unlicensed books, to the contempt of an Imprimatur, first broke that triple ice clung about our hearts, and taught the people to see day; I hope that none of those were the persuaders to renew upon this bondage which they themselves have wrought so much good by contemning. But if neither the check that Moses gave to young Joshua, nor the countermand which our Saviour gave to your John [*Luke*, ix, 49, 50] who was so ready to prohibit those whom he thought unlicensed, be not enough to admonish our elders how unacceptable to God their testy mood of prohibiting is; if neither their own remembrance what evil hath abounded in the church by this let of licensing, and what good they themselves have begun by transgressing it, be not enough, but that they will persuade, and execute the most Dominican part of the Inquisition over us, and are already with one foot in the stirrup so active at suppressing, it would be no unequal distribution, in the first place, to suppress the suppressors themselves; whom the change of their condition hath puffed up, more than their late experience of harder times hath made wise. . . .

This I know, that errors in a good government and in a bad are equally almost incident; for what magistrate may not be misinformed, and much the sooner, if liberty of printing be reduced into the power of a few; but to redress willingly and speedily what hath been erred, and in highest authority to esteem a plain advertisement more than others have done a sumptuous bribe, is a virtue, honored Lords and Commons, answerable to your highest actions, and whereof none can participate but greatest and wisest men.

Milton, *Areopagitica*, ed. John W. Hales (London: Clarendon Press, many editions with differing pagination). The extracts are the third from last and last paragraphs respectively.

tion. The Independents, while they were in opposition, stood firmly for the right of religious groups to worship God as they wished. Though in their brief tenure of power they showed a readiness to persecute, they were never firmly enough in the saddle to make England into a seventeenth-century version of Calvin's Geneva. At least on sect, the Quakers, led by George Fox (1624-1691), held to the idea and practice of religious toleration as a positive good. The Quakers denounced all worldy show, finding even buttons ostentatious. They found the names of the days and months indecently pagan, the polite form "you" in the singular a piece of social hypocrisy, and the taking of legal oaths impious. Hence they met for worship on what they called the First Day, rather than the day of the sun god, they addressed each other as "thee" or "thou," and they took so seriously the Protestant doctrine of the priesthood of the believer that they eliminated any formal ministry. In the Religious Society of Friends, as they were properly known, any worshiper who felt the spirit move might testify—give what other sects would call a sermon. The Friends felt too deeply the impossibility of forcing anyone to see the "inner light" for them to force people to accept their faith. They would abstain entirely from force, particularly from war, and would go their own way in Christian peace.

The Restoration, 1660-1688

The Restoration of 1660 left Parliament essentially supreme, but attempted to undo some of the work of the Revolution. Anglicanism was restored in England and Ireland, though not as a state church in Scotland. Protestants who would not accept the Church of England were termed dissenters. Although they suffered many legal disabilities, dissenters remained numerous, especially among artisans and middle-class merchants. As time went on they grew powerful, so that the noncomformist conscience became a major factor in English public life. Indeed, the three-century progression of names by which these non-Anglican Protestants were called shows their rise in status: the hostile term "dissenter" became "nonconformist" in the nineteenth century, and "Free Churchman" in the twentieth.

The Restoration was also a revulsion against Puritan

ways. The reign of Charles II (1660-1685) was a period of moral looseness, of lively court life, of Restoration drama with its ribald wit, and of the public pursuit of pleasure, at least among the upper classes. But the new Stuarts were not as adept at public relations as the Tudors had been. Charles II dissipated some of the fund of good will with which he started by following a foreign policy that seemed to patriotic Englishmen too subservient to Louis XIV. Yet Charles's alliance with Louis in 1670 did result in the extinction of any Dutch threat to English seapower, and it confirmed an important English acquisition, that of New Amsterdam, now New York, first taken in the Anglo-Dutch War of 1664-1667.

What really undid the later Stuarts and revealed their political ineptitude was the Catholic problem. Charles II had come under Catholic influence through his French mother and probably became a Catholic before he died in 1685. Since he left no legitimate children, the crown passed to his brother, James II (1685-1688), who was already an open Catholic. To enlist the support of the dissenters for the toleration of Catholics, James II issued in 1687 a Declaration of Indulgence, granting freedom of worship to all denominations in England and Scotland. While this was, in the abstract, an admirable step toward full religious liberty, to the majority in England Catholicism still seemed a great menace, and it was always possible to stir them to an irrational pitch by an appeal to their fear of "popery." Actually, by the end of the seventeenth century the few remaining Catholics in England were glad to accept the status of the dissenters and were no real danger to an overwhelmingly Protestant country. In Ireland, however, the Catholics remained an unappeasable majority, and Ireland posed a genuine threat.

The political situation was much like that under Charles I: the Crown had one goal, Parliament another. Although James II made no attempt to dissolve Parliament or to arrest its members, he went over Parliament's head by issuing decrees based on what he called the "power of dispensation." Early in his reign he had used a minor rebellion by the duke of Monmouth, a bastard son of Charles II, as the excuse for two ominous policies. First, his judges punished suspected rebel sympathizers with a severity that seemed out of all proportion to the extent of the rebellion. Second, he created a standing army of thirty thousand men, part of whom he stationed near London in what appeared as an attempt to intimidate the capital. To contemporaries it looked as though James were plotting to force both Catholicism and divine-right monarchy on an unwilling England.

The Glorious Revolution and Its Aftermath, 1688-1714

The result was the Glorious Revolution, a coup d'état engineered at first by a group of James's parliamentary opponents who were called Whigs, in contrast to the Tories, who tended to support at least some of the policies of the later Stuarts. The Whigs were the heirs of the moderates of the Long Parliament, and they represented an alliance of the great lords and the prosperous London merchants.

James II married twice. By his first marriage he had two daughters, both Protestant—Mary, who had married William of Orange, the Dutch opponent of Louis XIV, and Anne. Then in 1688 a son was born to James and his Catholic second wife, thus apparently making the passage of the crown to a Catholic heir inevitable. The Whig leaders responded with propaganda, including rumors that the queen had never been pregnant, that a baby had been smuggled into her chamber in a warming pan so that there might be a Catholic heir. Then the Whigs and some Tories negotiated with William of Orange, who could hardly turn down a proposition that would give him the solid assets of English power in his struggle with Louis XIV. He accepted the invitation to take the English crown, which he was to share with his wife, the couple reigning as William III (1689-1702) and Mary II (1689-1694). On November 5, 1688, William landed at Torbay on the Devon coast with some fourteen thousand soldiers. When James heard the news he tried to rally support in the West Country, but everywhere the great lords and even the normally conservative gentry were on the side of a Protestant succession. James fled from London to France in December 1688, giving William an almost bloodless victory.

Early in 1689 Parliament (technically a convention, since there was no monarch to summon it) formally offered the crown to William. Enactment of a Bill of Rights followed. This document, summing up the constitutional practices that Parliament had been seeking since the Petition of Right in 1628, was, in fact, almost a short written constitution. It laid down the essential principles of parliamentary supremacy: control of the purse, prohibition of the royal power of dispensation, and frequent meetings of Parliament.

Three major steps were necessary after 1689 to convert Britain into a parliamentary democracy in which the Crown is the purely symbolic focus of patriotic loyalty. These were, first, the concentration of executive direction in a committee of the majority party in the Parliament, that is, a Cabinet headed by a prime minister, achieved in the eighteenth and early nineteenth centuries; second, the establishment of universal suffrage and payment to members of the Commons, achieved in the nineteenth and twentieth centuries; and third, the abolition of the power of the House of Lords to veto legislation passed by the Commons, achieved in the early twentieth century. Thus democracy was still a long way off in 1689, and William and Mary were real rulers with power over policy.

Childless, they were succeeded by Mary's younger sister Anne (1702-1714), all of whose many children were stillborn or died in childhood. The exiled Catholic Stuarts, however, did better; the little boy born to James II in 1688 and brought up near Paris grew up to be known as the "Old Pretender." Then in 1701 Parliament passed an Act of Settlement that settled the crown—in default of heirs to Anne, then heir presumptive to the sick William III—not on the Catholic pretender, but on the Protestant Sophia of Hanover or her issue. Sophia was a granddaughter of James I and the daughter of Frederick of the Palatinate, the "Winter King" of Bohemia in the Thirty Years' War. On Anne's death in 1714, the crown passed to Sophia's son George, first king of the house of Hanover. This settlement made it clear that Parliament, and not the divinely ordained succession of the eldest male in direct descent, made the kings of England.

To ensure the Hanoverian succession in both Stuart kingdoms, Scotland as well as England, the formal union of the two was completed in 1707 as the United Kingdom of Great Britain. Scotland gave up its own parliament and sent representatives to the parliament of the United Kingdom at Westminster. Although the union met with some opposition from both English and Scots, on the whole it went through with ease, so great was Protestant fear of a possible return of the Catholic Stuarts.

The Glorious Revolution did not, however, settle the other chronic problem—Ireland. The Catholic Irish rose in support of the exiled James II and were put down at the Battle of the Boyne in 1690. William then attempted to apply moderation in his dealings with Ireland, but the Protestants there soon forced him to return to the Cromwellian policy. Although Catholic worship was not actually forbidden, many galling restrictions were imposed on the Catholic Irish, including the prohibition of Catholic schools. Moreover, economic persecution was added to religious, as Irish trade came under stringent mercantilist regulation. This was the Ireland whose deep misery inspired the writer Jonathan Swift (1667-1745) in 1729 to make his satirical "modest proposal," that the impoverished Irish sell their babies as articles of food.

Absolutism was thus almost universal in Europe. On the Continent enlightened despots ruled with an often intelligent but determined hand. In England a tenuous balance had been struck, though for those outside the United Kingdom the rule of the monarch was no less absolute and perhaps less enlightened. While writers of genius might criticize governments, Everyman still had no way of doing so, save through peasant revolts.

III CENTURY OF GENIUS/ CENTURY OF EVERYMAN

In the seventeenth century the cultural, as well as the political, hegemony of Europe passed from Italy and Spain to Holland, France, and England. Especially in literature, the France of the *grand siècle* set the imprint of its classical style on the West through the writings of Corneille, Racine, Molière, Boileau, Bossuet, and a host of others. Yet those writers who exerted the greatest influence on modern culture were not exclusively French and were philosophers and scientists (see Chapter 13). Their arguments were expressed in political and economic constructs that justified or attacked the conventional wisdom of the age. In all fields of intellectual endeavor the seventeenth century saw such a remarkable flowering that historians have called it "the century of genius."

Progress and Pessimism

Scientists and rationalists helped greatly to establish in the minds of the educated throughout the West two complementary concepts that were to serve as the foundations of the Enlightenment of the eighteenth century: first, the concept of a "natural" order underlying the disorder and confusion of the universe as it appears to unreflecting people in their daily life; and, second, the concept of a human faculty, best called reason, which is obscured in most of humanity but can be brought into effective play by good—that is, rational—perception. Both of these concepts can be found in some form in the Western tradition at least as far back as the ancient Greeks. What gave them novelty and force at the end of the seventeenth century was their being welded into the doctrine of progress—the belief that all human beings can attain here on earth a state of happiness, of perfection, hitherto in the West generally thought to be possible only in a state of grace, and then only in a heaven after death.

Not all the great minds of the seventeenth century shared this optimistic belief in progress and in the infallibility of reason. The many-sided legacy of this century of genius is evident, for example, in the contrast between two of the most important political writings issuing from the English Revolution: Thomas Hobbes's *Leviathan* and John Locke's *Second Treatise of Government*. Published in 1651 and much influenced by the disorders of the English Civil War, *Leviathan* was steeped in Machiavellian pessimism about the inherent sinfulness of human beings. The state of nature, when people live without government, is a state of war, Hobbes argued, where people prey upon each other and human life is "solitary, poor, nasty, brutish, short." The only recourse is for people to agree among themselves to submit absolutely to the Leviathan—an all-powerful state that will force peace upon humankind.

Hobbes (1588-1679) turned the contract theory of government upside down by having people consent to give up all their liberties; Locke (1632-1704) put the contract right side up again. Locke was a close associate of the Whig leaders who engineered the Glorious Revolution. In his *Second Treatise of Government*, published in 1690 as a defense of their actions, Locke painted a generally hopeful picture of the state of nature, which suffers only from the "inconvenience" of lacking an impartial judicial authority. To secure such an authority, people contract among themselves to accept a government—not an omnipotent Leviathan—that respects a person's life, liberty, and property; should a king seize property by imposing unauthorized taxes, then his subjects are justified in overthrowing their monarch. Locke's relative optimism and his enthusiasm for constitutional government nourished the major current of political thought in the next century, culminating in the American and French revolutions. But events after 1789 brought Hobbesian despair and authoritarianism to the surface once more.

Meantime, exponents of the older Christian tradition continued to flourish on the Continent. One example is Blaise Pascal, a one-man personification of the complexities of the century of genius. He won an important place in the history of mathematics and physics by his work with air pressure and vacuums and, at the practical level, by his invention of the calculating machine and his establishment of the first horse-drawn bus line in Paris. Yet he was also profoundly otherworldly and became a spokesman for the high-minded, puritanical Jansenists, whose doctrines he defended with skill and fervor. He dismissed as unworthy the concepts of God as mere master geometer or engineer and sought instead for the Lord of Abraham and the Old Testament prophets. He advocated acts of charity, especially by those with wealth and status, for God's incomprehensible love had placed on them the obligation to look after the weak and poor. One night in November 1654, he underwent a great mystical experience in which he felt with absolute certainty the presence of God and of Christ. He spent his final years in religious meditation.

Another example is Baruch Spinoza (1632-1677), the century's most controversial thinker, who was the son of a Jewish merchant in Amsterdam. Spinoza tried to reconcile the God of Science and the God of Scripture. He constructed a system of ethical axioms as rigorously Cartesian and logical as a series of mathematical propositions. He also tried to reunite the Cartesian opposites—

This is the illustration from the title page of Hobbes's *Leviathan*. While it shows the ruler in absolute control over the land, his body symbolically consists of all those individuals whose self-interest is served by their consent to accept the collective rule of the state for the general welfare. All look to him, and each loses individuality; but the mass is, nonetheless, composed of individual figures. This title page is considered to be a masterpiece, summarizing a philosopher's view in a single illustration. The Latin quotation from the book of *Job* translates, "Upon the earth there is not his like."

Non est potestas Super Terram quæ Comparetur ei Iob. 41. 24.

PASCAL ON ERROR

Pascal left unfinished at his death one of the most remarkable works of Christian apologetics in existence, the *Pensées* ("Thoughts"). In it he wrote:

> Man is but a being filled with error. This error is natural, and, without grace, ineffaceable. Nothing shows him the truth; everything deceives him. These two principles of truth, reason and the senses, besides lacking sincerity, reciprocally deceive each other. The senses deceive reason by false appearances: and just as they cheat reason they are cheated by her in turn: she has her revenge. Passions of the soul trouble the senses, and give them false impressions. They emulously lie and deceive each other.

Thoughts, Letters, and Opuscules, trans. O. W. Wight (New York: Hurt and Houghton, 1869), p. 192.

matter with mind, body with soul—by asserting that God was present everywhere and in everything. His pantheism led to his ostracism in Holland by his fellow Jews and also by the Christians, who considered him an atheist; his rejection of rationalism and materialism offended intellectuals. Spinoza found few admirers until the romantic revolt against the abstractions and oversimplifications of the Enlightenment over a century later.

Literature

Just as Henry IV, Richelieu, and Louis XIV brought greater order to French politics after the civil and religious upheavals of the sixteenth century, so the writers of the seventeenth century brought greater discipline to French writing after the Renaissance extravagance of a genius like Rabelais. It was the Age of Classicism, which insisted on the observance of elaborate rules, on the authority of models from classical antiquity, and on the employment of a more polite, stylized vocabulary. In the early 1600s the example of greater refinement in manners and speech was set by the circle who met in the Paris *salon* (reception room) of an aristocratic hostess, the marquise de Rambouillet (1588-1665). Later proper behavior was standardized by the court ceremonial at Versailles, and proper vocabulary by the famous dictionary of the French language that the experts of the academy founded by Richelieu finished compiling in the 1690s, after more than half a century of labor. Nicholas Boileau (1636-1711), the chief literary critic of the day, set the rules for writing poetry with his Cartesian pronouncement, "Think well, if you wish to write well." Exaggerated notions of propriety outlawed from polite usage the French counterparts of such terms as *spit* and *vomit* and obliged writers to seek euphemisms for dozens of commonplace activities. Indeed, many of our concepts of which words are vulgar or obscene derive from this time, though they were later reinforced by Victorian prudery and class concern for "nicety" in the nineteenth century. Already there were indications of the social divisions that would produce the Revolution of 1789 in the enormous gap between the classical French speech of the court and the plainer, coarser language of the average French person.

On the other hand, the linguistic standards of the seventeenth-century court also brought substantial benefits to literature. Without its discipline, French would not have won its unique reputation for clarity and elegance. The leading tragic dramatists of the *grand siècle* made observance of all the classical do's and don'ts not an end in itself but a means to probe deeply into the endless variety of human personalities. Pierre Corneille (1606-1684) and Jean Racine (1639-1699) created moving portraits of people upholding exalted ideals of honor or crushed by overwhelming emotion. The French tragedies of the seventeenth century were worthy successors to the Greek dramas of the fifth century B.C., not merely because of their classical form but also because of their powerful rhetoric, complex structure, psychological insight, and clarity of expression.

As a writer of comedies, Jean Baptiste Molière (1622-1673), the other great French dramatist of the age, was less constrained to employ a dignified vocabulary and to heed the other rules of classicism. The main characters of his satirical comedies were not only sharply etched personalities but social types as well—the overrefined pedantic ladies of the salons, the hypocrite in *Tartuffe* (1664), the ignorant and self-important newly rich in *Le Bourgeois Gentilhomme* (1670). In Molière, as in all good satire, there is more than a touch of moralizing, and didactic overtones are also present in two other characteristic works of the Great Century: the *Fables* of Jean de La Fontaine (1621-1695) reworked in lively fashion tales borrowed from antiquity; the *Maxims* of the duc de la Rochefoucauld (1613-1680) were even more disenchanted in their estimates of human nature. "Judged by most of its reactions, love is closer to hatred than to friendship." "Men would not get on for long in society if they did not fool one another." "In general, we give praise only that we may get it." But la Rochefoucauld could also write, "Perfect courage means doing unwitnessed what we would be capable of with the world looking on," and "The fame of great men should always be judged by the methods they employed to achieve it."*

Seventeenth-century English literature also had its cynics, notably William Wycherley (c 1640-1716), William Congreve (1670-1729), and other playwrights who wrote witty, bawdy, and disillusioned Restoration comedies. Under Charles II and his successors the pendulum of public taste and morality made a particularly violent swing as a reaction to the midcentury Puritans who had closed down the theaters as dens of sinfulness. One of those Puritans, John Milton, the secretary of Oliver Cromwell, produced his major work of literature, *Paradise Lost* (1667), the only English epic in the grand manner that still attracts many readers, after going blind. Though Milton was a classical scholar of great learning, his often complex style and his profound belief in Christian humanism really made him a belated representative of an earlier literary age, the last great writer of the English Renaissance.

What was needed to prepare for the classical age of English letters was the modernization of the English language by pruning the elaborate flourishes, standardizing the chaotic spelling, and eliminating the long flights of rhetoric characteristic of Elizabethan and early seventeenth-century prose. Under the influence of John Dryden (1631-1700), English began to model itself on French, adopting a straightforward word order, comparatively brief sentences, and the polish, neatness, and clarity of the French school. English letters were entering the Augustan Age, which lasted through the first half of the eighteenth century.

The Baroque Era

Baroque, the label usually applied to the arts of the seventeenth century, probably comes from the Portuguese *barroco*, an irregular or misshapen pearl. Some critics have seized upon the suggestion of deformity to criticize the impurity of seventeenth-century art in contrast with the purity of the Renaissance. Especially among Protestants, the reputation of baroque suffered because it was identified with the Counter-Reformation, and many of its leading artists appeared to be propagandists for Rome. Many viewers were also repelled by the flamboyance of baroque works.

Baroque art was closely associated with the Jesuits, with the successors of Philip II in Spain, and above all with Rome during the century following the Council of Trent. Catholic reformers enlisted the arts in propagating the faith and endowing it with greater emotional intensity. But not all the baroque masters were Catholic—Rembrandt, for instance, was a Mennonite, and Sir Christopher Wren an Anglican—nor were all their patrons Catholic prelates or grandees. Portraits of the Protestant Charles I of England brought Van Dyck fame and wealth; and in the Dutch Republic, where the Calvinist churches frowned on all ornamentation, painters won support from the business community and sometimes became prosperous businessmen themselves.

The unprecedented financial success of some artists is one of the distinguishing characteristics of the baroque period. Rubens, Van Dyck, Wren, and Bernini lived like lords, in contrast to the relatively austere existence of such Renaissance masters as Leonardo and Michelangelo. A second characteristic is the baroque stress on sheer size, as exemplified by the vast canvases of Rubens, the immense palace of Versailles, and Bernini's decorative canopy over the high altar in Saint Peter's in Rome. A third characteristic is theatricality, as painters intensified the illusion of brilliant lighting and placed figures in the immediate foreground of a canvas to draw the spectator into the scene. A final characteristic is the realistic depiction of a wide range of humanity—clowns, beggars, gypsies, card sharps, cripples, and dwarfs, as well as ordinary people, praying, laughing, or eating. In France, for example, Georges de La Tour (1593-1652) took everyday subjects and people—a woman retrieving a flea as she undresses, a hurdy-gurdy player, and, at the height of the seventeenth century devotional cult of Mary Magdalen, a painting of her

Diego Velásquez (1599-1660) painted many portraits of Spain's King Philip IV, but perhaps his most famous royal painting is "The Maids of Honour." Here is Princess Margarita, only four years old, dressed as the times and her station required. With her are two young noblewomen, the court jester, a female dwarf, and others. The child is receiving cold, perfumed water to drink.

The Maxims of La Rochefoucauld, trans. Louis Kronenberger (New York: Random House, 1959), maxims 72, 87, 146, 216, 157.

pensively contemplating a candle—and executed them in a nighttime setting that permitted dramatic contrasts of light and shadow.

Painting The most restrained baroque painter was probably Diego Velásquez (1599-1660), who spent thirty-four years at the court of Philip IV of Spain. Velásquez needed all his skill to soften the receding chins and thick lips of the Hapsburgs and still make his portraits of Philip IV and the royal family instantly recognizable. His greatest feat of technical wizardry is *The Maids of Honor* (see p. 423). A little princess, having her portrait painted, is surrounded by a pet dog, dwarfs, and other attendants; it is the moment when the royal parents are looking in on the scene, but only their reflections are seen in a mirror at the rear of the room. As Velásquez turns to greet them and looks at the viewer, the latter realizes he is standing where the royal couple must have stood. Painted with the adroit use of mirrors, *The Maids of Honor* is a splendid example of baroque attempts to make the spectator an active participant.

Unlike the aristocratic Velásquez, the Flemish Peter Paul Rubens (1577-1640) was the baroque counterpart of the Renaissance universal man. A diplomat, a linguist, and a student of antiquity and archaeology, he amassed a fortune from his painting and collected such impressive honors as being knighted by Charles I of England and elevated to the nobility by the king of Spain. Rubens made his studio, with its two hundred students, a factory of art. He himself is estimated to have contributed to over two thousand pictures, whose subjects ranged from simple portraits to ambitious political themes. He was commissioned by Marie de' Medici, widow of Henry IV of France, to execute a series of canvases glorifying Henry and herself. As monarchs by divine right, Henry and Marie were portrayed more as mythological figures than as mere mortals.

One of Rubens's pupils was a fellow Fleming, Anthony Van Dyck (1599-1641), whose portraits of Charles I captured the casual elegance and confident authority of the Stuart monarch. Although courtly style was not highly valued by the Flemings' northern neighbors in the Netherlands, the officers of Dutch civic guards, the governing boards of guilds, and other important organizations of Dutch merchants liked to be portrayed for posterity. Dutch middle-class families favored small,

Peter Paul Rubens (1577-1640) painted his "Massacre of the Innocents" about 1635. The painting shows King Herod's decree that all children under age two should be killed in order to eliminate the new-born Christ, being carried out with ruthless bloodshed. But Rubens was also recording current events, for in 1635 France prolonged the Thirty Years' War by its entry. Thus, a historical and biblical scene, a contemporary scene, and an allegory were all represented in a single painting, for in the background Rubens showed angels with flowers, to suggest that a heavenly hand still guided earthly events.

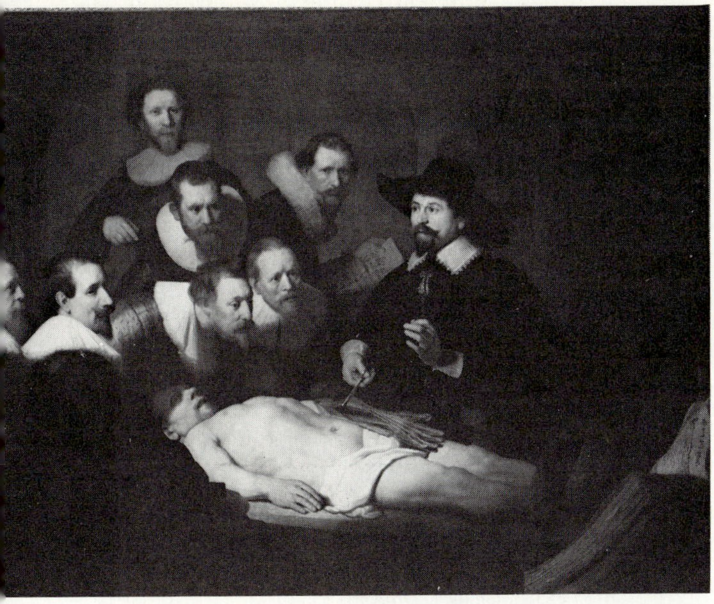

Rembrandt used light and facial expression as well as the position of the figures in his paintings to capture a sense of psychological truth. Here, in "The Anatomy Lesson of Dr. Tulp," the first commission he completed after moving from Leiden to Amsterdam, he showed a demonstration given by the leading professor of anatomy of the time. Those around him are members of the surgeons' guild. Each figure is individually realized, as Rembrandt draws attention to the developing science of pathology.

cheerful pictures, preferably showing the leisure activities cherished by these hard-working people. The consequence was a veritable explosion of artistic output that coincided with the heyday of Dutch prosperity during the first two-thirds of the century. With the French invasion of the 1670s, both the economic and artistic hegemony of the Dutch began to fade.

Seventeenth-century Dutch painters were admired both for their subtle depiction of light and color in landscapes and for their realistic representations of the interiors of Dutch houses, with their highly polished or well-scrubbed floors and their strong contrasts of light and shade. The best-known baroque painters in the Netherlands were Frans Hals (c 1580-1666) and Rembrandt Van Rijn (1606-1669). Hals used bold strokes to paint cheerful contingents of civic guards, laughing musicians, and tavern drunks. As he aged, he himself became a chronic drinker; yet in his eighties, a penniless inmate in a poorhouse, he painted the most remarkable group portrait in baroque art—*The Women Regents of the Haarlem Hospital*—dour, formidable, and aging matrons in all their Calvinist severity.

Rembrandt too attained fame early, then slipped into obscurity and poverty; he documented his troubles in a series of moving self-portraits. He also executed famous group portraits—*The Night Watch* and *The Syndics of the Drapers' Guild*. Rembrandt painted an exceptional scientific subject, *The Anatomy Lesson of Dr. Tulp*, in which a physician is explaining the structure of blood vessels and tendons in the arm of an executed criminal, the only kind of cadaver available to anatomists.

Architecture and the Art of Living Baroque architecture and urban planning were at their most flamboyant in Rome, where Urban VIII (1623-1644) and other popes sponsored churches, palaces, gardens, fountains, avenues, and piazzas in their determination to make their capital once again the most spectacular city in Europe. The Church of Saint Peter's, apart from Michelangelo's dome, is a legacy of the baroque rather than the Renaissance.

In the last third of the century the France of Louis XIV set the trends in architecture, landscape gardening, town planning, and furniture—especially at Versailles and in Paris. Vienna, Munich, Madrid, Warsaw, and

In the famous church of St. Peter's at Rome, the proportions of Michelangelo's Greek-cross design were altered when a greatly lengthened nave was constructed in the early 1600s. With the vast space of the nave leading into the space beneath the dome, it was imperative to find a way of filling the latter. Urban VIII entrusted the commission to a young architect, Gian Lorenzo Bernini (1598-1680), who hit upon the ingenious solution of the *baldachin*, or tabernacle, an enormously magnified and strengthened version of the canopy used to cover the sacrament. This 85-foot structure made elaborate use of the Barberini family symbols and was supposedly modeled on Solomon's temple. To obtain bronze for the columns and canopy, Urban VIII had the bronze roof of the Pantheon—the best preserved of Rome's ancient monuments—melted down.

The great Piazza Obliqua was added to St. Peter's by Bernini in 1657-1666, completing a masterpiece of the baroque. This was the first large open space within a city, in contrast to the enclosed squares typical of the Renaissance, the great colonnades providing a massive space that focuses on St. Peter's itself.

St. Paul's Cathedral in London, b between 1673 and 1710, becam architectural model for much pub architecture well into the ninetee century.

Prague also became major baroque cities, though their styles tended to be imitative of the Italian or French. Great architectural feats sometimes took two generations or more, and the post-1630 period (known as high baroque) was marked by constant building, even in lesser cities like Würzburg or Dresden.

In England baroque building was much diluted by classicism. Under Charles II the chief architect was Sir Christopher Wren (1632-1723), a talented engineer and astronomer who was deluged with commissions after a great fire destroyed much of London in 1666. Saint Paul's Cathedral, in particular, drew upon his capacity to fuse varying styles into a harmonious whole.

The arts of good living made substantial progress in the seventeenth century, despite the ravages of disease and famine that reduced the European population by at least 15 percent between 1648 and 1713. The expansion of Europe overseas made available the new beverages of coffee, tea, and cocoa, the new cotton fabrics, and luxuries like Chinese porcelain and lacquer ware. Exotic tropical woods were used to inlay and veneer furniture. On the whole, furniture was becoming more specialized: dining chairs replaced dining benches; chairs were made both with arms and, to accommodate hoopskirts, without. Table napkins came into use; individual plates and glasses replaced communal bowls and goblets. Families of moderate means could afford these innovations, as well as a teapot, a pitcher, and a few items of plain silver, and thus shared in what amounted to a revolution in domestic arrangements.

Music Baroque composers, especially in Italy, moved further along the paths laid out by their Renaissance predecessors. In Venice Claudio Monteverdi (1567-1643) wrote the first important operas. The opera, a characteristically baroque mix of music and drama, proved so popular that Venice soon had sixteen opera houses, which focused on the fame of their chief singers rather than on the overall quality of the supporting cast and the orchestra. The star system reached its height at Naples, where conservatories (originally institutions for "conserving" talented orphans) specialized in voice training. Many Neapolitan operas were loose collections of songs designed to show off the talents of the individual stars. The effect of unreality was heightened by the custom of having male roles sung by women and some female roles sung by *castrati*, male sopranos who had been castrated as young boys to prevent the onset of puberty and the deepening of their voices.

In England Henry Purcell (c 1659-1695), the organist of Westminster Abbey, produced a masterpiece for the graduation exercises of a girls' school, the beautiful and moving *Dido and Aeneas.* Louis XIV, appreciating the obvious value of opera in enhancing the resplendence of his court, imported from Italy the talented Jean-Baptiste Lully (1632-1687). In his operas Lully united French and Italian musical, dance, and literary traditions, and took over the artificiality, gaiety, and weight of court ballet. No artist of the time was more representative, and none was more distant from the concerns of the people who, though they might admire the majesty of the court from a distance, could know no part in it—the common people, who saw little if any of the art and architecture, read none of the literature, and heard none of the music of baroque high society.

Social Trends

Throughout the seventeenth century the laborer, whether rural or urban, faced repeated crises of subsistence, with a general downturn beginning in 1619 and a widespread decline after 1680. Almost no region escaped plague, famine, war, depression, or even all four. Northern Europe and England suffered from a general economic depression in the 1620s; Mediterranean France and northern Italy were struck by plague in the 1630s; and a recurrent plague killed 100,000 in London in 1665. The "little ice age"—a gradual onset of acute cold too severe for most crops—began in the late sixteenth century and made harvests unpredictable until 1650, and for a decade there was a perceptable advance of glacial ice. Population increase slowed dramatically, and general stagnation was the norm, despite important regional exceptions. Given the emphasis on high fashion at the French court, the gap between the rich and the poor was perceived as growing.

HISTORY AND CHANGE

In his *Pensées* Pascal remarked upon the transitions in history:

> Rivers are roads which move, and which carry us wither we desire to go.
>
> When we do not know the truth of a thing, it is of advantage that there should exist a common error which determines the mind of man, as, for example, the moon, to which is attributed the change of seasons, the progress of diseases, etc. For the chief malady of man is restless curiosity about things which he cannot understand; and it is not so bad for him to be in error as to be curious to no purpose.

Thoughts, Letters, and Opuscules, trans. O.W. Wight (New York: Hurt and Houghton, 1869), p. 211.

In France and Russia the sixteenth century was marked by peasant revolts. In France the revolts were directed against the tax collectors, who raised revenues "for the needs of the state"—needs which were felt to be a pretext for enriching a few private persons. The peasants especially resented the tax-farmer, who was a vigorously efficient tax collector because he kept part of what he raised. They also resented the tendency toward centralization which the new taxes, and most especially the *gabelle*, a tax on salt, represented. Peasant revolts in 1636, 1637, 1639, and 1675 underscored the general discontent.

Discontent and fear also help explain the renewal of the search for witches. Witches had once been part of the general belief in magic and religion. In the fifteenth century a substantial handbook on the detection and interrogation of witches had been widely read, and by 1669 it was in its twenty-ninth edition. Witchcraft combined sorcery and heresy; the first was to be feared and the second condemned. Though skeptics and rationalists doubted the existence of witches or the Devil, theologians and the great mass of people did not. Moreover, both law and medicine accepted witchcraft, and even the English jurist Blackstone would seriously discuss witchcraft as an issue in the 1730s.

Between 1580 and 1650 witchcraft trials were commonplace; there probably were nearly 100,000 such trials, amounting to epidemics of mass hysteria. Even in England, where the common law prohibited torture to extract confessions, there were over a thousand trials. Although concern for witches was almost universal, the greatest number of executions took place in Calvinist areas. Historians are not agreed on why an outbreak of witch persecutions would occur in one place rather than another—in Scotland and New England, in Switzerland and France—except to say that where popular magic was commonplace, so was the fear of witches. Trials also usually followed a period of fear about the future and concern over apparent changes in ordered and stable conditions. Nor were the educated spared—indeed, they were often in the lead when a community sought out a witch.

In 1691, in Massachusetts, the strange behavior of two small girls led the community of Salem into a mass witchhunt that did not stop until twenty persons had been executed. Historians believe the hallucinations of the children thought to be under the influence of witches were induced by ergot poisoning from a fungus that grows on barley in a moist season. Elsewhere fertility cults were accused of performing black magic. In southern France witchcraft may simply have been a form of rural social revolt in which the Mass could be mocked and the church hierarchy challenged.

The clergy did not have all the needed answers for the peasant, and were often challenged by astrologers, village wizards, "cunning folk." Popular magic often seemed to provide a more ready remedy for illness, theft, unhappy personal relationships, or a world in which meanings were shifting. In the seventeenth century magic declined in relation to religion; increased popular literacy, improved communications, the slow recognition that diseases such as epilepsy were open to human investigation instead of partaking of the supernatural, the failures of divination, and perhaps reaction against the horrors of the witchcraft craze, all contributed to the turn toward rationalism that occurred first in the cities.

Still, there was continuity amid change. The old traditional rhythms continued in marriage, child-rearing, death, and burial. As feast and famine alternated, people continued to try to explain insecurity, sought for stability, and realized that their lives were racked by events not only beyond their control but beyond their understanding. These fears were also true of the upper classes. Indeed, in some matters the lower classes had more control over their lives. The children of those who owned no property were freer to choose a spouse, since their parents had little economic leverage over them, having nothing to bequeath to them, than were the children of the aristocracy, who had to make carefully calculated marriage alliances to hold on to or increase family property.

By the seventeenth century the position of women with respect to property was improving. On the Continent perhaps 20 percent of families had daughters and no sons; when women inherited land, the social implications were far-reaching, since ownership might pass to a different family at every generation. By the eighteenth century the "female presence" in land holding had become very important in England, finally matching the position women had held in ancient Sparta. Marriages were thereby encouraged between persons of similar status and wealth, hardening class lines. Since a second spouse would diminish the interest of the first, the economy joined the church in working against polygamy. The marriage of a widow had become of great importance to her adult children, since it would influence the estate.

When other siblings were excluded from the land, younger children had to be given an equivalent share in some other way. Thus the custom grew of a younger son's buying a commission in the army, or of entering the church, or of joining the faculty of a university, or of being given a stake in business. However, since the family name remained attached to the land, the aristocracy remained one of land rather than of wealth or of intelligence, so that being a "counter jumper" (a merchant, or "in trade") might lead to far more income but much less prestige. Since common people were unlikely to be able to break into the aristocracy of prestige, successful commoners cast their lot with the merchant class and with capitalism, which was increasingly open to talent rather than to inherited wealth.

Increasingly, the law was used to hold society in balance: to keep people in their place, to assure that the poor did not poach upon the land of the rich, to define acts of social unrest as crimes. The growth in individualism—whether among contributors to the "century of genius" or among those who emerged from "Every-

WHO BUILT THE TOWERS OF THEBES?

In the seventeenth century the underclasses, that unspoken for and, for the historian who relies solely on written records, unspeaking mass of humankind, began to speak and to answer the questions posed in the twentieth century by a radical German dramatist and poet, Bertolt Brecht (1898-1956):

Who built Thebes of the seven gates?
In the books you will find the names of kings.
Did the kings haul up the lumps of rock?
And Babylon, many times demolished
Who raised it up so many times? In what houses
Of gold-glittering Lima did the builders live?
Where, the evening that the Wall of China was
  finished
Did the masons go? Great Rome
Is full of triumphal arches. Who erected them?
  Over whom
Did the Caesars triumph? Had Byzantium, much
  praised in song
Only palaces for its inhabitants? Even in fabled
  Atlantis
The night the ocean engulfed it
The drowning still bawled for their slaves.

The young Alexander conquered India.
Was he alone?
Caesar beat the Gauls.
Did he not have even a cook with him?

Philip of Spain wept when his armada
Went down. Was he the only one to weep?
Frederick the Second won the Seven Years' War.
Who Else won it?

Every page a victory.
Who cooked the feast for the victors?
Every ten years a great man.
Who paid the bill?

So many reports.
So many questions.

B. Brecht, "Questions from a Worker Who Reads," trans. Michael Hamburgh, in John Willett and Ralph Manheim, eds., *Bertolt Brecht Poems* (London: Eyre Methuen, 1976), pp. 252-53.

man"—led to greater variation in human behavior. As a result, there was a perceived need to use laws to define appropriate behavior, with greater interference by the state (as well as the church) in matters relating to sexuality, bastardy, and marriage. Mere nakedness was not yet considered indecent, nor was drunkenness thought to be a public vice. Destruction of the family unit, however, by failing to observe the laws of inheritance was a clear offense against continuity and propriety. It remained one small area of stability that rich and poor could, to some extent, control.

Perhaps we speak today of the seventeenth century as "the century of genius" because so much that is still central to our thought—in politics, economics, literature, art, and science—can be traced most immediately to the great thinkers of that century. But the seventeenth century was also the century of the inarticulate, of the far-less-than-great, of common people who labored for themselves, their families, their church, and, often and increasingly, for their nation. The Fronde was not a popular uprising, but there were many peasant revolts in the seventeenth century and thereafter. The English Civil War was not a "war of people," but the people were intimately touched by its events.

"The past is a foreign country: they do things differently there."* The past summarized so scantily in this volume is indeed, to the twentieth century, a vast foreign land—more different by virtue of the distance of time than modern countries may be from another despite the distances imposed by language and technology. In 1513 Nicolò Machiavelli had written in *The Prince*, "There is nothing more difficult to take in hand, more perilous to conduct, or more uncertain in its success, than to take the lead in the introduction of a new order of things." Soon the introduction of a new order of things would become frequent, even seem commonplace, as the pace of known history—of recorded events that bear directly upon our understanding of the present—speeded up dramatically. To tread on the dust of the past, as the early nineteenth-century English poet Lord Byron wrote, is to feel the earthquake waiting below.

*The twentieth-century English novelist L.P. Hartley.

SUMMARY

The seventeenth century was dominated by France. During the reign of Louis XIII, Cardinal Richelieu created an efficient centralized state. He eliminated the Huguenots as a political force, made nobles subordinate to the king, and made the monarchy absolute. Louis XIV built on these achievements during his long reign. Louis XIV moved his capital from the turbulence of Paris to Versailles, where he built a vast palace and established elaborate court rituals that further limited the power of the nobles.

From Versailles, the Sun King demanded unquestioning obedience from his subjects, seeing himself as the representative of God on earth and ruling by divine right. In religion, Louis XIV encouraged the evolution of the Gallican church. In 1685, he revoked the Edict of Nantes, ending toleration of Huguenots. Mercantilism, practiced by Colbert, was central to French economic policy. Colbert's policies promoted foreign trade and the expansion of industry.

Hoping to expand France to its "natural frontiers," Louis XIV pursued an aggressive foreign policy that embroiled the nation in numerous wars. In the War of the Spanish Succession (1701-1714), England, Holland, the Holy Roman Empire, and German states joined forces to prevent a union of Spain and France. The treaty of Utrecht (1713) preserved the balance of power in Europe but left many unresolved issues.

In England, the Stuart monarchs James I and Charles I violated traditions limiting royal authority and protecting individual rights. Their attempts to rule without Parliament brought matters to a revolution between the Crown and Parliament. During the Civil War (1640-1648), England was split between royalists and parliamentarians. Under Puritan leader Oliver Cromwell, the New Model Army decisively defeated the king. Radicals in the Rump Pariament tried and condemned the king to death in 1649.

During the Interregnum, England was a republic dominated by Oliver Cromwell and the Puritans. They faced opposition at home and abroad. In 1660, the monarchy was restored. But the Interregnum marked the first successful challenge to a monarch by a politically active citizenry. Moreover, the events of the Civil War affirmed the existence of an unwritten constitution rooted in English common law. Belief in freedom of speech and religious toleration also emerged in this period.

During the Restoration, Parliament was supreme. The Catholic sympathies of James II so alienated his subjects that he was toppled by the Glorious Revolution of 1688, which put William of Orange on the throne. Parliament then enacted the Bill of Rights of 1689 that embodied the principles of parliamentary supremacy. In the next three hundred years, England would become a parliamentary democracy.

The seventeenth century was an age of intellectual ferment dominated by France, Holland, and England. Two concepts underlay thought: the idea of a natural order and the importance of reason. In England, Thomas Hobbes in the *Leviathan* (1651) and John Locke in his *Second Treatise of Government* (1690) set out ideas on government and human nature that would greatly influence political thought. On the continent, Pascal and Spinoza made equally significant contributions to Western thought.

During the Age of Classicism, French dramatists such as Corneille, Molière, and Racine dominated literature just as the court of Louis XIV influenced all of Europe. In *Paradise Lost,* John Milton combined classical scholarship and profound Christian faith.

Baroque masters produced flamboyant works of art that emphasized size and theatricality. Flemish and Dutch painters including Rubens, Rembrandt, and Van Dyck won widespread acclaim.

In the seventeenth century, laborers faced hardships of plague, famine, and warfare. An epidemic of witchhunts and witch trials reflected a pervasive fear. Yet belief in popular magic declined as literacy spread. The property rights of women were recognized, thereby helping to improve their position. Despite gradual change, traditional patterns of life continued, and law was used to affirm social rights and traditions.

SUGGESTED READINGS

Lists of supplementary or additional readings are usually intended to offer the student guidance into fuller, more specialized, or more advanced historical literature. These lists also include sources—that is, primary documentary materials—for students who want to enter into the spirit of the period under study by reading of that period in the words of contemporaries. Because footnotes have been used throughout the text to provide information on the origins of quotations, the following list is not intended to serve as a formal bibliography of books used in preparing the text. No titles are included that author Robin Winks has not read, but titles are not supplied to support all potentially controversial statements made in the text. Rather, the purpose of these lists, which are broken down by chapter and general subject matter, is to provide the student with a way to learn more about the major subjects.

Information listed refers to the latest edition available at the time this text went to press. Obviously there are dozens, even hundreds, of books on any of the subjects discussed in the text. The criteria for selection, therefore, have had to be clear: books, preferably short, written in a manner likely to be of interest to students of history, and when possible, books that are in print and in paperback editions. Clarity, accuracy, and availability were the primary tests. The most recent book on a subject is not always the best, though many titles published in the 1970s and 1980s have been included if they met the criteria. The authors believe that this list of suggested readings is therefore both up to date and useful, and books that have been included should be available in any good college library.

THE VALUE OF HISTORY AND OF HISTORICAL CONTROVERSY

Our first controversy was to define "civilization," and this was done in the introductory chapter. Readers wishing to pursue this thorny problem further might best begin with Robert Redfield, *The Primitive World and its Transformations* (Ithaca: Cornell University Press, 1953); move on to Lloyd Warner, *A Black Civilization*, rev. ed. (New York: Harper & Row, 1958); A. L. Kroeber, *The Nature of Culture* (Chicago: University of Chicago Press, 1952); and Arnold Toynbee, *Civilization on Trial* (Oxford: Oxford University Press, 1953), of which Kroeber was critical. Then explore Glyn Daniel, *The First Civilizations: The Archaeology of Their Origins* (New York: T. Y. Crowell, 1968) and *The Idea of Prehistory* (Cleveland: World Publishing Co., 1962).

CHAPTER ONE: THE FIRST CIVILIZATIONS

General Accounts

William F. Albright, *From the Stone Age to Christianity*, 2nd ed. (New York: Doubleday, 1957). Superb survey of a field that has been much altered by modern scholarship.

Rushton Coulborn, *The Origins of Civilized Societies* (Princeton, N.J.: Princeton University Press, 1959). A scholarly, readable, and stimulating study.

Alexander Marshack, *The Roots of Civilization* (New York: McGraw-Hill, 1972). Magnificently illustrated (and controversial) account of new research into the artifacts and mental processes of Paleolithic (Old Stone Age) people.

James Mellaart, *Catal Hüyük* (London: Thames & Hudson, 1967). The discoverer's account of the Neolithic settlement of 6500 B.C. in southern Turkey.

Stuart Piggott, *Approach to Archaeology* (New York: McGraw-Hill, 1965). Short, up-to-date account of the problem of creating through archaeology time scales that can be used by historians.

Karl A. Wittfogel, *Oriental Despotism* (New York: Random House, 1981). Famous controversial statement of the thesis that hydraulic societies strive for total power.

The Near East

Geoffrey Bibby, *Four Thousand Years Ago* (New York: Knopf, 1962). A most readable account of the crucial millennium from 2000 to 1000 B.C.

James H. Breasted, *History of Egypt* (New York: Scribner's, 1979). By a celebrated Egyptologist of another generation; though dated, still a classic worth reading.

Christiane Desroches-Noblecourt, *Egyptian Wall Paintings from Tombs and Temples* (New York: Mentor, n.d.). An informative sampler.

Louis Finkelstein, ed., *The Jews: Their History, Culture and Religion*, 4th ed., 2 vols. (New York: Schocken Brooks, 1970). Comprehensive; popular in the best sense.

Henri Frankfort, *The Birth of Civilization in the Near East*, 5th ed. (New York: Barnes & Noble, 1968). A brief and stimulating essay by an expert in the area.

Henri Frankfort, et al., *Before Philosophy* (Baltimore: Penguin, 1972). Admirable essays on the intellectual history of the ancient Near East.

Cyrus H. Gordon, *Forgotten Scripts*, rev. ed. (New York: Basic Books, 1982). Lively and up-to-date survey of the history of decipherment.

Oliver R. Gurney, *The Hittites*, 2nd ed. (Baltimore: Penguin, 1972). Authoritative survey of a people rescued from almost total oblivion by archaeology.

William W. Hallo and William K. Simpson, *The Ancient Near East: A History* (New York: Harcourt, 1971). Up-to-date survey; not always easy to read.

Donald Harden, *The Phoenicians* (New York: Praeger, 1962). Clear summary.

Samuel N. Kramer, *History Begins at Sumer* (Philadelphia: University of Pennsylvania Press, 1981). Introduction by an expert.

J. Lassoe, *People of Ancient Assyria* (New York: Barnes & Noble, 1963). An attempt to show the Assyrians as more than mere militarists.

Sabatino Moscati, *The Face of the Ancient Orient: A Panorama of Near Eastern Civilization in Pre-Classical Times* (Garden City, N.Y.: Anchor, 1962). Good introductory survey.

H. M. Orlinsky, *The Ancient Jews*, 2nd ed. (Ithaca, N.Y.: Cornell University Press, 1960). A good introductory manual.

Henry B. Parkes, *Gods and Men: The Origins of Western Culture* (New York: Knopf, 1959). Perceptive survey of early religions.

Reader's Digest Atlas of the Bible (New York: Reader's Digest Association, 1981). A popular though accurate history interspersed with useful maps.

Chester G. Starr, *Early Man* (New York: Oxford University Press, 1973). Well-illustrated, simple introduction.

John A. Wilson, *The Culture of Ancient Egypt* (Chicago: University of Chicago Press, 1956). One of the best single-volume studies of the subject.

Leonard Woolley, *Beginnings of Civilization* (New York: Mentor, n.d.). Sequel to the popular survey by Jacquetta Hawkes, *Prehistory*.

Crete and Early Greece

C. W. Blegen, *Troy and the Trojans* (New York: Praeger, 1963); and Lord William Taylor, *Mycenaeans* (New York: Praeger, 1964). Clear, scholarly introductions.

John Chadwick, *The Decipherment of Linear B* (Cambridge: Cambridge University Press, 1970). By Michael Ventris' collaborator.

M. I. Finley, *Early Greece: The Bronze and Archaic Ages*, 2nd ed. (New York: Norton, 1982). Authoritative, detailed survey.

Geoffrey S. Kirk, *Homer and the Epic* (Cambridge: Cambridge University Press, 1962). The most recent summary; nontechnical and authoritative.

Denys L. Page, *History and the Homeric Iliad* (Berkeley: University of California Press, 1959). Readable, scholarly set of lectures.

Leonard R. Palmer, *A New Guide to the Palace of Knossos* (London: Faber & Faber, 1969). A clear statement of our present knowledge.

Leonard R. Palmer, *Mycenaeans and Minoans,* 2nd ed. (Westport, Conn.: Greenwood, 1980). Controversial reassessment in the light of the Linear B tablets.

Emily Vermeule, *Greece in the Bronze Age* (Chicago: University of Chicago Press, 1964). Excellent.

CHAPTER TWO: THE GREEKS

General Accounts

M. M. Austin and P. Vidal-Naquet, *Economic and Social History of Ancient Greece* (Berkeley: University of California Press, 1978). Sober, thorough examination, with many extracts from and commentaries on sources.

André Bonnard, *Greek Civilization,* 3 vols. (New York: Macmillan, 1957–1961). Stimulating chapters on many aspects of Greece by a European scholar.

J. B. Bury, *A History of Greece to the Death of Alexander the Great,* 4th ed. rev. (New York: St. Martin's, 1975). Another celebrated, somewhat idealized, older account; stresses war and politics.

Robert M. Cook, *The Greeks till Alexander* (London: Thames & Hudson, 1961). Well-illustrated survey stressing material accomplishments.

Eric R. Dodds, *The Greeks and the Irrational* (Berkeley: University of California Press, 1951). A fine balance to the tendency to overrationalize the Greeks.

M. I. Finley, *The Ancient Economy* (Berkeley: University of California Press, 1973). Brief, clear analysis; especially good on the difference between town and country.

M. I. Finley, *The Ancient Greeks* (New York: Penguin, 1977). Compact, up-to-date, and perceptive introduction to Greek life and thought.

M. I. Finley, *Studies in Ancient Society* (London: Routledge & Kegan Paul, 1978). Key essays on the Romans as well as the Greeks, demagogues, peasants, and Greek and Roman thought.

M. I. Finley, *Economy and Society in Ancient Greece* (London: Penguin, 1983). Excellent on slavery, debt, inflation, and property.

William G. Forrest, *The Emergence of Greek Democracy* (New York: McGraw-Hill, 1966). A clear, general account focusing on the years from 800 to 400 B.C.

William G. Forrest, *A History of Sparta, 950–192 B.C.* (New York: Norton, 1969). Best general history.

N. G. L. Hammond, *A History of Greece to 332 B.C.,* 2nd ed. (Oxford: Clarendon Press, 1967). A good, up-to-date survey.

Donald Kagan, *The Outbreak of the Peloponnesian War* (Ithaca, N.Y.: Cornell University Press, 1969). A rethinking of the evidence by a scholar interested in the causes of war.

Donald Kagan, *The Archidamian War* (Ithaca, N.Y.: Cornell University Press, 1974). The fullest reconstruction.

H. D. F. Kitto, *The Greeks* (Chicago: Aldine Publishers, 1964). Lively, though opinionated, introduction.

G. E. Robinson, *Hellas: A Short History of Greece* (Boston: Beacon, n.d.). Good survey by a scholar who has written extensively on Greek history.

M. I. Rostovtzeff, *Greece* (Oxford: Oxford University Press, 1963). A famous older account by a distinguished Russian scholar; now somewhat out of date on details.

Morton Smith, *The Ancient Greeks* (Ithaca, N.Y.: Cornell University Press, 1960). Very short summary of the generally accepted views.

Special Studies: The Polis

Antony Andrewes, *The Greek Tyrants* (New York: Humanities Press, 1956). Informative comparative survey of emerging Greek constitutions.

Andrew R. Burn, *Pericles and Athens* (New York; Collier Books, n.d.). Popular introduction to the Athenian Golden Age.

Victor Ehrenberg, *The Greek State,* 2nd ed. (New York: Methuen, 1974). A solid scholarly introduction.

Kathleen Freeman, *Greek City-States* (New York: Norton, 1963). Excellent overview; focuses on interesting examples usually neglected in the concern for Athens and Sparta.

Gustave Glotz, *The Greek City and Its Institutions* (New York: Barnes & Noble, 1965). Celebrated study by a French scholar; now somewhat out of date.

A. H. M. Jones, *Athenian Democracy* (Oxford: Blackwell, 1969). An up-to-date interpretation.

Humfrey Michell, *Sparta* (Cambridge: Cambridge University Press, 1964). A comprehensive survey; somewhat more favorable in tone than most treatments of the subject.

A. G. Woodhead, *The Greeks in the West* (New York: Praeger, 1962); and John M. Cook, *The Greeks in Ionia and the East* (New York: Praeger, 1965). Volumes in the series Ancient Peoples and Places; highlight the often-neglected geographical outposts of the Greek world.

Alfred E. Zimmern, *The Greek Commonwealth* (Oxford: Oxford University Press, n.d.). A celebrated older account; highly sympathetic in tone.

Special Studies: Greek Civilization

Cecil M. Bowra, *The Greek Experience* (New York: New American Library, 1961). Stresses interpretation rather than fact; by a literary scholar.

Cecil M. Bowra, *Classical Greece* (New York: Time-Life, 1965). A beautifully illustrated short history.

Emile Bréhier, *The Hellenic Age* (Chicago: University of Chicago Press, 1963). The first volume of a detailed history of philosophy by a French scholar.

J. B. Bury, *The Ancient Greek Historians* (New York: Macmillan, 1909). Appraisal by a celebrated English historian.

Rhys Carpenter, *The Esthetic Basis of Greek Art* (Bloomington: Indiana University Press, 1959). Analysis by an expert.

Francis M. Cornford, *Before and After Socrates* (Cambridge: Cambridge University Press, n.d.). First-rate short introduction to Greek science and philosophy.

J. K. Davies, *Athenian Propertied Families* (Oxford: Oxford University Press, 1971). Covers the years from 600 to 300 B.C.

J. K. Davies, *Democracy and Classical Greece* (New York: Humanities Press, 1978). Clearest reexamination of the present state of our knowledge about democratic concepts in Athens and Sparta.

Aubrey de Sélincourt, *The World of Herodotus* (Berkeley: North Point Press, 1982). Loving, careful evocation of the Greece on which Herodotus reported.

G. E. M. de Ste. Croix, *The Class Struggle in the Ancient Greek World* (Ithaca, N.Y.: Cornell University Press, 1982). Controversial examination of labor in archaic Greece.

G. Lowes Dickinson, *The Greek View of Life* (Ann Arbor: University of Michigan Press, 1958). Greek culture appraised from an older point of view.

K. J. Dover, *Greek Homosexuality* (Cambridge, Mass.: Harvard University Press, 1978). Exploration of a generally neglected subject.

William K. Guthrie, *The Greeks and Their Gods* (Boston: Beacon, 1955). Detailed but stimulating study of the origins and the nature of Greek religion.

Moses Hadas, *A History of Greek Literature* (New York: Columbia University Press, 1950). Helpful survey.

Edith Hamilton, *Mythology* (New York: New American Library, 1971). Brief introduction, centered on Greek myths.

Edith Hamilton, *The Greek Way to Western Civilization* (New York: Avon, 1973). Enthusiastic popular treatment by a great admirer of the Greeks.

Werner Jaeger, *Paideia,* 3 vols. (Oxford: Oxford University Press, 1939–1944). (Volume 1 also in paperback.) An advanced study of Greek civilization and ideals.

H. I. Marrou, *A History of Education in Antiquity* (Madison: University of Wisconsin Press, 1982). Useful account; also treats the Romans and early Christians.

Martin P. Nilsson, *Greek Folk Religion* (Philadelphia: University of Pennsylvania Press, 1972). Informative lectures on popular beliefs and practices.

J. J. Pollitt, *Art and Experience in Classical Greece* (Cambridge: Cambridge University Press, 1972). A succinct reexamination of what we know about Greek art.

Special Studies: The Hellenistic World

Emile Bréhier, *The Hellenistic and Roman Age* (Chicago: University of Chicago Press, 1965). Another volume of the French scholar's history of philosophy.

Andrew R. Burn, *Alexander the Great and the Hellenistic World* (London: English Universities Press, 1964). Brief popular account.

Kurt Emmrich, *Alexander the Great* (London: Thames & Hudson, 1970). Beautiful pictures of the remains and scenery of Alexander's world

Peter Green, *Alexander of Macedon, 356–323 B.C.*, rev. ed. (Hammondsworth: Penguin, 1974). A generally critical examination of Alexander's record.
Moses Hadas, *Hellenistic Culture* (New York: Norton, 1972). Good evaluation.
Bernard M. Knox, *The Heroic Temper* (Berkeley: University of California Press, 1965). Focuses on Sophocles to examine the concept of tragic heroism.
Russell Meiggs, *The Athenian Empire* (Oxford: Oxford University Press, 1979). Excellent account of the rise and fall of the empire; a model of how to draw knowledge from ancient inscriptions.
M. I. Rostovtzeff, *The Social and Economic History of the Hellenistic World* (Oxford: Clarendon, 1941). Detailed study by a great historian.
W. W. Tarn, *Alexander the Great* (Boston: Beacon, 1956). A sympathetic (and not always convincing) study by one of the foremost experts on the subject.
W. W. Tarn, *Hellenistic Civilization,* rev. ed. (New York: New American Library, 1961). Comprehensive survey of civilization under Alexander's successors.

Sources

Note: The following list includes only the most famous works, many of which are available in other translations and editions.

W. H. Auden, ed., *The Portable Greek Reader* (New York: Penguin, 1977). Excellent short anthology.
The Dialogues of Plato, trans. B. Jowett (New York: Random House, 1937). New edition of a famous (and controversial) old translation.
Herodotus, *The Histories,* trans. Aubrey de Sélincourt (New York: Penguin, 1954).
Homer, *The Iliad.* Two of many translations; that of Richard Lattimore (Chicago: University of Chicago Press, 1961) is a good poetic translation; that of W. H. D. Rouse (New York: New American Library, 1954) is in modern English prose.
W. J. Oates and E. O'Neill, Jr., eds., *The Complete Greek Drama* (New York: Random House, 1938). A selection of dramas by the same editors may be found in *Seven Famous Greek Plays* (New York: Random House, 1955).
Thucydides, *History of the Peloponnesian War* (New York: Oxford University Press, 1960). A standard translation.
A. J. Toynbee, ed., *Greek Civilization and Character,* 2nd ed. (Boston: Beacon, 1950), and *Greek Historical Thought* (New York: New American Library, 1964). Two volumes of excerpts from Greek writers that afford a kaleidoscopic view of Greek attitudes.
The Works of Aristotle, ed. W. D. Ross (Oxford: Oxford University Press, 1908–1931). Selections by the same editor are also available (New York: Scribner's, n.d.).
Xenophon, *Anabasis: The March Up Country,* trans. W. H. D. Rouse (Ann Arbor: University of Michigan Press, 1958). Very readable.

CHAPTER THREE: THE ROMANS

General Accounts

Reginald H. Barrow, *The Romans* (London: Penguin, 1955). Sound popular introduction.
A. E. R. Beak and William G. Sinnigen, *A History of Rome to 565 A.D.,* 6th ed. (New York: Macmillan, 1977). A detailed study.
Tenney Frank, *A History of Rome* (Darby, Penn.: Darby Books, 1981). Useful, though opinionated, survey by an American scholar.
Michael Grant, *The World of Rome* (Chicago: World, 1960). General introduction to imperial Rome; handsomely illustrated.
Theodore Mommsen, *The History of Rome* (New York: Meridian, n.d.). A detailed study by a great German scholar of the nineteenth century; still worth reading, though its interpretations are often out of date.
M. I. Rostovtzeff, *Rome* (New York: Oxford University Press, 1960). Excellent survey by a famous scholar.

The Etruscan Background and the Roman Republic

Ernest Badian, *Roman Imperialism in the Late Republic,* 2nd ed. (Ithaca, N.Y.: Cornell University Press, 1971). Readable, brief lectures on whether the Senate was for or against imperial expansion.
John P. Balsdon, *Roman Women: Their History and Habits* (Westport, Conn.: Greenwood, 1975). A relaxed, clear description.
Raymond Bloch, *The Etruscans* (London: Cresset, 1969), and *The Origins of Rome* (New York: Praeger, 1960). Two volumes in the series Ancient Peoples and Places. The first volume is a general introduction, generously illustrated; the second takes the story of Rome to the early fifth century B.C.
Michael Grant, *The Etruscans* (New York: Scribner's, 1981). Highly readable, up-to-date, popular history.
Massimo Pallottino, *Etruscologia,* 3rd ed., trans. J. Cremona (London: Penguin, n.d.). The best academic introduction to the subject.
T. G. E. Powell, *The Celts* (London: Thames & Hudson, 1980). Informative survey.
Howard H. Scullard, *Roman Politics, 220–150 B.C.* (Westport, Conn.: Greenwood, 1982), and *From the Gracchi to Nero* (New York: Methuen, 1976). The first is a detailed study of the era when Rome began to dominate the Mediterranean world; the second, a clear, balanced history of the later republic and early empire.
A. N. Sherwin-White, *Racial Prejudice in Imperial Rome* (London: Cambridge University Press, 1970). Short, clear lectures on the rise of racial tension, especially between Romans and the "barbarians."
Richard E. Smith, *The Failure of the Roman Republic* (New York: Arno Press, 1975). A provocative essay critical of the Gracchi.
Lily R. Taylor, *Party Politics in the Age of Caesar* (Boston: Peter Smith, 1962). Analytic as well as descriptive study of the way in which Roman politics worked; learned and stimulating.
Malcolm Todd, *The Northern Barbariana, 100 B.C.–A.D. 300* (New York: Hutchinson, 1976). An excellent corrective to the biased impressions handed down from the time of Caesar.
Otto-Wilhelm von Vacano, *The Etruscans in the Ancient World* (New York: St. Martin's, 1960). Scholarly study carefully based on archaeological evidence.

The Roman Empire

John P. Balsdon, *Romans and Aliens* (Chapel Hill: University of North Carolina Press, 1980). Lively, often amusing look at how one could become a Roman.
P. A. Brunt, *Italian Manpower, 225 B.C.–A.D. 14* (Oxford: Clarendon Press, 1971). Authoritative, careful inquiry into all the issues relating to the supply of manpower for the fields, cities, and armies; makes excellent use of census figures.
J. H. d'Arms, *Commerce and Social Standing in Ancient Rome* (Cambridge, Mass.: Harvard University Press, 1981). The latest available information on trade and class.
Emilio Gabba, *Republican Rome, The Army and the Allies* (Berkeley: University of California Press, 1977). A series of essays on the professional army.
Michael Grant, *From Alexander to Cleopatra* (New York: Scribner's, 1982). Fine survey of the meaning of the Hellenistic world.
William V. Harris, *War and Imperialism in Republican Rome, 327-70 B.C.* (Oxford: Oxford University Press, 1979). A reexamination of Roman attitudes toward war and the controversial question of self-defense.
Keith Hopkins, *Conquerors and Slaves* (Cambridge: Cambridge University Press, 1981). Fine study of slavery in the Roman empire.
A. H. M. Jones, *The Later Roman Empire,* 4 vols. (Oxford: Basil Blackwell, 1964). Magnificently detailed master work.
Ramsay MacMullen, *Roman Government's Response to Crisis, A.D. 235-337* (New Haven: Yale University Press, 1976). Thoughtful, balanced short account; especially good on the "perception of decline."
Ramsay MacMullen, *Roman Social Relations, 50 B.C. to A.D. 284* (New Haven: Yale University Press, 1981). Excellent short examination of rural and urban differences.
William H. McNeill, *Plagues and People* (Garden City, N.Y.: Doubleday, 1977). Brilliantly argued, controversial book on the relationship between disease and demography.
Fergus Millar, *The Emperor in the Roman World: 31 B.C.–A.D. 337* (Ithaca, N.Y.: Cornell University Press, 1977). Impressive, massive study of the scope and function of the emperor and his relations to his subjects.
Stewart Perowne, *Hadrian* (Westport, Conn.: Greenwood, 1976). Entertaining modern treatment.
Henry T. Rowell, *Rome in the Augustan Age* (Norman: University of Oklahoma Press, 1971). Sympathetic appraisal fo Augustus and his work.
Ronald Syme, *The Roman Revolution* (London: Oxford University Press, 1939). Detailed study of the transformation of the Roman state and society under Caesar and Augustus.
K. D. White, *Roman Farming* (Ithaca, N.Y.: Cornell University Press, 1970). A book that has substantially revised previous views on the subject.

CHAPTER FOUR: JUDAISM AND CHRISTIANITY

General Accounts

Christopher H. Dawson, *Religion and the Rise of Western Culture* (New York: AMS Press, 1977). Excellent survey to the thirteenth century.

L. M. O. Duchesne, *Early History of the Christian Church,* 3 vols. (New York: Longmans, 1912–1924). A lengthy standard account; very readable.

Kenneth Latourette, *History of Christianity* (New York: Harper & Row, 1975). A short survey, balanced and sympathetic.

Hans Lietzmann, *The Beginnings of the Christian Church, The Founding of the Church Universal, From Constantine to Julian, and the Era of the Church Fathers,* trans. B. L. Woolf (Guildford: Lutterworth, 1949–1951). A learned and well-written survey of the early church.

Arthur C. McGiffert, *A History of Christian Thought,* Vol. 1 (New York: Scribner's, 1932). A good, brief account from a Protestant position.

Henry B. Parkes, *Gods and Men: The Origins of Western Culture* (New York: Knopf, 1959). A clear and sympathetic account; includes a fine reading list.

Richard M. Pope, *The Church and Its Culture* (St. Louis: Bethany, 1965). A brief, sympathetic account; includes a full bibliography.

Special Studies

Peter R. L. Brown, *Augustine of Hippo* (Berkeley: University of California Press, 1967). A brilliant, learned, and well-written biography; takes all modern scholarship into account.

Peter R. L. Brown, *The World of Late Antiquity* (New York: Harcourt, 1971). A lively exploration of A.D. 150 to 750.

Rudolf Bultman, *Primitive Christianity in Its Contemporary Setting,* trans. R. H. Fuller (Philadelphia: Fortress, 1980). An up-to-date, scholarly treatment.

Millar M. Burrows, *The Dead Sea Scrolls* (Grand Rapids, Mich.: Baker Books, 1978). Of the many books on the subject this is perhaps the most useful for the student of general history.

Franz Cumont, *The Oriental Religions in Roman Paganism* (New York: Dover, 1911). A classic introduction to the general religious climate in which Christianity took root.

Jean Danielou, *The Theology of Jewish Christianity,* trans. and ed. John A. Baker (London: Darton, Longman & Todd, 1964). The fullest treatment of the subject by a great modern authority.

John Ferguson, *The Religions of the Roman Empire* (Ithaca, N.Y.: Cornell University Press, 1970). Up to date and comprehensive.

W. H. Frend, *Martyrdom and Persecution in the Early Church* (Grand Rapids, Mich.: Baker Books, 1981). A scholarly yet readable account; includes a full bibliography.

Maurice Goguel, *Jesus and the Origins of Christianity, The Birth of Christianity,* and *The Primitive Church,* trans. H. C. Snape (New York: Humanities Press, 1964). Highly scholarly studies of Christianity through the year A.D. 150.

Erwin R. Goodenough, *The Church in the Roman Empire* (Totowa, N.J.: Cooper Square, 1970). A brief, balanced account directed to the beginning student.

Michael Grant, *The Jews in the Roman World* (New York: Scribner's, 1973). A short, though full, account.

Michael Grant, *The Fall of the Roman Empire: A Reappraisal* (New York: Crown, 1976). An interesting exploration of the ways in which Christianity contributed to social disunity.

Timothy E. Gregory, *Vox Populi: Popular Opinion and Violence in the Religious Controversies of the Fifth Century A.D.* (Columbus: Ohio State University Press, 1979). An excellent analysis of the explosion of popular violence, especially over the councils of Ephesus and Chalcedon.

Richard S. Kirby, et al., *Engineering in History* (New York: McGraw-Hill, 1956). An excellent survey, especially good on the Romans.

David Knowles, *Christian Monasticism* (New York: McGraw-Hill, 1969). The best general history; carries the story to the present.

J. H. Liebeschuetz, *Continuity and Change in Roman Religion* (New York: Oxford University Press, 1979). Largely about the late Roman Republic and early empire; especially enlightening on cults, magic, and astrology.

Ramsay MacMullen, *Constantine* (New York: Dial Press, 1969). A readable, short biography that provides the most recent views on the various controversies.

Sigmund Mowinckel, *He That Cometh* (London: Oxford University Press, 1956). A study of the Jewish concept of the Son of man.

Arthur D. Nock, *St. Paul* (Oxford: Oxford University Press, 1955). A classic treatment; originally published in 1938.

Arthur D. Nock, *Early Gentile Christianity and Its Hellenistic Background* (New York: Harper & Row, 1964). An important essay with two shorter studies, of which one, "Hellenistic Mysteries and Christian Sacraments," is also a landmark.

Jaroslav Pelikan, *The Christian Tradition: A History of the Development of Doctrine* (Chicago: University of Chicago Press, 1977). The first two volumes of this massive study examine the growth of doctrinal argumentation to A.D. 600.

Reader's Digest Atlas of the Bible (Pleasantville, N.Y.: Reader's Digest Association, 1981). Good maps and informative illustrations are combined with accurate popular histories of the events recounted in the Old and New Testaments.

Albert Schweitzer, *The Quest of the Historical Jesus,* rev. ed. (New York: Macmillan, 1968). An excellent introduction to the question.

A. J. Toynbee, ed., *The Crucible of Christianity* (New York: World, 1969). Learned essays by leading scholars, including the editor, on Judaism, Hellenism, and the historical background of Christianity; splendidly illustrated.

F. W. Walbank, *The Awful Revolution: The Decline of the Roman Empire in the West* (Toronto: University of Toronto Press, 1969). A controversial book that emphasizes slavery rather than political disunity, inflation, or religion as the engine of Rome's destruction.

Sources

The New Testament is the best source reading. The inquisitive reader may wish to compare several versions: the Authorized version (many editions) is substantially the King James version; the Revised Standard version (Nelson, 1952) has created some unfavorable comment both from literary reviewers and from fundamentalist Protestants; a recent American edition of the Douay (Roman Catholic version) was published in 1950 (Catholic Book Publishing Company); finally, there is an American Protestant version by Smith and Goodspeed (University of Chicago, 1939).

Next to the New Testament may be ranked the writings of St. Augustine: his spiritual autobiography, *The Confessions,* trans. J. F. Sheed (New York: Sheed & Ward, 1947), and *The City of God,* trans. G. E. McCracken, 6 vols. (Cambridge, Mass.: Harvard University, Loeb Classical Library, n.d.).

H. S. Bettenson, ed., *Documents of the Christian Church,* 2nd ed. (Oxford: Oxford University Press, 1963). An excellent collection, accompanied by enlightening summaries and editorial comments; useful not only for the early period but also for the whole history of Christianity.

P. R. Coleman-Norton, ed., *Roman State and Christian Church,* 3 vols. (London: S.P.C.K., 1966). Translations of the key legal documents through 535.

CHAPTER FIVE: THE EARLY MIDDLE AGES IN EUROPE

General Accounts

Geoffrey Barraclough, *The Medieval Papacy* (New York: Norton, 1979). Lively general survey.

Marc Bloch, *Slavery and Serfdom in the Middle Ages* (Berkeley: University of California Press, 1975). Corrects the long-maintained notion that the Church systematically opposed slavery.

Christopher Dawson, *The Making of Europe* (New York: New American Library, 1956). A scholarly account.

Alfons Dopsch, *The Economic and Social Foundations of European Civilization* (New York: Gordon Press, 1969). An influential German work that emphasizes the continuity between the fifth and eleventh centuries rather than a specific beginning period for the "Middle Ages," as defined by others.

Georges Duby, *Rural Economy and Country Life in the Medieval West* (Columbia: University of South Carolina Press, 1968). Translation of Duby's work on the manorial economy.

Lina Eckenstein, *Woman Under Monasticism* (New York: Russell, 1963). Covers the years 500 to 1500 in detail.

Robert Folz, *The Concept of Empire in Western Europe from the Fifth to the Fourteenth Century* (Westport, Conn.: Greenwood, 1980). Especially informative on Charlemagne and the law.

Harold V. Livermore, *The Origins of Spain and Portugal* (London: Allen & Unwin, 1971). Covers the later Roman empire, the Hispano-Gothic kingdom of Toledo, and the Muslim invasions.

Robert S. Lopez, *The Birth of Europe* (New York: M. Evans, 1967). Fine, original summary.

P. H. Sawyer, *From Roman Britain to Norman England* (New York: St. Martin's, 1979). Significantly alters earlier views on the Mercians and Vikings.

Western Europe

J. B. Bury, *The Invasion of Europe by the Barbarians* (New York: Norton, 1967). A helpful short account.

The Cambridge Medieval History, 2nd ed. (Cambridge: Cambridge University Press, 1964-1968). One of the few scholarly surveys of the whole period in a single volume.

Christopher Dawson, *The Making of Europe* (New York: New American Library, 1956). A scholarly account.

Deno J. Geanakoplos, *Medieval Western Civilization and the Byzantine and Islamic Worlds* (Lexington, Mass.: D. C. Heath, 1979). Perhaps the best general history on the interaction of the three centuries.

James Graham-Campbell and Adfydd Kidd, *The Vikings* (New York: Morrow, 1980). Well-illustrated; incorporates the most recent views.

Archibald R. Lewis, *The Development of Southern French and Catalan Society, 718–1050* (New York: AMS Press, 1981). Excellent on the Carolingians.

Ferdinand Lot, *The End of the Ancient World and the Beginnings of the Middle Ages* (New York: Knopf, 1931). A balanced survey by a French historian.

Lucien Musset, *The Germanic Invasions: The Making of Europe, A.D. 400–600* (University Park: Pennsylvania State University Press. 1975). A fine translation of a judicious French work.

Joseph F. O'Callaghan, *A History of Medieval Spain* (Ithaca, N.Y.: Cornell University Press, 1975). Full and fine coverage from 415 to 1479.

E. A. Thompson, *The Early Germans* (Oxford: Clarendon Press, 1965). A brief, up-to-date general survey.

John M. Wallace-Hadrill, *The Barbarian West: The Early Middle Ages, A.D. 400-1000* (New York: Harper & Row, 1967). Brief up-to-date account. account.

Special Studies

Peter H. Blair, *Roman Britain and Early England, 55 B.C.–871 A.D.* (New York: Norton, 1966). Supplements Stenton (see later entry) and is equally scholarly.

Marc Bloch, *Feudal Society,* 2 vols. (Chicago: University of Chicago Press, 1961–1964) The masterpiece of a great French scholar.

Ernest Brehaut, *An Encyclopedist of the Dark Ages: Isidore of Seville* (New York: B. Franklin, 1967). A revival of a long-neglected figure.

Christopher N. Brooke, *The Saxon and Norman Kings* (London: Batsford, 1963). The first nine (of thirteen) chapters relate the story of the kingship from the reign of Canute in authoritative, up-to-date, crisp prose.

Raymond W. Chambers, *Beowulf: An Introduction to the Study of the Poem,* suppl. C. L. Wrenn, 3rd ed. (Cambridge: Cambridge University Press, 1959). A full compendium of the scholarship on the poem.

J. H. Clapman and Eileen Power, eds., *The Cambridge Economic History, Vol. 1* (Cambridge: Cambridge University Press, 1941). A scholarly study of agrarian life in the Middle Ages.

Lowrie J. Daly, *Benedictine Monasticism: Its Formation and Development through the Twelfth Century* (New York: Sheed & Ward, 1965). A general account of a major monastic order.

Samuel Dill, *Roman Society in Gaul in the Merovingian Age* (Totowa, N.J.: Rowman, 1970), and *Roman Society in the Last Century of the Western Empire* (Philadelphia: R. West, 1979). Useful older social and cultural accounts.

Alfons Dopsch, *The Economic and Social Foundation of European Civilization* (New York: Harcourt, 1937). An important work which revises earlier notions of the breakdown that occurred after the "fall" of Rome.

Heinrich Fichtenau, *The Carolingian Empire: The Age of Charlemagne* (Toronto: University of Toronto Press, 1979). A competent study.

Charles H. Haskins, *The Normans in European History* (New York: Ungar, 1966). A readable and sympathetic introduction; largely covers the later period.

Edward James, *Visigothic Spain: New Approaches* (Oxford: Clarendon, 1980). Fascinating collection of essays; good on freedmen and on Isadore of Seville.

Gwyn Jones, *The Norse Atlantic Saga* (New York: Oxford University Press, 1964), and *A History of the Vikings* (Oxford: Oxford University Press, 1968). Two excellent studies.

David Knowles, *Christian Monasticism* (New York: McGraw-Hill, 1969). Readable short history.

Max L. Laistner and H. H. King, *Thought and Letters in Western Europe, A.D. 500–900,* 2nd ed. (Ithaca, N.Y.: Cornell University Press, 1966). A good scholarly study.

K. J. Leyser, *Rule and Conflict in an Early Medieval Society: Ottonian Saxony* (Bloomington: Indiana University Press, 1980). An original, well-researched case study.

Otto J. Maenchen-Helfer, *The World of the Huns* (Berkeley: University of California Press, 1973). Scholarly, detailed, authoritative work.

Henri Pirenne, *Mohammed and Charlemagne* (New York: Barnes & Noble, 1968). Propounds and defends the highly controversial thesis that the Arab conquest of the Mediterranean harmed western Europe more than the German invasions had done.

Edward K. Rand, *Founders of the Middle Ages* (Cambridge, Mass.: Harvard University Press, 1928). Excellent essays on early medieval men of letters.

F. M. Stenton, *Anglo-Saxon England* (New York: Gordon Press, 1977). A standard account.

Carl Stephenson, *Medieval Feudalism* (Ithaca, N.Y.: Cornell University Press, 1967). A quite simple introductory manual.

Dorothy Whitelock, *The Beginnings of English Society* (London: Penguin, 1964). A briefer introduction to Anglo-Saxon England.

David M. Wilson, *The Anglo-Saxons,* rev. ed. (London: Penguin, 1971). An excellent summary account of Anglo-Saxon archaeology.

Richard Winston, *Charlemagne: From the Hammer to the Cross* (New York: Harper & Row, 1968). An excellent biography.

Sources

Bede the Venerable, *A History of the English Church and People,* trans. Leo Sherley-Price (New York: Penguin, 1955). A readable new edition.

Beowulf, trans. Kevin Crossley-Holland (New York: Farrar, Straus & Giroux, 1968). A good, recent translation.

Arthur J. Grant, ed., *Early Lives of Charlemagne* (London: Chatto & Windus, 1922). Extracts.

Gregory of Tours, *History of the Franks,* ed. O. M. Dalton (Oxford: Clarendon Press, 1927). The account of a sixth-century historian.

Sidonius, *Poems and Letters,* trans. W. B. Anderson (Cambridge, Mass.: Harvard University Press, 1936). The observations of a fifth-century Roman aristocrat.

CHAPTER SIX: BYZANTIUM AND ISLAM

General Accounts

Wilson B. Bishai, *Humanities in the Arabic-Islamic World* (Dubuque, Iowa: William C. Brown, 1973). Concise, learned, up to date.

The Cambridge Medieval History, Vol. IV: *The Byzantine Empire.* Part I: *Byzantium and Its Neighbours,* ed. J. M. Hussey (Cambridge: Cambridge University Press, 1966). Collaborative work with contributions by many excellent scholars; includes full bibliographies.

Norman Daniel, *The Arabs and Medieval Europe,* 2nd ed. (New York: Longmans, 1979). A fine survey of how the Latin West dealt with the Muslim world.

Michael T. Florinsky, *Russia: A History and an Interpretation, Vol. I* (New York: Macmillan, 1954). A good textbook, solid and accurate.

Hamilton A. Gibb, *Mohammedanism: An Historical Survey* (New York: Oxford University Press, 1953). An excellent, somewhat dated essay by a leading Western authority on the subject.

Alfred Guillame, *Islam* (London: Pelican, 1956). Very clear, balanced account; especially good on the Koran.

P. K. Hitti, *History of the Arabs from the Earliest Times to the Present,* 10th ed. (New York: St. Martin's, 1970). A detailed treatment; useful for reference.

Joan M. Hussey, *The Byzantine World* (Westport, Conn.: Greenwood, 1982). Useful shorter sketch.

V. O. Kluchevsky, *A History of Russia,* 5 vols. (London: Dent, 1911–1931). The greatest single work on Russian history; its usefulness is impaired, however, by a poor translation.

Bernard Lewis, *The Arabs in History,* 3rd ed. (New York: Harper & Row, n.d.). A reliable, short treatment.
Harry J. Magoulias, *Byzantine Christianity: Emperor, Church, and the West* (Chicago: Rand McNally, 1970). Good, brief account of the religious aspects of Byzantine history.
John Julius Norwich, *A History of Venice* (New York: Knopf, 1982). Superb major reexamination.
Georgeije Ostrogorsky, *History of the Byzantine State,* rev. ed., trans. Joan M. Hussey (New Brunswick, N.J.: Rutgers University Press, 1969). A brilliant historical synthesis; includes a rich bibliography.
Fazlur Rahman, *Islam,* 2nd ed. (Chicago: University of Chicago Press, 1979). Sound comprehensive introduction; excellent on religious disputes.
Alexander A. Vasiliev, *History of the Byzantine Empire, 324–1453,* 3 vols. (Madison: University of Wisconsin Press, 1952). A good, comprehensive work.
Gustave E. von Grunebaum, *Medieval Islam,* 2nd ed. (Chicago: University of Chicago Press, n.d.). A learned essay on Islamic culture; in part controversial.
W. Montgomery Watt, *Muhammad: Prophet and Statesman* (London: Oxford University Press, 1974). Clear and informative study.
T. Cuyler Young, ed., *Near Eastern Culture and Society* (Princeton, N.J.: Princeton University Press, 1966). Fine essays on Islamic literature, science, and religion.

Special Studies

Sigfus Blondal, *The Varangians of Byzantium,* trans. Benedikt S. Benedikt (New York: Cambridge University Press, 1979). The best account of the origins and functioning of the Varangian corps.
Peter R. L. Brown, *The Cult of the Saints: Its Rise and Function in Latin Christianity* (Chicago: University of Chicago Press, 1982). Fresh study.
Robert Browning, *Byzantium and Bulgaria: A Comparative Study across the Early Medieval Frontier* (Berkeley: University of California Press, 1975). A fine, fresh review of the "ethnic mosaic" that shaped the relationship.
J. B. Bury, *A History of the Later Roman Empire, 395–802,* 1st ed., 2 vols. (New York: Macmillan, 1889). This is the first edition of a work later revised only through 565. The second edition (New York: Dover, 1957) is one of the best works on the period from 395 to 565.
Charles Diehl, *Byzantine Portraits* (New York: Knopf, 1927). A collection of excellent essays on important Byzantine personalities.
George Every, *The Byzantine Patriarchate, 451–1204,* 2nd rev. ed. (New York: AMS Press, 1978). A good summary.
George P. Fedotov, *The Russian Religious Mind* (Woodside, N.Y.: Northland, 1976). A study of the Kievan period of Russian history from an unusual point of view.
Deno J. Geanakoplos, *Byzantine East and Latin West: Two Worlds of Christiandom in Middle Ages and Renaissance* (New York: Harper & Row, 1966). Short, able restatement of the influences of Byzantine culture on the West.
Deno J. Geanakoplos, *Interaction of the "Sibling" Byzantine and Western Cultures in the Middle Ages and Italian Renaissance (330–1600)* (New Haven: Yale University Press, 1976). A well-written examination of cultural interaction which draws in part on sociology.
André Grabar, *Byzantine Painting* (New York: Rizzoli International, 1979). Superb reproductions of mosaics and frescoes.
Joan M. Hussey, *Church and Learning in the Byzantine Empire, 867–1185* (London: Oxford University Press, 1937). Good introduction to the subject.
R. J. H. Jenkins, *Byzantium: The Imperial Centuries,* A.D. *610–1071* (New York: Random House, 1967). Reliable narrative.
A. H. M. Jones, *Constantine and the Conversion of Europe* (Toronto: University of Toronto Press, 1979). A sensible and helpful introduction.
Paul Lemerle, *Le premier humanisme Byzantin* (Paris: Presses Universitaires de France, 1971). Though not yet available in English, this is an exceptional reexamination of Byzantine humanism to the tenth century.
Guy Le Strange, *Baghdad during the Abbasid Caliphate* (New York: Barnes & Noble, 1972). A standard work.
Muhsin Mahdi, *Ibn Khaldun's Philosophy of History* (Chicago: University of Chicago Press, 1971). A fine study of the *Muqaddimah,* a pioneering work in sociology and the philosophy of history.
Roy P. Mottahedeh, *Loyalty and Leadership in Early Islamic Society* (Princeton, N.J.: Princeton University Press, 1980). Fine study of how the Hadith—the traditional sayings and actions of Muhammad as reconstructed by Islamic dogmatists—shaped early Islamic society.
Donald M. Nicol, *Church and Society in the Last Centuries of Byzantium* (Cambridge: Cambridge University Press, 1979). Fine, short study of the "inner" and "outer" wisdom in Byzantine religious thought.
Dimitri Obolensky, *The Byzantine Commonwealth: Eastern Europe, 500–1453* (New York: Praeger, 1971). Thorough, well-argued reconstruction of Balkan history.
David T. Rice, *The Art of Byzantium* (London: Thames & Hudson, 1959). A beautiful picture book.
Steven Runciman, *History of the First Bulgarian Empire* (New York: AMS Press, 1980). Lively and reliable.
George Vernadsky, *Kievan Russia* (New Haven: Yale University Press, 1973). Vol 11 of the Yale History of Russia; authoritative and complete.

Sources

Charles M. Brand, *Icon and Minaret* (Englewood Cliffs, N.J.: PrenticeHall, 1969). A well-chosen series of excerpts from Byzantine and medieval Islamic sources.
Digenes Akrites, trans. J. Mavrogordato (Oxford: Clarendon Press, 1956). The first English translation of a Byzantine frontier epic; includes a good introduction.
Procopius, trans. H. B. Dewing, 7 vols. (Cambridge, Mass.: Harvard University Press, 1914–1940). The writings of a major historian who lived through the events he recounts. His work includes histories of Justinian's wars and of his activities as a builder, and also a scurrilous secret denunciation of Justinian. There is a one-volume Penguin abridgement of the *Secret History.*
Michael Psellus, *Chronographia,* trans. E. R. A. Sewter (New Haven: Yale University Press, 1953). A contemporary account of eleventh century history.
The Russian Primary Chronicle, Laurentian Text, ed. S. H. Cross and O. P. Sherbowitz-Wetzor (Cambridge, Mass.: Mediaeval Academy, 1953). The oldest source for early Russian history.
Saint John Damascene, *Barlaam and Ioasaph,* trans. G. R. Woodward and H. Mattingly (Cambridge, Mass.: Harvard University Press, 1967). The transformed life of Buddha. The attribution to Saint John of Damascus is no longer regarded as correct. See D. M. Jang's introduction and bibliography.

CHAPTER SEVEN: THE MEDIEVAL WEST: THE CHURCH AND THE EMPIRE

Social and Economic Foundations

William J. Brandt, *The Shape of Medieval History: Studies in Modes of Perception* (New Haven: Yale University Press, 1966). On the aristocratic, clerical, and "scholarly" views of human nature.
The Cambridge Economic History, Vols. I and II (Cambridge: Cambridge University Press, 1944, 1952). Detailed investigations of the medieval European economy; includes chapters by scholarly specialists.
Georges Duby, *The Three Orders: Feudal Society Imagined,* trans. Arthur Goldhammer (Chicago: University of Chicago Press, 1980). A stunning examination of an intellectual problem.
Jean Gimpel, *The Medieval Machine: The Industrial Revolution of the Middle Ages* (New York: Penguin, 1980). Especially good on changing energy resources.
David Herlihy, *The Social History of Italy and Western Europe, 700–1500* (London: Variorum, 1980). A superb reassessment of a range of controversial social subjects.
Paul Hohenberg, *A Primer on the Economic History of Europe* (New York: University Press of America, 1981). A clear survey based on the idea of "the economic surplus."
Anne Hollander, *Seeing Through Clothes* (New York: Avon, 1980). A full and lively probing of what one may learn about a society from its attitudes toward clothing.
Robert S. Lopez, *The Birth of Europe* (New York: Evans, 1967). Basic work by a distinguished economic historian.
Robert S. Lopez, *The Commercial Revolution of the Middle Ages* (Cambridge, Eng.: Cambridge University Press, 1976). Short summary presentation of a controversial argument which suggests steady growth from the tenth century.
Sidney Painter, *Mediaeval Society* (Westport, Conn.: Greenwood, 1982). Useful introduction.
Henri Pirenne, *Medieval Cities* (Princeton, N.J.: Princeton University Press, 1952). Classic essay by a notable scholar.
Lynn White, Jr., *Medieval Technology and Social Change* (New York: Oxford University Press, 1966). Scholarly, readable, and full of original insights.

The Church, the State, and the Medieval Empire

John W. Baldwin, *The Scholastic Culture of the Middle Ages, 1000–1300* (Lexington, Mass.: D. C. Heath, 1971). An excellent students' introduction.

Geoffrey Barraclough, *The Origins of Modern Germany* (Oxford: Blackwell, 1957). A good general treatment of medieval Germany.

Geoffrey Barraclough, ed., *Mediaeval Germany, 911–1250,* 2 vols. (New York: AMS Press, 1975). A series of scholarly essays by German historians, conveniently translated and commented upon.

James B. Bryce, *The Holy Roman Empire* (Darby, Penn.: Arden Library, 1978). A brilliant undergraduate essay whose conclusions have been much modified by recent investigation.

Ernst Kantorowicz, *Frederick the Second, 1194–1250* (New York: Ungar, 1957). Scholarly and imaginative treatment.

Richard W. Southern, *Western Society and the Church in the Middle Ages* (New York: Penguin, 1970). Volume II of the Pelican History of the Church, 1970. Authoritative, well written; a fine introduction to the subject.

Gerd Tellenbach, *Church, State, and Christian Society at the Time of the Investiture Controversy,* trans. R. F. Bennett (New York: Humanities Press, 1979). Useful and intelligent.

Walter Ullman, *Medieval Papalism: The Political Theories of the Medieval Canonists* (New York: Methuen, 1949), *The Growth of Papal Government in the Middle Ages,* 2nd ed. (New York: Methuen, 1968), *Principles of Government and Politics in the Middle Ages* (New York: Barnes & Noble, 1961), *A History of Political Thought in the Middle Ages* (New York: Pelican, 1965). By one of the leading scholars in the field, whose views are highly controversial.

Church and Civilization

Frederick B. Artz, *The Mind of the Middle Ages, A.D. 200–1500,* 3rd ed. (Chicago: University of Chicago Press, 1980). A useful survey.

M. D. Chenu, *Toward Understanding St. Thomas* (Chicago: Regnery, 1964). Standard work translated from the French.

A. C. Crombie, *Medieval and Early Modern Science,* 2nd ed. (Cambridge, Mass.: Harvard University Press, 1963). Good introductory account.

Christopher H. Dawson, *Religion and the Rise of Western Culture* (New York: AMS Press, 1977). An admirably sympathetic but also realistic survey in terms of cultural history.

Maurice De Wulf, *Philosophy and Civilization in the Middle Ages* (Westport, Conn.: Greenwood, 1979). Popular lectures by a great medieval scholar of an older generation.

Etienne Gilson, *The Spirit of Medieval Philosophy* (New York: Scribner's, 1936), and *Reason and Revelation in the Middle Ages* (New York: Scribner's, 1968). By a distinguished French scholar, author of many other important works sympathetic to the Middle Ages.

Charles H. Haskins, *The Renaissance of the Twelfth Century* (Cambridge, Mass.: Harvard University Press, 1971), and *The Rise of Universities* (Ithaca, N.Y.: Cornell University Press, 1957). The first is an important work, stressing "modern" elements in medieval civilization; the second is a delightful series of short essays.

David Knowles, *The Evolution of Medieval Thought* (New York: Random House, 1964). Stresses the continuity between classical and scholastic thought.

K. J. Leyser, *Rules and Conflict in an Early Medieval Society* (Bloomington: Indiana University Press, 1980). Revised views on Ottonian Saxony.

D. D. R. Owen, *The Vision of Hell: Infernal Journeys in Medieval French Literature* (Edinburgh: Scottish Academic Press, 1970). A fascinating examination of how Hell was depicted in medieval French literature.

Eileen Power, *Medieval People* (New York: Anchor, n.d.) An admirable set of brief biographical sketches of a half-dozen people from various walks of medieval life.

Hastings Rashdall, *The Universities of Europe in the Middle Ages,* new ed., 3 vols. (Oxford: Clarendon, 1936). The classic account; full and readable.

Henry Daniel Rops, *Bernard of Clairvaux* (New York: Hawthorne, 1964). An excellent account translated from the French.

H. O. Taylor, *The Mediaeval Mind,* 2 vols. (Cambridge, Mass.: Harvard University Press, 1949). Sympathetic and objective in its treatment of the Middle Ages, but in some respects outdated.

Sources

B. J. Kidd, *Documents Illustrative of the History of the Early Church* (London: Macmillan, 1941). Multi-volume, advanced collection.

J. M. Powell, ed., *Innocent III, Vicar of Christ or Lord of the World?* (Lexington, Mass.: D. C. Heath, 1963). Succinct collection of excerpts from original sources.

James Bruce Ross and Mary Martin McLaughlin, eds., *The Portable Medieval Reader* (New York: Viking Press, 1956). Broad coverage.

Brian Tierney, *The Crisis of Church and State, 1050–1300* (Englewood Cliffs, N.J.: Prentice-Hall, 1964). A valuable collection of excerpts from original sources; includes particularly authoritative commentary.

CHAPTER EIGHT: THE BEGINNINGS OF THE SECULAR STATE

The Medieval West (see also Chapter Seven)

R. H. C. Davis, *A History of Medieval Europe: From Constantine to St. Louis* (London: Longmans, 1972). Clear, succinct, and up to date.

Joseph and Francis Gies, *Life in a Medieval City* (New York: Harper & Row, 1981). Lively, humanizing account.

Special Studies: France

Marc Bloch, *French Rural History,* trans. Jane Sondheimer (Berkeley: University of California Press, 1966). A classic work.

Joan Evans, *Life in Medieval France,* 3rd ed. (London: Phaedon, 1969). Good picture of French society.

Robert Fawtier, *The Capetian Kings of France* (New York: St. Martin's, 1960). An up-to-date account.

Amy R. Kelly, *Eleanor of Aquitaine and the Four Kings* (Cambridge, Mass.: Harvard University Press, 1966). A learned and lively treatment; one of the best in English.

Achille Luchaire, *Social France at the Time of Philip Augustus* (New York: Gordon Press, 1976). A well-written account, perhaps overemphasizing the seamy side of life.

Charles E. Petit-Dutaillis, *The Feudal Monarchy in France and England from the Tenth to the Thirteenth Century,* trans. E. D. Hunt (New York: AMS Press, 1980). A clear political analysis.

General Accounts: England

Helen M. Cam, *England before Elizabeth* (London: Hutchinson's University Library, 1950). Excellent overview.

A. R. Myers, *England in the Late Middle Ages* (New York: Penguin, 1952). A useful introduction at the popular level.

Austin L. Poole, *From Doomsday Book to Magna Carta, 1087–1216* (London: Oxford University Press, 1955). Well-written, sometimes criticized, general examination.

Frederick M. Powicke, *Mediaeval England, 1066–1485* (London: Home University Library, 1948), and *The Thirteenth Century, 1216–1307,* 2nd ed. (Oxford: Oxford University Press, 1962). Though revised on significant matters of detail, still standard works.

Richard W. Southern, *Western Society and the Church in the Middle Ages* (Baltimore: Penguin, 1979). Superbly balanced, judgmental examination.

Doris M. Stenton, *English Society in the Early Middle Ages* (Baltimore: Penguin, 1952). A good, quite short history.

Special Studies: England

Frank Barlow, *William I and the Norman Conquest* (London: English Universities Press, 1965). Popular.

Reginald A. Brown, *The Normans and the Norman Conquest* (London: Constable, 1969). Well-written, authoritative, recent introduction to the subject; excellent for students.

David C. Douglas, *William the Conqueror: The Norman Impact upon England* (Berkeley: University of California Press, 1964). Scholarly.

George L. Haskins, *Growth of English Representative Government* (Boston: Peter Smith, 1948). A clear account of a most difficult and vital subject.

C. Warren Hollister, *Anglo-Saxon Military Institutions on the Eve of the Norman Conquest* (London: Oxford University Press, 1964), and *The Military Organization of Norman England* (London: Oxford University Press, 1965). Excellent scholarly monographs which settle many disputed questions.

James C. Holt, *Magna Carta* (Melbourne, Fla.: Krieger, 1982). The best shorter analysis; challenged on some points.

George C. Homans, *English Villagers of the Thirteenth Century* (New York: Norton, 1975). Interesting study of social organization and behavior.

Sydney K. Mitchell, *Taxation in Medieval England* (Hamden, Conn.: Shoe String, 1977). Discusses central organization and local machinery of taxation.

Sidney Painter, *French Chivalry* (Ithaca, N.Y.: Cornell University Press, 1957). Lively examination of courtly love.

Frederick M. Powicke, *King Henry III and the Lord Edward* (Oxford: Clarendon Press, 1947). Scholarly.

P. H. Sawyer, *From Roman Britain to Norman England* (New York: St. Martin's, 1979). Excellent review of the most recent research.

George O. Sayles, *The Medieval Foundations of England* (New York: A. S. Barnes, 1961). Excellent basic study. With H. G. Richardson, Sayles is coauthor of *The Governance of Medieval England from the Conquest to Magna Carta* (Edinburgh: Edinburgh University Press, 1963), a brilliant and provocative analysis.

John A. F. Thomson, *Popes and Princes, 1415–1517* (London: Allen & Unwin, 1980). The popes in politics in the late Middle Ages.

Bertie Wilkinson, *The Constitutional History of England, 1216–1399* (London: Longmans, 1952–1963). Uses the latest scholarly investigations of a much-debated subject.

Literature

C. S. Lewis, *The Discarded Image: An Introduction to Medieval and Renaissance Literature* (Cambridge: Cambridge University Press, 1968). Original and provocative.

Erwin Panofsky, *Gothic Architecture and Scholasticism* (New York: New American Library, 1957). Controversial and readable.

Helen Waddell, *The Wandering Scholars,* 7th rev. ed. (New York: Barnes & Noble, 1968). Lively account.

Sources

Andreas Capellanus, *The Art of Courtly Love,* trans. J. J. Parry (New York: Columbia University Press, 1941). Materials from Marie de Champagne.

The Chronicle of Jocelin of Brakelund, trans. H. E. Butler (London: Nelson, 1949). Medieval monastery life.

D. C. Douglas and G. W. Greenway, eds., *English Historical Documents, 1042–1189* (London: Oxford University Press, 1953). Volume II of a monumental series still in publication.

Joinville and Villehardouin: Chronicles of the Crusades (Baltimore: Penguin, 1977). A fine translation by M. R. B. Shaw.

The Song of Roland, trans. Patricia Terry (Indianapolis: Bobbs-Merrill, 1977). Captures the drumlike rhythm and the high spirits of the story.

CHAPTER NINE: THE LATE MIDDLE AGES IN EASTERN EUROPE

General Accounts

E. S. Creasy, *History of the Ottoman Turks,* 2 vols. (1854–1856), new ed., intro. Z. Zeine (Beirut: Khayats, 1961). Despite its age, still a good general account in English; based on a ten-volume German work.

A History of the Crusades, Vol. I: *The First Hundred Years,* ed. M. W. Baldwin; Vol. II: *The Later Crusades, 1189–1311,* ed. R. L. Wolff and H. W. Hazard; 2nd ed., K. M. Setton, general ed. (Madison: University of Wisconsin Press, 1969). Collaborative work with authoritative contributions by many scholars; includes good bibliographies.

Steven Runciman, *A History of the Crusades,* 3 vols. (Cambridge: Cambridge University Press, 1951–1954). The fullest treatment of the subject by a single scholar; goes well beyond the Crusades.

Special Studies

Aziz A. Atiya, *The Crusade in the Later Middle Ages* (Millwood, N.Y.: Kraus, 1965). A study of the propaganda and the expeditions that marked the decline of the crusading movement.

J. W. Barker, *Manuel II Palaeologus, 1391–1425* (New Brunswick, N.J.: Rutgers University Press, 1969). Good monograph on a late Byzantine emperor.

Charles M. Brand, *Byzantium Confronts the West, 1180–1204* (Cambridge, Mass.: Harvard University Press, 1968). Scholarly study of the diplomacy of an important period.

Claude Cahen, *Pre-Ottoman Turkey* (New York: Taplinger, 1968). The only recent survey work in English on the subject; by the leading authority on the period before 1330.

Anwar G. Chejne, *Muslim Spain: Its History and Culture* (Minneapolis: University of Minnesota Press, 1974). Full inquiry into Spain's political and cultural history; strong on Granada.

J. L. I. Fennell, *Ivan the Great of Moscow* (New York: Macmillan, 1961). Valuable monograph.

H. A. R. Gibb and H. Bowen, *Islamic Society and the West,* Vol. I, Parts 1 and 2 (London: Oxford University Press, 1950, 1956). A useful survey of Ottoman institutions.

Herbert A. Gibbons, *The Foundation of the Ottoman Empire* (Totowa, N.J.: Biblio Distributors, 1968). An older work whose conclusions are again finding favor.

Halil Inalcik, *The Ottoman Empire: The Classical Age, 1300–1600* (London: Weidenfeld & Nicolson, 1973). Recent monograph by a distinguished Turkish scholar; lacks interpretation.

Norman Itzkowitz, *Ottoman Empire and Islamic Tradition* (Chicago: University of Chicago Press, 1980). Excellent brief introduction covering the period to the end of the eighteenth century.

Angus MacKay, *Spain in the Middle Ages: From Frontier to Empire, 1000–1500* (New York: St. Martin's, 1977). Excellent summary with fresh insights into the Inquisition.

Barnett Miller, *Beyond the Sublime Porte* (New Haven: Yale University Press, 1931), and *The Palace School of Mohammed the Conqueror* (Salem, N.H.: Arno, 1973). Studies of the Ottoman imperial palace and the Ottoman educational system, respectively.

Joshua Prawer, *The Crusaders' Kingdom* (New York: Praeger, 1972). A fine study of the Crusader states as European colonies.

Donald E. Queller, *The Fourth Crusade: The Conquest of Constantinople, 1201–1204* (Philadelphia: University of Pennsylvania Press, 1977). A fine, fresh look at the reasons for the Crusaders' attack on the Byzantine capital.

D. M. Vaughan, *Europe and the Turk: A Pattern of Alliances, 1350–1700* (Liverpool: Liverpool University Press, 1954). Role of the Ottoman Empire in European diplomacy.

George Varnadsky, *The Mongols and Russia* (New Haven: Yale University Press, 1953). Volume III of the Yale History of Russia.

Speros Vryonis, *The Decline of Medieval Hellenism in Asia Minor and the Process of Islamization from the Eleventh through the Fifteenth Century* (Berkeley: University of California Press, 1971). The title describes well the subject of this massive, scholarly study.

Paul Wittek, *The Rise of the Ottoman Empire* (London: Royal Asiatic Society, 1938). A suggestive essay on the elements that helped to advance the Ottoman state.

Sources

An Arab-Syrian Gentleman and Warrior in the Period of the Crusades: Memoirs of Usamah ibn-Munquidh, trans. P. K. Hitti (New York: Columbia University Press, 1929).

Anna Comnena, *The Alexiad,* trans. E. A. S. Dawes (New York: AMS Press, 1976). The life and reign of Emperor Alexius Comnenus (from 1081 to 1118), by his daughter.

Foucher of Chartres, *Chronicle of the First Crusade,* trans. M. E. McGinty (Philadelphia: University of Pennsylvania Press, 1941). Readable.

William, Archbishop of Tyre, *A History of Deeds Done Beyond the Sea,* trans. E. A. Babcock and A. C. Krey, 2 vols. (New York: Columbia University Press, 1943). The greatest contemporary account of the Crusaders' Levant.

CHAPTER TEN: THE RISE OF THE NATION

The West: General Accounts

Philippe Ariès, *Centuries of Childhood,* trans. Robert Baldick (New York: Random House, 1965), and *Western Attitudes Toward Death,* trans. Patricia M. Ranum (Baltimore: Johns Hopkins University Press, 1975), present many data and much speculation on two subjects frequently ignored by historians.

Margaret Aston, *The Fifteenth Century: The Prospect of Europe* (New York: Norton, 1979). An overall view emphasizing social and cultural history; abundantly illustrated.

Edward P. Cheyney, *The Dawn of a New Era, 1250–1453;* and Myron P. Gilmore, *The World of Humanism, 1453–1517* (both New York: Harper & Row, n.d.) Good introductory accounts with full bibliographies; part of the Rise of Modern Europe series, edited by W. L. Langer.

Wallace K. Ferguson, *Europe in Transition, 1300–1520* (Boston: Houghton Mifflin, 1963). Another useful survey.

Denys Hay, *Europe in the Fourteenth and Fifteenth Centuries* (New York: Holt, 1966). Excellent social, political, and economic survey with useful bibliographical footnotes.

George Holmes, *Europe: Hierarchy and Revolt, 1320–1450* (New York: Harper & Row, 1976). Clear, up-to-date look at the fourteenth century in particular.

Johan Huizinga, *The Waning of the Middle Ages* (New York: St. Martin's, 1924). Celebrated recreation of the atmosphere of a whole era; emphasizes France and the Low Countries.

Frederic C. Lane, *Venice: A Maritime Republic* (Baltimore: Johns Hopkins University Press, 1973). Tough-minded account, by an economic historian, of the rise and slow decline of Venice.

M. M. Postan, *Medieval Trade and Finance* (Cambridge: Cambridge University Press, 1973). A complex inquiry into the uses of credit and the sources of capital formation.

Philip Ziegler, *The Black Death* (New York: Harper & Row, 1971). Graphic details of the havoc wrought by the plague.

National Monarchies

Stanley B. Chrimes, *English Constitutional History* (New York: AMS Press, 1975). Reliable manual.

J. H. Elliott, *Imperial Spain, 1469–1716* (New York: New American Library, 1977). A sound recent survey.

James C. Holt, *Robin Hood* (London: Thames & Hudson, 1982). Inquiry into the origins and meaning of a famous medieval legend.

John E. A. Jolliffe, *Constitutional History of Medieval England* (New York: Norton, 1967). Good on the "new feudalism" to 1485.

P. S. Lewis, *Later Medieval France: The Polity* (New York: St. Martin's 1968); and P. M. Kendall, *Louis XI* (New York: Norton, 1971). Stimulating studies.

John Lynch, *Spain under the Hapsburgs,* Vol. 1 (New York: New York University Press, 1981). Begins with a good, brief evaluation of the work of Ferdinand and Isabella.

J. H. Mariejol, *The Spain of Ferdinand and Isabella,* ed. B. Keen (New Brunswick, N.J.: Rutgers University Press, 1961). Celebrated older study by a French scholar; edited to bring it abreast of twentieth-century scholarship.

Garrett Mattingly, *Renaissance Diplomacy* (Boston: Houghton Mifflin, 1971). Stimulating study of the origins of modern diplomatic techniques.

May McKisack, *The Fourteenth Century;* and Ernest F. Jacob, *The Fifteenth Century* (both Oxford: Clarendon, 1959, 1961). Detailed, scholarly volumes in the Oxford History of England.

A. R. Myers, *England in the Late Middle Ages, 1307–1536* (Baltimore: Penguin, 1952). Handy, shorter account.

Edward Perroy, *The Hundred Years' War* (New York: Capricorn, 1965). The standard work on the subject and the best introduction to the late medieval history of France.

Robin L. Storey, *The Reign of Henry VII* (New York: Walker, 1968). Revisionist study; questions traditional estimates of Henry's personality and policies.

Barbara W. Tuchman, *A Distant Mirror: The Calamitous 14th Century* (New York: Knopf, 1979). Beautifully witten, rich account of the times; focuses on the life of a French knight, Enguerrand de Coucy VII.

Charles W. S. Williams, *Henry VII* (London: Barker, 1937). Standard older assessment.

Germany and Italy

Cecilia M. Ady, *Lorenzo de'Medici and Renaissance Italy* (New York: Collier, 1962). Brief, popular account.

Hans Baron, *The Crisis of the Early Italian Renaissance* (Princeton, N.J.: Princeton University Press, 1966). Monograph incorporating recent scholarship and affording many insights into Renaissance politics.

Geoffrey Barraclough, *The Origins of Modern Germany* (Oxford: Blackwell, 1957). The best general treatment of late medieval Germany in English.

Marvin B. Becker, *Florence in Transition,* 2 vols. (Baltimore: Johns Hopkins University Press, 1967–1968). Up-to-date study of Florence in the fourteenth century. Consult also *Medieval Italy* (Bloomington: Indiana University Press, 1981), a study of the relationship between religious and secular thought.

Gene A. Brucker, *Renaissance Florence* (Melbourne, Fla.: Krieger, 1975). Recent introduction.

Jacob Burckhardt, *The Civilization of the Renaissance in Italy,* 2 vols. (New York: Harper & Row, n.d.). Famous interpretation now more than a century old; its contention that the modern state originated in Renaissance Italy is no longer generally accepted.

F. L. Carsten, *Princes and Parliaments in Germany from the Fifteenth to the Eighteenth Century* (Oxford: Clarendon, 1959). Scholarly study of Wurttemberg, Saxony, Bavaria, and other states.

Federico Chabod, *Machiavelli and the Renaissance* (Cambridge, Mass.: Harvard University Press, 1960). Pithy, sympathetic evaluation, which may be contrasted with the more critical Herbert Butterfield, *The Statecraft of Machiavelli* (New York: Collier, 1962).

John R. Hale, *Machiavelli and Renaissance Italy* (New York: Harper & Row, n.d.). Good brief account.

Giuseppe Prezzolini, *Machiavelli* (New York: Farrar, Straus & Giroux, 1967). Detailed survey of his work and its reception over the centuries.

Sources

Jean Froissart, *Chronicles of England, France, Spain, Etc.* (Baltimore: Penguin, 1978). A great narrative source of late medieval history.

S. Kinser and I. Cazeaux, *The Memoirs of Phillippe de Commynes* (Columbia: University of South Carolina, 1969). Well-edited translation. Another recent translation is by M. Jones: Commynes, *Memoirs* (Baltimore: Penguin, 1972).

Niccolo Machiavelli, *The Chief Works and Others,* 3 vols., trans. Allan Gilbert (Durham, N.C.: Duke University Press, 1965). A new scholarly translation. Older translations of *The Prince* and *The Discourses* are available in many paperback editions.

Arthur J. Slavin, *The "New Monarchies" and Representative Assemblies: Medieval Constitutionalism or Modern Absolutism?* (Lexington, Mass.: D. C. Heath, n.d.). Illuminating exploration of the pros and cons about the degree of newness in the new monarchies.

CHAPTER ELEVEN: THE RENAISSANCE

General Accounts

Jacob Burckhardt, *The Civilization of the Renaissance in Italy,* 2 vols. (New York: Harper & Row, 1958). The classic statement of the view that the Renaissance was unique and revolutionary.

Peter Burke, *Culture and Society in Renaissance Italy, 1420–1540* (New York: Scribner's, 1972). Major look at how "taste" developed in Renaissance terms; by a leading inquirer into the methods of popular culture studies.

Federico Chabod, *Machiavelli & the Renaissance* (New York: Harper & Row, n.d.). The chapter "The Concept of the Renaissance" is especially good on the problem of continuity.

E. P. Cheyney, *The Dawn of a New Era, 1250–1453;* and Myron P. Gilmore, *The World of Humanism, 1453–1517* (both New York: Harper & Row, n.d.). The first two volumes in an important series, the Rise of Modern Europe. Gilmore's is particularly informative.

Karl H. Dannenfeldt, ed., *The Renaissance: Medieval or Modern?* (Lexington, Mass.: D. C. Heath, 1973). A collection of essays directed to the question.

Elizabeth L. Eisenstein, *The Printing Press as an Agent of Change* (Cambridge: Cambridge University Press, 1979). Fundamental, brilliant examination of how print revolutionized the world.

Lucien Febvre, *Life in Renaissance France,* trans. Marian Rothstein (Cambridge, Mass.: Harvard University Press, 1979). Short, provocative "silhouette of a civilization."

Lucien Febvre and Henri-Jean Martin, *The Coming of the Book: The Impact of Printing, 1450–1800,* trans. David Gerard (New York: Schocken, 1976). Develops a basis for seeing the Renaissance in two major phases; looks at the introduction of paper and at the book as a commodity.

Wallace K. Ferguson, *The Renaissance in Historical Thought: Five Centuries of Interpretation* (New York: AMS Press, 1977). Valuable and stimulating monograph.

J. R. Hale, *Renaissance Europe: Individual and Society, 1480–1520* (Berkeley: University of California Press, 1978). Exceptional history that shows us how the individual viewed the world.

J. R. Hale, ed., *A Concise Encyclopaedia of the Italian Renaissance* (Oxford: Oxford University Press, 1981). Thorough, well-organized coverage by topics and persons.

Denys Hay, ed., *The Renaissance Debate* (Melbourne, Fla.: Krieger, 1976). Excerpts illustrating contrasting points of view.

Denys Hay, *The Italian Renaissance in Its Historical Background* (Cambridge: Cambridge University Press, 1977). Valuable treatment of the historiography of the topic.

Robert S. Lopez, *The Three Ages of the Italian Renaissance* (Charlottesville: University Press of Virginia, 1970). Fine lectures which argue for three states of Renaissance developments.

J. Russell Major, *The Age of the Renaissance and Reformation* (New York: Harper & Row, 1970); and Eugene F. Rice, Jr., *The Foundations of*

Early Modern Europe, 1460–1559 (New York: Norton, 1970). Good general introductions.

Garrett Mattingly, et al., *Renaissance Profiles* (New York: Harper & Row, n.d.). Lively sketches of nine representative Italians, including Petrarch, Machiavelli, Leonardo, and Michelangelo.

The New Cambridge Modern History, Vol. 1: *The Renaissance* (Cambridge: Cambridge University Press, 1957). Chapters by experts in many fields; uneven but useful for reference.

Leonardo Olschki, *The Genius of Italy* (Ithaca, N.Y.: Cornell University Press, 1954). Scholarly essays on many aspects of the Renaissance.

J. H. Plumb, *The Italian Renaissance* (New York: Harper & Row, 1965). Concise historical and cultural survey.

The Economy

Fernand Braudel, *Capitalism and Material Life, 1400–1800,* trans. Mariam Kochan (New York: Harper & Row, 1974). A rich look at the detail of fashion, housing, food, and drink.

The Cambridge Economic History of Europe, *Vol. 2:* Trade and Industry in the Middle Ages; *Vol. 3:* Economic Organization and Policies in the Middle Ages *(Cambridge: Cambridge University Press, 1954, 1965). Advanced scholarly work and a mine of information.*

Richard Ehrenberg, *Capital and Finance in the Renaissance: A Study of the Fuggers and Their Connections* (New York: Kelley, 1963). Another instructive case history.

Richard W. Unger, *The Ship in the Medieval Economy, 600–1600* (London: Croom Helm, 1980). Brings together the most recent reinterpretations on the significance of medieval shipping.

Literature and Thought

R. R. Bolgar, *The Classical Heritage and Its Beneficiaries from the Carolingian Age to the End of the Renaissance* (Cambridge: Cambridge University Press, 1977). On the question of continuity.

Natalie Z. Davis, *Society and Culture in Early Modern France* (Palo Alto, Calif.: Stanford University Press, 1975). Especially good on attitudes toward women.

Eugenio Garin, *Italian Humanism* (Westport, Conn.: Greenwood, 1976). Good scholarly survey.

Gilbert Highet, *The Classical Tradition: Greek and Roman Influences on Western Literature* (London: Oxford University Press, 1949). Lively, somewhat dated, general survey.

George Holmes, *The Florentine Enlightenment, 1400–1450* (New York: Pegasus, 1969). Informative monograph on humanists obsessed with classicism.

Johann Huizinga, *Erasmus and the Age of the Reformation* (New York: Harper & Row, 1957). Excellent analysis by a distinguished Dutch scholar.

Walter Kaiser, *Praisers of Folly* (Cambridge, Mass.: Harvard University Press, 1963). Folly and fools in the writings of Erasmus, Rabelais, and Shakespeare.

Paul O. Kristeller, *Renaissance Thought and Its Sources* (New York: (Columbia University Press, 1981). Valuable study; stresses diversity.

N. A. Robb, *Neoplatonism of the Italian Renaissance* (New York: Octagon, 1968). Good treatment of an intellectual common denominator of the age.

Roberto Weiss, *The Spread of Italian Humanism* (New York: Hutchinson's University Library, 1964). Lucid, brief introduction.

Science

Marie Boas, *The Scientific Renaissance, 1450–1630* (New York: Harper & Row, 1962). Helpful, detailed account.

Herbert Butterfield, *The Origins of Modern Science, 1300–1800,* rev. ed. (New York: Free Press, 1965). A controversial interpretation; minimizes the scientific contribution of the Renaissance.

A. C. Crombie, *Medieval and Early Modern Science,* 2nd ed. (Cambridge, Mass.: Harvard University Press, 1963). Volume 2 of this standard survey treats the Renaissance.

Eugenio Garin, *Science and Civic Life in the Italian Renaissance* (Boston: Peter Smith, n.d.). A helpful, scholarly survey.

Emmanuel Leroy Ladurie, *The Mind and Method of the Historian,* trans. Siân and Ben Reynolds (Chicago: University of Chicago Press, 1981). Contains a fine essay on "the unification of the globe by disease" in the fourteenth to seventeenth centuries.

George Sarton, *Six Wings: Men of Science in the Renaissance* (Bloomington: Indiana University Press, 1957), *The Appreciation of Ancient and Medieval Science during the Renaissance* (Philadelphia: University of Pennsylvania Press, 1955), and *The History of Science and the New Humanism* (Cambridge, Mass.: Harvard University Press, 1937). Clear studies by a pioneering historian of science.

Charles Singer, et al., *A History of Technology* (Oxford: Oxford University Press, 1954–1958). Volumes 2 and 3 relate to the Renaissance. Singer has also written *A Short History of Anatomy and Physiology* (New York: Dover, 1957).

Lynn Thorndike, *Science and Thought in the Fifteenth Century* (New York: Hafner, 1963). By a specialist on medieval science.

Music

Edward J. Dent, *Music of the Renaissance in Italy* (London: British Academy, 1954). Meaty lecture by a great authority.

Gustave Reese, *Music in the Renaissance* (New York: Norton, 1959). Detailed study.

Religion

Roland H. Bainton, *Erasmus of Christendom* (New York: Scribner's, 1969). Sets Erasmus solidly into the tradition of religious thought.

Gene Brucker, *Renaissance Florence* (New York: Wiley, 1969). Contains a well-balanced analysis of the role of the church at the center of culture.

Herbert Butterfield, *The Statecraft of Machiavelli* (New York: Collier, 1962). Brief, still-valuable look at "the science of statecraft."

Albert Hyma, *The Christian Renaissance* (Hamden, Conn.: Shoe String, 1965). Reprint of an older work; stresses an aspect of the Renaissance that is often neglected.

Roberto Ridolfi, *Savonarola* (Westport, Conn.: Greenwood, 1976). Biography of the Florentine preacher-dictator.

Fine Arts

Frederick Antal, *Florentine Painting and Its Social Background* (New York: Harper & Row, 1975). Suggestive attempt to relate art to social and economic currents.

Otto Benesch, *The Art of the Renaissance in Northern Europe* (Cambridge, Mass.: Harvard University Press, 1945). Examines the interrelations of art, religion, and intellectual developments.

Kenneth Clark, *Leonardo da Vinci* (New York: Penguin, 1976). Lively and perceptive assessment of his art.

Walter S. Gibson, *Bruegel* (New York: Oxford University Press, 1977). Fine, short work with many illustrations.

Creighton Gilbert, *History of Renaissance Art throughout Europe* (New York: Abrams, 1973). Comprehensive and profusely illustrated introduction.

Michael Levey, *The Early Renaissance* (New York: Penguin, 1978). Stresses the interrelations of art and civilization in general.

Bates Lowry, *Renaissance Architecture* (New York: Brazillier, 1962). Brief introduction.

Erwin Panofsky, *Renaissance and Renascences in Western Art* (New York: Harper & Row, 1972), *Studies in Iconology: Humanistic Themes in the Renaissance* (New York: Harper & Row, 1972), *The Life and Art of Albrecht Dürer* (Princeton, N.J.: Princeton University Press, 1955). Stimulating studies by an eminent scholar.

Rudolf Wittkower, *Architectural Principles in the Age of Humanism* (New York: Norton, 1970). Important study of the links between humanism and design.

Heinrich Wölfflin, *Classic Art: An Introduction to the Italian Renaissance,* 3rd ed. (London: Phaidon, 1968). An older and still very useful interpretation.

Note: More detailed scholarly accounts may be found in various volumes of the Pelican History of Art (New York: Penguin, various dates): J. White, *Art and Architecture in Italy, 1250–1400* (1966); L. Heydenreich and W. Lotz, *Architecture in Italy, 1400–1600* (1974); C. Seymour, *Sculpture in Italy, 1400–1500* (1966); S. J. Freedberg, *Painting in Italy, 1500–1600* (1971); and A. Blunt, *Art and Architecture in France, 1500–1700* (1980).

Sources

The Autobiography of Benvenuto Cellini, trans. John Addington Symonds (London: Penguin, 1956). An engrossing, inflated look into the life and ideas of the brilliant artist.

Ernst Cassirer, et al., *The Renaissance Philosophy of Man* (Chicago: University of Chicago Press, 1956). Excerpts from Petrarch, Pico, Valla, and other humanists; includes helpful commentary.

Paul M. Coremans and A. Janssens de Pisthoven, *Van Eyck: L'adoration de l'Agneau mystique* (Antwerp: Nederlandsche Boekhandel, 1948). Contains 209 remarkable plates by which one can study the smallest detail of the great altarpiece.

Desiderius Erasmus, *The Praise of Folly* (New Haven: Yale University Press, 1979). Scholarly, clear edition.

W. L. Gundesheimer, ed., *The Italian Renaissance* (Englewood Cliffs, N.J.: Prentice-Hall, n.d.). Selections from eleven representative writers, including Valla, Pico, Leonardo, and Castiglione.

Samuel Putnam, ed., *The Portable Rabelais: Most of Gargantua and Pantagruel* (New York: Penguin, 1977). Well condensed.

James B. Ross and Mary M. McLaughlin, *The Portable Renaissance Reader* (New York: Penguin, 1977). Wide selection.

CHAPTER TWELVE: THE PROTESTANT REVOLUTION

General Accounts

Roland H. Bainton, *The Reformation of the Sixteenth Century* (Boston: Beacon, 1956). Excellent introduction by a Protestant scholar who has written several more specialized works on the period.

Owen Chadwick, *The Reformation* (New York: Penguin, 1964). A comprehensive survey addressed to the general reader.

Arthur G. Dickens, *Reformation and Society in Sixteenth-Century Europe* (New York: Holt, n.d.). Informative, broad survey; includes many illustrations.

G. R. Elton, *Reformation Europe, 1517–1559* (New York: Harper & Row, 1968). A lively survey summarizing many of the findings in the more ponderous *New Cambridge Modern History: The Reformation* (Cambridge: Cambridge University Press, 1958), which Elton edited.

E. Harris Harbison, *The Age of Reformation* (Westport, Conn.: Greenwood, 1982). A brief, perceptive introduction.

H. G. Koenigsberger and George L. Mosse, *Europe in the Sixteenth Century* (London: Longmans, 1971). Up-to-date, scholarly survey; includes excellent biographies.

E. William Monter, *Calvin's Geneva* (Melbourne, Fla.: Krieger, 1975). Examines the relationship between an environment and the development of a body of thought.

Eugene F. Rice, Jr., *The Foundations of Early Modern Europe, 1460–1559* (New York: Norton, 1970). Recent, brief introduction.

Guy E. Swanson, *Religion and Regime* (Ann Arbor: University of Michigan Press, 1967). A challenging and controversial "sociological account of the Reformation."

Luther

Roland H. Bainton, *Here I Stand: A Life of Martin Luther* (New York: New American Library, 1962). Sympathetic, scholarly, readable.

Karl Brandi, *The Emperor Charles V* (Norwood, Pa.: Telegraph, 1981). Comprehensive study of Luther's antagonist.

E. H. Erikson, *Young Man Luther* (New York: Norton, 1962). Luther's "identity crisis" persuasively presented.

Hartmann Grisar, *Martin Luther: His Life and Works* (New York: AMS Press, 1971). From the Catholic point of view.

Hajo Holborn, *A History of Modern Germany,* Vol. 1: *The Reformation* (Princeton, N.J.: Princeton University Press, 1982). Scholarly and readable.

Ernest G. Schwiebert, *Luther and His Times* (St. Louis: Concordia, 1952). From the Lutheran point of view; particularly useful for the setting and the effects of Luther's revolt.

Gerald Strauss, *Luther's House of Learning* (Baltimore: Johns Hopkins University Press, 1979). On Luther's educational ideas and the indoctrination of the young.

The Other Founders

Jacques Courvoisier, *Zwingli: A Reformed Theologian* (Atlanta: John Knox, 1963). Good study of an important and often-neglected figure.

Arthur G. Dickens, *The English Reformation* (New York: Schocken, 1968). Detailed study through 1559; includes a useful biography.

Arthur G. Dickens, *The German Nation and Martin Luther* (London: Arnold, 1974). A close look at the problem of the cities, printing, and nationalism.

G. Harkness, *John Calvin: The Man and His Ethics* (New York: Gordon Press, 1977). A good, short introduction.

Franklin H. Littell, *The Anabaptist View of the Church,* 2nd ed. (Boston: Starr King, 1958). Perceptive, brief introduction.

John D. Mackie, *The Early Tudors, 1485–1558* (Oxford: Clarendon, 1972). Authoritative and thorough; especially good on Henry VIII.

James Mackinnon, *Calvin and the Reformation* (London: Longmans, 1936). Substantial, longer study.

Bernd Moeller, *Imperial Cities and the Reformation* (Durham, N.C.: Labyrinth Press, 1982). Translation of three complex, highly influential essays on how the cities forced Luther to retreat to a more medieval position.

Steven E. Ozment, *The Reformation in the Cities* (New Haven: Yale University Press, 1980). Fresh emphasis on the role of German and Swiss municipalities in furthering the social ethic of Protestantism.

T. M. Parker, *The English Reformation to 1558,* 2nd ed. (New York: Oxford University Press, 1966). Excellent short account.

J. J. Scarisbrick, *Henry VIII* (Berkeley: University of California Press, 1968). A major scholarly assessment.

François Wendel, *Calvin, The Origins and Development of His Religious Thought* (New York: Harper & Row, 1963). Translation of a solid study by a French scholar.

George H. Williams, *The Radical Reformation* (London: Westminster, 1977). Encyclopedic study of the Anabaptists and other left-wing reformers.

The Catholic Reformation

Henry Daniel-Rops, *The Catholic Reformation* (New York: Dutton, 1962). Admirable study by a French Catholic scholar.

Arthur G. Dickens, *The Counter-Reformation* (New York: Norton, 1979). Comprehensive survey by an English Protestant scholar.

René Fulop-Miller, *Jesuits: History of the Society of Jesus* (New York: Capricorn, n.d.); and Heinrich Boehmer, *The Jesuits* (Secaucus, N.J.: Castle, 1928). By a Catholic and a Protestant, respectively.

Pierre Janelle, *The Catholic Reformation* (Milwaukee: Bruce, 1951). Scholarly account by a Catholic.

Beresford J. Kidd, *The Counter-Reformation* (Westport, Conn.: Greenwood, 1980). Scholarly account by an Anglican.

Protestantism and "Progress"

Steven E. Ozment, ed., *The Reformation in Medieval Perspective* (New York: Quadrangle, 1971). Excellent on issues of theology.

Lewis W. Spitz, ed., *The Reformation: Basic Interpretations* (Lexington, Mass.: D. C. Heath, 1972). Useful introduction to divergent scholarly views.

Richard H. Tawney, *Religion and the Rise of Capitalism* (Boston: Peter Smith, 1963). Turns the Weber thesis around to emphasize economic motivation.

Paul Tillich, *The Protestant Era* (Chicago: University of Chicago Press, 1957). Abridged from a longer study by a ranking modern theologian.

Ernst Troeltsch, *Protestantism and Progress* (Boston: Beacon, 1958). By a leading modern religious philosopher.

Max Weber, *The Protestant Ethic and the Spirit of Capitalism* (New York: Scribner's, 1958). Advances the famous thesis on the interrelationship of religion and economics.

Sources

Henry S. Bettenson, ed., *Documents of the Christian Church,* 2nd ed. (New York: Oxford University Press, 1963). Admirable compilation; particularly valuable for the Reformation.

H. J. Hillerbrand, *The Reformation in Its Own Words* (New York: Harper & Row, n.d.). Another useful compilation of primary material.

Robert M. Kingdon, ed., *Transition and Revolution* (Minneapolis: Burgess, 1974). Excellent collection of sources on Reformation issues.

E. G. Rupp and Benjamin Drewery, eds., *Martin Luther* (New York: St. Martin's, 1970). An anthology of his significant writings; includes helpful editorial comment.

CHAPTER THIRTEEN: THE GREAT POWERS IN CONFLICT

General Accounts

J. H. Ball, *Merchants and Merchandise: The Expansion of Trade in Europe, 1500–1630* (New York: St. Martin's, 1977). Excellent short survey of sixteenth-century trade.

Fernand Braudel, *Capitalism and Material Life, 1400–1800* (New York: Harper & Row, 1974). Fine, debatable examination of trends in population, climate, and daily life.

The Cambridge Economic History of Europe, Vol. 4: *The Economy of Expanding Europe in the Sixteenth and Seventeenth Centuries* (Cambridge: Cambridge University Press, 1967). Scholarly chapters by experts on selected aspects of the economy.

J. H. Elliott, *Europe Divided, 1559–1598* (Ithaca, N.Y.: Cornell University Press, 1982). Useful introduction to the Age of Philip II.

H. G. Koenigsberger and George L. Mosse, *Europe in the Sixteenth Century* (London: Longmans, 1971). An excellent survey with useful bibliographical footnotes.

Marvin R. O'Connell, *The Counter Reformation, 1559–1610* (New York: Harper & Row, 1974); and Carl J. Friedrich, *The Age of the Baroque, 1610–1660* (New York: Harper & Row, 1952). Comprehensive volumes with full biographies; in the Rise of Modern Europe series.

Theodore K. Rabb, *The Struggle for Stability in Early Modern Europe* (New York: Oxford University Press, 1975). A brief, thoughtful inquiry into the use of "crisis" terminology and analysis as the unifying principle for the seventeenth century.

Eugene F. Rice, Jr., *The Foundations of Early Modern Europe, 1460–1559* (New York: Norton, 1970); and Richard S. Dunn, *The Age of Religious Wars, 1559–1689* (New York: Norton, 1979). Enlightening surveys.

Lacey Baldwin Smith, *The Elizabethan World* (Boston: Houghton Mifflin, 1967). Popular, balanced look at the Elizabethans in the context of European history generally.

Hugh Trevor-Roper, ed., *The Age of Expansion* (New York: McGraw-Hill, 1968). Sumptuously illustrated collaborative volume which touches on many topics in European and world history from the midsixteenth to midseventeenth centuries.

War and Diplomacy

Charles H. Carter, *The Secret Diplomacy of the Habsburgs, 1598–1625* (New York: Columbia University Press, 1964). An instructive case study in diplomatic history.

Ludwig Dehio, *The Precarious Balance: Four Centuries of the European Power Struggle* (New York: Knopf, 1962). A German historian interprets the shifting balance of power beginning with the sixteenth century.

Henry Kamen, *The Rise of Toleration* (London: World University Library, 1972). A short, clear account of changing attitudes toward religious toleration.

Garrett Mattingly, *Renaissance Diplomacy* (Boston: Houghton Mifflin, 1971). A stimulating and indispensable look at the invention of diplomacy through resident ambassadors.

Charles W. Oman, *A History of the Art of War in the Sixteenth Century* (New York: AMS Press, 1975). Highly interesting examination of a less-studied aspect of history.

Spain

Karl Brandi, *The Emperor Charles V* (Norwood, Pa.: Telegraph, 1981). Thorough study of the ruler of a troubled dynastic conglomerate.

Fernand Braudel, *The Mediterranean and the Mediterranean World in the Age of Philip II*, 2nd ed. (New York: Harper & Row, 1976). An important geographical and socioeconomic study of Spain's involvement with Italy and the Ottoman empire.

Cecil John Cadoux, *Philip of Spain and the Netherlands* (Hamden, Conn.: Shoe String, 1969). A sharp attack on Philip II and a defense of William of Orange.

R. T. Davies, *The Golden Century of Spain* (London: Macmillan, 1937), and *Spain in Decline, 1621–1700* (New York: St. Martin's, 1957). Popular accounts addressed to the general reader.

J. H. Elliott, *The Old World and the New, 1492–1650* (Cambridge: Cambridge University Press, 1970). A thoughtful reevaluation of arguments about the impact of bullion on the European and especially the Spanish economy.

John Lynch, *Spain under the Hapsburgs*, 2 vols. (New York: New York University Press, 1981). A thorough and up-to-date scholarly study; the first volume treats the sixteenth century, the second, the seventeenth.

Antonio Dominguez Ortiz, *The Golden Age of Spain, 1516–1659,* trans. James Casey (New York: Basic Books, 1971). Balanced account with excellent sections on the economy, religious life, and cultural developments.

Geoffrey Parker, *Philip II* (Boston: Little, Brown, 1978). Perhaps the best short biography. *The Army of Flanders and the Spanish Road, 1567–1659* (Cambridge: Cambridge University Press, 1972). Close study of the disastrous consequences for the Spanish economy of keeping a vast army in the field. *The Dutch Revolt* (Ithaca, N.Y.: Cornell University Press, 1977). Fresh interpretation based on wide-ranging sources.

R. A. Stradling, *Europe and the Decline of Spain* (London: Allen & Unwin, 1981). Up-to-date, methodologically fashionable look at "the Spanish system" from 1580 to 1720.

France

Albert L. Guerard, *France in the Classical Age: The Life and Death of an Ideal* (New York: Brazillier, 1956). Lively, provocative, and highly personal interpretation of French history from the Renaissance to Napoleon.

Q. Hurst, *Henry of Navarre* (New York: Appleton, 1938). A standard biography.

Alexandra D. Lublinskaya, *French Absolutism: The Crucial Phase, 1629–1690* (Cambridge: Cambridge University Press, 1969). Good on Richelieu.

J. E. Neale, *The Age of Catherine de'Medici* (Lawrence, Mass.: Merrimack, 1978). Excellent short introduction to the French civil and religious books.

W. J. Stankiewicz, *Politics and Religion in Seventeenth Century France* (Westport, Conn.: Greenwood, 1976). Goes back to the *politiques* of the late sixteenth century.

John W. Thompson, *The Wars of Religion in France, 1559–1576* (Chicago: University of Chicago Press, 1909). A detailed narrative; still very useful.

G. R. R. Treasure, *Seventeenth Century France* (London: John Murray, 1981). Balanced, full survey.

England

Stanley T. Bindoff, *Tudor England* (Baltimore: Penguin, 1967). Sound, short introduction.

Antonia Fraser, *Mary, Queen of Scots* (New York: Delacorte, 1978). Popular biography of Elizabeth's impulsive antagonist.

W. P. Haugaard, *Elizabeth and the English Reformation* (Cambridge: Cambridge University Press, 1968). Excellent scholarly assessment.

Elizabeth Jenkins, *Elizabeth the Great* (New York: Coward, 1959). Sound biography focused more on the person than on the office.

Wallace T. MacCaffrey, *Queen Elizabeth and the Making of Policy, 1572–1588* (Princeton, N.J.: Princeton University Press, 1981). Intricate analysis of Elizabeth's policy, focusing (as she did) on the Netherlands.

Wallace T. MacCaffrey, *The Shaping of the Elizabethan Regime* (Princeton, N.J.: Princeton University Press, n.d.). Able study of Elizabeth's early years in power.

John D. Mackie, *The Earlier Tudors, 1485–1558;* and J. B. Black, *The Reign of Elizabeth, 1558–1603* (both London: Clarendon, 1952, 1960). Comprehensive, scholarly volumes in the Oxford History of England.

Garrett Mattingly, *The Armada* (Boston: Houghton Mifflin, n.d.). A beautifully written work of history.

J. E. Neale, *Queen Elizabeth I: A Biography* (New York: Doubleday, 1957). By the author of *The Elizabethan House of Commons* (London: J. Cape, 1949), and *Elizabeth I and Her Parliaments,* 2 vols. (New York: Norton, 1966).

Conyers Read, *The Tudors* (New York: Norton, 1969). Excellent introduction to the interrelations of personalities and politics. Read also published *The Government of England Under Elizabeth* (Charlottesville, Va.: University of Virginia Press, n.d.), and scholarly studies of her chief ministers.

J. J. Scarisbrick, *Henry VIII* (Berkeley: University of California Press, 1968). A fine scholarly biography; may be supplemented with a psychological study by Lacey Baldwin Smith, *Henry VIII: The Mask of Royalty* (Lawrence, Mass.: Merrimack, 1980).

The Dutch Republic

Violet Barbour, *Capitalism in Amsterdam in the Seventeenth Century* (New York: AMS Press, 1978). Illuminating study of an important factor in Dutch success.

Pieter Geyl, *The Revolt of the Netherlands, 1555–1609* (New York: Barnes & Noble, 1980), and *The Netherlands in the Seventeenth Century,* 2 vols. (New York: Barnes & Noble, 1964). Detailed studies by a Dutch historian. A briefer statement may be found in his *History of the Low Countries* (New York: St. Martin's, 1964).

Johan Huizinga, *Dutch Civilization in the Seventeenth Century and Other Essays* (New York: Harper & Row, n.d.). The title essay is a thoughtful evaluation by another distinguished Dutch historian.

C. V. Wedgewood, *William the Silent* (New York: Norton, 1968). Sound biography of the Dutch national hero.

Germany and the Thirty Years' War

Hajo Holborn, *A History of Modern Germany,* Vol. 2: *The Reformation* (Princeton, N.J.: Princeton University Press, 1982). This authoritative study covers through 1648.

Erich Kahler, *The Germans,* trans. Robert and Rita Kimber (Princeton, N.J.: Princeton University Press, 1974). Good on the problem of German particularism; strong on the Reformation issues.

Georges Pages, *The Thirty Years' War* (London: Black, 1970). Translation of an older French study; stresses the diplomatic side of the war.

Theodore K. Rabb, ed., *The Thirty Years' War: Problems of Motive, Extent, and Effect* (New York: University Press of America, 1981). Sampler of differing views of these controversial questions.

Michael Roberts, *Gustavus Adolphus: A History of Sweden, 1611–1632,* 2 vols. (New York: Longmans, 1953–1958). Sympathetic, detailed biography.

Sigfrid H. Steinberg, *The "Thirty Years' War" and the Conflict for European Hegemony, 1600–1660* (New York: Norton, 1967). Briefer, more recent account.

C. V. Wedgewood, *The Thirty Years' War* (New York: Methuen, 1981). Full and generally well-balanced narrative.

Science

Fulton H. Anderson, *Francis Bacon: His Career and His Thought* (Westport, Conn.: Greenwood, 1977). Good appraisal of an important figure.

Herbert Butterfield, *The Origins of Modern Science, 1300–1800,* rev. ed.

(New York: Free Press, 1965). Older, controversial survey; beautifully written.

Giorgio de Santillana, *The Crime of Galileo* (Chicago: University of Chicago Press, 1955). Stimulating examination of how Galileo's thought constituted a heresy for the Church.

E. J. Dijksterhuis, *The Mechanization of the World Picture* (Cambridge: Cambridge University Press, 1961). Able study of the intellectual impact of science.

Stillman Drake, *Galileo Studies: Personality, Tradition, and Revolution* (Ann Arbor: University of Michigan Press, 1970). Excellent set of essays on the range of Galileo's interests.

Alfred R. Hall, *The Scientific Revolution, 1500–1800* (Boston: Beacon, 1966). A solid account, somewhat dense with detail.

Hugh Kearney, *Science and Change, 1500–1700* (New York: McGraw-Hill, 1971). Succinct, wide-ranging introduction to a still much-debated subject.

Thomas S. Kuhn, *The Copernican Revolution: Planetary Astronomy in the Development of Western Thought* (Cambridge, Mass.: Harvard University Press, 1957). Complex, path-breaking study.

Franklin Le Van Baumer, *Religion and the Rise of Skepticism* (New York: Harcourt, n.d.). Assesses the spiritual impact of science.

Sources

G. R. Elton, *The Tudor Constitution: Documents and Commentary* (Cambridge: Cambridge University Press, 1972). Fine selection of the key documents.

Hiram Haydn, ed., *The Portable Elizabethan Reader* (New York: Viking, n.d.). A good anthology.

Samuel Putnam, ed., *The Portable Cervantes* (New York: Putnam, 1977). Selections from the editor's admirable translation of Don Quixote.

Nancy Roelker, ed., *The Paris of Henry of Navarre* (Cambridge, Mass.: Harvard University Press, 1958). Selections from the informative *Memoires-journaux of Pierre de l'Estolle,* a rich source of social history.

Hans J. C. Von Grimmelshausen, *Simplicius Simplicissimus* (Indianapolis: Bobbs Merrill, 1965). Picaresque but realistic novel written in the seventeenth century and set against the background of war-ravaged Germany.

Charles Wilson and Geoffrey Parker, eds., *An Introduction to the Sources of European Economic History, 1500–1800* (Ithaca, N.Y.: Cornell University Press, 1977). Valuable compilation of contemporary data on economic developments.

CHAPTER FOURTEEN: EXPLORATION AND EXPANSION

Background and General Accounts

J. N. L. Baker, *A History of Geographical Discovery and Exploration* (Totowa, N.J.: Cooper Square, 1972). A standard work.

The Cambridge Economic History, Vol. 4 (Cambridge: Cambridge University Press, 1967). Scholarly essays on expanding Europe in the sixteenth and seventeenth centuries.

Helen Delpar, ed., *The Discoverers: An Encyclopedia of Explorers and Exploration* (New York: McGraw-Hill, 1980). Less inclusive than the title suggests, but with good short essays on the exploration of specific world regions.

J. H. Elliott, *The Old World and the New, 1492–1650* (Cambridge: Cambridge University Press, 1970). Stimulating lectures on the impact of the New World upon the Old.

Holden Furber, *Rival Empires of Trade in the Orient, 1600–1800* (Minneapolis: University of Minnesota Press, 1976). Thorough, informative look at the conflicting nature of trading empires.

Edward J. Goodman, *The Explorers of South America* (London: Macmillan, 1972). Excellent summary.

Gwyn Jones, *The Norse Atlantic Saga* (London: Oxford University Press, 1964). A reliable summary of Viking exploration.

Samuel Eliot Morison, *The European Discovery of America: The Northern Voyages, A.D. 500–1600* (New York: Oxford University Press, 1971), and *The Southern Voyages, A.D. 1492–1616* (New York: Oxford University Press, 1974). Full, carefully argued, beautifully written explorations.

Charles E. Nowell, *The Great Discoveries and the First Colonial Empires* (Westport, Conn.: Greenwood, 1982). Handy, brief introduction.

John H. Parry, *The Age of Reconnaissance* (Berkeley: University of California Press, 1981), and *The Establishment of the European Hegemony, 1415–1715: Trade and Exploration in the Age of the Renaissance* (New York: Harper & Row, 1963). Excellent introductions by an expert in the field.

Boles Penrose, *Travel and Discovery in the Renaissance, 1420–1620* (New York: Atheneum, 1962). Informative survey with accounts of voyages not easily available elsewhere.

Hugh Trevor-Roper, ed., *The Age of Expansion: Europe and the World, 1559–1660* (New York: McGraw-Hill, 1968). Less comprehensive in treatment than the title suggests, but with enlightening chapters on the Spaniards, the Dutch, and the Far East.

Walter P. Webb, *The Great Frontier: An Interpretation of World History* (Austin: University of Texas Press, 1964). Assigns the New World a crucial role in the developing wealth and power of the Old.

John Noble Wilford, *The Mapmakers* (New York: Knopf, 1981). A fine retelling of the story of the pioneers of cartography.

The Portuguese

Charles R. Boxer, *The Portuguese Seaborne Empire, 1415–1825* (New York: Knopf, 1969). Admirable study in the History of Human Society series. Boxer has also written a succinct survey covering the same period: *Four Centuries of Portuguese Expansion* (Berkeley: University of California Press, 1965).

Henry H. Hart, *Sea Road to the Indies* (Westport, Conn.: Greenwood, 1971). Deals with da Gama and other Portuguese explorers.

Charles M. Parr, *So Noble a Captain* (Westport, Conn.: Greenwood, 1976). A scholarly treatment of Magellan and his circumnavigation.

Elaine Sanceau, *Henry the Navigator* (Hamden, Conn.: Shoe String, 1969). A good biography of the Portuguese sponsor of exploration.

The Spaniards

Lewis B. Hanke, *The Spanish Struggle for Justice in the Conquest of America* (Boston: Little, Brown, 1965). Study of an important and often-neglected side of the Spanish record.

Charles Gibson, *The Aztecs under Spanish Rule* (Palo Alto, Calif.: Stanford University Press, 1964). A case study.

Samuel E. Morison, *Admiral of the Ocean Sea,* 2 vols. (Boston: Little, Brown, 1942). The best book on Columbus; by an historian who retraced Columbus' route in a small ship. Morison has also published the briefer *Christopher Columbus, Mariner* (Boston: Little, Brown, 1955).

John H. Parry, *The Spanish Seaborne Empire* (New York: Knopf, 1966). Excellent account in the useful History of Human Society series.

William H. Prescott, *The Conquest of Mexico* and *The Conquest of Peru* (many editions). Celebrated narratives written more than a century ago; may be sampled in various abridgments, among them *The Portable Prescott* (New York: Viking, 1964).

The Dutch

Charles R. Boxer, *The Dutch Seaborne Empire, 1600–1800* (New York: Humanities Press, 1980). Full, up-to-date survey; another volume in the History of Human Society series.

George Masselman, *The Cradle of Colonialism* (New Haven: Yale University Press, 1963). Fine, balanced account of the development of the Dutch empire in Southeast Asia.

The French and the British

John B. Brebner, *The Explorers of North America, 1492–1806* (New York: Meridian, n.d.). Good, brief survey.

Angus Calder, *Revolutionary Empire* (New York: Dutton, 1981). An ambitious, very readable effort to encompass the entire rise of the English-speaking empires from the fifteenth century to the 1780s.

Michael Foss, *Undreamed Shores: England's Wasted Empire in America* (New York: Scribner's, 1974). On the failure to take advantage of the work of Gilbert and Raleigh.

Gustave Lanctot, *History of Canada,* 2 vols. (Cambridge, Mass.: Harvard University Press, 1963–1964). Detailed study to 1713; by a French-Canadian scholar.

Samuel E. Morison, ed., *The Parkman Reader* (Boston: Little, Brown, 1955). Selections from the celebrated multivolume *France and England in North America* by the nineteenth-century historian Francis Parkman.

J. H. Rose, ed., *The Cambridge History of the British Empire,* Vol. 1 (Cambridge: Cambridge University Press, 1929). Detailed survey to 1783.

Marcel Trudel, *The Beginnings of New France, 1524–1663,* trans. Patricia Claxton (Toronto: McClelland and Stewart, 1973); W. J. Eccles, *Canada under Louis XIV* (Toronto: McClelland and Stewart, 1964). The best short histories of the rise of the French empire in North America.

Africa, Asia, and the Pacific

Arthur L. Basham, *The Wonder That Was India* (New York: Taplinger, 1968). A survey of Indian history up to the Muslim invasions.

Basil Davidson, *The African Slave Trade,* rev. ed. (Boston: Little, Brown, 1981). By a prolific writer on African history.

Réne Grousset, *The Rise and Splendor of the Chinese Empire* (Berkeley: University of California Press, 1953). An enlightening study of Chinese culture.

Henri Labouret, *Africa before the White Man* (New York: Walker, 1963); Basil Davidson, *Africa in History* (New York: Macmillan, 1974); Roland Oliver and J. D. Fage, *A Short History of Africa* (New York: New York University Press, 1962). Three helpful introductions. Fage has also written *A History of West Africa,* 4th ed. (Cambridge: Cambridge University Press, 1969), and other useful books on the continent.

Kenneth S. Latourette, *China* (Englewood Cliffs, N.J.: Prentice-Hall, 1964). Excellent introduction.

William Napier, et al., *Eastern Islands, Southern Seas: A History of Discovery and Exploration* (London: Aldus Books, 1973). A handsomely illustrated survey.

Edwin O. Reischauer and John K. Fairbank, *East Asia: The Great Tradition* (Boston: Houghton Miffiin, 1960). An expert survey of China, Japan, and Korea from the beginnings. Reischauer has also written *Japan: The Story of a Nation* (New York: Arno, 1974).

George B. Sansom, *A History of Japan, 1334–1615,* and *A History of Japan, 1615–1867* (both Palo Alto, Calif.: Stanford University Press, 1961, 1963). Perceptive, readable accounts; a bit dated.

The Americas

Charles M. Andrews, *The Colonial Period of American History,* Vols. 1, 2, 3 (New Haven: Yale University Press, 1934–1937). Detailed study of the European settlements.

Daniel J. Boorstin, *Americans: The Colonial Experience* (New York: Random House, 1958). A provocative briefer treatment.

Alfred W. Crosby, *The Columbian Exchange: Biological and Cultural Consequences of 1492* (Westport, Conn.: Greenwood, 1973). Provocative inquiry into the disease frontier and related matters.

Francis Jennings, *The Invasion of America* (New York: Norton, 1976). Excellent examination of the Europeans as invaders rather than explorers or settlers.

A. P. Newton, *The European Nations in the West Indies, 1493–1688* (New York: Barnes & Noble, 1967). Still an excellent study of a great arena of colonial rivalry.

Jacques Soustelle, *Daily Life of the Aztecs on the Eve of the Spanish Conquest* (Palo Alto, Calif.: Stanford University Press, 1961). Instructive study by an anthropologist.

Stanley J. and Barbara H. Stein, *Colonial Heritage of Latin America* (London: Oxford University Press, 1970). Essays stressing its economic dependence on the parent countries.

Louis B. Wright, *Cultural Life of the American Colonies, 1607–1763* (New York: Harper & Row, 1957). An especially good volume in the New American Nation series.

Sources

Irwin R. Blacker, ed., *The Portable Hakluyt's Voyages* (New York: Viking, n.d.). Excerpts from the famous late sixteenth-century collection.

Eugene D. Genovese and Laura Foner, *Slavery in the New World* (Englewood Cliffs, N.J.: Prentice-Hall, 1969). Materials on the comparative slave policies of the imperial powers.

George Alexander Lensen, *Russia's Eastward Expansion* (New York: Spectrum, 1964). Source materials.

Joseph R. Levenson, *European Expansion and the Counter-Example of Asia* (Englewood Cliffs, N.J.: Prentice-Hall, 1967). Materials on technology, religion, social structure, and "spirit."

ILLUSTRATIONS

INDEX

[**Boldface** figures indicate major discussions; *m* = map; *n* = footnote; C = century.]

Pronunciations have been adapted from *Webster's Third New International Dictionary* (1976), *Webster's Biographical Dictionary* (1971), *Webster's Geographical Dictionary* (1962), *The Columbia Encyclopedia*, 4th ed. (1975), *The Oxford Universal Dictionary on Historical Principles* (1955), and the *BBC Pronouncing Dictionary of British Names* (London: Oxford University Press, 1971).